YOUR PASSPORT TO THE GLOBAL BUSINESS

Oded Shenkar's and Yadong Luo's INTERNATIONAL BUSINESS will introduce you to b_____ other countries. To truly understand their unique perspectives, you need a geographic understanding of different places and peoples around the globe.

Now you can get a working knowledge of where things are with the enclosed GeoDiscoveries CD! With this CD, you will explore various countries throughout the world through multimedia, videos, text, art, and animations.

Photographs, area and demographic maps, an audio pronunciation guide, and much more will assist you in becoming geographically and culturally literate, and arm you with invaluable insights into global business practices and the perspectives of other countries!

GEODISCOVERIES MODULES

These learning activities allow you to explore important concepts in more depth. Each module has a three-part structure:

- Presentations that use videos, animation, and other resources to focus on key concepts from the chapter.
- Interactivities that engage students in concept-based exercises.
- Assessment self-tests that allow students to measure their comprehension of the concept being explored.

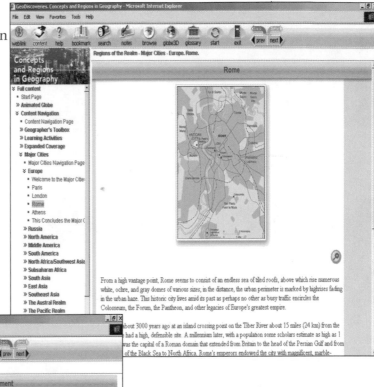

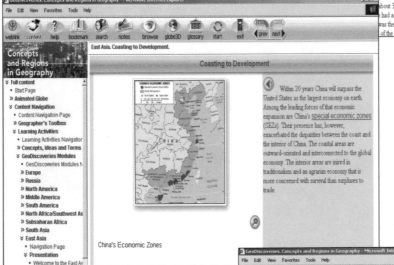

China's Economic Zones

MAJOR CITIES ON CD

This feature reflects the growing process and influence of urbanization worldwide. More than thirty profiles of the world's leading cities are presented, each accompanied by specially drawn maps.

MAP QUIZZES

For each region of the world, GeoDiscoveries offers three game-formatted place-name activities that quiz:

- Countries, States, and Provinces
- Cities
- Physical Features

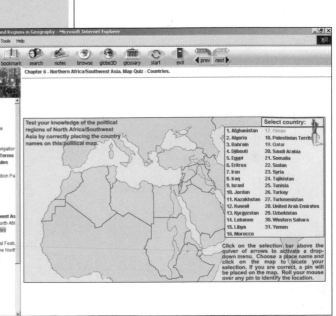

International Business

Oded Shenkar
Ohio State University

Yadong Luo
University of Miami

WILEY

John Wiley & Sons, Inc.

PROJECT EDITOR	David Kear
MARKETING MANAGER	Charity Robey
SENIOR PRODUCTION EDITOR	Petrina Kulek
DEVELOPMENT EDITOR	Caroline Ryan
SENIOR DESIGNER	Harry Nolan
INTERIOR DESIGN	Delgado Design, Inc.
COVER DESIGN	Harry Nolan
ILLUSTRATOR EDITOR	Anna Melhorn
PHOTO EDITOR	Sara Wight
PHOTO RESEARCHER	Elyse Rieder
NEW MEDIA EDITOR	Allie Keim

This book was set in 9.5/12.5 Stone Serif by TechBooks and printed and bound by Von Hoffmann. The cover was printed by Von Hoffmann.

COVER PHOTOS
Clockwise: Pottery seller in doorway of his humble shop, Midoun, Djerba, Tunisia. Interior of a Shopping Mall, Baltimore, Maryland. Ndebele tribe doorway, South Africa. Bank of Communications, Shanghai. Brazil, Sao Paolo Torii Gate to Liberdade, Japanese arr. as market farm, 1908. Entrance to 50 Rockefeller Plaza. Bar in Dublin. Entrance of multistory Bancosorno building in the Chilean capital of Santiago. Please see Photo Credits at the end of this book.

This book is printed on acid free paper. ∞

ISBN (domestic) 0-471-38350-3
ISBN (WIE) 0-471-42937-6

Printed in the United States of America

To Miriam, Keshet, Joshua and Rakefet; and to the
memory of my parents, Bluma and Joshua—OS

To my family, Cuihua, Edward, and Rosalie—YL

About the Authors

Oded Shenkar holds the Ford Motor Company Chair in Global Business Management and is Professor of International Business at the Fisher College of Business, the Ohio State University. He is a member of six editorial boards, including the three leading journals in international business (*Journal of International Business Studies, Management International Review,* and *Journal of International Management*), and has authored over 70 refereed journal articles and four books. Based on major journal publications, he was ranked among the 300 most prolific management authors (*Organization Science*), the 30 top international strategy authors (*Journal of International Management*), and first among Chinese management scholars (*Journal of Business Research*). He was the first Andersen Fellow at the Judge Institute of Management, Cambridge University, and the first holder of the Ford Motor Company Chair at the Fisher College. Oded is a member of the Conference Board Council for Business Development and Integration Executives, and is also on the board of the Hang Lung Center for the Study of Chinese Management (Hong Kong University of Science and Technology) and the School of Business at Zhejiang University (China). He taught in Hong Kong (The Chinese University of Hong Kong and HKUST), mainland China (Peking University, the University of International Business and Economics), Japan (International University of Japan), the UK and Israel, among others. He has been a consultant to governments, international organizations, and multinational enterprises as well as to small and start-up global firms.

Yadong Luo is Professor of International Business and Strategy and holds the Emery Means Findlay Distinguished Chair in Graduate Business Studies in the School of Business, University of Miami. He has authored about 100 refereed journal articles, mostly on international business, and over 10 books, mostly on multinational corporations in emerging markets. Yadong's recent articles have appeared in leading journals such as *The Administrative Science Quarterly, The Academy of Management Journal, The Strategic Management Journal, The Journal of International Business Studies, The Journal of Applied Psychology, Organization Science, The Journal of Management, The Journal of Management Studies, The Journal of International Management, The Journal of World Business,* and *Management International Review,* among others. He is the recipient of nearly a dozen research and teaching awards at the University of Miami and the University of Hawaii, where he taught before moving to Miami. He has been a consultant to governments, law firms, and large corporations. Prior to coming to the United States, Yadong was a provincial official in charge of international business in China.

Preface

The Key to Success in an Interconnected World

In a global environment, it is impossible to understand and succeed in business without understanding the repercussions of business realities and developments in other countries. *International Business* goes beyond a U.S.-centered perspective to take into consideration business realities in other countries and their unique perspectives. Presenting the latest thinking in the field as well as recent events around the world, this action-oriented text helps students relate the material to current events as well as to their own daily lives and, most importantly, broaden their understanding of the global business environment and its influence on the role of the business executive.

The book is directed at both undergraduate and graduate students and is written so as to be accessible and motivational to both. We have done this by (a) presenting rigorously researched material in a readable form, (b) defining all new terms as they appear, (c) providing related knowledge, including that of current events, as necessary (rather than assuming knowledge, whether of basic geography or of recent world events), (d) providing a balance as well as a clear link between theory and practice, and (e) supplying cases that vary from the introductory to the complex and advanced. These features also make the book accessible to students in the variety of disciplinary areas in which international business is taught. Relevant to all audiences is the 'real-world' feel that conveys the excitement of cross-border business.

The book takes a fresh and unique perspective on international business:

- **First,** believing that students need to learn to look at the world from diverse perspectives, we provide a truly global rather than United-States–centered view, offering balanced coverage of business in many parts of the world and from both developed and developing-country perspectives.
- **Second,** we have written the book from an action-oriented, executive perspective to help students see the relevance of the main topics in international business to their future roles as managers and entrepreneurs.
- **Third,** in order to help students develop the skills they need to address various issues in international business, we offer an integrated approach, making connections among different concepts and functions and across cultures. Through this cross-functional emphasis, we believe students can gain a broad understanding of the environments, players, and policies at work in both the core and functional areas of international business. In addition, we provide problem-solving strategies designed to give students the analytical skills and tools they will need to meet the many challenges in today's international business environment.
- **Fourth,** we include in-depth coverage of key topics such as culture, global e-commerce, and global ethics and corruption that we believe are essential for students entering the international business arena.

Organization

The organization of this text is geared to provide a modular yet integrative usage, so that it is possible to use a selection of sections and chapters without losing the sense of cohesiveness and wholeness that is critical in an integrative area such as international business. This is done, for instance, by providing links to related chapters and topics in each and every chapter so the student does not feel lost and can quickly identify where to supplement his/her knowledge as necessary.

We begin with an introductory chapter focusing on the foundations of international business in the context of a rapidly evolving global business environment. This sets the stage for the rest of the book and serves to align the expectations of students and their instructors.

Following the Introduction, in Part 1 we examine what we view as the core phenomena in international business: international trade, foreign direct investment, and multinational and international firms. We believe that it is essential to present these topics early in the book so students can begin to develop an executive mindset and apply their knowledge of these areas throughout the book. To give students a firm understanding of these concepts, we integrate theory and practice, presenting them side-by-side and pinpointing when reality supports theory, as well as when it does not and why. In this section, as in the rest of the book, we reflect on the most recent trends in international business; for example, we provide coverage not only of the traditional multinational enterprise but also of the multinational corporation from developing countries and the small international firm.

In Part 2 we focus on the environment of international business, placing emphasis on two prominent features. We begin with a unique chapter on country competitiveness that ties environmental analysis to earlier topics such as trade and comparative advantage as well as to topics that follow such as international strategy. A second feature of this section is our extensive coverage of cultural, political, and legal environments, all presented within the context of the challenges facing the multinational and international company. Most importantly, elements from these environments are addressed again in later chapters, providing genuine integration and giving students a clear sense of how they are related.

The subsequent discussions in Part 3 of global business institutions, monetary systems, and financial markets further solidify the relationship among the international business environment, the nation and the firm. Here, too, the coverage is both extensive and integrative. For example, students will find coverage of almost every region of the world and its regional integration, using the terms and concepts introduced earlier in the text. Another unique feature of this section is the provision of detailed strategic responses to economic integration and changes in financial markets. As in other sections, we make ample use of recent and current events to illustrate our points.

Part 4 deals with international business strategies, providing an integrative approach with chapters on strategy, organization design, alliances, and R&D all tied to a unifying theme that recognizes the intertwined position of strategy and implementation in a global environment. Thus, Chapter 11 discusses not only organization design options but also how structure is driven by global strategy, while Chapter 12 discusses both the strategic and managerial aspects of alliances.

The chapters on functional business areas in Part 5 enable students to look at international business phenomena from the perspective of the functional expert, using their knowledge from prior functional courses as well as the topics covered earlier in the book. These chapters provide extensive coverage of each functional area but also show how they fit together and how they link with other topics. For example, when covering global human resource management, we explain its control function and its relation to a firm's global strategy; when covering marketing, we show the impact of culture on consumption patterns.

Finally, this book is unique in offering extensive treatment of two emerging areas: global e-commerce and global ethics and corruption. Each of these two areas has received considerable attention lately, and in these chapters we provide students with up-to-date coverage of key emerging issues in international business. This last section underscores the general thrust of the book in highlighting current events that affect the role and operation of executives in a global and changing business environment.

Key Features In developing and writing this book, we have included a number of features for a comprehensive, up-to-date introduction to international business. Among the key features of the text are:

- **Global Perspective:** Describes business realities and processes in many parts of the world, covering both developed and developing countries. Students will learn to look at the world from diverse perspectives, including those of small and midsize international companies and developing country multinationals, as well as understand the motives and needs of their global competitors, customers and partners.
- **Currency and Relevance:** Presents the latest concepts and models as well as recent events that help students relate the material to daily life. Spells out new developments in the global environment and shows how they impact the task of the business executive.
- **Integrated Approach:** Features an approach that helps students make connections among different concepts and goes beyond the traditional silos that characterize much of current IB learning tools.
- **Cross-Functional Emphasis:** Provides students with a broad, cross-functional understanding of the environments, players, and policies at work in both the core and functional areas of international business.
- **Problem-Solving Strategies:** Outlines strategies, policies, and tools for solving international business challenges, and develops problem-solving aptitude and skills.
- **Cultural, Legal, and Environmental Coverage:** Highlights the role of these factors in all aspects of international business. In addition to a chapter devoted to culture and one to the political and legal environment, these elements are integrated into other chapters.
- **Opening Cases:** Each chapter begins with motivational questions followed by a brief case illustrating the core concepts presented in the chapter. This attunes the student to the material that follows, making subsequent reading more efficient.
- **Country and Industry Boxes:** Additional short cases in each chapter serve to illustrate and zoom in on phenomena that may at first look abstract, enabling the student to find relevance to their areas of interest.
- **Special Cases:** The last section of the text features cases corresponding to all chapters of the book. These cases, of varying length and complexity, provide a comprehensive framework that can be adjusted to student level and progress. Together with cutting-edge technology, these cases provide an all-inclusive learning package.
- **Superior Technology:** The text promotes geographic literacy with an innovative and highly interactive CD offering a global interface that transports students to various countries around the world through multimedia, videos, text, photos, art, and animations.

Ancillary Package

International Business features a full line of teaching and learning resources for students and professors:

- *Instructor's Manual:* Prepared by Ralph Jagodka, Mt. San Antonio College, this comprehensive manual includes the following material for each chapter: Learning Objectives, Teaching Notes/Suggestions, Chapter Summary, Sample Syllabi, Case Recommendations/Teaching Notes, Internet or written exercises.
- *Test Bank:* Douglas Peterson, Indiana State University, prepared this extensive Test Bank, including Multiple Choice, True/False, Short-Answer Questions, and Essay Questions. Section references throughout provide the appropriate section of the chapters for the answer.
- *Computerized Test Bank:* Available in both IBM and Windows format, this contains all the Test Bank material within a Test-Generating Program that allows instructors to customize exams.
- *PowerPoint Presentations:* These include both lecture outlines and text art for each chapter of the text.
- *Videos:* The integrated Video Series contains clips corresponding to each chapter. In addition, a special integrative video on Vietnam is included.
- *Web site: www.wiley.com/college/shenkar* an extensive Web site, provides a variety of resources for students as well as electronic versions of the Instructor's Manual, Test Bank, and PowerPoint Presentations for instructors.
- *CD-ROM:* This state-of-the-art interactive geography-based system anchors topics within a geographic context. The CD features multimedia, videos, text, photos, art, and animations.

Acknowledgments

In developing this book, we have benefited from the insightful comments and suggestions of many colleagues, to whom we remain indebted. We especially wish to thank the reviewers listed below for their invaluable feedback on the manuscript:

Juan Alacer, University of Michigan

Josiah Baker, University of Central Florida

Dharma DeSilva, Wichita State University

Krishna Dhir, Pennsylvania State University

Les Dlabay, Lake Forest College

Subhash Durlabhji, Northwestern State University

James Foley, Bradley University

Ellen Kaye Gehrke, United States International University

Randal Gunder, Gosher College

Nicholas Gurney, San Francisco State University

Y. Paul Huo, University of Puget Sound

Ralph Jagodka, Mt. San Antonio College

John Kmetz, University of Delaware

Gary Knight, Florida State University

David Leapard, Eastern Michigan University

Joseph Leonard, Miami University

Bijou Yang Lester, Drexel University

Roger Levy, St. Thomas Aquinas College

Kamlesh Mehta, Sierra Nevada College

Sam Okoroafo, University of Toledo

Peter Olson, Rensselaer Polytechnic Institute

Russell Reston, George Mason University

Douglas Ross, Towson University

Hugh Sloan, University of Mississippi

Jennifer Spencer, University of Houston

John Stanbury, George Mason University

Paul Tiffany, University of California—Berkley

Michael Weininger, Florida Atlantic University

Alan Wright, Henderson State University

William Ziegler, Bethune-Cookman College

We would also like to acknowledge the support of the CIBER at the Fisher College of the Ohio State University and the research help of Asli Arikan, Ilgaz Arikan and Yaping Gong, all about to become or already scholars in their own right.

Last but not least, we would like to acknowledge the Wiley staff that has accompanied this text from initiation through implementation to completion, tending to both the predictable and the unforeseen. Along the way, Barbara Heaney, David Kear, Petrina Kulek, Amy Goldberger and many others whom we have met or who were there behind the scenes contributed their knowledge and efforts to seeing this project through. The same is true of Wiley's senior leadership. Without them, this book would not have become a reality.

Brief Contents

Contents

PART FIVE Functional IB Areas 355

CHAPTER 14 Financial Management for Global Operations 356

CHAPTER 15 International Accounting for Global Operations 386

CHAPTER 16 Global Marketing and Supply Chain 410

CASES

MAPS

International Business in an Age of Globalization

DO YOU KNOW

1. What is globalization, and why is it important, even to domestic firms? How does globalization affect you, the domestic consumer?

2. In what ways is globalization perceived as a benefit, and in what ways is it considered a threat?

3. Can you differentiate between international business, international transaction, international trade, and international investment? Can you distinguish between the multinational enterprise (MNE) and the international firm?

4. What differences do you observe between international business and domestic business? Why?

5. Why do firms expand globally? What gains can they achieve and what hazards will they confront? Does every firm seek identical goals or face the same threats in this process?

OPENING CASE The Coca-Cola Company

Atlanta-based Coca-Cola Company is often hailed as the model for a global company. The company has 239 beverage brands sold around the world and Coke, its flagship beverage, has become the symbol of a global product. Although ninety-third on the Fortune 500 list for the year 2000 (immediately followed by its archrival PepsiCo) with roughly twenty and a half billion dollars in revenue, Coca-Cola's visibility across the globe is second to none. Studies show that the Coca-Cola brand has the highest name recognition in the world. Only 30 percent of the unit case volume of the company is sold in North America. Twenty-six percent is sold in Latin America while Europe (including Eurasia), Asia Pacific, and Africa/Middle East account for 21, 16, and 7 percent, respectively. In 1999, Coca-Cola acquired the beverage brands of U.K.-based Cadbury Schweppes that sell in 155 countries.

Coca-Cola produces Coke in essentially the same way across the globe: It sells concentrate to local bottlers that make the drink and distribute it in their markets. But while preserving a coherent global theme, it also adapts taste as well as operations to local markets. Its 2000 annual report states: "We have to maintain our special place in local cultures, recognizing the differences between countries and regions." The company's famous slogan "think globally and act locally" embodies what may be the central dilemma in international business: the need to maintain global strategic focus and control while allowing for adaptation to local circumstances in everything from management to distribution. The company's most global function—advertising— avoids themes that would be controversial in any of its local markets. This is in contrast to its rival Pepsi, which, for example, irked religious circles in Israel with ads showing monkeys as human ancestors.

Coca-Cola's global success has ruffled some feathers, however. The European Commission recently rejected its bid to acquire a French beverage maker, pointing out that it already had a majority share in the EU markets. The company's argument that it merely had a tiny share of the market—defined as all liquids consumed, including water—has fallen on deaf ears. The company's efforts to promote a global image have not prevented it from being identified as an American icon, and it has become a frequent lightning rod for attacks by anti-U.S. and anti-globalization activists. In 2001 alone, Coca-Coca's facilities have been bombed by Moslem rebels in India and by Maoist guerillas in Nepal. ■

Source: Company press releases; 2000 annual report; *Fortune Magazine* 500 list.

AN AGE OF GLOBALIZATION

"Globalization" has become one of the key buzzwords of modern times. While globalization means different things to different people, its manifestations are found all around us. You can buy a Coke in almost every country of the world. In some countries (e.g., Chile), Coca Cola has more than half of the market share for nonalcoholic, ready-to-drink beverages. Its equivalent market share in China is 10 percent, but it grew at the breakneck rate of 29 percent in 1999. When traveling abroad you will see not only Coke but also McDonald's familiar golden arches and other staples of the American consumer.

Measured in constant prices, the value of world exports in 2000 more than tripled between 1980 and 2000, while foreign investment grew more than twentyfold during the same period. These numbers suggest that even a firm without international aspirations may soon find that its domestic market is under threat from foreign competition. Time and time again this has happened to established but unsuspecting domestic firms that have been complacent in monitoring and reacting to foreign competition. U.S. automakers in the 1970s and 1980s faced an onslaught from Japanese competitors with Chrysler almost driven to bankruptcy.

Countries differ in their globalization levels. Exhibit 1–1 ranks the twenty most global countries according to their overall globalization level as well as according to the four components which make up the Globalization Index—economic integration, personal contact, technology, and political engagement. Exhibit 1–2 provides the complete rankings of the 62 countries included in the study.

What Does Globalization Mean for You?

To the consumer, globalization means more choices, lower prices, and an increasingly blurred national identity for products and services. Buy a Whopper at a local Burger King and you will have contributed to the revenue of U.K.-based Diageo. Purchase a General Motors (GM) or a Ford car or truck, and you will find out that the car is either made in Canada or Mexico or contains numerous foreign components. Chrysler, the smallest of the "Big Three," is no longer a U.S. company, having been acquired by Germany's Daimler. Buy a car carrying the logo of a foreign manufacturer, and you may find out that it is manufactured in the United States—Honda Civics in Ohio, Mercedes M Class in Alabama, Nissan pickup trucks in Tennessee. If you are a Canadian who prefers to buy Canadian, you will have to choose between the foreign brands assembled in Canada or settle for the Mercedes M class, made in the United States but advertised in Canada as "made by a Canadian—alluding to the U.S. plant manager. If you are an Australian consumer who wants to buy a locally produced vehicle, you will be able to choose between three locally produced foreign brands: Holden (a GM brand whose design is influenced by its German subsidiary Opel), a Ford, or a Mitsubishi.

Similar trends can be observed in the service sector. The mortgage on your U.S. property might be underwritten by Dutch bank ABN Ambro; your life insurance by French insurer AXA. Your retirement funds might be invested in Swiss food giant Nestlé or managed by the German-based Deutsche Bank. The advertisement

Exhibit 1–1
The global top 20
countries

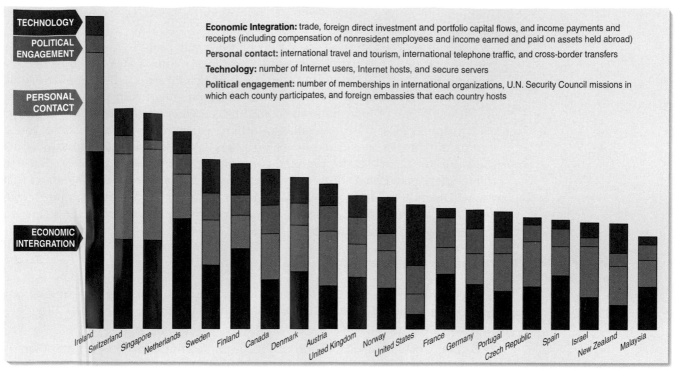

Source: A.T. Kearney, "Globalization's Last Hurrah?", *Foreign Policy*, Jan./Feb. 2002.

Exhibit 1–2
Globalization index
rankings

1 Ireland	22 Slovak Republic	43 Sri Lanka
2 Switzerland	23 Hungary	44 Argentina
3 Singapore	24 Italy	45 Egypt, Arab Rep.
4 Netherlands	25 Croatia	46 Morocco
5 Sweden	26 Greece	47 Kenya
6 Finland	27 Poland	48 Bangladesh
7 Canada	28 Panama	49 India
8 Denmark	29 Botswana	50 Mexico
9 Austria	30 Slovenia	51 Thailand
10 United Kingdom	31 Korea, Rep.	52 Philippines
11 Norway	32 Taiwan	53 China
12 United States	33 Nigeria	54 South Africa
13 France	34 Chile	55 Turkey
14 Germany	35 Uganda	56 Pakistan
15 Portugal	36 Tunisia	57 Venezuela, RB
16 Czech Republic	37 Saudi Arabia	58 Brazil
17 Spain	38 Japan	59 Indonesia
18 Israel	39 Russian Federation	60 Colombia
19 New Zealand	40 Senegal	61 Peru
20 Malaysia	41 Romania	62 Iran
21 Australia	42 Ukraine	

Source: A.T. Kearney, "Globalization's Last Hurrah?", *Foreign Policy*, Jan./Feb. 2002.

enticing you to buy Cincinnati-based P&G's Pampers will have been created by the U.K.'s Saatchi & Saatchi. In fact, the student sitting next to you may be of a foreign nationality, as might be the patient waiting next to you in the hospital clinic. You are also more likely to take your vacation in a foreign destination—the number of international arrivals reached almost 700 million in 2000, up from less than 460 million a decade ago.[2]

Globalization also impacts your career choices and progression. It is increasingly possible that upon graduation you will be working for one of the many foreign companies in the United States or that you will work in another country for a U.S., local, or another foreign firm. If you are considering employment with a foreign firm, one of the first pieces of information you will need is whether the recruiting company tends to open its senior-most ranks to other than its own nationals. If in doubt, look for foreign names on the list of members of the board of directors. Whether you work for a domestic or a foreign corporation, it is increasingly likely that you will be sent abroad on a short- or long-term assignment by your employer and that you will spend time negotiating, entertaining, coaching, and learning from foreign executives and employees. How well you perform this assignment may be an important benchmark for your career progress.

Interim Summary

1. Globalization is evident in the consumer products and services you find all over the world. The Globalization Index shows a continuous advance of globalization in recent years.
2. To the consumer, globalization can mean more choices, lower prices, and an increasingly blurred national identity for products and services.

THE FACE OF GLOBALIZATION

Globalization is sometimes viewed as a threat, affecting even disinterested observers. The effort to combat it, however, is difficult and probably futile. Rather than fighting globalization, we should acknowledge it, study it, and seek the best ways to obtain positive outcomes for the largest possible number of constituencies, not least the most vulnerable.

Who Benefits from Globalization?

Globalization has its winners and losers, and it allegedly comes at the cost of poorer nations. Before we discuss the argument itself, let us take a look at the relationship between development level and globalization. While globalization is higher among the G-7 nations than among the developing and emerging economies, it is clear (see Exhibit 1–2) that some developed nations (e.g., Japan) are low on globalization, while some developing (e.g., Botswana) and emerging economies (e.g., the Czech Republic) are quite high.

In 2000, the share of developing countries in world merchandise trade rose to its highest level in 50 years. The trade growth of the 49 least developed countries (LDCs) exceeded the global average. Furthermore, many of the manifestations of globalization in wealthy nations end up helping poorer economies. For instance, when a Singaporean tourist is visiting Laos, he is in effect increasing the export sales of that country by purchasing such services as hotel stays and tours. Finally, 95 percent of the 78 million new births a year occur in developing nations. For instance, in 2016 India's population will exceed the combined population of all the developed countries.[3] This suggests that sooner or later developing economies will provide the bulk of both production and consumption, profiting even more from international trade

Exhibit 1–3

Globalization and social expenditure

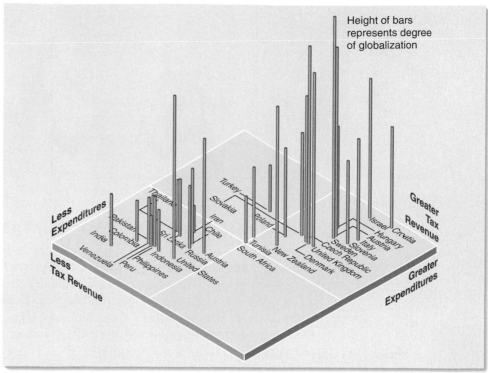

Source: Taxation and expenditure data from World Development Indicators (Washington World Bank, 2001). Cited in A. T. Kearney, "Globalization's Last hurrah?" Foreign Policy, Jan./Feb. 2002

and investment. Employees of foreign affiliates in developing countries already enjoy wages far in excess of those paid by domestic firms. While large multinational firms remain a somewhat exclusive club of rich nations, they are joined by multinationals from developing economies. In 2000, for the first time ever, multinational firms from developing countries made it into the ranks of the top 100 global multinationals.[4]

Exhibit 1–3 shows that globalization is not necessarily synonymous with low levels of public expenditure or with a lack of social safety net, as is sometimes argued by opponents of globalization. Countries such as Sweden and Denmark provide good examples.

Globalization and the Monopoly Power of Large Corporations

Another common complaint is that globalization will deprive nations of their sovereignty. This will supposedly occur because of the growing stature of international organizations such as the World Trade Organization (WTO) whose officials are not elected by popular vote, and because to some people, globalization simply means Americanization and hence a threat to their identity and values. Related to this argument is the complaint that globalization enhances the monopoly power of large multinational corporations.

These arguments too are only partially accurate. The WTO may have assumed a conflict resolution role that was previously the domain of bilateral negotiations, but international trade remains very much a government-to-government domain. Similarly, while mega multinational corporations abound, small firms remain viable players that have a role in the global economy. For instance, as you will see in Chapter 4, small firms in the United States have actually been increasing their share of U.S. exports over the last decade.

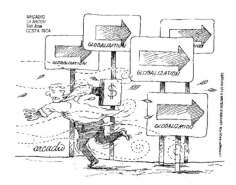

Images of Globalization.

Globalization and the Environment

Another common complaint against globalization is that it comes at the expense of the environment. Environmentalists cite firms that relocate their operations solely for reasons of escaping tough pollution rules in their home country, an argument often titled as "the race to the bottom" or "the lowest common denominator." This argument too is only partially true. Although some firms may seek to lower cost regardless of environmental responsibilities, others adhere to strict codes of environmental protection. Some multinationals, e.g., Dow Chemicals, have actually been credited with much of the environmental cleanup in eastern Europe and former East Germany. Further, the reality is that for most firms, environmental standards are only one of many criteria used in determining their investment and location decision.

Globalization: The Social Balance

We will show throughout this book that globalization is a complex phenomenon whose repercussions are often less than crystal clear. Globalization carries both promises and threats and has both winners and losers at the national, regional, organizational, and individual (e.g., employee) level. For instance, while we will show that trade benefits all participants and while globalization is correlated with higher overall economic growth, this would be of little consolation to an employee who loses his job as a result of foreign competition. Keep in mind that globalization is not the only factor influencing job loss and wage levels. Research shows that it is technology rather than globalization that puts the bulk of downward pressures on the wages of unskilled labor.[5] Still, this reality will not mitigate the devastating community impact of a major employer moving its facilities to foreign shores. The globalization challenge is one of maintaining a balance between the public interest and that of those who suffer its consequences in the short range.

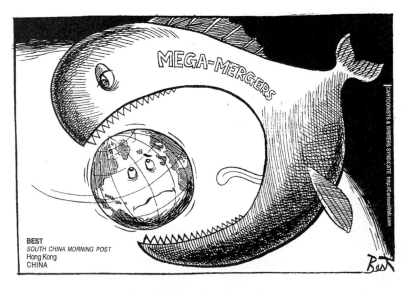

Are ever-growing multinationals taking over the global economy?

Globalization is associated with other, potentially negative repercussions. Global capital flow makes less regulated emerging economies such as Mexico, Thailand, and Argentina vulnerable to volatilities of international capital or foreign exchange markets (thus could contribute to a financial or currency crisis in these countries). When prices of commodities, especially raw materials and natural resources, are undervalued due to market control or influence by transnational cartels or by barriers imposed by importing nations, developing countries that export these commodities to developed countries lose many economic gains that would otherwise occur. While asking for market access into developing countries, some developed nations themselves erect new barriers against developing country imports.

Globalization also exposes national economies to the uncertainties of the global economy; ironically, the most open economies are also the most vulnerable to a global slowdown of the sort commencing in 2001. However, the most global economies also appear to have the most even income distribution;[6] hence, the hardships as well as the benefits are likely to be shared by all segments of society.

A balanced view acknowledging both the bright and dark sides of globalization is called for, in order to focus attention on constructive solutions to the foreign trade and investment debate. Globalization could offer even more advantages to participating economies, rich or poor, if globalization infrastructure is better developed. **Globalization infrastructure** concerns institutional frameworks (e.g., multilateral agreements in trade, investment, and service) and market efficiency (e.g., efficiency of international capital markets or foreign exchange markets) that support fair and transparent transactions of products or services and streamline flows of commodities, capital, labor, knowledge, and information. As discussed in Chapter 8, international economic organizations such as the International Monetary Fund (IMF), the World Bank, and the World Trade Organization (WTO) play a fundamental role in facilitating such infrastructure. We also need to consider the role of different actors (firms, governments, regional blocs, and international organizations) in the course of globalization.

Finally, a balanced view of globalization requires a recognition that it is merely one of many factors affecting the well-being of a population. Exhibit 1–4 shows that globalization is not necessarily correlated with subjective well being, which can be high for highly global countries (e.g., Ireland) as for those least global (e.g., Ghana).

Interim Summary

1. It is best to understand globalization in a balanced light, recognizing its positive and negative aspects, so as to focus attention on constructive solutions to the foreign trade and investment debate.

2. International economic organizations such as the International Monetary Fund, the World Bank, and the World Trade Organization provide added infrastructure to support globalization.

GLOBALIZATION AND INTERNATIONAL BUSINESS

It is sometimes suggested that globalization means the advance of a homogeneous civilization and a uniform business system that would no longer require adjustment to different business environment. This erroneous assumption might lead firms to believe that their strategies, practices, and products or services have universal applicability with no need to distinguish between domestic and international business. Nothing could be further from the truth. While globalization marches on, pressures to maintain national identity and solidarity are not subsiding. On the contrary, the growing interaction between different systems makes people more rather than less aware of the differences among them and perceive foreign inputs as potentially threatening to their group.

Exhibit 1–4
Globalization and
happiness

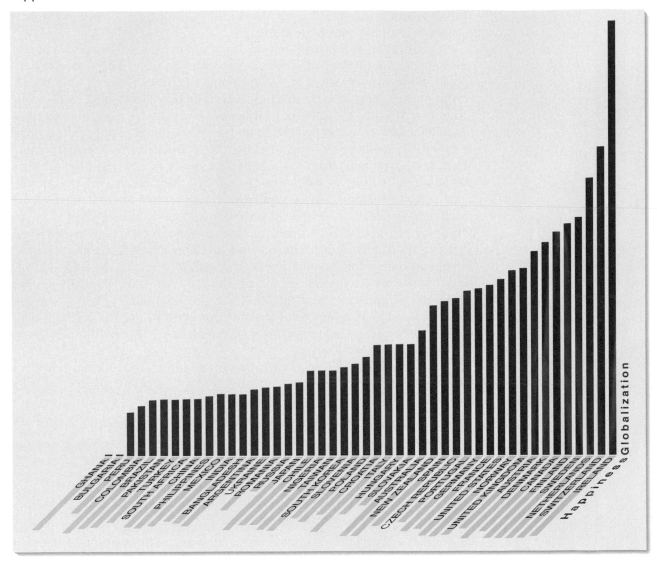

Source: A.T. Kearney; "Globalization's Last Hurrah?", *Foreign Policy,* Jan./Feb. 2002. Scores from "Subjective well-being" (happiness), *World Values Survey* (Ann Arbor: Institute for Social Research, 1996).

Throughout this book, you will be made aware of this simultaneous existence of global and local forces and their interaction in the realm of international business. Examples are how to leverage the global resources of the multinational enterprise yet compensate for its unfamiliarity with the foreign environments in which it operates; how to extract economies of scale by selling a product in multiple locations while making product adjustments and adaptations to reflect different tastes and selling methods; or how to maintain a globally unified compensation system for employees while taking into account the vast differences in practices, values, and taxation systems across the globe. Please note that we use the term "nation" to denote boundaries of economic and political units that are not necessarily sovereign states, such as, Hong Kong, which is part of China but is a separate entity for foreign trade and investment purposes.

What Is International Business?

International business refers to business activities that involve the transfer of resources, goods, services, knowledge, skills, or information across national boundaries. The resources that make up this flow are raw materials, capital, and people. Goods may be semifinished and finished assemblies and products. Services include accounting, legal counsel, banking, insurance, management consulting, trade service, education, healthcare, and tourism, among others. Knowledge and skills include technology and innovation, organizational and managerial skills, and intellectual property rights such as copyrights, trademarks, and brand names. Information flows include databases and information networks. The parties involved may be individuals (e.g., tourists and individual investors buying foreign stocks or bonds), companies (private or public), company clusters (e.g., alliances), government bodies (e.g., central banks), and international institutions (e.g., the World Bank, the International Monetary Fund). Of these, companies are the dominant player. They are the primary economic agent facilitating and gaining (or suffering) from globalization. Their activities crossing national boundaries are often called **international transactions.** Their international transactions are manifested mainly in international trade and international investment. **International trade** occurs when a company exports goods or services to buyers (importers) in another country. **International investment** occurs when the company invests resources in business activities outside its home country.

Any firm, regardless of its size, that is engaged in international business is defined in this book as an **international firm.** A firm that has directly invested abroad and has at least one working affiliate in a foreign country (e.g., a factory, a branch office) over which it maintains effective control, is defined in this book as a **multinational enterprise,** or **MNE.** Please note that there are multiple definitions of the MNE, which are mostly arbitrary (for instance, one definition requires presence in at least six foreign locations, another that the firm has a presence in all major regions—North America, Europe, and Asia). For the sake of clarity, however, we provide a standard working definition.

International companies are the beneficiaries of, as well as the reason for, the growing interdependence among nations. Motorola has 1,100 facilities in 45 countries, employing 140,000 people worldwide. In 1999, 57 percent of its revenues came from foreign operations. Companies like Motorola can be listed and raise capital in financial markets around the world, including New York, London, Paris, Zurich, Singapore, Tokyo, and Hong Kong. Both large and small firms can benefit from competitively priced labor, cheap resources, and enormous market opportunities by shifting their production facilities to emerging economies such as China, India, Brazil, and Russia, while benefiting from the high skill level available in places such as Europe and Israel to do much of their development and design work there. Levi Strauss jeans and other apparel are made by subcontractors in Bangladesh, and are then sold in markets throughout the world. IBM and Microsoft software is written by Indian software developers based in both India and the United States. Such activities involve the movement of capital, people, knowledge, and products from one country to another. They are a consequence of, as well as the facilitator of, the interdependence among nation-states of the world.

International versus Domestic Business

International business is the outgrowth of domestic business. In fact, most major corporations that are active in today's international scene started their operations in the domestic market. Leading Japanese automakers such as Toyota, Honda, and Mitsubishi started their operations in their domestic market before beginning to export to other countries. As the magnitude of their operations grew, they found it profitable or otherwise necessary to build their plants and facilities in other countries, most notably, the United States. By the end of 1999, Japanese carmakers were manufacturing about one million vehicles in North America. Companies or individuals that actively invest and operate in another country without a home base are called **international entrepreneurs.** They may set up international new ventures abroad and operate these ventures using their experience, networks, expertise, and flexibility. Many Hong Kong investors in mainland China, for example, do not have any home base (hence nicknamed "suitcase company") in Hong Kong, but are active in trade and investment activities on the mainland. Recent years saw the emergence of "born international" firms, especially in the high-tech sector, which exported their products before selling anything in their domestic market. Nasdaq-traded Israeli firm Checkpoint, a leader in the software security segment, is one such company.

Although international business is often an extension of domestic business, it is significantly different from the latter, mainly due to the differences in **environmental dynamics** and **operational nature.** Environmentally, the diversity that exists between countries with regard to their currency, inflation and interest rates, accounting practices, cultures, social customs, business practices, laws, government regulations, and political stability is among the many reasons for the complexity of international business. Therefore, international business is usually riskier than domestic business. For instance, variations in inflation, currency, taxation, and interest rates among different nations have a significant impact on the profitability of an international firm. For a firm that is borrowing and investing in a foreign country, higher interest rates, tax rates, and inflation rates mean higher cost of operation and lower profitability. On the other hand, for a firm that is depositing money in a foreign bank, higher interest rates mean a higher return. Similarly, when the euro goes down in value against the U.S. dollar, U.S. exporters to the EU will receive (unless hedging their currency risk) a lesser amount of dollars for their transaction denominated in euro, while U.S. importers of EU goods will be able to either lower the cost of the imports or increase their profitability. Cultural clash is not rare in international business. For instance, when a general manager of Tropical Food Ltd, a small American food processing business, visited Madagascar seeking opportunities to import spices to the United States, his first few days in the country were characterized by culture shock as he endeavored to understand the workings of this society.

International companies also face different industrial environments than domestic companies. Coca-Cola receives payment in multiple currencies and needs to convert and protect its values; it must decide on effective tax strategies in environments with different accounting methods; select the most appropriate human resources for each market, and so forth. These issues are indicative of those of other international companies, as well as their consumers, employees, regulators, and competitors. Market demand and supply conditions in a foreign country are inevitably different from those in a home country. These differences and complexities create more opportunities as well as more risks and uncertainties for international companies than for domestic businesses. However, if one is concerned with the diversification of his/her financial portfolio (e.g., stocks or bonds) or product portfolio, presence abroad may sometimes helps mitigate risks for investors or firms. Broadly, **risk** refers to unpredictability of operational and financial outcomes. **Uncertainty** refers to the unpredictability of environmental or organizational conditions that affect firm performance. Uncertainty about environmental or organizational conditions increases the unpredictability of corporate performance, and therefore, increases risk.

Operationally, international business tends to be more difficult and costly to manage than economic activities in a single country. Benefits might not be realized if an international firm cannot run a complex business effectively. Local employees and expatriates (i.e., people who were sent to a foreign location from the home headquarters) may have trouble getting along with each other because of cultural and language differences. The cultural diversity encountered when operating in several countries may create problems of communication, coordination, and motivation. Organizational principles and managerial philosophies may differ widely across nations, thus heightening the complexity of operation and management of international business. The extent of differences varies. For example, operational complexities arising from cultural differences may be greater for American executives in most of Asia or Africa than in Europe.

Why Do Firms Expand Internationally?

Generally, the motivations for conducting international business include **market motives, economic motives,** and **strategic motives.** The motives will vary from one business activity to another, producing multiple motivations for the international firm with a broad scope of activities in different parts of the globe.

Market Motives

Market motives can be **offensive** or **defensive.** An offensive motive is to seize market opportunities in foreign countries through trade or investment. Amway, Avon, and Mary Kay all entered China in the early 1990s in search of opportunities in China's direct marketing business. During 1995–1998, for instance, Amway earned more than $178 million in sales there. Besides having the largest population and one of the fastest-growing economies in the world, China's strong culture of personal connections and the pervasiveness of close-knit families and friends helped make the country the world's biggest direct-selling market. That the Chinese government later outlawed direct selling altogether exemplifies the inherent risk in doing business abroad.

Formerly a rice paddy, Pudong, China, has been a magnet for foreign investment in the last decade.

A defensive motive is to protect and hold a firm's market power or competitive position in the face of threats from domestic rivalry or changes in government policies. Dell, the world's leading personal computer-systems company, invested in Europe, Asia, Latin America, and Africa partly because of strong competition in the U.S. domestic market. Similarly, the voluntary restriction of exports to the United States of Japanese automobiles in 1980 prompted Toyota, Honda, and Nissan to build car manufacturing plants in the United States. Similarly, many North American and Asian companies in computer and electronics industries have invested heavily in European countries in order to bypass various barriers against imports from non-European Union members. (As of 2000, the Union members were Great Britain, Ireland, France, Germany, the Netherlands, Belgium, Luxembourg, Italy, Greece, Spain, Denmark, Portugal, Austria, Sweden, and Finland.)

Economic Motives

Firms go internationally to increase their return through higher revenues and/or lower costs. International trade or investment is a vehicle enabling the company to benefit from the differences in costs of labors, natural resources, and capital, as well as the differences in regulatory treatments, such as taxation, between domestic and foreign countries. For example, more than 2,000 plants have sprung up near the U.S.–Mexican border. These plants take advantage of cheap labor to assemble American-made components for re-export to the United States. Similarly, many companies have expanded into Asia, seeking cheap labor or cheap resources. Fossil, a leading producer of wrist watches, opted to locate its overseas manufacturing headquarters in East Asia rather than in its home country, the United States. Firms such as Motorola, Boeing, Microsoft, Lucent Technology, Compaq, Intel, Kodak, Otis, and Coca-Cola established production facilities in China's special economic zones or open coastal cities in order to attain a significantly lower taxation rate than that applicable in the United States.

Strategic Motives

Firms often participate in international business for strategic reasons. They may intend to capitalize on their distinctive resources or capabilities already developed at home (e.g., technologies and economy of scale). By deploying these resources or capabilities abroad or increasing production through international trade, firms may be able to increase their cash inflows. Firms may also go international to be the first-mover in the target foreign market before a major competitor gets in. This may create some strategic benefits for the company such as technological leadership, brand image, customer loyalty, and competitive position. Additionally, firms may benefit from vertical integration involving different countries. For example, a company in the oil exploration and drilling business may integrate "downstream" by acquiring or building an oil refinery in a foreign country that has a market for its refined products. Conversely, a company that has strong distribution channels (e.g., gas stations) in a country but needs a steady source of supply of gasoline at predictable prices, may integrate "upstream" and acquire an oil producer and refiner in another country.

Yet another strategic motive is to follow the company's major customers abroad (often termed "piggybacking"). Japanese tire maker Bridgestone found itself in the U.S. market when its customers—Japanese car makers—exported their cars, with Bridgestone tires mounted on them. Other suppliers of Honda, Nissan, and Toyota followed suit, many eventually establishing manufacturing operations in the United States. Bridgestone took over U.S. tire manufacturer Firestone to become one of the leading global tire makers. Since responsiveness and product adaptation are becoming increasingly critical for business success, proximity to foreign customers is an important driver of overseas investment.

Interim Summary

1. Globalization does not simply allow a firm to apply its strategies and policies to another country. Pressures to maintain national identity and solidarity must be considered when adapting to the global market.

2. International business refers to business activities that involve the transfer of resources, goods, services, knowledge, skills, or information across national boundaries.

3. International business is usually more complex than domestic business due to the differences in environmental dynamics and operational nature.

4. If an international business is not run effectively, the benefit of doing business internationally may turn into a drawback because of the costs and difficulties associated with managing activities in many countries.

THE STRUCTURE OF THIS BOOK

This book is not about globalization per se but about conducting international business in a global and rapidly changing environment. It will teach you the basic concepts, principles, procedures and practices in international business, as well as provide you with an understanding of the environments in which it is conducted. This should enable you to "play the game" of international business effectively, responsibly, and ethically.

The structure of this book is based on a vision of international business as a proactive managerial undertaking. Thus, the sequence consists of a description of the major international activities and the players that pursue them, the environments in which they operate, the institutions governing their transactions, their strategies and design, and the various functional areas that conduct specialized international business activities. A more detailed outline of the chapters follows.

Part 1 introduces three core topics in international business: international trade in Chapter 2 (imports/exports), foreign direct investment in Chapter 3 (e.g., establishing foreign subsidiaries), and the major "players" in international business in Chapter 4 (the more traditional multinational enterprise hailing from a developed country, the rising multinationals from developing economies, and the small- and medium-size international company).

Part 2 discusses the environment of international business. Understanding the environment is essential if we are to understand the motivations and nature of home and host country firms as well as explain the features that draw or inhibit trade and investment in a host country. We start with country competitiveness (Chapter 5), a link to trade, foreign investment, and the multinational firm, but also a product of the endowments described in this part and the strategies undertaken by nations, industries, and firms. We proceed with culture (Chapter 6), a somewhat intangible yet crucial facet of international business that is too often underestimated. We also discuss the political and legal environments that establish the ground rules within which international business operates (Chapter 7).

Part 3 focuses on global markets and institutions. It covers international economic integration and organizations (Chapter 8), the international monetary system, and financial markets (Chapter 9). These global institutions are key elements of globalization infrastructure. They affect either regulatory frameworks or market efficiency for cross-border transactions. Global institutions are part of the environments in which they operate but they also participate in shaping the international business environment within which transactions take place.

Part 4 deals with international business strategies, the starting point for a firm's operations in international markets. It begins with a chapter on international entry strategies (Chapter 10), followed by a chapter on the organization design of the multinational firm, namely how it organizes its operations in order to execute its set strategy (Chapter 11). Chapter 12 focuses on building and managing global strategic alliances, an increasingly popular yet problematic type of organization. Finally, Chapter 13 is on global research and development (R & D), a crucial element in an increasingly knowledge-based economy.

Part 5 deals with the separate international business functions. The aim is to illustrate the main challenges international business poses to each of the functional business areas. Thus, we present chapters on finance (e.g., raising capital) (Chapter 14), accounting (e.g., transfer pricing issues) (Chapter 15), marketing (e.g., advertising, pricing) and supply chain (logistic issues such as distribution modes) (Chapter 16), and human resource management (e.g., staffing) (Chapter 17).

Part 6 highlights emerging issues in international business. One emerging topic is global e-commerce (Chapter 18). Despite the bursting of the "tech bubble," e-commerce continues to be important and is likely to grow in the years ahead. The nature of e-commerce challenges some of the key ways of doing business internationally and the regulatory systems that govern them. E-commerce also exposes firms that hitherto have engaged in domestic business only to the vagaries of international commerce. The other emerging topic, ethics and corruption, has long been associated with international business, especially in developing economies. In recent years, however, it became more visible and more openly debated. Part of the reason is increased transparency, the other, a possible increase in the scope of the phenomenon. Technological advances and increased globalization have opened the door to piracy, counterfeiting, and similar phenomena on an unprecedented scale. This assault on property rights is having a major influence on a firm's global strategy and operational performance. It is also correlated with globalization: the more global the country, the less likely it is to engage in corrupt practices. As Chapter 19 will show, however, ethics and corruption are key ingredients for the workings of any economy.

The book emphasizes the integration of topical areas. For instance, although culture is discussed in a separate chapter, its impact on environments, institutions, and firms is apparent throughout. Thus, when we discuss accounting, we note the correlations of certain accounting and auditing systems with cultural patterns, and when we discuss human resource management, we examine the role of cultural differences on expatriate adjustment. The manager's role is, after all, integrative, and this book reflects this reality. Other integration mechanisms are the **country box** and **industry box** in each of the subsequent chapters. These boxes provide a more in-depth glimpse into a particular national market and into a particular industry, respectively. Readers should use these boxes not only to learn about the country or industry being highlighted but also to question whether things would have been different in another country or for another industry.

The book is based on keen awareness of the changing and intensifying nature of globalization and global competition. Whereas some observers see globalization as leading to a more homogeneous world, we view it as a continually changing mosaic whose diverse pieces come in more frequent contact with each other, affecting each and every piece in a unique manner. The role of management is to monitor, understand, and respond to this changing environment with sensitivity and respect for those differences and with a realization that international business decisions influence a great variety of constituencies in multiple locations. This book is a reflection of this philosophy.

CHAPTER SUMMARY

1. The signs of globalization are all around us, apparent in the products we buy, the services we consume, and the companies we work for. Globalization brings more interdependence among nations but does not necessarily make them more similar to each other.

2. Globalization is a complex phenomenon that carries both negative and positive consequences. It has winners and losers depending on region, industry, profession, and skill level.

3. Globalization intensifies the ongoing tension between forces for standardization and consolidation on the one hand, and a need for localization and adaptation on the other hand. This tension

represents one of the main challenges of doing business internationally.

4. International business consists of business activities and resource transfer across national boundaries undertaken by international firms. Firms that have directly invested in at least one foreign market are considered multinational enterprises (MNEs) in this book.

5. International business is significantly more complex than domestic business and often requires different types and scale of resources and capabilities. Many firms have been successful domestically but failed to replicate that success abroad.

CHAPTER NOTES

[1] WTO Statistics on Globalization, 2001.
[2] A. T. Kearney, "Globalization's last hurrah?", *Foreign Policy,* Jan./Feb. 2002.
[3] WTO Statistics on Globalization.
[4] World Investment Report 2000 (UNCTAD).
[5] W. R. Cline, Institute of International Economics, cited in *The Economist,* September 29, 2001.
[6] A. T. Kearney, "Globalization's last hurrah?", *Foreign Policy,* Jan./Feb. 2002.

PART ONE

Concepts and Theories in International Business

CHAPTER 2: International Trade Theory and Application

CHAPTER 3: Foreign Direct Investment Theory and Application

CHAPTER 4: The Multinational Enterprise

International Trade Theory and Application

DO YOU KNOW

1. What are the major theories of international trade? In your opinion, what is the applicability of those theories in today's environment?

2. How do governments limit trade with other countries, and what are their reasons for doing so?

3. How do different technological levels define a country's trade relationships, and why do countries with similar levels of technology trade more than countries with disparate technology levels?

OPENING CASE   The Banana War

In April of 1999, the World Trade Organization (WTO) ruled that the European Union (EU) violated international trade law by establishing quotas and tariffs on bananas from Latin America imported by U.S.-based Chiquita Brands International, Dole Foods, and Fresh Del Monte Produce. At the same time, the EU allowed licensed access for bananas from former colonies in Africa, Asia, and the Caribbean. According to the WTO ruling, the arrangement cost the United States $191 million in trade opportunities.

The banana business is hardly lucrative. Retail prices and sales of bananas have been falling for years, margins are narrow, the crop is susceptible to disease, and transportation is tricky. While European banana prices are double those in the United States, the growers hardly benefit. The Center for Interna-

tional Economics in Canberra, Australia estimates that only $150 million of the $2 billion this arrangement costs European consumers finds its way to the banana growers. The main beneficiaries are the firms that hold the banana import licenses.

Still, bananas represent a major export for many developing nations. In the small Caribbean nation of St. Lucia, bananas bring in 56 percent of export revenues. Such nations find it difficult to substitute bananas' high output with other crops. Bananas are also labor intensive, providing a crucial source of employment. The Latin American nations whose banana exports have been restricted in Europe are hopeful that the WTO ruling will eventually bear fruit. In the spring of 2001, the United States and the EU finally reached an agreement that would alter the tariff and quota structure until their removal in 2006, ending nine years of the Banana War—or so it seemed. During the Doha meeting of the WTO in the fall of 2001, Ecuador brought up the issue again during an all-night session, only to be thwarted by a stunned WTO official repeating "They are talking about bananas. They are talking about bananas." ■

Source: G. Fairclough and D. McDermott, "The Banana Business Is Rotten, So Why Do People Fight Over It?" *Wall Street Journal* August 9, 1999; N. Dunne, "U.S. Lists Sanctions over Bananas," *Financial Times*, April 10, 1999, p. 4; A. DePalma, "U.S. and Europeans Agree on Deal to End Banana Trade War," *The New York Times*, April 12, 2001, C1; H. Cooper and G. Winestock, "Tough Talkers," *Wall Street Journal*, November 15, 2001, A1.

INTERNATIONAL TRADE THEORIES

International (or foreign) trade is the exchange of goods and services across borders. The opening case suggests that bananas represent the major export commodity for some Latin American countries and that their economies are susceptible to international market conditions on bananas and other agricultural commodities. Industrialized countries such as EU members and the United States have a markedly different export structure. Their primary exports are technology-intensive (e.g., PCs), knowledge-intensive (e.g., software), capital-intensive (e.g., construction machinery and equipment), or a combination of all of the above (e.g., telecom products, pharmaceuticals, airplanes, and automobiles). You may wonder why export structures vary across countries, why nations do not mimic each other, and why they have different vulnerabilities to trade conditions. The answers can be found in the following international trade theories. Following their introduction, we will comment on the merits and limitations of each theory.

The Mercantilist Doctrine

Emerging in England in the mid-sixteenth century, **mercantilism** is the first (or preclassical) theory of international trade. The doctrine placed great faith in the ability of a government to improve the well-being of its residents using a system of centralized controls. Under mercantilism, the government had two goals in foreign economic policy. The first goal was to increase the wealth of the nation by acquiring gold. Mercantilists identified national wealth with the size of a nation's reserves of precious metals (which could then be used to hire mercenary armies). The second policy goal was to extract trade gains from foreigners through regulations and controls so as to achieve a surplus in the balance of trade through maximizing exports (e.g., subsidies) and minimizing imports (e.g., tariffs and quotas).

In modern economy, however, gold reserves are merely potential claims against real goods on foreigners. In addition, as demonstrated by David Hume in 1752,[1] an influx of gold would increase the domestic price level and boost the price of exports. Hence, the country holding the gold would lose the competitive edge in price that had enabled it to acquire the gold earlier by exporting more than it imported. In contrast, the loss of gold in the foreign nation would reduce prices there and reinforce its exports. Today, gold reserves represent a minor portion of national foreign exchange reserves. Governments use such reserves to intervene in foreign exchange markets (e.g., selling some of these reserves in exchange for local currencies) so as to influence foreign exchange rates.

Mercantilism also overlooked other sources of a country's wealth accumulation such as the quantity of its capital, the skill of its work force, and the strength of other production inputs such as land and natural resources. In Chapter 5 we explain in detail that a country's wealth today is accumulated mainly through superior competitiveness, which is in turn determined not only by the abundance of resources but also by national policies, industrial structure, firm efficiency, and individual productivity.

Absolute Advantage Theory

In his 1776 landmark treatise, *An Inquiry into the Nature and Causes of the Wealth of Nations*,[2] Adam Smith from the United Kingdom introduced the doctrine of **laissez-faire** to international trade. Laissez-faire means literally "let make freely" or, more generally, "freedom of enterprise and freedom of commerce." Elimination of the ubiquitous regulation was the keystone of nineteenth-century liberalism. Smith argued that all nations would benefit from unregulated, free trade that would

Exhibit 2–1
Labor hours required to produce one unit of a good

	Wheat (1 unit)	Coffee (1 unit)
United States	2	8
Colombia	10	2

Colombia remains one of the main coffee growers in the world.

permit individual countries to specialize in goods they were best suited to produce because of natural and acquired advantages. Smith's theory of trade has come to be known as the theory of absolute advantage. This theory stated that a nation's imports should consist of goods made more efficiently abroad while exports should consist of goods made more efficiently at home. According to this theory, Caribbean countries should export bananas (which have absolute advantage at home) and import apples from the state of Washington (which have absolute advantage in the United States).

The absolute advantage theory holds that the market would reach an efficient end by itself. Government intervention in the economic life of a nation and in trade relations among nations (e.g., in the form of tariffs) is counterproductive. A nation would benefit from free trade simply because imports would cost less than domestic products it otherwise had to produce. Unlike the mercantilist doctrine that a nation could only gain from trade if the trading partner lost (i.e., zero-sum game), the absolute advantage theory argued that both countries would gain from the efficient allocation of national resources globally.

Exhibit 2–1 provides a simple illustration of how a country gains from free trade. It shows that the United States has an absolute advantage in producing wheat whereas Colombia has an absolute advantage in producing coffee. It takes 2 labor hours to produce a unit of wheat in the United States whereas it takes 10 hours to produce a unit of wheat in Colombia. Therefore, the United States should specialize in the production of wheat. Similarly it takes 8 hours to produce a unit of coffee in the United States and 2 hours to produce a unit of coffee in Colombia. Therefore, Colombia should specialize in the production of coffee. Smith argued that in a situation such as this, both countries benefit from specialization and trade. World production would increase if both countries specialized in the production of the good in which they have an absolute advantage and then traded to obtain the other goods in which they have an absolute disadvantage.

Comparative Advantage Theory

The absolute advantage theory could not explain a situation where, for example, one country is more efficient than another in producing *all* goods. Would it still pay for both countries to trade if one country were more efficient than the other in production of all goods? David Ricardo, a nineteenth-century English economist, answered this question in his 1817 landmark book *On the Principles of Political Economy and Taxation.* He stated that both countries would gain from trade even if one were more efficient in all goods.[3] Thus, it was the **comparative advantage** of a nation in producing a good relative to the other nation that determined international trade flows. To illustrate this, Ricardo used the example in Exhibit 2–2. In England a gallon of wine costs 120 and a yard of cloth 100 hours of work, while in Portugal the real cost (labor cost) of wine and cloth amounts to 80 and 90 hours of work, respectively. Portugal thus has an absolute advantage over England in the production of wine as well as in the production of cloth, because the labor cost of production for each unit of the two commodities is less in Portugal than in England.

Exhibit 2–2

Labor hours required to produce one unit of a good

	Wine (1 gallon)	Cloth (1 yard)
England	120	100
Portugal	80	90

To demonstrate that trade between England and Portugal will, even in this case, lead to gains for both countries, it is useful to introduce the concept of **opportunity cost.** The opportunity cost for a good X is the amount of other goods which have to be given up in order to produce one unit of X. Exhibit 2–3 shows the opportunity costs for producing wine and cloth in Portugal and England, based on the information given in Exhibit 2–2.

A country has a comparative advantage in producing a good if the opportunity cost for producing the good is lower at home than in the other country. Exhibit 2–3 shows that Portugal has the lower opportunity cost of the two countries in producing wine, while England has the lower opportunity cost in producing cloth. Thus Portugal has a comparative advantage in the production of wine and England has a comparative advantage in the production of cloth. Once trade between the two countries is launched, England will export cloth and import wine. As long as the opportunity costs for the same commodities differ between countries, open trade will result in gains for each country through specialization in producing a commodity (or commodities) in which a country has comparative advantage vis-à-vis its trading partner(s).

It is important to understand the *sources* of comparative advantages. The immediate source of trade is a difference in the price of the same commodity between different countries, thus the difference in opportunity costs. But why does such a difference arise? Price is essentially determined by the interaction of supply and demand. Therefore, a price differential derives from differences in demand conditions, supply conditions, or both. On the demand side, differences in tastes and incomes will cause differences in patterns of demand, and hence, prices. When two countries share similar income levels and consumer tastes, however, income is unlikely to be a major source of demand differences. Similarly, differences in tastes are unlikely to account for significant demand differences—and thus for trade—between countries belonging to the same social-cultural matrix. On the supply side, we know that differences in supply patterns result from differences in the patterns of production costs.

Thus, in today's world economy, comparative advantage must be explained by reference to differences in **comparative production cost,** which further depends on the commodity's production process (especially the state of technology) and on the prices of **production factors** such as labor, land, capital, and natural resources. Factor prices, in turn, are related to the availability of those factors in the national economy. Economists refer to inputs to the production process as production factors. They then refer to conditions (availability and cost) of factors of production as the country's factor endowment. In today's global economy, quality levels of production factors (e.g., knowledge and productivity of workers or service and efficiency of a banking sector) become even more important for improving a country's exports

Exhibit 2–3

Opportunity costs for producing wine and cloth

	Opportunity Cost for Wine	Opportunity Cost for Cloth
England	120/100 = 12/10	100/120 = 10/12
Portugal	80/90 = 8/9	90/80 = 9/8

or attracting foreign investments. In today's international business environment, therefore, factor endowment should also include the quality of production factors. However, because inter-country differences in technology were relatively minor in the nineteenth century, international variations in comparative advantage were attributed primarily to different national endowments in terms of availability and cost. This was the theoretical root of the **Heckscher-Ohlin theorem.**

Heckscher-Ohlin Theorem

The Heckscher-Ohlin (or H-O) theorem is named for its authors, Eli Heckscher (in 1919) and Bertil Ohlin (in 1933), both Swedish economists. It explained the link between national factor endowments and comparative advantage of nations.[4] The theorem states that a country has a comparative advantage in commodities whose production is intensive in its relatively abundant factor, and will hence export those commodities. Meanwhile, a country would import commodities whose production is intensive in the country's relatively scarce factor of production. Thus, differences in comparative advantage are attributed to the differences in the structure of the economy. A country is relatively more efficient in those activities that are better suited to its economic structure and does best with what it has most of. If, for example, the United States is more abundant in capital relative to labor than other countries, it will export such commodities (e.g., motor vehicles) whose production requires a greater use of capital than other products do, and will import labor-intensive commodities (e.g., clothing).[5]

Several assumptions underlie the Heckscher-Ohlin theorem. First, it is assumed that countries vary in the availability of various factors of production. Second, while each commodity is assumed to have its own specific production function, the production function is assumed to be identical anywhere in the world. **Production function** shows the amount of output that can be produced by using a given quantity of capital and labor. In other words, this theorem assumes that the same amount of the same input will produce the same output in any country. Third, the theorem holds that technology is constant in all trading countries and that the same technology is used in all those countries. Finally, it assumes that the conditions of demand for production factors are the same in all countries. With identical demand conditions, differences in the relative supply of a factor of production will lead to differences in the relative price of that factor between the two countries.

The H-O theorem also implied international equalization of the prices of production factors under free trade—the so-called **Heckscher-Ohlin law of factor price equalization.** It argued that the exchange of goods between agricultural and industrial countries would result in an increase in the previously relatively low levels of land rents and a drop of the high level of industrial wages in the agricultural country. In the industrial country, however, the opposite change in factor prices occurs—an increase in industrial wages and a decrease in land rents. In addition to identical production factors across different countries, the theorem assumed other conditions under which free commodity trade equalizes factor prices: (1) free competition in all markets; (2) absence of transportation costs; and (3) all commodities continue to be produced in both countries after free trade has begun.

The implications of the H-O theorem for world trade are highlighted below:

1. Trade as well as trade gains should be greatest between countries with the greatest differences in economic structure;

2. Trade should cause countries to specialize more in producing and exporting goods that are distinctly different from their imports;

3. Trade policy should take the form of trade restrictions rather than trade stimulation;

4. Countries should export goods that make intensive use of their relatively abundant factors;

5. Free trade should equalize factor prices between countries with fairly similar relative factor endowments but not between countries with markedly different endowments;

6. Factor prices should be nearly equal between countries with more liberal mutual trade;

7. International investment should be stimulated by differences in factor endowments, and international trade and international investment should be negatively correlated.

The Leontief Paradox

The central notion of the H-O theorem is that a country exports goods that make intensive use of the country's abundant factor and imports goods that make intensive use of the country's scarce factor. Wassily Leontief, the 1973 winner of the Nobel Prize in Economics, attempted in 1953 to test this proposition for the United States. Using input-output tables covering 200 industries and 1947 trade figures, he found that U.S. exports were apparently labor-intensive and its imports capital-intensive. Since this result contradicted the predictions of the H-O theorem, it has become known as the **Leontief paradox**. The Leontief study motivated further empirical research. The empirical evidence accumulated since then shows many paradoxical results and contains serious challenges to the general applicability of a factor-endowments explanation in other countries such as Germany, India, Canada, and Japan.

Exhibit 2–4 shows the principal findings of Leontief's study in 1953. Since the ratio of imports to exports in terms of capital per worker-year (18,184/14,015) was about 1.30, U.S. exports were less capital-intensive (or more labor-intensive) than U.S. import replacements. Instead of capital-intensive exports and labor-intensive import replacements, Leontief showed that a representative bundle of U.S. import replacements required 30 percent more capital per worker-year to produce than a representative bundle of U.S. exports.

The Leontief paradox stimulated a search for explanations, among them:[6]

- *Demand bias for capital-intensive goods.* The U.S. demand for capital-intensive goods is so strong that it reverses the U.S. comparative cost advantage in such goods.
- *Existence of trade barriers.* U.S. labor-intensive imports were reduced by trade barriers (e.g., tariffs and quotas) imposed to protect and save American jobs.

Exhibit 2–4
Capital position in U.S exports and imports

	Exports	Import Replacements
Capital (in 1947 $)	2,550,780	3,091,339
Labor (worker-years)	182	170
Capital per worker-year ($)	14,015	18,184

Source: W. Leontief, 1953. Domestic production and foreign trade: The American capital position reexamined. *Proceedings of the American Philosophical Society*, vol. 97 (Nov.), pp. 332–349.

- *Importance of natural resources.* Leontief considered only capital and labor inputs, leaving out natural resource inputs. Because natural resources and capital are often used together in production, a country that imports capital-intensive goods may be actually importing natural resource-intensive goods. For example, the United States imports crude oil, which is capital-intensive.
- *Prevalence of factor-intensity reversals.* A **factor-intensity reversal** occurs when the relative prices of labor and capital change over time, which changes the relative mix of capital and labor in the production process of a commodity from being capital-intensive to labor-intensive (or vice versa).

Human Skills and Technology-Based Views

The aforementioned explanations were subsequently found to have offered only a partial explanation of the Leontief paradox.[7] Searching for better explanations of the sources of comparative advantage, several scholars challenged the conventional theory of trade which assumed technology and human skills equivalence among different nations.[8] Rather than a separate theory, the human skills and technology-based view is regarded as a refinement of the conventional theory of trade. It added two new factors of production, namely **human skills** and **technology gaps,** to the explanation of comparative advantage sources.

Human skill theorists explained the source of comparative advantage in terms of the comparative abundance of professional skills and other high-level human skills. According to Donald B. Keesing, these include (1) scientists and engineers, (2) technicians and draftsmen, (3) managers, (4) other professionals, and (5) skilled manual workers. Keesing argued that U.S. export industries employ higher proportions of highly skilled labor than do import-competing industries. Thus, the U.S. exports more skill-intensive manufactures than do other countries. Studies treating professional and skilled human resources as capital reversed the Leontief paradox and found that U.S. exports were actually capital-intensive.[9] The relative abundance of professional and other highly skilled labor in the United States is thus a major source of its comparative advantage in manufacturing products.

Technology theorists argued that certain countries have special advantage as innovators of new products. They also postulated that there was an **imitation lag** that prevents other countries from immediately duplicating the new products of the innovating country. These two conditions gave rise to **technology gaps** in those products that afford the innovating country an export monopoly during the period of imitation lag.[10] In other words, for the duration of the imitation gap, the innovator is the only exporter on world markets. Similarly, when a firm discovers a different and more advanced production technique, it will enjoy a cost advantage and dominate the world market for a while (especially if its innovation is legally protected from imitators by the international patent system). For example, it was found that transportation, electrical machinery, instruments, chemicals, and nonelectrical machinery were the five strongest industries in the United States in terms of R&D, which performed 89.4 percent of U.S. total R&D in 1962. These five industries accounted for 72 percent of U.S. exports of manufactures in the same year.[11] As long as technological progress is made, the technology gap would serve as a major source of comparative advantage. As such, technology, like human skills, is a separate factor of production whose relative abundance or scarcity in a country determines comparative advantage or disadvantage in technology-intensive products. This notion, despite being more than four decades old, still has strong implications for country competitiveness (as discussed in Chapter 5), competitive advantage of MNEs (Chapter 4), and global R&D management (Chapter 13).

The Product Life-Cycle Model

Closely related to the technology gap view is the **product life-cycle model**, proposed by Raymond Vernon in the mid-1960s.[12] Vernon's theory further developed the imitation-gap approach by suggesting that changes occur in the input requirements of a new product as it becomes established in a market and standardized in production. As the product cycle develops, the cost advantage will change accordingly, and a comparative advantage in innovative capacity may be offset by a cost disadvantage. To explain the behavior of U.S. exports of manufactures, Vernon developed a four-stage model assuming that the export effects of product innovation are undermined by technological diffusion and lower costs abroad. This life-cycle model includes the following four stages:

1. The United States has an export monopoly in a new product;
2. Foreign production of this product begins;
3. Foreign production of this product becomes competitive in export markets;
4. The United States becomes an importer of this no-longer-new product.

Vernon postulated that U.S. producers are likely to be the first to exploit market opportunities for a technology-intensive new product. They will first produce this new product in the United States regardless of the costs of production inputs in other countries because of close proximity to customers and suppliers. In this first stage, U.S. producers have a monopoly in export markets and they proceed to build up sales with no concern for foreign competition. During the second stage, producers in other industrial countries start to manufacture the product whose design and production is now standardized. Consequently, the overall growth rate of U.S. exports declines. During the third stage, foreign producers displace U.S. exports in the remaining export markets. Finally, foreign producers achieve sufficient competitive strength arising from economies of scale and lower labor costs to export to the U.S. market.

Exhibit 2–5 graphically presents the product cycle model of international trade for the innovating country (e.g., the United States) and an imitating country (e.g., Germany or Mexico), respectively. As Exhibit 2–5 shows, the innovating country starts production of the new product at time 0, but it does not export that product until time A when production exceeds domestic consumption. At time B, foreign production begins to compete against the innovating country's exports which, in turn, begin to fall. Exports come to an end at time C as the innovating country becomes an importer of this no-longer-new product.

Exhibit 2–5
Product cycle model of international trade— innovating country

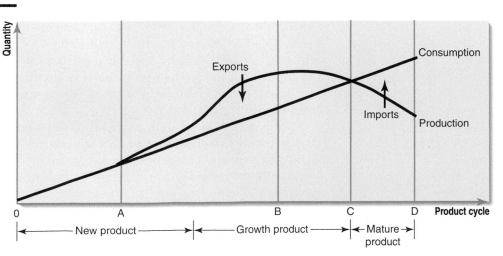

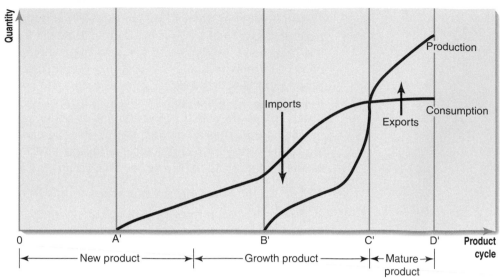

Exhibit 2–6 shows that an imitating country starts to import the new product from the innovating country at time A'. If this imitating country is a high-income, advanced country (e.g., Germany), then time A' most likely coincides with time A in Exhibit 2–5. If, however, it is a low-income, developing country (e.g., Mexico), then time A' will come after time A. Local production begins at time B' when the local market grows to sufficient size and cost conditions favor production against imports. If the imitating country is an advanced country, then B' will coincide with B in Exhibit 2–5. If it is a developing country, B' will come after time B. At time C', when production begins to exceed consumption, the imitating country begins to export, and may export first to third countries and later to the innovating country.

Vernon's theory also suggests that the product cycle model of international trade is associated with the life-cycle stage of the product itself. As the product moves through its life cycle, the life cycle of international trade will change. The *new-product stage* is associated with the first production of the product in the innovating country (0-A) and the early portion of the export monopoly stage (A-B). During this stage, production functions are unstable and techniques used in production are rapidly changing. No economy of scale is reached. This phase is also characterized by a small number of firms and no close substitute products. The *growth-product stage* is associated with the later portion of the export monopoly (A-B) and the start of foreign production (C). During this stage, mass-production methods are used to exploit expanding markets, and therefore high returns are achieved from economy of scale and market growth. Finally, the *mature-product stage* is associated with the third and fourth stages of the product cycle model of international trade (C-D). This last stage is characterized by production of standardized products with stable techniques and intense price competition.

The product life-cycle theory helps to explain changes in production and trade in new product lines. It is generally true that the United States has been the principal innovator and production has spread rapidly to other countries that have been technically competent (e.g., Germany) and to those which have had a comparative advantage in terms of cheap labor (e.g., Mexico). It is also useful to remember that since the development of the model in the 1960s, the share of the United States in global GDP declined substantially, with other countries, such as Germany and Japan emerging as innovators. Also, some countries (e.g., the United Kingdom) were innovators of major products such as the passenger jet but failed to dominate the market for those products.

Several facts emerged in connection with product cycles:

1. The export performance of the mature, principal innovating country is better for new products than it is for products approaching maturity;

2. Technology is simplified as the maturing process continues, and products that are initially produced with skilled labor can later be produced by an increased use of automation combined with the use of unskilled labor;

3. The relationship between innovating and imitating countries changes over time. Countries that were once the principal innovators might fall into relative decline. Britain, for example, was the first country to build railways, at the time with a narrow gauge and small goods wagons. Later, this investment proved to be a drag on progress and subsequent imitators like Germany and the United States adapted their railways more successfully to new technological and economic conditions;

4. International trade may increase in the later stages of the product cycle. As a consumer good matures and income rises, products once seen as luxury (e.g., cell phone) become a necessity. General growth of *per capita* incomes broadens the market for mass production.

Linder's Income-Preference Similarity Theory

When you observe the actual pattern of international trade since the 1970s (described in the second part of this chapter), you will find a prominent feature: Developed countries trade more with other developed countries. Overall, developed countries among themselves generate about three fourths of total world exports. This fact, by itself, is an indictment of Heckscher-Ohlin's factor-endowment theory. According to the H-O theorem, the incentive to trade is greatest among nations of radically different factor endowments. This means that trade would take place in larger part between developed manufacturing countries and developing countries producing primary products (i.e., natural resource commodities such as oil and petroleum) and labor-intensive goods.

Staffan B. Linder, a Swedish economist, divided international trade into two different categories: primary products (natural resource products) and manufactures.[13] Linder asserts that differences in factor endowments explain trade in natural resource-intensive products but not in manufactures. He argues that the range of a country's manufactured exports is determined by *internal demand*. International trade in manufactures takes place largely among developed nations because nations will only export those goods they manufacture at home and will only manufacture at home those goods for which there is a strong domestic demand. Note, however, that Chapter 4 on the MNE will introduce "born national" enterprises whose very first products are destined for foreign markets.

Linder also contends that the more similar the demand preferences for manufactured goods in two countries (e.g., the United States and the United Kingdom), the more intensive is the potential trade in manufactures between them. If two countries have the same or similar demand structures, then their consumers and investors will demand the same goods with similar degrees of quality and sophistication, a phenomenon known as **preference similarity**. This similarity boosts trade between the two industrialized countries. To explain the determinants of the demand structure, Linder argues that average *per capita* income is the most important one. Countries with high *per capita* income will demand high-quality, "luxury" consumer goods (e.g., motor vehicles) and sophisticated capital goods (e.g., telecommunications equipment and machinery), while low *per capita* income countries will demand low quality, "necessity" consumer goods (e.g., bicycles) and less sophisticated capital goods (e.g., food processing machinery). Consequently, a rich country that has a comparative advantage in the production of high-quality, advanced manufactures will find its big export markets in other affluent countries where people demand such products. Similarly, manufactured exports of the poor countries should find their best markets in other poor countries with similar demand structures. Linder also acknowledged that the effect of *per capita* income levels on trade in manufactures may be constrained or distorted by entrepreneurial ignorance, cultural and political differences, transportation costs, and legislative obstacles such as tariffs.

The New Trade Theory

The set of ideas sometimes referred to as the **new trade theory** was originally expounded in a series of papers by Dixit and Norman, Lancaster, Krugman, Helpman, and Ethier.[14] These theorists argue that countries do not necessarily specialize and trade solely in order to take advantage of their differences; they also trade because of *increasing returns,* which makes specialization advantageous per se. Although this theory is not totally "new," it makes several contributions to the understanding of international trade.

First, the new trade theorists introduce an industrial organization view into trade theory, and include real-life imperfect competition in international trade. They argue that because of economies of scale, there are increasing returns to specialization in many industries. **Economy of scale** is reduction of manufacturing cost per unit as a result of increased production quantity during a given time period. For instance, manufacturing the one-hundred thousandth car is much cheaper than making the first. Because of the presence of substantial scale economies, world demand will actually support only a few firms in an industry (e.g., only Boeing and Airbus remain as makers of large passenger jets).

Second, the new trade theory suggests that *inter-industry trade* (international trade between different industries in different nations) continues to be determined by Heckscher-Ohlin theory. In contrast, *intra-industry trade* (international trade involving the same industry) is largely driven by increasing returns resulting from specialization within the industry. This suggests that comparative advantage from factor endowment differences and increasing returns from economy of scale can coexist because they differ in the application of inter- versus intra-industry trade.

Finally, the new trade theory realizes the importance of externality in international specialization and trade. **Externality** occurs when the actions of one agent directly affect the environment of another agent. For example, firms that cause pollution or noise would have an adverse impact on local residents. In international trade, externalities include government policies, political relations between two countries, history of the importing or exporting country, consumption differences between different cultures, accident and luck (e.g., first entrant of the industry), among others. The new trade theorists contend that these externalities could be the alternatives to comparative advantage as the factors influencing actual patterns of international trade.

The new trade theory has a number of implications. First, it helps explain the Leontief paradox by bringing in the economies-of-scale concept. The theory argues that firms engage in trade because they expect increasing returns from larger economies of scale; such economies may not necessarily be associated with factor endowment differences between importing and exporting countries. Scale economies will likely lead countries to specialize and trade with a similar country in terms of income level or consumption preference. Second, this theory helps explain intra-industry trade, which is a substantial two-way trade (i.e., import and export) that takes place with goods that belong to the same industry. Trade is intended to realize economies of scale, and may not be correlated with differences in factor endowments. Finally, this theory helps explain intra-firm trade, which occurs when import and export activities take place between the subsidiaries of the same MNE. Driven by the prospect of increasing returns, MNEs see intra-firm trade as a facilitator of global integration of upstream and downstream activities. Chapter 4 discusses the MNE in more detail.

INDUSTRY BOX

THE GLOBAL AUTOMOTIVE INDUSTRY

Global trade in the automotive industry is a century old. Almost as soon as the first products appeared, some of the manufacturers (e.g., the Ford Motor Company) began to export their cars. Today, the major exporters of automotive products are also the major importers (e.g., the United States, Germany), supporting Linder's Income-Preference Similarity theory (see table). The largest volume of trade in automotive products involves trade among the countries of western Europe. The numbers are not necessarily balanced, however. For example, as noted earlier in this chapter, Japan exports (and manufactures) many more cars in the United States than the United States exports to and manufactures in Japan, suggesting the impact of other, non-tariff barriers.

Although Mexico's increasing role as a car exporter seems to challenge the view of developed nations exporting to other developed nations, it is in line with the new trade theory, which suggests that intra-industry trade is driven mainly by increasing returns resulting from specialization within the industry. Mexican car exports to the United States contain a substantial content of components imported from the United States. The result, according to Lucinda Vargas of the Federal Reserve Bank of Dallas, is that "in some respects, each country is sending the other essentially the same product but at a different stage of production."

Exports and imports of automotive products of selected economies (million dollars and percentage)

	Exports				Imports		
	Value		Share[a]		Value		Share[a]
	1990 ($Mil)	2000 ($Mil)	2000		1990 ($Mil)	2000 ($Mil)	2000
World	318940	571320	9.2	Argentina	183	—	12.0
Argentina	200	—	7.7	Austria	5521	7745	11.3
Austria	3526	7789	12.2	Belgium-Luxembourg	18481	—	13.9
Belgium-Luxembourg	18046	—	14.2	Brazil	532	4314	7.4
Brazil	2034	4682	8.5	Canada	24640	46276	19.3
Canada	28442	60656	21.9	Finland	2595	2373	7.0
Finland	797	1257	2.8	France	21595	30532	10.0
France	26194	39885	13.4	Germany	30856	42241	8.4
Germany	69955	92167	16.7	Hungary	715	2481	7.7
Hungary	648	4765	17.0	Italy	18090	25314	10.9
Italy	13017	18363	7.7	Japan	7315	9957	2.6
Japan	66230	88082	18.4	Korea, Rep. of	929	—	1.2
Korea, Rep. of	2301	15368	8.9	Mexico	5268	18816	10.3
Mexico	4708	30645	18.4	Netherlands	8244	12606	6.4
Netherlands	4673	8655	4.1	Spain	10133	26308	17.1
Spain	11729	28127	24.7	Sweden	4585	7565	10.4
Sweden	7719	10771	12.4	Turkey	1177	5831	10.8
Turkey	153	1517	5.7	United Kingdom	22821	36078	10.9
United Kingdom	14087	25557	9.0	United States	79320	172727	13.7
United States	32547	67901	8.7				

Source: WTO International Trade Statistics, 2001; "This trade deficit was made in the USA", *The Wall Street Journal*, August 7, 2000, A1.

[a]"Share" refers to the percentage in economy's total merchandise exports or imports.

Theory Assessment

Although none of the theories is capable of explaining the entire range of motives for international trade, they collectively provide invaluable insights into why international trade occurs. With reference to the sources of comparative advantage, differences in factor endowments (i.e., Heckscher-Ohlin theorem) survive as the most general explanation of the pattern of "old" trade (e.g., labor-intensive products). The comparative advantage theory, despite its diminishing power in explaining today's international trade, is still capable of explaining international trade in natural resource products such as bananas (see opening case). When we extend the factor endowments by including skilled labors and technologies, the Heckscher-Ohlin theorem applies to current import and export activities between developed and developing countries. As an example, let us look at trade between Europe and Southeast Asia. Major exports from Europe are technology-intensive, including power generation equipment, petroleum processing machinery, medical equipment, and transportation equipment, whereas exports from Southeast Asia are mostly labor or skill-labor intensive, such as garments, furniture, shoes, rubber products, arts and crafts, and standardized electric and electronics products.

Meanwhile, the technological gap (i.e., human skills and technology-based views) and the product life cycle theories emerge as powerful explanations of trade in "new" products (i.e., manufactures made by skilled workforce using technologies). These skills and technologies are the key stimulus to improving a country's terms of trade, the major concern of both developed and developing countries today. The **terms of trade** is the relative price of exports, that is, the unit price of exports divided by the unit price of imports. The terms of trade improve if the country exports more goods that are associated with advanced human skills and technologies. In this case, the contribution of foreign trade to the nation's economic growth will be stronger. Although the product life-cycle model is less applicable today than at the time of its inception, it still explains key patterns in the evolution of international trade. A nation's import and export structures change over time. Similarly, every new product has its life stages in the global marketplace.

The Leontief paradox and Linder's income-preference similarity theory provide insights on the triggers of international trade for sophisticated manufacturing products and on trade between regions with similar income levels and consumption preferences. These theories view market demand (income levels and demand structure) as important parameters of international trade. Indeed, international trade today is driven not only by national differences in factor endowments but also by national differences in market demand. Intra-regional trade still accounts for a high proportion of world trade because of similarities in income levels and demand structures as well as efficiencies arising from reduced uncertainty and transaction costs. The limitation of these theories is that they did not illuminate how trade activities would take place between two nations sharing similar income levels but with different consumption preferences. Because of this weakness, they seem unable to explain the increasing trade between developed countries and newly industrialized (e.g., Singapore, South Korea, Taiwan, and Hong Kong) or emerging markets (e.g., China, Brazil, India, Russia, and Mexico). These countries are not in the same region, nor do they share similar consumption preference with the Western world. Increasing income and elevated purchasing power seem to be the key driver of this trade phenomenon.

Finally, the new trade theory enriches our understanding of intra-industry and intra-firm trade. It links national factor endowments with firm behavior and firm incentives in explaining international trade. As Chapter 4 shows, this link is important because firms rather than countries conduct international trade and investment. The efficiency of international trade is maximized if both national factor endowment differences and economies-of-scale advantages of firms are combined and realized simultaneously. Since the MNE's role in international trade and investment is highly visible, the new trade theory has attracted more attention in recent years. The limitation of this theory, however, is that it overlooks other incentives beyond increasing returns from economy of scale. MNEs seek geographical diversification and accumulate knowledge about the target market from international trade. Chapter 4 articulates these issues in more detail.

Can we expect new theoretical development about international trade in the future? We believe so. As the following sections of this chapter demonstrate, patterns and characteristics of today's international trade are quite different from those of trade activities in the last century and even those of two decades ago, a period when the last trade theory emerged. The most important thrust for a new line of theoretical development will be a shift from the analysis of country comparative advantages to the assessment of country capabilities (or competitiveness). Factor endowment conditions (including human resources, technology, and information) are a critical aspect of country competitiveness, and factor endowment differences between two nations remain an important foundation for international trade. However, other aspects of country capabilities also shape international trade. For example, an importing country's macroeconomic soundness, demand conditions, local competition, government policies, support of related industries (e.g., banking service and foreign exchange hedging systems) as well as culture are expected to affect trade activities. At the same time, an exporting country's infrastructure, business rivalry, openness, and innovation are important factors influencing the volume of, and gains from, export activities. Chapter 5 focuses on country competitiveness. A nation generally gains more from international trade if its competitiveness in the world market is higher than that of other countries. Japan, for instance, is not rich in terms of factor endowments, but its competitiveness in innovation, adaptability, and business management made it a major player in international trade.

Interim Summary

1. Many theorists have created models to show the reasons, rationales, gains, or complexities of international trade. Some older theories such as the mercantilist doctrine and the absolute advantage theory, while accurate for their time, are inaccurate in today's world, due to drastic changes in technological diffusion, information exchange, and capital flow as well as the enhanced role of MNEs.

2. The Heckscher-Ohlin theorem, the most general explanation of the "old" trade, is not entirely obsolete. By integrating advanced technology and a skilled workforce into systems of comparative advantage between countries, modern international trade can be modeled relatively accurately by the theorem.

3. When a new technology is created, the innovating country has a massive trade advantage until the imitation gap is overcome.

4. The new trade theory explains intra-industry and intra-firm trade. Theories of international trade must be continually revised as new technology and new political and economic realities create a different global climate.

INTERNATIONAL TRADE PATTERNS

International Trade Volume and Growth

International trade continues to grow briskly, outpacing the growth in economic output. In 2000, global merchandise exports reached $6.2 trillion, an increase of 12.5 percent over 1999. Global exports of commercial services reached $1.4 trillion, an increase of 6 percent over the prior year.[15] The increase slowed in 2001, but if recent decades are an indication, it will soon resume. From a historical perspective, however, it is useful to recall the late nineteenth century when rapidly growing trade growth was reversed by high tariff regimes raised in the name of domestic interests, in particular employment. This is a reminder of how trade is intertwined with other realities, such as domestic and global political interests, which will be explored later in this book.

Exhibit 2–7 shows the growth in international merchandise trade from 1950 to 2000. The exhibit shows that the increase in merchandise trade has been more pronounced in manufacturing than in mining and agricultural products, a pattern partially explained by trade barriers discussed later in this chapter. Trade in services will be discussed separately. While overall trade has been growing steadily, there has been, over time, a considerable change in the share of various world regions (see Exhibit 2–8). In exports, the Americas went from about half of the total in 1948 to less than one quarter in 2000, while Africa lost more than two thirds of its share. In contrast, Asia and western Europe increased their global share. In imports, Asia has dramatically increased its intake while other regions had either small gains (North America) or substantial declines (Latin America).

Exhibit 2–7

World merchandise trade by major product group, 1950–2000

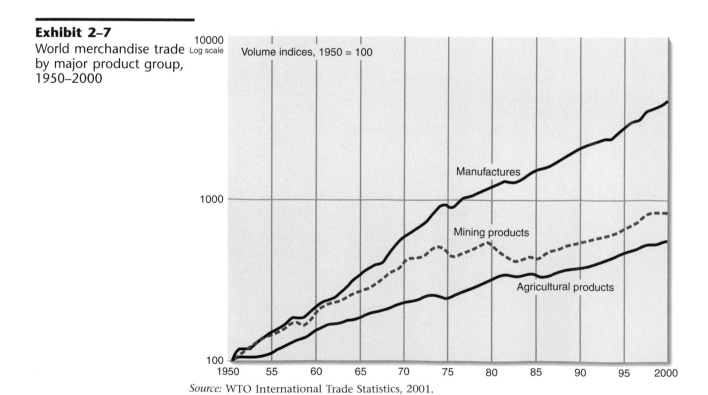

Source: WTO International Trade Statistics, 2001.

Exhibit 2–8
World merchandise trade
by region and selected
economy, 1948, 1953,
1963, 1973, 1983, 1993
and 2000 (billion dollars
and percentage)

	1948	1953	1963	1973	1983	1993	2000
				Export Value			
World	58.0	84.0	157.0	579.0	1835.0	3641.0	6186.0
				Share			
World	100.0	100.0	100.0	100.0	100.0	100.0	100.0
North America	27.3	24.2	19.3	16.9	15.4	16.8	17.1
Latin America	12.3	10.5	7.0	4.7	5.8	4.4	5.8
Mexico	1.0	0.7	0.6	0.4	1.4	1.4	2.7
Brazil	2.0	1.8	0.9	1.1	1.2	1.1	0.9
Argentina	2.8	1.3	0.9	0.6	0.4	0.4	0.4
Western Europe	31.5	34.9	41.4	45.4	38.9	43.7	39.5
C./E. Europe/Baltic States/CIS[a]	6.0	8.1	11.0	9.1	9.5	2.9	4.4
Africa	7.3	6.5	5.7	4.8	4.4	2.5	2.3
South Africa	2.0	1.7	1.5	1.0	1.0	0.7	0.5
Middle East	2.0	2.7	3.2	4.1	6.8	3.4	4.2
Asia	13.6	13.1	12.4	14.9	19.1	26.3	26.7
Japan	0.4	1.5	3.5	6.4	8.0	10.0	7.7
China	0.9	1.2	1.3	1.0	1.2	2.5	4.0
India	2.2	1.3	1.0	0.5	0.5	0.6	0.7
Australia and New Zealand	3.7	3.2	2.4	2.1	1.4	1.5	1.2
Six East Asian traders	3.0	2.7	2.4	3.4	5.8	9.7	10.5
GATT/WTO Members	60.4	68.7	72.8	81.8	76.0	86.9	90.7
				Import Value			
World	66.0	84.0	163.0	589.0	1881.0	3752.0	6490.0
				Share			
World	100.0	100.0	100.0	100.0	100.0	100.0	100.0
North America	19.8	19.7	15.5	16.7	17.8	19.8	23.2
Latin America	10.6	9.3	6.8	5.1	4.5	5.2	6.0
Mexico	0.8	1.0	0.8	0.6	0.7	1.8	2.8
Brazil	1.7	1.6	0.9	1.2	0.9	0.7	0.9
Argentina	2.4	0.9	0.6	0.4	0.2	0.4	0.4
Western Europe	40.4	39.4	45.4	47.4	40.0	42.9	39.6
C./E. Europe/Baltic States/CIS[a]	5.8	7.6	10.3	8.9	8.4	2.9	3.7
Africa	7.6	7.0	5.5	4.0	4.6	2.6	2.1
South Africa[b]	2.2	1.5	1.1	0.9	0.8	0.5	0.5
Middle East	1.7	2.0	2.3	2.8	6.3	3.2	2.6
Asia	14.2	15.1	14.2	15.1	18.5	23.4	22.8
Japan	1.0	2.9	4.1	6.5	6.7	6.4	5.8
China	1.1	1.7	0.9	0.9	1.1	2.8	3.5
India	3.1	1.4	1.5	0.5	0.7	0.6	0.8
Australia and New Zealand	2.6	2.4	2.3	1.6	1.4	1.5	1.3
Six East Asian traders	3.0	3.4	3.1	3.7	6.1	9.9	9.5
GATT/WTO Members	52.9	66.0	74.2	89.1	83.9	91.0	92.0

Source: WTO International Trade Statistics, 2001.

[a]Figures are significantly affected by (i) changes in the country composition of the region and major adjustment in trade conversion factors between 1983 and 1993; and (ii) the inclusion of the Baltic States and the CIS mutual trade between 1993 and 2000.

Note: Between 1973 and 1983 and between 1993 and 2000 export and import shares were significantly influenced by oil price developments.

Service Trade

Trade in services currently accounts for about one quarter of global trade, but as developed countries move to service-based economies, its share is rapidly growing. **Service trade** encompasses the import and export of financial services, information services, the provision of education and training, travel and tourism, health

Exhibit 2–9

Trade in commercial services of the United States, 2000 (billion dollars and percentage)

	Exports			Imports		
	Value	Share		Value	Share	
	2000	1995	2000	2000	1995	2000
Total commercial services	274.6	100.0	100.0	198.9	100.0	100.0
Transportation	51.2	22.7	18.6	64.6	32.3	32.5
Sea transport	5.1	2.8	1.9	20.0	9.2	10.0
Air transport	26.7	11.2	9.7	28.3	13.5	14.2
Other transport	19.4	8.6	7.1	16.4	9.6	8.2
Travel	100.5	37.7	36.6	67.3	35.7	33.9
Other commercial services	122.9	39.7	44.8	67.0	32.0	33.7
Communication services[a]	4.1	1.8	1.5	6.5	6.0	3.2
Construction services[a]	4.3	1.3	1.6	0.5	0.3	0.3
Insurance services[a]	2.7	0.7	1.0	6.6	4.1	3.3
Financial services[a]	17.9	3.5	5.5	5.1	1.9	2.5
Computer and information services[a]	4.3	1.2	1.6	0.7	0.2	0.3
Royalties and licence fees	38.0	15.3	13.8	16.3	5.4	8.2
Other business services	45.7	14.7	16.7	31.0	14.0	15.6
Personal, cultural, and recreational services	6.0	1.3	2.2	0.3	0.1	0.1

Source: WTO International Trade Statistics, 2001.

[a]Excludes transactions between affiliates, which are recorded under "Other business services"

care, consulting and advisory services, and so on. Because of their advantage in services, developed countries tend to push much more aggressively for a removal of barriers to trade in services.

Exhibit 2–9 shows U.S. service exports and imports for 1995 and 2000. For 2000, US service exports exceed imports by more than US $75 billion. Imports are divided roughly equally between transportation, travel, and other services. US exports are higher for other commercial services than for travel and transportation.

Trade Measurement

The United States has systematically recorded its imports and exports since 1821. Since 1989, it has used a harmonized system for classifying trade that facilitates comparability of data with the country's major trade partners. With the exception of Canada (where the United States is substituting Canadian import figures for U.S. exports), export data are compiled from Shipper's Export Declarations filed by exporters, forwarders, and carriers. Import data are compiled from U.S. customs forms. Trade data are used not only by governments but also by firms and research institutions to gauge such measures as market penetration and share.

While most trade statistics in this chapter appear in the aggregate, it is useful to remember that they are available for different categories, for example, domestic exports (produced or materially transformed in the United States) versus re-exports (commodities of foreign origin that have not been materially changed in the United States); or foreign imports (of foreign origin or those returned to the United States in their original form) versus American Goods Returned to the United States after Processing and/or Assembly. Additional data, for example, on transportation mode (see Chapter 16 on Global Marketing and Supply Chain) are also available.[16]

Major Exporters and Importers

Exhibit 2–10 shows the largest exporters and importers of merchandise trade and commercial services, respectively. In merchandise trade, the top seven importers and top six exporters are developed countries. In commercial services, the top nine importers and top eight exporters are developed economies. One reason for the gap is that commercial services such as financial services, global transportation, consulting, and healthcare are knowledge intensive and hence less likely to be either produced or consumed in a developing economy.

Exhibit 2–10a

Top 10 leading exporters and importers in world merchandise trade, 2000 (billion dollars and percentage)

Rank	Exporters	Value	Share	Annual percentage change	Rank	Importers	Value	Share	Annual percentage change
1	United States	781.1	12.3	11	1	United States	1257.6	8.9	19
2	Germany	551.5	8.7	1	2	Germany	502.8	7.5	6
3	Japan	479.2	7.5	14	3	Japan	379.5	5.7	22
4	France	298.1	4.7	−1	4	United Kingdom	337.0	5.1	5
5	United Kingdom	284.1	4.5	6	5	France	305.4	4.6	4
6	Canada	276.6	4.3	16	6	Canada	244.8	3.7	11
7	China	249.3	3.9	28	7	Italy	236.5	3.5	7
8	Italy	237.8	3.7	1	8	China	225.1	3.4	36
9	Netherlands	212.5	3.3	6	9	Hong Kong, China	214.2	3.2	19
10	Hong Kong, China	202.4	3.2	16	10	Netherlands	198.0	3.0	4

Source: WTO International Trade Statistics, 2001.

Exhibit 2–10b

Top 10 leading exporters and importers in world trade in commercial services, 2000 (billion dollars and percentage)

Rank	Exporters	Value	Share	Annual percentage change	Rank	Importers	Value	Share	Annual percentage change
1	United States	274.6	19.1	10	1	United States	198.9	13.8	13
2	United Kingdom	99.9	7.0	−3	2	Germany	132.3	9.2	0
3	France	81.2	5.7	0	3	Japan	115.7	8.1	1
4	Germany	80.0	5.6	1	4	United Kingdom	82.1	5.7	−1
5	Japan	68.3	4.8	13	5	France	61.5	4.3	−2
6	Italy	56.7	4.0	−6	6	Italy	55.7	3.9	−3
7	Spain	53.0	3.7	0	7	Netherlands	51.1	3.6	2
8	Netherlands	52.3	3.6	−1	8	Canada	41.9	2.9	9
9	Hong Kong, China	42.1	2.9	13	9	Belgium-Luxembourg	38.3	2.7	6
10	Belgium-Luxembourg	42.0	2.9	4	10	China	35.9	2.5	16

Source: WTO International Trade Statistics, 2001.

U.S. Trade Partners

Exhibit 2–11 shows U.S. merchandise trade with various regions and countries. Canada is the United States' largest trade partner, followed by the EU, Mexico, and Japan. How can these patterns be explained? With the exception of Mexico, three of the United States' four major trading partners are developed economies, which supports Linder's income-preference similarity theory. Canada, the major partner of the United States, has additional advantages in terms of trade with the United States: geographic proximity, relative cultural similarity, and NAFTA membership. More than 100,000 U.S. companies export to Canada, more than double the number to Mexico, the second-ranked destination. Mexico, the only emerging economy among the four major partners, also benefits from its proximity to the United States and from NAFTA membership. Since NAFTA's establishment in 1994, Mexico's exports have grown threefold, with the United States and Canada, accounting for much of the growth. The United States' fifth major partner is also an emerging economy— China (for imports) and South Korea (for exports).

Following the Heckscher-Ohlin theorem, it is easy to see why U.S. eateries import agricultural products and processed foods from Mexico, where expenses are low and wages start at about $50 a week;[17] or why pencil imports, mostly from China, now account for half of the U.S. market versus 16 percent just a decade ago.[18] Similarly, it is clear why Africa exports mostly mining products to North America but very few manufacturing products.[19] The overall trade picture, however, is more complex.

Let's start with the numbers. With increased globalization, more and more exported products contain a myriad of inputs from other countries, including those that end up importing the final product. The IBM plant in El Salto, Mexico, incorporates United States components in products that are then exported to the United States or sold in other export markets. They are registered as Mexican exports. Between 1995

Exhibit 2–11

Merchandise trade of the United States by region and economy, 2000 (billion dollars and percentage)

Destination	Exports					Origin	Imports				
	Value	Share		Annual percentage change			Value	Share		Annual percentage change	
	2000	1990	2000	1999	2000		2000	1990	2000	1999	2000
World	781.8	100.0	100.0	2	13	World	1257.6	100.0	100.0	12	19
Asia	214.6	30.3	27.4	3	17	Asia	469.3	39.5	37.3	11	15
Western Europe	181.4	28.7	23.2	2	9	Western Europe	248.5	21.9	19.8	11	13
North America	179.4	21.2	22.9	6	9	North America	238.4	18.1	19.0	13	18
Latin America	170.0	13.7	21.7	0	20	Latin America	216.0	13.0	17.2	15	25
Middle East	19.2	2.9	2.5	−11	−9	Middle East	40.3	3.9	3.2	32	50
Africa	11.0	2.0	1.4	−11	11	Africa	28.5	3.3	2.3	6	59
C./E. Europe/						C./E. Europe/					
Baltic States/CIS	5.9	1.1	0.8	−24	5	Baltic States/CIS	16.6	0.5	1.3	7	36
Selected Economies						*Selected Economies*					
Canada	178.9	21.1	22.9	6	9	Canada	238.3	18.1	19.0	13	18
European Union (15)	165.2	26.3	21.1	1	9	European Union (15)	227.2	20.0	18.1	10	13
Mexico	111.3	7.2	14.2	10	28	Japan	151.3	18.1	12.0	8	12
Japan	64.9	12.4	8.3	−1	13	Mexico	140.4	5.9	11.2	16	26
Korea, Rep. of	27.8	3.7	3.6	39	21	China	103.3	3.1	8.2	17	18

Source: WTO International Trade Statistics, 2001.

and 1998, exports to countries other than the United States by the Mexican affiliates of U.S. corporations have tripled.[20] The same is true for information technology exports out of the Philippines, Malaysia, and Thailand that represent a probable value added of no more than 20 percent given the importation of semiconductors and other manufacturing inputs that go into the exported products.[21] Exports from China to the United States include manufacturing goods; however, many of those are made by firms from developed economies, including the United States, Japan, and the EU, which use China as an export platform and incorporate foreign inputs. Vietnam stood to benefit only modestly from the abolition of U.S. tariffs on its textile exports because those are made with imported raw material.

Exhibit 2–12a and b presents the trade flow by product between the United States and Japan, a flow that has been described by some observers as the world's most important, both politically and economically. Some components of the flow are easily explained; for example, the flow of foodstuff from the United States to Japan can be explained by factor endowments. Other components of the flow,

Exhibit 2–12a
U.S. Exports to Japan (Top ten commodities)

	Millions of U.S. Dollars			% Share			% Change
Description	1997	1998	1999	1997	1998	1999	99/98
Total exports to Japan	33,587	29,408	28,288	9.89	8.59	8.40	−3.81
1 Machinery	5,346	4,267	4,114	15.92	14.51	14.54	−3.59
2 Electrical machinery	4,464	4,103	4,049	13.29	13.95	14.31	−1.31
3 Aircraft, spacecraft	2,054	2,526	2,612	6.11	8.59	9.23	3.39
4 Optic, NT B544; Med. instr.	2,613	2,495	2,458	7.78	8.48	8.69	−1.46
5 Meat	1,204	1,197	1,202	3.58	4.07	4.25	0.40
6 Cereals	1,555	1,254	1,165	4.63	4.26	4.12	−7.10
7 Vehicles, not railway	1,773	1,329	1,147	5.28	4.52	4.05	−13.69
8 Tobacco	955	991	1,001	2.84	3.37	3.54	1.00
9 Wood	1,427	790	791	4.25	2.69	2.80	0.15
10 Organic chemicals	791	623	656	2.36	2.12	2.32	5.28

Source: U.S. Dept. of Commerce, Bureau of the Census.

Exhibit 2–12b
U.S. Imports from Japan (Top ten commodities)

	Millions of U.S. Dollars			% Share			% Change
Description	1997	1998	1999	1997	1998	1999	99/98
Total imports from Japan	59,272	60,427	61,883	14.23	13.59	12.93	2.41
1 Vehicles, not railway	15,079	16,272	18,276	25.44	26.93	29.53	12.31
2 Machinery	16,237	16,026	15,370	27.39	26.52	24.84	−4.09
3 Electrical machinery	12,135	11,540	11,970	20.47	19.10	19.34	3.73
4 Optic, NT 8544; Med, instr.	3,773	3,803	3,590	6.37	6.29	5.80	−5.60
5 Organic chemicals	1,267	1,353	1,138	2.14	2.24	1.84	−15.83
6 Special other	842	883	994	1.42	1.46	1.61	12.56
7 Toys and sports equipment	1,105	995	961	1.86	1.65	1.55	−3.38
8 Rubber	694	753	848	1.17	1.25	1.37	12.71
9 Plastic	741	791	772	1.25	1.31	1.25	−2.36
10 Aircraft, spacecraft	604	658	728	1.02	1.09	1.18	10.59

Source: U.S. Dept of Commerce, Bureau of the Census.

however, are not easily explained. For example, Japanese vehicle exports to the United States are 10 times bigger than U.S. vehicle exports to Japan. Since the United States has the largest motor vehicle industry in the world and has (through its subsidiaries) a substantial share of a competitive market such as the EU, it is difficult to explain the large gap via comparative advantage or scale economy. Other factors must be at play, among them: trade barriers (described in the next section) that limit the access of U.S. firms to the Japanese market, currency exchange rates that have made U.S. vehicles expensive in Japan, and externalities such as rising fuel prices that made Japanese vehicles more attractive in the United States.

Recall that the new trade theory suggests that while inter-industry trade was governed by the Heckscher-Ohlin theorem (trade between countries with different factor endowments), intra-industry trade was not. When we look at U.S. textile imports for 2000, we can see that they come from the EU, Canada, China, Mexico, and India (in that order). In other words, although textiles are a labor-intensive product, the imports come from developed as well as developing economies. But the products that come in are different, with those from developed countries being of higher price and quality. Similarly, Canada imports textiles from the United States, the EU, China, Korea, and India, with exports from the United States constituting about three times the other sources combined. NAFTA member Mexico is a distant eighth. In that case, proximity and re-exports account for much of the import numbers.[22]

The Leontief paradox asks why the United States exported labor-intensive products when it had no advantage in labor rates. Labor migration is one reason. In this case, it is labor moving in the pursuit of capital rather than the other way around. Rather than moving south of the border, U.S. carpet manufacturers rely on Mexican migration to northwest Georgia to lower labor costs and remain competitive. While labor costs are still higher relatively to Mexican plants, transportation costs to U.S. customers are much lower, making domestic production cost effective.[23] With the wages of U.S. trading partners rising as a percentage of U.S. wages (about doubling from 1960 to 1992),[24] wage differentials are not the only factor determining the location of production, although they remain a vitally important criterion.

Trade Balance

The **balance of trade** is calculated as exports minus imports of goods and services. The United States has by far the largest trade deficit of any country though as a percentage of GDP its deficit is much lower than that of many other nations (Exhibit 2–13). The U.S. deficit in merchandise trade persisted since the early 1980s, and has been especially pronounced in trade with Japan during the 1980s and early 1990s and with China in the late 1990s. In both cases, considerable anxiety arose surrounding the possible repercussions of the deficit to U.S. competitiveness and national security.

In contrast to its deficit in merchandise trade, the United States enjoys substantial surplus in services. Between 1992 and 1998, U.S. service exports grew at an average rate of 8 percent, reaching U.S. $246 billion in 1998. The surplus balance ($73.13 billion as of the end of 1998) explains why the United States is in the forefront of those fighting to reduce barriers in service trade. For instance, the United States has been a major proponent of "open skies" agreements that liberalize the markets for commercial aviation and has fought hard for the opening of hitherto closed markets (e.g., China) for financial services. India, a country that has been dramatically increasing its service exports, has become a center for software export. This success played a role in the Indian government's decision to open up its own market to realize the benefits of free trade.

Exhibit 2–13
Balance of trade

Balance Of Trade		2001
US$ billions (minus sign = deficit)		
Ranking		US$ billions
1	GERMANY	76.5
2	JAPAN	54.6
3	RUSSIA	49.7
4	CANADA	34.0
5	IRELAND	32.5
6	INDONESIA	25.5
7	NORWAY	25.5
8	CHINA	23.1
9	NETHERLANDS	22.0
10	TAIWAN	15.7
11	MALAYSIA	14.1
12	SWEDEN	12.7
13	FINLAND	11.3
14	BELGIUM	10.9
15	VENEZUELA	9.8
16	KOREA	9.5
17	ITALY	7.5
18	ARGENTINA	6.3
19	DENMARK	6.3
20	SINGAPORE	5.8
21	THAILAND	4.0
22	PHILIPPINES	2.2
23	SOUTH AFRICA	0.6
24	CHILE	0.5
25	COLOMBIA	0.1
26	BRAZIL	−0.0
27	AUSTRALIA	−0.5
28	NEW ZEALAND	−0.6
29	ICELAND	−0.7
30	SLOVAK REPUBLIC	−0.8
31	ESTONIA	−0.8
32	SLOVENIA	−0.8
33	SWITZERLAND	−2.0
34	HUNGARY	−2.1
35	LUXEMBOURG	−2.5
36	CZECH REPUBLIC	−3.1
37	FRANCE	−3.5
38	AUSTRIA	−3.6
39	ISRAEL	−6.1
40	INDIA	−6.7
41	TURKEY	−9.2
42	HONG KONG	−11.6
43	PORTUGAL	−13.9
44	POLAND	−14.5
45	GREECE	−16.1
46	MEXICO	−17.6
47	SPAIN	−33.6
48	UNITED KINGDOM	−59.1
49	USA	−449.6

Balance Of Trade		2001
Percentage of GDP		
Ranking		%
1	IRELAND	30.91
2	INDONESIA	19.61
3	MALAYSIA	16.15
4	RUSSIA	16.04
5	NORWAY	15.57
6	FINLAND	9.31
7	VENEZUELA	7.85
8	SINGAPORE	6.74
9	SWEDEN	6.06
10	NETHERLANDS	5.78
11	TAIWAN	5.55
12	CANADA	4.86
13	BELGIUM	4.73
14	GERMANY	4.15
15	DENMARK	3.85
16	THAILAND	3.55
17	PHILIPPINES	3.10
18	ARGENTINA	2.29
19	KOREA	2.26
20	CHINA	1.99
21	JAPAN	1.32
22	CHILE	0.78
23	ITALY	0.69
24	SOUTH AFRICA	0.52
25	COLOMBIA	0.18
26	BRAZIL	−0.01
27	AUSTRALIA	−0.14
28	FRANCE	−0.27
29	SWITZERLAND	−0.81
30	NEW ZEALAND	−1.28
31	INDIA	−1.51
32	AUSTRIA	−1.89
33	MEXICO	−2.77
34	SLOVAK REPUBLIC	−4.05
35	UNITED KINGDOM	−4.14
36	HUNGARY	−4.15
37	USA	−4.41
38	SLOVENIA	−4.41
39	ISRAEL	−5.53
40	CZECH REPUBLIC	−5.57
41	SPAIN	−5.78
42	TURKEY	−5.80
43	HONG KONG	−7.15
44	ICELAND	−7.67
45	POLAND	−8.27
46	PORTUGAL	−12.12
47	LUXEMBOURG	−12.76
48	GREECE	−14.22
49	ESTONIA	−14.54

Source: The World Competitiveness Yearbook, 2002.

Knowledge is often the most valuable contribution toward a competitive advantage in services. This can be seen clearly in the distribution of U.S. service exports. The United States exports to Europe intellectual property (paid as royalties and license fees) and legal services, while in the Asia Pacific region it sells mostly education and engineering services. U.S. freight services are sold mainly in the Asia Pacific and Africa/Middle East regions, while Latin America absorbs U.S. exports in advertising, insurance, communications, and travel services.[25]

1. World trade levels have shifted dramatically in the last 50 years, with merchandise trade more pronounced in manufacturing than in mining and agricultural products. Also, the balance of trade between countries and regions has altered significantly.

2. Highly developed countries often have services as a major export. The United States is a prominent example.

3. The considerable US surplus in service trade is outweighed by its much bigger deficit in merchandise trade.

OPPOSITION TO FREE TRADE

Generally speaking, trade theories show the benefits to be derived from international trade but dwell less on its potential drawbacks. This is particularly true for the theories of absolute and comparative advantage, which point out that trade allows for the efficient deployment of national resources from which everyone benefits. At the same time, opponents of free trade have been wrangling for years, most recently in their strong opposition to "globalization." Most countries have taken the position that trade needs first and foremost to protect the interest of their citizens. For example, the U.S. Foreign Trade Anti-Trust Improvement Act permits price-fixing agreements among exporters if neither U.S. consumers nor U.S. competitors are harmed.[26]

Opinion surveys (see also Chapter 7 on the political and legal environment) show that the American public is divided on the benefits of free trade. An opinion survey conducted for the Institute of International Economics shows that by a margin of 48 to 34 percent, Americans believe that foreign trade is bad for the U.S. economy.[27] How can we reconcile the two views? One answer rests with the gap between the macro and micro views. Although trade may be good for the overall national economy, its impact varies across regional, occupational, and other lines. The aforementioned survey shows that unskilled workers are much less likely to support free trade, because they are threatened by a shift of their jobs to lower cost locals. In contrast, skilled and highly educated people are more likely to benefit from trade at least in the short term, and hence tend to support free trade. Other studies confirm that people with lower incomes tend to be more negatively disposed toward trade. This is ironic because, as the head of the WTO noted, poor people are more adversely affected by protectionism because it increases the price of consumer goods.[28] Union membership may not have much impact on attitudes toward trade, as is often assumed.[29] The schism between social groups regarding trade may in itself trigger opposition to trade on the part of governments that are worried about its economic, social, and political impact.

To deal with the uneven impact of trade, the U.S. government provides trade adjustment assistance in the form of extended unemployment benefits and retraining funds for workers who lose their jobs to overseas competition. Congress recently considered a bill that would provide wage insurance for workers who lose their jobs as a result of foreign competition, even when securing a new job at a lower pay level. It is estimated that an employee who loses his/her job to imports and gets another job will receive on average a 13 percent lower wage with a quarter suffering a 30 percent cut.[30]

The Sovereignty Argument

Another source of opposition to trade is the supposed threat it represents to national sovereignty. According to this argument, the shift in production to the most efficient location deprives a country the base it needs to be a viable economic entity. In turn, this will make a country too dependent on nations that may challenge its national interests. This argument is particularly salient in industries considered key to national security, either directly (e.g., the arms industry) or indirectly (e.g., airlines). The United States, like many other countries, prohibits non-U.S. firms from acquiring a majority stake in a U.S. airline on the pretext that the aircraft need to be mobilized should an emergency occur. For similar reasons, countries sometimes curb the exports of certain products to designated countries.

Free trade sometimes is opposed as a threat to national culture and institutions. You will be reminded of that when you read about cultural industries in the culture chapter (6). Some countries, notably France and Canada, impose restrictions on the introduction of foreign media under the pretext that open importation would endanger their culture and language. As we will see in our discussion of tariffs below, countries may establish particularly high tariffs on products that they see as essential to their way of life (e.g., rice in Japan).

The Lowest Common Denominator Argument

Still another source of opposition to free trade has to do with its potentially adverse consequences for the environment, safety, and such. This is the "lowest denominator" argument whereby production will shift to nations with the least protection since they will offer the lowest cost base, but eventually, everyone else will end up paying for the adverse impact in the form of environmental degradation, global warming, and such. As you may recall from Chapter 1, the lowest common denominator argument has been one of the main complaints lodged by the antiglobalization movement.

Trade Reciprocity

Although trade theories assume benefits even when a country opens its borders to free trade unilaterally, additional benefits can be gained from reciprocity. Those additional benefits are not only economic (e.g., the ability to export the goods and services in which it has a comparative advantage) but also political and social in that it is difficult to build domestic support for unilateral opening. For instance, if the U.S. government were to permit Chinese imports unilaterally, it might be supported by some consumer groups but opposed by almost everyone else. In contrast, the pressure it applied on China to open its borders to U.S. exports brought it the support of U.S. exporters who were instrumental in pushing through the administration's Most Favored Nation (MFN) agenda. Reciprocity also appeals to our sense of fairness (itself a key U.S. value). In a *Business Week* survey, only 10 percent of respondents identified themselves as "free traders."; 37 percent identified themselves as "protectionists" while the rest identified as "fair traders."[31]

Trebilcock and Howse distinguish between two kinds of reciprocity, passive and active. **Passive reciprocity** is a position taken by a country where it refuses to lower or eliminate its barriers to trade until the other party(ies) does the same. **Active or aggressive reciprocity** may be conducted through the threat of retaliation. For example, the withdrawal of previous commitments and concessions, or the undertaking of other retaliatory measures until the other party fulfills its obligations. An example is "super 301" which may be invoked by the United States in the case of "unreasonable and discriminatory" trade behavior by a foreign country.[32] Adam Smith suggested that retaliation should be considered a possible response to protectionism although he was concerned that this could harm the retaliating nation as well.

Indeed, reciprocity and retaliation are an integral part of the international trade scene. Countervailing duties and subsidies are commonly used by nations to retaliate or compensate for the value produced by preferences provided foreign manufacturers or service providers.

Interim Summary

1. Free trade and globalization are hot-button issues. Some argue that protectionism is the best stance, whereas most economists feel that free trade is the only path to a healthy economy in the long-term.

2. There are many reasons for a nation to be cautious when entering into free trade with other nations. For example, a country must balance protection of its workforce, national security, and national culture and identity with the benefits brought about by free trade.

3. A major concern with free trade and globalization is the potential for environmental damage from firms operating in poorly regulated markets.

4. Trade reciprocity can bring about additional benefits to countries engaged in free trade.

TYPES OF TRADE BARRIERS

Barriers to trade are typically divided into tariff and non-tariff barriers. **Tariff barriers** are official constraints on the importation of certain goods and services in the form of a total or a partial limitation or in the form of a special levy. **Non-tariff barriers** are indirect measures that discriminate against foreign manufacturers in the domestic market or otherwise distort and constrain trade. While tariff barriers have been significantly reduced during the several decades of the General Agreement on Tarrifs & Trade (GATT) regime, debate continues on whether similar progress has been made vis-à-vis non-tariff barriers that are by definition much more difficult to measure.

Although some non-tariff barriers (e.g., subsidies) have been targeted and reduced, others have emerged in their place. Sometimes, both tariff and non-tariff barriers are applied in tandem. India, which was once one of the most protective markets in the world, called the combination "swadeshi," or "nationalist policies."[33] This meant, for instance, prohibiting foreign firms from bidding on strategic defense projects (a tariff barrier) while preventing those firms from winning less sensitive bids by failing to disclose essential requirements or by publicizing the bids in obscure local outlets unlikely to be scrutinized by foreign firms (a non-tariff barrier).

Together, tariff and non-tariff barriers pose a serious obstacle to international trade. In a survey of Minnesota businesses, regulations and tariffs were considered the most serious barriers to entry into international trade, ahead of lack of information, cost and financing, qualified employees, language, and culture.[34]

Tariff Barriers

Tariff barriers include mainly tariffs and quotas and their derivatives as well as export controls and anti-dumping laws.

Tariffs

Tariffs are surcharges that an importer must pay above and beyond taxes levied on domestic goods and services. Tariffs are transparent (listed in the Harmonized Tariff Schedule) and are typically set *ad valorem*, that is, based on the value of the product or service. Tariffs were used widely in the nineteenth century but were incrementally reduced over time. The Smoot-Hawley Act in 1930 reversed this trend, pushing tariffs to a level of almost 60 percent of import value. Predictably, they brought on retaliatory measures by major trade partners of the United States.

In the decades that followed, tariffs in the United States and later in other nations declined substantially, reaching single digits for most products. Nevertheless, U.S. tariffs on some products (e.g., sugar) remain very high. Examples of particularly high tariffs include a 300 percent tariff on butter in Canada, a 179 percent tariff on sweet powdered milk in the United States, a 215 percent tariff on frozen beef in the EU, and a 550 percent tariff on rice in Japan.[35] The Japanese tariff on rice is particularly interesting, since the Japanese government maintains its rationale is to uphold a social and cultural way of life that is linked with rice cultivation. The more prosaic reason is the political strength of the farm lobby within Japan's ruling Liberal Democratic Party (LDP). The result, as trade theories would predict, is that the Japanese consumer pays much more for rice than do consumers in the United States and in most other countries.

Not surprisingly, tariffs have been on the agenda of virtually all rounds of trade negotiations through GATT (the predecessor of WTO), and remarkable progress has been made toward their elimination or reduction. Nevertheless, a hike in tariff is not unheard of. The United States and other nations often use punitive tariffs as a way to retaliate or obtain reciprocity. India, while generally reducing tariffs, has recently increased tariffs on such goods as whiskey from an already high level of 104 to 220 percent to 550 percent.[36] Not surprisingly, companies have been investing efforts in circumventing tariffs. Heartland By-Products, a small Michigan firm, circumvents the high U.S. tariff on sugar by buying sugar-molasses from its Canadian sister company, which makes it from sugar bought at world prices; it then reverses the process and turns the molasses into sugar syrup it sells to U.S. makers of ice cream, cereals, and candy.[37]

Generally, however, tariff rates are relatively low today, especially among developed countries. Exhibit 2–14 shows average import tariff rates among some of the nations discussing a possible free trade area of the Americas.

With overall tariffs low, governments often attempt to shift a product into a higher tariff category while firms develop strategies to benefit from the lower tariff category. The EU imposes a 288 percent tariff on imported vegetables, which is geared toward protecting the farm lobby in the Union, and only a 20 percent tariff on sauces. The EU decided to apply the very high tariff to imported sauces containing more than 20 percent of "lumps of fruits and vegetables" but now faces the ire of European firms such as Nestlé whose own sauces have faced retaliatory tariffs in other countries.[38] Similarly, the United States imposes 12.5 percent (if water packed) and 35 percent (if oil packed) tariffs on imported tuna in cans or pouches but only 1.5 percent on cooked non-canned fish. Bumble Bee, a unit of Conagra Foods, takes advantage of the gap by importing cooked tuna to automated processing plants in California and Puerto Rico, thereby qualifying for the lower tariff. Its rival Starkist, a unit of Heinz, which imports canned tuna from Ecuador, is fighting to reduce the tariff.[39]

Optimal Tariff

The **optimal tariff theory** assumes that by imposing a tariff, governments can capture a significant portion of the manufacturer's profit margin. In other words,

Exhibit 2–14
Average import tariff rates

Peru — 20.2%
Brazil — 16.6
Argentina — 12.9
Mexico — 12.5
Colombia — 12.4
Venezuela — 10.9
Chile — 10.9
Canada — 3.6
U.S. — 2.5

Sources: J.P. Morgan Chase, U.S. Commerce Department

assuming that the exporter cannot raise prices at will, domestic customers will not have to pay higher prices while their government manages to obtain part of the proceeds that otherwise would have been obtained by the exporter. The optimal tariff theory assumes however that the exporter can absorb the lower prices and will not simply shift its efforts into other markets. The theory also does not take into account the fact that high tariffs are likely to trigger smuggling (see Chapter 19 on Ethics and Corruption) that eventually reduce government revenue. An example is the importation of cigarettes, traditionally a high-tariff item, where even the manufacturers themselves have been accused of rampant smuggling to circumvent tariffs.

Infant Industries

The **infant industry** argument for tariffs is that an industry new to a country, especially a developing one, needs to be protected by tariff walls or risk being squashed by established global players before it is given a chance to grow and develop. The argument was vigorously raised by the United States throughout the nineteenth century, by Japan after World War II, and by Korea in the 1960s. These countries wanted to encourage the development of their domestic industry while generating revenues for the state, at the expense of foreign manufacturers. The interest of consumers, amply demonstrated by theories of international trade, was not considered. When U.S. motor vehicles were kept out of both Japan and Korea through high tariffs and other barriers, the result was higher local prices. The same was true for U.S. "voluntary quotas" set in the mid-1970s, which limited the number of Japanese cars sold in the United States and cost the U.S. consumer more than $1,000 per car. Here the argument was not one of infant industry (U.S. car manufacturers have been in business since early in the twentieth century) but rather that the industry needed time to recuperate from the Japanese onslaught and restructure to produce more fuel-efficient cars. The "import surge" protection has since become an acceptable WTO protection.

Quotas

Quotas are quantitative limitations on the importation of goods typically spelled in terms of units (e.g., 10,000 shirts) or value (ad valorem). Some quotas allow for

COUNTRY BOX

THE UNITED STATES AND STEEL IMPORTS

The United States, once the world's major producer of steel, now trails both China and Japan in steel production. The United States now imports steel from other countries, including Japan, Russia, Ukraine, South Korea, and Brazil. The U.S. steel industry has been trying to mobilize support to curb steel imports.

The second argument is more industry specific, and probably gained more prominence in the wake of the September 11, 2001, terror attacks. According to this argument, steel is a vital input in armaments, and the United States can ill-afford to become dependent on other nations for its supply. Steel is also a vital input in such industries as motor vehicles, so its price and availability would have a ripple effect in the economy. At the same time, the ad below makes the argument that the U.S. steel industry is competitive and would not be in trouble if not for dumping and subsidies for foreign producers.

The U.S. International Trade Commission recommended in early December 2001, to levy additional tariffs, ranging from 5 to 40 percent, on key steel products. The position was strongly supported by President Bush, who is also concerned about the political fallout in steel-producing states such as Ohio, Pennsylvania, and West Virginia. The EU Trade Commissioner, on his part, threatened to launch a complaint before the WTO. He blames the rising imports on the U.S. steel industry whose outdated management and labor practices. In March 2002, the Bush administration imposed a 30 percent tariff on a range of steel imports, which was followed up by an EU plan for counter sanctions not yet announced when this book went to print.

The following are some advertisements used by the industry in a bid to curb imports:

• *During the past year, America lost more than 1.1 million manufacturing jobs. We think the loss of 1.1 million good paying manufacturing jobs matters.*

• *Many workers lost their jobs because domestic factories have shifted their operations to low-wage, nonregulation countries. In other industries foreign producers have seized market share from U.S. producers.*

• *Manufacturing assures our national defense. It makes possible our global leadership. It undergirds the living standards of more than seventeen million workers.*

• *How could this paradox exist—a high and growing domestic demand, a productive domestic industry, and yet bankruptcies occur among these domestic producers? The answer is massive global overcapacity and equally massive foreign subsidies. Most of the steel imported into America today is selling below its cost of production—often far below.*

• *Other nations need dollars and jobs. Subsidizing their steel exports is an easy way to get both. Longer-term, subsidized imports by foreign countries will destroy a vital American industry and good-paying, high-quality U.S. jobs.*

• *In an uncertain and dangerous world, moreover, does America really want to become dependent on Russia, Japan, China, Brazil and developing countries for something so basic as steel?*

Source: Crafted with Pride in USA Council. *Wall Street Journal*, November 9, 2001, A15; November 26, 2001, A19.

Source: R. G. Matthews "A big stick: The US won't take 'no' for an answer at Paris steel summit," *Wall Street Journal*, December 14, 2001, A1.

a preset increase, for example, an annual increase of 3 percent. Some quotas allow for a preset decrease, as contained in the NAFTA agreement and most recently in China's admission into the WTO that will trigger stepwise tariff reductions. Quotas may also be established in terms of a market share beyond which either tariff or cessation of imports are triggered. Quotas are widely used in the case of textile products although they are by no means restricted to those.

Unlike tariffs, quotas hold the promise of definitive, quantifiable protection of domestic producers. They may however yield unintended consequences. The "voluntary" quotas capping Japanese auto imports at roughly 1.8 million units (set in terms of units rather than value), encouraged Japanese manufacturers to move beyond the entry level cars they were exporting at the time into more expensive models so as to increase their dollar volume without violating the quotas. In contrast to tariffs, quotas do not have the potential to trigger the efficiencies that arise from the need to remain competitive with domestic producers. The unmet demand for Japanese cars was simply translated into higher margins for the dealers that sold them.

Rule of Origin

Both tariffs and quotas are administered on the basis of their country of origin for which the default is the first importing country. For example, a product that was manufactured in Belgium and exported to France and from there to the United States will be considered a Belgian product unless the product has undergone material change in France. It is also important to remember that **rule of origin** terms may differ between different types of tariffs and supports. For instance, under GSP (Generalized System of Preferences), only 35 percent of a product's value needs to be from a developing nation to be granted duty-free treatment, whereas under the Buy American Act, a product needs to be made in the United States from at least half U.S. content.

Rule of origin is often an issue of contention, however, because the value added to the product in the transient country may be debatable. For instance, the French government once returned a shipment of U.S.-made Honda cars, arguing that the cars were in fact Japanese and hence fell under the quota for Japanese car imports into the country, which had already been exceeded. The U.S. government recently suspected that many garments imported from Hong Kong were in fact manufactured in Mainland China but had their origin concealed to circumvent the quota regime. The United States demanded that it be allowed to post inspectors at the Mainland–Hong Kong border, something the Hong Kong authorities saw as a threat to their sovereignty.

To remedy the problem, the WTO issued a first ever agreement on rules of origin. It requires that the rules be transparent, that they be applied in a consistent and impartial manner, that they be based on a positive rather than a negative standard (i.e., state what confers origin rather than what does not), and that they will not restrict, distort, or disrupt trade.

Export Controls

Many countries limit the type of products that can be exported to other countries, particularly those that are considered enemy nations or a security risk. **Export controls** are typically activated against products with a national security potential (e.g., armaments), but also to so-called dual-use products such as computers and trucks that can have both security and civilian uses. An example is the sale of aerospace equipment to China by McDonnell Douglas Corporation (which has since been acquired by Boeing). The company was fined $2.1 million by the Commerce Department because some of the machining tools it sold for use in a joint venture for the manufacturing of commercial aircraft parts were later found in a facility that was to manufacture military aircraft.[40]

In emergency situations, export controls can be used to prevent the export of goods that are vital to domestic industry and armed forces—for example, oil. Export controls are different from most other trade barriers in that they are placed by the exporting country rather than by the importing one. Exporting companies often pressure their government to ease export controls, arguing that the importing country will get the products from a competitor whose country does not apply strict controls. Finally, export controls affect not only manufacturers in the home country but also those in a third country. This is especially relevant in the case of countries with a substantial surplus in technology balance of payments such as the United

States. For instance, the United States has often warned Israel to make sure that it does not use sensitive U.S. technologies in its sales to China.

Dumping and Anti-Dumping

Dumping is defined by the WTO as selling a product at an unfairly low price, with the "fair price" defined as the domestic price, the price charged by an exporter in another market, or a calculation of production costs. Because it distorts pricing, dumping interferes with free trade flow. Dumping undermines the principle of comparative advantage because it may cause the exporting country to specialize in a product or service in which it has no advantage over the importing country.

Because of its adverse impact on trade, the WTO allows remedies against dumping but only where "material injury" to the domestic industry has been demonstrated. In theory, the extra duties that can add up to 40 percent of product price will bring the price back to a realistic level, restoring a level playing field and permitting the more efficient producers to sell their goods. The problem is that the retaliation, in the form of anti-dumping duties, is often used to protect inefficient domestic producers, thereby producing the opposite impact.

In 1999, a total of 1,200 anti-dumping measures were initiated by 28 nations. If the measures were once almost exclusively applied by developed nations, they are now taken by developed and developing nations alike. For example, India, which had no anti-dumping cases in 1993, became the number-one user of anti-dumping measures in 1999, with 68 cases, and its number-one target for anti-dumping measures was China, with 310 cases brought against it in the last decade.[41] It is easy to see why: The country has abundant low-cost labor and is a world leader in labor intensive exports such as toys and apparel. The case of China also shows how anti-dumping can distort trade. Before signing NAFTA in 1992, Mexico imposed anti-dumping duties on 4,000 Chinese products, basically covering all Chinese-made goods, even those not produced in Mexico. For 2002, the Mexican textiles and apparel industries extended anti-dumping tariffs of 557 percent on Chinese-made clothing and 1,100 percent on Chinese-made shoes, effectively keeping them off the retail shelf.[42]

Interim Summary

1. Tariff barriers are an obvious and transparent means of controlling trade. Tariff barriers include quotas and their derivatives, as well as export controls.

2. In using tariffs, countries must account for the fact that rate increases will likely trigger retaliation.

3. Quotas and tariffs are applied to goods based on their country of origin. However, what defines a country of origin can change based on individual bodies of law. A clear definition of country of origin is difficult because a product may pass through many countries and contain inputs from many others.

NON-TARIFF BARRIERS

By definition, **non-tariff barriers** are obstacles to trade, not anchored in laws and official regulations and therefore are not transparent. It is difficult to fight non-tariff barriers because often the offending party will not admit that a barrier is in place and therefore will not enter into negotiations for its removal. Some barriers are especially difficult to detect and monitor. For instance, a change in domestic product standards will typically be publicized only in that country with the result that foreign manufacturers may not be aware of it and may take a long time to make adjustment so that their products comply with the new standards. When a developing country limits the importation of used cars, the stated argument is safety even though the imports may be safer than the vehicles currently on the road. The idea is to protect local manufacturers and/or obtain the higher duties obtained from selling new vehicles, or to reduce imports altogether since most consumers cannot afford a new import.

There is great variety of non-tariff barriers, and their combined effect can be substantial. For instance, Brazil's foreign minister, Celso Lafer, estimates that 60 percent of Brazil's exports to the United States face non-tariff barriers.[43] The following section outlines some of the key barriers.

Administrative Barriers

Many administrative requirements result in the erection of barriers to trade. Often a government will use an administrative measure to block the entry of products while continuing to argue that no barrier exists. In one case, the French government tried to protect its domestic VCR manufacturer against Japanese competition by channeling those imports through a tiny custom station. This caused enormous delays and increased the cost of the Japanese exports without the French government having to accept responsibility for a policy violating trade agreements.

Labeling is one example of an administrative barrier. Most countries require product labels in the local language, which is a reasonable requirement but one that puts an additional burden on the small exporter who may not find it economically feasible to do so. A U.S. requirement to list the nutritional value of a food product may seem simple and reasonable but may represent a substantial burden to a small exporter from a developing country where the requisite analysis is not easily obtained. Even for a large exporter, the need to make substantial adjustment in a small market may not make economic sense.

Another example of an administrative barrier described in Chapter 16 on Global Marketing and Supply Chain is the United States barring Mexican trucks from entering the United States on safety grounds. This alleged violation of the NAFTA agreement hurts not only Mexican truck companies that are unable to export their services into the United States but also increases the cost to Mexican manufacturers (including the Mexican affiliates of U.S. firms) that export to the United States.

An interesting case of an administrative barrier involves the dispute resolution mechanisms themselves. The Canadian government complained to the WTO that the United States was dragging its feet in appointing representatives to the WTO panel which is supposed to investigate U.S. sanctions against soft wood imports from Canada.[44]

Production Subsidies

Subsidies are payments provided by a government or its agencies to domestic companies in order to make them more competitive vis-à-vis foreign competitors at home and/or abroad. A case in point is Airbus Industries, which receives subsidies from the EU and national governments to support the development of its aircraft. It has also been alleged that national airlines such as Air France received government support with the understanding that they will utilize Airbus products. Airbus countered that Boeing received subsidies as well through military procurement by the U.S. government. Airbus also accused Boeing of signing "exclusive supplier" agreements with some airlines (e.g., Continental) that were designed to keep Airbus out of the market.

Subsidies introduce an artificial incentive into the production equation of domestic manufacturers, funneling resources away from their optimal deployment. In contrast to tariffs, however, subsidies do not distort consumer decisions because they do not raise prices beyond their global level.[45] The WTO distinguishes three types of subsidies: prohibited, actionable, and non-actionable. Prohibited subsidies require the recipient to meet export targets or to use domestic rather than foreign goods. Actionable subsidies are disallowed only when damage to national interests (of the complaining country) is demonstrated. Non-actionable subsidies include support for disenfranchised regions (e.g., China's western provinces), to help companies comply with more stringent environmental laws (up to one fifth the cost) and R&D assistance not exceeding one half (for basic research) or one quarter (for applied research) of total R&D cost. Countervailing duties cannot be imposed on non-actionable subsidies.

Countervailing duties, designed to protect against the distortion of dumping and other forms of subsidies, often result in a barrier of their own. Such duties are set to counter the impact of the subsidies, thus leveling the playing field, but this can result in a recurring retaliatory game that is likely to dampen trade.

Emergency Import Protection

The WTO recognizes remedies against a **surge in imports**, defined as a sudden and dramatic increase in imports or in market share that can cause material damage to the domestic industry. Although the remedies cannot be targeted at a particular country, they can establish a quota formula to allocate supply among different exporting countries. In general, developing countries are held to a lower standard in the application of remedies. A variation of emergency restrictions can be seen in the setting of "voluntary quotas." These quotas, such as those imposed by the U.S. government to stem the rising tide of Japanese auto imports, are often anything but voluntary, since the importing country threatens other measures if the quotas are not heeded.

Although emergency import protection can be seen to disrupt the flow of free trade, it may be justified in that it can safeguard competition by preventing existing players from exiting the market because of a one-time surge, allowing them to regroup and remain viable competitors.

Foreign Sales Corporations

In February 2000, the WTO ruled in response to an EU complaint that the U.S. use of "foreign sales corporations" (FSCs) represented a subsidy to exports and that the United States had to remedy the situation or face sanctions. Such sanctions would take the form of retaliatory tariffs on U.S. products, producing an additional trade barrier in the opposite part of the trade flow. At the time of this book's writing, the U.S. Congress was debating a change to the tax law that would replace the tax break with a broad-based exemption for foreign-source income whether generated by exports or by foreign plants. This would be comparable to exemptions granted by EU countries such as France and the Netherlands.

Foreign sales corporations are offshore corporations that market the products and/or services of firms in foreign countries. The benefit to the firms is that part of the income generated by the foreign sales corporation is excluded from U.S. taxes. The U.S. Treasury estimates that the arrangement saves U.S. firms more than $4 billion a year. Between 1991 and 1998, Cisco Systems saved $203.4 million. Boeing alone saved $230 million in 1999. That reactions to the FSC issue are mixed is a testament to the complex reality of global business. For instance, British jet engine manufacturer Rolls-Royce was hurt by the FSC because it supported its archrival Pratt & Whitney, but also benefited from it through sales from its Illinois plant. Rolls-Royce was also worried by the specter of a global trade war that would severely harm its business.[46]

Recent attempts in the U.S. House of Representatives to replace the Extraterritorial Income Exclusion with other tax breaks encountered stiff opposition on the part of large U.S. exporters such as Boeing, whose benefits from the break amounted to more than $1.2 billion between 1991 and 2000, and General Electric, whose benefits for the same period are estimated at more than $1.15 billion.[47]

Embargoes and Boycotts

Embargoes and boycotts interfere with the free flow of trade by halting trade that would otherwise take place. Both seek to damage a country by withdrawing the benefits of international trade. **An embargo** is the prohibition on exportation to a designated country. In recent years, the United States has applied an embargo primarily to rogue states such as Iraq and Iran. In contrast to export controls, most embargoes are applied across the board. **A boycott** is the blank prohibition on importation of all or some goods and services from a designated country. The United States has anti-boycott legislation that is seldom found in other countries. In one publicized case, Baxter, a U.S. medical equipment company, was fined for supporting the Arab boycott against Israel. Boycotts often constitute non-tariff barriers as firms deny their existence. For instance, with the exception of Fuji Heavy Industries (manufacturer of Subaru cars), Japanese car makers refused to sell their cars in Israel but argued that the decision was made for economic reasons (e.g., too small a market). As soon as one other major manufacturer entered Israel without triggering Arab retaliation, however, other manufacturers jumped into the market.

Boycotts are usually initiated by national governments. Examples are the U.S. embargo on Cuba or France's embargo on Israel after the 1967 war. They are sometimes also initiated by Non-Government Organizations (NGOs), such as, business associations and consumer groups in the importing country. Supported by domestic growers, Japanese consumers organized protests against U.S. agricultural imports, at one time suggesting that U.S. oranges were sprayed with Agent Orange, an herbicide used during the Vietnam War that got its name from its coloring and had nothing to do with oranges.

Finally, **buy local campaigns** are efforts to curb all imports, regardless of the country of origin. Korean consumer groups held frequent demonstrations suggesting that buyers of imported products were undermining the national interest. This was especially true during economic hard times and, whether organized by the producers or at a genuine grass-roots level, had a chilling effect on imports. In the United States, "Buy American" campaigns are often held, sometimes pointing out that the purchase of foreign products might put one's neighbors out of work. In all those cases, the campaigns constitute a non-tariff barrier in that the free flow of trade is being interfered with, resulting in discrimination against foreign producers. Such campaigns should be distinguished from the Buy American Act that obliges federal agencies and the recipients of certain federal support to purchase U.S. products and services unless no U.S. products are available (e.g., a flight to a destination not served by a U.S. carrier) and, in certain instances, unless the U.S. product is substantially more expensive. The Act creates a tariff barrier in the sense that it establishes a transparent and formal constraint on the free trade in goods and services.

Technical Standards

Technical standards are provisions made by government agencies in various countries that pertain to a large array of areas, for example, safety, pollution, technical performance, and the like. Companies that wish to sell in that country are then required to demonstrate that their products meet those standards. Whether an intentional byproduct or not, the existence of domestic standards that are at variance with those of other countries, represents a trade barrier. A group appointed by the U.S. National Research Council and headed by Gary Hufbauer concluded:

(1) Standards that differ from international norms are employed as a means to protect domestic producers; (2) restrictive standards are written to match the design features of domestic products, rather than essential performance criteria; there remains unequal access to testing and certification systems between domestic producers and exporters in most nations; (3) there continues to be a failure to accept test results and certifications performed between domestic producers and exporters in most nations; (4) there continues to be a failure to accept test results and certifications performed by competent foreign organizations in multiple markets; and (5) there is significant lack of transparency in the systems for developing technical regulations and assessing conformity in most countries.[48]

An example of regulations that represent non-tariff barriers are the EU's bans on the importation of hormone-treated beef and genetically modified corn and soybeans, which adversely affects U.S. producers. In both cases, the official reason was a potential health risk although there is little in the form of scientific evidence to support it. On the contrary, the spread of mad cow and foot-and-mouth disease in Europe has made U.S. beef probably less risky than the domestic European variety. More recently, the EU banned the import of certain Chinese foods, arguing that they contained traces of a banned antibiotic. The Chinese, on their part, now require special safety permits for the import of genetically modified foods.[49]

We should note that the WTO agreement "encourages" countries to use international standards where appropriate, but does not obligate them to do so. The organization does however enforce import licensing procedures that require import licenses to be "simple, transparent and predictable." The goal is to ensure that the administrative process will not in itself restrict or distort imports.

Corruption

Corruption, discussed separately in Chapter 19 of this book, is another barrier to trade. For instance, firms from countries with anti-bribing legislation such as the United States may refrain from doing business in a country where bribes are expected. Exporters may also refrain from selling in markets where intellectual property is not respected. For example, many U.S. publishers avoid selling books to Chinese customers, fearing that the books will be copied and then sold in bootlegged editions. Trebilcock and Howse argue that intellectual property is a case where the interests of developed and developing countries do not coincide, challenging a key assumption in international trade theories that trade benefits all participants. They suggest that intellectual property protection serves the interests of innovating countries such as the United States but not the interest of economies like Korea and Taiwan, which tend to be "imitators" of new knowledge developed elsewhere.[50]

Ironically, the efforts to fight corruption can also represent trade barriers. An example is "pre-shipment inspection," a practice in many developing countries presumably aimed at preventing capital flight, tax evasion, and fraud by subjecting incoming imports to rigorous inspection by contracted private companies. In many instances, such inspections are used to delay or block imports in order to protect domestic producers that may be associated with the inspectors.

Barriers to Service Trade

Barriers to trade in services are quite different from those affecting merchandise trade. Because knowledge plays such a key role in a service economy, any limitations on the free flow of information, including constraints on individual mobility (e.g., immigration controls) represent barriers to service trade. Some barriers to trade in services are similar in nature to tariff barriers. For example, the regulation of landing rights for airlines constitutes a tariff barrier governed mostly by bilateral treaties. Progress toward "open skies" has been made, especially within the EU, but elsewhere this remains a relatively distant goal.

Trebilcock and Howse note that in the absence of global standards and regulation, free trade in services may actually result in a reduction in global welfare. A case in point is lax regulation in the banking industry of one country that is damaging to depositors from another country, resulting in a net reduction in global welfare.[51] Opponents of globalization will argue that a similar situation exists in merchandise trade, where manufacturers transfer production to countries with lax environmental standards, resulting in global warming and other adverse consequences, with a net reduction in global welfare.

Interim Summary

1. Non-tariff barriers to trade include government and business measures as well as other phenomena that discourage trade between countries (e.g., culture).

2. Since non-tariff barriers are not transparent, they may be much more difficult to respond to and offer an advantage to domestic businesses.

3. Barriers to service trade are different than those to merchandise trade. Because service is based on individuals, rather than goods, any limitation on individual movement is a non-tariff barrier.

CHAPTER SUMMARY

1. International trade is the exchange of goods and services across borders. Theories explaining trade flows include the mercantilist doctrine, the absolute advantage theory, the comparative advantage theory, the Heckscher-Ohlin theorem, the product life cycle model, Linder's Income-Preference Similarity Theory, and the new trade theory.

2. Although none of the theories is capable of explaining the entire range of motives for international trade, they collectively provide good insights into why international trade occurs. Differences in factor endowments as explained by the Heckscher-Ohlin theorem are still largely valid in explaining trade in labor-intensive or natural resource products, whereas theories of technological gap and product life cycle are more useful in explaining trade of technology-intensive products. The new trade theory clearly documents intra-industry and intra-firm trade.

3. Further theoretical development for international trade is needed because many new factors that affect trade today have not been taken into account in extant theories. Examples of these factors include fast-paced flows of human, capital, information, and

technological resources across nations and the increased importance of country capabilities such as openness of the economy and competitiveness in process innovation.

4. International trade has grown dramatically in recent decades; global trade in services is growing especially rapidly among the most developed nations and is likely to become more important as time passes.

5. International trade is becoming more difficult to measure and analyze as more and more products and services contain inputs that originate in a variety of nations. Consequently, it is difficult to pinpoint the origin of a product or a service and the rules under which it is to be traded.

6. There are two types of trade barriers, tariff and non-tariff. Tariff barriers include tariffs, quotas, export controls, and dumping regulations. Non-tariff barriers are less transparent and include administrative barriers, technical standards, foreign sales corporations, and corrupt practices, among others. Because of their nature, non-tariff barriers are more difficult to argue and negotiate.

CHAPTER NOTES

[1] D. Hume, Of the balance of trade. In *Essays, Moral, Political and Literary*, vol. 1, Oxford: Oxford University Press, 1973.
[2] A. Smith, *An Inquiry into the Nature and Causes of the Wealth of Nations.* Book IV, Oxford: Clarendon Press, 1869, 29–31.
[3] D. Ricardo, *On the Principles of Political Economy and Taxation.* New York: Dutton, 1948.

[4] E. Heckscher, "The effects of foreign trade on the distribution of income." Reprinted in H. Ellis and L. Metzler (eds.), *Readings in the Theory of International Trade*. Homewood, IL: Irwin, 1949; Ohlin, B. *International and interregional trade*. Cambridge, MA: Harvard Economic Studies, 1933; revised edition, 1967.

[5] W. Stolper, and P. A. Samuelson, "Protection and real wages," *Review of Economic Studies*, Vol. 9, November 1941, pp. 58–73.

[6] R. E. Baldwin, "Determinants of the commodity structure of U.S. trade," *The American Economic Review*, March 1971, 126–146; J. Vanek, "The natural resource content of foreign trade, 1870–1955, and the relative abundance of natural resources in the United States," *Review of Economics and Statistics*, May 1959, 146–153.

[7] P. B. Kenen, "Nature, capital, and trade," *Journal of Political Economy*, October 1965, 437–460; I. B. Kravis, "Wages and foreign trade," *Review of Economics and Statistics*, February 1956, 14–30.

[8] D. B. Keesing, "Labor skills and comparative advantage," *The American Economic Review*, May 1966, 249–258; R. E. Baldwin, "Determinants of the commodity structure of U.S. trade," *The American Economic Review*, March 1971, 126–146; W. H. Gruber, D. Metha, and R. Vernon. "The R&D factor in international trade and international investment of United States industries," *Journal of Political Economy*, February 1967, 20–37; M. Posner, "International trade and technical change," *Oxford Economic Papers*, vol. 13, October 1961, 323–341.

[9] P. B. Kenen, "Nature, capital and trade," *Journal of Political Economy*, October 1965, 437–460; R. E. Baldwin, "Determinants of the commodity structure of U.S. trade," *The American Economic Review*, March 1971, 126–146.

[10] G. C. Hufbauer, *Synthetic Materials and the Theory of International Trade*. Cambridge, MA: Harvard University Press. 1966; M. Posner, International trade and technical change. *Oxford Economic Papers*, vol. 13, October 1961, 323–341.

[11] W. H. Gruber, D. Metha, and R. Vernon, "The R&D factor in international trade and international investment of United States industries," *Journal of Political Economy*, February 1967, 20–37;

[12] R. Vernon, "International investments and international trade in the product life cycle," *Quarterly Journal of Economics*, May 1966, pp. 190–207.

[13] S. B. Linder, *An Essay on Trade and Transformation*. New York: Wiley, 1961.

[14] A. Dixit and V. Norman. 1980. *Theory of International Trade*. Cambridge: Cambridge University Press; K. Lancaster, 1980. Intra-industry trade under perfect monopolistic competition. *Journal of International Economics*, 10: 151–75; P. Krugman, 1979. Increasing returns, monopolistic competition, and international trade. *Journal of International Economics*, 9:469–479; P. Krugman, 1980. Scale economies, product differentiation, and the pattern of trade. *American Economic Review*, 70:950–959; P. Krugman, 1981. Intraindustry specialization and the gains from trade. *Journal of Political Economy*, 89:959–973; E. Helpman, 1981. International trade in the presence of product differentiation, economies of scale, and monopolistic competition—A Chamberlinian-Heckscher-Ohlin approach. *Journal of International Economics*, 11:305–340; W. Ethier, 1982. National and international returns to scale in the modern theory of international trade. *American Economic Review*, 72:389–405.

[15] World Trade Organization Press Release, October 19, 2001.

[16] U.S. Commerce Department, U.S. Trade Online, Guide to Foreign Trade Statistics.

[17] J. Millman, "Mexico's newest export: your meal." *Wall Street Journal*, January 19, 2000, B1.

[18] A. Carrns, "A pencil icon tries to get a grip," *Wall Street Journal*, December 24, 2000, A1.

[19] WTO, 2001 International Trade Statistics, p. 78.

[20] "This trade deficit was made in the USA," *Wall Street Journal*, August 7, 2000, A1.

[21] P. Bowring, "Pessimism unwarranted," *International Herald Tribune*, April 6, 2001, p. 17.

[22] WTO, International Trade Statistics 2001, p. 145.

[23] J. Millman, and W. Pinkston, "Mexicans transform a town in Georgia—and an entire industry," *Wall Street Journal*, August 30, 2001, A1.

[24] International Labor Office, Yearbook of Labor Statistics, Geneva, Switzerland, 2000.

[25] International Trade Administration, U.S. services trade highlights, December 1999.

[26] For a broader discussion, see M. J. Trebilcock and R. Howse, *The Regulation of International Trade*, London: Routledge, 2000.

[27] D. S. Broder, "U.S. opinion on free trade is divided," *International Herald Tribune*, March 17–18 2001, p. 10.

[28] "The human face of globalization," *The Economist*, 2000.

[29] "Protests: Face of future or just a blast from the past," *Wall Street Journal*, December 2, 1999, A8.

[30] "Trade balance: Tipping scales to help workers," *Wall Street Journal*, August 30, 2001, A1.

[31] "Globalization: What Americans are worried about," *Business Week*, April 24, 2000, p. 44.

[32] M. J. Trebilcock, and R. Howse, *The Regulation of International Trade*. Routledge, England, 2000 2nd ed.

[33] P. Constable and R. Lakshmi, "India braces for flood of imports," *International Herald Tribune*, April 6, 2001.

[34] "What business thinks," *Twin Cities Business Monthly*, August 24–27 Survey, 2000.

[35] *The Economist*, October 3, 1998.

[36] P. Constable, and R. Lakshmi, "India braces for flood of imports," *International Herald Tribune*, April 6, 2001, p. 13.

[37] "Sugar solution," *The Economist*, April 22, 2000, 58.

[38] "One lump or two?" *The Economist*, January 5, 2002, 61.

[39] N. King, Jr. "Tale of the tuna: Grocery rivalry fuels tariff spat," *Wall Street Journal*, April 20, 2002, B1.

[40] Y. J. Dreazen, "McDonnell Douglas to pay fine for problems with sale to China," *Wall Street Journal*, November 15, 2001, A4.

[41] S. Sakuma, "What's unfair?—The WTO rules on dumping." *Japan Economic Currents*, Keizai Koho Center, No. 9, June 2001.

[42] T. Beal, "A Mexican standoff with China, The Asian," *Wall Street Journal*, June 1–3 2001, 6.

[43] J. Karp, "Brazil to be vocal in America's trade talks," *Wall Street Journal*, April 19, 2001, A13.

[44] I. Jacj, and P. Morton, "Ottawa protests U.S. delays over lumber to WTO," *Financial Post*, January 23, 2002, FP6.

[45] Trebilcock and Howse, *The Regulation of International Trade*, Routledge, England, 2000. pp. 113–114.

[46] G. Winestock, "U.S., EU risk trade war over export tax shelters," *Wall Street Journal*, September 5, 2000, A26; (no author) "U.S. export subsidy has some fans in Europe," *Wall Street Journal*, September 29, 2000, A17.

[47] J. D. McKinnon, "Exporters attack tax proposal," *Wall Street Journal*, May 1, 2002, A2.

[48] Standards, Conformity Assessment and Trade, cited in Trebilcock & Howse p. 132.

[49] "Is EU's vision of free trade blurred by protectionism?" *Wall Street Journal*, March 29, 2002, A10.

[50] Trebilcock and Howse, *The Regulation of International Trade*, Routledge, England, 2000. p. 311.

[51] Trebilcock and Howse, *The Regulation of International Trade*, Routledge, England, 2000. p. 274.

Foreign Direct Investment Theory and Application

DO YOU KNOW

1. What are the types of foreign direct investment (FDI) and what strategic goals encourage an MNE to engage in such investment?

2. Assuming you are a senior manager at Nike while your friend works for Boeing, do you share strategic goals in pursuing FDI? And, are you both looking for the same benefits that may arise from FDI?

3. If you were the head of the investment authority of India, what benefits would you cite to MNE executives to attract them to establish a subsidiary in your country?

4. What drives FDI distribution and patterns, and why is Africa left out of the FDI mix? What will it take to change that?

OPENING CASE "The McDonald's of Thai Food"

"We want to be the McDonald's of Thai food," says Thailand's deputy commerce minister, explaining his government's launch of a venture that would place 3,000 Thai restaurants around the world, 1,000 in the United States. The restaurants will be divided in three levels, from the fast-food Elephant Jump to the mid-priced Cool Basil to the upscale Golden Leaf. The effort comes in addition to the Thai government's successful campaign to promote Thai food abroad via cooking fairs and food shows. The Thai government will have a minority stake in the venture, leaving day-to-day management to foreign franchisees.

Why is the Thai government investing in Thai restaurants in foreign countries? The popularity of Thai restaurants abroad has generated a huge domestic industry exporting more than $6 billion annually in foodstuff and supplies, including Buddha sculptures. The popularity of Thai food has also encouraged more tourists to visit Thailand, with the government using restaurants as a platform to promote tourism. The government will use its stake to ensure that the restaurants serve genuine Thai food and that they buy at least 70 percent of their supplies from Thailand.

The expansion has already encountered some obstacles, among them, a critical shortage in Thai chefs. Opposition from private operators based in Thailand and others based in foreign countries is also beginning to mount. The Thai government is confident however that its foreign investment, possibly the first of its kind by a government, will give a welcome boost to the Thai economy, which has yet to fully recover from the devastating Asian Financial Crisis of 1998. ■

Source: Based on Robert Frank, "Thai food for the world?" *Wall Street Journal,* February 6, 2001, B1.

DEFINITION AND TYPES OF FOREIGN DIRECT INVESTMENT

As the opening case shows, increasing globalization has captured the attention of not only entrepreneurs and businesspeople but also government officials who are searching for international business advantages in an ever-changing world. The establishment of Thai restaurants overseas in response to increasing offshore demand has resulted in enormous benefits for the Thai economy, including its domestic businesses, which stand to benefit from exporting to the new restaurants. The message of this case is clear: Markets are moving toward borderless competition and firms, whether from developed or developing countries, need to expand globally to seize more opportunities. To this end, they have to engage in foreign direct investment. As we will see in this chapter, as well as in Chapters 4 and 10, investment in foreign markets is potentially lucrative but also full of potential pitfalls. The complexities involved in controlling and coordinating foreign affiliates that are situated far from headquarters and from each other, and the uncertainty of operating in unfamiliar environments that differ culturally, legally, and politically, represent major challenges to firms. Failed international expansions such as Swissair, Gateway Computers, and, more recently, energy giant Enron serve as reminders of the difficulty of investing and operating abroad.

Foreign direct investment (FDI) occurs when a firm invests directly in production or other facilities in a foreign country over which it has effective control. Companies can enter a foreign market either through exporting or FDI. Exporting, further described in Chapter 10, is a relatively low-risk and simple vehicle with which to enter a foreign market because it does not involve actual presence in the target market. While lower in risk, exporting does not enable the firm to maintain control over foreign production and operations nor benefit from opportunities available only through actual presence in a foreign market, which FDI permits. Manufacturing FDI requires an establishment of production facilities abroad (e.g., Coca-Cola had built bottling facilities in about 200 countries by 2001), whereas service FDI requires either building service facilities (e.g., Walt Disney built Disneyland Europe in 1992) or establishing an investment foothold via capital contribution and building office facilities (e.g., Citigroup in 1997 acquired Confia, which owns 300 branches in Mexico providing banking and financial services). These overseas units or entities are broadly called **foreign subsidiaries** (or foreign affiliates). The country in which a foreign subsidiary operates is termed the **host country.**

One needs to distinguish between the flow of FDI and the stock of FDI. The **flow of FDI** refers to the amount of FDI undertaken over a given time period (e.g., a year). The **stock of FDI** refers to the total accumulated value of foreign-owned assets at a given time. With regard to the flow of FDI, it is important to differentiate between outflow and inflow FDI. **Outflows of FDI** mean the flow of FDI out of a country, that is, firms undertaking direct investment in foreign countries. **Inflows of FDI** mean the flow of FDI into a country, that is, foreign firms undertaking direct investment in the local country. We will later present the patterns and characteristics of FDI flows and stocks involving major countries in the world.

FDI versus Foreign Portfolio Investment

Foreign portfolio investment (or foreign *in*direct investment) is investment by individuals, firms, or public bodies (e.g., governments or nonprofit organizations) in foreign financial instruments such as government bonds, corporate bonds, mutual funds, and foreign stocks. In other words, FDI is the investment in real or **physical assets** such as factories and facilities, whereas portfolio investment is the investment in **financial assets** comprising stocks, bonds, and other forms of debt denominated in terms of a foreign country's national currency. As such, FDI involves control over foreign production or operations undertaken by the multinational enterprise (MNE) but portfolio investment does not. To understand foreign portfolio investment, one must be familiar with portfolio theory. **Portfolio theory** describes the behavior of individuals or firms administering large amounts of financial assets in search of the highest possible risk-adjusted net return. Fundamental to this theory is the idea that a guaranteed rate of return (say, 9 percent per year fixed over the next five years) is preferable to a rate of return which is higher on average but fluctuates over time (e.g., average 9.5 percent per year but with high volatility during this five-year period). The variability of the rate of return over time is referred to as the **financial risk** in portfolio investment. The key task of portfolio management is to reduce the variability (or risk) of a *group* of stocks so that the variability of the whole is less than that of its parts. If it is possible to identify some stocks whose yields will increase when the yields of others decrease, then, by including both types of securities in the portfolio, the portfolio's overall variability will be reduced. This is why some people interpret this theory as "putting eggs in different baskets rather than one basket." This logic also applies to the establishment of a conglomerate corporation that diversifies into many product lines rather than specializing in a single one. More detailed discussions on portfolio investment appear in Chapters 9 and 14.

Types of FDI

In defining FDI, we distinguish between horizontal and vertical FDI. **Horizontal FDI** occurs when the MNE enters a foreign country to produce the same product(s) produced at home (or offer the same service that it does at home). It represents, therefore, a geographical diversification of the MNE's established domestic product line. Most Japanese MNEs, for instance, begin their international expansion with horizontal investment because they believe that this approach enables them to share experience, resources, and knowledge already developed at home, thus reducing risk. If FDI abroad is to manufacture products *not* manufactured by the parent company at home, it is called **conglomerate FDI.** For example, Hong Kong MNEs often set up foreign subsidiaries or acquire local firms in mainland China to manufacture goods that are unrelated to the parent company's product portfolio. The main purpose is to seize emerging market opportunities and capitalize on their established business and personal networks with the mainland that western MNEs do not have. **Vertical FDI** occurs when the MNE enters a foreign country to produce intermediate goods that are intended for use as inputs in its home country (or in other subsidiaries) production process (this is called "backward vertical FDI"), or to market its homemade products overseas or produce final outputs in a host country using its home-supplied intermediate goods or materials (this is called "forward vertical FDI"). An example of backward vertical FDI is offshore extractive investments in petroleum and minerals. An example of forward vertical integration is the establishment of an assembly plant or a sales branch overseas.

Horizontal FDI is used by both developed and developing country MNEs. It enables the MNE to quickly establish its competitive advantage in the host country. This is because the company's key competencies, whether technological or organizational, are generally more transferable and applicable to the host country operations through horizontal FDI than through conglomerate or vertical FDI. All companies will inevitably face an additional cost when investing in a foreign market. The **liability of foreignness** represents the costs of doing business abroad that result in a competitive disadvantage vis-à-vis indigenous firms. An example of this liability is the lack of adaptation to European customs, from transportation models to food, by the Walt Disney Company when establishing its first park in Europe, Eurodisney (renamed Disneyland Europe since then).

Liability of foreigness in Eurodisney.

Source: © *The New Yorker Collection*, 1987. Frank Modell from cartoonbank.com. All Rights Reserved.

Utilizing established competencies abroad in the same product or business as that at home helps the firm overcome the liability of foreignness, and thus reduces the risks inherent in foreign production and operations. Conglomerate FDI is relatively less popular because it involves more difficulties in establishing market power and competitive position in the host country. These difficulties arise from the firm's inability to share distinctive competencies developed at home. Finally, vertical FDI, whether backward or forward, can create financial and operational benefits (e.g., transfer pricing, high profit margin, market power, and quality control) but requires global coordination at headquarters.

Entry Mode

The manner in which a firm chooses to enter a foreign market through FDI is referred to as **entry mode.** Entry mode examples include international franchising, branches, contractual alliances, equity joint ventures, and wholly foreign-owned subsidiaries. While Damon's, for example, used franchising to enter the Panama market, Lucent Technologies preferred a contractual alliance (i.e., co-production) to minimize investment risks when it entered this market in the early 1980s. While GE (the United States) and SNECMA (France) decided to form a joint venture to produce civilian jet engines, Mercedes-Benz (Germany) chose to establish a wholly owned subsidiary in Alabama to manufacture sports utility vehicles. Once the entry mode is selected, firms determine the specific approach they will use to establish or realize the chosen entry mode. Specific investment approaches include (a) greenfield investment (i.e., building a brand-new facility), (b) cross-border mergers, (c) cross-border acquisitions, and (d) sharing or utilizing existing facilities. Entry modes and investment approaches are detailed in Chapter 10, which explains international entry strategies.

The Strategic Logic Behind FDI

Different MNEs might have different strategic logic underlying FDI. **Resource-seeking FDI** attempts to acquire particular resources at a lower real cost than could be obtained in the home country. Resource-seekers can be further classified into three groups: those seeking physical resources; those seeking plentiful supplies of cheap and/or skilled labor; and those seeking technological, organizational, and managerial skills. **Market-seeking FDI** attempts to secure market share and sales growth in the target foreign market. Apart from market size and the prospects for market growth, the reasons for market-seeking FDI include (1) the firm's main suppliers or customers have set up foreign producing facilities abroad and the firm needs to follow them overseas; (2) the firm's products need to be adapted to local tastes or needs, and to indigenous resources and capabilities; and (3) the firm may consider it necessary, as part of its global production and marketing strategy, to maintain a physical presence in the leading markets served by its competitors. **Efficiency-seeking FDI** attempts to rationalize the structure of established resource-based or marketing-seeking investment in such a way that the firm can gain from the common governance of geographically dispersed activities. MNEs with this motive generally aim to take advantage of different factor endowments, cultures, economic systems and policies, and market structures by concentrating production in a limited number of locations to supply multiple markets. Finally, **strategic asset-seeking FDI** attempts to acquire the assets of foreign firms so as to promote their long-term strategic objectives, especially advancing their international competitiveness. MNEs with this intention often establish global strategic alliances or acquire local firms. Many

MNEs today pursue pluralistic goals and engage in FDI that combines characteristics of several of the preceding categories. Procter & Gamble, for instance, has sales in over 140 countries and on the ground operations in over 70 countries. Its strategic aims behind product and geographical diversifications include better resources, larger markets, and higher efficiency.

Interim Summary

1. Although FDI involves a higher risk than exportation, it allows a company greater control over its products or services in foreign markets as well as access to specialized opportunities not available to exporters.

2. In addition to FDI in the form of subsidiaries and other physical plants, many MNEs engage in foreign portfolio investment whereby they purchase stocks, bonds, or other securities in a foreign market.

3. The strategic logic of FDI is fourfold: resource-seeking, market-seeking, efficiency-seeking, and strategic asset-seeking.

4. FDI can take a number of forms based on the needs of the parent corporation. Horizontal FDI is a safe way to enter a foreign market because it produces the same product as the parent company, so experience and infrastructure are easily shared. If the investment produces a product entirely unrelated to the parent's products, it is a conglomerate FDI. Vertical FDI acts as an intermediary or finishing stage in the production process, offering either inputs to the parent or final access to a foreign market.

HOW MNEs BENEFIT FROM FOREIGN DIRECT INVESTMENT

Enhancing Efficiency from Location Advantages

In Chapter 2 we introduced the concept of comparative advantage of nations. Firms can realize these advantages not only through international trade but also through FDI. In fact, FDI is potentially a better vehicle than trade for firms in terms of leveraging factor endowment differences between home and host countries. This is because through FDI the firm owns and controls actual operations overseas, and can consequently capture the entire profit margin that otherwise must be shared between an importer and an exporter. **Location advantages** are defined as the benefits arising from a host country's comparative advantages accrued to foreign direct investors. Firms are prompted to invest abroad to acquire particular and specific resources at lower real costs than could be obtained in their home country. The motivation for FDI is to make the investing firm more profitable and competitive in the markets it serves or intends to serve. In addition to natural endowments, location specific advantages include created endowments such as economic systems and investment incentives. PepsiCo Inc., for example, invested heavily in Brazil, Argentina, and Mexico to seek out benefits resulting from economic liberalization in these economies. Generally, MNEs such as RCA that use cost-leadership strategies will choose the location that minimizes total costs. Labor cost differentials, transportation costs, tariff and non-tariff barriers, as well as governmental policies (e.g., taxes affecting investment in a host country) are important determinants of location choice. MNEs use their knowledge and information-scanning ability to locate manufacturing activities in countries that are the most advantageous from the standpoint of cost or other strategic considerations.

Improving Performance from Structural Discrepancies

Structural discrepancies are the differences in industry structure attributes (e.g., profitability, growth potential, and competition) between home and host countries. Through FDI, MNEs are likely to achieve higher performance than firms operating domestically because they benefit from such structural discrepancies by investing those distinct resources that can enhance competitive advantages vis-à-vis their rivals in indigenous markets. Compaq undertook FDI in the Middle East, Latin America, and Europe partially because the overseas competition in the computer industry is less intense than that in the United States. Moreover, Compaq's technological capabilities create a strong competitive position for the firm in these markets. Because national markets vary in industry life-cycle stages and in consumer purchasing power, market demand and sophistication are heterogeneous across borders. For instance, many emerging economies present vast market opportunities for MNEs to attain above-average returns from pent-up demand long stifled by government intervention. Levi Strauss, for example, invested in Mexico, Brazil, Argentina, China, Indonesia, the Philippines, South Korea, and Israel to benefit from growing demand there, because the jeans market is almost mature in the United States.

Increasing Return from Ownership Advantages

Ownership advantages are benefits derived from the proprietary knowledge, resources, or assets possessed only by the owner (the MNE). The possession of intangible assets (e.g., reputation, brand image, and unique distribution channels) or proprietary knowledge (e.g., technological expertise, organizational skills, and international experience) confers on their foreign owners competitive advantages. FDI serves as an instrument that allows firms to transfer capital, technology, and organizational skills from one country to another. FDI expands the market domain from which the MNE can deploy, exploit, and utilize its core competence developed at home. **Core competence** is skill(s) within the firm that competitors cannot easily match or imitate. These skills may exist in any of the firm's value-creation activities, such as production, marketing, R&D, human resources, and the like. Such skills are typically expressed in product or service offerings that other firms find difficult to imitate; the core competencies are thus the bedrock of a firm's competitive advantage. They enable an MNE to reduce the costs of value creation and/or create value in such a way that premium pricing is possible from product or service differentiation. FDI is hence a way of further exploiting the value-creation potential of skills and product offerings by applying them to new markets. IBM, for example, generates significant income from its voice recognition software used by many Chinese. This software, first developed in the United States, did not generate sizable income until a Chinese version was developed by the company's subsidiary in Beijing.

Ensuring Growth from Organizational Learning

FDI creates the diversity of environments in which the MNE operates. This diversity exposes the MNE to multiple stimuli, allows it to develop diverse capabilities, and provides it with broader learning opportunities than are available to a domestic firm. Organizational learning has long been a key building block and major source of competitive advantages. Sustainable competitive advantages are only possible when firms continuously reinvest in building new resources or upgrading existing resources. FDI provides learning opportunities through exposure to new markets, new practices, new ideas, new cultures, and even new competition. These opportunities result in the development of new capabilities that may be applicable to operations in similar markets. For example, many early movers entering China such as Motorola, Kodak, Philips, Sony, and Occidental Petroleum realize that the relationship-building (personal ties with local business community) skills they learned in China apply in their business in Russia, Hungary, Egypt, Southeast Asia, and Latin America. Moreover, host country environments are often characterized by both market opportunities and tremendous uncertainties. These force MNEs to learn how to respond to local settings. Further, through global alliances, FDI offers opportunities to acquire distinctive skills from foreign businesses or rivals. A global alliance can provide a firm with low-cost, fast access to new markets by "borrowing" a partner's existing core competencies, innovative skills, and country-specific knowledge. Chapter 12 discusses global alliances in detail.

The benefits suggested above are not guaranteed, however, since FDI is undertaken in a highly uncertain environment. As Chapter 1 indicates, MNEs encounter many challenges and risks. Additional costs arise from unfamiliarity with the cultural, political, and economic dimensions of a new environment. The impact of a host country's regulatory and industrial environment on FDI is substantial. In an uncertain foreign environment, regulatory factors (e.g., FDI policies, taxation and financing regulations, foreign exchange administration rules, threat of nationalization, earnings repatriation, and price controls) are especially important. The effect of uncertainty is particularly significant in formerly centrally planned economies undergoing transition and emerging markets undergoing drastic privatization, despite their promising potentials.

Interim Summary

1. Location advantages of a host country are its comparative advantages for FDI in relation to other countries. These include cheaper and/or quality resources such as labor, capital, and natural resources (known as factor endowments) as well as investment incentives (known as created endowments) that affect the cost of production and operation.

2. National markets vary in industry life-cycle stages, market growth potential, competition intensity, consumer purchasing power, and many other factors. These variations can be used to the advantage of the MNE when undertaking FDI.

3. FDI expands the market domain in which an MNE capitalizes on its core competencies, thus generating more income from existing resources, capabilities, or knowledge.

4. FDI is also a means of organizational learning. Being actively involved in FDI grants the MNE more learning opportunities that would not have been available otherwise.

THE IMPACT OF FDI ON THE HOST (RECIPIENT) COUNTRY

The impact of FDI on social welfare is best assessed from the perspective of the home and host countries, although those too vary internally by region and constituency. While nationals of the Netherlands, Finland, and the United States find foreign investment and globalization the least threatening, those from Colombia, the Philippines, and Venezuela perceive it as a threat.[1] Many of the factors that make FDI attractive to a host country may make it detrimental to the home country. For instance, although FDI benefits employment in the host country, this is often accompanied by job losses in the home country. A case in point would be any labor-intensive industry in the United States (e.g., garment) that moved much of their operations to Mexico following the NAFTA agreement.

Employment

When U.S. firms such as Xerox, Staples, and Cendant establish a customer-service call center in Canada, they do so in order to capitalize on abundant and less expensive workforce vis-à-vis the United States.[2] While this enhances employment in Canada, the emphasis of most host governments today is placed on jobs requiring knowledge and high added value. Host governments are especially keen on attracting firms that will augment such employment, and home governments are especially worried about losing such jobs. One consequence of the increased diversity of functional areas for FDI is a frequent criticism of FDI as a mere deployment of the less desirable segments of the production process abroad while retaining the most attractive portions, especially R&D, at home. Understandably, the same factor is noted as a negative by U.S. constituencies that emphasize the loss of jobs and the downward pressure on wages that result in the United States. As already noted in Chapter 2, when a job moves abroad, the displaced workers are unlikely to find a higher paying job than the one they lost.

FDI Impact on Domestic Enterprises

Thanks to their resource endowment, foreign invested enterprises are likely to be more productive than their local counterparts. The contribution of foreign affiliates to exports tends to be much higher than their proportional share in a national economy would suggest. FDI often gives rise to enhanced capabilities among local companies. Since the establishment of NAFTA, the number of Mexican firms undertaking outbound FDI has grown manifold. Mexican food firm Bimbo used its supplier relationship with McDonald's to piggyback on the U.S. firm and establish supply bases throughout Latin America. Chinese manufacturers such as appliance-maker Haier are now exporting to developed countries and have begun to establish manufacturing plants there, a step that was inconceivable before a massive FDI flow into China changed work practices and standards there. As discussed in Chapter 4, FDI tends to create innovation and knowledge, which are eventually dispersed throughout the many levels of the local economy. The extent to which local firms can take advantage of this depends on a host of other factors (e.g., local infrastructure and government policies).

UNCTAD (United Nations Center for Trade and Development) documented the various relationships between MNEs and domestic firms, ranging from purchasing to joint ventures to various contractual relationships (Exhibit 3–1). The key point is that the spillover from FDI is substantial. In typical developed economies, for example, MNE affiliates realize between 10 to 20 percent of their input locally and there is some evidence that local procurement increases over time. Such relationships are also important to the MNE in that they permit more flexibility than internalized operations would have allowed.

Meanwhile, FDI could adversely affect domestic enterprises. MNE superiority is sometimes rooted in favorable treatments (e.g., lower taxation rate or tax break) offered by host governments but not accorded to local firms. Thus local firms may be institutionally discriminated against, resulting in lesser competition in the industry.

Exhibit 3–1

Backward linkages between foreign affiliates and local enterprises and organizations

Form	Relationship of foreign affiliate to local enterprise			Relationship of foreign affiliate to non-business institutions
	Backward (sourcing)	**Forward (distribution)**	**Horizontal (co-operation in production)**	
Pure market transaction	• Off-the-shelf purchases	• Off-the-shelf sales		
Short-term linkage	• Once-for-all or intermittent purchases (on contract)	• Once-for-all or intermittent sales (on contract)		
Longer-term linkage	• Longer-term (contractual) arrangement for the procurement of inputs for further processing • Subcontracting of the production of final or inter-mediate products	• Longer-term (contractual) relation-ship with local distri-butor or end-customer • Outsourcing from domestic firms to foreign affiliates	• Joint projects with competing domestic firm	• R&D contracts with local institutions such as universities and research centers • Training programs for firms by universities • Traineeships for students in firms
Equity relationship	• Joint venture with supplier • Establishment of new supplier-affiliate (by existing foreign affiliate)	• Joint venture with distributor or end-customer • Establishment of new distribution affiliate (by existing foreign affiliate)	• Horizontal joint venture • Establishment of new affiliate (by existing foreign affiliate) for the production of same goods and services as it produces	• Joint public-private R&D centers/training centers/universities

Spillover	• Demonstration effects in unrelated firms
	  - Spillover on processes (incl. technology)
	  - Spillover on product design
	  - Spillover on format and on tacit skills (shopfloor and managerial)
	• Effects due to mobility of trained human resources
	• Enterprise spin-offs
	• Competition effects			

Source: UNCTAD, 2001.

China, for example, tried in 2001 to equalize such policy treatments to all firms, which were previously favorable to foreign investors. Additionally, heightened competition contributed by FDI may nurture a host country's overall competitiveness but could injure individual local firms in such areas as shrinkage of market share, layoffs, profit reduction, and even closure of facilities and factories. Such negative effects were felt in Nigeria, the sixth largest oil producer in the world, when the competitive giants Shell (Anglo-Dutch), Chevron (U.S.), and Texaco (U.S.) started operations there. Local firms such as the Nigerian National Petroleum Corporation (NNPC) have now yielded the market leader position to those MNEs. In response, local enterprises improve productivity and strengthen competitiveness on their own or through allying with other local firms or with MNEs. In this situation, whether or not local governments protect individual local firms through regulations depends on careful calculations of the gains and losses arising from this protection. We will discuss this further in Chapter 5.

Interim Summary

1. Job shift to the host country is one of the benefits of FDI to that country. Nevertheless, some more desirable jobs such as product design, basic research, applied research, and product development may be retained in the MNE's country of origin.

2. MNEs are powerful competitors to local businesses. However, depending on the business environment of the host country, local companies may be able to learn from the techniques employed by the MNE and become more globally competitive.

CURRENT THEORIES ON FDI

Product Life-Cycle Theory

International product life-cycle theory (first introduced in Chapter 2) provides theoretical explanation for both trade and FDI. The theory, developed by Raymond Vernon, explains why U.S. manufacturers shift from exporting to FDI. The manufacturers initially gain a monopolistic export advantage from product innovations developed for the U.S. market. In the *new* product stage, production continues to be concentrated in the United States even though production costs in some foreign countries may be lower. When the product becomes standardized in its *growth* product stage, the U.S. manufacturer has an incentive to invest abroad to exploit lower manufacturing costs and to prevent the loss of the export market to local producers. The U.S. manufacturer's first investment will be made in another industrial country where export sales are large enough to support economies of scale in local production. In the *mature* product stage, cost competition among all producers, including imitating foreign firms, intensifies. At this stage, the U.S. manufacturer may also shift production from the country of the initial FDI to a lower-cost country, sustaining the old subsidiary with new products.[3]

Vernon's theory is more relevant to manufacturers' initial entries into foreign markets than to MNEs that have FDI already in place. Many MNEs are able to develop new products abroad for subsequent sale in the United States, thus standing the product life-cycle model on its head. For example, Procter & Gamble employed more than 8,000 scientists and researchers in 2000 in 18 technical centers in 9 countries. Many new products in the health-care and beauty-care segments were developed in these offshore research centers and subsequently marketed in the United States and other foreign countries. MNEs can also transfer new products from the United States directly to their existing foreign subsidiaries, thereby skipping the export stage. Otis Elevator, a wholly owned subsidiary of United Technologies Corp., offered its products in 222 countries and maintained 28 major manufacturing facilities in 17 countries as of 1998. Despite being headquartered in the United States, 80 percent of Otis's revenues were generated elsewhere (50 percent from Europe and 20 percent from Asia Pacific). Most of Otis's new elevators, escalators, moving walkways, and shuttle systems were first developed in the United States and then transferred to and manufactured by its foreign subsidiaries in the target overseas markets.

Monopolistic Advantage Theory

The monopolistic advantage theory suggests that the MNE possesses monopolistic advantages enabling it to operate subsidiaries abroad more profitably than local competing firms.[4] **Monopolistic advantage** is the benefit incurred to a firm that maintains a monopolistic power in the market. Such advantages are specific to the investing firm rather than to the location of its production. Stephen H. Hymer found that FDI takes place because powerful MNEs choose industries or markets in which they have greater competitive advantages such as technological knowledge not available to other firms operating in that country. These competitive advantages are also referred to as firm-specific or ownership-specific advantages.

According to this theory, monopolistic advantages come from two sources: *superior knowledge* and *economies of scale*. The term "knowledge" includes production technologies, managerial skills, industrial organization, and knowledge of product. Although the MNE could possibly exploit its already developed superior knowledge through licensing to foreign markets, many types of knowledge cannot be directly sold. This is because it is impossible to package technological knowledge in a license, as is true for managerial expertise, industrial organization, knowledge of markets, and such. Even when the knowledge can be embodied in a license, the local producer may be unwilling to pay its full value because of uncertainties about its utilization. Given these reasons, the MNE realizes that it can obtain a higher return by producing directly through a subsidiary than by selling the license.

Besides superior knowledge, another determinant of FDI is the opportunity for achieving economies of scale. Economies of scale occur through either horizontal or vertical FDI. An increase in production through horizontal investment permits a reduction in unit cost of services such as financing, marketing, or technological research. Because each overseas plant produces the same product in its entirety, horizontal investment may also have the advantage of allowing the firm to even out the effects of business cycles in various markets by rearranging sales destinations across nations. Through vertical investment in which each affiliate produces those parts of the final product for which local production costs are lower, the MNE may benefit from local advantages in production costs while achieving maximum economies of scale in the production of single components. Such an international integration of production would be much more difficult through trade because of the need for close coordination of different producers and production phases.

Internalization Theory

Internalization theory advocates that the available external market fails to provide an efficient environment in which the firm can profit by using its technology or production resources. Therefore, the firm tends to produce an internal market via investment in multiple countries, and thus creates the needed market to achieve its objective.[5] A typical MNE consists of a group of geographically dispersed and goal-disparate organizations that include its headquarters and different national subsidiaries. These MNEs achieve their objectives not only through exploiting their proprietary knowledge but also through internalizing operations and management. **Internalization** is the activity in which an MNE internalizes its globally dispersed foreign operations through a unified governance structure and common ownership. Internalization theorists argue that internalization creates "contracting" through a unified, integrated intra-firm governance structure. It takes place either because there is no market for the intermediate products needed by MNEs (e.g., Falk, a global power transmission manufacturer, must use intermediate goods such as couplings and backstops produced by its Brazilian subsidiary owing to the unavailability from any outside source) or because the external market for such products is inefficient (e.g., IBM's speech recognition technology is "transacted" internally among different units because the external market has not been developed enough to properly value and protect such expertise). The costs of transactions conducted at arm's length in an external market (i.e., a fair price in an open market) may be higher than transactions within an intra-organizational market. The incentives to internalize activities are to avoid disadvantages in external mechanisms of resource allocation or to benefit from an internally integrated and intra-organizational network.

Internalization theory also specifies that the common governance of activities in different locations (e.g., Rubbermaid's subsidiary in China uses materials supplied by its sister subsidiary in Thailand, and then ships products to the United States, Europe, and Japan) is likely to result in transaction gains. In many industries, MNEs are no longer able to compete as a collection of nationally independent subsidiaries. Rather, competition is based in part on the ability to link or integrate subsidiary activities across geographic locations. To summarize, internalization advantages includes the following:

1. To avoid search and negotiating costs;
2. To avoid costs of moral hazard. **Moral hazard** refers to hidden detrimental action by external partners such as suppliers, buyers, and joint venture partners.
3. To avoid cost of violated contracts and ensuing litigation;
4. To capture economies of interdependent activities;
5. To avoid government intervention (e.g., quotas, tariffs, price controls);
6. To control supplies and conditions of sale of inputs (including technology);
7. To control market outlets;
8. To better apply cross-subsidization, predatory pricing, and transfer pricing.

Through internalization, global competitive advantages are developed by forming international economies of scale and scope and by triggering organizational learning across national markets. Operational flexibility can leverage the degree of integration. The allocation and dispersal of resources (both tangible and intangible) serve as a primary device for maintaining operational flexibility in global business activities. Essentially, by directing resource flows, an MNE may shift its activities in response to changes in tax structures, labor rates, exchange rates, governmental policy, competitor moves, or other uncertainties. Thus, resource flows are a necessary condition for achieving either location-specific or competitive advantages in global business. Resource flow requires internalization within an MNE network because it involves interdependence among subsidiaries. Internalization, in turn, requires centralized decision-making responsibility and authority. Nevertheless, control should be segmented by product line and distributed among different subsidiaries, depending on particular capabilities and environmental conditions.

The Eclectic Paradigm

The eclectic paradigm offers a general framework for explaining international production.[6] This paradigm recognizes the importance of three variables: Ownership-specific (O), Location-specific (L), and Internalization (I), all identified in earlier theories of trade and FDI. This paradigm is also called **OLI framework.** It stands at the intersection between a macroeconomic theory of international trade (L) and a microeconomic theory of the firm (O and I). It is an exercise in resource allocation and organizational economics. The key assertion is that all three factors (OLI) are important in determining the extent and pattern of FDI. Ownership-specific variables include tangible assets such as natural endowments, manpower, and capital but also intangible assets such as technology and information, managerial, marketing and entrepreneurial skills, and organizational systems. Location-specific (or country-specific) variables refer to factor endowments introduced in the preceding chapter as well as market structure, government legislation and policies, and the political, legal, and cultural environments in which FDI is undertaken. Finally, internalization refers to the firm's inherent flexibility and capacity to produce and market through its own internal subsidiaries. It is the inability of the market to produce a satisfactory deal between potential buyers and sellers of intermediate products that explains why MNEs often choose internalization over the market route for exploiting differences in comparative advantages between countries.

The eclectic paradigm distinguishes between *structural* and *transactional* market failure. Structural market failure is an external condition that gives rise to monopoly advantages as a result of entry barriers erected or increased by incumbent firms or governments. Structural market failure thus discriminates between firms in terms of their ability to gain and sustain control over property rights or to govern geographically dispersed valued-added activities. Transactional market failure is the failure of intermediate product markets to transact goods and services at a lower cost than that incurred via internalization.

Overall, the eclectic paradigm provides a more comprehensive view explaining FDI than do the product life-cycle theory, the monopolistic advantage theory, and the internalization theory. It combines and integrates country-specific, ownership-specific, and internalization factors in articulating the logic and benefits of international production. Although today's international business environment and MNE behavior differ markedly from that of two decades ago when the theory first emerged, the OLI advantages are still vital to explaining why FDI takes place and where MNEs' superior returns come from. The eclectic paradigm, like other theories of FDI, has some limitations, however. First, it does not adequately address how an MNE's ownership-specific advantages such as distinctive resources and capabilities should be deployed and exploited in international production. Possessing these resources is indeed important, but it will not yield high returns for the MNE unless they are efficiently deployed, allocated, and utilized in foreign production and operations. Second, the paradigm does not explicitly delineate the ongoing, evolving process of international production. FDI itself is a dynamic process in which resource commitment, production scale, and investment approaches are changing over time. The product life-cycle theory is also deficient in revealing the insights of these dynamics *within* the process of foreign direct investment. Third, the conventional wisdom seems inadequate in illuminating how geographically dispersed international production should be appropriately coordinated and integrated. The internalization perspective addresses how an MNE could circumvent or exploit market failure for intermediate products and services but does not discuss how a firm could integrate a multitude of sophisticated international production and balance global integration with local adaptation. To redress these deficiencies, several new theoretical perspectives have emerged in recent years. We introduce these perspectives next.

Interim Summary

1. The product life-cycle theory is an adequate descriptor for the manner in which companies with a new product become MNEs and engage in FDI. Unfortunately, it fails to describe the actions of existing MNEs with substantial FDI, which may skip steps in the model or even reverse the process.

2. Monopolization theory suggests that the core competencies of an MNE are products that it essentially holds a monopoly over. FDI occurs when it is more cost-effective to directly exploit and market these monopolies rather than license them to a local company.

3. Internalization theory states that one of the major reasons for MNEs to engage in FDI is to internalize most parts of the production process. This significantly reduces normal business risks and gives the MNE economy-of-scale advantages. The eclectic paradigm restates this concept and integrates it with corporate monopolization and national comparative advantage.

NEW PERSPECTIVES ON FDI

The Dynamic Capability Perspective

This perspective argues that ownership-specific resources or knowledge are necessary but insufficient for the success of international investment and production. This success depends not only on whether the MNE possesses distinctive resources but also on how it deploys and uses these resources in an efficient manner.[7] For example, IBM's breakthrough development in voice recognition systems did not generate much income until this system was deployed and adapted to such markets as Singapore, Hong Kong, Taiwan, China, and Korea through its subsidiaries there. FDI itself is not a single transaction, nor a one-step activity. Rather it is a dynamic process involving continued resource commitment. The ability of an MNE to thrive in today's turbulent international environment depends on its dynamic capabilities during international investment, production, and operations. **Dynamic capabilities** refer to a firm's ability to diffuse, deploy, utilize, and rebuild firm-specific resources in order to attain a sustained competitive advantage. Dynamic capability requires a capacity to extract economic returns from current resources (i.e., **capability exploitation**) as well as a capacity to learn and develop new capabilities (**capability building**). In other words, dynamic capabilities take MNE resources beyond their role as static sources of inimitable advantage toward becoming aspects of sustainable, evolving advantage.

Resource deployment is the first step in efficient capability exploitation. Capability deployment involves both quantity- and quality-based resource commitment and allocation. **Quantity-based** deployment refers to the amount of critical resources deployed in a target foreign market. **Quality-based** deployment involves the distinctiveness of resources allocated to a target market. To optimally deploy distinctive resources, MNEs need to know what factors affect the efficiency of deployment. Resources will generate stronger competitive advantages when they are applied through an appropriate configuration with external and internal dynamics in a competitive environment. Chapter 4 explains how this configuration should be made and how capability deployment may lead to competitive advantages for international expansion.

Resource deployment requires an MNE to transfer critical resources within a globally coordinated network. This transfer is the *process* whereby the MNE draws on some or all of its distinctive resources or capabilities from its home base or integrated network to give its operations in a foreign country a competitive advantage. **Transferability** is the extent to which MNE resources or knowledge developed at home can be transferred to a foreign sub-unit to result in competitive advantage or contribute to business success in the target foreign setting (industry, segmented market, or host country). Although foreign subsidiaries could rely on local resources or self-developed capabilities as needed in a local setting, this is usually inefficient because indigenous firms are already more effective at developing such capabilities. In other words, a foreign business can only gain an advantage if it is able to transfer critical capabilities unavailable to local players. For instance, McDonald's overseas success has been built on the firm's ability to rapidly transfer the capacity to operate its entire complex business system to foreign entrepreneurs. Similarly, KFC's superior knowledge in organizing and managing fast-food chains is largely transferable to its operations in foreign markets such as Australia, Europe, and Russia.

Transferability may vary for different resources or capabilities. While Toyota's "Just in Time" (JIT) system applies equally well to all its global sub-units, its centralized management style prohibits the company from adapting it quickly to changes in a volatile market. Technological capabilities are generally more transferable than organizational skills. For instance, in globalizing its R&D (research and development) activities, Sony did not encounter difficulties in transferring core technologies to overseas R&D units but was uncertain about which R&D management approach to use. Sony later realized that the top-down management approach used at home did not apply abroad and changed to a bottom-up approach. Furthermore, financial capabilities are more transferable than operational capabilities. Capital or cash flow management skills may be more mobile than workforce-related capabilities. Home country experience and reputation are also not easily transferred abroad, but international experience and global reputation are transferable across borders. Possession or control of a superior distribution network in the home market is another resource that cannot be shifted overseas. Knowing how to establish and manage a distribution network is, however, a critical capability that can be transferred to a foreign country. Finally, because environmental conditions differ across nations, transferability of the same resource or capability may also vary across nations. For example, Avon's direct selling skills may be effective in Japan or Europe but not in China, whose government banned direct selling in the late 1990s.

The dynamic capability perspective holds that FDI requires resource commitment but also creates opportunities for acquiring new capabilities. Through FDI, an MNE becomes a social community that specializes in the creation and internal dissemination of knowledge. It uses relational structures and shared coding schemes to enhance the transfer and communication of new skills and capabilities within this community. FDI, especially by forming foreign alliances, also helps the MNE acquire external knowledge. Through alliances, the MNE increases its store of knowledge by internalizing knowledge not previously available within the organization. Within the MNE network or community, a firm may establish several centers of excellence with job rotation in and out of the center in order to transfer expertise among major regional headquarters. **Centers of excellence** are foreign units equipped with the best practice of managing knowledge. At the heart of each center of excellence is the leading-edge knowledge of a small number of individuals responsible for the continual maintenance and upgrading of the knowledge base in question. Other managerial actions to facilitate knowledge transfer within the community may include building more flexible and up-to-date information systems, encouraging external benchmarking and communications, and sharing information and success stories.

It is increasingly common to find FDI in a range of functions, from back-office activities (e.g., bookkeeping and cash management) to R&D. For example, many financial service MNEs use Ireland and increasingly India as a place for conducting certain back-office operations, whereas high-tech firms such as Intel are locating R&D operations in Israel. This enables MNEs an effective use of location advantages across the spectrum of corporate operations. Indeed, one of the main criticisms of the global corporation is that it places its activities wherever it is more economical to do so. One byproduct of this trend is a phenomenon also discussed in other chapters (e.g., Chapters 2, 4, and 16), namely the increasing difficulty in determining company domicile and product country of origin.

The Evolutionary Perspective

The evolutionary perspective of FDI claims that international investment is an ongoing, evolutionary process shaped by an MNE's international experience, organizational capabilities, strategic objectives, and environmental dynamics. At the core of this perspective is the **Uppsala (or Scandinavian) model,** named after a group of scholars at Uppsala University of Sweden who published a series of articles about the international expansion process.[8] This perspective views international expansion as a process involving a series of incremental decisions during which firms develop international operations in small steps. The basic assumptions of the model are that lack of knowledge is an important obstacle to the development of international operations, but that the necessary knowledge can be acquired through time-based experience with operations abroad. Accumulated knowledge about country-specific markets, practices, and environments helps firms increase local commitment, reduces operational uncertainty, and enhances economic efficiency. The internationalization process evolves around the interplay between the development of knowledge about foreign markets and operations on the one hand, and an increasing commitment of resources to foreign markets on the other.

Two kinds of knowledge are distinguished in the model: *objective* (which can be taught) and *experiential* (which can only be acquired through personal experience). A critical assumption is that market knowledge, including perceptions of market opportunities and problems, is acquired primarily through experience in current business activities in the market. Experiential market knowledge can bring in more business opportunities and is a driving force in the internationalization process. Experiential knowledge is also assumed to be the primary way to reduce market uncertainty. Thus, the firm can be expected to make stronger resource commitments incrementally as it gains experience from current activities in a given market. This experience is to a large extent country-specific and may not be applicable to other markets.

The internationalization process model explains two patterns of internationalization of the firm. The first pattern is that the firm progressively engages in a target market. During the first stage, export starts to take place via independent representatives (trading companies). During the second stage, sales subsidiaries are set up in the foreign market, specializing in marketing and promotion. During the third stage, manufacturing facilities are established overseas, involving a multitude of activities such as production, R&D, marketing, outsourcing, and reinvestment. This sequence of stages indicates an increasing commitment of resources to the market as well as market experience accumulation. While the first stage provides almost no market experience, the second allows the firm to receive fairly regular but superficial information about market conditions. The subsequent business activities lead to more differentiated market experience.

Kenich Ohmae, a management consultant, further extends this three-stage process by including a fourth (insiderisation) and fifth stage (complete globalization). In the insiderisation stage, MNEs shift major functions such as engineering, R&D, customer financing, personnel, and finance from headquarters to local subsidiaries which then become virtual microcosms in managing and running overseas activities. In the fifth (last) stage of internationalization, MNEs coordinate common functions such as global branding, information systems, corporate finance, and R&D, while foreign subsidiaries share common purposes, corporate missions, and corporate philosophies. This coordination substantially reduces fixed costs in research, development, and administration and fosters knowledge sharing among subsidiaries in different locations or businesses. At the same time, local activities and operations are fully decentralized and local subsidiaries are totally autonomous in dealing with local markets and customers. The Industry Box shows some evolutionary experience of global automakers such as Ford and Toyota.

Another pattern stemming from the internationalization process model is that firms entering new markets involve successively greater psychic distance. **Psychic distance** is defined as differences in language, culture, political systems, and such, which disturb the flow of information between the firm and the market. Thus firms start internationalization in those markets where they can easily understand the environment, spot opportunities, and control operational risks. Overall, the model has gained some empirical support. This second pattern is an extension of **familiarity**

MNEs AND FDI IN THE AUTOMOTIVE INDUSTRY

In the Industry Box of the preceding chapter, we reviewed the global automotive industry. Now, let us look at FDI in this industry.

The automotive industry was at the forefront of FDI early in the twentieth century. Initially, FDI in automotives was mainly the result of high tariff barriers that prevented exportation into the host market. When the Ford Motor Company was founded in Detroit in 1903, it immediately recognized neighboring Canada as a promising market, but a 35 percent tariff forced it to establish a joint venture with a Canadian firm to assemble its Canada-bound cars in Windsor, Ontario. Today, Ford is spread throughout the world, growing from 65 foreign affiliates by 1970 to 140 by 1985 and 270 by 2000.

Because of its visibility, automotive FDI has always triggered strong emotions. The investment of Japanese automakers, starting with Honda and then continued by Nissan, Toyota, Mazda, and others prompted an outcry in the United States. Japanese car makers were accused of bringing low-added value jobs to the United States, while maintaining the production of sophisticated components, such as computer-controlled fuel injection systems at home.

However, if automotive FDI was initially prompted by tariff walls, subsequent investment sought to realize advantages of economies of scale and host country competitive advantage, whether in labor costs, component availability, or proximity to market. As part of this evolution, R&D, finance and other high knowledge functions started to migrate to foreign locations. For example, a number of Japanese car producers now have major design studios in the United States. Toyota has a design studio in Newport Beach, California. It also has research and development centers in Ann Arbor, Michigan; Costa Mesa, California; and Timmins, Ontario.

theory, a theory which held that firms would rather invest in host countries that are relatively close to it culturally (see Chapter 6) and that they were likely to be more successful in such relatively familiar environments.

The Integration-Responsiveness Perspective

For large MNEs, FDI is a complex process requiring coordinating subsidiary activities across national boundaries. Businesspeople often talk about "thinking globally but acting locally." But how? Prahalad and Doz offer a theoretical framework on how such balance can be achieved.[9] The framework, known as the global integration (I) and local responsiveness (R) paradigm (or the **I-R paradigm**), suggests that participants in global industries develop competitive postures across two dimensions. These dimensions represent two imperatives that simultaneously confront a business competing internationally. The first dimension, **global integration,** refers to the coordination of activities across countries in an attempt to build efficient operations networks and maximize the advantage of similarities across locations. The second, **local responsiveness,** concerns response to specific host country needs. MNEs choose to emphasize one dimension over another or compete in both dimensions, resulting in three basic strategies: *integrated, multifocal,* or *locally responsive.* Integrated strategy requires strong worldwide coordination, whereas multidomestic strategy necessitates strong national adaptation. The required degree of internalization is highest for integrated strategy, followed by multifocal strategy, and finally by locally responsive strategy (for details, see Chapter 11).

Bruce Kogut enriched the I-R paradigm by incorporating the strategic flexibility view.[10] The view is composed of two related, complementary concepts: *operational flexibility* and *strategic options.* The key notion in operational flexibility is that the balance of global integration and local responsiveness lies less in designing long-term strategic plans than in instilling flexibility. Flexibility permits a firm to exploit future changes in competition, government policies, and market dynamics. This flexibility is gained by decreasing the firm's dependence on assets already in place. This suggests that managers will alter their decisions when such changes are justified by emerging conditions in an uncertain and dynamic environment. If a decision made now has a chance of being altered later in response to new information, then the economic consequences of such change should be properly accounted for when evaluating the current decision. For example, if the establishment of a joint venture with a local partner may lead to acquisition of the partner's stake in the future, the evaluation of the joint venture ex ante should take into account the economic impact of the possible acquisition. Kogut summarizes the five opportunities arising from strategic flexibility as follows:

1. Production movement. This permits the firm to respond to shifts in market and cost factors, especially exchange rates;

2. Tax avoidance. An MNE can adjust its markup on intra-company sales of goods in order to realize profits in a low tax jurisdiction;

3. Financial arbitrage. MNEs can circumvent many host government instituted restrictions on finance, remittance, and foreign exchange balance with some innovative financial products;

4. Information transfer. Strategic flexibility enables MNEs to benefit from identifying more opportunities, scanning world markets to match sellers and buyers, and avoiding tariff and non-tariff barriers to trade;

5. Competitive power. This flexibility enables MNEs to differentiate prices according to their world competitive posture. Different links in the international value-added chain also provide leverage on enforcing equity claims or contracts in national markets.

Interim Summary

1. According to the dynamic capability perspective, FDI is not a one-time occurrence. It is a dynamic attribute of adaptability that an MNE possesses in conjunction with an understanding of its own capabilities as a company.

2. A similar model is the evolutionary perspective, which suggests that as the company changes, its pattern of FDI will change, presumably for the better. This is driven by the simultaneous development of knowledge regarding foreign markets and increased amounts of resources dedicated to those markets.

3. Global integration and local responsiveness are important to large MNEs, because their size and multinationality make coordination between subsidiaries complex. In general, an MNE will emphasize one of these two aspects over the other, but it is possible to build flexibility into both strategy and structure.

PATTERNS OF FDI

In this section, we describe the patterns of FDI throughout the world. Our focus is on FDI rather than on portfolio investment. We should note, however, that the U.S. portfolio investment liability, the largest in the world, is two and a half times the size of its portfolio of investment assets. In

Exhibit 3–2
The growth of sales and
gross product associated
with international
production, GDP and
exports, 1982–1999

(Index, 1982 = 100)

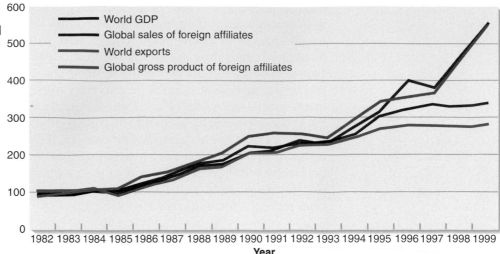

- World GDP
- Global sales of foreign affiliates
- World exports
- Global gross product of foreign affiliates

Source: UNCTAD, World Investment Report, 2001.

contrast, Germany, which has the second largest liability, has roughly the same amount in portfolio investment assets. This suggests that U.S. assets are more attractive to outsiders than foreign assets are to U.S. investors, but this is also the result of the large U.S. trade deficit described in the preceding chapter. Another observation regarding portfolio investment is that its high liquidity makes it less stable than FDI. For instance, FDI did not collapse in the aftermath of the Asian crisis.[11]

Exhibit 3–2 shows the growth of sales and gross product associated with international production (FDI), GDP, and exports. The exhibit shows global sales and global gross product of foreign affiliates growing faster than world GDP and exports— the latter have been growing as well but at a slower pace.

FDI continues to register dramatic growth. In 1980, the global FDI stock was 10 percent of global GDP; by 1999 it grew to 31 percent. At the end of 1999, FDI stock stood at $5 trillion. In that year alone, FDI inflows reached $865 billion, a 27 percent increase over the previous year.[12] In 2000, FDI inflows amounted to $1.271 trillion. FDI inward stock reached $6.314 trillion.[13]

Exhibit 3–3 shows the growth of selected FDI indicators in the 1980s and 1990s. Note, for instance, that between 1982 and 2000, FDI inflows grew twentyfold, whereas FDI outward stock grew more than tenfold. Sales of foreign affiliates grew almost sevenfold.

The composition of FDI also continues to change. Increasingly, service investment in the form of financial services, tourism establishments, retail operations, health-care centers, and the like is visible. Wal-Mart, the world's leading retailer, has a Mexican subsidiary with 520 stores and annual sales approaching $9 billion. Mexican operations bring in about one third of the $1.1 billion annual operating profit Wal-Mart earns abroad.[14] The University of Pittsburgh recently invested in a joint venture transplant center in Sicily, Italy. Citibank has opened a representative office in Israel and is looking forward to expanding its operations there when regulatory changes and political circumstances permit.

Exhibit 3–3

Selected indicators of FDI and international production, 1982–2000

Item	Value at current prices (Billions of dollars)			Annual growth rate (Percent)					
	1982	1990	2000	1986–1990	1991–1995	1996–1999	1998	1999	2000
FDI inflows	57	202	1 271	23.0	20.8	40.8	44.9	55.2	18.2
FDI outflows	37	235	1 150	26.2	16.3	37.0	52.8	41.3	14.3
FDI inward stock	719	1 889	6 314	16.2	9.3	18.4	19.8	22.3	21.5
FDI outward stock	568	1 717	5 976	20.5	10.8	16.4	20.9	19.5	19.4
Cross border M&As	...	151	1 144	26.4	23.3	50.0	74.4	44.1	49.3
Sales of foreign affiliates	2 465	5 467	15 680	15.6	10.5	10.4	18.2	17.2	18.0
Gross product of foreign affiliates	565	1 420	3 167	16.4	7.2	11.0	3.2	27.2	16.5
Total assets of foreign affiliates	1 888	5 744	21 102	18.2	13.9	15.9	23.4	14.8	19.8
Export of foreign affiliates	637	1 166	3 572	13.2	14.0	11.0	11.8	16.1	17.9
Employment of foreign affiliates (thousands)	17 454	23 721	45 587	5.7	5.3	7.8	16.8	5.3	12.7
GDP at factor cost	10 612	21 475	31 895	11.7	6.3	0.7	−0.9	3.4	6.1
Gross fixed capital formation	2 236	4 501	6 466	12.2	6.6	0.6	−0.6	4.3	...
Royalties and license fees receipts	9	27	66	22.1	14.1	4.0	6.1	1.1	...
Export of goods and non-factor services	2 124	4 381	7 036	15.4	8.6	1.9	−1.5	3.9	...

Source: UNCTAD, World Investment Report 2001.

Note: The net differences between FDI inflows and outflows and between FDI inward stock and outward stock figures on the worldwide basis are not zero due to differences in measurement and recording by various countries (e.g., a recipient nation may record reinvestment from a foreign investor's retained earnings as FDI inflow but the firm's home country may not record it as FDI outflow).

FDI OUTFLOWS From the FDI theories described earlier in this chapter it should come as no surprise that developed countries account for most of the outflow of FDI. MNEs from developed countries are more likely to possess ownership or monopolistic advantages, more likely to be innovators (and hence at the beginning of the product life cycle), more likely to be able to extract advantages from internalization, and more likely to have the dynamic capabilities necessary for successful venturing abroad. Indeed, in the 1998–2000 period, the Triad countries (United States, Europe, and Japan) accounted for 85 percent of FDI outflow and 78 percent of outward FDI stock, with much of it going to other Triad countries. **Concentration ratio,** which is the proportion of FDI outward stock held by the 10 top investor countries, was somewhat lower, however, in 2000 than in 1985, at 81.2 and 89.8, respectively.[15] Exhibit 3–4 shows outward FDI stock by region, from 1989 through 2000.

Exhibit 3–5 shows FDI outflows from developed countries for 1999 and 2000. Note that the United States placed third behind the United Kingdom and French firms. The United States remains first in terms of FDI outward stock, however, with more than $1.1 trillion of outstanding FDI, almost double that of the UK. The EU, as a whole, had by far the highest FDI outflow, but this included FDI by member countries in each other. In contrast, FDI flows from Japan declined from an already low 1999 level.[16]

The theory of familiarity suggests that MNEs prefer investments in countries and regions that are relatively similar to their own. Thus, most FDI from Spanish firms targets Latin America, most outward FDI from Hong Kong targets mainland China, and so forth. The first wave of FDI in many eastern and central European nations following the collapse of the Soviet Union was by Americans and European citizens of Hungarian, Polish, and Czech ancestry, who quickly spotted the opportunities available. These individuals and their small businesses had a competitive advantage in having acquired free market knowledge while being familiar with the investment target culture and language.

As you recall from the theoretical discussion, the Scandinavian school suggests that FDI occurs incrementally, with firms gradually moving away from familiar to less familiar markets. P&G is a good example. The company's first foreign operation, and for 15 years its only one, was established in Canada, a destination especially close given P&G's location in Cincinnati, Ohio. The company's second foreign operation was established in 1930, in the United Kingdom, whose "psychic distance" from the United States is relatively small. The third investment, in 1935, was in the Philippines, then under U.S. control, followed by Puerto Rico (1947) and Mexico (1948).

Exhibit 3–4
Outward FDI stock, 1985 and 2000 (millions of dollars)

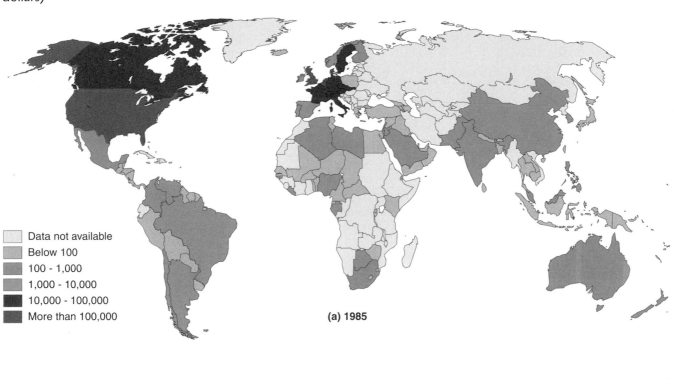

Data not available
Below 100
100 - 1,000
1,000 - 10,000
10,000 - 100,000
More than 100,000

(a) 1985

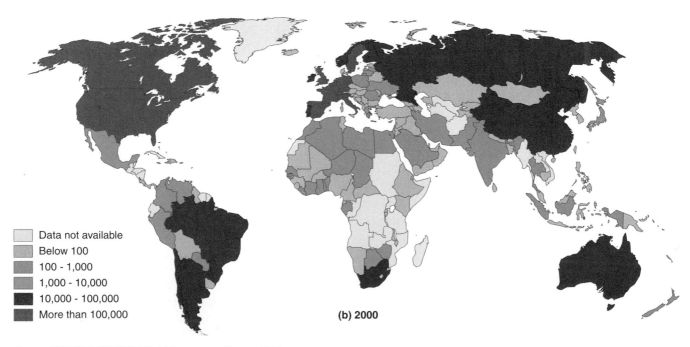

Data not available
Below 100
100 - 1,000
1,000 - 10,000
10,000 - 100,000
More than 100,000

(b) 2000

Source: UNCTAD. FDI/TNC, World Investment Report 2001.

Exhibit 3–5

Developed countries: FDI outflows, 1999 and 2000 (billions of dollars)

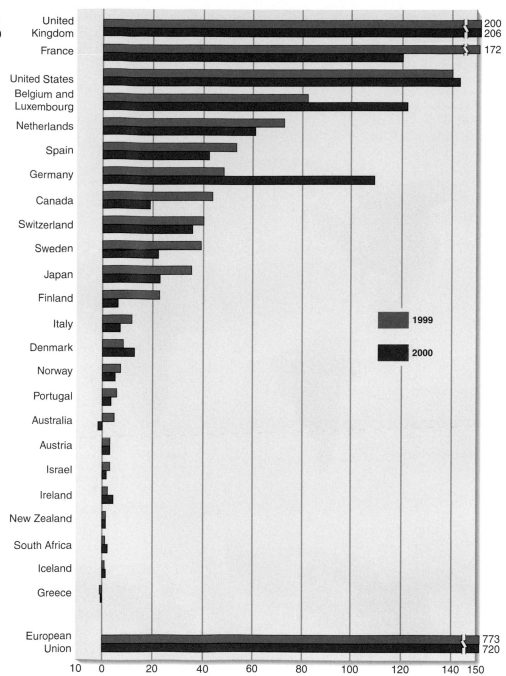

Source: UNCTAD, World Investment Report 2001.

Developing countries remain a secondary yet generally growing source of FDI. From 1980 to 1999, the share of developing countries in outflow FDI grew from 3 to 8 percent. Contributing to this outflow were mostly Asian firms, although Latin American firms also increased their FDI outflow.[17] In terms of growth in outward FDI stock in 1998, Portugal ranked first, followed by Turkey and Chile.[18] Chapter 4 discusses in detail the investment rationale and strategy of MNEs from developing countries. It notes that such MNEs rely on a different kind of competitive advantage and are often motivated by a search for knowledge rather than by a desire to leverage existing knowledge resources.

FDI INFLOWS Exhibit 3–6 shows inward FDI stocks for 1985 and 2000, respectively. Notice the significant growth in overall FDI, with only a few areas in the world today lacking much investment. Notice also the significant increase in FDI levels between the two periods in such locations as Latin America and South, East, and Southeast Asia.

Exhibit 3–6

Inward FDI stock, 1985 and 2000 (millions of dollars)

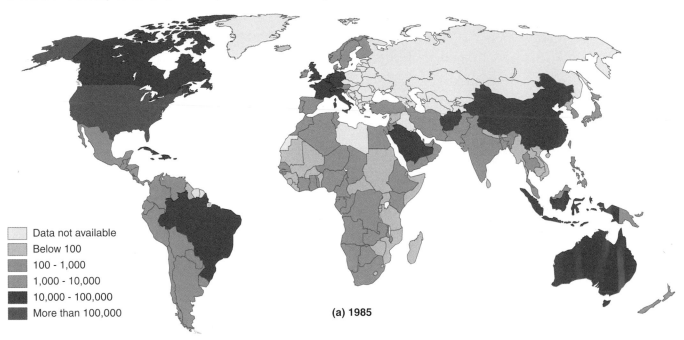

Data not available
Below 100
100 - 1,000
1,000 - 10,000
10,000 - 100,000
More than 100,000

(a) 1985

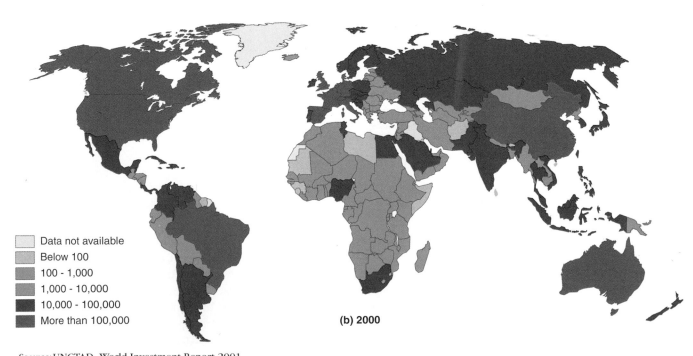

Data not available
Below 100
100 - 1,000
1,000 - 10,000
10,000 - 100,000
More than 100,000

(b) 2000

Source: UNCTAD, World Investment Report 2001.

Exhibit 3–7
Share of developing
countries in world FDI,
1980–2000 (percentage)

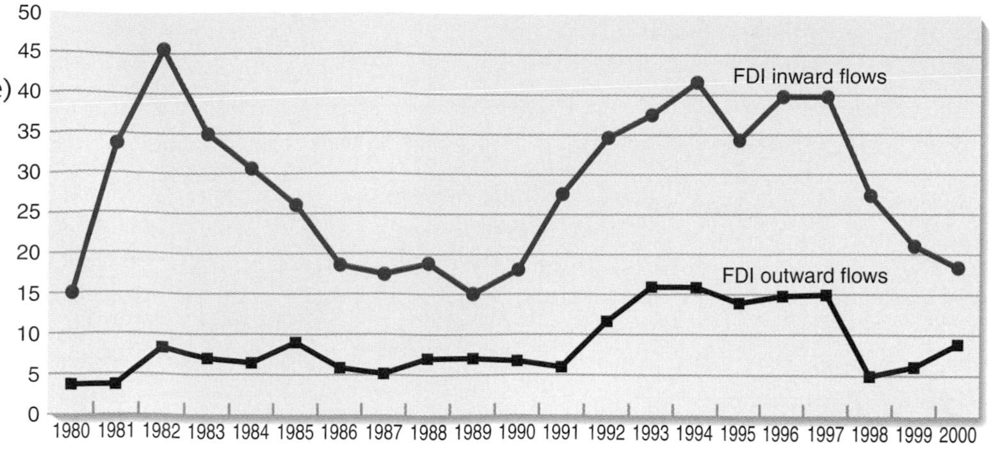

Source: UNCTAD, World Investment Report, 2001.

In the 1998–2000 period, 59 percent of incoming stock and 75 percent of inflow went into major developed economies. The concentration ratio for inflow stock was 67.7 in 2000, somewhat lower than the 70.4 registered for 1985. In 2000, inflows into developed economies exceeded $1 trillion, whereas inflows into developing economies reached $240 billion, a substantial increase over 1999 yet a lower 19 percent share of total investment, down from a peak of 41 percent in 1994. Interestingly, the curve for FDI inflows into developing countries increasingly tracks the curve for FDI outflows for those countries (see Exhibit 3–7), suggesting that the general environment of those countries has an important impact on their FDI involvement as both home and host countries.

Exhibit 3–8 lists the largest foreign investments in the United States. Note that the investments are spread across a wide range of industries, and that virtually all the high-ranked investors come from developed countries. Among the investments, there are some that might surprise you. For instance, you will notice that Burger King is owned by a U.K.-based conglomerate (see Chapter 1); or that heavy truckmaker Freightliner is owned by DaimlerChrysler. At the same time, keep in mind that no country has a larger stock of FDI than the United States. This is the reality of globalization with which we started this book.

Inflows into Developing Countries

How can the declining share of developing countries in FDI inflow be explained? First, the growing share of services in developed economies makes them ripe for investment in services, a growing portion of total FDI. More than half of the outflow from major investor countries is in the service sector, whether by retailers such as Wal-Mart and Home Depot, airlines such as British Airways (which holds a 25 percent stake in Qantas, the Australian airline), Houston-based construction firm Hines, or financial institutions such as Deutsche Bank (which purchased U.S. Bankers Trust). Second, the decline in the value of labor and commodities in overall product price erodes the competitive advantage of many developing economies that offer cheap labor pools and access to raw materials. A stable environment (low political risk), low corruption, a large market whose customers have high disposable income and a skilled workforce make a developed country attractive to foreign investors in today's knowledge economy. The same advantages seem to impact the propensity of economies to engage in outward FDI. The United States, with the largest outstanding FDI stock, was also the largest recipient of FDI. The United Kingdom, which was the first in outflow in 1999 and 2000, was the second in inflow in 1999, and third in 2000.

Exhibit 3–8
The 20 largest foreign investments in the U.S.

Rank	Foreign Investor	Country	US Investment	% Owned	Industry	Revenue (SMIL)	Income (SMIL)	Assets (SMIL)
1	DaimlerChrysler AG*	Germany	DaimlerChrysler Corp	100	automotive	73,144	NA	82,722
			Freightliner	100	commercial vehicles	10,469	NA	3,601
			Mercedes-Benz US Intl	100	automotive	2,458	NA	901
						86,071		
2	BP Amoco Plc*	UK	BP Amoco	100	energy	38,786	3,001	27,348
			Atlantic Richfield	100	energy	13,055	2,509	26,272
						51,841		
3	Royal Ahold*	Netherlands	Ahold USA	100	supermarkets	19,344	954	7,226
			US Foodservice	100	food service distribution	6,198	212	2,013
						25,542		
4	Sony*	Japan	Sony Music Entertainment	100	music			
			Sony Pictures Entertainment	100	film	21,117	918	NA
			Sony Electronics	100	consumer electronics			
5	Royal Dutch/ Shell Group*	Netherlands/ UK	Shell Oil	100	energy, chemicals	18,438	2,486	26,111
6	Toyota Motor*	Japan	Toyota Motor Mfg	100	automotive	10,600	NA	NA
			New United Motor Mfg	50	automotive	4,700	NA	NA
	Denso	Japan	Denso International America	100	automotive systems	2,563	NA	1,888
						17,863		
7	Diageo*	UK	Burger King	100	fast food	10,900	NA	NA
			Pillsbury	100	food processing	5,936	NA	NA
			Utd Distillers & Vintners (US)	100	wines and spirits	703	NA	NA
						17,539		
8	ING Group*	Netherlands	ING North America Insurance	100	insurance	14,197	442	NA
			ING Barings (US)	100	financial services	800	−75	NA
						14,997		
9	Deutsche Bank AG*	Germany	Deutsche Bank Americas	100	financial services			
			DB Alex Brown	100	financial services	14,500	NA	270,000
10	Tyco International*	Bermuda	Tyco International (US)	100	diversified mfg & services	14,409	NA	21,434
11	Siemens AG*	Germany	Siemens US	100	electronics	14,350	NA	NA
12	Vodafone AirTouch*	UK	Verizon Wireless	45	telecommunications	14,000	NA	NA
13	AXA Group*	France	AXA Financial*	60	financial services	13,371	2,491	207,554
14	Petróleos de Venezuela	Venezuela	Citgo Petroleum	100	refining, marketing	13,317	305	5,907
15	Honda Motor*	Japan	Honda of America Mfg	100	automotive	13,100	NA	NA
16	Nestlé SA*	Switzerland	Nestlé USA	100	food & beverage			
			Alcon Laboratories	100	pharmaceuticals	10,399	NA	NA
	L'Oréal	France	Cosmair (US)	100	cosmetics	2,400	NA	NA
						12,799		
17	Nortel Networks*	Canada	Nortel Networks (US)	100	telecommunications	12,758	NA	NA
18	Delhaize Le Lion SA	Belgium	Delhaize America*	44	supermarkets	10,879	588	3,973
			Super Discount Markets	60	supermarkets	315	7	NA
						11,194		
19	E.ON*	Germany	VEBA (US)	100	energy, chemicals	8,212	74	NA
			Viag (N America)	100	logistics, chemicals	2,920	NA	3,455
						11,132		
20	Aegon NV*	Netherlands	Aegon USA	100	insurance	11,083	NA	131,590

Source: Forbes, July 24, 2000.

Note: * publicly traded in the U.S. in shares or ADRs.

Exhibit 3–9

Share of the largest recipients of FDI flows among developing economies, 1985 and 2000 (percentage)

Economy	1985[a]	Economy	2000[b]
Saudi Arabia	20.4	China	19.2
Mexico	11.3	Hong Kong, China	16.0
Brazil	9.2	Brazil	14.4
China	7.0	Argentina	6.5
Singapore	6.9	Mexico	5.6
Malaysia	5.5	Korea, Republic of	4.0
Egypt	4.7	Singapore	3.1
Bermuda	4.6	Bermuda	2.8
Hong Kong, China	4.3	Chile	2.7
Argentina	2.7	Cayman Islands	2.4
Top 10 total	**76.6**	**Top 10 Total**	**76.7**

Source: UNCTAD, World Investment Report 2001.

[a]Average 1983–1985.

[b]Average 1998–2000.

FDI flows into developing countries are concentrated in a relatively small number of countries, such as China in Asia or Poland, Hungary, and the Czech Republic in central Europe. Inflows into Latin America and the Caribbean increased to $90 billion in 2000. In contrast, the entire continent of Africa received only 1.2 percent of global FDI inflows, although investment in some countries (e.g., Angola) was high in relation to gross domestic capital formation.[19] (See the concluding section on FDI in Africa). New FDI targets have become prominent in recent years. Examples are Egypt, with its market and investment liberalization, and Israel, where much of FDI has been directed to the high-tech industry.

Additional hints on the factors motivating investments in developing economies can be found on the list of major FDI recipients for 1985 and 2000 (see Exhibit 3–9). Note that in 1985, the largest recipient was Saudi Arabia whose economy is dominated by oil. By 2000, the major developing economy recipient was China (and the second Hong Kong, a Special Administrative Region of China), which offers both a low-cost export platform and an enormous and fast-growing domestic market. However, among the major recipients are small economies that are either service-based entrepots (Singapore and Hong Kong) or tax havens (Bermuda and Cayman Islands).

The Transnationality of Host Economies

When we account for the size of the economy in terms of output, employment, and the like, the impact of FDI looks quite different. UNCTAD calculated a **Host Economy Transnationality Index** as the average of four shares: FDI inflows as a percentage of gross capital formation, FDI inward stock as a percentage of GDP, value added of foreign affiliates as a percentage of GDP, and employment of foreign affiliates as a percentage of total employment. The results, presented in Exhibit 3–10, show the United States—the largest nominal recipient of FDI—near the bottom of the index, with only Italy and Japan below it. Among developing economies, Hong Kong ranks first.

FDI via Mergers and Acquisitions (M&As)

In recent years, the proportion of M&As in total FDI has been growing at the expense of greenfield investments (building new facilities from scratch). Completed M&As rose in value from less than $100 billion in 1987 to $720 billion in 1999.

Exhibit 3–10
Transnationality of host economies, 1998 (percentage)

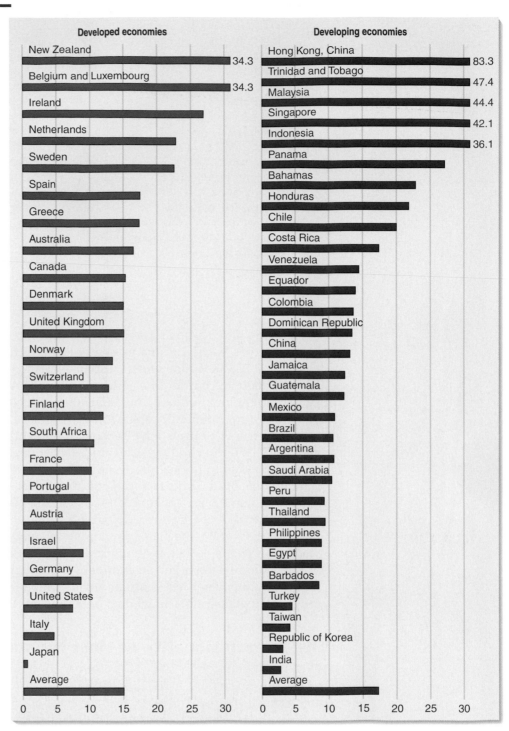

Source: UNCTAD, World Investment Report 2001.

The share of M&As in total FDI flow has grown from 52 percent in 1987 to 83 percent in 1999. The trend has been criticized by FDI opponents who say that M&As do not add to the capital stock and may stifle competition.[20] Proponents of FDI respond that acquisitions bring new technologies and better management that enable the acquired firm to survive and prosper under stiff global competition. They point out that at least in transition economies, greenfield and acquisition investments do not substitute for each other but rather play a different role, the former providing new facilities and capacities, the latter contributing to the restructuring and improvement of existing facilities and capacities.[21]

Although the acquisition of major local firms in developing nations draws frequent media attention, the most common form of M&A is one originating in and targeting developed country firms. Many large firms have embarked on multiple acquisitions. Examples are Ford Motor's acquisition of U.K.-based Jaguar and more recently Swedish company Volvo and the Land Rover division of the U.K.-based Rover group, formerly owned by German automaker BMW; the acquisition and partial acquisition of Chrysler and Mitsubishi by Daimler; and the controlling interest taken in Nissan by French automaker Renault. This wave is not limited to the car industry. Swedish paper manufacturer Svenska Cellulosa acquired both Pennsylvania-based Tuscarora and an Atlanta-based unit of Georgia Pacific in early 2001.[22] British utility National Grid completed three international acquisitions in 2000. Yet, preliminary figures for 2002 suggest that the process may have started to reverse, with many MNEs divesting some of their foreign holdings.

Although acquisitions by developing country MNEs are much less numerous than those by developed country MNEs, they are increasing. Mumbai-based Silverline Technologies acquired New Jersey-based SeraNova in 2000 for $99 million. Like other Indian high-tech firms with recent U.S. acquisitions, the company sought to gain an understanding of the U.S. market, which increasingly sources software in India.[23]

Intra-Regional Patterns

In most host countries, the distribution of FDI is uneven, triggering criticism that only a few benefit from the investment and that the beneficiaries are concentrated in areas that are already relatively affluent. Exhibit 3–11 shows the distribution of production by foreign affiliates in the United States. Although the exhibit shows the concentration of investment in a small number of states, it does not provide the whole picture. While four states (California, Michigan, New Jersey, and Massachusetts) had only a quarter of manufacturing employment of Japanese affiliates in the United States; they had fully two thirds (157 of 251) of their R&D facilities.[24] Thus, these states enjoyed the benefits of high wage, knowledge-based employment of FDI much more than other states. FDI in services is even more skewed toward investment on the East Coast (primarily), followed by California and to a lesser extent Texas.[25] This reality explains some of the political undercurrents of trade and investment discussed in Chapter 7, on the Political and Legal Environment.

In China, FDI was initially confined to special economic zones and remains concentrated along coastal areas and in a small number of other regions. This pattern is beginning to change, however. The Chinese government, like many others, is offering special incentives to firms willing to invest in less developed regions. Such incentives to disadvantaged regions are allowable under WTO rules. In Israel, the government offers extra incentives for foreign investors willing to locate in rural towns, as it recently did for Intel. In the United States, state governments have been competing with each other in offering FDI incentives in the hope of attracting investors into their state. Ohio provided such incentives to Honda, Tennessee to Nissan, and Alabama to BMW.

The regional distribution of FDI is often correlated with the investor country of origin, which again may be predicted by the theory of familiarity. In China, much of the initial investment from Hong Kong (now a Special Administrative Region of China but a separate entity for investment purposes) was concentrated in Guandong province, which is adjacent to Hong Kong and shares regional culture and dialect; Taiwanese investment was proportionally higher in Fujian province, which shares culture, language, and ethnicity with many Taiwan residents; and South Koreans were more likely to invest in areas of China with a large Korean minority. As familiarity theory predicts, such investment gradually expanded into other regions.

Exhibit 3–11

Distribution of production of foreign affiliates in the United States, by state (1992) (billions of dollars)

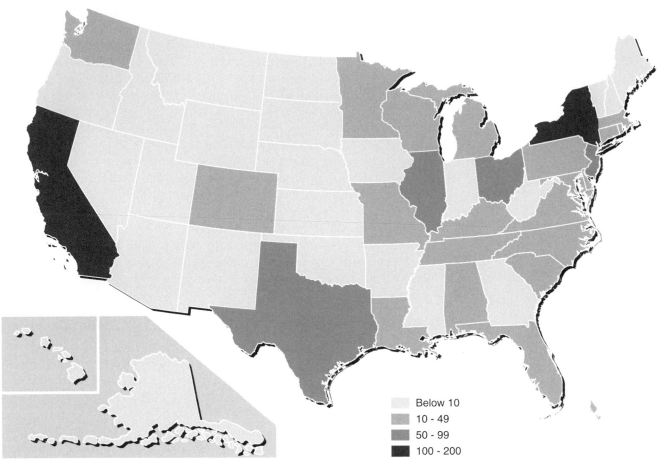

Below 10
10 - 49
50 - 99
100 - 200

Source: UNCTAD, World Investment Report 2001 based on United States, Department of Commerce, 1997.

Interim Summary

1. FDI amounts continually increase while the type of companies engaging in FDI is becoming more diverse. However, FDI outflow is overwhelmingly from the Triad countries, mostly into other Triad countries.

2. The bulk of FDI entering into developing countries goes to a short list of nations with exceptionally attractive investment environments.

3. Recently, M&As outpaced greenfield investments given their advantages such as quicker access to local markets or better use of local firms' established supply or distribution channels. FDI tends to concentrate in limited areas within host countries, generating uneven benefits.

THE INVESTMENT ENVIRONMENT

With most nations keen on attracting FDI, liberalization of markets and openness to FDI have been on the increase. In the 1991–2000 period, there were a total of 1,185 regulatory changes pertaining to FDI across the globe, of which 1,121 favored investors. In 1999 alone, 150 regulatory changes were made in 69 nations, and 147 of those were positive to FDI.[26] Many of the recently signed bilateral investment and double taxation treaties contain supportive FDI provisions.[27] The nations with the most liberal FDI environment in terms of freedom to control domestic firms are Luxembourg, Ireland, Argentina, and Hong Kong. The nations with the least open environment in this respect are China, Russia, Malaysia, and Slovenia. Russia offers by far the least protection for the foreign investor.[28]

Increased liberalization should not be confused with the uncertainty that continues to characterize international operations in developing and in transition economies (Country Box: FDI in Israel—shows an example). Weak property rights,

COUNTRY BOX
FDI in Israel

In 1994, foreign investment in Israel stood at roughly $500 million. By 2000, it grew tenfold, reaching one of the highest per capita figures for any economy. How this transformation has come about reveals a lot about the factors that motivate FDI. Israel is a country that lacks natural resources, has a tiny land area, and has a relatively small population of about 6 million. However, Israel has a highly skilled workforce and one of the highest ratios of scientists and engineers in the world (almost double that of the United States), further boosted by the immigration of thousands of scientists from the former Soviet Union. Israel ranks third after the United States and Japan in the number of patents per capita.

MNEs flocked to take advantage of this knowledge resource as well as Israel's sophisticated infrastructure and a supportive tax and investment environment. National Semiconductor, Cisco, and Motorola have all opened R&D facilities in Israel. Other firms investing in the country include Pratt & Whitney, Kimberly Clark, Intel, and IBM (all from the United States); Siemens, Unilever, and British Telecom (Europe); Sony, Toyo Ink, and Hutchison Telecom (Asia). The investment was often done through the acquisition of Israel firms, such as the purchase of ICQ by AOL for $407 million.

The following chart shows the growth of FDI in Israel from 1994 to 2000. In 2001, FDI in Israel fell considerably, a decline which is attributed mainly to two factors: first, the global decline in the technology sector in which Israel has had a competitive advantage; second, the deterioration in the security situation has devastated certain sectors such as tourism and lowered the country's appeal as a regional headquarters for the Middle East. The resulting uncertainty kept many potential investors at bay even in such industries as software that have not been directly affected.

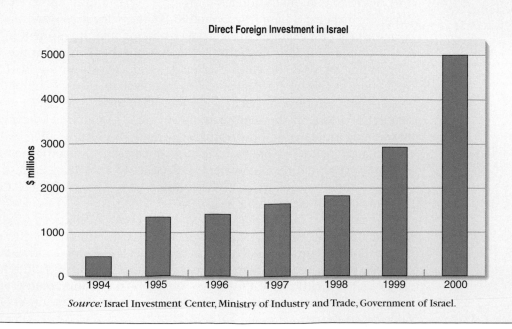

Direct Foreign Investment in Israel

Source: Israel Investment Center, Ministry of Industry and Trade, Government of Israel.

political upheaval, wild currency shifts and the like, make the international environment an uncertain terrain. However, liberalization means that FDI is less often made with the sole purpose of circumventing tariff barriers but rather for more fundamental economic and strategic reasons. With rapid globalization, product life-cycle assumptions have also been increasingly questioned. If in the past an MNE could simply utilize its older products in another, especially developing market, it is now often demanded, or necessary (owing to internal efficiencies or competitive pressures), to transfer more technology to foreign affiliates at an early stage.

Global competition to attract FDI leads many countries to offer not only a liberalized investment market but also an array of incentives to the foreign investor. Such incentives include tax holidays, tariff concessions, direct and indirect financial subsidies, training support, infrastructure improvement, capital repatriation rights, and a host of other incentives. Countries offering the most attractive incentives to foreign investors include Ireland, Singapore, Luxembourg, and the Netherlands. Russia, Slovenia, New Zealand, and Venezuela offer the fewest investment incentives.

High-tech investment that involves substantial employment is particularly in demand, enhancing the bargaining power of the MNE. Intel was thus able to extract substantial concessions from governments in various parts of the world. In Costa Rica, Intel received an eight-year tax holiday (and several more years at a reduced rate), unlimited fund repatriation rights, and infrastructure support in the form of a power station supplying power to the Intel plant at a reduced rate. Advanced Micro Devices (AMD) was similarly able to extract an array of incentives from the German government, especially since it agreed to locate its plant in the depressed eastern part of the country.[29]

FDI Decision Criteria

In the theory section, we discussed the location advantages of host countries as a major drive for FDI. We have noted that such advantages include natural endowments (e.g., mineral resources) and creative endowments (e.g., consumer purchasing power, skilled workforce), and government incentives. We have also noted that these endowments vary by region and by industry and that they tend to shift over time. For example, many foreign firms that were enticed to invest in the United Kingdom as their EU base (the United Kingdom is the preferred EU entry point for Japanese firms, for example) have been rethinking their investment in the aftermath of the United Kingdom not joining the euro mechanism. With the British pound appreciating vis-à-vis the euro, U.K.-made products sold in the EU have either become more expensive for consumers or less profitable for their producers.

A recent Deloitte and Touche study identified the following factors driving global location decisions in the high-tech industry, a sector that is knowledge-based and increasingly attractive to host countries because of its knowledge transfer and high wage characteristics.[30] Note that the most important criteria for high-tech investors are unrelated to natural endowments but rather to knowledge infrastructure, access to capital and even quality of life. Also important is the existence of other firms in the same domain (see Exhibit 3–12).

The preceding factors may change in importance, however, when other industries are involved. For instance, in industries based on monopolistic advantage, agglomeration in terms of existence of competitors is a negative rather than a positive. Low-tech labor-intensive industries (e.g., most garment manufacturers) typically regard wages as a critical location factor. Similarly, tire manufacturers are much more concerned with transportation costs than electronic chip producers for whom the value-to-weight ratio is much higher.

Exhibit 3–12

Foreign investment location criteria

ESSENTIAL CRITERIA
1. Access to skilled and educated workforce
2. Proximity to world class research institutions
3. An attractive quality of life
4. Access to venture capital

IMPORTANT CRITERIA
5. Reasonable costs of doing business
6. An established technology presence
7. Available bandwidth and adequate infrastructure
8. Favorable business climate and regulatory environment

DESIRABLE CRITERIA
9. Presence of suppliers and partners
10. Availability of community incentives

Source: Deloitte and Touche

Nor is the relationship between cost of production and location simple. As you may recall from Chapter 2, the Leontief paradox showed that the United States, a country with high capital endowment, was also exporting many labor-intensive products. The United States is also domestically manufacturing low-tech products despite wages that are often more than 10 times higher vis-à-vis alternative locations. For example, most lightbulbs sold in the United States are made locally, sometimes by foreign firms such as German-based Siemens. The reasons are transportation costs, capital intensity (i.e., automation), the importance of quick delivery and on-site service, local tastes, trade barriers, skills that are not easily transferable, and the ability to quickly implement innovation.[31]

Similarly, Conference Board data show that U.S. manufacturers are more likely to choose a high- rather than a low-wage country for investment, and that this holds in North America, Asia, and Europe. In 1997, Motorola chose to invest in Germany despite its having the highest labor costs and one of the highest tax regimes in the EU. Quality and productivity supplemented by local incentives have turned the decision in Germany's favor.[32]

National boundaries do not always provide a good indication of key criteria for the location decision. As an example, wage costs can vary substantially across regions of the same country due to varying levels of development (e.g., it is much more expensive to do business in Shanghai than in the Chinese inland) or due to special arrangement in free trade zones or territorially contiguous areas. For instance, Ohio-based firm R.G. Barry opened a footwear plant in Laredo, Texas, thanks to the Twin Plant plan that allowed it to employ Mexican workers at a fraction of its U.S. domestic cost. The plant was, however, moved to Mexico in 2002 when the further wage savings were no longer offset by tariffs, thanks to the NAFTA agreement.[33] Chapter 10 provides a detailed framework with which to analyze locational decisions.

Interim Summary

1. Global competition to attract FDI promotes liberalization of global markets and opening of the world economic environment. Many countries offer a host of incentives to foreign investors.

2. For high-tech investors, FDI concerns are less related to natural endowments and turn to creative endowments such as knowledge infrastructure, access to capital, consumer purchasing power, and government incentives.

THE LOST CONTINENT: FDI IN AFRICA

Africa is often lamented as a lost opportunity for foreign investors. Despite its considerable size and wealth of resources, the continent draws a minute 1.2 percent share of global FDI. Yet, an UNCTAD report[34] suggests that not all is bleak in the African FDI picture.

The report makes a number of important observations:

1. FDI in Africa has been on the increase, admittedly at a lower pace than that of other developing regions. FDI in Africa doubled from about $3 billion in 1988–1992 to $6 billion in 1993–1997, whereas FDI into developing countries as a whole almost quadrupled. As a result, Africa's share in FDI inflow into developing nations dropped from more than 11 percent in 1976–1980 to 4 percent in 1996–1997. Although in 1970 Africa had more FDI per $1,000 of GDP than Asia and Latin America, it has fallen behind and stayed behind since then.

2. Since 1994, per-capita income in Africa (including sub-Saharan Africa) has been on the increase, reversing an earlier trend of declining figures. This creates FDI opportunities that did not exist in the past, because they necessitate a minimal income level.

The tourist industry in Kenya is a growing one, as evidenced by this photo of vacationers outside the Nairobi Hilton.

3. As in other world regions, there are significant variations from country to country in African FDI performance. There are more than 50 countries in Africa, and some of them, notably South Africa, Egypt, and Nigeria, attracted significant investment. In recent years, countries such as Tunisia, Botswana, Namibia, Ghana, and Mozambique were also able to attract considerable investment.

4. While traditional investment in Africa came from France, the United Kingdom (former colonial masters), Germany, the United States, and Japan, new investors have emerged in recent years. Canada, Italy, the Netherlands, Norway, Portugal, and Spain have joined the ranks of investors, as did some developing countries, notably from Southeast Asia.

5. Inward FDI originating in other African countries is taking place, especially from South Africa. Anglo-American and Barlow Rand are examples, as are Moroccan food firm Conserverie Cherifiennes and Zambian mining concern Consolidated Copper Mines.

6. FDI in Africa has been expanding from traditional investment sectors such as mining and energy into manufacturing and services. This is true even in oil producer Nigeria, where in 1992 manufacturing accounted for almost half of FDI stock, and services accounted for about 20 percent. In Egypt, almost 50 percent of FDI in 1995 was in services and 47 percent in manufacturing.

7. Perhaps the most startling finding in the report is that FDI in Africa has proven profitable, in fact much more profitable than in other developing economies. Since 1990, the return on African investment averaged 29 percent. With one exception, each of the years in the 1983–1997 period produced returns in excess of 10 percent for U.S. firms in Africa.

Unfortunately, more recent data suggest that progress in Africa's FDI remains fragile. Dragged by the fall in investment into South Africa and Angola, FDI in the continent fell from $10.5 billion in 1999 to $9.1 billion in 2000. As a result, Africa's share in total FDI flows dropped below 1 percent. In a competitive global environment, Africa remains less attractive to foreign investors, despite the high profitability of existing investments. Political and military strife, AIDS, corruption, and violence combine to form an environment that does not encourage FDI. Africa remains one of the last frontiers of FDI yet to be explored.

CHAPTER SUMMARY

1. Foreign direct investment (FDI) involves investment in a manufacturing facility, service provision facility (e.g., a bank branch, an aircraft maintenance facility), or other assets in a foreign market over which the firm maintains control.

2. FDI can be horizontal (same product or service as the one produced or rendered in the home country) or vertical (investment in inputs preceding or following in the firm's value chain).

3. MNEs benefit from FDI by generating efficiencies from location advantages, leveraging structural discrepancies, getting returns from ownership advantages, and learning and then leveraging their experiences in diverse markets.

4. Conventional FDI theories emphasize monopolistic advantage, internalization, and/or location advantage. The monopolistic advantage perspective suggests that MNEs possess monopolistic power, enabling them to operate subsidiaries abroad more profitably than local competing firms. The internalization perspective suggests that it is more efficient for MNEs to internalize (e.g., vertical integration or knowledge transfer) overseas operations through a unified governance structure than otherwise to trade through open markets (if exist). The OLI paradigm integrates these perspectives with country-specific comparative advantages.

5. Among emerging perspectives, the dynamic capability view suggests that global success depends not only on a firm's distinctive resources but also how it deploys, uses, and upgrades these resources in an efficient manner and in a new international setting. The evolutionary perspective holds that internationalization is an evolutionary process, generally starting from export, to building foreign branches, to relocating facilities overseas, to insiderisation, and finally to complete globalization. The I-R paradigm addresses the balance between global integration and local responsiveness.

6. The United States has the highest stock of both outflows and inflows of FDI in the world. However, its share of the fast-growing pie of global FDI is shrinking and today it is no longer the biggest investor.

7. In recent years, more FDI has been channeled via mergers and acquisitions rather than via "greenfield" investment.

8. The global investment environment continues to liberalize, reflecting increasing competition for investment dollars. This trend suggests that most governments view FDI as being beneficial to their economies despite the problems associated with it.

CHAPTER NOTES

[1] A. T. Kearney, Globalization Ledger, Global Business Policy Council, April 2000; Measuring globalization, *Foreign Policy*, Jan/Feb. 2001.

[2] L. M. Greenberg, Canada answers the call for U.S. firms. *Wall Street Journal*, Oct. 1, 1999, A13.

[3] R. Vernon, "International investments and international trade in the product life cycle," *Quarterly Journal of Economics*, May 1966, pp. 190–207.

[4] The first systematic presentation of this theory was made by S. H. Hymer in his doctoral dissertation in 1960. See S. H. Hymer, *The International Operations of National Firms*, Cambridge, MA: The MIT Press, 1976. Follow-up efforts to reiterate this theory include C. P. Kindleberger, *American Business Abroad*, New Haven: Yale University Press, 1969; R. Z. Aliber, "A theory of direct foreign investment." In *The International Corporation: A Symposium*, edited by C. P. Kindleberger, Cambridge, MA: The MIT Press, 1970; and R. E. Caves, International Corporations: The Industrial Economics of Foreign Investment, *Economica*, February 1971, pp. 1–27.

[5] P. J. Buckley and M. Casson, *The Future of the Multinational Enterprise*, New York: Holmes and Meier, 1976; A. M. Rugman, *Inside the Multinationals*, New York: Columbia University Press, 1981.

[6] J. H. Dunning, 1980, "Toward an eclectic theory of international production: Some empirical tests," *Journal of International Business Studies*, 11(1): pp. 9–31; J. H. Dunning, 1981, *International Production and the Multinational Enterprise*, London: Allen and Unwin; J. H. Dunning, 1988, *Explaining International Production*, London: Unwin Hyman.

[7] D. J. Collis, 1991, "A resource-based analysis of global competition: The case of the bearings industry," *Strategic Management Journal*, 12: 49–68; Y. Luo, 2000, "Dynamic capabilities in international expansion," *Journal of World Business*, 35(4): 355–378; S. Tallman, 1991, Strategic management models and resource-based strategies among MNEs in a host market, *Strategic Management Journal*, 12: 69–82; U. Zander and B. Kogut, 1995, "Knowledge and the speed of the transfer and imitation of organizational capabilities," *Organization Science*, 6(1): 76–92; D. J. Teece, G. Pisano, and A. Shuen, 1997, "Dynamic capabilities and strategic management," *Strategic Management Journal*, 18(7): 509–533.

[8] See J. Johanson and J. Vahlne, 1977, "The internationalization process of the firm: A model of knowledge development and increasing foreign market commitment," *Journal of International Business Studies*, 8: 23–32; R. Luostarinen, 1980, *Internationalization of the Firm*. Helsinki School of Economics, Helsinki, Finland. Follow-up efforts include W. Davidson, 1980, "The location of foreign direct investment activity: Country characteristics and experience effects," *Journal of International Business Studies*, 11: 9–22; B. Kogut, 1983, "Foreign direct investment as a sequential process." In C. P. Kindleberger and D. Audretsch (eds.), *The Multinational Corporation in the 1980s*, pp. 35–56, Cambridge, MA: MIT

Press. O. Andersen, 1993, "On the internationalization process of firms: A critical analysis," *Journal of International Business Studies*, 24(2): 209–231; S. J. Chang, 1995, "International expansion strategy of Japanese firms: Capability building through sequential entry," *Academy of Management Journal*, 38: 383–407; Y. Luo and M. W. Peng, 1999, "Learning to compete in a transition economy: Experience, environment, and performance," *Journal of International Business Studies*, 30(2): 269–296, among others.

[9] See C. K. Prahalad and Y. Doz, 1987, *The Multinational Mission: Balancing Local Demands and Global Vision*. New York: The Free Press. Contributions to this perspective also come from C. A. Bartlett and S. Ghoshal, 1989, *Managing across Borders*. Boston, MA: Harvard Business School Press; K. Roth and A. J. Morrison, 1991, "An empirical analysis of the integration-responsiveness framework in global industries," *Journal of International Business Studies*, 21(4): 541–564; S. J. Kobrin, 1991, "An empirical analysis of the determinants of global integration," *Strategic Management Journal*, 12 (Summer): 17–32; G. S. Yip, 1995, *Total Global Strategy*, Englewood Cliffs, NJ: Prentice-Hall.

[10] See B. Kogut, 1985a, "Designing global strategies: Comparative and competitive value-added chains," *Sloan Management Review*, Summer: 15–27; B. Kogut, 1985b, "Designing global strategies: Profiting from operational flexibility," *Sloan Management Review*, Fall: 27–38; B. Kogut, 1990, "Joint ventures and the option to expand and acquire," *Management Science,* 37(1): 19–33; B. Kogut, 1994, "Options thinking and platform investments: Investing in opportunity," *California Management Review*, Winter: 52–71.

[11] See O. Shenkar, and M. Serapio, (eds.), "Tamed tigers: Restructuring, liberalization and changing business systems in the East Asian economies," *Management International Review*, 4, 1999.

[12] *World Investment Report—2000*. UNCTAD.

[13] *World Investment Report—2001*. UNCTAD.

[14] D. Luhnow, "Crossover success: How NAFTA helped Wal-Mart dominate the Mexican market," *Wall Street Journal*, August 31, 2001, A1.

[15] *World Investment Report—2001*, 9.

[16] *World Investment Report—2001*, 29, 35.

[17] *World Investment Report—2000*, 16.

[18] *The World Competitiveness Yearbook* 2000, 388.

[19] *World Investment Report—2000*.

[20] *World Investment Report—2000*.

[21] *Transnational Corporations*, 10, 3, UNCTAD 2002.

[22] C. Terhune, "Swedish concern to expand in the U.S. through two deals," *Wall Street Journal*, January 23, 2001.

[23] J. Pesta, "Indian companies buy passage to U.S.," *Wall Street Journal*, January 22, 2001, A16.

[24] *World Investment Report—2001*, 82.

[25] L. Nachum, "Economic geography and the location of TNCs: Financial and professional service FDI to the US," *Journal of International Business Studies*, 31, 3, 2000, 367–385.

[26] *World Investment Report—2001*, 6.

[27] *World Investment Report—2000*.

[28] *The World Competitiveness Yearbook—2000*, 390.

[29] C. M. Yee, "Let's make a deal," *Wall Street Journal*, September 25, 2000, R10.

[30] C. M. Yee, "Let's make a deal," *Wall Street Journal*, September 25, 2000, R10.

[31] "The strange life of low-tech America," *The Economist*, October 17, 1998, 73.

[32] C. Rhoades, "A contrarian Motorola picks Germany," *Wall Street Journal*, October 10, 1997, A18.

[33] J. Millman, "Mexican workers suffer as plants relocate South of the border," *Wall Street Journal*, March 26, 2002, A20.

[34] *Foreign Direct Investment in Africa: Performance and Potential*. UNCTAD 1999.

The Multinational Enterprise

DO YOU KNOW

1. Who are the players in the international business arena? How can you tell the degree of a firm's internationalization? Do you think that a higher degree of internationalization will necessarily lead to higher corporate performance? Why or why not?

2. What advantages and disadvantages do MNEs have when they operate overseas compared to local firms? What are the essential capabilities with which MNEs must be equipped?

3. What are the typical features of developing country MNEs? How do they differ from developed country MNEs? What do you advise these companies as well as small international firms if they want to compete with the developed country MNE in an international market?

OPENING CASE Johnson & Johnson

Incorporated in 1887, Johnson & Johnson is the most comprehensive manufacturer and service provider of health-care products in the world today. Consisting of 190 operating companies located in 51 nations, the company sells its products in more than 175 national markets. About half of its US $29.1 billion in sales in 2000 have been derived from foreign sales and almost 60 percent of its 99,100 strong workforce reside outside the United States. In the 1990s, however, foreign operations brought a lower share of the profit than domestic sales.

Johnson & Johnson has been conducting international operations for decades. The company established its first affiliate in Canada in 1919, followed by the United Kingdom in 1924. Affiliates were established in Australia in 1931, Sweden in 1956, Japan in 1961, South Korea in 1981, and Egypt in 1985. Johnson & Johnson used both greenfield investment and acquisitions to expand its global reach. It acquired Belgian pharmaceutical firm Janssen Pharmaceutica in 1961, German sanitary protection manufacturer Dr. Carl Hahn in 1974, and German baby toiletries maker Penaten in 1986.

The company has made significant strides in its efforts to leverage its global reach. In Europe, for example it has moved to establish "global platforms" consolidating production facilities in one country from which neighboring countries are served. It also embarked on a global human resources strategy, ranging from international recruitment to global management development. Many challenges remain, however, including how to expand in emerging markets while sustaining growth in established locations, how to coordinate the global network of member companies with different national and corporate cultures, and how to respond to changes such as health-care regulatory reforms in the multiple environments in which it operates. In the last several years, a strong dollar weighed heavily on the profitability of Johnson & Johnson's overseas operations by depressing its earnings when converted from foreign currencies into U.S. dollars. ∎

Source: Johnson & Johnson; Developing a global mindset at Johnson & Johnson—1998, IMD case GM791, 01.06.99.

WHAT IS A MULTINATIONAL ENTERPRISE?

When reading about international business, you will encounter many terms describing a company with significant international operations and presence. These include:

- The **internationally committed company** is a firm with at least one majority-owned plant or a joint venture abroad but which lacks representation in all major regions of the world such as Asia, Europe, and the Americas.[1]
- The **internationally leaning** firm is one with foreign sales and possibly a representative office and/or a licensing agreement, but no ownership of foreign production sites.[2]
- The **multidomestic** firm is an enterprise with multiple international subsidiaries that are relatively independent from headquarters.
- The **global** firm consists of closely integrated international subsidiaries controlled and coordinated from central headquarters.
- The **transnational** firm consists of subsidiaries that fulfill varying roles, with some subsidiaries playing a strategic role that in the global firm is reserved for headquarters.[3]
- The **multinational** firm, or MNE, according to the OECD, is "an enterprise that engages in FDI and owns or controls value-adding activities in more than one country." An MNE typically:

  (a) Has "multiple" facilities around the globe. According to the Conference Board, an *MNE* owns a majority stake in plants in North America, Europe, and the Pacific Rim.

  (b) Derives a "substantial" portion of revenues from foreign operations.

  (c) Runs subsidiaries that possess a common strategic vision and draw from a common pool of resources.

  (d) Places foreign nationals or expatriates at the board level and/or in senior management posts.

Firms such as Johnson & Johnson, Ford Motor, and Nestlé meet all of those criteria. Others may meet some or most but are still commonly referred to as MNEs. For instance, even though French dairy producer Danone has only two foreign nationals on its board, it has vast global presence, a common vision, and substantial foreign revenue. As a result, we will use a less confining definition of MNE in this book.

Throughout this textbook we use the term **Multinational Enterprise (MNE)** to denote a firm with foreign direct investment, whether in manufacturing or in services, over which it maintains effective control. A firm might have investment in only one foreign market, but if this investment is effectively controlled by it, we will call it an MNE. A firm engaged in trade activities but without an FDI component will be called an **international firm.** For example, a U.S.-based company that specializes in import and export management services such as export logistics, or an Italian firm that is exclusively an importer or exporter, is referred to as an international firm. Likewise, a firm that has a 10 percent equity stake in a single foreign investment and has no control over its operation and management, is an international firm and not an MNE.

In this chapter, we first discuss "traditional" MNEs, that is, large firms based in developed nations and present in most parts of the world. Johnson & Johnson belongs to this group. The second group consists of MNEs from developing and emerging economies (DMNEs), such as South Korea and Taiwan. The third group includes small and midsize enterprises engaged in international business. Most of these firms do not have FDI presence and hence do not qualify as MNEs under our definition. They are therefore called **Small and Midsize International Enterprises,** or SMIEs.

The Degree of Internationalization

The level of MNE internationalization can be gauged by the **transnationality index (TNI)**. This index, which should be distinguished from the term transnational corporation (TNC), is calculated as the average of three ratios: (a) foreign assets to total assets, (b) foreign sales to total sales, and (c) foreign employment to total employment.[4] Among the highest ranked on the index in 2000 are Swiss food firm Nestlé, Swedish appliance maker Electrolux, and Canadian media firm Thomson. No U.S. firm is among the top 10. Exhibit 4–1 shows the average transnationality index for the world's largest MNEs. Empirical evidence has been inconclusive regarding the generally-viewed positive link between the degree of transnationality and corporate performance. Overly globalized firms often face daunting challenges such as lack of core competencies in every battle field, enormous costs in intracorporate coordination, and financial difficulties in controlling liquidity and leverage for global operations.

History of the MNE

The MNE is not a new phenomenon. In their book *The Birth of the Multinational,* Moore and Lewis trace the origin and evolution of the MNE during the Pheonician, Carthage, Greek, and Roman empires. Formed as stock ownership companies, these firms appeared in Assyria shortly after 2000 B.C. They deployed their resources from the capital Ashur into foreign markets using both domestic and foreign employees engaged in value-adding activities. These early MNEs had to overcome many of the same obstacles facing current MNEs, such as tariffs and nationalist opposition to foreign trade and investment, using their competitive advantage and market power to prevail.[5]

MNEs continued to flourish and expand their reach in modern times. In the eighteenth and nineteenth centuries, the British-based East India Company took advantage of England's colonial rule and control of shipping lanes to become a formidable force in Asia. When the company lost its monopoly on trading with China in the 1830s, competitors quickly emerged. Jardine-Matheson, formed in Canton (today's Guangzhou), China at that time, opened an office in the newly established colony of Hong Kong. A decade later it became the first foreign trading firm to open

Exhibit 4–1
Average transnationality
of the world's 100 largest
MNEs 1990–1998

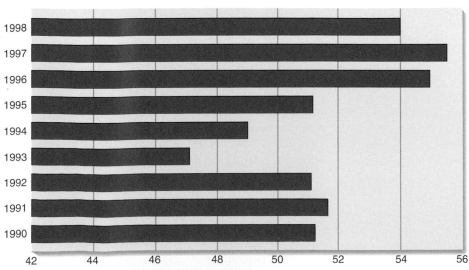

Source: UNCTAD, World Investment Report 2000.

an office in Japan. Jardine is now a diversified MNE listed in Bermuda but conducting most of its business from Hong Kong. In recent decades, the number of MNEs has expanded dramatically. The same 15 developed countries that had 7,276 MNEs at the end of 1960 were home to 39,650 multinationals by the second half of the 1990s.

Today, the MNE is a key player in the global economy. Consider this:

- The world's largest 1,000 industrial firms, most of which are MNEs, account for roughly 80 percent of global industrial output.[6]
- In a Conference Board survey of 1,250 publicly listed large firms, MNEs represented only 13 percent of the sample but had 53 percent of total sales.[7]
- Roughly 40 to 50 percent of world trade is conducted between MNEs and their affiliates. One third of U.S. trade consists of internal transfers among units of the same MNE. Interestingly, while the United States as a whole has a large trade deficit, U.S. MNEs export more to their foreign affiliates than they import from them.[8]
- The annual sales of each of the 10 largest industrial MNEs exceed the tax revenues of Australia.[9] In Ireland, foreign firms account for two thirds of national output and almost 50 percent of employment.

Interim Summary

1. There are many different types of international companies and multiple definitions of a multinational firm. In this book, we use the term multinational enterprise (MNE) to refer to a company that has FDI.

2. The degree of an MNE's internationality can be determined by calculating its transnationality index—a rating system based on a number of business attributes that show how global a company is.

THE WORLD'S LARGEST MNEs

In 1998, the top 100 global non-financial MNEs (ranked by foreign assets) accounted for 13 percent of all foreign assets or $1.9 trillion, an increase of 7 percent from 1997; 19 percent of all foreign sales or $2.1 trillion; and 18 percent of total foreign employment or 6,547,719 employees.[10] Exhibit 4–2 shows the top 50 list for 1999. There were few changes from 1998, among them the ascent of the merged ExxonMobil to second place and the entry of such newcomers as Aventis.

Almost 90 percent of the companies on the UNCTAD 100 list are from Triad countries, namely the United States, the EU, and Japan, which together accounted for 85 percent of FDI outflows in 1999. Variation is substantial within each region, however. For example, although France and Germany had 13 and 12 firms, respectively, on the 100 list in 1999, Belgium had none. Transnationality was generally higher for the EU than for U.S.- and Japan-based MNEs (see Exhibit 4–3) and, not surprisingly, for countries with small domestic markets such as Switzerland.

Exhibit 4–4 lists the 10 largest U.S. MNEs at the end of 1999. The percentage of total foreign revenues varies greatly from 13.8 percent for Wal-Mart stores to 71.8 percent for oil giant ExxonMobil. However, Wal-Mart's increase in foreign revenues is the highest in the group, suggesting that it is likely to catch up fast.

Exhibit 4–2
The world's 50 largest non-financial MNEs (ranked by foreign assets)*

Ranking 1999 by: Foreign assets	TNI	Ranked in 1998 by: Foreign assets	TNI	Corporation	Country	Industry
1	75	1	75	General Electric	United States	Electronics
2	22	5	19	ExxonMobil Corporation	United States	Petroleum expl./ref./distr.
3	43	3	45	Royal Dutch/Shell Group	The Netherlands/United Kingdom	Petroleum expl./ref./distr.
4	83	2	85	General Motors	United States	Motor vehicles
5	77	4	76	Ford Motor Company	United States	Motor vehicles
6	82	6	60	Toyota Motor Corporation	Japan	Motor vehicles
7	51	9	59	DaimlerChrysler AG	Germany	Motor vehicles
8	21	32	27	TotalFina SA	France	Petroleum expl./ref./distr.
9	50	7	54	IBM	United States	Computers
10	18	8	21	BP	United Kingdom	Petroleum expl./ref./distr.
11	2	10	3	Nestlé SA	Switzerland	Food/beverages
12	45	11	51	Volkswagen Group	Germany	Motor vehicles
13	11	—	—	Nippon Oil Co. Ltd.	Japan	Petroleum expl./ref./distr.
14	41	19	52	Siemens AG	Germany	Electronics
15	90	14	73	Wal-Mart Stores	United States	Retailing
16	55	—	—	Repsol-YPF SA	Spain	Petroleum expl./ref./distr.
17	13	17	17	Diageo Plc	United Kingdom	Beverages
18	59	87	84	Mannesmann AG	Germany	Telecommunications/engineering
19	58	13	63	Suez Lyonnaise des Eaux	France	Diversified/utility
20	32	23	40	BMW AG	Germany	Motor vehicles
21	3	15	8	ABB	Switzerland	Electrical equipment
22	42	20	41	Sony Corporation	Japan	Electronics
23	9	34	1	Seagram Company	Canada	Beverages/media
24	8	12	7	Unilever	UK/The Netherlands	Food/beverages
25	49	—	—	Aventis	France	Pharmaceuticals/chemicals
26	85	24	81	Mitsubishi Corporation	Japan	Diversified
27	6	27	13	Roche Group	Switzerland	Pharmaceuticals
28	38	21	34	Renault SA	France	Motor vehicles
29	27	18	38	Honda Motor Co Ltd.	Japan	Motor vehicles
30	73	52	86	Telefónica SA	Spain	Telecommunications
31	14	22	12	News Corporation	Australia	Media/publishing
32	44	51	62	Motorola Inc	United States	Electronics
33	35	33	14	Philips Electronics	The Netherlands	Electronics
34	68	25	67	Nissan Motor Co. Ltd.	Japan	Motor vehicles
35	7	69	5	British American Tobacco Plc	United Kingdom	Food/tobacco
36	67	38	80	ENI Group	Italy	Petroleum expl./ref./distr.
37	79	39	91	Chevron Corporation	United States	Petroleum expl./ref./distr.
38	48	74	66	Johnson & Johnson	United States	Pharmaceuticals
39	52	36	53	Hewlett-Packard	United States	Electronics/computers
40	54	29	56	Elf Aquitaine SA	France	Petroleum expl./ref./distr.
41	33	26	33	Bayer AG	Germany	Pharmaceuticals/chemicals
42	26	47	25	Coca-Cola Company	United States	Beverages
43	25	42	42	Alcatel	France	Electronics
44	69	44	77	Texas Utilities Company	United States	Utility
45	86	37	78	Mitsui & Co. Ltd.	Japan	Diversified
46	36	40	46	BASF AG	Germany	Chemicals
47	80	53	83	Vivendi SA	France	Utility/media
48	74	—	—	Hutchison Whampoa Ltd.	Hong Kong, China	Diversified
49	62	43	65	Peugeot SA	France	Motor vehicles
50	72	56	79	Fujitsu Ltd.	Japan	Electronics

Source: UNCTAD, World Investment Report 2001.
*TNI rankings are within the 100 largest.

Exhibit 4–3

Home country of the world's largest 100 MNEs by Transnationality Index (TNI) and foreign assets, 1990, 1995, and 1999

Economy	Average TNI (%)			Share of top 100 in total of foreign assets (%)			Number of entries		
	1990	1995	1999	1990	1995	1999	1990	1995	1999
European Union	**56.7**	**66.0**	**58.7**	**45.5**	**43.8**	**43.0**	**48**	**39**	**46**
France	50.9	57.6	55.7	10.4	8.9	11.6	14	11	13
Germany	44.4	56.0	49.6	8.9	12.2	12.3	9	9	12
United Kingdom	44.4	56.0	49.6	8.9	12.2	12.3	12	10	8
The Netherlands	68.5	79.0	68.2	8.9	8.2	5.3	4	4	5
Italy	38.7	35.8	50.1	3.5	2.3	2.6	4	2	4
Sweden	71.7	80.6	71.8	2.7	1.7	1.3	5	3	3
Finland	—	—	72.5	—	—	0.5	—	—	1
Spain	—	—	44.8	—	—	2.5	—	—	2
Belgium	60.4	70.4	—	1	0.9	—	1	2	—
North America	**41.2**	**46.0**	**46.2**	**32.5**	**35.9**	**35.2**	**30**	**34**	**28**
United States	38.5	41.9	42.7	31.5	33.3	33.3	28	30	26
Canada	79.2	76.5	92.0	1	2.7	1.9	2	4	2
Japan	**35.5**	**31.9**	**38.4**	**12**	**15.1**	**15.4**	**12**	**17**	**18**
Remaining countries	**73.0**	**66.9**	**70.4**	**10**	**9.0**	**7.5**	**10**	**10**	**9**
Switzerland	84.3	83.6	93.1	7.5	6.6	4.6	6	5	4
Australia	51.8	—	69.3	1.6	—	1.5	2	3	2
Hong Kong, China	—	—	38.5	—	—	0.3			1
Mexico	—	—	54.6	—	—	0.8			1
Venezuela	—	44.4	29.8	—	0.4	0.4	—	1	1
New Zealand	62.2	—	—	0.5	—	—	1	—	—
Norway	58.1	—	—	0.4	—	—	1	—	—
Republic of Korea	—	47.7	—	—	0.7	—	—	1	—
Total of all listed MNCs	**51.1**	**51.5**	**52.6**	**100**	**100**	**100**	**100**	**100**	**100**

Source: UNCTAD, World Investment Report, 2001.

Exhibit 4–4

The largest 10 U.S. MNEs (at the end of 1999)

Bank	Company	Revenue		Net Profit		Assets	
		Foreign ($MIL)	Foreign as % of Total	Foreign ($MIL)	Foreign as % of Total	Foreign ($MIL)	Foreign as % of Total
1	ExxonMobil	115,464	71.8	5,310	62.7	60,130	63.9
2	IBM	50,377	57.5	3,825	49.6	14,969	43.7
3	Ford Motor	50,138	30.8	NA	NA	22,014	44.2
4	General Motors	46,485	26.3	3,279	55.3	12,641	38.0
5	General Electric	35,350	31.7	3,926	22.8	19,447	47.4
6	Texaco	32,700	77.1	637	54.1	7,109	45.2
7	Citigroup	28,749	35.1	NA	NA	239,889	41.0
8	Hewlett-Packard	23,398	55.2	1,801	58.0	2,231	51.5
9	Wal-Mart Stores	22,728	13.8	817	8.2	25,330	36.0
10	Compaq Computer	21,174	55.0	577	101.4	917	28.2

Source: Forbes, July 24, 2000.

The Industry Composition of MNEs

Exhibit 4–5 shows the industry composition of the top 100 non-financial MNEs. The list is dominated by a limited number of industries, in particular electronics/electrical equipment, motor vehicles, and petroleum exploration and distribution.[11] Some of these industries (e.g., motor vehicles) rank much lower on the transnationality index than others (e.g., food and beverages). See Exhibit 4–6.

Note that the list does not include financial institutions, many of which are important MNEs. U.S.-based Citigroup placed 11 on the Forbes list of top 100 world firms. Bank of America placed 43 on the same list. U.K.-based HSBC (Hong Kong and Shanghai Banking Corporation) placed 46. Other banks and insurance companies can also be found on that list.[12] The next section describes the growth of non-manufacturing MNEs.

The Growth of Service MNEs

Recent years saw a significant growth of MNEs in media, education, transportation, information services, travel, tourism, health care, and professional services. There are several reasons for the growth, as follows:

- *Economic transformation.* As developed nations shifted into service economies, their service firms sought to leverage their scale and resources toward new growth venues in foreign markets. For instance, large U.S. airlines such as United and American entered international routes to serve the increasingly global destinations of their customers as well as to utilize these carriers' expertise and cost advantages.
- *Globalization and liberalization of regulatory systems.* Because many service MNEs are "location-bound," that is, production and consumption must take place in the same location, they are especially dependent on global regulatory

Exhibit 4–5

Industry composition of the largest 100 MNEs, 1990, 1995, and 1999

Industry	Number of entries			Average TNI per industry (Percent)		
	1990	1995	1999	1990	1995	1999
Media	2	2	2	82.6	83.4	86.9
Food/beverages/tobacco	9	12	10	59.0	61.0	78.9
Construction	4	3	2	58.8	67.8	73.2
Pharmaceuticals	6	6	7	66.1	63.1	62.4
Chemicals	12	11	7	60.1	63.3	58.4
Petroleum exploration/refining/ distribution and mining	13	14	13	47.3	50.3	53.3
Electronics/electrical equipment/computers	14	18	18	47.4	49.3	50.7
Motor vehicle and parts	13	14	14	35.8	42.3	48.4
Metals	6	2	1	55.1	27.9	43.5
Diversified	2	2	6	29.7	43.6	38.7
Retailing	—	—	4	—	—	37.4
Utilities	—	—	5	—	—	32.5
Telecommunications	2	5	3	46.2	46.3	33.3
Trading	7	5	4	32.4	30.5	17.9
Machinery/engineering	3	1	—	54.5	37.9	—
Other	7	5	4	57.6	59.4	65.7
Total/average	100	100	100	51.1	51.5	52.6

Source: UNCTAD, World Investment Report, 2001.

Exhibit 4–6
The largest 5 MNEs in
each industry, 1990,
1995, and 1999

Industry	Year	Transnationality index	Assets		Sales		Employment	
			Foreign	Total	Foreign	Total	Foreign	Total
Petroleum	1990	57.7	15.1	10.6	15.8	11.9	5.5	4.2
	1995	64.8	12.9	8.0	13.6	10.0	4.0	3.1
	1999	70.1	13.6	8.3	13.5	9.8	4.1	2.8
Motor vehicles	1990	34.7	11.9	15.3	10.4	11.8	9.7	14.2
	1995	38.6	14.0	17.3	9.6	13.4	9.7	13.5
	1999	41.4	13.3	18.5	15.4	15.8	12.2	13.1
Electronics/electrical equipment	1990	36.1	6.4	7.4	4.7	6.3	6.5	9.6
	1995	61.1	11.1	10.4	7.8	6.9	13.2	10.7
	1999	59.6	12.7	13.0	9.5	8.3	13.6	10.5
Pharmaceuticals	1990	47.1	1.5	1.3	1.6	1.4	2.4	2.3
	1995	68.0	3.8	2.5	2.4	1.7	3.4	2.5
	1999	67.3	4.7	2.8	3.1	2.5	4.7	3.3
Chemicals	1990	51.6	5.3	4.2	5.9	4.5	4.8	5.4
	1995	61.1	6.2	3.9	5.0	4.0	5.5	4.9
	1999	53.9	3.1	2.9	3.8	3.1	3.3	3.2
Food/beverages	1990	60.8	7.2	5.6	5.8	5.0	11.7	7.6
	1995	76.9	6.7	4.8	7.4	5.2	12.9	7.1
	1999	88.7	6.3	3.3	6.1	3.2	10.5	5.1

Source: UNCTAD, World Investment Report, 2000.

Note: This table reports averages in TNI, assets, sales, and employment of the largest 5 MNEs in each industry. "Foreign" or "Total" columns refer to the top 5's percentage in top 100 MNEs' total.

regimes as well as on the domestic regulations in each market in which they operate. New "open skies" aviation agreements allowed U.S. carriers to serve more foreign markets and opened domestic markets to foreign competition. The globalization of accounting standards made it possible for large U.S.-based accounting firms to operate abroad. The extension of shopping hours in Germany permitted Wal-Mart to make better use of its scale and resources. The relaxation of the "Big Store" law in Japan permitted Toys 'R' Us to operate the large-scale retail operations it has come to master in the United States.

■ *Communications advances.* Progress in communications and computer technologies enable service MNEs to coordinate knowledge-intensive operations across borders. As an example, consulting firms can exchange information and transfer knowledge quickly and efficiently.

The growth of service MNEs has been especially pronounced in the United States, which is widely regarded as having the most competitive service sector as a result of relative openness and intense domestic competition in comparison with the European and Japanese service industries. The United States runs a substantial trade surplus in services vis-à-vis a chronic deficit in its merchandise trade. In 1998, the United States exported $246 billion in commercial services with many more sold by and exported by the overseas subsidiaries of U.S. MNEs.

Exhibit 4–7

The world's top 20 banks 2001 (based on total assets)

1	Mizuho Financial Group (Japan)
2	Citigroup (U.S.)
3	Deutsche Bank (Germany)
4	JP Morgan Chase (U.S.)
5	Bank of Tokyo-Mitsubishi (Japan)
6	HSBC Holdings (U.K.)
7	HypoVereinsbank (Germany)
8	UBS (Switzerland)
9	BNP Parlbas (France)
10	Bank of America Corp (U.S.)
11	Credit Suisse Group (Switzerland)
12	Sumitomo Bank (Japan)
13	ABN AMRO (The Netherlands)
14	Crédit Agricole Groupe (France)
15	Industrial and Commercial Bank (China)
16	Norinchukin Bank (Japan)
17	Royal Bank of Scotland (U.K.)
18	Barclays Bank (U.K.)
19	Dresdner Bank (Germany)
20	Commerzbank (Germany)

Source: The Banker, July 2001

U.S. firms do not dominate all service sectors, however. Exhibit 4–7 shows the list of the world's 20 largest banks by assets in 2001. It contains only three U.S. banks (Citigroup, JP Morgan Chase, and Bank of America) vis-à-vis four each from Japan and Germany, two each from Switzerland, France, and the United Kingdom, and one each from China and the Netherlands. Although this is partly the result of U.S. limitations on interstate banking, it does provide a fairly even playing ground in terms of bank scale and reach.

In advertising, in contrast, U.S. and European agencies are the leaders, whereas the Japanese lag far behind. Dentsu—Japan's dominant advertising agency—generates less than 10 percent of its $15 billion in revenue outside its home country. This is not for lack of trying. Dentsu opened a New York office in 1959, and in 1999 it took a 20 percent stake in U.S.-based Bcom3 Group, a merger of Leo Burnett and D'arcy Masius Benton & Bowles. The United States also leads in airlines. As you can see in Exhibit 4–8, the six largest airlines in terms of passenger traffic are U.S. based; however, this is mostly the result of the size of the U.S. domestic aviation market and does not reveal much about the stiff competition U.S. airlines face in international markets.

Interim Summary

1. With a few exceptions, the largest MNEs are based in the Triad countries of the EU, United States, or Japan and have annual revenues larger than the tax incomes of some countries.

2. The largest MNEs represent a relatively limited number of industries, primarily electronics, motor vehicles, and petroleum (although banking institutions and other service MNEs are increasing).

3. Using an extensive network of MNE affiliates, the United States exports more services than any other country. The U.S. trade surplus in services is offset by a much larger merchandise trade deficit though this is not the case for internal transfer of US-based MNEs.

Exhibit 4–8

The world's top airlines, 2001

Rank	Airline	Passengers (000)
1	Delta	105,723
2	American	86,280
3	United	84,521
4	Southwest	63,678
5	US Airways	60,636
6	Northwest	58,722
7	All Nippon Group	49,887
8	Continental	46,896
9	Lufthansa	41,300
10	Air France	39,204
11	British Airways	38,261
12	Japan Airlines	33,857
13	Alitalia	26,697
14	TWA*	26,392
15	Iberia	24,543
16	Japan Air System	20,836
17	America West	19,954
18	Thai Int'l	18,038
19	Air Canada	17,655
20	China Southern	16,800
21	Malaysia Airlines	16,561
22	KLM	16,234
23	Singapore Airlines	14,874
24	Swissair	14,238
25	Alaska	13,525

Source: ATW Research: Direct airline reports. Financial data are for carrier's most recent financial year.

*Acquired by American in 2001

THE IMAGE OF THE MNE

The MNE in the Public Eye

Over the years, the MNE has been both lauded and vilified for its impact on its host (especially) and home countries. Although the MNE was vilified as monopolistic and a threat to national sovereignty in the 1970s, during the 1980s it was considered a dinosaur whose large size and inability to adapt would eventually doom it.

In the 1990s, the MNE emerged as a relatively benevolent provider of knowledge and capital.[13] Thanks to their technology, expertise, and network of global affiliates, MNEs were viewed as contributing to national productivity and exports. For instance, in 1996, foreign invested enterprises (FIEs) accounted for 41 percent of China's exports, up from 17 percent in 1991.[14] MNEs were also positively cited for being an agent of change, introducing new ways of doing business that would eventually be adopted by local firms. For example, the first industrial robots were introduced to Singapore by MNEs, with local firms adopting the technology later. Finally, MNEs have been noted for creating jobs. In Turkey, MNEs increased their staffing at a double-digit level in an otherwise stagnant labor market, and those jobs have been paying more than double the average wage.[15]

At the dawn of the twenty-first century, MNEs are once again seen as a threat to national sovereignty. *The Economist* suggests this is because the MNE is the most visible symbol of globalization. Many emerging nations want the MNE to bring in capital and technology but refrain from bringing in foreign ideas. The MNE is accused of having an unfair advantage, exploiting incentives granted exclusively to foreign firms to shift production to ever lower-cost locations. The MNE is also criticized for limiting knowledge transfer to "intermediate" technologies, constraining the host country's ability to become a global competitor. For instance, Motorola has been criticized for limiting its R&D efforts in Brazil to the adaptation of its existing technology to Latin American markets rather than creating new technologies.[16] A related criticism is that MNEs generate low-paying, low-tech jobs in the host country while keeping high value-added jobs at home.

The image of the MNE varies, among other factors, by country, industry, market orientation, and the constituency affected. The impact of the MNE in developed countries is assessed using different yardsticks than in developing countries. MNEs in extraction industries (e.g., oil, mining) are scrutinized more closely than those engaged in manufacturing, and those that bring advanced technology are treated differently from those that provide mere assembly ("screwdriver plants").[17]

In the current public eye, MNEs and host country governments involve both cooperation and bargaining elements in their interdependent relationships. They cooperate by contributing complementary resources. An MNE's technological resources, capital investment, global distribution, and managerial expertise add critical value to local economies, especially to developing countries. MNEs need support from local governments in developing investment infrastructure, creating a better environment for fair competition, and improving the quality of production factors such as labor (through training and education), information (through advancing the information technology industry), and capital (through improving the banking sector). Meanwhile, they bargain with each other, especially when a particular MNE's strategic goals are not compatible with those of the host country government. The government may want to control critical natural resources demanded by the MNE or to safeguard an infant local industry by posing many entry or operational barriers against the MNE. We further discuss MNE–government relations in Chapter 7.

The image of the MNE in its home country is also complex. On the one hand, it is often recognized that the MNE brings resources that are unavailable in the home country, lowering prices and enhancing variety for domestic consumers. Another plus is that MNE's successes in foreign markets allow suppliers and other host country firms to "piggyback" on the MNE, thus increasing national output and job creation at home. On the other hand, MNEs are criticized for shifting production from their home base to foreign locations, undermining employment and "hollowing-out" the production base of the home country.

The Borderless Corporation: Myth or Reality?

The rise of a borderless, transnational corporation, which owes allegiance to no one, has been a major theme in the popular media. This firm establishes its headquarters anywhere it sees fit, moves its operations at will to wherever it can garner the highest return, and adopts the form of governance and management that it finds most suitable. Proponents of this thesis point out that it is increasingly difficult to pinpoint country-of-origin for firms engaged in international business. Daimler-Chrysler, the result of the acquisition of U.S.-based Chrysler by German automaker Daimler Benz, is headquartered and registered in Germany although it maintains a U.S. headquarters for its North American operations and its shares are traded on the New York Stock Exchange with a large block held by U.S. investors. Rhombic Corp.

was founded in Nevada, is based in Vancouver, Canada, and the highest turnover of its shares is in Hamburg, Germany.

Opponents of the borderless thesis argue that the borderless corporation is a myth; that most MNEs maintain a clear national base and that enduring national and political realities shape their governance, financing, R&D, FDI, and intra-firm trading strategies.[18] MNEs based in different countries utilize various competitive advantages developed in response to factor and product market circumstances in their home countries.[19] Most MNEs still produce more than two thirds of their output and employ two thirds of their workforce in their home countries.[20] For instance, a recent study suggests that there remain significant differences among Triad firms in product strategy. While U.S. firms compete on "economy" (lower price, lower quality), Japanese MNEs highlight the superior value of their products (a combination of higher quality and lower prices), whereas Europeans emphasize the premium nature of their product (higher quality, higher price). Companies that align their global strategy with the national stereotype performed better than those that did not.[21]

Interim Summary

1. The image of MNEs varies according to time, country, and industry. The level of MNEs' contribution to the local economy is affected by whether or not MNEs and the local government share compatible goals and contribute complementary resources. MNEs and the government both cooperate and bargain with each other.

2. Despite a heightened tendency towards borderless activities and a growing contribution from foreign production and sales, most MNEs still maintain clear roots to a specific country or region.

THE COMPETITIVE ADVANTAGE OF THE MNE

When McDonald's opened its first restaurant in Moscow, the MNE increased the number of customers served there more than twentyfold over the number served in the Soviet-era cafeteria which occupied the site before. Thanks to its global scale and experience, the MNE has a large capital, human, brand, and technological resource base that it can effectively leverage in multiple countries. As the chairman and CEO of Toronto-based Four Seasons Hotels justifies its drive for foreign expansion, "we can double the size of the company, and then can double it again, without changing the product or brand." Procter & Gamble's operations in 140 countries allows it to spread development, manufacturing, and marketing costs. With almost five billion customers worldwide, the company can monitor the performance of each of its 300 brands and apply lessons from one market to another. Global spread also permits the MNE an effective response to trade and investment barriers. PepsiCo was able to profitably sell its cola in the Soviet Union despite the lack of a covertible currency by taking Russian vodka as payment and then using its U.S. distribution channels to market it. Similarly, KFC used its China revenues to commission uniforms for its branches in other Asian countries.

Global spread also provides MNEs with diversification, allowing them to compensate for low performance or uncertainties such as currency fluctuations in certain markets. This allows them to overcome entry barriers in the form of high start-up costs and be early entrants in emerging markets where return is often not realized for many years. Procter & Gamble, one of the most successful MNEs in China, entered the country in the 1980s but did not turn a profit until the mid-1990s. Most automotive MNEs are still only marginally profitable in China but are adamant that, as global players, they cannot afford not to be in this promising market.

Although the performance of MNEs varies by company and markets, as a group they have been consistently more profitable than local counterparts. However, this higher rate of return must be considered against the higher risk associated with foreign investment.[22] In contrast, the returns for internationally committed and internationally leaning firms were found to be quite comparable with those of domestic companies. Profitability was higher for firms operating in developing markets than for those in developed markets, a spread especially pronounced for internationally leaning firms.[23]

MNE's Capabilities

In Chapter 3, we introduced the dynamic capability theory. It suggests that, to prosper in today's turbulent international environment, the MNE cannot merely rely on its existing resources; it must develop "dynamic capabilities" to create, deploy, and upgrade resources in pursuit of sustained competitive advantage. It must instill its capabilities within its global operating units. If superior knowledge is the main source of its competitive advantage, the MNE must have an organization that extends and exploits its knowledge throughout its global operations.

MNE Capabilities

Firm capabilities include familiarity with national culture, industrial structure, and government requirements; and existing relationships with customers, suppliers, and regulators. These and various other aspects of doing business locally give a domestic business a potential edge over a foreign competitor. The MNE must have strategic and organizational capabilities to mitigate this disadvantage. Such capabilities include resources that are unique to the firm, difficult to imitate, and can generate economic returns and competitive advantage. Coca-Cola's vast number of bottling facilities worldwide is less critical than its ability to coordinate such a system. Its formulas (syrups and concentrates), however, are a key asset that gives the firm a leading edge.

Strategic capabilities include technological assets such as patents, trade secrets, proprietary designs, product development, and process innovation. IBM's Chinese speech recognition system ViaVoice has dominated the greater China market for years. The system uses IBM's most advanced voice recognition technology and can be adapted to standard Mandarin and a number of special dialects. The Body Shop's franchising skills with international retail operations, Merrill Lynch's relationships with Japanese financial institutions, and Kodak's extensive networking with Chinese government agencies have significantly contributed to each firm's success.

Managerial skills are part of the MNE capabilities. They are manifested in global human resource management as well as in information, organization design, and control systems. Kodak's skills in recruiting, evaluating, motivating, and training its 53,000 overseas employees provide a distinct advantage. Coca-Cola's ability to propagate a common human resources philosophy and develop a group of internationally minded midlevel executives also constitutes an advantage. Colgate's system of recruiting MBAs who speak at least one foreign language and have lived outside the United States is another example. Colgate does not assign foreign-born trainees to their native countries for initial postings, but rather to a third country.

International experience is essential to strategic and organizational capabilities. Gillette's 20 plus years experience in emerging markets and a century of experience in its industry helped the company become a global leader. This experience allows Gillette to select and enter foreign markets successfully. The same is true for

Starbuck's which leveraged its first experience in foreign forays into Tokyo in 1996 to expand into other foreign markets. Starbuck's expects to have about 1,500 foreign stores by 2003.[24]

Capability Deployment

To be successful, the MNE must transfer critical capabilities unavailable to local players. McDonald's and KFC's overseas success has been built on their ability to rapidly transfer the capacity to operate their entire complex business system to foreign entrepreneurs. Leveraging capabilities across markets is difficult, however. As market conditions in other countries vary, so does the effectiveness of those skills. Toyota's "Just in Time" (JIT) system yields benefits globally but the risks associated with reduced inventory levels are greater in countries where change and disruptions—from weather conditions to strikes—are common.

Technological and financial capabilities (e.g., cash flow management) are generally more transferable than organizational skills. Among strategic capabilities, both a superior market position and an oligopolistic market power are competitive edges that are not immediately transferable. The same is true for home country experience and reputation, although some firms and brands such as The Four Seasons, possess a global reputation that can be leveraged. A superior distribution network cannot be easily replicated overseas; however, knowing how to establish and manage a distribution network is transferable. Nestlé's applied promotion and distribution experience accumulated in China was helpful in other emerging markets such as Vietnam and Russia.

Capability Upgrading

Learning capability is the capacity to generate ideas and acquire new knowledge. It is generally more transferable than firm resources. Firms with the capacity to learn can gain more from experience and apply it to other relevant situations. This capacity helps mitigate the "liabilities of foreignness" during international expansion. To translate learning into competence, the MNE must convert it into firm-specific resources. This involves acquisition, sharing, and utilization. Knowledge acquisition accrues through internal development or external learning. Some MNEs offer seminars in which senior managers regularly share their best practices and knowledge about foreign markets across functional, divisional, and geographical boundaries. Measuring, benchmarking, tracking, and rewarding learning may also increase learning. Using the best practices of other firms as a benchmark is commonplace. Centers of excellence that represent the best practice of managing knowledge are another learning mechanism. An MNE can put together a list of best practices in core marketing activities; for example, the best database marketing is done in London, the best distribution logistics can be found in Singapore, and the best account management is in New York. Many MNEs have gained ideas and experience from foreign businesses that were early movers in a host country market. Next, firms must be able to generate innovative ideas useful in international expansion through competency acquisition, experimentation, and spanning boundaries. When learning through competency acquisition is coupled with a high capacity for change, MNEs tend to be more innovative, proactive, and willing to take risks. They react to market changes in different countries more quickly.

External knowledge acquisition through alliances is also an important vehicle for upgrading capabilities. Starbuck's takes a 20 percent stake in many of its overseas stores with the hope of learning about the local market and eventually increasing its stake.[25] Alliances enable firms to run product development programs in conjunction with their own internal development efforts or to broaden their access to new skills and insights. Motorola licensed some of its microprocessor technology to Toshiba and in return Toshiba licensed some of its memory chip technology to Motorola. The alliance experience can trigger learning but can also expose the MNE to technology loss. In the alliance between GE and SNECMA to build commercial aircraft engines, GE tried to reduce the risk of excess transfer by walling off certain sections of the production process. This modularization was supposed to cut off transfer of what GE felt was key competitive technology, but complete separation was found to be impractical and detrimental to the effectiveness of the venture.

Sharing and disseminating newly acquired knowledge among different subunits of an MNE will determine the efficiency of capability upgrading. Once new knowledge is acquired, firms integrate it with their existing skills. The integration depends on having an effective information transfer system, an incentive structure promoting external learning and experimentation, and an organizational implementing mechanism. Sharing experiences and mindsets through training programs, efficient communications systems, and clear information transfer is crucial, as is a governance structure that facilitates learning diffusion.

Interim Summary

1. MNEs have many advantages over local firms. They can draw on larger financial, knowledge and human resources, have broader experience than most local firms, and can afford to operate at a loss in unfavorable markets for a longer time before turning a profit. These factors, combined with research capabilities and a dynamic structure, make the MNE a challenge to local businesses even in otherwise hostile or difficult markets.

2. It is relatively easy to transfer capital and equipment to a new operation but much more difficult to transfer knowledge, skill, and experience. It is crucial for the MNE to be able to disseminate knowledge to new operations and to integrate information acquired from those operations into already existing procedures. Effective knowledge transfer is the most important capability for an MNE to develop.

THE MNE FROM EMERGING/ DEVELOPING ECONOMIES (DMNE)

For years, the term *MNE* was synonymous with the likes of General Motors, Coca-Cola, Siemens, and Matsushita—large firms from developed nations, mostly from the United States, Europe, and Japan. Firms from emerging and developing nations were rarely in a position to amass the resources and knowledge necessary for extensive forays into foreign markets. Although MNEs from developed nations still dominate global business, **developing nations'** MNEs (DMNEs), especially emerging economies, have become global competitors and even leaders in their field. Taiwan-based Acer is a leader in notebook computers. Thai conglomerate Charoen Pokphand is a major force in food production and processing in Asia.[26] Philippines' brewer San Miguel and Singapore Telecom are also global players.

Israel-based Teva was established in Jerusalem in 1901 as a drug distribution agency and started its pharmaceutical operations in the 1930s as a small-scale producer competing with foreign imports. Taking advantage of the immigration-driven growth in its domestic market as well as of the cessation of imports during wartimes, the company grew rapidly, then merged with its domestic competitors Asia and Zori and embarked on exports as a major thrust. Teva solidified its entry into the U.S. market via a joint venture with W. R. Grace in 1985 and the acquisition of Lemmon in 1986. In the 1990s, Teva embarked on aggressive acquisition strategy in the United States and Europe, eventually gaining a berth among the world's 50 largest pharmaceutical companies. By 2001, the company became the world's largest maker of generic drugs. The company shares are trading on the NASDAQ, the Tel-Aviv Stock Exchange, the Seaq International in London, and the Frankfurt Stock Exchange.[27]

Like Teva, many DMNEs start by competing on price, using "intermediary" technology that is not cutting edge, but represents sufficient improvement over local standards in developing markets. Such was the investment of South Korean firms in Southeast Asia and eastern Europe. Like Teva, DMNEs upgrade their capabilities. Today, South Korean conglomerates LG and Samsung sell their consumer electronics in the United States and the EU, while China-based Haier dominates the small refrigerator market in the United States. Brazilian regional jet manufacturer Embraer has been holding its own in this very competitive market contested by developed market players such as Canadian-based Bombardier. In the wake of the U.S. presidential election impasse in 2000, Brazilian Procomp (acquired by Ohio-based Diebold) offered electronic voting machines superior to those currently in use.[28]

The rise of DMNEs is intertwined with the increase in outward-FDI from developing countries. In 1960 the stock of FDI from developing countries amounted to a mere 0.8 percent of the global FDI stock, whereas it reached 1.2 percent in 1975 and 3.2 percent in 1992, with growth rate about double that from developed nations.[29] In Asia and eastern Europe, DMNEs represent a considerable proportion of FDI. Hong Kong and Taiwan are the largest foreign investors in mainland China, while Singapore and South Korea are major investors there.

The Largest Developing Country MNEs

Exhibit 4–9 lists the top 50 DMNEs in 1999. For the first time ever, the top three DMNEs are also represented in the global top 100 MNEs: Hutchison Whampoa, Petröleos de Venezuela, and Cemex (see Exhibit 4–10 for Cemex's global expansion).[30] A number of firms on earlier lists such as China's Shougang are no longer on the list; number six, Daewoo, may not survive.

DMNE Scale

Although the two highest-ranked firms on the list are not much smaller than the smallest global 100, the next four are. The median FDI holding for a top 50 DMNE in 1998 was $1.5 billion versus $14 billion for a global 100. Having started to invest at a later stage, the DMNE is also less transnational, although some of the biggest players have significant international presence. For instance, Korea-based LG has employees in more than 120 nations. As a group, the top 50 DMNEs had $109 plus billion in foreign sales and assets, and employed more than 400,000 foreign workers (out of a total workforce of over 1.5 million).

DMNE Industries

The most represented industries in the top 50 DMNEs can be found in Exhibit 4–11. In a sharp departure from developed country MNEs, the largest group consists of diversified firms, which is especially true in Asia. Other industries prominent on the list are electronics, petroleum, and food and beverages. Note that these areas do not always involve cutting-edge technology, and labor costs (a competitive advantage in developing economies) constitute a considerable portion of product cost.

Exhibit 4–9
The largest 50 MNEs from developing economies, 1999

Ranking by Foreign assets	TNI	Corporation	Economy	Industry
1	24	Hutchison Whampoa Ltd.	Hong Kong, China	Diversified
2	30	Petröleos de Venezuela	Venezuela	Petroleum expl./ref./distr.
3	10	Cemex SA	Mexico	Construction
4	39	Petronas—Petroliam Nasional Berhad	Malaysia	Petroleum expl./ref./distr.
5	34	Samsung Corporation	Korea, Republic of	Diversified/Trade
6	13	Daewoo Corporation	Korea, Republic of	Diversified/Trade
7	22	LG Electronics Inc.	Korea, Republic of	Electronics and electrical
8	45	Ssanyong Group	Korea, Republic of	Energy/Trading/Chemicals
9	43	New World Development Co., Ltd.	Hong Kong, China	Construction
10	42	Samsung Electronics Co., Ltd.	Korea, Republic of	Electronics and electrical
11	3	Neptune Orient Lines Ltd.	Singapore	Transportation
12	6	Sappl Ltd.	South Africa	Pulp and paper
13	8	First Pacific Company Ltd.	Hong Kong, China	Electronics and electrical
14	49	Petroleo Brasilero SA—Petrobras	Brazil	Petroleum expl./ref./distr.
15	19	Jardine Matheson Holdings Ltd.	Hong Kong, China	Diversified
16	40	Keppel Corporation Ltd.	Singapore	Diversified
17	46	Hyundai Motor Co., Ltd.	Korea, Republic of	Motor vehicles
18	14	Hyundai Engineering & Construction Co.	Korea, Republic of	Construction
19	1	Tan Chong International Ltd.	Singapore	Diversified
20	44	Singapore Telecommunications Ltd.	Singapore	Telecommunication
21	20	Citic Pacific Ltd.	Hong Kong, China	Diversified
22	9	Acer Inc.	Taiwan	Electronics and electrical
23	25	South African Breweries Plc.	South Africa	Food and beverages
24	2	Orient Overseas International Ltd.	Hong Kong, China	Transportation
25	17	Barlow Ltd.	South Africa	Diversified
26	27	Companhia Vale Do Ria Doce	Brazil	Mining/other
27	18	Gener SA	Chile	Electrical services (in 1997)
28	29	Metalurgica Gerdau SA	Brazil	Steel and iron
29	37	San Miguel Corporation	Philippines	Food and beverages
30	38	Pérez Companc SA	Argentina	Petroleum expl./ref./distr.
31	5	Guangdong Investment Ltd.	Hong Kong, China	Diversified
32	26	Savla SA de CV	Mexico	Diversified
33	33	Tatung Co. Ltd.	Taiwan	Electronics and electrical
34	7	Fraser & Neave Limited	Singapore	Food and beverages
35	36	Samsung Sdi Co., Ltd.	Korea, Republic of	Electronics and electrical
36	28	Singapore Airlines Limited	Singapore	Transportation
37	11	Gruma SA de CV	Mexico	Food and beverages
38	41	Pohang Iron And Steel Co., Ltd.	Korea, Republic of	Steel and iron
39	50	CLP Holding—China Light & Power Company Limited	Hong Kong, China	Electric utilities or services
40	21	Sime Darby Berhad	Malaysia	Diversified
41	47	Reliance Industries Limited	India	Chemicals & pharmaceuticals
42	35	Copec—Compana de Petröleos	Chile	Diversified
43	16	Companhia Cervejaria Brahma	Brazil	Food and beverages
44	32	Great Eagle Holdings Limited	Hong Kong, China	Hotel/Property
45	4	WBL Corporation Limited	Singapore	Electronics and electrical
46	31	Berjaya Group Berhad	Malaysia	Diversified
47	23	De Beers Consolidated Mines	South Africa	Mining/other
48	15	Hong Kong And Shanghai Hotels Ltd.	Hong Kong, China	Tourism and hotel
49	48	Telekom Malaysia Berhad	Malaysia	Telecommunication
50	12	Nalsteel Limited	Singapore	Steel and iron

Source: UNCTAD, World Investment Report, 2001.

Exhibit 4–10
Global expansion of Cemex SA 2001

Affiliate

Home country

Note: Based on 21 foreign affiliates identified. There is only one affiliate in each country except in the Philippines (where there are two).

Source: UNCTAD, based on information from www.cemex.com.

Exhibit 4–11
Industry composition of the largest 50 MNEs from developing economies

Industry	Number of entries			Average TNI per industry (Percent)		
	1993	1996	1999	1993	1996	1999
Diversified	12	11	14	25.6	32.3	44.3
Food and beverages	7	8	5	15.6	32.8	45.0
Construction	4	3	3	28.8	47.4	39.6
Petroleum expl./ref./distr.	3	6	5	3.1	19.4	21.6
Electronics and electrical equipment	7	5	6	28.1	35.6	41.5
Electric utilities or services	1	...	2	2.0	...	25.3
Steel and iron	5	1	3	11.6	37.6	34.2
Trade	...	4	...	...	44.6	...
Transportation	1	4	3	23.2	54.1	71.2
Chemicals and pharmaceuticals	1	1	1	17.0	7.7	9.6
Other	4	5	...	23.6	38.1	...
Pulp and paper	2	...	1	26.0	...	63.7
Tourism, hotel and property	3	2	2	33.1	33.2	37.9
Automotive	1	...	1	...	...	10.9
Media	1	...	...	...	...	...
Mining	...	...	2	...	...	36.4
Telecommunications	...	...	2	...	59.4	11.7
Average/total	**50**	**50**	**50**	**19.8**	**36.9**	**38.9**

Source: UNCTAD, World Investment Report, 2001.

Note: This list does not include countries from Central and Eastern Europe.

Exhibit 4–12
Country composition of
the largest 50 MNEs from
developing economies

Region/economy	Average TNI per country (Percent)			Share in total foreign assets of the largest 50 (Percent)		
	1993	1996	1999	1993	1996	1999
South, East and South-East Asia	21.8	31.8	39.1	70.6	65.7	72.1
China	...	30.0	...	...	8.2	...
Hong Kong, China	36.5	50.7	45.4	22.0	20.4	26.4
India	6.4	7.7	9.6	0.4	0.8	0.7
Korea, Republic of	20.2	45.6	27.8	24.8	24.4	23.2
Malaysia	20.0	34.4	24.1	4.7	3.2	7.0
Philippines	6.9	16.1	25.0	1.4	0.9	1.1
Singapore	43.0	38.1	58.9	5.3	3.7	11.2
Taiwan	19.6	32.1	43.9	12.3	4.2	2.4
Latin America	14.0	28.9	48.3	29.9	28.9	21.9
Argentina	...	19.5	24.5	...	2.6	1.1
Brazil	17.4	13.1	30.2	12.0	6.2	5.6
Chile	12.1	29.0	35.4	1.0	3.6	1.8
Mexico	12.5	48.7	48.0	16.9	7.5	7.3
Venezuela	...	44.9	29.8	...	8.6	6.2
Africa	...	40.2	46.0	...	5.4	5.9
Average/total	**19.8**	**35.1**	**38.9**	**100.0**	**100.0**	**100.0**

Source: UNCTAD, World Investment Report, 2001.

Note: This list does not include countries from Central and Eastern Europe.

The National Affiliation of DMNEs

As shown in Exhibit 4–12, companies from South, Southeast and East Asia dominate the top 50 DMNEs. Hong Kong, South Korea, and Singapore are the leading home countries on the list. Among central and east European nations, Russia, Croatia, Hungary, Slovenia, Poland, Slovakia, the Czech Republic, Latvia, Romania, and Moldova are homes of the top 50 DMNEs from this region. East and central European firms scored relatively low on the transnational index, with an average of 32.4 (Exhibit 4–13).

Obstacles Facing MNEs from Developing Economies

DMNEs face a number of obstacles in entering foreign markets, including:

- *Resource Constraints.* Teva initially focused on generic drugs, partly because it could ill-afford the huge capital investment involved in the development of new drugs. Lack of reputation and brand recognition are other obstacles faced by DMNEs. These obstacles can be surmounted via an alliance with a developed country MNE, at times selling the product under the MNE's name.
- *Lack of Knowledge.*[31] For Teva, the complex process involved in obtaining FDA approval in the United States—a prerequisite for selling pharmaceutical products in many markets—was a major hurdle. DMNEs lack experience in

Exhibit 4–13

The largest 25 non-financial MNEs based in central and eastern Europe, ranked by foreign assets, 1999 (millions of dollars)

Foreign assets	Corporation	Country	Industry	Sales Foreign/Total	TNI
1	Lukoil Oil Co.	Russia	Petroleum & natural gas	4 642.0/10 903.0	29.8
2	Latvian Shipping Co.	Latvia	Transportation	191.0/191.0	87.3
3	Hrvalska Elektroprivreda d.d.	Croatia	Energy	10.0/780.0	4.3
4	Podravka Group	Croatia	Food & beverages/ pharmaceuticals	119.4/390.2	32.6
5	Primorsk Shipping Co.	Russia	Transportation	85.3/116.5	59.4
6	Gorenje Group	Slovenia	Domestic appliances	593.3/1 120.6	33.3
7	Far Eastern Shipping Co.	Russia	Transportation	134.0/183.0	38.8
8	Pliva Group	Croatia	Pharmaceuticals	384.7/587.6	39.7
9	TVK Ltd.	Hungary	Chemicals	248.9/394.3	37.5
10	Motokov a.s.	Czech Rep.	Trade	260.2/349.1	64.8
11	Skoda Group Plzen	Czech Rep.	Diversified	150.7/1 244.5	10.6
12	Atlantska Plovidba d.d.	Croatia	Transportation	46.0/46.0	63.2
13	MOL Hungarian Oil & Gas Plc.	Hungary	Petroleum & natural gas	582.4/3 129.6	8.9
14	Krka d.d.	Slovenia	Pharmaceuticals	209.0/283.0	38.1
15	Adria Airways d.d.	Slovenia	Transportation	103.4/104.6	64.0
16	Petrol d.d.	Slovenia	Petroleum & natural gas	105.7/924.4	10.1
17	Slovnaft a.s.	Slovakia	Petroleum & natural gas	627.5/1 035.7	22.7
18	Zalakeramia Rt.	Hungary	Clay product & refractory	39.0/64.0	60.7
19	Matador i.s.c.	Slovakia	Rubber & plastics	34.0/203.4	11.3
20	Malev Hungarian Airlines Ltd.	Hungary	Transportation	274.1/367.5	32.4
21	KGHM Polska Miedz SA	Poland	Mining & quarrying	265.0/1 155.0	8.6
22	Croatia Airlines d.d.	Croatia	Transportation	60.2/77.9	30.8
23	Eleklrim SA	Poland	Diversified	42.0/374.0	2.2
24	Petrom SA National Oil Co.	Romania	Petroleum & natural gas	211.0/2 041.0	3.7
25	Intereuropa d.d.	Slovenia	Trade	17.0/136.0	15.4
	Averages			**377.4/1 068.1**	**32.4**

Source: UNCTAD, World Investment Report, 2001.

foreign operations. Many do not possess the production, marketing, and management skills that are necessary in competitive international markets.

- *A Sheltered Environment.* Teva was initially protected by duties on the foreign drugs with which it competed. Many DMNEs have been sheltered in their domestic market for a long time. They often had a domestic monopoly or a huge cost advantage thanks to protectionist measures, and did not have to develop globally competitive products. International activities (if any) were mediated by specialized government or quasi-government agencies (e.g., China's foreign trade corporations), which prevented those firms from developing the knowledge and expertise that result from conducting international business directly (e.g., feedback from international clients).

DMNE Advantage in Global Markets

Obstacles notwithstanding, DMNEs develop some unique advantages that position them well in the competition with established MNEs. Among them:

- *Home Government Support.* DMNEs enjoy the backing of their home government to an extent that may compensate for their ownership and location disadvantages.[32] A major reason for the support is their impact of the DMNE on the national economy. For instance, Embraer's exports of U.S.$1.7 billion in 1999 accounted for 3.52 percent of Brazil's exports. The WTO found the Brazilian government in noncompliance with its rules for subsidizing its aircraft maker Embraer (the Canadian government initially did the same for Bombardier). One form of indirect support and subsidy is local government procurement: Embraer accounts for 50 percent of the Brazilian Air Force fleet. In Thailand, government support for commercial chicken farming assists the animal feed business of Charoen Pokphand. Many DMNEs benefit from monopolized access to a natural resource, such as oil. They have access to low-cost capital, subsidies, and incentives as well as to competitively priced labor, although their wage advantage tends to erode as their home economies develop. When that happens, exchange rates become less favorable, and DMNEs move production to other low-cost locations.

  Government support is a two-edged sword, however. It shields the firm from the marketplace, thereby acting as a damper on its capability development. The price for the support is often government interference in such key decisions as the domain and location of investment, hence limiting the strategic freedom of the firm. One reason for the development of "bogus blue-eyed" ventures in mainland China—ventures that are funded by the Chinese firms themselves through a foreign registered entity—is to circumvent government control and involvement.

- *Flexibility.* While reducing scale advantages, the lower production scale of the DMNE permits flexibility and adaptation that are critical in international markets. Often newly formed, DMNEs have less investment sunk in older plants and technologies and can leapfrog into cutting-edge technologies. DMNEs develop a competitive advantage in their ability to "mediate" technologies for use in developing markets by downscaling, simplifying, substituting local inputs, and increasing the labor intensity of production.[33] The entry-level models produced by Korean automakers do not require the sophisticated testing and service equipment that are unlikely to be available in developing markets. DMNEs also have experience in customizing technologies and products, capabilities that serve them well especially in other developing markets.[34]

Typical Features of DMNEs

DMNEs differ along national lines. For example, Li found that, compared to their Taiwanese counterparts, South Korean MNEs put more emphasis on market share or revenue growth than on profit margins (although the Asian crisis has probably narrowed the differences) and focused more on cost reduction than on value maintenance and enhancement. While Korean MNEs favored mass and domestic markets, Taiwanese MNEs favored niche and international markets, relied more on core competencies, and were less centralized than their Korean counterparts.[35] Because many of these differences can be attributed to cultural and institutional factors, it is reasonable to assume that as DMNEs mature, they will follow a different path.

At the same time, some generalities seem to hold for most DMNEs, as follows:

- *Internationalization Patterns.* Some of the motivations of DMNEs are similar to those of MNEs from developed economies. Both groups seek to exploit their firm-specific advantages, overcome obstacles to exports in the form of tariff and non-tariff barriers, escape stringent environmental limitations at home, and obtain lower cost production bases. Although both groups seek to enter new and promising markets, DMNEs have a number of unique reasons to pursue foreign trade and investment:

  1. To develop ownership advantages. Although traditional MNEs move abroad to exploit their ownership and skill advantages, DMNEs often do so to develop and gain such advantages.[36] A survey of outward FDI by Chinese enterprises found that learning manufacturing and marketing techniques was a key reason for internationalization.[37] DMNEs also seek to exploit their advantage in intermediate technologies.

  2. To serve as intermediaries. DMNEs intermediate in the flow of technologies from industrialized to developing countries.[38] For instance, Korean VCR makers relied on Japanese technology to develop low-cost VCRs which they then exported to developing (and also developed) markets.

  3. To overcome import quotas in developed markets.[39] Quotas represent a key barrier to exports of labor-intensive goods such as textiles. By locating FDI in developed markets or in a developing market that has a trade agreement with a developed country, this barrier can be overcome. Note, for example, the proliferation of Asian textile assemblies in the Northern Marianas—an American commonwealth therefore allowing free trade with the United States.

  4. To reduce risk via diversification.[40] By shifting assets abroad, DMNEs based in regions characterized by political risk and volatility can effectively reduce risk exposure and protect some of their capital base. FDI in this case serves as a substitute for portfolio investment that is limited owing to foreign exchange controls in many developing countries.

- *Focus on Other Developing Markets.* DMNEs are more likely to have a greater share of FDI in other developing markets where their combination of intermediary technology and low cost provide a competitive advantage (see Country Box: Asian MNEs in China). For instance, Brazilian companies sell arms to other developing countries. However, DMNEs often find it necessary to eventually enter developed markets to increase scale and improve learning.
- *Reliance on Third Parties.* To compensate for their resource shortage, DMNEs tend to heavily rely on other entities in their international activities, whether as alliance partners, export intermediaries, government organizations, and the like.
- *Governance.* DMNEs are less likely to be publicly traded and are often tightly controlled by a founding family or the government. Hong Kong-listed Lippo is controlled by the founding Riady family, Indonesians with overseas Chinese roots. Some DMNEs eventually evolve into market entities, however. Embraer (Empresa Brasiliera de Aeronáutica) was founded in 1969 as a government company with the purpose of developing a local aircraft industry. Privatized in 1994, it was purchased by Bozano Simonsen, one of Brazil's biggest investment firms and by the country's two largest pension funds, PREVI and SISTEL. In 1999, Embraer formed a strategic alliance with a group of French aerospace companies—Aerospatiale-Matra, Dassault Aviation, Snecma, and Thomson-CSF—which jointly acquired 20 percent of Embraer's voting shares.
- *Industry Domain.* DMNEs are more likely to be in manufacturing, starting with labor-intensive production and gradually moving into technological and

COUNTRY BOX

ASIAN MNEs IN CHINA

Asian MNEs from Newly Industrialized Economies (NIEs) are generally more diversified than MNEs from developed Western countries but bear more similarity to large Japanese business groups. Thailand-based Charoen Pokphand operates nine business groups, ranging from agro-industry to automotive and industrial products to telecommunications. In China, it invested in areas ranging from feeding mills to motorcycle manufacturing.[106] In entering Hong Kong, the Indonesia-based Lippo group acquired a bank, a mortgage company, a property company, and an investment firm.[107] The Asian financial crisis has lowered the scope of diversification, however.

Asian MNEs (especially those from Hong Kong, Taiwan, and Singapore) have been major investors in China, taking advantage of their superior China-specific knowledge and lower social and cultural barriers. They have utilized mostly intermediate technologies in entering the Chinese market. Their gross profit margin and operating profit margin are lower than those of western MNEs. They have higher export growth but lower local sales and net profit growth than western MNEs. Although western MNEs use advertising and R&D to seek local market expansion, Asian MNEs adopt *guanxi* (relationship)-based strategy variables such as sales force marketing and credit granting. Moreover, the investment size of Asian MNEs is smaller. Whereas western MNEs focus on technologically advanced and domestic market-oriented projects, Asian MNEs opt for export-oriented projects.

Japanese MNEs are more risk-averse than both western and other Asian MNEs, which is in line with Japan's high uncertainty avoidance culture (see Chapter 6 on the Cultural Environment). Most Japanese firms have taken an evolutionary approach to China investment, starting with trade, continuing with a minority-equity position in cooperative arrangements, often using two or more Japanese partners, before attempting wholly owned subsidiaries. A similar evolution is also apparent in Japanese MNEs' location strategy. Until the early 1990s, about half of Japanese investment was located in northeast and northern China, a reflection of a historical and geographical link between Japan and these areas. They gradually expanded to other coastal areas. Investment size also increased gradually. Japanese firms rarely initiate a vast amount of capital in the early stage of investment. They rely heavily on personal management strategies such as establishing a sense of obligation, and make greater use of staff control in managing their subsidiaries, compared to western MNEs.

Korean MNEs are generally less risk-averse than Japanese MNEs and have been growing faster. The LG Group, for instance, established 20 projects in China within two years after entering the market. Most Korean invested projects are more technologically intensive than those of Greater China MNEs and reflect long-term investment strategies. Since Korean businesspeople prefer transactions with those they know and trust, they tend to rely heavily on investment intermediaries. Many Korean investments are concentrated in one town or even on one street. Most projects are vertically integrated, ranging from parts and components to final products.

---

marketing-intensive products often based on imported technology.[41] Some emerging market MNEs can be found in services (e.g., Singapore Airlines, consistently ranked at the top of the industry in terms of service and profitability).

- *Bargaining Power.* DMNEs are less likely to export from their foreign affiliates; when they do export from them, however, they do not target their home markets the way traditional MNEs do.[42] DMNEs lack bargaining power in the host country. Although their home governments are very supportive, they usually cannot offer much assistance in the form of pressuring the host government to purchase the DMNE's products or accord it favorable investment terms. DMNEs sometimes have bargaining power intra-regionally (e.g., a Brazilian firm investing in Venezuela). A DMNE advantage is that it is often perceived in other developing economies to be less intimidating than developed country MNEs.

■ *Strategy.* DMNEs are more likely to compete on price than on product differentiation.[43] Activity often begins with manufacturing for private brands and continues with low-end branded products.

DMNEs also tend to pursue niche strategies. Having already entered other developing markets, China-based Haier has been pursuing the U.S. market for small office refrigerators, products initially abandoned by domestic manufacturers such as GE and Amana. Embraer specializes in regional aircraft ranging from 30 to 108 seats, one of the fastest-growing segments in the industry, but one in which Boeing and Airbus currently do not compete. DMNEs are less likely to be the innovator but rather quickly offer a lower priced version of an original product introduced in a developed market. With the entry of competitors from less developed markets, however, DMNEs seek to go up the value chain. This is what happened to Taiwanese TV and computer makers with the advance of mainland Chinese firms (in which many Taiwanese firms invested). Taiwanese computer maker Acer started by selling components that were used in computers sold by such firms as Hitachi and Siemens, but then proceeded to sell computers under its own name. Korean electronics maker LG (then Lucky Goldstar) started by selling under private label but eventually developed its own brand name and now sells most of its products under it. When Korean firms first began selling TV sets in the United States in the 1970s, they focused on the low-end, offering limited-feature sets priced substantially below their Japanese and U.S. competitors. However, rises in wages and the currency exchange rate in their home country put pressure on costs and forced Korean firms to move up-market.

DMNEs are also less likely to be vertically integrated than MNEs from developed economies.[44] This strategy has been viewed as an advantage in changing global markets and has been adopted to a considerable extent by established MNEs. DMNEs are more likely to establish alliances and to take a minority stake both for lack of resources and because of a lesser need to protect proprietary technology.

Craig and Douglas outline six strategies that MNEs from developing economies can pursue: (1) *Low-cost commodity,* where a firm competes only on price and exports out of its domestic base; (2) *manufacture for private label,* where a company manufactures a product but sells it under a retailer's brand name; (3) *component manufacturing,* where a company manufactures inputs to be assembled and marketed by the developed country firm; (4) *low-cost leader,* where the emerging market MNE sells an assembled product but competes mostly on cost; (5) *first-generation* or *market-specific* technology, where the emerging market firm focuses on a market with characteristics similar to its domestic market; and (6) *a specialized niche,* whether in a given country or region or worldwide.[45] Some emerging market MNEs continue with the same strategy for a long period. For example, Mexican cement maker Cemex continues to compete on cost, whereas others move through those strategies as they mature.

For the DMNE, the shift away from cost leadership implies developing its own technological base, emphasizing profitability, expanding foreign sales, locating production abroad, and moving toward a product organization design.[46] The Asian financial crisis created additional changes. In an effort to reduce debt and improve profitability, both Samsung and LG have been divesting entire subsidiaries and product lines at home and abroad. Their scale has diminished with resources deployed toward the achievement of strategic goals. Other emerging-market MNEs are setting higher goals. Bimbo, Mexico's largest and the world's third largest baker, expanded first into South America where it now sells bread, snacks, and candy in almost all of the countries on the continent. It also entered Texas and California, which have the largest Hispanic markets in the United States. Now Bimbo is eyeing other Latino markets in the United States as well as the broader U.S. market. It is seeking to acquire a major U.S. bakery with an extensive distribution system that will allow it to further penetrate and serve that market.[47]

DMNEs need to contend with the threats to competitiveness that accompany development and liberalization. Higher wages erode their competitive advantage with lower-priced competitors from "new tigers" such as Malaysia and Indonesia and require substantial investment in capital equipment and new production techniques. Greater openness at home means that the home market is not as well protected as it was and cannot serve as an assured base from which to launch foreign expansion. Rapid changes in technology require capital investment that is more difficult to obtain since the Asian crisis, as creditors have become much more careful in scrutinizing investment projects.

Interim Summary

1. DMNEs are often competitive with developed country MNEs and may enhance their competitive position over time. The main difference between MNEs and DMNEs is the scale of DMNE holdings, which are substantially smaller and have higher diversification as compared to the market focus of developed country MNEs.

2. DMNEs face many hurdles when moving into foreign markets. Most notably, they lack the capital resources of other MNEs as well as experience in dealing with foreign institutions and the rigors of international competition.

3. DMNEs have some advantages in the global market. Often, their home government goes out of its way to protect their edge in the home market while assisting their expansion abroad. The DMNE's comparatively small size allows for flexibility in taking advantage of new products, technologies and market opportunities.

4. The successful DMNE takes advantage of its unique features and does not try to compete head on with an already strong MNE.

THE SMALL AND MEDIUM-SIZE INTERNATIONAL ENTERPRISE (SMIE)

Small and medium-size enterprises (SMEs) have been major participants in international business since the 1920s. Between 1987 and 1997 the number of U.S. small business exporters tripled from 65,900 to 202,185.[48] The value of small business exports rose 300 percent between 1992 and 1997.[49] This success, symbolized by the addition of the Small Business Administration (SBA) to the President's Export Council in 1996, challenges the "common wisdom" that "to compete globally you have to be big."[50]

What Is an SMIE?

Before we discuss the international small and midsize company or SMIE, we need to define a small and midsize company or a SME. There are numerous definitions of a small and medium-size enterprise. A common definition of "small" business in the United States is a firm with fewer than 100 employees and less than $5 million in annual revenues. Midsize firms, according to the Conference Board, are firms with annual revenues in the range of $100 to $500 million. Although this may sound like a lot, keep in mind that large MNEs are in a different league. Ford Motor Company, for instance, has annual revenues in excess of $160 billion.

The 24 million U.S.-based SMEs represent 99.7 percent of all employers in the country and employ 53 percent of private workforce[51] in both manufacturing and services.[52] They account for approximately 50 percent of U.S. GDP and, remarkably,

55 percent of technological innovations,[52] providing almost all of the nearly 20 million net new jobs added between 1992 and 1997 in the U.S. economy.[53] The SBA notes that every $1 billion in exports of manufactured goods creates an estimated 15,000 new jobs; two to three times that number of additional jobs emerge to support the new products and personnel (e.g., restaurants, housing).[54] SME exporters pay 15 percent higher wages and 11 percent higher benefits than their counterparts that do not export,[55] are 20 percent more productive and 9 percent more likely to stay financially solvent. They also experience a 20 percent greater job growth than non-exporters.[56]

The importance of the SME sector varies by country. For example, they are a formidable force in Taiwan and Korea, where they account for more than 40 and 46 percent of output, respectively.[57] In contrast, in Indonesia and the Philippines, SMEs account for less than 10 percent and 13 percent of output, respectively; in Singapore, SMEs account for 15 percent. The contribution of SMIEs to national exports also varies. In France and Italy, the export contribution of SMIEs approaches that of large MNEs. In Italy, 45 percent of exports were attributed to SMIEs.[58] In Korea, they accounted for 42.6 percent of total merchandise export in 1998.[59] In contrast, Japanese SMEs contributed merely 13 percent of the country's merchandise exports in 1990.[60]

SME involvement in international business is likely to grow rapidly in the coming years, especially in services and technology-related areas, the fastest growing sectors in the economy, where SMEs tend to be concentrated.[61] Their potential is still largely untapped. Just a shade over 200,000 of the 24 million U.S. SMEs are currently exporting.[62] In 1999, 205,577 SMEs with fewer than 100 employees and 18,104 medium-sized (100–499 employees) firms were exporters.[63] SMEs account for 47 percent of total domestic sales but only 31 percent of total exports. Nearly two-thirds of SMIEs send their products to just one country with total exports of less than $1 million.[64]

A study by PricewaterhouseCoopers found that access to international markets was viewed as an important benefit by SMEs from many nations.[65] The internet may lower entry barriers into international markets (see also Chapter 18 on Global internet and E-commerce). Technological developments such as Flexible Manufacturing Systems are also making it possible for a small firm to profitably produce relatively small batches of goods. Developments in financial services have had a similar effect.

Size and Internationalization

In one study, only a quarter of SMIEs considered their size a constraint.[66] Indeed, the fastest export growth occurred among very small businesses—those with fewer than 20 employees. These firms made up 65 percent of all U.S. exporting firms in 1997, up from 59 percent in 1992. Even among firms with sales of $1,000–$99,000, almost half were exporting.[67] Other studies, however, suggest size matters. Even among small international firms, the larger the firm, the more likely it was to engage in international business and to have an international strategy. Size was significantly correlated with exports; 82 percent of larger (more than $50 million in sales) firms were exporters versus 48 percent of the small firms.[68]

Midsize firms ($100 million to $500 million annual sales) seem to have an especially appropriate balance of size and agility for international operations. The Conference Board found that such firms reported a significant percentage of foreign sales and early manufacturing presence overseas. Foreign sales accounted for 22 percent of total annual turnover for firms in the midsize category. Small international firms grew three times as fast as companies their size that did not internationalize and twice as fast as the large MNEs. Those with sales below $100 million grew at an annual rate of 67 percent with a 35 percent annual return in the 1986–1991 period.

Exhibit 4–14
Small companies can be international

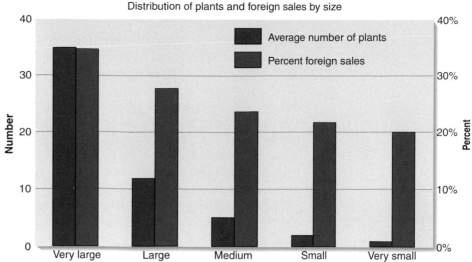

Distribution of plants and foreign sales by size

Legend:
- Average number of plants
- Percent foreign sales

Source: U.S. Manufacturers in the Global Marketplace. The Conference Board, Report #1058-94-RR, 1999.

Exhibit 4–14 displays distribution of exports and foreign investment by company size in the Conference Board survey, showing that while size matters, even very small firms can be international.

Obstacles to SMIE Internationalization

Exhibit 4–15 lists entry barriers to international trade identified in a survey of SMEs in Minnesota. Note that some of the obstacles noted in the exhibit (e.g., culture) are not different, in principle, from those encountered by established MNEs. How-

Exhibit 4–15
Entry barriers to international trade for Minnesota SMIEs

	A serious obstacle	Somewhat of an obstacle	A minor obstacle	Not an obstacle
• Integration with a country's business culture	10.4%	31.2%	24.4%	29.2%
• Lack of information	16.0%	30.0%	26.4%	24.8%
• Cost and financing	15.6%	24.8%	24.4%	32.0%
• Qualified employees	14.8%	26.8%	19.6%	36.4%
• Regulations and tariffs	21.2%	37.2%	23.6%	15.6%
• Language	12.4%	35.2%	26.4%	25.2%
• Lack of expertise	10.4%	28.8%	21.2%	34.8%
• Brokers	2.8%	12.8%	14.8%	61.6%
• Partners	5.2%	20.0%	17.6%	52.0%
• Port of entry	4.4%	16.0%	19.2%	55.6%

Source: Twin Cities Business Monthly. What Business Thinks. 2001, p. 14.

ever, much of the challenge presented by SME entry into international markets involves the unique character of the smaller enterprise.[69] A study examining the concerns of U.S.-based SMIEs expanding into Europe found that their concerns differed considerably from those of large MNEs. For example, managing foreign exchange risk was ranked the most minor concern of the large MNE but is a concern for the SMIE, which lacks the resources to effectively manage risk or geographical diversity. Similarly, international communications was an important concern for smaller firms but not for the larger ones. In contrast, developing a manufacturing strategy was a concern for large MNEs but not for the SMIEs, possibly because of lack of awareness of the need for formal planning on the SMIEs' part.[70]

A UN report states that internationalizing SMEs face problems relating to management, training, and quality control as well as market and infrastructure problems, such as the lack of capital and intense competition. However, it considers the greatest obstacle the barriers created or permitted by governments, such as regulatory impediments or corruption. Some of the main obstacles for the internationalizing SME are listed below.

Scale and Transaction Constraints

The small scale and limited reach of the SMIE constrain its production and service delivery options and costs. The transaction costs of the SMIE are substantially higher than those of the large MNE, which internalizes much of its operations. While large MNEs conduct much of their trade via internal networks, SMIEs have to go through the complex process of cross-border trade flow that can add as much as 10 percent to the final value of goods.[71] Relying on export intermediaries is an option, but it is costly and implies distance from the customer.

Access to Capital

An important roadblock on the internationalization route for the SME is shortage of capital[72] and its correlates (e.g., inability to obtain reliable market information and lack of training for traders and expatriates). Public institutions judged financial strength the single most important problem for internationalizing SMEs.[73] Much of the problem has to do with lack of access. The SBA reports that only about 150 to 200 of the 9,000 banks operating in the United States offer significant financing for SMIEs.[74] At the same time, the globalization of financial services is rapidly changing the patterns of access to capital and opening new opportunities for raising capital. This is true not only in the United States, where venture capital has created many opportunities for SMEs (especially in high tech), but also in countries like Japan where in the past banks would rarely extend loans to SMEs.

Lack of Knowledge

A critical resource for SMEs entering foreign markets is knowledge.[75] Lacking a track record in exporting and foreign investment, such firms usually do not possess the relevant knowledge ranging from how to conduct market research in foreign locations to how to address currency fluctuations. Tiny Hatteras Yachts was hard hit by the Euro's decline in value against the U.S. dollar because it did not employ sophisticated hedging techniques and lacked the ability to source globally.[76] SMEs also face problems when having to transfer their knowledge to foreign recipients. More than in large MNEs, the knowledge possessed by SMIEs tends to be less codified and more tacit and embedded. Combined with weak information processing, SMIEs find it hard to "level the playing field" with larger players.[77]

To compensate for its knowledge deficiency, the SMIE is often compelled to look to others for assistance. UNCTAD recommends that governments assist SMIEs with information on market conditions, opportunities, and government regulations and requirements. Channels include commercial attachés and embassies, trade missions, trade shows, networking systems, chambers of commerce, international agencies, technology-exchange programs, international forums and conferences, Web sites, market-research consultants, and national trade promotions. A U.S. Chamber of Commerce survey shows that 66 percent of SMIEs utilized at least one form of government export assistance, while 50 percent used two or more agencies.

Another way to compensate for knowledge deficiency is by learning from the experience of others in a similar situation in the industry.[78] An important source is the knowledge shared by executives with experience in foreign markets. SMIEs with internationally experienced management teams obtained foreign sales more quickly than those without such teams.[79]

Lack of Market Power

Lack of market power is another key deficiency for smaller firms, which often find themselves powerless against trade barriers. They are too small to bargain with local governments and cannot produce the large quantities that would trigger local suppliers to manufacture to their specifications.[80] They are also "very vulnerable to trade barriers," according to SBA administrator Alvarez. The SBA is required to aggressively advance the interests of U.S. small business in international trade under the Small Business Export Promotion Act of 1980.

Vulnerability to Intellectual Property Violations

U.S. SMIEs are very concerned with intellectual property rights such as patents, copyrights, and trademarks. This issue is particularly important to SMIEs because they are overrepresented in high-tech areas but lack the resources to pursue violators across the globe. The same is true for the uniform application of product standards. Finally, given the importance of e-commerce for SMIEs, a tax moratorium on that activity is very important to them.

SMIE Advantages in Internationalization

The many obstacles noted previously notwithstanding, SMIEs have been successful in the global marketplace owing to a number of distinct advantages. Innovativeness, creativity, entrepreneurial spirit, lower overhead costs, and the ability to move fast to take advantage of new opportunities are all important factors in the global marketplace, and are relatively common at SMIEs. Some of the advantages noted for DMNEs, such as lack of investment in outdated technologies and hence the ability to "leapfrog" technologically, also apply to SMIEs.

SMIE Internationalization Features

Internationalization Motivation

A UNCTAD survey identified a number of drivers of SME internationalization, including push factors, pull factors, management factors, and chance. The push factors are competitive pressures in its domestic market, which "push" the SME to increase the scale of its operations via exports so as to reduce unit cost, or to reduce its labor costs by moving operations to low-cost countries. Another push factor is decline in domestic demand. For instance, facing an economic downturn in the early 1990s, architectural firms in Hawaii doubled their efforts to penetrate Asian markets. Pull factors make foreign locations more attractive (e.g., rapidly expanding markets, growth potential, or lower production costs). Management factors include managerial commitment and resources devoted to international activity. Finally, chance factors are unforeseen circumstances that create internationalization opportunities. According to the survey findings, when SMIEs invest in other SMEs, management and chance factors are the most important, followed by push factors. For larger enterprises investing in foreign SMEs, management and pull factors are the most important, whereas push factors are relatively less important.[81]

Brush[82] found that the manager's personal knowledge of markets, personal contacts, and expertise were important factors influencing the export decision of young firms. However, these factors were linked to the perceived market opportunity in terms of demand and growth potential, an opportunity often expressed in the form of unsolicited orders from foreign customers. Personal contacts, owner/manager's expertise and competencies (often acquired earlier in another venture or another firm), product innovation, and foreign market information were key factors behind internationalization.

For established SMIEs, perceived market demands and managerial factors were less instrumental than the desire for expansion and growth. Host country transportation and distribution were also more important for established firms than for newer firms. Established firms were also more likely to use export intermediaries or piggyback on large exporters and investors. They tended to sell more products to a wider array of countries and derive more overall revenues from export than the younger firms. Exhibit 4–16 lists FDI motivations by SMIEs of different world regions.

Internationalization Patterns

Controlling for industry, significant differences have been found between the foreign expansion strategies of large and small firms.[83] SMIE internationalization is often not incremental. Newer, high-tech, small firms in particular tend to "leapfrog" into international markets before gaining a foothold in their domestic markets. This has been found to be the case for small software firms.[84] Other SMIEs go through a number of stages but follow a different route than that of large MNEs, often starting with inward investment before moving to outward investment.

More than large MNEs, SMIEs rely on exports rather than on FDI. This is understandable in light of the SMIE resource constraints, as well as the fact that SMIEs are often in an early phase of the internationalization process. SMIEs are also more likely to rely on export intermediaries such as export agents, export merchants, export management firms, and export trading firms. Like their larger counterparts, SMIEs often use foreign markets as an export platform to third countries.[85] This is probably more true for Japan and other high labor cost countries faced with a decline in their export competitiveness at home. Indeed, manufacturing SMIEs are more likely to internationalize in the more labor intensive areas of textiles, clothing, and mechanical equipment.

SMNE Exporter Profile

According to research conducted for the SBA and the U.S. Department of Commerce, 97 percent of U.S. exporters are small businesses. Of 209,500 U.S. exporters in 1997, 202,185 were SMIEs. Their share of U.S. merchandise exports has risen from 26 percent in 1987 to almost 31 percent in 1997. In 1992, SMIEs accounted for 13.4 percent of manufacturing exports but for more than 60 percent of non-manufacturing exports.[86] Because many exports consist of intra-company transfers within subsidiaries of the same MNE, the proportion of SMIEs in inter-company exports is considerably larger. According to the U.S. Central Budget Office, small exporters were more likely to export 50 percent or more of their product than large exporters. Some

Exhibit 4–16

Motivations for foreign direct investment by small and medium-sized corporations, by host region 1998 (percentage)

	Motivation	North America	Europe	Asia	Latin America	World
				Host region		
(1)	Outside proposal (initiative in this venture came from outside the firm in host country, host-country governments, or third party, such as international organizations etc.)	1.9	1.3	3.2	50.0	3.3
(2)	To secure raw materials	9.6	3.8	14.0	50.0	11.2
(3)	To secure supply of materials (intermediate goods)	3.9	6.3	6.5	16.7	5.8
(4)	Low-cost labor in host country	3.9	3.8	31.2	16.7	14.5
(5)	Protection measures by host-country government	3.9	3.8	17.2	—	9.9
(6)	Expectation of growth in local market	5.8	44.3	52.7	16.7	50.0
(7)	Access to and growth in third-country markets	15.4	24.1	29.0	33.3	24.4
(8)	Lower production costs for exporting to third countries and to home country	3.9	2.5	21.5	—	9.9
(9)	Information gathering	28.9	22.8	16.1	—	20.6
(10)	Presence of other foreign firms or firms of the same home country in the same industry in the host country	11.5	11.4	10.8	—	11.2
(11)	Small market in home country	5.8	20.3	8.6	—	11.2
(12)	Risk diversification	3.9	16.5	9.7	—	10.7
(13)	High return in host country	—	2.5	6.5	16.7	5.0
(14)	Home-country government incentives	—	1.3	·	—	0.4
(15)	Host-country government incentives	—	2.5	11.8	—	5.4
(16)	To acquire technology	7.7	1.3	2.2	—	2.9
(17)	To acquire managerial expertise	—	·	1.1	—	0.4
(18)	To diversify production lines	3.9	2.5	7.5	—	5.0
(19)	To strengthen competitive capacity	25.0	29.1	31.2	16.7	27.3
(20)	To strengthen financial capability (fund-raising)	—	1.3	2.2	—	1.2
(21)	Favorable tax schemes (tax holiday)	—	1.3	15.1	—	7.0
(22)	Others	7.7	10.1	4.3	—	6.6
	Number of foreign affiliates observed	52.0	79.0	91.0	6.0	242.0

Source: M. Fujita. The transnational activities of small and medium-sized enterprises. Boston: Kluwer, 1998.

22.8 percent of self-employed exporters (i.e., with no hired employees) exported half or more of their product, compared with 3.7 percent of the exporters with 100 or more employees.

The top 10 markets for U.S. SMIE exporters are Canada, the United Kingdom, Japan, Mexico, Germany, Australia, Hong Kong, France, Taiwan, and Singapore. The position of Canada and the United Kingdom shows that as in the case of traditional MNEs, cultural familiarity is a major factor in determining where SMIEs choose to invest. In the same vein, many French firms entering the North American market start with Quebec, the French-speaking province of Canada. This reality may be changing, however. The top 10 fastest-growing markets for U.S. small exporters are Brazil, Malaysia, China, Philippines, Canada, Thailand, Israel, Argentina, the United Kingdom, and Hong Kong. Thus, emerging markets are of growing importance to SMIE exporters. SMIEs accounted for 35 percent of the volume and value of U.S. exports to China in 1997, up 8 percent from 1992. Of 9,000 plus U.S. exporters to China, SMIEs constituted 82 percent.[87] This record is especially impressive since China is considered one of the most difficult markets for foreign investors.

Exporter Demographics. According to Central Budget Office data from 1992, 2.2 percent of firms owned by men and 1.1 percent of those owned by women were exporters. However, when women-owned firms did export, their exporting activities were more intensive: 30 percent exported 50 percent or more of the value of their product, compared with 21.9 percent of firms owned by men; 2.7 percent of Hispanic-owned firms, 2.3 percent of firms owned by Asian-Pacific, American Indian, or Aleut Eskimo business owners, 1.8 percent of Caucasian-owned firms, and 0.8 percent of African-American firms exported. Exporting firms owned by minorities exported more intensively than did non-minority-owned exporters: 50 percent of Hispanic-owned firms, 42.9 percent of Asian, Pacific, American Indian, or Aleut Eskimo-owned firms; 28.6 percent of African-American-owned firms while only 18.1 percent of Caucasian-owned firms exported half or more of the total value of sales.[88] States that had more exporters of goods overall—such as California, New York, and Florida—also had the highest percentages of small business exporters. SMIE share of exporters ranged from 92.5 percent in California to 61.3 percent in West Virginia.[89]

SMIE Foreign Investment Profile

Foreign investment by SMIEs is at present relatively small (which is why, as you may recall, most of these firms do not qualify as MNEs). In Japan, it accounts for more than half of the cases but only about 10 percent of the value of outward FDI. In the United States, SMIEs account for 6 percent of the number and 3 percent of the assets of foreign affiliates.[90] Still, as far back as 1988, American SMIEs controlled U.S.$15 billion in FDI stock. Western Europe is by far the largest target for U.S. SMIE foreign investment. In Singapore, Taiwan, and Vietnam, SMEs are the recipients of FDI by large foreign MNEs. "Small-package FDI" (<$1 million) accounts for 5–20 percent by value in Myanmar and less than half a percent in Vietnam. In the Philippines, it accounts for more than 60 percent of projects but only about 2–10 percent by value.

In recent years, FDI by SMIEs has been growing, often at a more rapid pace than FDI overall. A UN survey of Asian SMIEs found that factors considered important for their internationalization include improving the quality of products/services, local management and staff training and government relations. SMIEs were found to be three times more likely than MNEs to regard training of unskilled staff as very important to strategic success, more than twice as likely to regard the introduction or improvement of products or services as very important, and more than 50 percent more likely to regard local managers' training an increase in foreign earnings as very important.

Chance Expansion. SMIEs' exports and FDI are often not a systematically planned strategic move but rather a response to an incidental opportunity. In a survey of 100 U.S. entrepreneurial technology firms commissioned by the U.S. firm Protégé, 82 percent of CEOs acknowledged that their foreign expansion was not part of a broader strategy but rather an opportunistic pursuit of clients and an inexpensive way to achieve internationalization.[91] Chances for internationalization include, for example, a customer expanding into a foreign location ("piggybacking"). The piggybacking may occur at the initiative of an MNE that needs supply, components, and such for its international operations. For example, Japanese automotive suppliers followed Japanese auto manufacturers to the United States.[92] Pico Rivera, a shelving company that once sold only in the United States and Canada, followed its customer Disney to eastern Europe and other countries where Disney wanted to install the same shelves that it has in the United States.[93]

Nature of FDI by SMIEs

- ***Emphasis on Developed Markets.*** When engaging in FDI, SMIEs are more likely to invest in developed rather than developing markets. In Fujita's study, 80 percent of SMIEs located in developed countries. Host country red tape,

Hong Kong, a special administrative region of China, is home to numerous SMIEs.

economic instability, hard currency restrictions, procurement difficulties, and lack of domestic bank support were among the reasons why SMIEs avoided investment in developing markets. Japanese, Australian and Hong Kong firms are an exception, probably because most markets in their area are developing.[94] The trend is also true for medium-size firms. Conference Board data show that firms with more than 20 overseas plants were much more likely to invest in developing countries than firms with fewer than 10 foreign plants.[95] SMIEs are also more likely to establish new operations (greenfield investments) than to acquire existing operations. This is largely a product of their resource limitations.

- *Selective Globalization.* SMIEs tend to focus on one link in the supply chain (e.g., manufacturing) as well as on a selected market.[96] In one study, 17 percent of the large firms exported to more than 50 countries versus none among the small and medium-size firms.[97] In the Conference Board sample, very large firms ($5 billion and over) had an average of 36 plants in 14 foreign countries, compared with 13 plants in 6 countries for firms with $1–$5 billion in annual sales. Companies with sales of less than $100 million had 1 to 3 overseas plants.

- *Strategy.* SMIEs often adopt niche strategies, pursuing areas that are not covered by large firms due to neglect, lack of expertise, or high cost structure.[98] The Industry Box provides such an example. Investment tends to be in medium-technology industries because the scale provided by globalization is especially important in this sector. In making investment decisions, SMIEs are unlikely to be motivated by host country incentives,[99] which is not surprising given their lack of market power. However, SMIE investment is less likely to trigger the visibility and the resentment that sometimes accompanies FDI.

SMIEs rely more on cooperative strategies, often as a result of the local partner initiative to compensate for a resource shortfall. This is particularly true for those with experienced management.[100] In the UN survey, SMIEs are shown to engage a local partner in a joint venture in more than half of the cases. When Canadian Sleeman Brewing entered the highly competitive U.S. market, it teamed up with the Boston Beer Company, whose beer was already being sold in Canada, to launch a U.S. brand.[101]

Namiki lists effective export strategies for small firms as follows: competitive pricing and brand identification, speciality product manufacturing, technological advantage, and superior customer service. Exploiting niche markets is also very important.[102] Smaller firms often went abroad in order to avoid direct competition with large MNEs. This led them to develop in-depth narrow expertise that may be useful in developing "deep niche" strategies.[103]

The UNCTAD report recommends that governments encourage cross-border alliances between SMIEs. Governments can create a pool of suitable partners, initiate introductions and resolve conflicts. They can encourage investment and trade missions, conferences, and investment/trade shows designed to encourage business matching, electronic business-matching services, chambers of commerce and other facilitators, and clustering programs.

Born International

Some firms develop an international orientation very early. Those include "international market makers," namely multinational traders or import/export start-ups and "geographically focused start-ups," which utilize their knowledge of a particular world area. The most advanced form is the "global start-up," or **"born international,"** a "business organization that from inception seeks to derive significant competitive advantages from the use of resources and sale of output in multiple countries."[104]

While "born international" firms existed for many years (e.g., the East India Company, established in 1600), the phenomenon is associated mainly with the last two decades, particularly in the high-tech sector. Examples of "born international" are European and Israeli high-tech start-ups that generate most, and sometimes all, of their revenues abroad from the very start.[105] Oviatt & McDougall (p. 46) provide this interview with a United Kingdom executive:

We did not succeed because we tried to sell the product by starting up in England and then selling in the U.S., and by that time it was too late. We should have developed our products first of all for the U.S. market and then sold it back into England.

In his subsequent venture, this executive targeted the United States and Japan before turning his attention to the United Kingdom and continental Europe. According to the authors, successful global start-ups have global vision from inception; internationally experienced management; strong international business networks; use of preemptive technology or marketing, building on a unique intangible asset; incremental, closely linked extensions in product/service; and tight worldwide coordination.

Interim Summary

1. SMIEs are a powerful and growing economic force in many countries. Although each of them is small, they are collectively important. Increasingly, they seek access to international markets as part of their business strategy.

2. Company size matters in exporting, but the fastest export growth occurs among very small businesses. However, many SMIEs do not have a coherent international strategy.

3. SMIEs face many of the same difficulties that DMNEs experience in internationalization, and make up for their disadvantages with adaptability and the quick reaction time only a small company can offer.

4. SMIEs usually develop niche market strategies when going international, often following an established client base. However, some firms plan on exporting from the beginning without developing a local market until after they have found success abroad.

CHAPTER SUMMARY

1. The "players" in the international business scene include a great variety of companies, but only those with foreign direct investment over which the company maintains effective control are called in this book multinational enterprises (MNEs).

2. MNEs from developing and emerging economies (DMNEs) and small and medium-size international companies (SMIEs, which include "born international" firms) also play an important role in shaping world economy and global business. The MNE, DMNE, and SMIE significantly differ in their internationalization patterns, resources, and obstacles to international expansion.

3. MNEs, whether in manufacturing or service sectors, need strong competitive advantages to compete with established local firms. They need to effectively and efficiently build, deploy, exploit, and upgrade distinctive capabilities (technological, organizational, operational, and financial) if they want to prosper.

4. DMNEs often encounter obstacles in entering foreign markets, including resource constraints, lack of knowledge, and a sheltered environment. They,

however, enjoy some unique advantages such as flexibility and home government support. Nevertheless, they cannot simply mimic global strategies used by developed country MNEs.

5. SMIEs emphasize export rather than FDI due to their resource or experience limitations. They either directly export products to a foreign market or sell through export intermediaries. Recently, some SMIEs, including those offering high-tech products or services, have engaged in various FDI activities such as joint ventures, cooperative alliances, mergers, or acquisitions and skipped many of the evolutionary steps or stages that traditional counterparts followed.

6. The type of MNE does not necessarily determine international expansion success but strategy and capability do. Firms engaging in international expansion, regardless of their type, size, industry, or origin, need to formulate and execute appropriate strategies that match both external environments and internal capabilities in the course of internationalization.

CHAPTER NOTES

[1] *US manufacturers in the global market place.* The Conference Board *Report # 1058-94-RR, 1994.*

[2] The Conference Board, *US manufacturers in the global market place.* The Conference Board *Report # 1058-94-RR, 1994.*

[3] C. A. Bartlett, and S. Ghoshal, 1989, *Managing Across Borders: The Transnational Solution,* Harvard Business School Press.

[4] World Investment Report 2000, United Nations Conference on Trade and Development (UNCTAD).

[5] K. Moore and D. Lewis, *Birth of the Multinational,* Copenhagen Business School Press, 2000.

[6] The world view of multinationals. *The Economist,* Jan. 29, 2000, 21.

[7] The Conference Board, *US manufacturers in the global market place.* The Conference Board *Report # 1058-94-RR, 1994.*

[8] E. M. Graham, Institute for International Economics. Cited in *The Economist,* September 29, 2001, 9.

[9] "The world view of multinationals," *The Economist,* January 29, 2000, 21.

[10] UNCTAD, World Investment Report, 2001.

[11] UNCTAD, World Investment Report, 2001.

[12] *Forbes,* July 24, 2000.

[13] R. E. Caves, 1996, Multinational enterprise and economic analysis. Cambridge University Press.

[14] World Investment Report 1996, UNCTAD.

[15] The world view of multinationals, *The Economist,* January 29, 2000.

[16] P. Druckerman, The foreign Invasion, *Wall Street Journal,* September. 25, 2000, R21.

[17] L. T. Wells, "Multinationals and the developing countries." *Journal of International Business Studies,* 29, 1, 1998, 101–114.

[18] P. N. Doremus, W. W. Keller, L. W. Pauly, and S. Reich, The Myth of the Global Corporation, NJ: Princeton, University Press.

[19] D. J. Lecraw, "Performance of transnational corporations in less developed countries," *Journal of International Business Studies,* Spring/Summer 1983, 15–33.

[20] The world view of multinationals, *The Economist,* Jan. 29, 2000, 21.

[21] M. S. Roth and J. B. Romeo, "Matching product category and country image perceptions: A framework for managing country-of-origin effects," *Journal of International Business Studies,* 3, 1992, 477–497.

[22] D. J. Lecraw, "Performance of transnational corporations in less developed countries," *Journal of International Business Studies,* Spring/Summer 1983, 15–33.

[23] The Conference Board, "U.S. manufacturers in the global marketplace," Report #1058-94-RR.

[24] J. Ordonez, "Starbuck's to start major expansion in overseas markets," *Wall Street Journal,* October 27, 2000, B10.

[25] J. Ordonez, "Starbuck's to start major expansion in overseas markets," *Wall Street Journal,* October 27, 2000.

[26] P. Pananond and C. P. Zeithaml, "The international expansion of MNEs from developing countries: A case study of Thailand's CP group," *Asia Pacific Journal of Management,* 15, 1998, 163–184.

[27] Company publications.

[28] J. Karp, "Procomp hopes to bring Brazilian efficiency to Floridian chaos," *Wall Street Journal,* November 13, 2000, A27.

[29] H. W. C., Yeung, "Transnational corporations from Asian developing countries: Their characteristics and competitive edge," *Journal of Asian Business,* 10, 4, 1994, 17–58; World Investment Report-2001.

[30] UNCTAD, World Investment Report 2001, xv.

[31] D. J. Lecraw, "Performance of transnational corporations in less developed countries," *Journal of International Business Studies,* Spring/Summer 1983, 15–33.

[32] R. Aggarwal and T. Agmon, 1990, "The international success of developing country firms: Role of government directed comparative advantage," *Management International Review,* 30, 2, 163–180.

[33] L. T. Wells, *Third World Multinationals: The Rise of Foreign Investment from Developing Countries,* Cambridge, MA: MIT Press, 1983.

[34] H. Vernon-Wortzel, and L. H. Wortzel, "Globalizing strategies for multinationals from developing countries," *Columbia Journal of World Business,* Spring 1988.

[35] P. P. Li, 1994. "Strategy profiles of indigenous MNEs from the NIEs: The case of South Korea and Taiwan." *The International Executive,* 36, 2, 147–170.

[36] D. J. Lecraw, "Outward direct investment by Indonesian firms: Motivation and effects," *Journal of International Business Studies,* 3rd quarter, 1993, 589–600.

[37] H. Zhang and D. Ven den Bulcke, 1994. International Management Strategies of Chinese Multinational firms, University of Antwerp, E/17.

[38] S. Tallman and O. Shenkar, "International cooperative venture strategies: Outward investment and small firms from NICs." *Management International Review,* 34, 1994, 75–91.

[39] D. J. Lecraw, "Direct investment by firms from less developed countries," *Oxford Economic Papers,* 29, 3, 442–457.

[40] D. J. Lecraw, "Direct investment by firms from less developed countries," *Oxford Economic Papers,* 29, 3, 442–457.

[41] D. J. Lecraw, "Direct investment by firms from less developed countries," *Oxford Economic Papers,* 29, 3, 442–457.

[42] D. J. Lecraw, "Direct investment by firms from less developed countries," *Oxford Economic Papers,* 29, 3, 442–457.

[43] D. J. Lecraw, "Direct investment by firms from less developed countries," *Oxford Economic Papers,* 29, 3, 442–457.

[44] H. Vernon-Wortzel, and L. H. Wortzel, Globalizing strategies for multinationals from developing countries," *Columbia Journal of International Business,* Spring 1988, 27–35.

[45] C. S. Craig and S. P. Douglas, Managing the transnational value chain—strategies for firms from emerging markets," *Journal of International Marketing,* 3, 1997, 71–84.

[46] Y. H. Kim and N. Campbell, "Strategic control in Korean MNCs," *Management International Review,* 1, 1995, 95–108.

[47] G. Gori, "A strategy built on loaves throughout the land," *The New York Times,* December 24, 2000, bu4.

[48] US Small Business Administration, Office of International Trade: America's small business and international trade: a report. Nov. 1999.

[49] US Small Business Administration, Office of International Trade: A report. Nov. 1999.

[50] A. D. Chandler, Jr., "The enduring logic of industrial success," *Harvard Business Review,* March/April, 1990, 130–140.

[51] US Small Business Administration, Office of International Trade: A report. Nov. 1999.

[52] US Small Business Administration, Office of International Trade: A report. Nov. 1999.

[53] US Small Business Administration, Office of International Trade: A report. Nov. 1999.

[54] US Small Business Administration, Office of International Trade: A report. Nov. 1999.

[55] US Small Business Administration, Office of International Trade: A report. Nov. 1999.

[56] US Small Business Administration, Office of International Trade: A report. Nov. 1999.

[57] M. Fujita, *The Transnational Activities of Small and Medium-Size Enterprises.* Boston: Kluwer, 1998.

[58] Z. Acs, R. Morck, M. Shaver, and B. Yeung. "The internationalization of small and medium-size enterprises." In Z. Acs and

B. Yeung (eds.), *Small and Medium-Size Enterprises in the Global Economy*. Ann Arbor: The University of Michigan Press 1999.

[59] Korea Federation of Small Business (KFSB).

[60] M. Fujita, *The Transnational Activities of Small and Medium-Size Enterprises*. Kluwer, 1998.

[61] U.S. Department of Commerce News, August 17, 2001.

[62] U.S. Department of Commerce, August 17, 2001.

[63] U.S. Department of Commerce, August 17, 2001.

[64] U.S. Department of Commerce, August 17, 2001.

[65] Pricewaterhousecoopers. *Transforming a Business*. 2000.

[66] M. Fujita, *The Transnational Activities of Small and Medium-Size Enterprises*. Kluwer, 1998.

[67] U.S. manufacturers in the global marketplace. A Conference Board Research Report #1058-94-RR 1994.

[68] J. L. Calof, "The relationship between firm size and export behavior revisited," *Journal of International Business Studies*, 25, 2, 367–387, 1994; S. Baird, M.A. Lyles, and J. B. Orris, "The choice of international strategies by small business," *Journal of Small Business Management,* January 1994, 48–59.

[69] J. C. Shuman and J. A. Seeger, "The theory and practice of strategic management in smaller rapid growth companies," *American Journal of Small Business*, 11, 1, 7–18; N. E. Coviello and A. McAuley," "Internationalization and the smaller firm," *Management International Review*, 3, 223–256.

[70] R. Klassen and C. Whyback, "Barriers to the management of international operations," *Journal of Operations Management*, 11, 1994, 385–397.

[71] World Investment Report—1993. UNCTAD.

[72] G. Fairclough and M. Murray, "Small banks expand their trade financing for exports," *Wall Street Journal*, February 24, 1998, B2.

[73] M. Fujita, *The Transnational Activities of Small and Medium-Size Enterprises*. Kluwer, 1998.

[74] G. Fairclough and M. Murray, "Small banks expand their trade financing for exports," *Wall Street Journal*, February 24, 1998, B2.

[75] P. Liesch and G. A. Knight, "Information internalization and hurdle rates in small and medium enterprise internationalization," *Journal of International Business Studies*, 30, 1, 383–394.

[76] C. Cooper, "Euro drop is hardest for the smallest," *Wall Street Journal*, October 2, 2000.

[77] E. Prater and S. Gosh, "The globalization process of U.S. small and medium-sized firms: A comparative analysis." Working paper # 97–005. DuPree School of Management, Georgia Institute of Technology.

[78] E. Prater and S. Gosh, "The globalization process of U.S. small and medium-sized firms: A comparative analysis." Working paper #97-005. DuPree School of Management, Georgia Institute of Technology.

[79] A. R. Reuber and E. Fischer, "The influence of the management team's international experience on the internationalization behaviors of SMEs," *Journal of International Business Studies*, 28, 4, 1997, 807–825.

[80] M. Fujita, *The Transnational Activities of Small and Medium-Size Enterprises*. Kluwer, 1998.

[81] UNCTAD, World Investment Report. 1999.

[82] C. A. Brush, *International Entrepreneurship: The Effect of Firm Age on Motives for Internationalization*. New York: Garland, 1995.

[83] J. W. Ballantine, F. W. Cleveland and C. T. Koeller, "Characterizing profitable and unprofitable strategies in small and large businesses," *Journal of Small Business Management,* April 1992, 13–24.

[84] H. Boter and C. Holmquist, "Industry characteristics and internationalization processes in small firms," *Journal of Business Venturing*, 11, 1994, 471–487; B. M. Oviatt and P. P. McDougal, "Toward a theory of international new ventures," *Journal of International Business Studies*, 25, 1, 45–64; Bell, J. "The internationalization of small computer software firms—a further challenge to stage theories," *European Journal of Marketing*, 29, 8, 60–75.

[85] M. Fujita, *The Transnational Activities of Small and Medium-Size Enterprises*. Kluwer, 1998.

[86] SBA Exporting by Small Firms April 1998; SBA America's Small Businesses and International Trade: A Report, November 1999; SBA and U.S. Department of Commerce publications.

[87] Export America 1999; SBA and Department of Commerce publications.

[88] Characteristics of Business Owners. 1992. U.S. Government Printing Office.

[89] These percentages are lower than the national SMIE figures because businesses are counted in every state in which they operate.

[90] M. Fujita, *The Transnational Activities of Small and Medium-Size Enterprises*. Kluwer, 1998.

[91] C. Fleming, "U.S. tech firms press on with global expansion," *Toronto Globe and Mail* (by agreement with the *Wall Street Journal*), August 17, 2001, B7.

[92] K. Banejri and R. Sambharya, "Vertical Keiretsu and international market entry: The case of the Japanese automobile ancillary industry," *Journal of International Business Studies*, 27, 1, 89–113, 1996.

[93] S. Doggett and A. Haddad, "Global savvy," *Los Angeles Times*, February 21, 2000.

[94] M. Fujita, *The Transnational Activities of Small and Medium-Size Enterprises*. Kluwer, 1998.

[95] U.S. manufacturers in the global market place. The Conference Board, Report #1058-96-RR

[96] K. Roth, "International configuration and coordination archetypes for medium-sized firms in global industries," *Journal of International Business Studies*, 3, 533–549; P. W. Beamish, A. Goerzen, and H. Munro, "The export characteristics of Canadian manufacturers: a profile by firm size." Working paper # 824, School of Business and Economics, Wilfred Laurier University, 1984.

[97] J. L. Calof, "The relationship between firm size and export behavior revisited," *Journal of International Business Studies*, 25, 2, 367–387, 1994.

[98] D. L. Balcome, "Choosing their own paths: Profiles of the export strategies of Canadian manufacturers." International Business Research Center Report 06–86, Conference Board of Canada, 1986.

[99] M. Fujita, *The Transnational Activities of Small and Medium-Size Enterprises*. Kluwer, 1998.

[100] B. Gomes-Casseres, "Alliance strategies of small firms." In Acs and Yeung, *Small and Medium-Sized Enterprises in the Global Economies*. Ann Arbor: The University of Michigan Press, 1999.

[101] E. Cherney, "Canadian brewery seeks export success to U.S. market," *Wall Street Journal*, July 24 2001, B2.

[102] N. Namiki, "Export strategy for small business," *Journal of Small Business Management*, 26, April 1988, 32–37.

[103] N. Namiki, "Export strategy for small business." *Journal of Small Business Management*, 26, April 1998. 32–37; B. Gomes-Casseres and T. Kohn, "Small firms in international competition: A challenge to traditional theory?" In P. Buckley et al., *International Technology Transfer by Small and Medium-Size Enterprises: Country Studies*, 280–296. New York: St., Martin's Press, 1997.

[104] B. M. Oviatt and P. P. McDougal, "Toward a theory of international new ventures," *Journal of International Business Studies*, 25, 1, 1994, 45–64.

[105] T. Almor, "Ownership structure of small high tech global companies: The case of Israel." Discussion paper #99.8, The College of Management, Tel-Aviv, Israel, 1999.

[106] P. Paranond and C.CP. Zeithaml, "The international expansion of MNEs from developing countries: A case study of Thailand's CP group," *Asia Pacific Journal of Management*, 15, 1998, 163–184.

[107] "Enter the lippo-potamus," *The Economist*, July 16, 1994.

PART TWO

Endowments and Environments of International Business

Country Competitiveness

DO YOU KNOW

1. Why do countries differ in their overall competitiveness in the global marketplace?

2. Why is a country's competitiveness more salient in some industries? For example, why do Swiss watches or pharmaceuticals dominate the world market, as do German upscale cars or Italian gold and silver jewelry?

3. What roles should firms and individuals play in shaping country competitiveness? For example, can Japanese firms' total quality management improve their country's competitiveness?

4. How does a foreign country's competitiveness influence the strategies and decisions of MNEs?

OPENING CASE Singapore's Competitive Advantage in the Hard Disk Drive Industry

Singapore is known as one of the most competitive nations in the world. Between 1995 and 2001, the country ranked second in the national competitiveness scoreboard released by Swiss-based IMD (International Institute for Management Development). Hard disk drive (HDD) production in Singapore reached about $10 billion and accounted for approximately 70 percent of the world's production of HDDs in 1999.

HDDs are highly standardized and easily transportable. Demand is primarily driven by their technical and operating characteristics. This allows manufacturing to be located in distant locations away from consumers. Many world MNEs and domestic companies use Singapore as the platform of HDD manufacturing and as the gateway to international markets, particularly to other Asian countries. Seagate, a world leader in the industry and the largest industrial employer in Singapore, has built a $130 million facility there for assembling disk drives and making printed circuit boards.

Singapore's workforce was rated the best in the world by the Business Environment Risk Intelligence (BERI), based on such factors as relative productivity, worker attitude, technical skills, and legal framework. Although not rich in natural resources, Singapore is situated in a strategic location on a major trading route across continents and is a focal point for Southeast Asian shipping routes. Singapore is also a thriving financial center served by 149 commercial banks, 77 merchant banks, and 8 international money brokers. Additionally, Singapore has first-class infrastructure in telecommunications and communications. The National Science and Technology Board (NSTB) was established in Singapore in 1991 in order to promote R&D through a financial assistance program, coordinating with several research institutions such as the Institute of Microelectronics (IME) and the Institute of Manufacturing Technology (IMF).

To promote growth and productivity in the electronics industry, the Singaporean government established several major agencies. Apart from the NSTB, the Economic Development Board (EDB) devises incentives to attract competitive companies into the nation's electronics sector. In addition, the National Computer Board (NCB) was created to drive Singapore to excel in the information age and to exploit the information technology (IT) niche. The NCB spearheads the implementation of Singapore's national IT master plan—IT2000. The government also initiated eight large-scale industrial parks in China, Indonesia, India, and Vietnam. These flagship projects, each of which is geographically concentrated in the same area, are positioned as premier investment locations, not only for Singaporean investors but also for other foreign firms and local enterprises. Singapore is increasingly dependent on the value-added edge that a highly skilled workforce brings. Therefore, through research aid and program development, the government assists higher educational institutions in providing a skilled workforce. ■

DEFINING COUNTRY COMPETITIVENESS

The preceding chapters explained that MNEs are a dominant force in today's international business activities (Chapter 4) and that activities such as trade and FDI are largely determined by comparative advantages of nations (Chapters 2 and 3). So how are MNEs and comparative advantages of nations linked? How do national advantages in a foreign country influence MNE strategies? If these advantages are important to national wealth, social welfare, and business operations, then how are these advantages determined, established, and maintained? We explain these issues from a country competitiveness perspective.

Competitiveness is the relative strength that one needs in order to win in competition against rivals. **Country competitiveness** is the extent to which a country is capable of generating more wealth than its competitors do in world markets. It measures and compares the effectiveness of countries in providing firms with an environment that sustains the domestic and international competitiveness of those firms. In the opening case, the Singaporean government created several institutions and offshore zones to help local businesses excel in international competition in the information industry. The core of country competitiveness centers on productivity. **Productivity** is the value of the output produced by a unit of labor or capital. It is the prime determinant of a nation's long-term standard of living and is the root source of national per capita income. The level of productivity depends on both the quality and features of products and services and the efficiency with which they are produced or provided. As such, increasing productivity is key to enhancing country competitiveness. Many factors (such as a nation's educational and scientific strengths) influence productivity, which in turn determines a country's capabilities.

Country competitiveness is associated with, but different from, country comparative advantages. As introduced in Chapter 2, conventional wisdom suggests that comparative advantages of nations are based on factor endowment conditions (abundance and costs of production factors such as labor, land, natural resources, and capital). The resultant conclusion is that a nation's competitiveness is high if it possesses an abundance of labor, capital, and/or natural resources at low prices.[1] This theory falls short of explaining the reality that we see today: there are many countries with abundant resources that are characterized by poor economies, and vice versa. Germany, Switzerland, and Sweden have prospered, despite having high wages and labor shortages. Similarly, Japan, South Korea, and Singapore have limited natural resources, but are very successful in maintaining their high competitiveness. In today's world where raw materials, capital, and even labor move across national borders, endowed resources can influence, but in and of themselves do not fully determine a nation's competitiveness. Country comparative advantages (e.g., cheap land and labor in developing countries) may influence the level of competitiveness in industries that are labor-intensive or cost-sensitive. However, a nation's comparative advantage in production factors alone is far from sufficient in determining its international competitiveness, that is, its competitive advantage in the global marketplace.

International trade and investment can both improve a nation's competitiveness and threaten it. They increase national productivity by allowing a nation to specialize in industries where its companies are more productive and to import where its companies are less productive. No nation can be competitive in everything. The ideal is to deploy the nation's limited human and other resources into their most productive use. Yet, international trade and FDI are likely to threaten productivity growth because they can expose a nation's industries to the test of international productivity standards. A country's industry will suffer if its productivity is not sufficiently higher than a foreign rival's productivity. If a nation loses the ability to compete in a range of high-productivity industries, its standard of living is threatened. In several industrialized countries, the rapid development of information technology has led to increased productivity and higher economic growth. Meanwhile, large disparities in the global economy continue to exist. Of major concern to international managers is why such national disparities exist and how companies should respond to them.

Interim Summary

1. Country competitiveness measures and compares how effective countries are in providing firms with an environment that sustains the domestic and international competitiveness of those firms. Productivity is the core of country competitiveness.

2. Country competitiveness is associated with, but different from, country comparative advantages. Germany, Switzerland, and Sweden have all prospered, despite having high wages and labor shortages.

COUNTRY COMPETITIVENESS AND MNEs

In a world of increasing global competition, nations have become more, rather than less, influential in international business operations. Differences in national values, culture, economic structures, institutions, and histories all contribute to competitive success. The national environment influences national competitiveness through the development of particular profiles of resources and capabilities (e.g., Italian footwear and textiles or Japanese semiconductors and electronics). The national environment also influences national competitiveness through its impact on the conditions for innovation. For example, as concern for product safety has grown in many industrialized countries, Swedish companies such as Volvo and Atlas Copco have succeeded by anticipating the market opportunities in this area. The impacts of country competitiveness on MNEs are fourfold.

First, *country competitiveness affects an MNE's selection of its global operations location*. Nike, for example, utilizes China as one of its major offshore production centers in order to benefit from cheap labor, abundant materials, and large market demand.

Second, *country competitiveness affects an MNE's industry selection*. For diversified MNEs, it is important to choose a foreign industry that will fit with the firm's global product portfolio and benefit from industry structure differences between home and host countries. A country's competitiveness is industry-specific, meaning that no nation can, nor should, maintain high competitiveness in every industry. Japan, for example, while very competitive in motor vehicles, has large sectors of its economy (i.e., aircraft, chemicals, and banking) that lag far behind the world's leading competitors. Thus, a more important question that concerns international managers is which industry of the target country is superior in terms of environment and competitiveness.

Third, *country competitiveness affects an MNE's innovation and capability building.* Trade and FDI patterns often reflect the sectors favored by a country's organizing and technological strengths (e.g., Japan's VCRs and Singapore's hard disk drives), and these patterns promote further expansion and investment in these capabilities. The variations in country competitiveness pertain to differences in organizational and institutional capabilities. By investing and operating in a country with superior organizing and technological strengths, MNEs can learn more from local partners and the business community.

Finally, *country competitiveness affects an MNE's global strategy.* A country's competitiveness is reflected in different elements, including rich resources, strong market demand, efficient governmental administration, and superior infrastructure for innovation. This diversity enables MNEs to globally differentiate their dispersed functions and businesses so as to leverage the advantages of various countries' competitiveness. Several Taiwanese companies (e.g., Acer) have greatly benefited from this differentiated process in which R&D is located in Taiwan and the United States, products are manufactured in mainland China, financing is obtained in Hong Kong, and worldwide distribution is channeled through Singapore or Hong Kong.

Interim Summary

1. Country competitiveness affects an MNE's location selection and industry selection. For example, Nike chose China because it benefits from cheap labor and abundant resources needed for its production.

2. Country competitiveness affects an MNE's capability building and global strategy. For example, India has lured many software MNEs because it offers a favorable environment for developing software, which is then marketed globally.

COUNTRY-LEVEL DETERMINANTS

Country competitiveness improves via increased productivity, which is driven by a large array of *country-level, industry-level, firm-level,* and *individual-level* factors. Sustained productivity growth requires that an economy continuously upgrade itself. International managers search for those decisive characteristics of a nation that allows its companies to create and sustain competitive advantage in particular fields (industries or sectors). Country competitiveness necessitates competitive strength across all these four levels (see Exhibit 5–1).

Economic growth and stability cannot be sustained without political/social stability, a well-constructed and enforced legal system, and sound macroeconomic conditions. This chapter emphasizes economic essentials required for country competitiveness and leaves the discussion of the importance of the social/cultural and political/legal environments to the next two chapters. Economic fundamentals have long been considered the cornerstone for economic development. As summarized in Exhibit 5–2, these country-level fundamentals include (1) science, education, and innovation; (2) economic soundness; (3) finance; and (4) internationalization.

Exhibit 5–1
Determinants of country competitiveness

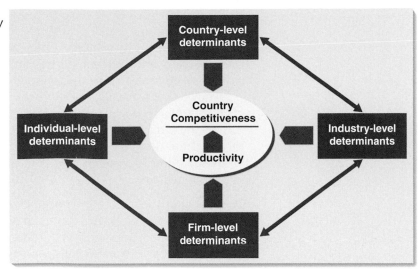

Science, Education, and Innovation

Technological innovation has long been seen in all economies as central to the process of raising productivity and thus improving country competitiveness. By increasing the range of choices with respect to new products and production processes, technological progress raises the potential for economic expansion and, in general, fosters human and economic development. Conversely, technological deficiencies are one of the major reasons for low incomes in some developing countries. To build and maintain a strong record of innovation, a country has to develop and promote science and education. Technological innovation and diffusion is a complex process, requiring support from a set of institutions. The United States, for example, has developed a rich set of institutions in both the public and private sectors to support a high level of technological innovation. Innovation depends on a complex interplay between basic science and new technologies and on commercialization of those

Exhibit 5–2
Country-level determinants of country competitiveness

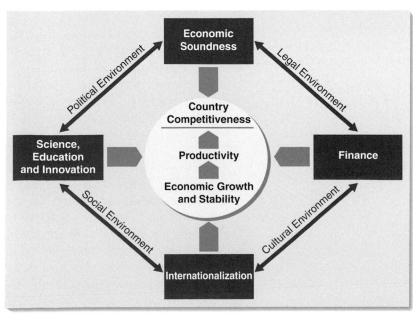

technologies in new products and production processes. Basic science is not exclusively a market-driven activity, because it is difficult to ensure payoff. Thus, nonmarket institutions usually carry out most projects in basic science. Examples include government laboratories (such as the National Institutes of Health in the United States) and academic centers such as universities. Some corporations sponsor basic scientific research in their laboratories as well.

The level of technological innovation depends largely on the commercialization of new products and processes. Several developing countries, most notably Russia, China, and India, have a large number of world-class scientists in basic science. However, because they lack a developed commercialization system, the competitiveness of these countries remains low. An effective commercialization process requires several ingredients:

1. There must be a close interface between basic scientists and R&D managers in the corporate world. In the United States, the education system has allowed scientific faculty to participate in private-sector R&D undertakings, and has allowed universities to own patents for products developed by their faculty. This pattern of close business-university linkage is quite distinct from the situation in Poland or Ukraine, for instance, in which universities belong to state institutions and have minimal contact with industry sectors.

2. There must be strong support for developing intellectual property rights in order to encourage enterprises to make large outlays in R&D activities before a product is introduced to market. About 1 percent of the U.S. GDP is provided as the seed money for basic science in many crucial areas such as information technology, biotechnology, and material sciences.

3. The economy must be flexible enough to support the rapid adoption and diffusion of new technologies. For example, venture capital funds should be available to innovative firms to commercialize new technologies.

Apart from commercialization, technological innovation can also be improved by adopting and assimilating technology from foreign countries. There are several channels through which this can be done. First, a country can attract investments from MNEs, thereby bringing advanced technological innovation into its economy. For example, Mexico has dramatically upgraded its production technology through the rapid inflow of U.S. investments in key sectors such as automotive, electronics, textiles, and pharmaceuticals. International joint ventures with MNEs (discussed in Chapter 12) are a quick and effective means for the host country to acquire foreign technologies and innovation expertise. Second, technology (e.g., robots) can be bought from a foreign country, or licensed from a foreign patent holder for use in the borrowing country. In fact, international trade in technology via licensing, franchising, export, or lease has been growing since the early 1990s. Finally, the technology can be engineered by an adopting country and suitably modified by local engineers for domestic production and use. Generally, knowledge acquisition from foreign firms is a better strategy for relatively small but newly industrialized countries, since they usually lack the scientific and technological base to innovate on their own, yet still have the ability to absorb technologies introduced in advanced countries. The competitiveness growth of the four mini-dragons, namely Singapore, South Korea, Taiwan, and Hong Kong, largely ascribes to this strategy.

It is difficult to think about competitiveness and technological innovation without considering education. Education has become the prerequisite for entry into the knowledge-based economy, while technology has become the prerequisite for bringing education to society. The excellence in basic skills required in a good primary and secondary school system is important, but by itself is not very helpful in pushing countries up the ladder of country competitiveness if it is not matched by superior higher education in technology and management. Vietnam, for example, is one of the top-ranking countries with regard to the math skills exhibited by its elementary and high school students. Its weakness in higher education, however, hampers the nation's competitiveness. The executives of the twenty-first century require not only business savvy, but also strong technical, communication, project-management, and human resource management skills. This is the new formula for grooming leaders who can handle the business world's increasingly complex problems.

Macroeconomic Soundness

Economic soundness is the key economic foundation and a major source of country competitiveness. It occupies an important place in the assessment of country competitiveness because it influences an economy's capacity to grow, the health of the trade sector, the balance of payments, and the attractiveness of investment by foreign businesses. **Economic soundness** can be defined as the extent to which an economy has been equipped with all the economic prerequisites for sustained economic growth. Macroeconomic soundness concerns both economic growth and economic stability, which are two distinct, but not mutually exclusive, fundamentals of the macroeconomic environment. An economy may be stable, but the policies that are in place may not be conducive to growth. Long-term growth and sustained competitiveness can be accomplished only if economic stability is maintained. Generally, economic stability is reflected in a low rate of inflation. In high-inflation situations, the loss of competitiveness and the emergence of balance-of-payments difficulties may interrupt economic growth. Rising public expenditures and the resultant budget deficits are often a principal cause of inflation. Expansionary public policies may initially stimulate economic growth, but as capacity limits are reached, output fails to keep up with rising expenditures, which eventually results in increased difficulty in financing the deficits.

Specific elements of economic soundness include *investment, consumption, real income level, economic sectors' performance, and infrastructure development.* First, investment by domestic firms and foreign businesses plays an important role in stimulating economic growth. Investment does not just augment a factor of production, it is also the means by which new technologies are put into practice. In addition, investment in one sector stimulates investment in others and encourages technological progress. When an economy slows down, investments from public or private sectors are important forces driving economic growth. In the late 1990s, for example, the United States, Japan, and most European nations employed a more favorable policy toward such investments.

Second, real income per capita and consumption per capita levels are also important because an economy's sustained growth depends partly on its citizens' final consumption. "Real" means that inflation has been subtracted from this indicator. The real interest rate is a key component linking the real income and consumption levels because this rate acts to adjust consumption relative to savings. The Federal Reserve, the central bank of the United States, for example, cut this rate several times in 2001 in an effort to stimulate domestic consumption.

Third, the performance of economic sectors, including both the manufacturing and service sectors, is a driving force for country competitiveness because it represents the strength of economic development. This performance consists of many facets such as innovativeness, efficiency, profitability, stability, and quality of products and service. The reason why the competitiveness of many developing countries (especially those in Africa) is relatively low is that their manufacturing and service sectors have not yet been developed nor are they performing well.

Finally, the development levels of basic infrastructure (e.g., transportation, utility, and energy) and technological infrastructure (e.g., telecommunications and university graduates in science and engineering) influence country competitiveness

Exhibit 5–3
The strength of macro-
level domestic economy
(Top 20)

Country	2001 Rank	2002 Rank
United States	1	1
Luxembourg	2	2
China Mainland	7	3
Ireland	4	4
United Kingdom	18	5
Norway	15	6
Australia	22	7
France	14	8
Switzerland	13	9
Denmark	23	10
Japan	5	11
Netherlands	16	12
Iceland	30	13
Canada	10	14
Spain	26	15
Italy	21	16
Germany	9	17
Korea	8	18
Austria	27	19
Estonia	29	20

Source: The World Competitiveness Yearbook 2002, p. 30. Lausanne, Switzerland: The International Institute for Management Development (IMD).

because they are a key segment of the external environment in which businesses operate. The supportiveness of these infrastructures affects production and business operations. The high growth rate of the Chinese economy in the 1990s, for example, was supported by its infrastructure improvement. Foreign investors there previously complained about an inadequacy of electric power and freight transportation but today these infrastructure elements have expanded to a point where capacities are actually underutilized in some provinces.

Building on the preceding criteria, the *World Competitiveness Yearbook,* prepared and published by the International Institute for Management Development (IMD), based in Lausanne, Switzerland, reported the country rankings in terms of economic soundness in 2001 and 2002 (see Exhibit 5–3).

Finance

Finance is an important macroeconomic fundamental affecting economic stability and growth, and thus country competitiveness. Specific finance indicators that affect competitiveness include *currency valuation, solvency of the banking system,* and *short-term external debt.* First, **currency valuation** concerns the extent to which a country's home currency is valued or priced properly to reflect the situation of market supply and demand pertaining to this currency. The price level in one country naturally rises along with this country's income. A country with a price level exceeding its income level is said to have an *overvalued currency.* A country with an income level exceeding its price level is said to have an *undervalued currency.* High overvaluation or undervaluation can be a source of instability and is unhealthy for long-term economic growth (see Chapter 9 for details). One of the factors leading to the collapse of the Thai baht and the Korean won in 1997 involved overvaluation of their currencies.

ECONOMIC GROWTH

arcadio

LATIN AMERICA

DEBT

ARCADIO
LA NACION
San Jose
COSTA RICA

Second, a weak banking system can be a source of instability as well. The nature of banking itself—borrowing short and lending long—always leaves banks vulnerable to abrupt and unanticipated losses on deposits. This can happen internationally just as it can happen domestically. If the creditors of the bank happen to be foreign, then perceptions of exchange rate vulnerability can interact with perceived banking vulnerability to produce a particularly volatile mixture. While the Netherlands, Luxembourg, and Australia are considered to have the most solvent banks, banks in Indonesia and Thailand are considered the most vulnerable, which is one of the major causes of the banking crisis that began in the region in 1997 (see Chapter 9 for details).[2]

The last indicator of financial vulnerability is a high amount of short debt in relation to the hard currency reserves of a country's central bank. This indicator is more relevant for a country defending its fixed exchange rate. If foreign creditors discover that a country does not have enough hard currency to meet its short-term liabilities, then the country is at risk of a bank-run situation, where each creditor wishes to get its money out before the hard currency runs out. Taiwan, for example, was not considered high risk during the Asian financial crisis because its central bank had enough hard currency reserves to cover these liabilities. Hong Kong, although recognized as one of the world's most expensive cities, still remains competitive thanks to its solid financial system, its advanced financial markets, and its position as one of the largest financial centers in the world. Hong Kong also enjoys very high foreign exchange reserves and also benefits from the high reserves held by mainland China.

Internationalization

Internationalization associated with country competitiveness refers to the extent to which the country participates in international trade and investment. (As you may recall from Chapter 1, this participation is one of the key indicators on the Globalization Index). This internationalization is influenced by a nation's strength in the following areas: (1) exports (both goods and services) and related current account balance (see Chapter 9), (2) exchange rate systems, (3) foreign investment (both FDI and portfolio investment), (4) foreign exchange reserves, and (5) openness of the economy. A high degree of competitiveness requires a high degree of internationalization of that economy, because competitiveness measures a nation's competitive advantage in an international marketplace compared to other countries. A strong domestic economy may or may not translate into a strong international competitiveness; it depends on the economy's openness and strength of foreign trade and investment as reflected in its current account and foreign exchange reserves. This openness is in turn dependent upon a nation's economic soundness as well as the government's policies pertaining to foreign trade, investment, and exchange rate. A country's **openness** refers to the extent to which its national economy is linked to world economies through the flow of resources, goods, services, people, technologies, information, and capital. In a competitive nation, this flow means both inflow and outflow. The inflow of goods, capital, services, and the like is determined not only by an economy's attractiveness but also by the extent of its national protectionism. **National protectionism** reflects the level of barriers that foreign goods, capital, services, and other inputs of production are confronted with when moving into the focal country. As introduced in Chapter 2, examples of these barriers include import tariffs, quotas, voluntary export restraint, and commodity inspection standards, among others. For developing countries in which economic foundations and systems are underdeveloped, a certain degree of protectionism during an early stage of economic development is necessary for ensuring trade balance and economic stability. For this reason, the World Trade Organization (WTO) permits a few developing country members such as Poland, Hungary, and the Czech Republic to have a higher bar against foreign imports.

Interim Summary

1. Country competitiveness is determined by four levels of factors: country-level, industry-level, firm-level, and individual-level. They affect competitiveness individually as well as jointly.

2. Country-level determinants include (a) science, education, and innovation; (b) macroeconomic soundness; (c) finance; and (d) internationalization.

3. Macroeconomic soundness is determined by investment, consumption, real income level, economic sectors' performance, and infrastructure development.

INDUSTRY-LEVEL DETERMINANTS

Sound country-level foundations such as macroeconomic fundamentals and science and innovation are necessary for enhancing country competitiveness. However, they are not sufficient to ensure a prosperous economy. Although country-level determinants influence overall competitiveness of a nation and are important to improving national productivity, no country can build and maintain high competitiveness in every industry. Within a country, different industries are not the same in terms of comparative advantages. Economically, it is neither necessary nor realistic to expect high competitiveness in every industry of the economy. This industry-specific perspective is especially important for international managers because it is often a target country's *industrial,* rather than national, environment that directly impacts firm decisions and operations. Of course, for a nation's government, the more industries with high international competitiveness, the greater the overall country competitiveness. Governments should devote more resources to improving infrastructures of those industries (or sub-industries) in which their nations are potentially already competitive.

When you look closely at any national economy, you will see enormous differences among a nation's industries in the area of competitive success. International advantage is often concentrated in particular industry sectors or segments within a given economy. For example, U.S. commercial aircraft and defense industries have dominated the world market, while Japanese semiconductors and VCRs have led as well. In the automobile industry, German exports are heavily skewed toward high-performance cars, whereas Korean exports are clustered at the low end of the market. The assessment of country competitiveness therefore is about competitive advantage of a nation in particular industries or industry segments. To help assess this competitiveness, classical theory explains the successes of nations in certain industries based on production factors (or inputs) such as land, labor, and natural resources. A nation gains comparative advantages in industries that make intensive use of the factors it possesses in abundance. This classical view, however, has been overshadowed in advanced industries and economies by the globalization of competition and the power of technology. A new perspective called the "diamond framework," developed by Michael E. Porter, offers an analytical tool for international managers to appraise a country's competitive advantage in particular fields.[3]

According to Porter's diamond framework, there are four broad attributes, which individually and collectively constitute the diamond of national advantage in particular fields:

1. *Factor Conditions.* This concerns the nation's position in factors of production, including basic factors such as labor, capital, land, and natural resources, and sophisticated factors such as skilled workforce, scientific base, infrastructure, and information. Each country may be abundant in certain factors while lacking in others. For example, Hungary's optical instrument industry is abundant in skilled workers but lacks a well-developed supplier infrastructure. The same is true for China's copy-machine industry. Low design costs and growing market demand for copier machines are also major considerations luring foreign companies such as Xerox to invest there. Country competitiveness is likely to be higher in industries in which the country has superior factors of production. Basic factors are generally important in obtaining competitive advantage in labor-intensive industries but do not constitute an advantage in knowledge-intensive industries that require sophisticated factors of production. The contribution of factor conditions to country competitiveness changes over time. The stock of factors that a nation enjoys at a particular time is less important than the rate and efficiency with which it creates, upgrades, and deploys them in particular industries.

2. *Demand Conditions.* This involves the nature of market demand for the industry's product or service. International companies often enter a foreign market because of promising opportunities arising from strong market demand. Strong market demand drives an economy's gross domestic product (GDP) upward and facilitates the improvement of productivity in a competitive environment. In addition to the size of market demand, the character of demand is also critical. Nations can gain competitive advantage in industries where the market demand gives their companies a clearer or earlier picture of emerging buyer needs as well as where demanding buyers pressure companies to innovate faster and achieve more sophisticated competitive advantages than their foreign rivals. If domestic buyers are the world's most sophisticated and demanding buyers, then a nation's companies in this sector are more likely to gain competitive advantage through constantly improving and upgrading their products or services. As an example, Japanese firms have pioneered compact, quiet air-conditioning units powered by energy-saving rotary compressors. This is largely because the firms have responded to the needs of Japanese consumers, most of whom live in small, crowded homes in a country where humid summers are the norm.

3. *Related and Supporting Industries.* This refers to the presence and support level of a nation's suppliers or other related industries. For foreign investors, the availability and supportiveness of local suppliers as well as other related industries such as banking, foreign exchange services, and infrastructure services are fundamental to their routine operations. For the country itself, the competitiveness of related industries provides benefits of information flow and technical interchange among related industries, which in turn speeds up the rate of innovation and upgrading. For example, Switzerland's success in pharmaceuticals evolved from previous international success in the dye industry. Having home-based suppliers that are internationally competitive can create advantages in downstream industries. Italian gold and silver jewelry companies lead the world in part because other Italian companies supply two-thirds of the world's jewelry-making and precious-metal recycling machinery. In addition, suppliers and end-users located near each other can take advantage of short lines of communication, quick and constant flow of information, and an ongoing exchange of ideas and innovations. Through close working relationships, companies have the opportunity to influence their suppliers' technical efforts and can serve as test sites for R&D work, accelerating the

Milan is home to one of the most successful clusters in the fashion industry.

pace of innovation. When suppliers, manufacturers, and even distributors are located near each other or concentrated in the same area (a city or part of the city), we call this geographical concentration a **cluster.** Examples include: Silicon Valley in California for the semiconductor and software industry, Milan in Italy for fashion garments, Hamamatsu in Japan for motorcycles and musical instruments, Pusan in South Korea for footwear products, and Zhongguanchun in Beijing for electronics.

4. *Rivalry and Business Practice.* This entails the nature of domestic rivalry in addition to the conditions governing how businesses are organized, managed, and operated in a nation. International investors may select a country in which local rivalry is low. However, in terms of competitiveness, the presence of strong local rivals is a powerful stimulus to the creation and persistence of national competitive advantage. This is especially true for small countries such as Switzerland, where the rivalries among its pharmaceutical companies—Ciba-Geigy, Sandoz, and Hoffman-La Roche—contribute to global leadership. Domestic rivalries exert pressure on companies to innovate and improve. Local rivals force each other to lower costs, improve quality and service, and create new products and processes. Domestic rivals compete not only for market share but also for people, for technical excellence, and more importantly, for product quality, customer responsiveness, and innovation. Business and management practice is relevant to country competitiveness because competitiveness in a specific industry results from convergence of management and business policy with the sources of competitive advantage in the industry. In industries where Italian companies are among the world's leaders—such as lighting, furniture, footwear, woolen fabrics, and packaging machines—a company strategy that emphasizes customized products, niche marketing, rapid adaptation, and great flexibility fits well, both with the dynamics of the industry and with the character of the Italian management system. Successful Italian international competitors also tend to be small or medium-sized companies (SMEs) that are privately owned and operated like extended families. In Germany, companies tend to be hierarchical in organization and management practices, and top managers usually have technical backgrounds. This system works well in technical or engineering-oriented industries (e.g., optics, chemicals) where complex products demand precision manufacturing as well as a highly disciplined management. Germany's success, however, is quite limited in consumer goods and services where image marketing and product innovation are important to competition. In the greater China region, including the P.R.C., Taiwan, Hong Kong, Macao, and Singapore, successful companies are technologically innovative as well as skillful in cultivating and developing personal ties with government officials and with top managers of other firms. Personal relations (or *guanxi* in Mandarin) may be conducive to improving competitiveness in such industries where the regulatory environment is highly unpredictable.

Exhibit 5–4 highlights the diamond framework of national competitive advantage. The four determinants in this framework create the national environment into which companies are born and in which they learn to compete. Each point on the diamond—as well as the diamond itself as a system—produce essential ingredients for achieving international competitive success. In general, companies gain a competitive advantage when a national environment (1) permits and supports the most rapid accumulation of specialized assets and skills, (2) affords better ongoing information and insight into product and process needs, and (3) pressures companies to innovate and invest. It is also important to note that the diamond factors create an environment that may promote competitiveness of other related industries. Japan's

Exhibit 5–4
Industry-level
determinants of country
competitiveness

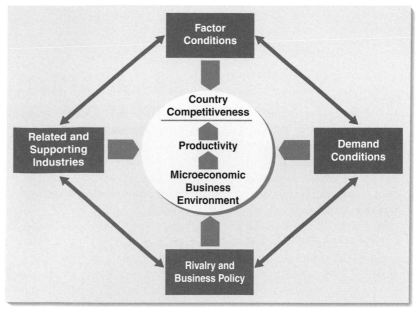

Source: M. E. Porter, "The competitive advantage of nations." *Harvard Business Review,* March–April 1990, pp. 73–93.

strength in consumer electronics, for example, drove its success in semiconductors toward the memory chips and integrated circuits these products use.

The four diamond attributes together serve as the microeconomic business environment that affects country competitiveness. Exhibit 5–5 lists the top 20 countries in terms of the strength of their microeconomic business environments from

Exhibit 5–5
The microeconomic
competitiveness
scoreboard (top 20)

Country	1998 Rank	1999 Rank	2000 Rank
Finland	2	2	1
United States	1	1	2
Germany	4	6	3
Netherlands	3	3	4
Switzerland	9	5	5
Denmark	8	7	6
Sweden	7	4	7
United Kingdom	5	10	8
Singapore	10	12	9
Australia	15	13	10
Canada	6	8	11
Belgium	19	15	12
Austria	16	11	13
Japan	18	14	14
France	11	9	15
Hong Kong	12	21	16
Iceland	24	22	17
Israel	21	20	18
New Zealand	17	16	19
Norway	14	18	20

Source: M. E. Porter, "The current competitiveness index: Microeconomic foundations of prosperity." In *The Global Competitiveness Report 2000,* Geneva, Switzerland: World Economic Forum, p. 44.

E-COMMERCE AS AN ELEMENT OF COUNTRY COMPETITIVENESS

E-commerce capabilities can help boost a country's competitiveness in many ways. First, the Internet is a global network, enabling people and businesses to connect to the rest of the world. Second, the Internet provides easy access to the global market, matching buyers and sellers across national boundaries. Third, the Internet is an efficient distribution tool, saving transaction costs. Fourth, the Internet lets small businesses play in the big business arena. Finally, the internet shortens a company's time to market.

However, many countries lag behind in the e-business race, and in many cases, the e-business laggards are at the bottom of the competitive rankings. The reasons are three-fold: language, education, and technical infrastructure. But many governments are taking steps to address these issues because they understand that the Internet presents developing nations the opportunity to bolster their competitiveness and economy. Asia-Pacific Economic Cooperation (APEC) leaders, for instance, acknowledged during their meetings in Vancouver on November 25, 1997, the need to promote Asian economies to construct and utilize a global information infrastructure. For governments, adequate regulations and supervision also need to be in place to ensure that private enterprises are playing their part in innovating and implementing the global systems and needed infrastructure. International companies such as GE Capital and Infotech Global have made investments in emerging markets. For example, both companies have announced expansion of their services in India.

Source: Adapted from E. Sprano and A. Zakak, "E-Commerce capable: Competitive advantage for countries in the new world e-economy," *Competitiveness Review,* 10(2), 2000, 114–131.

1998 to 2000, appraised using the preceding diamond framework. Unless there is appropriate improvement at the microeconomic environment, the country-level determinants (i.e., macroeconomic business environment) as discussed earlier will not bear full fruit.[4] National productivity is ultimately set by the productivity of a nation's companies. Companies need appropriate conditions for rapid and sustained productivity growth. The country-level determinants create the potential for improving national prosperity, but wealth is actually created at the microeconomic (industrial) level—in the ability of firms to create valuable goods and services productively. A country's economy cannot be competitive unless the companies operating within it are competitive, whether they are domestic or foreign company subsidiaries. To conclude, the improvement of country competitiveness is a process of successive upgrading, in which a nation's business environment evolves to support and encourage increasingly sophisticated and productive ways of competing and innovating. This chapter's Industry Box illustrates how e-business may shape country competitiveness in the future. Chapter 18 provides more detailed information on global e-commerce.

Interim Summary

1. It is neither possible nor necessary to expect *every* industry in a country to be competitive. Industry-level fundamentals determine a country's microeconomic business environment.

2. The "diamond framework" is often used to assess country competitiveness in particular industries or fields. This framework consists of four factors—factor conditions, demand conditions, related and supporting industries, and rivalry and business practice.

3. A cluster is a geographical concentration in which suppliers, manufacturers, and even distributors are located near each other. Cluster can help improve country competitiveness.

FIRM-LEVEL DETERMINANTS

An economy's product competitiveness stems from companies within that nation. It is firms that produce products and provide services. Thus, country competitiveness is also associated with firm-level factors that can characterize country-unique organizational, innovational, and operational strategies employed by most firms of that nation. These strategies, principles, or approaches should differentiate one country's firms from those of other countries, and more importantly, create competitive advantages for both the nation and firms to which they belong. For example, most Japanese firms have obtained their competitive advantages vis-à-vis American and European companies through superior process innovations, quality control systems, and unique manager-employee relationships. These firm-level policies have become Japan's national standards and have been widely applied by most Japanese firms. Country competitiveness can thus be partly explained by differences in country capabilities in terms of technologies and organizing principles. These technologies and organizing principles diffuse more slowly across borders than within a nation. In other words, these unique firm-level factors are virtually embedded in Japanese firms. This embeddedness helps Japan maintain strong country competitiveness.

Organizing principles of technological innovation and production are particularly important because they are not easily diffused across nations. National economic leadership of a country is not driven by technological investments alone, but also by the efficiency of a country's dominant organizing principles.[5] The superiority of U.S. competitiveness in relation to that of European countries is attributable not only to the country's creation of technologies (as measured by patents) but also to its adoption of new methods of management. Although the basic research skills of Japanese firms are generally inferior to those of U.S. firms, organizing principles such as lean flexible production, total quality management, just-in-time manufacturing, and multi-sourcing strategy used by Japanese firms add substantial value to the international competitiveness of Japanese products.

The contribution of technologies and organizing principles to creating competitive advantages for both firms and the country cannot last forever. Technology, and even organizing principles, are inevitably diffused across nations, and eventually imitated by foreign rivals. Through technology transfer, foreign direct investment, and global strategic alliances, one nation's firms can learn both technologies and organizing principles that were developed and employed by counterparts in another nation. This suggests that firms ought to continuously upgrade their technological skills and organizing approaches if they wish to sustain competitive advantages that help maintain their country's competitiveness in the long run. Constant and rapid technological progress, rather than one single innovation, is the secret to retaining competitive advantage.

Firms can also influence the environment that impacts country competitiveness. Companies do not simply accept the status quo of factor development in the nation but instead seek to upgrade it. For example, Italian industry associations invest in marketing information, process technology, and common infrastructure in such industries as woolens, ceramic tiles, and lighting equipment. Swiss and German firms widely participate in apprenticeship programs. In Britain, successful industries such as chemicals and pharmaceuticals are characterized by close ties with universities and government research institutes. Firms can, and must, invest directly in factor creation through their own training, research, and infrastructure building. Internal efforts at factor creation lead to the most specialized, and often most important, factors. Competitive firms often have well-developed internal training programs and, compared to their rivals, set aside higher amounts of resources for R&D. Leading U.S. and Japanese companies usually have their own universities or schools. Yamaha, for example, faced a shortage of skilled piano technicians in Japan, so it founded its own educational program for acoustics training that is now highly regarded internationally. The benefits flow to Yamaha as well as to the entire Japanese industry.

Firms can also join with, or participate in, the efforts of government entities, educational institutions, and the local communities, in order to influence factor creation or improvement. Nestlé, for example, founded and supports Geneva-based IMI, which has become a leading European business school. Nestlé has benefited from a steady flow of talented management as well as ongoing management training. German chemical companies have established relationships with all of the major German universities and also sponsor institutes devoted to chemical research, contributing to advancements in the industry. In addition, they sponsor students or their staff to study at the universities. They also play an active role in helping institutions identify the needs of the industry by assisting with planning curriculum, placing graduates, and providing financial support for facilities and scholarships. Exhibit 5–6 outlines the firm-level determinants of country competitiveness.

Interim Summary

1. It is firms that directly create national wealth, and thus the productivity of firms is central to country competitiveness.

2. Technologies and organizing principles (e.g., process innovation and quality control systems) are two firm-level fundamentals. When unique and productive organizing principles and technological skills become national standards or permeated throughout the nation, they will substantially heighten country competitiveness.

Exhibit 5–6
Firm-level determinants of country competitiveness

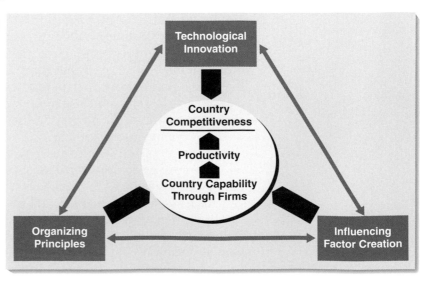

INDIVIDUAL-LEVEL DETERMINANTS

Individual-level determinants are people or human resources associated with country competitiveness. They include workers, entrepreneurs, professional managers, designers and engineers, educators and intellectuals, and politicians and government officials (see Exhibit 5–7). Human resources affect productivity (the core of country competitiveness) by shaping the environment for developing competitiveness and by combining and arranging the preceding physical competitiveness determinants at both the country and industry-levels.

Workers: Workers' productivity affects country productivity. For example, skillful and diligent workers in Singapore are an important force in improving its country-level productivity. In addition to the wage level and the size of labor pool, other important factors associated with worker productivity include educational level, loyalty to organizations, passion for work, self-motivation, learning skills, and discipline. In Denmark, Finland, and Sweden, superior education and passion for work is an important reason for the superior productivity of workers. In Japan, workers' loyalty to organizations and learning skills are partly responsible for its competitiveness.

Entrepreneurs: **Entrepreneurs** venture into new businesses despite a high degree of risks arising from uncertainty about the future. They are a special group of businesspeople taking risks in the development of new products, new markets, or new technologies. They create new businesses, stimulating a nation's economic development. A nation's competitiveness is strengthened in the course of their efforts and commitments to take high risks and maximize returns. Singapore's high level of competitiveness can in large part be attributed to the high percentage of entrepreneurs in its total population.

Managers: Experienced and skillful managers in various enterprises, whether public, private, or state-owned, play an important role in increasing country

Exhibit 5–7
Individual-level determinants of country competitiveness

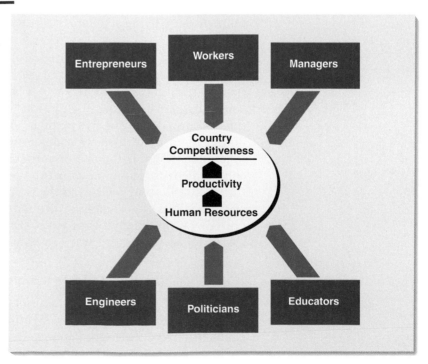

R&D capabilities are a critical competitiveness ingredient.

competitiveness. Production and operation processes are becoming increasingly complex and interrelated among different value-chain activities (e.g., from inbound logistics and operations to outbound logistics, marketing, and service; or from human resource management to technological development and procurement). As a result, a country with a large pool of educated and experienced managers who are well-versed in production, operation, and organization will have a much better chance of creating and sustaining high competitiveness. Several newly industrialized economies such as South Korea and Taiwan have successfully secured and retained a large number of Western-educated and experienced managers who were educated abroad. This greatly helps to raise the level of national competitiveness in these countries.

Engineers: Engineers and designers stand at the forefront of country competitiveness. They are key players in improving a nation's productivity because they create value through production innovation and process innovation. A country's expertise in these two types of innovations is a crucial element for elevating its competitiveness. Because international competitiveness involves worldwide consumers, it is important for engineers and designers to have a global vision. Engineers in Switzerland and the Netherlands have a strong educational background, industrial experience, and global vision, which in turn helps stimulate the competitiveness of these nations.

Educators: Educators and intellectuals represent a prime force for strengthening education and science. High competitiveness of an economy requires the creation and dissemination of knowledge needed for improving productivity. Although intellectuals are the major source of knowledge creation, educators at various levels (from elementary to higher education) are a prominent source for knowledge dissemination. For countries moving to knowledge-based economies, growth depends heavily on the contributions of educators and intellectuals. A country's productivity and competitiveness are generally positively correlated with the salary level, or more broadly, living standards, of educators and intellectuals.

Politicians: The role of politicians and government officials in supporting competitiveness cannot be underestimated simply because government policies and administrative efficiency exert a significant effect on other determinants of country competitiveness. Nations with politicians who select economic development as a priority or are willing to give up their political ambitions for their nations' economic development tend to create competitiveness. South Korea in the 1970s is a manifestation of how a national economy can benefit from political leaders with a strong commitment to economic growth even under a non-democratic regime. Government officials apply policies to the economy. Their role can be compared to that of an automobile's transmission: the most efficient transmission would convey the power with minimum loss of power. Officials who can implement politicians' policies in the most efficient way can enhance their nation's competitiveness.[6]

Interplay of the Four-Level Determinants

The preceding four levels of determinants are not exclusive of each other. Country-level determinants provide an overall national foundation for developing country competitiveness. This foundation provides a general economic and technological environment, which can directly or indirectly influence industrial, organizational,

Italy

CAN BERLUSCONI RENEW THE NATION?

Hundreds of thousands of anxious entrepreneurs voted on May 13, 2001, for media baron Silvio Berlusconi in the hope this new prime minister would carry out his promise to reverse Italy's declining competitiveness. The country's entrepreneurs survived and even thrived by remaining small and nimble. In the northern industrial districts, manufacturers of the same products, such as textiles or shoes, clustered together like virtual keiretsu, purchasing supplies jointly, for example, but skirting inflexible labor laws by employing fewer than 15 workers each. They bridged the gaps in skills or education with extensive in-house training. The result has been an army of small and midsize companies that boast global strength in fashion, industrial design, machinery, and other niche sectors.

But now, Italy's stalwart exporters face a series of obstacles that is proving insurmountable for many of them. They are caught in the middle of two new forces: cheap Asian goods of steadily improving quality are flooding global markets, posing competition Italians have never experienced. At the same time, the rest of Europe is leaping ahead into the digital economy, with companies producing some of the most sophisticated software and telecom products in the world. And Italy? Its businesses, by and large, simply lack the size and research muscle to go against bigger competitors in these technology-driven industries.

Meanwhile, in Italy, taxes, labor costs, and labor-market regulation have become even more burdensome and restrictive over the past 15 years. Aging roads and railroads are obstacles to growth. Half-hearted liberalization has left markets in the grip of former monopolies. Worst of all is a serious deterioration in the quality of education at every level and the power of courts to function properly.

Source: Adapted from G. Edmondson, K. Carlisle, and S. Pierce, "Italy: Can Berlusconi Renew the Nation?" *Business Week*, May 28, 2001, 46.

and individual determinants of competitiveness. For example, a nation's education system (a country-level determinant) affects the qualifications of workers, managers, and engineers (individual-level determinants). Conversely, politicians and officials (individual-level determinants) have the power to change country-level determinants such as economic policies and financial systems. Industry-level determinants jointly create a microeconomic business environment that impacts companies' productivity. They are a central force linking a nation's comparative advantage with firms' competitive advantages in wealth creation. While country-level and industry-level determinants together provide a context for improving country competitiveness, firm-level and individual-level determinants are direct "hands" in creating and improving this competitiveness. These "hands" can be stronger or weaker, depending on both country-level and industry-level conditions. This chapter's Country Box provides an illustrative case in which Italy's country competitiveness is jointly influenced by various determinants at the individual-level (e.g., politicians, entrepreneurs, workers), firm-level (e.g., flexibility, cluster, small size) industry-level (competition, factor conditions, related industries), and country-level (infrastructure, education, legal system, economic soundness).

Interim Summary

1. Individual-level determinants are people or human resources that affect country competitiveness. They include workers, entrepreneurs, managers, engineers and designers, educators and intellectuals, and politicians and government officials.[6]

2. Human resources affect country competitiveness in such a way that they determine a country's expertise, creativity, and efficiency.

3. Multilevel fundamentals also interactively affect country competitiveness. Country- and industry-level determinants provide an important context in which firms and individuals directly create national wealth. Firms and individuals are also able to reshape this context so that macro- and microeconomic business environments become more favorable for productivity.

GOVERNMENT ROLE

Government plays an important role in shaping country competitiveness. It can affect all four levels of determinants outlined previously. Through policy making and intervention, government can impact investment, savings, and trade. Through a combination of trade liberalization and exchange rate adjustment, government can strengthen the balance of payments and improve international competitiveness. The experiences of several newly industrialized nations (NIEs) in the early 1980s suggest that a certain amount of governmental control over macroeconomic problems is necessary. In that particular instance, when macroeconomic fundamentals grew seriously out of line, governments acted promptly to bring the situation under control. They were also committed to export expansion rather than import substitution as a means of relieving balance-of-payment constraints.

Governments can also exert influence on the microeconomic business environment and on human resource development. Such influence is normally exerted through a set of industrial policies. **Industrial policies** can be defined as all forms of conscious and coordinated government interventions to promote industrial development. Such forms include, but are not limited to: import protection, financial subsidies, regulatory changes, and interventions in capital, labor, technology, and natural resource markets. For example, a government can shape factor conditions through its training and infrastructure policies. Factor conditions are also affected through subsidies and policies aimed at the development of capital markets. Furthermore, market demand conditions are influenced by regulatory standards and processes, government purchasing, and openness to imports. Governments are often a major buyer of many products, including defense goods, telecommunications equipment, aircraft for a national airline, and such. Governments can shape the circumstances of related and supporting industries through control of advertising media and also regulation of supporting services such as banking and foreign exchange. Finally, government policy also influences competition and business practices through such means as capital market regulation, tax policy, and antitrust laws.

The effect of government policies on country competitiveness can be positive (stimulating competitiveness) or negative (obstructing competitiveness). Too much dependence on direct help or interference from the government may hurt companies in the long run and only lead to them becoming more dependent. On the other hand, a government that has a hands-off policy may miss on the benefits of shaping the macro- and micro-economic business environment and institutional structure that can stimulate companies to gain competitive advantage. Thus, the appropriate role that a government should play is one of a catalyst and challenger—it should encourage, or even push, companies to aspire to higher levels of competitive performance, even though this process may be difficult. Governments cannot directly create competitive industries; only companies can do that. Government policies that succeed are those that create an environment in which companies can gain competitive advantage.

There are several principles that governments should embrace in order to play a supporting role in national competitiveness:

1. *They should emphasize competitiveness infrastructure.* Governments have critical responsibilities for developing and improving infrastructure such as education, science, research, transportation, and information technology.

2. *They should enforce strict product, safety, and environmental standards.* Stringent standards for product performance, product safety, and environmental control pressure companies to improve quality, upgrade technology, and provide features that respond to consumer and social demands.

3. *They should deregulate competition.* Regulation through maintaining a state monopoly, controlling entry to industry, or fixing prices hampers rivalry and innovation.

4. *They should adopt strong domestic antitrust policies.* These policies, especially when applied to horizontal mergers, alliances, and collusive behavior, are fundamental to innovation. Government policy should generally favor new entry over acquisition.

5. *They should boost goal-setting that leads to sustained investment.* Governments can indirectly affect the goals of investors, managers, and employees though various policies. For instance, the tax rate for long-term capital gains is a powerful tool for adjusting the rate of sustained investment in industry as it affects the level of new investment in corporate equity.

This chapter concludes with the World Competitiveness Scoreboard (1998–2002), identified in the *World Competitiveness Yearbook* (Exhibit 5–8). This yearbook ranks nations' environments according to their ability to provide an environment in which enterprises can compete. Similar to the aforementioned determinants at multiple levels, the yearbook assesses country competitiveness based on eight competitiveness input factors: domestic economy, science and technology, people, firm management, internationalization, infrastructure, finance, and government. Since 2001, these factors have been re-grouped into four main categories, including economic performance, government efficiency, business efficiency, and infrastructure.

Interim Summary

1. Government is a critical force impacting country competitiveness and can influence virtually all determinants discussed previously.

2. In order to improve country competitiveness, governments should be committed to upgrading competitiveness infrastructures, encouraging competition, enforcing strict product, safety, and environmental standards, and motivating firms and individuals for better innovation and creativity.

Exhibit 5–8

The world competitiveness scoreboard 1998–2002

Country	1998 Rank	1999 Rank	2000 Rank	2001 Rank	2002 Rank
USA	1	1	1	1	1
Finland	6	5	4	3	2
Luxembourg	3	3	6	4	3
Netherlands	4	4	3	5	4
Singapore	2	2	2	2	5
Denmark	10	9	13	15	6
Switzerland	9	7	7	10	7
Canada	8	10	8	9	8
Hong Kong, China	5	6	12	6	9
Ireland	7	8	5	7	10
Sweden	16	14	14	8	11
Iceland	18	13	9	13	12
Austria	24	18	15	14	13
Australia	12	11	10	11	14
Germany	15	12	11	12	15
United Kingdom	13	19	16	19	16
Norway	11	16	17	20	17
Belgium	23	21	19	17	18
New Zealand	17	17	18	21	19
Chile	27	25	25	24	20
Estonia				22	21
France	22	23	22	25	22
Spain	26	20	23	23	23
Taiwan	14	15	20	18	24
Israel	25	22	21	16	25
Malaysia	19	28	27	29	26
South Korea	36	41	28	28	27
Hungary	28	26	26	27	28
Czech Republic	37	37	40	35	29
Japan	20	24	24	26	30
China (Mainland)	21	29	30	33	31
Italy	31	30	32	32	32
Portugal	29	27	29	34	33
Thailand	41	36	35	38	34
Brazil	35	34	31	31	35
Greece	33	32	34	30	36
Slovak Republic				37	37
Slovenia		39	36	39	38
South Africa	42	43	43	42	39
Philippines	32	31	37	40	40
Mexico	34	35	33	36	41
India	38	42	39	41	42
Russia	43	46	47	45	43
Colombia	45	45	45	46	44
Poland	44	40	38	47	45
Turkey	39	38	42	44	46
Indonesia	40	47	44	49	47
Venezuela	46	44	46	48	48
Argentina	30	33	41	43	49

Source: The World Competitiveness Yearbook 2002, Lausanne, Switzerland: The International Institute for Management Development (IMD), p. 23.

CHAPTER SUMMARY

1. Country competitiveness is the extent to which a country is capable of generating more wealth than its competitors in world markets. The central force for improving country competitiveness is productivity. There are four levels of specific determinants of country competitiveness: country-level, industry-level, firm-level, and individual-level.

2. Country competitiveness can be analyzed by governments for consummating competitiveness infrastructures, by local firms for selecting a more favorable environment in which sustained competitive advantages can be developed, or by MNEs for electing optimal foreign locations and industries.

3. Country-level determinants of competitiveness comprise (a) science, education, and innovation; (b) economic soundness; (c) finance; and (d) internationalization. These fundamentals are the cornerstone for economic development and the building blocks of macroeconomic business environment for country competitiveness.

4. Industry-level determinants of competitiveness comprise (a) factor conditions; (b) demand conditions; (c) related and supporting industries; and (d) rivalry and business practice. They affect country competitiveness individually as well as collectively. MNEs operating in foreign countries are often impacted more directly by these industry-level determinants than by country-level determinants.

5. Firm-level determinants are country-unique organizational, technological, or operational strategies, policies, and practices employed by most firms in that nation. Country competitiveness can be partly explained by differences in national capabilities in terms of technologies and organizing principles (e.g., lean flexible production, total quality management, just-in-time manufacturing, and multi-sourcing strategy used by Japanese firms).

6. Individual-level determinants are human resources that shape the environment for developing competitiveness. Major players include workers, entrepreneurs, managers, engineers, educators, politicians, and government officials. Country competitiveness is positively correlated with the productivity or creativity of these individuals.

7. Governments significantly shape country competitiveness through industrial policies and the development of a competitiveness infrastructure. Governments should serve as catalysts in providing a stimulating environment for companies to gain a competitive advantage in international markets.

CHAPTER NOTES

[1] B. Ohlin, *Interregional and International Trade.* Cambridge, MA: Harvard University Press 1952; W. W. Leontief, "Domestic production and foreign trade: The American capital position reexamined." *Proceedings of the American Philosophical Society,* 1953.

[2] *The Global Competitiveness Report 1999.* Geneva, Swizerland: World Economic Forum, 1999, 14–27.

[3] M. E. Porter, *The Competitive Advantage of Nations.* New York: The Free Press 1990; also see M. E. Porter, "The competitive advantage of nations," *Harvard Business Review,* March–April, 1990, 73–93.

[4] M. E. Porter, "The current competitiveness index: Measuring the microeconomic foundations of prosperity," *The Global Competitiveness Report 1999,* Geneva, Switzerland: World Economic Forum.

[5] B. Kogut, "Country capabilities and the peameability of borders," *Strategic Management Journal,* 12 (summer special), 1991, 33–47.

[6] D. S. Cho, "From national competitiveness to bloc and global competitiveness," *Competitiveness Review,* 8(1) 1998, 11–23.

The Cultural Environment

DO YOU KNOW

1. In what ways do cultural differences, language, and religion influence international investment and trade?

2. How does corporate culture interact with local and national culture? Is corporate culture primarily homogeneous throughout an MNE?

3. What are the major models for comparison of different cultures? Do these models succeed in their mission, and is it even possible to fully define and measure culture?

OPENING CASE The Goodyear–Sumitomo Alliance

When Ohio-based tire manufacturer Goodyear acquired a majority stake and took control of the tire operations of Japanese manufacturer Sumitomo, it took pains to portray the transaction as an alliance of equals rather than as a takeover by the U.S. firm. Why has Goodyear been willing to term the deal "a global alliance" while in effect it was taking control of Sumitomo's assets?

By presenting the alliance as a marriage of equals, Goodyear prevented its Japanese partner from "losing face." If Goodyear were to appear as the controlling partner in the alliance, it would imply an acknowledgment of failure on Sumitomo's part. Further, letting the U.S. firm appear to be in charge of running the operations would position the Japanese firm as the junior partner in the venture, something embarrassing in a culture that puts great emphasis on hierarchy. ■

Source: Based on "From Egypt to Europe to Ohio, a CEO finds his home," *Wall Street Journal*, December 22, 1999, 41.

The concept of "face" is ingrained in many Asian societies, and has ramifications for many facets of international business. In conducting negotiations, for example, Japanese buyers will rarely inform a vendor that they are not interested in his/her product, but rather that they "will think about it." Americans, misinterpreting the response, will often complain that the Japanese are "beating around the bush," that is, wasting time and effort by not providing a clear and straightforward answer. In the human resources area, "face" implies that negative performance feedback is rarely provided in Asian societies such as China except indirectly (e.g., through a trusted third person and not in the presence of peers and subordinates).

WHAT IS CULTURE?

The *Oxford Encyclopedic English Dictionary* defines **culture**—in terms of its usage in this book—as:

The art and other manifestations of human intellectual achievement regarded collectively; The customs, civilization, and achievement of a particular time or people; The way of life of a particular society or group

Culture has been defined in literally hundreds of ways[1]—a testament both to its importance and to its elusive and intangible nature. Anthropologists Herskovits and Harris define culture as "the man-made part of the environment" and "the learned patterns of thought and behavior characteristic of a population or society," respectively. Huntington, a political scientist, distinguishes "culture" from "civilization"—both civilization and culture refer to a people's way of life, values, norms and modes of thinking; however a civilization is the broadest cultural entity.[2] Among modern management scholars, Hofstede defines culture as "the collective programming of the human mind," whereas Trompenaars and Hampden-Turner define culture as "the way in which people solve problems and recognize dilemmas." Whitely and England synthesized more than 100 definitions of culture to arrive at this working definition, which is also the definition we use in this book.[3]

The knowledge, beliefs, art, law, morals, customs and other capabilities of one group distinguishing it from other groups.

Different definitions notwithstanding, there is a broad consensus regarding the main features of culture, as follows:

- *Culture is shared;* it is not an individual but a group property. Multiple group affiliations (e.g., with a nation, a firm) create multiple cultural memberships. Individuals vary however in the extent to which they adhere to cultural prescriptions.
- *Culture is intangible.* Culture is not only about "things," be they products or customs, but, importantly, about meaning. Meanings are not very visible; thus, many aspects of culture must be inferred.[4]
- *Culture is confirmed by others.* To understand a culture, you need to step back and look at it from the outside. This is why some of the most astute observers of a given culture are members of another culture.

CULTURE AND INTERNATIONAL BUSINESS

The importance of culture to international business cannot be overestimated. For instance, culture is a key ingredient in the "liability of foreignness" described earlier as an obstacle to the MNE's success abroad. The impact of culture at the firm level ranges from strategy formulation to FDI and organization design.[5] As the Goodyear case shows, culture can impact the way strategic moves are presented; however, it can also influence the decisions themselves. Organization behavior processes such as perception, motivation, and leadership as well as human resource management, are also influenced by culture, as are management style, decision making, and negotiations. More that 70 percent of the articles on international organization behavior and international human resource management used the concept of culture.[6] As you will discover throughout this book, the impact of culture is not limited to management, however. Marketing, accounting, the management of the supply chain, and virtually all other functions of business are influenced by culture. Culture also plays a key role in international alliances and mergers.

In Japan, culture and business are closely intertwined.

According to Huntington, the role of culture will not be reduced in the global era, on the contrary:[7]

In this new world the most pervasive, important and dangerous conflicts will not be between social classes, rich and poor, or other economically defined groups, but between people belonging to different cultural entities.

Thus, says Huntington, "culture is both a divisive and a unifying force." It is a force of cohesion among members but a source of friction between them and others. Culture can also be a source of internal friction, where strict adherents struggle with others whom they see as betraying the cultural heritage. Often, foreign cultural imports such as movies and TV programs are a subject of contention in such disputes.

Culture Does Not Explain Everything

Although we should not ignore the important role culture plays, we should not commit the opposite error of treating culture as a "residual variable," namely as the explanation for anything that is different. Uncertain of what drives a foreign competitor strategy, it is tempting to conclude that culture is behind it. But the strategy could well be the result of other factors. In the 1980s, the ascent of Japan and later that of the "four tigers" of Taiwan, Korea, Hong Kong, and Singapore, was attributed by many to Confucian values of frugality and discipline. The best-sellers that drove this explanation forgot to mention that Confucianism also contains elements that can be considered negative for progress. As for the Japanese, many of them overplayed the role of culture in their economic success and as a result failed to make economic and structural adjustments that would have made Japanese firms more competitive.

To avoid the pitfall of treating culture as a residual variable, it is essential to consider the possible impact of other, non-culture environmental variables. The research design in Exhibit 6–1 shows how this can be done.

In addition to comparing Japanese-Americans with Anglo-Americans and Japanese managers, Kelley and his associates also compared Japanese, Chinese, and Mexican managers with their ethnic American counterparts.[8] Shenkar and Ronen compared managerial values in mainland China, Hong Kong, Taiwan, and Singapore, so as to isolate the role of culture from that of political, economic, and social variables.[9]

Exhibit 6–1
Research design for the isolation of culture

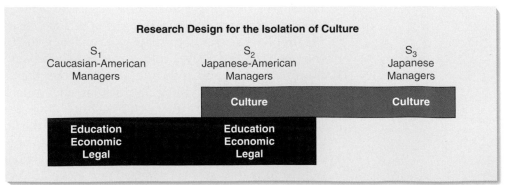

Source: L. Kelley, A. Whately and R. Worthley, 17–31. "Assessing the effects of culture on managerial attitudes: A three-culture test," *Journal of International Business Studies,* Volume 18, 2, 1987.

CORRELATES OF CULTURE

Culture is correlated with other variables that vary cross-nationally (e.g., language and religion). It is useful to remember, however, that culture often cuts across linguistic and religious boundaries, and that the latter cut across national borders. For example, Switzerland, Belgium, and Nigeria are countries with multiple official languages. South Korea has a large Christian minority (although this does not necessarily imply that this minority has developed a meaningful subculture). Lebanon has a large Christian minority while Northern Ireland has both Protestant and Catholic communities.

Language

Webster's Dictionary definition of **language** is "a systematic means of communicating ideas or feelings by the use of conventionalized signs, gestures, marks, or especially articulate vocal sounds." Language is one of the defining expressions of culture. It instills basic socialization themes and determines how values and norms are expressed and communicated. Just as culture is both a unifying and dividing force, so is language. Exhibits 6–2 and 6–3 show the major families of languages and the number of speakers in the most commonly spoken languages.

Because of fundamental differences between languages in structure and in the usage of slang and dialects, language blunders are common. Such mistakes as launching a hair product by the name of "Mist Stick" in Germany where "mist" is slang for manure are humorous but the consequences for the manufacturer may be dire. Coca-Cola was originally translated into Chinese as "bite the wax tadpole" only to be outdone by Pepsi whose jingle, "(Pepsi) comes alive" was translated into "brings your ancestors from their burial place." Name evaluation, where natives examine the proposed product or service name, is a good way to avoid the problem.

Differences in grammatical and structural format produce radically different types of discourse. In contrast to the preference for subject-predicate format in English and other European languages, most Chinese utterances are of the topic-comment type (i.e., is, the topic precedes the comment). Young's recording of a budget meeting illustrates the point (literal translation from the Chinese original):[10]

Exhibit 6–2

Language families of the world. Generalized map of the world distribution of language families

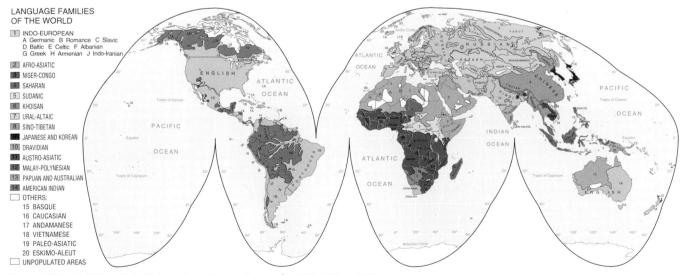

Source: H. J. de Blij and A. B. Murphy. *Human Geography.* NY: Wiley, 1999.

Exhibit 6–3

Numbers of speakers of major languages of the world (estimated)

Language Family	Major Language	Number of Speakers (Millions)
Indo-European	English	405
	Spanish	300
	Hindi	300
	Bengali	195
	Russian	205
	Portuguese	165
	German	100
	Punjabi	90
	French	90
	Italian	60
Sino-Tibetan	Chinese	1160
	Thai	50
	Burmese	35
Japanese-Korean	Japanese	125
	Korean	75
Afro-Asiatic	Arabic	170
Dravidian	Telugu	80
	Tamil	75
Malay-Polynesian	Indonesian	150

Source: H. J. de Blij and A. B. Murphy. *Human Geography.* NY: Wiley, 1999.

Chairman: So by purchasing the new machine, do you think we need to recruit additional workers or our existing workforce will cope with our requirement?

Subordinate: I think that with this new machine, the production time will be shortened or will become more efficient. And the number of staff required, I think we can utilize the existing staff for the time being, and no more new staff is necessary. So that we can solve the problem in recruiting the new staff.

And, again in the following example:

One thing I would like to ask. Because most of our raw materials are coming from Japan and this year is going up and up and uh it's not really I think an increase in price but uh we lose a lot in exchange rate and secondly I understand we've spent a lot of money in TV ad last year. So, in that case I would like to suggest here: chop half of the budget in TV ads and spend a little money on Mad Magazine.

Note that the "punch line" does not appear until the last minute, which is typical of Chinese discourse. This is contrary to Western discourse that tends to start with a preview statement providing tone and direction for the rest of the conversation. Young notes that the main points were often lost on native English speakers listening to these examples. This explains why patience and listening skills are promoted as key negotiation skills with the Chinese. Listening patiently is especially critical because the most important points will come at the end rather than at the beginning of a conversation.

Finally, non-verbal language is an important means of communication that varies across languages and cultures and is more important in some cultures than in others. Variations in the meaning of non-verbal cues may lead to embarrassing gaffes. For instance, the hand gesture used in many Western cultures to implore someone to come over is reserved in Korea for pets—not a good way to leave a positive impression on a Korean executive.

The Emergence of English as "Lingua Franca"

The term **lingua franca** comes from the Franks—people originating in southern France who traded with other people in the Mediterranean who spoke a variety of languages—Arabic, Italian, Greek, Spanish, and Portuguese. The Franks developed a language that was a mixture of the preceding languages and became the language of commerce in the Mediterranean. Today, the term lingua franca denotes any knowledge shared by people of different national and linguistic origins.

English has become the business world's lingua franca, the number-one foreign language taught in non-English-speaking countries. Germans and French speakers are more likely to converse with each other in English than they are in each other's language. Only 20 percent or so of Germans learn French as a foreign language, whereas roughly 60 percent choose English. This is resented in some countries as "cultural imperialism." France is an example. In 1975, the country banned the use of foreign words in commercials as well as in TV and radio broadcasts. In 1992, the constitution was amended to declare French the official language, and in 1994, the use of foreign words was banned. In 1988, Quebec, a province of Canada with a French majority, enacted a law requiring the use of French in all commercial signs.

The dominance of English does not imply that knowledge of other languages is not necessary. On the contrary, knowledge of foreign languages is often viewed as a distinct advantage. Much has been said of the advantage enjoyed by Europeans who typically master at least one foreign language. Utah has become attractive to international firms because of the abundance of multilingual residents. Moncton in New Brunswick, Canada, has become the call center of choice in Canada because it enjoys bilingual fluency while Canada's maritime provinces attract U.S. firms with the "neutral accent of their residents."[11] However, multilinguism also has its drawbacks. Multilingual states such as Belgium (Flemish versus Walloons) and Canada are often ripe for tension and conflict. Indeed, there tends to be a correlation between multilingualism and political risk.

While English is a lingua franca, its adoption might have a symbolic and even a strategic meaning. When Korean car manufacturer Daewoo Motor was acquired by General Motors, the Korean executives quickly embarked on the study of English, figuring that this will now be the enterprise's working language.[12] The adoption of English as a working language in an Italian-British joint venture helped the British get the upper hand because it meant adopting their working routines.[13]

Religion

Religion contains key values and norms that are reflected in adherents' way of life. The impact of religion extends to the secular segment of the population, albeit to a lesser extent. Globally, Christianity claims the most adherents, while Islam is the fastest growing. De Blij and Murphy term the two together with Buddhism "global religions," whereas religions that dominate a single national culture are termed "cultural religions." (See Exhibits 6–4 and 6–5.)

Religion influences international business in many ways. National institutions (in particular) and business firms try to adopt practices that will satisfy religious decrees without undermining modern business practice. For instance, because bank interest is generally prohibited under Islamic law, banks in Moslem countries issue shares to depositors and charge borrowers fees and commissions to maintain profitability without charging interest. Religion and its associated customs also influence marketing. In China, birth rates tend to rise during the year of the dragon in the Chinese 12-year calendar, creating opportunities for manufacturers of children's clothes and toys. In Moslem countries from Saudi Arabia to Indonesia, believers do not eat during daylight hours during the month of Ramadan, curtailing lunch business at restaurants but creating opportunities for traditional buffet dinners after dark.

Exhibit 6–4
Religions of the world

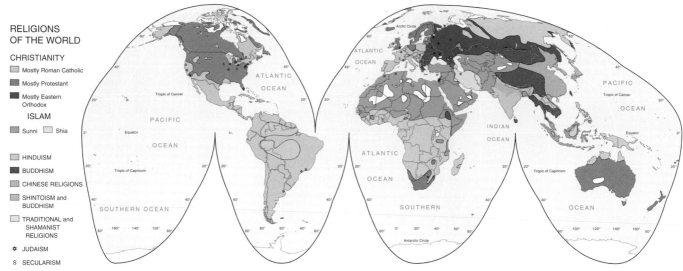

Source: H. J. de Blij and Patero Muller. *Concepts and Regions in Geography,* NY: Wiley, 2002.

Interim Summary

1. Culture plays an important role in international business. Culture affects not only how employees interact, but the overall strategy that the business employs.

2. Language and religion create difficulties as well as opportunities for MNEs. Employees with different cultures, languages, or religions may form subcultures in the MNE, while at the same time they are valuable as a means of bridging the gap between the corporate culture and local cultures.

Exhibit 6–5
Adherents to major world religions, by geographic region, 1996 (in millions)*

	Americas				Subsaharan Africa	N. Africa/ Southwest Asia	Asia			Russia	Pacific	Totals
Religion	North	Middle	South	Europe			South	Southeast	East			
Christianity	208.1	140.8	296.2	409.6	253.1	5.0	24.7	90.5	50.0	110.7	15.3	1,604.0
R. Catholic	94.7	128.6	281.8	255.3	109.1	0.3	5.5	69.7	13.0**	4.9	6.9	969.8
Protestant	107.4	12.1	14.2	107.2	114.6	4.3	19.2	20.8	37.0**	9.1	7.9	453.8
Orthodox	6.0	0.1	0.2	47.1	29.4	0.4	—	—	—	96.7	0.5	180.4
Islam	6.1	0.2	0.3	13.9	171.9	401.3	327.1	182.6	29.3	3.2	0.2	1,136.1
Sunni	6.0	0.2	0.3	11.9	164.5	260.4	319.4	180.1	29.3	3.2	0.2	975.5
Shiite	0.1	—	—	2.0	7.4	140.9	8.7	2.5	—	—	—	160.6
Hinduism	1.0	0.3	0.4	0.7	1.7	2.3	741.3	5.9	0.3	—	0.4	754.3
Buddhism	0.6	0.1	0.4	0.3	—	0.1	22.5	168.7	151.2	0.9	—	343.9
Chinese religions	0.1	—	0.1	0.1	—	—	0.1	9.1	253.0	—	—	262.5
Sikhism	0.3	—	—	0.2	—	—	20.1	—	—	—	—	20.6
Judaism	7.4	0.2	0.7	2.1	0.1	5.1	—	—	—	2.5	0.1	18.2

Source: H. J. de Blij and A. B. Murphy. *Human Geography.* NY: Wiley, 1999.

NATIONAL CULTURE CLASSIFICATIONS

To international business scholars and practitioners, nation is the most visible layer of culture. This is not to say that culture and nation are synonymous—cultural and national boundaries overlap only partially—but the national unit represents a convenient way of assessing culture together with other environmental sectors such as the economic and the political. The following are the key classifications of national culture.

Hofstede's Dimensions of Culture

By far the most used (and, some would say, abused) work on culture is that of Hofstede, who studied more than 100,000 IBM employees throughout the world.[14] The study, controlling for employee function and level, was also noteworthy for its attempt to correlate its findings with a host of other predictors (e.g., climate). Hofstede's survey yielded four underlying dimensions: power distance, uncertainty avoidance, individualism/collectivism, and masculinity/femininity.

Power Distance (PD)

Power distance (PD) is the extent to which hierarchical differences are accepted in society and articulated, for example, in the form of deference to senior echelons. Exhibit 6–6 shows a number of countries that are very high or very low on PD as well as the organizational implications of their position on the construct.

PD should not be confused with the actual distribution of wealth and power in a nation. For instance, Israel is very low on power distance although its income inequality is among the highest in the developed world. In contrast, Japan is relatively egalitarian in terms of wealth and income distribution (though some Japanese now describe Japan's "middle-class society" as a myth) yet is relatively high on power distance. In Japan, seating arrangements reflect one's position. The highest in rank typically sits at the head of the table and enjoys other status distinctions, as shown in Exhibit 6–7. MNEs from cultures high on power distance (e.g., Mexican cement maker Cemex), are less likely to delegate much authority to their subsidiaries.

Exhibit 6–6
Power distance: country examples and organizational implications

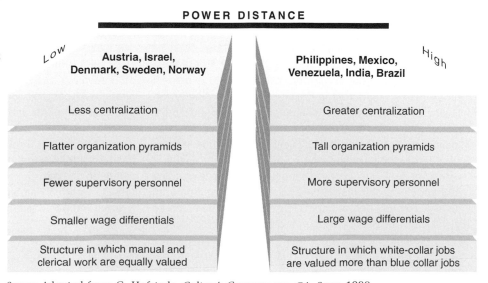

POWER DISTANCE

Low — Austria, Israel, Denmark, Sweden, Norway	High — Philippines, Mexico, Venezuela, India, Brazil
Less centralization	Greater centralization
Flatter organization pyramids	Tall organization pyramids
Fewer supervisory personnel	More supervisory personnel
Smaller wage differentials	Large wage differentials
Structure in which manual and clerical work are equally valued	Structure in which white-collar jobs are valued more than blue collar jobs

Source: Adapted from G. Hofstede. *Culture's Consequences.* CA: Sage, 1980.

Exhibit 6–7
Rank distinctions among the Japanese

Recognizing the Highest Ranked	Recognizing Rank by Car Manners
• His business card will generally be presented by a subordinate. Sometimes he will not even carry a card. • He drinks his tea first. • He speaks last. • He sits the farthest to the rear. • He speaks the least. • No one minds if he nods off. • Climbing stairs, the highest ranked walks last. • Coming down, he walks first.	• The highest ranked sits deepest in the back seat. • When the owner is driving, the highest ranked sits in the passenger's seat. • More recently, he rides where it is easiest to get in and out. • If the owner's wife is along, she sits in the passenger's seat.

Source: Japan External Trade Organization.

Uncertainty Avoidance (UA)

Uncertainty Avoidance (UA) refers to the extent to which uncertainty and ambiguity are tolerated. Exhibit 6–8 includes country examples and organizational implications of uncertainty avoidance. Japan's high score on uncertainty avoidance is reflected in the attempt to standardize behavior and rules, as in the following example:

> *The design and construction of Japanese parks is highly regulated. The rules cover not only how many trees each park must contain, but how many of them must be small, medium-sized and large, and at what density they should be planted.*[15]

COUNTRY BOX

KOREA—POWER DISTANCE IN THE COCKPIT

A chilling example of the potential influence of power distance comes from descriptions of recent crashes of Korean Air's planes: "Did aspects of Korean national culture, such as respect for authority, play a role in the crash by preventing lower-level crew members from challenging the captain's decisions? . . . South Korean military discipline still pervades many Korean Air cockpits. Even after altitude alarms sounded in their cockpit, the co-pilot and flight engineer on a Korean Air Boeing 747 that eventually crashed killing 228 people, didn't insist the pilot abort his landing until just six seconds before impact. Discipline can be enforced physically: The report cites an incident in which a captain hit his co-pilot with the back of his hand for making a mistake." . . . A Korean Air official disputed suggestions that the Korean tradition of respecting authority played a role in the crash. But he also announced that the airline had extensively revised pilot training to encourage co-pilots to speak up and offer advice to the captain . . . The airline now teaches co-pilots to repeat their concern if a captain ignores them . . ."

"Veteran pilots and industry experts say the problems described in the Korean Air report can be found in varying degrees at airlines throughout Asia . . . Some Asian airlines need to address the hierarchical culture in the cockpit, where no one questions the pilot even if he's making a mistake," says Ross Hamony, manager of the FAA's Asia Pacific flight-standards office in Singapore.

Source: "Korean airlines faulted on safety by internal study," Wall Street Journal, April 8, 1999; "Korean Air sees no culture link in Guam crash," International Herald Tribune, March 27, 1998, 6, see also November 3, 1999, A6; April 8, 1999, A15.

Exhibit 6–8

Uncertainty avoidance:
country examples and
organizational implications

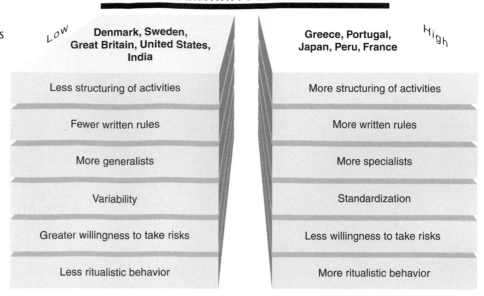

UNCERTAINTY AVOIDANCE

Low — Denmark, Sweden, Great Britain, United States, India

Greece, Portugal, Japan, Peru, France — High

Low	High
Less structuring of activities	More structuring of activities
Fewer written rules	More written rules
More generalists	More specialists
Variability	Standardization
Greater willingness to take risks	Less willingness to take risks
Less ritualistic behavior	More ritualistic behavior

Source: Adapted from G. Hofstede. *Culture's Consequences.* CA: Sage, 1980.

Hofstede believes that uncertainty avoidance is probably the most critical dimension for foreign investment because of its implication for risk taking and investment. For instance, MNEs from cultures high on uncertainty avoidance are likely to take a more incremental approach to internationalization. For instance, Japanese car manufacturers such as Nissan lagged behind their European and U.S. counterparts in establishing production facilities in China.

Individualism/Collectivism (I/C)

Individualism/Collectivism (I/C) refers to the extent to which the self or the group constitutes the center point of identification for the individual. To some scholars, this is the most important dimension of culture. High collectivism does not mean that individuals do not seek self-interest. Rather, it means that the pursuit is conducted within acceptable group frameworks with group norms guiding individual behavior and with group harmony being an important endeavor. Gannon distinguishes between different types of collectivism, for example, the Chinese family altar and the Israeli kibbutz.[16]

Exhibit 6–9 shows examples of countries high or low on individualism as well as some key organizational implications. Of all the countries surveyed, the United States received the highest score on individualism.

McClelland used children's literature to study national cultures. He assumed that such literature helps us learn about the patterns of acculturation—the process by which the basic values of culture are instilled into its members. The following illustration, taken from a Chinese children's book, shows how collectivism is weaved into a story:

> *"What are you looking for, Mom?*
> *"A sweater for you to take to kindergarten. It may be windy today."*
> *"Two new friends have come to our class . . . They won't know about the wind."*
> *Mom nods and smiles. She puts three sweaters in Qin's satchel.*
> *"Good child," says the teacher. "So little, but you already know about helping others."[17]*

Exhibit 6–9

Individualism/collectivism: country examples and organizational implications

INDIVIDUALISM-COLLECTIVISM

Low
Venezuela, Colombia, Taiwan, Mexico, Greece

High
United States, Australia, Great Britain, Canada, the Netherlands

Organization as "family"	Organization is more impersonal
Organization defends employee interests	Employees defend their own self-interest
Practices are based on loyalty, sense of duty and group participation	Practices encourage individual initiative

Source: Adapted from G. Hofstede. *Culture's Consequences*. CA: Sage, 1980.

MNEs from highly collectivistic cultures, e.g., Taiwan's Acer, tend to be more paternalistic. For instance, they are less likely to lay off employees during a downturn. However, such protection does not always extend to overseas subsidiaries.

Masculinity-Femininity (M/F)

Masculinity-Femininity (M/F) describes the extent to which traditional masculine values such as aggressiveness and assertiveness are emphasized. Exhibit 6–10 shows the organizational implications of masculinity ratings. However, there are implications in other domains, such as marketing. De Mooij found that masculinity-femininity explained differences in consumer behavior. For instance, consumers in feminine European cultures preferred coupé cars in 1990 and hatchbacks in 1996.[18]

MNEs from feministic cultures, e.g., car makers Volvo and Saab (now owned by Ford and GM, respectively), tend to emphasize social rewards and benefits in the workplace that are sometimes viewed as excessive by their parent firms.

Long-Term Orientation (LTO)

Originally termed **"Confucian Dynamism"** because of its anchoring in the Confucian value system, this dimension has been renamed **"long-term orientation**

Exhibit 6–10

Masculinity/femininity: country examples and organizational implications

MASCULINITY-FEMININITY

Low
Sweden, Denmark, Thailand, Finland, Yugoslavia

High
Japan, Austria, Venezuela, Italy, Mexico

Sex roles are minimized	Sex roles are clearly differentiated
Organizations do not interfere with people's private lives	Organizations may interfere to protect their interests
More women in more qualified jobs	Fewer women are in qualified jobs
Soft, intuitive skills are rewarded	Aggression, competition, and justice are rewarded
Social rewards are valued	Work is valued as a central life interest

Source: Adapted from G. Hofstede. *Culture's Consequences*. CA: Sage, 1980.

Exhibit 6–11

Country scores on Confucian dynamism (long-term orientation)

Score rank	Country or region	LTO score
1	China	118
2	Hong Kong	96
3	Taiwan	87
4	Japan	80
5	South Korea	75
6	Brazil	65
7	India	61
8	Thailand	56
9	Singapore	48
10	Netherlands	44
11	Bangladesh	40
12	Sweden	33
13	Poland	32
14	Germany	31
15	Australia	31
16	New Zealand	30
17	United States	29
18	Great Britain	25
19	Zimbabwe	25
20	Canada	23
21	Philippines	19
22	Nigeria	16
23	Pakistan	0

Source: Chinese Cultural Connection. "Chinese values and the search for culture-free dimensions of culture," *Journal of Cross-Cultural Psychology*, 18, 143–164.

(LTO)." It represents such values as thrift and persistence as well as traditional respect of social obligations. In high LTO cultures, organizations are likely to adopt a longer planning horizon, with individuals ready to delay gratification. Organizations in long-term cultures may also find it difficult, however, to change deeply rooted traditions and practices.

MNEs who hail from cultures high on LTO, are more likely to be willing to defer return on investment for a long time. This tendency, however, has often led to disregard of basic principles of economic return, as in the case of the Korean conglomerate Daewoo.

The LTO is not one of the original dimensions unveiled in Hofstede's 1980 book. Rather, it is the result of his cooperation with Michael Bond and his associates (known as The Chinese Cultural Connection) who developed the **Chinese Values Survey (CVS).** The Connection used an innovative technique. A group of Chinese social scientists was asked to name at least 10 "fundamental and basic values for Chinese people." Supplemented by readings of Chinese philosophy and social science, this produced a list of 40 values that made up the survey. The survey was then distributed to students in 22 countries. Country rankings on LTO are shown in Exhibit 6–11.

Criticism of Hofstede

Partially due to its broad dissemination, Hofstede's framework has been often singled out for criticism. Not all the criticism is valid. Sondergrad[19] reviewed the empirical studies which used Hofstede's framework and concluded that Hofstede's results were

Exhibit 6–12
Criticisms of Hofstede

- **A single company's data:** Hofstede's survey was conducted at IBM, an MNE with a strong corporate culture. IBM employees might not be representative of their compatriots in other firms and industries. A counterargument is that the use of single firm data permits control of corporate culture, allowing for an equivalent inter-country comparison. Also, finding significant national variations in a firm with a strong corporate culture shows the importance of national culture.

- **Time-dependent results:** Hofstede's results are an artifact of the time of data collection and analysis. Data were collected between 1967 and 1973, and analyzed in the late 1970s.[21] Most subsequent studies confirmed the results.

- **Business culture, not values:** A number of scholars argue that the dimensions reflect business culture rather than underlying values.[22] The counterargument is that it is precisely this layer that is of interest to business scholars and practitioners and that business behavior is embedded in broader societal values.

- **Non-exhaustive:** Schwartz[23] argues that Hofstede's dimensions do not cover the entire spectrum of the culture phenomenon. This is true but the framework is meant to provide a mere blueprint of some of culture's main building blocks. Such dimensions as time and spatial orientation are not included in Hofstede's dimensions.

- **Partial geographic coverage:** Hofstede covered only a portion of the world's countries, possibly missing other dimensions underlying culture. But over the years, information has been collected on additional countries.

- **Western bias:** The meaning of items used in Hofstede's instrument might vary from one culture to another and therefore is culturally biased. The work of the Chinese Cultural Connection shows this concern to be partially valid.

- **Attitudinal rather than behavioral measures:** This general criticism of attitudinal classifications of culture objects to the making of inferences from attitude to behavior.[24]

- **Ecological fallacy:** The interpretation of Hofstede's national level data as if it were about individuals. This criticism applies more to the interpretations and uses of Hofstede rather than to the original framework.[25]

generally confirmed and the dimensions validated. The individualism-collectivism dimension received the broadest support, followed by power distance, then uncertainty avoidance and lastly masculinity/femininity. Hoppe replicated Hofstede's masculinity/femininity dimension among business elites in 19 countries, and obtained a rank order that was strongly correlated with Hofstede's results.[20] Exhibit 6–12 lists some of the main criticisms of Hofstede's classification.

Schwartz's Classification

Originating in psychology, this framework has been used to a limited extent in the business literature. Schwartz arrived at his classification by a conceptualization of values prior to their sampling and measurement. His data are more recent than Hofstede's, having been collected in the 1980s and 1990s. Schwartz and his colleagues have collected data on a fairly large number of countries (including sub-regions).[26]

Schwartz and his associates identify three polar dimensions of culture, producing the following dimensions:

I. Embeddedness versus Autonomy

(1) Embeddedness (conservatism) implies emphasis on social relationships and tradition
(2) Autonomy implies finding meaning in one's own uniqueness and be encouraged to express one's own attributes.

There are two kinds of autonomy:

(a) Intellectual autonomy—self-direction, creativity
(b) Affective autonomy—the pursuit of stimulation and hedonism

II. Hierarchy versus Egalitarianism

(3) Hierarchy means legitimacy of hierarchical role and resource allocation
(4) Egalitarianism means transcendence of self-interests and promoting others' welfare

III. Mastery versus Harmony

(5) Mastery implies mastering the social environment via self-assertion (success, ambition)
(6) Harmony implies being "at peace" with nature and society. Organizations are viewed as part of the broader social system.

Exhibit 6–13 presents some examples of countries that are very high or very low on Schwartz's dimensions.

There is partial overlap between Schwartz's classification and that of Hofstede. For instance, autonomy in Schwartz's model is close to Hofstede's individualism/collectivism dimension, whereas hierarchy is similar to Hofstede's power distance. Mastery is close to masculinity in that both emphasize goal achievement. Harmony is relatively similar to uncertainty avoidance; Schwartz found positive correlation between them. Egalitarian commitment overlaps with femininity; a positive correlation was found between the two.

Trompenaars and Hampden-Turner's Classification

This classification found followers especially in the practitioner community. The classification consists of seven dimensions largely drawn from previous literature but validated, according to the authors, by large-scale practitioner surveys.

- *Universalism versus particularism* (rules versus relationships): In universal cultures, rules are assumed to apply in all situations and legal solutions are prominent. Countries high on universalism include the United States, Canada, the United Kingdom, the Netherlands, Germany, and the Scandinavian countries. Cultures high on particularism (e.g., Arab) typically provide more benefits to employees in return for commitment.
- *Communitarianism versus individualism* (the group versus the individual): In individualistic cultures, people see themselves primarily as individuals, whereas in communal cultures they see themselves as members of a group. Countries high on individualism are Israel, Canada, Nigeria, Romania, the United States, the Czech Republic, and Denmark. Countries high on communitarianism are Egypt, Nepal, Mexico, India, and Japan.

Exhibit 6–13
Sample country rankings
on Schwartz's dimensions

	Embeddedness	Affective Autonomy	Intellectual Autonomy	Hierarchy
High	Singapore Taiwan Poland Turkey	France Switzerland Germany Denmark	Switzerland France Slovenia Spain	China Thailand Turkey Zimbabwe
Low	Japan United States Brazil China	Turkey Brazil China Hungary	Hong Kong Poland Greece Turkey	Italy Slovenia Denmark Greece

	Egalitarianism	Mastery	Harmony
High	Estonia Mexico Australia Hungary	Hong Kong Switzerland Brazil Spain	Italy Mexico Finland Spain
Low	Thailand China Malaysia Taiwan	Finland Estonia Slovenia France	Israel Malaysia Hong Kong United States

Source: L. Sagiv and S. H. Schwartz. "A new look at national culture: illustrative applications to role stress and managerial behavior." In N. N. Ashkanasy and M. F. Peterson (eds). *The Handbook of Organizational Culture and Climate.* CA: Sage, 2000.

■ *Neutral versus emotional:* In neutral cultures, interactions are impersonal and objective; in emotional cultures they are laden with emotions. Countries high on neutral expression include Ethiopia, Japan, Poland, and New Zealand; they prefer indirect, non-confrontational response, and emphasize control. Countries high on emotional expression include Kuwait, Egypt, Oman, and Spain; they prefer direct, emotional response, and avoid social distance.

■ *Diffuse versus specific:* In specific cultures, interaction is confined to a narrow domain and private life is kept separate from work. Countries high on specific involvement—the United States and Germany—allow more outspoken expression and encourage transparency. Countries high on diffuse involvement include Japan, Mexico, and France. Such cultures have no clear separation between different life domains. Response is situational, depending on the person and other circumstances.

■ *Achievement versus ascription:* In achievement cultures, status is based on achievement and people are evaluated by performance. In ascriptive cultures, status is bestowed by birth, kinship, and age. Countries high on achievement—the United States and Canada—permit individuals to make commitments in the name of their company, and make use of detailed technical data to support their position. Countries high on ascription—Kuwait and Saudi Arabia—make ample use of titles and show respect for superiors.

■ *Attitudes to time:* Countries emphasizing the short term—the United States, Ireland, and Brazil—plan for a shorter time horizon than countries with long time horizon—Portugal and Pakistan. Countries with orientation toward the past—Hong Kong, Israel, and China—emphasize heritage and reputation more than the present or future. Countries with sequential time perception, such as the United States, adhere to planning more than those with synchronic culture, such as Italy and Spain.

- *Attitudes toward the environment*: Countries geared toward controlling the environment—the United States, Israel, and Spain—appreciate control and dominance, whereas countries not geared toward such control—Venezuela, Nepal, and Russia—accept that many life events cannot be controlled.

The Trompenaars and Hampden-Turner's classification bears partial resemblance to Hofstede's model. The long- versus short-term orientation is similar to the fifth dimension (LTO) in Hofstede's model. The communitarianism versus individualism dimension is similar to Hofstede's collectivism versus individualism. There is no equivalent in Hofstede's scheme to the specific/diffuse dimension; however, in individualistic cultures interpersonal relationships tend to be more specific, whereas in collectivist cultures they tend to be diffuse. Achievement versus ascription has no direct match in Hofstede's model; however, people with achievement orientation are likely to emphasize success and goal attainment, whereas high-power distance cultures are more likely to contain ascriptive assumptions.

Other Dimensions of Culture

The classifications presented here do not cover all aspects of culture. For instance, Hall distinguishes cultures as being "high context" or "low context." High-context cultures such as Japan do not emphasize verbal communications, tend to require a strong leader, and have a polychromatic perception of time (i.e., they will handle various issues and groups at the same time). In contrast, low-context cultures, such as the United States, have a monochronic time perspective (i.e., they usually attend to various issues sequentially).[27]

National Culture Clustering

Culture clustering is the grouping of cultures based on their relative similarity. Two groupings appear below.

Ronen and Shenkar

The Ronen and Shenkar classification is based on a synthesis of eight earlier studies.[28] Note that the degree of similarity between countries is relative (see Exhibit 6–14). The regions presented encompass many regions although some countries, noticeably (former) communist and African nations, are not included. For those countries, it is possible to predict work values on the basis of geography, language, and religion, three dimensions that underlie the clusters formed. However, four countries—Brazil, Israel, Japan and India—are classified as "independents" since they do not fit any of the groupings.

Like Hofstede's classification, the Ronen and Shenkar's scheme was utilized to predict MNE strategies (e.g., entry mode, as in Chapter 10) and organization design (see Chapter 11).

Huntington

Based on historical and political observations (although not quantitative empirical research), Huntington distinguishes seven civilizations: Sinic, Japanese, Hindu, Islamic, Western, Latin American, and African[29] (see Exhibit 6–15; there, Sinic in-

Exhibit 6–14
Ronen and Shenkar's culture clustering

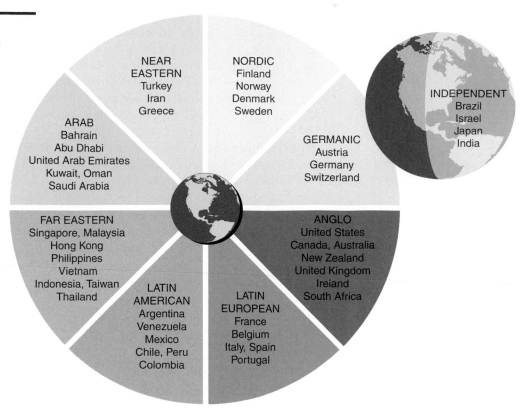

Source: S. Ronen & D. Shenkar, "Clustering countries on attitudinal dimensions: A review and synthesis." *Academy of Management Review,* 10, 3, 1985, 435–654.

Exhibit 6–15
Huntington's civilization clustering

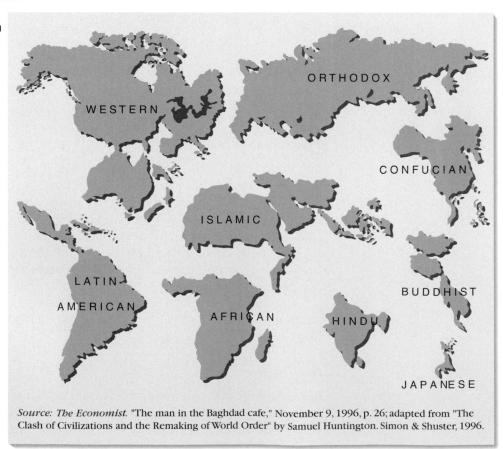

Source: The Economist. "The man in the Baghdad cafe," November 9, 1996, p. 26; adapted from "The Clash of Civilizations and the Remaking of World Order" by Samuel Huntington. Simon & Shuster, 1996.

cludes Orthodox, Confucian, and Buddhist civilizations). Huntington's grouping has received more attention since September 11, 2001, partly because of the probable clash he sees between Western and Islamic civilizations.

Interim Summary

1. Hofstede attempted to develop a universal, objective means of measuring differences between cultures. This task is problematic due to the subjectivity of culture in general, and he faced a great deal of criticism regarding his system of classification.

2. The most important criticisms of Hofstede's work relate to his having dealt only with employees from a single corporation during a specific period. Thus, he may have been offering a snapshot of the culture at that moment which could not be extended to predict future attitudes and especially behavior. Also, the cultures being studied may have been altered by the IBM corporate culture, rendering the data less representative of national cultures.

3. Other theorists have offered alternative systems of cultural classification. These systems contain some measures that are similar to Hofstede's classifications and some that are not. Culture clustering solves some of the methodological problems associated with the various dimensions.

CORPORATE CULTURE

Corporate culture is the culture adopted, developed, and disseminated by a company. It is of tremendous importance, for instance, for an MNE that adopts a global strategy and uses corporate culture as an integrator of its various units. Corporate culture can deviate from the "national norm." For example, Honda is often described as being different from the "typical" Japanese firm in that it is less immersed in tradition and more open to change. Hofstede points out that corporate culture is more superficial than national culture, because the imprints on the latter alone reside in deeply embedded values. While national culture forms *values* through early socialization, corporate culture involves the subsequent acquisition of organizational *practices* and symbols in the firm.

Hofstede and his colleagues who studied corporate cultures in two countries, the Netherlands and Denmark, found differences in values but more considerable differences in practices among the firms they studied. They proposed that national and corporate cultures are distinctive—if related—constructs.[30] Laurent proposes that corporate culture can modify (a) behavior and artifacts and (b) beliefs and values but the deeper level of underlying assumptions is derived from national culture.[31] Laurent found that national differences in beliefs regarding firm practices were considerably greater in a single MNE than in multi-firm samples, leading Schneider to suggest " . . . a paradox that national culture may play a stronger role in the face of a strong corporate culture. The pressures to conform may create the need to reassert autonomy and identity, creating a national mosaic rather than a melting pot."[32]

Classifications of Corporate Culture

Two of the authors who provided classifications of national cultures did the same for corporate culture. Exhibit 6–16 presents the classifications.

Exhibit 6–16
Corporate culture classifications

Hofstede et al.:

I Value dimensions (factors):

    Need for security
    Work centrality
    Need for authority

II Practices

    Process-oriented vs. results-oriented
    Employee-oriented vs. job-oriented
    Parochial vs. professional
    Open system vs. closed system
    Loose control vs. tight control
    Normative vs. pragmatic

Source: G. Hofstede, B. Neuijen, D. D. Ohayv and G. Sanders. "Measuring organizational cultures: A qualitative and quantitative study across twenty cases." *Administrative Science Quarterly*, 35, 1990, 286–316.

Trompenaars and Hampden-Turner:

a. The Family: Personal, hierarchical, power-oriented
b. The Eiffel Tower: Specific relations, ascribed status, rational authority
c. The Guided Missile: Egalitarian, impersonal, and task oriented
d. The Incubator: Individual self-fulfillment, personal and egalitarian relations

Source: F. Trompenaars and C. Hampden-Turner. *Riding the Waves of Culture: Understanding Diversity in Global Business.* NY: McGraw-Hill, 1998.

Other Layers of Culture

Ethnicity

Significant ethnic communities exist in many countries. In the United States, Hispanic and various Asian communities have been growing rapidly, creating subcultures within the U.S. culture. In Asia, Chinese have long constituted much of the business elite in countries such as Thailand, Malaysia, and Indonesia. Such variations must be recognized by the MNE as they are likely to affect a myriad of issues, from consumption patterns to employee relations.

Industry

While relatively little researched, it is clear that industry is an important layer of culture. For instance, the high-tech industry is considered flexible, informal, and innovative. It is also probably the most "global" industry in the sense of people having shared values, and (albeit electronic) interaction. Profession also provides an important source of cultural affiliation. Common values and norms shared by, say, marketers, across the markets in which the MNE operates, can facilitate global integration.

Demographics

Hofstede et al. found that education, age, seniority, and hierarchical level strongly affected differences in values, although not differences in practices.[33] For instance, Ralston et al.[34] found the new generation of Chinese managers to be considerably

Exhibit 6–17
Motive scores in Chinese societies

	Republican China	Taiwan	Mainland China
Achievement	.86	1.81	2.24
Affiliation	.38	.43	1.05
Power	1.29	1.00	1.81

Source: D. C. McClelland. "Motivational patterns in Southeast Asia with special reference to the Chinese case." *Social Issues,* 19, 1963, 6–19.

more individualistic and adhere less to Confucianism than the previous generation. These subcultures also vary geographically, making the country unit less homogeneous and making the MNE's integration challenge more complex.

Ideology

An important though less stable layer of culture is ideology. In China, for example, Maoist ideology provided many of the beliefs and values in the country from the mid-1950s to the mid-1970s. Ideologies are not always consistent with cultures and can vary along time and across regions.

McClelland, the motivational theorist mentioned earlier in this chapter, studied the strength of achievement, affiliation, and power motivations during different periods and locations in Chinese history: Republican (or Nationalist) China, which existed between 1911 and 1949; Taiwan, which has been ruled by the Nationalist regime since 1949; and mainland Communist China.[35] (See Exhibit 6–17.) The differences could be attributed, among other factors, to changes in the prevailing ideologies—for example, between relatively free-market Taiwan and the Communist mainland. Ideological as well as political and legal differences between the Chinese mainland and Taiwan imply that countries with a similar culture may still require the MNE to adopt different operational modes and practices.

Interim Summary

1. Corporate culture is embedded in national culture, but is also notably different in many cases. However, corporate culture is less deeply imprinted on the individual than national culture. Essentially, corporate culture is an add-on to national culture, which overlays the basic cultural patterns.

2. Culture is composed of many layers in addition to corporate culture. These layers, such as ethnicity and demographic background of employee, are all modifiers of the base culture of the individual.

3. The various layers of culture affect MNE strategy and operations in both the home and host country.

KEY CULTURAL ISSUES

Cultural Etiquette

Each culture has values, beliefs, and norms that distinguish it from other cultures. **Cultural or business etiquette** is the manners and behavior that are expected in a given situation, be it business negotiations, a supervisor-subordinate discussion of a raise, or the behavior expected outside the workplace and after business hours. Violation of business culture is considered more offensive in some cultures, especially those that are high on uncertainty avoidance and emphasize ritualistic behavior.

Exhibit 6–18 will let you test some of your business etiquette knowledge. It is a good idea to acquire such knowledge, whether through formal training or otherwise, before taking on a business assignment in a foreign country as well as prior to other encounters with foreign business people, e.g., when serving as a host to a foreign buyer or supplier.

Cultural Stereotypes

Our view of other people's culture is a function of our perceptions and stereotypes. To an extent, we are all **ethnocentric,** that is, we look at the world from a perspective shaped by our own culture and upbringing. Ethnocentrism, in turn, shapes

---

Exhibit 6–18

Testing your business etiquette

Going Global? Before you buy your plane tickets, test your business etiquette knowledge (some questions have more than one answer):

1. During business meetings, use first names in:
   a) Great Britain, because everyone is oh, so chummy.
   b) Australia, because informality is the rule.
   c) China, because the first name is the surname.
   d) Japan, because the last names are easy to mispronounce.

2. In China, offer expensive gifts to your hosts:
   a) Every time they ask for one.
   b) When you need help getting out of the country.
   c) Never—if they can't reciprocate, they'll lose face.

3. In which country is a business card an object of respect?
   a) Japan: An executive's identity depends on his employer.
   b) Taiwan: It explains a person's rank and status.
   c) France: Especially cards describing a man's mistress.

4. When doing business in Japan, never:
   a) Touch someone.
   b) Leave your chopsticks in the rice.
   c) Take people to pricier restaurants than they took you.
   d) All of the above.

5. Power breakfasts are inappropriate in all but:
   a) Italy: They like to bring the family along.
   b) Mexico: They don't bother to get to work till 10 a.m. anyway.
   c) United States: We invented them.
   d) France: They're at their most argumentative in the morning.

6. In some countries, colors are key. Which is true?
   a) For Koreans, writing a person's name in red signifies death.
   b) In China and Japan, gifts wrapped in white or black should only be presented at funerals.
   c) Purple suits in Great Britain represent lack of taste.

7. Which of these choices are obscene gestures?
   a) The okay sign in Brazil.
   b) A hearty slap on the back in Switzerland.
   c) Doing anything with the left hand in Saudi Arabia.
   d) Thumb between second and third finger in Japan.

Answers: 1-b, c; 2-c; 3-a, b; 4-d; 5-c; 6-a, b; 7-a, c, d

Source: Business World, May 1990, p. 27.

our **mental maps,** namely our perceptions of the world around us and even our perceptions of geographic realities. Note the following interview with a Japanese executive on how his firm made its site location selection in the United States:

> In picking a site . . . companies like Mazda or Nissan look for areas in which the population is relatively well educated, and where there is not a lot of competition for labor. Asked which part of America the Japanese were eyeing now, he replied, "the Northeast."—The Northeast? Where land is expensive and the demand for skilled labor particularly intense? "No, no," he replied, "I mean up around Washington, Oregon, around there . . ." The Northeast, that is, viewed from Tokyo, Beijing, and Seoul.[36]

Although we may not always believe our culture is superior, we use it as an anchor when looking at ourselves as well as when interacting with others. **Stereotypes** are our beliefs about others, their attitudes and behavior. **Auto-stereotypes** are how we see ourselves as a group distinguished from others. The following are auto-stereotypes of U.S. culture according to Adler and Jelinek:[37]

1. Distrust of others combined with a belief that individual change is possible.

2. Man mastering a predictable environment. Situations are problems to be resolved.

3. The individual above all else—hence, impermanence of relationships.

4. Emphasis on doing rather than on being.

5. A present to slightly future orientation; immediate gratification but change is constant.

According to Graham and Sano Americans are:[38]

Informal—not bound by rules
Materialistic
Non-deterministic
Egalitarian
Individualistic
Achievement/action oriented
Open/direct
Practical/efficient
Litigious
Culturally ignorant/monolingual

Hetero-stereotypes are how we are seen by others. In Exhibit 6–19, Americans are described by Chinese observers. Note that the Chinese tend to notice precisely those elements that are different in their culture. For instance, the "me first" attitude is salient to someone who comes from a collectivistic culture.

Stereotypes are important because they affect how MNE staff at headquarters and in various locations perceive other MNE employees. For instance, if headquarters staff believe that employees in a given country are not self-motivating, they may be reluctant to delegate authority to that subsidiary.

In Exhibit 6–20, a group of U.S. employees protest using their stereotype of Japanese firms.

Cultural Distance

In an international business context, the most important question may be not how cultures differ but what happens when they interact with each other. **Cultural distance** is a measure of the extent to which cultures differ from each other; however, such measures that are typically built as an aggregate of Hofstede's dimensions are

Exhibit 6–19
Americans from A to Z

Americans from A to Z

A Americans are Westerners.
B Busy folks, whether blue or brown eyed.
C Competition in business.
D Dollars are an uncommonly common goal.
E Enter and exit human relations quickly.
F Friendly to good friends.
G 'Go for it' is a motto.
H Hypertension goes with high income and high living.
I Impatience is a trait.
J Jamboree may jeopardize your health.
K Kiss and ride, a sign in a subway.
M 'Me first' attitude.
N Nosiness is tabooed.
O Oops is an exclamation or interjection.
P Penny wise and pound foolish in value judgments.
Q Quest for influence.
R Risk is the foundation of the firm.
S Salesmanship is a benign tumor.
T Teasing is a sign of being liked.
U Unemployment breeds foreclosures.
V Vulnerable to temptations.
W Woo fame and fortune.
X A movie classification for sex and violence.
Y Yen for yen, the Japanese currency.
Z Zest for fun and pleasure.

Source: Wang. *Westerners Through Chinese Eyes.* Beijing: Foreign Languages Press, 1990.

Exhibit 6–20
Nikko Hotel pamphlet

To: The General Public
From: Hotel Employees & Restaurant Employees International Union
1216 28th Street N.W. Washington D.C. 30007

Japanese Airlines (JAL) owns the Nikko Hotel in Chicago. The Nikko Hotel signed a neutrality agreement with Hotel Employees and Restaurant Employees Union Local 1, in Chicago.

Essentially, the agreement provided that Nikko Workers would have the right to Join Local 1, if they so choose, without any interference from the company. Moreover, if a majority of the workers joined Local 1, the Nikko would recognize Local 1 as the bargaining agent and would begin negotiating a labor contract.

However, when the workers began signing union cards, the Nikko blatantly broke their word to the Union by doing all it could to discourage the workers from organizing.

We thought the Japanese companies honored their agreements as part of their culture. Apparently, we Americans were wrong.

Please don't patronize JAL or the Nikko Hotel.

From a leaflet distributed by picketing workers in New York City, August 8, 1988

Global communications networks do not necessarily herald a convergence of cultures.

problematic. For instance, Hofstede suggested that some of his dimensions were more important than others for certain purposes. As mentioned earlier, he stated that uncertainty avoidance was the most important dimension for FDI because it involved different perceptions of risk.[39] Other studies confirmed the variability in the impact of various dimensions.[40] Trompenaars and Hampden-Turner elaborated on the encounters of different cultures and the problems likely to arise from such encounters.[41]

Cultural distance plays a key role in MNE strategies and foreign investment. Recall, for instance, familiarity theory (discussed in Chapter 3) that suggests that firms incrementally invest in culturally distant locations. Cultural distance also affects entry mode (see Chapter 10) and alliance performance (see Chapter 12), among others.

Convergence and Divergence

The debate surrounding "convergence" versus "divergence" presents two competing theses: The **convergence hypothesis** assumes that the combination of technology and economics is making countries more alike, and that with global integration of markets and the diffusion of MNC practices, convergence will accelerate.[42] The **divergence hypothesis** assumes that countries will continue to maintain their distinctive characteristics, and that those differences may even be accentuated over time. The case for convergence is often made in terms of the proliferation of "global products" that are widely recognized throughout the world and sold with little or no adaptation; examples are McDonald's and Coca-Cola, though, as you will see in Chapter 16, even those products are tinkered with in different markets. Trompenaars and Hampden-Turner suggest that even "global goods" are subject to cultural variations. This is because these products and services have different meanings to the people in each culture. Nor do global products imply harmony among diverse cultures and civilizations. John Bolton has pointed out in the *Washington Times* that the Kosovo conflict punctured the myth that "no two countries which both have a McDonald's will ever go to war with each other."[43]

There are of course also strong forces for convergence. Those include migration, developments in communications (especially the Internet), transportation, and travel. It is useful to remember however that at the end of the nineteenth century, many countries were doing almost as much trade as a proportion of GNP as they do today, yet cultures remained highly differentiated. According to Huntington, the world is moving toward greater divergence: "Global politics has become multipolar and multicivilizational." Rather than taking over, the West, currently the most powerful civilization, is gradually losing power to non-Western civilizations.[44] The events of September 11, 2001, have focused much attention on that view.

Interim Summary

1. Cultural stereotypes are an important force in international business. For instance, they influence how headquarters and subsidiary staff perceive each other.

2. Cultural distance affects MNE's decisions such as internationalization, entry mode, product adjustments and staffing.

INDUSTRY BOX

CULTURAL INDUSTRIES

Cultural industries—movies, radio and television programming, book publishing and distribution, are especially susceptible to protectionism in countries that see their culture endangered by a dominant and close neighbor (Canada) or by a dominant language (France; the Canadian province of Quebec). For example, Canada has a heritage minister, whose role is to protect the national heritage of the country and restrict foreign ownership of cultural industries. The Canadian government tried to limit the sale of U.S. magazines without "sufficient" Canadian content but publishers, who in the past have had their trucks stopped at the border, used new technology to beam the content to their print plants in Canada. Most recently, Canada's supreme court ruled that foreign satellite television signals could not be picked up legally in the country.

The French government has been concerned for a long time with the permeation of English words such as "le weekend" and with the decline in consumption of the famous French baguette. Among other things, the French limit the foreign content of TV broadcasting. Canada and France advanced a proposal that would exempt cultural industries from the Multilateral Agreement on Investment. Maude Barlow, chairwoman of the Council of Canadians, called the Agreement "the largest threat to Canadian culture ever."

Source: Adapted from M. Heinzl. "Foreign satellite-TV signals barred by Canada's high court," *Wall Street Journal,* April 29, 2002, B5; *Wall Street Journal,* February 4, 1998; R. Tamburri. "Canada considers new stand against American culture," *Wall Street Journal,* February 4, 1998, A18.

CHAPTER SUMMARY

1. Culture is an extremely important force in international business. However, culture does not explain everything and we should not assume that all differences observed across nations are to be attributed to culture.

2. When interacting with other cultures, individuals and firms use their own culture as an anchor for interaction with other cultures.

3. Language and religion are important correlates of culture that also exert direct influence on international business strategies and operations.

4. There are various classifications of national culture, including those of Hofstede, Schwartz, and Trompenaars-Hampden-Turner, among others. Using the Ronen and Shenkar framework, it is possible to cluster countries according to the relative similarity of their cultures.

5. Based on the preceding classifications, it is possible to calculate the "cultural distance" among countries; however, this concept is more complex than it may appear. Cultural distance, in turn, influences the MNE's internationalization process, and its strategic decisions.

6. In addition to the national level, we should be aware of corporate culture as well as of differences in culture by industry, ethnicity, and ideology, among other factors.

7. Key cultural issues include stereotypes (e.g., how we see others), cultural distance, and convergence/divergence.

8. The question of difference between cultures is not as important in an international business context as is the question of what happens when those cultures interact.

9. "Cultural industries" (e.g., media) are usually more sensitive to cultural issues, for example, to criticism of "colonization" by a foreign culture.

CHAPTER NOTES

[1] R. S. Bhagat and S. J. McQuaid, 1982, "The role of subjective culture in organizations: A review and direction for future research," *Journal of Applied Psychology Monograph,* 67, 5, 635–685.
[2] S. P. Huntington, *The Clash of Civilizations and the Remaking of World Order.* New York: Simon & Schuster, 1996.

[3] W. Whitely and G. W. England, "Managerial values as a reflection of culture and the process of industrialization," *Academy of Management Journal,* 20, 3, 1977, 439–453.
[4] C. Geertz, "Thick description: Towards an interpretative theory of culture." In *The Interpretation of Culture.* New York: Basic Books, 1973.

[5] S. Ronen, 1986, *Comparative and Multinational Management*. NY: Wiley.

[6] N. J. Adler and S. Bartholomew, "Academic and professional communities of discourse: Generating knowledge on transnational human resource management," *Journal of International Business Studies*, 23, 3, 1992, 551–569.

[7] S. P. Huntington, *The Clash of Civilizations and the Remaking of World Order*. New York: Simon & Schuster, 1996.

[8] L. Kelley and R. Worthley, "The role of culture in comparative management: A cross-cultural perspective," *Academy of Management Journal*, Volume 24, 1, March, 1981; L. Kelley, A. Whately, and R. Worthley, "Assessing the effects of culture on managerial attitudes: a three-culture test," *Journal of International Business Studies*, Volume 28, 2 Summer, 1987, 17–31.

[9] O. Shenkar and S. Ronen. "Structure and importance of work goals among managers in the People's Republic of China," *Academy of Management Journal*, 30, 3, 1987, 564–576.

[10] L. W. Young, "Inscrutability revisited," In J. J. Gumperz (ed.), *Language and Social Identity*. New York: Cambridge University Press, 1982.

[11] L. M. Greenberg, "Canada answers the call for U.S. firms." *Wall Street Journal*, October 1, 1999, A13.

[12] Ki-tae Kim, "Daewoo Motor staff engrossed in English learning," *Korea Times* On-Line, September 29, 2001.

[13] J. Salk and O. Shenkar, "Social identities in an international joint venture: An exploratory case study," *Organization Science*, 12, 2, 161–178, 2001.

[14] G. Hofstede, *Culture's Consequences*. Thousand Oaks, CA: Sage, 1980.

[15] "A land fit for consumers," *The Economist*, November 27, 1999, 16.

[16] M. J. Gannon, et al. *Understanding Global Cultures: Metaphorical Journeys Through 17 Countries*. Thousand Oaks, CA: Sage, 1994.

[17] S. Wang, *Three Sweaters*. Beijing: Foreign Languages Press, 1976.

[18] M. De Mooj, "Masculinity/femininity and consumer behavior." In G. Hofstede with W. A. Arrindell, *Masculinity and Femininity The Taboo Dimension of National Cultures*, 1998.

[19] M. Sondergraad, "Hofstede's consequences: A study of reviews, citations and replications," *Organization Studies*, 15, 3, 1994, 447–456.

[20] M. H. Hoppe, "Validating the masculinity/femininity dimension on elites from 19 countries." In G. Hofstede, with W. Arrindell, *Masculinity and Femininity: The Taboo Dimension of National Cultures*. Thousand Oaks, CA: Sage, 1998.

[21] H. Baumgartel, and T. Hill, G. Hofstede "Culture's consequences: International differences in work related values," *Personnel Psychology*, 35, 1, 1982, 192–196; M. Warner, "Culture's consequences," *Journal of General Management* 7, 1, 1981, 75–78; E. A. Lowe, "Culture's consequences," *Journal of Enterprise Management*, 3, 3, 1981, 312.

[22] H. H. Baligh, "Components of culture: Nature, interconnections, and relevance to the decisions on the organization structure," *Management Science*, 40, 1994, 14–27; Schwartz, S. H. "Are there universals in the content and structure of values?" *Journal of Social Issues*, 50, 19–45.

[23] S. H. Schwartz, "Are there universals in the content and structure of values?" *Journal of Social Issues*, 50, 19–45.

[24] Triandis, H. "Culture's consequences," *Human Organization*, 41, 1, 1982, 86–90.

[25] G. Hofstede, M. H. Bond, and C. Luk, "Individual perceptions of organizational cultures: A methodological treatise on levels of analysis," *Organization Studies*, 14, 4, 1993, 483–503.

[26] S. H. Schwartz, "A theory of cultural values and some implications for work." *Applied Psychology: An International Review*, 1999, 48-1, 23–47.

[27] E. T. Hall, *Beyond Culture*. New York: Doubleday, 1976; *The Silent Language*. Greenwich, CT: Fawcett, 1959.

[28] S. Ronen and O. Shenkar, "Clustering Countries on Attitudinal Dimensions: A review and synthesis," *Academy of Management Review*, 10, 3, 1985, 435–454.

[29] S. P. Huntington, *The Clash of Civilizations and the Remaking of World Order*. New York: Simon & Schuster, 1996.

[30] G. Hofstede, B. Neujen, D. D. Ohayv and G. Sanders, "Measuring organizational cultures: a qualitative and quantitative study across twenty cases," *Administrative Science Quarterly*, 35, 1990, 286–316.

[31] A. Laurent, "The cross-cultural puzzle of international human resource management," *Human Resource Management*, 25, 1, 1986, 91–102.

[32] S. Schneider, "National vs. corporate culture: Implications for human resource management," *Human Resource Management*, 27, 2, 1988, 231–246.

[33] G. Hofstede, B. Neujen, D. D. Ohayv and G. Sanders, "Measuring organizational cultures: a qualitative and quantitative study across twenty cases," *Administrative Science Quarterly*, 35, 1990, 286–316.

[34] D. A. Ralston, C. P. Egri, S. Stewart, R. H. Terpstra, and Y. Kaicheng, "Doing business in the 21st century with the new generation of Chinese managers. A study of generational shifts in work values in China," *Journal of International Business Studies*, 30, 2, 1999, 415–428.

[35] D. C. McClelland, "Motivational patterns in Southeast Asia with special reference to the Chinese case," 1963. *Social Issues*, 19, 1963, 6–19.

[36] *Newsweek*, February 22, 1988, 14.

[37] N. J. Adler and M. Jelinek, "Is 'organization culture' culture bound?" *Human Resource Management*, 25, 1, 1986, 73–90.

[38] J. L. Graham and Y. Sano, *Smart Bargaining: Doing Business with the Japanese*. Cambridge, MA: Ballinger, 1984.

[39] G. Hofstede, "Organizing for cultural diversity," *European Management Journal*, 7, 1989, 390–397.

[40] O. Shenkar and Y. Zeira, "Role conflict and role ambiguity of chief executive officers in international joint ventures," *Journal of International Business Studies*, 23, 1992, 55–75.

[41] F. Trompenaars and C. Hampden-Turner, *Riding the Waves of Culture: Understanding Diversity in Global Business*. NY: McGraw-Hill, 1998.

[42] J. T. Dunlop, F. H. Harbison, C. Kerr, and C. A. Myers, *Industrialism and Industrial Man Reconsidered*. Princeton, NJ: Princeton University Press; K. Ohmae, *The Borderless World*. New York: Harper Row, 1990; F. Mueller, "Social effect, organizational effect, and globalization." *Organization Studies*, 15, 1994, 407–428.

[43] Cited in *The Economist*, July 31, 1999, p. 8, "That thing that won't go away."

[44] S. P. Huntington, *The Clash of Civilizations and the Remaking of World Order*. New York: Simon & Schuster, 1996.

The Political and Legal Environment

DO YOU KNOW

1. How do politics affect international trade and foreign investment? Can you distinguish between different types of political risk?

2. How can an MNE engage the political organizations and constituencies that most affect its operations and performance?

3. What are the challenges of working in countries such as Bulgaria and Vietnam, whose legal systems are different from that of the MNE's home country?

4. What levels of jurisdiction need an MNE be concerned with? How do laws regarding competition, product liability, and the like affect the MNE's operations and competitive advantage?

OPENING CASE Burger King Israel

Burger King Corporation, owned by U.K.-based Diageo, operates in almost 60 countries and territories. Its independent franchise in Israel has been successful from the outset, operating 46 restaurants by 1999. In that year, Burger King opened a new restaurant in Ma'aleh Adumim, a suburb that extends beyond the "green line" demarcating the 1967 border between Israel and the West Bank, which is now part of Jerusalem under Israeli sovereignty.

The Ma'aleh Adumim branch drew both Jewish and Arab customers seeking brand-name fast food. However, soon after its opening, the company argued that it was unaware the restaurant was located outside Israel's 1967 borders and informed the franchise holder that their agreement covered only pre-1967 Israel—which the Israeli franchisee disputed—and that its authority to operate the branch was being revoked. The decision was prompted by Arab political pressure (the company has restaurants in Bahrain, Jordan, Kuwait, Lebanon, Oman, Qatar, Saudi Arabia, and the United Arab Emirates), as well as by pressure from Moslem groups in Asia, Europe, and the United States, who threatened a boycott of the company. Israelis and American Jewish groups decried the company's bowing to Arab pressure and called for a worldwide boycott on their part. In the meantime, the restaurant remained open pending the outcome of international arbitration to which Burger King and its franchisee agreed to submit. The prolonged delay prompted U.S. Moslem groups to renew the boycott threat. ■

Source: Company reports and Web sites; M. Henry, "Burger King yields to boycott threat, drops Ma'aleh Adumim franchise," *The Jerusalem Post Internet Edition,* August 27, 1999.

The political-legal environment provides a critical context for the MNE at home and abroad. As the Burger King case illustrates, political constraints and political risk are part and parcel of conducting business across national boundaries. Facing multiple national constituencies, it is often difficult to meet the demands of one constituency without aggravating another. The MNE must not only respond to pressures exerted by those constituencies, but also be proactive in identifying and responding to their concerns.

If the political environment identifies key constituencies, the legal environment sets the "rules of the game" as well as the range within which legitimate business activity is conducted. Since, at least in democratic systems, laws are enacted by elected legislative bodies, political processes both determine legal issues and are guided by them. Under U.S. law, boycotting Israel altogether would not be an option for Burger King despite its ownership by a British conglomerate. The company and the franchisee eventually agreed to binding arbitration to determine whether their agreement allowed for the opening of branches outside the green line. The arbitration is to be conducted in the United States, as is customarily the case in international franchise agreements.

THE POLITICAL ENVIRONMENT

Political behavior is defined as "the acquisition, development, securing, and use of power in relation to other entities, where power is viewed as the capacity of social actors to overcome the resistance of other actors."[1] Although not unique to international operations, the political processes faced by the MNE, whether compliance, evasion, negotiation, cooperation, coalition building, and cooptation,[2] are more complex and problematic than is typically the case for domestic operations. The number of political constituencies—governments, political parties' interest groups, unions, and public opinion—is multiplied in the international business environment. The MNE is often viewed as a foreign implant, prompting coalitions of domestic forces that unite against the "foreign invasion."

Political processes are viewed by economists as constraints on the free flow of production factors, intermediary and final goods, that distort supply and demand. Political processes do not represent only constraints, however.[3] Government incentives, preferential subsidies, and other political acts alter the transaction costs of the firm and influence its strategic decisions. For instance, high import tariffs imposed by a government may lead an MNE to launch foreign investment that it would not have otherwise pursued. Being politically astute—having superior political intelligence and influence skills[4]—is a key skill for MNEs, many of which have placed "government liaisons" in senior positions.

The nature of international business activity influences the political constraints and the political agenda. For instance, while importers are typically concerned with achieving such goals as tariff reduction, exporters may seek to reduce limitations on high-technology exportation. Foreign investors, on their part, seek a more favorable investment climate in a host country. Domestic firms utilize political pressure to keep foreign competitors out of their home turf or to create obstacles to their operation.

The Institutional Context

The historical landscape of political institutions and relations both between and within countries constitute a crucial layer of the political environment. For example, some 40 years after the end of French colonial rule, former colonies in western

Africa still import many of their needs from France. Air France enjoys a virtual monopoly on many west African routes that have been very lucrative for the French state-owned airline. In addition to linguistic, cultural affinity, personal relationships, and vast knowledge of the local market (hence lower "liability of foreignness"), the trade and investment dominance of former colonial powers is the result of political pressure, often in the form of economic aid packages requiring the recipient to spend the money on purchases from donor country firms. For instance, in Latin America, Spanish banks dominate foreign investment in the financial industry. The endurance of political ties is also evident in the recently settled "banana war" in which European governments increased tariffs on Latin American bananas in order to protect former colonies and present allies in Africa and the Caribbean. This triggered a backlash on the part of the United States whose firms dominate Latin American banana plantations and who is more closely aligned with Latin American nations (see opening case in Chapter 2).

Affinity or **animosity** between nations reflect how closely aligned, or estranged, nations are based on both history and political reality. It is an important determinant of international business relations.[5] Countries who share a common historical bond and political affinity, such as the United States and the United Kingdom, tend to have high levels of mutual trade and investment. In contrast, trade and investment among hostile countries is often prohibited. U.S. firms are not allowed to invest in Cuba, and Syrian citizens are prohibited from doing business in Israel. Even where trade and investment are not legally banned, animosity can still have a serious effect. Trade and investment flows between Turkey and Greece are much smaller than they would be if not for the historical hostility between the two nations. Animosity, and trade barriers in general, also create opportunities for those that act as middlemen between the foes or that have special access to one of the trading partners. Prior to the opening of the Chinese mainland, Hong Kong benefited from its position as gateway to China. Jordan benefits from transferring Israeli goods to and from Indonesia as well as from handling Iraqi goods that cannot enter the international trade system owing to the UN-imposed sanctions on Iraq.

Political considerations also influence third countries. The U.S. administration successfully lobbied the Israeli government to cancel the sale of airborne aircraft warning systems to China, threatening to withhold economic aid to Israel if it were to consummate the deal. The pressure reflected geopolitical considerations—the United States feared the equipment could tempt China to mount an attack on Taiwan. Israel argued that the intervention was aimed at protecting U.S. firms from competition and that another foreign supplier would emerge in the event it withdrew from the deal. Israel finally caved in to U.S. pressure, and now faces an angry Chinese government who is less enthusiastic about promoting Israeli trade and investment. Trade is also used to influence political outcomes. Such is the effort by some EU members to deny duty-free access to Israeli products made in the territories held by Israel since 1967. To further dissuade importers, some EU officials warned that duties might be levied retroactively.[6]

Political relations among nations not only influence trade and investment but are also influenced by them. According to John Bolton of the American Enterprise Institute, the myth that "no two countries which both have a McDonald's" will go to war with each other has exploded with the Kosovo crisis (see also Chapter 6).[7] A study shows, however, that countries belonging to the same preferential trade agreement (PTA) were 30 to 45 percent less likely to become involved in military disputes than countries that did not have such agreements. When PTA members did have military disputes, they were less likely to go to war over them. Only 2 percent of such disputes led to war among signatories of PTA agreements vis-à-vis 11 percent for non-signatories. When not accompanied by a PTA, trade flows did not contribute to reduced hostilities, however.[8]

THE MNE–GOVERNMENT RELATIONSHIP

The relationship with governments in its host and home countries is probably the most important political challenge for the MNE. Governments affect the economic and legal environment in which the MNE operates, for example, via setting monetary and tax policies, setting price controls, enacting, endorsing, and enforcing intellectual property legislation, and influencing labor relations. Governments are also responsible for trade and investment policies, capital and exchange controls, and transfer-pricing policies.[9] In parliamentary democracies, the executive branch plays a less important legislative role than in countries lacking strict separation of powers.[10] In Vietnam, the government is a regulator, a competitor, a customer, and a potential partner. With no clear separation of the executive and the judiciary, the Vietnamese government also influences legal procedures and plays the key role in enforcement decisions.

The MNE Relationship with the Host Government

Three models have been used in the past to analyze the government–MNE relationship, *Sovereignty at Bay, Dependency,* and *Neo-Mercantilism.* All three assume a powerful MNE at odds with a less powerful, developing country government over market access if not over broader sovereignty issues. The *Sovereignty at Bay* model goes the furthest by viewing the MNE as a threat to the national sovereignty of the host country. The *Dependency* model also sees a cooperative relationship but only between the MNE and its home government.[11]

At the beginning of the twenty-first century, the nature of the relationship between MNEs and host governments can perhaps be best described as **coopetition,** that is, cooperation and competition simultaneously function in increasingly interdependent MNE–government relations. Cooperation reflects the elements of mutual accommodation and collaboration, with the government and the MNE seeking joint payoffs and goal accomplishment from their interdependent activities or resources. Competition reflects the elements of bargaining or control and related conflicts with the government and the MNE, seeking private gains at the expense of each other's interests. From a government's viewpoint, increasing pressure of global integration, heightened competition for inbound FDI, decelerated economic growth, and stronger needs for upgrading economic structure all encourage cooperation with MNEs. From an MNE's viewpoint, foreign operations increasingly depend on educational, technological, industrial, and financial structures built by host governments. For MNEs, whether a host government provides a stable set of rules for business players to act within and whether the rules can be adapted to changing conditions has become increasingly crucial for firm growth and international expansion. However, competition remains entrenched in MNE–government relations, and is mainly manifested in bargains and controls for resources or market access, despite its decreasing significance in countries with liberalized FDI policies.

MNE Political Objectives in the Host Country. Typically, the key political goal of the MNE in the host country is the establishment of a favorable trade and investment environment. This means nondiscrimination, namely equal (if not preferential) treatment of the foreign firm. Except where it seeks to block the entry of other MNEs, the MNE strives to remove limits on foreign ownership, to open access to local markets (i.e., few or no tariff and non-tariff barriers), and to have as few regulatory hurdles as possible. In short, it wishes to remove any obstacles that interfere with its freedom to locate,

The MNE must make its case to both its host and home governments.

manufacture, and sell where it can deploy its resources most effectively and obtain the highest return. MNEs also wish to reduce mandatory requirements for product or service adaptation, especially where they judge adaptation to be unnecessary in terms of competitive advantage or customer preferences.

Another important goal for the MNE in the host environment is to obtain **legitimacy.** Legitimacy is the acceptance of the MNE as a natural organ in the local environment. It is not transferable across borders[12] and as the Burger King example shows, legitimacy in one market may constitute a liability in another. The MNE will often try to convince political constituencies that it operates as a domestic company, contributes to the local economy and takes social responsibility seriously. Airbus often buys full-page advertisements in U.S. newspapers to highlight its use of U.S. suppliers. When McDonald's opened its first Russian restaurant, children from a local orphanage were invited to head the customer line. In Saipan, part of the Northern Marianas (a U.S. commonwealth), MNEs improved roads and local schools. Research shows that such positive corporate citizenship is a good investment that improves the MNE's bargaining power.[13]

Pressure for good citizenship can also come from outside the host country, and is particularly strong when the MNE operates under regimes with poor political records. Canadian oil firm Talisman has been accused that its operations in Sudan bring the host government revenues that are then being used to fund a civil war with the southern part of the country. To pacify the critics, Talisman funds community programs in Sudanese villages, builds hospitals, and digs watering ponds for cattle.[14]

Local Government Objectives. Host governments are primarily interested in protecting national interests, especially where "vital interests" such as national security are concerned. In Venezuela, the dependence on oil as the major foreign exchange earner means considerable government intervention in the form of taxation, government participation in the industry, and the protection of external markets and prices.[15] In the past, this has also meant opposition to FDI. Host governments have been found to discriminate against MNEs, especially during the later stages of industry competition.[16] Today, when competition for FDI is keen, host government efforts are directed at technology transfer and exports.

Increasingly, local governments are also concerned with protecting their environment from pollution, unsustainable logging, and the like. Host nations, especially (but not only) developing economies, are also concerned with MNE interference with the political process either directly or by way of introducing foreign values and lifestyles that erode the standing of current political actors and tip the balance of political forces.

The Bargaining Power of the MNE and the Host Government. When the political objectives of the MNE and the host nation diverge, their relative bargaining power will, to a significant extent, determine the outcome. When a nation offers an attractive environment that is unmatched by other locations, its bargaining power is high, especially when competition among investors is intense.[17] When investment opportunities emerged in eastern and central Europe, the Chinese government relaxed its investment requirements in order to remain an attractive investment target. When the country later became the investment target of choice among emerging markets, however, it withdrew some of the special incentives it previously offered to foreign investors. In the end, however, the outcome of the bargaining is not only the result of such advantages but also of the success of the parties in building political coalitions that will enlist support for their cause in both the host and the home country.

The bargaining power of the MNE tends to be greater when it offers a differentiated, technologically advanced product that others cannot or are unwilling to provide. Extractive industries usually provide the foreign investor with considerable leverage with both home and host government, but this advantage fast erodes once the investment has been consummated. The MNE also has a stronger bargaining position when the subsidiary is complex to operate and manage, when its volume of exports is large, and when the ratio of expatriates is high.[18]

While "traditional" MNEs operating in developing markets command substantial marketing power vis-à-vis their host governments, developing country MNEs (DMNEs) do not. DMNEs are usually not in a position to pressure host governments for concessions and favorable investment terms, although they can insist on reciprocity in host countries that are substantial investors in their home market. For small and mid-sized international firms (SMIEs), the probability of pressuring host governments is even lower, though they may build alliances and coalitions that will create such pressure. Some of the liabilities of SMIEs and DMNEs can be seen as advantages, however. Both are considered less of a menace to national sovereignty and are less likely to arouse nationalist sentiments in the host country.

Government Investment Support. (See also Chapter 3). In an era of keen competition for FDI, governments compete with each other and are willing to bargain with the MNE over the provision of investment incentives. These incentives typically are administered by a designated investment agency whose main roles are to solicit potential investors, weigh project feasibility and contribute to national goals, as well as to assure compliance with investment requirements. Incentives range from outright grants and investment allowances to subsidies for infrastructure development, preferential tax treatment (tax holidays, reduced rates, accelerated depreciation), import duties exemption, loans and loan guarantees, and interest subsidies.[19] For example, it is estimated that to entice Mercedes-Benz into Alabama, the state offered the automaker $253 million—$169,000 for every job the company promised to create.[20]

Special support is often provided to MNEs willing to invest in troubled areas, such as Northern Ireland, or in priority regions, such as the former East Germany. Domestic firms often complain that they are being discriminated against and are not provided the same support and incentives available to the foreign investor. Domestic firms may build political coalitions to counterbalance incentives granted to foreign firms or may conclude that it is better to invest as a foreign entity. This is one reason why "bogus blue-eyed" ventures, domestic firms disguised as foreign investors, are established in China and in other developing countries.

Investment incentives are more likely to be offered when competition among potential sites is intense, when the investment at stake is considered vital, and when a country perceives itself to be at a disadvantage owing to worsening economic conditions or political and social turmoil. Research conducted in the Caribbean shows that the attractiveness of various FDI incentives offered by host governments varies with market orientation and the type, size and location of the investment, its timing and the type of product involved. Import duty concessions were seen as the most desirable by exporters in that region because of the high ratio of imported components in the exported product.[21]

The MNE and Its Home Government

Despite globalization, the MNE remains firmly grounded in its host environment.[22] The state continues to charter and steer the MNE, shape its operating environment, and remains the only potent entity to conduct international affairs, including international trade and investment policies. Nor is the government role diminishing. In developed nations, the ratio of government expenditure as percentage of GDP now stands at five times World War I level. MNEs are engaged in lobbying their home governments in support of their cause, as U.S. MNEs did in the 1990s to end the trade embargo on Vietnam and lift the restrictions on investment there.

The home government plays an important role in facilitating the MNE political objectives. When Saudi Arabia was deciding whether to buy new aircraft from Boeing or Airbus, President Clinton personally called the Saudi king on behalf of Boeing. Obviously, not every deal is accorded the same treatment. The bigger the magnitude and visibility and the bigger the perceived threat to the country's MNE, the more likely are political leaders to intervene. The stated rationale for the intervention is usually to protect the national interest and preserve jobs, goals that have broad political appeal. In contrast, when French cheeses were included in the U.S. retaliatory measures in the "banana war," the president of the French Cheese Association noted, "We represent the flower of French gastronomy, but we have no political clout."[23]

While political pressure is often applied in the opening of foreign markets, it is also applied in the closure of the home market to foreign competition. In the late 1970s and 1980s, U.S. car manufacturers sought to limit Japanese imports to the United States. The media decried the "buying up of America," suggesting that the United States was becoming a low-tech platform for Japanese firms, which were keeping high value-added production at home. As a result, the U.S. government was persuaded to set "voluntary" quotas on Japanese car imports. In South Korea, activist groups pressured their government not to open its market to foreign goods, stalling international efforts to open the country's economy.

Exhibit 7–1 lists steps taken by governments to assist their firms operating in foreign markets, ranging from using diplomatic and political pressure to the linking of educational and health programs to trade issues. Exhibit 7–2 shows respondents' questions about what nations are associated with the application of such practices. In the eyes of respondents, the United States is the leader in applying political tactics to assist its firms in foreign markets.

Exhibit 7–1

Governmental means used to secure "unfair" advantage

Means Used	Percent Responding
Diplomatic or political pressure	53%
Commercial pressure/dumping/pricing	49%
Financial pressure: differential taxes, tariffs, custom barriers, subsidies	45%
Tied aid	36%
Favors/gifts	36%
Tied defence/arms deals	28%
Absence of laws/regulations/pressures on legal issues	23%
Tied scholarships/educational or healthcare programs	16%
Other means	11%
Not stated	2%

Source: Transparency International 9/26/2000. Percent responding to the question "What means do you see governments using to secure unfair business advantages for companies from their own countries?" posed by Gallup International.

Exhibit 7-2
Country rankings on helping their MNEs obtain "unfair" advantage

Country	Percent Responding	Country	Percent Responding
United States	61%	Taiwan	16%
France	34%	Singapore	13%
Japan	34%	Belgium	9%
China/Hong Kong	32%	Australia	8%
Germany	27%	Canada	8%
Italy	24%	Netherlands	8%
South Korea	23%	Sweden	8%
United Kingdom	23%	Austria	7%
Spain	17%	Switzerland	6%
Malaysia	16%	Other	18%
Country of residence of respondent			28%

Source: Transparency International 9/26/2000. Percent responding to the question "What governments do you principally associate with these practices?" posed by Gallup International.

Coalition Building and Influence Tactics

Nations and governments are not unitary entities but rather collections of individuals, political parties, interest groups, and agencies that negotiate internally as much as externally to define and achieve their objectives, and that have different agendas. Singapore, Finland, and Ireland are examples of governments with more policy consensus than the United States; Slovenia, the Philippines, and Russia have a much lower policy consensus.[24] In the United States elite groups are more favorably disposed toward trade, whereas isolationists and lower income groups tend to support mercantilism.[25] Political interests influence not only the general approach toward trade but also the treatment of specific goods and services. In the aftermath of September 11, 2001, for example, the United States expressed a willingness to abolish tariffs on the importation of cotton yarn from Pakistan and ease restrictions on bed linen from that country. It refused to do the same for textiles, fearful of

INDUSTRY BOX

EU RETALIATION AGAINST U.S. STEEL TARIFFS

When the United States established protective tariffs on its steel industry in early 2002, the European Union (EU) sought how to retaliate against the move that hurt its producers by curtailing EU exports to the United States and by diverting Asian exports from the United States to the EU. It came up with the idea of targeting products that are not only symbols of U.S. industry (e.g., Harley-Davidson motorcycles) but are also manufactured in states that are particularly important to George W. Bush's reelection prospects: Florida, Wisconsin, Pennsylvania, and West Virginia. For example, retaliatory tariffs have been put on U.S. steel from Pennsylvania and West Virginia although these two states export only a small portion of their steel production. By putting pressure on these future political battlegrounds, the EU was hoping to get the U.S. president to retreat from the tariffs that are due for a review in the fall of 2003. The practice is increasingly common, especially in trade disputes between the United States and the EU. "Counter-measures are there to leverage change of decision. You have to do that in sectors and places where you can build a coalition," said Pascal Lamy, the EU Trade Commissioner.

Source: Based on G. Winestock and N. King, "EU designs retaliation against Bush's tariffs on steel," *Wall Street Journal*, March 22, 2002, A2.

angering the House Ways and Means chairman whose congressional district includes a large textile manufacturer.[26] Political activities in the United States include constituency building, political action committee contributions, advocacy advertising, lobbying, and coalition building.[27]

The appointment of executives with political experience and contacts is evidence of the importance of political activities. For example, Boeing appointed Thomas Pickering, former Undersecretary of State for Political Affairs, as senior vice president for Political Affairs. To build political goodwill, firms channel investment into regions and industries supported by a political party or an influential constituency. Political contributions are made with a similar purpose even though they are prohibited or restricted in many nations. Coalition building often involves bringing on board local constituencies, sometimes in the form of alliance partners.

Political Risk

Political risk is the probability of disruption to an MNE's operations from political forces and events and their correlates. For instance, with the increasing separatist sentiment in the Aceh province in Indonesia, Mobil's gas field there came under guerrilla attack. Political risk is not only about political stability, it is also about a stable society, the economic and regulatory climate, policy continuity, and the likelihood of unforeseen problems for the trader and investor. The prospect of an arbitrary decision by a government (e.g., retroactive change in investment rules) and the undermining of property rights by the court system are also political risk factors.

Political risk is a problem for the foreign trader and investor, but especially for the latter, who commits resources to the host country. Political risk narrows the decision-making span of the foreign investor, in effect transferring decision-making power to the host government. It may lead the MNE to refrain from investing or to seek a high premium to compensate for the risk.

The events of September 11, 2001 drew attention to the risk of terrorism. The risk comes not only from outside elements but also from within. A study by the *Wall Street Journal* and the Heritage Foundation found a negative correlation between economic freedom and domestic terrorism: The lesser the government freedom, the higher the probability of terrorism developing in the country. Exhibit 7–3 provides the 2002 rankings on economic freedom. The rankings are useful not only in determining political risks but also in deciding effective influence tactics.

Although in general democratic regimes are considered more stable, a country does not need to be democratic to rank as a low-risk prospect. Nor is political risk the exclusive realm of developing countries. Prospects for the breakup of Canada triggered by Quebec's possible secession represent a political risk for investors who may find their investment located in a different political entity than the one they initially targeted for investment.

The Measurement of Political Risk

The inherent problem in the measurement of political risk is that the political landscape is notoriously difficult to forecast. Change may come as a result of a decision by an autocratic ruler, such as Saddam Hussein's invasion of Kuwait. It may be a political misstep; for instance, Credit Suisse First Boston Corp. was removed from a foreign underwriting team for a lucrative share offering in China after company executives hosted conferences attended by senior Taiwanese officials.[28] Political risk can also materalize as a result of a shifting power or balance. Coca-Cola partnered with the son-in-law of the president of Uzbekistan who became the president of its

Exhibit 7-3
Index of Economic Freedom, 2002

FREE		MOSTLY UNFREE		REPRESSED

FREE
1 Hong Kong
2 Singapore
3 New Zealand
4 Estonia
   Ireland
   Luxembourg
   Netherlands
   United States
9 Australia
   Chile
   United Kingdom
12 Denmark
   Switzerland
14 Finland

MOSTLY FREE
15 Bahrain
   Canada
17 Bahamas
   El Salvador
   Sweden
20 Austria
   Belgium
   Germany
23 Cyprus
   Iceland
   United Arab
   Emirates
26 Barbados
   Portugal
   Spain
29 Italy
   Lithuania

Taiwan
32 Czech Rep.
   Hungary
   Thailand
35 Japan
   Norway
   Trinidad &Tobago
38 Argentina
   South Korea
   Latvia
41 Uruguay
42 Cambodia
43 Costa Rica
   Israel
45 Armenia
   Belize
   Bolivia
   France
   Jordan
   Malta
   Panama
   Poland
53 Kuwait
   Peru
55 Greece
   Guatamaia
   Sri Lanka
58 Colombia
   Tunisia
60 Botswana
   Ivory Coast
   Jamaica
   Mali

Mexico
Mongolia
Namibia
Oman
Slovak. Rep.
South Africa
70 Philippines
   Qatar

MOSTLY UNFREE
72 Dominican Rep.
   Mauritius
   Saudi Arabia
   Uganda
76 Central
   African Rep.
   Morocco
   Mozambique
79 Algeria
   Brazil
   Djlbouti
   Gambia
   Madagascar
   Malaysia
   Paraguay
   Slovenia
   Swazlland
88 Benin
   Cape Verde
   Honduras
   Lebanon
   Nicaragua
93 Burkina Faso
   Guyana

Kenya
Senegal
97 Cameroon
   Gabon
   Macedonia
   Zambia
101 Albania
   Guinea
   Mauritania
   Pakistan
105 Indonesia
   Moldova
   Turkey
108 Bulgaria
   Croatia
   Fiji
   Georgia
   Ghana
   Lesotho
   Nepal
   Rwanda
   Tanzania
117 Ecuador
118 Azerbaijan
   Malawl
   Niger
121 China
   Egypt
   Ethiopia
   India
125 Chad
   Kazakhstan
   Kyrgyz Rep.

Nigeria
Togo
130 Venezuela
131 Bangladesh
   Romania
   Russia
134 Congo Rep.
   Yemen
136 Halti
137 Tajlkistan
   Ukraine
   Vietnam
140 Bosnia
   Equatorial
   Guinea
142 Guinea Bissau
   Suriname

REPRESSED
144 Yugoslavia
145 Burma
   Syria
147 Zimbabwe
148 Belarus
   Uzbekistan
150 Turkmenistan
151 Iran
   Laos
153 Cuba
   Libya
155 Iraq
   North Korea

Source: G. O'Driscoll, K.R. Holmes and M.A. O'Grady, 2002 Index of Economic Freedom. Washington DC: The Heritage Foundation (with the *Wall Street Journal*).

local bottling company. When the son-in-law separated from the president's daughter, the company found itself harassed by the authorities.[29]

The importance of political risk creates demand for its assessment. The various ways to measure the risk can be roughly classified into five categories: (1) qualitative approaches, (2) aggregates of expert opinions, (3) scenario approaches, (4) decision-tree methods, and (5) quantitative techniques that result in political risk indices. Many MNEs use their own customized instruments to gauge political risk; others rely on independent assessments e.g., by the Economist Intelligence Unit (EUI) or Business International (BI).

Exhibit 7-4 shows the risk of political instability according to the World Competitiveness Yearbook.

Exhibit 7–4
Risk of political instability

Ranking		
1	FINLAND	9.71
2	LUXEMBOURG	9.63
3	AUSTRALIA	9.58
4	SWITZERLAND	9.42
5	DENMARK	9.38
6	USA	9.25
7	IRELAND	9.17
8	SWEDEN	9.15
9	UNITED KINGDOM	9.04
10	SPAIN	9.00
11	NORWAY	8.97
12	CANADA	8.95
13	NETHERLANDS	8.91
14	CHILE	8.82
15	ICELAND	8.65
16	SINGAPORE	8.63
17	GERMANY	8.60
18	NEW ZEALAND	8.56
19	AUSTRIA	8.23
20	HONG KONG	8.19
21	GREECE	8.03
22	HUNGARY	7.85
23	FRANCE	7.70
24	CZECH REPUBLIC	7.56
25	MALAYSIA	7.55
26	THAILAND	7.27
27	BELGIUM	7.21
28	BRAZIL	7.20
29	SOUTH AFRICA	7.12
30	MEXICO	6.87
31	ITALY	6.58
32	ESTONIA	6.51
33	SLOVENIA	6.43
34	JAPAN	6.40
35	CHINA	6.23
36	INDIA	5.92
37	PORTUGAL	5.69
38	KOREA	5.64
39	ISRAEL	5.05
40	RUSSIA	4.81
41	TAIWAN	4.61
42	COLOMBIA	4.27
43	PHILIPPINES	4.25
44	SLOVAK REPUBLIC	4.09
45	TURKEY	3.75
46	POLAND	3.65
47	INDONESIA	2.52
48	ARGENTINA	0.89
49	VENEZUELA	0.68

Source: The World Competitiveness Yearbook 2002, Lausanne, Switzerland; IMD.

Types of Political Risk

The three types of political risk include ownership, operational, and transfer. **Ownership risk** represents a threat to the current ownership structure or to the ability of the MNE to select or shift to a given governance structure. Its most extreme form is outright expropriation, namely the forced divestment of assets as a result of a host government decision to nationalize or otherwise transfer ownership. Such divestment may or may not carry compensation, but even when it does, this rarely compensates the MNE for actual damages, especially in opportunity cost. Expropriation risk has been traditionally higher in extractive industries such as oil and mining.

Milder forms of ownership risk include pressure toward or a formal change in investment rules that force firms to reduce their stake (e.g., sharing ownership with a local firm). In the early 1970s, the Indian government established such rules that resulted in a strategic shift toward unrelated diversification and eventually to the exodus of many foreign MNEs.[30] Ownership risk has been lowered in recent years because of competition for investment dollars and because of the development of institutions such as the WTO that make such unilateral steps prohibitively difficult. Ironically, WTO membership can force divestment on the part of MNEs who hitherto had a monopoly position. A case in point is AIG in China, which remains the only foreign insurer allowed to do business in the country via a wholly-owned subsidiary. Other countries often bow to domestic pressure to keep MNEs at bay. For instance, the Polish parliament has been debating a law that would require local ownership of all pharmacies.

Operational risk includes any change to the "rules of the game" under which the foreign firm operates (e.g., new and arbitrary taxation), especially when foreign firms are singled out. Operational risk is less tangible than ownership risk but may be equally damaging should it limit strategic freedom and autonomy. For example, Amway has recently faced an effort on the part of the Japanese authorities to curb the direct selling practices which are at the core of its business model. Finally, **transfer risk** involves impediments to the transfer of production factors e.g., newly imposed capital controls. The three risk types are interrelated. For instance, if a government prohibits the placement of expatriates in key positions, this may present an operational risk compromising efficient operation and technology protection.

Political risk declined during the 1990s. According to UNCTAD, between 1986 and 1995, more than 80 countries liberalized their FDI policies. Between 1991 and 2000, 1,121 changes in FDI regimes were introduced, with more than 95 percent of those geared toward liberalization (see also Chapter 3). Host governments have been moving away from a confrontational stance to a partnership where bargaining is focused on the value-added activities of the MNE.[31] The level of risk in many nations remains substantial, however. Furthermore, due to increased global integration, MNE operations in one market are often used as leverage by political groups at home or in third countries.

Political risk also affects outward investment. Firms and individuals in countries with a high level of political risk often seek "safe haven" investment locations such as the United States as a way of protecting capital.[32] This trend is more apparent for portfolio investment than for FDI, although data for the former are notoriously unreliable.

Finally, as in other facets of business, risk is often associated with opportunities. U.S.-based AES is fueling much of its growth by acquiring utilities in global hot spots, many of them in Latin America, where its competitors are reluctant to enter or have pulled back. To do that, AES relies on cultivating close relationships with host governments and their leaders, as it recently did in Venezuela where it bought the leading utility.[33] A similar strategy was considered by Taiwan-based Grace T.H.W. Groups when seeking a semiconductor venture in mainland China, whose investors would include the son of President Jiang Zemin.[34]

Strategies for Managing Political Risk

Despite the decline in expropriation, political risk remains a vital concern for the MNE. The successful MNE is not only educated about political risk but also knows how to proactively manage it. To manage political risk, MNEs can:

- Minimize outright investment, leasing rather than buying and relying where possible on government incentives
- Sign bilateral or multilateral treaties that protect mutual investment

- Identify or create reciprocal settings where investment from the host country can be seized in case of expropriation
- Avoid high-visibility acquisitions, especially of firms or assets viewed as national icons
- Reduce exposure by utilizing host country financing
- Accelerate profit repatriation
- Develop a staggered technology transfer policy
- Source locally, reducing the host country incentive to harm the foreign firm
- Opt for strategic alliances with a local partner, reducing the foreign investor outlays and pacifying nationalist sentiment
- Utilize agencies such as the Overseas Private Investment Corporation (OPIC) which insure companies against political risk
- Build political support at home and in the host nation through lobbying, public relations, and a proactive social responsibility
- Monitor political and economic development so as to prepare, avoid, or counter intervention

Regional Level Politics

Although the national government is the most influential in the political arena, it is not the only one to do so. Regional and federated organizations are partners for dialogue with the MNE. This is especially apparent where economic integration is accompanied by political integration, as is the case in the EU (see Chapter 8).

Below the national level there are relevant political entities with whom the MNE interacts. For instance, Hong Kong, a Chinese Special Administrative Region, has its own trade and investment agreements with foreign countries that are separate from those of its national sovereign, China. We have already mentioned the incentives offered by various American states to lure foreign car manufacturers such as Mercedes-Benz, Toyota, Nissan, BMW, and Hyundai. Most states maintain trade and investment offices in foreign countries and often compete with each other on attracting FDI. In Canada, provincial governments play a substantial role in trade and investment regulation. In China, provincial governments often act as quasi-independent fiefdoms with powers often beyond the reach of the central government. In 1974, Freeport-McMoran Copper & Gold signed a land-rights agreement with the Amungme and Kamoro tribes in its Indonesian West Papua province. The recently expanded agreement established the relationships with the tribes without infringing on the firm's contract with the Indonesian government.[35]

Micro-Region Political Processes

Even municipalities play a role in international business. A conference of mayors from France, Germany, and the United States convened in Lyons, France, in April 2000, to discuss the problems and opportunities stemming from globalization. They concluded that like nations and firms, cities were now in a global competition for investment and skilled employees. According to Alain Juppe, the mayor of Bordeaux and a former French prime minister, "governments are too small to deal with the big problems and too big to deal with the small problems. Cities are now competing with each other to attract people who can choose to live where they wish, but also cooperate and establish alliances with each other."[36]

"Micro regions" (below state level) take a stronger interest in foreign investment issues since they realize that such investment is vital to their economic future and is seldom distributed evenly. Exhibit 7–5 shows European investment in the Greater Columbus, Ohio area. It is evident that the vast majority of the investment is in the urban Franklin County, while the more rural counties received very little investment.

Exhibit 7–5

European investment in the greater Columbus, Ohio area

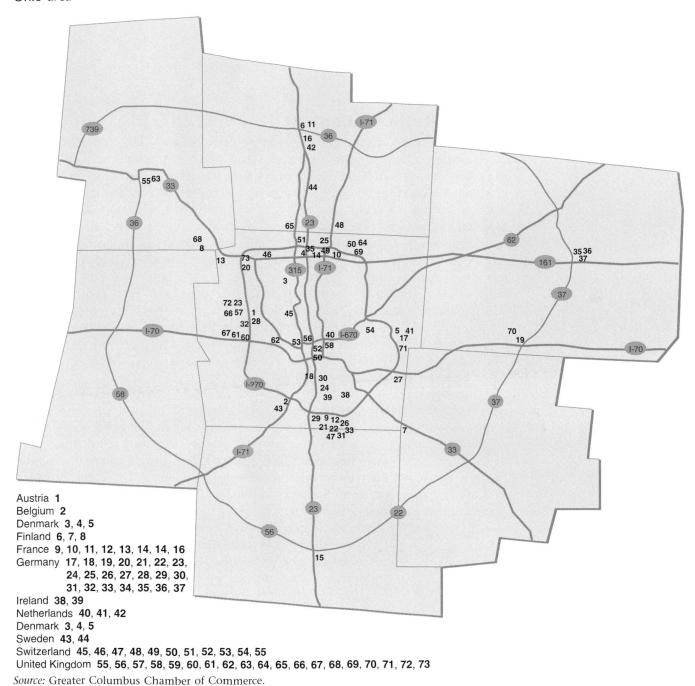

Austria **1**
Belgium **2**
Denmark **3, 4, 5**
Finland **6, 7, 8**
France **9, 10, 11, 12, 13, 14, 14, 16**
Germany **17, 18, 19, 20, 21, 22, 23,**
           24, 25, 26, 27, 28, 29, 30,
           31, 32, 33, 34, 35, 36, 37
Ireland **38, 39**
Netherlands **40, 41, 42**
Denmark **3, 4, 5**
Sweden **43, 44**
Switzerland **45, 46, 47, 48, 49, 50, 51, 52, 53, 54, 55**
United Kingdom **55, 56, 57, 58, 59, 60, 61, 62, 63, 64, 65, 66, 67, 68, 69, 70, 71, 72, 73**

Source: Greater Columbus Chamber of Commerce.

Interim Summary

1. Often viewed as a foreign implant, MNEs may be opposed by coalitions who apply a variety of political means.

2. MNEs often appoint government liaisons to senior positions. Also, they try to retain bargaining power and influence politics.

3. There are three types of political risk: Ownership, operational, and transfer. Ownership risk, while potentially the most substantial, has declined in recent years.

4. Sub-regions (e.g., states and municipalities) are increasingly involved in inward foreign investment.

THE LEGAL ENVIRONMENT

The Institutional Context

The origins of legal systems can be traced to past centuries. The United States and other former British colonies such as Australia and New Zealand, rely on a **common law** system, which originated in England. Common law is associated with an independent judiciary relying on case precedents. Most of continental Europe and Latin America use a *civil law* system that originated in the Roman Empire. **Civil law** relies almost exclusively on the legal code and is applied universally. It is therefore considered less flexible than the common law system. The implications of those differences are substantial. For instance, in common law, ownership rights are affected by actual use and are generally better protected. Common law also limits the range of events that justify noncompliance to "acts of God" such as a natural disaster. Civil law is associated with higher government intervention.

An additional type of legal system is **theocratic law,** a system that relies on religious code. Among the countries using theocratic law are Iran and Saudi Arabia, which rely on Islamic law as the basis of their legal system. Countries such as Indonesia use limited elements of Islamic law.

There are other important differences in legal systems that go beyond the common versus civil law distinction. One other fundamental difference is the independent status of the judiciary. Even in civil law systems, where the law is administered by public officials, there is clear separation of powers. In contrast, in China, "rule by man and not by law" has been a longtime tradition, and although the country has now developed the contours of a modern legal system, much of that tradition lives on. The same is true in Vietnam. Another key difference between legal systems is enforcement. In many developing nations, enforcement is often lax and inept. Canadian insurer, Manufacturers Life Insurance, has had great difficulty enforcing its ownership rights after its bankrupt Indonesian partner protested the sale of its stake. Furthermore, it was targeted by Indonesian police and was prevented from obtaining effective recourse from the Indonesian justice system.[37] (See Country Box). In the Ukraine, a small investor in a pharmaceutical factory won a legal battle to recover assets pillaged by his joint venture partner only to have the ruling overturned following pressure by the country's president, who, in a televised visit to the factory, said:

I often say . . . we must obey the law. But there is something slightly higher than the law: The country's national interest. And this means the interests of our people, not someone else's.[38]

"This is no longer a legal case, this is a political case," said the exasperated investor.

Finally, legal environments differ in the tendency to rely on the court as the primary conflict resolution mechanism. This is clearly the case in the United States, which is considered one

" 'Season's Greetings' looks O.K. to me. Let's run it by the legal department."

of the most litigious societies in the world. Japan, in contrast, is a "non-contractual" society, relying more on such mechanisms as third-party mediation, to resolve conflicts. Unlike the United States, in Japan a signed contract reflects mostly general understanding that is subject to change should circumstances so demand.

Exhibit 7–6 shows country rankings on the fair administration of justice, based on survey results, according to the *World Competitiveness Yearbook*. At the bottom of the list you will find mostly developing and emerging economies.

Legal Jurisdiction

When a Concorde crashed outside Paris, victims' families filed suit in the United States because the plane, while co-produced in France and the United Kingdom and flown by national carrier Air France with mostly German passengers on board, was bound for New York, and because a Continental Airlines jet was implicated in the investigation. The more generous awards meted by U.S. courts were an incentive, but it is the nature of the service that provided the opportunity to argue for American jurisdiction in an otherwise German and French affair.

Legal jurisdiction is the legal authority under which a legal case can be adjudicated. It is often difficult to determine legal jurisdiction in international business. The MNE is subject to the laws of both its home and host countries and, less often, to the laws of a third country. These laws may be in conflict—compliance with one legal jurisdiction could invoke noncompliance or violation of the other. For instance, as noted in the opening case, compliance with the Arab boycott of Israeli products is a violation of U.S. law. As Chapter 18 illustrates, jurisdictional issues come to the fore even more prominently in electronic trade, where it is increasingly difficult to determine the origin of manufacturing, distribution, and consumption.

Exhibit 7–6
Fair administration of justice

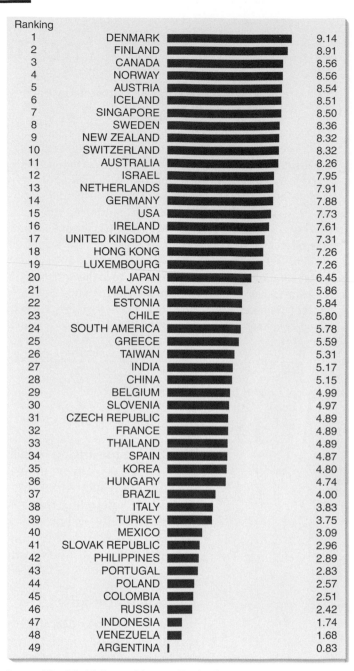

Ranking		
1	DENMARK	9.14
2	FINLAND	8.91
3	CANADA	8.56
4	NORWAY	8.56
5	AUSTRIA	8.54
6	ICELAND	8.51
7	SINGAPORE	8.50
8	SWEDEN	8.36
9	NEW ZEALAND	8.32
10	SWITZERLAND	8.32
11	AUSTRALIA	8.26
12	ISRAEL	7.95
13	NETHERLANDS	7.91
14	GERMANY	7.88
15	USA	7.73
16	IRELAND	7.61
17	UNITED KINGDOM	7.31
18	HONG KONG	7.26
19	LUXEMBOURG	7.26
20	JAPAN	6.45
21	MALAYSIA	5.86
22	ESTONIA	5.84
23	CHILE	5.80
24	SOUTH AMERICA	5.78
25	GREECE	5.59
26	TAIWAN	5.31
27	INDIA	5.17
28	CHINA	5.15
29	BELGIUM	4.99
30	SLOVENIA	4.97
31	CZECH REPUBLIC	4.89
32	FRANCE	4.89
33	THAILAND	4.89
34	SPAIN	4.87
35	KOREA	4.80
36	HUNGARY	4.74
37	BRAZIL	4.00
38	ITALY	3.83
39	TURKEY	3.75
40	MEXICO	3.09
41	SLOVAK REPUBLIC	2.96
42	PHILIPPINES	2.89
43	PORTUGAL	2.83
44	POLAND	2.57
45	COLOMBIA	2.51
46	RUSSIA	2.42
47	INDONESIA	1.74
48	VENEZUELA	1.68
49	ARGENTINA	0.83

Source: The World Competitiveness Yearbook 2002, Lausanne, Switzerland; IMD.

Jurisdictional Levels

A number of jurisdictional levels govern MNE operations. At the international level, a firm is subject to international law and to a rapidly internationalizing regulatory system. At the regional-global level, a firm is subject to the laws and regulations of a regional entity, such as the EU, or of a trade framework (e.g., ASEAN). The more integrated the region, the more important are the laws enacted at that level (see Chapter 8). The national level, whether in its home, host country, and sometimes third country, remains the most important and relevant for the MNE. Which national jurisdiction is in force is often difficult to determine, however.

Recently, the WTO has become more proactive in deciding matters of jurisdiction and contradictory laws. For instance, it has ruled that a U.S. law denying protection to trademarks held by businesses confiscated in Cuba contradicted trade rules, thereby allowing Pernod Ricard to sue a U.S. firm over the rights to Havana Club rum.[39]

International Jurisdiction. Because international law relies on customs and treaties, it is rarely enforced. The International Court of Justice in The Hague (Netherlands) is a UN institution that has no jurisdiction in most cases unless the governments involved agree to submit the matter to the court (this is beginning to change, however, in regard to war-related violations). Parties to international business contracts often agree in advance to an arbitration authority, such as the International Court of Arbitration, the Inter-American Commercial Arbitration Commission, or the Canadian-American Commercial Arbitration Commission, each specializing in arbitrating between firms from their region and U.S. companies. Parties can also choose a body such as the International Center for Settlement of Investment Disputes, which specializes in FDI.

Recent years saw a remarkable globalization of international business regulation, evolving around a number of key principles, chief among them transparency.[40] The United States and the EU have been the most active supporters of the globalization of regulation, while other countries and firms have been active in niche areas. For instance, Lloyd's of London has been a major driving force behind the globalization of marine insurance. International organizations also play a major role in the globalization of regulation. Much of the global regulatory work takes place in technical committees of such organizations as the WTO (see Chapter 8).

In the aircraft industry, the United States has often taken the regulatory lead. National regulators typically await certification by the U.S. Federal Aviation Administration (FAA) before sending in their teams to Boeing's Seattle facilities largely to rubber-stamp that decision. Similarly, although inspection orders issued by the FAA are binding only for U.S. carriers and, in some instances, for aircraft flying to the United States, they are often followed by other carriers wishing to uphold safety and sustain their reputation. Similarly, while approval by the Federal Drug Administration (FDA) is required for any drug sold in the United States, authorities in many other countries require such approval as an indication of product safety and effectiveness.[41]

Regional Jurisdiction

Increasingly, regional bodies are taking responsibility for the enactment and enforcement of laws. At times, considerable uncertainty prevails as to whether regional jurisdiction supersedes national jurisdiction. For example, the European Court of Justice ruled that no EU country could limit trade in a product imported into the EU. In this case, the court found that French rules prohibiting such trade were incompatible with European laws.[42]

National Jurisdiction

The MNE must comply with both domestic jurisdiction at home and foreign jurisdiction abroad; many of its foreign operations fall under domestic jurisdiction as well. One example is the Foreign Corrupt Practices Act that holds U.S. MNEs responsible for bribery and related activities in their foreign operations (see Chapter 19). Recently, activist groups in the United States resurrected a 1789 law enacted to protect foreigners from sea pirates to prosecute U.S.-based MNEs accused of unethical business practices. In one case, 18 U.S.-based retailers and garment manufacturers were sued on behalf of 50,000 garment workers in Saipan.[43] Such alien-tort precedents may mean that in the future, MNEs will become more vulnerable to suits filed at home concerning their foreign operations.

Legal Issues of Interest to the MNE

Legal issues that are of particular concern to the MNE include the protection of corporate and individual property, contract law (the United Nations Convention on Contracts for the International Sale of Goods sets standards for the formulation and enforcement of contracts among its signatories), as well as restriction on foreign asset ownership. For instance, the United States does not permit foreign entities to own a majority-share in a U.S. airline, in case its aircraft are needed for emergency deployment of American troops. This rule was used to block British Airways' attempt to acquire a controlling stake in US Air, a U.S. carrier (later renamed US Airways). In a related case, the United States ordered an immediate halt to the operations of Discovery Airlines, a Hawaii-based inter-island carrier, when it was discovered that the airline owner, while U.S. registered, was a Japanese corporation. On similar grounds, the United States also does not permit foreigners to own television and radio stations. Rupert Murdoch, an Australian citizen and owner of News Corporation (which operates the Fox television network), has overcome the restriction by becoming a naturalized American citizen.

In the following pages, a number of other key legal issues are discussed. In addition, labor laws are discussed in Chapter 17 and taxation law is referred to in Chapter 9.

Rule of Origin Laws

Knowing **product origin** is important for determining duties or for measuring local content, a frequent requirement in trade and FDI (see also Chapters 2, 3, and 16). Local content is an especially important issue in developing economies. For instance, India requires substantial local content for cars produced domestically by foreign manufacturers.

Determining product origin is increasingly complex. The U.S. Federal Trade Commission determined that for a product to be labeled "Made in the USA," it must be "all or virtually all" made in the United States and should contain "no—or negligible—foreign content"; however, it is unclear what "negligible" means. The EU, on its part, uses 60 percent local value as a threshold.

Competition Laws

(a) Antitrust Legislation and Enforcement

U.S. antitrust legislation is among the most advanced and a model emulated by several countries. For example, Japan's antitrust legislation dates back to the Allied occupation and its American heritage is evident. In contrast to the United States, however, antitrust laws are seldom enforced in Japan. The United States poses the most stringent transparency requirements and is willing to enforce its authority abroad. For instance, the Securities and Exchange Commission filed a suit alleging fraud on the part of German-based, U.S. traded E.On for failing to disclose merger intentions.[44] Chrysler's biggest shareholder sued DaimlerChrysler for allegedly concealing its takeover of Chrysler as a "merger of equals." Nevertheless, when asked whether competition laws prevented unfair competition in their country, respondents from Finland, the Netherlands, Germany, and Norway gave their legal systems a better grade than the United States, as did respondents in 15 other countries. Indonesia, Argentina, and Russia ranked lowest.[45]

In recent years, the European Commission has become an aggressive enforcer of antitrust legislation. The commission derailed the purchase of a French beverage company by Coca-Cola on the grounds that it would give the Atlanta-based company a monopoly position in the European market. The commission is also investigating Coca-Cola's sales and distribution practices following allegations by its U.S. archrival PepsiCo that Coca-Cola is paying retail outlets to refrain from stocking Pepsi's products. The commission recently rejected the acquisition of Honeywell by General Electric, both U.S. companies, arguing that it would lower competition in the European aviation market.

Antitrust and takeovers are one area where legal provisions vary significantly, even within the EU. Take the case of France Telecom, which recently purchased a 54 percent stake in Equant NV. Because Equant was incorporated in the Netherlands, France Telecom did not have to make the same or better offer to all shareholders, as it would have to do if the acquired firm was located in the United Kingdom or Germany.[46]

The United States has recently undertaken a major effort to adopt a global approach to antitrust regulation and enforcement. It proposed the establishment of an independent international agency to oversee mergers and acquisitions, whose increasingly global scope involves multiple jurisdictions. The EU endorses the idea but would like to see such an agency operate within the WTO.[47]

(b) Subsidies

EU rules prohibit government subsidies that give an unfair edge to a firm from one country over another. The commission tried (but failed) to prevent the French government from providing a hefty subsidy to Air France, the then ailing national French carrier. The commission seems less concerned however with infringements detrimental to non-EU firms. Boeing contends that Airbus, a European consortium, holds an unfair advantage because it has been receiving subsidies from the German, French, Spanish, and British governments of its partner firms. Airbus counters that the award of military contracts to Boeing by the U.S. government amounts to a subsidy because it permits the company to use research and development and manufacturing techniques developed for the military in their civilian aircraft production (see also Chapter 2).

Marketing and Distribution Laws

National laws determine allowable practices in distribution, advertising, and promotion. For instance, TV cigarette advertising is prohibited in many countries. Norway does not permit two-for-one promotions. In France, a manufacturer cannot offer a product it does not manufacture as an inducement to buy one of its products. In Germany, comparative advertising is prohibited; in China, it is prohibited if the comparison reflects negatively on the other product.

Of special interest to MNEs, especially in the EU, is a recent ruling by the European court in favor of San Francisco-based Levi Strauss & Co. The court ruled against British retailer Tesco, which imported Levi's jeans from outside the EU, where they are cheaper, and undercut the prices charged by Levi Strauss in the EU (see Chapter 16).[48] The decision, which has yet to be enforced, is key to the strategy of MNEs, which often position their brands differently in different locations.

Product Liability Laws

Product liability laws are stringent in the United States and the EU and many other developed countries, but are lax or not enforceable in many developing economies. In Japan, product liability cases are rarely brought to court, partly because it is more difficult to prove negligence. When a case is brought to court outside the United States, restitution rarely includes the punitive damages that are common in the

United States and can increase an award manifold. The Bridgestone/Firestone controversy revealed just how much the United States and Japan differed on product liability enforcement. Where the United States had 47 people in the National Highway Traffic Safety administration working on tire issues, Japan had only 2, and they lacked authority to investigate and press for recalls.[49]

Many foreign countries accept U.S. certification of product safety as a substitute for their own, making it easier for U.S. firms to export their products. Some countries (e.g., Japan) often do not accept U.S. product certification however, making it necessary for the MNE to do costly testing and product adaptation. To the MNE, divergence in the rigor and enforcement of product liability legislation presents a temptation to reduce standards and a possible ethical dilemma in the case of safety standards, such as the use of fire-retardant material.

The World Competitiveness Yearbook ranks the United States at the bottom, with only Russia and Korea ranked lower in terms of restriction on business represented by product liability laws.[50] Apparently, the stringent U.S. system is seen as much of a handicap as the lack of such a system in Russia. In addition, U.S. product liability law makes a distinction between domestic and foreign markets. For instance, as the recent Firestone/Ford controversy has shown, the U.S. laws do not cover overseas recall, preventing regulatory agencies from analyzing data of potential interest to U.S. consumers.

Treaties

Treaties are agreements signed by two (bilateral) or more (multilateral) nations. In the United States, treaties require senate approval but **executive agreements** do not. A multilateral treaty that is ratified by many countries with a joint interest in the issue at hand is called a **law-making treaty.** Some of the international institutions described in Chapters 8, 17, and elsewhere, such as the International Labor Office (ILO), have their origins in multilateral treaties. **Treaties of Friendship, Commerce and Navigation (FCN)** provide firms from the signatory countries with the same rights and privileges enjoyed by domestic businesses in the other country. Many of those treaties contain a **Most Favored Nation (MFN)** clause that entitles the signatory state to a treatment as favorable as that provided to other countries (see Chapter 8). The UN Convention on the Recognition and Enforcement of Foreign Arbitration Awards facilitates the enforcement of arbitration rulings. When a judgment is issued and not performed, the plaintiff can pursue a court judgment in a foreign or domestic court, although an award by the latter may have little impact unless the company in question has substantial assets in the home country that can be seized.

Other treaties of importance include those involving the protection of intellectual property rights, for example, the Paris Convention for the Protection of Intellectual Property, the Berne Convention, the Madrid Trademark Convention, the Universal Copyright Convention, and the Geneva Phonograph Convention. The Berne Convention for the Protection of Literary and Artistic Work automatically extends protection of a copyright holder in one signatory country to all others, so that the copyright needs to be registered in only one office of a signatory country. For work done on or after January 1, 1987, protection is typically extended for up to 50 years after the death of the author. (this may be extended to 70 years in the future). The Paris Convention for the Protection of Industrial Property recognizes the use of a trademark in one signatory country as a substitute for its use in another signatory country. For instance, because both the United States and Canada are signatories to the Convention, a Canadian firm that has used a trademark in Canada will be granted the use of the same trademark in the United States without having to show prior use of this trademark in the U.S. One of the obstacles for a smaller firm, especially one that lacks substantial resources, is that trademark information is often available only in the native language.

Patent Laws

Patent registration is nationality based—a patent issued in the United States does not provide protection from infringement in other countries. Separate patent applications must be made in each country, a costly and time-consuming investment. Most patent systems outside the United States operate on a "first to file" rather than a "first to invent" principle which underlies U.S. patent laws. A **first to invent** system grants patent protection to the person, or entity, who first invented the technology or the product. A **first to file** principle means that the first to file a patent in a given country is awarded the patent without the need to prove he/she has been the inventor. Some countries, notably Japan, require such detailed disclosure as part of the application process that the technology may be compromised. Finally, patents are granted for a limited number of years, which varies from one country to another, providing "arbitrage" opportunities.

Two international treaties govern patent protection. The first is the Paris Convention for the Protection of Industrial Property, which has been ratified by many countries but not by some Newly Industrialized Economies (NIEs) that are among the main violators of such rights. The Convention guarantees equal treatment of applicants from member countries. It sets a one-year grace period from the time of application in one country during which the filer enjoys priority in registering the patent in other signatory countries. It also prevents automatic expiry of patent in all member countries when a patent has expired in one. The second international treaty governing patent protection is the Patent Cooperation Treaty, which permits a one-stop application for patents in all signatory countries.

Interim Summary

1. Legal systems in different countries vary in their underlying principle (common, civil, or theocratic) as well as in independence, transparency and enforcement.

2. The nation remains the most potent level for legal jurisdiction, although the regional and international levels have made strides in recent years.

3. MNEs study, adapt, and leverage national variations in competition, product liability, marketing, and rule-of-origin laws, among others.

CHAPTER SUMMARY

1. The political environment in both the home and host countries influences international trade and investment in multiple ways.

2. The institutional context is an imprint of history and political relations that represents both a constraint and an advantage for MNE operations in a given market.

3. Managing the relationship with the home and host governments is probably the most important political challenge for the MNE.

4. Political risk is the probability of disruption to MNE operations; however the MNE has numerous strategies at its disposal to reduce its effects.

5. The type of legal system used in a country, i.e. common, civil, or theocratic, determines, for instance, the protections available to MNE's assets.

6. Jurisdictional issues are more complex in the context of international business than in domestic business. MNEs often face conflicting demands from overlapping jurisdictions but can also manipulate jurisdictions in a bid to further their interests.

7. Among the main legal issues in international business are rule of origin, competition, marketing and distribution, product liability, treaties, and patent laws.

CHAPTER NOTES

[1] W. G. Astley and P. S. Sachdeva, Structural sources of inter-organizational power: A theoretical synthesis. *Academy of Management Review*, 9, 1984 104–113.

[2] J. J. Boddewyn and T. L. Brewer, "International business political behavior: New theoretical directions," *Academy of Management Review*, 1994, 19, 119–143.

[3] J. J. Boddewyn and T. L. Brewer, "International business political behavior: New theoretical directions," *Academy of Management Review*, 1994, 119–143.

[4] J. J. Boddewyn, "Political aspects of MNE theory," *Journal of International Business Studies*, Fall 1988, 341–363.

[5] S. B. Tallman, "Home country political risk and foreign direct investment in the United States," *Journal of International Business Studies*, Summer 1988.

[6] H. Keinon, "Israel fighting EU on duty-free products," *The Jerusalem Post Internet Edition*, November 14, 2001.

[7] American Enterprise Institute. 2001 (press release).

[8] E. D. Mansfield, J. C. Pevehouse, and D. H. Bearce, "Preferential trading arrangements and military disputes," *Security Studies*, 9, January 2, 2000.

[9] T. L. Brewer, "Government policies, market imperfections, and foreign direct investment," *Journal of International Business Studies*, 1, 1993, 101–120.

[10] A. Hillman and G. Keim, "International variation in the business-government interface," *Academy of Management Review*, January 1995.

[11] T. L. Brewer, "An issue area approach to the analysis of MNE-Government relations," *Journal of International Business Studies*, 2, 1998, pp. 295–309.

[12] J. N. Behrman, J. J. Boddewyn, and A. Kapoor, *International Business—Government Communications*. MA: Lexington Books, 1975.

[13] W. C. Kim, "The effects of competition and corporate social responsiveness on multinational bargaining power," *Strategic Management Journal*, 9, 1988, 289–295.

[14] T. Carlisle, "For Canadian firm, an African albatross," *Wall Street Journal*, August 17, 2000, A19.

[15] M. V. Makhija, "Government intervention in the Venezuelan petroleum industry: An empirical investigation of political risk," *Journal of International Business Studies*, 3, 1993, 531–555.

[16] K. W. Chan, "Industry competition, corporate variables, and host government," *Management International Review*, 1988.

[17] W. C. Kim, "Industry competition, corporate variables, and host government intervention in developing nations," *Management International Review*, 28, 2, 1988.

[18] N. Fagre and L. T. Wells, "Bargaining power of multinationals and host governments," *Journal of International Business Studies*, Fall 1982, 9–23; T. A. Poynter, "Government intervention in less developed countries: The experience of multinational companies," *Journal of International Business Studies*, Spring/Summer 1982, 9–25.

[19] R. Mudambi, "Multinational investment attraction: principal-agent considerations," *International Journal of Economics and Business*, February 1999.

[20] R. Brooks, How big incentives won Alabama a piece of the auto industry, *Wall Street Journal*, April 3, 2002, A1.

[21] R. J. Rolfe, D. A. Ricks, M. M. Pointer, and M. McCarthy, "Determinants of FDI incentive preferences of MNEs," *Journal of International Business Studies*, 3, 1993, 335–355.

[22] P. N. Doremus, W. W. Keller, L. W. Pauly, and S. Reich, *The Myth of the Global Corporation*. Princeton, NJ: Princeton University Press, 1998.

[23] G. Winestock, "Why US trade sanctions don't faze Europe," *Wall Street Journal*, September. 8, 2000, A15.

[24] The World Competitiveness Yearbook 2000, Lausanne, Switzerland: International Institute of Management Development (IMD).

[25] R. K. Herrmann, P. E. Tetlock, and M. N. Diascro, How Americans think about trade: Combining ideas about politics and economics. Working paper, The Mershon Center, Ohio State University.

[26] H. Cooperm and G. Winestock, "Domestic interests limit U.S., EU bargaining at WTO," *Wall Street Journal*, November 12, 2001, A24.

[27] G. D. Keim and C. P. Zeithaml, "Corporate political strategy and legislative decision making: a review and contingency approach," *Academy of Management Review*, 11, 4, 1986, 828–843.

[28] "CSFB pays a steep price for offending Beijing," *Wall Street Journal*, August 31, 2001, A4.

[29] S. LeVine, and B. McKay, "Coke finds mixing marriage and business is tricky in Tashkent," *Wall Street Journal*, August 21, 2001, A1.

[30] Y. L. Doz, "How MNEs cope with host government intervention," *Harvard Business Review*, March–April 1980, 149–157.

[31] J. H. Dunning, "An overview of relations with national governments. New political economy," Abingdon, July 1998.

[32] S. B. Tallman, "Home country political risk and foreign direct investment in the United States," *Journal of International Business Studies*, Summer 1988.

[33] P. Druckerman, "How to project power around the world," *Wall Street Journal*, November 13, 2000, A23.

[34] R. Flannery, "Chip plant venture discussed by firms in China, Taiwan," *Wall Street Journal*, August 21, 2000, A13.

[35] C. Cummins, "Freeport signs accord with Indonesian tribes," *Wall Street Journal*, August 21, 2000, A10.

[36] "Mayors not stopping at city limits," *International Herald Tribune*, April 8–9, 2000, p. 1.

[37] T. Mapes, "Manufacturers Life learns Indonesian hardball," *Wall Street Journal*, December 11, 2000, A32.; company press releases.

[38] T. Warner, "Lessons for foreign investors in Ukraine," *Wall Street Journal*, August 16, 2000, A18.

[39] "WTO panel says U.S. trademark law violates trade rules," *Wall Street Journal*, August 7, 2001, A11.

[40] J. Braithwaite and P. Drahos, *Global Business Regulation*. Cambridge, UK: Cambridge University Press, 2000.

[41] J. Braithwaite and P. Drahos, *Global Business Regulation*. Cambridge, UK: Cambridge University Press, 2000.

[42] "Trade ban fails trademark test," *Financial Times*, March 25, 1997.

[43] "Go global, sue local," *The Economist*, August 14, 1999, p. 54.

[44] V. Fuhrmans, "Foreign firms trading in U.S. get a warning on deception," *Wall Street Journal*, September 29, 2000, A12.

[45] The World Competitiveness Yearbook 2000, Lausanne, Switzerland: International Institute of Management Development (IMD), p. 418.

[46] A. Raghavan, "Netherlands remains cool to investors' concerns," *Wall Street Journal*, December 22, 2000, C1.

[47] B. Mitchener, "U.S. endorses a global approach to antitrust," *Wall Street Journal*, September 15, 2000, A15.

[48] *The Plain Dealer*, November 21, 2001, C1.

[49] P. Dvorak and T. Zaun, "To grasp the tire case, pay a visit to Mr. Seki, a very mild regulator," *Wall Street Journal*, September 8, 2000, A1.

[50] The World Competitiveness Yearbook 2000, Lausanne, Switzerland: International Institute of Management Development (IMD), p. 416.

PART THREE

Global Markets and Institutions

International Economic Integration and Institutions

DO YOU KNOW

1. Why have world markets become more integrated today? How has this integration taken place? Why, for example, did the U.S. government push hard to form NAFTA with Canada and Mexico?

2. What roles do the WTO, the World Bank, and the IMF play in the world economy? Are they "clubs" of rich nations? If not, why did thousands of people in Seattle protest against the WTO meeting?

3. Why do people debate whether regional blocs (e.g., the European Union or MERCOSUR) are compatible with globalization? If you are an export manager in an Australian company, would you like to see the advent of more blocs in other regions?

4. How should MNEs strategically respond to regional integration? Why, for example, have Siemens and Nokia proactively diversified their geographical presence throughout Europe since 1992, while Hitachi and Toshiba have substituted FDI in Europe for export to Europe?

OPENING CASE 3M's Response to European Market Integration

 M, a U.S. supplier of branded industrial and consumer products, derives about one quarter of its total revenues from its European operations. 3M integrated its Europe-wide production network in the early 1980s, specializing each plant to manufacture certain products for the entire European market. Even before the European Union was announced, the company had already integrated its upstream activities (e.g., outsourcing, supply base, and inbound logistics) to attain economies of production scale on a regional level. However, its downstream activities—marketing, sales, distribution, and after-sale service remained fragmented, with local sales forces and advertising geared toward a national, rather than a regional (European), market. By removing many costly barriers to cross-border flows of goods, information, capital, and services (such as advertising and after-sale support), the harmonized market program in Europe makes it possible for 3M to achieve scale economies not just in production but in customer-related activities as well. 3M took advantage of this development by consolidating the company's downstream activities within Europe. The manager of marketing communications at 3M Europe calls the company's new marketing approach "Pan-European communication," in which marketing and selling expenses are spread over a regional customer base, creating economies of scale in advertising and distribution. Part of the strategy involves creating Euro-brands and uniform products and services whose brand image, packaging, attributes, and advertising are standardized throughout Europe. The reason why 3M is able to pursue such a strategy is that it sells relatively standardized products. Moreover, many of 3M's products enjoy high brand-name recognition. Substantial competitive advantages can accrue to the market leaders in this type of market segment—through significant economies of scale—after a large share of the market has been captured. 3M is in a position to take advantage of globalizing its operations—selling a single, standardized product to global markets—thereby maximizing profitability through worldwide economies of scale. ■

INTERNATIONAL ECONOMIC INTEGRATION

The preceding case suggests that MNEs are facing a new landscape in the international market: increasing economic integration among countries. International managers must understand the influence of such integration on their worldwide operations and, more importantly, strategically respond to this integration as 3M did. International economic relations are governed by a variety of institutions and a complex web of principles, most of which have been established by treaties and agreements signed since World War II. These institutions (e.g., the International Monetary Fund and the World Bank), treaties or agreements (e.g., the General Agreement on Tariff and Trade, or GATT, and the International Multifiber Agreement) have helped boost global economic integration and erase barriers to free trade, investment, and services among nations. Meanwhile, many regions or sub-regions, from Europe and North America to Latin America and the Caribbean, have established harmonized blocs within their respective territories. Intra-regional trade and investments significantly increase as a result of reduction or elimination of various trade barriers. While MNEs have to realign international expansion strategies with increasingly integrated environments, they themselves are also a critical force steering international economic integration. MNEs are more committed today to intra-organizational trade and global vertical integration. This intra-MNE activity heightens cross-border and inter-regional flows of products, services, capital, technology, and human resources. Consequently, the world is entering a new era of economic integration which is simultaneously altering global political and social systems. This integration is characterized by high levels of both globalization and regionalization.

Economic integration is concerned with the removal of trade barriers or impediments between at least two participating nations and the establishment of cooperation and coordination between them. Economic integration helps steer the world towards globalization. As explained in Chapter 1, **globalization** refers to the growing economic interdependencies of countries worldwide through the increasing volume and variety of cross-border transactions in goods and services and of international capital flows, as well as through the rapid and widespread diffusion of technology and information. The following forms of economic integration are often implemented:

1. **Free trade area** involves country combination, where the member nations remove all trade impediments among themselves but retain their freedom concerning their policy making vis-à-vis non-member countries. The Latin American Free Trade Area, or LAFTA, and the North American Free Trade Agreement, or NAFTA are examples of this form.

2. **Customs union** is similar to a free trade area except that member nations must conduct and pursue common external commercial relations such as common tariff policies on imports from non-member nations. The Central American Common Market (CACM) and the Caribbean Community and Common Market (CARICOM) are examples of this form.

3. **Common market** is a particular customs union that allows not only free trade of products and services but also free mobility of production factors (capital,

labor, technology) across national member borders. The Southern Common Market Treaty (MERCOSUR) is an example of this form.

4. **Economic union** is a particular common market that involves unification of monetary and fiscal policies. Participants introduce a central authority to exercise control over these matters so that member nations virtually become an enlarged single "country" in an economic sense.

5. **Political union** requires the participating nations to become literally one nation in both an economic and political sense. This union involves the establishment of a common parliament and other political institutions.

Along the above sequence from 1 to 5, the degree of economic integration increases. One form may shift to another over time if all the participating nations agree. For example, the European Union, or EU, started as a common market and shifted over the years to an economic union and now to a partial political union (e.g., citizens vote for both national and European parliaments).

The above forms reflect economic integration between or among nations within a region. Global economic integration also occurs through **multilateral cooperation** in which participating nations are bound by rules, principles, or responsibilities stipulated in commonly agreed agreements. Unlike the preceding five forms that all lead to regional economic integration, multilateral agreements are largely used to promote worldwide economic exchanges. They may be designed to govern either general trade, service, and investments (e.g., the World Trade Organization), capital flows and financial market stability (e.g., the World Bank and the International Monetary Fund), or specific areas of trade such as dealing with particular commodities (e.g., the International Coffee Agreement).

Economic integration has the potential to generate economic gains for participating nations. Efficiency in production may be enhanced by increased specialization in accordance with the law of comparative advantage.[1] The increased size of the market improves economies of scale, which in turn elevates production levels. Further, the collective bargaining power of member nations is increased vis-à-vis non-participating nations. This power may lead to better terms of trade, that is, lower prices on imports from the non-participating countries and higher prices on products exported to those countries.[2] It should be noted, however, that these gains are not guaranteed, nor will each member country benefit equally from integration. The unification of monetary and fiscal policies, for instance, may exert a different impact on participating countries that experience different macroeconomic conditions and varying levels of economic growth. Free mobility of production factors such as labor and capital may create different pressures on employment levels, inflation rates, income distribution, or trade balance for nations that are in different economic stages or have a varying dependence on the goods and services of other nations. Although there are legitimate reasons for possible economic gains from integration, integration in and of itself is not a panacea to cure all economic ills.

International economic integration is propelled by three levels of cooperation: *global, regional,* and *commodity.* Global-level cooperation occurs mainly through international economic agreements or organizations (e.g., WTO); regional-level cooperation proceeds through common markets or unions (e.g., NAFTA); and commodity-level cooperation proceeds through multilateral commodity cartels or agreements (e.g., OPEC). To international managers, it is important not only to understand how economic integration impacts their international expansion but, more importantly, to realign their resources and strategies to cope with increasingly borderless regions. Exhibit 8–1 lists these issues which are described in detail in the following sections.

Exhibit 8–1
Forces stimulating
international economic
integration

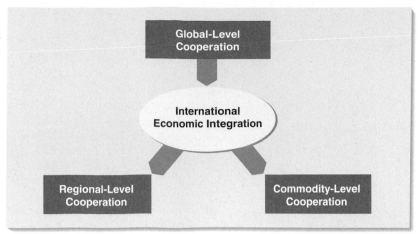

Interim Summary

1. World markets are more integrated today because of (a) the formation of regional blocs such as the European Union and NAFTA; (b) the contribution of international economic organizations such as the WTO, the IMF, and the World Bank; and (c) increased intra-organizational investments, trade, and production undertaken by MNEs.

2. International economic integration takes several forms, including free trade area, customs union, common market, economic union, political union, and multilateral cooperation. Economic integration occurs at three levels including global, regional, and commodity.

3. Economic integration is likely to generate economic gains for participating nations. However, these gains are not necessarily equally distributed to all participating nations, nor will every individual or organization within a participating nation be equally impacted by integration.

GLOBAL-LEVEL COOPERATION AMONG NATIONS
The World Trade Organization (WTO), the World Bank, and the International Monetary Fund (IMF) are the three fundamental institutions affecting the global-level cooperation of nations. While the World Bank and IMF serve as the institutional foundation of the international monetary and financial system, the WTO represents the institutional foundation of the international trade system.

The World Trade Organization (WTO)

Background and Structure

The **World Trade Organization** (WTO) is a multilateral trade organization aimed at international trade liberalization. It came into being on January 1, 1995, as the successor to the General Agreement on Tariffs and Trade (GATT), which was established in the wake of World War II. GATT was the result of the first round of tariff negotiations at the 1947 Geneva conference on the proposed International Trade

Exhibit 8-2

Multilateral negotiations under GATT

Round	Year	No. of Members	Average Tariff Cut (%)
Geneva Round	1947	23	35
Annecy Round	1949	13	na
Torguay Round	1950–51	38	25
Geneva Round	1955–56	26	na
Dillon Round	1961–62	45	na
Kennedy Round	1963–67	62	35
Tokyo Round	1973–79	99	33
Uruguay Round	1986–94	117	36

Note: In WTO's ministerial meeting in November 2001, some nations proposed a new round of negotiations. Other nations objected and asked that past commitments be honored by all members before holding new talks.

Organization (ITO). GATT evolved through periodic rounds of multilateral negotiations on tariff cuts and non-tariff reductions. Exhibit 8–2 summarizes these negotiations.

Prior to the *Kennedy Round,* early negotiations dealt primarily with reducing tariffs. These tariff cuts facilitated postwar trade liberalization, pushing average trade growth to 8.1 percent per year. By the end of the *Tokyo Round* in 1979, the need to confront the increasing use of non-tariff barriers, particularly by developed countries, led to the adoption of a number of codes dealing with specific practices. The *Uruguay Round* sought to broaden the scope of the GATT and reintroduced the idea of a comprehensive international trade organization to coordinate international economic activities including those involving a large number of developing countries.

Taking effect in 1995, the Uruguay Round agreement specified several liberalization measures that affected the opportunities and threats for international companies. First, members agreed to slash domestic agricultural price supports by 20 percent and export subsidies by 36 percent. These subsidy reductions have benefited major food exporters such as Australia, Canada, New Zealand, Thailand, and the United States. Second, the Uruguay Round instituted several principles concerning trade in services. For instance, government controls on services trade should be administered in a non-discriminatory manner. Third, the Uruguay Round agreement substantially strengthened the protection of intellectual property rights which include patents, copyrights, trademarks, brand names, and expertise.

As successor to the GATT, the WTO's main objective is the establishment of trade policy rules that help international trade expand and raise living standards. These rules foster non-discrimination, transparency, and predictability in the conduct of trade policy. The WTO pursues these objectives by:

- Administering trade agreements
- Acting as a forum for trade negotiations
- Settling trade disputes
- Reviewing national trade policies
- Assisting developing countries on trade policy issues, through technical assistance and training programs
- Cooperating with other international organizations

The WTO had 144 members as of January 1, 2002, accounting for about 95 percent of world trade. About 30 applicants are negotiating to become members. Russia is not yet a member of the WTO. In November 2001, China's membership was officially approved, ending 15 years of marathon negotiations with WTO members

HENG
LIANHE ZAOBAO
Singapore
SINGAPORE

(most notably the United States). China must slash import tariffs to 8 percent from 21 percent and reduce subsidies for farmers and state-owned enterprises (see the Country Box for more details). Decisions on admission into the WTO are made by the entire membership, not by the WTO itself.

The WTO's top-level decision-making body is the Ministerial Conference, which meets at least once every two years. In the intervals between sessions, the highest-level WTO decision-making body is the General Council where member nations are usually represented by ambassadors or the heads of delegations. The General Council also meets as the Trade Policy Review Body and the Dispute Settlement Body. Reporting to the General Council are the Goods Council, Services Council, and Trade-Related Aspects of Intellectual Property Council. In addition, numerous specialized working groups or committees deal with individual agreements and other important areas such as the environment, development, membership applications, regional trade agreements, trade and investment, trade and competition policy and transparency in government procurement. Electronic commerce is also being studied by various councils and committees.

Functions and Measures

In addition to reduction in import duties, which is the dominant function of the WTO, the organization has several other functions. The first function is the *elimination of discrimination*. The two main principles designed to eliminate discrimination are the *most-favored-nation* treatment and the *national treatment*. The

---

COUNTRY BOX

China

CHINA JOINS WTO

China, one of the 23 original contracting parties of the GATT, has rejoined the world trade forum. It signed the accession agreement at the WTO's fourth Ministerial Meeting in Doha on November 10, 2001. This accession process took 15 long and difficult years beginning with its application in July 1986. The road was so arduous that some people even called the WTO the "World Torture Organization" for the process that applicants must go through.

As the world's largest consumer market and fastest growing economy, China's entry is viewed with both optimism and caution. Since 1978, the Chinese economy has registered a growth rate of 10 percent annually and doubled its per capita income every 10 years. This record has not been matched by any other country. Under the WTO, MNEs will enjoy nondiscriminatory treatment. Barriers to imports will fall. China will limit its domestic subsidies on agriculture to 8.5 percent of the aggregate value of farm output. Import duties on cars will fall drastically to 25 percent. Foreign investors will also be allowed to enter China's infrastructure sector (i.e., railways). Foreign banks can han-

dle both foreign exchange and Chinese yuan (RMB) transactions for Chinese companies and individuals. China will also open other service industries such as telecommunications, insurance, and tourism. MNEs have already made their move. South Korea's LG group launched a new joint venture with Changhong Electronics in a bid to become China's leading manufacturer of household appliances. Nissan initiated a new partnership with Dongfeng Automobile in an effort to make China its largest manufacturing and export base.

It remains to be seen, however, whether China will honor all its obligations. China has a long history of according priority to its own national interests. It is also a leading international competitor in labor-intensive products. Current members of the WTO are obligated to phase out quantitative restrictions against Chinese goods in accordance with a mutually agreed-upon timetable. Above all, China's accession provides a new impetus for worldwide trade and investment growth, especially at a time when the world economy is slowing down following the tragic September 11, 2001 events in New York.

most-favored-nation (MFN) treatment means that any advantage, favor, or privilege granted to one country must be extended to all other member countries. For example, if Canada reduces its tariff on imports of German cars to 20 percent, it must cut its tariffs on cars imported from all other member nations to 20 percent. The **national treatment** means that once they have cleared customs, foreign goods in a member country should be treated the same as domestic goods.

Several exceptions to the MFN principle should be noted. First, the WTO allows members to establish bilateral or regional *customs unions* or free trade areas. For example, following China's admission into the WTO, the Association of Southeast Asian Nations (ASEAN) and China embarked on a plan to form the world's largest free trade area (1.7 billion in population) within a decade. Members in such unions or areas may enjoy more preferential treatment than those outside the group. Second, the WTO allows members to *lower tariffs to developing countries* without lowering them to developed countries. For example, the United States offers such treatment to developing countries (they must be GATT members) through what is called the *Generalized System of Preferences (GSP)*. Because of this system, U.S. companies that are more vulnerable to import competition from developing countries face greater pressure on cost reduction. If a developing country is not a GATT member, it cannot enjoy such preferences. The third exception are the *escape clauses* permitted by the WTO. **Escape clauses** are special allowances permitted by the WTO to safeguard infant industries or nourish economic growth for newly admitted developing countries. These countries may (1) withdraw or modify concessions on customs duties if this is required for the establishment of a new industry that will improve standards of living; (2) restrict imports in order to keep the balance of payments in equilibrium and to obtain the necessary exchange for the purchase of goods for the implementation of development plans; and (3) grant governmental assistance if this appears necessary to promote the establishment of enterprises. The purpose of escape clauses is to help developing country members safeguard their economies. The term "safeguard" is used to denote government actions in response to imports that are believed to cause serious "harm" to the importing country's economic or domestic competing industries.

The second function of the WTO is to *combat various forms of protection and trade barriers*. In addition to the reduction of import duties as shown in Exhibit 8–2, the WTO is devoted to elimination of quantitative restrictions (i.e., quotas) maintained for agricultural products or for balancing foreign exchange reserve by a member government. Quantitative restrictions are also levied on industrial products by slapping an anti-dumping duty on them. **Dumping** is the sale of imported goods either at prices below what a company charges in its home market or at prices below cost. Other forms of protection include import deposit without interest, customs valuation, excise duties, subsidies, and countervailing duty (see Chapter 2 for more details). The Uruguay Round was particularly effective in combating non-tariff barriers. The WTO's Trade Policy Review Body regularly monitors the trade policies of its members. These efforts significantly enhance the degree of market access to members' markets.

The third function of the WTO is to *provide a forum for dealing with various emerging issues* concerning the world trade system such as intellectual property, the environment, economic development, regional agreements, unfair trade practices, government procurement, and special sectors such as agriculture, telecommunications, financial services, and maritime service. Many new rules have been derived from such forum discussions. For example, the Trade-Related Intellectual Property Agreement (TRIP) brings new discipline to the protection of patents, copyrights, trade secrets, and similar intellectual property components.

Finally, the WTO functions as *a united dispute settlement system for members* through its *Dispute Settlement Body (DSB)* consisting of representatives from every

WTO member. The DSB has the sole authority to establish dispute settlement panels for cases, to adopt panel reports, to monitor the implementation of its rulings, and to authorize suspension of rights if its rulings are not acted upon by the member(s) in a timely fashion. Since the WTO's obligations extend only to member governments, non-members may neither take advantage of the WTO nor are they subject to its requirements. In this regard, the WTO's judicial reach differs from that of the International Court of Justice, in which non-members of the United Nations may be parties as applicant, respondent, and perhaps intervenor. For example, the DSB established a panel to examine the European Union's complaint against Section 304 of the U.S. Trade Act of 1994. Section 304 is often used by the United States to redress trade policies not covered by the WTO. The EU claimed that Section 304 violates WTO principles because it allows the U.S. Trade Representative Office to unilaterally decide whether another WTO member has violated WTO rules *before* the DSB has ruled on the matter.

The WTO, and its predecessor the GATT, have been viewed as the "club of rich nations" by some developing countries. While beneficial to world trade as a whole, benefits depend in large part on the bargaining power of a member nation or a group of nations. Developing countries often believe they are victims of unfair trade policies and practices adopted by rich nations. Developing countries have long been asking affluent nations to honor commitments to open more markets or remove unfair treatments. At WTO's ministerial meeting in Doha, the capital of Qatar, in November 2001, several developing countries such as Malaysia and India voiced the opinion that rich nations have no right to call for a new round of talks until they have honored past commitments.

The International Monetary Fund (IMF)

The IMF and the World Bank together are often called the *Bretton Woods Institutions*, because they were both established at Bretton Woods, New Hampshire, in July 1944. The overall objectives of the IMF are to promote international monetary cooperation and expansion of international trade and to reduce the disequilibrium in members' balances of payments. To accomplish these goals, the IMF seeks to promote exchange stability, maintain orderly exchange arrangements, avoid competitive exchange depreciation, and provide confidence to member states by placing the general resources of the Fund at the disposal of nations facing an economic crisis, subject to adequate safeguards. As the key institution in the international monetary system, the IMF was established to render temporary assistance to member countries trying to defend their currencies against cyclical, seasonal, or random fluctuations. It also assists countries having structural trade problems if they take adequate steps to correct their problems. If persistent deficits occur, however, the IMF cannot save a country from eventual devaluation.

The IMF is headed by a Board of Governors, composed of representatives from all member countries (160 as of the end of 1999). In order to facilitate the exchange of goods, services, and capital, and to provide conditions necessary for financial and economic stability, the IMF requires all members to collaborate with the Fund in promoting a stable system of exchange rates. Each member should avoid manipulating exchange rates for the purpose of preventing effective balance-of-payments adjustments or as an attempt to gain an unfair competitive advantage. Although members may apply the exchange arrangements of their choice, they must follow exchange policies compatible with these undertakings. While the financing role played by the IMF has diminished for industrial countries, this role remains significant for the vast majority of developing countries.

The world community has been increasingly using the IMF as an important forum for multilateral surveillance and coordination of national fiscal and monetary

The IMF is also a forum for the coordination of monetary and fiscal policy.

policies. Developing countries have a particularly strong stake in this process: it is only in a multilateral forum that major countries' policies are likely to be coordinated in a manner that accords due weight to the impact and implications of these policies on the rest of the world community.

The growing integration of the world's money and capital markets and the inevitable increased role of private capital can at times greatly complicate the task of orderly economic management, particularly in developing countries with limited policy instruments at their disposal. As demonstrated by the Asian financial crisis, one has to take particular note of the volatility and unpredictability of portfolio capital flows. The world needs credible international safety nets, while preserving the freedom of capital markets, to protect the integrity of their development programs in the face of sudden outflows of private capital. In a rapidly changing and uncertain world, the IMF has already begun, and should continue, to develop greater flexibility to respond purposefully and quickly to constantly changing economic conditions.

In order to carry out the tasks of monitoring the international monetary system and supplementing foreign exchange reserves, the IMF created the **Special Drawing Right** *(SDR)*. As an international reserve asset, SDR serves as a unit of account for the IMF and other international and regional organizations, and is also the base against which some countries peg the rate of exchange for their currencies. Defined initially in terms of a fixed quantity of gold, the SDR was later the weighted value of currencies of the five IMF members that had the largest exports of goods and services: U.S. dollar (39 percent), German mark (21 percent), Japanese yen (18 percent), French franc (11 percent), and British pound sterling (11 percent).

SDRs are not circulated internationally. Individual countries hold SDRs in the form of deposits in the IMF. These holdings are part of each country's international monetary reserves, along with each country's official holdings of gold, foreign exchange, and reserve position at the IMF. Members may settle transactions among themselves by transferring SDRs.

The World Bank Group

The World Bank refers to the *International Bank for Reconstruction and Development (IBRD)*. The World Bank, together with its three affiliates, the *International Development Association (IDA)*, the *International Finance Corporation (IFC)*, and the *Multilateral Investment Guarantee Agency (MIGA)*, are sometimes referred to as the **World Bank Group.** The common objective of these institutions is to help raise standards of living in developing countries by channeling financial resources to them from developed countries.

Established in 1945, the World Bank is owned by the governments of 160 countries. Its capital is funded from the subscription of its member countries. The World Bank finances its lending operations primarily through its own borrowing in the world capital markets. A substantial contribution to the World Bank's capital resource also comes from its retained earnings and the flow of repayments on its loans. World Bank loans generally have a grace period of five years and are repayable over 15 to 20 years. Loans are geared toward developing countries that are in relatively more advanced stages of economic and social growth. The interest rates on these loans are calculated based on the cost of their borrowing, which makes them lower than market interest rates.

The World Bank's charter spells out basic rules that govern its operations. It must lend only for productive purposes and must stimulate economic growth in the recipient developing countries. It must pay due regard to the prospects of repayment. Each loan is made to a government or must be guaranteed by the government concerned. The use of loans cannot be restricted to purchases in any particular member country.

While the World Bank has traditionally financed all kinds of capital infrastructure (such as roads and railways, telecommunications, and port and power facilities), the centerpiece of its development strategy emphasizes investment that can directly affect the well-being of the masses of impoverished people in developing countries by making them more productive and by integrating them as active partners in the development process.

The International Development Association, or IDA, established in 1960, concentrates on assisting the least developed nations. The terms of IDA credits, which are traditionally made only to governments, are 10-year grace periods, 35- or 40-year maturities, and no interest. The International Finance Corporation, or IFC, was established in 1956 for the purpose of assisting the economic development of developing countries by promoting growth in the private sector of their economies and helping to mobilize domestic and foreign capital for this purpose. Finally, the Multilateral Investment Guarantee Agency, or MIGA, established in 1988, specializes in encouraging equity investment and other direct investment flows to the developing countries through the mitigation of non-commercial investment barriers. To carry out this mandate, MIGA offers investors guarantees against non-commercial risks, advises developing country governments on the design and implementation of policies concerning foreign investments, and sponsors a dialogue between the international business community and host governments on investment issues.

Since the late 1990s, cooperation between the WTO, the IMF, and the World Bank has increased significantly. This includes participation at meetings, information sharing, contacts at staff level, and the creation of a *High Level Working Group on Coherence* that oversees the process and prepares an annual joint statement on Coherence. In 1998, the WTO Secretariat cooperated with the staff of the IMF and the World Bank to assist developing countries in stimulating their foreign trade and their participation in the multilateral trading system. Such cooperation was also addressed in a Joint Statement by the director-general of the WTO, the managing director of the IMF, and the president of the World Bank, which was issued at the time of the *Seattle Ministerial Conference*. The Joint Statement calls upon ministers to make substantial progress on all three fronts, noting that such efforts represent the essence of adopting a more coherent approach to global economic policy making.

Other International Economic Organizations

The Organization for Economic Cooperation and Development (OECD)

The OECD was established in December 1960, replacing the former OEEC (the Organization for European Economic Cooperation) and includes non-European countries such as the United States, Canada, Japan, Australia, New Zealand, and Mexico. Its mission is to aid in the achievement of the highest and soundest possible growth in economies of member countries and also of non-member states. Its emphases are placed on economic development, employment expansion, living standard improvement, financial stability, and extension of world trade on a multilateral and non-discriminatory basis. The Council is the highest authority in the OECD. In the past, the OECD has made efforts to lower barriers to the exchange of goods, services and capital, stabilize financial fluctuations that may endanger economies of members or those of other countries, and promote scientific research and vocational training. The OECD, however, does not have specific provisions on the liberalization of goods, invisible transactions, and capital. Thus, the OECD has not made many concrete decisions, though it has issued many publications on international business. Coordination of economic policies of all developed countries became the principal aim of the OECD after the European Union was formed.

The United Nations Conference on Trade and Development (UNCTAD)

Prior to the first UNCTAD held in Geneva in June 1964, most international economic organizations concerned the economic interests of the developed countries. UNCTAD is in many ways a forum for an examination of economic problems plaguing developing countries as well as for formulating, negotiating, and implementing measures to improve the development process for these countries. This forum is essential to achieve the demand for "a new international economic order" involving more trade and capital concessions on the part of developed countries, which have generally benefited more from global trade and investment. Specifically, developing countries hope to solve three problems via the UNCTAD:

1. Their share in world trade is decreasing and their terms of trade with developed countries are deteriorating.

2. Markets of developed countries are not sufficiently open to manufactured products of developing countries.

3. Although the aid given by developed countries has increased, it remains inadequate. In fact, many developing countries are still struggling with huge burden of foreign debts.

Exhibit 8–3 summarizes other international economic organizations by their function or objective.

Exhibit 8–3

Summary of specialized
international economic
organizations

Special Area	Name of Organization	Major Function/Objective
Food	Food and Agriculture Organization (FAO) of the United Nations, founded in 1945	Collect, analyze, interpret, and disseminate information on nutrition, food, and agriculture
Health	World Health Organization (WHO) Founded in 1946	Assist all people in achieving the highest level of health
Labor training	International Labor Organization (ILO), founded in 1919	Promote employment, living standard, improve working conditions, social security
Standard-ization	International Organization for Standardization (ISO) Founded in 1947	Promote the development of standardization to facilitate exchange of goods and services throughout the world
Intellectual property	World Intellectual Property Organization (WIPO), founded in 1967	Promote the protection of intellectual property through cooperation among nations and intellectual property unions
Tourism	World Tourism Organization (WTO), founded in 1970	Promote and develop tourism to contribute to economic growth, international understanding and peace
Environment	United Nations Environment Program (UNEP), founded in 1972	Preserve the environment and natural resources through international cooperation

Interim Summary

1. The WTO, IMF, and the World Bank are the three major international economic organizations affecting global-level cooperation of nations. The WTO aims to facilitate trade through reducing trade barriers and eliminating discrimination, whereas the IMF and the World Bank focus on the monetary (currency stability) and fiscal (financial funding) system, respectively.

2. Although these organizations are supposed to help raise standards of living in member countries, developing countries often find their voice weak in these organizations, especially the WTO, and ask affluent nations to remove unfair trade policies or honor commitments for further opening their markets.

REGIONAL-LEVEL
COOPERATION AMONG NATIONS
Multilateral trade liberalization after World War II has been paralleled by a process of integration through regional agreements. A total of 109 agreements were reported to the GATT, from 1947 through the end of 1994.[3] These agreements have, for the most part, involved countries in the same geographic region (see Exhibit 8–4).

Postwar Regional Integration

Three features characterize postwar regional integration. First, postwar regional integration has been centered primarily in western Europe. The creation of the

Exhibit 8–4

Selected regional integration agreements (as of September, 2002)

EUROPE
    European Union (EU)

Austria	Germany	Netherlands
Belgium	Greece	Portugal
Denmark	Ireland	Spain
Finland	Italy	Sweden
France	Luxembourg	United Kingdom

    EC Free Trade Agreements with

Estonia	Latvia	Norway
Iceland	Liechtenstein	Switzerland
Israel	Lithuania	

    EC Association Agreements with

Bulgaria	Hungary	Romania
Cyprus	Malta	Slovak Rep.
Czech Rep.	Poland	Turkey

NORTH AMERICA
    Canada-United States Free Trade Agreement (CUFTA)
    North American Free Trade Agreement (NAFTA)

LATIN AMERICA AND THE CARIBBEAN
    Caribbean Community and Common Market (CARICOM)
    Central American Common Market (CACM)
    Latin American Integration Association (LAIA)
    Southern Common Market (MERCOSUR)

MIDDLE EAST
    Economic Cooperation Market (ECO)
    Gulf Cooperation Council (GCC)

ASIA
    Australia-New Zealand Closer Economic Relations Trade
      Agreement (CER)
    Asia-Pacific Economic Cooperation Forum (APEC)
    Association of South East Asian Nations (ASEAN)
    Great China Circle

OTHER
    Israel-United States Free Trade Agreement

European Economic Community (EEC) in 1958 and of the *European Free Trade Association (EFTA)* in 1960 initiated a process of enlarging the scope of regional integration among European countries and with other countries. Integration through preferential trade agreements has also been a significant feature of the trade policies of non-European countries. If APEC's objective of achieving open trade and investment by the year 2020 is formalized as a free trade area, all WTO members will be parties to at least one trade agreement. In other words, all WTO members will simultaneously be insiders to at least one trade agreement and outsiders to other agreements.

Second, many developing countries, particularly in Latin America and Asia, have renewed their interest in regional integration since the Uruguay Round began. As part of their adoption of outward-oriented policies, regional integration can help broaden the openness and internationalization of developing economies while avoiding overdependence on world markets. Moreover, continued economic reforms, especially more developed macroeconomic and exchange rate policies, suggest that the overall policy environment has become more conducive to regional integration objectives.[4]

Third, the level of economic integration varies widely among different agreements. Most regional integration agreements involve free trade areas, and the number of customs union agreements is small. Among free trade agreements, it is useful to distinguish between *reciprocal agreements* and *non-reciprocal agreements*. In a reciprocal agreement, each member agrees to reduce or eliminate barriers to trade. In a non-reciprocal agreement, some developed countries may reduce trade barriers, allowing more exports from some developing countries without a request for reciprocity from the latter.

North America: The North American Free Trade Agreement (NAFTA)

The leaders of Canada, Mexico, and the United States signed a historic trade accord, the North American Free Trade Agreement (NAFTA), on December 17, 1992, creating a tri-national market area of more than 360 million people with a combined purchasing power of approximately $6.5 trillion. NAFTA is the first ever reciprocal free trade accord between industrial countries and a developing nation (Mexico), which explains why this pact is of special interest to developing countries, particularly those located in Latin America. NAFTA helps enhance the ability of North American producers (especially U.S. companies) to compete globally. By improving the investment climate in North America and by providing companies with a larger market, NAFTA also helps increase economic growth despite the fact that this increase is not equal among the three members.

NAFTA went into effect on January 1, 1994, uniting the United States with its largest (Canada) and third-largest (Mexico) trading partners. Based on the earlier U.S.-Canada Free Trade Agreement, NAFTA dismantled trade barriers for industrial goods and included agreements on services, investments, intellectual property rights, and agriculture.

NAFTA also includes side agreements on labor adjustment, environmental protection, and import surges. The side agreement on labor adjustment came in response to American workers' concerns that jobs in the United States would be exported to Mexico because of Mexico's lower labor wages, weak child labor laws, and other conditions that afford Mexican labor an economic advantage over its American counterpart. The side agreement is an attempt to manage the terms of the potential change in labor markets. The agreement involves such issues as restrictions on child labor, health and safety standards, and minimum wages. In addition to signing the labor side agreement, the Mexican government has pledged to link increases in the Mexican minimum wage to productivity increases.

The side agreement on environmental cooperation explicitly ensures the rights of the United States to safeguard the environment. NAFTA upholds all existing U.S. health, safety and environmental standards. It allows states and cities to enact even tougher standards, while providing mechanisms to encourage all parties to raise their standards. The side agreement on import surges creates an early warning mechanism to identify those sectors where a sudden, explosive trade growth may do significant harm to the domestic industry. It also establishes that in the future, a working group can provide for revisions in the treaty text based on the experiences with the existing safeguard mechanisms. During the transition period, safeguard relief is available in the form of a temporary retreat to pre-NAFTA duties if an import surge threatens to seriously damage a domestic industry. These three side agreements were negotiated to alleviate the fears of U.S. labor and industry groups that felt threatened by the possible immediate adverse impact on their members.

With the integration of the Canadian, U.S., and Mexican markets, many companies have changed their business strategies and plans in order to serve the integrated North American market more efficiently. Many companies in Mexico, the United States, and Canada closed inefficient plants and concentrated production where it could generate highest possible returns. Whether it is the Mexican company Cemex, the Canadian company Alcan Aluminum, or the American company Ford, each can take advantage of cheaper labor or resources for certain components and products. In the foreseeable future, assuming that Mexican worker productivity is equal to or close to that of the U.S. or Canadian worker, one would expect that labor-intensive production would be performed in Mexico where workers' hourly wages are less than half of those in the United States.

Europe: The European Union (EU)

The postwar efforts to establish the European Union have been a long process, beginning with the formation of the *European Economic Community (EEC)* in 1957. After three enlargement efforts ended on January 1, 1995, the *European Community (EC)* was formed, consisting of 15 member states: Belgium, the Netherlands, Luxembourg, France, Germany, Italy, Denmark, Ireland, the United Kingdom, Greece, Spain, Portugal, Finland, Sweden, and Austria. These EC member states constitute the core as well as the deepest level of the European economic integration. The outer

The opening ceremony of the Association of Southeast Asian Nations and European Union ministerial meeting in Singapore.

Exhibit 8–5
The European Union

EUROPEAN SUPRANATIONALISM

- Original EEC members (joined 1958)
- Later EC/EU members (joined 1973–1995)
- "First Wave" applicants
- Countries anticipating negotiations to join EU
- Countries voting against membership

€ Euro adopters as of 2001

| 0 | 200 | 400 | 600 Kilometers |
| 0 | 100 | 200 | 300 Miles |

Source: de Blij & Muller, Concepts and Regions in Geography 1e, figure 1–10, p. 44. Wiley: New York, 2002.

tier of trade and economic liberalization around the European Community is composed of countries in central and eastern Europe, as well as Mediterranean countries (e.g., Slovenia, Malta, and Turkey), with which the European Community has concluded reciprocal trade agreements. (See Exhibit 8–5.)

The most fundamental step in strengthening economic and political ties among EC member states occurred with the *Treaty on European Union* (or the "Maastricht" Treaty). Signed in February 1992, the treaty was enforced in November 1993. This treaty not only promotes economic and trade expansion within a common market, but also embraces the formation of a monetary union, the establishment of a common foreign and security policy, common citizenship, and the development of cooperation on justice and social affairs. Its significance was marked by the adoption of the new name "European Union" (EU). The Maastricht Treaty contains several high-impacting provisions, such as:

1. It creates a common European currency, known as the *European Currency Unit (ECU)*;

2. Every citizen in each member state in the EU is eligible to obtain a European passport, which bestows the right to move freely from one country to another within the Union;

3. It contains provisions on cooperation in the fields of justice and domestic affairs;

4. It empowers the Union to play a more active role in areas such as trans-European transport and environmental protection;

5. It increases the power of the European Parliament to enact legislation;

6. It removes all restrictions on capital movements between member states;

7. Finally, it establishes a European Central Bank responsible for monetary policy, and transforms the European Union into the European Economic and Monetary Union (EMU) under which the currencies of the member states are tied irrevocably to one another at the same exchange rate.

The European Currency Unit (ECU, or euro) is a "basket" of specified amounts of each EC currency. The amounts are determined in accordance with the economic size of the member countries, and are revised every five years. The value of the ECU is determined by using the spot market rate of each member currency. The ECU has already become a popular unit for international payment, bond issuance, security investment, bank deposits, commercial loans, and traveler's checks since it was created in 1999.

The EU is run by five institutions, each playing a specific role:

- European parliament (elected by the people of the member states);
- Council of the Union (governments of the member states);
- European Commission (executive body);
- Court of Justice (compliance with the law);
- Court of Auditors (lawful management of the EU budget).

Apart from the European Union, there are several other trade unions in Europe. For instance, in December 1992, several central and east European countries (the Czech Republic, Slovakia, Hungary, and Poland) created the *Central European Free Trade Agreement (CEFTA)*, which provides for the establishment of a free trade area by the end of 1997. Also in 1992, Finland, Norway, Sweden, and Switzerland concluded free trade agreements with each of the Baltic states (Estonia, Latvia, and Lithuania).

Asia Pacific

The Asia-Pacific Economic Cooperation Forum (APEC), founded in November 1994, consists of Australia, New Zealand, Canada, Mexico, the United States, Chile, China, Hong Kong, Japan, South Korea, Papua New Guinea, Chinese Taipei (Taiwan), Indonesia, Malaysia, the Philippines, Singapore, Thailand, and Brunei. In the 1994 summit declaration, members agreed to build on the commitments they made in the Uruguay Round of the GATT, by accelerating their implementation, and broadening and deepening these commitments. Compared to other regional unions or

Exhibit 8–6
The Asia-Pacific Economic
Cooperation (APEC)

areas, APEC is cross-regional, spanning Asia, North and South America, and the Pacific. Moreover, APEC is unique in terms of the mix of members involved, encompassing large and small, rich and poor, as well as politically divergent nations (See Exhibit 8–6).

Relative to APEC, the *Association of South East Asian Nations (ASEAN)* is much older, established on August 8, 1967 by Indonesia, Malaysia, the Philippines, Singapore, and Thailand (Brunei joined in 1984). The aim of ASEAN is to promote peace, stability, and economic growth in the region. Since January 1995, member countries began earmarking products for low-duty status from a list of 3,141 items. In order to become a free trade zone by the year 2003, when the average tariffs will be reduced to 2.6 percent, ASEAN countries have cut the tariffs on various products such as cement, ceramics, chemicals, pharmaceuticals, and dozens of others. Although located in the same region, ASEAN members are diverse in terms of economic, geographical, political, and cultural backgrounds. This diversity sometimes increases the difficulty in achieving the specific goals or implementing plans set by ASEAN members.

Accounting for one-fifth of the world trade, Asia is distinctive in several ways. First, many countries in the region have accelerated their trade liberalization at the subnational level by authorizing export processing zones or special investment areas within each country. In China, for instance, the Standing Committee of the National People's Congress approved in August 1980 the establishment of four special economic zones, namely, Shenzhen, Zhuhai, Shantou, and Xiamen. Thailand, Vietnam, Indonesia, Malaysia, India, Bangladesh, and the Philippines, to name a few, also established such zones within their own territories.

Second, many geographically proximate neighbors in Asia reached less formal trade agreements. For example, members of the *South Asian Association for Regional Cooperation (SAARC)*—Bhutan, India, Maldives, Nepal, Pakistan, and Sri Lanka—concluded a trade agreement in April 1993. Similarly, the *China Circle* is now an extremely dynamic region exerting substantial impacts on world trade and investment. This circle, which includes Hong Kong, Macau, Taiwan, and mainland China, comprises—from the standpoint of degree of economic integration—three concentric layers. The core consists of the Hong Kong-Guangdong economic nexus; the inner layer, "Greater South China," embraces Hong Kong, Guangdong, Fujian, and Taiwan; and the outer layer, "Greater China," includes Hong Kong, Taiwan, and China. Hong Kong is the pivot for integration of the China Circle and plays a role in each of its three layers.

Finally, numerous subregional economic zones have emerged. Intense trade and investment flows have grown among geographically contiguous but politically separated border areas, taking advantage of the complementarity in factor endowment and technological capacity among countries at different stages of economic development. These zones are alternately called *transnational export processing zones, natural economic territories,* or *growth triangles.* They include the *Tumen River Area Development Project* in northeast Asia, composed of the Russian Far East, Mongolia, northeast China, and the Korean peninsula and Japan; the *Baht Economic Zone,* encompassing Thailand and the contiguous border areas of southwest China, Myanmar, Laos, Cambodia, and Vietnam; the *Mekong River Basin Project,* involving the riparian countries of Thailand, Myanmar, Vietnam, Laos, Cambodia, and southwest China; and three growth triangles in ASEAN—the *Southern Growth Triangle* (Singapore, the Johor state in Malaysia, and Batam island in Indonesia), *Northern Growth Triangle* (western Indonesia, northern Malaysia, and southern Thailand), and *Eastern Growth Triangle* (Brunei, eastern Indonesia, southern Philippines, and Sabah and Sarawak in eastern Malaysia).

Latin America

Attempts to form free trade blocs in Latin America were made as early as 1960 when the *Latin American Free Trade Association (LAFTA)* (involving Argentina, Bolivia, Brazil, Chile, Colombia, Ecuador, Mexico, Paraguay, Peru, Uruguay, and Venezuela) and the *Central American Common Market (CACM)* (consisting of Costa Rica, El Salvador, Guatemala, Honduras, and Nicaragua) were initiated. Both failed to achieve their objectives because of different economic conditions and economic policies among member countries that worked against regional economic integration.

LAFTA was superseded in 1980 by the Montevideo Treaty, which established the *Latin American Integration Association (LAIA).* Its goal was to increase bilateral trade among the member countries, carried out on a sectoral basis. In 1991, Argentina, Brazil, Paraguay, and Uruguay signed the *Southern Common Market Treaty (MERCOSUR),* which called for a common market among the four countries with free circulation of goods, services, capital, and labor. The member countries also aimed to coordinate macroeconomic policy and to harmonize legislation to strengthen the integration process. Since January 1, 1995, MERCOSUR members have used a common tariff structure and common external tariff rates.

Other LAFTA members, including Bolivia, Colombia, Ecuador, Peru, and Venezuela, formed the *Andean Free Trade Area* in 1992 with a common external tariff. Since 1995, these members adopted a four-tier external tariff structure of 5, 10, 15, and 20 percent, when trading with other members of this agreement. The *Central American Common Market (CACM)* reactivated its objectives and established a customs union on January 1, 1993. Countries in the Caribbean region started the *Caribbean Community and Common Market (CARICOM)* in 1973. The major objective of this treaty is to achieve economies of scale in the regional production of services, such as transportation, education, and health, and to pool financial resources for

Exhibit 8–7
Free trade blocs in the
Americas

investment in a regional development bank. This treaty also targets the coordination of economic policies and development planning (See Exhibit 8–7).

Africa and the Middle East

The Economic Community of West African States (ECOWAS), established in 1975, is composed of Benin, Burkina Faso, Cote d'lvoire, Mali, Mauritania, Niger, Senegal, Guinea, Liberia, Sierra Leone, Cape Verde, Gambia, Ghana, Guinea-Bissau, Nigeria, and Togo. ECOWAS eliminated duties on unprocessed agricultural products and handicrafts in 1981, and implemented free trade for all unprocessed products in 1990. Other activities of the community have included progressive liberalization of industrial products, steps to avoid the use of hard currencies in intra-member trade through a regional payments-clearing system, and cooperation on industrial and agricultural investment projects.

Established in 1966 in former French Africa, the *Central African Economic and Customs Union (UDEAC)* consists of Congo, Gabon, Chad, the Central African Republic, Equatorial Guinea, and Cameroon. EDEAC provides a framework for the free movement of capital throughout the area and for the harmonization of fiscal incentives, as well as the coordination of industrial development. A common external tariff was introduced in 1990 by four members of the community—Cameroon, Congo, Gabon, and the Central African Republic.

In former British East Africa, the establishment of the *East African Economic Community (EAEC)* in 1967 by Kenya, Tanzania, and Uganda formalized the common market. The EAEC was dissolved in 1979 and the three members later joined with other states (Angola, Burundi, Comoros, Djibouti, Ethiopia, Lesotho, Malawi, Mauritius, Mozambique, Namibia, Rwanda, Somalia, Sudan, Swaziland, Zambia, and Zimbabwe) to establish the Preferential Trade Area for eastern and southern African States (PTA) in 1981. Its goals include the establishment of a common market and the promotion of trade and economic cooperation among its members.

In the Middle East, Kuwait, Saudi Arabia, Bahrain, Oman, Qatar, and the United Arab Emirates established the *Gulf Cooperation Council (GCC)* in 1981. A free trade area covering industrial and agricultural products (excluding petroleum products) was established. In 1989, the *Arab Maghreb Union* was also established by Algeria, Libya, Mauritania, Morocco, and Tunisia to lay the foundations for a Maghreb Economic Area.

Regionalization vs. Globalization

Does regionalization work? Let us look at how the preceding regional blocs or agreements have actually contributed to the increased share of intra-regional trade. Indeed, intraregional trade increased in western Europe (e.g., from 53 percent in 1958 to 70 percent in 1999), as it has done in North America. For example, Canada expanded its exports to the United States by 18 percent between 1997–1999 and Mexico's exports and imports, heavily linked to the U.S. market, grew by 20 percent over 1997–1999. This seems to support a view that regionalization can increase the share of regional trade. However, the uniqueness of the European Union and the NAFTA—in terms of the structure and commitment to carry integration—differs markedly from what has been envisaged in other regional integration agreements. Caution is required in generalizing the unique experiences of NAFTA and the European Union to other regional agreements (e.g., MERCOSUR experienced a contraction of its intra-trade by about one quarter during 1997–1999). In fact, many developing countries encountered problems when implementing these agreements. Moreover, as Asia's experience indicates (e.g., despite absence of any bilateral trade agreements, China's trade with Japan and Korea has steadily increased in the late 1990s), regional integration agreements are not a prerequisite for rising share of intraregional trade. Economic growth, commodity structure, and demand-supply situations seem to be more profound factors affecting the level of intraregional exchanges.[5]

Many people, from government officials and corporate executives to labor union leaders and business instructors, ask whether regionalization is compatible with globalization. To answer this question, we first need to know how the WTO rules regulate regionalization.

Both regional integration agreements (regionalization) and multilateral trading systems (globalization) share the general objective of achieving, within their respective spheres, substantial reduction of tariffs and other barriers to trade. The WTO requires that (1) under the MFN (Most-Favored-Nations) rule, any privilege promised to another regional member as specified in a regional agreement must extend unconditionally to all other WTO members (bilateral or regional obligations thus transform into multilateral or global obligations); (2) members of a regional integration agreement must have a common trade policy with respect to third countries (outsiders), and this policy should not be more restrictive than policies of individual members prior to the agreement; and (3) WTO's dispute settlement mechanisms provide a platform to solve disputes between members concerning discrepancies between regional agreements and global trading rules. For WTO members, these rules make it possible for regional integration and global trading systems to mutually support (rather than conflict with) each other in reducing tariffs and other trade barriers.

The complementarity between regionalization and globalization in dismantling trade barriers is also manifested in other areas. With the exception of the EU, few regional agreements have specified the rules of non-tariff barrier reduction, intellectual property protection, and service trade. Multilateral trading systems such as the WTO, however, serve as an important framework for them to follow in these areas. In other words, members of regional agreements still benefit from the enhanced transparency and procedural guarantees for dealing with these issues in intraregion trade as well as in trade with third countries as covered under the WTO agreements in which they participate. On the other hand, implemented policies or measures taken by certain regional integration agreements (e.g., environmental rules, competition regulations, and investment policies enacted by the EU) help lay the foundation for progress in multilateral trading systems. Finally, the WTO has been provided with a strengthened dispute settlement system and a monitoring function, which together bring increased transparency and predictability to trade and economic policies. As a result, parties to regional integration have ensured—by virtue of being members of the WTO—the adoption of an enhanced set of policies and procedures for their trade and economic relations.

The preceding complementarity, however, holds true for WTO members only under the assumption that the multilateral trading rules will be fully enforced. For non-WTO members, regionalization of foreign markets may increase the barriers to their foreign trade, thus conflicting with their efforts towards global integration. Rules and procedures for trade-related policies are the essence of the world trading system. If these rules are not completely and strictly implemented by all members, the compatibility between regionalization and globalization will be obstructed.

Interim Summary

1. Regionalization, such as the formation of NAFTA and European Union, is a prominent feature of the world economy today. In the near future, all WTO members will simultaneously be insiders of at least one regional bloc or agreement and outsiders of others.

2. Regional integration takes several different forms, including common markets (e.g., European Union and MERCOSUR), free trade areas (e.g., NAFTA and LAFTA), customs unions (e.g., CACM and CARICOM), economic cooperation forums (e.g., APEC and GCC), and economic and political associations (e.g., ASEAN).

3. Regionalization is generally compatible with globalization. However, insiders gain many more benefits than outsiders from economic integration.

COMMODITY-LEVEL COOPERATION AMONG NATIONS

The emergence of many international commodity agreements or organizations is a natural development in international economic relations. Countries may also cooperate with one another to control the production, pricing, and sale of goods that are traded internationally. A **commodity cartel** is a group of producing countries that wish to protect themselves from the wild fluctuations that often occur in the prices of certain commodities traded internationally (e.g., crude oil, coffee, rubber, or cocoa). Cartel members may also seek higher, as well as more stable, prices for their goods. By assigning production quotas to individual countries and limiting overall output, a commodity cartel can raise the price of its good in international markets. The two most important commodity cartels influencing the world economy are OPEC and the Multifiber Arrangement.

Organization of Petroleum Exporting Countries (OPEC)

The most notable and critical commodity cartel today is the *Organization of Petroleum Exporting Countries (OPEC)*. OPEC is not a commercial entity, but an intergovernmental organization. It consists of 13 members, including Iran, Iraq, Kuwait,

Exhibit 8-8

OPEC cartel members

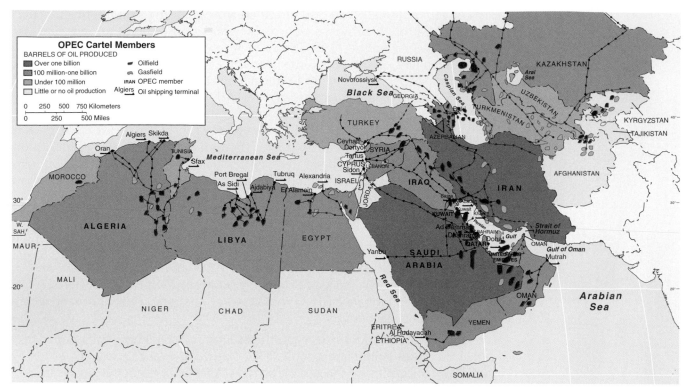

Source: de Blij & Muller, Concepts and Regions in Geography 1e, figure 6–8, p. 187. Wiley: New York 2002.

Saudi Arabia, Venezuela, Algeria, Ecuador, Gabon, Indonesia, Libya, Nigeria, Qatar, and the United Arab Emirates (See Exhibit 8–8). OPEC is the strongest collective force impacting prices in the international oil market. OPEC controls the price of oil in world markets by assigning to its members production quotas that limit the overall amount of crude oil supplied internationally. This organization successfully augmented oil prices for the benefit of its members in the 1970s and successfully overcame crises facing it in the 1980s. Currently, OPEC members control more than 40 percent of the world's oil production.

OPEC became a catalyst for action by developing countries to ensure remunerative export earnings from their raw materials and tropical products. For instance, the *International Bauxite Association (IBA)* and the *Intergovernmental Council of Copper Exporting Countries (CIPEC)* were formed in the 1970s by the major developing countries producing these commodities, both following the model of OPEC.

The Multifiber Arrangement (MFA)

The Multifiber Arrangement (MFA), originally signed in 1972, is an agreement between exporting and importing countries to control exports of textiles and apparel from developing countries to developed countries. The MFA takes advantage of an exemption in GATT rules that allows individual importing countries to establish quotas and other restrictions on textile and apparel exports on a country-by-country basis. About two-thirds of textile and apparel products that are traded internationally are covered by the MFA. The United States currently imposes quotas on imports from 41 countries.

The MFA has been renewed several times for lack of a better solution to the conflict between developing and developed nations over the textile and apparel trade.

For example, the United States and China renegotiate yearly over the quota (restricted quantity) of Chinese exported textiles and garments. The process is lengthy because of conflicts over issues on which neither party is willing to compromise. Generally, this type of conflict results from the nature of the production of these goods: it requires much labor, little capital, and simple technology. Thus it presents one of the major opportunities for less developed, low-wage countries to export manufactured goods to developed countries. Yet, because it is labor-intensive, domestic political forces in developed countries often organize to protect domestic jobs from low-wage foreign competition. As a result, many developed countries have imposed high tariffs or low quotas on the importation of textiles and apparel, thereby severely restricting trade. The MFA's complex barriers to trade are set to be dismantled by the year 2005 as a result of the Uruguay Round.[6]

Other multilateral commodity agreements include *The Wheat Trade Convention (WTC)*, *The International Sugar Agreement (ISA)*, *The International Coffee Agreement (ICA)*, *The International Cocoa Agreement (ICCA)*, The *International Tin Agreement (ITA)*, and *The International Natural Rubber Agreement (INRA)*.

Interim Summary

1. International economic integration also occurs at the commodity-level via the establishment of commodity cartels (e.g., OPEC and CIPEC) or multilateral arrangements (e.g., MFA and ISA).

2. OPEC is an intergovernmental organization and the strongest collective force impacting supply and price in the international oil market.

STRATEGIC RESPONSES OF MNEs

International economic integration profoundly affects the operations of MNEs. So how should MNEs properly respond to, and further benefit from, increasing integration? As a result of heightened integration of the world economy, national boundaries have become increasingly irrelevant in the definition of market and production spaces, while at the same time regions, rather than countries, are emerging as the key economic policy arenas.

Economic integration triggers MNE activities, which then increase FDI in the integrated region. This is not surprising because MNEs quickly make adjustments to the new environment in which intraregional trade barriers have been eliminated.[7] Three strategies can be identified in response to regional economic integration. The *defensive export substituting investment* is a strategy by which MNEs defend their pre-existing market share achieved through exports by switching to direct production inside the region. Many Japanese MNEs such as Sony and Nissan employed this strategy in response to the European market integration in the early 1990s, in part to protect themselves against the possibility of future barriers to Japanese exports. In comparison to the U.S. MNEs, Japanese MNEs were latecomers to the European market and had a trade-based rather than an investment-based commercial relationship with the European community. As a result of defensive export substituting investment, Japanese MNEs are now in a strong position to compete in the EU. As another example, both Du Pont and Dow Chemicals increased investments in their Canadian export-oriented operations in reaction to NAFTA.

The *offensive export substituting investment* is a strategy by which MNEs choose to ensure market penetration by investing directly in the region before the region is officially integrated. This strategy is intended to gain early position in the market, which is anticipated to grow rapidly as a result of an integration program. In order to gain an early foothold in the European market, Coca-Cola, which has an 80 percent share of the European cola market, used this strategy and invested more than $100 million in new European plants. Similarly, Campbell Soup and Quaker Oats have used this strategy to expand their operations in Canada. Aggressive acquisitions activities by these U.S. MNEs in the Canadian market occurred in response to the passage of NAFTA.

The *rationalized foreign direct investment* is a strategy by which MNEs increase investment in, and heighten resource commitment to, the integrated region in pursuit of greater economic efficiency through scale economies and market expansion. IBM, for example, has been operating in Europe for about eight decades and is the industry leader in the European data-processing market. It used rationalized FDI strategy in response to the European market integration by establishing 12 new manufacturing plants, 9 R&D facilities, 7 scientific centers, and a network of local sales and support offices. To benefit from NAFTA, IBM also invested more than $1 billion to upgrade its Canadian facilities, and now exports all high-technology components and software manufactured in Canada to overseas markets, while importing computers for sale in the Canadian market.

Finally, the *reorganization investment* is a strategy by which MNEs realign their organizational structures and value-added activities to reflect a regional market. Firms realign investment capital among members of the trading bloc once protective barriers have been removed altogether. Under this strategy, an MNE's cross-border investment activity within the region increases, while the aggregate level of investment stock may not necessarily increase. Several European MNEs, for example, used this strategy to respond to European market integration. Philips, one of Europe's largest MNEs in the electronics industry, was reorganized as a collection of autonomous national subsidiaries. It restructured to create an integrated set of Europe-wide, product-based companies. To prepare for a single European market, Siemens launched a radical corporate reorganization in 1987, with plans to concentrate on high-growth segments of its core electronics/electrical businesses, while expanding geographically in the European Community through a series of acquisitions (see the Industry Box for details). In North America, Gillette and Whirlpool closed some of

INDUSTRY BOX

SIEMENS SHARPENS ITS FOCUS TO RESPOND TO THE SINGLE MARKET

Siemens, Germany's largest electronics firm, is an example of an MNE from the European Community that was forced to reorganize and expand geographically in the region. Before the single market was formed, Siemens was highly dependent on government purchases and concentrated in regulated markets such as telecommunications equipment, nuclear power and energy, and defense-related equipment. After 1992, Siemens and other former "national champions" in Europe faced deregulated markets in which they competed with MNEs such as AT&T, GE, and IBM. In response, Siemens diversified its geographical presence in Europe and refocused its product lines on those that had competitive advantages. It chose the United Kingdom and France as locations for major new markets in the Community. It integrated vertically to produce end products that share a common core in advanced semiconductor technology in high-growth sectors. Siemens decentralized from 7 product-based divisions to 15 smaller independent units, making the company more flexible in a fast-changing environment. It acquired Plessey of the United Kingdom, which gave it a foothold in the United Kingdom and a 10 percent world market share for public branch exchange products. Siemens also entered into alliances with BASF in mainframes, Bendix in automotive electronics, and Westinghouse in factory automation and controls. All of these efforts helped Siemens to become a premier MNE in Europe in the electronics, semiconductor, computer, and software industries.

their Canadian facilities as a response to free trade in the region. They committed more production to their home markets and then exported to Canada from the United States.

As shown in the preceding examples, strategic choice depends on a company's current position in the regional market, the length of time it has had presence in the region, and the industry to which it belongs. In response to economic integration, MNEs, including those from developing economies such as South Korea, Taiwan, Singapore, and Brazil, have been actively employing cross-border strategic alliances. These alliances allow them to enter a new market far more rapidly than do mergers and acquisitions. Brazil, for example, is now one of the largest investors in the Portuguese economy, mostly with joint ventures in industries such as construction, textiles, and shoes.

Interim Summary

1. MNEs need to strategically respond to economic integration, whether at the regional or global level, if they want to survive in an increasingly competitive environment.

2. MNEs can emphasize one of the three strategies to cope with economic integration: defensive export substituting investment, offensive export substituting investment, and rationalized FDI. The selection of this strategy depends on an MNE's goals, experience, and capabilities.

3. MNEs, whether insiders or outsiders, can expand their presence within a regional block through acquisitions, alliances, or the building of new facilities.

CHAPTER SUMMARY

1. International economic integration involves the discriminatory removal of all trade impediments as well as the establishment of some elements of cooperation among several nations. This integration fosters globalization.

2. Economic integration takes several forms, including free trade area, customs union, common market, economic union, political union, and multilateral cooperation, and occurs at three levels—global, regional, and commodity.

3. Global level cooperation among nations proceeds through international economic organizations such as the WTO, the IMF, and the World Bank. While the WTO sets the institutional foundation for the global trading system, the IMF and the World Bank serve as the foundation of the global monetary and financial systems.

4. The WTO attempts to not only reduce tariff and non-tariff barriers in trade (commodity and service) but also to help solve problems associated with economic development, intellectual property, environmental protection, unfair practices, and dispute settlement.

5. Regional integration has become a prominent characteristic of the world economy. From the EU to NAFTA, from APEC to LAFTA, or from GCC to ECOWAS, most countries already belong to at least one regional bloc or agreement. Within a regional bloc, subregional integration such as a free trade area or a common market becomes increasingly pervasive.

6. From the world economy perspective, regionalization is an integral part of globalization. From the firm perspective, regionalization substantially benefits insiders but not outsiders. Outsiders may shift exports to FDI because an actual investment within the region bypasses trade barriers against outsiders' exports and enables these firms to gain from free flows of products, capital, service, or human resources within the integrated region.

7. Commodity-level cooperation is reflected in commodity cartels or arrangements. The most important cartel is OPEC, which controls more than 40 percent of the world's oil production.

CHAPTER NOTES

[1] M. A. G. Van Meerhaeghe, *International Economic Institutions.* Boston, MA: Martinus Nijhoff Publishers, 1985; A. M. El-Agraa, *Economic Integration Worldwide.* New York: St. Martin's Press, 1997.

[2] B. Hoekman and M. Kostechi, *The Political Economy of the World Trading Systems: From GATT and the WTO.* Oxford, UK: 1995; J. Groome, *Reshaping the World Trading System: A History of the Uruguay Round.* Geneva: World Trade Organization, 1996.

[3] *Regionalism and the World Trading System.* Geneva: World Trade Organization, 1995.

[4] J. H. Jackson, *The World Trading System.* Cambridge, MA: MIT Press, 1997; B. Hettne, A. Inotai, and O. Sunkel, *Globalism and the New Regionalism.* New York: St. Martin's Press, 1999.

[5] Regionalism and Its Place in the Multilateral Trading System. France: OECD, 1996; R. Gibb and W. Michalak (eds). *Continental Trading Blocs: The Growth of Regionalism in the World Economy.* Chichester, UK: Wiley, 1994.

[6] M. R., Mendoza, P. Low, and B. Kotschwar (eds.), Trading Rules in the Making: Challenges in Regional and Multilateral Negotiations. Washington, DC: Brookings Institution Press, 1999; B. Colas, (ed.), *Global Economic Cooperation: A Guide to Agreements and Organizations.* Cambridge, MA: Kluwer Law and Taxation Publishers, 1994.

[7] N. A. Phelps, *Multinationals and European Integration: Trade, Investment and Regional Development.* London, UK: Jessica Kingsley Publishers, 1997; H. Mirza, *Global Competitive Strategies in the New World Economy.* Cheltenham, UK: Edward Elgar, 1998.

The International Monetary System and Financial Markets

DO YOU KNOW

1. What exchange rate systems are available today? Why don't nations use the same exchange rate system? For example, why does Cameroon peg its currency (CFA franc) to the French franc whereas Romania allows its currency (leu) to independently float?

2. Why do some currencies fluctuate more than others? Why do some currencies depreciate while others appreciate? How do you determine and predict the foreign exchange rate?

3. What constitutes international financial markets? How do speculators earn profits from international foreign exchange markets? Is this speculation one of the reasons leading to the Asian financial crisis? How do MNEs finance global operations via international capital markets?

OPENING CASE The Mexican Crisis During 1994 and 1995

Mexico experienced a financial crisis during 1994–1995. Mexico's exchange rate regime was modified a number of times but it was consistently aimed at price stabilization. It started as a strict peg to the U.S. dollar in 1988 and shifted to a crawl policy in early 1989. Be-

ginning in 1992, an asymmetrical band was adopted, allowing for gradual depreciation but placing a ceiling on the peso in relation to the dollar. Though steady from mid-1992 to early 1994, the Mexican peso became overvalued. The real effective exchange rate appreciated steadily as inflation exceeded the rate of the peso's depreciation. Between 1990 and December 1993, the peso depreciated by about 17 percent in nominal terms. However, consumer price inflation amounted to 56 percent from 1990 to 1993. Thus, the real effective exchange rate rose by nearly 35 percent over that period. The result was an increase in the current-account deficit from $7.5 billion in 1990 to $29.4 billion in 1994, which amounted to 7 percent of Mexico's GDP.

The year 1994 was an election year and a period of political mishaps in Mexico. Both the presidential candidate and the secretary-general of the majority party were assassinated. These and other events led to a slowdown in capital inflow and withdrawals of capital that had been invested in short-term government securities *(cetes)*. Reserves decreased by $11 billion in April 1994. The government then issued short-term peso obligations *(tesobonos)* with interest and principal linked to the dollar. The interest rate on these securities was considerably lower than it was on peso securities without a dollar link. Many

Mexican residents shifted out of pesos into dollars, further escalating the peso devaluation. This crisis differs slightly from the one that occurred during the 1980s. In the previous crisis, Mexico fought to keep the peso fixed to the U.S. dollar. In order to discourage investors from withdrawing funds from Mexico to avoid losses when the devaluation eventually occurred, the Mexican government had to maintain high interest rates. These high rates were the indirect consequence of fixed exchange rates, and they consequently stifled investment and job creation. The problem of high interest rates due to delayed devaluation with fixed exchange rates became known as "the peso problem." ∎

HISTORY OF THE INTERNATIONAL MONETARY SYSTEM

The preceding case shows that a country's currency value is not always stable, and therefore, its exchange rate with other countries' currencies can change. International businesses operate in an uncertain environment in which exchange rates have been increasingly volatile over the past quarter century. Volatile exchange rates increase risk for international companies. To manage foreign exchange risk, management must first understand how the international monetary system works. As the opening case demonstrates, there are many new terms associated with this system (e.g., peg or crawl policies, nominal or real exchange rate). This chapter is designed to explain these concepts and related monetary system and financial markets.

The **international monetary system** refers primarily to the set of policies, institutions, practices, regulations, and mechanisms that determine foreign exchange rates. This system is comprised of currencies from individual countries as well as some composite currency units such as the *European Currency Unit (ECU)* and the *Special Drawing Right (SDR)* as illustrated in Chapter 8. **Foreign exchange** refers to the money of a foreign country, such as foreign currency bank balances, banknotes, checks, and drafts. A **foreign exchange rate** (or simply, exchange rate) is the price of one currency expressed in terms of another currency (or gold). If the government of a country (e.g., Iraq) regulates the rate at which the local currency (e.g., Iraqi dinar) is exchanged for other currencies, the system is classified as a **fixed or managed exchange rate system.** When a country's currency (e.g., Iraqi dinar) is tied or fixed to another country's currency (U.S. dollar), this is called **pegged exchange rate system.** The rate at which the currency is fixed is often referred to as its **par value.** If the government does not interfere in the valuation of its currency, it is classified as **floating or flexible exchange rate system** (e.g., U.S. dollar). The **real exchange rate** is the exchange rate after deducting an inflation factor. The **nominal exchange rate** is the exchange rate before deducting an inflation factor.

Changes in exchange rates may move in one of two directions. Associated with the fixed or managed exchange rate system, **devaluation** of a currency refers to a drop in the foreign exchange value of a currency that is pegged to another currency or gold. In other words, the par value is reduced. The opposite of devaluation is **revaluation.** Associated with the floating exchange rate system, **depreciation** (or weakening, deterioration) means a drop in the foreign exchange value of a floating currency. The opposite of depreciation is **appreciation** (or strengthening), which means a gain in the exchange value of a floating currency. The media often use the terms devaluation and depreciation (or revaluation and appreciation) interchangeably, without distinctions, which is incorrect.

The choice of foreign currencies used by international companies affects their cash flows and even their income levels. For example, firms in countries with soft currencies often use hard foreign currencies in export businesses. A **soft or weak**

currency is one that is anticipated to devalue or depreciate relative to major trading currencies. Conversely, a currency is considered **hard or strong** if it is expected to revalue or appreciate relative to major currencies. In daily life, the term hard currency is also used to denote the fully convertible currency of a major developed country (e.g., the U.S. dollar, the U.K. pound, or the Japanese yen).

A brief review of the history of the international monetary system can help us better understand the present monetary system and also appraise the strengths and weaknesses of different foreign exchange systems.

The Gold Standard Period (1876–1914)

Since the days of the pharaohs (about 3000 B.C.), gold was used as a medium of exchange and a store of value. The gold standard gained acceptance as an international monetary system in the 1870s. Under this system, each country pegged its money to gold. For example, if the German Bank fixed the price of gold at 50 deutsche mark (DM) per ounce of gold, it effectively stood ready to buy and sell gold at this rate. The same applied to the United States if the U.S. Federal Reserve (the Fed) fixed the price of gold at $20 per ounce. The exchange rate, then, is simply the ratio of the two prices: DM50/$20 means an exchange rate of DM2.5 per U.S. dollar.

The government of each country using the gold standard agreed to buy or sell gold on demand at its own fixed parity rate. Thus, the value of each individual currency in gold terms and the fixed parities between currencies remained stable. Under this system, it was very important for a country to maintain adequate gold reserves with which to back its currency's value. The gold standard worked adequately until the outbreak of World War I interrupted trade flows and the free movement of gold. As a result, the major trading nations suspended the gold standard.

The Inter-War Years and World War II (1914–1944)

During World War I and the early 1920s, currencies were allowed to fluctuate over fairly wide ranges in terms of both gold and another currency. This created arbitrage opportunities for international speculators. Such fluctuations hampered world trade in the 1920s, thereby contributing to the Great Depression in the 1930s.

The United States returned to a modified gold standard in 1934, when the U.S. dollar was devalued to $35/ounce of gold from the $20.67/ounce price in effect prior to World War I. Although the United States returned to the gold standard, gold was traded only with foreign central banks, not with individual citizens. From 1934 to the end of World War II, exchange rates were determined, in theory, by each currency's value in terms of gold. During World War II and its immediate aftermath, however, many of the main trading currencies lost their convertibility into other currencies. The dollar was the only major trading currency that continued to be convertible.

The Bretton Woods System (1944–1973)

This period, commencing a year prior to the end of World War II, was characterized by a fixed exchange system. Under the provisions of the *Bretton Woods Agreement* signed in 1944, the government of each member country pledged to maintain a fixed, or pegged, exchange rate for its currency vis-à-vis the dollar or gold. Because one ounce of gold was set equal to $35, fixing a currency's gold price was equivalent to setting its exchange rate relative to the dollar. For example, the deutsche mark was set equal to 1/140 of an ounce of gold, meaning it was worth $0.25 ($35/DM140). Participating countries agreed to try to maintain the value of their currencies within a 1 percent band by buying or selling foreign exchange or gold as needed. Devaluation was not to be used as a competitive trade policy, but if a currency became too weak to defend, a devaluation of up to 10 percent was allowed without formal approval by the IMF.

During this period, the U.S. dollar was the main reserve currency held by central banks and was the key to the web of exchange rate values. Unfortunately, the United States ran persistent and growing deficits on its balance of payments. A heavy capital outflow of dollars was required to finance these deficits and to meet the growing demand for dollars from investors and businesses. Eventually the heavy overhang of dollars held abroad resulted in a lack of confidence in the ability of the United States to meet its commitment to convert dollars to gold. On August 15, 1971, the United States responded to a huge trade deficit by making the dollar inconvertible into gold. A 10 percent surcharge was placed on imports, and a program of wage and price controls was introduced. Many of the major currencies were allowed to float against the dollar. The dollar then began a decade of decline.

Under the *Smithsonian Agreement,* which was reached among the world's leading trading nations in Washington, D.C. in December 1971, the United States agreed to devalue the dollar to $38 per ounce of gold. In return, the other countries present agreed to revalue their own currencies upward in relation to the dollar by specified amounts. Actual revaluation ranged from 7.4 percent by Canada to 16.9 percent by Japan. Furthermore, the allowed floating band around par value was expanded from ±1 to ±2.25 percent.

Because of high inflation in the United States, the dollar devaluation remained insufficient to restore stability to the system. By 1973, the dollar was under heavy selling pressure even at its devalued rates. By late February 1973, a fixed-rate system appeared no longer feasible given the speculative flows of currencies. The major foreign exchange markets were actually closed for several weeks in March 1973. When they reopened, most currencies were allowed to float to levels determined by market forces.

The Post-Bretton Woods System: 1973–Present

This period is characterized by a floating exchange rate system. Since March 1973, exchange rates have become much more volatile and less predictable than they were during the "fixed" exchange rate period. The system became increasingly volatile as it approached the oil crisis of the fall of 1973. As mentioned in the preceding chapter, October 1973 marked the beginning of successful efforts by the *Organization of Petroleum Exporting Countries (OPEC)* to raise the price of oil. By 1974, oil prices had quadrupled. Several nations, most notably the United States, tried to offset the effect of higher energy bills by boosting spending. The results were high inflation and vast deficits in the balance of payments, which eventually caused the dollar crisis of 1977–1978.

Although the U.S. dollar strongly rebounded during 1981–1985, largely because of President Reagan's economic policy (high interest rates, foreign capital inflow, and economic expansion), the dollar resumed its long downhill slide. The slide was attributed mainly to changes in U.S. government policy and a slowdown in the U.S. economy. Believing that the dollar had declined enough, the United States, Japan, West Germany, France, Britain, Canada, and Italy—also known as the **Group of Seven** (or G-7)—met in February 1987 and agreed to slow the dollar's fall. This agreement, also known as the **Louvre Accords,** called for the *G-7 nations* to support the falling dollar by pegging exchange rates within a narrow, undisclosed

Exhibit 9–1
World currency events
1973–2002

Date	Event	Impact
February 1973	U.S. dollar devalued	Devaluation pressure increases on U.S.$ forcing devaluation to $42.22/oz of gold.
February–March 1973	Currency markets in crisis	Fixed exchange rates no longer considered defensible; speculative pressures force closure of international foreign exchange markets for nearly two weeks; markets reopen with floating rates for major industrial currencies.
June 1973	U.S. dollar depreciation	Floating rates continue to drive the new free floating U.S.$ down by about 10 percent by June.
Fall 1973–1974	OPEC oil embargo	Organization of Petroleum Exporting Countries (OPEC) imposes oil embargo, eventually quadrupling world price of oil; because oil prices are stated in U.S.$, the U.S.$ recovers some of its former strength.
January 1976	Jamaica Agreement	IMF meeting in Jamaica results in the "legalization" of the floating exchange rate system already in effect; gold is demonetized as a reserve asset; IMF quotas are increased.
1977–1978	U.S. inflation rate rises	Rising U.S. inflation causes continued depreciation of the U.S.$.
March 1979	EMS created	European Monetary System (EMS) is created, establishing a cooperative exchange rate system for participating members of the EEC.
Summer 1979	OPEC raises prices	OPEC nations raise oil prices once again.
Fall 1979	Iranian assets frozen	President Carter responds to Iranian hostage crisis by freezing all Iranian assets held in U.S. financial institutions.
Spring 1980	U.S. dollar begins rise	Worldwide inflation and early signs of recession coupled with real interest differential advantages for dollar-denominated assets contribute to rising demand for dollars.
August 1982	Latin American debt crisis	Mexico informs U.S. Treasury that it will be unable to make debt service payments; Brazil and Argentina follow suit; the debt crisis begins.
February 1985	U.S. dollar peaks	U.S. dollar peaks against most major industrial currencies, hitting record highs against the deutsche mark and other European currencies.
September 1985	Plaza Agreement	Group of Five members, meeting at the Plaza Hotel in New York, sign an international cooperative agreement to control the volatility of world currency markets and establish currency target zones.
February 1987	Louvre Accords	Group of Seven members state they will "intensify" economic policy coordination to promote growth and reduce external imbalances.
September 1992	EMS crisis	High German interest rates induce massive capital flows into Germany and deutsche mark-denominated assets, eventually causing the withdrawal of the Italian lira and British pound from the EMS's Exchange Rate Mechanism (ERM).
July 31, 1993	EMS realignment	EMS adjusts allowable deviation band to +/− 15% for all member currencies (except the Dutch guilder); U.S. dollar continues to weaken against other major currencies; Japanese yen reaches ¥100.25/$ in August 1993.

continued

Date	Event	Impact
1994	EMI founded	European Monetary Institute, the predecessor to the European Central Bank, is founded in Frankfurt, Germany.
December 1994	Peso collapses	Mexican peso suffers major devaluation as a result of increasing pressure on the managed devaluation policy; peso falls from Ps3.46/$ to Ps5.50/$ within days. The peso's collapse results in a fall in most major Latin American exchanges (tequila effect).
August 1995	Yen peaks	Japanese yen reaches an all-time high versus the U.S. dollar of ¥79/$; yen slowly depreciates over the following two-year period, rising to over ¥130/$.
June 1997	Asian financial crisis	First afflicting Thailand in June 1997, then quickly spreading to South Korea, Indonesia, Malaysia, the Philippines, and other Southeast and East Asian countries.
August 1998	Financial turmoil in Russia and Latin America	Influenced by the Asian crisis, Russia devaluates the ruble and unilaterally restructures its debts. The situation worsens following the devaluation in Brazil in January 1999.
January 1, 1999	Euro launched	Official launch date for the single European currency, the euro. Participating states' exchange rates will be irrevocably locked; European Monetary Institute will be succeeded by the European Central Bank, establishing a single monetary policy for Europe.
January 1, 2002	Euro coinage	Euro coins and notes are introduced in parallel with home currencies; transition period to last no more than six months.

range. They agreed that exchange rates had been sufficiently realigned and pledged to support stability of exchange rates at or near their current levels. Although the dollar declined further during 1987, it rallied in early 1988, thereby ending for the moment its dramatic volatility during the period 1980–1987. The U.S. dollar fell again in 1990 but then stayed basically flat during 1991–1992. It began falling again in 1993, especially against the Japanese yen and DM.

The turmoil that rocked Asian foreign exchange markets since June 1997 was the third major crisis of the 1990s. Its two predecessors were the crisis in the European Monetary System (EMS) of 1992–1993 and the Mexican peso crisis of 1994–1995 (see opening case). The collapse of the Thai currency, the baht, started the Asian crisis in June 1997. In one month, the baht lost 20 percent of its value against the dollar. The currencies of the Philippines, Malaysia, and Indonesia all weakened as well. Malaysian Prime Minister Mahathir Mohamad blasted "rogue speculators." Later he called billionaire hedge-fund manager George Soros a "moron" for betting against Asian currencies. In August 1997, Indonesian authorities were forced to allow the national currency, the rupiah, to move freely against other currencies. In December 1997, the IMF put together a $58.4 billion international bailout for Korea, the largest ever. The Koreans decided to let the won float. Faced with rapidly deteriorating foreign currency reserves, the Russian authorities devalued the ruble in August 1998. The U.S. Federal Reserve responded to fear of a U.S. credit crunch by lowering interest rates three times in quick succession during the course of the fall, including a rare unilateral move by Fed Chairman Alan Greenspan. Other industrialized countries such as Canada, Japan, and most of the European nations also eased monetary policies in September 1998. In October 1998, the world's rich nations, the G-7, endorsed a U.S. plan to allow the IMF to lend to countries before they get into financial difficulties. Exhibit 9–1 lists major events related to the international monetary system during 1973–2002.

1. The international monetary system has undergone several phases, including the gold standard period (1876–1914), the interwar years and World War II (1914–1944), the Bretton Woods system (1944–1973), and the post-Bretton Woods system (1973–present).

2. The fixed exchange rate system was a staple of the international monetary system prior to March 1973 and the floating exchange rate system was dominant after March 1973.

CONTEMPORARY EXCHANGE RATE SYSTEMS

Fixed-Rate System

Under a **fixed-rate system,** governments (through their central banks) buy or sell their currencies in the foreign exchange market whenever exchange rates deviate from their stated par values. A purely fixed-rate system is employed currently by only a few centrally planned economies such as Cuba and North Korea. In these economies, it is generally mandatory that a local firm's foreign exchange earnings be surrendered to the central bank, which in return pays the firm a corresponding amount in local currency. The central bank often allocates these foreign exchange incomes to state-owned users on the basis of governmental priorities. Exhibit 9–2 presents typical foreign exchange control measures used by governments under fixed or managed foreign exchange systems.

Despite drawbacks such as resource misallocation, distortion of foreign exchange demand and supply, and a drag on company performance, the fixed-rate system may help economies stabilize their economic environment, emphasize priority projects that need foreign exchange, and control foreign exchange reserves. In a broader, international context, fixed rates provide stability in international prices for the conduct of trade, which in turn lessens risks for international companies.

Exhibit 9–2
Frequently used foreign exchange control measures

1. Import restrictions such as license or quota systems
2. Restrictions on remittance of foreign exchange such as profit, dividends, or royalty
3. Surrender of hard-currency export earnings to the central bank
4. Mandatory government approval for using a firm's retained foreign exchange earnings
5. Pre-deposit of foreign exchange expenditure for import business in interest-free accounts with the central bank for a certain period
6. Credit ceilings for foreign firms
7. Restriction or prohibition on offshore deposit or investment of hard currencies
8. Use of multiple exchange rates simultaneously for different items of the balance of payment

Crawling Peg System

The peg system is situated between the fixed-rate and float-rate systems. The **crawling peg** is an automatic system for revising the exchange rate, establishing a par value around which the rate can vary up to a given percentage point. The par value is revised regularly according to a formula determined by the authorities. Once the par value is set, the central bank intervenes whenever the market value approaches a limit point. Suppose, for example, that the par value of the Mexican peso is 3,000 pesos for one dollar, and that it can vary ±2 percent around this rate, between 3,060 pesos and 2,940 pesos. If the dollar approaches the rate of 3,060 pesos the central bank intervenes by buying pesos and selling dollars. If the dollar approaches 2,940 pesos, the central bank intervenes by selling pesos and buying dollars. If it hovers around a limit point for too long, causing frequent central bank intervention, a new par value closer to this point is established. Suppose the dollar was hovering around 3,060 pesos. The government might then establish the new par value at 3,060 pesos with new limit points at 3,121 and 2,999.

A government can peg its currency to either another single currency (see the Country Box for illustration) or to a "basket" of foreign currencies. Today, 62 of the 167 members of the IMF peg their currency to some other currency. The U.S. dollar is the base for 20 other currencies (e.g., Argentina, Iraq, Panama, Venezuela, Dominica, Hong Kong). The French franc is the base for 14 currencies (all issued by former French colonies in Africa). Similarly, six of the new countries created with the breakup of the Soviet Union peg their currency to the Russian ruble.

Other countries peg their currency to a composite basket of currencies, where the basket consists of a portfolio of currencies of their major trading partners. The base value of such a basket is more stable than any single currency. Under this regime, a country can peg its currency to the standard basket such as the Special Drawing Rights, or SDR (e.g., Libya and Myanmar), or to its own basket, designed to fit the country's unique trading and investing needs (e.g., Bangladesh, Cyprus,

---

COUNTRY BOX

Hong Kong

CAN THE HONG KONG DOLLAR RETAIN THE FIXED PEG TO THE U.S. DOLLAR?

Many analysts question whether or not Hong Kong can retain the fixed peg to the U.S. dollar. Several factors are in Hong Kong's favor. First, in addition to Hong Kong's foreign exchange reserves of some U.S.$75 billion, the Chinese government is also prepared to use its U.S.$140 billion of reserves to defend the HK dollar. China has a vested economic and political interest in preserving Hong Kong's exchange rate and financial stability. Second, the overall economy of Hong Kong remains strong, as reflected in recurring fiscal and balance-of-payments surpluses, an extremely long foreign debt service ratio (1.3 percent), and an efficiently regulated and supervised banking system. Non-performing loans account for less than 1 percent of advances and capital adequacy ratios are over 13 percent.

The risk is that coming off the peg now would lead to more frequent and intense speculation in the future in both the foreign exchange and equity markets, given the openness of these markets and the lack of exchange controls. A very small economy like Hong Kong, which serves as a regional financial and trading center, needs stability and certainty, which the peg provides. With the manufacturing sector accounting for less than 10 percent of GDP, the benefits of devaluation would be minimal. The peg system was established in 1984 to counter the uncertainty following the U.K.—PRC declaration of 1997 handover.

Source: Adapted from *Accountancy (International Edition)*, First Quarter 1998, anonymous, pp. 27–29.

Czech Republic, Iceland, Jordan, Kuwait, Nepal, Thailand, and Morocco). In the latter approach, the basket normally contains currencies of major trading partners, weighted according to trading relations with the focal country.

The peg system is not a panacea. When pegged rates become overvalued, countries are forced to deplete their foreign exchange reserves to defend the currency peg. With reserves depleted, countries try to manipulate interest rates but are often eventually forced to devalue, repegging at a lower rate or giving up the peg altogether. With a floating rate system, countries can maintain their foreign reserves and thereby maintain a defense against financial panic which often plagues pegged exchange regimes. Foreign creditors understand that the central bank has sufficient reserves to repay short-term debts, thereby eliminating the possibility of a self-fulfilling creditor panic. Also, governments are not forced to break their word when international or domestic events force change in market exchange rates. For example, in April 2002, undergoing economic meltdown and five changes of president in two weeks, Argentina (under the floating regime) declared the world's largest debt default and devalued its peso by more than 70 percent.

Target-Zone Arrangement

Target-zone arrangement is virtually a joint float system cooperatively arranged by a group of nations sharing some common interests and goals. Under a target-zone arrangement, countries adjust their national economic policies to maintain their exchange rates within a specific margin around agreed-upon, fixed central exchange rates. Such an arrangement exists for the major European currencies participating in the European Monetary System (EMS). Members of the European Union have a cooperative agreement to maintain their currencies within a set range against other members of their group. The **EMS** is, in essence, a peg of each country's currency to all the others, as well as a joint float of all member currencies together against non-EMS currencies. The target-zone arrangement helps minimize exchange rate instability and enhance economic stability in the group (zone). Exhibit 9–3 shows EMS's current Euro members and its eastward march.

Let us use the EMS to illustrate this type of arrangement. As part of the EMS, the members established the *ECU* (and later the *euro*), which plays a central role in the functioning of the EMS. Taking effect January 1, 1999, the **euro** is a composite currency for European Union countries (Denmark, the United Kingdom, and Sweden didn't join the euro as of 2002), with foreign exchange rates of the participating national currencies being irrevocably fixed against one another and against the euro. The euro now functions as a unit of account, a means of settlement, a reserve asset for the members of the European Union and a real currency. At the heart of the EMS is an exchange-rate mechanism, which allows each member to determine a mutually agreed central exchange rate for its currency; each rate is denominated in currency units per euro (e.g., DM2.05853 per euro). Central rates establish a grid of cross-exchange rates between currencies. For example, 2.05853 deutsche marks per euro, divided by 6.90403 French francs per euro, equals 0.29816 DM per French francs. Member nations pledged to keep their currencies within a ±2.25 percent margin around their central cross-exchange rates (Spain has a 6 percent margin).

The **European Central Bank** (ECB), based in Frankfurt and established in June 1998, is the central bank in the euro zone. It is as powerful in Europe as the Federal Reserve is in the United States. This central bank sets interest rates for the euro zone. However, the ECB is not a duplicate of the U.S. Fed. One of the most important differences between the two is their respective mandates. The Fed's goal is to balance the objectives of price stability with those of employment and economic growth. The ECB, on the other hand, has a narrower focus patterned on the

Exhibit 9–3
The Euro's eastward march

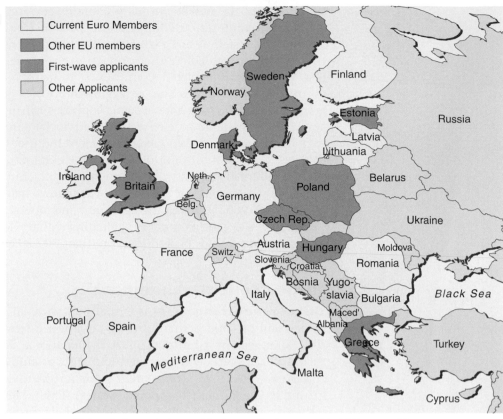

Source: The ECB heads for turbulence, *The Economist,* January 29, 2000, page 82.

Bundesbank (Germany's former central bank). It is only responsible for keeping prices stable. In addition, the Fed deals with only one government, whereas the ECB is faced with all member governments each with their own fiscal policies. Finance ministers from the currency-union members hold informal meetings regularly to coordinate fiscal policies.

The target-zone arrangement is not without problems. Owing to the divergence of national policies, the level of economic development, and the trade structure, it is difficult for every member to maintain the central exchange rate for a long period of time. Moreover, when currency speculators attack one of the zone currencies, defense is more costly. In fact, the euro's exchange rate mechanism had to be realigned in 1992, as a result of attacks by speculators against the Nordic currencies (Finland, Sweden, and Norway) as well as the French franc, British pound, and Italian lira, successively.

Managed Float System

The **managed float,** also known as a *dirty float,* is employed by governments to preserve an orderly pattern of exchange rate changes and is designed to eliminate excess volatility. Each central bank sets the nation's exchange rate against a predetermined goal, but allows the rate to vary. In other words, rate change is not automatic but is based on the government's view of an appropriate rate in the context of the country's balance-of-payments position, foreign exchange reserves, and rates quoted outside the official market. Rather than resist the underlying market forces, the authorities occasionally intervene by buying or selling domestic currency

The euro has become a real currency since January 2002.

to smooth the transition from one rate to another. At other times they intervene to moderate or counteract self-correcting cyclical or seasonal market forces. The rationale for the managed float is to improve the economic and financial environment by reducing uncertainty. For instance, government intervention may reduce exporters' uncertainty caused by disruptive exchange rate changes. Currently, about 40 countries (e.g., Brazil, China, Egypt, Hungary, Korea, Israel, Poland, Turkey, Russia) maintain a managed float system. The challenge behind this approach is to define just what is meant by "excess volatility." It is also questionable if governments are more capable than markets in determining what is fundamental and what is temporary and self-correcting.[1]

Independent Float System

Approximately 55 countries currently allow full flexibility through an **independent float,** also known as a *clean float.* Under this system, an exchange rate is allowed to adjust freely to the supply and demand of this currency for another. Consequently, there is usually no need for an economy to undergo the painful adjustment process set in motion by a decrease or increase in the money supply. This category contains currencies of both developed (e.g., USA) and developing (e.g., Peru) countries. Central banks of these countries allow exchange rates to be determined by market forces alone. Although some central banks may intervene in the market from time to time, such intervening usually attempts to alleviate speculative pressures on their currency. Further, central banks intervene only as one of many anonymous participants in the free market in an occasional, non-continuous manner. Exhibit 9–4 shows sample countries and their exchange rate systems.

Advantages and Disadvantages of the Floating System

The float-rate system, whether managed or independent, is the dominant system in the beginning of the twenty-first century, utilized by about 100 countries. The flexible exchange rate system provides a less painful adjustment mechanism to trade imbalances than do fixed exchange rates and prevents a country from having large

Exhibit 9–4
Sample countries using different exchange rate systems

Independent Float	Managed Float	Target Zone	Crawling Peg	Fixed
United States	Singapore	Austria	Argentina	North Korea
Peru	Afghanistan	Belgium	Iraq	Cuba
Philippines	Brazil	France	Panama	
Romania	Australia	Germany	Hong Kong	
South Africa	China	Ireland	Cameroon	
Yemen	Canada	Luxembourg	Chad	
Zambia	India	Netherlands	Togo	
Denmark	Japan	Portugal	Estonia	
Yemen	Israel	Spain	Libya	
Zimbabwe	Korea	Finland	Bangladesh	
Paraguay	Malaysia	Italy	Czech Republic	
Sudan	Poland	Greece	Kuwait	
Tanzania	Russia	United Kingdom	Iceland	

persistent deficits. Unlike the fixed-rate system, which requires a recession to reduce real (inflation-adjusted) income or prices when trade deficits arise, flexible exchange rates will only lower the foreign exchange value of the currency. In a fixed rate system, reducing local currency income (wages) is likely to be painful for political and social reasons even though this reduction (and thus the decline in the value of this nation's currency) can improve trade balance.[2]

Moreover, flexible exchange rates do not require central banks to hold foreign exchange reserves because there is no need to intervene in the foreign exchange market. This means that the problem of insufficient liquidity (foreign exchange reserves) does not exist with truly flexible rates. Further, flexible exchange rates avoid the need for strict import and export regulations such as tariffs, foreign exchange control, and import restrictions. These regulations are not only costly to enforce but also prone to criticism and even retaliation from trade partner countries.

Finally, floating exchange rates can help ensure the independence of trade policies. For example, if the United States allows rapid growth in the money supply, this will tend to raise U.S. prices and lower interest rates (in the short run), the former causing a deficit or deterioration in the current account and the latter causing a deficit or deterioration in the capital account. If, for example, the Canadian dollar were fixed to the U.S. dollar, the deficit in the United States would most likely mean a surplus in Canada. This would put upward pressure on the Canadian dollar, forcing the Bank of Canada to sell Canadian dollars and hence increase the Canadian money supply. In this case an increase in the U.S. money supply would cause an increase in the Canadian money supply. However, if exchange rates were flexible, the U.S. dollar would simply depreciate against the Canadian dollar.

The role of flexible rates, however, is limited in balancing trade after a certain period of time. A depreciation or devaluation of currency will help the balance of trade if it reduces the relative prices of locally produced goods and services. However, after a short period of time, domestic prices of tradable goods will rise following depreciation or devaluation. This will increase the cost of living, which puts upward pressure on wages.[3] For example, if 1 percent depreciation raises production costs by the same percentage point, and if real wages are maintained, then nominal wages must rise by the amount of depreciation or devaluation. If wages rise 1 percent when the currency falls by 1 percent, the effects are offsetting, and changes in exchange rates will be ineffective. In addition, flexible rates could make it more difficult for governments to control inflation and also create less motivation for governments to combat it.[4] Finally, free float rates may cause more uncertainty, which may in turn hamper the growth and stability of economies vulnerable to international financial and export markets. Under the floating system, international speculators can cause wide swings in the values of different currencies. These swings are the result of the movement of "hot money chasing better returns and the enormous speed of capital flows whose scale dwarfs that of trade flows."[5]

Interim Summary

1. Countries utilize the crawling peg system, target-zone arrangement, managed float system, or independent float system in a rising sequence of flexibility and volatility.

2. Countries select different exchange rate systems because they have different goals, different levels of internationalization, and different capabilities of managing foreign exchange volatility.

DETERMINATION OF FOREIGN EXCHANGE RATES

The determination of a national currency's exchange rate should answer two basic questions: (1) *how is the base rate between this nation's currency and foreign currencies determined?* That is, what is the underlying criterion used to determine the base level *(stocks)* of exchange rate of a currency vis-à-vis others? and (2) *how does a nation's exchange rate change over time (flows)?* That is, what are the conditions under which the exchange rate should change, and how?

Under the gold standard regime (1876–1914), the base level of a currency's exchange rate was determined by the stated value of gold per unit of the currency. Assuming, for example, one deutsche mark is worth 0.02 ounce of gold while one U.S. dollar is worth 0.048 ounce of gold. The gold equivalent then becomes the underlying criterion used in determining the base rate of the deutsche mark against other currencies, such as the U.S. dollar (DM2.4/$1 in this case).

Under other foreign exchange regimes, however, there is no direct way to value one currency against others in terms of both stocks and flows. Moreover, the present international monetary system is characterized by a mix of free floating, managed floating, pegged or target zone, and fixed exchange rates. No single general theory is available to forecast exchange rates under all conditions. Nevertheless, it is widely agreed that the purchasing power parity principle helps explain both the stocks and the flows of exchange rates. Other principles or approaches to analyze foreign exchange movements include interest rate parity and international Fisher parity. The **purchasing power parity** (PPP) approach emphasizes the role of prices of goods and services in determining exchange rates, whereas the **interest rate parity** focuses on the role of capital movements. Although these two perspectives are insufficient to explain exchange rate changes, they are useful building blocks of foreign exchange determination.

Purchasing Power Parity (PPP)

The purchasing power parity principle suggests that the exchange rate between two currencies should, in the long run, reflect purchasing power differences; that is, the exchange rate should equalize the price of an identical basket of goods and services in the two countries. This principle has absolute and relative perspectives toward purchasing power parity. **Absolute PPP** states that the exchange rate is determined by the relative prices of similar baskets of goods or services. In other words, the ratio of one currency's price of a bundle of goods and services to another currency's price of the same bundle should be the exchange rate between the two. For example, if the identical basket of goods cost ¥1000 in Japan and $10 in the United States, the PPP-based exchange rate would be ¥100/$1.

The PPP principle in the absolute, or static, form offers a simple explanation for exchange rate determination. However, it is difficult in practice to compute the price indices. Different baskets of goods are used in different countries, given the different demand structures and consumption behaviors. To avoid this deficiency, **relative PPP** focuses on the relationship between the change in prices of two countries and the change in the exchange rate over the same period. The relative **PPP** suggests that if the exchange rate between two countries starts in equilibrium, any change in the differential rate of inflation between them tends to be offset over the long run by an equal but opposite change in the exchange rate. If the domestic inflation level is rising faster than the foreign inflation level, the exchange rate is depreciating. If the foreign inflation level is rising faster than the domestic inflation level, the exchange rate is appreciating. If the exchange rate does not change in this situation, the country's exports of goods and services will become less competitive with comparable products produced elsewhere. Imports from abroad will also become more price-competitive than higher-priced domestic products.

The PPP principle offers an economic foundation for determining and adjusting the exchange rates. In the real business world, however, PPP conditions may not always hold. The exchange rates are thus not always determined by the purchasing power parity. Reasons for departures from PPP include:

1. The PPP principle assumes that goods or services can move freely across borders. In practice, however, we see many restrictions on movement of goods and services (e.g., tariff and non-tariff barriers). These barriers affect both the price and quantity of exports and imports.

2. Many of the items that are often included in the commonly used price indexes do not enter into international trade (e.g., land and buildings). These non-traded items can allow departures from PPP to persist.

3. The PPP principle fails to consider cross-border transportation costs which enlarge the PPP deviations.

4. The PPP principle fails to consider the reality that different items have different weights in various nations' price indexes.

Interest Rate Parity (IRP)

The PPP principle focuses only on goods and services and omits the importance of capital flows in the determination of exchange rates. To redress this limitation, the **interest rate parity** (IRP) principle provides an understanding of the way in which interest rates are linked between different countries through capital flows. The IRP principle suggests that the difference in national interest rates for securities of similar risk and maturity should be equal to, but opposite in sign of, the forward rate discount or premium for the foreign currency. A **forward rate** is the rate at which a bank is willing to exchange one currency for another at some specified future date. If this exchange takes place immediately, this rate is called a spot rate. A forward rate discount (premium) measures the percentage by which the forward rate is less (more) than the spot rate at a specific date. The IRP implies that the interest rate differential between two countries will be matched by the forward premium of the exchange rate. This relation holds due to efficient arbitrage in risk-free assets. It can be applied to international investments as well as to international lending. The rationale underlying the IRP is that for investment projects, investors compare the return from the domestic market with the return from the foreign market; the latter is the return from the foreign asset plus the forward premium. For financing projects, borrowers compare the costs from the domestic market with those from the foreign market. Equilibrium will be achieved when interest parity is established.

Consider, for example, the case in which the one-year interest rate in New York is 8.75 percent, and in London 11.75 percent. This seems to suggest that investors will earn an excess return of 3 percent if the funds are invested in the London bond market (or that borrowers will acquire funds more inexpensively in New York). However, if the prevailing current spot rate is $1.6375/£1 and the one-year forward rate is $1.5883/£1, then investors who convert their proceeds back to U.S. dollars will have to pay a 3 percent forward discount on the pound sterling in the forward market. We see that the interest rate advantage is offset by the forward discount on the pound. If the investors did not use the forward market, they may suffer a loss greater than 3 percent, because the actual spot rate between dollar and pound a year later may drop more than 3 percent.

Like PPP, IRP also face deviations due to transaction costs and tax factors in financial markets. Political risks can also cause deviations from interest parity between countries because investors expect to be compensated for the greater risk of investing in a foreign country. The forward market and related terms will be discussed in detail later in this chapter.

The IRP is generally applicable to securities with maturities of one year or less, since forward contracts are not routinely available for periods longer than one year. Similar to the IRP principle but involving securities with maturity that could be longer than one year, the **international Fisher effect** addresses the relationship between the percentage change in the spot exchange rate over time and the differential between comparable interest rates in different national capital markets. Specifically, the international Fisher effect states that the spot exchange rate should change in an equal amount but in the opposite direction to the difference in interest rates between two countries. For example, if a dollar-based investor buys a 10-year yen bond earning 4 percent annual interest, compared with 6 percent interest available on dollars, the investor must be anticipating the yen to appreciate vis-à-vis the dollar by at least 2 percent per year during the 10 years.

Implications for MNEs: Foreign Exchange Forecasting

Because future exchange rates are uncertain, participants in international financial markets can never know for sure what the exchange rate will be one month or one year ahead. As a result, forecasts must be made. Some forecasters believe that for the major floating currencies, foreign exchange markets are "efficient" and forward exchange rates are unbiased predictors of future spot exchange rates. However, empirical studies rejected this hypothesis.[6] Although referencing to the forward rate (see next section) is still necessary and useful, and can be viewed as a baseline in forecasting a foreign exchange rate, international managers should take into account many economic and noneconomic factors in predicting foreign exchange rates, especially long-term rates (over one year).

Economic fundamentals that influence long-term exchange rates include balance of payments, foreign exchange reserves, relative inflation rates, relative interest rates, and the long-run properties of purchasing power parity. The strength of a focal country's economy, which is often reflected in its GDP (gross domestic product), GNP (gross national product), national income, investment growth, and export growth, among others, also influences the country's long-term exchange rates. Because governments differ in the extent to which they exert influence on foreign exchange rates, even under the floating system, managers should be aware of government declarations and agreements regarding exchange rate goals. Noneconomic fundamentals that may affect exchange rates include political or social events, bilateral relations between the two countries, market speculations against the currency, the confidence of market participants, and natural disasters.

In emerging markets with foreign exchange control set by the government, there often exist foreign exchange black (or parallel) markets in which buyers and sellers transact foreign currencies using the market rate, which is generally different from the official rate. Because this "market" rate is often a "shadow" price that reflects the demand and supply equilibrium in the foreign exchange market, it is often used as the reference rate in predicting managerial floating exchange rates. In predicting exchange rates, international managers also look at the country's foreign exchange rate system. If, for example, a country pegs its currency to that of another major trade partner, then the exchange rate prediction will emphasize the partner country's currency. To predict a long-term fixed rate, managers also need to see if the government is capable of controlling domestic inflation, in order to generate hard currency reserves to use for intervention, and to run trade surpluses. To predict a long-term floating rate, managers must focus on inflationary fundamentals and PPP as well as indicators for economic health such as growth and stability.

Time-series analysis of prior years, together with anticipated new factors about future changes, is a widely applied technique for predicting foreign exchange rates, particularly short-term trends. The accuracy of these forecasts depends on whether the foreign exchange market is efficient. The more efficient the market, the more likely it is that exchange rates are "random walks" (e.g., with past price behavior providing no clues to the future). The less efficient the foreign exchange market, the higher the probability that forecasters will find a key pattern that holds, at least in the short run. If the pattern is truly consistent, however, others will soon discover it and the market will become efficient again with respect to that information.

Interim Summary

1. The purchasing power parity (PPP) principle holds that the exchange rate between two currencies is determined in the long run by the price of an identical basket of goods and services. The interest rate parity (IRP) principle holds that the interest rate differential between two countries will be matched by the premium of their forward exchange rate.

2. To predict or forecast foreign exchange rates, international managers analyze both economic and noneconomic fundamentals, while making reference to forward or black market exchange rates.

THE BALANCE OF PAYMENTS

The exchange rate system is a necessary tool for international transactions involving different currencies. The national goal of these transactions is to accomplish gains from trade and investment activities, which are recorded in the balance-of-payments account. The **balance of payments** is an accounting statement that summarizes all the economic transactions between residents (individuals, companies, and other organizations) of the home country and those of all other countries. That is, it reports the country's international performance in trading with other nations and the volume of capital flowing in and out of the country. Balance of payments accounting uses the system of **double-entry bookkeeping,** which means that every debit or credit in the account is also represented as a credit or debit somewhere else. In a balance-of-payment sheet, currency inflows are recorded as *credits* (plus sign), whereas outflows are recorded as *debits* (minus sign).

A standard balance of payments includes *current account, capital account,* and *official reserves account.* Each category is made of several subcategories. To maintain the balance of the total credit and total debit, the statistical discrepancy is also included in a balance of payments. Statistical discrepancy reflects net *errors and omissions* in collecting data on international transactions. Exhibit 9–5 illustrates the United States' balance of payments sheet for 2000.

Current Account

The **current account** records flows of goods, services, and unilateral transfers (gifts). It includes exports and imports of merchandise (trade balance) and service transactions (also known as invisible items). The service account includes various service income and fees (e.g., interest, dividends, and royalty). Tourism income, financial charges (i.e., banking and insurance), and transportation charges (i.e., shipping and air travel) are part of service income. The investment income account separates

Exhibit 9–5
The U.S. balance of payments, 2000 (in billions of dollars)

CURRENT ACCOUNT		
Goods		
Exports	+772.21	
Imports	−1224.42	
Balance of Merchandise Trade	−452.21	
Services		
Exports	+293.49	
Imports	−217.02	
Balance of Services Trade	+76.47	
Investment Income		
Received	+352.87	
Paid	−367.66	
Balance of Investment Income	−14.79	
Unilateral Transfer (Net)	−54.14	
Balance on Current Account		−444.67
CAPITAL ACCOUNT		
Portfolio		
New Investment/Lending in		
United States	+736.56	
New U.S. Investment/Lending		
Abroad	−428.22	
Foreign Direct Investment		
New FDI in United States	+287.66	
New U.S. FDI Abroad	−152.44	
Balance on Capital Account		+443.56
OFFICIAL RESERVES ACCOUNT		−0.29
Gold	0	
SDRs	−0.72	
Reserve in the IMF	+2.31	
Foreign Currencies	−1.88	
ERRORS AND OMISSIONS		+1.40
NET BALANCE		0

Source: Bureau of Economic Analysis, U.S. Department of Commerce, Washington, D.C. (www.bea.doc.gov).

investment income from service income, and it records income receipts on the country-owned assets abroad and income payments on foreign-owned assets within the country. Unilateral transfers include pensions, remittances, and other transfers for which no specific services are furnished.

Capital Account

The **capital account** records private and public investment or lending activities and is divided into portfolio (short- and long-term) and foreign direct investment. Foreign branches, wholly-owned subsidiaries and joint ventures are typical forms of direct investments. Foreign bonds, notes, or mutual funds are examples of portfolio investment insofar as they confer no management or voting rights on their owners. The portfolio account includes both short-term (e.g., cash, deposits, and bills) and long-term investments or lending (e.g., securities with a maturity longer than one year, bank loans, and mortgages). Government borrowing and lending are also included in the capital account.

Official Reserves Account

The **official reserves account** records net holdings of the official reserves held by a national government. Reserves include gold, special drawing rights (SDRs), reserve positions in the IMF, and convertible foreign currencies. To most countries, foreign currency is by far the largest component of total international liquidity. Each government normally keeps foreign exchange reserves in the form of foreign treasury bills, short-term and long-term government securities, euros, and the like.

Note that the implications of the balance of payments, especially trade deficits or surplus under current account, may change over time and is subject to interpretation. Today many imports are actually "exported" by the country's own companies operating in a trading partner country. But, statistically, they are still "imports" recorded in the balance of payments. The United States had, for example, a $52.67 billion merchandise trade deficit with China, followed by 45.67 with Japan, 37.57 with Canada, and 19.86 with Mexico, as of August 2001. However, a sizable percentage of imports entering the United States were in fact "exported" by American companies (e.g., RCA, HP, Pepsi, GE, Xerox, and Rubbermaid) investing and operating in these partner countries. One-third of China's total exports ($249 billion in 2000), for instance, are undertaken by foreign investors in the country. From a wealth creation perspective, these "imports" may be viewed as a plus, rather than minus, sign in the balance of payments.

Interim Summary

1. The balance of payments records economic transactions between one country and the rest of the world. It contains current account, capital account, and official reserves balance.

2. A nation's trade deficits (such as those in the United States) may be reinterpreted if a large number of MNEs from this nation invest abroad and export back their products.

INTERNATIONAL FOREIGN EXCHANGE MARKETS

The international monetary systems introduced earlier are not the only influence on foreign currency movements. International financial markets also play a crucial role. International monetary systems and international financial markets are inherently linked such that the former impact company decisions or firm operations through the latter. International firms face many opportunities as well as threats arising from the international financial markets, which are determined at least partly by the monetary systems. International financial markets are composed of *international foreign exchange markets* and *international capital markets*. International capital markets further include (a) international money markets, (b) international stock markets, (c) international bond markets, and (d) international loan markets (see Exhibit 9–6).

Exhibit 9–6
International financial markets

INTERNATIONAL FINANCIAL MARKETS				
International Foreign Exchange Market	International Capital Markets			
	International Money Market	International Stock Market	International Bond Market	International Loan Market

Landscape of the International Foreign Exchange Market

The **foreign exchange market** is where foreign currencies are bought and sold. It is the physical as well as institutional structure through which currencies are exchanged, exchange rates determined, and foreign exchange transactions completed. A **foreign exchange transaction** is an agreement between a buyer and seller for the delivery of a certain amount of one currency at a specified rate in exchange for some other currency. The 1999 survey of foreign exchange markets conducted by the BIS (Bank of International Settlements) illustrated that average daily turnover in the international foreign exchange market was about $1.5 trillion. The U.S. dollar was the most actively traded currency, reflecting its liquidity, its use as a settlement currency, and its predominance in trade-related transactions. The dollar was involved in over 80 percent of all foreign exchange transactions in 2001. The second and third most traded currencies were the deutsche mark and Japanese yen, respectively.

The global foreign exchange business is concentrated in four centers, which together account for about two-thirds of total reported turnover. These four centers are London, New York, Tokyo, and Singapore. Other important exchange markets are located in Paris, Frankfurt, Hong Kong, Amsterdam, Milan, Zurich, Toronto, Brussels, and Bahrain. A larger share of U.S. dollar turnover and deutsche mark turnover is conducted in London than in either New York or Frankfurt. The foreign exchange market is dominated by dealers, and is becoming increasingly automated and concentrated.

Market Participants and Functions

A market for foreign exchange consists of *individuals, corporations, banks,* and *brokers* who buy or sell currencies. Currency trading in each country is conducted through the intermediation of foreign-exchange brokers, who match currency bids and offers of banks and also trade directly among themselves internationally. Banks in each country and throughout the world are linked together by telephone, Internet, telex, and a satellite communications network called the **Society for Worldwide International Financial Telecommunications (SWIFT)** based in Brussels, Belgium. Despite the long distance separating market participants, this computer-based communication system makes all significant events virtually instantaneously impacting everywhere in the financial world. This in turn contributes to a worldwide market with narrower spreads for participants.

Although the market is global, the exchange market in each country has its own identity and institutional and regulatory framework. An efficient communication system can substitute for participants' need to convene in a specific location *(bourse)*. Indeed, the U.K.–U.S. type of market is based on communication networks, whereas the European approach remains traditional, based on the physical meeting of the participants, usually at the bourse. Daily meetings take place in some markets such as those in Frankfurt and Paris, where representatives of commercial banks and central banks meet and determine a rate, known as the fixing rate. In those countries, the posted fixing rates serve as a guide for pricing small to medium-sized transactions between banks and their customers. Among major industrial countries, Japan, Germany, France, Italy, and the Scandinavian and the Benelux countries have a daily fixing. The United Kingdom, Switzerland, Canada, and the United States do not.

Foreign exchange is traded in a 24-hour market. As the market in the Far East closes, trading in the Middle Eastern financial centers has been going on for a couple of hours, and trading in Europe is just beginning. As the London market closes, the one in New York opens. A few hours later, the market in San Francisco opens and trades with the East Coast of the United States and the Far East as well. Banks dominate the foreign exchange market, with about 90 percent of foreign-exchange trading constituting interbank trading. Nonbank participants in foreign-exchange trading include commodities dealers, multinational corporations, and nonbank financial institutions.

The foreign-exchange market performs three major functions:

1. It is part of the international payments system and provides a mechanism for exchange or transfer of the national currency of one country into the currency of another country, thereby facilitating international business.

2. It assists in supplying short-term credits through the Eurocurrency market (see next section) and swap arrangements.

3. It provides foreign-exchange instruments for hedging against exchange risk. Although most commercial banks handle actions for their clients, many banks also act as market-makers, with each prepared to deal with other banks at any time. This activity constitutes interbank market, where portfolio positions are adjusted and exchange rates determined.

Foreign-exchange trading expanded sharply under the floating exchange rate system, and the number of banks participating in the market increased significantly as they entered the market to service their corporate clients. Increased hedging by companies of their cash flows and balance sheets was accompanied by the entry of new corporate participants into the market.

Foreign Exchange Rate Quotations

A foreign exchange quotation is the expression of willingness to buy or sell at a set rate. There are several pairs of quotations being used in foreign exchange businesses. Correctly interpreting the meaning of these quotations is important, as they are easy to confuse.

Direct and Indirect

A **direct quote** is a home currency price of a foreign currency unit (e.g., C$1.489/U.S.$1 in Canada), whereas an **indirect quote** is a foreign currency price of a home currency unit (U.S.$0.67182/C$1 in Canada). Under a direct quote, an increase of the exchange rate (e.g., from C$1.489 to C$1.589 per dollar) means depreciation of the home currency (C$) or appreciation of the foreign currency (U.S.$). Conversely, under an indirect quote, an increase of the exchange rate (e.g., from U.S.$0.67182 to U.S.$0.68182 per Canadian dollar) means the appreciation of the home currency (C$) or depreciation of the foreign currency (U.S.$). In most countries, banks use a direct quote.

Exhibit 9–7

Spot and forward quotations between U.S. dollar and deutsche mark (DM)

	American Terms ($/DM)		European Terms (DM/$)	
	Bid	Offer	Bid	Offer
Spot	0.6396	0.6400	1.5625	1.5635
Forward-1 month	0.6419	0.6424	1.5567	1.5579
Forward-3 months	0.6466	0.6472	1.5450	1.5466
Forward-6 months	0.6536	0.6543	1.5283	1.5301

Note: 1 euro = DM1.95583 (euro fixed exchange rate)

Bid and Offer

A **bid** is the exchange rate in one currency at which a dealer (usually bank) will buy another currency. An **offer** (also referred to as *ask*) is the exchange rate at which a dealer (usually a bank) will sell the other currency. The difference between the bid and offer prices, also known as the **bid-ask spread,** is the compensation for transaction cost for the dealer. For example, a Canadian bank's quotation for the U.S. dollar (U.S.$/C$) may be: 0.6718 (bid) and 0.6748 (offer). For widely traded currencies such as the U.S. dollar, euro, yen, or pound, the spread ranges from 0.05 to 0.08 percent.

Spot and Forward

This pair of quotes is used for foreign exchange transactions between dealers in the interbank market. A **spot rate** is the exchange rate for a transaction that requires almost immediate delivery of foreign exchange (normally before the end of the second business day). A **forward rate** is the exchange rate for a transaction that requires delivery of foreign exchange at specified future date (e.g., 30-day, 90-day, or 180-day). See Exhibit 9–7 for some examples.

Cross Rates

The **cross rate** is the exchange rate between two infrequently traded currencies, calculated through a widely traded third currency. For example, an Argentine importer needs the Hong Kong dollar to pay for a purchase in Hong Kong. The Argentinean peso is not quoted against the Hong Kong dollar. However, both currencies are quoted against the U.S. dollar. Assuming:

Argentinean Peso:	Arg$0.998/US$1
Hong Kong Dollar:	HK$7.798/US$1
Cross Rates Between Arg$ and HK$:	Arg$0.998/HK$7.798 = Arg$0.128/HK$
	or HK$7.798/Arg$0.998 = HK$7.814/Arg$

Transaction Forms

Spot Transactions

Spot transactions include bank notes transactions for individuals and spot transactions between banks. Bank notes transactions such as currency changes for individuals are exchanged for each other instantaneously over the counter. Spot transactions between banks, however, are normally settled on the second working day after the date on which the transaction is concluded. The interbank foreign exchange market is by far the world's largest financial market. On the *settlement date* (also referred to as *value date*), most dollar transactions in the world are settled through the computerized **Clearing House Interbank Payments Systems (CHIPS)** in New York, which provides for calculation of new balances owed by any one bank to another and for payment by 6:00 P.M. the same day in Federal Reserve Bank of New York funds. This system, owned by large New York clearing banks, has more than 150 members, including the U.S. agencies and subsidiaries of many foreign banks. It handles over 150,000 transactions a day, together worth hundreds of billions of dollars. Similar systems also exist in other major foreign exchange centers where currencies other than the U.S. dollar are settled.

When a company (or individual) needs foreign exchange to be paid to a foreign company, it can use either customer drafts or international wire transfers through a bank. The bank sells this company a foreign exchange draft payable to the stated foreign company. For example, if a U.S. business needs to make a Japanese yen payment to a Japanese company, it can buy a yen draft from a U.S. bank, where this draft is drawn against the U.S. bank's yen account at a Japanese bank. A wire transfer is the fastest settlement for international companies, paying foreign exchange to their foreign creditors. Under a wire transfer, the payment instructions are sent via SWIFT or similar electronic means.

Forward Transactions

A **forward transaction** occurs between a bank and a customer (company, broker, or another bank), calling for delivery at a fixed future date, of a specified amount of foreign exchange at the fixed forward exchange rate. This exchange rate is established at the time of agreement, but payment and delivery are not required until maturity. Customers such as international companies may either buy a foreign currency forward from a bank (e.g., in an import business) or sell a foreign currency forward to a bank (e.g., in an export bank). If the initial transaction represents an asset or future ownership claim to foreign currency, this position is described as a **long position.** If the cash market position represents a liability or a future obligation to deliver foreign currency, this position is described as a **short position.** Chapter 14 will describe forward transactions to avoid foreign exchange risks for MNEs.

Swap Transactions

A **swap** is an agreement to buy and sell foreign exchange at prespecified exchange rates where the buying and selling are separated in time. In other words, a **swap transaction** involves the simultaneous purchase and sale of a given amount for two different settlement dates. Both purchase and sale are carried out by the same counter-party. Two common types of swap transactions are spot-forward swaps and forward-forward swaps.

In a **spot-forward swap,** an investor sells forward the foreign currency maturity value of the bill, and simultaneously buys the spot foreign exchange to pay for the bill. Since a known amount of the investor's home currency will be received according to the forward component of the swap, no uncertainty from exchange rates exists. Similarly, those who borrow in foreign currency can buy forward the foreign currency needed for repayment of the foreign currency loan at the same time that they convert the borrowed foreign funds on the spot market.

A **forward-forward swap** involves two forward transactions. For example, a dealer sells Euro1,000,000 forward for dollars for delivery in three months at U.S.$0.94/Euro, and simultaneously buys Euro1,000,000 forward for delivery in six months at U.S.$0.94/Euro. The difference between the buying price and the selling price is equivalent to the three-month interest rate differential between the deutsche mark and the U.S. dollar.

The two preceding types of swaps are particularly popular with banks, because it is difficult for them to avoid risk when making a market for many future dates and currencies. For some dates and currencies, a bank may be in a long position, which means that it has agreed to purchase more of the foreign currency than it has agreed to sell. For other dates and currencies, the bank may be in a short position, which means that it has agreed to sell more of these currencies than it has agreed to buy. Swaps help the bank to balance its position and reduce financial risk.

Foreign Exchange Arbitrage

In the foreign exchange market, price information is readily available through computer networks, which makes it easy to compare prices in different markets. As such, exchange rates tend to be equal worldwide but temporary discrepancies do exist. These temporary discrepancies provide profit opportunities for simultaneously buying a currency in one market (at lower price) while selling it in another (at higher price). This activity is known as **arbitrage.** Arbitrage will continue until the exchange rates in different locales are so close that it is not worth the costs incurred in further buying and selling.[7]

For example, suppose Citibank is quoting the German mark/U.S.dollar exchange rate as 1.4445–55 and Dresdner Bank in Frankfurt is quoting 1.4425–35. This means that Citibank will buy dollars for 1.4445 marks and will sell dollars for 1.4455 marks. Dresdner will buy dollars for 1.4425 marks and will sell dollars for 1.4435 marks. This presents an arbitrage opportunity. We could buy $10 million at Dresdner's ask price of 1.4435 and simultaneously sell $10 million to Citibank at their bid price of 1.4445 marks. This would earn a profit of DM0.0010 marks per dollar traded, so DM 10,000 would be the total arbitrage profit. If such a profit opportunity exists, the demand to buy dollars from Dresdner will cause it to raise its ask price above 1.4435, while the increased interest in selling dollars to Citibank at its bid price of 1.4445 marks will cause it to lower its bid. In this way, arbitrage activity pushes the prices of different traders to levels where no arbitrage profits are earned.

Arbitrage could also involve three or more currencies. Let us temporarily ignore the bid-ask spread and associated transaction costs. Suppose that in London $/£ = 2.00, while in New York $/DM = 0.40, then £/DM = 0.40/2.00 = 0.2. If we observe a market where one of the three exchange rates— $/£, $/DM, £/DM—is out of line with the other two, there is an arbitrage opportunity. Suppose that in Frankfurt the exchange rate is £/DM = 0.2, while in New York $/DM = 0.40, but in London $/£ = $1.90. A trader could start with dollars and use $1.9 million to buy £/1 million in London since $/£ = $1.90. The pounds then could be used to buy marks at £/DM = 0.2, so that £1,000,000 = DM5,000,000. The DM 5 million could then be used in New York to buy dollars at $/DM = $0.40, so that DM5,000,000 = $2,000,000. Thus the initial $1.9 million could be turned into $2 million with the triangular arbitrage action earning the trader $100,000.

Black Market and Parallel Market

As a result of government restrictions or legal prohibitions on foreign exchange transactions, illegal markets in foreign exchange exist in many developing countries in response to business or private demand for foreign exchange. These illegal markets are known as **black markets.** Such illegal markets exist openly in some countries (e.g., Brazil and Venezuela), with little government interference. In some other countries however, foreign exchange laws are strictly enforced and lawbreakers receive harsh sentences when caught (e.g., China before 1985).

Often, governments set an official exchange rate that deviates widely from that which the free market would establish. If a government will purchase foreign exchange only at the official rate, but private citizens are willing to pay the market-determined rate, there will be a steady supply of foreign exchange to the black market. Obviously, government policy creates the black market. The demand arises because of legal restrictions on buying foreign exchange, and the supply exists because government-mandated official exchange rates offer less than the free market rate. Ironically, governments defend the need for foreign exchange restrictions based on conserving scarce foreign exchange for high-priority uses. But such restrictions work to reduce the amount of foreign exchange that flows to the government as traders turn to the black market instead.

When the black market is legalized by the government, this market is referred to as the **parallel market** and operates as an alternative to the official exchange market. In many countries facing economic hardship, the parallel markets allow normal economic activities to continue through a steady supply of foreign exchange. For instance, Guatemala had an artificially low official exchange rate of one quetzale per dollar for more than three decades; however, a black market where the exchange rate fluctuated daily with market conditions was allowed to operate openly in front of the country's main post office. In Mexico, this parallel market thrived during times of crisis when the official peso/dollar exchange rate varied greatly from the market rate. For instance, in August 1982, the Mexican government banned the sale of dollars by Mexican banks. Immediately, the parallel market responded. The official exchange rate was 69.5 pesos per dollar, but the rate on the street ranged from 120 to 150 as the parallel market demand increased with the ban on bank sales. Private currency trades between individuals were legal, so trading flourished at the Mexico City airport and other public places.

Interim Summary

1. A foreign exchange market consists of individuals, corporations, banks, and brokers who buy or sell currencies. Major foreign exchange markets in the world include London, New York, Tokyo, and Singapore. International foreign exchange markets offer spot transactions, forward transactions, and swap transactions.

2. It is possible to earn profits from foreign exchange arbitrage—simultaneously buying a currency in one market at a lower price while selling it in another market at a higher price. This type of activity escalates volatility in international foreign exchange markets.

INTERNATIONAL CAPITAL MARKETS

International Money Markets

International money markets are the markets in which foreign monies are financed or invested (e.g., Hitachi and Matsushita borrowed U.S. dollars from several U.S. banks in Tokyo to finance their worldwide operations). MNEs use international money markets to finance global operations at a lower cost than is possible domestically. They borrow currencies that have low interest rates and are expected to depreciate against their own currency. They incur the risk that the currencies borrowed may appreciate, however, which will increase their cost of financing. Investors, on the other hand, may achieve substantially higher returns in foreign markets than in their domestic markets when investing in currencies that appreciate against their home currency. However, if these currencies depreciate, the effective yield on the foreign investments will likely be lower than the domestic yield, and may even be negative. Investors attempt to capitalize on potentially high effective yields on foreign money market securities, while reducing the exchange rate risk by diversifying the investments across currencies.

Often, transactions in international money markets are conducted via the Eurocurrency market. The **Eurocurrency market** consists of commercial banks that accept large deposits and provide large loans in foreign currencies (e.g., banks in Zurich lend U.S. dollars or banks in Frankfurt provide loans in Japanese yen). Those banks offering Eurocurrency services are either local banks or foreign bank subsidiaries in a host country. Growing international trade and capital flows as well as cross-border differences in interest rates are the primary reasons for the growth of the Eurocurrency market. In this market, Eurodollar deposits are intensively transacted.

Eurodollars represent U.S. dollar deposits in non-U.S. banks. When interest rate ceilings were imposed on dollar deposits in U.S. banks, corporations with large dollar balances often deposited their funds overseas to receive a higher yield. These deposits were used by local banks to provide loans to other corporations that needed U.S. dollars. Eurodollar deposits are not subject to reserve requirements, so banks can lend out 100 percent of the deposits. For these reasons, the spread between the interest rate paid on large Eurodollar deposits and charged on Eurodollar loans is relatively small. Deposits and loan transactions in Eurodollars are typically $1 million or more per transaction.

Two popular Eurodollar deposits are *Eurodollar fixed-rate certificate of deposits (CD)* and *Eurodollar floating-rate certificate of deposits*. Investors in fixed-rate Eurodollar CDs receive guaranteed interest but are adversely affected by rising market interest rates. To neutralize this problem, floating-rate Eurodollar CDs provide the rate that is adjusted periodically to the *London Interbank Offer Rate (LIBOR)*—the rate charged on interbank dollar loans. The floating-rate CDs allow the borrower's cost and investor's return to reflect prevailing market interest rates.[8]

International Bond Markets

International bond markets are the markets where government bonds or corporate bonds are issued, bought, or sold in foreign countries (e.g., China International Trust and Investment Corporation, or CITIC, issued its corporate bonds in Japan, Europe, and the United States during the 1980s and 1990s). The growth of international bond markets is attributed to some unique features offered by international bonds that are not offered by domestic bonds (see the Industry Box). The development of international bond markets is partially attributed to tax law differentials across countries. Until 1984, foreign investors who purchased bonds that were placed in the United States paid a 30 percent withholding tax on interest payments. However, various tax treaties between the United States and other countries reduced the withholding tax. Interest payments to non-U.S. investors were exempt from the withholding tax, triggering lower interest rates and allowing U.S. firms to issue bonds at a higher price. The withholding tax on U.S.-placed bonds was eliminated in 1984, causing an even larger increase in the foreign demand for U.S.-placed bonds.

Bonds placed in international bond markets are typically underwritten by a syndicate of investment banking firms. Many underwriters in the *Eurobond* market (i.e., bonds in one foreign currency are issued in the country that uses this currency) are subsidiaries of U.S. banks that have focused their growth on non-U.S. countries, since they were historically banned by the Glass-Steagall Act from underwriting corporate bonds in the United States.[9] Some recent issuers of bonds in the Eurobond market include DaimlerChrysler Financial, Citicorp, General Motors Acceptance Corp., and the World Bank. DaimlerChrysler Financial Corp. now obtains about one-fourth of its funds from the Eurobond market. Its bonds have been denominated not only in dollars but also in Swiss francs, German marks, and Australian dollars. Citicorp now borrows about half of its funds overseas.

International Stock Markets

International stock (or equity) markets are where company stocks are listed and traded on foreign stock exchanges (e.g., Nokia of Finland issued stock on the New York Stock Exchange, or *NYSE*). Firms in need of financing use foreign stock markets as additional sources of funds. Investors use foreign stock markets to enhance their portfolio performance. This financing source allows MNEs to attract more funds without flooding their home stock market, avoiding a decline in share price. A large number of MNEs also issue stock in foreign markets in order to circumvent regulations, since regulatory provisions differ among markets. Firms may also believe that they can achieve worldwide recognition among consumers if they issue stock in various foreign markets. Further, listing stock on a foreign stock exchange not only enhances the stock's liquidity but also increases the firm's perceived financial standing when the exchange approves the listing application. It can also protect a firm against hostile takeovers because it disperses ownership and makes it more difficult for other firms to gain a controlling interest. For instance, when Daimler-Benz AG announced its listing on the New York Stock Exchange, its share price quickly increased by 30 percent.

The *Euroequity market* (e.g., issuing U.S. dollar-denominated stocks on non-U.S. exchanges) has developed and grown at a rapid pace since the 1980s. The stocks issued in the Euroequity market are specifically designed for distribution among foreign markets. They are underwritten by a group of investment banks and purchased primarily by institutional investors in several countries. Many of the underwriters

The trading floor of the New York Stock Exchange, one of the world's leading stock markets.

are U.S.-based investment banks, such as First Boston (now part of Credit Suisse First Boston, or CSFB), Merrill Lynch, and Salomon Brothers.

The ability of firms to place new shares in foreign markets depends partially on the stock's perceived liquidity in that market. A secondary market for the stock must be established in foreign markets to enhance liquidity, and makes newly issued stocks more attractive. There are some costs of listing on a foreign exchange, such as translating a company's annual financial report from the local currency into the foreign currency, and making financial statements compatible with the accounting standards used in that country.

International Loan Markets

International loan markets involve large commercial banks and other lending institutions providing loans to foreign companies. Unlike international money markets that deal only with foreign money, loan markets are not restricted to foreign currency transactions. As regulations across Europe, Japan, and the United States are standardized, the markets for loans and other financial services are becoming more globalized. As a result, some financial institutions are attempting to achieve greater economies of scale on the services they offer. Even financial institutions that are not planning global expansion are experiencing increased foreign competition in their home markets. U.S. banks have been particularly interested in foreign markets because U.S. regulations restrain banks from spreading across state lines.

Banks from all countries perceive *international lending* as a means of diversification. A portfolio of loans to borrowers across various countries is less susceptible to a recession in the bank's home country. International lending also allows banks to develop relationships with foreign firms, which create a demand for the banks' other services. In addition, a large portion of international lending is to support *international acquisitions*. Commercial banks and investment banks serve not only as advisers but also as financial intermediaries by placing stocks and bonds or by providing loans. One common form of participation has been to provide direct loans for financing acquisitions, especially for *leveraged buyouts (LBOs)* by management or some other group of investors. Since LBOs are financed mostly with debt, they result in a large demand for loanable funds. Many LBOs are supported by debt from an international syndicate of banks. In this way, each bank limits its exposure to any particular borrower. Because the firms engaged in LBOs are often in diversified industries, a problem in any given industry does not create a new lending crisis. In addition, the debt of each individual firm is relatively small, so that most borrowers would not have sufficient bargaining power to reschedule debt payments. For this reason, international bank financing of LBOs is perceived to be less risky than providing loans to governments of developing countries, another group of major borrowers in international loan markets.

Lending to developing countries often requires credit checking. International commercial banks and other lending institutions do so based on analysis by *credit rating agencies* such as *Standard & Poor's* and *Moody's*. Notably, political risk and overall pressures on the balance of payments and macroeconomic conditions are the focus of analysis (see also Chapter 7). Exhibit 9–8 provides an illustrative example.

Exhibit 9–8

Factors used in sovereign rating by Standard & Poor's

Political Risk
1. Form of government and adaptability of political institutions
2. Extent of popular participation
3. Orderliness of leadership succession
4. Degree of consensus on economic policy objectives
5. Integration into global trade and financial system
6. Internal and external security risks

Economic Factors
1. Income and economic structure
2. Economic growth prospects
3. Fiscal flexibility
4. Public debt burden
5. Price stability
6. Balance-of-payments flexibility
7. External debt and liquidity

Issuer Credit Ratings (or ICR) are offered by credit-rating agencies based on the preceding analysis. ICR apply to both *Corporate Credit Service* (company-level) and *Sovereign Credit Ratings* (country-level). Under the Standard and Poor's system, the long-term issuer credit ratings are classified into the following:

AAA   An obligor (debtor) has extremely strong capacity to meet its financial commitments.

AA   An obligor has very strong capacity to meet its financial commitments. It differs from the highest-rated obligor (AAA) only in small degree.

A   An obligor has strong capacity to meet its financial commitments but is somewhat more susceptible to the adverse effects of changes in circumstances and economic conditions.

BBB   An obligor has adequate capacity to meet its financial commitments. However, adverse economic conditions are more likely to weaken this capacity.

BB   An obligor is less vulnerable in the near term than other lower-rated obligor. However, it faces major ongoing uncertainties and exposure to adverse business, financial, or economic conditions which could lead to the obligor's inadequate capacity to meet its financial commitments.

B   An obligor is more vulnerable than in the case of BB, but currently has the capacity to meet its financial commitments. Adverse business, financial, or economic conditions will likely impair the obligor's capacity or willingness to meet its financial commitments.

CCC   An obligor is currently vulnerable, and is dependent upon favorable business, financial, and economic conditions to meet its financial commitments.

CC   An obligor is currently highly vulnerable.

The preceding ratings may be modified by the addition of a plus or minus sign to show relative standing within each rating category.

Interim Summary

1. MNEs can finance their global operations from international money markets, bond markets, equity markets, and loan markets. They can borrow money from money markets or loan markets, or issue corporate bonds (bond markets) or stocks (equity markets).

2. Banks and corporations actively participate in Eurocurrency markets (e.g., banks in Amsterdam lend U.S. dollars), Eurobond markets (e.g., issue U.S. dollar bonds in Brussels), and Euroequity markets (e.g., issue U.S. dollar stocks on Singapore Stock Exchange) to benefit interest rate differentials or regulatory differences.

THE ASIAN FINANCIAL CRISIS

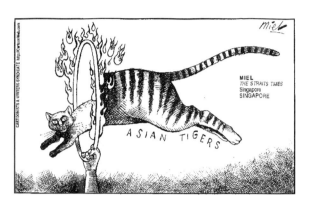

The Asian financial crisis shows how a crisis could occur in international financial markets (foreign exchange market, stock market, money market, and loan market) and how this crisis relates to businesses (domestic and foreign), governments, financial institutions, and international financial markets. First afflicting Thailand in June 1997, the Asian financial crisis quickly spread to South Korea, Indonesia, Malaysia, the Philippines, and other Southeast and East Asian countries. The crisis initially took the form of a financial meltdown, with currencies, stock markets, and property prices tumbling across the region. Economic aftershocks ensued. The crisis was soon to affect markets and economies across the world from Europe to Latin America. The nations of East and Southeast Asia, accustomed to high single or double-digit growth rates, shifted to slow or negative growth. These poor economic conditions prevailed in most of these nations until early 1999. Exhibit 9–9 shows how the Asian financial crisis drastically affected both the foreign exchange rates and stock markets in five major emerging economies. Explanations concerning the causes of the crisis fall into three broad perspectives,[10] namely: (1) financial, (2) political/institutional, and (3) managerial.

The Financial Perspective

The financial perspective views the Asian financial crisis as resulting primarily from financial-sector weakness and market failure. From a financial perspective, two interrelated factors stand out as having contributed to financial-sector weakness and market failure. The first is the maintenance of pegged exchange rates that came to be viewed as implicit guarantees of exchange, constraining monetary remedies. The second is excessive private-sector short-term and dollar-denominated borrowing. For example, Thailand pegged its currency to the U.S. dollar, prompting dollar-denominated borrowing underpinned by higher interest rates for baht-denominated loans. From 1988 to 1994, international bank loans to Thai borrowers more than doubled. By the end of 1997, Thai foreign debt reached $89 billion, of which $81.6 billion was owed by private corporations. About half of the debt carried a maturity date of under a year. In 1997, the value of private sector foreign liabilities was estimated at 25 percent of GDP. Thailand's weakening exports, growing current account deficit, and exploding dollar-denominated short-term private company debt began to weigh on foreign investors and lenders in late 1996. Attacks by currency speculators in the first half of 1997 were followed by loan defaults by several property companies, a downgrade of Thailand's long-term debt, and the unraveling of the Thai stock market. The situation quickly deteriorated and on June 27, 1997, the government floated the baht.[11]

The financial perspective additionally emphasizes the effects of contagion on the crisis. Contagion fueled the crisis through the dynamics of competitive devaluation and the so-called *wake-up-call* effect. The former pertains to the pressures faced by Asian countries to devalue their currency to match devaluation by

Exhibit 9–9

The effect of the Asian financial crisis on five emerging economies

Foreign Exchange
Change in dollar value of currencies (Jan. 1, 1997 = 100)

- South Korea
- Thailand
- Brazil
- Indonesia
- Russia

Stock Markets
Stock-market performance (Jan. 1, 1997 = 100)

- Brazil
- South Korea
- Indonesia
- Thailand
- Russia

Source: The *Wall Street Journal,* April 26, 1999, page R4.

neighboring Asian countries. The latter explains the tendency of most foreign investors to treat all Asian countries as one and pull out investments from a country regardless of its economic or market fundamentals. Undoubtedly, contagion played a major role in accelerating the pace by which the crisis spread from Thailand to South Korea, Indonesia, Malaysia, and throughout Southeast and East Asia.

The Political/Institutional Perspective

Political/institutional-based explanations contend that the causes of the Asian crisis extend much deeper than financial sector weaknesses and market failure, the latter often seen as symptoms rather than causes. The political and institutional perspective points to crony capitalism, irresponsible domestic governance, weak national and political institutions, corruption in the public and private sectors, a misguided and poorly enforced regulatory environment, and other political and institutional-related factors as the principal forces behind the crisis.

The crisis exposed key weaknesses in the political/economic systems and institutions of several Asian countries. The widespread practice of crony capitalism and the incestuous relationship between government, banking, and business in such countries as Indonesia, Malaysia, and Thailand led to an overextension of credit to undeserving companies with close ties to the political and military leadership. In addition, politicians and government bureaucrats have been largely ineffective in responding to the crisis due to conflicting business interests. In the case of Indonesia, for example, the Suharto government backpedaled in implementing the IMF reforms because of their possible adverse impact on the business interests of the ruler's extended family and cronies.

The IMF noted three political and institutional-related considerations as contributing forces to the Asian financial crisis:[12]

1. In financial systems, weak management and poor control of risks, lax enforcement of providential rules and inadequate supervision, and government direct lending practices led to a sharp deterioration in the quality of banks' loan portfolios.

2. Problems of data availability and lack of transparency hindered market participants from maintaining a realistic view of economic fundamentals, and at the same time added to uncertainty.

3. Problems of governance and political uncertainties exacerbated the crisis of confidence, the reluctance of foreign creditors to roll over short-term loans, and the downward pressure on currencies and stock markets.

The Managerial Perspective

The third group of explanations maintains that micro-mismanagement was at the heart of the crisis. Encouraged by a booming economy in the 1990s, many industrial companies in East and Southeast Asia pursued risky overdiversification. To fund their expansion, these companies relied heavily on short-term debt financing. In 1996, the five largest South Korean conglomerates or "chaebols" (i.e., Samsung, Hyundai, Lucky Goldstar, Daewoo, and Sunkyong) controlled over 250 subsidiaries in more than four dozen (mostly unrelated) lines of business. The combined liabilities of the five amounted to about 70 percent of South Korea's gross domestic product in 1996.

Overdiversification and extended leveraging created a vicious cycle for many companies. Firms pursued risky ventures in order to earn larger returns on their investments and service their expensive, short-term debt. When these risky projects failed, they turned to more borrowing to keep their operations afloat. These companies were able to maintain this practice for as long as banks were willing and able to extend credit. When the financial crisis hit, and banks refused or were unable to roll over their loans, many of these industrial companies, particularly the undercapitalized firms, were forced into bankruptcy.

Rising labor costs, falling commodity prices, contracting export markets, and other external pressures compounded the problems faced by industrial companies during the months preceding the financial crisis. Instead of addressing these external pressures by improving productivity, cutting costs, and focusing on the bottom line, the large majority of companies opted for growth and diversification into unrelated businesses. This strategy proved costly when the financial crisis hit and funds dried up. In contrast, firms that remained focused on their core competencies—enhanced productivity, cut costs, and focused on profitability—were able to weather the storm. Most notable among them are South Korea's Pohang Steel Company (POSCO) and Ayala Land Corporation in the Philippines.

Banks and financial institutions extended credit to undeserving companies. When those companies were unable to repay, the banks agreed to roll over the loans and extend them new credit. The financial perspective views the process as a market failure, but hardly explains its roots. The political/institutional perspective blames the decision to overextend credit on such factors as direct government lending, crony capitalism, close relationships between banks and industrial companies, and lack of transparency in financial reporting. The management perspective attributes such overextension of credit to the lack of management sophistication, as well as the absence of the administrative apparatus to conduct proper analysis and oversight. In addition, the management perspective sees a behavioral process of escalation, with banks increasing credit to justify earlier credit decisions.

Interim Summary

1. The Asian financial crisis provides an illustrative case showing how a financial crisis is simultaneously reflected in international foreign exchange markets and international capital markets.

2. The Asian financial crisis derived from political, financial, and managerial reasons. This crisis is a reminder that the growth of an emerging economy requires strong economic fundamentals, an efficient banking sector, transparent political institutions, counter-fluctuation capabilities, and clearly defined business-government relations.

CHAPTER SUMMARY

1. The international monetary system is made up of the policies, institutions, regulations, and mechanisms that determine foreign exchange rates. Most countries today use the peg system, managed float system, target-zone system, or free float system.

2. Each foreign exchange system has its merits and drawbacks. The floating exchange rate is less costly for the government or its central bank to adjust trade imbalances and can facilitate independence of trade policies. It may lead, however, to immense market fluctuations that hamper economic growth and cannot help the country balance trade for a long period.

3. In the long run, the purchasing power parity (PPP) tends to be a proper foundation to determine the foreign exchange rate. In the short run, the demand and supply in the foreign exchange market are crucial in determining changes in the floating rate.

4. The balance of payments summarizes a country's currency inflows and outflows and documents current account, capital account, and official reserves. Official reserves are made of gold, special drawing rights (SDRs), and foreign currencies. Many imports are actually "exported" by a nation's own companies investing abroad, making current account balance statistically less meaningful.

5. International financial markets consist of international foreign exchange markets and international capital markets. International capital markets in turn comprise money markets, bond markets, equity markets, and loan markets.

6. Foreign exchange markets perform three functions, including international payment, short-term supply of foreign currencies, and hedging against foreign exchange risks. These markets also offer opportunities for foreign exchange arbitrage.

7. International money markets are where foreign capital (such as Eurodollars) is financed or invested. Eurodollars are U.S. dollar deposits in non-U.S. banks. International loan markets deal with loans in any international currency provided by large commercial banks that must assess corporate credit or sovereign credit ranked by credit rating agencies.

8. International stock (or equity) markets are the places where company stocks are listed and traded on foreign stock exchanges. International bond markets are the places where corporate or government bonds are issued and traded in foreign countries. These markets not only provide financing for global operations but can also improve organizational recognition.

9. The Asian financial crisis demonstrates that international foreign exchange markets and capital markets can present risks destabilizing emerging economies that depend on international markets. This crisis also reveals the importance of transparent and efficient institutions (governments, banking sector, and legal systems) that govern financial markets.

CHAPTER NOTES

[1] See T. Agmon, R. G. Hawkins, and R. M. Levich, *The Future of the International Monetary System*. Lexington, MA: Lexington Books, 1984; R. N. Cooper, *The International Monetary System: Essays in World Economics*. Cambridge, MA: MIT Press, 1987.

[2] E. Sohmen, *Flexible Exchange Rates: Theory and Controversy*. Chicago: University of Chicago Press, 1969; I. Friedman, *Reshaping the Global Money System*. Lexington, MA: Lexington Books, 1987.

[3] W. J. McKibben and J. D. Sachs, "Comparing the global performance of alternative exchange agreements," *Journal of International Money and Finance,* 7(4), 1988, 387–410; J. R. Shafer, and B. E. Loopesko. "Floating exchange rate after ten years," *Brookings Papers on Economic Activity,* Washington, D.C.: Brookings Institution, 1983.

[4] G. Dufey and I. H. Giddy, *The International Money Market.* 2nd ed., Englewood Cliffs, NJ: Prentice-Hall, 1994; V. Koromzay, J. Llewellyn, and S. Potter. "The rise and fall of the dollar: Some explanations, consequences, and lessons," *Economic Journal,* March 1987, 23–43.

[5] R. I. McKinnon, "The rules of the game: International money in historical perspective," *Journal of Economic Literature,* March 1993, 1–44; E. Sohmen, *Flexible Exchange Rates: Theory and Controversy.* Chicago: University of Chicago Press, 1969.

[6] G. Dufey and I. H. Giddy, Ibid.

[7] R. M. Kubarych, *Foreign Exchange Markets in the United States.* New York: Federal Reserve Bank of New York, 1983.

[8] K. A. Chrystal, "A guide to foreign exchange markets," *Federal Reserve Bank of St. Louis Review,* March 1984, 5–18.

[9] R. G. F. Coninx, *Foreign Exchange Dealer's Handbook.* Homewood, IL. Dow Jones-Irwin, 1986; I. Gregory and P. Moore, Foreign exchange dealing, *Corporate Finance,* October 1986, 33–46.

[10] M. G. Serapio and O. Shenkar, "Reflections on the Asian crisis," *Management International Review,* April 1999 (special issue), 3–10; *Far East Economic Review,* Deep Impact: The Asian Crisis (Special Report), July 16, 1998, 40–52.

[11] Ibid., 209–210.

[12] International Monetary Fund, *World Economic Outlook,* Washington, D.C., May 1998.

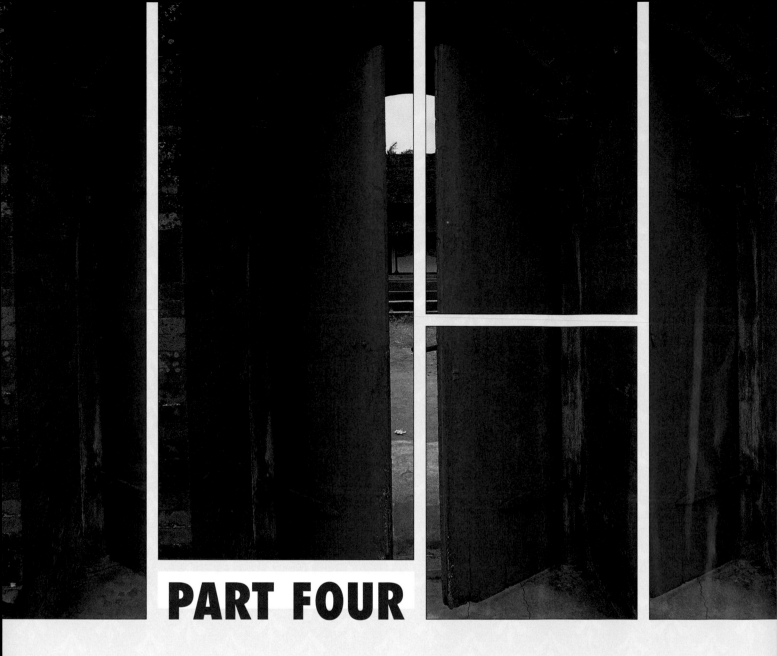

PART FOUR

International Business Strategies

International Entry Strategies

DO YOU KNOW

1. What factors should managers take into account in choosing locations for FDI projects? Why has Rio de Janeiro in Brazil lured hundreds of large MNEs to invest there? How should location selection be associated with the firm's goals and experience? Why does Nike often locate its projects in underdeveloped areas but Oracle does not?

2. How do MNEs benefit when they enter foreign markets as first movers? What challenges do early movers normally face? Why have some early movers such as Motorola and Siemens been quite successful in China but other early movers there such as Peugeot and Occidental Petroleum have not?

3. What entry modes are available to companies interested in investing in another country? How do such entry modes vary in terms of expected risks and returns as well as required commitment? If you are concerned with organizational control over overseas operations, what entry modes would you elect?

OPENING CASE DuPont's Entry Strategies into China

DuPont is one of the oldest and largest industrial corporations in the world. Since 1989 DuPont has set up 12 joint ventures, 4 wholly-owned subsidiaries and 4 representative offices, with a total investment of more than $300 million in China. Some joint venture exam-
ples include partnerships with Shanghai Photomask Precision Company to produce photomasks and with China Worldbest Development Corporation to manufacture Lycra spandex fiber. It has also formed joint ventures there with other foreign companies such as BASF Akitengesellschaft. DuPont's use of joint ventures was aimed at garnering greater loyalty by Chinese consumers. Joint ventures also allowed DuPont to overcome trade barriers and gain access to distribution channels. Meanwhile, the company set up wholly-owned subsidiaries to produce those products that involve very sensitive technologies and require strong control over production and chemical patent protection.

DuPont was an early entrant to China's chemical and energy industries. As an early entrant, it was able to establish strong market power and create entry barriers for followers. It faced little competition because there were only a few companies in the country that participated in the same industry. DuPont also had the advantage of being the first company to make use of some of China's raw materials. DuPont took advantage of these factors to build a strong foundation for itself while increasing its presence in China, gaining technological leadership, and establishing its brand name. Of course, the company also faced many operational risks as an early entrant. DuPont had to deal with high anti-imitation costs. In 1991, a local entrepreneur took one of DuPont's fiber formulas and started a rival firm to produce the same product. It was not until 1993 that new laws were introduced to supplement and strengthen China's patent regulations, extending patent protection from 10 to 20 years and requiring patents to be registered in China.

DuPont chose China for its low labor costs, high demand, and abundant raw materials. It selected areas such as Shenzhen, Shanghai, and Guangdong where the tax rates were lower. Shenzhen and Guangdong, for example, are coastal cities offering tax rates of only 15 percent. Shanghai was chosen because it is a major industrial and financial center. Shanghai and other eastern coastal provinces such as Jiangsu, Shandong, and Zhejiang form the heart of China's chemical industry. A new chemical industrial zone is being built on the outskirts of Shanghai at Caojing on Hangzhou Bay. In 1998, DuPont formed DuPont (China) Ltd. in Beijing to coordinate its entire operations in China. ∎

INTERNATIONAL LOCATION SELECTION *(WHERE)*

The preceding case illustrates that several important decisions have to be made when entering a foreign market. **International entry strategies** concern where (location selection), when (timing of entry), and how (entry mode selection) international companies should enter and invest in a foreign territory during international expansion. These entry strategies are important because they determine an MNE's investment environment, operation treatment, resource commitment, and evolutionary path. In the opening case, DuPont views China as a strategic location not only in terms of being the primary offshore market but also by virtue of being the major manufacturing center of products marketed elsewhere. Even though it encountered tremendous uncertainty in the early 1980s, DuPont decided to enter this market as an early mover seeking market leadership. The company's ambitious investments, however, were incremental. DuPont started with exports to China, followed by minority joint ventures, then majority joint ventures, and eventually wholly-owned subsidiaries. This evolutionary entry path balances well its experience and capability with the risks and hazards it has faced in the past. This chapter details these issues, beginning with international location selection (e.g., for DuPont, why China? And why Shanghai and Shenzhen within China?)

International location selection involves country selection *and* regional selection (e.g., state, province, or city) within the chosen country for an MNE's foreign direct investment project(s). The country selection determines the macro-environment for operations in a specific site. Siemens, for example, chose Brazil as an important platform for Latin America and the Caribbean nations. The company selected the city of Rio de Janeiro, rather than São Paulo, as its major production base since Rio de Janeiro provides cheaper and more abundant resources (labor and supplies) and a superior infrastructure. Similarly, Motorola chose the city of Tianjin instead of Beijing or Shanghai as its major production base in China. This location strategy seems to have worked well, because the sales revenue generated by this base accounted for more than 10 percent of its worldwide revenue in 2002. To select an appropriate country and a region within that country, international managers should first appraise locational determinants that are likely to influence future operations and expected returns. These determinants as well as the decision framework elaborated below are generally applicable to both country selection and region (city or province) selection. The only distinction between them is that the breadth of locational determinants differ. Country selection should emphasize nationwide factors whereas site selection should focus more on related factors that are specific to that region.

You may recall that we discussed country competitiveness in Chapter 5 and explained the relevance of country competitiveness to an MNE's location selection.

The analysis of country competitiveness helps us better understand a host country's national environment and is thus valuable to country selection. Nevertheless, location selection requires analyses and comparisons of specific factors (i.e., locational determinants) associated with the costs and revenues of investment in a specific site. For this purpose, we outline specific locational determinants managers need to consider when they calculate expected costs and payoffs from a potential foreign location.

Locational Determinants

Locational determinants can be categorized into the following groups: (1) cost/tax factors; (2) demand factors; (3) strategic factors; (4) regulatory/economic factors; and (5) sociopolitical factors. The importance of each of these factors to a specific firm depends on the firm's objectives and the business nature of the FDI project. For instance, high-tech FDI may depend more on strategic factors while labor-intensive projects may be more susceptible to cost/tax factors. Local market-focused investments may rely more on demand factors whereas export market-focused investments may be impacted more by cost/tax conditions.

Cost/Tax Factors

1. *Transportation costs:* For country selection, MNEs should consider the costs incurred in transporting materials from a home (or foreign) country to a host country or transporting products from a host country to a home or international market. When an MNE's home country is the source of product components as well as the market for finished products, transportation costs associated with this two-way flow become even more important. For site selection, MNEs need to calculate the convenience and costs of the various transportation channels (air, sea, railway, and highway) from the candidate site to destinations of major local and foreign customers. When the Ford Motor Company entered the United Arab Emirates (UAE), it chose Dubai because of its convenience and low cost connections to the rest of the country and the world.

2. *Wage rate:* Labor costs constitute a substantial proportion of total production costs. Foreign production is more likely to occur when production costs are lower abroad than at home. Labor costs sway investment location decisions, particularly for firms in labor-intensive industries. The decision by many MNEs to locate assembly plants in developing countries is heavily influenced by prevailing wages. Nike located its 13 footwear and 14 apparel factories along the Pearl River Delta in China because of the low wage rate of workers relative to their productivity.

3. *Availability and costs of land:* Availability of suitable plant sites, the cost of land, space for expansion, and local government policy on renting or purchasing land have been recognized by international managers as critical factors in the early stages of project development and late stages of project operation. In some cases, this consideration may overwhelm other location factors, since it influences other costs such as transportation and construction. Mercedes-Benz selected Alabama in 1993 as its site for producing its sport-utility vehicles (SUVs) because the Alabama state government provided the company with 1,000 acres of land between Tuscaloosa and Birmingham.

4. *Construction costs:* This cost accounts for a substantial part of capital investment. Different sites vary in the cost of construction materials, labor, land, equipment rental, and quality of construction. Burger King had opened 1,640 restaurants in Europe by the end of 2001, 1,397 of which were franchise-owned operations. A major factor behind the franchise strategy is high construction costs in Europe.

5. *Costs of raw materials and resources:* MNEs are increasing the percentage of local outsourcing in total production. This localization reduces foreign exchange risks from devalued currencies and improves relationships with local governments and indigenous firms. Under these circumstances, the costs of local materials and resources needed in production will affect the firm's gross profit margin. IKEA, a leading furniture MNE based in Sweden, buys 90 percent of what it sells from closely monitored suppliers in many countries—mostly developing countries such as Poland and China. One of the major reasons the company chose these countries is the relatively low cost of raw materials.

6. *Financing costs:* The cost and availability of local capital are a major concern for MNEs because local financing provides much of the capital needed for mass production and operations. Financing by local banks and financial institutions also helps an MNE mitigate possible financial risks arising from fluctuations in foreign exchange rates and uncertain foreign exchange policies as well as political risk in a host country. Merck entered Brazil, sited specifically in São Paulo, Rio de Janeiro, Recife, Curitiba, and Campinas, because local banks are very supportive in financing Merck's investments or expansion.

7. *Tax rates:* Both statutory and effective tax rates influence a firm's profitability. **The statutory tax** rate determines the general level of the tax burden shouldered by firms. The **effective tax rate** on corporate income, which is the statutory corporate rate adjusted for all other taxes and subsidies affecting an MNE's taxable income, determines the company's net return from its revenues. Depending on the extent of these subsidies and other taxes, the statutory corporate tax rate may differ substantially from the effective corporate tax rate because the latter is adjusted to include tax-related incentives such as investment tax credits, tax breaks, and accelerated depreciation. MNEs need to assess both the statutory and the effective tax rate. Because regions within a diverse nation such as Brazil, China, and Indonesia may vary in terms of the statutory and/or effective rates, investors should compare these rates at both the country- and region-level. Since FDI projects are still subject to import or export tariffs when importing regulated materials or export licensed products, firms should also be aware of the level of these tariffs.

8. *Investment incentives:* Many countries, especially developing ones, are competing to attract FDI to support their domestic economies. In so doing, they often offer preferential incentives to foreign investors. Although these are country-specific, an array of investment incentives that attract FDI include (see also Chapter 3):

   (a) Tax breaks and/or reductions on corporate income taxes;
   (b) Financial assistance such as preferential terms of financing, wage subsidies, investment grants, or low-interest loans;
   (c) Tariff concessions including exemption from or reduction of duties on imports, or additional duties on imports of competing goods, or rebates of duties on imported inputs;
   (d) Business assistance such as employee training, research and development support, land grants, site improvements, and site selection assistance;
   (e) Other incentives such as infrastructure development and access, legal services, business consultation, and partner selection assistance.[1]

9. *Profit repatriation:* Repatriation restrictions have a negative impact on the net income or dividends remitted to foreign headquarters. Restrictions can involve a remittance tax on the cash repatriated to a home country or a ceiling on the cash amount. In other cases, investors must obtain approval from the central bank or foreign exchange administration department to repatriate dividends. These restrictions can become a deterrent to FDI. Today, profit repatriation restrictions have been gradually removed in many developing countries. Nonetheless, restrictions on foreign exchange flows still abound (e.g., currency conversion at formally set exchange rate in Russia, China, and India).

Demand Factors

1. *Market size and growth:* Although different MNEs may not emphasize the same level of marketing in a host country, it is rare for them not to consider local consumers. At the national level, the size and growth rate of markets signal market opportunities and potentials. Pfizer selected India to produce multi-vitamins targeting India's 300 million middle-class consumers. In 1990, Toys-"R"-Us chose Japan whose retail market expanded greatly in the 1980s as a result of the strong Japanese economy and increased consumer spending. At the subnational level, per capita consumption and the growth rate of consumption in respective regions (state, province, city) may be more accurate parameters for measuring market potential and growth. Average income growth among consumers in a target region is also an appropriate measure (see also Chapter 16).

2. *Presence of customers:* MNEs may find it desirable to locate their manufacturing sites in the area where they have longstanding customers. The closer operations are to major buyers, the better the cost efficiency and marketing effectiveness. Coca-Cola and PepsiCo both selected east coast provinces of China as project sites because the majority of their consumers are located there. Similarly, UPS (United Parcel Service) elected Cologne in Germany and Taipei in Taiwan as its European and Asia-Pacific air hubs, respectively, because of the ease of reaching customers.

3. *Local competition:* The intensity of competition in a host country or specific region is important because it directly impacts a firm's market position and gross profit margin from local sales.[2] In general, MNEs locate sites in places where competition is relatively low unless they have sufficient advantages to ensure their competitive edge in the market. Competition may come from local rivals as well as from other foreign rivals. When Coca-Cola made substantial new investments to strengthen its market position in east coast provinces of China in the early 1990s, PepsiCo began to expand to inland provinces in order to pioneer in this new territory.

Strategic Factors

1. *Investment infrastructure:* Today, MNEs attach increasing importance to infrastructure conditions. This is especially true for companies investing in knowledge or technology-intensive projects. Singapore attracted many of those MNEs mainly because of its ideal infrastructure. Major infrastructure variables include transportation (highways, ports, airports, and railroads), telecommunications, utilities, and governmental efficiency. The infrastructure also includes the availability of international seaports and import/export facilities since most FDI projects have operational linkages with home and other international markets. When Hewlett-Packard (HP) entered Mexico, it did not choose Mexico City but instead Ciudad Juarez, near the metropolitan area, which has excellent infrastructure conditions (access to roads and airports, strong support from local authorities, a superb export-processing environment, and the availability of an information-technology industry).

2. *Manufacturing concentration:* One of the major determinants of location selection is the strength of existing manufacturing activities. Cost savings can result from manufacturers locating in close proximity. A country or region with a strong concentration of manufacturing activity in certain industries or products is more likely to have an adequate labor pool and supply network supporting production or operations.[3] Just-in-time systems require a supplier base that is capable, reliable, and physically close. Otis opted for Leningrad as its primary manufacturing center in Russia because it has a well-established supply network for materials and components and has many skilled laborers and technicians for producing elevators and escalators.

3. *Industrial linkages:* The nature and quality of complementary industries and special services (distribution, consulting, auditing, banking, insurance, marketing services, etc.) are also important as MNE operations interact actively with these sectors in a host country. Industrial linkages with these businesses affect the firm's ability to pursue value creation and addition. Mary Kay Cosmetics located its business center in Buenos Aires, which serves Argentina, Uruguay, and Chile, having considered the favorable industrial linkages in this city.

4. *Workforce productivity:* As a result of increasing technological permeation and process innovation, international production requires high workforce productivity and superior labor skills. The labor requirements of new systems and techniques are driving the need for a better educated direct-labor workforce. Just-in-time and total quality management systems place greater importance on the flexibility of workers and their ability to operate under growing autonomy. The increasing sophistication of product and process technologies has also increased skill requirements. The availability of a skilled managerial, marketing, and technical workforce is also crucial, because they are primary forces in gaining competitive advantages in the market.

5. *Inbound and outbound logistics:* Typical inbound (input) logistics include proximity to suppliers and sources of raw materials and inputs. Since MNEs have a tendency to rely more on local input sources, this type of logistics should be among the critical considerations for international managers. Outbound (market) logistics are based largely on proximity to major buyers and end consumers. This factor can heavily influence the effectiveness of customer responsiveness. When the firm pursues market penetration and product specialization strategies, the firm's profitability will be strongly associated with market logistics. A main reason why Procter & Gamble (P&G) chose Mexico City as its major production base for North America was the effective inbound and outbound logistics, which satisfy P&G's needs for production and marketing.

Regulatory/Economic Factors

1. *Industrial policies:* In many countries, industrial policies are used to control new entrants (both foreign and local firms), net profit margins, degree of competition, structural concentration, and social benefits. Typical industrial policies include antitrust rules, project approval and registration, categorization of industries and treatment differences among categories, and varying value-added tax among others (also see the last section of Chapter 4). In selecting a location, MNEs need to make sure that the target country or region allows foreign business entry and that industrial policies are reasonably favorable or at least not a hindrance. Industrial policies generally have a more direct impact on MNE operations than do macroeconomic policies of a host government.[4] Lucent Technologies moved into Brazil after the Brazilian government announced the "Real Plan" in 1994, which devalued its currency (*real*), privatized telecom services, and offered more favorable treatments to new entrants into the telecom infrastructure sector.

2. *FDI policies.* In determining a foreign location (country and region), MNEs need to learn how FDI policies there will impact their plans and payoffs. First, they should know what entry mode(s) are allowed. They might be allowed to

FEDERAL EXPRESS SELECTS SUBIC BAY

In December 1992, the United States closed down its naval shipyard in Subic Bay, the Philippines, which was its largest overseas base. The departure of the military put Subic Bay in a deep economic slump and left 47,000 Filipinos unemployed. It also left an $8 billion facility unused, so the Philippine government decided to turn Subic Bay into a self-sustaining commercial investment center. It was immediately declared a free-trade zone area with unlimited duty-free imports and a hassle-free export system. In 1993, the management team from Federal Express went to Subic Bay to investigate the area for its central hub location. The government presented many investment incentives to FedEx, offering liberal air traffic rights, streamlined customs clearance procedures to accommodate the quick turnaround time of express carriers, and help in dealing with the bureaucracy. This all happened in a nation known for bureaucratic red tape and favoritism toward local companies. In September of 1995, FedEx opened its Pacific Asian hub facility in Subic Bay at a cost of about U.S.$100 million. This strategic event enabled it to obtain a 24-hour use of airport facilities, and employ the low-paid, well-educated, English-speaking laborers already located there. Hong Kong and Taipei did not have the 24-hour airport facilities critical to hub operations. Singapore was too far south, and Osaka of Japan was too far north. Federal Express's decision to open the regional hub in Subic Bay created an excellent strategic advantage for the company. It now connects 13 major economic and financial centers in the region.

enter into certain sites or industries only through certain entry modes such as minority joint ventures. Second, a host government may require MNEs to locate projects in certain geographical regions to help boost regional economies. Projects in different locations may be taxed differently. Third, MNEs should check content localization requirements. A foreign company is often required to purchase and use local materials, parts, semi-products, or other supplies made by indigenous firms for the production of its final outputs. The required level of localization varies across countries or industries. Fourth, MNEs need to identify any geographical restrictions imposed on the breadth of the market. For example, prior to China's entry into the WTO, foreign banks were allowed to provide services only in the city in which they were located. Finally, MNEs must appraise foreign exchange control measures in a host country. These measures may hinder the free inflow and outflow of foreign capital and income.

3. *Availability of special economic zones:* One way many countries (especially in the developing world) attempt to attract FDI is through the establishment of special zones such as free trade zones (FTZs), special economic zones (SEZs), economic and technological development zones (ETDZs), high-tech development zones (HTDZs), open economic regions (OERs), bonded areas, and so on. In general, these zones provide preferential treatment in terms of taxation, import duties, land use, infrastructure access, and governmental assistance to MNEs. However, many of these zones are regulated regarding eligibility for preferential treatment. For instance, MNEs located in Chinese ETDZs must export 75 percent of output or bring in advanced technologies as verified by governmental authorities.

Sociopolitical Factors

1. *Political instability:* This factor reflects uncertainty over the continuation of present political and social conditions and government policies that are critical to the survival and profitability of a firm's operations in the host country. Changes in government policies may create problems related to repatriation of earnings, or, in extreme cases, expropriation of assets. Although international lobbying on foreign country policies has become pervasive, the magnitude of politically induced environmental uncertainty still overwhelms transaction-related risks affecting MNE operations.

2. *Cultural barriers:* Another trigger of uncertainty are differences in culture between the home and host countries. This factor determines a firm's receptivity and adaptability to the social context of a host country.[5] Language barriers are also an important consideration underlying location selection. Although every foreign business can recruit local people, communications with headquarters as well as between employees within the company are crucial to business success (see also Chapter 6).

3. *Local business practices:* Culture-specific business practices often constitute key forms of knowledge that MNEs must acquire. In fact, a prominent logic behind formation of international cooperative ventures with developing country enterprises is to gain such country-specific knowledge. Superior technological and organizational skills cannot guarantee the success of international operations unless the firm is able to integrate country-specific knowledge with its firm-specific knowledge. The ability to integrate these two types of knowledge often determines the survival and growth of MNEs in foreign markets.

4. *Government efficiency and corruption:* International managers often perceive the "soft" infrastructure (e.g., regulatory environment and government efficiency) as having a greater and more enduring impact on firm operations than the "hard" infrastructure (e.g., transportation and communication). Efficient governments are more responsive to an MNE's requests or complaints, take shorter time periods for ratifying projects, and provide superior assistance and support in various matters. Governmental corruption implies not only low efficiency and excessive red tape, but also high costs of bribery in setting up governmental linkages in order to get project approval, infrastructure access, and acquisition of scarce resources (see Chapter 19).

5. *Attitudes toward foreign business:* Social and governmental attitudes toward foreign businesses often have visible or invisible influences on MNE operations and management. If the society and government of a host country are somewhat friendly to foreign business, MNEs will benefit from the congenial environment. This attitude has an enduring effect on both firm operations and the commitment of employees to the foreign firm. Burger King selected the Dominican Republic as its major site in the Caribbean (22 restaurants as of July 2001) because Dominicans (both government and the public) have a very positive view of the United States and American products. The country is now the Caribbean's largest democratic country and has a long-standing and close relationship with the United States (where many Dominicans legally immigrate).

6. *Community characteristics:* Site selection must include considerations of community environment aspects such as community size, educational facilities, housing facilities, police and fire protection, climate, suitability for expatriates and their families, facilities for children, the social environment for spouses, hotel accommodations, crime level, and other quality of life indicators. This environment is highly relevant because it affects costs, quality, and security of living for foreign expatriates and their families.

7. *Pollution control:* Environmental protection laws and regulations in the target location influence the choice and cost of investments. Before making a location decision, an MNE should appraise these laws and regulations, assess whether the firm is able to comply with them, and evaluate whether it is financially feasible to invest in pollution control. Rubbermaid entered Poland in 1995 and now views the country as its central site in eastern Europe. A relatively low standard in pollution control (thus lower costs to comply with this standard) is one of the factors that attracted Rubbermaid to invest there.

Exhibit 10–1 summarizes the major locational determinants explained previously. Overall, site selection within a diverse country should be based on micro-context factors, whereas country selection should be made after a careful analysis of both micro-context and macro-context factors.

Decision Framework

The preceding section presented locational determinants that must be assessed in the course of choosing a location. These determinants constitute the core in the framework of a location decision-making process. Aside from this core, MNEs also need to take into account their strategic objectives, global integration, and market orientation.

Location and Strategic Objectives

If an MNE wishes to pursue market growth and a competitive position in a host country, demand factors and strategic factors appear to be its most critical considerations. Because these factors generally concern long-term investments and operations, macroeconomic and sociopolitical factors also have a moderate impact on location selection. If an MNE seeks short- or mid-term profitability, it should attach more value to cost and taxation factors. Infrastructure conditions and investment incentives may also play a role. The costs of production factors and operational expenses will determine the gross profit margin, whereas income tax rates will affect the net return. Remittance taxes or profit repatriation restrictions have a great

Exhibit 10–1
Locational determinants

Micro-Context	**Macro-Context**
Cost/Tax Factors Transportation costs Wage rate Land availability and costs Construction costs Costs of raw materials and resources Financing costs Tax rates Investment incentives Profit repatriation	*Regulatory Factors* Industrial policies FDI policies Availability of special zones *Sociopolitical Factors* Political instability Cultural barriers Local business practices Government efficiency and corruption Attitudes towards foreign business
Demand Factors Market size and growth Customer presence Local competition	Community characteristics Sustainable development (e.g., pollution control and recycling requirements)
Strategic Factors Investment infrastructure Manufacturing concentration Industrial linkages Workforce productivity Inbound and outbound logistics	

impact on the level of dividends that the parent firm finally receives. If an MNE strives to diversify risks or operate in a stable environment, sociopolitical factors become fundamental to the decision. Because some macroeconomic factors such as exchange rate and the inflation rate are related to environmental uncertainty, they should also be included in the analytical framework. Finally, if an MNE intends to secure innovation, learning, and adaptation from international expansion, strategic factors often outweigh other groups of factors in affecting location choice. Nevertheless, industrial linkages, competition intensity, cultural distance, and attitudes toward foreign businesses may also influence the accomplishment of this goal.

Location and Global Integration

The location decision should be framed within the design of global integration. As the world economy becomes increasingly regionalized (see Chapter 8), MNEs may first decide which regional bloc they should enter. In this situation, location selection involves regional bloc selection, country selection, and site selection. In considering regional bloc selection, managers can review the preceding determinants at the integrated bloc level (e.g., the EU vs. NAFTA) and find out how removed or lessened inter-country barriers within the bloc reduce cost/tax burdens and change regulatory/economic environments (thus identifying new opportunities and new threats). Other groups of determinants such as demand, strategic, and sociopolitical factors are less affected by the formation of a regional bloc. Today, MNEs use host country sites to achieve global integration and/or regional integration. MNEs tend to locate labor-intensive processes in sites that are relatively well endowed with abundant labor or locate an R&D facility in an area where abundant technological capabilities exist. Linking activities across locations is fundamental to capturing international scale and scope. It is important for international managers to locate projects in such sites that provide an ideal environment for integrating operations with the rest of the MNE network. When Cisco entered France, it built distribution centers in Toulouse, which serve not only France but also the Middle East. Today Cisco sells its products in approximately 115 countries, distributed mostly through consolidated sites in respective regions.

Location and Market Orientation

Market orientation is concerned mainly with whether an MNE primarily targets a host country market, export market (home or other foreign markets), or both. Naturally, different market orientations vary in their relationship with locational determinants. Local market-oriented projects are highly sensitive to demand and strategic factors in the local environment. Some regulatory/economic factors are also relevant because they affect a firm's stability and the exposure of its operations to environmental turbulence. Certain sociopolitical variables including cultural distance, government efficiency or corruption, and political stability are likely to have a stronger effect on a local market orientation than on an export orientation. The latter, by contrast, relies more on cost/tax factors. Plants producing for an export market can be located with little regard for domestic demand. Therefore, cost/tax factors, together with strategic factors such as investment incentives, input logistics, labor productivity, and infrastructure, are prominent micro-contextual determinants underlying this location strategy. For example, many U.S. companies relocate their production facilities just south of the U.S.-Mexico border. These factories, called *maquiladoras,* assemble imported, duty-free components into finished goods, most of which are then re-exported to the United States. In addition to benefiting from lower labor costs, these companies enjoy reduced transportation costs, eliminated

Exhibit 10–2

Maquiladoras in the
Mexico-U.S. border zone

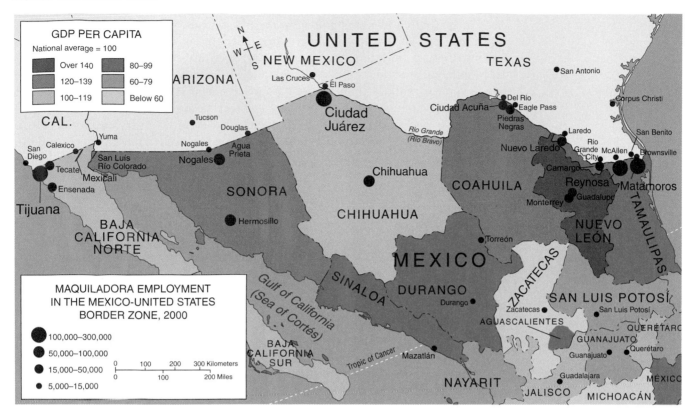

Source: de Blij & Muller *Concepts and Regions in Geography* 1e, Wiley, 2002; Figure 4–11, p. 142.

tariff burdens, and logistics convenience. Currently, approximately 4,000 maquiladoras with over 1.2 million employees operate along the border zone, accounting for nearly one-third of Mexico's industrial jobs and 45 percent of its total exports. (See Exhibit 10–2.)

Finally, the dual-emphasis orientation may be influenced by all five group factors. In other words, the dual-emphasis orientation necessitates the most comprehensive scheme in the appraisal of locational determinants. Levi Strauss & Company's three manufacturing facilities in Mexico, located in Aguascalientes, Naucalpan, and Teziutlan, respectively, are ideal for this dual pursuit. All these facilities are close to Mexico City and physically close to California (the U.S. headquarters). About a half of the jeans made in these facilities are exported back to the United States while the other half targets local consumers (about 25 percent market share in Mexico).

Interim Summary

1. When selecting a foreign location, managers need to consider not only cost and tax factors but also market demand, investment infrastructure, regulatory and economic environments, and sociopolitical factors.

2. Managers should choose a foreign location that not only provides a favorable investment environment but also helps fulfill the firm's objectives underlying international entry.

TIMING OF ENTRY (WHEN)

Timing of entry involves the sequence of an MNE's entry into a foreign market vis-à-vis other MNEs (i.e., first mover, early follower, and late mover). Timing of entry is important because it determines the risks, environments, and opportunities the MNE may confront.[6] In today's increasingly integrated global marketplace, where demand level, consumption sophistication, and rivalry intensity are all changing drastically, the decision on when to embark on international expansion is critical for transnational operations. Transnational investors are likely to have more preemptive investment opportunities in foreign markets than in their home markets. This is largely because of the different market and industry structures between home and host economies. By investing in a foreign market, a later mover in the home country could become an early entrant in the host country. It could enjoy more favorable business opportunities in sectors that are in early stages of the industry life cycle in the host country market, or in industries in which it has distinctive competitive advantages. Aside from noticing an opportunity, the decision on when to invest is broadly based upon an entrant's assessment of entry barriers erected by a host government and existing firms, relative to the factors promoting entry. Potential entrants weigh the expected benefits and costs of entry; entry occurs when the former outweigh the latter.

Early-Mover Advantages

When entering a foreign market, pioneering MNEs (**first mover** or **early followers**) generally have advantages such as greater market power, more preemptive opportunities, and more strategic options over late entrants. These advantages might be ultimately reflected in higher economic returns compared with later movers. First, pioneering investors tend to outperform later entrants in acquiring *market power*. Early movers are able to invest strategically in facilities, distribution networks, product positioning, patentable technology, natural resources, and human and organizational expertise. If imitation of its product is expected to be expensive or involve a long time lag, a preemptive investment can be leveraged into significant long-run benefits for early movers. Moreover, market pioneers may benefit from the advantages of holding technical leadership, seizing scarce resources, and creating buyer switching costs.[7] Because of such switching costs, and because most customers are more loyal to an early mover's successful products and services, customer loyalty tends to be stronger for early-mover products than for late-mover products. This loyalty fortifies an early-mover's market power and competitive position. Citibank and Bank of America were both early movers into Latin America in both the prewar and postwar periods, relative to other foreign banks such as Barclays from Britain and the Bank of Nova Scotia from Canada. By 1929, for example, Citibank and Bank of America had branches or offices in Mexico City, Buenos Aires, São Paulo, and Santiago. By the 1970s, these two U.S. banks had branches or offices in almost every Latin American country. They have dominated these markets largely because of the market power they obtained from an early-entry position (loyal customers, close relations with local banks and governments, and established technological and service standards). This market power was further strengthened when they erected entry barriers against later movers in the form of acquiring local banks, partnering with Visa International, creating innovative banking approaches such as internet banking and banking services via cable TV, and extending their network-type presence almost everywhere.

Second, early movers gain from *preemptive opportunities*. Early movers have the right to preempt marketing, promotion, and distribution channels, while gaining product image, organizational reputation, and brand recognition. Toys "R" Us entered Japan in May 1990 right after MITI (The Japanese Ministry of International Trade and Industry) relaxed regulations and restrictions in the retail toy industry.

"I've always found enough to keep me busy right here on the Atlantic Rim."

Source: © 2003, *The New Yorker Collection* from cartoonbank.com. All Rights Reserved.

By the end of 1996, it had opened 35 stores throughout Japan, with approximately $20 million annual sales per store compared with $10 million per U.S. store. The company's success involves, in part, the first-mover opportunities it seized such as preemptive marketing and promotion as well as brand recognition and pioneer reputation. Similarly, Otis entered Russia as the first mover in the elevator industry and preempted the distribution channels previously built by the Russian government and used by local state-owned enterprises. It is incorrect to assume that foreign market opportunities are limitless, however. The window of opportunity opens only for a time and is therefore available only to early movers.[8] For example, to pursue economic reform and political stability, China's State Council set up a ceiling on the number of FDI projects in the automobile industry. Today, Volkswagen dominates China's small car market while GM does well in the luxury sedan market. They were all first movers in their respective categories.

Third, early movers benefit from many *strategic options*. Pioneer investors often have more strategic options in selecting industries, locations, and market orientations (e.g., import-substitution, local market-oriented, export-market oriented, infrastructure-oriented, etc.). In addition, early movers are often given priority access to natural resources, scarce materials, distribution channels, promotional arrangements, and infrastructure. As early movers into Poland, Matsushita and Philips were better able to access scarce or governmentally-controlled resources such as local financing and state-instituted wholesale networks than later movers such as Toshiba and Samsung. Moreover, early investors have a superior option to select better local firms for equity/contractual joint ventures or for supply-purchase business relations. Charoen Pokphand (CP), one of the world's largest agro-industrial MNEs from Thailand, entered China in 1979 as the first mover into the Chinese agriculture sector. By 2000, the company had set up 170 projects throughout 28 provinces. Most of these projects are joint ventures with the best local firms in respective regions. Further, early movers enjoy low competition before late movers come in. The only competition comes from local firms (if any). Wal-Mart was among the first foreign superstores established in Korea, China, Costa Rica, Argentina, Germany, Puerto Rico, and Brazil, to name a few. The only competition the company faced during early years was from some indigenous department stores in major metropolitan areas. When later movers are about to enter, early movers and local firms tend to establish alliances to drive out new entrants or maintain strong competitive power in the industry. Even when not forming alliances, early movers are still in a better position to deal with competition from local firms than late entrants. They can position their competitive advantage in businesses, industries, and markets where competition from local firms is weak or where they have better technological and organizational competencies.

Early-Mover Disadvantages

Early movers, however, also suffer from some disadvantages compared to late entrants. Pioneer investors may be confronted with greater environmental uncertainty and operational risks. Environmental uncertainty generally comes from (1) underdeveloped FDI laws and regulations in a host country, (2) the host government's lack of experience in dealing with MNEs, and (3) infant or embryonic stages of the industry or market in a host country. Operational risks originate from (1) a shortage of qualified supply sources and other production inputs such as talented managers and R&D workforce; (2) under-developed support services such as local financing, foreign exchange, arbitration, consulting, and marketing; (3) poor infrastructure in transportation, utilities, and communications; and (4) an unstable market structure in which market demand and supply are misaligned and local governments often interfere with MNE operations.

In contrast with early movers, **late investors** do not suffer, or suffer less, from the preceding uncertainties and risks.[9] When late movers arrive, the host-country environment is usually more stable, regulatory conditions are more favorable, and the market infrastructure is already developed. Korean MNEs (*chaebol*) are all late movers entering China relative to western MNEs. They did not enter until 1994 when Hyundai, Samsung, LG, and Daewoo started their FDI in China, especially on the Shandong peninsula. In that year China significantly deepened economic reforms and liberalization, broadened the industries and geographical areas for MNE operations, and enacted various laws and regulations concerning inbound FDI. As late movers, Korean MNEs benefited greatly from these improved environments. Facing reduced uncertainty and a more stabilized environment, Korean *chaebol* were aggressive late movers who waited patiently until the best time but committed aggressively after entry to seize emerging opportunities. LG Group, for example, built 20 projects in China, amounting to $688 billion in the first two years after entering the country in 1994.

Early movers also tend to pay higher costs in learning and adapting to local environments and in countervailing imitation. Many early movers are compelled to invest more in building industrial infrastructure (e.g., supply bases and distribution networks) and technological or service standards. When Sharp and Hitachi entered China in the early 1980s to produce fax machines, they had to establish these standards and construct supply bases because the fax machine industry had not yet emerged in the country prior to their entry. It also cost early movers more in training local workers, technicians, and managers. Such human resources might be unavailable or lack skill before early FDI is undertaken. Late entrants, however, can benefit greatly from a pool of skilled laborers and favorable industrial infrastructure established by early entrants. In addition, early movers pay more to learn about the local environment (cultural, social, economic, legal, and political), unique business practices, social norms and customs, and consumer behavior. Conversely, later movers who use a wait-and-see strategy gain from lessons from early movers. In particular, they benefit from mimicking an early mover's business policies and strategies that have proved to be successful in a host country. For example, when the Franklin Templeton Group, a U.S. financial service company, entered Brazil in 1998 as a late mover, it learned a great deal about viable strategies from early movers such as Citibank. As of December 2000, its mutual fund assets in Brazil reached $1.17 billion.

Finally, early movers may have to fight followers who imitate their strategies or innovations, counterfeit their products, or infringe on their industrial (e.g., trademark and brand) or intellectual property rights (e.g., patent, expertise, software). This cost is especially high when early movers invest in a country with underdeveloped and under-enforced legal systems in protecting these rights. Philip Morris entered Russia's tobacco market (Russians consume 300 billion cigarettes per year) in 1974 as a first mover. However, it has proved to be very costly for the company to protect its leading brands such as Marlboro and Parliament because about 30 percent of these brands sold on the street are counterfeits. When followers imitate a first-mover's products or strategies, the latter needs to commit more to new innovations, new developments, and new strategies. When followers infringe on a first-mover's property rights, the latter has to spend on litigation, investigation, lobbying, or arbitration. In addition to direct costs of anti-imitation, early movers have to pay higher switching and start-up costs. Later movers can piggyback on early investment if imitation is easy, thereby gaining profit without having to pay as much as innovators.

Because of the preceding uncertainties, risks, and costs, pioneer MNEs tend to select the joint venture mode for FDI entry. In the joint venture business, however, the objectives of local partners usually diverge from those of their foreign partners.

Exhibit 10–3

Advantages and disadvantages of early movers

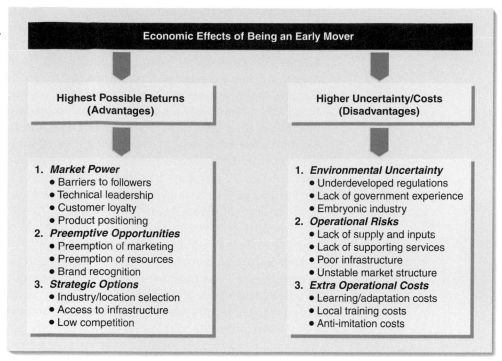

Economic Effects of Being an Early Mover	
Highest Possible Returns (Advantages)	**Higher Uncertainty/Costs (Disadvantages)**
1. *Market Power* • Barriers to followers • Technical leadership • Customer loyalty • Product positioning 2. *Preemptive Opportunities* • Preemption of marketing • Preemption of resources • Brand recognition 3. *Strategic Options* • Industry/location selection • Access to infrastructure • Low competition	1. *Environmental Uncertainty* • Underdeveloped regulations • Lack of government experience • Embryonic industry 2. *Operational Risks* • Lack of supply and inputs • Lack of supporting services • Poor infrastructure • Unstable market structure 3. *Extra Operational Costs* • Learning/adaptation costs • Local training costs • Anti-imitation costs

The pursuit of self-interest rather than common goals, as well as lack of autonomy among local partners, can result in significant uncertainty for joint venture operations. This internal uncertainty is generally difficult for MNEs to control. Since late investors can usually choose to establish wholly-owned subsidiaries, this uncertainty is less substantial than that faced by early movers.

Exhibit 10–3 summarizes the advantages and disadvantages of being an early mover. In general, the advantages of early movers are the disadvantages of late movers, and vice versa.

Decision Framework

Entry decisions must be based on rigorous cost-benefit analysis and then prudently timed. After assessing the advantages and disadvantages of the timing choice (e.g., early mover), international managers consider other factors in formulating timing strategy. These include: (1) the MNE's technological, organizational, and financial resources or capabilities; (2) the host-country environment in terms of infrastructure, industry structure, market demand, and governmental policies; and (3) potential competition from late foreign entrants as well as local entrants.

An MNE's resources and capabilities determine its ability to reduce early-mover risks and seize preemptive investment opportunities. A pioneer entrant must wait for a feasible opportunity for investment, the appearance of which depends on the investor's foresight, skills, resources, and good fortune. Not every MNE is competent to be a pioneer mover. One prerequisite, for instance, is the firm's international experience and its ability to cultivate relationships with local authorities and handle environmental changes overseas. Motorola has been capable of being the first mover into many emerging markets due to its accumulated experience in a large number of developing countries, especially its experience in dealing with local governments and communities.

The real balance between costs and benefits or between risks and returns for a timing decision depends on actual dynamics and specific characteristics of the host-country environments. As explained in Chapter 5, the microeconomic business environment (industrial conditions and market situations) often impacts MNE activities more directly than the macroeconomic environment. The host-country conditions in infrastructure, technology, factor endowments, market demand, industry structure, and government policies are all likely to affect an MNE's timing of entry and its eventual success. Moreover, anticipated first-mover opportunities may disappear, or unanticipated new opportunities may emerge, because of environmental changes in a host country. The transformation of national economies, market structures, and government policies is often so uncertain in foreign countries that pioneer MNEs may need to have second or even third backup plans. When Philip Morris (PM) entered Russia as the first mover, it built two projects, PM Izhora in Leningrad and PM Kuban in Krasnodar. The two projects were set in such a way that PM Kuban would switch from producing cigarettes to processing raw tobacco for PM Izhora if local suppliers were unable to supply processed tobacco and/or if the local market became more restricted.

The option of being a first mover is not entirely under the firm's control. Preemptive investment opportunities may be observed and reacted upon by local rivals as well as foreign competitors. The responses and actions of the firm's competitors need to be carefully examined. The MNE must study the strengths and weaknesses of potential rivals in areas such as technology, production, marketing, and capital. When an opportunity presents itself, the investor must decide whether it should enter the foreign territory as a first mover or early entrant, and then whether it has the capacity to build a sustainable advantage from its entry timing. If the answers are "yes", the firm must then decide how to enter the host market and best exploit the opportunity, the critical issue being discussed next. Once a pioneering strategy is chosen, the investor must react faster than its rivals, commit to its own pioneering opportunities, and take measures to sustain its first-mover advantages. If the investor chooses not to be an early mover, or if a rival has preempted this position, then the investor must decide whether, how, and when to follow.

Interim Summary

1. Compared to late entrants, early movers benefit from stronger market power, greater preemptive opportunities, and more strategic options, but suffer more from environmental uncertainty, operational risks, and extra operational costs.

2. Not every early mover can succeed abroad, nor should every firm be the first mover. The timing decision depends not only on the opportunity-risk balance but also on the firm's capabilities, the local environment, and new competition.

ENTRY MODE SELECTION (*HOW*)

Entry Mode Choices

An MNE seeking to enter a foreign market must make an important strategic decision concerning which entry mode to use. **Entry modes** are specific forms or ways of entering a target country to achieve strategic goals underlying international presence in that country. Entry mode choices fall into three categories: *trade-related*, *transfer-related*, and *FDI-related*. Along this sequence, the levels of resource commitment, organizational control, involved risks, and expected returns all increase. Within each category, these levels differ somewhat between specific modes.

Trade-Related Entry Modes

Trade-related entry modes include exporting, subcontracting, and countertrade.

Exporting

It is natural for most firms to get their start in international expansion through exporting in which the firm maintains its production facilities at home and sells its products abroad. Through exporting, the firm gains valuable expertise about operating internationally and specific knowledge concerning the individual countries in which it operates. Export offers the advantage of not requiring a very substantial presence in foreign countries. Generally, exporting is a type of international entry open to virtually any size or kind of firm, whereas other types of entry modes tend to demand greater resources and involve more risks. Over time, accumulated experience with exporting often prompts a firm to become more aggressive in exploiting new international exporting opportunities or consider FDI in the country to which it previously exported.

A firm can either export goods directly to foreign customers or buyers or through export intermediaries. **Export intermediaries** are third parties that specialize in facilitating imports and exports. These intermediaries may offer limited services such as handling only transportation, documentation, and customs claims, or they may perform more extensive services, including taking ownership of foreign-bound goods and/or assuming total responsibility for marketing and financing exports. Typical export intermediaries are export management companies. An **export management company** (EMC) is an intermediary that acts as its client's export department. Small firms may use an EMC to handle their foreign shipments, prepare export documents, and deal with customs offices, insurance companies, and/or commodity inspection agencies. EMCs are generally more knowledgeable about the legal, financial, and logistical details of exporting and importing and thus free the exporter from having to develop such expertise in-house.

Managers involved in exporting must know the terms of sale (or terms of price). **Terms of sale** are conditions stipulating rights/responsibilities and costs/risks borne by exporter and importer. These terms have been harmonized and defined by the International Chamber of Commerce as standards, and thus are widely used in export transactions. Major terms of price include:

- *FOB* (Free on Board): A term of price in which the seller covers all costs and risks up to the point whereby the goods are delivered on board the ship in a designated shipment (export) port, and the buyer bears all costs and risks from that point on. This means that the buyer is responsible for the insurance and freight expenses in transporting goods from the shipment port to the destination port.
- *FAS* (Free Alongside Ship): A term of price in which the seller covers all costs and risks up to the side of the ship in a designated shipment (export) port. The buyer bears all costs and risks thereafter.
- *CIF* (Cost, Insurance, and Freight): A term of price in which the seller covers cost of the goods, insurance, and all transportation and miscellaneous charges to the named foreign port in the country of final destination.
- *C&F* (Cost and Freight): Similar to CIF except that the buyer purchases and bears the insurance.

Export managers should also be familiar with key documentation in exporting. The key documents frequently used include the letter of credit, the bill of lading, the bank draft, the commercial invoice, the insurance certificate, and the certificate of origin. **A letter of credit** (L/C) is a contract between an importer and a bank that transfers liability for paying the exporter from the importer to the importer's bank (for details, see the first section of Chapter 14). A **bill of lading** (B/L) is the document issued by a shipping company or its agent as evidence of a contract for shipping the merchandise and as a claim to ownership of the goods. In Chapter 14, we explain in detail how export managers deal with international payment, import and export financing, foreign exchange risk reduction, and collection of export accounts receivable.

International Subcontracting

Subcontracting has been used extensively by MNEs seeking low labor costs in a host country. Generally, **subcontracting** is the process in which a foreign company provides a local manufacturer with raw materials, semi-finished products, sophisticated components, or technology for producing final goods that will be bought back by the foreign company. In most subcontracting businesses, local manufacturers are responsible only for processing or assembly in exchange for processing fees. In this situation, the local manufacturer does not own the property rights of materials or parts supplied by the foreign counterpart. Nike, for example, is still using subcontracting as its primary mode in China, Vietnam, Thailand, Indonesia, and Bangladesh. The company provides raw materials and technology, maintains proprietary rights over materials and products, controls production processes and product quality, and pays processing fees to local factories.

In the beginning of the twenty-first century, when falling trade barriers and increasing competition prompted large firms to cut costs, many MNEs producing sophisticated products began shrinking their manufacturing function by using the **original equipment manufacturing (OEM)** method. OEM is one specific form of international subcontracting, in which a foreign firm (i.e., original equipment manufacturer) supplies a local company with the technology and sophisticated components so that the latter can manufacture goods that the foreign firm will market under its own brand in international markets. Flextronics, a Singapore-based company, was during the 1990s a small contract assembler of circuit boards, but is now the world's third largest subcontractor in electronics, providing cost-efficient manufacturing services that free its OEM clients (e.g., Honeywell, GE, Pratt & Whitney, Compaq, Nortel) to concentrate on design, engineering, R&D, and global marketing. I-Berhad, a Malaysian subcontractor in PC assembly, has assembly plants in Shah Alam, Selangor, and Perak that provide subcontracting services (manufacturing and assembling) for many international brands such as Sanyo, Sharp, Toshiba, and Singer. China's Kelon now serves as GE's largest subcontractor for its household appliance products. This subcontracting helps Kelon utilize its existing production capacity, benefit from technology transfer from GE, and learn managerial skills from the foreign firm. It helps GE reduce production costs, rationalize its production process, and expedite large volume productions. Today, other MNEs such as Motorola, Ericsson, Siemens, Acer, HP, IBM, Boeing, Lucent, and Northern Telecom are using OEM to cut costs while maintaining their competitive edge in the global marketplace.

Countertrade

Countertrade is a form of trade in which a seller and a buyer from different countries exchange merchandise with little or no cash or cash equivalents, changing hands. Because of this nature, it is also viewed as a form of flexible financing or payment in international trade. Informed estimates suggest that countertrade accounts for about 20 percent of world trade.[10] Countertrade has evolved into a diverse set of activities that can be categorized as four distinct types of trading arrangements:

- Barter
- Counterpurchase
- Offset
- Buyback (or compensation)

Barter is the direct and simultaneous exchange of goods between two parties without a cash transaction. Barter trade occurs between individuals, between governments, between firms, or between a government and a firm, all from two different countries. Barter may be the oldest form of trade but it is certainly not history. For example, France shipped 138,067 tons of soft wheat to Cuba during the first quarter of 2001, half of which was through the wheat-for-sugar barter arrangement under which French trading companies purchase sugar and agricultural commodities from Alimport, Cuba's government-run food trading company. Because firms using barter run the risk of having to accept goods that may be difficult to market or earn a satisfactory profit margin from, it is important for a party to ensure that trading-in products are heavily demanded in its own market.

A **counterpurchase** is a reciprocal buying agreement whereby one firm sells its products to another at one point in time and is compensated in the form of the other's products at some future time (e.g., Russia purchased construction machinery from Japan's Komatsu in return for Komatsu's agreement to buy Siberian timber). Counterpurchase is more flexible than barter in facilitating many transactions because the volume of trade does not have to be equal, i.e., the dollar amount of goods exported need not be equal to the dollar amount of goods taken back. In this situation, two parties can either set up an escrow account or use cash to finally settle the differences. Unlike barter, which involves a single contract, a counterpurchase agreement usually involves three separate contracts—the sales contract, the purchase contract, and the protocol contract. The protocol contract serves as a protection contract, which explains what each party will do and what each party should expect.

An **offset** is an agreement whereby one party agrees to purchase goods and services with a specified percentage of its proceeds from an original sale. Like counterpurchase, offset involves three contracts including sales, protocol, and purchase. Unlike counterpurchase whereby exchanged products are normally unrelated, products taken back in an offset are often the outputs processed by this party in the original contract. For example, the Shanghai Aircraft Manufacturing Corp., China, may buy jets from Boeing using its proceeds from manufacturing the tail sections of the jets for Boeing. Offset is particularly popular in sales of expensive military equipment or high-cost civilian infrastructure hardware. General Dynamics sold several hundred F-16 military jets to Belgium, Denmark, Norway, and the Netherlands by agreeing to allow those countries to offset the cost of the jets through co-production agreements whereby 40 percent of the value of the aircraft was produced in these countries.

Finally, **buyback** (or compensation arrangement) occurs when a firm provides a local company with inputs for manufacturing products (mostly capital equipment) to be sold in international markets, and agrees to take a certain percentage of the output produced by the local firm as partial payment. A buyback agreement involves two contracts including the sales contract and the purchase contract. In a buyback arrangement, the equipment supplier gets a cash portion in addition to the goods. For example, a steel producer might send its goods to a foreign company, which would use the steel to manufacture a product such as shelving. The steel producer would then buy back the shelves at a reduced price, in effect partially paying the manufacturer with the raw steel. Buybacks help developing country producers upgrade technologies and machinery and ensure after-sale service. Chinatex, a Shanghai-based clothing manufacturer, and Japan's Fukusuke Corp., arranged a buyback whereby the latter sold 10 knitting machines and raw materials to the former in exchange for 1 million pairs of underwear to be produced on the knitting machines.

Because the buyback links payment with output from the purchased goods, China-tex benefited from Fukusuke's instructions on how to use the equipment and its excellent after-sale services.

Transfer-Related Entry Modes

Transfer-related entry modes are those associated with transfer of ownership or utilization of specified property (technology or assets) from one party to the other in exchange for royalty fees. They differ from trade-related entry modes in that the user in a transfer-related mode "buys" certain rights of transacted property (e.g., use of technology) from the other party (owner). These modes are extensively employed in technology-related or intellectual/industrial property rights-related transactions. This category includes the following entry modes:

- International leasing
- International licensing
- International franchising
- Build-operate-transfer (BOT)

International Leasing

International leasing is an entry mode in which the foreign firm (lessor) leases out its new or used machines or equipment to the local company (often in a developing country). International lease arises largely because developing country manufacturers (lessee) do not have financial capability or lack foreign currency to pay for the equipment. In many cases, the leased equipment sits idle but is in good operational condition, thus having a market in developing countries. In this mode, the foreign lessor retains ownership of the property throughout the lease period during which the local user pays a leasing fee. The major advantages of this mode for MNEs include quick access to the target market, efficient use of superfluous or outmoded machinery and equipment, or accumulating experience in a foreign country. From the local firm's perspective, this mode helps reduce the cost of using foreign machinery and equipment, mitigates operational and investment risks, and increases its knowledge and experience with foreign technologies and facilities. In the late 1970s, Japan's Mitsubishi leased 100 new and used heavy trucks to Chinese companies in such industries as construction, mining, and transportation.

International Licensing

International licensing is an entry mode in which a foreign licensor grants specified intangible property rights to the local licensee for a specified period of time in exchange for a royalty fee. Such property rights may include patents, trademarks, technology, managerial skills, and so on. They allow the licensee to produce and market a product similar to the one the licensor has already been producing in its home country without requiring the licensor to actually create a new operation abroad.

Generally, an MNE may use international licensing to: (1) obtain extra income from technical expertise and services, spread around the costs of company research and development programs or maximize returns on research findings and accumulated expertise; (2) retain established markets that have been closed or threatened by trade restrictions, reach new markets not accessible by export from existing facilities, or expand into foreign markets quickly with minimum effort or risk; (3) augment limited domestic capacity and management resources for serving foreign markets, provide overseas sources of supply and services to important domestic customers, or develop market outlets for raw materials or components made by the

McDonald's, in Egypt since 1994, offers franchise opportunities to investors and operators.

domestic company; (4) build goodwill and acceptance for the company's other products or services, develop sources of raw materials or components for the company's other operations, or pave the way for future investment; or (5) discourage possible infringement, impairment, or loss of company patents or trademarks, or acquire reciprocal benefits from foreign expertise, research, and technical services.

Income from licenses, however, is generally lower than from franchising and FDI entry modes. Loss of quality control can be another major disadvantage of this entry mode. It is often difficult for the licensor to maintain satisfactory control over the licensee's manufacturing and marketing operations. This can result in damage to a licensor's trademark and reputation. Moreover, a licensee overseas can also become a competitor to the licensor. If the original licensing agreement does not stipulate the region within which the licensee may market the licensed product, the licensee may insist on marketing the product in third-country markets in competition with the licensor. Further, a local licensee may benefit from improvements in its technology, which it then uses to enter the MNE's home market.

International Franchising

International franchising is an entry mode in which the foreign franchisor grants specified intangible property rights (e.g., trademark or brand name) to the local franchisee, which must abide by strict and detailed rules as to how it does business. Compared to licensing, franchising involves longer commitments, offers greater control over overseas operations, and includes a broader package of rights and resources, which is why service MNEs such as KFC often elect franchising (whereas manufacturing firms often use licensing). Production equipment, managerial systems, operating procedures, access to advertising and promotional materials, loans, and financing may all be part of a franchise. The franchisee operates the business under the franchisor's proprietary rights and is contractually obligated to adhere to the procedures and methods of operation prescribed in the business system. The franchisor generally maintains the right to control the quality of products and services so that the franchisee cannot damage the company's image. In exchange for the franchise, the franchisor receives a royalty payment that amounts to a percentage of the franchisee's revenues. Sometimes the franchisor mandates that the franchisee must buy equipment or key ingredients used in the product. For example, Burger King and McDonald's require the franchisee to buy the company's cooking equipment, burger patties, and other products that bear the company name.

The merits and limitations of international franchising are similar to those of licensing. The main advantages include little political risk, low costs, and fast and easy avenues for leveraging assets such as a trademark or brand name. For example, McDonald's has been able to build a global presence quickly and at relatively low cost and risk by using franchises. Nevertheless, the franchisee may damage the franchisor's image by not upholding its standards. Even if the franchisor is able to terminate the agreement, some franchisees still stay in business by slightly altering the franchisor's brand name or trademark.

Build-Operate-Transfer (BOT)

Build-operate-transfer (BOT) is a "turnkey" investment in which a foreign investor assumes responsibility for the design and construction of an entire operation, and, upon completion of the project, turns the project over to the purchaser and hands over management to local personnel whom it has trained. In return for completing the project, the investor receives periodic payments that are normally guaranteed. BOT is especially useful for very large-scale, long-term infrastructure projects such as power-generation, airports, dams, expressways, chemical plants, and steel mills. Managing such complex projects requires special expertise. It is thus not surprising that most are administered by large construction firms such as Bechtel (the United States), Hyundai (Korea), or Friedrich Krupp (Germany). Large companies sometimes form a consortium and bid jointly for a large BOT project. Iran's first BOT power plant, the 900MW combined cycle/gas fired Parehsar project, was launched in 2001 through an international consortium consisting of Italy's Sondel, Germany's Dillinger Stahl (DSD), and Iran's Mapna International. The foreign partnership has a 70 percent stake in the project. Like other big BOT projects, a part of the financing for this project was sourced from export credit agencies instituted by the German and Italian governments. The Iran government ensured that sovereign guarantees would be in place for repayment of loans and payment for electricity delivered locally. The plant is scheduled to open in 2004 and will be operated by the consortium for 20 years, before being handed back to Iran's state power company Tavanir.

Due in part to the difficulties of working out financing and equity arrangements, the BOT approach is often used in combination with other entry modes. Foreign businesses may set up BOT project firms by means of either equity or cooperative joint ventures with local partners. Because of their ability to provide foreign investors with returns in excess of their proportional contributions to the venture's total registered capital, contractual joint ventures have been the vehicles of choice for BOT infrastructure projects. For example, in 2001, Frankfurt Airport Corp, from Germany, was awarded by the Philippine government a BOT contract for the construction of the third passenger terminal at the Ninoy Aquino International Airport. It then formed a contractual joint venture, named Fraport, with Philippines International Airport Transport Company, to construct this project.

FDI-Related Entry Modes

In contrast to the preceding trade-related and transfer-related entry modes, FDI-related entry modes involve ownership of property, assets, projects, and businesses invested in a host country. Accordingly, firms undertaking FDI will control overseas operations and economic activities. FDI-related entry modes are more sophisticated than trade-related modes, and involve higher risk and longer-term contribution than both trade- and transfer-related choices. Compared with the latter, FDI-related modes underline the firm's long-term strategic goals of international presence and necessitate continuous contribution and commitment to investments and operations abroad. FDI-related entry modes include:

- Branch office
- Cooperative joint venture
- Equity joint venture
- Wholly-owned subsidiary
- Umbrella holding company

The Branch Office

A **branch office** is a foreign entity in a host country in which it is not incorporated but exists as an extension of the parent and is legally constituted as a branch.

Corporate law in many countries allows foreign companies to open branches that engage in production and operating activities. Unlike representative offices which by law are prohibited from engaging in direct, profit-making business activities (they instead serve as liaisons, establishing contacts with governments and handling market research and consulting activities), branch offices are entitled to run businesses within a specified scope or location. A foreign subsidiary can also open a branch office in another region of the host country to expand its operations there. Branch offices are particularly utilized by transnational banks, law firms, and accounting or consulting companies. For example, British's Standard Bank had 1,000 branches in South Africa in 2001, and was ranked the largest foreign bank in that country. It also had branch offices in 14 other sub-Saharan countries. Because of South Africa's traditionally strong financial infrastructure, and its long-established presence in the major financial centers of Africa, the bank is a match for foreign entrants in retail banking technology as well as wholesale payments, clearing, and custody. In most cases, branch offices may offer a relatively simple means for establishing or expanding a presence in a target country, but since they do not have legal-person status, the foreign parent company is liable if civil charges are brought against the branch. To shield the parent company from unlimited damage claims, foreign companies interested in establishing branch offices may designate an offshore subsidiary as the parent. For instance, the first McDonald's restaurant in Russia was launched by its Canadian subsidiary.

The Cooperative (or Contractual) Joint Venture

The **cooperative joint venture** (also known as contractual joint venture) is a collaborative agreement whereby profits and other responsibilities are assigned to each party according to a contract. These do not necessarily accord with each partner's percentage of the total investment. Each party cooperates as a separate legal entity and bears its own liabilities. Most cooperative joint ventures do not involve constructing and building a new legally and physically independent entity. As such, cooperative joint ventures normally take the form of a document (cooperative agreement), whereas equity joint ventures take the form of a new entity.

Many cooperative programs today involve joint activities without the creation of a new corporate entity. Instead, carefully defined rules govern the allocation of tasks, costs, and revenues. Joint exploration (e.g., offshore oil exploration consortia), research partnership, and co-production are typical forms of cooperative joint ventures. Others include joint marketing, long-term supply agreements, or technological training and assistance. Boeing entered China in the late 1970s through a co-production agreement with the Xian Aircraft Manufacturing Company which co-produced 737 vertical fins, horizontal stabilizers, and forward access doors; and another co-production agreement with the Shenyang Aircraft Manufacturing Company which co-produced 737 tail sections and 757 cargo doors. Chapter 12 details forms and features of various cooperative arrangements.

The Equity Joint Venture

The most common foreign entry for MNEs has been through equity joint ventures. An **equity joint venture** entails establishing a new entity that is jointly owned and managed by two or more parent firms in different countries. To set up an equity joint venture, each partner contributes cash, facilities, equipment, materials, intellectual property rights, labor, or land-use rights. According to joint venture laws in most countries, a foreign investor's share must exceed a certain threshold of the total equity (25 percent in many nations). Generally, there is no upward limit in deregulated industries in most countries, whether developed and developing.

However, in governmentally controlled or institutionally restricted sectors, foreign investors are often confined with respect to equity arrangements.

Broadly, cooperative joint ventures and equity joint ventures are together called global strategic alliances (GSAs). The proliferation of such alliances among MNEs from different countries is transforming the global business environment. These alliances are gaining importance worldwide as global competition intensifies for access to markets, products, and technologies. Most large MNEs such as Motorola, Siemens, Sony, GM, Daimler, and Toyota have built such alliances. In Japan alone, for example, Royal Dutch Shell has established more than 30 joint ventures. As a means of survival and growth, GSAs have become a fundamental element of many MNEs' key global business strategies. GSAs are explained in Chapter 12.

The Wholly-Owned Subsidiary

The **wholly-owned subsidiary** is an entry mode in which the investing firm owns 100 percent of the new entity in a host country. This new entity may be built from scratch by the investing firm (i.e., greenfield investment) or in acquiring a local business (i.e., cross-border acquisition). This mode offers foreign investors increased flexibility and control. It allows international managers to make their own decisions without the burden of an uncooperative partner. Wholly-owned subsidiaries also allow foreign investors to set up and protect their own processes and procedures, which leads to more careful strategic and operational oversight. During the 1990s, Japan's Kao Corporation established a large number of wholly-owned manufacturing and marketing subsidiaries overseas. For example, it established a wholly-owned subsidiary in Singapore for the following reasons:

- Coming out of a deeply-rooted Japanese corporate culture, Kao's head office prefers tight control over its subsidiaries. Kao's preference for wholly-owned operations clearly follows from this cultural bias.
- A wholly-owned subsidiary gives a firm the tight control over operations in different countries that is necessary for global integration, thus leading to greater global value.
- A wholly-owned subsidiary reduces the risk of losing control of a firm's technological expertise.
- A wholly-owned mode better ensures that Kao's foreign operations will benefit from the detergent-producing skills that its domestic operation has possessed for decades.

Nevertheless, the establishment of a large, wholly-owned project abroad, such as the Mercedez-Benz plant in Alabama, can be a complex, costly, and lengthy process. MNEs must choose between the importance of protecting core technology and manufacturing and marketing processes on the one hand, and the costs of establishing a new operation on the other. Many MNEs choose this alternative only after expanding into markets through other modes that have helped them accumulate host-country experience.

Wholly-owned subsidiaries have traditionally been viewed by many host-country governments, particularly those of developing economies, as offering little in the way of technology transfer or other benefits to local economies. Recently, this entry mode has become more attractive to them. When domestic credit is tight, this mode provides host countries with a means of attracting foreign investment. Nevertheless, governmental support for this mode often trails far behind that of joint ventures in many countries.

Some notes of caution should be stated. First, wholly-owned subsidiaries must rely on indigenous agents to make liaisons on their behalf and help procure land, materials, and services. Second, wholly-owned foreign subsidiaries may not be allowed to invest and operate in industries that are vital to the host-country economy. Third, since wholly-owned subsidiaries operate without the control of local partners, investment approval authorities often hold them to higher standards on pollution control, technological level, capital contribution, foreign exchange administration, and the like. Finally, wholly-owned subsidiaries are more vulnerable to criticism relating to cultural and economic sovereignty. Managers in wholly-owned subsidiaries should recognize and address this concern. One way is to localize production, that is, to buy as many parts and components as possible from local suppliers, and to localize human resources (i.e., hire local managers).

The Umbrella Holding Company

The **umbrella holding company** is an investment company that unites the firm's existing investments such as branch offices, joint ventures, and wholly-owned subsidiaries under one umbrella so as to combine sales, procurement, manufacturing, training, and maintenance within the host country. Many foreign companies are now seeking better integration of these functions for a broad range of products and services within a single but important country (such as China and Brazil). Such coordination becomes necessary as each production division sets up its own foreign subunits separated from other divisions' foreign subunits in the same host country. DuPont faced this problem in China because some joint ventures there belong to, and are controlled only by, its pharmaceutical division, whereas others belong to its plastic or petroleum divisions. In 1989 it established DuPont China Ltd. as its holding company to unite and integrate existing investments originally undertaken by respective production divisions. The umbrella model is thus particularly useful for MNEs that are multidivisional, where each division enters and runs differently while the holding company coordinates them. The umbrella mode helps improve the cash flow and capital structure of various investments by acting as a clearinghouse for intra-group financing. With a holding company in a host country, profits can be more easily transferred among different strategic business units (SBUs) and taken out of the country. It can also smooth the establishment of new investments. Like all legally independent subsidiaries, an umbrella company has legal person status in a host country. To establish an umbrella company, MNEs may need to comply with certain conditions set by the host-country government. In China, for example, the foreign investor must have established a minimum of 10 subunits in the country and engaged in manufacturing or infrastructure construction to which it has contributed at least $30 million in registered capital.

A foreign investor may consider establishing an umbrella enterprise to achieve some or all of the following objectives: (1) investment in subsidiary projects; (2) facilitation of cash flow or foreign exchange balance for all local activities; (3) centralized purchase of production materials for subsidiary projects; (4) provision of product maintenance services and technical support; (5) training of subsidiary project personnel and end users of products; (6) coordination and consolidation of project management; and (7) marketing of subsidiary products.

Exhibit 10–4 highlights the implications of various entry modes in terms of risk, return, control, and commitment. These dimensions serve as base points for MNE managers considering various entry modes. Overall, risk, return, control, and commitment all increase along this sequence with the exception that BOT may involve even more commitment (especially capital and technology) and take even longer to build a new project than some FDI-related entry modes such as branch offices and joint ventures.

Exhibit 10–4
International entry modes

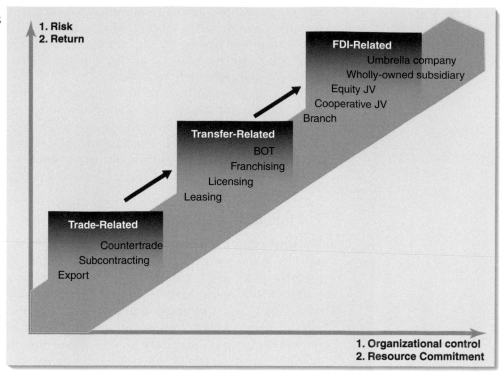

Decision Framework

To select an appropriate entry mode, MNEs should make sure they know all possible options for the entry into a target country before determining the best one. Once a foreign investor decides to pursue an FDI project, its choice of entry mode will depend on a wide range of considerations. Broadly, these can be classified into *country, industry, firm,* and *project* factors.

Country-Specific Factors

A number of host-country-specific factors have an impact on entry mode choice. First, *government FDI policies* may directly or indirectly influence entry mode selection. The laws in some countries mandate that foreign firms must choose joint ventures, as opposed to wholly-owned subsidiaries, as an entry mode.[11] Second, *infrastructure conditions* affect the extent to which a MNE plans to commit distinctive resources to local operations, and the degree to which it perceives operational uncertainty and contextual unpredictability. These in turn influence the entry mode option. Third, *property right systems* and other legal frameworks in a host country appear to be increasingly important to entry mode selection. Without sufficient legal protection, an MNE's property rights such as trademarks, brand names, expertise, patents, and copyrights will be exposed to possible infringement and piracy by local firms. In such circumstances, the MNE may have to use a high-control entry mode such as a wholly-owned subsidiary or dominant equity joint venture. Fourth, *host-country risks* including general political risks (e.g. instability of political system), ownership/control risks (e.g. price control, local content requirements), and transfer risks (e.g. currency inconvertibility, remittance control) may affect entry mode.[12] Licensing and joint ventures may be favored when country risk is high. Finally, *cultural distance* between home and host countries influences foreign entry decision and process. The greater the perceived distance between home and host countries, the more likely it is that the MNE will favor licensing/franchising or a joint venture over a wholly-owned subsidiary.

Industry-Specific Factors

Several industry-specific factors are important considerations underlying entry mode selection. First, *entry barriers* into a target industry in the host country constitute a significant impediment to entry mode selection. Contractual or equity joint ventures may be an effective vehicle to bypass these barriers. Second, *industrial uncertainty and complexity* may lead MNEs to use high control or low commitment entry modes such as representative or branch offices, licensing, franchising, loosely structured cooperative joint ventures with little resource commitment, or minority equity joint ventures. Last, *availability and favorability of supply and distribution* in the industry will determine the rationalization of value chain linkages needed for an MNE's local operations and the vertical integration of other units within the MNE network. When an MNE relies more on local resource procurement and/or emphasizes the local market, it is more vulnerable to industrial linkages with suppliers and distributors. Entry modes involving partners are superior when the MNE needs but lacks such linkages in the host country.

Firm-Specific Factors

Entry mode selection is contingent on several firm-specific traits as well. First, a firm's *resource possession* influences the firm's ability to explore market potential and earn a competitive edge in the global marketplace. A firm that lacks distinctive resources (technological, organizational, operational, and financial) but wishes to share in the risks associated with having them, is often compelled to enter the market through a joint venture where its resource commitment will be minimized.[13] Second, *the leakage risk of technologies* may affect entry mode. If this risk is high, a wholly-owned subsidiary mode increases the firm's ability to use and protect these technologies. Third, a firm's *strategic goals* for international expansion are one of the foremost determinants underlying entry mode selection. When an MNE attempts to pursue local market expansion, high commitment choices such as cooperative or equity joint ventures, wholly-owned subsidiaries, and umbrella companies are preferable because they enable the firm to have a deeper, more diverse involvement with the indigenous market, creating more opportunities to accumulate country-specific experience. If an MNE aims only to exploit factor endowment advantages, low commitment entry modes such as subcontracting, compensation trade, co-production, cooperative arrangement, and minority equity joint venture may be superior to other options because risks and costs are low. Finally, *international or host country experience* influences entry mode selection. MNEs with little or no experience with international or host-country business may prefer low control/low resource commitment entry modes such as export, subcontracting, international leasing or franchising, or countertrade.[14] In contrast, MNEs with significant multinational experience prefer high control/high resource commitment entry modes such as cooperative or equity joint ventures, wholly-owned subsidiaries, and umbrella investment companies.

Project-Specific Factors

In the course of entry mode selection, MNEs also need to consider some attributes of the FDI project itself. First, firms may shy away from a wholly-owned entry mode in favor of a joint venture when the *project size* is large. A large investment implies higher start-up, switching, and exit costs, thus involving higher financial and operational risks. Second, *project orientation* influences an MNE's resource dispersal and entry mode. MNEs investing in import-substitution projects may be inclined to establish partnerships with local government agencies or state-owned enterprises holding monopoly positions because this type of FDI project is vulnerable to host government control. If a project is local market-oriented, the MNE may choose the cooperative or equity joint venture mode, because the local partner can provide distinctive supply and distribution channels, governmental networks, and culture-specific business knowledge and experience. If a project is technologically advanced, the firm may opt for a wholly-owned subsidiary mode to protect its expertise, or a joint venture mode if it needs complementary technologies or knowledge from a partner firm. Finally, when a project is infrastructure-oriented, the MNE may apply the build-operate-transfer mode if it plans on having only a short-term run, or a majority joint venture mode if it has a long-term strategic plan and is willing to take risks. Finally, *the availability of proper local partners* for a particular project may affect an MNE's entry ability and choice. An MNE's ability to establish a joint venture or any other form of non-integrated entry mode depends upon the availability of capable, trustworthy partners. In the absence of acceptable local partners, the MNE may be forced to start a wholly-owned subsidiary.

Greenfield Investment, Acquisition, and Merger

An MNE can set up a wholly-owned subsidiary, through either greenfield investment or international acquisition. A **greenfield investment** is an initial establishment of fully-owned new facilities and operations undertaken by the company alone. An **international acquisition** is a cross-border transaction in which a foreign investor acquires an established local firm and makes the acquired local firm a subsidiary business within its global portfolio. International acquisition of a local firm or another foreign company with local ventures is the quickest way to expand one's investment in the target country. An acquisition is particularly useful for entering sectors formerly restricted to state-owned enterprises. Moreover, cash flow may be generated in a shorter time than in the case of greenfield investment, since the acquired firm, by definition, does not have to be built from scratch. Furthermore, acquisition deals may be more attractive than greenfield investment because acquisitions offer immediate access to a local acquiree's existing resources such as land, manufacturing facilities, distribution channels, supply networks, skilled labor and customer base. Foreign investors generally target enterprises with strong market niches in sectors with potential for growth. MNEs interested in acquisition must evaluate various risks. Gaining government approval for the transfer of ownership and clearance of property titles is often a difficult hurdle. Foreign investors should be careful to obtain accurate information, particularly concerning existing liabilities, when buying into an indigenous entity.

An **international merger** shares the logic of equity joint ventures and is a cross-border transaction in which two firms from different countries agree to integrate their operations on a relatively co-equal basis because they have resources and capabilities that together may create a stronger competitive advantage in the global marketplace. An example is the 1998 merger between Daimler-Benz of Germany (Stuttgart) and Chrysler of the United States (Detroit), the largest international corporate marriage in history (though this, too, as in many mergers, eventually turned out to be an acquisition by the German firm). Like joint ventures, cross-border mergers can generate many positive outcomes:

- Interpartner learning and resource sharing
- Elevating economies of scale or scope
- Reducing costs by eliminating expenditures for redundant resources
- Capturing greater market share by providing more comprehensive offerings
- Increasing revenue by cross-selling products to cross-border customers

The major difference between equity joint ventures and mergers is that the former involves formation of a third entity (equity joint venture) whose duration is often limited and specified in the contract, whereas the latter does not form any third party nor does it specify any duration. Joint venture parents remain independent after forming a venture but two parties are integrated into a single organization after a merger. Also, mergers combine all of the partners' assets (though some may be spun off later), while a joint venture involves only some of those assets.

International mergers and acquisitions inevitably confront many challenges, especially during early operations. The fundamental challenges are often rooted in cross-national differences in culture, managerial styles, and corporate values (the Industry Box illustrates Unilever's experience in Brazil). To overcome these challenges, international managers should develop a new corporate mission, vision, and strategic objectives. It is also imperative to integrate communications and human resources. The new organization must develop mechanisms to identify the most appropriate organizational structures and management roles so as to enhance administrative efficiency and operational effectiveness.

The Evolutionary Path

In many circumstances, international entry is not a one-step action but rather an evolutionary process involving a series of incremental decisions during which firms increase their commitment to the target market by shifting from low to high commitment entry modes.[15] Although some firms may bypass some steps or speed up the entire process, many MNEs follow the learning curve of accumulating competence, knowledge, and confidence in the international entry process. They move sequentially from no international involvement to export, to overseas assembly or sales subsidiaries (subcontracting, branches, or franchising), to overseas production via contractual or equity joint ventures (also from minority to majority), and, ultimately, to overseas penetration and integration through wholly-owned subsidiaries or umbrella companies.[16] Increasing levels of involvement in foreign markets relate

INDUSTRY BOX

UNILEVER'S ACQUISITIONS IN LATIN AMERICA

Unilever, the Anglo-Dutch conglomerate and one of the world's oldest MNEs, describes itself as a purveyor of products ranging from tea and ice cream to shampoo and toothpaste. Unilever's acquisition of Kibon (Brazil) in 1997 marked another expansion of the company's already strong presence in Latin America. Its management of human resources illustrates the firm's ability to mix internationally savvy executives with the best local talent and practices. The company's approach is a mix of taking the best of the local culture and combining it with the firm's global intentions. Its success with Kibon stems from a deliberate but gradual integration process, particularly with regard to personnel changes. Rather than immediately imposing control from the top, Unilever's strategy centers on two important initial stages.

It promoted dialogue with Kibon's staff during the initial period after the acquisition, then defined its priorities and assumed leadership. Management zeroed in on two priority areas: the ice-cream manufacturing process and R&D. Its preliminary studies of Kibon's best operations helped management make appropriate decisions about future layoffs and restructuring. Despite removing Kibon's entire board of directors, Unilever made a special effort to keep key personnel in priority areas, namely production and R&D. Once the groundwork was laid, Unilever did not hesitate to make changes. After carefully studying the acquired company, it quickly set out to forge a new identity and strategy and to rationalize production.

to a firm's accumulation of experiential and local knowledge. While relevant knowledge and experience are acquired predominantly through actual presence and activities in a foreign market, joint ventures with local firms represent bridges between no equity involvement and equity involvement in a host country. In fact, many MNEs start an equity joint venture and a wholly-owned subsidiary in sequence. This way, a foreign investor will obtain initial entry as part of an equity joint venture for a fixed period stipulated in the duration clause of the contract. Then, at the end of the stipulated term, it can take over the assets from the local partner and continue to run the operation as a wholly-owned subsidiary. This is an attractive alternative if the added value of the local partner is significant but limited to the early stages of the venture. Some equity joint ventures have included this option in the termination clause of the joint venture contract.

Large and experienced MNEs may combine several entry modes at the same time. For instance, selecting between an equity joint venture and a wholly-owned subsidiary is not necessarily an either–or decision. Sometimes a local partner has a strong distribution network or operates in a restricted sector that is attractive to a foreign investor. In such situations, foreign companies can, for instance, surround their wholly-owned subsidiary production operation with equity joint ventures that supply resources, or market and sell their products in the host market. Siemens did exactly that in Brazil, where it owned 4 wholly-owned manufacturing plants, surrounded by 7 joint ventures with either local firms or other MNEs such as Bosch GmbH or Philips as supply bases, and had 13 sales and service branch offices throughout the nation as of the end of 2001.

Interim Summary

1. Entry modes available to international companies include trade-related (exporting, subcontracting, and countertrade), transfer-related (leasing, licensing, franchising, and BOT), and FDI-related (branch, cooperative joint venture, equity joint venture, wholly-owned subsidiary, and umbrella holding companies). The levels of involved risks, anticipated returns, resultant control, and required commitment generally increase along the preceding sequence.

2. International acquisition is a way to form a wholly-owned subsidiary. Compared to greenfield investment, international acquisition generates some advantages such as quicker access, bypass of entry barriers, and utilization of an acquiree's existing resources.

CHAPTER SUMMARY

1. International entry strategies concern where, when, and how firms should enter in their international expansion. Location selection concerns not only country selection but also project location within this country. Managers need to consider various locational determinants such as cost/tax factors, demand factors, strategic factors (e.g., investment infrastructure, manufacturing concentration, industrial linkage, workforce productivity, and inbound and outbound logistics), regulatory and economic factors, and sociopolitical factors.

2. The decision on location selection is also contingent on the firm's strategic objectives of expansion, required global integration between this location and the rest of the MNE network, and the project's market orientation (local market vs. export market). The firm may also take into account its familiarity with the location, geographical market coverage, competitors' location pattern, and regional block effects (e.g., European Union).

3. Each timing option, whether early mover or late entrant, has distinct advantages and disadvantages.

Entry occurs when the firm anticipates gains to exceed risks or costs. Early movers benefit from greater market power (barriers for followers, technological leadership, customer loyalty, and product positioning); greater preemptive opportunities in marketing, resources, and branding; and greater strategic options (site selection, infrastructure access, and low competition).

4. Early-mover disadvantages are late-mover advantages. Early movers tend to face greater uncertainty derived from variable regulations and rules and unstable industrial and market structures; greater operational risks as a result of less developed infrastructure, and a lack of supporting services and resources; and greater operational costs arising from adaptation, training, learning, and anti-imitation.

5. Firms can enter a target country through numerous entry modes, ranging from trade-related modes (export, subcontracting, and countertrade), to transfer-related modes (leasing, licensing, franchising, and BOT), to FDI-related modes (branch, cooperative joint venture, equity joint venture, wholly-owned subsidiary, and umbrella company). Levels of risk, control, and commitment vary significantly across categories and across entry modes within each category.

6. Most international companies, whether large or small, still actively participate in import and export businesses. Export intermediaries specialize in import and export management. Managers should familiarize themselves with key concepts such as terms of price (e.g., FAS, CIF, C&F, and FOB) and key documents (e.g., L/C and B/L) involved in import and export processes.

7. Original equipment manufacturing (OEM) is an increasingly popular mode used by many large MNEs looking for cheaper production overseas. Countertrade methods such as barter, counterpurchase, offset, and buyback offer more flexibility than conventional import and export since the former do not involve hard currency cash flows. Transfer-related entry modes are widely used in technological, intellectual, or industrial property right transfers or transactions.

8. Joint venture and wholly-owned subsidiary are the two major entry modes embedded in FDI. The joint venture enables the firm to share risks and costs with others, acquire new knowledge from others, bypass entry barriers in a host country, and capitalize on the partner's reputation, experience, networks, and marketing skills. The wholly-owned entry mode provides the firm with stronger organizational control and knowledge protection.

CHAPTER NOTES

[1] J. H. Dunning, *Multinational Enterprises and the Global Economy.* Reading, MA: Addison-Wesley, 1993.

[2] M. E. Porter, *Competition in Global Industries.* Boston, MA: Harvard Business School Press, 1986.

[3] C. G. Culem, The locational determinants of foreign direct investments among industrial countries. *European Economic Review,* 32(4), 1988, 885–894; J. Friedman, D. A. Gerlowski, and J. Silberman. "What attracts foreign multinational corporations: Evidence from branch plant location in the United States," *Journal of Regional Science,* 32(4), 1992, 403–418.

[4] J. F. Hennart and Y. R. Park, "Location, governance, and strategic determinants of Japanese manufacturing investment in the United States," *Strategic Management Journal,* 15(6), 1994, 419–436.

[5] W. H. Davidson, "The location of foreign direct investment activity: Country characteristics and experience effects," *Journal of International Business Studies,* 11(2), 1980, 9–22.

[6] M. Lambkin, "Order of entry and performance in new markets," *Strategic Management Journal,* 9, 1988, 127–140; M. B. Lieberman and D. B. Montgomery, "First-mover advantages," *Strategic Management Journal,* 9, 1988, 41–58.

[7] B. Mascarenhas, "Order of entry and performance in international markets," *Strategic Management Journal,* 13, 1992, 499–510; W. Mitchell, "Whether and when? Probability and timing of incumbents' entry into emerging industrial subfields," *Administrative Science Quarterly,* 34, 1989, 208–230.

[8] Y. Luo, "Timing of investment and international expansion performance in China," *Journal of International Business Studies,* 29, 1988, 391–408.

[9] P. J. Buckley and M. Casson, "The optimal timing of a foreign direct investment," *The Economic Journal,* 91, 1981, 75–87.

[10] D. West, "Countertrade," *Business Credit,* 103(4), 2001, 64–67.

[11] B. Gomes-Casseres, "Firm ownership presences and host government restrictions: An integrated approach," *Journal of International Business Studies,* 21(1), 1990, 1–21.

[12] F. R. Root, *Entry Strategies for International Markets.* Washington, DC: Lexington Books, 1994.

[13] S. Agarwal and S. N. Ramaswami, "Choice of foreign market entry mode: Impact of ownership, location, and internalization factors," *Journal of International Business Studies,* 23(1), 1992, 1–27.

[14] C. W. L. Hill, P. Hwang, and W. C. Kim, "An eclectic theory of the choice of international entry mode," *Strategic Management Journal,* 11, 1990, 117–128; J. Johanson and J. E. Vahlne, "The internationalization process of the firm: A model of knowledge development and increasing foreign market commitments," *Journal of International Business Studies,* 8(1), 1977, 23–32.

[15] S. J. Chang, "International expansion strategy of Japanese firms: Capability building through sequential entry," *Academy of Management Journal,* 38, 1995, 383–407.

[16] E. Anderson and H. Gatignon, "Modes of foreign entry: A transaction cost analysis and propositions," *Journal of International Business Studies,* 17, Fall 1986, 1–26.

Organizing and Structuring
Global Operations

DO YOU KNOW

1. Is the organizational design of the MNE (or international firm) a function of its strategy or vice versa? Why do MNEs need to organize and coordinate global operations?

2. If you were a top manager in a subsidiary in Mexico, would you expect that your subsidiary would be similar to peer subsidiaries in London, Singapore, or Sydney in terms of authority, knowledge flow, or strategic importance? Why or why not?

3. What types of structure are available to MNEs for organizing global operations? Can you establish a link between an MNE's international strategy and its organizational structure?

4. If you were an executive at Sony's headquarters, how would you integrate overseas activities?

OPENING CASE   Aetna

In January of 2000, Aetna announced that it was merging its domestic and international operations, creating two business units, Global Financial Services and Global Health. The new structure, replacing a design where all non-U.S. business was handled by an international division, was devised to facilitate knowledge transfer between the United States and the firm's international operations. By removing the compartmentalization between domestic and international activities, the firm hoped to improve knowledge flow within each of its two new business units. The new structure was consistent with changes made earlier by such firms as the Ford Motor Company and Procter & Gamble. It reflected the growing prominence of international operations in U.S. companies and was devised to reap the synergies of global operations. Pressure from investors and analysts dismayed by the company's performance and sagging share price played a role in Aetna's move.

The reorganization was a clear indication that Aetna made a firm commitment not to divest its international operations, a strategic decision pushed by its CFO but rejected by the board. Aetna's chairman and CEO, Richard L. Huber, pointed out that although the company's international business was responsible for merely one tenth of revenues, it has doubled over the previous four years. It would be wrong to sell long-term international assets for a short-term gain, said Mr. Huber, who was accused by some analysts of objecting to the sale of international operations in order to protect his vision of a "global empire."■

Source: Adapted from C. Gentry, "Aetna to merge global, U.S. divisions," *Wall Street Journal,* January 10, 2000, E3.

INTERNATIONAL STRATEGY AND ORGANIZATION DESIGN

The objective of organizational design is to provide, maintain, and develop the organizational structure that works best toward the achievement of the company's strategic goals. It is aimed at providing a blueprint with which to translate the firm's vision and strategic objectives into workable assignments of rights, duties, and responsibilities for the various units and individual positions that make up the organizational apparatus.

Although organizational structures are driven by corporate strategy, they also drive it. In other words, the structure can represent a constraint on the firm's mode of operations and in turn on its strategic thinking and strategy execution. For instance, when Japan emerged as an economic power in the 1980s, it was noted that having a Japanese unit report to an Asian-Pacific regional division distracted corporate attention to this market. Suggestions have hence been made to separate Japan from the regional division, with direct reporting to corporate headquarters as a way to elevate its strategic visibility.[1] Aetna's compartmentalization of international operations in a separate unit meant that the managers of the much larger domestic businesses rarely paid attention to global operations. The same was true for the Ford Motor Company (prior to its Ford 2000 global structure) and General Motors, whose European subsidiaries, Opel in Germany and Vauxhall in the United Kingdom, were run as stand-alone operations. This permitted better understanding of local conditions but forfeited potential synergies across locations, resulting in duplication of resources and efforts.

Why is it important for MNEs to globally organize, structure, and coordinate geographically dispersed businesses? First, each subunit is subject to its own interests, goals, and environmental demands which leads subunits to pursue their own strategies. To overcome these forces, the executives of MNEs must maintain a structure that will provide maximum contribution to corporate performance while allowing subunits the necessary flexibility to adapt to their particular environments. Second, in many industries, MNEs are no longer able to compete as a collection of independent subsidiaries. Heightened requirements for economies of scale and technological developments have led many MNEs to integrate the value chain activities performed in their subsidiaries around the world. Integrating these activities means raising the level of interdependence among subsidiaries, thus demanding global coordination. Competition has become based in part on the ability of the corporation to link its subsidiary activities across geographic locations. Third, inter-unit sharing, learning, and resource flows require extensive coordination and careful organization within an MNE. To encourage such sharing, many MNEs assign different global mandates to different subsidiaries. For example, Siemens's subsidiary in Japan, in partnership with Asahi Medical, has worldwide responsibility for modeling compact magnetic resonance image machines, while its peer subsidiary in Singapore has worldwide responsibility over the distribution and marketing of these machines. To execute such globally interdependent operations, parent firms need to have organizing and integrating mechanisms in place. Finally, financial management for global operations such as the use of transfer pricing (to reduce taxation or tariff) and the use of internal bank (for intracorporate financing, foreign exchange hedging, and cash-flow management) necessitates global coordination and integration. Transfer pricing, for instance, cannot be smoothly implemented if such coordination is absent.

Global Integration and Local Responsiveness

Given the increasing globalization of the competitive environment, the dual imperatives of global integration (I) and local responsiveness (R) (also known as I-R balance) are becoming more critical than ever for the survival and growth of MNEs.

Global integration refers to the coordination of activities across countries in an attempt to build efficient operation networks and take maximum advantage of internalized synergies and similarities across locations. **Local responsiveness** concerns the attempt to respond to specific needs within a variety of host countries. Local responsiveness needs usually stem from diversity of market conditions and social and political environments found in various countries in which the firm operates. Responsiveness is necessary for responding to diverse consumer tastes, distribution channels, advertising media, and government regulations and constraints. MNEs can choose to emphasize integration over responsiveness or vice versa or compete in both dimensions, resulting in three basic responses: integrated, multifocal, or locally responsive. Firms that perceive a high level of pressure to integrate use a strategy of global integration. Globally integrated businesses link activities across nations in an attempt to minimize overall costs, reduce taxes, or maximize income. Locally responsive businesses are more tuned to local characteristics and needs. Multifocal businesses attempt to respond simultaneously to pressures for integration and responsiveness.

The relative strength of global integration and local responsiveness pressures can be analyzed at different levels such as industries, divisions, or subsidiaries. Levels of global integration and local responsiveness vary among different MNEs and even different divisions or subsidiaries within the same MNE. It is important that international managers identify factors that determine these levels. In general, pressures to integrate globally derive from industrial and organizational forces that necessitate worldwide business resource deployment. Strategic decisions are made to maximize the collective organization so that activities are integrated across national boundaries. In contrast, local responsiveness pressures are industrial, national, and objective forces that necessitate context-sensitive strategic decisions. Among market and industrial characteristics, the following features tend to trigger global integration: (1) customer needs tend to be the same or similar across borders or require relatively low responsiveness, (2) major competitors are few but global, and (3) economy of scale is essential to global success. Features leading to higher local responsiveness include (1) diverse market structures, (2) nation-specific distribution channels, (3) heterogeneous market demands and customer needs, and (4) stronger requirements for product differentiation and customer responsiveness. Among sociopolitical characteristics, the following tend to boost local responsiveness: (a) the host environment is volatile and complex; (b) government regulations are opaque, cumbersome, or arbitrarily changed; and (c) there is a strong and unique local business culture.

Among organizational characteristics, the level of global integration is likely to be high if the firm (1) attempts to use transfer pricing, tax minimization, or transaction cost savings; (2) focuses on risk reduction or internalized financing; (3) emphasizes global vertical integration and global value chain control; (4) needs to control key functions such as global branding, R&D, global distribution, and engineering; and (5) requires extensive sharing between corporate members in information, resources, and knowledge. In contrast, local responsiveness is likely to be high if the firm (1) targets local market expansion or building presence in highly uncertain markets; (2) aims at seizing market opportunities overseas or developing a sustained competitive position in the host country; (3) seeks acquisition of local firms' knowledge and experience; or (4) tries to improve organizational legitimacy through localization and adaptation.

MNE Strategy and Design

For the MNE, which operates in a highly complex, diverse, and rapidly changing environment, the organization design challenge is to configure a structure that works well in diverse locations but also brings them together in a coordinated fashion with the capability for rapid redeployment. Aetna's adoption of a global structure was aimed at altering a setup where international and domestic operations were run as two separate organizations, missing on the synergies between the two; but it also reflected a strategic vision that recognized the major growth potential of the international arena.

Because organization design is a vehicle for strategy formulation and implementation, MNE strategy in organizing global operations is the key input in devising its structure. The type of international strategy used by MNE headquarters to organize and coordinate worldwide businesses is threefold. A **multi-domestic** strategy is one in which strategic and operational decisions are delegated to strategic business units in each country. This permits customization but interferes with economies of scale and intraorganizational learning and sharing. A **global strategy** indicates relative standardization across national markets, allowing strategic and operational control. A global strategy leverages economies of scale and can quickly disseminate innovations across borders; however, it lacks in responsiveness to local markets. A **transnational (or hybrid) strategy** seeks to achieve both global efficiency and local responsiveness. It requires shared vision and commitment through an integrated network. Under this strategy, the roles and responsibilities of subsidiaries are varied to reflect differences in their external environment and internal capabilities.

The MNE maintaining a high level of overall global integration follows a global strategy, whereas the MNE maintaining a high level of local responsiveness over various overseas subunits exercises a multidomestic strategy. The MNE maintaining high levels of both overall integration and overall responsiveness follows a transnational strategy. Under a global strategy, foreign subunits operating in each country are assumed to be interdependent and the home office attempts to achieve integration among these businesses. Thus, a global strategy is one in which standardized products are offered internationally while the competitive strategy is dictated by the home office. A multidomestic strategy focuses on competition within each country, tailoring products and services to each local market in a bid to maximize competitive response to idiosyncratic requirements. The transnational strategy, where the roles and responsibilities of subsidiaries are varied to reflect differences in external environments and internal objectives, provides an asymmetrical treatment in coordinating worldwide businesses within the MNE network.

Subsidiary Roles and Imperatives

Subsidiary Autonomy

Subsidiary roles play a key part in balancing integration and local responsiveness. In an **autonomous** role, the subsidiary performs most activities of the value chain independently of headquarters, selling most of its output in the local market. In a **receptive role,** most subsidiary functions are highly integrated with headquarters or with other business units, for example, exporting most of the subsidiary production to the parent company or other subsidiaries, while importing multiple products or components from them. In an **active role,** many activities are located locally but carried out in close coordination with other subsidiaries. The autonomous role is typical of MNE subsidiaries employing a multidomestic strategy. The receptive role is typical of MNE subsidiaries using global strategy. The active role is often assigned to MNE subsidiaries following transnational strategy, with strong mandate from headquarters[2] combined with leeway for adaptation. Among different subsidiaries of the same MNE, however, the level of autonomy may vary due to the different roles or mandates among them. It is possible, for instance, that most subsidiaries in a firm (using a global strategy) be receptive while a subsidiary serving as the center of excellence in design is active or autonomous.

Subsidiary Knowledge Flow

Another way of looking at subsidiary role is as knowledge flow across the MNE units.[3] The expertise transferred can be input (e.g., purchasing skills), throughput (e.g., product, process, and packaging design), or output (e.g., marketing knowledge, distribution expertise) oriented. MNE subsidiaries can be classified by the extent to which each (a) receives knowledge *inflow* from the rest of the corporation and (b) provides knowledge *outflow* to the rest of the corporation. Four generic subsidiary roles are generated: **global innovator** (high outflow and low inflow), **integrated player** (high outflow and high inflow), **implementor** (low outflow and high inflow), and **local innovator** (low outflow and low inflow). In the global innovator role, the subsidiary is the fountainhead of knowledge for other units. The integrated player role implies responsibility for creating knowledge that can be utilized by other subsidiaries. In the integrated player role, the subsidiary exchanges knowledge with headquarters and with other subsidiaries on an ongoing basis. In the implementor role, the subsidiary engages in very little knowledge creation and relies heavily on knowledge inflows from either the parent or peer subsidiaries. Finally, the local innovator role implies that the subsidiary has almost complete local responsibility for the creation of relevant expertise; however, this knowledge is too idiosyncratic to be used outside its local market.

Subsidiary Importance and Competence

The strategic importance of the local environment and competence of the foreign subsidiary are two key considerations in determining subsidiary roles.[4] The **strategic leader** role is played by a highly competent national subsidiary located in a strategically important market. The subsidiary serves as partner to headquarters in developing and implementing strategy. **Contributor subsidiaries** operate in small or strategically less important markets but have distinctive capabilities. **Implementor subsidiaries** operate in less strategically important markets but are competent to maintain local operations. Their market potential is limited, as reflected in corporate resource commitment. The efficiency of an implementor is as important as the creativity of its strategic leaders because it provides the strategic leverage that affords MNEs their competitive advantage. Implementors create opportunities to capture economies of scale and scope that are crucial to global strategies. Finally, **black hole subsidiaries** operate in important markets where they barely make a dent, but their strong local presence is essential for maintaining global position.

In subunits with lead roles, the head office ensures that strategies fit the overall goals and priorities of the MNE. Corporate management's major function is to support those with strategic leadership responsibility by giving them the resources and freedom needed for the innovative, entrepreneurial role they have been asked to play. If the unit is placed in a contributory role, the head office should redirect local resources to programs outside the unit's control. If a unit is in an implementor role, the head office maintains tighter control to capture the benefits of scale and learning. Finally, if a unit acts as a black hole, corporate management develops resources and capabilities to make it more responsive to the local environment.

Interim Summary

1. MNEs need to organize, structure, and coordinate their global operations because each subunit may have its own interests, competing goals, and differential demands, leading it to pursue its own strategies. Heightened requirements

for economies of scale, technological advancement, intra-corporate resource sharing, and global corporate finance also propel this need.

2. The dual imperatives of global integration and local responsiveness are becoming more critical than ever, requiring appropriate balance between the two. Firms in different industries or environments and with different strategies or capabilities may have varying levels of integration and responsiveness.

MNE ORGANIZATIONAL STRUCTURES

The organization design decision can be summarized as a choice between differentiation and integration. The need for differentiation is rooted in the diverse requirements of different locals and business units. The need for integration comes from the managerial imperative to maintain overall coordination and control to monitor strategy implementation and reap synergies via optimal resource deployment. In electing an optimal design, firms position themselves along the globalization to localization continuum as well as choose among different forms of differentiation and various mechanisms for coordination, integration, and control.

Large MNEs maintain multiple forms of differentiation. For example, they may utilize a product structure for manufacturing operations and a geographic design for sales and marketing. Below the primary lines of differentiation, other forms usually exist. In the Aetna case, the firm did not do away with geographical and other forms of differentiation but rather subjected them to product line authority. Typically in such changes, executives with specific international specialization (e.g., central Europe) are retained either in staff capacity, providing advice to line personnel, or in a subordinate position, reporting to product or a divisional manager. The one exception to such prioritization is the matrix structure, where two or three bases of differentiation intersect to form a matrix of responsibilities.

As a company internationalizes, its structure changes to accommodate the increasing volume and scope of business as well as the increasing diversity of its constituencies. Phase of evolution, however, is only one of the factors affecting structural choice. Strategy, home and host country environments, projected market growth, the nature of business, and the human resources available to the firm, are among the factors influencing the choice of structure. It is not uncommon to find different structures among firms otherwise similar in product and geographical spread. MNE management has considerable leeway in design choices and continuously monitors the suitability of the structure as its operations evolve and as its business environment changes.

The National Subsidiary Structure

Until the early 1970s, many MNEs used a national subsidiary structure. In this arrangement, also called a "mother-daughter" design, national subsidiaries reported directly to headquarters and were in a position to attract the firm's attention without having information filtered through an intermediary. Once a firm had expanded beyond a handful of subsidiaries, however, coordination and control in this structure became difficult. Each subsidiary developed its own way of conducting business, and corporate headquarters were hard pressed to guide them within the overall corporate objectives.

The International Division Structure

The international division structure (see opening case) lets the firm's core structure focus on domestic business by shifting all foreign operations into a semi-independent division. The international division is in turn organized by function, product, or again by geography (e.g., country units within a region). In some firms, the international division was cast in a staff capacity, that is, it played an advisory role supporting line operations. The establishment of the international division was the result of the growing scope of international activities and a realization that foreign markets often offered the most promising growth opportunity.

The international division format was used mainly by firms with a low ratio of foreign to domestic revenues and low foreign product diversity, but is still in use today. Wal-Mart gave its Arkansas-based International Support Division such responsibilities as new store development, but has now delegated this task to its foreign subsidiaries. The company also moved to combine international and domestic buying, increasing its bargaining power with suppliers.[5] Japanese and Korean firms maintain an international division devoted to marketing, sales, and distribution. The division maintains responsibility for new business development and sales in the firm's foreign outposts. However, other foreign activities (e.g., finance) report to functional counterparts in the home country.

As companies pursued strategies of increased product diversification and attempted to maximize gains from activities around the world, the international division structure became less popular. The international division structure is still very common in developing country multinationals (DMNEs) that are in the first phases of internationalization. Chunlan Corporation, one of the 50 largest enterprises in China, is a good example. A manufacturer of electric appliances, motor vehicles, and electronics, Chunlan is also involved in trade and investment. Exhibit 11-1 shows the organizational structure of the Chunlan Group. The international division of Chunlan is incorporated as Chunlan Overseas Group. It includes two centralized units for trade and development, respectively, and ten branches in the United

Exhibit 11–1
Chunlan Corporation's organizational chart

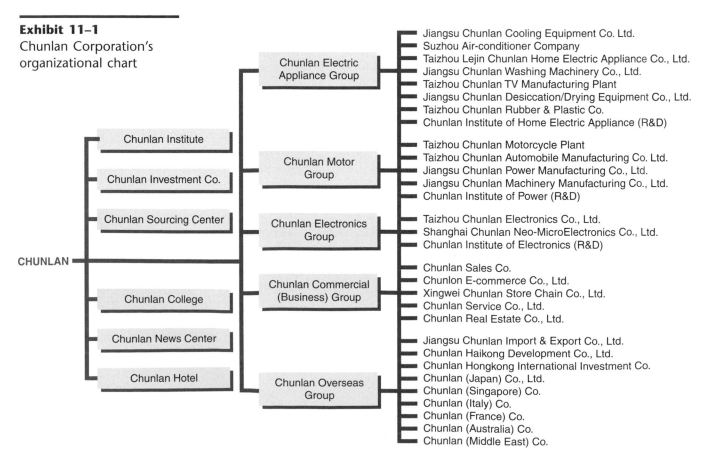

Source: Chunlan Corporation, 2002.

States, Japan, France, Italy, Australia, the Netherlands, Singapore and the Middle East, seven of which are incorporated. The branches are in turn grouped into five business regions: Europe, Americas, the Middle East, Southeast Asia, and East Asia. European MNEs such as Nestlé, Royal Dutch/Shell, and Unilever were among the first to shift away from an international division structure, with U.S. MNEs following suit later, the result of the much larger U.S. domestic market

The Global Functional Structure

Functional compartmentalization into research and development, marketing, production, human resources, and such can be found in all organizations, including those differentiated primarily along product line, customers, or geographical lines. In firms using function as a primary differentiation mode, functional divisions maintain responsibility for worldwide operations, with functional managers reporting directly to headquarters. This allows for centralized control and the accumulation of functional expertise. Functional structures are usually adopted by MNEs with narrow, integrated product lines (e.g., Caterpillar). The design was widely used in the automobile industry but as firms grew internationally they have been replaced by geographic and then product line designs.

The Global Geographic Structure

In a geographic structure, regional divisions or headquarters are responsible for all products or services rendered within an area. Corporate headquarters retain responsibility for worldwide planning and control, whereas coordination is handled by central staff. Geographic divisions are based not only on political borders but also on cultural similarities, economic realities, business prospects, regional integration (e.g., the EU), and tax and logistic considerations. Regional units are in turn segmented into geographic (i.e., country units within a region), product, or functional sub-units. Regional and country managers can also operate in a staff capacity. In the early 1970s geographic structures accounted for two thirds of MNEs, but the number was down to one third by the mid-1980s. Persistent cultural, social, and economic diversities continue to underpin the geographic structure and many MNEs with other structures incorporate geographical elements within their design. Regional integration may alter the boundaries of geographic units but does not necessarily challenge their necessity. Indeed, geographic structures are enjoying renewed popularity today.

Geographic structures enable rapid response to changing local tastes, regulatory regimes, and volatile rates of exchange and tariffs. The format is useful for a company that is marketing oriented and requires substantial adaptation of its product or service to local markets. Firms that are relatively new to international markets or are in the midst of expansion into such markets will also benefit from that structure.[6] Although in the past they were used mostly by firms with homogeneous, mature, and stable product lines, today geographic structures also appeal to firms with differentiated product lines, a changing technological environment, and those farther down the internationalization route.[7]

Nestlé is a world leader in foods and beverages and is also engaged in the production and distribution of pharmaceuticals and cosmetics. Showing profitability in all but two of its 123 years of existence, this Swiss-based company gets almost all of its revenues from foreign markets. Hailing from a small domestic market, Nestlé started on the internationalization route early on, opening a factory in Brazil in 1921.

Nestlé's geographic structure reflects the vital importance of localization in its core food business, in which customer preferences in taste, presentation, packaging

Nestlé, the world's largest food company, uses a global geographic structure to remain close to its markets the world over.

and the like vary across national boundaries, as does their emotional link to a given product. Nestlé deviates from this geographic departmentalization when it comes to businesses where product adaptation requirements are much smaller, such as pharmaceuticals and pet food. (The latter is not yet reflected in the current organizational chart.) Nestlé also centralizes across all businesses such functions as R&D, finance, purchasing and back-office operations, where scale advantages are especially substantial. (See Exhibit 11-2.)

Underneath Nestlé's three main geographic regions are subregions encompassing countries that are geographically contiguous, and, most importantly, share culture, language, and historical ties. Examples include Scandinavia (Sweden, Denmark, Norway, and Finland) and Iberia (Spain and Portugal) in the European region or Canada and the United States in the Americas region. Below the sub-regions are country units, each headed by the all-important country manager. The country manager directs all food and beverage operations in his/her region in coordination with Nestlé's strategic business units of Dairy, Coffee & Beverages, Chocolate, Confectionary & Biscuits, Ice Cream, Food, Petcare, and Food Services. As in all geographic structures, however, the major operational responsibility rests with the country manager.

The geographic structure simplifies regional strategy and defines accountability. Lines of authority are logical and provide easier channels for communication and

Exhibit 11–2
Nestlé's organization chart

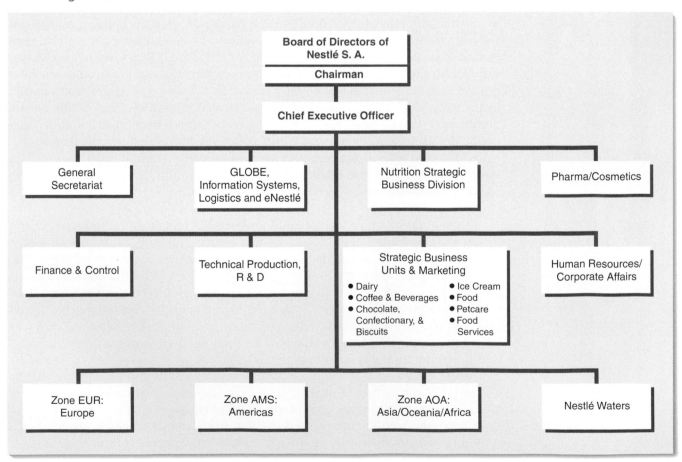

Source: Nestlé, 2002.

evaluation of individual performance. This structure also facilitates coordination of technical and functional capability across countries within a region. The structure facilitates consolidation of regional knowledge and expertise with executives becoming highly familiar with the region under their jurisdiction. Regions are easily expanded to accommodate new acquisitions, a key advantage in today's business environment. From a career development perspective, geographic structures provide opportunities for broad management training. Charles Strauss, president and CEO of Unilever US, describes how his geographical responsibilities prepared him for his current leadership role:

> My last job (was) group president in Latin America. I was heading an operation across a wide geography, and the many product categories required that I focus on the strategy portfolio, the people and the development of organizational capability.[8]

The major disadvantages of the geographic structure are operating problems in a context of diverse product lines and marketing characteristics. Product emphasis is weak, which interferes with information flow between manufacturing and marketing. It is also difficult to transfer technology and ideas across regions. Systems and policies diverge and lose consistency, and there is costly duplication of functional and product specialists. The result may be less than optimal deployment of resources and core competencies. Scale and synergy are reduced, although they can be maintained at the regional level.

A number of conditions need to be considered in the choice of a geographical structure. For example, what is the value-to-transport cost ratio? When the ratio is low, a geographic structure makes more sense. Similarly, a geographic design is more desirable when the firm needs to deliver service and support on-site, when it wants to be perceived as a local entity (e.g., due to nationalistic sentiments), and where geographical boundaries coincide with market segmentation.[9] The Otis Elevator Company manufactures 39,000 elevators and escalators annually, but it also maintains 800,000 of those around the world. It provides service and technical support on-site. Its country managers report to regional managers and supervise a team of functional specialists.[10]

Combined Forms Using Geographic Areas

Some regional structures are run in line capacity as profit and loss centers, whereas other are run in staff capacity and provide vision and more informal coordination. Companies can also opt for mixed formats. Union Carbide (recently acquired by Dow Chemical) used product structure at home and regional structure abroad, in order to deal with the increasing interdependence between function, regional area, and product.

Another mixed geographic structure is the Front-Back design that separates sales and service from R&D, manufacturing, and logistics. Such structures become more appealing when back-office operations are transferred to lower-cost locations. In India, local workers perform billing for British Airways and auditing for Ford's Asian subsidiaries, and call General Electric customers in the United States who are late making their payments.[11] The combined form maintains internal cohesion while permitting firms to tap market opportunities, accommodate local regulatory environments, and coordinate and control multiple sources of diversity.

Region-Specific Factors in Geographic Structures

Effective drawing of regional boundaries minimizes duplication of functional and product efforts and facilitates interregional coordination. The MNE maintains most of the advantages of a national subsidiary structure while pursuing a globally coordinated course. To achieve local responsiveness, regional divisions include countries

THE EU VERSUS ASIA

The advent of the European Union created powerful forces toward standardization and homogenization. This makes a European divisional structure more feasible and facilitates coordination and control among country units. It is also in line with other developments in the region, for example, the consolidation of distribution centers (see Chapter 16). In contrast, the level of integration in Asia is much lower. ASEAN is only a free trade area and it excludes some of the most important Asian economies. APEC is not scheduled to eliminate barriers to trade and FDI until 2020. This fragmentation creates pressures toward regional differentiation. Indeed, in a Conference Board survey, Asia is the one world region in which MNEs are not abandoning regional headquarters.

The Conference Board reports a number of factors responsible for success in using Asia Pacific regional designs: an appropriate strategic and operational role for the regional headquarters, effective use of country managers, whose authority is adjusted to a country's uniqueness, balanced differentiation and integration, use of joint ventures, and attendance to staffing and other human resource issues. Interestingly, information technology was not found to play an important role in the Asian-Pacific area, possibly because of the primacy of personal relations in the region (see Chapter 6).

Source: Organizing for global competitiveness: The Asia-Pacific regional design. The Conference Board #1133-95-RR, 1995.

that share political, economic, and logistic attributes while reflecting strategic considerations in terms of scale and product diffusion. Visa includes eastern Europe, the Middle East, and Africa (CEMEA) in a regional division encompassing 92 countries on three continents. In contrast, its other international regions—Asia-Pacific, the European Union, Canada, and Latin America and the Caribbean are by and large contiguous. Visa's Miami-based Latin American and Caribbean region contains 44 countries and territories. Using employee attitudes to draw divisional boundaries improves knowledge flow between regional headquarters and subsidiaries. In Chapter 6, we introduced the clustering of countries on the basis of employee attitudes. This clustering produced eight regions: Anglo-American, Nordic, Germanic, Latin European, Latin American, Near Eastern, Arab, and Far Eastern. The Anglo-American is the most geographically dispersed cluster, producing control and coordination challenges. There also remains the question of how to handle "independents," which are countries that do not fit culturally into a cluster, including Japan, Brazil, India, and Israel.

A related decision in geographic structures is the location of regional headquarters. For instance, firms with an Asia-Pacific division can choose between Hong Kong, Singapore, Tokyo, Sydney, and Honolulu, among others, as locations for their regional headquarters. In making the decision, firms consider multiple factors, among them: proximity to major markets (e.g., Hong Kong is much closer to the Chinese mainland than the other cities), cost of doing business (cheaper in Sydney), communications, quality of life, and cultural barriers.[12] The success of Singapore, now home to 170 regional MNE headquarters,[13] shows the importance of infrastructure and human resources relative to geographic proximity. Even though the island nation is in Southeast Asia, it attracts firms whose main operations are in East Asia, many miles away.

The Global Product Structure

A firm embarks on a global strategy when it decides to locate manufacturing and other value-creation activities in the most appropriate global location to increase efficiency, quality, and innovation. In seeking to obtain gains from global learning, a company must cope with greater coordination and integration problems. It has to find a structure that can coordinate resource transfers between corporate headquarters and foreign divisions while providing the centralized control that global strategy requires.

The Global Product Design

In this format, global product divisions are responsible for developing, producing, and/or marketing a product (or group of products) worldwide. Similar designs may be organized along customer groups or markets. Product units are responsible for planning, design, production, and sales and hence must contain all functional resources, though they may occasionally pool resources across product lines. Product managers report to their corresponding divisions, which allows for integration of development, production, and marketing. MNEs that utilize product structures typically accommodate country-specific knowledge as staff capacity sometimes within a staff international division and at other times in a combination of line and staff within corporate headquarters. A product group headquarters coordinates the activities of the domestic and foreign divisions within the product group. Product group managers in the home country are responsible for organizing all aspects of value creation on a global basis.

The product group structure allows managers to decide how best to pursue a global strategy. For example, they decide which value-creation activities, such as manufacturing or product design, should be performed in which country to increase efficiency. Increasingly, U.S. and Japanese companies are moving manufacturing to low-cost countries like India or China, but establishing product design centers in Europe or the United States to take advantage of their respective capabilities. In contrast, Japanese and South Korean MNEs tend to avoid the global product design altogether.

INDUSTRY BOX

GLOBAL PRODUCT DESIGN AT THE FORD MOTOR COMPANY

Effective January 1, 1995, Ford Motor Company shifted from a geographic structure to a global product design. The company established five Vehicle Program Centers (VPCs): one in Europe split between Dunton, UK, and Merkenich, Germany, for small front-wheel drive, and four in Dearborn, Michigan, for large front-wheel drive cars, rear-wheel drive cars, personal use trucks, and commercial trucks. Each VPC was assigned worldwide responsibility for the design, development, and engineering of the vehicles assigned to it.

In changing its structure from geographic to product-based, Ford was hoping to avoid duplication and cut costs. As Alex Trotman, chairman and CEO at that time, suggested: "By integrating all our automotive processes and eliminating duplication of effort, we will use our creative and technical resources most effectively in our pursuit of total customer satisfaction . . . This new way of doing business . . . through simplification of engineering, supply, technical and other processes, will substantially reduce the cost of operating the automotive business."

While integrating North American and European product development processes, Ford decided to maintain separate Asian and Latin American operations for the time being. Apparently, these two markets were considered not only substantial in their future potential but also sufficiently unique to merit the continuation of a geographical structure where country and regional adaptation are more easily obtained. Ford also maintained Jaguar and Aston Martin, its two acquisitions up to that time, as separate corporate entities, underlying the importance of maintaining their brand-name appeal.

FORD 2000 ORGANIZATION (1995)

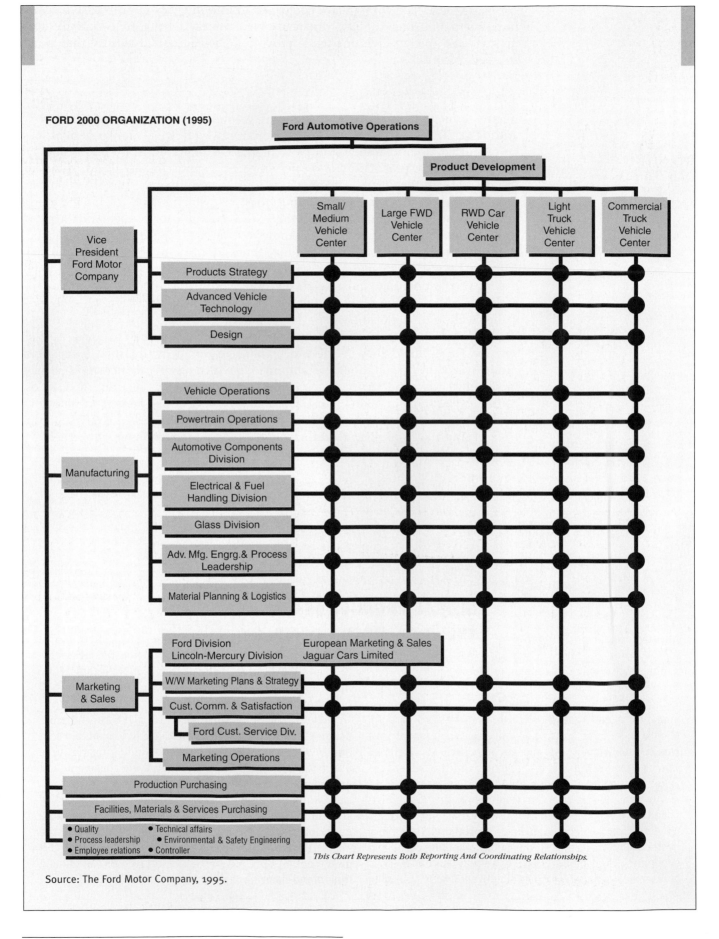

Source: The Ford Motor Company, 1995.

The global product format is a response to the growing need to serve customers across borders. Skyrocketing investment in product development that firms wish to spread across the largest possible number of markets and customers is also driving global product structures. The format is considered especially useful for diversified companies managing a portfolio of businesses in a rapidly changing environment. Advances in communication technologies and decline in travel cost have made global product structures more attractive by making it possible to establish multinational teams consisting of individuals who are physically separated.

Types of Global Product Structure

The three basic types of product structures include the **related divisional format,** the **cluster format,** and the **unrelated holding company** format. In the related divisional format used in such firms as Interpublic (United States) and Sandvik (Sweden), product divisions report directly to headquarters. In the cluster format, used by AlliedSignal (United States) and Rhone-Pulenc (France; prior to its merger), a business reports to a cluster headquarters that is accountable to corporate headquarters for business results. In the unrelated holding company or conglomerate format, businesses are managed as investment rather than profit centers with wide reporting variations.[14]

Fiat, a diverse industrial enterprise that is Italy's largest private sector enterprise, is organized in a conglomerate type structure, with divisions (operational sectors) reporting to a corporate head office that defines and oversees group strategy and resource deployment. Corporate headquarters also controls financial resources and is responsible for relations with internal and external constituencies. For Fiat, the holding company format is an advantage as it reorganizes in the face of growing competition at home and abroad. This structure makes it relatively easy to dispose of non-core assets while strengthening core assets.

The main advantages of product-based structures are a global vision and the ability to leverage resources across regions. This encourages strategic focus and flexibility. Other advantages are simplicity, clear accountability, standardized product introduction, and enhanced speed and quality of decisions. New product lines are introduced on a self-contained basis, reducing interference in other operations. From a human resource perspective, product structures support the early testing of talented individuals.

On the negative side, a global product structure makes it difficult for different product groups to trade information and knowledge and thus obtain the benefits of cooperation. The structure is costly to maintain because its self-contained nature generates duplication, fragments organizational resources, and erodes functional specialization. Communications become difficult; for example, when Procter & Gamble shifted to a global product structure, establishing five global business units such as "food and beverage," it created a setting where Cincinnati-based employees report to a Venezuela-based manager. Employees complained about lack of communication with their bosses, having to hold videoconferences at inconvenient times, and so on.[15]

Ominously, product designs are slow to adapt to local conditions. Firms can compensate for that deficiency by establishing a staff international division to handle business development, interact with key constituencies, and support line divisions. U.S.-based General Electric maintains an international division in London headed by a vice-chairman to support its product structure and engage in new business development, including search for potential alliance partners. The division places country executives in more than 40 countries, although these are not full-fledged country managers, which is the option sought by some other product-based MNEs. Still another solution to enhance the geographical sensitivity within a product structure is to establish a mixed product/geography format.

The Global Matrix Structure

Matrix designs are unique in that they contain simultaneous, intersecting differentiation bases, with many employees reporting to two or more supervisors simultaneously. MNEs that use global matrix structures select either a two-dimension (e.g., Caterpillar, ABB) or three-dimension designs (e.g., IBM). Two-dimension designs involve combinations of product and geography or product and function.

The Dow Chemical Company is a U.S.-based manufacturer of thousands of product families. The company used a three-way matrix structure combining product, function and region since 1992. In the mid 1990s, the company moved towards a more global structure, downplaying geography vis-à-vis business areas and function while maintaining the three-way matrix. As you can see in Exhibit 11-3(a), the main two axes of the matrix are business groupings (on the right hand of the chart), which are responsible for strategy and resource allocation and oversee operations; and functional areas (on the left hand of the chart), which are responsible for overall corporate oversight in their respective areas. Geographic coordination is achieved via the Global Geographic Council.

Exhibit 11-3(b) shows the Dow structure for a sample country and business group. Since the sample country has a major importance in the company, the site manager doubles as a country manager. As a site manager, he/she reports to the head of their global business unit (which, in turn, reports to the head of the business group) as well as to the respective corporate headquarters function (e.g., R&D). As a country manager, he/she reports to the Global Cooperation Council. Country managers within the same region (e.g., Europe), periodically meet to discuss and coordinate operations however the regional groups have lost the importance they have held prior to the mid 1990s change. As is the case for other matrix structures, numerous Dow employees report to two or more supervisors in the company.

Changes of the sort orchestrated by Dow are designed to better leverage and deploy resources in capital intensive industries (see also the Ford 2000 change). At the same time, the matrix enables continuous sensitivity and faster response to local variations and new developments.

Once thought the wave of the future, the matrix structure has lost some of its luster over the years; it has been criticized for its complexity and ambiguity.[16] The design is costly because it involves duplication of functions across units. Coordination difficulties undermine strategic focus and divert many resources to coordination tasks. Multiple, intersecting levels of authority slow decision making and undermine accountability and performance evaluation, reducing the incentive for executives to undertake risks. The complexity of operation is especially manifested in an international context because of employee diversity across country units. Yet, companies such as Dow Chemical have developed the proficiency to run matrix structures effectively.

Matrix structures provide a way for a MNE to simultaneously handle globalization and localization. The structure is designed "to help management cope with a highly complex, constantly changing global business environment by allowing the marshaling of diverse resources in multiple ways."[17] Among the advantages of the matrix structure are economies of scale and ease of transfer of technology to foreign operations and of new products to foreign markets and hence superior foreign sales performance. The matrix can also be used as an interim structure for a firm moving from an international division to a global structure. For instance, Deutsche Bank adopted a matrix structure to ease its shift from a geographic to a global product design.

Several large European (e.g., ABB, Royal Dutch/Shell) and U.S. (Dow Chemical, Caterpillar) MNEs use the matrix structure successfully. With the exception of ABB, these firms are not highly diversified and have product lines based on similar technologies. This is one reason why Japanese and Korean firms do not use the matrix structure, opting for functional structures combined with an international sales di-

Exhibit 11–3a
Organization chart of the
Dow Chemical Company

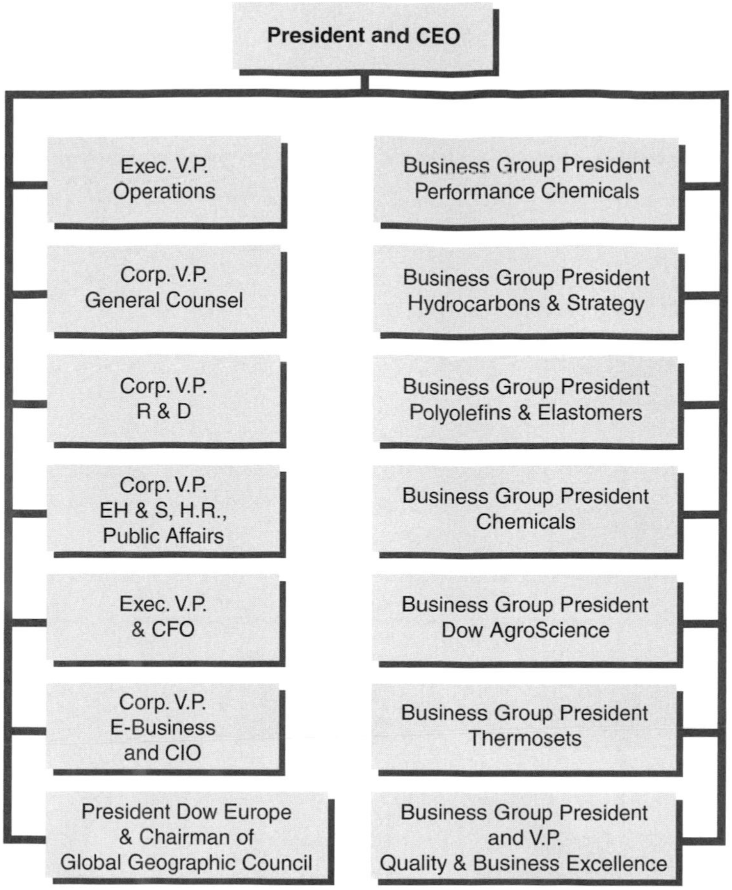

Exhibit 11–3b
Organization chart of the
Dow Chemical Company
(sample unit)

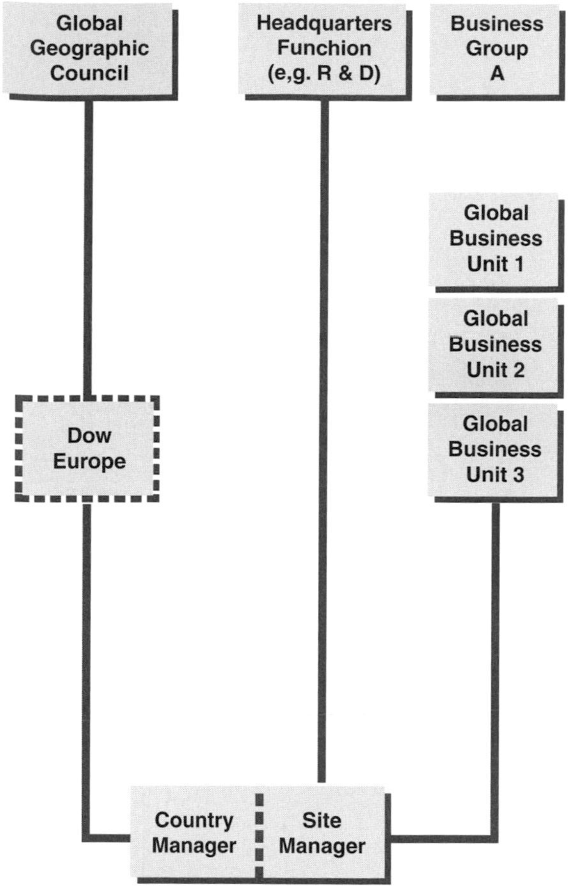

Source: The Dow Chemical Company, 2002.

vision. Successful matrix firms make sure they have coordinating mechanisms in place. ABB's motto is "delegation without abdication." While decisions are pushed down the line as much as possible, corporate headquarters monitors, advises, and "steers" operational units. A common reporting system and intense effort at communications compensate for the matrix weakness. In addition, most matrix-structured MNEs are led by strong CEOs with solid international business experience. With a related business portfolio (ABB being the exception) and international experience, they regard the matrix as a worthwhile investment whose return is a superior response to the complexity and diversity of global business. With the exception of ABB, most matrix-structured MNEs have a large cadre of executives who have spent most of their career in both foreign and domestic assignments with the same firm.

The Mixed Structure

The structure of a large MNE is almost always mixed, at least to some extent. Exhibit 11-4, on the following pages, shows the structure of the Ford Motor Company at the end of 2002. This current structure represents further evolution in the glob-

Exhibit 11–4
The Ford Motor
Company, 2002

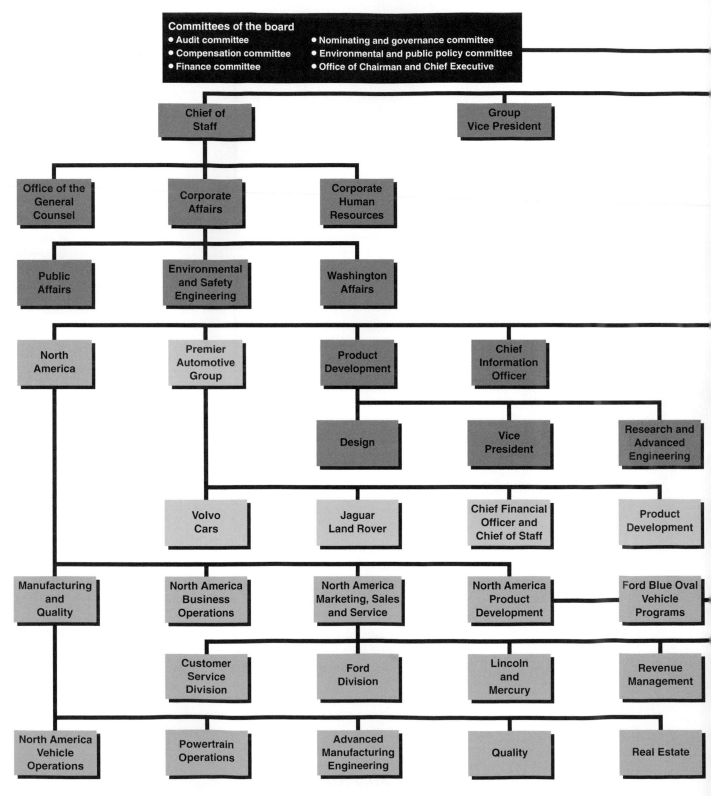

Committees of the board
- Audit committee
- Compensation committee
- Finance committee
- Nominating and governance committee
- Environmental and public policy committee
- Office of Chairman and Chief Executive

Chief of Staff

Group Vice President

Office of the General Counsel

Corporate Affairs

Corporate Human Resources

Public Affairs

Environmental and Safety Engineering

Washington Affairs

North America

Premier Automotive Group

Product Development

Chief Information Officer

Design

Vice President

Research and Advanced Engineering

Volvo Cars

Jaguar Land Rover

Chief Financial Officer and Chief of Staff

Product Development

Manufacturing and Quality

North America Business Operations

North America Marketing, Sales and Service

North America Product Development

Ford Blue Oval Vehicle Programs

Customer Service Division

Ford Division

Lincoln and Mercury

Revenue Management

North America Vehicle Operations

Powertrain Operations

Advanced Manufacturing Engineering

Quality

Real Estate

Source: The Ford Motor Company, 2002.

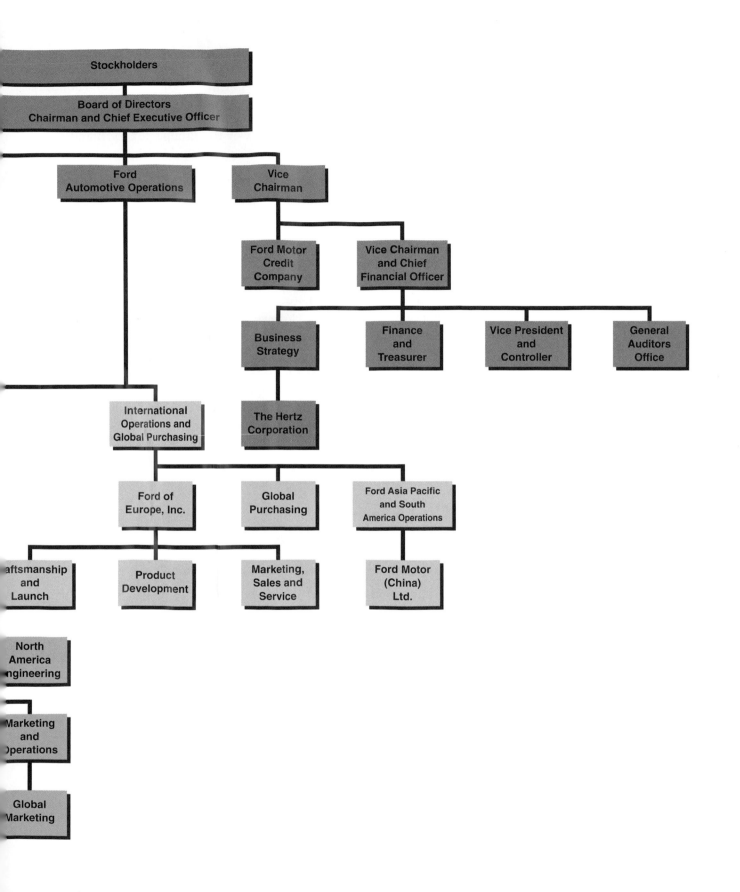

alization versus localization balance from the "Ford 2000" structure described in the Industry Box. Note, for instance, that Ford of Europe is a separate, incorporated entity, with its own product development, craftsmanship and launch, and marketing/sales/service units. This is most likely a reflection of regional integration in the EU as well as the scale and unique characteristics of its market. China, a potentially huge and unique market, is also a separate unit, reporting to Asia Pacific (and South America) operations. At the same time, purchasing is a global function aimed at producing scale advantages by establishing single source procurement. Ford's Premier Automotive Group pulls together the operations of the group's luxury brands in Sweden (Volvo) and England (Jaguar, Land Rover, and Aston Martin).

Interim Summary

1. As MNEs internationalize, they shift their structure from national subsidiary to international division and finally to global design.

2. MNEs select between functional, geographic, global-product and matrix structures. Over the last decades, MNEs have gradually shifted away from geographic to global product structures. However, geography continues to play a key role in MNE structure and may be enjoying a comeback.

3. Two-dimension matrix structures in MNEs involve interfacing geographic/ product or function/product combinations, while three-dimension structures are typically based on function/geographic/product differentiation. The matrix structure is the most complex to manage of all structural forms.

INTEGRATING GLOBAL OPERATIONS

The integration of subunits in foreign countries in a large MNE relies on processes of control, coordination, and orientation. **Control** is direct intervention in the operations of subsidiaries to ensure conformity with organizational goals. **Coordination** provides the appropriate linkage between different task units within the organization. It is associated with integrating activities dispersed across subsidiaries, and is less direct, less costly, and has a longer time span than control. MNE headquarters are often unable to use centralized decision-making processes to maintain global control. Finally, **strategic orientation** is the indirect exercise of corporate direction.

To control its subsidiaries, the MNE uses output (e.g., performance targets), bureaucratic (e.g., codified rules), and cultural mechanisms (e.g., the dissemination of corporate values). The diversity of countries, functions, and products makes centralized control difficult, however, making continuous monitoring necessary. Coordination helps the MNE deal with breadth (the number of units in the coordination network) and diversity (the number of functions coordinated). Formal coordination mechanisms include centralization, formalization, planning, output control, and behavioral control. Informal mechanisms include lateral relations, informal communication, and organizational culture. Coordination needs tend to be higher when international activities are more geographically dispersed. MNEs increasingly use strategic orientation in lieu of conventional controls to monitor the operation of foreign subsidiaries. Strategic orientation is less direct and less costly than control and coordination, and has the most sustained effect.

Tools for Global Integration

Delegating decision making to subsidiary managers abroad and/or product executives at headquarters without structuring processes and rules will reduce the effectiveness and efficiency of international expansion. Major tools that can be used to maintain global integration include: (1) data management and information systems; (2) managerial mechanisms and human resource administration; (3) communication intensity; (4) socialization practices; (5) expatriate dispatching; and (6) entry mode selection and sharing arrangements.

Data management tools can be used to control the kinds of information gathered systematically by members of the organization; how such information is aggregated, analyzed, and interpreted; how, in which form, and to whom it circulates; and how it is used in major decisions. Information systems must have a dual focus. Accounting and strategic data must be aggregated both for analytical purposes and to support integration (a portfolio of countries within a business) and responsiveness (a portfolio of businesses within a country). The flow of information can also be structured with sufficient asymmetry that individual managers will be encouraged to identify strongly with either responsive or integrative strategies, while others will develop more balanced perspectives.

Management tools can be used to set norms and standards of behavior as well as subunit objectives that are consistent with a desired strategic direction. Such tools work both directly—through their actual impact on managers—and indirectly—through the precedents they set and the meanings they assign to specific situations and choices. Management tools also include more usual human resource management components, such as shaping careers, reward systems, and management development. Less formal tools help develop norms, standards, and personal objectives. They help create an internal advocacy process that reflects the conflicting external needs for responsiveness and integration. Several managerial mechanisms can be used integrally. Planning processes can catalyze the process of strategic convergence and consensus building among executives whose initial perceptions and priorities differ. Management tools may create a climate in which managers will be encouraged to interact and will be motivated to undertake successful lateral relationships. Rewards may be based more on participation and contribution than on individual results. Managerial development activities may emphasize a corporate-wide perspective and flexible attitudes. Career paths create alternations between geographic and product-oriented responsibilities for individual managers so that they develop an empathy for both responsiveness and integration priorities.

Intensity of communication may be employed to balance integration-responsiveness relations. The intensity of communication between a focal subsidiary and the rest of the corporation can be treated as a positive function of the frequency, informality, openness, and density of communications between the subsidiary, the other units, and the head office. Frequent interunit communications facilitates the diffusion of innovations across subsidiaries. More intense communication patterns create higher information-processing capacity. This is especially desirable when subunits use differentiation strategies rather than harvest or cost-leadership strategies. Effective adaptation to environmental uncertainty requires unstructured decision-making processes involving open communications. Overall, frequency, informality, openness, and density of communication between a focal subsidiary and the rest of the corporation should be higher for subunits that play a greater part in global integration.

Corporate socialization of subsidiary managers can be an effective tool for global integration. **Corporate socialization** is the processes through which subsidiary managers' values and norms are aligned with those of the parent corporation. Such socialization is a powerful mechanism for building identification with and commitment to the organization as a whole, as distinct from the immediate subunit in which the manager is operating. Some of the key processes through which such socialization occurs are job rotation across foreign subsidiaries and management development programs involving participants from several subunits. Global corporate socialization of a subsidiary's top management team should vary across subsidiary strategic roles. Socialization should be high for integrated players, medium for global innovators and implementors, and low for local innovators.

Dispatching expatriates to foreign subsidiaries and manipulating the ratio of expatriates in the top management team of subsidiaries are also important for maintaining global integration. Host-country nationals are generally more familiar with the local environment, develop stronger rapport with local managers, and have a stronger identification with and commitment to the local subsidiary than to the parent MNE. Cognitively, host-country nationals are likely to have a more comprehensive understanding of the local sociocultural, political, and economic environments. By contrast, expatriate managers are likely to have a more comprehensive understanding of the MNE's overall global strategy. Motivationally, the local commitment of host-country nationals results from very limited prospects for their career progression outside of the local subsidiary. Expatriate managers do not operate under such a constraint. Therefore, the ratio of expatriates as a percentage of the top-management team should be higher for those subsidiaries that play a bigger role in the MNE's global integration.

Entry mode selection affects the MNE's ability to control local operations and integrate these businesses into its global network during subsequent operational stages. Other things being equal, the umbrella investment, wholly-owned subsidiary, and dominant joint venture modes enable the MNE to maintain greater control and integration than minority joint venture or other cooperative arrangements in which the MNE is a minority owner. Among other entry modes, franchising and build-operate-transfer modes enable the MNE to better control foreign operations than licensing and leasing. MNEs should align their entry mode selection with their needs for organizational control and global integration. In the case of joint ventures, the equity distribution between partners can make a substantial difference in control and integration. Majority equity ownership helps the MNE to not only protect its proprietary knowledge and control joint venture activities but also to mitigate the partner firm's possible opportunism while strategically orienting the joint venture to comply with the MNE's global mission.

The Transition Challenge

Changing an organization design is never easy. When Ford Motor Company adopted its "Ford 2000," its chairman and CEO said, "We are not simply changing lines on an organization chart; this is entirely about the processes that we use as we go about our business around the world." To meet the challenge, Ford assigned 27 senior executives to a transition team and embarked on a communications and training program for 1,700 senior and mid-level executives. The formal transition period lasted for eight months, although many of the change and integration processes continued for years. While generally considered a success, the implementation of Ford 2000 has not been without problems. British product developers had little understanding of the American consumer and found it difficult to come up with products that would appeal to that customer. For instance, they wondered why anyone would want a car with a red interior when that was long out of vogue in Europe. However, open communication lines enabled the company to overcome most of the obstacles.

The Role of Corporate Headquarters

An essential component of organizational structure in MNEs is the corporate headquarters. While relatively small—a Conference Board report suggests that well-managed firms cap their headquarters staff at 2 percent of total head count—the board is a key player in MNE management. It is from its headquarters that the firm leverages and manages its resources, controls and coordinates its far-flung international operations, and balances scale and standardization with needs for local adaptation. The corporate headquarters provides leadership and contributes to the development of company identity and vision. Even at ABB, where decisions are pushed down the line as much as possible, corporate headquarters monitors, advises, and "steers" operational units. In research and development, traditionally one of the most centralized functions, corporate headquarters now sets a general direction while shifting more and more responsibilities, including product development, to laboratories in foreign locations (see also Chapter 13).

Corporate headquarters' employees can be found not only at headquarters but also in divisional centers and in international locations where they provide added guidance to foreign subsidiaries and affiliates. Such guidance is especially important in the case of strategic alliances that are an increasingly popular mode through which firms enter or defend their position in a foreign market.

Interim Summary

1. MNE headquarters (or regional headquarters) integrate global operations through several mechanisms including output, bureaucratic mechanisms, and cultural mechanisms. Corporate culture (including values and philosophies) and information systems play an increasing integration role.

2. Global integration tools are diverse (e.g., reporting system, communication intensity, expatriate policy, and parent service). To choose these tools, MNEs need to ensure that they possess the organizational infrastructures to implement them effectively.

CHAPTER SUMMARY

1. Organizational design is driven by both strategy and a driver of strategy. It represents an opportunity to adapt the MNE's structure to its employees and to the multiple environments in which the MNE operates. Organizational design includes multidomestic, global, and transnational strategies. These strategies also indicate levels of global integration and local responsiveness.

2. The multidomestic strategy involves a decentralized system in which foreign subsidiaries in various countries are virtually independent. Under global strategy, foreign subunits are under centralized control from corporate headquarters, which seeks out standardized products suitable for a variety of markets. Under transnational strategy, foreign subunits coordinate their activities with headquarters and with one another; they also share knowledge and resources.

3. A subsidiary's role can be (a) autonomous, in which it enjoys a great deal of leeway, (b) receptive, in which it is closely integrated with headquarters, or (c), active, in which it coordinates with other subsidiaries. Subsidiary roles can also be classified by knowledge flow (global innovators, integrated players, implementers, and local innovators) and by subsidiary importance and competence (strategic leaders, contributors, implementers, and black holes).

4. MNE designs include the national subsidiary structure, the international division structure, the global functional structure, the global geographic structure, the global product structure, and the global matrix structure.

5. The main challenge of MNE design is to provide the appropriate balance in terms of differentiation and integration across functional, product, and regional lines. To balance these properly, the MNE should also devise effective mechanisms for global coordination and integration, without hindering the subsidiaries in their roles.

6. Global integration tools include data management, information system, communication, entry mode, expatriate assignment, planning, human resource management, and socialization, among others. Information and culture-based control are becoming more important than rigid or bureaucratic control.

CHAPTER NOTES

[1] J. C. Abegglen and G. Stalk, Jr. *Kaisha: The Japanese Corporation.* New York: Basic Books, 1985.

[2] J. C. Jarillo and J. I. Martinez, "Different roles for subsidiaries: The case of multinational corporations in Spain," *Strategic Management Journal,* 11, 7, 1990, 501–512.

[3] A. K. Gupta and V. Govindarajan, "Knowledge flow and the structure of control within multinational corporations," *Academy of Management Review,* 16, 4, 1991, 768–792.

[4] C. A. Bartlett and S. Ghoshal, *Managing across borders.* Boston, MA: Harvard Business School Press, 1989; C. K. Prahalad and Y. Doz, *The Multinational Mission: Balancing Local Demands and Global Vision.* New York: Free Press, 1987.

[5] E. Nelson, "International unit duties revamped at Wal-Mart stores," *Wall Street Journal,* August 20, 1999, B6.

[6] The Conference Board, "Organizing for global competitiveness: The business unit design." Report #1110-95-RR.

[7] R. A. Daft, *Essentials of Organization Theory and Design.* New York: Thomson, 2000.

[8] "Getting ahead," *Wall Street Journal,* August 22, 2000, B14.

[9] J. R. Galbraith, *Designing Organizations.* New York: Wiley, 1995.

[10] The Conference Board, "Organizing for Global Competitiveness: The business unit design." Report #1110-95-RR.

[11] D. Filkins, "Punching in the future: Technology puts India to work from afar," *International Herald Tribune,* April 8–9, 2000, p. 1.

[12] D. McClain and O. Shenkar, "Corporate downsizing, telecommunications and culture: Influence on Hawaii's competitiveness as a regional headquarters location." Report to the Department of Business, Economic Development and Tourism, State of Hawaii, 1995.

[13] B. Gordon, "Singapore in quest to lure Israeli talent," *The Jerusalem Post Internet Edition,* August 29, 2000.

[14] The Conference Board, "Organizing for global competitiveness: The product design." Report number 1063-94-RR, 1994.

[15] E. Nelson, "Rallying the troops at P&G, *Wall Street Journal,* August 31, 2000, B1.

[16] T. J. Peter and R. H. Waterman, *In Search of Excellence.* 1982.

[17] The Conference Board, "Organizing for global competitiveness: The matrix design." 1088-94-RR, 1994.

Note: This chapter borrows from various Conference Board reports. We are grateful to the Conference Board for permission to use this material.

Building and Managing Global Strategic Alliances (GSAs)

DO YOU KNOW

1. Why have so many firms chosen global strategic alliances (GSAs) to expand globally, and why have many GSAs failed? What types of GSAs can firms choose? Can you distinguish between equity joint ventures and non-equity (cooperative) joint ventures? Do you think allying between two competitors such as Toshiba and Philips is advisable?

2. How should firms select appropriate partners in another country? If you are planning to initiate an international joint venture, what criteria will underly your partner selection, and how should you prepare for negotiating joint venture contracts?

3. How will you decide the ownership level in an equity joint venture? Is a majority status necessarily better than minority or a 50–50 status? If your company is the minority party, what measures could you take to have more control over the joint venture?

4. In what ways can inter-partner cooperation be nurtured to maximize joint payoff? How do you balance the tension between cooperation and control? If you are in charge of Xerox's alliance with Fuji in Japan, how do you safeguard your proprietary knowledge? If you want to exit from this alliance, how should it be done?

OPENING CASE Motorola and Siemens AG in Germany

Semiconductor 300 is a global strategic alliance (GSA) in Germany established by Siemens AG and Motorola, Inc. Siemens AG, one of the world's largest and oldest electrical engineering and electronics companies based in Germany, is the market leader for the Chipcard IC. Motorola is a leading provider of wireless communications, advanced electronics, two-way radios, and data communications.

Given the strengths of each partner—Siemens's chip making and Motorola's semiconductor abilities—it is not surprising that these two companies joined forces to increase productivity and gain more advantages through the Semiconductor 300 GSA. This is not the first time the two have joined together for a project. In 1995, for example, Siemens and Motorola signed a memorandum of understanding to form a $1.5 billion GSA to establish a state-of-the-art eight-inch semiconductor plant in White Oak, Virginia. Siemens's and Motorola's successes in past cooperative relationships aided this new partnership. They were able to accelerate the decision-making process concerning issues such as ownership allocation and organizational form.

Semiconductor 300 is a 50–50 GSA (i.e., equal ownership). It seeks to develop the next generation of 300-mm 12-inch wafers, an important innovation for the semiconductor industry, which constantly requires more powerful integrated circuits at lower prices. The GSA provides both companies with first-mover advantages in the 300-mm memory chip technology arena. The Siemens and Motorola GSA also creates a valuable resource synergy. While Siemens provides Motorola with world-class technology, service, and global reach, Motorola brings expertise in advanced logic products and leading-edge manufacturing equipment development. In addition, Siemens provides leadership in dynamic, random access memory and logic products along with state-of-the-art 0.25-micron process technology. Teaming with Motorola, Siemens is able to expand its capacity to challenge the top five chipmakers and expand its telecommunications portfolio. ■

DEFINING GLOBAL STRATEGIC ALLIANCES

Types of GSAs

As the preceding case illustrates, the global strategic alliance (GSA) has become a popular vehicle for MNEs to expand globally and improve their global competitive advantage. Through Semiconductor 300, Siemens and Motorola each gain more than they would by working individually. **Global strategic alliances** are cross-border partnerships between two or more firms from different countries with an attempt to pursue mutual interests through sharing their resources and capabilities. Broadly, there are two basic types of GSAs: *equity joint ventures* and *cooperative (or contractual) joint ventures*. The former involve equity contributions, the latter do not.

The equity joint venture (EJV) is a legally and economically separate organizational entity created by two or more parent organizations that collectively invest financial as well as other resources to pursue certain objectives. In an international setting, these parent firms are from different countries. To set up an EJV, each partner contributes cash, facilities, equipment, materials, intellectual property rights, labor, or land-use rights. An EJV can be structured on a 50–50 ownership arrangement (e.g., the Prudential-Mitsui EJV in which both Prudential Insurance and Mitsui Trust & Banking each have 50 percent ownership), or a majority-minority basis (e.g., the U.S.'s Corning-Mexico's Vitro EJV in which Corning assumes majority ownership, 51 percent, whereas Vitro owns 49 percent).

The cooperative joint venture is a contractual agreement whereby profits and responsibilities are assigned to each party according to stipulations in a contract. Although the two firms entering into a contractual partnership have the option of forming a limited liability entity with legal person status, most cooperative ventures involve joint activities without the creation of a new corporate entity. Non-equity cooperative ventures have freedom to structure their assets, organize their production processes, and manage their operations. This flexibility can be attractive for a foreign investor interested in property development, resource exploration, and other projects in which the foreign party incurs substantial up-front development costs. Further, this type of venture can be developed quickly to take advantage of short-term business opportunities, then dissolved when its tasks are completed.

Cooperative joint ventures include several sub-forms: *joint exploration, research and development consortia*, and *co-production,* all of which are typical forms of contractual partnerships. Others include *co-marketing, long-term supply agreements,* and *joint management.*

Joint exploration projects (e.g., Atlantic Richfield's offshore oil exploration consortia in Brazil, Ecuador, and Indonesia) are a special type of non-equity cooperative alliance whereby the exploration costs are borne by the foreign partner, with development costs later shared by a local entity. Although such explorations allow the foreign firm to manage specific projects, this type of alliance does not necessarily result in the establishment of new limited liability enterprises. By comparison, the costs of a **research and development consortium** (e.g., Microsoft's R&D consortium with Cambridge University, England) may be allocated according to an agreed-upon formula, but the revenue of each partner depends on what it does with the technology created. In **co-production or co-service** agreements, such as the Boeing 767 project involving Boeing and Japan Aircraft Development Corporation (itself a consortium of Mitsubishi, Kawasaki, and Fuji), each partner is responsible for manufacturing a particular part of the product. Each partner's costs are therefore a function of its own efficiency in producing that part. However, revenue is a function of successful sales of the 767 by the dominant partner, Boeing. In the co-service arrangement between Delta Air Lines and Air France, the focus is on aligning commercial policies and procedures, coordinating transatlantic operations, and combining frequent-flier programs. Although Delta and Air France each retain independent fleets, together they look for ways to improve operating efficiencies.

The **co-marketing arrangement** provides a platform in which each party can reach a larger pool of international consumers. For example, Praxair (U.S.) and Merck KGA (Germany) established their global alliance in 1999 through which each uses the other's distribution channels to provide an offering combining Praxair's gases and Merck's wet chemicals to semiconductor customers. This co-marketing alliance gives both parties entry into the other's main markets. Praxair has a strong distribution infrastructure in North America but is a minor player in Europe and Asia. Merck, in contrast, is strong in Europe and Asia but absent from the U.S. wet chemical market. In a typical **long-term supply agreement,** the manufacturing buyer provides the supplier with updated free information on products, markets, and technologies, which in turn helps ensure the input quality. IKEA, for example, offers such information to its dozens of foreign suppliers and also provides them with free periodic training. As a result, many of IKEA's foreign suppliers are committed to becoming its long-term exclusive suppliers. Finally, a **co-management arrangement** is a loosely structured alliance in which cross-national partners collaborate in training (technical or managerial), production management, information systems development, and value-chain integration (e.g., integrating inbound logistics with production or integrating outbound logistics with marketing). Partnership provides a vehicle for firms to quickly and efficiently acquire skills that cannot be bought from a public market. Co-management arrangements occur because international companies often realize that they lack the managerial skills necessary for running foreign operations, while local companies often find that they can benefit from foreign counterparts' international experience and organizational skills. Therefore, foreign and local companies can benefit from complementary managerial expertise contributed through an alliance.

Rationales for Building GSAs

Although GSAs take several different forms, they share some common rationales. Firms team together seeking some synergy. **Synergy** means additional economic benefits (financial, operational, or technological) arising from cooperation between two parties that provide each other with complementary resources or capabilities. In practice, these synergies and related economic benefits can be the result of *risk reduction, knowledge acquisition, economies of scale and rationalization, competition mitigation, improved local acceptance, and market entry.*[1]

First, *a GSA allows a company to enter into activities that might be too costly and risky to pursue on its own.* If an investment project is too expensive or too risky for single firms to handle alone, they may join forces to share the risk. This is the case with oil exploration and commercial aircraft manufacturing where large, risky projects call for inter-firm collaboration. Having considered the fact that the design, development, and production of a new aircraft engine require more than 10 years at a cost of close to $2 billion, General Electric (U.S.) and Snecma (France) established CFM International, a 50–50 joint venture, to share the risks and costs involved in new aircraft engine development. Moreover, if the business environment in a host country is highly uncertain or unfriendly to foreign firms, a GSA with a local firm may allow an MNE to share political risks and defuse hostile local reactions. Finally, alliances can be used to cut the costs of leaving a business. Exiting an industry via an alliance also permits management to withdraw with the company's reputation intact. Minimizing exit costs is one of the considerations underlying Siemens's alliance with Toshiba and IBM to develop the 256-megabit dynamic random access memory chip.

Second, *a GSA allows a firm to acquire partner knowledge or resources to build competitive strength*. This knowledge acquisition may occur at significantly reduced costs—with capital investment much lower than if the firm either developed it alone or via an acquisition.[2] Access to a partner's technology enables a firm to enjoy the fruits of research and development while avoiding rapidly escalating R&D costs. Shell and ICI (Imperial Chemical Industries) share their complementary resources in producing rigid foam through a global alliance. ICI is highly regarded in the polyurethane market for its technical support and ability to bring new products to market, whereas Shell is a world leader in the technology for rigid polyether polyols.

Third, *a GSA allows a firm to enhance economies of scale or scope and to improve product rationalization*. By sharing financial resources that otherwise are not available to each individual partner, two smaller companies in an industry can form an alliance to achieve economies of scale similar to those that are enjoyed by their larger competitors. GSA partners may also cooperate to take advantage of pooled non-financial resources. The joint use of complementary resources, competencies, and skills possessed by different organizations can create synergistic effects, which none of the companies is able to achieve if acting alone. For example, Airbus aircrafts are manufactured under a consortium composed of France's Aerospatiale and Germany's Daimler-Benz Aerospace, British Aerospace, and Spain's Construcciones Aeronauticas. Because most aerospace projects require huge capital outlays, pooling both technological and financial resources is a rational step. (This consortium is in the process of transforming into an EJV.)

Fourth, *a GSA allows a firm to prevent or reduce competition (potential or existing) with a major rival*. Clark Equipment and Volvo formed an alliance producing earthmoving equipment; alone, neither could generate enough volume in their traditional home markets (United States and Europe) to survive against such global industry leaders as Caterpillar and Komatsu. Meanwhile, a GSA may be used in a more aggressive strategy. Caterpillar Tractor linked up with Mitsubishi in Japan to put pressure on the profits and market share that their common competitor Komatsu enjoyed in its Japanese market (about 80 percent of Komatsu's global cash flow was generated from Japan). Thus, while the alliance may be quite beneficial to Caterpillar, it may act as a thorn in Komatsu's side and reduce its competitiveness outside Japan.

GSAs can also be used to develop technological standards that help control the competition within an industry. For example, Sematech, a GSA among several electronic and semiconductor firms, facilitated the adoption of the UNIX standard operating system for workstation computer producers. Intel and Hewlett-Packard (HP) cooperated to offer a new chip that would process data in 64-bit chunks instead of Intel's Pentium standard 32 bits. The chip would be able to run today's Windows software as well as programs written for HP's version of UNIX, without modification. This innovation could take the microprocessor revolution to a new level, providing the partner firms a controlling position in the industry.

Fifth, *a GSA allows a firm to boost local acceptance as perceived by foreign consumers*. A foreign firm can piggyback on a local partner to gain access to the local market. The Ford Motor Company estimates that 60 percent of the automotive growth over the next 20 years will be in markets where Ford now has little or no presence. Ford's alliance with Mazda of Japan illustrates its efforts toward local acceptance in Asian markets. Without fully understanding the consumer behavior, distribution network, and effective marketing strategies and practices in a specific country, a foreign wholly owned subsidiary has a substantial potential for failure. The distinctive marketing and distribution practices in Japan encourage foreign companies to set up partnerships with Japanese companies as the most practical means of getting into the market. Similarly, many Japanese MNEs with little or no direct presence in Europe have moved aggressively to establish partnerships with their European counterparts.

Finally, *a GSA allows a firm to bypass entry barriers into a target foreign country*. Many governments, particularly in developing countries, pressure MNEs to conduct FDI in the form of equity joint ventures rather than wholly owned subsidiaries. To the foreign firm, an alliance with a local organization, either business or governmental, may be required in order to enter these countries. With Coca-Cola out, Pepsi entered India in the mid-1980s through a joint venture with the government-owned Punjab Agro Industrial Corporation (PAIC) and Voltas India Ltd. During that time, the Indian government imposed many restrictions on profit repatriation, technology transfer, and product distribution. Pepsi managed to overcome these obstacles through cooperation with local partners that contributed their market power, marketing channels, and strong ties with officials to the joint operations.

Challenges Facing GSAs

Not every firm should build GSAs to expand globally, nor is building GSAs necessarily a superior strategy to other investment choices under all circumstances. According to a survey by McKinsey & Company and Coopers & Lybrand, about 70 percent of GSAs fall short of expectations.[3] More complex than the single organization, GSAs involve multiple interorganizational relationships (between the parent firms, between alliance managers and the foreign parent, between alliance managers and the local parent, and between alliance managers nominated by different parents). Each of these relationships can be extremely difficult to manage. GSAs represent an intercultural and interorganizational linkage between two separate parent companies that join forces with different strategic interests and objectives. Interpartner conflict may arise from sources such as cross-cultural differences, diverging strategic expectations, and incongruent organizational structures. These conflicts in turn can lead to instability and poor performance of the alliance.

The aforementioned complexity generates problems and risks for using GSAs. First, *loss of autonomy and control* often creates inter-partner conflicts and alliance instability. Each partner may want to control the alliance's operations, so coordination and governance costs are generally higher. Cross-cultural partners may disagree on long-term objectives, time horizons, operating styles, and expectations for the alliance.

Second, the *risk of possible leakage* of critical technologies may be high and often difficult to avoid. Committing distinctive resources is often necessary for gaining a competitive edge in a foreign market. This, however, may lead to leakage of valuable intellectual property (known as *appropriability hazard*). Because distinctive resources are relatively difficult to specify, contract, and monitor, hazards associated with limited protection of such rights are particularly high for these resources, especially in developing countries where intellectual property rights systems have not yet been fully established. In the absence of strong control over alliance activities and self-protection mechanisms, local partners may disseminate the foreign investor's critical knowledge to third parties.

Third, inter-partner *differences in strategic goals* often lead to cumbersome decision-making processes, which may in turn cause strategic inflexibility. This may be compounded when the alliance managers do not share strategic directions and goals set by parent firms. In the absence of sufficient organizational control over alliance activities, GSAs may even be considered impediments to the flexibility of an MNE's global strategy. The MNE may need to maintain global integration of all parts of its network (outside the GSA) for strategic or financial purposes, but because of the inflexibility of the GSA, global optimization may not be possible for outsourcing, capital flows, tax reduction, transfer pricing, and rationalization of production.

Finally, local partners may *become global competitors* in the future, after developing skills and technology via the alliance. Japanese firms, for example, often plan ahead to increase the benefits they extract from a GSA, leaving the European or American partners in an inferior strategic position. In other words, they may look upon partnerships as a strategic competitive move, based on tactical expediency.[4] Reflecting on its GSA with NEC, one senior executive in Varian Associates (a U.S. producer of advanced electronics including semiconductors) concluded that "all NEC had wanted to do was to suck out Varian's technology, not sell Varian's equipment."[5]

Because of the preceding drawbacks, international managers should make a strategic assessment about the necessity of building GSAs in the course of a feasibility study. This assessment emphasizes value creation and thus is more beneficial than conducting a cost-benefit analysis. This is especially true when the alliance is used to learn about a new environment and thereby reduce the uncertainties present in a new territory. This calls for a strategic, rather than financial, view to capture value creation. Along with the increasing competition and technological development, a GSA is increasingly engaging multiple sophisticated businesses, calling for distinctive resources from multiple partners. This makes value-creation analysis for building GSAs more important and more difficult at the same time. Following this assessment, managers need to plan carefully for partner selection, contract negotiations, and alliance structuring (see Exhibit 12–1).

Exhibit 12–1
Key issues underlying building GSAs

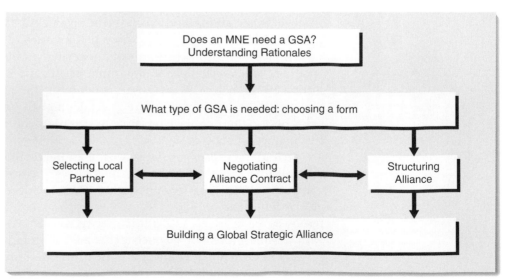

Interim Summary

1. There are two basic types of GSAs: equity joint ventures and non-equity (cooperative or contractual) joint ventures. Cooperative joint ventures include joint exploration, R&D consortium, co-production, co-marketing, joint management, long-term supply agreement, and so forth. Major advantages of building GSAs include cost/risk sharing, knowledge acquisition, product rationalization, competition reduction, local acceptance, and market access.

2. Many GSAs have failed, owing to inability to overcome inherent challenges such as loss of control, knowledge leakage, goal incongruence, cultural clashes, differences in managerial philosophies, and emerging competition between partners.

BUILDING GLOBAL STRATEGIC ALLIANCES

Selecting Local Partners

Partner selection is widely recognized as a vital factor in GSA success. All the benefits articulated in the preceding section may or may not be achieved depending on who has been selected as the partner. Benefits will accrue only through the retention of a partner that can provide the complementary skills, competencies, or capabilities that will assist the firm in accomplishing its strategic objectives.[6] Partner selection determines a GSA's mix of skills, knowledge, and resources as well as its operating policies, processes, and procedures.[7] During the process of GSA formation, foreign companies must identify what selection criteria should be employed as well as the relative importance of each criterion. Generally, five criteria (5-Cs) should be considered in partner selection:

- Compatibility of goals
- Complementarity of resources
- Cooperative culture
- Commitment
- Capability

Exhibit 12–2 highlights these 5-Cs for selecting appropriate local partners.

Exhibit 12–2
The Five-Cs scheme of partner selection

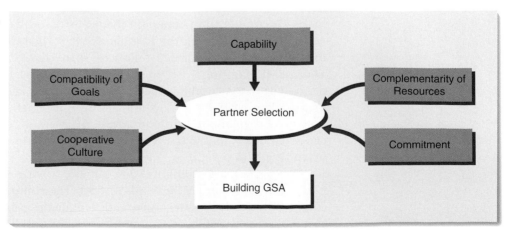

Goal Compatibility

Goal compatibility refers to the congruence of strategic goals set for an alliance between its parent firms. Goals for individual parents can be different, but goals set for the alliance must be compatible or congruent, because they represent collective gains for all parents involved. The success of the consortium between Boeing and three Japanese heavy industry companies to design and build the 767 is partially attributable to goal compatibility. Boeing sought foreign partners to ease its financial burden and operational risks, while the Japanese firms tried to expand their role in the aerospace industry. The Japanese are now significantly increasing their participation in the industry, providing an ever-increasing portion of production parts and assembly. Boeing has reduced the risks of development by adding more partners and by lowering the financial commitment required for production. When a GSA's collective goals set by different parents are incongruent, inter-partner conflicts are inevitable in the subsequent phase of operations. In this case, firms are more likely to use opportunistic rather than cooperative strategies during joint operations. For instance, foreign parents want joint ventures in China to target the local market, whereas Chinese parents may want these ventures to emphasize international markets or as a channel to acquire foreign technologies. This incongruence creates conflicts, as reflected in Peugeot's divorce with its local partner, Guanzhou Automotive Manufacturing Company.

To ensure goal compatibility, MNEs often partner with companies that have been cooperative in the past. For example, the GSA between Mitsubishi Electric and Westinghouse Corp. proceeded in an orderly fashion; partly because ties between the two companies date back to the 1920s. Previous relationships were also behind the partner selection process when LOF Glass and Nippon Sheet Glass (NSG) each spotted an opportunity in the nascent Korean auto industry. Similarly, NSG and Hankuk—which became the venture's local Korean partner—had technical and capital ties for 15 years. IBM and Siemens have also built on early ties to broaden and strengthen their alliance. Their cooperation dates back to a 1989 agreement to develop 16-megabit chips. This project was followed by joint manufacturing pacts in 1991 to launch volume production of 16-megabit chips.

Resource Complementarity

Resource complementarity is the extent to which one party's contributed resources are complementary to the other party's resources, resulting in synergies pursued by both. The greater the resource complementarity between foreign and local parents, the higher the new value added due to superior integration of complementary resources pooled by different parents. Resource complementarity also reduces governance and coordination costs and improves the learning curve.[8] For example, JVC was dependent on many different GSAs in its successful effort to make VHS (rather than Betamax) the industry standard for video. JVC stocked RCA with machines carrying the RCA label, set up licensing agreements with Japanese manufacturers, and formed alliances with Germany's Telefunken and Britain's Thorn-EMI Ferguson to help with manufacturing the video recorders. JVC's alliance with Thompson afforded it the knowledge necessary to succeed in the fragmented European market, while Thompson benefited from JVC's product technology and manufacturing prowess. As a result of these myriad GSAs, Sony conceded defeat in 1988, discontinued its production of Betamax, and began manufacturing VHS machines.

Complementary strengths were a major driving force behind the formation of Clark Equipment and Volvo's 50–50 GSA. The companies intended to operate and compete worldwide in the construction equipment business, but individually, neither partner had sufficient geographic presence and distribution capabilities to compete with the market leaders, Komatsu and Caterpillar. Volvo had roughly 70 percent of its sales in Europe and the Middle East, where Clark was very weak; Clark had 70 percent of its sales in North America, where Volvo had virtually no presence. Pooling their marketing resources resulted in a much broader geographic scope.

Cooperative Culture

Cooperative culture concerns the extent to which each party's corporate culture is compatible, thus leading to a more cooperative atmosphere during GSA operations. Normally, maintaining cooperation can become difficult for partners from different cultures. For instance, Americans tend to be individualistic; which is in sharp contrast to the Japanese emphasis on the group (see also Chapter 6). Such differences can be neutralized if both parties try to learn about each other's unique culture. Because both Toyota and GM were committed to learning about each other's corporate culture, the mix of Toyota's team approach and GM's corporate focus on innovation contributed significantly to enhanced productivity at their California-based GSA-NUMMI (New United Motor Manufacturing Company).

A company must take a close look at compatibility in organizational and management practices with a potential partner. For instance, it should ask: Are both companies centralized or decentralized? If not, are managers from these two parties flexible and committed enough to overcome potential conflict? How compatible are customer service policies and philosophies? In order to mitigate the differences in managerial and marketing practices with local Chinese partners, Hewlett-Packard hired as middle managers local people well versed in Chinese business culture.

Commitment

Commitment concerns the extent to which each party will constantly and continuously contribute its resources and skills to joint operations and be dedicated to enhancing joint payoff. Without this commitment, complementary resources, compatible goals, and cooperative culture are no guarantee of a GSA's long-term success. A partner's commitment also affects ongoing trust building. Commitment counters opportunism and fosters cooperation. When GSAs face unexpected environmental changes, commitment serves as a stabilizing device offsetting environmental uncertainties. Commitment is therefore even more critical in a volatile environment. Daewoo and GM each blamed the other for the lackluster performance of the Pontiac LeMans in the United States. Daewoo accused GM of failing to market the LeMans aggressively, while GM maintained that the initial poor quality of the LeMans and the unreliable supplies soured dealers on the car. Lack of commitment ended this GSA in 1992.

Capability

In the context of GSAs, capability concerns three categories: *strategic* (including technology), *organizational*, and *financial*. **Strategic capabilities** of a partner firm generally include such areas as market power, marketing competence, technological skills, relationship building, industrial experience, and corporate image. A partner's market power often represents its industrial and business background, market position, and established marketing and distribution networks. Market power also enables the firm to mitigate some industry-wide restrictions on output, increase bargaining power, and offer economies-of-scale advantages. A local partner's market experience and accumulated industrial knowledge are of great value for the realization of MNE goals. A local partner's history and background in a host market often results in a good reputation or high credibility in the industry. Lengthy industrial/market experience signifies that the local firm has built an extensive marketing and distribution network.

Organizational capabilities include organizational skills, previous collaboration, learning ability, and foreign experience. In a GSA, people with different cultural backgrounds, career goals, and compensation systems begin working together with little advance preparation. This "people factor" can halt the GSA's progress, sometimes permanently. Organizational skills are reflected not only in the ability to blend cultures and management styles, but also in job design, recruitment and staffing, orientation and training, performance appraisal, compensation and benefits, career development, and labor-management relations. Among these, the ability to overcome cultural barriers, recruit qualified employees, and establish incentive structures is especially important. The international experience of partners is critical to the success of intercultural and cross-border venturing activities. International experience affects the organizational fit between partners in the early stages of joint venturing and the changes of fit over time as the alliance evolves.

Financial capabilities are reflected in risk management, exposure hedging, financing and cash-flow management. A partner's risk management ability affects a GSA's vulnerability to external hazards and internal stability. Risk reduction in the form of hedging and risk sharing largely determines a GSA's stability and pattern of growth. During the host-country operations, currency fluctuations can accentuate the volatility of earnings and cash flows. Such volatility can in turn distort management information systems and incentives, hinder access to capital markets, jeopardize the continuity of supplier and customer relationships, and even force the company into bankruptcy. In many foreign markets, MNEs are constrained in obtaining local financing resources. A local partner who maintains superior relationships with local financial institutions and knows how to secure local financing is an important asset to both the venture and the MNE. This ability determines optional composition of debt and equity that will minimize costs and risks. It also affects the GSA's profitability, liquidity, working capital structure, leverage, and cash positions, all of which influence a firm's financial position and structure.

Negotiating Alliance Contracts

Familiarity with general terms negotiated and specified in an alliance contract is important. Major terms stipulated in an equity joint venture agreement are summarized in Exhibit 12–3.

Negotiating tactics affect the bargaining process as well as outcomes. Assembling the negotiating team is a critical element in creating a workable alliance. Qualified negotiators must be able to effectively convey what their parents expect to achieve from the GSA, the plans for structuring and managing the alliance, the value of the contributions each partner brings to the table, and practical solutions to potential problem areas. Good negotiators are also aware of the culturally rooted negotiating styles of the parties. Negotiations about forming a GSA become much easier when the discussions involve negotiators experienced in dealing with diverse cultures.

MNEs often include alliance manager candidates in the negotiating teams. For example, in the alliance activities of ICL, Fujitsu, Westinghouse, Glaxo, Tanabe, Philips, Montedison, and Hercules, the companies usually bring their alliance executive candidates to the negotiating table. This kind of inclusion offers several benefits. First, it provides the executives with an opportunity to learn whether they are compatible with their potential partners. Second, it provides continuity; a GSA manager involved in structuring the deal will be aware of its objectives, its limitations, and the partner's strengths and weaknesses. Third, the expertise of the individuals who will manage the alliance can be valuable in structuring a workable contract.

1. Joint venture name and its legal nature (e.g., limited liability company or not)
2. Scope and scale of production or operations
3. Investment amount, unit of currency, and equity (ownership) distribution
4. Forms of contribution (e.g., cash, technology, land, or equipment)
5. Responsibilities of each party
6. Technology or knowledge transfer
7. Marketing issues (e.g., focusing on export market or local market)
8. Composition of the board of directors (in EJVs)
9. Nomination and responsibilities of high level managers
10. Joint venture project preparation and construction
11. Labor management (e.g., various human resource issues)
12. Accounting, finance, and tax issues (e.g., the currency unit of accounting)
13. Alliance duration
14. Disposal of assets after expiration
15. Amendments, alterations, and discharge of the agreement
16. Liabilities for breach of contract or agreement
17. *Force majeure* (i.e., force or power that cannot be acted or fought against)
18. Settlement of disputes (e.g., litigation or arbitration)
19. Obligatoriness of the contract (e.g., when it will take effect) and miscellaneous issues

Finally, an alliance manager who takes part in creating the alliance is more likely to be committed to its success than one who has had the responsibility thrust upon him or her.

Another successful strategy for MNEs negotiating large, sophisticated alliance projects is to have two levels of negotiations. On one level, senior executives meet to define the general goals and form of cooperation. The negotiations concern broad strategy and whether the partners are committed to working together. At the second tier, operational managers or experts meet to work out the details of the alliance contract. Siemens, Toshiba, and IBM followed this strategy when they negotiated an R&D alliance to develop the 256-megabit DRAM chip. Senior executives at the three companies met and agreed on the principal objectives of the alliance contract. The three partners then organized a team to address many structural and managerial issues. Engineers and lower-level managers from each partner formed a single team to iron out the specifics of the development project and map out the work schedule and goals for the project.

Structuring Global Strategic Alliances

A critical decision underlying building GSAs, especially EJVs, is the ownership structure. The **ownership structure** is generally defined as the percentage of equity held by each parent. It is often interchangeably termed *equity ownership, sharing arrangement*, or *equity distribution*. This structure is particularly important for EJVs because the equity level determines the levels of control and profit sharing during the subsequent operations. Depending on contractual stipulations, the levels of control and profit sharing in non-equity cooperative alliances may or may not be the product of equity contribution. In the case of a two-party alliance (as earlier cases noted, alliances can have more than two partners), the joint venture is named a *majority-owned joint venture* when a foreign investor has a greater than 50 percent equity stake. It is a *minority-owned joint venture* if the investor owns less than a 50 percent equity stake. If ownership is equal to 50 percent, the joint venture is considered *co-owned* or *split-over*. Although there are other forms of joint ventures including those established between affiliated home-country based firms, between unaffiliated home-country based firms, or between home-country and third-country based firms, joint ventures that are launched by home-country based (foreign) and host-country based (local) firms are the dominant form of joint venture partnership.

A majority equity holding means that the partner has more at stake in the alliance than the other partner(s). Normally, the equity position will be associated with an equivalent level of management control in the venture. In other words, control based upon equity ownership is often direct and effective. Nevertheless, the correlation between holding equity and managerial control is not always precise. It is possible for a partner to have a small equity holding but exercise decisive control. This often occurs when a minority party maintains a greater bargaining power vis-à-vis the other party. For instance, because the other party depends on its resources, Burger King is able to control its joint venture operations in Moscow as a minority holder because the Russian partner relies on its expertise and experience in managing a large fast-food chain.

The ownership structure may end up equally split when both partners want to be majority equity holders. A 50–50 ownership split ensures that neither partner's interests will be compromised, other things being constant. A 50-50 split best captures the spirit of partnership and is particularly desirable in high-technology joint ventures as insurance that both partners will remain involved with technological development. In fact, equal ownership accounts for more than half of joint ventures in developed countries.[9] Split ownership can ensure equal commitment from each partner. Nevertheless, decision making must be based on consensus. This often means a prolonged decision process that can lead to deadlocks. The success of 50–50 equity ventures relies strongly on the synergy between partners over issues ranging from strategic analyses to daily management. It is important that partners speak a common language, have similar backgrounds, and share a set of short- and long-term objectives. By contrast, partners coming from diverse market environments, with different business backgrounds and conflicting goals often have a harder time making a 50–50 venture a success.

In a minority position, the partner may transfer expertise to the local partner without sufficient returns. More importantly, the ability to control alliance operations is weakened. Generally, the number of votes in board meetings is in equal proportion to actual equity stake. Thus, key decisions made by the board might be more favorable to the majority party. Protecting proprietary resources contributed to the venture also becomes more difficult for the minority party. Nonetheless, the minority status involves lower levels of risks, resource commitment, start-up or exit costs compared to a majority state.

Different MNEs attach varying importance to equity ownership level in joint ventures depending upon their strategic goals, global control requirements, resource dependence, firm experience, and alternatives for bargaining power, among others. A firm may not be interested in equity level because it has many other alternatives for gaining bargaining power and thus controlling joint venture activities. A firm lacking these alternatives, however, has to rely on equity arrangement for control purposes. Of course, high-equity ownership itself cannot ensure a party's satisfaction with joint venture performance. Venture performance depends more on successful management by both parties. This management, however, is challenging owing to inter-party differences in culture, language, philosophy, goals, and managerial style, as shown in Fujitsu's alliance in Spain (see Country Box).

Spain

FUJITSU IN SPAIN: BARRIERS TO ALLIANCE MANAGEMENT

Japan-based Fujitsu established a majority joint venture, SECOINSA (Sociedad Espanola de Communicationes e Infomatica, S.A.), partnering with the National Telephone Company of Spain and various Spanish banks. Fujitsu soon found that alliances are not a panacea. Communication proved to be difficult, and both firms had to rely on English as the common language although it is the second language for both. The Japanese felt they could not disclose their true feelings in written English; they favored a more interpersonal and fluid rapport that adapted to issues as they arose. The Spanish managers, on their side, believed the Japanese were too business oriented and were hiding behind a barrage of company talk that prevented friendships or personal rapport. They also felt that the Japanese were not well rounded because their at-work and after-work personas merged into one. Spanish people favor a distinct separation between job and leisure. The Japanese rarely adapted to the ways of the Spanish, which made the Spanish believe that the Japanese looked down on local ways.

Disharmony also existed in management. Decision making at Fujitsu was through the *ringi-sho* system, in which an idea is documented and distributed to all relevant parties for approval. *Ringi-sho* is a conservative approach that could minimize risks but is time consuming. Further, the Spanish are inclined to assume that authority is earned through ability and merit, and that authority automatically leads to power, whereas the Japanese treat age as the determining factor in earning power and authority. Finally, Fujitsu wanted to maintain stringent control over its products and prevent imitation. It wanted all the components tested at its facilities in Japan, but because manufacturing was done in Spain, SECOINSA favored Spanish-made components. SECOINSA suggested that the work could be done in Europe if Fujitsu would supply the specifications, testing, and quality control methods. Fujitsu was willing to provide the needed information, but refused to reveal it to any outside parties and would not pass along any information in writing, thus making quality control difficult to ensure.

Interim Summary

1. Five criteria must be considered in partner selection (5Cs): compatibility of goals, complementarity of resources, cooperative culture, commitment, and capability. As the key criterion, capability should be assessed along strategic capabilities (e.g., market power, marketing competence, technological skills, corporate image), organizational capabilities (e.g., foreign experience, organizational skills, learning ability, and previous collaboration), and financial capabilities (e.g., risk management, exposure hedging, local financing, and cash management).

2. Many relatively standardized terms and clauses should be specified in joint venture contracts. Preparing for negotiations includes choosing a negotiating team, planning for multilevel negotiations, and knowing a partner's intention, strengths, and weaknesses.

3. Setting the ownership level in an equity joint venture is important because it infers, in part, control over the venture. Three strategic options are majority, minority, and equally-split. If the minority party has strong bargaining power, it can still dominate the venture.

MANAGING GLOBAL STRATEGIC ALLIANCES

The management issues involved in global strategic alliances include managing interpartner learning, exercising managerial control, accentuating cooperation and trust, and thinking ahead of exit (Exhibit 12–4).

Managing Inter-Partner Learning

In bringing together firms with different skills, knowledge bases, and organizational cultures, GSAs create unique learning opportunities for the partner firms.[10] By definition, alliances involve a sharing of resources. This access can be a powerful source of new knowledge that, in most cases, would not have been possible without the GSA. Learning opportunities are manifested in two areas: *operational* and *managerial*. *Operational knowledge* includes knowledge of technology, processes (including quality control), production, marketing skills, and operational expertise (e.g., relationship-building expertise). *Managerial knowledge* is comprised of organizational and managerial skills (e.g., leadership, human resource management, organizational structure, managerial efficiency, and employee participation); market (international and host country), industrial, and collaborative experience; and financial management (e.g., cost-control, tax-reduction, capital utilization, financing, risk-reduction, resource deployment, and asset management).

To acquire partner knowledge, a firm needs to first identify what knowledge it needs and then extract and transfer this knowledge from its partner to its own organization. Germany's Bosch established "strategy meetings" focusing on what and how the firm can learn from its Japanese partners. Bosch sends trained German technicians and marketing managers to the Japanese joint ventures to help acquire partner skills and knowledge, including tips on how to improve customer satisfaction in Japan. The acquired knowledge is then shared by all members of the Bosch group who are trying to get access to Japanese clients. Similarly, when Chrysler joined forces with Mitsubishi Motors in 1986 to create Diamond Star Motors (DSM), its major objective was to gain firsthand knowledge of Japanese management and manufacturing principles. Chrysler deliberately ceded management control for daily operations to Mitsubishi to learn how that firm handled the complex engineering, functional, and operational tasks involved in launching and manufacturing a new range of midsized models.

Each party is expected to learn a certain amount about the other's capabilities. *Openness* is thus crucial to knowledge sharing or transfer between partners, because much of what the parties are trying to learn from each other or create together is difficult to communicate. This information is often embedded in a firm's practices

Exhibit 12–4
Managing global strategic alliances

and culture, and it can only be learned through working relationships that are not hampered by constraints. In order to enhance inter-partner trust, commitment from each party is necessary. However, to the party whose knowledge is very sensitive or constitutes its core competence (e.g., Coca-Cola's formula), knowledge protection becomes necessary. There are several ways to protect core knowledge from uncompensated leakage to partner firms:

First, *the design, development, manufacture, and service of a product manufactured (or a service rendered) by an alliance may be structured so as to protect the most sensitive technologies*. For example, in the GSA between GE and Snecma to build commercial aircraft engines, GE tried to reduce the risk of excess transfer by keeping certain sections of the production process secret. This modularization cut off the transfer of what GE felt was key competitive technology, while permitting Snecma access to final assembly. Similarly, in the GSA between Boeing and the Japanese to build the 767, Boeing walled off research, design, and marketing functions (considered more central to Boeing's competitive position), but allowed the Japanese to share production technology. Boeing also separated those technologies not required for 767 production.

Second, *contractual safeguards can be written into an alliance agreement*. For example, TRW has three strategic alliances with large Japanese auto component suppliers to produce seat belts, engine valves, and steering gears sold to Japanese-owned auto assembly plants in the United States. TRW has clauses in each of its GSA contracts that bar the Japanese companies from competing by introducing component parts. These protect TRW against the possibility that the Japanese companies may enter into alliances to gain access to TRW's home market and become its competitor.

Third, *both parties to a GSA can agree in advance to exchange specific skills and technologies that ensure equitable gain*. Cross-licensing agreements are one way of achieving this goal. For example, in the case of the alliance between Motorola and Toshiba, Motorola has licensed some of its microprocessor technology to Toshiba and in return Toshiba has licensed some of its memory chip technology to Motorola.

Finally, *avoiding undue dependence on an alliance can help mitigate the leakage risk*. This is particularly important when an MNE establishes GSAs with competitors or uses its own core knowledge in alliances. GM limited its dependence on its Asian allies in its Saturn project in an attempt to independently replenish the knowledge critical to its business. When GSAs do involve core knowledge, managers must guard against shifts in the balance of power, maneuvering by other parties, and the taking of vital knowledge. Moreover, an MNE may reduce dependence on an alliance by creating several similar GSAs or by seeking to be the senior partner in each relationship. For instance, Toyota and Daewoo provided GM with different versions of high-quality, low-cost, small cars. Toyota exercises a dominant influence over its family of suppliers; it usually buys a large portion of their output, often helps finance them, and provides equipment and managerial advice.

Exercising Managerial Control

Parent control is the process through which a parent company ensures that an alliance is managed in a way that conforms to its own interest. The partners often have differing agendas for forming the alliance and their strategic objectives are not identical. In this case, the alliance's efforts and outcomes valued by one partner are not necessarily appreciated by the other. Therefore, for each partner, achieving hands-on control over the alliance's operation confers the right of participation in the alliance's decision making, through which it ensures its strategic goals will be vigorously pursued by the alliance management.[11]

Parent control is realized through equity control and managerial control. We explained earlier that the majority equity holder is generally able to maintain greater equity control over the GSA and this equity control is often reflected in the voting power in board meetings. In routine management, however, it is managerial control rather than equity control that matters. **Managerial control** is the process in which a party influences alliance activities or decisions in a way that is consistent with its own interests through various managerial, administrative, or social tools. The really dominant party in alliance management is the one that dominates managerial control. As noted earlier, the minority equity holder may be able to exercise greater managerial control if it holds a stronger bargaining power over the majority counterpart.[12]

As Exhibit 12–5 shows, mechanisms of managerial control include the following.

1. *Nomination and appointment of key personnel:* Control requires knowledge of events and circumstances. Such knowledge is most readily available to the alliance's parents if it supplies key personnel to run or monitor operations or critical functions such as marketing, R&D, or corporate finance. The appointment of key staff as a control mechanism is especially important to parents that are geographically remote or occupy a minority position.

2. *Meetings of board of directors:* Although a majority equity holder is in an advantageous position in terms of composition and representation on the board, a minority partner can manipulate the frequency of meetings and agenda coverage. In addition, a majority parent cannot consistently overrule or refuse to compromise with its partner without building ill-will and risking the long-term survival of the relationship. Further, minority parents can prevent the majority partner from implementing unilateral decisions by negotiating the inclusion in the alliance contract of veto right over decisions important to their interests (e.g., dividend policy, new investment, transfer pricing, divestment, and selection of key managers). Finally, control at the board level is not simply a matter of votes. It also results from the ability to influence other board members on important issues. This is to a large extent a matter of bargaining power and negotiation skills.

3. *Managerial policies and procedures:* The behavior of executives in a GSA is influenced by various managerial policies and procedures devised by the owners. Since an alliance contract usually does not stipulate these policies and procedures, a minority partner can be more proactive by playing a larger part in formulating and adjusting such policies and procedures. Reward and report systems are particularly effective for the purpose of control. The former determines the incentive structure and performance evaluation, and the latter the information flow, dissemination, and accuracy.

Exhibit 12–5
How to maintain managerial control over alliance activities

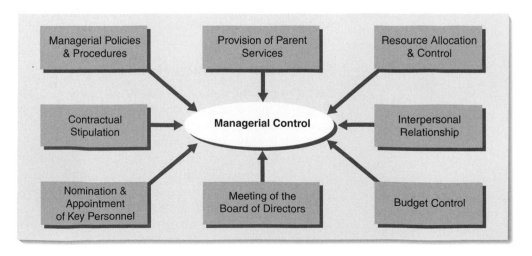

4. *Budget control:* Five aspects of budget control can be implemented: (1) emphasis on the budget during performance evaluations, that is, using quantitative criteria in evaluating divisional manager performance; (2) participation in the budget process, that is, the partner's degree of involvement during budget development; (3) budget incentives, that is, linking pay and promotion prospects to meeting budget goals; (4) budget standard setting difficulty, that is, the difficulty surrounding the setting of budget goals; and (5) budget controllability filters, that is, extenuating factors that are brought into the performance evaluation process. In general, minority partners can use all five budget control mechanisms to increase their overall or specific control over GSA operations and management.

5. *Provision of parent services:* In order to increase the likelihood that specific tasks in the alliance are performed in conformity with their expectations, parent firms may offer staff services and training, sometimes at no cost to the alliance. Such services can be provided irrespective of equity ownership level. Increased control accrues to parent firms in the following ways: (1) greater awareness of the parent to conditions within the GSA because of enhanced dialogue with the alliance employees; (2) increased loyalty from alliance employees who identify more with the parent and have assimilated its ethos; and (3) increased predictability of behavior in the GSA because its managers are more likely to use the guidelines within which they have been trained.

6. *Contract stipulations:* As one of the major mechanisms by which conflicts may be overcome and performance enhanced, contract stipulations serve to reduce managerial complexity in coordinating activities for collective goals; this is an institutionalized mechanism for mitigating opportunism and increasing forbearance. A minority partner can maintain greater control over subsequent GSA operations and management if terms and clauses in the contract are more favorable to that firm. Greater bargaining power and superior negotiation skills result in such favorable conditions. Of various terms and conditions, RRB (responsibility-rights-benefits), managerial rules, and strategic goals are of particular relevance for the minority party that aims to increase control using this approach.

7. *Resource allocation and control:* While resource competence leads to bargaining power, resource allocation and utilization contribute to managerial control. In other words, allocation and control of key resources needed by the GSA are an effective mechanism for a minority party attempting to exert control over the GSA's business activities and management process. This control mechanism is often sustained because control of key resources makes both the GSA's success and the partner company's goal accomplishment dependent upon the firm. Local knowledge is the contribution most consistently associated with a minority share in the original GSA agreement.

8. *Interpersonal relationship:* An MNE can increase its control if it builds and maintains a trustworthy, enduring personal relationship with upper-level managers representing the partner firm. This approach has helped many MNEs, as minority parties, successfully control their GSAs in developing countries. By arranging for managers from local firms to work at foreign headquarters, helping solve personal difficulties they face, or offering favors as needed, foreign companies are able to solidify relationships with local executives who will, in turn, remain loyal to the foreign company. This will eventually promote the foreign company's managerial effectiveness.

Heightening Cooperation

When a GSA is formed, alliance success will depend largely on inter-partner cooperation during subsequent operations and management. Cooperation, however, requires organizational commitments from both parties. Two important mechanisms nurturing cooperation include personal attachment and conflict reduction.

Personal Attachment

Governance mechanisms such as contractual stipulations and managerial control systems are insufficient for controlling opportunism and increasing cooperation. Ongoing business relationships often intermingle with social content, which generates strong expectations of trust. **Personal attachment** reflects socialization and personal relations between senior GSA managers from each party during their involvement in exchange activities. Personal attachment counters the pressure for dissolution, improves trust, and increases alliance duration and stability. Personal attachment is driven by interpersonal relationships as well as interpersonal learning of individual skills and knowledge. Personal attachment can be developed in the following ways:

First, *it is important that friendly personal contact is maintained between the leaders of the cooperating organizations.* This means planning for personal visits between partner chief executives at least once a year. Apart from the intrinsic merit such visits have in ironing out any differences between the partners and laying down broad plans for the future, they are very important in setting an example and establishing a climate of cooperation for the people working within the alliance.

Second, *careful consideration should be given to the length of appointment of key personnel to an alliance.* If this is short, say two years or under, the chances of achieving mutual bonding are reduced. Not only is there personal unfamiliarity to overcome, but, if a language has to be learned or improved, this clearly takes time as well. Personnel with longer-term appointments are also more likely to invest in establishing relationships within the alliance, for they see it as a more significant part of their overall career path. Western, and especially American, companies tend to assign people to alliances on contracts of four years maximum, whereas Japanese companies tend to appoint their people for up to eight years.

Like other alliances, the Fujitsu-Siemens alliance benefits from a close relationship between its leaders.

Third, *careful selection of people who are to work in an alliance will also improve the prospects for mutual bonding.* They should be selected not merely on the basis of technical competence, important though this is, but also on an assessment of their ability to maintain good relationships with people from other organizational and national cultures. Track records can reveal a lot in this respect. Some global companies have, for this reason, now created opportunities for successful alliance and expatriate managers to be able to remain in inter-organizational and international assignments without detriment to their long-term advancement within the home corporation.

Finally, *it is important for the alliance to encourage socializing between the partners' personnel.* Activities such as sports and social events as well as charitable and sponsorship activities in the local community can be helpful in overcoming social barriers. They help to bring about an acceptance of the alliance within its local community, and a strengthening of its external identity.

Reducing Conflicts

Most MNEs concede that conflict in GSAs is inevitable, given the rich diversity of capabilities, cultures, and constraints of each partner. There is likely to be a string of disputes over "hard" financial or technological issues and frictions of a "softer" cultural and interpersonal nature. In both cases, it is important to have mechanisms in place for resolving such conflicts from the very outset of the alliance's existence.

First, *it is important to understand and analyze the actions and/or positions of the partner firm from their perspective, rather than from one's own.* This helps one better appreciate the partner's position on issues and options available to that partner. This approach helped Fuji and Xerox overcome the common dividend dilemmas between the U.S. and Japanese firms. U.S. MNEs generally prefer high dividend payout due to pressure from Wall Street and institutional investors, whereas Japanese shareholders accept low payout in return for profits reinvested for growth. So, by understanding the constraints of both sides, each partner was more willing to opt for the middle ground: Fuji Xerox dividends generally hover around 30 percent of earnings.

Second, *having alliance executives jointly set milestones and principles helps mitigate possible conflicts.* Because many conflicts stem from unclear or misread signals between partners, it is important to jointly develop a set of operating principles for the alliance and establish effective communication systems. The communications system in Fuji Xerox includes a co-destiny task force, presidential summit meetings, functional meetings, resident directors meeting, and personnel exchanges. Such communications channels bridge the differences between Fuji and Xerox. Having regular meetings is an important step to jointly set principles for alliance operations. These meetings should establish the facts of any matters at issue and record the discussion and any solutions proposed. The records of such meetings provide a basis by which problems can be addressed at a higher level between the partners.

Third, *parent firms should steer the alliance clear of the goals and strategies of the parents.* Many executives view conflicts between an alliance and its parent organizations as a potential minefield. A GSA should steer clear of its parents' strategies, geographic expansion, and product lines. For example, many of the difficulties and tensions in the Rolls-Royce, Pratt & Whitney venture of forming International Aero Engines to manufacture V2500 engines stemmed from competitive conflicts with the parents. The V2500, a competitor of CFM International's own products, also compete directly with two Pratt & Whitney (P&W) engines—the JTAT 200 series and the P&W 2037, as well as Rolls-Royce's RB211 engine.

Fourth, *maintaining flexibility is crucial for avoiding conflicts.* It is important to have a formal specification of rules and guidelines that clarify important issues such as financial procedure and technology sharing for those working within the alliance. However, because market and environment conditions change, partners must be adaptable. Although a contract may legally bind partners together, an adherence to a rigid agreement may hamper adaptations. Cultivating a corporate culture that embraces adaptation is important.

Finally, *an understanding of human resource groups in alliances and their typical concerns is key to preventing or mitigating conflicts.* This understanding motivates alliance managers with different cultural backgrounds to be more committed to joint operations and more cooperative with their counterparts. Chapter 17 provides a detailed account of those issues.

Thinking Ahead of Exit

Because GSAs are not required to continue indefinitely, GSA divorce does not necessarily signal failure. It may mean in some cases that the business logic for the alliance no longer applies. Thus, the best scenario of alliance dissolution is that the *venture has already met its strategic goals set by both parties.* In particular, when each party aims to acquire knowledge from the other, this alliance does not have to maintain its longevity. For instance, Hercules and Montedison, two former competitors in polyprophylene products, established an alliance and pooled together $900 million in assets to create Himont in November 1983. Each side enjoyed a competitive advantage in the industry that the other lacked and wanted. Through research and technological breakthroughs, Himont added new properties and applications for polyprophylene and grew worldwide to include more than 3,000 employees, 38 manufacturing plants, and distribution capabilities in 100 countries. As a leader in the chemical industry with a return on equity of 38 percent, Himont earned at least $150 million per annum from new products. After successfully fulfilling its objectives (i.e., learning technologies), Hercules sold its equity stake in Himont to its partner.

In many other cases, nevertheless, GSAs are terminated owing to conflicts or failure to achieve alliance goals. *Differences in strategic or operational objectives often lead to divorce.* In several U.S.–Japanese alliances producing auto parts, U.S. partners often have a narrow focus—to gain access to the Japanese auto transplants in the United States. Their counterparts, however, have broader goals—to secure a foothold in the U.S. market. Similarly, a former alliance between Corning and Ciba-Geigy of Switzerland derailed because of growing differences in the two partners' ambitions and operational objectives.

Differences in managerial styles can be a cause for termination. In the case of the Corning–Vitro alliance, the two partners had different ideas about how to define and provide "service" to customers. Corning was concerned about prompt service to retailers, such as Wal-Mart and Kmart. Vitro, having operated for years in a closed Mexican economy with little competition, was concerned only with product reliability.

Exit may also be attributed to differences in conflict resolution. In many alliances in China, for instance, the Chinese partners prefer not to pre-specify explicit conflict resolution terms, especially judiciary or arbitration resolutions, in an alliance contract. From their perspective, leaving these terms ambiguous may encourage interpartner cooperation in the long term. When partnering with Western firms, however, this ambiguity can lead to alliance termination. For example, in 1994, Lehman Brothers sued Sinochem and Sinopec, the two giant state-owned Chinese firms, for failing to honor their obligations in swap transactions. This accusation, however, was rejected by the Chinese partners who argued there was no explicit stipulation on these transactions in the agreement. As a result of this open confrontation, the partnership between Lehman Brothers and the two Chinese giants ended.

Other reasons underlying the end of GSAs include *inability to meet shifting targets* (e.g., DuPont and Philips terminated their alliance in optical media for this reason), *inability to meet financial requirements* (e.g., financial strains prompted Chrysler to sell its stake in Diamond Star Motors to Mitsubishi), *inability to predict partner competencies* (e.g., AT&T ended its partnership with Philips when it found that Philips NV's clout did not extend far beyond the Dutch market), and *inability to predict regulatory policies* (e.g., Rohm and Hass terminated its electronic chemical alliance with Tokyo Okha Kogyo to accommodate European regulatory concerns about possible overlaps with its pending acquisition of Morton International).

There are generally three forms of termination—*termination by acquisition* (equity transfer), *termination by dissolution,* and *termination by redefinition* of the alliance. In the first case, the alliance is terminated with one of the partners acquiring the stake of the other partner. Termination by acquisition could also take the form of one partner selling its equity stake in the alliance to another company (e.g., British Aerospace selling its equity stake in Rover to BMW), or both partners selling their shares to a third company. Most MNEs prefer reallocation of alliance ownership between existing parent firms. These changes in ownership and resource commitments are a function of both firms' evolving relationships to the venture. Termination by acquisition is most common in international equity alliances. For instance, New Japan Chemical recently agreed to buy out its partner Hercules's share in their alliance, Rika Hercules. After this acquisition, the two partners intend to maintain a friendly relationship including technological exchanges.

In lieu of termination, partners to a GSA may agree to redefine or restructure their original agreement. For example, Matsushita Electric Industries, Co. of Japan (MEI) and Solbourne Computer, Inc. of Colorado entered into an ambitious partnership in 1987 to compete with Sun Microsystem's SPARC computers. When the venture failed, MEI and Solbourne agreed in 1992 to redraft their initial agreement into a more limited partnership arrangement. In this case, redefinition or restructuring of an old alliance may imply creation of a new alliance. In other words, the life cycle of the old alliance has ended while the life cycle of the new alliance has just begun.

To end this chapter, see what CEOs of Corning Incorporated and Emerson Electric say about their experience involving GSAs (see Industry Box).

Interim Summary

1. A GSA is, among other things, a learning tool enabling the investing firms to acquire knowledge from foreign partners. Firms must identify what knowledge they seek and how complementary it is to existing knowledge. To protect sensitive technology from leakage, firms can use walling-off, contractual specification, and cross-licensing techniques.

2. Firms can execute non-equity based control to influence GSAs. The tools of this control include appointment of key personnel, board meetings, managerial policies and procedures, budget control, provision of parent services, contract codification, resource control, and interpersonal relationship.

3. Cooperation can be facilitated by personal attachment between key managers from the parties. Firms should plan ahead for exit strategies with such options as termination by acquisition, termination by dissolution, and termination by redefining the alliance.

INDUSTRY BOX

EXPERIENCE OF BUILDING GSAs IN CORNING AND EMERSON

James R. Houghton, chairman and CEO of Corning Incorporated, identified seven criteria that have helped Corning reach decisions to enter into alliances:

1. Start with a solid business opportunity.

2. Both partners should make comparable contributions to the new alliance.

3. The new alliance should have a well-defined scope and no major conflicts with either parent.

4. Trust is the most important ingredient of the alliance.

5. Management of each parent firm should have the vision and confidence to support the alliance.

6. An autonomous operating team should be formed.

7. Responsibility for alliances cannot be delegated. It must include the CEOs or board-level individuals from one or both partners who can make decisions.

Charles F. Knight, chairman and CEO of Emerson Electric, suggested five rules as pre-venture guidelines:

1. Do not go into business with a company in a turn-around situation.

2. Do not do business with a company that does not have good management.

3. Stick to core competencies.

4. Do a lot of due diligence work.

5. Involve the alliance management in every business plan and deal, and have them report annually to the board of directors.

Source: The Conference Board, 1994. Making International Strategic Alliances Work, Report #1086-94-CH.

1. GSAs have become a pervasive vehicle for MNEs to further their globalization. Whether in the form of equity joint ventures or cooperative joint ventures, GSAs provide MNEs with possible gains such as access to foreign markets, learning from foreign firms, sharing start-up costs and project risks, reducing global competition, and improving local acceptance. Nonetheless, there exist many challenges in forming and managing GSAs.

2. GSAs cannot succeed in the absence of good partners. In selecting local partners, firms must seek a fit between a candidate's capabilities (strategic, organizational, and financial) and their own. Goal compatibility, resource complementarity, cooperative culture, and commitment are also important criteria underlying partner selection.

3. Many GSAs are unstable due to governance problems. Contract specifications and ownership arrangement are two critical ex ante mechanisms counteracting this problem. To what extent a joint venture contract should be specified and covered and in what level the equity ownership should be sought depend on the firm's strategic needs, bargaining power, and market uncertainty.

4. GSAs are like game fields in which both cooperation and control coexist. Firms exercise managerial control to direct GSAs to suit their needs. The minority equity holder can elevate its managerial control as long as it has bargaining power vis-à-vis the other party. Managerial control is achieved through both formal methods (e.g., appointing key personnel, managerial policies, budget control, and contract stipulation) and informal methods (e.g., interpersonal relations and setting board meeting agenda and locations).

5. Interpartner learning is sometimes an overriding intention behind GSAs, especially those in developed countries. After acquiring a partner's knowledge, the firm must integrate it with its own knowledge base. No firm can build a sustained competitive advantage solely on the basis of acquired knowledge.

6. Joint payoffs from GSAs depend in part on trust building and ongoing cooperation. Continued commitment, parent support, mutual compromise and understanding, as well as satisfactory resolution of conflicts are necessary steps toward this end. Informal steps such as socialization (e.g., personal attachment between senior managers from different parties) also encourage cooperation.

7. GSAs are transitional, not permanent, in nature. Thus, firms should be prepared in advance with exit options and procedures. GSAs may be terminated as a result of achieving initial goals for all parties or failing to achieve these goals due to differences in managerial styles, conflict resolution, or strategic orientation. Equity transfer from one party to the other (or third party) is a common approach for termination.

CHAPTER NOTES

[1] A. See Yan and Y. Luo, *International Joint Ventures: Theory and Practice.* Armonk, NY: M. E. Sharpe, 2000; F. J. Contractor and P. Lorange, *Cooperative Strategies in International Business,* Lexington, MA: Lexington Books, 1988; and Y. L. Doz and G. Hamel, *Alliance Advantage.* Boston, MA: Harvard Business School Press, 1998.

[2] Y. L. Doz and G. Hamel, *Alliance Advantage: The Art of Creating Value through Partnering.* Boston, MA: Harvard Business School Press, 1998; J. Bleeke and D. Ernst, "The way to win in cross-border alliances," *Harvard Business Review,* 69(6), 1991, 127–135.

[3] R. M. Kabterm, *When Giants Learn to Dance.* New York: Simon & Schuster, 1989; Y. L. Doz, "The evolution of cooperation in strategic alliances: Initial conditions or learning processes?" *Strategic Management Journal,* 17, Summer 1996; 55–85.

[4] R. B. Reich, "Japan Inc., U.S.A," *The New Republic,* November 26, 1984, 19–23; F. J. Contractor and P. Lorange, "Competition vs. cooperation: A benefit/cost framework for choosing between fully-owned investment and cooperative relationships," *Management International Review,* Special Issue, 1988, 5–18; G. Hamel, "Competition for competence and interpartner learning within international strategic alliances," *Strategic Management Journal,* 12, Summer Special Issue, 1994, 83–103.

[5] S. Goldenberg, *International Joint Ventures in Action: How to Establish, Manage, and Profit from International Strategic Alliances.* London, UK: Hutchinson Business Books, 1988; G. Hamel, Y. L. Doz, and C. K. Prahalad, "Collaborate with your competitors and win," *Harvard Business Review,* January-February, 1989, 133–139.

[6] G. Hamel, "Competition for competence and interpartner learning within international strategic alliances," *Strategic Management Journal,* 12, Summer Special Issue, 1991; 83–103; K. R. Harrigan, *Managing for Joint Venture Success.* Lexington, MA: Lexington Books, 1986.

[7] K. R. Harrigan, *Strategies for Joint Ventures.* Lexington, MA: D. C. Heath, 1985; J. P. Killing, *Strategies for Joint Venture Success.* New York, NY: Praeger, 1983.

[8] P. Lorange and J. Roos, *Strategic Alliances: Formation, Implementation, and Evolution.* Cambridge, MA: Blackwell, 1992; B. Kogut, "Joint ventures: theoretical and empirical perspec-

tives," *Strategic Management Journal,* 9(4), 1988, 319–332; A. C. Inkpen, *The Management of International Joint Ventures: An Organizational Learning Perspective.* London: Routledge, 1995.

[9] P. W. Beamish, "The characteristics of joint ventures in developed and developing countries," *Columbia Journal of World Business,* Fall, 1995, 13–19. P. W. Beamish, *Multinational Joint Ventures in Developing Countries,* New York: Routledge, 1988.

[10] J. L. Badaracco, *The Knowledge Link: How Firms Compete through Strategic Alliances.* Boston: Harvard Business School Press, 1991; G. Hamel, "Competition for competence and inter-partner learning within international strategic alliances," *Strategic Management Journal,* 12, 1991, 83–103; D. Lai, J. W. Slocum, and R. A. Pitts, "Building cooperative advantage: Managing strategic alliances to promote organizational learning," *Journal of World Business,* 32(3), 1997, 203–223.

[11] J. M. Geringer and L. Hebert. "Control and performance of international joint ventures," *Journal of International Business Studies,* 20(2), 1989; 235–254; A. Parkhe, "Strategic alliance structuring: A game theoretic and transaction cost examination of interfirm cooperation," *Academy of Management Journal,* 36, 1993, 794–829.

[12] A. See Yan and Y. Luo, *International Joint Ventures: Theory and Practice.* Armonk, NY: M. E. Sharpe, 2000; Y. Luo, *Entry and Cooperative Strategies in International Business Expansion.* Westport, CT: Quorum Books, 1999; S. H. Park, "Managing an interorganizational network: A framework of the institutional mechanism for network control," *Organization Studies,* 17, 1996, 795–824.

Managing Global Research and Development (R&D)

DO YOU KNOW

1. Why do firms increasingly globalize R&D? What benefits and challenges can you outline for firms that locate and operate R&D laboratories in different countries?

2. What types of foreign R&D units are available for firms to choose from? If you work at Honeywell's corporate technology center in Minneapolis, what type do you think this center belongs to? If this center plans to build a new but specialized lab in Asia, what factors should you consider in opting for its location?

3. How should firms structure and integrate global R&D activities? Can you differentiate, for instance, between polycentric decentralized structure model and global central lab model? If you are a senior manager at Ericsson, which model may you recommend for the company?

4. How do managers of MNEs define autonomy of global R&D units, and what areas of human resource management are particularly important for managing global R&D?

OPENING CASE Managing Global R&D at Nestlé

Nestlé is a research and development leader in the world's food industry. It dedicates 700 million Swiss francs (about US$410 million) per year to basic research and technological development, which are carried out in the Nestlé Research Center (NESTEC), near Lausanne, Switzerland

and in 17 R&D centers around the world. All R&D activity is incorporated into NESTEC, which provides technical assistance to all Nestlé operating units throughout the world. NESTEC brings together more than 550 researchers working in many disciplines such as food science, bioscience, plant science, food technology, food safety, and nutrition. R&D management sets research priorities that determine Nestlé's long-term competencies (category I projects), while Nestlé's strategic business units (SBU) are responsible for prioritizing and monitoring R&D work linked to new product and process developments (category II projects). SBUs have close working relationships with the R&D network as well as with the operating businesses, and take a multifunctional (marketing, research and development, production) approach to setting priorities. SBU R&D coordinators assign the related research project to the most competent R&D group within the network and monitor progress. NESTEC also asked 17 R&D center directors to take on an additional responsibility as product area managers, in order to improve coordination across various R&D centers working in the same product area (milk, chocolate, pet foods, etc.). The product area manager leads the R&D groups and helps them meet their assigned project tasks and deadlines. For example, R&D on pet care is carried out in two R&D centers (in the United States and in France). The U.S. research and development director carries the title of product area manager and is responsible for leading the programs of both units, even though he does not have line responsibility in France. Based on his proposals, human resources may be reallocated across projects. Cross-fertilization is considered the top priority in global R&D management. For example, extrusion (a food processing technology) was originally developed for confectionery and was later adopted by CPW, the breakfast cereal joint venture with General Mills. With the acquisition of Carnation in 1985, Nestlé entered the pet care business. Through NESTEC, it applied extrusion, especially its expertise in die technology, to pet food. The pet care R&D group succeeded in further improving the die technology, which is now being applied to the breakfast cereal joint venture. ■

Source: Abbreviated from The Conference Board, 1995. The Changing Global Role of the Research and Development Function (Report #1123-95-RR).

WHY GLOBALIZE R&D?

Like Nestlé, many MNEs are increasingly dedicating their important resources (financial, technological, and human) to global research and development (R&D) in search of sustained competitive advantages in the global marketplace. At the dawn of the twenty-first century, R&D has been fundamentally globalized, with core innovative capabilities remaining close to corporate headquarters in the home country. Many western MNEs are extending their R&D activities not only in other developed countries but also in developing countries, especially emerging markets (e.g., IBM's R&D center in Beijing, China). At the same time, MNEs from newly industrialized nations such as Asia's mini-dragons (South Korea, Singapore, Taiwan, and Hong Kong) have begun to relocate many R&D activities abroad.

Globalizing R&D is a process of locating and operating R&D laboratories in different countries, under a coordinated and integrated system by the company's headquarters, in order to leverage the technical resources of each facility to further the company's overall technological capabilities and competitive advantage. For example, Exxon developed a synthetic base stock for formulating high-performance engine oils through the collaboration of process research laboratories in Canada and Louisiana, and a product development laboratory in the United Kingdom. While the two terms are often used interchangeably, *globalizing R&D* differs from *internationalizing R&D*. The former requires global integration of geographically dispersed R&D laboratories or centers, but the latter does not. From this standpoint, internationalizing R&D is an early stage of globalizing R&D, which evolves as a firm's international expansion grows larger and more complex in scale and scope. The R&D function serves as the key avenue for building and sustaining a company's global competitive advantage. MNEs with a well-designed strategy on globalizing R&D tend to achieve superior sales and profit performance.[1]

R&D intensity (i.e., total R&D expenditure relative to total sales during the same period) has been steadily increasing in many industries such as electronics, pharmaceuticals, chemicals, and medical equipment. For instance, the average R&D intensity relative to sales by global pharmaceutical MNEs was about 4.7 percent in 1977 but 14 percent in 2000. While American MNEs lead in innovation in many high-technology industries such as automobiles, computers, software, health care, and advanced materials, MNEs from Europe, Canada, Japan, and newly industrialized countries such as Korea, Taiwan, and Israel also demonstrate high R&D level and inventive productivity. The number of patents developed by worldwide MNEs surged in recent years (see Exhibit 13–1). The main thrust of global firms has been to increase the patent output per unit of R&D spending.[2]

Managing global R&D receives greater attention by international business managers for these reasons: First, *technology is recognized as a major source of global competitive advantage*. International R&D expands and augments the overall R&D process

Exhibit 13–1

Top patenting MNEs in 2000 and 2001

Rank in 2001	Firm	Number of Patents Granted in 2001	Rank in 2000	Number of Patents Granted in 2000
1	IBM	3411	1	2886
2	NEC	1953	2	2021
3	Canon	1877	3	1890
4	Micron	1643	7	1304
5	Samsung	1450	4	1441
6	Matsushita	1440	11	1137
7	Sony	1363	6	1385
8	Hitachi	1271	13	1036
9	Mitsubishi	1184	14	1010
10	Fujitsu	1166	10	1147

Source: U.S. Patent & Trademark Office, Washington, DC, 2002.

of the firm. Second, *the nature of the technological innovation process has changed.* Technological innovations are often the result of the integration of technologies from different disciplines (an example is the convergence of electronic, telecommunication, and information technologies). As illustrated in Chapter 5, countries differ in their competitive advantage, and the globalization of R&D enables firms to tap these various sources of strength. Third, *time is a critical competitive factor in a number of industries.* R&D activities are decentralized to accelerate the process of innovation and adaptation. Finally, *the growth of network and information exchange systems facilitates long-distance communication,* which lowers coordination costs associated with globalizing R&D activities.

Globalizing R&D is also a strategic response to changes in international markets. Along with a shortened product life cycle in many industries, foreign customers demand higher levels of technical service and customized products. Targeting and

R&D investment has paid off for Asian manufacturers who are global market leaders in plasma TVs.

developing regional markets, such as the European Union, LAFTA (Latin American Free Trade Association), and CACM (Central American Common Market) may offer greater rewards for modifying products to meet market requirements. To gain access to cutting-edge technologies developed by foreign companies or improve the adaptability of their own innovations, MNEs send their own engineers and scientists to on-site laboratories. The globalization process is moving up the R&D value chain from technology support to product development and further to technology development. This indicates the increasingly important role assumed by foreign facilities in the creation of knowledge. Leading MNEs such as IBM, Philips, and Matsushita are expanding their networks worldwide. IBM, for instance, recently announced that it will open a new center of excellence in India which will focus on key technologies such as electronic commerce, cellular and mobile telephony, and distance learning.

Two distinctive patterns pertaining to globalizing R&D have emerged. First, while in the past the technology flow was unidirectional from the parent company to the affiliate abroad, *firms are now considering foreign R&D units as a critical source of knowledge and technology.* These units are assigned new tasks associated with the parent firm's global strategy. A part of these new tasks may involve deriving distinctive new product variants as part of a regional or world product mandate, or if a unique global product is envisaged, providing research input into its development. Second, *interorganizational technology cooperation has become a widespread practice.* Such cooperation exists not only between the firms, but also between firms and academic institutions at home and abroad. Apart from cost and resource sharing rationale, such cooperation is compelled by the increasing demand for skilled scientists and R&D personnel who are in short supply in the home countries (e.g., Japan).

Benefits and Challenges of Global R&D

The following benefits may be generated from globalizing R&D:

First, *globalizing R&D may provide a vehicle for access to, or extract benefits from, a target country's technical resources, scientific talent, or local expertise.* Israel, for instance, counts twice as many scientists (as a percentage of the population) as the United States, and is a very attractive country for companies that seek skilled engineers and researchers. MNEs such as IBM have established joint ventures or set up labs there, despite a fairly small local market for their products. MNEs may also receive benefits such as tax breaks and low interest financing offered by host governments (e.g., Indonesia, Malaysia, and Thailand) when they set up R&D centers overseas. The Country Box illustrates how India's rich pool of software engineers has lured many world-class MNEs to build global R&D centers there.

Second, globalizing R&D *may enhance a firm's global competitive advantage.* Building and maintaining a competitive position abroad necessitates localizing R&D in target countries, which improves proximity and responsiveness to local customers. Setting up research facilities in a host country signals long-term commitment to the local economy. For example, General Motors was selected, among several world-class automakers, by the Chinese government to build midsize cars in a joint venture with the Shanghai Automotive Industry Corporation because the U.S. company offered to set up a technology institute in China. Today, GM's R&D center in Warren, Michigan, coordinates and integrates the work being conducted at six Chinese universities and seven joint ventures. By locating R&D activity abroad, an MNE is able to improve its responsiveness to local needs both in terms of time and relevance. Hoffmann-LaRoche, the Swiss-based pharmaceutical company, established an R&D facility in Japan to become more aware of and responsive to consumption differences in Asia. Increased investments by MNEs in India, Brazil, Poland, and Mexico created a strong need for technical support and local adaptation abroad, which in many cases requires the presence of a permanent R&D group for expanded operations.

India

R&D CENTERS OF
GLOBAL COMPANIES IN INDIA

Since 1997, a large number of global firms, especially those in the information technology (IT) industry, have started R&D centers in India to access research resources there, particularly a large pool of software engineers. Most global R&D centers are concentrated in Bangalore (e.g., IBM, Lucent, HP, Sony, Siemens, Telesoft, Philips, Texas Instruments, LG, Sun Micro, Verifone, SAP, Huawei), with several others located in Hyderabad (e.g., Motorola, Nokia, Bell Labs, Microsoft), Mumbai (e.g., Gateway, Informix, Shimadzu, E-gain), or Delhi (e.g., Oracle and Adobe). MNEs in Bangalore serve both as producers and consumers of software, turning the city into an international gateway for trained manpower. Bangalore has become the largest IT cluster in India, attributable to the presence of educational institutions, state support, venture capital, and an extensive network of technology developers and providers. Many prestigious research institutes such as the Indian Institute of Science, Jawaharlal Center for Advanced Scientific Research, National Aerospace Laboratory, Central Manufacturing Technology Institute, Aeronautical Research Center, and Central Power Research Institute are located in Bangalore.

The growth of Bangalore as an IT cluster was catalyzed by the founding of the first global R&D center by U.S. firm Texas Instruments (TI). Originally founded in 1985, the center consists of 500 engineers specially trained in the design of circuits. In 1998 this center began to design digital signal processors (DSPs), the fastest growing sector of the global semiconductor market. It also designs chips, specifically Application Specific Integrated Circuits (ASICs). Fabrication is carried out in TI's U.S. facility, with the designs being encrypted and transmitted from India through a dedicated satellite link. The establishment of the TI India R&D center was one of the reasons for Bangalore becoming a software hub, since TI gave R&D contracts to other firms such as Wipro and Sasken, thus acting as a catalyst for knowledge networking. Wipro is a leading Indian IT firm and a major exporter of software from India. Wipro has a R&D division consisting of 3,000 engineers exclusively working on telecom.

Finally, *globalizing R&D may enable the MNE to enjoy the benefits arising from international division of labor in R&D among multiple foreign countries or regions.* A well-coordinated MNE is able to allocate specific responsibilities to different yet integrated R&D subsidiaries depending upon their expertise, knowledge, and external resources. This multilateral cooperation enables the firm to obtain a more varied flow of new ideas, products, and processes, providing greater input into a firm's innovation process. This also creates a synergy earned from comparative advantages in R&D resources from each participating nation. Canon, for example, built technical centers in Shanghai (China), interactive systems in Surrey (United Kingdom), software systems in California (United States), imaging technology in Sydney (Australia), telecommunications in Rennes (France), and process development centers in Japan. This individually specialized yet globally integrated network nurtures synergy creation from global research and development.

Globalizing R&D is a complex process involving a series of challenges and difficulties. Globalizing R&D generally creates the following challenges:

First, *maintaining minimum efficient scale in foreign R&D operations is not always easy.* It may be difficult to staff the foreign labs with enough qualified people to achieve the minimum efficient scale. In addition, splitting up an MNE's most qualified people over numerous international R&D sites might dilute the critical mass at the home-based, centralized R&D facility. Further, government controls and political risks in a host country may increase the uncertainty of R&D operations. It may create a schism between an MNE's motivations and those of a local government. In certain developing countries where import restrictions exist, it may also be difficult to import the necessary research materials. Hiring local employees may also be subject to governmental control.

Second, *the leakage of proprietary knowledge poses a serious threat when R&D is globalized.* This may arise because of the presence of a foreign joint venture partner, lax patent laws in the country, or perhaps the likelihood of foreign nationals being hired away by indigenous firms after they have acquired much of the MNE's expertise. McDonnell Douglas and Boeing faced such leakage risks when they partnered with Japanese firms on the F-15 Eagle fighter and the Boeing 767. Maintaining the confidentiality of technical information and knowledge is difficult and costly.

Finally, *globalizing R&D inevitably increases coordination and control costs.* An MNE may face coordination issues such as allocating research tasks among dispersed R&D centers, exchanging information among different R&D centers, and developing products that are responsive to market needs in different countries. The more decentralized and distant an MNE's R&D facilities, the more costly the coordination and control necessary for the arrangement to succeed. If R&D is done in just one country, there are fewer language and cultural barriers to surmount as well as a shorter distance to be covered in order to hold face-to-face meetings. Lack of coordination and control can easily lead to costly duplication of effort since different facilities may not be fully aware of what others are doing. In addition, cultural and business differences between home and host countries may intensify the difficulty in running R&D activities overseas. For example, the relationship between engineers and managers is very different in the United States, Japan, and Europe. In the United States, managers traditionally hold less authority over engineers working under them than is the case in Japan and Europe. Problem solving also differs across countries. In Europe, it is customary to discuss problems and solutions before cost figures are considered, whereas Americans first wish to know whether a program is financially feasible.

Despite these challenges, we have witnessed increased globalization of R&D activities as MNEs become more internationalized. To most of them, overseas R&D activities have added net value to their growth in the global marketplace and created sustained competitive advantages over local and international competitors.[3] To obtain the advantages of global R&D while attenuating its disadvantages requires well-prepared design and structuring in the building phase and well-established systems of management, coordination, communication, and control in the operational phase. Managing global R&D activities is difficult and complex, requiring the consideration of multiple factors in formulating strategies and policies concerning R&D dispersion and control. These factors include not only the dynamics of external environments, such as market demands and governmental policies, but also the requirements of organizational development, such as the firm's strategic goals and internal rationales behind research and development. A firm's global R&D system should be structured to fulfill organizational needs while taking advantage of external opportunities. Internally, the R&D function faces an ongoing task of managing coordination and control across the company's international network of R&D laboratories. Externally, corporate R&D is increasingly called upon to create and manage technological cooperation with universities, research consortia, and even competitors in order to stay abreast of leading edge developments. It is equally essential for the firm to manage such critical areas as communication and coordination, human resource management, technology transfer, and collaboration with local firms, among others. Without such management, the economic return of R&D dispersion cannot be ensured. We elaborate on these issues in the following section.

Interim Summary

1. An increasing number of MNEs have globalized R&D to take advantage of the expertise available in foreign markets as well as to be responsive to the demands of those markets. Firms view foreign R&D units as a critical source of knowledge and an important vehicle for intra-MNE knowledge sharing and utilization.

2. Globalizing R&D involves challenges such as high costs, knowledge leakage, and coordination difficulty. Overcoming these challenges necessitates a well-designed global structure and a carefully planned organizational scheme.

DESIGNING AND STRUCTURING GLOBAL R&D

Type of Foreign R&D Units

Defining the type of a planned foreign R&D program is the first step in globalizing R&D. In relation to the role of foreign R&D units, R&D subsidiaries can be categorized into (1) *corporate technology units,* (2) *specialized or regional technology units,* (3) *global technology units,* (4) *technology transfer units,* and (5) *indigenous technology units.*

A *corporate technology unit* is designed to generate basic, long-term technology of exploratory nature for use by the corporate parent. *A specialized technology unit* is set to develop specialized technologies, products, or processes predefined by headquarters to serve either the global or regional market. *A global technology unit* is generally established for developing new products and processes for major world markets. *A technology transfer unit* focuses on facilitating the transfer of the corporate parent's technology to a subsidiary and providing local technical services. Finally, *an indigenous technology unit* is formed overseas to develop new products specifically for the local market.

Technology transfer units and indigenous technology units are both locally adapting laboratories. The major function of these two units is to help the production and marketing facilities in a host country make the most efficient use of the MNE's existing technology. They may also assist the process of technology transfer by advising on necessary adaptation of the manufacturing technology. They may act as technical service center by examining why a product may not fully satisfy a local market and by adapting it to better meet local needs. Exxon, CPC International, and Otis, for example, used this technique in the development of products for the European market. When indigenous technology units are designed to serve a key foreign market, they become locally integrated laboratories and involve some fundamental development activities. The particular host market (e.g., China) may be considerably large, diverse, and fast-growing and may necessitate a nationwide R&D head office to coordinate and integrate host-country R&D activities. IBM's R&D center in Beijing or Xerox's R&D center in Shanghai are playing such a role.

Corporate technology units and global technology units are both globally interdependent laboratories. These two types of labs provide inputs into a centrally defined and coordinated R&D program, with no necessary connection with host-country production operations. Their major function focuses on research and development, rather than improvement and adaptation. They link mainly to corporate and divisional R&D, not local manufacturing. CPC International's R&D affiliates in Italy and Japan, and Eastman Kodak's R&D unit in Australia are examples of successful corporate technology units. IBM, on the other hand, has established several global technology units worldwide (each focusing on certain product-technology area) developing a product or process that will have universal applicability in all major foreign and domestic markets. This approach has served IBM well since the 1970s.

Specialized technology units are globally controlled yet individually differentiated laboratories. Each of these specialized units is focused on specific technological areas defined by headquarters. Daimler-Benz (now DaimlerChrysler), for example, has its corporate research center in Stuttgart, Germany. Its R&D center in Palo Alto, near Stanford University in Silicon Valley, focuses on applying the latest communication technologies in the company's vehicles. Its R&D center in Bangalore, India, emphasizes the development of multimedia, telematics, and manufacturing solutions. In Shanghai, the automaker's joint R&D center was established to focus on microelectronics and electronic packaging. These R&D activities are tightly coordinated with microelectronics research in Germany, and scientists are exchanged between China and Germany on a regular basis. Regional technology units are regionally integrated laboratories. In contrast to specialized units that focus on specific technological areas, regional units are responsible for respective geographical areas. Both specialized and regional units are subject to the control and coordination of headquarters.

R&D unit designation may change over time as international expansion increases, the R&D subsidiary grows, or the MNE's strategy changes. The global R&D function may evolve in stages, along the degree of the MNE's internationalization. In the initial stage, firms may dedicate few technical resources overseas, and maintain domestically oriented management structures and a highly ethnocentric management group. As their commitment to overseas markets grows, companies build up technical capabilities abroad to respond to local market conditions, either by modifying the parent's products or by generating products for sale only in the local market. When the headquarters realizes that the overseas labs have achieved a level of technical competence beyond that of the rest of the company, it may switch its overseas laboratories' orientation from the host-country markets to the world market. The headquarters may assign new product development projects to overseas labs to take advantage of their specialized technical skills. In this situation, foreign R&D units benefit simultaneously from a wide variety of environmental conditions that stimulate new product development as well as from intracompany collaborations that create synergetic returns for the company as a whole.

Selecting R&D Location

Choosing a R&D location is an important and complex decision because external parameters such as market conditions, resource availability, and governmental policies vary across countries and even locations within a country. Once a laboratory is built, the costs of switching from one location to another are enormous. The location selection framework presented in Chapter 10 is generally applicable to the R&D site decision. Nevertheless, the following factors are specific in the location choice of overseas R&D:

First, *location selection depends on an R&D subsidiary's strategic role set by the parent company*. If the subsidiary is designed to serve a home market, managers should consider the availability of scientific knowledge and talent from foreign universities. For a subsidiary targeting the world market, location factors include accessibility to foreign scientific communities and availability of adequate infrastructure and universities.[4] When the subsidiary serves only as a technology transfer center, it should be located in countries where the company already has a substantial investment in marketing and/or manufacturing. R&D generally follows marketing and manufacturing in the globalization process. In cases where the labs are established to perform basic research or develop new products for the global market, they should be situated in places in which there is a concentration of advanced innovation and technology resources. This concentration is an important reason why MNEs tend to cluster their technology development centers into several hot spots, as illustrated in the examples in Exhibit 13–2.

Second, *host governmental policies may influence location decision.* Some of these policies include: government requirements to increase the local technological content of the firm's activities; work permit regulations for expatriate scientists, engineers, and managers; efficient patent laws; and tax subsidies to support the foreign firm's R&D activities. In the 1990s, many developing countries established high-tech development zones to attract MNEs' R&D investments. These zones offer a series of incentives to foreign companies such as tax exemption for a certain number of years, financing support from government-owned banks, reduction of land rent expenses, and priority in acquiring local resources. Government itself may also organize some high-profile research consortia soliciting foreign participation. In the United States, for example, the Microelectronics and Computer Technology Corporation, Semiconductor Research Corporation, and Semateck consortia focus on technologies in microelectronics and semiconductors. In Europe, broader consortia were fostered through the European Strategic Program for Research and Development in Information Technology (ESPRIT), Research Development in Advanced Communications Technology for Europe (RACE), and European Research Coordinating Agency (EUREKA), to name a few.

Third, *the local infrastructure and technological level of a foreign country are critical.* A threshold of technological capability must exist in the country to permit R&D to take place. Some MNEs may wish to start tapping into technology that is more advanced. For example, Germany is a world leader in such areas as chemistry, physics, metallurgy, and medicine, while Britain has traditionally spent heavily in chemicals and pharmaceuticals. The presence of research universities or local firms with advanced technology becomes important in these circumstances (see the Industry Box about Ford in Aachen).

Finally, *sociocultural factors may affect location selection.* MNEs have shown a preference for locating R&D facilities in nations with a similar culture and language,[5] which makes sense considering the difficulties associated with operating any busi-

Exhibit 13–2
Hot spots in the U.S. for technology development

Location	Technology	Major Companies
Albuquerque, NM	Chips	Intel, Motorola, Philips, Honeywell
Austin, TX	Computers, software biotechnology	IBM, Samsung, Motorola, TI, 3M
Boston, MA	Computers, telecom, biotechnology	Hundreds of start-ups
Orange County, CA	Computers, Electronics	Over 300 high-tech start-ups
Huntsville, AL	Aerospace	Cummings, Honeywell, Hughes Lockheed, UTC
Portland, OR	Electronics	Intel, Tektronix, US West
Research Triangle Park, NC	Pharmaceuticals, micro-electronics, computer, telecom, biotechnology	98 research companies
San Francisco Bay	Software, computers, electronics	HP, Intel, Xerox, Oracle, Sun, Silicon Graphics
Seattle, WA	Aerospace, communications biotechnology, software	Boeing, Microsoft

Source: Adapted from V. Comello. Hot high-tech locations, in www.rdmag.com. 1998.

FORD LOCATES ITS R&D CENTER IN AACHEN, GERMANY

Ford chose Aachen in Germany as its new European R&D location partly because of its proximity to one of the most industrialized regions in Europe. Aachen is centrally positioned in the heart of Europe, allowing for close cooperation with more than 40 universities in 16 different countries. Aachen is also home to one of the major prestigious technical universities in Europe (RWTH Aachen), enabling Ford to easily recruit highly qualified scientists and engineers. Technical cooperation with local universities and institutes facilitates the acquisition of new technologies and supports strategic technology monitoring. Aachen, which is located close to the Netherlands, Belgium, and France, serves as an ideal listening post for the notoriously diverse European tastes and expectations. Ford finds it easier to design and develop product variants or to monitor European Community politics from Aachen than from other locations. Today, there are about 130 researchers from 20 different countries, working on sophisticated technologies to meet the growing demand for personal mobility, safety improvement, and emission control.

ness in a different cultural and social environment. It can be frustrating to operate in an environment where the most basic cultural, social, and business practices (which are taken for granted in one's home country) are quite different. Furthermore, the decision makers in headquarters should consider the attractiveness of the foreign country's lifestyle to the staff that will be assigned overseas. If the general consensus is that the location is undesirable, it may be difficult to find qualified people willing to work abroad. Because R&D development largely depends on the creativity and efficiency of human resources, the working and living conditions overseas may determine the expatriates' incentives and commitments (see also Chapter 17).

Structuring Global R&D Activities

In order to ensure global R&D success, MNEs must design an appropriate organizational structure governing R&D activities. Two critical factors should be considered in structuring global R&D operations: (1) *the level of authority an MNE plans to provide to its foreign R&D activities,* and (2) *the scope of geographical market to be covered.* Building on these two axes (autonomy level and market breadth), five models can be identified. They are: (1) *ethnocentric centralized,* (2) *polycentric decentralized,* (3) *specialized lab,* (4) *global central lab,* and (5) the *globally integrated network.* Exhibit 13–3 displays these five forms. You may note that these are choices about overall organizational structure governing an MNE's worldwide R&D, whereas the five types of global R&D units illustrated earlier are choices about a role played by a specific R&D laboratory within an MNE's global R&D network. A specific R&D lab is positioned within this network to help fulfill an MNE's overall goal in research and development. Each of these forms serves as an organizational framework in which different R&D units may be designed with different roles and types.

In the *ethnocentric centralized* R&D structure, all major R&D activities are concentrated in one home country. This structure contains a corporate technology unit at home, and may also include a few technology transfer units to distribute centralized R&D results to local operations. In this model, the core technologies are viewed as a national treasure in the home country base, designing products that are subsequently manufactured in other locations and distributed worldwide. This structure ensures technology protection and enhances returns to scale in R&D. Its dis-

Exhibit 13-3
Organizational models for global R&D

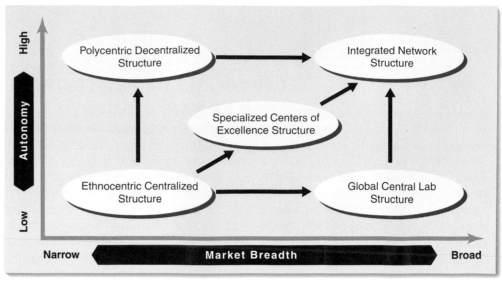

advantage is the lack of sensitivity to signals from foreign markets and insufficient consideration of local market demands. MNEs choose this structure only if they manufacture global, standardized products and do not consider differentiating between foreign markets. Nippon Steel of Japan, for example, has adopted this structure because its products are highly standardized in international markets. The company has four centralized R&D laboratories near Tokyo (about 1,000 researchers). This structure helps the company reduce costs considerably.

The *polycentric decentralized* R&D structure is characterized by a decentralized federation of R&D sites with no supervising corporate R&D center. This structure contains a number of indigenous technology units in major foreign markets. Foreign R&D laboratories are highly autonomous with little incentive to share information with other R&D units or central R&D. Overseas R&D laboratories emphasize product or process development in response to localization requests and local consumer demands. Royal Dutch/Shell, for example, used this structure during 1984–1997 to develop Carilon, a multiple-application polymer, in Shell's three decentralized R&D units, including Amsterdam R&D center, Westhollow Research center in Houston, and Belgium R&D laboratory. In this structure, efforts to preserve autonomy and national identity may impede cross-border coordination, and therefore lead to inefficiency on a corporate level and to duplication of R&D activities. The company may also lose its focus on a particular technology. Shell, therefore, restructured this R&D system in 1998 and authorized the Westhollow Research Center in Houston to lead in developing Carilon with other centers focusing on commercialization.

In the *specialized laboratory* structure, foreign R&D units are assigned global mandates. The aim is to improve the global efficiency of the product development process, concentrating in a single location the resources relevant to development operations in a particular product category. This structure contains several specialized technology units in respective product areas. When there exists a leading market in terms of size and presence of customers, the MNE will assign the global responsibility for developing and manufacturing the product to the laboratories and plant in that country. This approach makes it possible to achieve economies of scale in R&D and to place the product development operations close to the company's key customers. For example, Alcatel acquired Rockwell Company's R&D laboratory in the United States, the most sophisticated telecom market, and used it as the primary research base for its transmission systems. Because there are costs in transferring R&D to a manufacturing plant that is farther away from the R&D center, global development laboratories are often selected on the basis of their proximity to the manufacturing plants. For instance, Ericsson specializes its R&D facilities on the basis of their historical background and major area of technical specialization; for example, R&D on silicon technology and chip design is done in Australia, Italy, and Finland; and R&D on mobile telephone systems is carried out in Germany, France, Spain, and Greece. Similarly, the organization of R&D at Siemens is based on worldwide centers of competence laboratories selected on the basis of their traditional scientific specialization and competence, and given worldwide responsibilities. Siemens' Italian subsidiary is a worldwide competence center for microwave radio systems and cellular telephones.

The *global central lab* structure is used to leverage a company's centralized technical resources to create new global products. Although it is also centralized, R&D under this structure covers a much broader market domain than R&D in the ethnocentric centralized model. In this structure, there may be more than one global technology unit to generate worldwide innovation. In this model, companies concentrate their technical resources in their country of origin. To make this structure work, it is important to create an effective market information network that provides a flow of information from the decentralized production or marketing units to the parent company. This enables the central development laboratories to generate products suitable for the global market and/or to adapt different product versions to individual markets. Nissan, for example, implemented this model in the early 1990s. In the development of the Primera automobile, targeted for the European market, Nissan formed a core project team in western Europe. Back in Japan, this team was supported by some 100 engineers who had all experienced European culture during numerous visits.

The *globally integrated network* structure may be filled by a number of foreign R&D units with different roles and types, such as global technology unit, corporate technology unit, specialized technology unit, and indigenous technology unit. In this model, home R&D is no longer the center of control for all R&D activities, but rather one among many interdependent R&D units that are closely interconnected by means of flexible and varied coordination mechanisms. A central coordinating body exercises the necessary supervision to prevent duplication and to integrate the diverse contributions. Development processes whose results can be exploited across a number of markets involve resources from the different facilities whose work is coordinated according to a common plan. Each unit in the network specializes in a particular product, component, or technology area, and perhaps a set of core capabilities. At times, this unit takes over a lead role as a competence center, and is then responsible for the entire value generation process, not just for product-related R&D. Schindler Lifts, the worldwide leader in escalators and second in elevators, established its integrated R&D network in 1996. Its R&D is dispersed over several units in Switzerland, France, Spain, Sweden, and the United States. In order to avoid duplication and to realize synergy, its management has started to identify the core competencies in R&D. Each of the designated competence centers in the integrated R&D network assumes strategic roles for the entire company and is engaged in defining strategies and business development. Various MNEs, including Nestlé, Philips, and Bayer, moved from a polycentric decentralized organization toward an integrated R&D network.

Interim Summary

1. Foreign R&D units can be defined as one of the following types: corporate technology units, specialized or regional technology units, global technology units, technology transfer units, and indigenous technology units. To select an

R&D location, managers must consider an intended role of the R&D unit, host government policies, and infrastructural, technological, and sociocultural conditions.

2. Structuring global R&D depends on the level of decentralization offered to foreign R&D activities and the scope of geographical market covered by foreign units. Five structuring models are: ethnocentric centralized model; polycentric decentralized model; specialized lab model; global central lab model; and globally integrated network model.

MANAGING AND OPERATING GLOBAL R&D

The increasing dispersion of R&D laboratories in foreign markets forces MNEs to take a global view in managing their research operations through such areas as human resource management, autonomy specification, global planning, and communications improvement.

Human Resource Management

Chapter 17 discusses human resource management policies, many of which are applicable to managing human resources in global R&D. Nevertheless, R&D human resources should be managed in a way that fulfills the unique needs of global research and development. First, *selecting key personnel should be linked to the role or type of a foreign R&D unit*. If the laboratory belongs to an indigenous technology unit, for example, then well-qualified local talents should be considered for both R&D and management positions. If the lab is to accept technology from the parent company or belongs to a specialized or global technology unit, then qualified expatriates are preferable. Second, *personnel policies for foreign labs should be relatively standardized to the extent allowed by local laws and customs*. Promotions, titles, and reward and recognition programs should be as similar as possible. Because there should be frequent contact between home and overseas lab personnel, this uniformity of titles and managerial positions can help make foreign labs feel they are equal partners with the parent laboratories. Reward and recognition programs that are instituted at headquarters should be extended to include all the overseas laboratory personnel. Third, *maintaining some regular contacts and visits between foreign R&D units and the home lab center is useful*. This can take several forms: a visit to exchange information, an extended visit to work out a particularly difficult problem or to exploit a new discovery, or a regularly scheduled planning conference. 3M, for example, schedules regular conferences between U.S. R&D and Japanese engineering groups. In addition, 3M's Japanese R&D subsidiary often sends its laboratory and production personnel to their counterpart labs and factories in the United States for up to six months of training on equipment similar to what is being built in Japan.

Autonomy Setting

In the context of this chapter, autonomy means an R&D unit's decision-making power concerning R&D activities. *The autonomy of a foreign R&D unit depends largely on the role it plays within the MNE network*. For example, managerial autonomy in a lab that serves as a specialized global competence center should be delegated greater power. In general, autonomy should be higher if the lab's technical resources are scarce, need to be located together in a center of excellence to attain critical mass, or should be put to use where they would create the most leverage for the company as a whole. When a foreign R&D unit serves as a technology transfer unit for the

MNE network, its autonomy will be low and the decision-making authority will be centralized at headquarters. In this situation, the unit plays a role as effective adopter of new products and processes created by the parent company. If the unit functions as an indigenous, specialized technology laboratory, or global technology center, it requires a high level of autonomy and a low level of formalization (i.e., specifying the necessary behaviors in the form of rules, procedures, or programs). The subsidiaries require increased degrees of freedom and more resources dispensed by the parent companies. Some R&D subsidiaries of companies such as Unilever, ITT, and Philips enjoy considerable strategic and operational autonomy, although headquarters exercises administrative control through the budgeting and financial reporting systems. These relatively autonomous subsidiaries were found to be generally more productive than other R&D units in these companies.[6]

The autonomy of a foreign R&D unit is subordinating an MNE's strategic needs for global integration. There are positive associations between creation, adoption, and diffusion of innovations by a subsidiary and the extent to which the subsidiary is normatively integrated with the parent company and shares its overall strategy, goals, and values. Such integration is typically the result of a high degree of organizational socialization and is achieved through extensive travel and transfer of managers between the headquarters and the subsidiary, and through joint-work in teams, task forces, and committees. Ericsson, Procter and Gamble (P&G), and NEC are convinced that these activities have helped them in developing a common context that significantly improves subsidiary contributions to the entire innovation processes.

Resource allocation is a crucial vehicle in balancing global integration and local autonomy for managing dispersed R&D units abroad. Generally, resources allocated to global technology units or specialized technology units may be those involved in a core competency, strategic and exploratory research, global market coverage, or significant investment areas. Resources likely to be duplicated in regional R&D centers are those that focus primarily on product development as opposed to technology development. In addition to technological factors, considerations such as financial and geopolitical factors play a large role in determining proper allocation of resources. For example, Philips has set up an R&D facility in Palo Alto, California, as a window on Silicon Valley for all of its divisions and business units. Finally, in aligning resources, it is important to consider the interface between human resources and physical resources in a new information technology environment. Networks connecting a company's facilities throughout the world enable researchers to work on one project from many locations. The major innovations that have been made in modeling and simulation technology allow more development and testing to be done in simulation, reducing the time and money spent on manufacturing prototypes or running tests on finished products.

Global Planning

The corporate R&D office has the important task of coordinating an increasingly dispersed global network of R&D laboratories. Global planning serves as a primary means of information exchange among decentralized R&D laboratories and projects. In the planning process, corporate headquarters outlines a strategic intent to globalize R&D and communicate it to foreign R&D units. Matshushita, for example, established a three-pillars blueprint, including:

- Construction of a tri-pole R&D *network* between laboratories in North America and Europe and domestic research laboratories to establish advanced technological bases and create products for the global market
- Improved *efficiency* of R&D activities through expansion of collaborative relationships with international research institutions

■ Increased *speed* of R&D globalization through effective communications and superior management across borders

R&D planning activities can also contribute to learning throughout the MNE if they routinely solicit the participation of all scientists and technicians. The central R&D office can transform planning into an educational process. For example, Lucent holds biennial internal scientific conferences in which scientists exchange information with one other, and with strategic planning and business units. Planning activities can also facilitate global integration. Johnson & Johnson's Global Product Category Planning Groups provide a mechanism for incorporating foreign markets' product development priorities, which were often ignored in the past. Although budgeting is considered increasingly difficult because development cycles are five years long or more, global planning is easier owing to the ability to disseminate information and establish priorities.

Planning can help align the technological and business strategies of a company. Once the technology strategy is set, this alignment can be carried into specific project areas. A key aspect of R&D alignment on business objectives is cross-functional planning and execution. With the participation of marketing, manufacturing, and sales, R&D groups can optimize their process of project assessment, selection, and project portfolio balancing. Progress on R&D projects can also be evaluated more regularly and reported to multi-function teams. Nestlé's research center at Swiss headquarters sets budget and planning priorities through multi-functional strategic business units in close collaboration with operating businesses. After evaluating incoming development and product proposals through extensive information sharing, strategic business units (SBUs) set short- and medium-term priorities. Annual R&D work programs are updated and corrected on a rolling basis throughout the year.

It is usually impractical to combine product development, manufacturing, and R&D within the same organizational unit. This is particularly true in very large companies. Corporations such as IBM, General Foods, and Xerox have established committees or boards with coordination responsibility throughout the entire corporation. Membership in these committees is composed of representatives from business units, manufacturing, and R&D. AT&T has begun to experiment with having research managers at AT&T Labs report to both research management and product units. This new alignment is intended to improve the coupling between business and research. It is also designed to reduce the "time to market" between invention and product introduction.

Communication Improvement

Geographic distance poses a major challenge for communication across an international network of R&D labs. Cross-border communication breakdowns occur frequently, lowering R&D productivity. Moreover, the role of informal communication is especially important because much of the work can be accomplished only in teams. An effective communication system is needed not only within the R&D function but also between R&D and other functional activities such as marketing, manufacturing, and sales. To improve communication within a global R&D network, international managers need to be aware of the following issues.

Rules and Procedures

For overseas laboratories, careful reporting and documentation of research progress can help keep R&D personnel aware of research activity across the company. At Nestlé, progress reports are filed every six months and circulated to interested parties. In any given year, several hundred reports enter into the reporting system. Re-

Videoconferencing facilitates cross-border teamwork in various functions

search progress reports supplement the communication flows related to the planning cycle, which can also serve an educational purpose.

Electronic Communication

Videoconferencing images, facsimiles of visual and written material, electronic mail, and computer conferencing all offer greater possibilities for communication than a simple telephone call. They provide an essential infrastructure for accomplishing cross-border teamwork. However, they cannot replace the face-to-face informal communication that builds trust. Misunderstandings and excessively slow contact or feedback of information erode the climate of trust necessary for teamwork. Along with electronic means of communication, periodic meetings through direct, face-to-face contact are necessary.

Boundary Spanners

Headquarters R&D staff often perform the role of boundary spanners between the dispersed R&D laboratories. They travel frequently to each site location to share development elsewhere in the global R&D network and to discuss progress at the particular site. They may also divulge sensitive information across the network about developments with customers, joint-venture partners, or suppliers. At Johnson & Johnson, the head office R&D group consists of "internal scouts" who are always on the lookout for opportunities to cross-fertilize research project ideas from one laboratory to another. At Nestlé, the corporate R&D staff visits foreign laboratories to optimize long-term research priorities, to develop personal contacts, and to identify potential key personnel.

Informal Network

Communication through informal networks is often an efficient means for teamwork. The central R&D group can stimulate informal networks, which may be created both inside and outside the company, locally or internationally.[7] An external local network consists of local suppliers, customers, and research institutions that provide the opportunity for learning from foreign environments. The central office R&D group can organize an external international network of academics who work on company projects. Private conferences bring these academics together to present their research and to exchange information. Locating and funding outside academic researchers can be supervised by the central office. Johnson & Johnson finances R&D projects in universities through a program called Focused Giving Program. The program funds $3 million of academic research in and outside of the United States, and gathers the recipients together once a year to deliver findings. An MNE's internal network can be activated most directly with international project teams. Project team members stay in their respective laboratories most of the time, and collaborate on projects using electronic means and personnel transfers.

Cultural Adaptation

Often, international R&D project teams must overcome cultural differences. Although many researchers can speak English, there is no assurance that the members of a multicultural R&D team understand one another. Research shows significant cross-cultural differences among R&D professionals on the dimensions of power (respect for hierarchy), risk avoidance, individualism, and masculinity/femininity (see also Chapter 6).[8] The Japanese believe that a manager who champions an innovation should work within the organizational rules, procedures, and hierarchy, whereas Americans do not hold this belief. Often, an effective means of reducing cultural differences is to socialize R&D professionals through a wide range of activities. International training seminars help create a shared corporate culture as well as a network of colleagues who can communicate on a much more informal basis. International assignments not only deepen the understanding of the individual transferred, but the host and home laboratories gain a much clearer picture of internal workings of other laboratories through this individual.

Interim Summary

1. Incentive systems such as recognition and reward should be as uniform as possible among different R&D units. Also, it is useful to maintain a regular program of exchange and visitation between global R&D units so as to foster unity and cooperation. Communication is important not only within an R&D unit and between R&D units but with other functional divisions such as marketing and sales as well.

2. Autonomy of foreign R&D units should be based on their strategic roles in overall corporate strategy and requirements for global integration. Having clear business and technology strategies within the company makes integration of research much easier. Once the technology strategy is set, it can be carried into specific project areas, giving everyone a common frame of reference.

TECHNOLOGY TRANSFER ACROSS BORDERS

A popular alternative to establishing foreign-based R&D labs or centers is to use technology transfers and collaborative agreements with foreign partners. This approach is especially attractive to those firms or projects that require large investments and involve high uncertainties. In Chapter 12 we illustrated a number of issues on how to build and manage global alliances. The discussion in this section focuses only on technology transfer.

International technology transfer is a process by which one firm's technology or knowledge is passed on to another firm in a different country for economic benefits. Through technology transfer, a firm can acquire needed technology or knowledge from a foreign provider. Frequently used methods of technology transfer include international licensing, non-equity or equity joint ventures, turnkey operations, and countertrade (see Chapter 10 which explains these modes). Generally, firms acquiring technology through international transfer seek increasing competitiveness, increasing profits by reducing development costs, enhancing technological position in the market, or reducing prices while maintaining quality. If firms want to transfer own their technology to foreign companies, they need to consider such factors as protection of proprietary technology, competition, impact on a firm's existing market power, and earning of royalties from remote markets.

Technology transfer is a complex, ongoing activity, as demonstrated by the fact that many license relationships have been in effect for more than 50 years. Moreover, variations prevail across industry, company, or market lines. Even within an MNE network, policies and management of technology transfer differ according to subsidiaries, type of technologies, and stages of the technology life cycle. As such, it would be inappropriate for a firm to try to police it through uniform rules.

A frequent problem with technology transfer across borders is that much of the technological capability is not easily transferable from one partner to another. This is simply because the successful operationalization of many technologies depends to a great extent on the acquired experiences and expertise of critical personnel such as key scientists, engineers, equipment operators, suppliers, and such. The ways in which interdependent technologies are "fine-tuned" to work effectively within a complex system are often implicit or tacit in nature, relying on overall experiences, skills, and understandings that have been learned over time and internalized. Because of this, it is essential to check the absorptive capability of a transferee (e.g., a buyer of the technology). The **absorptive capability** concerns a firm's ability to acquire, assimilate, integrate, and exploit knowledge and skills that are transferred from others. This capability often depends on the level of the firm's related technology or skills already developed, the effectiveness of organizational learning systems, and the ability to combine a firm's own skills with newly acquired skills.

Effective technology transfer, especially via a joint venture, requires coordinating mechanisms linking two parties, which are often labeled bridges. There are three categories of bridges—procedural bridges, human bridges, and organizational bridges.[9] *Procedural bridges* involve the joint planning and joint staffing of activities, particularly around the time of the transfer of the technology. The emphasis in procedural bridges is on collaboration through joint planning, problem solving, and implementation. *Human bridges* rely on establishing direct interaction between individuals from different organizational areas, typically through the transfer and rotation of personnel. Such personal contact allows both responsibility and enthusiasm to be transferred from one person to another, and it establishes a common social and work-related context that should facilitate more learning and cooperative efforts. The success of the joint venture technology transfer project between British GEC Sensors and French Alcatel is attributable to formal communication and informal social networks at the senior manager, project manager, and operational staff levels. *Organizational bridges* use dedicated transfer teams to establish more formal ties between organizational areas. These groups are created to build a more formal structure and common context for the effective transfer of experience. When British Celltech and American Cyanamid cooperated through joint venture-based technology transfer, for example, they faced many communication problems. Cyanamid is a vast, complex organization, and it took Celltech a number of years to understand where executive power lay, and with whom it had to negotiate to get decisions made. These problems were later solved by forming several transfer teams to build formal ties between project managers from the two parties.

Interim Summary

1. Cross-border technology transfer between different firms is an alternative to foreign R&D projects that involve large investments and/or high uncertainty. Licensing and joint ventures are especially common ways of achieving this transfer.

2. Effective technology transfer requires coordinating mechanisms linking two parties. These linkages include human bridges, procedural bridges, and organizational bridges.

CHAPTER SUMMARY

1. Globalizing R&D is a process of distributing and operating R&D facilities in different countries under a coordinated system by headquarters. It is an important strategic response to changes in foreign market demands and global competition. Globalizing R&D provides an access to other countries' technical or scientific resources or talents, strengthens competitive advantage and local adaptation, and facilitates interfirm knowledge sharing.

2. Globalizing R&D is a complex process involving many challenges, including high costs and risks. Counteracting these challenges requires appropriate design, coordination, and management of various foreign R&D units. These units can be structured as corporate technology units, global technology units, specialized or regional technology units, technology transfer units, or indigenous technology units. Of these, the first two are more centralized and globally interdependent laboratories, whereas the last two are more decentralized and locally adapting units.

3. Carefully selecting location for foreign R&D units can lower the levels of risks, costs, and uncertainties. Location choice depends on a R&D unit's strategic role, foreign government policies, local infrastructure and technological level, and socio-cultural considerations.

4. The governance of global R&D often determines how much it contributes to global success. If an MNE adopts an ethnocentric structure, all major R&D activities will be concentrated in its home country. If it follows a polycentric structure, these activities will be scattered overseas with no supervising corporate R&D center. If it uses specialized laboratory structure, each foreign R&D unit will be assigned global mandates. If it adopts a global central lab structure, major R&D activities are centralized in the home center, which serves a broad range of markets. Today, more MNEs follow globally integrated network structure, which entails many interconnected foreign R&D units with different roles and types.

5. Personnel policies affect the productivity of foreign R&D units. These policies should be standardized to the extent allowed by local laws and customs. Unit members should be motivated to develop, share, and commercialize new knowledge. Parent firms should delegate sufficient autonomy to R&D units such that the latter can fulfill their goals effectively. Both formal and informal communication systems should be developed to spur inter-unit sharing of information, experience, and technology.

6. International technology transfer enables MNEs to acquire technology from foreign providers. This lowers research and development costs and expedites knowledge acquisition. Firms must develop absorptive capability and foster a learning environment for technology to be effectively transferred, exploited and integrated with their own.

CHAPTER NOTES

[1] V. Chiesa, "Strategies for global R&D," *Research Technology Management,* 39(5), 1996, 19–25.

[2] B. Bowonder and S. Yadav, "R&D spending patterns of global firms," *Research Technology Management,* Nov.–Dec., 1999, 44–55; *The Changing Global Role of the Research and Development Function,* The Conference Board, 1995, 7.

[3] M. E. Porter, "Competition in global industries: A conceptual framework." In *Competition in Global Industries,* M. E. Porter (ed.), 15–60, Boston, MA: Harvard Business School Press, 1986; J. H. Dunning, "Multinational enterprises and the globalization of innovatory capacity." In *Technology Management and International Business: Internationalization of R&D and Technology,* O. Granstrand, L. Hakanson, and S. Sjolander, (eds.), Sussex, UK: John Wiley & Sons, 1992, 19–51.

[4] J. N. Behrman and W. A. Fischer, *Overseas R&D Activities of Transnational Companies.* Cambridge, MA: Oelgeschlager, Gunn & Hain, 1980; S. D. Julian and R. T. Keller, "Multinational R&D siting," *Columbia Journal of World Business,* Fall 1991, 47–57.

[5] S. D. Julian and R. T. Keller, "Multinational R&D siting, corporate strategies for success," *Columbia Journal of World Business,* 26(2) 1991, 46–57; J. Howells, "The location and organization of research and development: New horizons," *Research Policy,* 19 1990, 133–146.

[6] A. De Meyer, "Management of an international network of industrial R&D laboratories." In: R&D Management Conference Proceedings, "Managing R&D Internationally," Manchester, UK: Manchester Business School, July 1992; R. Nobel and J. Birkinshaw, "Innovation in multinational corporations: Control and communication patterns in international R&D operations," *Strategic Management Journal,* 19 1998, 479–496.

[7] W. Kuemmerle, "Building effective R&D capabilities abroad," *Harvard Business Review,* March–April 1997 61–70; R. D. Pearce, *The Internalization of Research and Development by Multinational Enterprises.* New York: St. Martin's Press, 1989.

[8] S. A. Shane, "Cultural influences on national rates of innovation," *Journal of Business Venturing,* 8, 1993, 59–73; R. D. Pearce and S. Singh, *Globalizing Research and Development.* New York: St. Martin's Press, 1992.

[9] R. Katz, E. S. Rebentisch, and T. J. Allen, "A study of technology transfer in a multinational cooperative joint venture," *IEEE Transactions on Engineering Management,* 43(1) 1996, 97–105.

PART FIVE

Functional IB Areas

Financial Management for Global Operations

DO YOU KNOW

1. In what ways does financial management influence the global success of MNEs? What are the major financial management issues that are especially important for global operations?

2. How do payment methods differ between domestic and international transactions? By what means are global payments most commonly conducted?

3. Where does financing for global business and export projects come from? If you are a manager of Siemens, which plans to list its stocks on the Nasdaq, what are the major stages and procedures you ought to know?

4. What steps do MNEs take to reduce risk from foreign exchange fluctuations? Can you distinguish between foreign exchange risk and foreign exchange exposure? If you work for GE, whose operations often involve foreign exchange risks, by what measures, internally or externally, can you reduce or eliminate such risks?

OPENING CASE Minimizing Exposure in RTZ

R TZ, a $10 billion international mining company based in Britain, has revamped its foreign exchange policies following a radical review of the relationship between exchange risk management and shareholder value. After realizing that currency fluctuations can erode shareholder wealth, the company decided to abandon traditional short-term hedging strategies in favor of a dynamic, forward-looking focus on long-term results. Al-

though RTZ's costs are largely denominated in the currencies of the countries where it operates, an analysis of its revenue structure showed that the U.S. dollar, the Japanese yen, and the euro were the major currencies determining the price of its products. RTZ views its global net exposure as a portfolio of currency positions similar to a fund manager's treatment of a portfolio of equities. It tries to avoid excessive concentration of risk in any single currency. RTZ maintains a positive exposure in currencies that affect its revenues directly and a negative exposure in currencies in which it denominates its costs. When the firm needs liquidity, it borrows (usually long-term, to balance long-term exposure) in currencies where it has the greatest positive exposure, while holding surplus cash in currencies in which it has large negative exposure. In addition, some of RTZ's positive exposure offsets imports of commodities such as diesel fuel, which are denominated in major currencies. To facilitate implementation of this approach to foreign exchange risk management, corporate headquarters sets debt policies and handles most of the firm's borrowing operations. This centralized borrowing practice allows the corporate finance group and treasury to hedge the company's strategic exposure. Moreover, treasury controls the day-to-day management of the company's exposure. The finance director, a member of the executive committee, informs the CEO and other top executives about RTZ's exposure and actions taken to reduce risk. ■

WHY LEARN FINANCIAL MANAGEMENT?

International business decisions today are hardly associated with financial management. Financial management should not be viewed as the domain of financial managers alone, but rather as required knowledge for all international business managers. For example, what does "exposure" mean? Is it true that foreign exchange risks involve only foreign currencies, and the domestic currency is risk free in international business? Why did RTZ centralize its foreign exchange risk/exposure management associated with worldwide business? If you are a marketing manager in an overseas subsidiary, how would you deal with headquarters' requirement for using currencies that may not be attractive to your clients? To answer these questions, we need to know the major functions of financial management for global operations.

Financial management is one of the major business functions. Financial management for global operations is, however, much more complex than its domestic equivalent because management must cope with different financial environments, markets, and systems. As the RTZ case shows, effective financial management for international business has become more significant as a result of greater risks and more opportunities. Financial management of MNEs' global operations occurs in an environment characterized by volatile foreign exchange rates, a variety of restrictions on capital flows, various levels of country risk, different tax systems, and a wide spectrum of institutional settings.

Increasing globalization of financial markets, the rise of global e-commerce, and heightened pressure for acting locally while thinking globally have fundamental implications for MNE corporate finance. In this environment, management's ability to seize opportunities and avoid unnecessary risk depends on its knowledge of the international environment and its financial management skills. Increasing global competition is causing senior financial managers such as *CFOs* (*Chief Financial Officers*) to review the cost structure, orientation and strategic role of the finance function. Many are taking steps to reduce the cost of financial work, including automating the collection and processing of information, developing shared financial service facilities with higher transaction volumes, and improving automated systems. By emphasizing service over enforcement, they also initiate and motivate a role change from corporate policeman to business advocate and strategic partner. They often lead the global strategy process through their priority activities such as budgeting/planning, acquisition or investment decisions.

As MNEs continue to expand globally, their assets are increasingly widely dispersed and specialized. Philips Electronics (Europe's largest electronics company), for example, has operating units in 60 countries, some of which are large, fully integrated companies developing, manufacturing, and marketing a diverse range of products from lightbulbs to defense systems. Although other companies may be less diversified, the trend toward a broader configuration of assets continues. As a result, headquarters management in many MNEs is obligated to shift from exercising centralized control toward managing a network of established foreign subsidiaries. Accordingly, formal financial coordination and control processes are now being supplemented by investment analysis, risk reduction, global mobilization of financial resources, and optimization of capital structure.

Knowledge of international financial management helps a global business in two important ways. First, it helps the financial manager decide how international events (e.g., changes in foreign exchange rates) will affect a firm and what steps can be taken to exploit positive developments and insulate the firm from harmful ones. Second, it helps the manager anticipate events and make profitable decisions before the events occur. Today, it is difficult to think of any firm, international or domestic, that is not affected in some way by the international financial environment. A wide variety of firm decisions are tied to exchange rates and other developments in the global financial environment.

Financial management for global operations deals with the following major issues:

- International trade finance
- Financing global operations
- Managing foreign exchange risk and exposure
- Working capital management

Interim Summary

1. Modern international business is inextricably linked to financial management. For MNEs, financial management is much more complex than for other companies since they face multiple financial environments, systems, and markets.

2. Adequate international financial management helps an MNE maneuver past international events in the most beneficial way possible as well as to anticipate these events. This is important because many decisions are tied to exchange rates, which can have serious effects on the real income of a company.

INTERNATIONAL TRADE FINANCE

International Trade Payment

The widely used payment methods in international trade include (1) *cash in advance*, (2) *letter of credit (L/C)*, (3) *documentary collection*, and (4) *open account terms*. For an exporter, the risk of being unable to receive an importer's payments increases along this sequence.

Cash in Advance

Cash in advance affords the exporter the greatest protection because payment is received either before shipment or upon arrival of the goods. It is often used in a country where there is political instability or where the buyer's credit is shaky. Political crises or foreign exchange controls in the purchaser's country may cause payment delays or even prevent fund transfers, leading to a demand for cash in advance. In addition, in a circumstance where production of contracted products requires a vast amount of capital investment, prepayment is usually demanded, both to finance production and to reduce marketing risks.

Letter of Credit (L/C)

The majority of international trade uses letter of credit (L/C) as the payment method. The **letter of credit** is a letter addressed to the seller, written and signed by a bank acting on behalf of the buyer. In the letter, the bank promises it will honor drafts drawn on itself if the seller conforms to the specific conditions set forth in the (L/C). These conditions usually conform to those stipulated in an export contract or sales agreement. If they are not in conformity, the exporter must comply with conditions specified in the L/C. Through an L/C, the bank substitutes its own commitment to pay for that of its customer (the importer). The letter of credit, therefore, becomes a financial contract between the issuing bank and a designated beneficiary that is separate from the commercial transaction.

Most advantages of L/C for an exporter include:

- L/C *eliminates credit risk* if the bank that opens it is of good standing. It also reduces the risk that payment will be delayed or withheld due to exchange controls or other political acts.
- L/C *reduces uncertainty.* The exporter knows all the requirements for payment because they are clearly stipulated in the L/C.
- L/C can help *stabilize production.* The exporter that manufactures under contract a specialized piece of equipment runs the risk of contract cancellation before shipment. Opening a letter of credit will provide protection during the manufacturing phase.
- L/C *facilitates financing* because it ensures the exporter a ready buyer for its product.

While the L/C issuance often requires an importer to pre-deposit or have a savings account in the issuing bank (thus may forgo interest earnings in another investment), the importer also gains some benefits from this method, including:

- Because payment is made only under compliance with the L/C's conditions, the importer is able to ascertain that the merchandise is actually shipped on or before a certain date by requiring an on-board bill of lading (B/L). An L/C also helps ensure that the quality and quantity of exporting merchandise conform to regulations described in the L/C.
- The bank bears responsibility for any oversight on checking the documents that are required in the L/C (a phenomenon known as *document discrepancies*). In commercial L/C transactions, banks deal in documents and not in goods. The importer can refuse to accept the bill of lading and decline to pay if it finds any, and even very minor, oversight in any of the requirement documents.
- Using L/C heightens the importer's bargaining power, and allows the importer to ask for a price reduction from the exporter.
- If prepayment is required, the importer should deposit its money with a bank rather than with the seller because it is then easier to recover the deposit if the seller is unable or unwilling to make a proper shipment.

Exhibit 14–1 shows the process of using an L/C in an export business from a Chinese trading company to a U.S. importer. After a Chinese exporter in Shanghai has shipped the goods, it draws a draft against the issuing bank (Citibank) and presents it, along with the required documents, to its own bank, the Bank of China. The Bank of China, in turn, forwards the bank draft and attached documents to Citibank in New York; Citibank pays the draft upon receiving evidence that all conditions set forth in the L/C have been met.

Because there are several types of L/Cs, each export contract must specify which type should be used. Most L/Cs issued in connection with commercial transactions are **documentary**—that is, the exporter must submit, together with the draft, any necessary invoices and other documents such as the custom invoice, certificate of commodity inspection, packing list, and certificate of country of origin. L/Cs without the requirement for presentation of documents are called **clean L/Cs.** A clean L/C may be used for overseas bank guarantees, escrow arrangements, and security purchases. However, it is rarely used in import/export business.

The letter of credit can be revocable or irrevocable. A **revocable L/C** is a means of arranging payment, but it does not carry a guarantee. It can be revoked, without notice, at any time up to the time a draft is presented to the issuing bank. An **irrevocable L/C,** in contrast, cannot be revoked without the specific permission of

Exhibit 14–1
Process of using letter of credit (L/C)

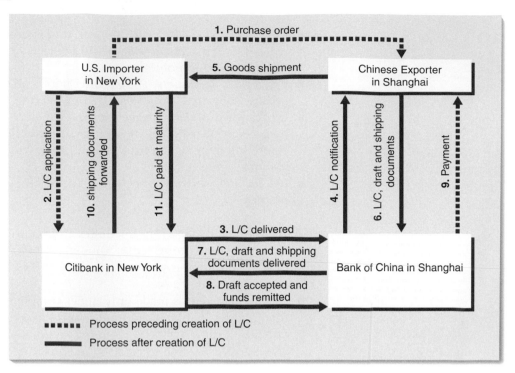

all parties concerned, including the exporter. Most credits between unrelated parties are irrevocable.

A letter of credit can also be confirmed or unconfirmed. A **confirmed L/C** is issued by one bank and confirmed by another, obligating both banks to honor any drafts drawn in compliance. An **unconfirmed L/C** is the obligation of only the issuing bank. Naturally, an exporter will prefer an irrevocable letter of credit by the importer's bank with confirmation by another (domestic or foreign) bank. In this way, the exporter need look no further than a bank in its own country for compliance with terms of the letter of credit. For example, if the Bank of China had confirmed the letter of credit issued by Citibank, and Citibank, for whatever reason, failed to honor its irrevocable L/C, a Chinese exporter could collect its accounts receivable from the Bank of China.

There are also special types of L/Cs that are used for specific purposes of an exporter. A **transferable L/C** is one under which the beneficiary has the right to instruct the paying bank to make the credit available to one or more secondary beneficiaries. No L/C is transferable unless specifically authorized in the letter of credit; moreover, it can be transferred only once. The stipulated documents are transferred along with the L/C. In effect, the exporter is the intermediary in a transferable credit, and usually has the credit transferred to one or more of its own suppliers. When the credit is transferred, the exporter is actually using the creditworthiness of the opening bank, thus avoiding having to borrow or use its own funds to buy the goods from its own suppliers.

A **back-to-back L/C** exists where the exporter, as beneficiary of the first L/C, offers its credit as security in order to finance the opening of a second credit in favor of the exporter's own supplier of the goods needed for shipment under the first or original credit from the advising bank. The bank that issues a back-to-back L/C not only assumes the exporter's risk but also the risk of the bank issuing the primary L/C. If the exporter is unable to produce documents or the documents contain discrepancies, the bank issuing the back-to-back L/C may be unable to obtain payment under the credit because the importer is not obligated to accept discrepant documents of the ultimate supplier under the back-to-back L/C. Thus, many banks are reluctant to issue this type of L/C.

A **revolving L/C** exists where the tenor (maturity) or amount of the L/C is automatically renewed pursuant to its terms and conditions. An L/C with a revolving maturity may be either cumulative or noncumulative. When cumulative, any amount not utilized during a given period may be applied or added to the subsequent period. If noncumulative, any unused amount is simply no longer available. If a revolving L/C is used, it must be explicitly stipulated in the export contract.

Documentary Collection

The **documentary collection** is a payment mechanism that allows exporters to retain ownership of the goods until they receive payment or are reasonably certain that they will receive it. In a documentary collection, the bank, acting as the exporter's agent, regulates the timing and sequence of the exchange of goods for value by holding the title documents until the importer either pays the draft— termed **documents against payment** (D/P)—or accepts the obligation to do so— termed **documents against acceptance** (D/A). The introduction of D/P and D/A is detailed in the "Uniform Rules for Collections" enacted by the International Chamber of Commerce (ICC).

The two principal control documents in a documentary collection are a *draft* and a *bill of lading (B/L)*. The *draft* is written by the drawer (exporter) to the drawee (importer) and requires payment of a fixed amount at a specific or determinable date to the payee (usually the exporter himself). A draft is a negotiable instrument that normally requires physical presentation as a condition for payment. A draft may be either a *sight draft* (i.e., payable upon presentation) or a *time draft* (i.e., payable at a determinable future date as specified in the draft). As introduced in Chapter 10, *bill of lading* is the document of title (property rights of the shipped products), the document for shipment (usually ocean transportation), and the carrier's receipt for the goods being shipped. Exhibits 14–2 and 14–3 present a step-by-step procedural flow for D/P and D/A, respectively.

A sight draft is commonly used for D/P payment. Nevertheless, for export sales that take several months in ocean transportation, exporters and importers may agree to use D/P at 30, 60, 90, or 180 days, and the like. Bear in mind that sight drafts are not always paid exactly at presentation, nor are time drafts always paid at maturity. Firms can get bank statistics on the promptness of sight and time draft payments, by country, from bank publications such as Chase Manhattan's Collection Experience Bulletin.

In practice, D/A at sight is seldom used. D/A is usually accompanied with a time draft ranging from 30 days up to perhaps two years, which is why time draft-based collections are also viewed as an important commercial or corporate financing approach that is granted by the exporter to the importer. The flip side of this method is the high risk of receivable collection for the exporter. D/A is a riskier collection method than D/P because the importer can claim the title of goods under the "promise" of payment rather than actual payment. For this reason, most bad debts accumulated in international trade have been transactions that used D/A as terms of payment.

Open Account

Open account selling involves shipping goods first and billing the importer later. The credit terms are arranged between the importer and the exporter, but the exporter has little evidence of the importer's obligation to pay a certain amount at a certain date. Sales on open account, therefore, are made only to a foreign affiliate

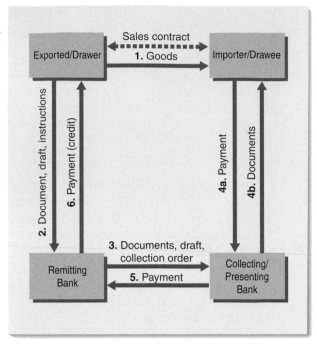

Exhibit 14–2
Documents against payment (D/P) flow

Sales contract

Exported/Drawer — **1.** Goods → Importer/Drawee

2. Document, draft, instructions
6. Payment (credit)
4a. Payment
4b. Documents

Remitting Bank — **3.** Documents, draft, collection order → Collecting/Presenting Bank
5. Payment

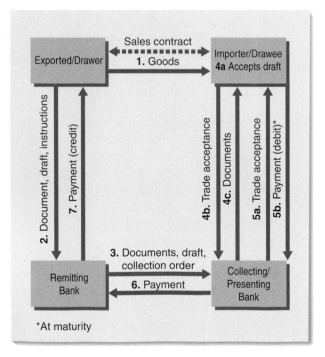

Exhibit 14–3
Documents against acceptance (D/A) flow

Sales contract

Exported/Drawer — **1.** Goods → Importer/Drawee **4a** Accepts draft

2. Document, draft, instructions
7. Payment (credit)
4b. Trade acceptance
4c. Documents
5a. Trade acceptance
5b. Payment (debit)*

Remitting Bank — **3.** Documents, draft, collection order → Collecting/Presenting Bank
6. Payment

*At maturity

or to a customer with which the exporter has a long history of favorable business dealings. However, open account sales have greatly expanded because of the major increase in international trade, more accurate credit information about importers, and the greater familiarity with exporting in general. The benefits include greater flexibility (no specific payment dates are set) and lower costs, including fewer bank charges than with other methods of payment. As with shipping on consignment, the possibility of currency controls is an important factor because of the low priority in allocating foreign exchange normally accorded this type of transaction.

Means of Payment Remittance

Remittance can be made by several means. In documentary L/Cs or collections, the primary means of remittance is airmail payment order in which an instruction is mailed from an importer's bank to an exporter's bank. These banks may also use *Telex/SWIFT (So-ciety for Worldwide Information and Funds Transfer)* capabilities to settle the payment. For cash in advance or open account terms, the importers/buyers may use company check, bank draft, or bank money order to remit the payment. Company check is also widely used for goods purchased on *cash with order (CWO)* or *cash on delivery (COD)*. Today, interbank e-mail systems have been extensively applied in lieu of airmail payment orders between cross-border banks (especially between those in developed countries).

Export Financing

Export financing is important because many export projects require a large amount of start-up costs. External sources of export financing are twofold, including *private sources* and *governmental sources*. Of private sources, the institutions that provide trade financing include commercial banks, export finance companies, factoring houses, forfeit houses, international leasing companies, in-house finance companies, and private insurance companies. These sources offer different types of financing for exporters.

Private Sources

Bank Financing Commercial bank financing for foreign trade business includes bank guarantees, bank line of credit, and buyer credit. A **bank guarantee** is a financial instrument that guarantees a specified sum of payment in the event of nonperformance by an exporter or by a foreign importer in the event of a payment default for goods purchased from a foreign supplier. Apart from regular bank guarantees, there are three other types of guarantees involved with commercial banks. These include (1) the *loan guarantee,* which grants a loan conditional on security provided by the borrower; (2) a *distraint guarantee,* which helps a debtor recover control over its seized assets; and (3) a *bill of lading guarantee,* which ensures that the carrier will hand over the goods to the consignee when individual bills of lading are lost.

Bank line of credit is a sum of money allocated to an exporter by a bank or banks that the exporter can draw from in order to finance its export business. This could also be structured to finance an export transaction from the foreign customer's side. In effect, the bank line of credit allows the exporter to extend competitive credit terms to foreign customers. **Buyer credit** exists where one or more financial institutions in an exporter's country extend credit to a foreign customer of the exporter. Although most buyer credit financing is arranged to finance capital equipment purchases, other goods with payment terms of up to one year can be financed by buyer credits. Buyer credits are normally arranged under an export credit insurance program.

Export Factoring and Forfaiting

Export factoring is particularly suited for small and medium-sized exporters. This technique proceeds through factoring houses. **Factoring houses** not only provide financing but can perform credit investigations, guarantee commercial and political risks, assume collection responsibilities, and finance accounts receivable. In addition, these houses can perform such services as letters of credit, term loans, marketing assistance, and all other necessary services a small to medium-sized exporter cannot afford to handle. Often, a factoring house's service charges are quoted on a commission basis. Commissions can range anywhere between 1 to 3 percent of total transaction value.

Although factoring is a well-known export financing technique in the United States, forfaiting has been widely used for export financing in Europe. **Forfaiting,** a term derived from the French term *a forfeit,* is a transaction in which an exporter transfers responsibility of commercial and political risks for the collection of a trade-related debt to a forfaiter (often a financial institution), and in turn receives immediate cash after the deduction of its interest charge (the discount). The forfait market consists of a primary and secondary market. The primary market consists of banks and forfait houses that buy properly executed and documented debt obligations directly from exporters. The secondary market consists of trading these forfait debt obligations among themselves.

In general, a forfait financing transaction involves at least four parties to the transaction: an exporter, the forfaiter, the importer, and the importer's guarantor. The financial instruments in forfaiting are usually time drafts or bills of exchange and promissory notes. Forfaiting is used to finance the export of capital equipment where transactions are usually medium term (i.e., 3–8 years) at fixed rate financing. The discount used by the forfaiter is based on its cost of funds plus a premium, which can range anywhere from 0.5 to 5 percent depending on the country of importation and level of risks involved.

Bankers Acceptance

The **bankers acceptance** (*BA*) is a time draft drawn on and accepted by banks. It is a two-armed instrument with one branch in financing and the other in investment. The bank first creates the BA by stamping "accepted" on the face of a draft presented by its customer (i.e., the drawer), then discounts the BA (i.e., it pays the drawer a sum less than the face value of the draft), followed by selling (rediscounting) the BA to an investor in the acceptance market. At maturity the bank settles the BA when it debits the drawer for the full amount of the BA and pays the full value to the investor who presents it. By definition, a bankers acceptance is a time draft (30, 60, 90, up to 180 days after sight or date) drawn on and accepted by a bank. The fee charged by the accepting bank varies depending on the maturity of the draft as well as the creditworthiness of the borrower. BA is mainly used for the export trade in raw materials, components, and general commodity financing. A deep secondary market for bankers acceptances combined with the lack of reserve requirements often enables the bank to obtain funding for eligible transactions at a cost significantly lower than alternative sources.

Corporate Guarantee

A **corporate guarantee** is where one company undertakes to pay if the principal debtor does not pay a matured debt obligation to a creditor. Typically in global business, creditors will ask the corporate or parent company to guarantee an obligation of one or more of its overseas subsidiaries or offshore affiliates that the creditor may consider not creditworthy for the export-related financing or credit limit. Because the parent company is often located outside of the exporting country, it is important to state in the financing contract by which country's law the guarantee will be governed.

Governmental Sources

Export-Import Bank Financing Many countries have put in place export-import financing programs that are similar in most respects to programs of the Export-

Import Bank of the United States (Eximbank). Japan's Eximbank, for instance, is an independent governmental financial institution providing yen financing for exports, imports, and overseas investments. Exports are supported by parallel lending with these banks in the form of yen loans for major borrowing with medium- to long-term terms. South Korea Eximbank provides direct loans to both foreign and domestic firms. The loans are low-cost with medium- to long-term financing arranged in conjunction with larger commercial banks throughout the world. Their purpose is to encourage the export of capital goods and services, overseas investment, and major resource development. South Korea's Eximbank offers such services as direct lending to both suppliers and buyers, relending facilities to foreign financial institutions, and the issuance of guarantees and export insurance.

In the United States, the primary function of its Eximbank is to give U.S. exporters the necessary financial backing to compete in other countries. Today this is done through a variety of different export financing and guarantee programs (e.g., direct loans, discount loans, guarantees, and export credit insurance) to meet specific needs. All are designed to be in direct support of U.S. exports, whether the eventual recipient of the loans or guarantees are foreign or domestic firms. Generally, export-import banks do not compete with private sources of export financing. Their main purpose is to step in where private credit is not available in sufficiently large amounts at low rates or long terms, to allow home country exporters to compete in a foreign market.

Foreign Credit Insurance

Many industrialized and developing countries have set up foreign credit insurance or guarantee programs to assist their exporting companies. Even branches of foreign companies located in that country are often eligible for assistance. These programs are usually run by and dependent on the government. In the United States, such insurance programs are offered by both Eximbank and the Foreign Credit Insurance Association. In Canada, these services are provided by Export Credits Insurance Corporation (ECIC). In Asia, Japan's International Trade Bureau (Export Insurance Section), Hong Kong's Export Credit Insurance Corporation, India's Export Credit & Guarantee Corporation Ltd, and Taiwan's Central Trust of China are all overseeing and offering these programs. In Latin America, similar programs can be found (e.g., in Compania Argentina de Seguros de Credito in Argentina and Instituto de Resseguros do Brasil in Brazil). Europe has an even longer history in providing export credit insurance. Les Assurances du Credit in Belgium, Export Credit Council in Denmark, Export Guarantee Board in Finland, Compagnie Francaise D'Assurance pour le Commerce Exterieur in France, Hermes Kreditversicherungs in Germany, and Instituto Nazionale delle Assicuranioni in Italy, for example, are all leading institutions offering foreign credit insurance and backed by their respective governments.

Because the services provided by these institutions are basically similar, let us use the case of the United Kingdom to illustrate the process and scope of these services. In the United Kingdom, commercial credit and political risks connected with exports can be insured with the Export Credits Guarantee Department (ECGD), a separate department of the British government. Even though ECGD is an arm of the British government, it is commercially independent. Risks covered by ECGD include commercial credit and political risk. More specifically, commercial credit risks include insolvency of the buyer, buyer's failure to pay within six months of due date for goods already accepted, and the buyer's failure to accept goods that have been shipped (provided this nonacceptance was not caused by an action or noncompliance on the part of the exporter). Political risks covered by ECGD include government action that blocks payment to the exporter, cancellation of a valid import license in the buyer's country, war or any cause of loss not within the control of the exporter or the buyer, or cancellation of an export license or imposition of new licensing restrictions. Generally, ECGD covers 95 percent of any loss resulting from political risk and 90 percent of the loss arising from most commercial risks.

Interim Summary

1. There are a number of accepted payment forms in international trade, ranging from cash in advance, to letter of credit (L/C), documentary collection (e.g., D/P and D/A), and to open account terms. L/C is particularly desirable for the exporter because it eliminates credit risk, reduces uncertainty, and facilitates financing, whereas it ascertains the quality and quantity of a purchase for the importer.

2. Documentary collection is a riskier payment form than L/C for the exporter. In this system, a draft is delivered either upon receipt of goods or with a time-based maturity clause. The International Chamber of Commerce details uniform rules for documentary collection.

3. There are various means of acquiring bank financing. For smaller exporters, factoring, whereby a financing house fronts money for transactions on a commission basis, is a good choice. Capital may also be acquired from governmental sources which offer many of the same services as private banks, but are specifically intended to aid traders from their home country.

FINANCING FOR GLOBAL BUSINESS Compared to financing for foreign trade activities, financing for MNEs' global productions, investments, and operations involves more choices but is more complex. Broadly, the sources of financing for global investments and operations include intercompany financing, equity financing, debt financing, and local currency financing (see Exhibit 14–4).

Intercompany Financing

Intercompany financing from the parent company or sister subsidiaries is a common means of financing for overseas subsidiaries or affiliates, which is done in the following ways:

- Allowing the subsidiary to keep a higher level of retained earnings.
- Obtaining financing from the parent company in the form of equity, loans, trade credit (e.g., longer maturity or extension for accounts payable), or borrowing with a parent guarantee.
- Arranging trade credit from other subsidiaries to this affiliate.

Parent loans are sometimes preferable to parent equity financing by MNEs, for several reasons. First, intercompany loan payments may be more readily remittable in the future than dividends. Second, loan interests reduce the tax burden. A subsidiary borrowing these loans will pay lower local corporate income tax after deducting interest expenses from the total taxable incomes. Third, the loan provided to the parent or a sister subsidiary and the loan received from the parent or another subsidiary are eliminated on consolidation. Cash has moved within the corporation without affecting the consolidated debt or equity accounts. Finally, short-term intercompany loans may be used to stabilize the subsidiary's working capital struc-

Exhibit 14–4
Sources of financing
global operations

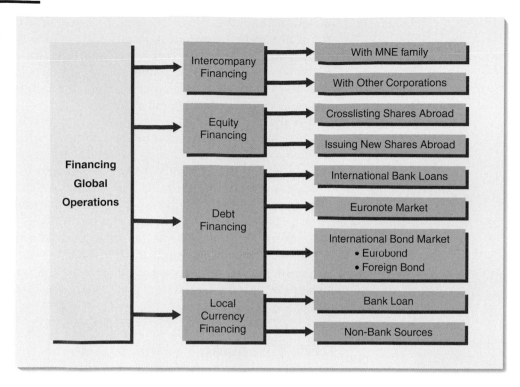

ture, and long-term intercompany loans may be used to reduce its dependence on external banks. **Working capital** is the net position whereby a firm's current liability is subtracted from its current assets.

Equity Financing

Financing through equity markets can be realized in an MNE's home country, a foreign affiliate's host country, and/or a third country. An MNE's equity financing can take the form of either *crosslisting shares abroad* or *selling new shares* to *foreign investors*. Many U.S.-based MNEs, for instance, have secured listing of their companies on foreign stock exchanges.

Crosslisting an MNE's shares on foreign stock exchanges may provide many benefits:

- Improve the liquidity of existing shares by making it easier for foreign shareholders to trade in their home markets and currencies.
- Increase the share price by overcoming mis-pricing in a segmented, illiquid, home capital market.
- Increase the firm's visibility and political acceptance to its customers, suppliers, creditors, and host governments.
- Create a secondary market for shares that can be used to compensate local management and employees in foreign affiliates.[1]

Crosslisting is frequently accompanied by depositary receipts. In the United States, foreign shares are usually traded through **American depositary receipts** (or **ADRs**). These are negotiable certificates issued by a U.S. bank in the United States to represent the underlying shares of stock, which are held in trust at a foreign custodian bank. ADRs are sold, registered, and transferred in the United States in the same manner as any share of stock. Because ADRs can be exchanged for the underlying foreign shares, or vice versa, arbitrage keeps foreign and U.S prices of any given share the same. To crosslist stocks abroad, an MNE must be committed to full disclosure of operating results and balance sheets. Today, the major liquid markets are London, New York (NYSE and Nasdaq), Tokyo, Frankfurt, and Paris. To decide where to crosslist, an MNE should consider its ownership expansion objectives, the size of the target stock market, the sophistication of market-making activities, and host governmental regulations.

An alternative to seeking international ownership through parent listings is the issuance of equity by local subsidiaries. Some countries require levels of minority or even majority ownership by local nationals. Firms typically have difficulty in achieving a broad-based ownership of their subsidiaries in the very thin capital markets of most developing countries. U.S. MNEs, in particular, prefer the flexibility of operations that sole ownership affords. Firms that are technology-based are concerned with the loss of control over proprietary technology that taking on an equity partner or partners might portend. MNEs of other countries, however, sometimes want to take on local equity, especially in their U.S. subsidiaries, thereby taking advantage of the remarkably broad and sophisticated U.S. equity market. Exhibit 14–5 illustrates what foreign MNEs must know when selling stocks in the U.S., the largest capital market in the world.

Debt Financing

Chapter 9 introduced international capital markets, which are in fact the major source of a MNE's debt financing. Debt financing for global operations can be made through *international bank loans, the Euronote market,* and *the international bond market.* International bank loans are often sourced in the **Eurocurrency markets,** that is, in countries not using the denomination currency (e.g., a Japanese firm obtained yen loans from banks in the United States and Europe). As such, international bank loans are often called **Eurocredits.** Because of the large size of these loans, the lending banks usually form a syndicate in order to diversify their risk. The basic borrowing interest rate for Eurocurrency loans has long been tied to the *London Interbank Offered Rate (LIBOR),* which is the deposit rate applicable to interbank loans within London.

The **Euronote market** is the collective term used to describe short- to medium-term debt instruments sourced in the Eurocurrency markets. The Euronote is generally a less expensive source of short-term funds than syndicated loans, because the notes are placed directly with the investor public. Euronotes can be *underwritten* or *non-underwritten.* In an underwritten Euronote, there are normally one to three lead banks that organize a group of participating banks to take shares of the total com-

Exhibit 14–5

Tapping Wall Street: three stages for non-U.S. MNEs to be traded in the United States

- *Set up an ADR program.* With ADRs (American Depository Receipts), U.S. depository banks maintain custody of deposited foreign securities at their overseas branches and issue receipts as proof of ownership. The receipt is transferable in the United States. Registration is made under either the Securities Act of 1933 or the Securities Exchange Act of 1934, or both.

- *Listing.* Some MNEs permit their ADRs to be traded in the pink sheets, which list quotes for ADRs of nonlisted companies. Others are listed on Nasdaq or on an exchange from the outset. Firms listing on NYSE or Nasdaq face the same legal requirement. NYSE listings have two separate standards for domestic and foreign entities, with the latter facing more stringent requirements.

- *Public offerings.* In a public offering, the foreign firm turns over its ordinary shares to its depository bank. The depository bank then issues ADRs, and it delivers them to the underwriters for resale and distribution.

mitment. The lead and participating banks stand ready to buy the borrower's notes in the event the notes could not be placed in the market at previously guaranteed rates. The non-underwritten Euronotes include *Euro-Commercial Paper (ECP)* and *Euro-Medium-Term Notes (EMTNs)*. ECP is a short-term debt obligation of a corporation or bank. Maturity is typically 1, 3, and 6 months, while EMTNs' typical maturity ranges from as short as 9 months to a maximum of 10 years.

The international bond market is comprised of *Eurobonds* and *foreign bonds*. A **Eurobond** is underwritten by an international syndicate of banks and other securities firms, and is sold exclusively in countries other than the country in whose currency the issue is denominated (e.g., a bond issued by a Japanese firm residing in Tokyo, denominated in Japanese yen but sold to investors in Europe and the United States). Most Eurobonds use the straight fixed-rate, with a fixed coupon, set maturity date, and full principal repayment upon final maturity. Recently, convertible Eurobonds have emerged. These bonds resemble the straight fixed-rate issue in practically all price and payment characteristics, with the added feature that they are convertible to stock prior to maturity at a specified price per share. A **foreign bond** is underwritten by a syndicate composed of members from a single country, sold principally within that country, and denominated in the currency of that country (a Japanese firm issued corporate bonds in U.S. dollars and sold to U.S. investors by U.S. banks). Foreign bonds sold in the United States are also known as **Yankee bonds,** those sold in Japan as **Samurai bonds,** and those sold in the United Kingdom as **Bulldogs.**

Local Currency Financing

The preceding description focused on corporate-level financing. Local currency financing in a host country opens an avenue for subsidiary financing. Access to various local financial markets in which an MNE operates can be advantageous in lowering the overall cost of capital and reducing financial risks. Thus, international managers should evaluate local financing choices as well as opportunities for investing the firm's surplus funds.

Financing in a host country generally includes two sources: *bank loans* and *nonbank sources*. *Bank loans* contain overdrafts, discounting, and loans. In countries other than the United States, banks tend to lend through overdrafts. An **overdraft** is a line of credit against which drafts (checks) can be drawn (written) up to a specified maximum amount. **Discounting** is a short-term financing technique by which a local bank discounts a firm's trade bills. These bills can often be rediscounted with the central bank. Discounting is particularly popular in Europe and Latin America because, according to the commercial laws in these countries (i.e., Code Napoleon in Europe), the claim of the bill holder is independent of the claim represented by the underlying transaction, which makes the bill easily negotiable. *Loans* can be term loans, line of credit, or revolving credit agreements. **Term loans** are straight loans that are made for a fixed period of time and repaid in a single lump sum. For frequent borrowers, term loans are relatively expensive, so they may instead seek a line of credit. Line of credit, which is usually good for one year with renewals renegotiated every year, allows the company to borrow up to a stated maximum amount from the bank. Similar to a line of credit, a revolving credit agreement permits the company to extend credit up to the stated maximum. The difference is that under this agreement the bank is legally committed to providing credit up to the specified maximum. The company has to pay interest on its outstanding borrowing plus a commitment fee on the unused portion of the credit line.

Nonbank sources of funds include commercial paper, factoring (see the preceding section), and local bond or equity markets, and parallel loans with a foreign company. Stanley Works, the $1.9 billion U.S. manufacturer of hand and power tools, has seven joint ventures in Japan. Its local financing is made via listing on the Tokyo Exchange assisted by Nikko Securities Co. Goldman also assists Stanley to be listed in Hong Kong and Singapore where the company operates three manufacturing plants and several distribution centers. A **parallel loan** (also known as *back-to-back loan*) involves an exchange of funds between firms in different countries, with the exchange reversed at a later date. For example, a U.S. MNE's subsidiary in Brazil needs Brazilian reals while a Brazilian company's subsidiary in the United States needs dollars. The Brazilian firm can lend reals to the U.S.-owned subsidiary in Brazil while it borrows an equivalent amount of dollars from the U.S. parent in the United States.

Financing Decisions

Several considerations affect the financing decisions and choices for MNEs. These considerations include minimizing taxes, managing currency risk and political risk, and exploiting financial market distortions to raise money at below market rate.

Financing choices designed to minimize corporate taxes are often concerned with selecting the tax-minimizing currency, jurisdiction, and vehicle for issue and selecting the tax-minimizing mode of internal transfer of currency and/or profit. Many MNEs prefer parent loans rather than parent investment for funding subsidiaries because interest payments on debt are tax deductible but dividends are not. Nevertheless, the debt/equity ratio of subsidiaries must be maintained within a reasonable limit. This is necessary to fulfill operating needs as well as local government requirements in certain countries.

In general, an MNE should seek financing in such a way that it balances the currency risks inherent in the operation. For instance, firms may reduce the risk of currency inconvertibility by appropriate inter-affiliate financing. Parent funds may be invested as debt rather than as equity. Back-to-back loans may be arranged, and as much local financing as possible may be sought. To reduce political risk, financing may be sought directly from the host and other governments, international development agencies, and overseas banks. When an MNE's offshore projects are financed by these government-based financial institutions, the firm may benefit from both financing and networking. Kennecott, for example, used this approach to finance its copper mine project in Chile.

Given the uncertainty in international financial markets, MNEs should ensure that their financing is not dependent on any one single source. Diversity of financing sources can help the MNE gain more from differences between capital markets across nations.[2] These differences are largely attributable to government credit and capital controls, which is why the cost of international borrowing is likely to be lower than that of domestic funding. Novo, a Danish MNE that produces industrial enzymes and pharmaceuticals, for example, has crosslisted in both the Copenhagen Stock Exchange and the NYSE and has used a multitude of other financing tools such as Eurobonds, Euronotes, local currency loans, and intercompany financing, among others. This strategy enables Novo to escape the shackles of its segmented national capital market and make the company more visible to foreign investors. Novo eventually reaped the full benefit of dramatic share price increase by selling a directed equity issue in the United States.

Interim Summary

1. MNEs have a broad range of choices in financing their global investment projects, including intercompany financing, equity financing, debt financing, and local currency financing. These choices are often more complex than export financing.

2. Equity financing involves either crosslisting shares on foreign exchanges or selling new shares to foreign investors. Many U.S. MNEs finance their global operations through crosslisting their shares abroad. Three stages for non-U.S. MNEs to be traded in Wall Street include (a) setting up an ADR program, (b) listing, and (c) public offerings.

3. Debt financing is made through international bank loans, Euronote market, and international bond market. Subsidiaries can also obtain local currency financing through local banks or local bond or equity markets.

MANAGING FOREIGN EXCHANGE RISK AND EXPOSURE

Foreign Exchange Risk and Exposure

Exchange risk is a critical issue in international business. Any company that operates in more than one nation or currency area or has cash flows across nations will face foreign exchange risk and foreign exchange exposure. Foreign exchange risk and exposure are two different concepts. **Foreign exchange risk** concerns the variance of the domestic-currency value of an asset, liability, or operating income that is attributable to unanticipated changes in exchange rates.[3] This definition implies that foreign exchange risk is not the unpredictability of foreign exchange rates themselves, but rather the uncertainty of values of a firm's assets, liabilities, or operating incomes owing to uncertainty in exchange rates. Therefore, volatility in exchange rates is responsible for exchange-rate risk only if it translates into volatility in real values of assets, liabilities, or operating incomes. This makes foreign exchange risk dependent on foreign exchange exposure. A firm may not face foreign exchange risks unless it is "exposed" to foreign exchange fluctuations. For example, General Electric (GE) and Hitachi both invest and operate in Mexico. Unlike Hitachi, which imports many parts for its production plants in Mexico, GE has built up its own supply base within Mexico. In this case, GE faces lower foreign exchange risks than Hitachi because GE is not exposed to fluctuations of Mexican peso in the process of supply procurement.

   Foreign exchange exposure refers to the sensitivity of changes in the real domestic-currency value of assets, liabilities, or operating incomes to unanticipated changes in exchange rates.[4] This implies that exposure involves the extent to which the home currency value of assets, liabilities, or incomes is changed by exchange rate variances. The "real" domestic currency value means the value that has been adjusted by the nation's inflation. Domestic currency-denominated assets can be exposed to exchange rates if, for example, unanticipated depreciation of the country's currency causes its central bank to increase interest rates.

   Foreign exchange risk is a positive function of both foreign exchange exposure and the variance of unanticipated changes in exchange rates. Uncertainty of exchange rates does not mean foreign exchange risk for items that are not exposed. Similarly, exposure on its own does not mean foreign exchange risk if exchange rates are perfectly predicable. The levels of foreign exchange risk and exposure often differ between asset/liability items and operating income. Because current asset and current liability items, especially accounts receivables and payable, have fixed face value and are short-term oriented, they are extremely sensitive to the uncertainty of foreign exchange rates. Unlike these asset or liability items, operating incomes do not have fixed face values. Exposure of operating incomes depends not only on unexpected changes of exchange rates but also on such factors as the elasticity of demand for imports or exports, the fraction of input prices that depend on exchange rates, and the flexibility of production to respond to market demand changes induced by exchange rate movements.

Transaction and Economic Exposures

Because foreign exchange risk is determined by foreign exchange exposure (along with the uncertainty of foreign exchange rates), managers must analyze and monitor foreign exchange exposure. MNEs encounter three types of foreign exchange exposure:

- Transaction exposure
- Economic (or operating) exposure
- Translation (or accounting) exposure (discussed in Chapter 15)

Transaction exposure is concerned with how changes in exchange rates affect the value, in home currency terms, of anticipated cash flows denominated in foreign currency relating to transactions already entered into. It arises when commitments in foreign currency are subject to settlements to exchange rate gains and losses due to changes in the currency rates. A change in exchange rates between the home or functional currency and the currency in which a transaction is denominated increases or decreases the expected amount of the functional or reporting currency cash flow on settlement of the transaction. For example, a U.S. exporter expects to receive a payment of £200,000 in two months after it ships the products to the importer in London. With a current spot rate (£1 = $1.5), this export is worth $300,000. Two months later, however, the actual spot rate changes to £1 = $1.3, which reduces the actual dollar avenue to $260,000. This U.S. exporter thus will suffer a $40,000 foreign exchange loss if it does not take steps to hedge its foreign exchange exposure and risk.

Transactions that give rise to foreign exchange exposure include:

- Purchasing or selling on credit goods and services whose prices are stated in foreign currencies (thus recorded as account payable or account receivables).
- Borrowing or depositing funds denominated in foreign currencies (reflected in foreign debt and credit).
- Transacting a foreign-exchange contract.
- Various transactions denominated in foreign exchange.

Accordingly, transaction exposure can be a variety of foreign currency-denominated assets (export receivables or bank deposits), liabilities (account payable or loans), revenues (expected future sales), expenses (expected purchase of goods), or income (dividends).

Economic exposure, also called operating exposure, measures the change in the present value of the firm resulting from any change in the future operating cash flows caused by an unexpected change in exchange rates and macroeconomic factors. The change in value depends on the effect of the exchange rate change on future sales volume, prices, or costs. Unlike **translation exposure,** which refers to the potential for accounting-derived changes in owners' equity to occur because of the need to consolidate foreign currency financial statements, both transaction exposure and economic exposure exist because of unexpected changes in future cash flows. In contrast to transaction exposure, which is concerned with preexisting cash flows that will occur in the near future, economic exposure emphasizes expected future cash flows that are potentially impacted by unanticipated changes of exchange rates and macroeconomic conditions (e.g., unexpected changes in interest rates and inflation rates). Thus, economic exposure derives largely from economic analysis which requires integrated strategies in finance, marketing, outsourcing, and production.

An MNE's economic exposure is determined by several economic factors:

First, it is influenced *by pricing flexibility* (i.e., a firm's ability to raise its foreign currency selling price sufficiently to preserve its home currency profit margin in the case of foreign currency depreciation).[5] This price flexibility depends mainly on price elasticity of demand, which is in turn determined by the level of competition in the market and the degree of product differentiation provided by the firm. For example, Motorola's subsidiaries in Indonesia and Thailand successfully maintained their U.S. dollar gross profit margin for producing and selling cellular phones in these markets during the Asian financial crisis because of a local price increase, which was made possible by the high quality and superior innovation of their products. Similarly, with about 45 percent of the world's liquid-crystal-display market, Japan's Sharp Inc. increased its export price in 1995 by 5 percent in countries where it did not face real competition.

Second, economic exposure is influenced *by production/outsourcing flexibility,* that is, the ability to shift production and outsourcing of inputs among different nations. MNEs with worldwide production systems can cope with currency changes by increasing production in a nation whose currency has undergone a real devaluation and decreasing production in a nation whose currency has revalued in real terms. For example, to cope with *endaka* (which means the strong Japanese yen period), many Japanese MNEs used the yen's strength to quickly and inexpensively set up integrated manufacturing bases in Asian countries with currencies pegged to the dollar. In addition, their earlier investments in the United States, Mexico, and Europe allowed them to play both sides of the yen-dollar swings, using cheaper dollar-denominated parts and materials to offset higher yen-related costs. For instance, 75 percent of the parts for the Toyota Camry built in Georgetown, Kentucky, were from the United States, up from 60 percent when Toyota started manufacturing the car there in 1988. The Honda Accord built in Marysville, Ohio, had local content rising from 70 percent before 1993 to about 85 percent in 1995.

Finally, economic exposure is influenced *by an MNE's localization structure and export orientation.* The negative impact of host-country (local) currency devaluation will be lower if an MNE's localization of production inputs there is higher. The harmful effect of host-country currency depreciation is reduced in this situation because this depreciation lowers the subsidiary's dollar production costs, particularly those attributable to local inputs. In contrast, the higher the import content of production inputs, the less dollar production costs will decline. An MNE using its foreign subsidiary as an export platform will benefit from a host-country currency depreciation. Thus, exporting products made of localized supplies is preferable to targeting a local market using local supplies, as far as risk minimization is concerned. For risk minimization, targeting a local market using local supplies is in turn better than targeting a local market but using imported supplies. Home currency depreciation also affects the operations of companies that focus on the home market using home supplies. This is because home currency depreciation reduces the competitive threat from foreign companies that may have a cost-leadership advantage. Exhibit 14–6 highlights major approaches that manage transaction exposure and economic exposure, respectively, which are further detailed below.

Exhibit 14–6

Framework of managing
foreign exchange
exposure

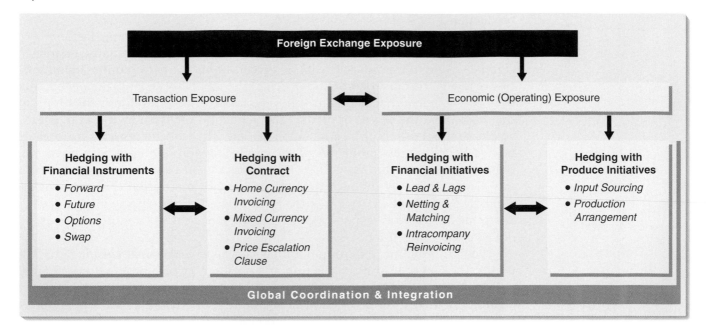

Managing Transaction Exposure

Hedging with Financial Instruments

Forward Market   Forward markets are available in most major currencies of the world. The period of forward contract coverage could extend to more than five years. Exhibit 14–7 shows how hedging via a forward contract works.

By the forward mechanism in this example, the U.K. exporter's accounts receivable is hedged, no matter what happens to the Canadian dollar/sterling spot and forward rates over the next two months. Once contracted, the forward is irrevocably fixed. In general, the expected cost of hedging is equal to the risk premium in the forward exchange rate plus forward transaction costs. The level of risk premium is reflected in the difference between the spot rate and the forward rate. The level of transaction cost is reflected in the spread on the particular forward rate. Since the forward rate is fixed in a completed forward contract, it is important for financial managers to accurately forecast currency appreciation or depreciation. The U.K. exporter mentioned earlier, for instance, sells the forward under the assumption that the Canadian dollar will depreciate or sterling will appreciate around the settlement date. If the realized spot rate actually moves in an opposite direction, this exporter will lose foreign exchange gains that it would otherwise have obtained.

Futures Market   Hedging via the futures market shares major principles with forward hedging. The difference is that in the forward market all the payment is made at the end, whereas with the futures market some of the payment is made through the margin account before the end. In the preceding example, for example, the expected two-month future spot rate is 2.2728. If it turns out at the maturity date of the futures contracts that the actual spot rate is 2.1728, then the U.K. exporter will find it has contributed £20,250 to its margin/future account. It will, of course, receive £460,236 (C$1 million/2.1728) at the due date, rather than £439,986 that

Exhibit 14–7
Forward hedging
example

Contract data

Exporter	United Kingdom exporter
Importer	Canadian importer
Contract date	January 1, 2001
Expected payment date	March 1, 2001
Invoice amount	C$1 million

**Exchange rate (C$/£) quotes
on January 1, 2001**

Spot rate	2.2765–2.2775
1 month forward/future	2.2730–2.2751
2 months forward/future	2.2705–2.2728
3 months forward/future	2.2681–2.2705

Mechanism of forward contract

January 1, 2001	U.K. exporter sells C$1 million 2-month forward at 2.2728 in the forward market (a bank handling foreign exchange transactions)
March 1, 2001	U.K. exporter receives C$1 million from Canadian importer, delivers C$1 million to the bank, and in return receives £439,986 at C$2.2728 per pound sterling

would have been received with a forward contract. However, after compensating for its contribution in the margin account, the U.K. exporter will be receiving £439,986, the same as if the Canadian dollar had been sold on the forward market. On the other hand, if the actual spot rate ends up at 2.3728, then the U.K. exporter will find it has gained £18,543 in its margin account. With this actual spot rate, it will receive £421,443. After adding its gains from the margin account, it will still receive £439,986. Thus we find that no matter what happens to the spot rate, the U.K. exporter still receives £439,986 from its C$1 million. In practice, the addition or subtraction to the margin account is done on a daily basis and is called *marking-to-market*. Because interest rates vary over time, it is unlikely that the amount in the margin account at the maturity of the futures contract will bring the eventual price of C$1 million to exactly £439,986. If interest rates are low when the margin account has a large amount in it, it is possible that slightly less than £439,986 is received. This is the marking-to-market risk of futures contracts.

Options Market   In the options market, a **call option** is to purchase a stated number of units of the underlying foreign currency at a specific price per unit during a specific period of time. Alternatively, a **put option** is to sell a stated number of units of the underlying foreign currency at a specific price per unit during a specific period of time. The *striking* (or *exercise*) *price* in this market refers to the price at which the option holder has the right to purchase or sell the price-underlying currency. A call whose strike price is above the current spot price of the underlying currency, or a put option whose strike price is below the current spot price of the underlying currency, is termed *out-of-the-money*. The reverse situation is called *in-the-money*. Although out-of-the money options have no intrinsic value, in-the-money options have intrinsic value. Intrinsic value reflects the extent to which an option would currently be profitable to exercise. Similar to forward and futures markets, an option holder has to pay risk premium and transaction cost to the banks offering options service. Buying options, however, is more costly than using forwards and futures.

Consider the case in which Dow Corning has to pay £1 million in three months for materials imported from the United Kingdom, and thus needs to hedge this account payable. If Dow Corning buys call options on pounds at a strike price of $1.5/£, the options will be exercised if the spot rate for the pound ends up above $1.50/£, but will not be exercised if the spot rate for the pound is below $1.5/£. This makes sense because it will cost Dow Corning less to buy the pounds at the actual spot rate when it is below $1.5/£. In other words, a call option provides an *option* that will be exercised if the pound becomes more expensive to buy, or will not be exercised (using the actual spot rate instead) if the pound becomes cheaper. In a put option as in the example of the preceding U.K. exporter, which needs to hedge its accounts receivable amounting to C$1 million, the put option will be exercised if the actual spot rate ends up below C$2.2728/£, or will not be exercised if the actual spot rate is above 2.2728, whatever generates more cash flow in pounds for the U.K. exporter.

Swaps **Swaps** involve the exchange of interest or foreign currency exposures or a combination of both by two or more borrowers. It is a transformation of one stream of future cash flows into another stream of future cash flows with different features. An interest rate swap is an exchange between two parties of interest obligations (payments of interest) or receipts (investment income) in the same currency on an agreed amount of the principal for an agreed period of time. Currency swaps involve counterparty A exchanging fixed rate interest in one currency with counterparty B in return for fixed rate interest in another currency. Swaps can be used for different purposes such as investment, speculation, and hedging.

When a firm needs to hedge its accounts payable (as in the situation of Dow Corning above), swaps hedging involves (1) borrowing, if necessary, in home currency; (2) buying the foreign exchange on the spot market; (3) investing the foreign exchange; and (4) repaying the domestic currency debt. For example, Dow Corning can hedge its import of £1 million of denim fabric with payment due in three months by borrowing dollars, buying pounds spot with the dollars, and investing the pounds for three months in a pound-denominated security in London. If this is done, then in three months Dow Corning repays a known number of dollars of domestic debt, and pays accounts payable in pounds using its investment principal and earnings.

Hedging with Contract Invoicing and Clause

Home Currency Invoicing Transaction exposure associated with international accounts receivables or payable can also be hedged via internal techniques. One of these techniques has to do with invoicing trade in their own (home) currency or a third-country currency whose value is stable and also acceptable to both parties. For example, if Dow Corning from the United States can negotiate the price of its imported denim fabrics in terms of U.S. dollars, or the U.K. exporter can manage the export contract by invoicing at sterling, they need not face any foreign exchange transaction exposure on their imports or exports. In general, when business convention or the power that a firm holds in negotiating its purchases and sales results in agreement on prices in terms of the home currency, the firm that trades abroad will not face foreign exchange risk and exposure.

Mixed-Currency Invoicing It is not unusual for both parties in an import/export contract to prefer invoicing the transaction using their own home currencies. As a compromise, both parties may agree to denominate the contract partly in an importer's currency and partly in an exporter's currency. For example, Dow Corning's £1 million import contract may be invoiced as £500,000 and $750,000. If this were done and the exchange rate between dollars and pounds varied, Dow Corning's transaction exposure would involve only half of the funds payable—those that are payable in pounds. Similarly, the British exporter would face exposure on only the dollar component of its receivables. Additionally, international trading companies often use composite currency units such as the *Special Drawing Right* (or *SDR*) and the *European Currency Unit (ECU)* to denominate the export contract. Because these composite units are constructed by taking a weighted average of a number of major world currencies, their values are considerably more stable than that of any single currency. Because they offer some diversification benefits, the composite currency units will reduce transaction risk and exposure, though not completely.

Price Escalation Clause   If using currency invoicing is not realistic for the two parties of an export contract, both parties may consider including and specifying a special term in the contract, known as a *price escalation clause*. Under this special clause, both parties agree to adjust the sales price in full or in a certain proportion of fluctuations of the invoice currency. When the weak currency denominated in the contract depreciates 1 percent, for example, the contract price will automatically increase by 1 percent or another percentage agreed upon by both. This clause is often applied in export contracts denominated in an importer's currency that is highly volatile and will continue to depreciate in the global foreign exchange market. To reduce the transaction exposure, an exporter uses this clause to fully or partially transfer foreign exchange risk to an importer. Another technique similar to this clause is a risk-sharing arrangement between a buyer and a supplier for long-term collaborations. Both parties agree to adjust the price or share the foreign currency risk when the contracted currency fluctuates beyond a certain reasonable range. For example, Ford (United States) and Mazda (Japan) may agree that all purchases by Ford will be made in yen at the current exchange rate, as long as the spot rate on the date of invoice is between, say, ¥105/$–¥125/$. If the exchange rate remains within this range, Ford may agree to accept whatever transaction exposure exists. If, however, the rate falls beyond this limit, Mazda may agree to share the difference equally.

Managing Economic (Operating) Exposure

Financial Initiatives

Several financial initiatives such as using leads and lags, risk-sharing arrangement, and intracompany netting are extensively employed to minimize foreign exchange risk and exposure. Because transaction exposure and economic exposure are sometimes inseparable, these financial initiatives can also be used to lower transaction exposure in some circumstances. Nevertheless, they are designed mainly to manage operating exposure to protect the net present value of the firm resulting from any change in the future operating cash flows caused by exchange rate changes and macroeconomic factors.

Leads and Lags   By timing or retiming the transfer of funds, firms can reduce operating exposure. To lead is to pay early; to lag is to pay late. **Leads** exist when a firm holding a soft currency with debts denominated in a hard currency accelerates by using the soft currency to pay the hard currency debts before the soft currency drops in value. **Lags** exist when a firm holding a hard currency with debts denominated in a soft currency decelerates by paying those debts late. Leads and lags may also be used to reduce transaction exposure. An international trading company can collect soft foreign currency receivables early or collect hard foreign currency receivables later. For instance, if the U.K. exporter mentioned previously expects that the Canadian dollar will depreciate against the pound sterling, it may ask its Canadian importer to lead in paying its export sales. Similarly, if Dow Corning in the preceding case predicts that the pound sterling will drop in value vis-à-vis the U.S. dollar, it may decelerate paying its accounts payable to its U.K. importer. This practice should proceed within the permitted range by a host government. Italy, for example, has placed a 180-day limit on export and import lags on trade payments with non-EU countries.

Intracompany leads and lags within an MNE network are easier to implement than those between two independent companies. Under parent control and by sharing common goals, MNE subsidiaries can rely on this financial technique to improve their respective foreign exchange position and optimize local currency cash flow. On the other hand, headquarters treasury managers must ensure that the timing of the intracompany settlement is functional from a group perspective rather than merely from a local one. They should also be aware that performance measurement may be affected if some subsidiaries are asked to lead and some to lag. The subsidiary that does the leading loses interest receivable and incurs interest charges on the funds led. To overcome this problem, evaluation of performance may be done on a pre-interest, pre-tax basis.

Netting and Matching **Netting** is a practice by which subsidiaries or affiliates within an MNE network settle inter-subsidiary indebtedness for the net amount owed during the post-transaction period. Gross intra-MNE trade receivables and payables are netted out. This approach not only reduces transaction and fund transfer cost and provides an opportunity for subsidiaries to manipulate their financial position but also helps foreign subsidiaries surpass the foreign exchange control barriers in respective countries. Netting occurs in either *bilateral* or *multilateral* form. *Bilateral netting* exists when two sister subsidiaries cancel out their receivables and payable and settle only the net payment. *Multilateral netting* involves three or more sister subsidiaries' inter-group debt and virtually necessitates the coordination of the headquarters treasury. For example, Pepsi's U.K. subsidiary buys $6 million worth of goods from the Swiss sister subsidiary, and the U.K. subsidiary sells $2 million worth of goods to the French sister subsidiary. During the same netting period, the Swiss subsidiary buys $2 million worth of goods from the French subsidiary. In this triangular case, the settlement of the inter-subsidiary debt within the three subsidiaries ends up involving a payment equivalent to $4 million from the U.K. subsidiary to the Swiss subsidiary.

For diversified MNEs, it is important to establish the netting center supervised by the headquarters treasury. Philips, for example, established what is called the Philips Multilateral Clearing System (PMC) in its headquarters to facilitate netting among affiliates (see Industry Box). Participating subsidiaries report all intra-MNE balances to the group treasury on an agreed date and the treasury subsequently advises all subsidiaries of amounts to be paid to and received from other subsidiaries on a specified date. Whether or not such netting operations function well largely depends on the effectiveness of information and communication systems and established discipline on the part of foreign subsidiaries.

Similar to netting, matching is often used for balancing accounts receivables and payable. However, it differs from netting in that matching may be used to match currency cash flows with firms outside the MNE network and occurs on the basis of the same foreign currency (netting may occur for different currencies). Specifically, **matching** is a mechanism whereby a company matches its foreign currency inflows with its foreign currency outflows in respect to amount, timing, and the currency unit. The prerequisite for a matching operation, either within or beyond the MNE network, is a two-way cash flow in the same foreign currency. For example, the U.S. firm focusing on exports to Canada can acquire its debt capital in the Canadian dollar markets and use the relatively predictable Canadian dollar cash inflows from export sales to service the principal and interest payments on Canadian

NETTING IN PHILIPS

Philips, the Dutch lighting and electronics giant, uses what is known as the Philips Multilateral Clearing System (PMC) to facilitate cash movements cross-border among its affiliates. This system is managed by the Amsterdam-based bank, Mendes Cans. Inter-subsidiary cross-border payments are made monthly through the PMC. Units worldwide notify treasury in Eindhoven of expected payments beginning 20 days prior to settlement. The system then generates payment instructions automatically several days before settlement date. Although most major international banks provide competent multilateral netting systems, Mendes Cans has long enjoyed a reputation as an innovator and high-quality partner in this regard.

Philips uses an internal, worldwide information exchange system called IFIS for purchase orders, invoices, and other communications related to inter-subsidiary transactions. IFIS is in effect an internal EDI (Electronic Data Information) system. Externally, Philips uses EDI for purchase orders and invoices with just a few trade partners; ironically, related payments and collections are still processed with different systems. Having spent a large part of his time in centralizing and improving funding and foreign exchange management, Corporate Treasurer Jean-Pierre Lac is now focusing on improving Philips's cash management. He is particularly concerned with the company's disbursement and collection methods. About 6,000 people in the company spend their time cutting checks, cashing checks, and doing related activities. Today, Philips is shifting from checks to electronic payments wherever possible. How quickly it can move depends on each country's payments system. In the Netherlands, for example, Philips delivers all of its payment orders to banks by tape; Germany and the Scandinavian countries have similar systems.

dollar debt. This U.S. exporter has thus hedged an operational cash inflow by creating a financial cash outflow, and so does not have to actively manage the exposure with contractual financial instruments. This technique is effective in eliminating operating exposure when the exposed cash flow is relatively constant and predictable over time. In addition to acquiring Canadian debt, there are several other ways to create cash outflow in the same foreign currency stated in the firm's cash inflow. For instance, the U.S. exporter could seek out potential suppliers in Canada as a substitute for raw materials or components previously procured from the United States. Another alternative is to pay foreign suppliers in a third country (e.g., Mexico or Venezuela) with Canadian dollars.

Intracompany Reinvoicing   This practice involves an establishment of a reinvoicing center within an MNE. The center is a separate corporate subsidiary that may be located in the MNE headquarters or in the country that is the center of financial intelligence for the MNE. Like the netting center, a reinvoicing center manages in one location all currency exposure from intracompany transactions. Thus, the reinvoicing center may be combined with or migrated into the netting center for some MNEs. The reinvoicing center often takes legal title of products but does not get involved in the physical movement of goods. In other words, it handles paperwork but has no inventory. For example, Acer's Korean subsidiary may ship goods directly to the Japanese sales affiliate. The invoice by the Korean subsidiary, which is denominated in Korean won, is passed on to Acer's reinvoicing center located in Singapore. The Singapore reinvoicing center takes legal title to the goods, then subsequently invoices the Japanese sales affiliate in Japanese yen. As a result, all operating subsidiaries deal only in their own currency, and all operating exposure lies with the reinvoicing center. In practice, such reinvoicing centers not only manage foreign exchange exposure for intracompany sales from one place but also oversee intracompany cash flows, including leads and lags. With a reinvoicing center, all subsidiaries settle intracompany accounts in their local currencies. The reinvoicing center need hedge only residual exposure for the entire MNE. Finally, in order to avoid some taxes such as interest withholding taxes or capital formation taxes, reinvoicing centers should avoid doing business with local suppliers or customers in the country of location. It is necessary for this special financial subsidiary to qualify for nonresident status, which helps the firm gain greater access to external foreign exchange markets and open bank accounts in foreign countries.

Production Initiatives

Input Outsourcing A firm can mitigate its economic exposure through input outsourcing in the same currency as the one used in export sales. To mitigate the risk from *endaka* in the 1990s, Japanese automakers protected themselves against the rising yen by purchasing a significant percentage of intermediate components from suppliers in Taiwan and South Korea. Because currencies of Taiwan and South Korea are closely linked to the U.S. dollar, the yen-equivalent prices of the intermediate supplies tend to decline with the dollar, and thus lessen the impact of a falling dollar on the cost of Japanese cars sold in the United States. In using this approach, MNEs should consider flexibility in making substitutions among various sources of goods and services. Maxwell House, for example, can blend the same coffee whether using coffee beans from Brazil, the Ivory Coast, or other producers. The more outsourcing flexibility, the easier it is for the firm to reduce operating exposure through offsetting accounts receivables against accounts payable in the same currency. This strategy, of course, must be weighed against the extra costs and the requirements of product differentiation in different markets.

Production Arrangement By production arrangement we mean that an MNE with worldwide production systems can adjust the quantity of its production in a specific location to respond to foreign exchange risk and exposure. An MNE may increase production in a nation whose currency has been devalued and decrease production in a country whose currency has been revalued. For example, with a well-developed portfolio of plants worldwide, Westinghouse Electric (United States) may ask its subsidiary in Spain to increase production of generators in response to a weakening peseta while arranging for another subsidiary in Canada to reduce generator production in response to a rising Canadian dollar. Similar examples can also be found at Ford and GM. These two companies have substantial leeway in reallocating various stages of production among their several plants in different countries, in line with relative production and transportation costs. Ford can shift production among the United States, Spain, Germany, the United Kingdom, Brazil, and Mexico. Obviously, this production initiative works better for MNEs whose products are standardized in the global market (see Chapter 16). Using the multiple production plants strategy to reduce currency risk must be weighed against the extra capital investment and operating costs. Standardized products benefit more from economies of scale and require fewer extra operating costs than specialized products.

Global Coordination of Exposure Management

Most of the techniques highlighted in Exhibit 14–6 cannot be instituted without headquarters coordination and guidance. Organizationally, an MNE's currency exposure should be coordinated and overseen by its netting and reinvoicing center which may or may not be located at headquarters. For MNEs without these centers, the treasurer's office at headquarters should play these roles. While most MNEs today are delegating more power in production and operations to overseas subsidiaries, they are using a centralized structure to manage currency exposure. Because of opportunities for offsetting exposures from different product divisions and/or different foreign subsidiaries, centralization of exposure management ensures offsetting

Latin America

EIGHT HEDGING TECHNIQUES IN LATIN AMERICA

1. Investing in dollar-related government assets, such as Argentina's bonex, Mexico's petrobonds, or Brazil's ORTN bonds.
2. Opening central bank dollar accounts, which normally pay monthly interest at LIBOR.
3. Using intercompany loans, that is, hedging excess cash by lending local currency to another company.
4. Investing in real estate, especially purchasing prime location office space as a long-term hedge.
5. Maintaining a portion of excess cash in gold.
6. Purchasing other commodities such as coffee and soybeans and exporting them to a home or third country.
7. Setting up a trading company there, which also handles risk management and receivable collection.
8. Converting debt/blocked funds to equity.

and self-hedging, which in turn reduces transaction costs and hedging expenses.[6] Centralization also increases benefits from economies of scale in purchasing financial instruments for hedging. It further facilitates the integration of hedging with other important aspects of international financial management such as global mobilization of cash flow, working capital management, and financing for global operations.[7] Finally, centralization does not diminish the importance of having valuable insights and necessary feedback from local managers. Incorporating a local perspective into the decision framework for exposure management helps diffuse conflicts between subsidiaries and headquarters. In situations where hedging can only be available at a local level, the role of the treasury at headquarters should transform from centralization to assistance. The electronic systems available today can greatly assist the management of currency exposure in terms of both strategy formation and ongoing control. Financial EDI (Electronic Data Information) systems have been already used by some MNEs such as Merck, SmithKline Beecham, Xerox, GE, and PepsiCo. EDI systems significantly improve the effectiveness of information flows within an MNE network. At the same time, EFT systems (electronic funds transfer) as applied by Philips, Siemens, and BMW have made cash flow shifts within an MNE network quicker and easier. The improved effectiveness of both information and cash flows in turn reduces the costs for exposure management and hastens the management process. Finally, global coordination should not rule out the importance of unique hedging techniques used in specific host countries. Local practices in exposure management may be more cost-effective. In Latin America, for example, many firms maintained a portion of excess cash in either gold- or dollar-related government bonds to hedge operating exposure during an inflationary period. The Country Box summarizes these techniques in Latin America.

Interim Summary

1. MNEs with resources built up in foreign countries encounter transaction exposure, economic (operating) exposure, and translation (accounting) exposure. Transaction and operating exposures are caused by real changes in the value of a company's cash flows or assets, whereas accounting exposure is not caused by this real change but the use of differing exchange rates when financial statements in multiple currencies are consolidated.

2. There are a number of ways of handling risks related to transaction exposure. These include hedging with financial instruments (forward, futures, options, and swaps) and hedging with contract invoicing and special clauses. Managing operating exposure is achieved through financial initiatives (leads and lags, netting and matching, intracompany reinvoicing), and production initiatives (input outsourcing and product arrangement).

WORKING CAPITAL MANAGEMENT

Quantitatively, working capital is equal to the amount of current assets minus the amount of current liabilities. In practice, working capital management concerns the efficiency enhancement of current assets such as cash, accounts receivable, and inventory. Because cash and accounts receivable are particularly vulnerable to the impact of currency fluctuations, potential exchange controls, and multiple tax jurisdictions, this section highlights the management of cash and accounts receivables.

Cash Management

Ideally, a global treasury would be a single finance company with the ability to disburse or collect all financial reserves worldwide instantaneously, and with the absolute minimum risk and transaction costs. In reality, however, there are many limits such as financial regulations, cash-flow restrictions, and idiosyncratic tax structures in foreign territories in which operations take place. The global cash management system includes three elements: home-country cash management, host-country cash management, and cross-border cash management. Most MNEs centralize at home such activities as borrowing, global liquidity management, international banking relations, and foreign exchange exposure management. Meanwhile, local disbursement and collection, local banking relationships, payroll, or management of trade credit and purchasing are generally managed overseas.

MNE cash concentration, known as *pooling,* generally occurs in two stages. First, cash is collected and pooled in local currency and used for local expenses. If a company has several subsidiaries in a single country, it is very efficient to use cash surpluses from one to fund the cash deficits of another. As introduced in Chapter 10, these activities are generally undertaken by the MNE's umbrella company, which plays a role as headquarters in the host country. Periodically, as net cash surpluses grow, unneeded funds are remitted. Siemens, for example, carefully manages national cash pools in each currency, using cash excesses from some units to fund the cash needs of others within the same host country. Treasury looks at balances and short-term cash projections for each national cash pool and decides how much to lend or draw out. Central borrowing is generally cheaper, but a special loan program or a high tax rate at the subsidiary level can sometimes make local borrowing more attractive. It is hence necessary to consider interest rates, tax rates, and the profitability of local operations when determining the most efficient funding route.

Another approach for global cash management is to build an efficient account structure, which also helps reduce banking fees and float. For example, Merck, a major U.S. pharmaceutical producer, uses a network of accounts held within a single bank's global network to transfer funds between national pools and the Merck treasury center in London. The system works in this way: The global bank maintains branches in each country of Merck's operation. At each branch, there is now both a national pool account and a treasury center account, with the treasury center wielding authority over both accounts. If a French subsidiary has "long" French francs, it can place the funds with the treasury center in the form of a deposit (a loan to the treasury). This subsidiary first transfers those funds into the French national pool account with the global bank's Paris branch. Then the treasury center debits the national pool account and moves the funds into its own account at the Paris branch. By transferring funds in this way, the company can avoid lifting charges levied by many European banks for transfers from resident to non-resident accounts.

Today, many diversified large MNEs have found that their financial resources and needs are either too large or too sophisticated for the financial services available in many locations where they operate. In response, many have established *in-house banks* to manage not only currency exposure but also cash flows. Such an in-house bank is not a separate corporation; rather, it is a set of functions performed by the existing treasury department. Acting as an independent entity, the central treasury of the firm transacts with its various business units. The purpose of the in-house bank is to provide bank-like services to the various units of the firm. The in-house bank may be able to provide services not available in many country markets, and may do so at lower cost when available. In addition to providing financing benefits, in-house banks allow for more effective currency risk management. Foreign subunits may sell their intra-MNE receivables to the in-house bank. The in-house bank is better equipped to deal with currency exposure and has a greater volume of international cash flow, allowing foreign subunits as a whole to gain from more effective use of netting and matching. This approach frees the units of the firm from struggling to manage transaction exposures and allows them to focus on their primary business activities. Volvo Construction Equipment's treasury center in Brussels acts as an in-house bank that maintains a network of bank accounts for all intra-organizational transactions. This network of accounts is used primarily for inter-subsidiary payments, and subsidiaries are responsible for making third-party payments and collections through local banks.

Foreign Receivable Management

A firm's operating cash flow comes primarily from collecting its accounts receivables. Managing foreign receivables requires appropriate measures in three stages: pre-transaction stage, transaction stage, and post-transaction stage. In the *pre-transaction stage,* a firm must investigate the buyer or importer's corporate credibility and financial capability. This is particularly imperative when dealing with a new client from a foreign country. Many large international companies categorize foreign clients into several clusters such as superior customers, priority customers, normal customers, and risky customers. This categorization and related client information are then disseminated to sales managers and treasury managers. Such clustering is usually built upon a client's previous record, company size, corporate image, financial strengths, and targeted markets. An exporter can obtain this information from previous collaboration, bank reports, archival research, or credit investigation agents. In general, the selection of currency unit, terms of payment, and the length of credit are all contingent on a foreign buyer's creditability and repayment ability.

In a *transaction stage,* the exporting company needs to decide in what currency the transaction should be denominated and what the terms of payment (including the length of time draft) should be. Ideally, the exporting transaction should be denominated in a hard currency together with a letter of credit at sight. In practice, however, this is largely determined by the exporter's bargaining power vis-à-vis the importer. The hedging instruments, hedging clauses, and invoicing techniques introduced earlier are useful in this stage.

International firms must establish organizational systems for tracking, managing, and collecting foreign accounts receivables in a *post-transaction stage.* In these systems, managers in the accounting or treasury department should be able to track the collection record and coordinate with the international sales or marketing department (when D/P or D/A is used) or the bank (when L/C is used). They should also share the information concerning the foreign exchange gains or losses and uncollected due receivables with the sales or marketing managers so that the latter could better evaluate past transactions and better prepare future businesses. In many firms, collecting foreign accounts receivables is linked with the reward system for sales managers. The level of bonus, commission, or reward does not depend on the amount of sales, but rather on the actual revenues collected.

Interim Summary

1. Cash and accounts receivable are particularly vulnerable to currency fluctuations, exchange controls, and multiple tax jurisdictions. Many MNEs have established in-house banks to manage cash flows and accounts receivables.

2. Most MNEs centralize at home borrowing, global liquidity management, international banking relations, and foreign exchange exposure management while leaving the management of local cash disbursement and collection, local banking relations, payroll, and trade credit management to local managers.

CHAPTER SUMMARY

1. Financial management for global operations occurs in an environment with foreign exchange risks, capital flow restrictions, country risks, and different tax systems. It deals with foreign trade finance, global financing, managing foreign exchange risk and exposure, and working capital management.

2. Payment for international transactions differs markedly from that for domestic transactions. To the exporter, bad debt risks ascend along cash in advance, letter of credit (L/C), documentary collection (D/P or D/A), and open account. Many uniform documents such as draft, bill of lading (B/L), and commercial invoice are needed in international payment.

3. Smaller international firms play an active part in international trade. To obtain export financing, they can use several channels, including private sources (commercial banks, factoring or forfeit houses, and corporate guarantee) and government sources (export-import banks and foreign credit insurance).

4. FDI involves more yet complex financing choices, including intercompany financing, equity financing, debt financing, and local currency financing. Intercompany loans from parent or peer subsidiaries can also be used for the purpose of avoiding taxation or foreign exchange control. Crosslisting firm stocks on exchanges in different countries is a major financing source for large MNEs because it increases liquidity and visibility.

5. Eurocurrency markets are the major source of international bank loans (i.e., Eurocredits). Yankee bonds are foreign bonds sold in the United States and Samurai bonds are foreign bonds sold in Japan. All financing decisions must consider currency risks, source diversity, taxation implications, and interest rates.

6. Foreign exchange risk and exposure are two related yet distinct concepts. The former concerns the variance of the home-currency value of an asset, liability, or income affected by unanticipated changes in exchange rates. The latter refers to the sensitivity of changes in the home-currency value of an asset, liability, or income to unanticipated changes in exchange rates. Risk is an increasing function of exposure and the variance of unanticipated changes in exchange rates.

7. MNEs encounter three types of foreign exchange exposure—transaction exposure, translation (accounting) exposure, and economic (operating) exposure. Transaction exposure can be hedged through financial instruments such as forward and options and production initiatives such as input sourcing.

8. Firms need to create a global management system for working capital, especially cash flow. Headquarters managers must clearly define what aspects of cash management are centralized and what should be decentralized. Meanwhile, they should formalize policies managing international account receivables.

CHAPTER NOTES

[1] See S. M. Saudagaran, "An empirical study of selected factors influencing the decision to list on foreign stock exchange," *Journal of International Business Studies,* Spring 1988, 101–128; D. K. Eiteman, A. I. Stonehill, and M. H. Moffett. *Multinational Business Finance.* New York: Addison-Wesley, 1998.

[2] J. J. Choi, "Diversification, exchange risk, and corporate international investment," *Journal of International Business Studies,* Spring 1989, 145–155; M. Adler and B. Dumas, "International portfolio choice and corporate finance: A synthesis," *Journal of Finance,* June 1983, 925–984.

[3] See M. D. Levi, *International Finance.* New York: McGraw-Hill, 1996, 302.

[4] See M. Adler and B. Dumas, "Exposure to currency risk: Definition and measurement," *Financial Management,* Summer 1984, 41–50; C. R. Hekman, "Measuring foreign exchange exposure: A practical theory and its application," *Financial Analysts Journal,* September/October 1983, 59–65.

[5] C. C. Y. Kwok, "Hedging foreign exchange exposures: Independent vs. integrative approaches," *Journal of International Business Studies,* Summer 1987, 33–52; L. Oxelheim, "Managing foreign exchange exposure," *Journal of Applied Corporate Finance,* 3(4), 1991, 73–82.

[6] L. Oxelheim, *Managing in the Turbulent World Economy—Corporate Performance and Risk Exposure.* New York: Wiley, 1997; L. A. Soenen and J. Madura, "Foreign exchange management—A strategic approach," *Long Range Planning,* 24(5), 1991, 119–124.

[7] D. R. Lessard and S. B. Lightstore, "Volatile exchange rates can put operations at risk," *Harvard Business Review,* July/August 1986, 107–114; R. M. Stulz, "Rethinking risk management," *Journal of Applied Corporate Finance,* 9(3), 1996, 8–24; W. R. Folks, Jr., "Decision analysis for exchange risk management," *Financial Management,* Winter 1972, 101–112.

International Accounting for Global Operations

DO YOU KNOW

1. What forces lead to different national accounting systems? How many accounting zones are there internationally and what are these zones based on? If you were a manager at Nokia, would you like to see international harmonization of such different systems? Why or why not?

2. Why is foreign currency translation so important yet difficult for MNEs? What are the major translation methods? Can U.S. companies such as Honeywell choose a specific method they like or switch methods every year?

3. What are the main benefits of intra-MNE transfer pricing practices and how do taxation agencies ensure that these transactions are fair? If you are a manager in large MNEs such as 3M, what do you take into account in choosing a transfer pricing practice?

OPENING CASE Compaq Won the Case

After a string of victories in the U.S. tax courts, the IRS (Internal Revenue Service) has lost a transfer pricing case. Not only did Compaq avoid the excess tax that the IRS had charged, it also received a positive adjustment of $21 million. This is the first reported case of a company receiving a positive adjustment. The case concerned the prices Compaq in the United States paid its Singapore subsidiary for circuit boards. The IRS claimed that the prices charged by the subsidiary did not reflect the *arm's-length price* (i.e., the price one independent company would charge another independent company for a good or service). Compaq's defense was that there was no other subcontractor in Singapore capable of manufacturing the boards to the required standards. Mark Oates, a Baker & McKenzie tax partner in Chicago represented Compaq. He commented: "As a technical proposition, Compaq was on the leading edge of circuit board technology and the Singapore subcontractors simply did not possess the capital-intensive equipment, the engineers, the processes or the experience required to produce and test the boards. As a factual matter, Compaq was able to prove that the Singapore subcontractors did not and could not produce the boards at issue." Compaq was indeed able to prove that the prices, after adjustment for minor physical differences, were comparable to those paid by Compaq to unrelated subcontractors in the United States. The IRS argument that the Singapore subsidiary made excess profits was rejected in favor of the price comparison method used by Compaq. The judge described the IRS's profits-based calculations as "arbitrary, capricious and unreasonable," and based on "unrealistic material, labor and overhead markups." ■

Sources: Adapted from Anonymous, "IRS loses key transfer pricing case," *International Tax Review,* September 1999, 10(8): 6–7; and D. Laro, "Economic substance: A view from the tax court," *Tax Executive,* January/February 2000, 52(1): 44–48.

COUNTRY DIFFERENCES IN ACCOUNTING

The Compaq case illustrates that MNEs should deal appropriately with accounting and tax issues that affect the firms' net incomes and cash flow. The aim of an *accounting system* is to identify, measure, and communicate economic information to allow informed judgments and decisions by users of the information. Today, the explosive expansion of cross-border transactions and the rapid growth of companies seeking capital in international markets have made international accounting issues a daily concern for international managers. **International accounting** involves accounting and taxation issues for companies that have internationalized their economic activities across countries in which accounting standards and practices vary. Four fundamental issues need to be understood by international business managers: (1) country differences in accounting and international harmonization; (2) foreign currency translation; (3) cross-border transfer pricing; and (4) tax havens, treaties, and strategies. We explain country differences in the next section.

Why Accounting Systems Differ Among Countries

To a large extent, accounting is a product of its external environment. It is shaped by, reflects, and reinforces characteristics peculiar to its national environment. No two countries have identical accounting systems. In a few cases—such as that of the United States and Canada, or the United Kingdom and Ireland—the differences are relatively few and minor. In other instances—for example, Germany and France, or China and India—the differences are much more fundamental.[1] In general, a country's accounting system is shaped by *institutions, societal culture,* and *external relations* with other countries. The institutions of the country, in particular how it organizes its economic, political, legal, taxation, and professional systems, are the central forces determining the development of the accounting system.

Institutions

Economic System. A country's economic system factors, such as the level of inflation, economic and industrial structures, and the complexity of business organizations, affect the accounting system. As inflation rates increase, the problems of historical cost accounting also increase. Developed countries rarely suffer severely from high inflation and thus tend to view inflation accounting with suspicion. Inflation continues to be a serious problem in countries such as Mexico, Chile, and Brazil. Obviously, when inflation is running at high levels, the historical cost of an asset quickly becomes irrelevant. Therefore, various forms of inflation accounting have been found in these countries. In Brazil, for example, a revised Corporation Law, introduced in 1976, regulated that official monthly price indices be employed to update the values of all assets, depreciation, cost of goods sold, and owner's equity.

Economic structure influences how such accounting issues as pensions, retained earnings, dividends, depreciation, and research and development (R&D) cost amortization are handled. For example, accounting for pensions is an important issue in the United States, which has a very complex and concrete pension standard. This reflects the particular institutional arrangements of the United States, where many companies oversee employee pension plans. In other regions such as Chile, Hong Kong and Singapore, pensions are run by the state or through private arrangements, and accounting for pensions becomes less important. In some transitional economies such as China, Russia, and Hungary, accounting for owner's equity items such as initial capital, retained earnings, and dividends vary according to ownership form, i.e., state-owned, collectively-owned, privately-owned, and foreign-owned enterprises. Similarly, accounting for depreciation and R&D expense amortization differs across countries that have different levels of economic development. More advanced economies such as Japan and the United States tend to use a faster amortization schedule.

Industrial structure affects the consistency of accounting standards and practices among different industries. Whether or not a country stipulates industry-specific accounting principles depends on the relative importance of that industry to the economy. For example, in Vietnam, accounting standards governing the foreign trade sector differ significantly from those governing other sectors. Similarly, accounting for the oil and gas industry has been a crucial and contentious issue in the United States and subject to unique accounting rules and practices. In the United Kingdom, the standard on research and development was strongly influenced by the potential impact of alternative accounting methods on companies in the aerospace and other R&D-dependent industries.

The complexity of the business organizations that dominate an economy affects the complexity of the internal accounting information system and management accounting in general. For instance, if most companies in a country are small or family-owned, then there is little need for external, sophisticated reporting systems, and there should be relatively few accounting regulations. As a company increases in size and complexity, the demand for sophisticated management accounting systems heightens, with problems of control, performance evaluations, and decision making gaining center stage. Typically, when business organizations become more complex, firms will start to arrange themselves into groups, with subsidiaries, branches, joint ventures, or strategic alliances all gaining in importance. Accounting standards and practices must reflect these changes. For example, greater focus will be placed on the regulation of group financial statements and extra disclosure requirements.

Political System. The political system is a critical determinant of national accounting because the accounting system will reflect political philosophies and objectives. The most common system found in western Europe, North America, Japan, and Australia, for instance, is the *liberal-democratic system.* A second important system is the *egalitarian-authoritarian political system* (e.g., North Korea and Cuba). Most transition economies such as Russia and eastern European countries fall somewhere in-between. In the egalitarian-authoritarian form, all production and operations are owned and controlled by governmental institutions. Accounting serves two roles in this circumstance: to help in centralized planning and to help in controlling the economy. Profit is essentially retained by the government instead of the firm. Therefore, "owner's equity" in state-owned enterprises actually reflects "state's equity" or "governmental equity." While dividend policy is important in western countries, it is meaningless in central-planning systems.

Legal System. The legal system determines the extent to which company law governs the regulation of accounting. In countries such as France, Germany, and Argentina, in which *codified Roman law* dominates, accounting regulations and rules appear to be concrete and comprehensive. This contrasts with countries using common law such as the United Kingdom and the United States. As such, many split the accounting world into two groups based on the pervasiveness of the legal approach: *legalistic orientation* toward accounting (i.e., using codified Roman law) and *nonlegalistic orientation* (i.e., using common law). Laws in codified Roman law countries are a series of *"thou shalts"* (you-shall) that stipulate the minimum standard of behavior expected. In most countries with a legalistic orientation, accounting principles are national laws and accounting practices are codified. Accounting rules tend to be prescriptive, detailed, and procedural. Because accounting standards and practices are set by legislators, whether or not they are adaptive and effective depends largely on the legislators' knowledge of accounting principles, practices, and implications.

By contrast, laws in countries with a nonlegalistic orientation are a series of *"thou shalt nots"* (you-shall-not) that establish the limits beyond which an activity or practice is unlawful. Within these boundaries, latitude and judgment are allowed and encouraged. Accounting practices in common law countries are in large part decided by accountants themselves. Thus they tend to be more flexible, innovative, and adaptive. Nevertheless, the legalistic approach may be used in a particular sector or a special circumstance in common law countries. For example, tax laws and the regulations enacted by the U.S. Securities and Exchange Commission represent the legalistic approach to accounting. In addition, certain laws not directly related to accounting may have strong implications for accounting practices. For example, the major accounting effect of the *Foreign Corrupt Practices Act* in the United States is that U.S. MNEs must establish a system of internal controls and an internal audit staff to ensure that bribes are not being offered (see Chapter 19).

Taxation System. The taxation system is an important factor in situations where accounting systems are strongly influenced by state objectives. In countries such as France and Germany, public accounting reports are used to determine tax liabilities. In the United States and the United Kingdom, published accounts are adjusted for tax purposes and submitted separately from the reports to shareholders. Overall, there are three types of tax systems that correspond to different financial reporting rules:

- Tax rules and financial reporting rules are kept entirely, or mostly, independent of each other (e.g., the United Kingdom and the United States).
- There is a common system, with many of the financial reporting rules also being used by the tax authorities (e.g., less developed British Commonwealth countries).
- There is a common system, with many of the tax rules also being used for financial reporting purposes (e.g., Austria and western Europe).

Professional System. The accounting profession is influential because the way in which the profession is organized and society's attitude toward accountants affect their ability to control or audit companies and their reporting systems. The extent to which auditors are independent and hold power relative to the companies they audit influences the perceived value of financial statements. The accountant's role in formulating regulation also affects the national accounting system. Even though this role is largely contingent on the country's legal system, accounting regulations can be influenced by the professional who may act as an adviser to the government, provide input into the regulatory process, and issue standards or recommendations in areas where there are no legal regulations. The French profession in the form of the OEC (Ordre des Experts Comptables) provides a good example of this approach.[2]

Societal Culture

Societal culture influences the accounting system. For example, the detailed accounting procedures instituted by the French government reflect France's statistical tradition. Australia's accounting requirements for public firms are generally permissive, reflecting the distrust of government power embedded in that country's individualistic, frontier culture. Cultural dimensions at the national level, initially identified by Hofstede,[3] which are particularly relevant to accounting development, are "uncertainty avoidance" and "individualism." As outlined in detail in Chapter 6, in a high uncertainty avoidance country, institutions will be organized in ways that minimize uncertainty. Rules and standards tend to be explicit, prescriptive, all-embracing, and rigid. Individualism affects preferences for earnings measurement rules and disclosure practices, and influences the willingness to accept uniform accounting rules in preference to a more permissive system involving the use of professional discretion. Recent studies by accounting scholars suggest that countries with low uncertainty avoidance cultures (e.g., the United Kingdom, the United States, and Sweden) tend to have strong independent auditing professions that audit a firm's accounts to ensure they comply with *GAAP (Generally Accepted Accounting Principles)*.[4]

External Relations

External relations, economically and/or politically, with other countries influence accounting practices and regulations through colonialism or regionalization. Historically, colonies adopted or were forced to adopt the accounting system of the colonial power, even though it may not have been particularly appropriate at the colony's stage of development. Thus the accounting standards and practices in the British colonies were significantly influenced by British accounting, and the influence remains today in Hong Kong, Australia, New Zealand, India, and Jamaica. The same can be said for former French colonies, Spanish colonies, and others. Regionalization harmonizes national differences in accounting systems. For example, since the passage of NAFTA, the accounting systems in the United States, Canada, and Mexico have converged on a common set of norms. Similarly, the member nations of the European Union, and the Central American Common Market (CACM) have expended great effort toward integrating their accounting systems.

As shown in Exhibit 15–1, the preceding forces, namely institutions, societal culture, and external relations jointly affect or explain a country's accounting system, especially accounting objectives, regulation mode, and regulation strictness. Accounting objectives refer to the extent they meet the needs of investors, creditors,

Exhibit 15–1
Forces shaping a country's accounting system

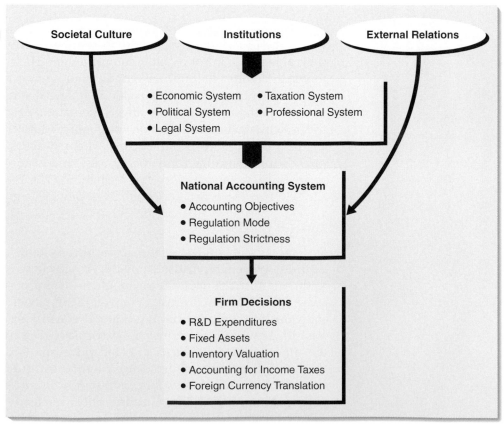

ACCOUNTING DIVERSITY IN VOLVO

Volvo is one of the largest industrial groups in the Nordic region. More than 80 percent of its sales occur outside Sweden. For a large MNE from a relatively small country, raising capital on foreign stock markets is an essential vehicle to access international capital and improve publicity. Currently, Volvo's shares are traded on the stock exchange of eight foreign countries, including the United Kingdom, Germany, Norway, France, the United States, Belgium, Japan, and Switzerland. The largest foreign market was London, where 17.8 million shares were traded, while in the United States 2.0 million ADRs were traded on Nasdaq. The London Stock Exchange requirements for listing demand that a company produce financial statements that are prepared and independently audited in accordance with standards appropriate for companies of international standing and repute. Any financial statements that comply with International Accounting Standards, U.K. or U.S. standards would automatically meet these requirements. In contrast, the SEC in the United States requires all foreign corporations to disclose, in their annual Form 20-F report, a U.S. GAAP reconciliation of their reported net income and shareholders' equity. Volvo, along with many other corporations subject to these requirements, voluntarily reproduces some financial information in its annual report and accounts together with an explanation of the U.S.-GAAP differences.

the government, or other users. The mode of regulation concerns whether accounting rules and standards are regulated by government, the profession, or other groups. Finally, the strictness of regulation is the extent to which accounting rules and standards are strict and comprehensive. The Industry Box exhibits accounting diversity in Volvo during its global expansion and operations.

The characteristics of a national accounting system influence many company decisions, especially those concerning research and development (R&D) expenditure, fixed assets, inventory valuation, accounting for income taxes, and foreign currency translation. For example, Germany and the United States require immediate expense recognition for R&D expenditure under all circumstances since they believe that there is a great deal of uncertainty as to whether the R&D will benefit future periods. Canada, France, the Netherlands, Switzerland, the United Kingdom, and *IAS (International Accounting Standards),* however, allow this recognition only where the technical feasibility of a product or process has been established.[5]

National Accounting Zones

Although no two countries share identical accounting standards and practices, countries can be grouped into a few clusters based on critical similarities. This is possible because factors that shape a country's accounting system, as discussed earlier, can be similar to those facing another country. In light of dramatic changes in both external environment and accounting systems in many countries, especially emerging economies, we list five accounting zones. This is a modified list, building on a recent study by Mueller and his associates.[6] As highlighted in Exhibit 15–2, these five zones are:

1. British-American (or Anglo-Saxon)
2. Continental
3. South American
4. Transitional Economy
5. Centrally Planned Economy

Exhibit 15–2
Selected economies using the four major accounting models

British-American Model

Australia	India	Panama
Bahamas	Indonesia	Papua New Guinea
Barbados	Ireland	Philippines
Benin	Israel	Puerto Rico
Bermuda	Jamaica	Singapore
Botswana	Kenya	South Africa
Canada	Liberia	Tanzania
Cayman Islands	Malawi	Trinidad & Tobago
Central America	Malaysia	Uganda
Colombia	Mexico	United Kingdom
Cyprus	Netherlands	United States
Dominican Republic	New Zealand	Venezuela
Fiji	Nigeria	Zambia
Ghana	Pakistan	Zimbabwe
Hong Kong		

Continental Model

Algeria	Germany	Norway
Angola	Greece	Portugal
Austria	Papua New Guinea	Senegal
Belgium	Italy	Sierra Leone
Burkina Fasso	Ivory Coast	Spain
Cameroon	Japan	Sweden
Denmark	Luxembourg	Switzerland
Egypt	Mali	Togo
Finland	Morocco	Zaire
France		

South American Model

Argentina	Chile	Paraguay
Bolivia	Ecuador	Peru
Brazil	Guyana	Uruguay

Transitional Economy Model

Armenia	Hungary	Russia
Azerbaidzhan	Kazakhstan	Serbia
Belarus	Kirgizia	Slovak Republic
Bosnia-Herzegovina	Latvia	Slovenia
Bulgaria	Lithuania	Tadzhikstan
Croatia	Moldavia	Turkmenistan
Czech Republic	Poland	Ukraine
Estonia	Romania	Uzbekistan
Georgia	China	

Centrally Planned Economy Model

Cuba	North Korea	Vietnam

In *Anglo-Saxon nations,* accounting is oriented toward the decision needs of investors and creditors. Countries in the *Continental zone* include most of continental Europe and Japan. Financial accounting is legalistic in its orientation, and practices tend to be highly conservative. Most countries in South America belong to the *South American zone,* with the exception of Brazil. A distinct feature in this zone is the persistent use of accounting adjustments for inflation. In the *transitional economy zone,* accounting standards vary according to ownership types. For collectively owned (e.g., township or village enterprises that are jointly owned by the local community, management, and workers) and privately owned enterprises, the accounting orientation moves toward a capitalist market, emphasizing information for investors, bankers, and taxation departments. State-owned enterprises (SOEs) that are no longer dominating their national economies operate under dual accounting systems. One provides information for managers used to the former system oriented toward a command economy which retains a heavy proportion of net profits earned by SOEs; the other employs a capitalist market orientation, trying to emulate the British-American accounting model. China is included in this zone because its SOEs no longer play a dominant role in shaping its growing economy. Chinese SOEs in many sectors have already adopted new accounting principles that are virtually similar to the GAAP in the United States. Finally, the accounting system in the *Centrally Planned economies,* in which central governments control production and resources of most enterprises, is characterized by high uniformity. Uniform accounting is necessary for tight central economic control. The primary users of financial statements are governmental planners. Assets are state-owned, and liabilities accrue through governmental arrangements via state banks. Initial or increased capital contribution was made and owned by the government. The overwhelming majority of net profits is either turned over to the state (often upper-level governmental authorities) or owned by the government. "Owner's equity" in a private sense does not exist.

International Accounting Harmonization

Having discussed national differences in accounting systems earlier, we can better appreciate the benefits that can be obtained from international harmonization and standardization. **Harmonization** is a process of increasing the compatibility of accounting practices by setting limits on how much they can vary. Harmonized standards minimize logical conflicts and improve the comparability of financial information from different countries.[7] The terms harmonization and standardization are often used interchangeably. Although highly related, these two concepts are not identical. **Standardization** means the imposition of a rigid and narrow set of rules and may even apply a single standard to all situations. Unlike harmonization, standardization does not necessarily accommodate national differences. As such, harmonization is a more appropriate term than standardization in the reconciliation of national differences in accounting standards. Accounting harmonization is comprised of three main components:

- Harmonization of accounting standards that deal with measurement and disclosure
- Disclosures made by publicly traded companies in connection with securities offerings and stock exchange listings
- Auditing standards

Not everyone agrees that national differences in accounting standards should be harmonized. Some argue that international standards setting was too simple a solution for a complex problem. They suspect that these standards could be adaptive enough to handle differences in social traditions, political systems, and economic environments among different countries. Along with the increasing integration of the world economy, however, the pressure for internationalizing and harmonizing accounting and auditing practices has been intensified. A growing body of evidence suggests that the need for international harmonization of accounting, disclosure, and auditing has been so widely accepted that the trend will accelerate. The globalized business community requires transparent, internationally comparable accounting practices consistent across borders. The two most notable developments that increase the necessity for harmonization are the evolution of MNEs and the development of international capital markets. For many MNEs, more than half of sales, profits, assets, or investments come from overseas operations. The heterogeneity of applicable accounting, auditing, and tax rules hampers an MNE's ability to prepare reliable financial information necessary for a careful analysis of various strategies. Meanwhile, the vast global capital market requires a common accounting language for the communication of financial information. In the absence of this common language, it is difficult to develop and maintain a truly efficient global capital market.

The major benefits of harmonization are threefold. First, comparable and transparent financial information helps enhance the reliability of foreign financial statements. It also helps in making informed decisions which, in turn, reduce risk for investors. Second, harmonized accounting reduces the costs of preparing financial statements and facilitates the task of investment analysts, investors, and other users in assessing business results. This saves on both the time and money currently spent consolidating divergent financial information. Third, many emerging and transitional economies regard uniform accounting as an efficient way of conforming to global norms. This is because they can avoid creating burdensome national standard-setting bodies of their own. For instance, China is about to issue a core set of accounting standards that are based on, and broadly comply with, International Accounting Standards (IAS).

International Accounting Standards

Harmonization proceeds through formulating and implementing international accounting standards. These standards have now been widely recognized and accepted in many countries throughout the world. For instance, a special television program was recently broadcast in Japan covering new accounting rules developed by IAS Committee and their impact on corporate financial reporting in Japan. The key players in setting international accounting standards and in promoting international accounting harmonization include the following:

1. International Accounting Standards Committee (IASC)
2. Commission of the European Union (CEU)
3. International Organization of Securities Commissions (IOSCO)
4. International Federation of Accountants (IFAC)
5. International Standards of Accounting and Reporting (ISAR), which is under the United Nations Conference on Trade and Development (UNCTAD)
6. Organization for Economic Cooperation and Development Working Group on Accounting Standards

IASC, the most dominant player in setting international accounting standards, was founded in 1973 by representatives of professional bodies in Australia, Canada, France, Germany, Japan, Mexico, the Netherlands, the United Kingdom, Ireland, and the United States. As of January 1999, IASC included 142 member bodies in 103 countries, representing more than 2 million accountants. IAS are used as a result of either international or political agreement (e.g., the European Union accounting-related directives), or voluntary compliance. When national and international standards differ, national standards usually take precedence. Companies that adopt more than one set of accounting standards must often issue one set of reports for each set of accounting standards they adopt. At the national level, some countries now use IAS as the basis for national standards, whereas others use them as a benchmark against which to compare national practices. The standard-setting bodies in many developing countries are now using IAS as the basis for national requirements although there are some who question the desirability of wholesale adoption without regard for differing economic circumstances. The Country Box offers an example in Australia.

An increasing number of MNEs report their accounting results by reference to IAS. When the accounting standards in a home country conform with IAS, accounting managers need not provide separate sets of financial statements; they just need to offer an explicit statement of conformity with IAS as well as national standards. Groupe Saint Louis (a French MNE), for example, provides such a note attached to its consolidated financial statements:

The Saint Louis consolidated financial statements have been prepared in accordance with French accounting principles relating to consolidated accounts. The principles and methods used are also in conformity with the pronouncements of IAS Committee.

When national and international standards differ, MNEs often include in the financial report a reconciliation showing the differences between national accounting practices and the requirements of IAS. Profit before taxation and shareholder's equity are usually reported twice, with one based on IAS and the other on the home country's standards. Some other companies provide full financial statements in conformity with IAS, either as the main financial statements or in addition to the financial statements complying with national accounting practices. Nokia (Finland),

---

COUNTRY BOX

Australia

ACCOUNTING IN AUSTRALIA

The Australian Accounting Standards Board (AASB), the main body governing accounting policies in Australia, has issued ED 102, International Harmonization and Convergence Policy. The proposals reflect the AASB's statutory responsibility to participate in, and contribute to, the development of a single set of worldwide accounting standards. The AASB's objective is to pursue, through participation in the activities of the International Accounting Standards Committee (IASC) and the International Federation of Accountants' Public Sector Committee (PSC), the development of an internationally accepted single set of accounting standards that can be adopted in Australia for both domestic and worldwide use. In the short term, however, AASB aims to converge the Australian standards with those issued by IASC, but only where such standards are "in the best interests of both the private and public sectors in the Australian economy."

As part of its work program, the AASB intends to work with the IASC and PSC to remove incompatibilities between international standards and the corresponding Australian standards. For instance, AASB's ED#49 somewhat differs from IAS#38 in measuring, amortizing, and recognizing intangible assets (including R&D expenditure). When AASB harmonizes with IAS#38, it results in a value decrease of many existing intangible assets, fewer new intangibles being recognized as assets, and lower costs that can be recognized as expenses in developing intangible assets. IAS#38 imposes many more restrictions in recognizing internally generated intangibles such as goodwill, brand names, mastheads, and publishing titles than does AASB's ED#49.

Source: Adapted from Jim Dixon, "Harmonization policy," *Accountancy*, October 1, 2001, Vol. 128, Issue 1298, pp. 1–2; Colin Parker and Daen Soukseun, "IAS 38: How tangible is the intangible standard," *Australian CPA*, December 1998, Vol. 68, Issue 11, pp. 32–33.

for example, prepares the financial statements according to IAS. At the same time, it provides a reconciliation between U.S. GAAP and IAS results.

Core standards as set forth by IAS include the following categories:

- General, which involves disclosure of accounting policies, changes in accounting policies, and information disclosed in financial statements.
- Income statement, which deals with such issues as revenue recognition, construction contracts, production and purchase costs, depreciation, taxes, government grants, retirements benefits, research and development, interest, and hedging.
- Balance sheet, which covers various issues such as leases, inventories, deferred taxes, foreign currency, investments, joint ventures, business combinations, intangible assets, and goodwill.
- Other standards, which involve how to account for consolidated financial statements, subsidiaries in hyperinflationary economies, equity financing, earnings per share, discontinued operations, fundamental errors, and segment reporting.[8]

Interim Summary

1. Accounting practices in each nation are shaped by that country's institutions, culture, and external relations. Institutions include economic, political, legal, taxation, and professional systems. Legal systems divide accounting into two broad groups: the legalistic orientation based in countries with codified Roman law and the nonlegalistic orientation found in countries with common law systems.

2. Based on national accounting systems and practices, countries can generally be grouped into five accounting zones, including Anglo-Saxon, Continental, South American, Transition Economies, and Centrally Planned economies. Within each group, countries share not only similar accounting systems but also similar economic and organizational structures.

FOREIGN CURRENCY TRANSLATION

Foreign currency translation is perhaps the most prominent accounting issue that directly and significantly affects the results revealed in MNE's financial statements. MNEs, regardless of their home countries, cannot prepare consolidated financial statements unless their accounts and those of their subsidiaries are expressed in a same, single currency. For instance, one cannot add Chinese yuan (RMB) or Japanese yen to U.S. dollars without a proper conversion of different currencies. Without foreign currency translation, MNE headquarters cannot appropriately plan, evaluate, integrate, and control overseas activities that should be coordinated within the network. The expanded scale of international investment activities also necessitates foreign currency translation. This occurs particularly when an MNE's subsidiary wishes to list its shares on a foreign stock exchange, contemplates a foreign acquisition or joint venture, or wants to communicate its operating results and financial position to its foreign stockholders.

Translation is the process of restating accounting data recorded in one currency (e.g., the currency of a foreign subsidiary in Italy) into another currency (e.g., the currency of the parent company in the United States) for the purpose of

Exhibit 15–3
Glossary of foreign currency translation terms

Conversion The exchange of one currency for another.

Current Rate The exchange rate in effect at the relevant financial statement date.

Discount When the forward exchange rate is below the current spot rate.

Exposed Net Asset Position The excess of assets that are measured or denominated in foreign currency and translated at the current rate over liabilities that are measured or denominated in foreign currency and translated at the current rate.

Foreign Currency Transactions Transactions (e.g., sales or purchases of goods or services or loans payable or receivable) whose terms are stated in a currency other than the entity's functional currency.

Foreign Currency Translation The process of expressing amounts denominated or measured in one currency in terms of another currency by use of the exchange rate between the two currencies.

Functional Currency The primary currency in which an entity conducts its operation and generates and expends cash. It is usually the currency of the country in which the entity is located and the currency in which the books of record are maintained.

Historical Rate The foreign exchange rate that prevailed when a foreign currency asset or liability was first acquired or incurred.

Local Currency Currency of a particular country; the reporting currency of a domestic or foreign operation.

Monetary Items Obligations to pay or rights to receive a fixed number of currency units in the future.

Reporting Currency The currency in which an enterprise prepares its financial statements.

Translation Adjustments Translation adjustments result from the process of translating financial statements from the entity's functional currency into the reporting currency.

Unit of Measure The currency in which assets, liabilities, revenue, and expense are measured.

aggregating data from different reporting entities. Translation differs from conversion; conversion refers to the physical exchange of one currency for another, whereas translation is simply a change in monetary expression, as when a balance sheet expressed in Italian lira is restated to U.S. dollar equivalents. No physical exchange occurs in the course of translation. Exhibit 15–3 outlines the definitions of other terms that are associated with foreign currency translation.

Countries are in different stages with respect to the financial statement consolidation requirement. Consolidation has long been a common practice in countries such as the Netherlands, the United Kingdom, and the United States, whereas it is a relatively recent phenomenon in many other European and Asian countries. For example, German MNEs have been required to present global consolidated financial statements since 1990. In Japan, consolidation is also quite recent with most companies not reporting full consolidated statements before the early 1980s. Today, consolidation has become much more widespread as a result of increasing globalization and heightened needs for information flow within and beyond the boundary of the MNE.

Commonly Used Translation Methods

There are four internationally accepted and commonly used translation approaches, which include:

- Current rate method
- Current/non-current method
- Monetary/nonmonetary method
- Temporal method

The primary distinction among these methods is the classification of assets and liabilities that would be translated at either the current or historical rate. All four methods, which can be found today in various countries, produce considerably different foreign currency translation results. At present, the IAS Committee and the U.S. GAAP both mandate use of the current rate method for translating the financial statements of a foreign entity.

1. Current rate method. A feature of this approach is that all assets and liabilities, both monetary and non-monetary, are translated at the current or closing rate. Foreign currency revenues and expenses are generally translated at exchange rates prevailing when these items are recognized (typically translated by an appropriately weighted average of current exchange rates for the period). All resulting exchange differences are classified as a separate component of equity of the reporting enterprise until disposal of the net investment in a foreign entity. The basis of this method is the "net investment concept," wherein the foreign subsidiary is viewed as a separate entity that the parent invested into, rather than being treated as part of the parent's operations. As an important consequence of this method, translating all foreign currency balances gives rise to translation gains and losses every time exchange rates change. Reflecting such exchange adjustments in current income could significantly distort reported measures of performance.

2. Current/non-current method. Current assets and liabilities are translated at the current rate, and non-current assets and liabilities at the applicable historical rates. Income statement items, with the exception of depreciation and amortization charges, are translated at average rates applicable to each month of operation or on the basis of weighted averages covering the entire period to be reported. A major weakness under this method is the treatment of inventory and long-term debt. As a current asset, inventory is translated at its current cost, which is a major departure from traditional GAAP. The translation of foreign denominated long-term debt under this approach may be misleading to users, because it is translated at its historical value. For example, from the perspective of a U.S. reporting entity, if the dollar weakens internationally, it will take more dollars to repay this obligation, a fact that would not be apparent from the reporting entity's financial statements.

3. Monetary/nonmonetary method. This method translates monetary assets and liabilities at the current rate. Non-monetary items such as fixed assets, long-term investments, and inventories are translated at historical rates. Income statement items are translated under procedures similar to those described for the current/non-current approach. Under the U.S. GAAP, if the foreign entity's local currency is the functional currency, it requires the current rate method. If the U.S. dollar is the functional currency, U.S. GAAP requires the re-measurement method which is essentially the same as the monetary/non-monetary framework. A limitation of this method is that not all items can be classified as monetary or non-monetary.

4. Temporal method. Monetary items such as cash, receivables, and payables are translated at the current rate. Non-monetary items are translated at the rates that preserve their original measurement bases. In other words, non-monetary assets carried on foreign currency statements at historical cost are translated at the historical rate. Non-monetary items carried abroad at current values are translated

Exhibit 15–4
Foreign currency
translation methods

Items/ Methods	Current	Current/ Non-current	Monetary/ Non-monetary	Temporal
Cash	CR	CR	CR	CR
Accounts receivable	CR	CR	CR	CR
Inventories				
Cost	CR	CR	HR	HR
Market	CR	CR	HR	CR
Investments				
Cost	CR	HR	HR	HR
Market	CR	HR	HR	CR
Fixed assets	CR	HR	HR	HR
Other assets	CR	HR	HR	HR
Accounts payable	CR	CR	CR	CR
Long-term debt	CR	HR	CR	CR
Common stock	HR	HR	HR	HR

\# CR = current rate; HR = historical rate.
* Example economies using the current method include Austria, Canada, France, Taiwan, Sweden, United States, and United Kingdom; Japan is an example using the current/non-current approach; Germany is an example using the monetary/non-monetary method; Before 1981, the United States used the temporal approach.

at the current rate. Revenue and expense items are translated at rates that prevailed when the underlying transactions occurred. The temporal method was the required method in the United States under SFAS (Statement of Financial Accounting Standards) #8 until it was superseded by SFAS #52, which requires the current rate method. The major points of the preceding four methods are summarized in Exhibit 15–4.

All translations of foreign currencies will inevitably result in gains or losses associated with translation adjustment. The way in which such gains or losses are accounted for affects the operating results as perceived, particularly by the stockholders of a parent company. Approaches to accounting for translation adjustment include deferral, partial deferral, and no deferral. With a deferral approach, translation adjustments are excluded from the income statement and are instead accumulated separately as a part of equity in the consolidated balance sheet. Under the partial deferral approach, translation losses are recognized in a consolidated income statement as soon as they occur, whereas translation gains are recognized only as they are realized. A final method is to recognize instantly translation gains or losses in the income statement. Inclusion of such "paper" gains or losses in current income brings up a random element to earnings that could generate substantial earning gyrations whenever exchange rates fluctuate. Nevertheless, it is a widespread view that, if the reporting currency of the parent company is the unit of measure for the translated financial statements, immediate recognition of translation gains or losses in income is advisable. From a parent company point of view, translation gains or losses reflect changes in the domestic currency equity of the foreign investment and should be recognized.

Harmonization of Translation Methods

MNEs employing different translation approaches could produce divergent consolidated financial statements, which in turn hinders financial comparison and strategic decision making. For example, because most continental EU countries have no standards, the practice is left up to the MNEs themselves. To harmonize the use of such methods, IAS #21 prepared by IAS Committee and SFAS #52 by *FASB (Financial Accounting Standard Board)* are presently the two most important standards widely applied by international companies. Although they are basically compatible, IAS #21 differs from SFAS #52 in that the former advocates the current rate method in all circumstances (as explained earlier) whereas the latter emphasizes functional currency, which will determine an applicable translation method. Today, an increasing number of internationally listed MNEs are following IAS, and the world's stock exchanges are pressured to allow IAS in lieu of domestic standards for foreign company listings. While domestic MNEs in the United States are asked to follow SFAS #52, foreign MNEs in the United States are permitted to follow IAS #21.

The core premise of SFAS #52 centers on *functional currency*. SFAS #52 stipulates that the assets, liabilities, and operations of a foreign entity shall be measured using the functional currency of that entity. An entity's functional currency is the currency of the primary economic environment in which it operates; normally that is the environment in which an entity primarily generates and expends cash. For an entity with operations that are relatively self-contained and integrated within a particular country, the functional currency generally would be the currency of that country (e.g., RMB for a Shanghai subsidiary of a U.S. parent). If a foreign entity keeps its accounts in a currency other than the functional currency (e.g., the German accounts of a U.S. subsidiary whose functional currency is actually British pounds), its functional currency is the third-country currency (pounds). If a foreign subsidiary is merely an extension of a U.S. parent company (e.g., Nike's assembly subsidiary in Thailand whose main function is to assemble shoes that will be exported to the United States), its functional currency is the U.S. dollar.

According to SFAS #52, if a foreign entity's books of record are not maintained in its functional currency, re-measurement into the functional currency is required before translation into the reporting currency. If a foreign entity's functional currency is the reporting currency, re-measurement into the reporting currency obviates translation. The re-measurement process is intended to produce the same result as if the entity's books of record had been maintained in the functional currency. This means that an entity needs to maintain two sets of records, one in the local currency and one in the functional currency when these two are different. To help understand the preceding issues, see the process tree (Exhibit 15–5) on currency translation accrued in a foreign subsidiary of a U.S. MNE.

International Accounting Information Systems

Consolidating financial statements is only one aspect of international financial reporting. As MNEs act more locally, accounting and financial reporting systems become increasingly critical. Global coordination has shifted from the previous rigid control mechanisms such as budget and bureaucratic control to information-based coordination, which is why international accounting information systems become fundamental. **International accounting information systems** (*IAIS*) involve accounting-related reporting systems, data management, and communication between various units of the same MNE. Financial controllers in MNE headquarters find themselves under increasing pressure to bring information to market more quickly, to deliver more extensive information than previously required, and to proactively manage business risk at a corporate level. Preparation of detailed MNE group information on a monthly basis is now the norm—with the result that headquarters' accountants and financial managers often spend most of their time preparing and monitoring information rather than working with the output or reformulating accounting plans. Many MNEs have set up computerized accounting information systems with overseas affiliates to furnish the accounting information needed to plan, evaluate, and coordinate all business activities. Microsoft, with 54

Exhibit 15–5
Process tree in foreign
currency translation

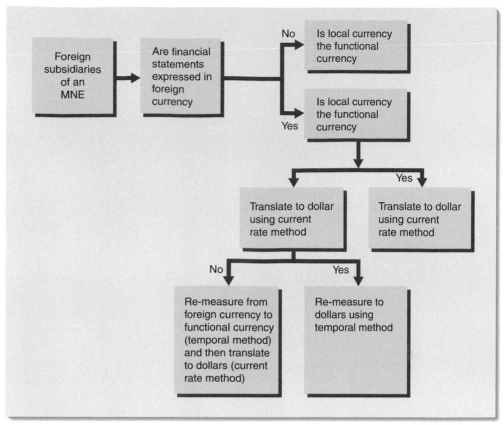

financial groups charged with providing financial support to more than 85 global subsidiary operations, has struggled with these challenges. Its answer is the financial *digital nerve system,* an intranet-based environment that links all of the company's financial groups into a single, coherent system that provides its employees with real-time access to information and financial reports through the Internet. An effective IAIS provides an MNE with a competitive advantage arising from operational flexibility and transnational coordination in this increasingly competitive and complex global environment.

In general, MNEs tend to make internal reporting systems in their foreign subunits uniform. This allows easy comparison of corporations throughout the world and augments the consolidation process at the home office. This uniform reporting system, however, must be accommodated by following considerations:

- Different managerial styles of users may impose different standards on the design. European managers are more conservative decision makers than most U.S. managers, which means European managers need more detailed accounting information to make decisions.
- Intraorganizational interdependence in information flow, capital flow, resource flow, and product flow is a key factor determining design. The greater the interdependence, the greater intense communication and information exchange is indispensable.
- Legislative and legal developments in both home and host countries may influence uniform reporting. For example, the Freedom of Information Act and Fair Credit Reporting Act in the United States prohibits the improper use of personal data. European countries with data protection legislation do not allow name-linked data to be transmitted outside national boundaries.

Interim Summary

1. Translation is not the actual exchange of hard currency, but a re-expression in another currency (e.g., an MNE's home country currency) for the purpose of consolidating financial statements.

2. The major translation approaches are: current rate method, in which all assets and liabilities are translated at the current rate; current/non-current method, by which current assets and liabilities are translated at the current rate and non-current assets and liabilities at the historical rates, income statements translated at average rates; monetary/non-monetary method, whereby monetary assets and liabilities are translated at the current rate, and non-monetary assets and liabilities at historical rates.

TRANSFER PRICING AND TAXATION STRATEGIES

Why Transfer Pricing?

As one of the major international tax issues facing MNEs, **transfer pricing** refers to the pricing of goods and services transferred between members of an MNE network. These transfers are also termed intra-MNE transactions. The essence of transfer pricing is to earn economic benefits such as tax avoidance by manipulating the price of intra-MNE transactions. Transfer pricing can achieve the following benefits for the MNE:

1. *Tax and tariff reduction.* Tax minimization is the main driver behind transfer pricing policies. When tax rates are different in two countries, MNEs favor low transfer prices for goods and services bought by, and high transfer prices for goods and services sold by, an affiliate in a low-tax jurisdiction. Consider this example: Subsidiary A assembles shoes in China, whose corporate income tax is 33 percent, and needs to sell $10,000 shoes to its sister subsidiary B in Japan, where the income tax is 55 percent. If these shoes were overpriced at $12,000, then it could lower subsidiary B's tax by $1,100 ($2,000@55%). Although subsidiary A had to pay $660 ($2,000@33%) more in taxes, the MNE network saved $440 ($1,100 − 660). Transfer pricing can also be used in a similar fashion to minimize import duties. The effect of tariffs could be reduced if the selling company underprices the goods it exports to the buying unit. For example, a product that normally sells for $100 has an import price of $120 because of a 20 percent tariff. If the invoice price were listed as $80 rather than $100, however, it would be imported for $96.

2. *Avoiding exchange controls.* Transfer pricing may be used to offset the volume effects of foreign exchange quotas. For example, if a government allocates a limited amount of foreign exchange for importing particular goods, a parent company may underprice products shipped to its subsidiary, thereby allowing a greater volume of imports. If an MNE wishes to move funds out of one country, it may consider charging higher prices on goods sold to its local affiliates. Similarly, an MNE may indirectly finance an affiliate by lowering the prices on goods sold to it.

3. *Increasing profits from joint ventures.* Transfer pricing enables the party to gain unilateral profit from controlling the joint venture's import and export activities. For example, some Hong Kong investors are not overly concerned with the reporting profits in their joint ventures in mainland China. This is because they have already made noticeable returns from overpricing materials imported for the joint ventures and/or by underpricing joint venture outputs exported to headquarters. They normally control the material importation and products export for the ventures as specified in joint venture agreements.

Internally, the underlying problem of transfer pricing is possible conflict between the goals of subsidiaries and those of the parent when subsidiaries are evaluated as separate profit or investment centers. Overpricing outputs or underpricing inputs for subsidiaries in high-tax countries reduces their accounting-based profits. Therefore, MNEs should prepare corporate policies on internal transfer pricing and use different criteria to assess subsidiary performance when this practice has been used. Furthermore, if a transfer price is too high, tax authorities in the purchasing affiliate's country forego income tax revenues. MNEs should check anti-taxation evasion measures adopted by related countries. This is explained below.

Transfer Pricing Techniques

From the tax authority perspective, intra-MNE transfer pricing must proceed following the arm's-length principle. The **arm's-length principle** in this context means that the transfer price struck between related companies should be the same as that negotiated between two independent entities acting in an open and unrestricted market. In the process of using transfer pricing, MNEs must become familiar with the methods used by taxation authorities in host and home countries to determine whether transfer pricing practices comply with the arm's-length principle. These methods delineate the legitimate range of transfer pricing that is allowed by tax authorities. Knowing these methods helps an MNE prepare appropriate transfer pricing policies. These methods are as follows:

- *Current open market prices:* Tax authorities generally view comparable open market prices as the most satisfactory method because it requires the fewest adjustments. If this method cannot be applied, they may compare the gross margin or operating profit the company earns from intercompany transactions with gross margins or operating profit earned in the open market. Differences between the terms of intercompany transactions and the terms of open-market transactions require adjustment before a true comparison can be made for taxation purposes.
- *Gross margin method:* This method relies on a certain range of gross margins achieved in comparable transactions between independent companies. The gross margin methods include (1) the resale price method and (2) the cost plus method. The *resale price method* is used for transfers of goods to distributors, which sell them without further processing. The price paid for a final product by an independent party is used as a baseline, on which a suitable markup is deducted to allow for the seller's expenses and reasonable profit. The *cost-plus method* is used when one group company transfers items that need additional processing by the other group company before they can be sold to a final customer. Cost-plus simply marks up the cost of producing the transferred goods and services commensurate with functions performed by the transferring company. In this case the effective comparison is with the margin earned on similar transactions occurring at arm's-length. In effect, the procedure is the opposite of the resale price method.
- *Operating profit methods.* The difficulty of finding comparable transactions or gross margins often leads companies to use *operating profit methods* that include (1) comparable profits method (CPM), (2) transactional net margin

method (TNMM), and (3) profit split method (PSM). The *comparable profits method,* as its name suggests, simply compares the period percentage operating profit (e.g., return on sales or return on assets) in the controlled subsidiary with percentages in similar uncontrolled entities on a whole company basis. The *transactional net margin* method is similar to CPM, but compares operating profit on transactions rather than on a whole-company basis. Often, intra-group trading of goods and services is unique to a particular group. In this situation no external operating profit comparisons can exist so the *profit split method* may have to be used in this situation. Group companies simply reach an agreement on how profits from the final product will be shared between them, based on a considered assessment of the contribution made by each party to the transaction.

Transfer Pricing Regulations and Penalties

Concurrent with the increase in transfer pricing is an increase in scrutiny by cross-border tax authorities who want to ensure that their countries receive their fair shares of tax revenues. Tax authorities are acutely aware of the potential revenue losses associated with intercompany transfer pricing policies. For this purpose, tax authorities are requiring more reporting and documentation, carrying out more comprehensive audits, and introducing more harsh penalty regimes. For example, the U.S. Tax Court fined DHL for misstatement of income for the tax years 1990, 1991, and 1992 about the trademark royalty paid by its Hong Kong affiliate, DHL International. The IRS had sought more than $160 million in back taxes, plus penalties. DHL and the IRS varied widely on the value of the DHL trademark. DHL estimated the value as low as $20 million to $50 million. The IRS said the DHL trademark was worth as much as six times that amount when DHL sold its trademark to DHL International at what the tax agency said was not an "arm's-length" transaction.

The issue of the *1995 OECD guidelines* and the *U.S. section 482 regulations* are the two most important guidelines regulating transfer pricing practices. The *OECD transfer pricing guidelines* (1995 version) provide information on the application of the arm's-length principle that the OECD hopes can be used by MNEs and tax authorities in all member countries. The OECD guidelines reject the use of splitting profits between jurisdictions on the basis of revenue and payroll. This latter method is considered to be against the arm's-length principles and is therefore considered an invalid transfer pricing method. *The U.S. section 482 guidelines* are similar to the OECD model. The arm's-length standard is affirmed as the basis of the Section #482 regulations but requires that the best method be used. Taxpayers must demonstrate that their chosen method produces the most reliable arm's-length result. This means that MNEs will have to give full and documented consideration to all possible methods before settling on the most appropriate. Unlike the OECD model, the U.S. rules accept the profit-based methods.

Both the OECD and U.S. guidelines require the taxpayer to provide the supporting documentation for its transfer price on a timely basis, or suffer, at worst, a non-deductible penalty of up to 40 percent in the United States and up to 100 percent in the United Kingdom. The strict U.S.-initiated transfer pricing model (with accompanying documentation requirements, penalties, and enforcement) is spreading quickly to other nations around the globe and adding to the strain. Since 1997, new legislation and rulings have taken effect in many countries, including Australia, Brazil, Canada, Denmark, France, Korea, Mexico and the United Kingdom. Most of these countries focus on the need to document adherence to the arm's-length standard, with the accompanying threat of large penalties for failure to do so.

To reduce the risk arising from transfer pricing/tax audit, many MNEs adopt an *advance pricing agreement (APA)* with the tax authorities of the countries in which an

MNE generates taxable income. **An advance pricing agreement** is an agreement between the tax authority and the taxpayer on the transfer pricing methodology to be applied to any apportionment or location of income, deductions, credits, or allowances between two or more members within an organization. An APA allows an MNE to negotiate an understanding with one or more tax authorities that approves a transfer pricing methodology for a given term, resolving the uncertainty about its acceptability and reducing audit risk. An APA may be unilateral (least preferred by most tax authorities), bilateral, or multilateral. Bilateral and multilateral agreements are more easily negotiated with tax authorities in countries that have existing tax treaties. The APA is also an alternative dispute resolution process that can reduce the number of transfer pricing cases requiring legal resolution, saving both time and money for the MNE and for the tax authority.

Interim Summary

1. Transfer pricing aims at gaining benefits through manipulation of prices of intra-MNE transactions on exchange controls, and increased profits from joint ventures. These benefits include tax and tariff reduction, foreign exchange control avoidance, and profit increase from joint ventures. Tax avoidance is the overriding intention behind this practice.

2. The legitimate range of transfer pricing allowed by tax authorities are determined by (1) current open market prices, (2) gross margin method, or (3) operating profit methods.

TAX HAVENS, TREATIES, AND STRATEGIES

Intra-MNE transfer pricing on tangible goods or intangible services is only one of the major vehicles to reduce worldwide taxation burdens for MNEs. Using tax havens and taking advantage of tax treaties between home and host countries have also served as important instruments for MNEs seeking tax reduction. Tax reduction or avoidance differs from tax evasion in that the latter is considered illegal but the former is acceptable, aimed at keeping tax burdens to the minimum.

Tax Havens

High tax rates in many countries have forced MNEs to seek refuge in tax havens. **Tax havens** are geographical locations in which taxation is substantially lower than that in a home country. To avoid high taxation in a home country, an MNE may incorporate or register a company in a tax haven that may impose little or no corporate income taxes. For example, Bermuda has become a home to 75 percent of Fortune 100 companies, due to virtually zero income taxes (plus meetings and conventions in Bermuda are 100 percent U.S. tax deductible for American corporations and associations). Because of low or no taxes on certain classes of income, thousands of so-called mailbox companies have sprung up in such exotic places as Liechtenstein, Vanuatu, and the Netherlands Antilles. Tax havens have the following categories:

- Traditional tax havens with virtually no taxes whatsoever: the Bahamas, Bermuda, the Cayman Islands, Andorra, Bahrain, Campione, Monaco (except for French citizens), the Turks, Tonga, and Vanuatu.

- Tax havens that impose a relatively low rate: the British Virgin Islands, the Channel Islands, Gibraltar, Liechtenstein, Switzerland (except a few regions), Angola, the Netherlands Antilles, Kiribati and Tuvalu, Montserrat, Norfolk Island, the Solomon Islands, and several other small islands.
- Tax havens that tax income from domestic sources but exempt all income from foreign sources, such as Hong Kong, Liberia, and Panama.
- Tax havens that allow special privileges, such as Brazil, Luxembourg, and the Netherlands.

To benefit from a tax haven, an MNE would ordinarily set up a subsidiary in the tax haven country through which different forms of income would pass. The goal is to shift income from high tax to tax haven countries. For example, a U.S. manufacturer could sell goods directly to a dealer in Japan and gather the profits in the United States, or it could sell the goods to its Bermuda subsidiary at cost and then sell the goods to the Japanese dealer, thus concentrating the profits in the Bermuda subsidiary. Specifically, MNEs can use tax havens through setting up holding companies, offshore banking, captive insurance companies, shipping companies, free-port manufacturing, or export and management companies. Most manufacturing MNEs seeking tax havens prefer the holding company mode. Companies can avoid tax in their home country by transferring assets to a holding company, over which they have control. The holding company then collects the income arising from the relevant assets (investments, loans, parent royalty, etc.). Ideal locations for such holding companies are countries that do not tax, or tax only lightly the income in question. In the finance sector, a remarkable phenomenon is that the international banking industry does not remain in well-established finance centers such as London, New York, Tokyo, Zurich, and Luxembourg but has moved offshore in search of more favorable climates for international banking operations (e.g., low tax, freedom from exchange controls, and freedom from withholding tax on interest). For example, the value of operations generated by U.S., Canadian, and European banks channeled through the Bahamas and Cayman Islands is still rising. Most banking institutions in the islands have highly reputable international connections. The majority are cubicle operations with neither offices nor staff of their own, but the amount of funds booked through these subsidiaries is phenomenal. For example, external assets of banks in the Bahamas amounted to $185 billion at the end of 1995.

Tax Treaties

Where income earned and taxed in one country is remitted to investors in other countries, the income may be subject to multiple taxation. This is a particular, but not peculiar, problem to U.S. investors, because the United States follows the worldwide concept of taxation. Two common approaches are used to avoid multiple taxation: *foreign tax credits* and *tax treaties*. The idea of the tax credit is that a company can reduce its tax liability by the amount of the credit. In determining the tax credit in the United States, for example, the predominant nature of the foreign tax must be that of an income tax as defined in the United States. With the spread of business worldwide, most nations in the world, both developed and developing, have signed numerous bilateral tax treaties. Accordingly, tax treaties have become the primary device for avoiding multiple taxation today.

The major purpose of international tax treaties is to eliminate international double taxation and render mutual assistance in tax enforcement (e.g., preventing tax evasion) and in reducing barriers to trade and investment. Many countries avoid international double taxation by not taxing their taxpayers on foreign source income (e.g., China). To a large extent, the income tax treaties determine the amount of tax to be paid to the country where the income is produced and the amount to be paid to the taxpayer's country of residence. It does this by offering reduced rates of tax or complete exemptions from tax for certain specified items of income. For example, under U.S. law, interest paid by a U.S. company to a foreign recipient is subject to a 30 percent U.S. withholding tax. Under the U.K.–U.S. income tax treaty, this tax is eliminated. Each treaty may also differ from the others and results from negotiation between the two countries. In order to prevent a resident of a non-treaty country from using, for example, the U.K. treaty to invest in the United States, anti-conduit provisions were also included. If a Saudi Arabian investor were to lend money to a U.K. corporation that lent it to the U.S. subsidiary, the anti-conduit provisions would treat the loan as coming directly from Saudi Arabia.

Other Tax Strategies for MNEs

1. *Setting up a holding company in a host country:* This technique for repatriating cash and reducing future taxes involves setting up a holding company in the same host country as a high-tax operating subsidiary. Funding is provided to that holding company to buy the shares of the operating company from the U.S. parent, allowing direct future earnings to be repatriated without withholding taxes. The consolidation of the return of the holding company and the operating company allows not only deduction of the new interest but also reduction of future foreign taxes. The U.S. law, through section 304 of the International Revenue Code, considers this taxation as a dividend distribution rather than a sale, because the ultimate ownership of the operating company has not changed. Foreign countries generally levied this as a sale by a foreign corporation, with no foreign tax on any capital gain.

2. *Establishing a holding company in an integrated region:* This approach involves a regional or other multicountry holding company. Given that intercompany dividends between European Union countries are tax free, a subsidiary in the country (e.g., the Netherlands) would borrow to buy shares of another subsidiary in another European country (e.g., Belgium). For this reason, MNEs need a holding company in a country that does not tax dividend income or capital gains and that has a low withholding rate on dividends back to the United States.

3. *Building a finance corporation:* In view of the tax incentives given to finance companies in some countries such as Belgium and Ireland, U.S. MNEs may establish finance companies in these countries to manage group cash and currency exposure and to channel funds within Europe without bringing them back to the parent. For example, if an MNE has excess cash in Germany, it may want to finance a subsidiary in exchange for preferred shares in the finance company. The German company reduces its cash, which may be particularly useful if it cannot pay dividends because of an insufficiency of earnings or reluctance to pay withholding tax.

4. *Locating projects in a low tax region within a host country.* A large proportion of MNEs entering developing countries often invest their projects in special technological, investment, or trade zones which impose substantially lower tax rates or provide preferential tax terms. China provides an excellent example. MNE manufacturing projects located in Shenzhen, one of the five special economic zones in China, enjoy a reduced 15 percent rate on corporate income tax (as opposed to 33 percent in normal cases). They also receive an exemption of income tax for the first two years and a 50 percent reduction of income tax during the third to fifth years, starting from the first profit-making year. MNEs located in coastal cities such as Tianjin, Shanghai, Dalian, Qingdao, and Guangzhou are entitled to a 24 percent corporate income tax levied on general manufacturing projects and a

15 percent corporate income tax for those MNEs that are technologically intensive. Similarly, if projects are hosted in an Economic and Technological Development Zone (ETDZ) designated by the central government, MNEs will enjoy a 15 percent corporate income tax. If the project is more than 10 years in duration, it enjoys a two-year exemption and a subsequent three-year 50 percent reduction of corporate income tax, and a 10 percent corporate income tax for MNEs with 70 percent of output exported, after a stipulated term.

In sum, there are several tax strategies used by MNEs in addition to transfer pricing or using tax havens and tax treaties. To deal with the complex international tax systems efficiently, MNEs set up holding companies or finance corporations in a foreign region (or country) or locate investment projects in special zones within a target foreign country. Because the taxation burden directly affects net profit that can be retained by the firm, these strategies add value to the firm's wealth and influence the firm's ability to reinvest overseas. Although the international taxation environment is much more complex than the domestic one, MNEs can benefit from opportunities arising from the differences in taxation rates and systems between countries. These benefits will not accrue unless MNEs have adopted realistic and viable strategies on taxation reduction.

Interim Summary

1. High tax rates in many countries often compel MNEs to incorporate or register a company in a tax haven. Bermuda is especially popular for American MNEs. Tax treaties and foreign tax credits are also used to avoid double taxation on the same income.

2. Other tax reduction strategies exist, dealing primarily with setting up holding companies to avoid taxation, creating finance firms in countries with tax incentives, and locating new projects in low-tax regions of host countries.

CHAPTER SUMMARY

1. Accounting is fundamental to MNEs because their ultimate success needs to be reflected in accounting reports and because their key decisions are often made based on accounting information. Some accounting practices such as transfer pricing, accounting information system, and cash-flow management can add important value to an MNE.

2. When firms expand globally, they face different accounting systems in different nations. Such differences exist owing to different economic, political, legal, cultural, and taxation systems. These differences can affect a firm's decisions on R&D expenditure, fixed assets, inventory valuation, foreign currency translation, and accounting for income taxes.

3. MNEs will benefit from harmonizing accounting standards and practices between nations. The International Accounting Standards Committee (IASC) is the leading institution in setting international ac-

counting standards. Increasing numbers of MNEs now report their accounting results by reference to IASC's standards.

4. Foreign currency translation can significantly affect the results in MNEs' consolidated financial statements. Widely accepted translation approaches include current rate method, current/non-current method, monetary/non-monetary method, and temporal method. IASC and the U.S. GAAP now both mandate to use the current rate method. SFAS #52 details how this method is advanced.

5. Transfer pricing provides MNEs with several gains, especially reducing corporate income taxes in heavily taxed countries in which MNE subsidiaries are located. However, firms must conform to various restrictions and rules imposed by home- or host-country taxation authorities. Tax havens and treaties offer additional opportunities for tax avoidance.

CHAPTER NOTES

[1] See C. Roberts, P. Weetman, and P. Gordon, *International Financial Accounting*. London: Financial Times Management, 1998, 8–9.

[2] H. H. E. Fechner and A. Kolgore, "The influence of cultural factors on accounting practice," *International Journal of Accounting*, 29(4), 1999, 265–277.

[3] G. Hofstede, *Culture's Consequences: International Differences in Work-related Values*. Beverly Hills, CA: Sage, 1980. For details, refer to Chapter 6.

[4] S. J. Gray, "Towards a theory of cultural influence on the development of accounting systems internationally," *Abacus*, 24(1), 1988, 1–15, and S. B. Salter and F. Niswander, "Cultural influences on the development of accounting systems internationally," *Journal of International Business Studies*, 26: 1995 379–397; R. J. Kirsch, "Towards a global reporting model: Culture and disclosure in selected capital markets," *Research in Accounting Regulation*, 8, 71–110.

[5] For a detailed discussion on these accounting issues, see W. E. Becker and P. Brunner, "A summary of accounting principle differences around the world." In F. D. S. Choi (ed.), *International Accounting and Finance Handbook*, 3, 1997, 1–33, New York: Wiley; and International Accounting Standards Committee, 1996, *International Accounting Standards 1996*. London.

[6] See G. G. Mueller, H. Gernon, and G. Meek, *Accounting: An International Perspective*. New York: Business One Irwin, 1994.

[7] F. D. S. Choi, C. A. Frost, and G. K. Meek, *International Accounting*. Upper Saddle River, NJ: Prentice-Hall, 1999.

[8] For details, see B. J. Epstein and A. A. Mirza, *IAS 2000*. New York: Wiley, 2000.

Global Marketing and Supply Chain

DO YOU KNOW

1. **How can you determine the market potential of a foreign country?**

2. **What adaptations, if any, are necessary for a product to sell in another country? For instance, if you were to sell a Ford Focus in Vietnam, what adjustments would you make in the car's appearance and technical specifications?**

3. **What influence can the manufacturing (or the service provider) country have on the image of a product? Would you buy a Malaysian-made Proton car?**

4. **How do you make channel decisions in a foreign market? What should you do when your main channel, e.g., direct marketing, is constrained in a foreign market?**

5. **What type of transportation dominates international trade?**

6. **If you were a manager at Mattel, what would you have done when California's ports shut down in the Fall of 2002?**

OPENING CASE Domino's Pizza

ounded in 1960 in Ypsilanti, Michigan, Domino's Pizza opened its first foreign store in 1983 in Winnipeg, Canada. It added Japan in 1984, the United Kingdom in 1985, and Mexico in 1989. By 2000, the firm owned and franchised 6,652 stores in the United States and in 63 international markets but it continued to expand its international presence. Later that year it acquired a controlling stake in a Dutch Pizza company that op-

erated 52 of its stores. Domino's successfully entered Hong Kong and Taiwan in 1984 and 1987, where it was not clear whether pizza would sell given the lack of milk-product tradition, and applied the lessons it learned in those markets when entering the Chinese mainland in 1994.

While prices in China are slightly lower than in the United States, store sales volume is more than double the U.S. average. Unlike in the United States, where home delivery is dominant, in China it accounts for only 10 to 15 percent of volume, with most orders placed in restaurants open from 9 A.M to 11 P.M. However, competitive pressures from Pizza Hut and local outlets are pushing Domino's toward an expansion of home delivery in the Chinese market. The menu is adapted to local tastes, with shrimp, scallops, and squid added to the conventional toppings. The pepperoni pizza is called the American Pizza, and print advertising demonstrates how to eat pizza with your hands.

Master franchisees in each country are key to Domino's marketing strategy. Many master franchisees and general managers are veterans of the U.S. market; for example, Taiwan's general manager was a Domino's employee who spent many years in the United States. Master franchisees contribute to product adaptation, determine pricing, and devise national promotion and advertising. In Japan, the master franchisee came up with the idea of using a customized scooter for delivery in narrow alleys. ∎

Source: Company publications; Domino's Pizza International, Inc. HEC case, 1998.

THE INTERNATIONAL
MARKETING CHALLENGE
International markets offer vast opportunities for firms with a product or a service potentially in demand abroad. As the Domino's case shows, even when the imported product deviates from local tastes and customs, it can penetrate a market. Newness, cultural attractiveness, and appropriate marketing strategies can make a product welcome in international markets. Some U.S. products do even better abroad than at home. U.S.-based Kenny Rogers Roasters filed for bankruptcy in 1998 and was purchased the following year by Nathan's Famous. However Kenny Rogers China, led by the former head of Kentucky Fried Chicken (KFC)'s operations there, continues to operate and expand in that country.

Unfortunately, this is not the norm. International markets contain many pitfalls and are littered with failed attempts at foreign expansion. Dunkin' Donuts closed its Chinese operations in 1999, as did Tex-Mex. Office Max closed down its Japan operations in early 2001, four years after its initial entry. Gateway Computers divested its foreign operations in 2001. Many otherwise successful brands do not sell well in certain foreign markets, such as Campbell's Soup in Brazil and McDonald's in Barbados. Initial success often proves elusive, when the novelty wears off or when pent-up demand slackens off.[1] Some products rarely sell at all. For years, both Japanese and U.S. manufacturers attempted unsuccessfully to market dishwashers in Japan. Local housewives felt guilty for not washing the dishes themselves and found the machine unwieldy when it came to Japanese staples such as sticky rice, raw eggs, and fermented soybeans. They also found the Japanese kitchen too small for the bulky machine. Some manufacturers are currently working on a smaller dishwasher, but it is not yet clear whether demand for the machine exists.[2]

What is clear is that globalization brings about intense competition in markets that have in the past been largely domestic in nature or limited to one import source. The following list from the Chicago-based Beverage Tasting Institute shows a list of the vodka brands sold in the United States, ranked according to one taste test. (Exhibit 16–1). In addition to the domestic competitors and those from countries with a vodka tradition (Russia, Poland, and Finland), you will notice competitors from countries including Brazil, the Netherlands, Sweden, and England. Indeed, the essence of international marketing, especially in more global industries, is that competition can come from anywhere on the globe. Being the country in which the product originated can help but is no guarantee of success.

Success in international markets depends on many skills: accurate assessment of market potential; selection of the right product mix, and appropriate adjustments in distribution, pricing, packaging, and advertising. Cultural values and social mores, rules and regulations, economic conditions and political realities constitute the context within which international marketing takes place. Often, the diversity associated with international operations spills over into the increasingly diverse domestic arena. Upstart Alo Vatan has become the third largest provider of phone service for the large Turkish community in Germany by being tuned to the Turk's linguistic, cultural, religious, and social sensitivities.[3]

Assessing Market Potential

To assess market potential, firms seek to identify the aggregate demand for a product (or a service) and estimate the costs associated with product introduction and distribution. Accessibility, profitability, and market size all play a role in deciding market priority. In and of itself, population size reveals little about short-term market potential. When China embarked on economic reforms in 1978, MNEs salivated at the prospect of "selling a toothbrush to every Chinese" in a country of well over a billion, only to discover that most Chinese had neither the desire nor the money to buy foreign products at that time.

Exhibit 16–1
"Best tasting vodkas" in the United States

Rank	Vodka	Country
96	Grey Goose Vodka	France
94	Canadian Iceberg Vodka	Canada
93	Stolichnaya Gold Vodka	Russia
92	Staraya Moskva Premium	Russia
91	Van Hoo Vodka	Belgium
91	Stolichnaya Vodka	Russia
90	Tanqueray Sterling Vodka	England
90	Rain 1995 Harvest Vodka	USA
89	Ketel One Vodka	Holland
88	Wyborowa Vodka	Poland
87	Kremlyovskaya Vodka	Russia
86	Finlandia Vodka of Finland	Finland
86	Alps French Vodka	France
85	Skyy Vodka	USA
82	Original Polish Vodka	Poland
82	Glenmore Special	USA
82	Fleischmann's Royal Vodka	USA
81	Mr. Boston Vodka	USA
80	Pole Star Vodka	Poland
80	Luksusowa Potato Vodka	Poland
80	Absolut Vodka	Sweden
78	Cardinal Vodka	Holland
78	Barton Vodka	USA
78	Barclay's Vodka	USA
78	Amazon Vodka	Brazil
76	Skol Vodka	USA
74	Smirnoff Vodka	USA
74	Crystal Palace Vodka	USA
74	Belvedere	Poland
72	Schenley	USA
69	Mr. Boston's Riva Vodka	USA

Source: www.tastings.com.

Population growth provides a coarse estimate of future market potential. For instance, Japan and many EU countries face low and even negative population growth forecasts, whereas most Asian nations are likely to rapidly grow their populations. This suggests many more potential customers in Indonesia, for example, but it also means rising health care expenditures in the EU. Furthermore, it is not at all clear that Indonesians will be able to afford foreign products. Indeed, probably the single most important indicator of market potential is economic development and its correlate of disposable income.[4] Nominal income figures say little about the consumers' ability to afford certain products and services. Purchasing Power Parity (PPP) is an index used to adjust nominal figures to the purchasing power of local consumers. The following Big Mac Index, published by *The Economist*, shows what a McDonald's Big Mac costs in selected locations around the world in both unadjusted and PPP terms[5] (Exhibit 16–2).

The United Nations (UN) developed a product cost measure in its International Comparison Project (ICP), published in its Atlas. In addition to income figures, per capita GDP figures are often used to gauge the potential in a given market. In Exhibit 16–3, the Boston Consulting Group (BCG) shows the direct relationship between GDP per capita and the penetration rate for refrigerators in Asia.

Exhibit 16–2

Big Mac prices in selected markets

	Big Mac prices		Implied PPP* of the dollar	Actual $ exchange rate 4/25/00	Under (−)/ over (+) valuation against the dollar, %
	In local currency	in dollars			
United States[†]	$2.51	2.51	—	—	—
Argentina	Peso2.50	2.50	1.00	1.00	0
Australia	A$2.59	1.54	1.03	1.68	−38
Brazil	Real2.95	1.65	1.18	1.79	−34
Britain	£1.90	3.00	1.32[‡]	1.58[‡]	−20
Canada	C$2.85	1.94	1.14	1.47	−23
Chile	Peso1,260	2.45	502	514	−2
China	Yuan9.90	1.20	3.94	8.28	−52
Czech Rep	Koruna54.37	1.39	21.7	39.1	−45
Denmark	DKr24.75	3.08	9.86	8.04	+23
Euro area	€2.56	2.37	0.98[§]	0.93[§]	−5
France	FFr18.50	2.62	7.37	7.07	+4
Germany	DM4.99	2.37	1.99	2.11	−6
Italy	Lire4.500	2.16	1,793	2,088	−14
Spain	Pta375	2.09	149	179	−17
Hong Kong	HK$10.20	1.31	4.06	7.79	−48
Hungary	Forint339	1.21	135	279	−52
Indonesia	Rupiah14,500	1.83	5,777	7,945	−27
Israel	Shekel14.5	3.58	5.78	4.05	+43
Japan	¥294	2.78	117	106	+11
Malaysia	M$4.52	1.19	1.80	3.80	−53
Mexico	Peso20.90	2.22	8.33	9.41	−11
New Zealand	NZ$3.40	1.69	1.35	2.01	−33
Poland	Zloty5.50	1.28	2.19	4.30	−49
Russia	Ruble39.50	1.39	15.7	28.5	−45
Singapore	S$3.20	1.88	1.27	1.70	−25
South Africa	Rand9.00	1.34	3.59	6.72	−47
South Korea	Won3,000	2.71	1,195	1,108	+8
Sweden	SKr24.00	2.71	9.56	8.84	+8
Switzerland	SFr5.90	3.48	2.35	1.70	−39
Taiwan	NT$70.00	2.29	27.9	30.6	−9
Thailand	Baht55.00	1.45	21.9	38.0	−42

*Purchasing-power parity; local price divided by price in United States   †Average of New York, Chicago, San Francisco and Atlanta   ‡Dollars per pound   §Dollars per euro
Source: The Economist, April 29, 2000.

Market potential is also affected by consumption patterns. The French drink six times more wine than the British do, whereas Germans consume six times the amount of beer the Italians do.[6] A poll showed that Venezuelans, Mexicans, Russians, Turks, and South Africans (in that order) care most about their appearance.[7] Venezuelans spend as much as 20 percent of their household income on personal care products, and hold the world record for deodorant use.[8] One-Hour Martinizing, a dry-cleaning franchise, decided to open its first foreign franchise in Ecuador after discovering that businessmen there changed their shirts as much as three times a day because of the hot, sticky weather.[9]

Consumption patterns are dynamic, and current patterns should be interpreted with caution. Although Coca-Cola's per capita consumption in the United States and Mexico is roughly similar, volume growth for carbonated soft drinks in Mexico is higher than in the United States.[10] Consumption is often driven by factors different than those in domestic markets. BCG research shows that in some developing economies such as Colombia or the Philippines, Coca-Cola is a substitute for non-drinkable water (see Exhibit 16–4).

Exhibit 16–3
Asian refrigerator
penetration vs.
GDP/capita

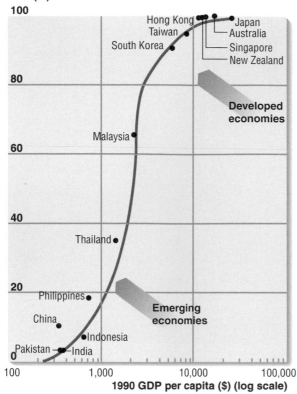

Exhibit 16–3
Asian refrigerator
penetration vs.
GDP/capita

Source: Reprinted with permission of George Stalk,
The Boston Consulting Group. 1995.

Exhibit 16–4
Consumption is not
driven by income alone

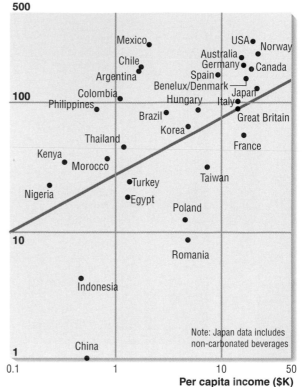

Source: Reprinted with permission of George Stalk,
The Boston Consulting Group. 1995.

In assessing market potential within the context of corporate strategy, firms undertake marketing research. The research is aimed at answering the following questions[11]: (a) What objectives should the firm pursue in the foreign market? (b) What foreign market segments should the firm pursue? (c) Which are the best product, distribution, pricing, and promotion strategies for the foreign market? and (d) What should the product-market-company mix be to take advantage of the available foreign marketing opportunities?

GLOBALIZATION AND LOCALIZATION IN INTERNATIONAL MARKETS

As in other functional areas of international business, striking a balance between globalization and localization is a key challenge. Lack of marketing globalization has proved to be detrimental to performance[12]; however, the same is true for indiscriminate standardization of marketing practices without attention to localization factors.[13,14] Here is how the globalization versus localization dilemma is described in a Conference Board report citing General Motors Europe:

Generally, the more closely defined the market segment, the less important are national stereotypes (German focus on ecology, Italians on performance). Across na-

tional markets, there is a trend toward greater similarity on product specifications, price and packaging. On the other hand, cultural and national differences exist and require flexibility in communication with customers.

Globalization, in a marketing sense, is the standardization of products (or services), brands, marketing, advertising, and the supply chain across countries and regions. **Localization**, in contrast, is the adjustment of one or more of the above elements to be idiosyncratic characteristics of a given national market.

Fine-tuning the globalization–localization balance is possibly the major challenge for the MNE. The challenge is approached and handled in different ways. Cees van der Hoven, CEO of Ahold NV, the number-three supermarket chain globally behind Wal-Mart and French Carrefour, summarizes his firm's strategy succinctly: "Everything the customer sees we localize, everything they don't see, we globalize." Partly as a result, Ahold recently posted better results than Carrefour, which prefers brand uniformity, substituting global brands for the local brands it acquires. However, Carrefour also tailors its products to local markets.[15]

Globalization Forces

Once the most localized and decentralized business function, marketing is increasingly coordinated on a global basis. Regional blocks such as the EU accelerate the trend. Although there were no grocery products available simultaneously in at least eight European countries in 1983, by 1992 there were at least 50 such products.[16] Dell Computer utilizes a Pan-European office to take advantage of increasing standardization of European rules and requirements.

Global Brands

Behind the globalization trend is an assumption that many industrial and (to a lesser extent) consumer products can be standardized. "There are pipes all over the world and there are water leaks all over the world," says Richard Rennick, owner of American Leak Detection, whose franchises span more than 60 countries.[17] Kellogg designated Corn Flakes, Special K, Frosted Flakes, Fruit Loops, and Nutri-Grain bars as "global brands" because of their wide name recognition and global sales volume.[18] Avon launched its "Far Away" fragrance as a global product reflecting inputs from most of its foreign subsidiaries, maintaining positioning, pricing, packaging, and advertising uniformity to the extent possible.[19]

Global products are products that enjoy worldwide recognition and are relatively unaltered in terms of brand and appearance when sold abroad.

But how many global products are out there? AC Nielsen, the marketing research firm, recently ranked 43 global brands of 23 manufacturers. To be designated global, products had to be sold throughout the world under the same name with more than $1 billion in sales and more than 5 percent of those sales outside the home market. The most global industry on this list is beverages, with snack and pet foods a distant second and third (see Exhibit 16–5 for the global brand leaders).

The chart shows brands that achieved at least $1 Billion in sales and had a geographic presence in each of four major regions of the world—North America, Latin America, Asia Pacific, and Europe/Middle East/Africa. Within those four regions, data was analyzed from 30 countries representing 90% of the world's gross domestic product. To be part of the list, a brand needed to have not only a geographic presence across all of the regions, but it must have had at least five percent of its sales outside of its home region. The list is in rank order based on revenue. The data was collected from each country in local currency and then converted into US$.

Each of the brands has been measured within a category. Brand franchises that cross category boundaries have not been aggregated across categories (e.g. Nivea is

Exhibit 16–5
Top 10 global brands

Company	Headquarters	Brand	Sales YE Q1 2001 (in constant US$)	Largest Market	Home Market	% Sales Outside of the Home
Philip Morris Companies Inc.	New York, NY	Marlboro	Over $15 billion	Europe, Middle East & Africa	NA	67%
The Coca-Cola Company	Atlanta, GA	Total Coke		Europe, Middle East & Africa	NA	77%
Pepsi-Cola Company	Purchase, NY	Total Pepsi	$5–10 billion	North America	NA	41%
Kellogg Company	Battle Creek, MI	Kellogg's		North America	NA	49%
Campbell Soup Company	Camden, NJ	Campbell's		North America	NA	6%
Anhauser-Busch Companies, Inc.	St. Louis, MO	Budweiser		North America	NA	27%
The Procter and Gamble Company	Cincinnati, OH	Pampers	$2.5–5 billion	Europe, Middle East & Africa	NA	63%
Nestlé S.A.	Vaud, Switzerland	Nescafe		Europe, Middle East & Africa	Europe	49%
The Gillette Company	Boston, MA	Gillette		North America & Europe	NA	61%
Philip Morris Companies Inc./ British American Tobaccco...	New York, NY; London, UK	Benson & Hedges		Europe, Middle East & Africa	Europe	28%

Source: ACNielson Global Services, September 2001.

a billion dollar brand within Moisturizers & Cleansers although it also has a smaller presence in other categories like Hair Care and Deodorants).

Local ACNielsen information wss used in the study. Therefore, the study is heavily weighted towards purchases from retail stores and generally excludes purchases in such outlets as restaurants, bars and vending machines.

Why Global Brands?

The primary motivation toward product and service globalization is to gain scale economies. Selling the same product using the same promotional message and distribution channels reduces cost. JC Penney closed its home-furnishing stores in Japan because so many products had to be made differently for the Japanese market that it was not profitable to operate there.[20] Globalization permits firms to leverage experience accumulated in one market toward another, using communications technologies to facilitate coordination and integration. In addition, the allure of a "global" product can be an important selling point for some consumers.

Marketing Repercussions of a Global Approach

What does the current trend toward globalization mean to the marketing function? Here are some of the key ramifications.[21]

■ Rapid roll-out of new products across major markets, preempting competitors from introducing similar products in new markets.

- Product prioritization and targeting across markets, limiting local product offerings.
- Globally uniform branding and advertising to create a consistent message, reassure customers with global reach, and reduce cost and duplication. This enhances entry into the increasingly crowded shelves of retailers that display only best-selling brands.
- Manufacturing relatively standardized products to scale economies.
- Transferring of marketing best practices across borders.

A Conference Board survey suggests that the greatest increase in globalization is set to occur in advertising, brand positioning, and package design. Further, such coordination seems to distinguish the successful from the less successful firms (see Exhibit 16–6). Successful firms also coordinate pricing to some extent, but not new product development.[22]

A by-product of the increased globalization of the marketing function is erosion in the authority of country managers (see also Chapter 11). Country managers today find themselves with less control over marketing budget, pricing, and other key marketing decisions. Although they usually maintain control over local brands and have some say in new product development, their influence over the marketing of global brands in their country of jurisdiction is clearly on the decline. National brand managers are more rare, and they often report directly to a global marketing group rather than the country manager.[23] The two may find themselves at odds, as shown in Exhibit 16–7. An innovative design solution is AMP's global account group,

Exhibit 16–6

International decision making: more vs. less successful companies

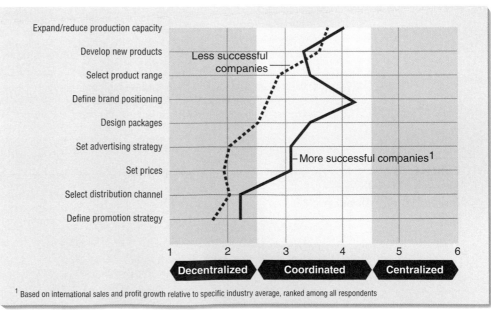

[1] Based on international sales and profit growth relative to specific industry average, ranked among all respondents

Source: The Conference Board, Report #1105-95-RR, based on Organizing for Global Success, McKinsey & Company, 1. Theuerkauf, D. Ernst, A. Mahini, 1993

Exhibit 16–7

Shared vision about global marketing activities between country managers and global marketing groups

Setting advertising strategy	2.85
Defining brand positioning	3.35
Package design	3.48
	N = 29

1–5 scale, 1 = no shared vision, 5 = strong shared vision
Source: The Conference Board Report #1105-95-RR

which assigns marketing executives to work directly with major clients in the United States, Japan, and Europe.[24]

While marketing globalization is evident throughout the world, there are significant differences in how MNEs from different countries approach it. Yip and Johansson found that U.S. firms were more likely to globalize branding than other marketing practices, probably a result of the global reach of English but also because their proportion of global sales was significantly lower than that of the Japanese (5 and 28 percent, respectively). (See Exhibits 16–8 and 16–9.)

Also, in contrast to U.S. firms, Japanese companies entrusted more selling and distribution autonomy to foreign marketing managers.

Exhibit 16–8
Use of globally uniform marketing practices

	U.S. Businesses	Japanese Businesses	Significance of Difference
Average	3.2	2.7	.10
Brand Names	4.6	4.4	n.s.
Packaging	3.9	4.1	n.s.
Absolute Pricing	2.5	2.6	n.s.
Relative Pricing	3.4	3.2	n.s.
Advertising	2.7	2.0	.05
Promotion	2.2	1.9	n.s.
Selling	3.3	1.8	.01
Distribution	3.2	2.1	.01

▨ = Significantly greater

Scale: Ranked from 1 to 5, with 5 being highest.
Source: The Conference Board Report #1105-95-RR, citing *Global Market Strategies of U.S. and Japanese Businesses.* Marketing Science Institute. G. Yip and J. Johansson. 1993.

Exhibit 16–9
Strength of (selected) individual globalization drivers

	U.S. Businesses	Japanese Businesses	Significance of Difference
Global Customers	5%	28%	.05
Global Channels	2%	16%	.05
Favorable Reaction to Foreign Brand Names	4.5	3.9	.10
Favorable Reaction to Foreign Promotion	2.2	2.8	.10
Favorable Reaction to Foreign Sales Personnel	1.6	2.3	.05
New Product Development Cost	5%	10%	.05

▨ = Significantly greater

Scale: Ranked from 1 to 5, with 5 being the highest. Percentages indicate facts rather than opinions. For instance, 28% of the customers of the Japanese firms in the survey are global versus only 5% in the United. States.
Source: The Conference Board Report #1105-95-RR, citing *Global Market Strategies of U.S. and Japanese Businesses.* Marketing Science Institute. G. Yip and J. Johansson. 1993.

Localization Forces

As earlier noted, localization forces represent pressures towards adjustment in product marketing or distribution to make it more appealing or to meet requirements particular to a foreign market.

Following a spate of alleged product contamination and other problems in foreign markets, Coca-Cola executives noted that the firm's motto "think globally and act locally" needed to be changed to "think locally and act locally." Indeed, despite globalization, local content and conditions remain paramount. In the global music market, the share of recording by local artists has risen from 58 percent in 1991 to 68 percent in 2000.[25] U.S. cable channels such as HBO now acknowledge that they grossly underestimated the need for adjustment in Asian markets, and that their operations there are marginally profitable as a result. Among other customization requirements, HBO has to satisfy Malaysian and Singaporean censors who demand editing out sensitive material.[26] Firms in other industries do not always fare better. Metro Cash and Carry was "taken to the cleaners" when it tried to import its South African wholesale model in Israel.[27] Carrefour, the French supermarket giant and the world's number-two retailer, is suffering huge losses in Japan where critics point out it never adjusted to the Japanese habit of purchasing small daily quantities of food to fit with their small kitchen appliances.[28]

Cross-national variations have a significant impact on marketing. Differences in income levels create different consumer requirements. Diverse regulatory regimes put different constraints on product design, packaging, and promotion. Even in the EU, where logotype and trademarks are relatively standardized, promotion, pricing, and media-mix are far from uniform.[29] Social attitudes and public opinion also make a difference. Kellogg's Nutri-Grain, successful in the United States, did not do nearly as well in the United Kingdom, where health consciousness had not been stressed at the time.[30] More recently, opposition to genetically modified foods, while muted in the United States, has been vocal in the EU and Canada.

Culture is also a major influence. Cultures high on power distance and uncertainty avoidance put more emphasis on appearance as a way to reaffirm one's status and to reduce uncertainty regarding others' positions. Members of high-power distance cultures are more likely to buy expensive watches, a status symbol. In cultures with high uncertainty avoidance, consumers buy more bottled water but fewer used cars because they want to minimize surprises. Jewelry purchase is more related to masculinity than to purchasing power.[31] Culture also influences sale practices. In high-power distance cultures, a sales pitch will be made in a formal manner whereas it is likely to be personalized in individualistic countries.[32]

Cultural and social mores also shape the context in which a product is used. In Hong Kong, Taiwan, and mainland China, McDonald's restaurants serve as bases for social activity for seniors in the late morning and for schoolchildren in the afternoon.[33] In this case, cultural rankings on collectivism are supplemented by physical realities: With residential space scarce, the restaurants provide an opportunity for social gathering.

Product Adaptation

Faced with a foreign market with different characteristics, a firm may choose not to offer a product or a service in that market, to offer the same product it offers in other markets, or adapt it to regional or country requirements. To make the decision, firms use "benefit/cost" and "user/need" models. **Benefit/cost models** assess the advantages and disadvantages of a product or distribution mode in a given market. **User/need models** test the needs of potential customers, including the circumstances in which the product or service are likely to be used. The analysis yields a decision to standardize or customize the product and/or its promotion and distribution.

In 1999, Ford offered the European version of the Escort in Argentina, Brazil, and Ecuador, and a South American version in 13 other South American nations.[34] In Colombia, the company did not offer any Escort product. Following disappointing sales of the Escort in India, Ford decided to develop "an Indian car," the first designed and built for a developing market. While using the Ford Fiesta basic platform to lower development costs, the car shows little resemblance to the Fiesta. Extras were cut to make possible a price tag that would appeal to value-conscious consumers, and local content beefed up to reduce costs and meet government requirements. Ford's designers and engineers drove many miles on India's roads with families of five, a key customer group, making the following adjustments to customer requirements:

> *Rear headroom was raised to make way for men in turbans, doors were adjusted to open wider than normal to avoid catching the flowing saris of women, air intake valves were fitted to avoid flooding during monsoon season, shock absorbers were toughened for pock-marked city streets, and air conditioning was revved up for summer heat.[35]*

The Volkswagen Beetle (not the New Beetle), manufactured in Mexico, is not exported to the United States because compliance with U.S. safety and emission standards would make it prohibitively expensive. Mitsubishi gave up on building a "global car" and redesigned its cars sold in the United States to be "more American." Toyota and Nissan increased engine size and interior space in their U.S. models following disappointing sales and moved much of the design and development to the United States to be closer to the market. Honda credits its U.S. market research with the addition of a third row of seats on its sports utility vehicle, something to which Japanese designers initially objected.[36]

COUNTRY BOX

THE KIMCHI DOCTORS

Kimchi is a Korean national dish of fermented cabbage, which is also popular in Japan and a number of other East Asian countries. The dish received mixed reviews in foreign markets, with many customers complaining about strong taste and offending smell. A group of Korean food scientists was recently recruited by Doosan, South Korea's leading kimchi producer, to develop a version that would appeal to Americans and displace imports from Japan which currently dominate international markets with a 70 percent share.

The Korean team (known as "the kimchi doctors") faces a challenge similar to that of other international marketers: How to develop a product that is attractive in a foreign market yet retains the unique characteristics and allure of its country of origin, and how to differentiate its product from its major competitors. The team succeeded in developing kimchi with longer shelf life and a smell more appealing to Westerners. In the summer of 2001, Korean kimchi manufacturers won an important victory when the Codex Alimentarius, which sets international food standards accepted by the WTO, adopted a global standard for kimchi that corresponds to the Korean method of preparing the dish.

Doosan also faces competition from other domestic manufacturers, among them a company previously allied with a kosher food manufacturer in New York that is now developing kimchi kraut for the European market and a kimchi-topped burger for McDonald's. Meanwhile, Pizza Hut has introduced a kimchi topping for its pizza that now accounts for 30 percent of its Korean sales.

Source: Adapted from J. Solomon, "Stinking national dish seeks smell of success and a global market," *Wall Street Journal*, August 17, 2001, A1.

Nor is adaptation limited to the automotive industry. Coca-Cola, the quintessential global brand, tinkers with its formula to suit local taste. Its diet Coke is sold in France as Coke Light. Kraft Foods sweetens the flavors of Tang for sale in Latin America. In Israel, Pizza Hut features special toppings not offered elsewhere in the world, including imitation shrimp. In Egypt, Chili's offers a version of the Sohur (a special midnight buffet) during the month of Ramadan when Moslems fast from daylight to sunset.[37] *Time* magazine, whose first international edition dates back to 1942, publishes different editions for the U.S., Asian, and European markets, among others, as does the *Wall Street Journal*. In both cases, regional editions share some common material but use local content as appropriate. As in other industries, this customization has been greatly aided by technological advances that enable simultaneous printing in different locations.

For the MNE, global marketing requires a fine balance. While making adjustments to local tastes and customs, it is equally important for the MNE to leverage its name recognition and global reputation.

McDonald's is the largest fast-food chain in the world, with more than 30,000 restaurants, about 17,000 of these in 121 foreign countries, employing over 314,000 people. With 60 percent of its profits coming from international sales, the firm's motto is "all business is local." As Jim Cantalupo, head of international operations, says, "We don't run Spain out of Portugal." McDonald's is selling Big Macs around the world, but in Seoul it also offers roast pork on a bun with garlicky soy sauce.[38] In selected Jerusalem outlets, Big Macs (minus the cheese) are kosher. In India, where cows are sacred, Veggie McNuggets are served. When the Indonesian rupiah collapsed during the Asian financial crisis, rice was added to the menu as a substitute for expensive fries. While offering local variants, as shown in Exhibit 16–10, McDonald's makes full use of its scale and spread. It serves a global brand, renowned for quality and cleanliness, which customers can find in multiple locations.

The adaptation challenge extends to all marketing aspects. In Japan, relationships with suppliers, distributors, and suppliers have been, until recently, long lasting. Despite a growing proliferation of larger stores and retail chains, Japanese retail trade continues to be dominated by non-affiliated independent organizations, with half of the retail establishments employing one or two people.[39] Office Depot and OfficeMax launched their Japanese outlets as replicas of the firms' U.S.-based large, warehouse type discount stores. They discovered that the global efficiencies derived were insufficient to compensate for local rents and reluctance to buy in an impersonal, warehouse-type store. The firms changed their strategies accordingly.[40]

Country-of-Origin Effect

Country-of-origin effect is the influence of the country of manufacturing image upon the buying decision. The effect consists of these dimensions: innovativeness, namely the use of new technology and engineering advances; design, namely appearance, style, color, and variety; prestige (i.e., exclusivity), status and brand name reputation; and workmanship, including reliability, durability, craftsmanship, and manufacturing quality.[41] There is strong evidence that country-of-origin influences buyers' perceptions.[42] The impact has more to do with perception than reality. For instance, British firms are not associated with many strong products and innovations they have actually created.[43]

Country-of-origin effect can change over time. In the 1960s, Japanese products had a reputation of shoddy quality and it was decades before the country established a reputation for quality manufacturing. Because products from developed nations tend to receive higher evaluation,[44] a country moving into the ranks of developed economies is also likely to enhance the reputation of its products. In the

Exhibit 16–10
Product adjustments at
McDonald's

Country	Adjustment
Switzerland	Veggie Mac, and ski-thru window in some restaurants
Singapore	Chicken rice, also reduced fat in foods, switched to vegetable oil in food preparation and in French fries
Saudi Arabia	Traditional first-floor; family section on the second floor, all Muslim employees, non-pork menus
Portugal	Traditional bica (like espresso) served in porcelain instead of foam cups. Pasties de nata (Portuguese style cakes) added to menus alongside traditional muffins and brownies
Paraguay	Use of computers and internet in select restaurants, McMacos, McFiesta added to menus (lower price and smaller size)
Netherlands	McKroket (100 percent beef ragout with crispy layer around it, topped with fresh mustard and mayonnaise sauce)
Mexico	McNifica, McBurrito à la Mexicana
Japan	Teriyaki McBurger (sausage patty on a bun with teriyaki sauce)
Italy	Salads featuring Mediterranean flavors. Marinara (shrimp and salmon in fresh lettuce), Vegetariana (veggie), Mediteranea (cheese and olive), Fiordiriso (rice, tuna, ham, mushrooms)
Ireland	Shamrock shake (available during St. Patrick's Day celebrations)
Hong Kong	Curry potato pie; shake fries, red bean sundae
Germany	Translating quarter pounder to metric system is difficult, so they named it McRoyal and Hamburger Royal
Argentina	McCafe (a variety of coffees, pastries, desserts), McSwing (ice cream with various toppings)
Australia	McCafe with formal cutlery, special napkins, china cups, chocolate desserts, uniforms of black and gold
Chile	McPalta (made from avocados)

Source: www.mcdonalds.com.

interim, firms from emerging economies often engage in reputation-enhancing activities. Giant Manufacturing, a Taiwanese bicycle maker, sponsors professional racing teams to build a reputation as a company staying on the leading edge of technology.[45]

Leveraging Positive Country Image

Country image varies across product categories.[46] German automotive firms take advantage of the country's reputation for advanced engineering, quality, and reliability. The same is true for Japanese automotive and electronics makers. Other countries may be noted for a single product, for example, Iranian carpets or Russian caviar. A British publication recently lamented the country's top ranking in merely one industry:

> The United States is rated best for many key sectors, including retail, computers, and telecom; Germany is top for sectors such as engineering, cars, and beer; France for cosmetics, food, health care, spirits; Japan for consumer electronics and domestic appliances; Britain is rated top for just one commercial area: air travel.[47]

A positive country image may lead to minimize customization that is not inherent to product use. The original appearance and packaging will be preserved to the extent permitted by law so as to highlight the product's national origin.

Leveraging Nationalist Sentiments

Country-of-origin may serve as a patriotic appeal to buy domestic products. Many countries have campaigns urging consumers to buy locally as a way of supporting local industry and employment. For example, a prospective car buyer may be reminded that by buying a domestic car he/she will prevent further deterioration of the ongoing U.S. trade deficit with Japan.

"Buy local" campaigns have been popular around the globe.

Support of domestic products may at times extend to the vilification of foreign products. Japanese farmers placed ads in local newspapers accusing U.S. orange growers of spreading "agent orange" on their fruit (agent orange was a chemical used by the U.S. armed forces in Vietnam to retard vegetation growth). Visible companies such as Coca-Cola and McDonald's are often singled out. When Yugoslav students demonstrated against U.S. interests, McDonald's and Coca-Cola topped the target list.[48]

Some foreign firms attempt to disarm nationalist sentiment by emphasizing the local content in their product. **Local content** is the portion of a product (or service) that includes locally made and procured inputs. Airbus, in its ads in the United States, outlines its U.S. suppliers. The aim is to "localize" the product, helping people feel that by buying the foreign product they are, in fact, supporting their countrymen. Finding a local angle is not always easy in an age when many products involve multiple nations and when the national flags of many countries are made abroad. Take, for example, the ad placed by German automaker Mercedes-Benz in a Canadian newspaper for its M-Class car manufactured in the United States. The firm touts that the plant's president is a Canadian.

Others may downplay the foreign origin of the product, using brand names and packaging that reflect local heritage. In Russia, "the beloved taste of real Russian butter" appears on the package of butter from New Zealand, while Zlato vegetable oil, featuring a Russian peasant family in its TV commercials, originates in Argentina. However, this phenomenon is not extended to other Russian products that are not held in high esteem by local consumers.[49]

MNEs often point out that local firms do not necessarily suffer from their entry. Burger Ranch, an Israeli burger chain, continued to prosper following the entry of McDonald's and Burger King, which greatly increased the overall market. In Latvia, Kvas, a traditional fermented drink, initially disappeared from the market under pressure from Coca-Cola and PepsiCo. Then, using modern production and marketing techniques and touting its healthy image, Kvas increased its market share from 4 percent in 1998 to 32 percent in the first half of 2000.[50] In Japan, locally-based Askul is successfully competing against Office Depot and OfficeMax with marketing that is better suited to the local environment.[51] A Siberian detergent manufacturer piggybacked on Procter & Gamble's campaign promoting its Ariel detergent over "ordinary powder" by introducing its Ordinary Powder brand. The local product, priced at about 15 percent of the foreign import, has already captured 1 percent of the Russian market.[52]

Branding

Branding is the process of creating and supporting positive perceptions associated with a product or service. In global markets, branding is especially complex given varying demand and environmental characteristics. Procter & Gamble entered China in 1988 with one product. Today, the company has 20 brands and a $1 billion volume in profitable sales there. Here is how the former head of P&G's China operations views the principles that led P&G to create successful brands in China:

- Selecting the right (Chinese) name
- In-depth understanding of the local market and willingness to make the necessary adaptations
- Fine-tuning the right size/price/value formulation of offerings
- Providing quality and reliability at a competitive price
- Holistic marketing using a variety of channels
- Turning trademarks into "trust-marks"
- Establishing leadership brands, changing social habits if necessary
- Selecting the right allies and partners

Exhibit 16–11 contains the rankings of Fortune's Global Most Admired Companies. The list is dominated by U.S. firms (obviously influenced by the respondent group) but also includes such firms as Nokia (Finland), Sony, and Toyota (Japan).

Exhibit 16–12 contains *Business Week's* top 100 global brands (only brands with at least 20 percent foreign revenues were included). Note that all but one of the top 10 are U.S. brands, and that the top 50 had merely one firm that is not from the United States or Europe. However, the exhibit also contains the top eight brand portfolios, five of which are owned by non-U.S. firms.

The global reach of some brands should not distract attention from the power of local brands. Ahold's CEO notes that discarding the Dutch company's Swedish brand ICA would be "ridiculous" since this brands ranks with Volvo as one of the best-known brands in Sweden.[53]

Channel Decisions

Channel decisions involve the length (the number of levels or intermediaries employed in the distribution process) and width (the number of firms in each level) of the channel used in linking manufacturers to consumers.[54] In business-to-business sales, channel decisions are often more important than brand name, advertising, and pricing.[55] A study of United Kingdom, Japanese, and German subsidiaries in the United States shows that they are more likely to localize channel decisions than product or pricing decisions. Localization is especially pronounced among U.K. affiliates, perhaps due to the assumption of cultural similarity.[56]

Intermediation

Many international sales are not made directly by firms but by export intermediaries. **Export intermediaries** are firms that mediate between firms, especially SMIEs, and their export markets, by providing logistic, documentation, and related services. Intermediaries play a central role for smaller firms, although some MNEs prefer to outsource this function. When SED International, a leading international distributor of microcomputer and wireless communication products throughout the

Exhibit 16–11
Fortune's global most admired companies

2002 Rank	2001 Rank	Company	Country
1	1	General Electric	U.S.
2	5	Wal-Mart Stores	U.S.
3	3	Microsoft	U.S.
4	14	Berkshire Hathaway	U.S.
5	9	Home Depot	U.S.
6	17	Johnson & Johnson	U.S.
7	74	FedEx	U.S.
8	18	Citigroup	U.S.
9	4	Intel	U.S.
10	2	Cisco Systems	U.S.
11	21	Merck	U.S.
12	20	Pfizer	U.S.
13	24	United Parcel Service	U.S.
14	N/A	Target	U.S.
15	26	Procter & Gamble	U.S.
16	61	PepsiCo	U.S.
17	40	AOL Time Warner*	U.S.
18	60	Anheuser-Busch	U.S.
19	35	Exxon Mobil	U.S.
20	15	Coca-Cola Enterprises	U.S.
21	34	J.P. Morgan Chase	U.S.
22	27	American Intl. Group	U.S.
23	7	Dell Computer	U.S.
24	8	Nokia	Finland
25	10	Toyota Motor	Japan
26	37	Northwestern Mutual	U.S.
27	62	Walgreen	U.S.
28	6	Sony	Japan
29	51	Eil Lilly	U.S.
30	48	Continental Airlines	U.S.
31	22	Walt Disney	U.S.
32	52	Bristol-Myers Squibb	U.S.
33	N/A	Duke Energy	U.S.
34	54	DuPont de Nemours (E.I.)	U.S.
35	N/A	Boeing	U.S.
36	70	Colgate-Palmolive	U.S.
37	67	Caterpillar	U.S.
38	N/A	Sun Microsystems	U.S.
39	39	Nestlé	Switzerland
40	46	SBC Communications	U.S.
41	29	Honda Motor	Japan
42	N/A	Oracle	U.S.
43	N/A	Deere	U.S.
44	58	Alcoa	U.S.
45	33	BP	Britain
46	19	Ford Motor	U.S.
47	N/A	BellSouth	U.S.
48	N/A	Kroger	U.S.
49	N/A	Texas Instruments	U.S.
50	31	Singapore Airlines	Singapore

*AOL Time Warner's previous rank is the 2000 rank of Time Warner. AOL did not appear in last year's Global Most Admired.
Source: Fortune Magazine, 2001.

Exhibit 16–12

The global brand scoreboard

Rank		2001 Brand Value $Billions	Country of Ownership	Rank		2001 Brand Value $Billions	Country of Ownership
1	COCA-COLA	68.95	U.S.	51	KFC	5.26	U.S.
2	MICROSOFT	65.07	U.S.	52	REUTERS	5.24	Britain
3	IBM	52.75	U.S.	53	SUN MICROSYSTEMS	5.15	U.S.
4	GE	42.40	U.S.	54	KLEENEX	5.09	U.S.
5	NOKIA	35.04	Finland	55	PHILIPS	4.90	Netherlands
6	INTEL	34.67	U.S.	56	COLGATE	4.57	U.S.
7	DISNEY	32.59	U.S.	57	WRIGLEY'S	4.53	U.S.
8	FORD	30.09	U.S.	58	AOL	4.50	U.S.
9	McDONALD'S	25.29	U.S.	59	YAHOO!	4.38	U.S.
10	AT&T	22.83	U.S.	60	AVON	4.37	U.S.
11	MARLBORO	22.05	U.S.	61	CHANEL	4.27	France
12	MERCEDES	21.73	Germany	62	DURACELL	4.14	U.S.
13	CITIBANK	19.01	U.S.	63	BOEING	4.06	U.S.
14	TOYOTA	18.58	Japan	64	TEXAS INSTRUMENTS	4.04	U.S.
15	HEWLETT-PACKARD	17.98	U.S.	65	KRAFT	4.03	U.S.
16	CISCO SYSTEMS	17.21	U.S.	66	MOTOROLA	3.76	U.S.
17	AMERICAN EXPRESS	16.92	U.S.	67	LEVI'S	3.75	U.S.
18	GILLETTE	15.30	U.S.	68	TIME	3.72	U.S.
19	MERRILL LYNCH	15.02	U.S.	69	ROLEX	3.70	Switzerland
20	SONY	15.01	Japan	70	ADIDAS	3.65	Germany
21	HONDA	14.64	Japan	71	HERTZ	3.62	U.S.
22	BMW	13.86	Germany	72	PANASONIC	3.49	Japan
23	NESCAFE	13.25	Switzerland	73	TIFFANY	3.48	U.S.
24	COMPAQ	12.35	U.S.	74	BP	3.25	Britain
25	ORACLE	12.22	U.S.	75	BACARDI	3.20	Bermuda
26	BUDWEISER	10.84	U.S.	76	AMAZON.COM	3.13	U.S.
27	KODAK	10.80	U.S.	77	SHELL	2.84	Brit./Neth.
28	MERCK	9.67	U.S.	78	SMIRNOFF	2.59	Britain
29	NINTENDO	9.46	Japan	79	MOET & CHANDON	2.43	France
30	PFIZER	8.95	U.S.	80	BURGER KING	2.43	U.S.
31	GAP	8.75	U.S.	81	MOBIL	2.42	U.S.
32	DELL	8.27	U.S.	82	HEINEKEN	2.27	Netherlands
33	GOLDMAN SACHS	7.86	U.S.	83	WALL STREET JOURNAL	2.18	U.S.
34	NIKE	7.59	U.S.	84	BARBIE	2.04	U.S.
35	VOLKSWAGEN	7.34	Germany	85	POLO/RALPH LAUREN	1.91	U.S.
36	ERICSSON	7.07	Sweden	86	FEDEX	1.89	U.S.
37	HEINZ	7.06	U.S.	87	NIVEA	1.78	Germany
38	LOUIS VUITTON	7.05	France	88	STARBUCKS	1.76	U.S.
39	KELLOGG'S	7.01	U.S.	89	JOHNNIE WALKER	1.65	Britain
40	MTV	6.60	U.S.	90	JACK DANIELS	1.58	U.S.
41	CANON	6.58	Japan	91	ARMANI	1.49	Italy
42	SAMSUNG	6.37	S. Korea	92	PAMPERS	1.41	U.S.
43	SAP	6.31	Germany	93	ABSOLUT	1.38	Sweden
44	PEPSI	6.21	U.S.	94	GUINNESS	1.36	Britain
45	XEROX	6.02	U.S.	95	FINANCIAL TIMES	1.31	Britain
46	IKEA	6.01	Sweden	96	HILTON	1.24	U.S.
47	PIZZA HUT	5.98	U.S.	97	CARLSBERG	1.08	Denmark
48	HARLEY-DAVIDSON	5.53	U.S.	98	SIEMENS	1.03	Germany
49	APPLE	5.46	U.S.	99	SWATCH	1.00	Switzerland
50	GUCCI	5.36	Italy	100	BENETTON	1.00	Italy

(continued)

Exhibit 16–12
continued

The Top Brand Portfolios			
	Company	**2001 Brand $Billions**	**Country**
1	JOHNSON & JOHNSON	68.21	U.S.
2	P&G	45.44	U.S.
3	NESTLE	41.69	Switzerland
4	UNILEVER	37.85	Brit./Neth.
5	L'OREAL	17.80	France
6	DIAGEO	15.00	Brit./Neth.
7	COLGATE-PALMOLIVE	14.36	U.S.
8	DANONE	13.58	France

Data: Interbrand, Citigroup, *Business Week,* August 3, 2001.

United States and Latin America, was designated a "Certified HP Top Value Reseller," it was given exclusive right to offer top-selling HP products in several international markets.[57] SED resells HP products, charging customers up to 5 percent over competitors in the direct distribution channel. Because of the amount of business it generates, HP prefers to deal with SED instead of handling multiple consumers.

Direct Marketing

Direct marketing involves direct sales to customers via individual agents who typically make a commission not only on their sales but also on the sales of other agents that they have recruited. The system was pioneered by cosmetic-makers Avon and Mary Kay and was eventually adopted by manufacturers of other products. More recently, Amway has become the world's largest direct seller, with operations in many countries.

Direct marketers face many problems abroad. The image of direct selling is quite low, especially in Asia. In China, the government ruled that direct sales constituted a "pyramid scheme" and banned such sales altogether. In Japan, Avon found that its system of selling to random groups was not effective, because people are reluctant to invite strangers into their home. However, once it tinkered with the system to rely on groups of friends and acquaintances, the operation prospered.

Niche Marketing

Niche marketing is narrowly directed towards a pre-defined segment of the market. In international markets, niche marketing may be directed not only to a product category (e.g., low end) but also to an ethnic or geographical segment. Big Boy in Thailand, Schlotzky's Delicatessen in Malaysia, Shakey's Pizza Restaurant in the Philippines, and Carl's Jr. in Mexico all target a specific niche in their target market.[58] Convencao, a small Brazilian soft-drink company, cut into the market share of industry giants Coke and Pepsi by offering lower-priced soft drinks in its home market.[59] A niche can also serve as a base for expansion, however. Timberland, originally known for its weather-proofed boots, now exports casual wear to more than 50 (mostly developed) countries, including Italy.[60]

Pricing

Pricing is the decision and process of setting a price to a product or a service. In international markets pricing is much more complex due to varying cost structures (e.g., transportation costs, tariffs) and market positioning. An equally equipped Ford Escort sells for about $10,000 in the United States but costs $20,000 in England,[61] about 10 to 12 percent more than in other EU markets.[62] (Ford recently moved to cut U.K. prices[63]). A British buyer seeking to buy the car elsewhere in the EU would not only find the steering wheel on the wrong side, but could also face a reluctant dealer, deterred by exclusive distribution agreements. The European Commission fined German automaker Volkswagen for turning back German customers who sought to buy their cars from Italian dealers to benefit from the weak lira (prior to the Euro introduction).

Price differentials facilitate market segmentation, allowing a firm to position its product differentially in different markets. Firms may hike prices where there is little competition and where consumer resistance to price increases is low. Or, they may price a brand higher so it can be positioned as "premium." Belgian brewer Interbrew markets its Stella beer in the United States under the slogan "reassuringly expensive."[64]

Even if desirable, price consistency is not easy to achieve. For instance, some subsidiaries provide a higher level of service than others.[65] Prices are also influenced by host government decisions. The Turkish government imposes an 80 percent import tax on all vehicle imports; this protects domestic manufacturers as well as the international firms that manufacture in Turkey. In the United States, pharmaceutical manufacturers have been lobbying to prevent cheaper medicine imports.[66] They argue that cheaper drugs lower the incentives for domestic manufacturing and expose consumers to the risk of fakes.

Predatory Pricing

Predatory pricing is the selling of goods below real cost so as to drive competitors out of the market (eventually raising prices). Matsushita allegedly priced its Panasonic TV sets below cost in the United States, subsidizing sales with its high margins in the Japanese market and driving U.S. manufacturers out of business.[67] A complaint by Zenith was dismissed on the grounds that if Matsushita had priced its products below cost, it would have gone out of business in the 20 years the case took to resolve.[68] A similar complaint was filed by Republic Engineered Steels and Timken, which argued that Brazilian exporters were selling steel at 40 percent below their home-market price, or the cost of manufacturing the product in Brazil[69] (see also Chapter 2).

Promotion

Globalization can yield substantial promotion savings. When United Distillers (now Diageo) bought control of its distributors, it was able to consolidate more than 50 campaigns worldwide into one.[70] General Motors Europe uses a unified promotional approach to drive brand identity; however, it recognizes the need for adaptation in some markets. When it launched its Omega sedan, it created a single European campaign but held a separate campaign for Germany and Switzerland.

Advertising

Like other marketing functions, and often more, advertising must be adjusted to local tastes, norms, and regulations if it is to be effective in international markets. When Lego exported its successful U.S. advertising into Japan, it quickly flopped.[71] Like other firms, Lego discovered that moving advertising across borders is difficult linguistically, culturally, and socially.[72,73] Missteps are common. DHL Worldwide Express had to apologize for an ad that Indonesians felt likened President Suharto to a courier. Nike was criticized for an ad showing the Brazilian national team playing a soccer match against the devil.[74] In another incident, Nike sold shoes with an imprint that could be interpreted as similar to the Arabic scripture for God. The perceived insult was especially severe because a shoe sole is considered impure (e.g., it should not be shown to a counterpart to a conversation) and Nike had to pull 37,000 shoes off the shelves in 1997. Even savvy MNEs such as Coca-Cola, which announced that it would stay away from controversial topics such as religion, politics, and disease,[75] can encounter difficulty. When a rumor spread in Egypt that its logo contained the Arabic words for "no Mohammed, no Mecca," Coca-Cola had to obtain a decree from Egypt's Mufti, the country's top religious authority, that the logo did not defame Islam.[76] In contrast, Benetton purposely includes religion and controversial subjects such as the death penalty and disease in its global advertising campaigns.

Swatch targets young, energetic people of all ages, and broadly defines their lifestyle; however, it airs its ads in markets with cultural and economic similarities.[77] Swatch ads show people of different races, ages, gender—plus Olympic track star Michael Johnson and supermodel Tyra Banks. The use of well-known stars helps European sales, and the use of American celebrities helps U.S. sales. The ad legend "Time is what you make of it" is easily comprehended in the two regions. Nike's ads in Europe feature soccer stars but those are not aired in the United States where soccer is less popular. Tang is marketed as a breakfast drink in the United States, but as a "throughout the day drink" in Latin America.

The temptation to standardize advertising is considerable. Standardization provides a coherent and consistent message and greatly reduces production cost by spreading it across multiple markets. McKinsey calculated that Gillette saved $20 million by creating a global campaign for its Sensor razor in 19 markets, out of a total advertising expense of $175 million.[78] Cable television and the Internet make a global campaign feasible. Coca-Cola and Benetton, and, more recently, Ford Motor Company, have all launched global advertising campaigns. However, as the Conference Board notes, advertising uniformity depends on "the similarity of consumer buying motivations and of competitors' messages; the existence of specific government restrictions on content; and the availability of desired media channels."[79] In Canada, for example, infomercials can only be aired after midnight. Other countries prohibit the use of brand names during programs. Indeed, Coca-Cola has recently abandoned its global ad campaign, although it maintains central "guidance, process, and strategy" for its advertising efforts.[80]

As they globalize their marketing, firms increasingly seek advertising agencies with global reach to provide a one-stop shop. Kellogg assigned responsibilities for three of its global brands to Leo Burnett and assigned two others to J. Walter Thompson. This is one reason for the consolidation of advertising agencies into global networks. Network members share the reach and brand recognition of the network while offering in-depth knowledge of the local market.

Marketing Alliances

International strategic alliances are a major market entry venue. Such alliances as well as mergers and acquisitions allow a firm to quickly establish itself in a foreign market (see also Chapters 10 and 12). Leuven (Belgium)-based Interbrew grew from a small family-owned brewery to the world's second largest brewer and the owner of more than 200 brands through a series of acquisitions. Its typical strategy: retain the existing local brands while leveraging distribution channels to market high margin specialty brands.[81] Similar moves by Coca-Cola to acquire smaller rivals and link their distribution channels with its own have raised concerns among competition authorities in the EU and Mexico.[82] Marketing alliances are also established between large firms; for example, IBM and Dai Nippon Printing cooperate in database marketing. Swiss food giant Nestlé and French retailer Casino cooperate in marketing, logistics, and sales. The two share and analyze bar code information to learn how to enhance customer loyalty while reducing costs.[83]

Not all marketing alliances prosper. In 1992, Timex established a marketing and distribution alliance with India's Titan. Timex provided low-end watches, whereas Titan focused on the high-end luxury watches that can be considered jewelry. Titan shops serviced Timex watches while Timex had access to Titan's 4,500 dealers and 60 showrooms. In return, Titan had access to low-cost–mass production market through Timex. As market conditions changed, the firms decided to move into other segments, and in 1997 announced that they were breaking up their alliance.[84,85]

Interim Summary

1. Market potential is a function of economic variables (e.g., disposable income) but also of cultural and social variables that affect consumption patterns.

2. Globalization forces include emergence of global brands as well as the potential for cost savings and efficiencies, technological advances, and lower trade barriers. Localization forces include a variety of country level factors that affect product introduction and adaptation. This is true not only for the product itself but also for marketing channels, pricing, and promotion.

3. Country-of-origin effect is a powerful force influencing purchase decisions.

4. Branding, channel decisions, and promotion all reflect the globalization–localization tension.

THE GLOBAL SUPPLY CHAIN

The term **global supply chain** covers both logistics and operations. It includes such activities as sourcing, procurement, order processing, manufacturing, warehousing, inventory control, servicing and warranty, custom clearing, wholesaling, and distribution. Supply chain management is a key component in a firm's global strategy, influencing major decisions such as plant and service location. A report published by the Conference Board states: "in today's world, it is supply chains that compete, not companies".[86]

In real terms, the cost of logistics has fallen in recent years. In the United Kingdom, distribution costs have fallen from 12 to 15 percent in the 1980s to 5.2 percent in 1991.[87] The decline reflects increased efficiencies, for example, the incorporation of Just-in-Time and the resulting decrease in inventory levels.[88] Amdahl, a U.S. subsidiary of Japan's Fujitsu, reduced logistic costs from 9 percent of revenues in 1991 to 3.5 percent in 1997.[89] Stride Rite Corp., a retailer of athletic and casual footwear, cut by one third the shipping time of shoes manufactured in Asia to its distribution center in Kentucky. The retailer cut 30 percent of its transportation cost and improved inventory turnaround time by 25 percent.[90]

E-commerce has so far failed to create a "seamless" supply chain. Among the 600 e-marketplaces seeking to match corporate buyers and suppliers in early 2000, "virtually none is capable of handling international logistics, credit verification and payment between companies in different countries." Issues such as international shipping costs, language, currency translation, customs documentation, and cross-border financial settlement are only beginning to be addressed.[91] Forrester Research found that most of the companies it surveyed failed to calculate the total cost of shipping an international order and many were losing money on shipments for failing to adjust pricing to reflect real costs (see also Chapter 18). Additionally,

Eighty-five percent of the companies noted that they could not fill overseas orders because of the complexity of shipping across borders. Of those that had problems

shipping overseas, 75 percent cited their system's inability to register international addresses accurately or to price total delivery cost.[92]

The Globalization of Supply Chains

To deliver a product or service effectively, firms increasingly consolidate production and distribution in a few strategic locations. This shift from domestic to global supply chains is driven by rapidly escalating capital costs and enhanced technologies as well as by regional integration. The evolution of flexible manufacturing systems enables mass customization to meet customer demands at reasonable cost. Transport industry consolidation facilitates seamless transportation (e.g., Canada National Railways and Illinois Central plan to merge in order to provide direct shipping between Canada, the United States, and Mexico). Developments in management information systems permit accurate tracking of variable customer demands and material flow. Suggests a logistics executive:

> *In the past, for technical reasons, it was impossible to enter an order in one country, process it in another, and ship the goods from a third country. Now with the installation of a new client/server-based order management system, all this is possible.[93]*

Where integration has progressed as in the EU, standardized regulations have been replacing local rules, enhancing the case for consolidation. French tire-maker Michelin shifted from local plants manufacturing a variety of products to regional or global plants specializing in one type of product. The company now manufactures a tire type in just one or two European sites.[94] Nike consolidated its distribution operations in Belgium, and Energizer (the European arm of Eveready Battery) consolidated its 60 distribution systems into six. With nations increasingly served by logistic centers in other countries, geographic designs become less of an option for MNEs (see Chapter 11). Becton Dickinson, a medical technology provider, developed a global supply chain as part of a broader shift from a decentralized geographical structure to a global one. Other repercussions of supply chain globalization are extended supply and distribution chains, increased transportation from and to transportation centers, and more small-volume transactions.[95]

The Challenge for SMIEs

SMIEs may not have the requisite economies to justify a specialized facility. One solution is **mutualization**—the sharing of logistic facilities by two or more partners.[96] SMIEs also form alliances with other firms, especially local companies. The local partner may already have a logistic component or a long-term logistic provider, which makes it difficult for the foreign firm to consolidate its supply chain locally. For instance, foreign investors in China found that their Chinese partner was not as helpful in resolving distribution obstacles as initially believed.[97] Sourcing logistic services from third parties is another solution for the SMIE that is also used by large firms such as Marks & Spencer and Phillips Semiconductors. In such alliances, the shipper takes the lead in strategy formulation while the provider leads day-to-day operations. There is a sole key provider (although some of those purchase services from subcontractors) with whom the manufacturer has a close working relationship.[98]

Global Sourcing

Global sourcing is the procurement of production or service inputs and components in international markets. Global sourcing provides the MNE with the opportunity to leverage its scale and competitive advantage in spotting procurement opportunities around the globe for use in its various divisions and locations. For example, because of its scale, Wal-Mart uses its huge volume to extract lower prices from suppliers; Ford Motor, because of its competitive advantage, can use parts produced in its Chinese joint venture in its Brazilian operations. Materials, components, and other value-added activities are sourced throughout the world. Toronto-based Canadian Tire sources in the United States and Asia, importing 8,000 and 4,000 container loads annually from these respective locations.[99] In 1997, fashion house Donna Karan International sourced 52 percent of its raw materials and finished products in Asia, 26 percent in Europe, and 22 percent in the United States.[100]

MNEs also increasingly use **outsourcing**, or the buying of inputs outside their network. Firms may even outsource the logistic function itself.

Logistic Providers

While one-stop, international provision of logistic provision remains an ultimate goal, national services are more likely to be replaced by regional providers. Texas Instruments Semiconductors Group contracts with a key logistic provider to manage forwarding and distribution in each region of the world.[101] TNT Logistics distributes parts for Italian car-maker Fiat throughout Europe, while Fritz Companies handles warehousing and distribution for General Motors' after-sale parts and accessories in Taiwan.[102]

Consolidation among providers is apparent, as in the merger between U.S.-based AEI and Switzerland's Danzas. However, in other countries the number of logistic providers is actually increasing. Between 1997 and 2000, the number of logistic service providers in Brazil has tripled.[103]

Customizing the Supply Chain

While the globalization of supply chain management proceeds, various factors require continuous attention to localization and customization. Three sets of factors support localization: The first is variation among national environments. The second is product customization that triggers logistic adjustments. The third is the existance of national borders that constrain the free flow of goods and services and hence limit global solutions. Advances such as the incorporation of suppliers' input at the product design phase heighten dependencies and the logistic challenges that accompany the need to coordinate and control them.

National Variation

World regions vary in size, terrain, and other characteristics that impact the supply chain. For example, the NAFTA land area is more than six times that of the EU, implying different logistic requirements and challenging the use of global "best practices." Skill level, quality of supplies, availability of process equipment and technologies, and the level of transportation and communications vary substantially among regions. Asia, Africa, large parts of the Middle East, and Latin America suffer from poor infrastructure. Yet, although overall Asian infrastructure is relatively weak, Singapore has superb infrastructure in terms of both air and shipping.

"We have ordered a lot of bicycles with cool boxes," says Paul Wright, the general manager for Commercial Development at TNT Logistics Asia, who noted that in many Asian locations "neither the technology nor the regulatory environment support logistics integration."[104] Energizer maintains central and eastern European operations separate in an otherwise integrated European supply chain, reflecting the significant differences in development levels and the lack of integration with the EU.

Even among developed nations, conditions often vary. For instance, in the United States it takes 3 weeks from the time of manufacturing for breakfast cereals to reach retailers' shelves, but it takes 11 weeks in France.[105] This may explain why domestic supply chains continue to dominate the transfer of goods. Furthermore, increased FDI in local production bases creates even more reliance on domestic supply chains.[106] Fragmented supply chains and a great number of intermediaries add to the problem.[107]

Product and Logistic Customization

Product customization challenges supply chain management characteristics because of its impact on modularity, packaging, transportation, tracking, shipping, and distribution. A "postponement" strategy, designed to delay customization to the latest possible value-adding phase is not always feasible without compromising product variety.[108] Meritor, which used to provide a variety of automotive parts (mostly in North America), now manufactures only roofs, doors, and suspension systems but provides them to car manufacturers across the globe from 28 facilities in 13 countries.[109] When McDonald's started operations in Russia, it consolidated all its processing operations in one large facility. This was a radical departure from McDonald's operations around the globe, but was necessary to overcome bottlenecks and supply disruptions that plagued the Soviet system.

Packaging

Standardization of packaging is appealing for logistic ease and because it promotes brand recognition. Kodak's yellow film box is recognized across the globe as is Fuji Film's green. Coca-Cola uses similar color and logo (albeit in different alphabets) to enhance its brand. Package standardization also produces savings in design and promotion costs.[110] Mattel is in the process of reducing the number of packages it prints for the same products from 14 to 3 in order to save on costs and create flexibility. The firm will now be able to ship toys from one market to another in mid-season.[111] Packaging size must often be adapted as well. Where space is scarce, as in the typical Japanese household, bulk packaging is less attractive to customers.

Some adaptations are necessary for logistic reasons, such as sturdier packaging to shield a product from outside elements in a harsh environment. Other adaptations are necessary to meet legal requirements. The 1991 German Packaging Ordinance requires manufacturers to use environmentally friendly, recyclable packaging material whenever feasible.[112] A similar law went into effect in Japan in 1996.[113] Various laws also govern safety (e.g., use of nonflammable material) requirements.

Labels in most countries must be printed in the local language (in Canada, labels must be printed in both English and French), adding time and cost to distribution. The United States requires all food products to carry labels indicating their nutritional value. Most countries also require clear labeling of the country source of the product. In the United States, U.S. content must be disclosed on cars, textile, wool, and fur products. Other producers need not specify U.S. content but must comply with Federal Trade Commission guidelines if they choose to do so. For instance, to merit a "Made in the USA" label, a product must be "all or virtually all" made in the United States with no, or "negligible" foreign content.[114]

Other packaging adaptations are necessary for cultural or religious reasons. For example, Hogla-Kimberly, a joint venture between Kimberly Clark and an Israeli manufacturer, sells diapers to the orthodox sector in Israel in a specially designed, easy-to-prop open packaging that meets religious requirements for doing no work on the Sabbath.

Transportation Modes

Meeting customer demand in a timely and cost-effective fashion depends on effective transportation. Globalization has been one of the driving forces behind **intermodal transportation,** a term denoting the combination of ocean vessels (including short sea shipping), river transport, rail, road links, and air transport within a seamless supply chain. Intermodality represents many challenges, however. Comparing the price of alternative transportation modes is difficult because price is based on many product (e.g., weight, value, space) and non-product (e.g., port of shipment, custom administrative procedures) factors. Intermodality also requires modularity and standardization to permit frequent transfer of goods from one mode to another.[115] Additional obstacles to intermodality and seamless logistics lie at the legal and political level. For instance, Thai regulations require transport and warehousing to be handled by separate companies. In China, approval must be obtained from authorities in each province along the supply chain.[116]

Maritime Transportation

Maritime transportation serves well over 90 percent of international trade.[117] Of the 29 border crossing points between the United States and Mexico, 9 ports handle most of US-Mexico trade.[118] Mexico-based Frigotux is building a refrigerated terminal in the hope of diverting some of the 90 percent share of Mexican agricultural exports now handled by trucking into marine shipping from Tuxpan to Philadelphia-Camden and Rotterdam (the Netherlands).[119]

Historically the most global in terms of use and regulation, impediments to further globalization of maritime transport include the issuance of "flags of convenience," that is the registering of ships in countries with less stringent regulations such as Liberia and Panama. Such registries not only provide for less stringent safety standards but also confer labor and tax benefits; however, they do raise opposition in some of the countries where MNEs operate.

The port of Houston, Texas ranks sixth in the world in total tonnage.

Port Facilities. Port facilities represent a crucial ingredient in the cost and convenience of maritime transport. According to a Conference Board report, the most competitive ports provide speed processing (cargo handling and administration), low cost, and superb intermodal links (road, rail, and air). There are four types of ports: (1) The maritime hub—dedicated to transshipment from an ocean vessel to another or to a feeder vessel; (2) the gateway port—an interchange between the maritime hub and maritime and/or land transport; (3) the logistic-industrial port—interchange between transport modes combined with logistic support; (4) The trade port—logistic activities combined with other value-added international trade services.

The two largest container ports in the world are Singapore and Hong Kong, which together have 44 percent of the world's container lifts.[120] UPS established an Asian hub in Taiwan while Federal Express established an Asian hub in the Philippines.[121] Non-hub ports can still compete, for example, by adopting niche strategies. One port strategy is to specialize in a particular product line so as to achieve economies of scale. For instance, the Port of Barcelona handles more than 500,000 cars a year.

One of the main challenges for ports as key links in the global supply chain has been to accommodate local distribution; for example, to integrate domestic and international shipping (now mostly separated) so as to accommodate situations such as when the final destination is closer to the port rather than to rail transportation.[122]

Exhibit 16–13 ranks nations based on their water transport infrastructure (including internal waterways such as canals).

The Inland Port. "Port Columbus" in land-locked central Ohio is an "inland port." It utilizes 86 million square feet of warehousing and distribution facilities on the grounds of a former air force base located "within a 10-hour drive of over 50 percent of the United States and Canadian populations." The port has arteries to airports, highways (there are 130 trucking firms in the area), and rail and coastal port access via agreements with the ports of New York/New Jersey, Virginia, and Los Angeles. Countries with vast, underdeveloped hinterland such as China are interested in the inland port concept as a way of improving access to less developed regions.

Trucking

Trucking plays an important role in international trade, particularly in Europe where distances are relatively short, as well as in geographically contiguous areas such Texas/Mexico and Hong Kong/Shenzhen in southern China. Trucks also play a crucial role in the domestic distribution of products delivered internationally by ship, rail, or air. The use of containers has made such intermodality substantially easier.

While the United States, Europe, and other, mostly developed countries have moved to standardize safety and other regulations pertaining to motor vehicles, there remain substantial obstacles to the standardization and globalization of truck transportation.[123] For example, there are different conventions regarding use of the manufacturer's fleet, rentals, and so forth. There are also differences in safety standards, a reason the United States gives for its refusal to comply with the NAFTA agreement and permit Mexican trucks to cross into the United States. Pressure from existing joint ventures between U.S. and Mexican truck firms as well as opposition from U.S. organized labor also played a role in the decision that the Bush administration was hoping to repeal,[124] but was made all the more difficult by the September 11 events.

Traffic congestion is costly to trucking in terms of deteriorating service quality, delayed shipments, higher energy costs, and lower productivity of vehicles and workforce. The problem is especially pronounced in Europe. In 1993, the cost of

Exhibit 16–13

Water transportation infrastructure

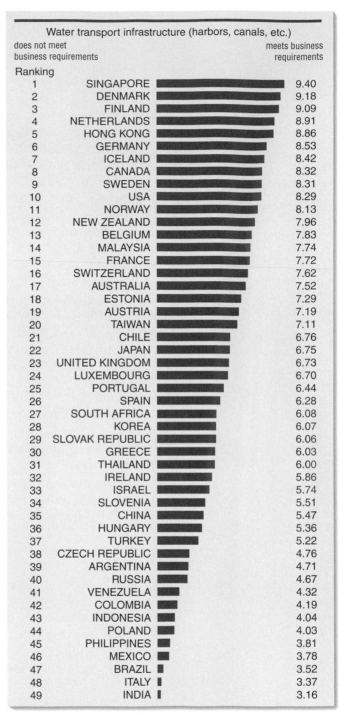

Water transport infrastructure (harbors, canals, etc.)

does not meet business requirements — meets business requirements

Ranking		
1	SINGAPORE	9.40
2	DENMARK	9.18
3	FINLAND	9.09
4	NETHERLANDS	8.91
5	HONG KONG	8.86
6	GERMANY	8.53
7	ICELAND	8.42
8	CANADA	8.32
9	SWEDEN	8.31
10	USA	8.29
11	NORWAY	8.13
12	NEW ZEALAND	7.96
13	BELGIUM	7.83
14	MALAYSIA	7.74
15	FRANCE	7.72
16	SWITZERLAND	7.62
17	AUSTRALIA	7.52
18	ESTONIA	7.29
19	AUSTRIA	7.19
20	TAIWAN	7.11
21	CHILE	6.76
22	JAPAN	6.75
23	UNITED KINGDOM	6.73
24	LUXEMBOURG	6.70
25	PORTUGAL	6.44
26	SPAIN	6.28
27	SOUTH AFRICA	6.08
28	KOREA	6.07
29	SLOVAK REPUBLIC	6.06
30	GREECE	6.03
31	THAILAND	6.00
32	IRELAND	5.86
33	ISRAEL	5.74
34	SLOVENIA	5.51
35	CHINA	5.47
36	HUNGARY	5.36
37	TURKEY	5.22
38	CZECH REPUBLIC	4.76
39	ARGENTINA	4.71
40	RUSSIA	4.67
41	VENEZUELA	4.32
42	COLOMBIA	4.19
43	INDONESIA	4.04
44	POLAND	4.03
45	PHILIPPINES	3.81
46	MEXICO	3.78
47	BRAZIL	3.52
48	ITALY	3.37
49	INDIA	3.16

Source: IMD World Competiveness Yearbook, 2002.

congestion in France was 17 billion French francs with 2010 estimates of 275 billion.[125] Developing countries such as China and Iran have less of a congestion problem but a much higher proportion of unpaved roads than in the United States and other developed countries, imposing serious constraints on the domestic transportation of goods. (See Exhibit 16–14.)

Exhibit 16–14
Road density

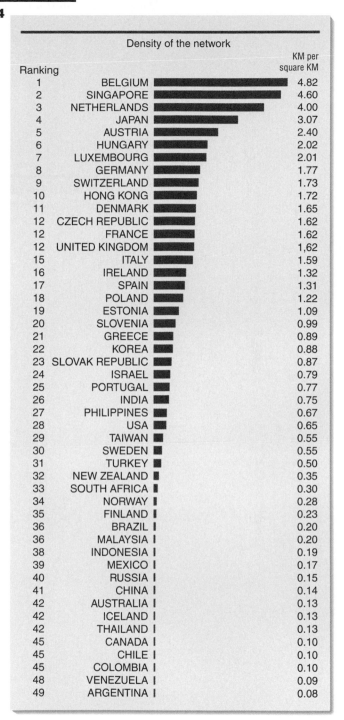

Ranking	Density of the network	KM per square KM
1	BELGIUM	4.82
2	SINGAPORE	4.60
3	NETHERLANDS	4.00
4	JAPAN	3.07
5	AUSTRIA	2.40
6	HUNGARY	2.02
7	LUXEMBOURG	2.01
8	GERMANY	1.77
9	SWITZERLAND	1.73
10	HONG KONG	1.72
11	DENMARK	1.65
12	CZECH REPUBLIC	1.62
12	FRANCE	1.62
12	UNITED KINGDOM	1,62
15	ITALY	1.59
16	IRELAND	1.32
17	SPAIN	1.31
18	POLAND	1.22
19	ESTONIA	1.09
20	SLOVENIA	0.99
21	GREECE	0.89
22	KOREA	0.88
23	SLOVAK REPUBLIC	0.87
24	ISRAEL	0.79
25	PORTUGAL	0.77
26	INDIA	0.75
27	PHILIPPINES	0.67
28	USA	0.65
29	TAIWAN	0.55
30	SWEDEN	0.55
31	TURKEY	0.50
32	NEW ZEALAND	0.35
33	SOUTH AFRICA	0.30
34	NORWAY	0.28
35	FINLAND	0.23
36	BRAZIL	0.20
36	MALAYSIA	0.20
38	INDONESIA	0.19
39	MEXICO	0.17
40	RUSSIA	0.15
41	CHINA	0.14
42	AUSTRALIA	0.13
42	ICELAND	0.13
42	THAILAND	0.13
45	CANADA	0.10
45	CHILE	0.10
45	COLOMBIA	0.10
48	VENEZUELA	0.09
49	ARGENTINA	0.08

Source: IMD World Competitiveness Yearbook, 2002.

Rail

A competitive time to cost ratio as well as road and sky congestion makes rail an attractive transportation mode domestically and internationally. For instance, about half of U.S. grain exports to Mexico are transported by rail. Where rails are not contiguous, railways can still play an important role as part of intermodal transportation. The Baltic state of Estonia wants to connect Europe and East Asia via the

Trans-Siberian railroad. It believes that it can cut the current marine shipping time of 33 days to 17 to 24 days using intermodal containers, thus tapping into the huge trade volume between Asia and Europe. (China alone exports more than $50 billion of goods annually to Europe.)[126]

Exhibit 16–15 shows the density of rail networks with Europe showing the highest density.

Exhibit 16–15
Railroad density

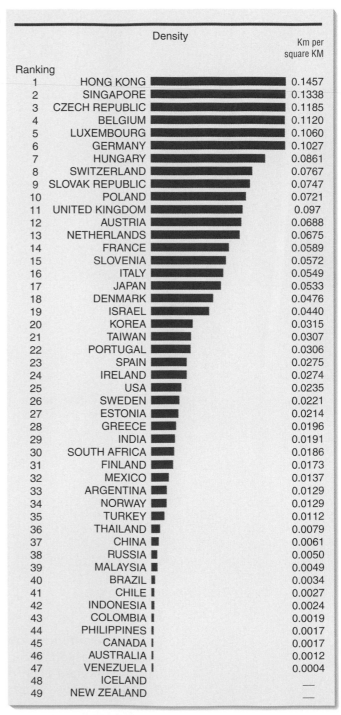

Density		Km per square KM
Ranking		
1	HONG KONG	0.1457
2	SINGAPORE	0.1338
3	CZECH REPUBLIC	0.1185
4	BELGIUM	0.1120
5	LUXEMBOURG	0.1060
6	GERMANY	0.1027
7	HUNGARY	0.0861
8	SWITZERLAND	0.0767
9	SLOVAK REPUBLIC	0.0747
10	POLAND	0.0721
11	UNITED KINGDOM	0.097
12	AUSTRIA	0.0688
13	NETHERLANDS	0.0675
14	FRANCE	0.0589
15	SLOVENIA	0.0572
16	ITALY	0.0549
17	JAPAN	0.0533
18	DENMARK	0.0476
19	ISRAEL	0.0440
20	KOREA	0.0315
21	TAIWAN	0.0307
22	PORTUGAL	0.0306
23	SPAIN	0.0275
24	IRELAND	0.0274
25	USA	0.0235
26	SWEDEN	0.0221
27	ESTONIA	0.0214
28	GREECE	0.0196
29	INDIA	0.0191
30	SOUTH AFRICA	0.0186
31	FINLAND	0.0173
32	MEXICO	0.0137
33	ARGENTINA	0.0129
34	NORWAY	0.0129
35	TURKEY	0.0112
36	THAILAND	0.0079
37	CHINA	0.0061
38	RUSSIA	0.0050
39	MALAYSIA	0.0049
40	BRAZIL	0.0034
41	CHILE	0.0027
42	INDONESIA	0.0024
43	COLOMBIA	0.0019
44	PHILIPPINES	0.0017
45	CANADA	0.0017
46	AUSTRALIA	0.0012
47	VENEZUELA	0.0004
48	ICELAND	—
49	NEW ZEALAND	—

Source: IMD World Competitiveness Yearbook, 2000.

GLOBAL LOGISTICS AT WAL-MART

The largest retailer in the world, Arkansas-based Wal-Mart had only 16 percent of its sales come from outside the United States in 2000; however 300,000 of its 1 million associates were abroad. Attesting to the difficulty in penetrating foreign markets, the company's operating profit abroad was significantly lower than at home. By the end of January 2000, the firm had 572 discount stores, 383 "supercenters," and 49 SAM'S Club stores located in 9 countries outside the United States. Much of the growth has been fueled by acquisitions, for example, ASDA with 232 stores in the United Kingdom and German chains Spar and Wertkauf's, with 74 and 21 stores, respectively. In 2002, Wal-Mart purchased a stake in Japanese retailer Seiyu.

Efficient, large-scale supply chain management has long been a Wal-Mart competitive advantage. The firm has 7,000 suppliers and averages 120,000 inquiries per week. In England, Wal-Mart had to adjust to ASDA's 65,000 square feet stores, roughly a third of Wal-Mart's domestic average. The different store size and product composition required adjustments in store layout and display, as well as in transportation, warehousing, and distribution. Wal-Mart also replaced ASDA's information system with its own so as to benefit from worldwide sourcing, buying power, and distribution scale.

In Argentina, Wal-Mart expanded aisle size initially set to U.S. standards to accommodate higher than expected customer traffic. As Joe Menzer, president and CEO of Wal-Mart International, suggested, "it wasn't such a good idea to stick to the domestic Wal-Mart blueprint in Argentina, or in some of the other international markets we've entered, for that matter." As 2000 drew to a close, Wal-Mart was fighting a bill introduced in the Buenos Aires legislature to limit hypermarkets' size to 20,000 square feet, a tenth of Wal-Mart's Supercenters.[135]

In entering a difficult and recession-plagued Japanese market, Wal-Mart will rely on a slow learning curve from its Japanese partner. It will also leverage capabilities that it developed through earlier entries. For example, Wal-Mart will use lessons it has learned from its Chinese operations about handling fresh produce, a critical category in Asia that Wal-Mart did not emphasize in its domestic operations.

Source: Wal-Mart Annual Report, 2000; Y. Ono and N. N. Zimmerman, "Wal-Mart enters Japan with Seiyu stake," *Wall Street Journal*, March 15, 2002, B5.

Air Transport

Air transportation has grown rapidly in recent years. Initially confined to perishable or high value items, air transport is increasingly used whenever speed of transportation is vital and where logistic infrastructure is in place. One impediment to globalization of air transport is the stringent safety standards imposed by developed nations, especially the United States and the EU, vis-à-vis the relatively lax regimes common in many developing countries. The United States does not permit the landing of foreign aircraft that do not comply with certain safety standards, but it is not always effective in enforcing these standards.

Crossing National Borders

Michelin calculates that 45.3 percent of its European sales come from import flows, meaning that almost half of the products it sells in one country are imported from another. For example, 67 percent of Michelin sales in the United Kingdom are imports.[127] It is difficult to establish a seamless supply chain spanning national borders. Customs inspection, processing, and other barriers associated with border crossing create unpredictable and costly delays.[128] In the aftermath of September 11, 2001, such delays have increased dramatically. The U.S. government is now in process of revising its import procedures, streamlining the process for firms that have improved the security of their supply chain.[129]

The NAFTA agreement provides for substantially non-tariff movement of goods across Canada, the United States, and Mexico, on the condition that the goods in question originate in one of the three countries. This requires substantial documentation to establish country-of-origin source. In addition, shortage of border-crossing points, bridges, rails, and docks undermine traffic expansion.[130] Paperwork, and the need to switch trailers have been identified as key reasons for delays in crossing the U.S. borders with Mexico and Canada (delays have been worse on the Mexican border).[131] In 1997, 88 percent of U.S.–Mexico trade passed through border-crossing points between the two countries, mostly in Texas but also in Arizona and California. One border crossing—Laredo—accounts for almost 40 percent of U.S.–Mexico trade (currently about $200 billion) and half of the U.S. agricultural, fishery, and forestry exports to Mexico.[132] Yet, crossing Laredo takes at least three hours as shipments are hauled by tractor through an antiquated system connecting the U.S. and Mexican border points.[133]

Every day, $1.72 billion worth of goods cross the U.S.–Canadian border, a number that has been increasing by 13 percent annually since 1994; 2,000 trucks pass through the Blaine border crossing between Washington and British Columbia daily. The cost associated with crossing the U.S.–Canadian border is estimated at 5 to 10 percent of product cost. In an effort to reduce the cost, constituencies on both sides of the border have been pushing for increased integration, with some proposing the elimination of the border altogether.[134]

Exhibit 16–16 ranks countries on the extent to which the bureaucracy of customs hinders the efficient transit of goods. Finland, Singapore, and Hong Kong are ranked best with the smallest hindrance, whereas Argentina, Venezuela, and Indonesia close the list.

In the aftermath of the events of September 11, 2001, border delays have worsened considerably in many parts of the world, including in major borders such as Canada–U.S. Similarly, the recent closure of California's port caused importers to resort to much more expensive air transportation or face delays in their holiday shipments. Although the delays have since been shortened, they show the vulnerability of global logistics to the problem of overlapping international boundaries and the unexpected contingencies that characterize the global supply chain as well as other facets of international business.

Interim Summary

1. Supply chains have undergone substantial globalization in recent years with firms consolidating sourcing and distribution operations; however, the trend has been more pronounced in some regions (e.g., the EU) than in others (e.g., Asia).

2. Customization remains an issue in such realms as packaging, although here too there is an attempt to reduce the number of variants.

3. Transportation modes need to be considered in terms of their cost and efficacy, with special attention given to intermodal transportation.

4. Border-crossing has become more cumbersome in the aftermath of 9/11.

CHAPTER SUMMARY

1. International markets are more complex and difficult yet represent tremendous potential for firms.

2. There are various ways to assess the potential of a foreign market. First and foremost is economic development and its correlate of disposable income; however, consumption patterns are determined by a myriad of other factors.

3. Companies standardize products and services as well as the methods in which they are advertised, sold, distributed, and serviced, in an attempt

Exhibit 16–16
Customs' authorities bureaucracy

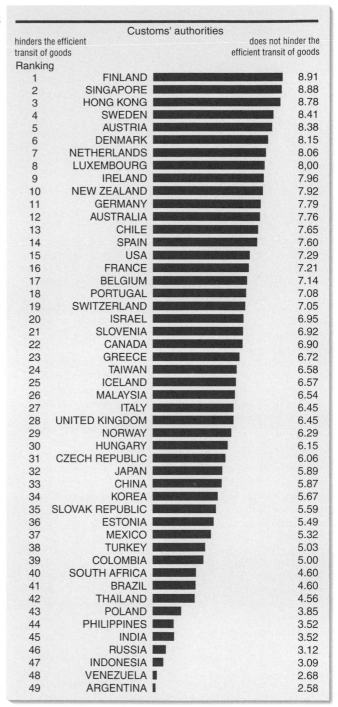

Customs' authorities		
hinders the efficient transit of goods		does not hinder the efficient transit of goods
Ranking		
1	FINLAND	8.91
2	SINGAPORE	8.88
3	HONG KONG	8.78
4	SWEDEN	8.41
5	AUSTRIA	8.38
6	DENMARK	8.15
7	NETHERLANDS	8.06
8	LUXEMBOURG	8,00
9	IRELAND	7.96
10	NEW ZEALAND	7.92
11	GERMANY	7.79
12	AUSTRALIA	7.76
13	CHILE	7.65
14	SPAIN	7.60
15	USA	7.29
16	FRANCE	7.21
17	BELGIUM	7.14
18	PORTUGAL	7.08
19	SWITZERLAND	7.05
20	ISRAEL	6.95
21	SLOVENIA	6.92
22	CANADA	6.90
23	GREECE	6.72
24	TAIWAN	6.58
25	ICELAND	6.57
26	MALAYSIA	6.54
27	ITALY	6.45
28	UNITED KINGDOM	6.45
29	NORWAY	6.29
30	HUNGARY	6.15
31	CZECH REPUBLIC	6.06
32	JAPAN	5.89
33	CHINA	5.87
34	KOREA	5.67
35	SLOVAK REPUBLIC	5.59
36	ESTONIA	5.49
37	MEXICO	5.32
38	TURKEY	5.03
39	COLOMBIA	5.00
40	SOUTH AFRICA	4.60
41	BRAZIL	4.60
42	THAILAND	4.56
43	POLAND	3.85
44	PHILIPPINES	3.52
45	INDIA	3.52
46	RUSSIA	3.12
47	INDONESIA	3.09
48	VENEZUELA	2.68
49	ARGENTINA	2.58

Source: IMD World Competitiveness Yearbook, 2002.

to reduce costs and increase efficiencies. At the same time, there remain strong pressures to adapt products and services to the local environment in which they are offered.

4. Country-of-origin remains a powerful force in marketing and consumer behavior. It can lead consumers to purchase a product (even if higher priced) or avoid the purchase.

5. Pricing pressures and economic integration push companies to consolidate their global supply chains from sourcing to delivery. Logistic providers respond by consolidating their own operations.

6. A trend toward "intermodal" transportation involves the simultaneous use of multiple transportation modes such as rail, sea, and air.

CHAPTER NOTES

[1] J. Micklethwait, "Washed up?" *The Economist*, 338, 1996, S23–27.

[2] Y. Ono, "Overcoming the stigma of dishwashers in Japan," *Wall Street Journal*, May 19, 2000, B1.

[3] W. Boston and K. Richter, "Telecom firms battle to serve Germany's Turks," *Wall Street Journal*, November 6, 2000, B7B.

[4] Keegan, W. J. *Global Marketing Management*, Englewood Cliffs, NJ: Prentice-Hall, 2001.

[5] Burgernomics beats reading the tea leaves. *The Economist*, April 29, 2000.

[6] H. Riesenbeck and A. Freeling, "How global are global brands?" *European Business Report*, Summer 1993, 13.

[7] *The Economist*, September 2, 2000, p. 98, citing RoperASW.

[8] *The Economist*, September 2, 2000, citing RoperASW.

[9] "Franchises head overseas," CNNfn, September 11, 2000:7:49 A.M. ET.

[10] M. Mulligan, "Brand arbitrage," *Forbes*, July 24, 2000, p. 350, citing Steven Dixon, manager of Global Beverage Fund at Arnhold & S. Cleichroeder.

[11] M. R. Czinkota and I. A. Ronkainen, *International Marketing*, Orlando, FL: Harcourt Brace, 1998.

[12] *The Changing Global Role of the Marketing Function*, The Conference Board 1105-95-RR.

[13] *The Changing Global Role of the Marketing Function*, The Conference Board 1105-95-RR.

[14] S. Samie and K. Roth, "The influence of global marketing standardization on performance," *Journal of Marketing*, April 1992, 1–17.

[15] S. Ellison, "Carrefour and Ahold find shoppers like to think local," *Wall Street Journal*, August 31, 2001.

[16] L. Mazur and J. Lannon, "Cross-border marketing: Lessons from 25 European success stories," *The Economist*, Intelligence Unit, 1993, 39.

[17] "Franchises head overseas," CNNfn Internet edition, September 11, 2000, 7:49 A.M. ET.

[18] A. Baar and A. McMains, "Kellogg realigns global brands," adweek.com. May 29, 2000, 5.

[19] "Launching a mass-market fragrance worldwide at Avon," The Conference Board 1105-95-RR, 15.

[20] Y. Ono, "U.S. superstores find Japanese are a hard sell," *Wall Street Journal*, February 14, 2000, B1.

[21] *The Changing Global Role of the Marketing Function*, The Conference Board 1105-95-RR.

[22] *The Changing Global Role of the Marketing Function*, The Conference Board 1105-95-RR.

[23] *The Changing Global Role of the Marketing Function*, The Conference Board 1105-95-RR.

[24] "Global accounts at AMP," The Conference Board 1105-95-RR p. 19.

[25] "Domestic recording artists boost share of market to 68%," *Wall Street Journal*, September 7, 2001, B6.

[26] M. Flagg, "Asia proves unexpectedly tough terrain for HBO, Cinemax channels," *Wall Street Journal*, August 23, 2000, B1.

[27] S. Bereger, "Expert: Metro Cash and Carry 'taken to the cleaners' in Israel," *The Jerusalem Post* (Digital Israel), September 14, 2001.

[28] M. Tanikawa, "French supermarket struggles to fit it," *Wall Street Journal*, October 5, 2001.

[29] J. N. Kapferer, "How global are global brands, ESOMAR seminar," cited in M. van Mesdag, "Culture-sensitive adaptation or global standardization—the duration of usage hypothesis," *International Marketing Review*, 1999, 17, 1, 74–84.

[30] H. Riesenbeck, and A. Freeling, "How global are global brands?" *The McKinsey Quarterly*, 1991, No. 4, 3–18.

[31] M. De Mooij, "Masculinity/femininity and consumer behavior." In 55–73.

[32] K. F. Winsted, "Evaluating service encounters: A cross-cultural and cross-industry exploration." *Journal of Marketing Theory and Practice*, Spring, 1999, 106–123.

[33] J. L. Watson, "China's Big Mac Attack," *Foreign Affairs*, 79, 3, 2000, 130.

[34] Ford Facts. Ford Motor Company, 1999.

[35] J. E. Hilsenrath, "Ford designs Ikon to suit Indian tastes," *Wall Street Journal*, August 8, 2000, A17, also cited in *Globe & Mail*, April 8, 2000.

[36] N. Shirouzu, "Tailoring world's cars to U.S. tastes," *Wall Street Journal*, January 15, 2001, B1.

[37] R. Martin, "Religion reshapes realities for US reastaurants in Middle East," *Restaurant News*, February 16, 1998.

[38] D. Barboza, "Market place: Pluralism under golden arches," *The New York Times*, 1999, C1.

[39] Euromonitor, Retail Trade International, 2000 (11th ed.).

[40] Y. Ono, "U.S. superstores find Japanese are a hard sell," *Wall Street Journal*, February 14, 2000, B1.

[41] M. S. Roth, and J. B. Romeo, "Matching product category and country image perceptions: a framework for managing country-of-origin effects," *Journal of International Business Studies*, 3rd quarter, 1992, 477–497.

[42] R. A. Peterson, and A. J. P. Jolibert, "A meta-analysis of country-of-origin effect," *Journal of International Business Studies*, 4th quarter, 1995, 883–900.

[43] C. Powell, "Why we really must fly the flag: Being cool isn't enough." *The Observer*, April 25, 1999, p. 4.

[44] R. Daedeke, "Consumer attitudes towards products 'made in' developing countries," *Journal of Retailing*, Summer 1973, 13–24.

[45] J. Baum, "Riding high: A Taiwanese bicycle maker races to success in the West," *Far Eastern Economic Review*, May 7, 1998, 58–59.

[46] M. S. Roth and J. B. Romeo, "Matching product category and country image perceptions: a framework for managing country-of-origin effects." *Journal of International Business Studies*, 3rd quarter, 1992, 477–497.

[47] C. Powel, "Why we really must fly the flag," *The Observer*, April 25, 1999, 4, citing a BMP DDB survey.

[48] J. L. Watson, "China's Big Mac Attack," *Foreign Affairs*, 79, 3, 2000,120.

[49] G. Vchazan, "Foreign products get Russian makeovers," *Wall Street Journal*, January 16, 2001, A23.

[50] B. Smith, "In Latvia, a traditional drink takes on Western production and Pepsi generation," *Wall Street Journal*, September 8, 2000, A17.

[51] Y. Ono, "U.S. superstores find Japanese are a hard sell," *Wall Street Journal*, February 14, 2000, B1.

[52] "Spin Cycle," *The Economist*, August 14, 1999, 52.

[53] S. Ellison, *Wall Street Journal*, August 31, 2001 A5.

[54] M. R. Czinkota and I. A. Ronkainen, *International Marketing*, 5th ed., Orlando, FL: Harcourt Brace, 1998.

[55] J. Kim and J. D. Daniels, "Marketing channel decisions of foreign manufacturing subsidiaries in the U.S.: The case of metal and machinery industries," *Management International Review*, 31, 1991, 123–138.

[56] J. Kim and J. D. Daniels, "Marketing channel decisions of foreign manufacturing subsidiaries in the U.S.: The case of the metal and machinery industries," *Management International Review*, 31, 1991/2, 123–138.

[57] SED International, Inc. announces status as certified HP top value reseller. *Business Wire*, April 9, 1998.

58 R. Frank, "Big Boy's adventures in Thailand," *Wall Street Journal,* April 12, 2000.

59 G. Dyer, "Brazil's regional drink makers *slake* thirst for value," *Financial Times,* June 16, 1999, 5.

60 D. Summers, "Boots for global trip," *Financial Times,* October 12, 1995, pp. 13.

61 R. Kuttner, "Globalization's dirty little secret," *Business Week,* September 7, 1998, 3594, 20.

62 "Ford Motor to cut prices in Britain," *Wall Street Journal,* October 3, 2000, A21.

63 "Ford Motor to cut prices in Britain," *Wall Street Journal,* October 3, 2000, A21.

64 "This Euro Brew's for you," *Business Week,* July 24, 2000, 120–122.

65 T. Burt and D. Hargreaves, "Crackdown pledge as VW fine is upheld," *Financial Times,* July 7, 2000.

66 L. McGinley, "Drug industry seeks to prevent importation of cheaper medicines," *Wall Street Journal,* July 19, 2000, A8.

67 C. W. L. Hill, *International Business: Competing in the Global Marketplace,* Boston, McGraw-Hill, 1999.

68 R. Belderbos and P. Holmes, "An economic analysis of Matsushita revisited," *Antitrust Bulletin,* 40, 1995, 825–857.

69 "Trade barriers," *Journal of Commerce,* June 10, 1992, 5A.

70 H. Riesenbeck and A. Freeling, "How global are global brands?" *European Business Report,* Summer, 1993.

71 K. Kashani, "Beware the pitfalls of global marketing," *Harvard Business Review,* September/October 1989, 92–93.

72 J. Lafayette, "Marketing: Picking the right ad agency," *International Business,* 5, 1992, 106–110.

73 D. Guthery, and B. A. Lowe, "Translation problems in international marketing research," *The Journal of Language for International Business,* 4, 1992, 1–14.

74 L. Himelstein, "The swoosh heard round the world," 1997, *Business Week,* May 12, 1990, 76.

75 S. Donaton, "Not always Coca-Cola's policy threatens integrity of magazines," *Advertising Age,* 70, 1999, 36.

76 M. Gjalwash, "In Egypt, rumors of blasphemy swirl around Coca-Cola," *Online Athens,* July 25, 2000.

77 D. Gellene, "Swatch makes the most of its airtime," *Los Angeles Times,* April 16, 1998, D4.

78 H. Riesenbeck and A. Freeling, "How global are global brands?" *European Business Report,* 7, Summer, 1993.

79 *The Changing Global Role of the Marketing Function,* The Conference Board, 1105-95-RR p. 14.

80 B. McKay, "Coke hunts for talent to re-establish its marketing might," *Wall Street Journal,* March, 2002, B4.

81 "This Euro brew's for you," *Business Week,* July 24, 2000, 120–122.

82 "Unquenchable thirst," *Financial Times London,* April 30, 1999, 19.

83 "The changing global role of the marketing function," CB 1105-95-RR.

84 S. Sidhva, "Foreign foray," *Far Eastern Economic Review,* 160, 1997, 64–66.

85 K. Guha, "Timex and Titan end Indian alliance," *Financial Times,* December 24, 1997.

86 "Meeting the Challenge of Global Logistics," The Conference Board Europe Report #1207-98-CR.

87 P. P Dornier, R. Ernst, M. Fender, and P. Kouvelis, *Global operations and logistics,* New York, Wiley, 1998.

88 Prologis company information, 1999.

89 B. Radstaak, and M. H. Ketelaar, Worldwide Logistics. Holland International Distribution Council, 1998.

90 E. Chabrow, "Supply chains go global," *Informationweek.com,* April 3, 2000, 51.

91 "Exchanges fall short on global e-commerce," *Internetweek,* May 8, 2000, 1.

92 UNCTAD, Electronic commerce and development, 2000.

93 The Conference Board, 1105-95-RR.

94 P. P. Dornier, R. Ernst, M. Fender, and P. Kouvelis, *Global Operations and Logistics,* 62, New York, Wiley, 1998.

95 The Conference Board, 1105-95-RR.

96 P. P. Dornier, R. Ernst, M. Fender, and P. Kouvelis, *Global Operations and Logistics,* 180, New York, Wiley, 1998.

97 S. M. Shaw and J. Meier, "Second generation' MNCs in China," *The McKinsey Quarterly,* 1993, 4, 3–16.

98 S. Lal, P. Van Laarhoven, and G. Sharman, "Current research: Making logistics alliances work," *McKinsey Quarterly,* 1995, 3, 188–190.

99 The Conference Board, 1105-95-RR.

100 B. Radstaak and M. H. Ketelaar, *Worldwide Logistics.* Holland International Distribution Council, 1998.

101 B. Radstaak, and M. H. Ketelaar, *Worldwide Logistics.* Holland International Distribution Council, 1998.

102 Dornier et al., ibid.

103 R. Morton, "Latin American business is looking up," *Transportation & Distribution,* October 2000, 52.

104 P. Wright "Logistics in Asia," Conference Board, ibid, p. 20.

105 "Nestlé on the win-win partnership with the retail trade," *The Conference Board* 1105-95-RR.

106 The Conference Board, 1105-95-RR.

107 P. P. Dornier, R. Ernst, M. Fender, and P. Kouvelis, *Global Operations and Logistics,* 226, New York, Wiley, 1998.

108 P. P. Dornier, R. Ernst, M. Fender, and P. Kouvelis, *Global Operations and Logistics,* 120–121, New York, Wiley, 1998.

109 M. Yost, "Innovation lifts Meritor's profile in auto-parts business," *Wall Street Journal,* November 15, 1999, B4.

110 The Conference Board 1105-95-RR p. 14.

111 L. Bannon, "New playbook: Taking cues from GE, Mattel's CEO wants toy maker to grow up," *Wall Street Journal,* November 14, 2001, A1.

112 S. Livingstone and L. Sparks, "The new German packaging laws: Effects on firms exporting to Germany," *International Journal of Physical Distribution & Logistics Management,* 24, 1994, 15–25.

113 P. L. Grogan, "European influence," *BioCycle,* 38, 1997, 86.

114 U.S. Department of Commerce, "Complying with the made in the USA standard."

115 The Conference Board, 1105-95-RR.

116 P. Wright, "Logistics in Asia," Conference Board, 19.

117 S. Mankabady, *The International Maritime Organization,* London: Croom-Helom, 1984.

118 T. Drennan, "Where the action's at: The U.S.-Mexican border. FAS on-line, U.S. Department of Agriculture, 1999, 2.

119 D. McCosh, "A cool place for Mexican shippers," *Journal of Commerce,* April 28, 1999, 1.

120 "Asian success built on bulk," *South China Morning Post,* December 15, 1999, 7.

121 The Conference Board, 1105-95-RR.

122 "Improving interchange management," *Intermodal Insights,* September 1999, 179.

123 J. Braithwaite, and P. Drahos, *Global Business Regulation,* New York: Cambridge University Press, 2000.

124 R. Gold, "Mexican trucks won't fill the U.S. soon," *Wall Street Journal,* February 16, 2001, A2; H. Cooper and K. Chen, "U.S. is told to let Mexican trucks enter," *Wall Street Journal,* February 7, 2001, A2, ibid.

125 P. P. Dornier, R. Ernst, M. Fender, and P. Kouvelis, *Global Operations and Logistics,* 19, New York, Wiley, 1998.

126 B. Smith, "Estonia mulls Beijing-Baltic rail link in bid to be gateway for Asian exports," *Wall Street Journal,* November 13, 2000, B19.

127 P. P. Dornier, R. Ernst, M. Fender, and P. Kouvelis, *Global Operations and Logistics,* 63, New York, Wiley, 1998.

[128] P. P. Dornier, R. Ernst, M. Fender, and P. Kouvelis, *Global Operations and Logistics,* New York, Wiley, 1998.

[129] G. R. Simpson, "U.S. to revise dealings with importers, reward those with enhanced security," *Wall Street Journal,* Nov. 27, 2001, A24.

[130] A. W. Mathews, "On the borderline. Nafta reality check: Trucks, trains, ships face costly delays," *Wall Street Journal,* June 3, 1998, A1.

[131] 1991 Intermodal Association of North America (IANA) Intermodal Index.

[132] T. Drennan, "Where the action's at: The U.S.-Mexican border. FAS on-line, U.S. Department of Agriculture," 1999.

[133] R. Gold, "Mexican trucks won't fill the U.S. soon," *Wall Street Journal,* February 16, 2001, A2; H. Cooper and K. Chen, "U.S. is told to let Mexican trucks enter," *Wall Street Journal,* February 7, 2001, A2.

[134] B. Cameron, "Just blow it up," *National Post* (Canada), August 18, 2001, B3.

[135] Adapted from Wal-Mart Inc. Web site; R. Koenig, "Wal-Mart Stores Inc. has struck a deal to enter Europe via a takeover of a German retail chain," *Journal of Commerce,* September 4, 2000; Prologis, October 18, 1999; A. Zimmerman, and M. Moffett, "Wal-Mart faces Latin floor-space squeeze," *Wall Street Journal,* November 28, 2000, A23.

Global Human Resource Management

OPENING CASE BP Amoco

Since acquiring 40 percent of Ohio-based Standard Oil in 1976 (the rest in 1987), British Petroleum embarked on a series of expansions, mergers, and acquisitions that transformed it into a global company. Following its merger with U.S.-based Amoco, the company was renamed BP Amoco. Most recently, it acquired Atlantic Richfield (ARCO), a group with vast Asian operations. BP Amoco is now listed on eight stock exchanges and operates in 100 countries.

Headquartered in London, England, BP Amoco's board consists of 14 non-executive directors and 7 executive directors. Of the first group, one is Canadian, one is Irish, and six are Americans. The remaining non-executive directors are British, although one of them has spent most of his career in Asia. Of the seven executive members, one is from New Zealand, one from the United States, and five are British—all with significant overseas experience.

BP Amoco believes that the breadth of experience and understanding brought by both non-national directors and directors with significant expatriate experience is invaluable. It provides the company with insights into different facets of its operations, from corporate governance to compensation systems. The company also uses the insights gained from international experience to develop human resource policies that maintain both consistency and equity among its employees worldwide. ■

Source: "Globalizing the board of directors: Trends and strategies." The Conference Board Report 1242-99-RR; company Web site.

International human resource management (IHRM) is the procurement, allocation, utilization, and motivation of human resources in the international arena. IHRM is critical to the strategy and success of global operations. A Conference Board Survey found that "culture and people issues" were the biggest roadblocks to global success.[1] Research by Booz, Alen, and Hamilton found that the problem of hiring quality personnel ranked as one of the main factors inhibiting expansion of U.S. foreign investment in Japan. The Japanese, on their part, named conflict between expatriates and the local workforce as their main globalization concern.[2] By appointing people with significant experience in foreign and international operations, BP Amoco hopes to avoid those problems and improve corporate performance worldwide.

The distinct features of IHRM are multiculturalism and geographic dispersion[3] as well as the need to address issues such as international taxation, relocation, and foreign culture orientation. IHRM also generates more involvement in personal life (e.g., expatriate housing and educational assistance in the host country).[4] IHRM implies multiple constituencies, including a great variety of employee groups. In 1997, Johnson & Johnson employed 42,946 people in the United States, 23,581 in Europe, 10,447 in the Western Hemisphere (excluding the United States), 11,962 in Asia, and 1,568 in Africa.[5] Canada-based Bombardier employs 52,700 employees in 12 countries to manufacture and service its regional aircraft, mass transit systems, and related products and services. Each of those countries has a different cultural and economic environment and its own set of labor laws and human resource practices. The challenge for Johnson & Johnson, Bombardier, BP Amoco, and other MNEs is to make proper adjustments in each of the markets in which it operates yet maintain system-wide consistency and equity that will enable global deployment of talent in line with the firm's strategy.

From a career perspective, it is useful to note that international experience increasingly opens doors from initial entry and up to the CEO suite. Johnson & Johnson explicitly seeks candidates with international experience (e.g., participation in a college exchange program) on the assumption that such individuals are better suited to the demands of a global business environment. J&J executives also go through Executive Development and Executive Conference programs which further develop their global mind-set.[6]

STRATEGIC IHRM

Strategic International Human Resource Management (SIHRM) is defined as "human resources, management issues, functions and policies and practices that result from the strategic activities of MNEs and that impact the international concerns and goals of these enterprises."[7] Compared to strategic human resource management in a domestic context, SIHRM is more complex because it concerns multiple environments and employee groups and because it must be aligned with the multi-faceted strategic considerations of the MNE. The SIHRM model has three orientations.

- The **adaptive** system imitates local HRM practices.
- The **exportive** system replicates the HRM system in the home country and other affiliates.
- The **integrative** system emphasizes global integration while permitting some local variations.

An optimal SIHRM is capable of balancing the different forces in the firm's environment, in particular, the tension between local responsiveness and global integration.[8] The overall SIHRM strategy chosen by the parent—together with the affiliate's specific conditions (e.g., the cultural distance from the parent) will deter-

Exhibit 17–1
Model of Strategic
International Human
Resource Management
(SIHRM)

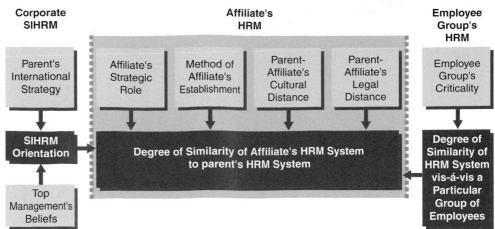

Source: S. Taylor, S. Beechler, and N. Napier, Toward an integrative model of strategic international human resource management. *Academy of Management Review*, 21, 4, p. 965.

mine the degree of similarity in SIHRM between the affiliate and headquarters. This, in conjunction with the criticality of the group, will determine the similarity of HRM practices for each employee group (see Exhibit 17–1).

Exhibit 17–2 shows the evolution in the firm's SIHRM system based on product life-cycle theory.[9] IHRM changes as firms go through the domestic, international, multinational, and global phases of internationalization. Exhibit 17–2 shows the phases and associated IHRM activities.[10]

Exhibit 17–2
Phases of
internationalization
and IHRM

Phase I Domestic: focus on home market and export
- Incidental brief visit to foreign agents/sales offices or short assignment on a project basis.
- Product and technical competence are the most important factor.
- Can scarcely speak of international HRM.

Phase II International: focus on local responsiveness and transfer of learning
- Managers are assigned to posts in foreign markets to provide general management, technical expertise, and financial control.
- In addition to technical competence, language skills, cross-cultural sensitivity, and adaptability are also important.
- Host-country nationals are frequently recruited for management positions in the areas of sales, marketing, and personnel.

Phase III Multinational: focus on global strategy, low cost, and price competition
- Selection in this phase focuses on recruiting the best managers for international positions, regardless of country of origin.
- Training and developing all members to share the same organizational values and norms are among HRM's most important tasks.
- Management development, career counseling, and periodic transfers to different assignments spearhead phase III HRM.

Phase IV Global: focus on both local responsiveness and global integration
- The major issue for IHRM is how to satisfy the requirements for global integration and national responsiveness.
- Large measure of cultural diversity.
- IHRM focuses on offering promising managers the opportunity to grow and gain experience so that an environment for continuous learning will be created throughout the entire organization.

Source: N. J. Adler, Strategic human resource management: a global perspective. In R. Pieper (Ed.), *Human Resource Management: An International Comparison*, Berlin: DeGruyter, 1990.

1. As the MNE shifts from domestic to global strategy, the criteria by which it selects management and its general HR policies naturally change. This shift tends to move the company toward broad-scale standardization while retaining local flexibility.

2. In advanced phases of internationalization, growth opportunities for managers expand both vertically and geographically.

STAFFING THE MNE

The Globalization of Boards of Directors

In 1998–99, the Conference Board conducted a global survey to assess how globalization affected the composition of boards of directors. It found that between 1995 and 1998 the percentage of firms with non-national directors increased from 39 to 60 percent. Companies with three or more non-national directors increased from 11 to 23 percent, with the majority of directors recruited in the last three years. By 1998, 10 percent of directors of surveyed firms were non-nationals, up from 6 percent three years earlier.

The survey found that entering new markets and exposure to new demands from customers and investors are the primary internal drivers for seeking non-national board members. The initiative often comes from new managers wishing to expand international operations where the credibility and expertise of non-national directors makes a difference. Firms that initially took on non-nationals for "cosmetic" reasons learned to appreciate their added value over time. For Deutsche Telekom, the addition of France Telecom CEO Michel Bon to its supervisory board cemented the ties between the two firms, raised Deutsche Telekom's profile in the French market, and brought a new business perspective.

INDUSTRY BOX

THE GLOBALIZATION OF THE BOARD OF DIRECTORS IN DIFFERENT INDUSTRIES

A Conference Board report shows significant differences in board globalization across industries. While firms in non-financial services draw half of their non-national directors from the same or similar industry, financial services companies prefer directors from a different industry. This is understandable as financial institutions, such as Citigroup, finance projects and operations in multiple industries across the globe and need board-level expertise to oversee those activities. Utility and mining companies recruit non-national directors exclusively from within their own industry; however, the number of non-national directors in these sectors is quite small. Manufacturing is the most "global" sector, with 82 percent of firms having non-national directors, followed by non-financial services (61 percent).

Source: The Conference Board Report #1242-99-RR

Selecting Global Board Members

Firms seeking to internationalize their boards typically begin by selecting someone who is culturally similar to existing members but has an international perspective. In the next phase, firms look for individuals with in-depth cultural and business experience in a given part of the world. Even then, the majority of appointments are made among those with experience working or living in the country in which the company is based. U.S.-based Du Pont appointed ABB's Percy Barnevik to its board in 1991 and Goro Watanabe, an executive vice president of Japan's Mitsui in 1996. Both have had substantial experience in the U.S. market.

Searches for non-national directors result—on average—in 9 to 10 rejections for one accepted. The extra commitment (U.S. and U.K. firms hold eight or nine annual board meetings, the average in continental Europe is four), different time zones, language and culture are barriers to the appointment of non-national directors, as is the board evaluation process. While Americans have had difficulty adjusting to a Japanese board that is seldom staffed by independent directors, Japanese directors serving on U.S. boards find them "frighteningly open" in terms of the information flow between management and board. The Conference Board recommends accommodating non-nationals by reducing the number of annual meetings, rotating locations, setting up orientation programs, and widening the definition of non-national director to include non-nationals living and working abroad who maintain strong ties with their home country.

Another obstacle for non-national directors is representation. U.S. institutional investors are concerned with having non-national directors in domestic firms as well as with national directors in non-U.S. firms. Because these institutions have a fiduciary duty to protect shareholder interests, they must consider limited representation of shareholders in the decision to elect directors. This works well in the United States or the United Kingdom, but not in continental Europe or Japan, where shareholders are only one of many constituencies represented by the board. Representation is more difficult when significant shareholders sit on the board, especially if

COUNTRY BOX

THE GLOBALIZATION OF BOARDS ACROSS THE GLOBE

Africa is the one region where all MNEs have non-national directors. This is followed by Europe, with 71 percent of companies reporting non-national directors, followed by North America with 60 percent. Sixty-five percent of directors in countries other than their own are European. Firms outside Europe recruit 73 percent of their non-national directors in Europe. Surprisingly, only 52 percent of non-national directors in European firms are European nationals.

Overall, companies in all regions bring in most of their non-national directors from a region other than their own, suggesting they seek for input from individuals with different cultural backgrounds and with business knowledge of different markets. In Europe, "roughly a third to a half of all our non-executive directorship searches are now for non-nationals," comments Peter Breen, a partner in Heidrick & Struggles, London. Another Heidrick executive adds that roughly three times as many U.S. or U.K. companies look for European or Asian directors as vice versa: "The majority are U.S. corporations that now want a continental European on their board instead of, or as well as, the customary Brit." But he expects the global drive to catch on in continental Europe: "Clearly attitudes are changing as more and more companies are looking for an international perspective on their board."

Source: The Conference Board Report #1242-99-RR.

they are family members, board members of companies with significant cross-share-holdings, board members of major suppliers, or labor or pension fund representatives. While U.S. shareholders are relatively dispersed, shareholders with major control blocks are common in Europe, Latin America, and Asia.

Staffing the MNE Ranks

Factors that affect MNE staffing include strategy, organizational structure, and subsidiary-specific factors such as its duration of operations, technology, production and marketing technologies, and host-country characteristics such as level of economic and technology development, political stability, regulation, and culture. The MNE can draw employees from the country in which it is headquartered (parent-country nationals or PCNs, who are by definition expatriates), where the overseas operation is located (host-country nationals or HCNs), or from a third country (third-country nationals or TCNs). Alternative philosophies of staffing abroad are ethnocentric, polycentric, regiocentric, and geocentric.[11]

In **ethnocentric staffing,** PCNs are selected for key positions regardless of location. Japanese companies tend to follow this mode more than European and U.S. firms.[12] Korean firms and most other DMNEs utilize ethnocentric staffing as well. Samsung, for instance, not only had an all-Korean senior management team until 1999, but 90 percent of those people graduated from Seoul National University.[13] For U.S. firms, the greater the cultural distance to the host nation, the greater the proportion of U.S. nationals in the subsidiary.[14] In **polycentric staffing,** HCNs are hired for key positions in subsidiaries but not at corporate headquarters. In **regiocentric staffing,** recruiting is conducted on a regional basis (e.g., recruit within Asia for a position in Thailand). In **geocentric staffing,** the best managers are recruited worldwide regardless of nationality. The value of this approach in introducing new perspectives and modes of operation is apparent. Firms which considered themselves as the most successful in globalization have had a significantly higher proportion of foreign citizens in senior management—20 to 25 percent versus 10 percent for other firms.[15]

Most MNE employees abroad are HCNs or "foreign employees," for a number of reasons. They are, in most instances, the most widely available. They are the easiest to employ legally and administratively (with the exception of illegal immigrants); for instance, they are likely to have local certification where needed. They also know more about the local environment. In addition, in the case of developing and emerging markets, HCNs are often cheaper to employ than home country nationals, even without adjusting for expatriate terms. You may recall from Chapter 3 on foreign direct investment that labor cost is an important consideration in location decisions especially for labor-intensive activities. Exhibit 17–3 provides comparative compensation costs for manufacturing workers in selected countries.

Among the largest 100 MNEs globally, foreign employment exceeded 6.5 million in 1998, about half of their total employment.[16] In 2000, roughly one of eight manufacturing employees in the United States was employed by a foreign affiliate. Honda alone expected to employ 20,000 U.S. "associates" by 2002. U.S. firms, on their part, employed more than seven million people in foreign countries. The availability of qualified candidates is often a decisive factor in selecting HCNs.[17] Foreign MNEs in Japan found it difficult to hire qualified Japanese employees although this situation has since improved. In some countries, hiring requires a government-controlled labor bureau that may assign employees to work for the MNE. In Singapore, high on the cultural dimensions of power distance and masculinity, it is legal to specify race, age, and sex requirements in job advertisements, which would violate American Equal Employment Opportunity law. The same is true in Hong Kong. Once an employee is hired, the MNE needs to deal with communication and integration challenges.

Exhibit 17-3
Hourly compensation
costs in U.S. dollars for
production workers in
manufacturing, 2001

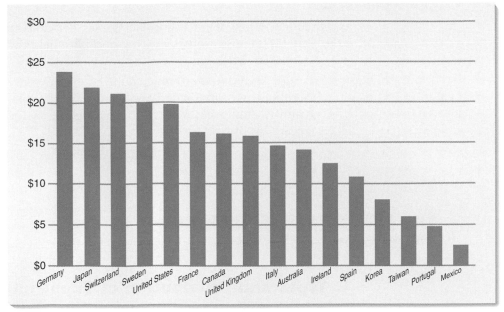

Source: U. S. Department of Labor; Bureau of labor Statistics, September 2001

The cultural challenges go beyond staffing. Sixty percent of Citigroup's workforce lack knowledge of English, a key obstacle to the firm's effort to leverage its global reach.[18] A formal career planning system in which people are evaluated in terms of skills, abilities, and traits that will be tested, scored, and computerized may appear to be impersonal in collective cultures. Individualistic societies use more cognitive testing because they emphasize performance, individual rights, and individual interests, whereas collective cultures emphasize loyalty and organizational compatibility that cannot be assessed via cognitive tests.[19] Personality profiles generated in the United States may be meaningless in Japan where assertiveness is not appreciated.

Finally, the MNE is expected to monitor employment conditions not only at home but also in its subsidiaries and among its subcontractors. Wal-Mart has been accused of buying from vendors that use child labor in Bangladesh, whereas Nike recently admitted to worker abuse occurring in its Indonesian factories ranging from verbal abuse to sexual coercion. The company has promised to remedy the problem.[20]

Country Specific Issues

As in other functional realms, the need for adjustment in corporate policies and practices is anchored in the variation of labor markets and employment conditions. In transition economies, older employees who have grown accustomed to a central planning system often have difficulty adjusting to the higher productivity expected in an MNE. For younger, highly skilled employees, the problem is different. Despite overall high employment in such economies, skilled employees are often in short supply due to lack of educational infrastructure. In China, for example, the greatest problem facing MNEs is very high turnover, a problem that undermines investment in recruitment and training. This is a "self-fulfilling prophecy" in the sense that high turnover discourages investment in HCNs, making jobs at the MNE less desirable.

To overcome the problem, MNEs in China customize solutions. For example, Ford Motor Company offers retention incentives to their Chinese workers, such as, a housing loan that is forgiven after seven years of service, and tuition to pursue an MBA degree. Ford is also deviating from its worldwide policy of preventing employees who have left the company to be rehired.

1. Entering new markets and facing new demands from customers and investors are the main reasons for hiring non-national personnel to the board of directors of an MNE.

2. MNEs from different home countries employ different strategies regarding staffing their subsidiaries. Some prefer to staff management with only parent-country employees, whereas others use mostly local talent and still others staff regardless of country of origin.

THE EXPATRIATE WORKFORCE

Types and Distribution of Expatriates

Expatriate numbers are small relative to total MNE employment. In 1997, Texaco had 6,000 employees and 15,000 contractors in Indonesia—only 80 of whom were expatriates. Many MNEs (e.g., Ford and Johnson & Johnson) have attempted to reduce the number of their expatriates as a cost reduction measure. Yet, with the growth of global operations and increased demand for their skills, expatriate numbers are growing. A survey of 130 MNEs in 1992 found half with more than 50 high-level expatriates and 25 percent with 200 to 2,000 expatriates each; a 1998 Windham survey showed continuous increase in expatriate assignments.[21]

There are different types of expatriates.[22] The **traditional expatriate,** older and experienced, is selected for his/her managerial or technical skills for a period of one to five years. Some of those are **international cadres,** individuals who move from one foreign assignment to another, seldom returning to their home country, sometimes becoming **permanent expatriates** who stay in overseas assignments for extended periods of time, or even permanently. **Young, inexperienced expatriates** are sent for six months to five years, usually on local hire terms. **Temporaries** go on short assignments, up to one year. Organization Resource Counselors (ORC) reports that 77 percent of 500 MNEs it surveyed expect to increase temporary assignments.[23] Still another type is the **expatriate trainee,** who is placed abroad for training purposes as part of initiation into an MNE. For instance, Johnson & Johnson places new executive recruits in another country for an 18-month period.[24]

A PricewaterhouseCoopers (PWC) survey of 270 European organizations employing 65,000 expatriates found a significant increase in "short-term, commuter, and virtual assignments" over the past two years. Short-term assignment increased by 54 percent whereas virtual assignments increased by 44 percent. Two thirds of the firms employ virtual expatriates, up from 44 percent earlier. The **virtual expatriate** takes on foreign assignments without physically relocating. A frequent flier, the virtual expatriate uses videoconferencing and telecommunications to stay in touch. Examples include Ian Hunter who manages the Middle East and Pakistan for London-based SmithKline Beecham and Gerals Lukomsli who manages Central Eastern Europe, the Middle East, and Africa for Motorola. Both manage from England. Rajiv Bhatia oversees hotels in Mexico and other countries from his New Jersey base for Cendant Corp., a franchisee for Howard Johnson and other U.S. hotel chains. Among the allures of the virtual expatriate are low cost, avoiding family adjustment, and not having to relocate.[25]

Using Expatriates: Pros and Cons

MNEs use expatriates "to get the business off the ground, put in the infrastructure, and, more importantly, have a plan to change the mix of expatriates versus nationals."[26] In many developing nations, locals are not yet ready to take over top management positions. For example, management localization in China is forecasted to be at least a decade away. In addition to contributing essential knowledge and experience, expatriates serve as a mechanism of control and as a way to transmit corporate culture and goals.[27] By rotating expatriates, MNEs establish and maintain informal networks that are conducive to the sharing of knowledge and coordination among units. Expatriation creates a global perspective and is essential to knowledge and technology transfer. A senior Corning executive observed:

> *Five to ten years ago, companies were using expatriates largely for command and control or to transfer specific knowledge. Today, in an effective local organization we are looking for learning that the expatriates can use in their jobs as they move around the globe.*[28]

Reasons for not using expatriates include the disincentive to the local workforce whose promotion is blocked and who would feel relatively deprived owing to their lower wage levels. Excessive use of expatriates can rob a company of the skills, insight, and initiative of local nationals. Another strike against expatriates is their high rate of failure, discussed in the next section.

Expatriate Failure

Expatriate failure occurs when the assignee returns prematurely to the home country or when performance does not meet expectations. Failure rates range from 15 to 80 percent, with many who stay on performing inadequately.[29] Japan and China show the highest failure rates for U.S. expatriates.[31] Failure rates for European and Japanese expatriates are reportedly lower than for U.S. expatriates.[30] The relative success of Japanese expatriates may be attributed to the country-specific training they receive for an entire year prior to their assignment.[31] However, Japanese expatriates are commonly evaluated on adjustment and host-country knowledge rather than on professional results. Also, because of culture (loss of "face") and other factors, Japanese firms are less likely to repatriate a low-performing expatriate.

The cost of expatriate failure is substantial, ranging from $55,000 to $150,000[32] in direct costs. The real cost of expatriate failure is considerably higher, however. It includes not only the cost of selection, training, preparation, and moving, but also the consequences of poor performance in lower revenues, lost business opportunities, and damage to the firm's reputation, which may undermine future ventures in the host country.

There are many reasons for expatriate failure. They include a spouse's unhappiness (including dual career issues which today involve almost three quarters of expatriates), inability to adjust to an unfamiliar physical and cultural environment, personality or emotional immaturity, inability to cope with the responsibilities and stress posed by overseas work, and lack of technical competence.[33] Lack of motivation to work overseas, especially where the firm attaches low value to international assignments, is also a problem.[34] More than 80 percent of firms surveyed by PWC had employees who refused overseas assignments due to dual-career and family concerns or the perceived career risk of being away. Still, more than half of the firms surveyed reported an increase in the overall number of international assignments. More willing to relocate are executives who have relocated domestically, who find the host country culturally or otherwise attractive, and those who find a match with their career plans. Spouse willingness to relocate also plays a major role. Older, better-educated spouses, often members of minority groups and with fewer children, are more likely to relocate.[35]

Despite the dramatic strides made by women up the corporate ladder, they remain underrepresented in the expatriate workforce. This is sometimes the result of an assumption that women will be ineffective in foreign cultures, especially those high on masculinity where women rarely occupy senior management positions. This view is not empirically supported, as evidence suggests expatriate women are viewed first and foremost as foreigners.[36]

Expatriates Selection

Among the attributes MNEs are looking for in an expatriate are cultural empathy, adaptability and flexibility, language skills, education, leadership, maturity, and motivation.[37] Adler specifies these competencies: a global perspective, local responsiveness, synergistic learning (integrating learning from multiple cultures), transition and adaptation, cross-cultural interaction, collaboration, and foreign experiences. Especially important is the ability to exercise discretion in choosing when to be locally responsive and when to engage in global integration.[38]

Successful expatriates need three sets of skills. The first set are **personal skills** that facilitate mental and emotional well-being, for example, stress orientation, reinforcement, substitution, physical mobility, technical competence, dealing with alienation, isolation, realistic expectation prior to departure. The second set are **people skills** such as relational abilities, willingness to communicate, non-verbal communication, respect for others, and empathy for others. The third set are **perception skills,** namely the cognitive process that helps executives understand the behavior of foreigners. This includes flexible attribution and breadth as well as being open-minded and non-judgmental.[39] Extroversion and being culturally adventurous are important for expatriate success in culturally distant countries.

Expatriate Selection Instruments

A number of instruments assist in the selection of expatriates. *The Prospector* assesses the potential of aspiring international executives on 14 dimensions: (1) cultural sensitivity, (2) business knowledge, (3) courage, (4) motivational ability, (5) integrity, (6) insight, (7) commitment, (8) risk taking, (9) seeking feedback, (10) using feedback, (11) culturally adventurous, (12) seeking learning opportunities, (13) open to criticism, and (14) flexibility.[40] Another instrument is the *Overseas Assignment Inventory* (*OAI*), developed by Tucker International. This instrument uses these predictors of success on a foreign assignment: expectations, open-mindedness, respect for others' beliefs, trust in people, tolerance, locus of control, flexibility, patience, social adaptability, initiative, risk taking, sense of humor, and spouse communication.[41]

Role-based simulations have become especially popular in recent years as a selection tool. These simulations are either generic or country-specific, such as Motorola's China program. They have proved quite effective. Danone, the French food giant, was able to reduce the failure rate among its expatriates from 35 to 3 percent in the three years it has been using such evaluation and selection programs.[42]

Preparing for Foreign Assignment

Expatriates entering a foreign country must adjust to new job responsibilities and to a new environment, including a different culture. The first adjustment phase is anticipatory and takes place before departure. In-country adjustment follows. Adjustment varies by individual factors (self-efficacy, relation, and perception skills), job-related factors (role clarity, role discretion, role novelty, and role conflict), organization culture (culture novelty, social support, and logistical help), organization socialization, and non-work factors such as culture novelty and family-spouse adjustment. Language fluency and previous assignments also influence adjustment.[43]

The U-Curve Theory suggests that individuals exposed to a new culture go through four stages of adjustment: In Stage 1, "honeymoon," they are fascinated by the new culture. In Stage 2, "culture shock," infatuation with the new culture is replaced by disillusionment and the frustration of having to cope with it on a daily basis. In Stage 3, "adjustment," individuals gradually adapt to the new culture and learn how to behave appropriately. In Stage 4, "mastery," individuals incrementally learn how to function smoothly in the new culture.[44]

Five determinants of cross-cultural adjustment have been identified:[45] Pre-departure cross-cultural training; previous overseas experience; multiple-candidate, multi-criteria selection; individual skills including self-dimension skills (to maintain mental health, psychological well-being, self-efficacy, and effective stress management), relational skills (to interact with host nationals), and perceptual skills (to correctly perceive and evaluate the host environment); and non-work factors such as cultural distance and spouse and family adjustment. Matching expatriates' previous cross-cultural experiences with the target countries and moving expatriates gradually from culturally similar countries to culturally distant countries have also been found to mitigate cultural adjustment.[46]

Expatriate Training

Expatriate failure was shown to correlate with absence of company training for the assignment.[47] However only 30 percent of U.S. firms conduct cross-cultural training versus 70 percent of European and Japanese firms. The reasons for the low U.S. showing include a belief that cross-cultural training programs are ineffective, trainee dissatisfaction, a short span between selection and relocation, and a perception that the short-term nature of many overseas assignments does not warrant the expense.[48]

Training for an overseas assignment has two components.[49] The first is information-giving, consisting of (a) practical information on living conditions in the destination country; (b) area studies, namely facts about the country's macro environment; and (c) cultural awareness information. There are no empirical studies that measure the effectiveness of practical information. Evidence suggests that areas studies training is generally useful although it is not very helpful in terms of equipping expatriates with the skills necessary to work effectively within the destination culture. Similar evidence applies to cultural awareness programs. The second set of activities in cross-cultural training consists of experiential learning, which combines cognitive and behavioral techniques. The goal is to acquire intercultural effectiveness skills that include transition stress management, relationship building, cross-cultural communication, and negotiation techniques.[50] A number of studies suggest that such training is valuable.[51]

Effective cross-cultural training requires an integrated approach consisting of both general cultural orientation and specific cultural development. Content and sequencing of training content are critical to success. Yoshida and Brislin[52] list five cultural training guidelines: First, *identify*—become aware of which skills you need to function well in the target culture. Second, *understand*—know why, where, when, to whom, and how the behavior is appropriate. Third, use *cultural informants to understand specifics*—observe and consult people from the target culture to make sure you are using the behaviors in the proper context and are delivering them appropriately. Fourth, *practice*—it is only through practice that proficiency in a new skill is gained. Fifth, *deal with emotions*—trainees should anticipate strong emotional reactions to cultural differences, as well as to the new behaviors they will be using.

Harrison proposes a two-stage cultural orientation.[53] The first stage is designed to focus trainees' *attention* and prepare them for cross-cultural encounters in general. This stage consists of (a) self-assessment of factors that may influence one's receptiveness to and propensity for effective cross-cultural assignments, and (b) cultural awareness of the general dimensions on which most cultures differ and the potential impact of these differences for expatriates. The second stage, specific cultural orientation, is designed to develop a trainee's ability to interact effectively within the specific culture to which he or she will be assigned. This stage also includes two phases: (1) knowledge acquisition (e.g., *retention*) of the language and customs in the specific culture, and (2) skill training (*reproduction*) in the application of appropriate behaviors in the specific culture.

Choosing a Training Method. Tung proposes a contingency framework for determining the nature and level of rigor of training based on the degree of interaction required in the overseas position and the cultural distance between the expatriate's native and new culture. If the expected interaction between expatriates and HCNS is low and the cultural distance is low, training should focus on task-related rather than culture-related issues, and the level of rigor required is relatively low. If expected interaction and cultural distance are high, training should focus on the new culture and on cross-cultural skill development as well as on the new task, and the level of rigor should be moderate to high.[54]

Another training model is based on social learning theory, with rigor defined as the degree of cognitive involvement by the trainee. The model distinguishes between processes-symbolic modeling, involving observation of modeled behavior, and participative modeling, which involves observing and participating in the modeled behaviors.[55] In addition to training methods and level of training rigor, duration of training relative to degree of interaction and cultural novelty is also derived in this model. For example, if the level of interaction and the cultural distance are low, the length of training should be less than a week and such methods as area or cultural briefings, films, and books provide appropriate level of training rigor. If the individual is going overseas for a period of 2 to 12 months and is expected to have some interaction with host nationals, the training rigor should be higher and longer (one to four weeks), and role-play would be appropriate. If the individual is going to a novel culture and the expected degree of interaction with host nationals is high, the level of training rigor should be high and training should last as long as two months. Sensitivity training and some field experiences would be appropriate.

Compensation

MNE compensation programs are geared to attract and retain qualified employees, facilitate transfer between HQ and affiliates, create consistency and equity in compensation, and maintain competitiveness.[56] Compensation systems derive from MNE international strategies (multi-domestic, international, global, and transnational) as well as its product and/or organizational life cycle. They also reflect the host-country laws, regulations, and cultural traditions. Research suggests that an appropriate compensation package should reduce expenses while enhancing commitment to the employer, job satisfaction, and willingness to relocate internationally.[57] Exhibit 17–4 shows compensation practices for local staff in India.

An effective compensation system starts with accurate performance appraisal. In the case of expatriates, difficulties include the choice of evaluator, difference in performance perceptions between home and host countries, communication difficulties with headquarters, inadequate recording of performance objectives, parent-country ethnocentrism, and indifference to the foreign experience of the expatriate. Other problems are difficulty in balancing local responsiveness and global

Exhibit 17–4

MNE's compensation practices for local staff in India (data in local currency as of April, 2001)

Typical Package (Mid-Size Company)	Director HR	CEO
Salary	620,000	1,045,000
Bonus	60,000	1,005,000
Mandatory Company Contribution	NA	NA
Voluntary Company Contribution	NA	NA
Perquisites	NA	NA
Long-Term Incentives	93,000	209,000

Compensation	Staff	Management
Annual Pay (# of Months)	12	12
Mandatory Bonus	No	No
Variable Bonuses Typical	No	Yes
Stock Options Prevalent	No	Yes

Salary Increases and Inflation	2001 (Estimated)	2002 (Projected)
Executives	14.00%	12.00%
Middle Mgmt/Professional	15.00%	12.00%
Technical/Administrative	6.00%	6.00%
Production	8.00%	8.00%
Inflation	5.00%	5.50%

Maximum Income Taxes	Max Tax Begins	Top Rate (%)
Federal	150000	32%
Local	None	None

Social Security	Max Annual Contribution	Rate %
Employer Contributions	No Maximum	17%
Employee Contributions	No Maximum	12%
Retirement Benefits	No State Benefit	
Health Care Benefits	Partial Benefit	
Survivors Benefits	No State Benefit	
Disability Benefits	No State Benefit	

Notes: There is no social security system per se; however, the state requires employers to provide Provident Fund.

Company Benefit Plans	Typical
Retirement Benefits	Yes
Health Care Benefits	Yes
Survivors Benefits	Yes
Disability Benefits	Yes

Executive Perks	
Annual Physical	Sometimes Provided
Club Membership	Sometimes Provided
Company Automobile	Most Prevalent
Entertainment Allowance	Sometimes Provided
Financial Counseling	Not Usual/Rare
Housing Assistance	Most Prevalent
Low-Interest Loans	Not Usual/Rare
Mobile Telephone	Most Prevalent

Source: Tower Perrin Website: www.Towers.com
Date: September 2002

integration, non-comparability of data from different subsidiaries/regions, and environmental variation across subsidiaries. Decisions need to be made regarding raters' location (home or host country) and their expatriate experience, and regarding the use of standard, customized, or hybrid evaluation forms.[58] Studies found that a balanced set of raters from host and home countries and more frequent appraisals relate positively to perceived accuracy of evaluation; however, most respondent firms did not follow these practices.[59] The use of balanced set of raters from host and home country increased accuracy as did the use of host-country raters.

Cost and Elements of Expatriate Compensation

The cost of employing expatriates is high, up to 3 to 5 multiples of domestic salary for a local hire.[60] The cost can easily reach U.S. $350,000 for the first year and much more in high-cost locations such as Japan. Recent data show an effort to reduce expatriate pay packages (rather than benefits) as well as a tendency to pay an end-of-term bonus.[61] Benefits are becoming more important, reaching 42 percent of total compensation in 1995.

Expatriate compensation is comprised of these elements:

- **Salary**—Base pay plus incentives (merit, profit sharing, bonus plans), determined via job evaluation or competency-based plans. Incentives—in the form of cash or deferred payment—may be based on home-country plans, host-country plans, or both. Payment may be deferred until return if the home-country's tax rate is lower.
- **Housing**—Most MNEs pay allowances for housing or provide company-owned housing for expatriates. Housing allowance is provided to maintain expatriates' living standard at their home country level.
- **Services allowance and premiums**—These are paid to compensate for differences in expenditures between the home and host country. Allowances are provided for higher cost of living in the host country, home leave (home-country visits), education (children's tuition, language classes), and relocation (moving, shipping, and storage, temporary living quarters). The balance sheet approach is the most widely used technique for equalizing the purchasing power of home- and host-country employees and to offset qualitative differences between locations.[62] The housing allowance is a function of the expected hardship in the host country and the job type, but it takes into account that the expatriate represents the employer in the host country. A hardship allowance is paid to compensate the expatriate for a variety of factors that make expatriate assignment difficult. Exhibit 17–5 shows a hardship evaluation for an expatriate in Montevideo, Uruguay.
- **Tax equalization**—Expatriates face two potential sources of income tax liability—home and host. The United States, unlike most other nations, taxes its citizens on foreign income although it exempts the first $78,000 (inflation adjusted) of foreign wages. Depending on tax treaties and duration of stay, the host country may tax the expatriate as well, but the tax is credited on the U.S. tax return. **Tax equalization** is an adjustment to expatriate pay to reflect tax rates in the home country.[63] Exhibit 17–6 shows a sample of how foreign compensation is calculated. Note that the net foreign compensation is more than double base salary.

Approaches to Expatriate Compensation

There are three approaches to expatriate compensation: home-based, host-based, and hybrid. All three assume that the employee will remain vested in home-country social security, pensions, and other retirement programs. All motivate employees

Exhibit 17–5

Hardship Evaluation:
Montevideo, Uruguay

	Maximum Score	Location Score
I: Assessment of Physical Threat to Employee and Family		
A. Potential or actual violence in area	15	3
B. Hostility of local population	10	2
C. Prevalence of disease	15	3
D. Limited medical facilities and services	10	3
Total threat category	**50 pts**	**11 pts**
II: Assessment of Discomfort to Employee and Family		
A. Difficult physical environment	10	2
B. Geographic isolation	10	4
C. Cultural or psychological isolation	10	2
Total discomfort category	**30 pts**	**8 pts**
III: Assessment of Inconvenience to Employee and Family		
A. Shortcomings in local education system	5	2
B. Restricted availability or low quality housing	5	2
C. Limited recreational or community facilities	5	2
D. Poor availability, quality, or variety of consumer goods	5	2
Total inconvenience category	**20 pts**	**8 pts**
TOTAL (all categories)	**100 pts**	**27 pts**

Source: www.air-inc.com. Sample from the Expatriate Compensation Report—Hardship Evaluation, September 2002.

Exhibit 17–6

Sample foreign compensation calculation

EMPLOYEE	Pierre Bertrand	*EXCHANGE RATE/*	0.1304
HOME COUNTRY	France	*FF = A$ BASE SALARY RESIDENTS AT FOREIGN LOCATION*	FF500,000
			4
FOREIGN LOCATION	Buenos Aires, Argentina		
DATE OF SURVEY	Feb-01	*HOME COUNTRY TAX EXEMPTIONS*	4

Computation of Foreign Compensation

FOREIGN PAY

BASE SALARY	FF500,000	
+ Hardship Premium (5%)	25,000	
− Home Country Income Tax		
French Tax and Social Security (less Family Allowance)	90,360	
FOREIGN PAY		FF434,640

EQUALIZATION COMPONENT

Total Foreign Spending on Goods & Services	FF394,020	
− Home Spending on Goods & Services	205,135	
Cost-of-Living Allowance (COLA)		FF188,885
Total Foreign Spending on Rent & Utilities	FF526,380	
− Home Spending on Rent & Utilities Rent & Utilities Allowance	84,530	
		FF441,850

NET FOREIGN COMPENSATION **FF1,065,375**

Source: www.air-inc.com. Sample from the Expatriate Compensation Report—Individual Report Date: September 2002.

to take the assignment, successfully complete it, and return without extraordinary loss or gain. A **home-country compensation system** links base expatriate salary to the salary structure of the home country. For instance, the salary of a U.S. executive transferred to Japan will be based on the United States rather than Japanese level.

In a **host country-based (localized) compensation system,** base salary for an expatriate is linked to the pay structure in the host country; however, supplemental compensation provisions are often linked to home-country salary structures. The combination produces an international compensation approach oriented toward the higher of host or home gross salary level and the lowest of host, home or third-country taxes.[64] Elements related to home country will be gradually phased out from the fourth to the sixth years in the host country. A study by Watson Wyatt Worldwide found that, of the U.S.-based foreign subsidiaries studied, 66 percent departed from their home country compensation plans to offer U.S.-style executive compensation plans. Exhibit 17–7 shows the percentage of firms from different countries making such adjustment.

Finally, a **hybrid compensation system** blends features from the home- and host-based approaches. The purpose is to create an international expatriate workforce that, while not coming from one location, is paid as if it were.[65] The simplest form of a hybrid system assumes that all expatriates, regardless of country of origin, belong to one nationality. Other forms involve the application of identical cost-of-living allowances to all nationalities, uniform premiums, and uniform housing and other local allowances.

Exhibit 17–8 summarizes the features, advantages, and disadvantages of the three approaches.

Other compensation approaches include the lump-sum/cafeteria and negotiation approaches. The lump-sum/cafeteria approach offers expatriates more choices. Salary is set according to the home-country system. Instead of breaking compensation into its component parts, firms offer a total allowance package and expatriates make their own choice. The logic is to avoid paying for items that expatriates do not value. The negotiation approach means that employer and employee find a mutually acceptable package. This approach is most common in smaller firms with very few expatriates. It creates comparability problems, and negotiation needs to be conducted on a case-by-case basis.

Culture and Compensation

Business performance improves when HRM practices are consistent with national culture (see also Chapter 6).[66] In masculine cultures, work units with more merit-based reward practices were found to perform better, while in feminine cultures,

---

Exhibit 17–7
Adoption of U.S.-style compensation by foreign firms in the United States

MNE's host country	Percent using US-style compensation
France	78%
Canada	56
Germany	56
Japan/Other Asian	56
Netherlands	71
Other Europe	30
United Kingdom	73

Source: Watson Wyatt Worldwide. *Management Review,* June 99, Vol. 88 Issue 6, p9.

Exhibit 17–8
Expatriate compensation
systems

	Home-based	Host-based	Hybrid
Features	■ Consistent treatment of expatriates of same nationality ■ Link with home-country structure/economy ■ Different pay levels for different nationalities ■ No relationship to local employee	■ Equity with local nationals ■ All nationalities paid the same ■ Simple administration ■ Variation in "value" by localities ■ No link to home-country structure/economy	■ All nationalities paid equitably ■ Some link to home-country structure/economy ■ No relationship to local employees
Applicable Conditions	■ Temporary international assignment (2–5 years) ■ Expatriates will ultimately be repatriated to their country of origin ■ The number of different nationalities in any one host location is relatively low ■ International staff predominate in higher-level host location jobs	■ International assignments are of indefinite duration ■ Expatriates tend to be assigned to high-pay countries and will ultimately be repatriated to their country of origin ■ The number of different nationalities in any one host location is relatively high ■ Host-country local staff predominate in higher-level host location jobs	
Advantages	■ Expatriates neither gain nor lose financially ■ Facilitates mobility ■ Eases repatriation	■ All employees operate on equivalent pay ■ System is easy to administer ■ All employees, including expatriates, are paid the same ■ Most suitable for international assignments of indefinite duration	■ All expatriate nationalities are paid equitably ■ Assists transfers and development of an international management cadre
Disadvantages	■ Expensive ■ No link to local pay structure ■ Expatriates of the same seniority from different origins will be paid differently ■ Administration can be complex	■ Complicates reentry ■ Most applicable when salary and living standards improve, thereby becoming expensive ■ Unprotected fluctuations in the exchange rate puts company and employee at additional risk ■ Certain host-country benefits are not applicable to expatriates ■ Difficult to transfer to lower-paying location	■ Complicated administration ■ Sometimes difficult to communicate ■ No link to local pay structure

Source: G. T. Milkovich and J. M. Newman, *Compensation*. Chicago: Irwin/McGraw-Hill,1999.

work units with fewer merit-based reward practices were higher performers. The propensity to use both seniority-based and skill-based compensation systems was positively correlated with uncertainty avoidance. Compensation practices based on individual performance were correlated with individualism. High masculinity was associated with lesser use of flexible benefits, workplace child-care programs, career-break schemes, and maternity-leave programs.[67] High collectivism was found to be negatively related to individual- and equity-based reward, and merit-based promotion system.[68] However, there are occasions where collectivists compromise cultural traditions to help their organization survive.[69]

The following recommendations have been made vis-à-vis compensation in different cultures:[70]

- In high-power distance cultures, MNEs should pursue hierarchical compensation for local managers, pay and benefits should be tied to the local managers' position, and a large pay differential between echelons is desirable.
- In cultures with high individualism, performance-based pay and extrinsic rewards are important. In cultures with low individualism, group-based pay and compensation packages that reflect seniority and family needs are more acceptable.
- In cultures with high masculinity, MNEs should pursue a compensation strategy for local managers that recognizes and reward competitiveness, aggressiveness, and dominance. In cultures with low masculinity, compensation should focus on social benefits, quality of work life, and equity.
- In cultures with high uncertainty avoidance, structured and consistent pay plans are preferred. Salary and benefits decision should be centralized, with no variable pay plans or discretionary salary allocation. Where uncertainty avoidance is low, pay should be closely linked to performance. In addition, the local manager's salary should be competitive to retain top talent.
- In high uncertainty-avoidance cultures it is better to have centralized pension systems with multiple controls and safeguards.
- Low uncertainty-avoidance cultures would be more open to defined contribution pensions with flexible plan implementation.
- Separate pension plans for different classes of employees would be acceptable in high-power distance cultures.
- In masculine cultures with moderate to high uncertainty avoidance, policies designed to protect job security would be welcome.
- Employees from feminine cultures with moderate to high uncertainty avoidance would prefer policies designed to protect income security.
- Employees from feminine cultures prefer family-friendly management practices as well as other policies designed to maximize quality of work life.
- Employees in low individualistic and low-power distance cultures will prefer flexible benefit programs.
- Health programs in low-power distance cultures would be uniform for all, while employee choice of health insurance providers is important in individualistic cultures.

Training and performance evaluation also vary across cultures. Management by Objectives (MBO), where subordinates and supervisors develop measurable goals, tends to fail in high-power distance culture. Similarly, in cultures with high uncertainty avoidance, it may be hard to get subordinates to commit to risky goals. Cultural differences also affect the relative importance of different dimensions of performance; for example, in collectivist cultures, group harmony and cohesiveness may be more important than task performance.

Repatriation

Repatriation represents an adjustment equally if not more difficult than the overseas assignment,[71] yet most returning employees are dissatisfied with the repatriation process. Most U.S. firms do not provide a written guarantee of reassignment prior to departure, and most returnees do not know what their next assignment will be prior to repatriation. Even those with a suitable reassignment often feel that their employers fail to make effective use of their foreign experience. With the exception of housing assistance, most firms do not provide spouse career counseling or other forms of family repatriation assistance. It is not surprising that one quarter of repatriated employees leave their firm within one year of repatriation,[72] and that many decline to undertake subsequent international assignments.

Interim Summary

1. MNEs use expatriate staff to get businesses off the ground, to import managerial experience into a foreign subsidiary to control the subsidiary, and as a development tool.

2. Although the expatriate manager is useful as a means of transmitting experience and corporate culture, many expatriates have difficulty adjusting to life in the new country, and the rate of expatriate failure is high.

3. Adaptability, as well as a non-judgmental stance toward other cultures, are the primary necessary attributes in expatriate employees. However, adjustment to working in another culture can take a long time. It is important for the company to prepare the expatriate prior to departure.

4. A great deal of thought must be put into determining appropriate compensation packages for expatriates, including salary, housing, and other benefits, since it is necessary to adjust this compensation based on the home country of the employee and/or the host country where he or she will be working.

HRM IN INTERNATIONAL AFFILIATES

Human resource issues and problems vary depending on the type of foreign affiliate involved. Although wholly owned subsidiaries (WOSs) employ up to three employee groups (expatriates, HCNs, and TCNs), IJVs employ multiple employee groups, as follows: (a) Foreign Parent(s) Expatriates (i.e., nationals of the country in which the headquarters of the foreign parent(s) is (are) located, assigned by that parent(s) to the affiliate); (b) Host Parent(s) Transferees (host-country nationals employed by the host parent(s) and transferred to the affiliate from the host-parent headquarters or one of its subsidiaries); (c) Host-Country Nationals (nationals of the host country, hired directly by the affiliate; (d) Third-Country Expatriates of the host parent(s) (third-country nationals who are neither nationals of the host country nor of the foreign parent('s) country(ies) and assigned by the host parent(s) to work in the affiliate); (e) Third-Country Expatriates of the foreign parent(s) (third-country nationals assigned by the foreign parent(s) to work in the affiliate); (f) Third-Country Expatriates of the affiliate (third-country nationals recruited directly by the affiliate, who are neither nationals of the parent(s) country(ies) nor of the country in which the affiliate operates); (g) Foreign Headquarters Executives (i.e., policymakers at the headquarters of the foreign parent(s), who play a major role in the functioning of the affiliate at headquarters or are board members of the affiliate); (h) Host Headquarters Executives (i.e., policymakers at the headquarters of the host parent(s), who play a major role in the functioning of the affiliate at headquarters or are board members of the affiliate).

Human Resource Problems in Foreign Affiliates

The following human resource problems can be expected in WOSs and IJVs.[73]

- *Staffing Friction*   Parent companies prefer to appoint their own transferees or expatriates to key positions in the affiliate as a control measure. When the staffing policy is not contractually specified, friction often ensues. In many cases, friction also develops regarding the level of staffing, with the host parent looking at the IJV as a way of "unloading" extra staff. In both WOSs and IJVs, host-country nationals are often deprived of opportunities to staff the most senior positions.

- *Blocked Promotion*   In both types of foreign subsidiaries, local employees can be frustrated by the lack of promotion opportunities if senior positions are reserved for "outsiders." This problem is especially serious in IJVs where the "outsiders" may be not only the foreign expatriates but also transferees of the host parent. When such "outsiders" are abundant, local personnel may be reluctant to join, stay, or contribute their best efforts to the affiliate.

- *Exile Syndrome and Reentry Difficulties*   Feeling "exiled" in an overseas assignment because of fear of interruption of the career track back home occurs in both WOSs and IJVs. WOSs are more closely integrated, however, so an assignment to a subsidiary might be less disruptive. Assignees in an IJV, on the other hand, may be working with, or supervised by, employees of another company. They will not report directly to their parent headquarters, nor will their supervisors be in a position to assess their performance. Exile syndrome may be damaging to the foreign affiliate because it may lead employees to bypass their supervisors in the affiliate, report achievements rather than failures, and take a short-term perspective.

- *Split Loyalty*   The problem of split loyalty is quite unique to IJVs. Employees recruited by the host or the foreign parent might remain loyal to that parent rather than shift their allegiance to the IJV. This happens especially when employees expect to return to the parent firm at the end of their assignment or when the IJV has a predetermined life span. The result is suspicion and low level of cooperation that prevents the venture from attaining its potential.

- *Compensation Gaps*   The problem of compensation gaps (e.g., HCNs receiving much lower pay than expatriates) occurs in both types of affiliates. For example, many U.S.-based executives of foreign MNEs earn more than their superiors in Europe or Asia. IJVs suffer from an additional problem of relative deprivation, however, where employees receive compensation packages that are not necessarily based on universal criteria, such as skills and experience, but on affiliation with a particular parent or the IJV itself. Each MNE has an established compensation policy, and in many cases, the differences are significant. Moreover, each employee group has a different perception about what is the most desirable package of benefits. The result is a feeling of deprivation and consequently reduced motivation and morale.

- *Blocked Communication*   Effective communication among parent(s) and between a parent and an affiliate can be hampered by a combination of cultural differences and variations in organizational procedures and norms. Because of differences in parents' objectives, communications may be distorted or withheld by their respective employees. Such communication blockages represent an impediment to decision making. The problem is especially serious in IJVs with a 50/50-equity distribution.

- *Limited Delegation*   Many parent companies try to maintain control of their affiliate by limiting the scope of authority and decision-making power they delegate. This is especially true when parents have conflicting goals, when they depend on the affiliate for scarce and vital resources, and when they feel that the affiliate's staff is loyal to the other parent. Under these conditions, the affiliate's management finds it difficult to operate effectively, especially in a fast-changing environment.

- *Screening of Information* Many firms are hesitant to pass information and technology to an affiliate, especially an IJV whose partner might be a present or a future competitor. The result is self-defeating, with the other parent(s) limiting information as well. The venture is then unable to operate effectively.
- *Unfamiliarity* Expatriates who join a foreign affiliate are unfamiliar, in most cases, with the environment in which the venture operates. In IJVs, most employees are also unfamiliar with the unique structure of this organization and with its conflict-prone nature.

Research provides some suggestions for alleviating some of the human resource problems in foreign affiliates. Among the solutions are organization development and training for working in an IJV structure; identifying and rewarding leadership; interpersonal and negotiation skills that are crucial in IJV systems; opening up communication channels among parent and venture organizations; and career planning that takes account of the overlapping yet diverse tracks among the member organizations. The following section provides a brief illustration of management education requirements according to the type of affiliate.

Preparing for an Assignment in a Foreign Affiliate

Although much has been written about expatriate selection, relatively little is known about the training and preparation required for operating effectively in a specific foreign affiliate. At the same time, we are only beginning to consider the adjustments when moving, say, from a WOS to an IJV. Exhibit 17–9 provides a starting point.

Interim Summary

1. WOSs and IJVs face many of the same staffing problems as any overseas venture, including resentment of expatriate staff by the local staff and feelings of being exiled on the part of expatriates.

2. IJVs are especially difficult to manage due to suspicion and loyalty issues, especially when the parent firms are competitors.

Exhibit 17–9
Management education requirements in two types of foreign affiliates

Educational Focus	Wholly-Owned Subsidiary	International Joint Venture
Cultural sensitivity/national	High	High
Cultural sensitivity/org. level	Low	High
Interpersonal skills	Low	High
Negotiation/bargaining skills	Med	High
Entrepreneurial skills	High	High
Leadership skills	High	High
Knowledge/global environment	High	High
Knowledge/regional	High	High
Knowledge/firm-specific	Med	Low
Knowledge/functional area	High	Med

Source: Adapted from E. Bailey, and O. Shenkar, "Management education for international joint venture managers," *Leadership and Organization Development Journal* 14, 1993: 15–20.

CHAPTER SUMMARY

1. Strategic international human resource management (SIHRM) (adaptive, exportive, or integrative) determines the degree of similarity between the HRM practices of the parent company and those of its foreign affiliates. IHRM changes as the firm develops its international presence and capabilities.

2. Boards of directors are becoming more global; that is, there is a significant increase in the proportion of non-native board members in most MNEs.

3. Although small in numbers, expatriate employees play a vital role in the operations of MNEs. Since expatriate failure rates are high, companies pay increased attention to their recruitment, selection, training, and compensation.

4. Approaches to expatriate compensation include home-based, host-based, and hybrid of both systems. Lump-sum/cafeteria and negotiation are additional approaches that offer more flexibility but are difficult to administer.

5. Companies are paying closer attention to their local workforce and making judgments regarding what practices they can standardize across their affiliates and what practices they need to adapt to the particular need of a local environment. Those are linked, in turn, to the firm's strategy.

6. Significant correlations exist between cultural dimensions and the human resource practices used in different countries. This represents a constraint on the MNE's ability to globalize its HRM policies and practices.

7. HRM problems in foreign affiliates vary by the type of affiliate (e.g., a wholly foreign-owned subsidiary versus an international joint venture), among other factors.

CHAPTER NOTES

[1] How The CEOs drive global growth, Conference Board 1184-97RR.

[2] *Wall Street Journal,* November 24, 1992, Citing Towers Perrin.

[3] N. J. Adler, "Cross-cultural management: Issues to be faced," *International Studies of Management and Organization,* 1983.

[4] F. Acuff, *International and Domestic Human Resources Functions: Innovations in International Compensation,* New York: Organization resources counselors, 1984.

[5] "Developing a Global Mindset at Johnson & Johnson—1998," IMD case #BM791, 01.06.99.

[6] "Developing a Global Mindset at Johnson & Johnson—1998," IMD case #GM791, 01.06.99.

[7] S. Taylor, S. Beechler, and N. Napier, "Toward an integrative model of strategic international human resource management," *Academy of Management Review,* 21, 4, 1996, 959–985.

[8] R. Schuller, P. Dowling, and H. DeCieri, "An integrative framework of strategic international human resource management," *International Journal of Human Resource Management,* 1, 1993, 717–764.

[9] R. G. Vernon, "International investment and international trade in the product cycle," *Quarterly Journal of Economics,* 1996, 190–207.

[10] N. J. Adler, F. Ghadar, Strategic human resource management: a global perspective. In R. Pieper, (Ed.), *Human Resource Management: An International Comparison.* Berlin: DeGruyter, 1990.

[11] H. V. Perlmutter, "The tortuous evolution of the multinational corporation," *Columbia Journal of World Business,* 4, 1969, 9–18.

[12] R. L. Tung, "Selection and training procedures of US, European, and Japanese multinationals," *California Management Review,* 25, 1982, 57–71.

[13] "Won Choi Hae, Korea's Samsung seeks a bit more worldliness," *Wall Street Journal,* March 22, 2002.

[14] N. Boyacigiller, "The role of expatriates in the management of interdependence, complexity and risk in multinational corporations," *Journal of International Business Studies,* third quarter, 1990, 357–381.

[15] "How the CEOs drive global growth," Conference Board 1184-97-RR.

[16] *World Investment Report,* UNCTAD, 2000.

[17] R. Kopp, "International human resource policies and practices in Japanese, European, and United States multinationals," *Human Resource Management,* 33, 1994, 581–599.

[18] P. Beckett, "Citigroup's Menezes plays key game to lift growth via emerging markets," *Wall Street Journal,* February 21, 2001, C1.

[19] N. Ramamoorthy, and S. J. Carroll, "Individualism/collectivism orientations and reactions toward alternative human resource management practices," *Human Relations,* 51, 1998, 571–588.

[20] "Nike admits worker abuse," CNNfn, February 22, 2001, 7:41 A.M. ET.

[21] Cited in P. M. Caligiuri, "The big five personality characteristics as predictors of expatriate's desire to terminate the assignment and supervisor-rated performance," *Personnel Psychology* 2000, 53, 67–88.

[22] D. R. Briscoe, *International Human Resource Management,* Englewood Cliffs, NJ: Prentice-Hall, 1995.

[23] Cited in *Wall Street Journal,* January 16, 2001, B12.

[24] "Developing a global mindset at Johnson & Johnson—1998," IMD case #GM791, 01.06.99.

[25] J. Flynn, "E-mail, cellphones and frequent flier miles let 'virtual' expats work abroad but live at home," *Wall Street Journal,* October 25, 1999, A26; J. Millman, "Exporting management savvy," *The Wall Street Journal,* Oct. 24, 2000, B1.

[26] "How The CEOs drive global growth," Conference Board 1184-97-RR.

[27] M. S. Fenwick, H. L. D. DeCieri, and D. E. Welch, "Cultural and bureaucratic control in MNEs: The role of expatriate performance appraisal," *Management International Review,* 39, 1999, 107–124.

[28] "How The CEOs drive global growth," The Conference Board, 1184-97-RR.

[29] L. Copeland and L. Griggs, *Going International.* New York: Plume, 1985; D. R. Briscoe, *International Human Resource Management.* Englewood Cliffs, NJ: Prentice-Hall, 1995.

[30] Windham International 1995 survey, cited in *The China Business Review,* May–June 1997, 30.

[31] R. L. Tung, "Selecting and training of personnel for overseas assignments," *Columbia Journal of World Business*, 16, 1981, 68–78. R. L. Tung, "Expatriate assignments: Enhancing success and minimizing failure," *Academy of Management Executive*, 1, 1987, 117–126.

[32] M. E. Mendenhall, E. Dunbar, and G. R. Oddou, "Expatriate selection, training and career pathing: A review and critique," *Human Resource Management*, 26, 1987, 331–345.

[33] R. L. Tung, "Expatriate assignments: Enhancing success and minimizing failure," *Academy of Management Executive*, 1, 1987, 117–126.

[34] M. E. Mendenhall and G. R. Oddou, "The overseas assignment: A practical look," *Business Horizons*, 31(5), 1988, 78–84.

[35] J. M. Brett, and L. K. Stroh, "Willingness to relocate internationally," *Human Resource Management*, 34, 1995, 405–424.

[36] N. Adler and D. N. Izraeli, Women managers: Moving up and across borders. In *Global perspectives of Human Resource Management*. Englewood Cliffs, NJ: PrenticeHall, 1994, 165–193. Shenkar. O. (ed.) *Business Week*, November 6, 2000, p. 14.

[37] K. E. Baumgarten, "A profile for international managers and its implications for selection and training." Thesis, Faculty of Applied Educational Science, University of Twente, Enschede, The Netherlands, 1992.

[38] N. J. Adler and S. Bartholomew, "Managing globally competent people," *Academy of Management Executive*, 6, 1992, 52–65.

[39] M. E. Mendenhall and G. R. Oddou, "The overseas assignment: A practical look," *Business Horizons* 31, 5, 1988, 78–84.

[40] G. M. Spreitzer, M. W. McCall Jr. and J. D. Mahoney, "Early identification of international executive potential," *Journal of Applied Psychology*, 1997, 82, 6–29.

[41] M. S. Schell and C. M. Solomon, *Capitalizing on the Global Workforce: A Strategic Guide to Expatriate Management*. Chicago: Irwin Professional Publications, 1997.

[42] D. Woodruff, "Distractions make global manager a difficult role," *Wall Street Journal*, November 21, 2000, B1.

[43] J. S. Black, M. Mendenhall, and G. Oddou, "Toward a comprehensive model of international adjustment: An integration of multiple theoretical perspectives," *Academy of Management Review*, 16, 1991, 291–317.

[44] J. S. Black and M. Mendenhall, "The U-curve adjustment hypothesis revisited: A review and theoretical framework," *Journal of International Business Studies*, 22, 1991, 225–247.

[45] M. E. Mendenhall and G. R. Oddou, "The overseas assignment: A practical look," *Business Horizons*, 31(5), 1988, 78–84.

[46] S. Ayree, Y. W. Char, and J. Chew, "An investigation of the willingness of managerial employees to accept an expatriate assignment," *Journal of Organizational Behavior*, 17, 1996, 267–283.

[47] R. L. Tung, "Expatriate assignments: Enhancing success and minimizing failure," *Academy of Management Executive*, 1, 1987, 117–126.

[48] M. E. Mendenhall, E. Dunbar, and G. R. Oddou, "Expatriate selection, training and career pathing: A review and critique," *Human Resource Management*, 26, 1987, 331–345.

[49] D. J. Kealey and D. R. Protheroe, "The cross-cultural training for expatriates: An assessment of the literature on the issue," *International Journal of Inter-cultural Relations*, 20, 1996, 141–165.

[50] D. J. Kealey and D. R. Protheroe, "The cross-cultural training for expatriates: An assessment of the literature on the issue," *International Journal of Inter-cultural Relations*, 20, 1996, 141–165.

[51] D. J. Kealey and D. R. Protheroe, "The cross-cultural training for expatriates: An assessment of the literature on the issue," *International Journal of Inter-cultural Relations*, 20, 1996, 141–165.

[52] T. Yoshida and R. W. Brislin, "Intercultural skills and recommended behaviors: The psychological perspective for training program," In O. Shenkar (Ed.), *Global Perspective of Human Resource Management*, Englewood Cliffs, NJ: Prentice-Hall, 1995, pp. 112–113.

[53] J. K. Harrison, "Developing successful expatriate managers: A framework for the structural design and strategic alignment of cross-cultural training programs," *Human Resource Planning*, 17, 1992, 17–35.

[54] R. L. Tung, "Expatriate assignments: Enhancing success and minimizing failure," *Academy of Management Executive*, 1, 1987, 117–126.

[55] M. E. Mendenhall, E. Dunbar, and G. R. Oddou, "Expatriate selection, training and career pathing: A review and critique," *Human Resource Management*, 26, 1987, 331–345.

[56] D. R. Briscoe, *International Human Resource Management*, Englewood Cliffs, NJ: Prentice-Hall, 1995.

[57] H. B. Gregersen, and L. K. Stroh, "Coming home to the Arctic cold: Antecedents to Finnish expatriate and spouse repatriation adjustment," *Personnel Psychology*, 50, 635–654; R. A. Guzzo, K. A. Noonan, and E. Elron, "Expatriate managers and the psychological contract," *Journal of Applied Psychology*, 79, 1994, 617–626.

[58] H. B. Gregersen, J. S. Black, and J. M. Hite, "Expatriate performance appraisal: Principles, practices, and challenges. In J. Selmer (Ed.), *Expatriate Management: New Ideas for International Business*. Westport, CT: Quorum Books, 1995.

[59] H. B. Gregersen and J. M. Hite, "Expatriate performance appraisal in US multinational firms," *Journal of International Business Studies*, fourth quarter, 1996, 711–738.

[60] The Conference Board 1148-96-RR.

[61] *Benefits Canada*, 20, 11, 1966, p. 11.

[62] Milkovich and Newman, *Compensation*. Chicago: Irwin/McGraw-Hill, 1999.

[63] Milkovich and Newman, *Compensation*. Chicago: Irwin/McGraw-Hill, 1999.

[64] J. B. Anderson, "Compensating your overseas executives, Part 2: Europe in 1992," *Compensation and Benefits Review*, 1995.

[65] M. S. Schell and C. M. Solomon, *Capitalizing on the Global Workforce: A Strategic Guide to Expatriate Management*. Chicago: Irwin, 1997.

[66] S. Schneider, "National vs. corporate culture: Implications for human resource management," *Human Resource Management*, 27, 231–246.

[67] R. S. Schuller and N. Rogovsky, "Understanding compensation practice variations across firms: The impact of national culture," *Journal of International Business Studies*, 29, 1, 1998, 159–177.

[68] N. Ramamoorthy and S. J. Carroll, "Individualism/collectivism orientations and reactions toward alternative human resource management practices," *Human Relations*, 51, 1998, 571–588.

[69] C. C. Chen, "New trends in reward allocation preferences: A Sino-U.S. comparison," *Academy of Management Journal*, 38, 1995, 408–424.

[70] P. S. Hempel, "Designing multinational benefits programs: The role of national culture," *Journal of World Business*, 33, 1998, 277–294.

[71] N. J. Adler, "Re-entry: Managing cross-cultural transitions," *Group & Organization Management*, 6, 1981, 341–356.

[72] J. S. Black, H. B. Gregersen and M. E. Mendenhall, "Toward a theoretical framework of repatriation adjustment," *Journal of International Business Studies*, 23, 1992, 737–760.

[73] Based on O. Shenkar, and Y. Zeira, "Human resource management in international joint ventures: Directions for research," *Academy of Management Review*, 12, 1987, 546–557.

PART SIX

Emerging Issues in International Business

CHAPTER 18: Global Internet and E-Commerce

CHAPTER 19: Ethics and Corruption in the Global Marketplace

Global Internet and E-Commerce

DO YOU KNOW

1. Do you shop on-line? If yes, do you know, or mind, in what country the seller is located?

2. Would having a Web site make your firm an international company? Why or why not?

3. Would global e-commerce avoid barriers to trade, tariff and non-tariff?

4. What are the prospects for global e-commerce in the years ahead? What are the opportunities and threats posed by e-commerce to the MNE and the SMIE?

OPENING CASE Otis Elevator

Founded in 1853, Otis Elevator—a wholly owned subsidiary of United Technologies Corporation—is the world's number one manufacturer of elevators and escalators. With 1.2 million installations in more than 200 countries, Otis has a 22 percent share of the global elevator market. Based in Connecticut, nearly 80 percent of its sales are outside the United States as are 55,000 of the company's 63,000 employees.

Integration of computer technology at Otis began in 1979, with the installment of microprocessors in elevators to detect problems and improve maintenance. In 1983, Otis started OTISLINE®, a computerized dispatch service for North American elevators. In 1988, REM® allowed the firm to monitor elevator performance from distant locations in North America. Otis then extended those innovations globally. In 1999, Otis introduced E*Display, an Internet-based information display in an elevator car, E*Direct, which allows customers to order elevators online, and E*Service, an on-line customer service Web site.

By the summer of 2000, Otis was taking on-line orders in 49 countries in 29 languages. The company expects on-line business to account for 25 percent to 30 percent of its growth between 2000 and 2003. In selected markets such as France, the Otis site permits architects to submit their building specifications and have Otis engineers determine the type of elevators required. ■

Source: M. Meehan, "Foreign markets draw B-to-B firms overseas," *Computerworld,* May 15, 2000; company Web sites.

The internet is a worldwide network of computer networks known as the World Wide Web (WWW). WWW constitutes all the resources and users on the internet that use Hypertext Transfer Protocol (HTP, or HTTP). HTP uses a set of rules for exchanging files such as: text, graphic images, sound, video, and other multimedia files on the WWW.

Electronic commerce (E-commerce) is the conduct of transactions to buy, sell, distribute, or deliver goods and services over the internet. E-commerce transactions are Business-to-Business (B2B), Business-to-Customer (B2C), or Customer-to-Customer (C2C). B2B, which currently drives 90 percent of the projected growth in global e-commerce, involves inter-firm transactions, including government procurement. B2C transactions are between firms and individuals purchasing goods or services over the internet. Ordering a book online from a vendor is an example of a B2C transaction. C2C transactions involve individual transactions, for example, via online auction. All three types now occur globally as well as domestically. **Global e-commerce** is the conduct of electronic commerce, whether B2B, B2C, or C2C across national boundaries (e.g., a U.S. customer purchasing pharmaceuticals from a Canadian site.)

The emergence of the internet and e-commerce created initial expectations for exploding global trade, expectations that have since been scaled down. The assumption was that "a firm marketing its products or services through the internet is, by definition, a global firm because consumers worldwide can access it."[1] Others acknowledged that "the internet won't magically ensure overseas success, but it can ease some of the pain of going global."[2] The Otis case illustrates that point. The company, which has been in international markets for over a century, uses the internet as a supplementary tool in its global sales and service. The technology has

Internet cafes are symbols as well as vehicles for the diffusion of the internet and e-commerce.

expedited the procurement process but has not come to substitute for its "bricks and mortar" business. For some small firms, the impact has been more pronounced. The Naushad Trading Company of Mombassa, Kenya (Web link: www.ntclimited.com), which sells African handcraft products, attributes much of its rapid growth from $10,000 to $2 million in sales within a few years to the Web.[3]

As in domestic markets, the main growth of global e-commerce has been in the B2B segment. Examples are the global automobile industry exchange established by the Ford Motor Company, General Motors, and DaimlerChrysler (with Toyota possibly joining as well) and the alliance of IBM, Nortel Networks, Toshiba, and cell phone makers Motorola, Nokia, and LM Ericsson. The alliance will link billions of dollars in annual purchasing in what could be the biggest business-to-business internet auction marketplace.[4]

INTERNET AND E-COMMERCE DIFFUSION
Exhibit 18–1 presents the percentage of internet users in selected countries. It shows the United States in second place after Denmark, followed by The Netherlands, Canada, Finland, Norway, and Australia.

Exhibit 18–2 further divides the countries into three groups based on their rate of internet penetration.

The "digital divide" between North and South has persisted for some time. While developed countries had an average 312 internet hosts per 1,000 residents back in 1999, developing countries had 6.[5] The entire continent of Africa had only 1.5 million users

Exhibit 18–1
Internet users around the world 2002

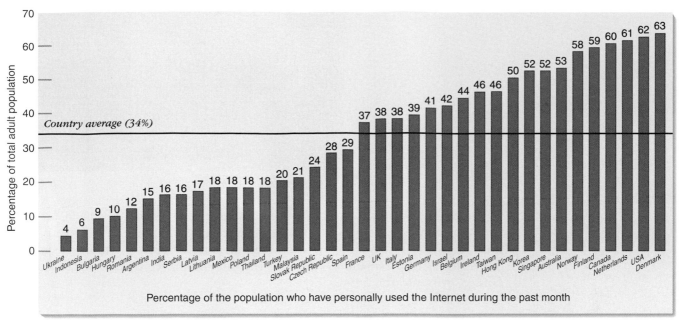

Source: *Taylor Nelson Sofres Interactive Global eCommerce Report*, 2002

in 2000, and 1 million of those were in South Africa.[6] Despite this gap, it has been estimated that by 2002 Non-English speakers will outnumber English speakers on the Web.[7]

Another indicator of the level of internet penetration is the abundance of country-level domain names. Exhibit 18–3 presents country rankings by domain name registrations. The United States is not listed because U.S. sites are not designated by a country domain name.

Exhibit 18–2
Internet Penetration, by Country

Low penetration	Medium penetration	High penetration
(less than 20% are users)	(20 to 40% are users)	(more than 40% are users)
■ Argentina	■ Czech Republic	■ Australia
■ Bulgaria	■ Estonia	■ Belgium
■ Hungary	■ France	■ Canada
■ India	■ Great Britain	■ Denmark
■ Indonesia	■ Italy	■ Finland
■ Latvia	■ Malaysia	■ Germany
■ Lithuania	■ Slovak Republic	■ Hong Kong
■ Mexico	■ Spain	■ Ireland
■ Poland	■ Turkey	■ Israel
■ Romania		■ South Korea
■ Serbia		■ Netherlands
■ Thailand		■ Norway
■ Ukraine		■ Singapore
		■ Taiwan
		■ USA

Source: *Taylor Nelson Sofres Interactive Global eCommerce Report*, 2002

Exhibit 18-3
Top country-level domains
(2000)

.uk	United Kingdom	1,938,740
.de	Germany	1,732,994
.nl	Netherlands	399,411
.kr	South Korea	325,203
.ar	Argentina	324,548
.it	Italy	283,860
.dk	Denmark	204,475
.jp	Japan	190,709
.au	Australia	150,505
.at	Austria	123,287
.ch	Switzerland	112,912
.ca	Canada	93,330

Source: DomainStats.com, 2000

Between 2001 and 2002, internet penetration growth slowed down and, for some countries, turned negative. This led to a scaling down of some of the overly optimistic forecasts of the late 1990's. Yet, high penetration rates for young age groups, as well as pent-up demand in emerging and developing economics, suggest continuous growth into the future.

Comparative Internet Demographics

User demographics within each country vary significantly. Exhibit 18-4 shows national distribution of internet usage by gender. Female usage is higher in the United States and Canada but lower in all other countries compared.[9] Thus, North America seems to be the exception in the gender distribution of internet users. In India, for example, women make up only one third of users. Such demographics are important in e-commerce and other uses of the internet in business.

Usage patterns also vary. While Americans spend on average 12.7 days a month on-line, Japanese spend 13.9 days while users in France spend 7.7 days. However, Americans spend 70.6 minutes per day on average while Japanese spend 44.9 minutes and the French only 35.4 minutes.[10] Asian B2C sites spend only 10 cents to attract a visitor vis-à-vis 41.50 cents in Europe and $2.30 in the United States; however,

Exhibit 18-4
Internet usage by gender

Country	Female	Male	Country	Female	Male
Argentina	45.4%	54.6%	**Japan**	42.3%	57.7%
Australia	46.9	53.1	**Mexico**	40.6	59.4
Austria	42.8	57.2	**Netherlands**	43.1	57.0
Belgium	40.5	59.5	**New Zealand**	49.6	50.4
Brazil	43.1	56.9	**Norway**	43.4	56.6
Canada	51.9	48.1	**Singapore**	45.0	55.0
Denmark	44.8	55.2	**South Africa**	43.1	56.9
Finland	47.0	53.0	**South Korea**	45.9	54.1
France	39.8	60.2	**Spain**	41.1	58.9
Germany	39.0	61.0	**Sweden**	44.9	55.1
Hong Kong	43.9	56.1	**Switzerland**	41.4	58.6
India	33.9	66.1	**Taiwan**	45.0	55.0
Ireland	45.2	54.8	**United Kingdom**	44.5	55.5
Israel	42.6	57.4	**United States**	51.4	48.6
Italy	36.4	63.6			

Source: Nielsen//NetRatings, January 2002, U.S., Home: Wall Street Journal, April 15, 2002, R4.

only 1.3 percent of Asian visitors complete a purchase vis-à-vis 2.3 percent in the United States and 2.5 percent on European sites.[11]

E-Commerce around the Globe

E-commerce has been the fastest growing segment of the internet economy.[12] Still, at less than one percent of total sales in the United States—the global leader—e-commerce is still not a major force in retailing, leading some observers to suggest that B2B transactions will be the main engine for e-commerce growth. While internet access is a prerequisite for e-shopping, it does not guarantee it. Over half of the internet users questioned by TNS Interactive in 2002 noted that they did not plan to buy anything on-line.[13]

Advertising, while delivering less than initially forecasted, is still projected to account for substantial on-line revenues. Exhibit 18–5 shows current and expected on-line ad spending by country in selected European nations.

E-commerce is forecasted to grow rapidly, however, eventually accounting for a substantial portion of global exports.[14] Growth has already been pronounced in selected segments such as travel and for digitalized (e.g., music) and electronic products. For instance, almost half of Dell's sales in the US in 1999 came through its Web site.[15]

Exhibit 18–6 shows what products are more likely to be purchased on-line in different countries, revealing remarkable differences. For instance, 8 percent of internet shoppers in Germany buy cars on-line, versus just 1 percent in the United States. Almost half of Israeli on-line shoppers purchase electronics and electrical goods on-line, and almost 40 percent of Taiwanese on-line shoppers use the internet to buy books.

The United States remains the global leader in e-shopping, with 32 percent of internet users shopping on-line (versus less than 2 percent in Bulgaria, Romania, and the Ukraine).[16] However, by 2003, the United States overall share of the global

Exhibit 18–5

Estimated online ad spending by country in 2001, in millions of euros

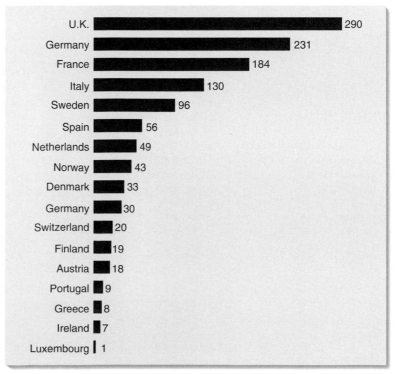

Source: Jupiter MMXI, 2002.

Exhibit 18–6

On-line purchases in selected countries, 2002 (percentage of total purchases)

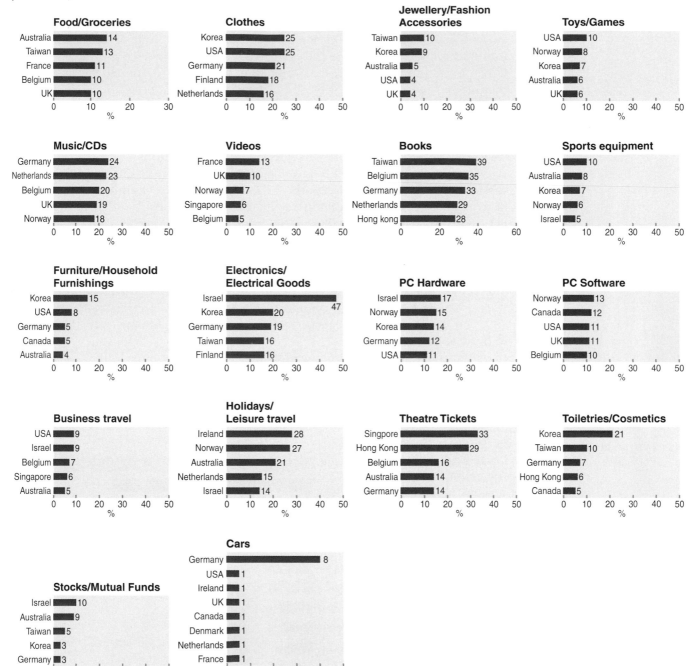

Source: Taylor Nelson Sofres Interactive Global eCommerce Report, 2002.

e-market was projected to decline to 44 percent from 61.7 percent in 1999, while Europe was projected to increase its share from 18.7 percent to 31.2 percent and Japan from 10.3 percent to 15.4 percent.[17] Some regions, such as Asia-Pacific, were also expected to show especially strong growth.[18]

Interim Summary

1. Although developed economies generally have higher internet/e-commerce usage than developing economies, there are significant variations in the rate and pattern of usage within each group.

2. The United States is the global leader in e-commerce, but its share is fore-casted to decline sharply in the years ahead.

E-READINESS

Nations vary dramatically in their preparedness for e-commerce. Developed countries are generally more prepared, although some, such as Japan, lag behind. Online spending in Japan amounted to $1.8 billion, 6 percent of the U.S. total in 1999.[19]

McConnell International developed a classification of e-readiness factors that includes Connectivity, E-Leadership, Information Security, Human Capital, and E-Business Climate.[20] This classification forms the basis for the following discussion, whereas scores for selected nations will be presented later in this section.

From high-tech telecommunications infra-structure to low-tech distribution, connectivity in China is a mixed bag.

Connectivity

Connectivity is the existence and affordability of a communication and transportation network. In 2000, the United States had 580 computers per 1,000 people, which is higher than the rates in Canada (522), Australia (566), Finland (573), and Switzerland (473).[21] The United States is less competitive when it comes to telephone systems. In Israel, Japan, China, and Germany, virtually all phones are connected to digital exchanges vis-à-vis about 90 percent in the United States. The United States ranks only twenty-third in the penetration of wireless communications, well behind Europe and Japan. Among developing nations, China has four times as many telephone lines and 18 times as many cellular phones as India.[22]

Exhibit 18–7
Access costs and usage of
the internet

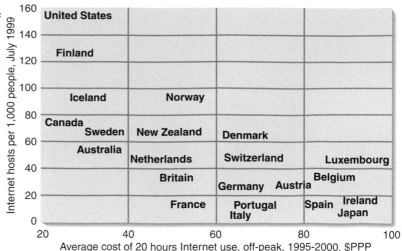

Average cost of 20 hours Internet use, off-peak, 1995-2000, $PPP

Source: The Economist, September 23, 2000; OECD.

The cost of accessing the internet is prohibitive in many countries, such as in most of Latin America. The price of 20 hours monthly internet connection in Mexico is equal to 14.8 percent of per capita GDP versus 1 percent in the United States.[23] The annual cost of using the internet in Kenya in 1997 was $1,681, a sum higher than the annual income of many Kenyans.[24] In the United Kingdom, the lower cost of dial-up internet connections is behind much of the dramatic increase in internet usage. Exhibit 18–7 shows the relationship between access cost and internet use for selected countries.

Distribution is another facet of connectivity. The wide variety of ground and overnight delivery services in the United States is unavailable or prohibitively expensive in many parts of the world. In developing countries such as China, even conventional, ground distribution is problematic outside a few urban areas.[25] Products are delivered by pedicarts and by bicycles with cash collected upon delivery.[26]

Information Security

Information security refers to the existence of security and other protections pertaining to information dissemination. Recent data show that security concerns remain the single most important obstacle in the way of an internet user who is considering shopping on-line.[27] Confidentiality is a product of the availability of secure servers (see Exhibit 18–8) as well as of transcription technologies. Not all governments are eager to assist. For instance, in order to ensure government monitoring, Chinese regulations forbid foreign-designed encryption software.[28] The Chinese government also assigns Chinese-language domain registration names exclusively to domestic firms, even though this is as much a barrier to foreign entrants as a security measure.

Privacy Protection

Many potential customers are reluctant to provide information and/or make purchases on-line out of fear that the information they provide (as well as information they do not voluntarily provide such as site visit patterns) will be used inappropriately or given to other vendors. Privacy laws facilitate e-commerce by alleviating those concerns, but may also be seen to limit the flow of information and the effective consumer targeting that are likely to increase the volume of on-line transactions.

Exhibit 18–8
Internet host penetration
and secure server
penetration

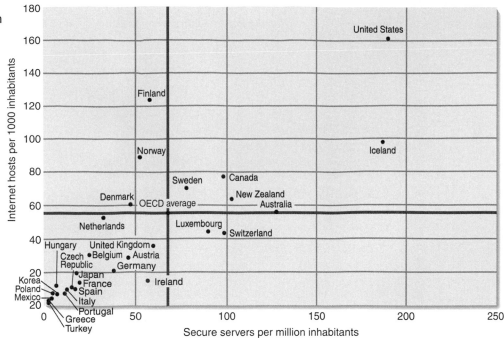

Note: Data on secure are from April 2000. Data on Internet hosts are from September 1999.
Source: OECD (www.oecd.org/dsti/sti/it/cm) based on Telcordia Technologies (www.netsizer.com)
and Netcraft (www.netcraft.com)

European laws give internet users more protection than do U.S. laws.[29] The European laws are based on "safe harbor" principles requiring that a company seek explicit agreement before transferring personal data to another company. Also, it gives the data subject reasonable access to personal data to review and possibly correct it. Data collection is permitted when (1) the subject has unambiguously given consent; (2) the data are needed to complete a contract, such as billing; (3) the data are required by law or needed to protect the subject's vital interests, or (4) the data are needed for law-enforcement purposes.

In 2000, the European Parliament ruled U.S. data privacy protection inadequate.[30] Under a tentative agreement negotiated by the U.S. Department of Commerce, U.S. firms can (1) subject themselves to the data-protection authority in one of the EU nations; (2) show that they are subject to similar U.S. privacy laws, such as those covering credit applications or videocassette rentals; (3) sign up with a self-regulatory organization, such as BBBOnline (Better Business Bureau), which provides an adequate level of privacy protection and is subject to oversight by the U.S. Federal Trade Commission; or (4) agree to refer privacy disputes to a panel of European regulators. When Citicorp entered the Bahn Credit Card project in 1993, it chose to adopt the strict German privacy laws. By complying with the German laws, Citicorp gained a large market share in this competitive market. In 1998, only 10 percent of the large American companies doing on-line business in Europe had complied with the EU standards on internet privacy.[31]

E-Business Climate

An **e-business climate** is composed of the institutional and regulatory frameworks that facilitate or hinder e-commerce. Credit card use is a critical ingredient in e-commerce. Use is low not only in developing nations such as China but also in

Exhibit 18–9

Global E-readiness among emerging economies 2000

	Country	Connectivity	E-Leadership	Information Security	Human Capital	E-Business Capital
The Americas	1. Argentina	A ↗	A	A	A	A
	2. Brazil	A	A ↗	A	A	R
	3. Chile	A ↗	A	A ↗	A	A
	4. Costa Rica	A	A ↗	R ↗	B	B
	5. Equador	R	R	R	R	R
	6. Mexico	R ↗	A	A ↗	A	A
	7. Peru	R	A ↗	A	R	A
	8. Venezuela	R ↗	R	R ↗	A	R
Asia/Pacific	9. China	R	A	R	A	A
	10. India	R	A ↗	A ↗	A	A
	11. Indonesia	R	R ↗	R	R ↗	R
	12. Malaysia	A ↗	B	A	A	A
	13. Pakistan	R	R ↗	R	R	R
	14. Philippines	R	R ↗	R ↗	A	R
	15. South Korea	A ↗	A ↗	A ↗	B	B
	16. Taiwan	A ↗	B	A ↗	B	B
	17. Thailand	R	A	R	R ↗	R
	18. Vietnam	R	R ↗	R	R	R
Europe	19. Bulgaria	R ↗	A	R	A	R
	20. Czech Republic	A ↗	A	A	A	R
	21. Estonia	A ↗	B	A	B	B
	22. Greece	A	R	A ↗	A	R
	23. Hungary	A ↗	A ↘	A	B	A
	24. Italy	A ↗	A	B	A ↗	A
	25. Latvia	R ↗	R ↗	A	A ↗	A
	26. Lithuania	A	A	A	A	A
	27. Poland	R	A	A	A ↗	A
	28. Portugal	A ↗	B	A ↗	A	A
	29. Romania	R	A	R	A	R
	30. Russia	R	R	R	A ↘	R
	31. Slovakia	A	R ↗	A ↗	A	R
	32. Slovenia	A ↗	A ↗	A	A	R
	33. Spain	A ↗	A ↗	A ↗	A ↗	A
	34. Turkey	A	A	R ↗	A ↗	A
	35. Ukraine	R	R	R	A ↘	R
Middle East / Africa	36. Egypt	R	A ↗	R	R	R
	37. Ghana	R	A	R	R	R
	38. Kenya	R	R	R	R	R
	39. Nigeria	R	R	R	R	R
	40. Saudi Arabia	R	R ↗	R ↗	R ↗	R
	41. South Africa	R ↗	A	A	R ↗	R
	42. Tanzania	R	R	R	R	R

LEGEND

↗ indicates improving relative to prior time periods

↘ indicates deterioration relative to prior time periods

A indicates improvement needed in the conditions necessary to support e-business and e-government

B indicates the majority of conditions are suitable to the conduct of e-business and e-government

R indicates substantial improvement needed in the conditions necessary to support e-business and e-government

Source: McConnell International, *EReadiness Report*

many developed countries. In some countries such as Japan, credit card processing fees are extremely high, deterring use of "plastic," which in other nations has the lowest transaction cost of any payment system. This creates a role for physical intermediaries; 7-Eleven uses its outlets in Japan to take payment and deliver products ordered over the internet. Like the Japanese, 80 percent of Germans do not have credit cards. Additionally, the reluctance to give credit card numbers over the internet has resulted in a small on-line market.[32]

National E-Readiness

Exhibit 18–9 compares emerging economies, on e-commerce readiness. **E-commerce readiness** is an index comprised of the three aforementioned criteria of connectivity, information security, and e-business climate, plus **e-leadership** (the extent to which e-commerce is a national priority) and **human capital** (the availability of human resources to support e-commerce). Wide variations are apparent. For instance, South Korea and Taiwan are among the most prepared economies, although, in general, Asian economies are hampered by data security problems.[33] Buoyed by inexpensive and widespread internet access, South Korea also enjoys strong government support in such realms as the acceptance of electronic signatures.

Another ranking, which includes both developed and developing economies, appears in *The Economist* (see Exhibit 18-10).

Exhibit 18–11 ranks countries by the ability of their technological infrastructure to support e-commerce. It is apparent that some of the low users today, such as Russia, have the technological capacity to eventually grow e-commerce substantially.

A recent survey of seven northern European cities found London and Copenhagen to be the best for e-business operations due to their labor availability and flexibility, foreign language proficiency, expatriate regulations, international and regional accessibility and office rental rates. Dublin, Ireland, received the lowest score.[34]

Interim Summary

1. A country's "e-readiness" is a product of many factors, among them internet connectivity and cost, information security, and privacy protection.

2. National "e-readiness" varies greatly and offers guidance in terms of the future growth of e-commerce in a particular country/region.

Exhibit 18–10
E-business readiness rankings

	Top ten		Bottom ten
1	United States	51	China
2	Sweden	52	Sri Lanka
3	Finland	53	Ecuador
4	Norway	54	Vietnam
5	Netherlands	55	Pakistan
6	Britain	56	Kazakhstan
7	Canada	57	Algeria
8	Singapore	58	Iran
9	Hong Kong	59	Nigeria
10	Switzerland	60	Iraq

Source: The Economist, June 10, 2000. 5.

Exhibit 18–11

Electronic commerce technological infrastructure

Number of hosts per 1000 people

Ranking		Number
1	USA	8.063
2	ICELAND	7.750
3	FINLAND	7.728
4	SINGAPORE	7.705
5	SWEDEN	7.653
6	AUSTRALIA	7.361
7	IRELAND	6.967
8	CANADA	6.918
9	NEW ZEALAND	6.786
10	NETHERLANDS	6.317
11	SWITZERLAND	6.306
12	TAIWAN	6.300
13	ISRAEL	6.275
14	RUSSIA	6.268
15	NORWAY	6.237
16	LUXEMBOURG	6.222
17	DENMARK	6.207
18	GERMANY	6.169
19	UNITED KINGDOM	6.162
20	KOREA	6.114
21	SLOVENIA	6.000
22	HONG KONG	5.917
23	AUSTRIA	5.695
24	SOUTH AFRICA	5.633
25	CHINA	5.533
26	BELGIUM	5.000
27	FRANCE	4.989
28	BRAZIL	4.979
29	HUNGARY	4.900
30	JAPAN	4.740
31	MALAYSIA	4.686
32	TURKEY	4.413
33	POLAND	4.400
34	PORTUGAL	4.370
35	ARGENTINA	4.311
36	CHILE	4.300
37	INDIA	4.025
38	INDONESIA	3.875
39	THAILAND	3.767
40	SPAIN	3.714
41	MEXICO	3.677
42	ITALY	3.647
43	GREECE	3.551
44	COLOMBIA	3.520
45	PHILIPPINES	3.509
46	CZECH REPUBLIC	3.362
47	VENEZUELA	2.810

Source: *The World Competitiveness Yearbook, 2000.*

CROSS-BORDER E-COMMERCE

Cross-border transactions already account for 25 percent of all e-commerce transactions by volume, and are predicted to grow to 54 percent or roughly $3.7 trillion by 2004. By various estimates, the ratio of e-commerce in international trade is poised to reach 10 percent to 25 percent by 2003.[35] Some small internet firms have already reached a level of globalization that would have been unthinkable a few years ago. U.K.-based The Internet Bookshop derives 80 percent of its sales from outside the United Kingdom.[36] Exhibit 18–12 shows the percentage of international traffic and transactions for a number of companies.

Exhibit 18–12
International on-line sales
for selected firms

Company	Industry	Primary Audience	Secondary Audience	International Business	
				Percentage of Traffic	Percentage of Transactions
Software net	Software	End customers	Suppliers	20%	30%
Wordsworth Books	Books	End customers	Publishers	25	25
CD Now	Music	End customers		20	20
Underground Music Archive	Music	End customers	Musicians	N/A	30
Zima	Liquor	End customers		6	N/A
CatalogSite	Catalogs	End customers	Catalog distributors	15	N/A
Individual Inc.	News service	Customers and subscribers	Advertisers, press employees	25	25
3M	Diverse business products	Business market end customers and distributors	Consumer market end customers	20	N/A
OnSale	Auction house	Buyers and sellers		20	20
Consulting Inc.	Consulting	Clients and job seekers	Partners and employees	20	N/A
American Venture Capital Exchange	Venture capital	Entrepreneurs and investors		5	3
Building Industry Exchange	Information	Buyers and suppliers		30	N/A

Source: J. A. Quelch and I. R. Klein, "The internet and international marketing", *Sloan Management Review*, Spring 1996, 60–75.

The President's report of July 1, 1997, describes the impact of the internet on global trade, especially in services:

> *Internet technology is having a profound effect on global trade in services. World trade involving computer software, entertainment products (motion pictures, videos, games, sound recordings), information services (databases, on-line newspapers), technical information, product licenses, financial services, and professional services (business and technical consulting, accounting, architectural design, legal advice, travel services, etc.) has grown rapidly in the past decade, now accounting for well over $40 billion of U.S. exports alone. An increasing share of these transactions now occurs on-line.*[37]

Web Site Categories

The advantages obtained from e-commerce's reach of international customers vary by audience focus and content. Exhibit 18–13 presents such variations. Quadrants

Exhibit 18–13
Categories of Web
sites

Web Site Content		
	Information Support/ Service Only	**Transactions**
Domestic	**1** • Apple Computer • Saturn • Reebok • CatalogSite	**2** • Software.net • Wordsworth Books • Mr. Upgrade • CD Now • Godiva Chocolates • LIGHTNING Instrumentation • Yvonne's Weinkabinett
Audience Focus **Global**	**3** • Building Industry Exchange • Federal Express • Sun Microsystems • ChinaWeb • Gateway to New Zealand • Digital Equipment Corp. • Eli Lilly & Co. • British Airways • Consulting Inc.	**4** • TRADE'ex • Underground Music Archive • American Venture Capital Exchange • Online BookStore • CapEx

Source: J. Quelch and L. Klein, "The Internet and International marketing," *Sloan Management Review,* Spring 1996, 60–75.

3 and 4 focus on international audiences. Quadrant 3 includes businesses in which reaching international audiences is the primary motivation for establishing a Web site and where international reach adds value. Quadrant 4 sites match buyers and sellers with global reach benefiting both parties.[38]

The Impact of e-Commerce on International Business

As a Forrester report suggests, "The Internet removes barriers to communication with customers and employees created by geography, time zones and location, creating a 'frictionless' business environment." However, for that to happen, barriers on both sides of the border need to be removed. For instance, the recent EU ruling that customers could sue non-EU retailers in their national courts could put a damper on the evolution of E-commerce there.[39]

Assuming that the internet and e-commerce create a "frictionless" environment and that their scope expands beyond their current minor share of international trade and investment, what would be the impact on international business? Quite possibly, the change could be far-reaching. Exhibit 18–14 shows the potential impact of "information and communication technology (ICT)," a somewhat broader class of phenomena than the internet and e-commerce, on MNE competitiveness according to de la Torre and Moxon. Among the possible changes are a fundamental change in the cost of market transactions versus internalization and change in location parameters.

Prospects for Large MNEs

For the larger MNE, the internet and e-commerce create an opportunity for rapid global dissemination of products but they also enable quicker imitation on the part of competitors. In theory, the internet creates pressure toward price parity, posing a

Exhibit 18–14
Potential impact of information and communications technology (ICT) on MNE competitiveness

Topic/ Construct	Elements Sensitive to ICT-Driven Transformation	Potential Direction of Change
Internalization advantages ■ market failure resulting in transacting costs which exceed coordination costs	■ search costs diminished ■ alternative sources of resources enlarged ■ increased value of intangible assets ■ lower coordination costs within network	Indeterminate since forces acting in different direction; drop in coordination costs may result in greater internalization and concentration simultaneous with more outsourcing
■ risk and uncertainty favors internalization ■ externalities, scope economies, etc.	■ market information easier to access and of higher quality ■ increased availability of alternative channels ■ greater resource availability and sources	Favors increases in outsourcing and market-based transactions Favors disintegration and market-based transactions
Locational advantages ■ differences in factor endowment and costs ■ transport costs and distance (physical and cultural)	■ information content of tasks more transferable ■ logistics, coordination and communications facilitated by ICTs	Favors greater dispersion of economic activities Fewer changes with respect to physical products; larger changes for intangibles
■ artificial barriers and market impediments	■ border controls increasingly difficult for digital products	Little change for physical products; large impact on digital products and content.
■ infrastructure and incentives	■ critical role of infrastructure and protection of intellectual property	The digital divide will favor locations with good infrastructure and IP protection
Ownership advantages ■ structural or asset-based, e.g., technology, trademarks, and other monopolistic advantages	■ digital piracy and greater availability of technical information shortens life cycles ■ increased permeability of borders to information ■ greater returns to scale	These effects would seem to enhance the relative power of MNEs and lead to greater concentration and integration in global industries
■ knowledge and organizational capabilities ■ political connections	■ virtual and internal communication networks expand capabilities ■ increased transparency and availability of political information	Increases the value of intangible assets and internal capabilities Should lead to a reduced advantage from "insider" positions or knowledge
The liability of foreignness ■ foreign firm faces higher operating costs due to lack of knowledge	■ increased availability of public and private information reduces liability of foreignness	Market integration and lower foreignness costs will lead to higher competitive advantage for MNEs

Source: de la Torre, J. and Moxon, R. W. *Introduction* to the Symposium E-Commerce & Global Business *Journal of International Business Studies,* 32, 4, 2001, 617–639.

problem for the MNE with different distributors charging different prices in different markets. There is evidence, however, that the internet may actually encourage collusion. Sony and Phillips were faced with legal problems in Germany when trying to stop on-line sales of Primus Online, offering less expensive Sony and Phillips' products.[40]

Exhibit 18–15 shows how the motivation to locate activities internationally might change under internet and e-commerce. Note that the traditional motivations have been discussed in Chapters 2 through 4. Among the potentially important impacts noted by Zaheer and Manrakhan are a reduction in transaction costs and improvement of monitoring and coordination by the MNE, and the ability to export human skills without incurring immigration and brain drain. Note also the differential impact on resource-, market-, efficiency- and capability-seekers, discussed earlier in this book. All in all, we are looking at the possibility of "virtual FDI," which could challenge basic assumptions about location decisions, among others.

Prospects for SMIEs

The reduction in barriers should, in theory, open doors to SMIEs especially from developing countries that have been shut out of international trade and investment. It should lower transaction costs for such firms and improve their international competitiveness.[41] Many SMIEs have taken advantage of the new opportunities. Small Latin American start-ups became SMIEs almost overnight, opening local offices in Spain, Portugal, Mexico, Hispanic U.S. and Latin America.[42] Latinexus is a Latin American electronic marketplace that aims to provide an even playing field for SMIEs by providing the same cost benefits and broad audiences available to blue chip firms.[43] Other SMIEs piggybacked on intermediaries such as Amazon or L.L. Bean to reach international customers.

For physical goods, however, barriers in the form of logistic challenges in dealing with multiple, dispersed customers remain significant for the smaller firm. There are suggestions that size and volume may matter even more in an e-commerce operation. The handling of a large and diverse number of customers may lie beyond the ability of many SMIEs that lack strategic and managerial capabilities. Shanghai Online Information Mailing (SOIM) is a Chinese start-up that serves local Chinese internet users. With its 400,000 subscribers, it provides its clients e-mails of e-zines, allowing them to read articles off the internet inexpensively. Phil Ren, founder of SOIM, acknowledges he does not know how to manage his workforce, or strategize for the growing Chinese market.[44] OECD data show that in most countries, internet penetration is substantially lower in smaller businesses, putting them at a disadvantage in B2B applications as well.[45]

Prospects for Intermediaries

Although it was initially believed that the internet would make intermediaries superfluous, the impact diverged. The number of intermediaries has indeed been reduced for digitalized products (e.g., software, music, movies, and certain educational and training programs) as well as services such as brokerage, retail, and auctions; however, intermediaries remained entrenched in other areas. Further, a new breed of value-adding intermediaries has emerged, no longer principally involved in the physical distribution of goods, but in the collection, collation, interpretation, and dissemination of vast amounts of information.[46] It has been estimated that intermediaries will account for more than a quarter of B2B transactions by 2002, and that the gross value of transactions completed by such "infomediaries" would exceed $200 billion in 2002.[47] One such intermediary is planetarySales.com, a division of SinoMetrics International, Inc. The company offers to deliver—from Web content to product delivery—in the target country language.

Exhibit 18–15

Motivations to locate
activities internationally:
Impact of remote
electronic access

	Traditional motivations for physical location in specific countries or markets	Fundamental assumptions on why physical co-location is necessary	How do assumptions change with remote electronic access?
Resource seekers	To acquire specific resources at lower real costs. Resources could include. ■ Physical resources ■ Labor ■ Technological capability, management skills, knowledge and intellectual capital	■ Immobility of resources ■ Cheaper to engage in FDI than import ■ Extractive type industries; preemptive lock-in ■ Capability cannot be acquired in market ■ Knowledge spillover and agglomeration effects are localized	■ Resources delivering digitized content can be remotely accessed (e.g., animation or graphic design labor) ■ Requires new forms of employment contracts and control mechanisms for remote telecommuters
Market Seekers	(1) Locate production and/or marketing to supply country or region, to: ■ Achieve sales growth, scale economies ■ Service global customers ■ Facilitate local adaptation, learning ■ Minimize production and transaction costs (2) Have a physical presence in leading markets served by competitors, for strategic blocking and knowledge spillovers	■ For locating downstream activities: Building customer relationships and servicing global customers requires physical co-location with them ■ For locating upstream activities: Access to markets restricted (e.g., tariff barriers), transportation costs, low scale economies ■ Strategic benefits and knowledge spillovers only derived from co-location	■ Customer relationships for simple products may be better built through digital channels (e.g., Amazon versus bricks and mortar bookstore), as may digitizable service elements, such as help desks ■ How local are knowledge spillovers? Tacit knowledge spillovers likely to remain localized, codified knowledge less so. Rate of knowledge spillovers likely to be higher in local rather than global arena
Efficiency Seekers	■ Rationalize structures to take advantage of differences across countries in cost of traditional or created factor endowments ■ Tends to take place in countries of broadly similar economic levels	■ Differential locational advantages (e.g., tax, performance incentives, labor market, living conditions) ■ Low coordination costs ■ Optimizing location portfolio ■ Cross-border markets are well developed and open ■ Knowledge spillover effects	■ Physical and regulatory locational advantages cannot be remotely accessed. ■ Coordination costs lower ■ More opportunities to optimize location portfolio (e.g., global relay strategies) ■ Extent of regulation of internet commerce? ■ Again, how local are knowledge spillovers?
Strategic Asset or Capability Seekers	■ Aim to capitalize on the benefits of common ownership of diversified activities/capabilities	■ Arise from market imperfections in asset markets in which the MNE operates	■ Information as a strategic asset ■ Will asset/capability markets become less susceptible to market failure?

Source: Zaheer, S. and Manrakhan, S., "Concentration and dispersion in global industries: Remote electronic access and the location of economic activities." *Journal of International Business Studies,* 32, 4, 2001, 667–686.

Other Impacts

E-commerce's impact extends to other realms. For example, it has made it more difficult to determine the origin of a product or a service, with concomitant implications for customs, tariffs, and taxation. This is because the server, the manufacturer, and the physical distributor may be located in different countries (see also section on Taxation). E-commerce should also accelerate the mobility of people as a production factor. Jobs in back-office and customer service are likely to shift to lower-cost countries, especially where language is no obstacle (e.g., from the United States to Canada, Ireland, and India). For instance, Washington-based Talisma Corporation outsources customer service functions to Bangalore, India, where an abundance of highly educated workers can be found at a fraction of the U.S. cost.[48]

Interim Summary

1. Cross-border e-commerce has the capability to reduce but not eliminate friction in international business transactions.

2. Although e-commerce opens new opportunities for SMIEs, many lack the resources to capitalize on its promise.

3. Cross-border e-commerce can alter the location decisions of MNEs.

GLOBAL E-COMMERCE CHALLENGES

Entering into global e-commerce is not easy. Dominant portals such as AOL found that penetrating Germany, the United Kingdom, and other European markets is difficult. In a departure from past patterns of MNE entry, AOL found that domestic competition on the part of European newcomers flared up almost immediately. Exhibit 18–16 shows Amazon's rank among retailers in a number of countries.

As in other realms of international business, finding the right balance between globalization and localization has proven difficult. The next section illustrates how.

Standardization Forces

Many consumers from other nations reach into U.S. sites. This is true for Canadians, who do 63 percent of their Canadian $3 billion on-line shopping on U.S. Web sites (although many resent buying from a U.S. firm and seem to shift purchases to Canadian e-sellers where possible).[49] (Canadian sites, on their part, have been quite successful in selling pharmaceuticals to U.S. citizens.) Latin Americans prefer to use

Exhibit 18–16
Amazon.com's market rankings worldwide

Country	Rank	Visitors (thousands)
Australia	1	461
Brazil	3	93
Canada	1	1,225
Denmark	4	69
France	3	70
Germany	5/1*	555/2,074
Japan	5	697
U.K.	2/1*	993/1,746
U.S.	1	14,499

*URL's Amazon.co.uk and Amazon.de
Source: The Wall Street Journal, 15, 2001, B10.

Exhibit 18–17

Language used on internet web pages. (1999)

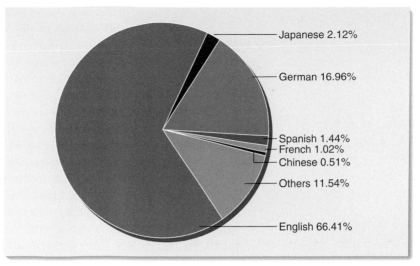

Source: Building Confidence, Electronic Commerce and Development. United Nations Conference on Trade and Development, 2000.

U.S. e-commerce sites over those developed in their own countries because of trust, convenience, and lower prices.[50] Yahoo found out that its U.S. site posted more traffic from China than its Chinese site.[51] Although this trend is expected to continue for some time, there is strong evidence of increasing diversity.[52]

Standardization at times appears appealing. The position of English as a lingua franca has been considerably strengthened on the internet, supported by the prevalence of English as a second language and by the dominance of U.S.-hosted Web sites. (See Exhibit 18–17.) While only half of internet users are native English speakers, 78 percent of all Web sites and 96 percent of e-commerce sites are in English.[53] However, as noted earlier, there are already predictions that other languages, primarily Chinese, will soon take over as the most popular internet language.

Localization Challenges

As with other international business activities, the risks of neglecting customization are substantial. Many U.S. firms underestimated the customization they would need to undertake in e-trading with foreign markets, whether tangible (tax, currencies, tariffs) or intangible (culture, buying habits).

Web Site Localization

Despite the promise of "instant globalization," MNEs engaged in internet and e-commerce soon discover the "liability of foreignness." AOL has struggled behind local providers in the Latin American market, although it has been closing the gap as of late. Still, AOL is not the primary provider in any of the many Latin American markets it serves.[54] E-Bay had to withdraw from the potentially lucrative Japanese market, admitting such missteps as emphasizing collectibles rather than new goods in the belief that the Japanese market would mirror the development of the U.S. site. It did not.[55] Still, e-Bay has been growing its international presence rapidly, with 2001 revenues of $115 million, up from $34 million in 2000.[56]

Cultural "faux pas" are common. A British consulting firm used snapshots of colorful liquorish candy to symbolize "miscellaneous," which was widely recognized in England but not in the United States, where a small yellow folder icon has been commonly used.[57] Auction house e-Bay posted prices in dollars on its British site. Language blunders are also common. "Getgift.com" may make sense in the United States but its Swedish translation is "go get poison for goats." When U.S. sites use

American spelling for words such as *favorite*, *behavior*, *theater*, *liter*, and so on, some British consumers perceive these as misspellings.

A key response to localization pressures has been to establish local Web sites. It is here that internet and e-commerce companies make a difference for MNEs—they need not establish physical premises in order to have local presence. Yahoo! has 21 international on-line properties in 12 languages, including localized English versions in Asia, Australia and New Zealand, Brazil, Canada, China, Denmark, France, Germany, Hong Kong, Italy, Japan, Korea, Mexico, Norway, Singapore, Spain, Sweden, Japan, the United Kingdom, and Ireland. It also has guides in Spanish and Chinese. As far back as 1997, Sony had 13 country-specific sites. UPS offers its services around the globe in multiple languages. Reebok has done the same after tracking its Web traffic.[58] A recent study shows the target countries for localized Web sites for a sample of U.S. internet firms (see Exhibit 18–18). The study found that firms with localized Web sites abroad were distinctly different from those that did not. Among other differences, those with localized Web sites had higher revenues, higher media visibility, wider global reach, and more alliances.[59]

The need for customization goes beyond language, however, to include local content, cultural awareness, and design. Exhibit 18–19 shows that most leading U.S. Web sites ignore the need for localization despite the many "hits" from other countries.

Some vendors have taken pains to localize their Web sites. Ikea, the Swedish furniture maker, designs its sites with an eye to national tastes. Its Italian site is stylish,

Exhibit 18–18
Target countries for foreign Web sites by U.S. internet companies (March 2000)

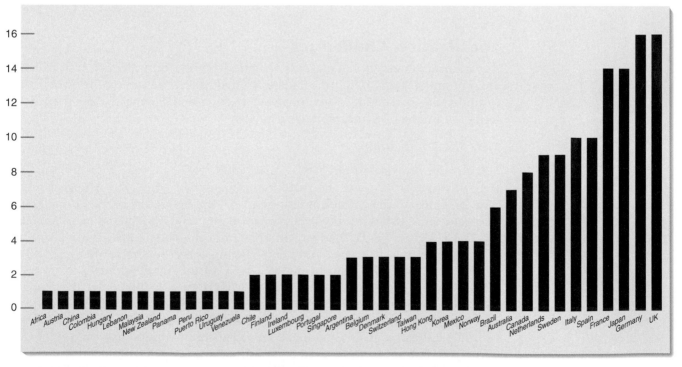

Source: S. Koth, V. R. Rindova, and F. T. Rotharmel. "Asset and actions: Firm-specific factors in internationalization of U.S. Internet firms, *Journal of International Business Studies, 32, 4, 769-791.*

Exhibit 18–19
Customization of leading
U.S. Web sites (2000)

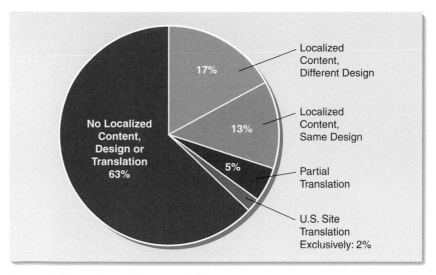

Source: Wall Street Journal, January 15, 2001, B10.

the German site is more traditional, and the Saudi Arabian site shows a reassuring family shopping scene. For its Danish site, the firm substituted red and white for its customary blue and yellow (the Swedish flag colors).[60] McDonald's adds pink and brown to its trademark red and gold on its Japanese Web sites. E-tailers such as Amazon established European operations with local partners who have helped them with the necessary customization. Yahoo! did the same in Japan.[61] Others have turned to specialists for help in tailoring their sites and sales practices to foreign nations. E-commerce globalization and customization has become a $47 billion a year consulting industry. A number of start-ups promise to help firms, especially SMEs, in customizing their internet ware. Thinkamerican.com assists small U.S. apparel brands to sell in Japan. In addition to language translation, the company translates sites into Japanese while watching for cultural errors. It also aims to cut costs by consolidating the shipments of multiple small vendors.[62] Yet, according to Forrester Research, just 37 percent of Fortune 100 companies have tailored their sites to different world markets.[63]

Logistics

Logistics represent a key area where many companies have failed to make the necessary adjustments in terms of global e-commerce in general or in terms of customizing the system to deal with the requirements in a given country. A Forrester study suggested:

> *Eighty five percent of the companies noted that they could not fill overseas orders because of the complexity of shipping across borders. Of those that had problems shipping overseas, 75 percent cited their system's inability to register international addresses accurately (one European customer had his on-line order rejected because he could not fill the "state" section on the U.S. order form[64]) or to price total delivery cost.[65]*

Taxation Issues

A recent study argued that if on-line taxes were in effect, internet sales would have been 25 to 30 percent lower.[66] In the United States, the Supreme Court ruled that states could not require an out-of-state company to collect a sales tax on goods coming into the state unless the company had a physical presence or "nexus" within that state. Some states suggested that local internet service providers should be considered the agents of electronic retailers and be subject to local taxation.[67] In 1998, Congress passed the Internet Tax Freedom Act, allowing policymakers to debate a permanent arrangement while establishing a three-year ban on new internet taxes (which has since been extended). A recent poll showed 73 percent of active internet users were opposed to an internet sales tax, and more than a third of registered voters who are active internet users would be less likely to vote for a political candidate who supports taxes on internet transactions.[68]

In the international arena, the implications of e-commerce taxation are more ominous. While cross-border catalog sales existed for many years, they have not been substantial enough to generate a strong interest among governments. E-commerce has changed that.[69] In the EU, value added taxes (VAT) ranging from 15 to 25 percent—representing a key portion of government revenues—are at risk. In itself, a Web site is not considered a fixed place of business that would trigger taxation but it could be considered as such in conjunction with server location and other company operations in that country. However, Web and server locations as well as other components of e-commerce operations are increasingly difficult to pinpoint. Furthermore, e-commerce makes it increasingly easy for MNEs to shift their domicile to low-tax locations and to offshore tax havens as it becomes difficult if not impossible for other nations to claim physical presence of the company in their territory. Problems such as transfer pricing become much more acute in this environment.

The internet raises many other taxation issues. For instance, the traditional distinction between income and royalty taxation may be impossible to determine when a consumer downloads software from a vendor.[70] Individual income tax may be largely avoided in countries with a territorial tax base, whereas the few countries with a global taxation base, such as the United States, may find it increasingly difficult to enforce their tax legislation.

To the MNE as well as the SMIE, e-commerce taxation represents a significant challenge. In Chapter 15, we discussed the tax strategies employed by MNEs, including tax havens, tax treaties, and the creation of a holding or a finance corporation. Global e-commerce creates additional strategic opportunities, such as placing servers in low-tax jurisdictions. However, it also creates additional risks: for instance, most tax treaties do not refer to e-commerce activities, and they may be open to challenge.

INDUSTRY BOX

TAXING DIGITIZED PRODUCTS

Digitized products that are downloaded by users are often singled out as being most open to jurisdictional and enforcement challenges. Although this is true, it is worthwhile to remember that "digitizable" products represent on average less than 1 percent of tariff revenue (although substantially higher in developed economies) and merely 0.06 percent of total tax revenue globally. The problem is potentially much more serious for services. It is estimated that the share of value added amenable to e-commerce represents 30 percent of GDP in service sectors.[72]

In the spring of 2002, the European Union bowed to pressure from its e-commerce firms, which, unlike their U.S. or Asian counterparts, pay a national sales tax on their sales, and decided to tax digitized or "downloadable" products. According to the new ruling, a non-EU provider will have to register in one of the EU 15 nations and pay taxes in that country (which will then be distributed to the countries in which the buyer resides). The move was widely perceived to be aimed at the competitive edge of U.S. firms.

Source: "EU set to tax downloadable products." The Wall Street Journal, May 7, 2002, A3; R. Perez-Esteve and L. Schuknect, "A quantitative assessment of electronic commerce." Geneva, Mimeographed, p. 11.

Interim Summary

1. The localization challenge in global e-commerce entails customization of Web sites as well as of the supply chain and distribution network.

2. Country-of-origin is especially difficult to determine in global e-commerce transactions. Both MNEs and SMIEs have to deal with the challenges and opportunities posed by this reality in taxation as well as in other realms.

CHAPTER SUMMARY

1. The proportion of cross-border transactions as a percentage of total e-commerce transactions continues to grow.

2. E-commerce could change some of the fundamental assumptions pertaining to trade and foreign investment, although it is too early to determine whether, for instance, it will "even the playing field" between the SMIE and the large MNE.

3. E-commerce is unlikely to terminate the role of global intermediaries but it is likely to divert their strategic positioning, often in the direction of knowledge analysis and dissemination. For instance, with their role as ticket issuers eliminated, travel agencies will need to focus on advice, niche or wholesale activities.

4. As in other international business realms, international e-commerce requires a balance of globalization and localization. While customers in some countries are logging onto U.S. sites, U.S. firms, like other international firms, take pains to localize their Web site in terms of language, culture, currency units, and so forth.

5. Taxation is looming large as an obstacle to the promise of free flow of goods and services on which e-commerce thrives. In the global arena, taxation could affect the competitiveness of U.S. purveyors.

6. MNEs must take account of the repercussions of global e-commerce in such realms as competitive advantage, location decisions and taxation.

CHAPTER NOTES

[1] J. A. Quelch, and L. R. Klein, "The internet and international marketing," *Sloan Management Review,* Spring 1996, 60–75.

[2] A. LaPlante, *Computerworld* online, October 1997.

[3] "E-commerce bonanza for African firms," *African Business,* October 1999, 54–55.

[4] S. Young, "Tech giants brew hefty B2B venture," *USA Today,* Money: Section B, May 30, 2000.

[5] ITU 1999 "Challenges to the network: Internet for development," cited in *Building Confidence* p. 74.

[6] State of the Internet 2000, International Technology Trade Associates, September 1, 2000.

[7] State of the Internet, 2000, International Technology Trade Associates, Sept. 1, 2000.

[8] Taylor, Nelson Sofres, Global e-commerce report, 2002.

[9] Taylor, Nelson Sofres, Global e-commerce report, 2002.

[10] Media Metrix, quoted in the *Wall Street Journal,* November 13, 2000, B14.

[11] C. Ling, "E-commerce in Asia shows efficiencies," *Wall Street Journal,* December 5, 2000, A10.

[12] State of the Internet, 2000, International Technology Trade Associates, Sept. 1, 2000.

[13] Taylor, Nelson Sofres, Global e-commerce report, 2002.

[14] Forrester Research, "Sizing global online exports," November 2000; Forrester Research, "Global online trade will climb to 18% of sales," December 26, 2001.

[15] "Electronic E-commerce in Japan is held back by retail traditions," *Wall Street Journal,* March 30, 2000.

[16] Taylor, Nelson Sofres, Global e-commerce report, 2002.

[17] State of the Internet, 2000, International Technology Trade Associates, Sept. 1, 2000.

[18] State of the Internet, 2000, International Technology Trade Associates, Sept. 1, 2000.

[19] "Net shopping: Why Japan won't take the plunge," *Business Week,* July 31, 2000.

[20] McCall International, "Risk E-business: Seizing the opportunity of global e-readiness," August 2000.

[21] *Computer Industry Almanac,* cited in *Wall Street Journal,* September 25, 2000.

[22] "Survey of the new economy," *The Economist,* September 23, 2000, 38.

[23] Building confidence: Electronic commerce and development, UNCTAD, 2000.

[24] United National Conference on Trade and Development, Policy issues relating to participation in electronic commerce, September 17, 1998.

[25] "China's tangled web: Will Beijing ruin the Net by trying to control it?" *BusinessWeek.*

[26] G. Fan, "Pedicarts link Shanghai's streets to the Internet," *The New York Times,* March 29, 2000.

[27] Taylor, Nelson Sofres, Global e-commerce report, 2002.

[28] S. Lawson, "RSA optimistic about encryption business in China," IDG News Service, Feb. 25, 2000.

[29] B. Mitchener and D. Wessel, "U.S. in tentative pact protecting Europeans' privacy," *Wall Street Journal,* February 24, 2000 B11;

"EU rejects U.S. data privacy protection as inadequate. CCN online July 7, 2000, 10:53 a.m. EDT.

[30] E. Bony, "EU rejects U.S. data privacy protection as inadequate," www.cnn.com, July 7, 2000.

[31] L. Didio, European Union directive: It's no joke. www.computerworld.com, 1998.

[32] S. McGrane, "3 Brothers, 4 months, 1 fortune in an early success in Germany," *The New York Times*, September 22, 1999.

[33] McConnell International Global E-Readiness Summary, August 2002.

[34] *Financial Times.com* February 2, 2001.

[35] Building confidence: Electronic commerce and development. UNCTAD, 2000.

[36] K. Essick, "Bookshop hits Web walls," *Computerworld*, October 6, 1997, 1.

[37] The White House, Office of the Press Secretary, Text of the President's message to Internet Users, July 1, 1997, 1.

[38] J. A. Quelch, and L. R. Klein, "The internet and international marketing," *Sloan Management Review*, Spring 1996, 60–75.

[39] B. Mitchener, "EU approves law that some fear will hurt e-tailing," *Wall Street Journal*, December 1, 2000, A12.

[40] N. E. Boudette, Germany's Primus Online faces legal challenge. *Wall Street Journal*, January 6, 2000, A17.

[41] Building confidence: Electronic commerce and development. UNCTAD, 2000.

[42] P. Druckerman, "Latin American Web concerns fight to stay in business," *Wall Street Journal*, October 9, 2000, A20.

[43] "Latin firms build online marketplace for business in major e-commerce push," *Wall Street Journal*, July 14, 2000.

[44] *BusinessWeek*, 1999. Big brother and E-revolution. October 4, 132.

[45] OECD, cited in *The Economist*, November 11, 2000.

[46] J. A. Quelch and L. R. Klein, "The internet and international marketing," *Sloan Management Review*, Spring 1996, 60–75.

[47] Business 2.0, September 99, cited in *Building Confidence*.

[48] *Wall Street Journal*, November 21, 2000, A1.

[49] R. Ricklefs, "U.S. E-tailors expand efforts north of the border," *Wall Street Journal*, January 31, 2000, A21.

[50] E. Rasmusson, "Targeting Global E-customers," *Sales & Marketing Management*, 2000, 78.

[51] K. L. Stout, "Yahoo! Asia top exec calls it quits," CNN.com February 19, 2001, 7:15 A.M.

[52] State of the Internet, 2000, International Technology Trade Associates, Sept. 1, 2000.

[53] State of the Internet, 2000, International Technology Trade Associates, Sept. 1, 2000.

[54] J. Karp, "AOL hangs tough in the dicey Latin market," *Wall Street Journal*, September 5, 2001, A22.

[55] N. Wingfield, "E-Bay, admitting missteps, will close its site in Japan," *Wall Street Journal*, February 27, 2002. B4.

[56] N. Wingfield, and C. Ling, "Unbowed by its failure in Japan, eBay will try its hand in China," *Wall Street Journal*, March 18, 2002, B1.

[57] E. F. Sheridan, and G. F. Simons, www.webofculture.com

[58] S. Kalin, "The importance of being multiculturally correct," *Computerworld*, October 6, 1997.

[59] S. Koth, V. R. Rindova, and F. T. Rothaermel, "Assets and actions: Firm specific factors in the internationalization of U.S. internet firms," *Journal of International Business Studies*, 32, 4, 769–791.

[60] B. Giussani, Europe's Internet lag: An American fabrication? *New York Times*, September 14, 1999.

[61] R. A. Guth, "Yahoo! Japan learns from parent's achievements, errors," *Wall Street Journal*, December 11, 2000, A28.

[62] L. Vickery, "Cultural portal could translate way to profit," *Wall Street Journal*, February 12, 2001, B6.

[63] B. Vivkers, "Firms give global Web businesses local appeal," *Wall Street Journal*, December 4, 2000, B17A.

[64] E. Rasmusson, "E-commerce around the world," *Sales & Marketing Management*, 1999, 94.

[65] Forrester Research, "Mastering E-Commerce Logistics," 1999. Cited in *Building Confidence*, 50.

[66] *The Economist*, "Globalization and tax: The mystery of the vanishing taxpayer," January 29, pp. 1–22.

[67] R. R. Burk, "Do you see what I see? The future of virtual shopping," *Journal of the Academy of Marketing Science*, 25, 4, 1997, 352–360.

[68] J. Clausing, "Internet tax panel faces thorny issues," *New York Times*, September 15, 1999.

[69] R. Dorenberg, and L. Hinnekens, *Electronic Commerce and International Taxation*. The Hague: Kluwer Law International, 1999.

[70] Dorenberg and Hinnekens, *Electronic Commerce and International Taxation*. The Hague: Kluwer Law International, 1999.

Ethics and Corruption in The Global Marketplace

DO YOU KNOW

1. **What are the main elements of the MNE code of conduct? How would you react if the only way to close a deal would involve violation of your company's code?**

2. **What characteristics of a nation can predispose it to corruption?**

3. **What are some of the drawbacks to corruption?**

4. **What are the most common corrupt practices in international business?**

OPENING CASE **Shell Group**

Shell Energy operates in 130 countries. The Shell Group often faced demands for "facilitation payments" from junior officials or for bribes from senior officials. It also faced the specter of criminal activity in procurement and contracting, such as in the North Sea. Shell has a clear anti-corruption policy specified in its Statement of General Business Principles. It does not sanction giving or receiving any type of bribe or illegal payment; an employee who is found to have done so is instantly fired and, if possible, prosecuted. Donations to political parties are prohibited even where legal and above board. Gifts of more than token value, received or given, must be declared.

To ensure enforcement, Shell companies are subject to internal and external audits, with the accounting system used to spot discrepancies between customer payments and vendor receipts. Any instances of fraud in, or against, a Shell company are reported to the Group Audit Committee, made up of external directors. Every CEO in a wholly- or majority-owned Group company must sign an annual "letter of representation," confirming that all accounts are accurate and that "neither the company nor its representatives has been party to the offering, paying, or receiving of bribes." It specifies that no payment made has knowingly violated the laws of the country of operation.

Shell believes that while in the short term, the no-bribe policy may place its companies at a competitive disadvantage, it is a sound long-term investment. "When a reputation for clean dealing gets around, the demands for bribes begin to disappear," say Shell officials who note that Shell's employees are no longer cited for bogus traffic offenses as a way to extract money. Other firms take a different approach. Shell's competitor BP admitted that it has been paying "facilitating payments" (recorded as "petty disbursements"), arguing they were necessary to safeguard competitiveness. Shell had its share of ethical challenges, however. The company was severely criticized for its attempt to dump an oil rig in the North Sea.[1] ■

ETHICS AND CORRUPTION IN INTERNATIONAL BUSINESS

The MNE (as well as the SMIE) is expected to conduct its business ethically. **Ethical behavior** implies not only following the rule of law but also attending to the values, norms, and concerns of the home and host environments. It also implies taking a proactive approach in identifying, preempting, and responding to ethical challenges. For instance, when the Ford Motor Company started production of its Transit vehicles in a joint venture in Nancheng, China, it donated the first vehicles to schools in the province of Jiangxi.[2]

Although ethical issues are not unique to international business, some ethical challenges are typical to or more common in international than in domestic business. Among such challenges are dealing with diverse legal and moral contexts, different expectations from corporate players, and the need to accommodate diverse and often conflicting values and norms under the same corporate umbrella. Nike and Wal-Mart triggered an outcry among U.S. watch groups regarding the employment environment provided by their Asian suppliers even though conditions there were arguably comparable or better than those common in those countries.

To deal with these and other ethical challenges, the OECD developed guidelines for MNEs that specify disclosure, employment practices, competition, the environment, and consumer interests, among others *(see the appendix to this chapter.)* The guidelines emphasize the need for the MNE to be a good citizen in the countries in which it operates. They "encourage the positive contributions that MNEs can make to economic, environmental and social progress and (are designed) to minimize the difficulties to which their various operations may give rise." Such guidelines are not binding, however, nor are they uniform. The International Chamber of Commerce estimates that there are more than 40 codes of conduct worldwide, including the UN-issued Global Compact signed by more than 180 nations.[3]

While ethical issues have been on the radar screen of MNEs for many years, corruption was often an issue not talked about. For almost three decades, the United States was virtually the only country to criminalize bribe paying when doing business abroad. Other countries looked the other way, viewing corruption as a necessary if unpleasant part of international business. Many nations treated corruption outside their national borders differently than at home, condoning the use of corrupt practices abroad while banning them at home. Drawing the line at one's borders is increasingly tenuous, however. As *The Economist* noted, "companies have learned the hard way that they live in a CNN world, in which bad behavior in one country can be seized on by local campaigners and beamed on the evening news to customers back home." As we will see later in this chapter, distinguishing between corruption at home and abroad is also becoming legally difficult.

Definition and Magnitude of Corruption

"Corruption often defies precise definition."[4] Most of the definitions of corruption view it as the illegitimate exchange of power into material remuneration mostly on the part of office holders who take advantage of their position to grant underserving favors. Not all corruption violates the law. Some corrupt activities merely defy "accepted norms" or "customs."[5] In this chapter, we will use the following definition of **corruption:**

> *An exchange between two partners (the "demander" and the "supplier" which (a) has an influence on the allocation of resources either immediately or in the future; and (b) involves the use or abuse of public or collective responsibility for private ends.[6]*

By definition, corruption is difficult to measure. Most nations do not gauge corruption, and companies are reluctant to provide information on activity that is by and large considered unethical if not illegal, and may seek to protect their government counterparts and prevent backlash. Nevertheless, estimates of corrupt activities and their economic impact are available. *The Economist* puts the "shadow" or "underground" economy at $9 trillion.[7] Even in some developed economies (e.g., Italy and Belgium) underground economic activity represents a quarter of GDP.[8] According to Stuart Eizenstat, undersecretary for Economic, Business, & Agricultural Affairs in the Clinton administration, in 1996 alone U.S. firms lost $30 billion worth of international contracts to firms whose countries did not adopt anti-corruption legislation.

Some industries are especially prone to corruption. The European Court of Auditors estimates that member states wasted $1.2 billion on fraudulent infrastructure projects.[9] Between May 1994 and April 1998, 239 international contracts totaling U.S.$108 billion were influenced by bribes. About half of those contracts involved military procurement; the others involved aerospace, communications, infrastructure, energy, and transportation.[10] It is estimated that leading exporters, especially in the arms and construction industries, traditionally pay upward of 10 percent to a senior official to win a contract.[11] The U.S. government cites a case in which a European aircraft maker offered agent commissions of 20 percent or more in an Asian market if its product was chosen.[12]

The Origins of Corruption

A number of conditions tend to increase the probability of corruption: First, developing and transitional economies are more prone to corruption, partly because of the lack of an adequate legal framework and weak enforcement. Hybrid or transitional economies are especially susceptible because their institutions tend to lag behind the reality of fast economic and social change. A study by Shleifer and Vishny shows that while in the Communist systems officials extorted small bribes, in the hybrid Russian systems they extort much larger sums because they have no concerns about other bribe takers.[13] One reason for the preponderance of bribe paying in hybrid and developing economies is the inadequate legal framework and the lack of open and independent media. There are other reasons, however. According to Transparency International (TI) data, factors supporting corruption include low public sector pay, immunity of public officials, secrecy in government, and media restrictions. Privatization, financial liberalization, and increase in FDI and trade—all factors associated with a transition economy—also play a role.[14] A second predictor of corruption is high level and scope of government involvement in and regulation of economic activity especially where public official pay is low and corruption is viewed as legitimate remuneration. Nigeria represents such an example. Finally, lack of transparency (e.g., public disclosure of financial information), more common in developing and hybrid economies but also evident in some developed economies (e.g., Italy), is associated with higher corruption levels.

Undersecretary Eizenstat identified eight key elements of reform in the anti-corruption fight: economic policy (including deregulation), transparency (including streamlining administrative processes affecting trade and investment), public sector/civil service reform (including downsizing bureaucracy and establishing a merit system), public finance (including accounting, auditing, and procurement reform), judicial (including independence and enforcement), commercial law (including regulation of securities, intellectual property, and the like), civil society, and law enforcement.

Culture is a predictor of corruption level; for instance, it was found to correlate with receptivity toward questionable accounting principles.[15] Uncertainty avoidance and masculinity were correlated with unethical decision making.[16] Husted formed a "cultural profile" of a corrupt country, high on uncertainty avoidance, masculinity, and power distance. Corruption is associated with high uncertainty avoidance because corruption is an uncertainty reduction mechanism. Masculinity creates corruption potential because it implies preference for material things. Power distance is associated with paternalism, a system where a superior grants favors to subordinates in return for loyalty, permitting arbitrary judgment and hence corruption.[17]

Drawbacks of Corruption

Ninety percent of the Asian executives surveyed by the *Far Eastern Economic Review* said that corruption slowed progress.[18] Corruption obstructs firm growth and development through the imposition of risk, the punishment suffered by violator firms, the damage to a firm's reputation, and the financial cost incurred in direct payments as well as in indirect costs. From an economic perspective, corruption causes misallocation of capital, diverting resources from constructive activities such as innovation and technological development. It also produces incomplete, distorted, and undisclosed information, allowing one party to take advantage of another, which undermines cooperation and potential synergies between partners. The damage is especially pronounced in emerging economies, where internal funds often constitute the single most important capital resource, discouraging legitimate investment. A recent headline in the *Wall Street Journal* read "Pakistani stocks surge since military takeover amid hopes less corruption will lift economy."[19]

Corruption undermines trade and FDI, depriving the host countries the benefits associated with trade and investment. Further, the prospect of obtaining personal benefits may lead officials to oppose trade liberalization. Foreign investors, on their part, may be reluctant to invest in an economy known for its corrupt practices.[20] Cited about his company's exit from Bulgaria, a Unilever official said in 1997:

> It was impossible for us to do business without getting involved in corruption. So we took the logical step and accepted the consequences. That meant packing our bags.[21]

Shang-jin Wei calculates that an increase in the level of corruption from the Singaporean to the Mexican level would be tantamount to an increase of more than 20 percent in the tax burden on foreign investment.[22]

Corruption Rankings

Established in 1993 by a former World Bank official, Transparency International (TI) publishes the **Corruption Perception Index (CPI),** a broad measure of corruption that is calculated from multiple survey responses. Exhibit 19–1 provides the 2002 scores for 102 countries for which data are available. TI notes that 70 of the 102 countries listed score below 5, out of a clean score of 10, showing the magnitude of the problem. The least corrupt countries, topped by a number of Scandinavian nations as well as New Zealand and Singapore, are mostly rich economies. Nigeria is among a group of countries where corruption is rampant. Exhibit 19–2 contains a warning by the Bank of Nigeria regarding a global fraud scam originating in the country.

Indonesia also ranks high on the corruption index. *The Economist* recently carried the story of Teten Masduki, a leader in fighting corruption in Indonesia.[23] According to Mr. Masduki, while wages accounted for 10 percent of company overhead in Indonesia, "invisible costs" often accounted for 30 percent of overhead. There are indications that the new Indonesian government is moving against corruption, but it remains to be seen how successful its efforts will be.

Exhibit 19-1

2002 Corruption Perceptions Index (CPI) rankings

Rank	Country	CPI 2002 score[a]	Rank	Country	CPI 2002 score[a]
1	Finland	9.7	52	Czech Republic	3.7
2	Denmark	9.5		Latvia	3.7
	New Zealand	9.5		Morocco	3.7
4	Iceland	9.4		Slovak Republic	3.7
5	Singapore	9.3		Sri Lanka	3.7
	Sweden	9.3	57	Colombia	3.6
7	Canada	9.0		Mexico	3.6
	Luxembourg	9.0	59	China	3.5
	Netherlands	9.0		Dominican Rep.	3.5
10	United Kingdom	8.7		Ethiopia	3.5
11	Australia	8.6	62	Egypt	3.4
12	Norway	8.5		El Salvador	3.4
	Switzerland	8.5	64	Thailand	3.2
14	Hong Kong	8.2		Turkey	3.2
15	Austria	7.8	66	Senegal	3.1
16	USA	7.7	67	Panama	3.0
17	Chile	7.5	68	Malawi	2.9
18	Germany	7.3		Uzbekistan	2.9
	Israel	7.3	70	Argentina	2.8
20	Belgium	7.1	71	Cote d'Ivoire (Ivory Coast)	2.7
	Japan	7.1		Honduras	2.7
	Spain	7.1		India	2.7
23	Ireland	6.9		Russia	2.7
24	Botswana	6.4		Tanzania	2.7
25	France	6.3		Zimbabwe	2.7
	Portugal	6.3	77	Pakistan	2.6
27	Slovenia	6.0		Philippines	2.6
28	Namibia	5.7		Romania	2.6
29	Estonia	5.6		Zambia	2.6
	Taiwan	5.6	81	Albania	2.5
31	Italy	5.2		Guatemala	2.5
32	Uruguay	5.1		Nicaragua	2.5
33	Hungary	4.9		Venezuela	2.5
	Malaysia	4.9	85	Georgia	2.4
	Trinidad & Tobago	4.9		Ukraine	2.4
36	Belarus	4.8		Vietnam	2.4
	Lithuania	4.8	88	Kazakhstan	2.3
	South Africa	4.8	89	Bolivia	2.2
	Tunisia	4.8		Cameroon	2.2
40	Costa Rica	4.5		Ecuador	2.2
	Jordan	4.5		Haiti	2.2
	Mauritius	4.5	93	Moldova	2.1
	South Korea	4.5		Uganda	2.1
44	Greece	4.2	95	Azerbaijan	2.0
45	Brazil	4.0	96	Indonesia	1.9
	Bulgaria	4.0		Kenya	1.9
	Jamaica	4.0	98	Angola	1.7
	Peru	4.0		Madagascar	1.7
	Poland	4.0		Paraguay	1.7
50	Ghana	3.9	101	Nigeria	1.6
51	Croatia	3.8	102	Bangladesh	1.2

[a]**CPI 2002 Score** relates to perceptions of the degree of corruption as seen by business people and risk analysts, and ranges between 10 (highly clean) and 0 (highly corrupt).
Source: Transparency International.

Exhibit 19–2
Fraud warning from the
Central Bank of Nigeria

CENTRAL BANK OF NIGERIA

PRESS STATEMENT ON ADVANCE FEE FRAUD/SCAM

DON'T BE FOOLED! MANY HAVE LOST MONEY!!
IF IT SOUNDS TOO GOOD TO BE TRUE THEN IT IS NOT TRUE!!!

1 The publicity campaigns by the Central Bank of Nigeria (CBN) and the Government of the Federal Republic of Nigeria have proved successful in sensitising the public about the menace of advance fee fraud and the falsehood of claims that easy money could be made in Nigeria. Consequently, the reported incidence of advance fee fraud (A.K.A. '419'), has declined significantly. Nevertheless, there are still some people who have continued to fall victim to the solicitations of advance fee fraudsters. This warning is, therefore, specifically intended for the benefit of those misguided people who, in the quest to make easy money at the expense of Nigeria, are defrauded by international fraudsters.

2 The advance fee fraud is perpetrated by enticing the victim with a bogus 'business' proposal which promises millions of US dollars as a reward. The scam letter usually promises to transfer huge amounts of money, usually in US dollars, purported to be part proceeds of certain contracts, to the addressee's bank account, to be shared in some proportion between the parties. A favourable response to the letter is followed by excuses why the funds cannot be remitted readily and subsequently by demands for proportionate sharing of payments for various 'taxes' and 'fees' supposedly to facilitate the processing and remittance of the alleged funds. The use of 'fake' Government, Central Bank of Nigeria. Nigerian National Petroleum Corporation, etc. documents is a common practice.

3 The fraudsters usually request that the transaction be done under the cover of confidentiality. Sometimes, the 'victims' are invited to Nigeria where they are given red-carpet reception and attended to by the fraudsters, posing as Nigerian Government officials. Quite often the fraudsters invent bogus Government committees purported to have cleared the payments. Also, it is not unusual for them to contrive fake publications in the newspapers evidencing purported approvals to transfer non-existent funds.

4 To consummate the transaction, the 'victim' would be required to pay 'advance fees' for various purposes: e.g. processing fees, unforeseen taxes, licence fees, registration fees, signing/legal fees, fees for National Economic Recovery Fund, VAT, audit fees, insurance coverage fees, etc. The collection of these 'advance fees' is actually the real objective of the scam!

5 A recent variant of the scam directed primarily at charitable organisations and religious bodies overseas involves bogus inheritance under a will. Again the sole aim is to collect the 'advance fees' already described above. A new strategy that has also been used to defraud the 'victims' is an offer to use chemicals to transform ordinary paper into United States dollar bills, which would be subsequently shared by the parties.

6 You are again warned in your own interest not to become yet another dupe to these fraudulent solicitations or schemes. Genuine and prospective investors in Nigeria are advised to consult their home Chambers' of Commerce and Industry, or Nigeria's Chambers' of Commerce and Industry, Manufacturers' Associations of Nigeria. Federal Ministries of Commerce and Industry, Nigerian Missions in their countries of origin, their embassies or High Commissions in Nigeria for proper briefing and advice.

7 The Central Bank and indeed, the Federal Government of Nigeria cannot and should not be held responsible for bogus and shady deals transacted with criminal intentions. As a responsible corporate body, the Central Bank of Nigeria is once again warning all recipients of fraudulent letters on bogus deals, that there are no contract payments trapped in the bank's vaults. They are once again put on notice that all documents appertaining to the payment, claims, or transfers purportedly issued by the bank, its senior executives or the Government of the Federal Republic of Nigeria for the various purposes described above are all forgeries, bogus and fraudulent.

8 Please join the Central Bank and the Federal Government of Nigeria to fight the criminal syndicates who play on the gullibility and greed of their victims by reporting any solicitation to your local law enforcement agencies or the local International Police Organisation (Interpol).

9 You have been warned several times before! You have been warned again!!

CENTRAL BANK OF NIGERIA
Samuel Ladoke Akintola Way, P.M.B. 0187, Garki, Abuja, NIGERIA

In rankings of the "shadow" economy, Nigeria again ranks very high, followed by Thailand, Egypt, the Philippines, Mexico, Russia, and Malaysia. Among developed nations, Italy, Spain, and Belgium have the highest ratio of underground economic activity.[24] The World Competitiveness Yearbook (2000) ranks Argentina, Russia, China, and Colombia (in that order) as nations where the "parallel" market seriously impairs the economy.[25] As in other instances, it is useful to be aware of internal variations within countries. For instance, *The Economist* ranks Chechnya, Dagestan, and Primorsky as having the highest level of corruption in Russia. The Samara region has the lowest.[26]

Interim Summary

1. Modern MNEs are expected to operate their business in an ethical manner in both their host and home countries. To facilitate this, the OECD produced a broad set of guidelines that encourage MNEs to be good citizens.

2. On an international scale it is difficult to clearly define what constitutes corrupt business practices. The primary difficulty involved is differing cultural understandings related to these issues and the coinciding laws and norms under which various societies operate.

3. Corruption slows progress. In addition to misallocation of capital resources for the paying of bribes, corrupt countries create an artificial, usually ossified, economic atmosphere that makes firms less capable of competing in open, international markets.

TYPES OF CORRUPT PRACTICES

International business corruption takes many forms: a request from an exporter to pay a fee to "expedite" custom clearance, a "consultant fee" demanded from a foreign investor by government officials involved in project approval, a bid awarded to regulators and their proxies. Common forms of corruption in international business are listed below.

Smuggling

Smuggling is the illegal trade and transportation of goods devised to circumvent custom duties, quotas, and other constraints on the movement of goods (e.g., safety transportation requirements that may add to cost at destination). Smuggling diminishes national control over trade policies. It damages legitimate importers that find themselves in competition with same or similar products sold at a lower cost, as well as the manufacturer whose reputation is tarnished by the sale of inferior imitations and/or inability to serve products that are not under genuine warranty.

Smuggling is especially likely to occur in economies sharing a contiguous border with substantial differences in the availability and cost of goods. A case in point: the Hong Kong border with southern China where local Mainland authorities often collude with the smugglers. In the past, this was a conduit for the smuggling of stolen cars into the Mainland (easily detected, because the steering wheel is on the right side). Nowadays, the flow consists more of counterfeit products into Hong Kong. (Since 1997, Hong Kong has been a Special Administrative Region of China but it continues to be a separate entity for trade and customs purposes.)

Cigarettes have been especially appealing to smugglers throughout the world due to high taxes and tariffs and the relative ease of transportation. The Canadian government recently alleged that cigarette makers have been exporting their Canada made cigarettes to the United States only to have them smuggled back into Canada

Brand name luxury goods are often subject to counterfeiting.

to avoid high taxes. The manufacturers, mostly affiliates of U.S. firms, deny any involvement but acknowledge the rampant smuggling of the product.[27]

Particularly appealing to smugglers are contraband goods such as drugs, liquor, and guns (where prohibited) because of the lack of competition from legitimate means of importation. Smuggling also occurs in products that seem difficult to ship and conceal, such as steel (see Chapter 2). Steel smuggling involves falsifying shipping documents to conceal the product source or its classification. There are about 100 nations that import steel to the United States, and because there are almost 1,000 different types of steel—two variables that determine the tariff level—there is substantial incentive to smuggle the metal and it is difficult for the U.S. Customs Service to monitor it.[28]

The smuggling of illegal immigrants has become especially lucrative. Driven by hardship at home and the prospect for a better life elsewhere, individuals are often lured into paying exorbitant sums to organized gangs with the promise of entry into a developed country, most notably the United States and the EU. It is estimated that almost half a million illegal immigrants are smuggled into the EU annually, whereas 300,000 make their way into the United States.[29]

Money Laundering

Money laundering involves concealing the source of ill-gotten funds by channeling them into legitimate business activities and bank deposits in other countries. Although not new, the phenomenon has been growing rapidly, partially because of a burgeoning drug trade and privatization in the former Soviet Union and other emerging economies. While it is impossible to accurately measure the extent of the problem, some estimates have put it as high as 5 percent of global GDP. The flow has been aided by electronic payment systems that made possible the transfer of huge sums of money at a lightning speed. The chairman of the Bank of New York acknowledged that the bank's recent money-laundering lapse was the result of a

"global payments system that put priority on speed rather than knowing whether the electronic money transfers are legal."[30]

The G-7 Financial Action Task Force listed 15 countries as centers for money laundering. The list includes the Bahamas, the Cayman Islands, Panama, Dominica, St Kitts and Nevis, St. Vincent and the Grenadines, the Cook Islands, the Marshall Islands, Nauru, Niue, Israel, Lebanon, Liechtenstein, Russia, and the Philippines. The task force is threatening retaliation if the countries involved do not clean up their act. The pressure is bearing fruit, with some governments (e.g., Dominica and Liechtenstein) tightening anti-money-laundering rules, and others (e.g., the Marshall Islands and the Philippines) voicing commitment to act.[31] The events of September 11, 2001 have drawn much more attention to money laundering as a vehicle in international terrorism, triggering much closer scrutiny of the phenomenon.

Piracy and Counterfeiting

Counterfeiting and piracy account for 5 to 7 percent of world trade, or $200 to $300 billion in lost revenues.[32] Counterfeiting and piracy are not the same. **Piracy** means using illegal and unauthorized means to obtain goods, such as copying software (see the Industry Box). **Counterfeiting** goes a step beyond, attempting to pass the copied product as an original, such as producing and selling a fake Gucci bag or a Rolex watch. Both phenomena have been growing rapidly and represent a substantial threat to the original manufacturers. In piracy, the most significant threat is probably in intellectual property, such as computer software, music, and videos.

The growth in piracy of such goods is explained by industry growth and the globalization of intellectual property products. For instance, the global appeal of new movies increases demand for bootlegged versions often released before the original (see Exhibit 19–3). Technological advances make pirating easier: the price of disk production machinery declined precipitously in recent years, facilitating a cottage industry of pirated disks in China, Vietnam, and other countries.

Counterfeit goods include not only videos and designer watches and handbags but, alarmingly, pharmaceuticals and aircraft spare parts. Counterfeit services can also be found in the form of unauthorized providers of automotive services, which put up the manufacturer's logo as a way to entice unsuspecting customers.

Exhibit 19–3
Example of movie piracy

Quick on the Draw

Despite Touchstone Pictures' best attempts at keeping its blockbuster under wraps, the pirated version of **Pearl Harbor** arrived in many Asian markets even before the official release.

PREMIERE		BOOTLEGS
June 21	**Hong Kong**	May 28
June 21	**Malaysia**	May 28
June 22	**Taiwan**	mid-May
August	**Sri Lanka**	May 31
December	**Pakistan**	June 1

Source: Time, June 11, 2001, p. 35.

INDUSTRY BOX

PIRACY IN THE GLOBAL SOFTWARE INDUSTRY

According to the Business Software Alliance, in 2000 the global piracy rate in software was 37 percent, amounting to $11.8 billion in losses. The Alliance calculates piracy rates on the basis of personal computer shipments, comparing projected to actual software sales. Computer software is a prime piracy target owing to cost, availability, ease of copying, and lax attitudes on the part of many foreign governments.

Asia is the leader in pirated software, with a 51 percent rate. Although software piracy has generally been on the decline, the figures for Asia represent an increase over 1999. Piracy rates were down for Malaysia from 71 to 66 percent, and the Philippines declined from 70 to 61 percent, probably as a result of aggressive government efforts.[42]

The top offenders and software piracy rates are presented below.

	1999	2000		1999	2000
Vietnam	98%	97%	Nicaragua	80%	78%
China	91%	94%	Oman	88%	78%
Indonesia	85%	89%	Bulgaria	80%	78%
Ukraine/Other CIS	90%	89%	Romania	81%	77%
Russia	89%	88%	Guatemala	80%	77%
Lebanon	88%	83%	Paraguay	83%	76%
Pakistan	83%	83%	Jordan	75%	71%
Bolivia	85%	81%	Honduras	75%	68%
Qatar	80%	81%	Costa Rica	71%	68%
Bahrain	82%	80%	Dominican Republic	72%	68%
Kuwait	81%	80%	Kenya	67%	67%
Thailand	81%	79%	Nigeria	68%	67%
El Salvador	83%	79%			

Source: International Planning and Research Corp.

Bribe Paying

Bribery, which often appears under such euphemisms as "fees," "commissions," "gratuities," and "sweeteners," is a perennial form of corruption in international business. Investigations by the Securities and Exchange Commission (SEC) during the 1970s found that more than 400 U.S. companies made questionable payments totaling more than $300 million to foreign government officials, politicians, and political parties. Between mid-1994 and mid-1996, U.S. firms lost 36 of 139 contracts, valued at $11 billion, to bribery.[33] Swiss authorities recently froze $100 million held by the government of Kazakhstan, allegedly used by American and European oil firms to bribe Kazakh officials in order to gain favorable exploration and use rights.[34]

TI publishes a Bribe Payers Index (BPI) that ranks countries according to the willingness to offer and pay bribes. The BPI ranks 21 countries on the propensity of their MNEs to pay bribes, or the "supply side of bribery." (See Exhibit 19–4.) The higher the score, the lower the propensity. Thus, MNEs from Australia, Sweden, and Switzerland are least likely to use bribery in foreign markets, while those from Russia and China are most likely to bribe. The United States scores a relatively modest 5.3, despite the Foreign Corrupt Practices Act, which is covered immediately after this

Exhibit 19–4
The Transparency
International Bribe Payers
Index 2002

Rank		Score	Rank		Score
1	Australia	8.5	12	France	5.5
2	Sweden	8.4	13	United States	5.3
	Switzerland	8.4		Japan	5.3
4	Austria	8.2	15	Malaysia	4.3
5	Canada	8.1		Hong Kong	4.3
6	Netherlands	7.8	17	Italy	4.1
	Belgium	7.8	18	South Korea	3.9
8	United Kingdom	6.9	19	Taiwan	3.8
9	Singapore	6.3	20	People's Republic of China	3.5
	Germany	6.3	21	Russia	3.2
11	Spain	5.8		*Domestic companies*	1.9

Source: Transparency International.

section. The survey shows that bribes are more likely to be solicited and accepted in the public-works, construction, and arms and defense industries, and least likely to occur in agriculture, fishery, and light industry.

China, with the second lowest score, is a good illustration of the costs, patterns, and underlying reasons for bribe paying. A 1993 internal report of the Chinese government estimated the state lost about U.S.$50 billion over the preceding decade from undervaluation of privatized assets by officials in return for payoffs. In the same year, Hong Kong's Independent Commission against Corruption estimated that gifts and bribes add 3 to 5 percent to operating costs in China.[35] The same commission also found in a survey of 50 Hong Kong companies doing business on the Mainland that 35 admitted paying bribes, such as the purchase of "inspection certificates" necessary for the exportation of goods[36] (see Country Box).

Bribe paying is also widespread in the former Soviet republics. Exhibit 19–5 shows the level of bribery in former Soviet republics in Asia and their annual cost.

Exhibit 19–5
"Hands under the table"
in the former Soviet
republics

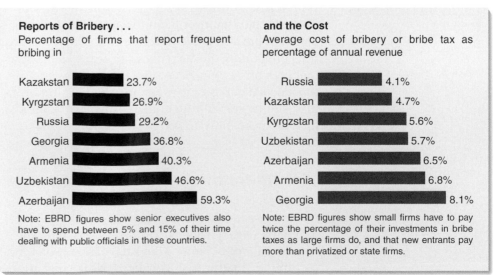

Reports of Bribery . . .
Percentage of firms that report frequent bribing in

Kazakstan 23.7%
Kyrgzstan 26.9%
Russia 29.2%
Georgia 36.8%
Armenia 40.3%
Uzbekistan 46.6%
Azerbaijan 59.3%

Note: EBRD figures show senior executives also have to spend between 5% and 15% of their time dealing with public officials in these countries.

and the Cost
Average cost of bribery or bribe tax as percentage of annual revenue

Russia 4.1%
Kazakstan 4.7%
Kyrgzstan 5.6%
Uzbekistan 5.7%
Azerbaijan 6.5%
Armenia 6.8%
Georgia 8.1%

Note: EBRD figures show small firms have to pay twice the percentage of their investments in bribe taxes as large firms do, and that new entrants pay more than privatized or state firms.

Source: European Bank for Reconstruction and Development cited in the *Wall Street Journal*, July 5, 2000.

The Foreign Corrupt Practices Act (FCPA)

The origin of the FCPA can be traced to the 1970s, when press reports alleged U.S. firms made questionable payments to foreign government officials. Payments were disbursed through hidden "slush funds" and financial records were often falsified to conceal them. The congressional investigations that ensued culminated in the enactment of the FCPA that was further amended in 1988. The FCPA criminalized the payment of bribes and other forms of special payment to foreign officials for the purpose of securing or retaining a deal (liability exists whether the deal has been consummated or not). It also required issuers of securities to meet accounting, record-keeping, and corporate control standards. Criminal and civil enforcement of the anti-bribery provisions with respect to domestic concerns is the responsibility of the Justice Department. The Securities and Exchange Commission (SEC) is responsible for civil enforcement of the anti-bribery provisions with respect to issuers.

Under the FCPA, the term "officials of a foreign government" includes executives in state-owned firms, foreign political parties, or candidates for office. A payment may be "in kind," such as a gratuitous trip. "Facilitating payments" made within the context of routine government operation (e.g., obtaining permits, issuance of license, providing utilities) are permissible under the Act's 1988 amendment, but must be reported on the company's financial statement. Bona fide payments (e.g., for necessary travel) that are legal in the host country, and are made for the purpose of product promotion or as part of contractual obligations, are also allowed under the 1988 amendment.

Subject to the FCPA are not only U.S. firms but also wholly owned U.S. subsidiaries and other U.S. entities controlled by foreign corporations, including their directors, employees, and agents. Actions taken abroad by U.S. citizens, nationals, or residents are covered under the FCPA even if conducted for a foreign corporation. The FCPA also prohibits indirect foreign payments, which can be interpreted as covering the foreign subsidiaries of U.S. corporations as well. However, it is not clear if the percentage of ownership in the subsidiary has a bearing on FCPA liability and if an international joint venture between a U.S. and a local company in a foreign country creates liability on the part of the local partner. This is an important question because firms often delegate functions with corruption potential (e.g., dealing with local government authorities) to their local partners. The FCPA also covers payment by intermediaries but requires proof that the U.S. MNE knew about the practice. It also prohibits payments to a third party with the knowledge that the payment will end up in the hands of a foreign official.

Violations of the FCPA can result in fines of up to $2 million to firms and $100,000 plus imprisonment for up to five years for individuals. Both firms and individuals are also liable to a civil fine if they violate the anti-bribery provisions. In suits brought by the SEC, fines can reach as much as $500,000. Under federal criminal laws other than FCPA, individuals may be fined up to $250,000 or up to twice the amount of the gain or loss incurred. A firm or individual who violates the FCPA may also be barred from doing business with the U.S. government. Other sanctions include ineligibility to receive export licenses and being barred from the securities business.

The Globalization of the Fight Against Corruption

Immediately following the passage of the FCPA, the United States tried to expand it to other nations. The efforts were initially unsuccessful, but since then many governments (e.g., Thailand, Zimbabwe, Poland, and China's Special Administrative Region, or SAR of Hong Kong) have established independent commissions against corruption. In the NAFTA-created NADBank, the United States successfully won agreement from its NAFTA partner Mexico in 1996, to require companies to certify that they have not engaged in bribery of foreign or domestic officials in projects funded by the bank. Companies must also have corporate policies that prohibit bribery and assert that they have not been convicted of bribery within five years of certification otherwise they will be barred from future participation in a NADBank funded or guaranteed project.

The OECD Convention

In 1994, the United States sponsored the 1994 OECD Recommendation on Bribery in International Business Transactions that called on member states to take "concrete and meaningful steps" to deter, prevent, and combat bribery of foreign public officials. In 1999, the OECD adopted the Combating Bribery of Foreign Officials in International Business Act (CBFOIB). The Act is substantially modeled after the U.S. FCPA. It makes the payment of bribes to elected or appointed foreign officials a criminal offense and abolishes its tax deductibility. The Act requires that sanctions against foreign corruption be comparable to those against public officials domestically. It also requires coordination in matters of jurisdiction, a key issue given the global nature of the phenomenon as well as coordination in legal matters (including extradition). Effective accounting and measures against money laundering are also set. As of October 1999, 18 of the 34 signatory nations, including the United States, had ratified the act. However, it is too early to determine if the pact will have the effect of curbing corruption in overseas business transactions among the 34 signatory nations even with the threat of country audits to follow.[37] Further, a TI survey shows that many businesspeople are not familiar with the Convention.

The 52-member Commonwealth has come forth in support of the OECD efforts to contain international business corruption, and on March 1996, 23 of the 34 member states of the Organization of the American States (OAS) signed the Inter-American Convention against Corruption. The treaty requires each signatory country to make bribery of foreign officials a crime and an extraditable offense. Signatories must update their domestic legislation to criminalize a set of specific corrupt acts related to bribery and illicitly obtained benefits. Cooperation among signatories is strengthened on extradition, mutual legal assistance, and asset forfeiture for corruption-related crimes.

By the end of 1998, 25 countries had signed the convention: Argentina, the Bahamas, Bolivia, Brazil, Chile, Colombia, Costa Rica, Dominican Republic, Ecuador, El Salvador, Guatemala, Guyana, Haiti, Honduras, Jamaica, Mexico, Nicaragua, Panama, Paraguay, Peru, Suriname, Trinidad and Tobago, the United States, Uruguay, and Venezuela. Ten countries have deposited their instruments of ratification with the OAS: Argentina, Bolivia, Costa Rica, Ecuador, Honduras, Mexico, Paraguay, Peru, Trinidad and Tobago, and Venezuela.

International Organizations' Anti-Corruption Efforts

International organizations also have been increasing their anti-corruption activities. In 1996, the board of the World Bank required that all commissions paid to agents be disclosed, giving the board the right to audit contractors and suppliers, and strengthened provisions for cancellation of bribe-tainted contracts and for debarment of violators from contracting. Anti-bribery amendments have been added to the Bank's loan conditions and procurement rules, and standard bidding documents were approved. The amendments require disclosure of commissions and gratuities paid or to be paid to agents relating to their bids or to contract execution on World Bank-financed contracts. The Bank will reject proposals for contract award or cancel the loan if the bidder or the borrower has engaged in fraud or corruption in the procurement or execution of the contract. Companies determined by the Bank to have engaged in corrupt or fraudulent practice will be blacklisted from participation in Bank-financed contracts, either indefinitely or for a stated period of time.

The International Monetary Fund has taken similar steps. The Council of Securities Regulators of the Americas (COSRA) adopted an anti-bribery resolution to ensure enforcement of and compliance with internal control and accurate books and records requirements. COSRA also agreed to facilitate closer cooperation among securities and banking regulators in investigations and in criminal prosecutions for bribery. In the WTO, the 1977 Government Procurement Agreement (GPA), while voluntary, assists in the anti-corruption drive although the signatories are predominantly industrialized countries, including the United States, Canada, the EU member states, Israel, Japan, Norway, the Republic of Korea, and Switzerland.

The United States introduced a proposal for a Declaration on Corruption and Bribery in Transnational Commercial Activities at the July 1996 session of the UN Economic and Social Council, which calls on member states to criminalize bribery (domestic or transnational) and prohibit tax deductibility of bribes. The United States also played a role in the development of the Model Procurement Law of the United Nations Commission on International Trade Law (UNCITRAL). The law is designed to promote transparency and objectivity in public procurement proceedings; it specifically requires the rejection of a tender, proposal, offer, or quotation if it is accompanied by a bribe from a supplier or contractor.

The Changing Tax Treatment of Bribe Paying

Under U.S. tax law, payments made to a foreign government official that are unlawful under the FCPA cannot be deducted as a business expense. However, in Germany, Greece, Luxembourg, Belgium, and France foreign bribe payments were tax deductible in whole or part. From a trade perspective, this amounted to an export subsidy. The OECD convention does not cover the tax deductibility of bribery although there exists a 1996 OECD recommendation to do so. As of 1999, Denmark, Norway, and Portugal completed the relevant legislative action, and 9 of 10 other countries have begun a legislative process to disallow the tax deductibility of bribes.

Exhibit 19–6 shows the changing tax treatment of bribes in OECD member countries.

Interim Summary

1. Corruption in international business appears in many forms. Although bribery may be the first corrupt practice that comes to mind, it is by no means the only one. Smuggling, for instance, is a means of increasing profit margin even on legitimate goods by avoiding customs duties, tariffs, import quotas, and any other constraints on the movement of goods. Liquor, guns, and cigarettes are particularly attractive to smugglers.

2. Money laundering is a corrupt practice that is receiving much greater scrutiny since 9/11.

3. Piracy of goods, especially intellectual property, and counterfeiting of everything from luxury clothing to aircraft parts and pharmaceuticals is also common, especially in developing economies.

4. The FCPA, passed in the 1970s, made it illegal for U.S. companies to bribe foreign officials. However, this fight against corruption did not become truly global and did not see ratification into international treaties until very recently.

Exhibit 19–6
Tax treatment of bribes in
OECD member countries
(as of July 30, 1999)

OECD Member countries that did not allow the tax deductibility of bribes to Foreign Public Officials before the 1996 OECD Recommendation and continue to deny such deductibility are: Canada, the Czech Republic, Finland, Greece, Hungary, Ireland, Italy, Japan, South Korea, Mexico, Poland, Spain, Turkey, the United Kingdom, and the United States.

OECD member countries that have repealed the Tax Deductibility of Bribes to Foreign Public Officials since the 1996 OECD Recommendation

Austria	According to legislation passed in late October 1998, bribes paid to foreign public officials are generally no longer deductible for income tax purposes.
Belgium	A bill aiming at the criminalization of bribes to foreign public officials and at denying the deductibility of so-called "secret commissions" paid in order to obtain or to maintain government markets or licenses has been adopted by the Senate on 9 July 1998 and by the House of Representatives on 4 February 1999. It entered into force on 3 April 1999.
Denmark	The Danish Parliament has adopted a bill from government denying the deductibility of bribes to foreign public officials. The new legislation entered into force on 1 January 1998.
France	The French Parliament passed legislation denying the tax deductibility of bribes to foreign public officials on 29 December 1997 as part of the Corrective Finance Bill for 1997.
Germany	With the entry into force of the OECD Convention, German income tax law will automatically exclude deductibility of bribes to foreign public officials as business expenses.
Iceland	Legislation was passed in June 1998 to deny the deductibility of bribes to foreign as well as domestic public officials and officials of international organizations.
Netherlands	A new law entered into force as of 1 January 1997 that denies the deductibility of expenses in connection with illicit activities if a criminal court has ruled that a criminal offense has been committed (Dutch criminal law will be amended in the near future to ensure that bribery of foreign public officials is a criminal offense).
Norway	Legislation was passed by the Norwegian Parliament on 10 December 1996 to disallow the deductions for bribes paid to foreign private persons or public officials.
Portugal	The Parliament has adopted on 20 December 1997 legislation effective from 1 January 1998 to disallow any deduction referring to illegal payments such as bribes to foreign public officials.

Update concerning the remaining OECD Member countries where legislation to deny Deductibility of Bribes to Foreign Public Officials has not yet passed

Australia	The legislation to criminalize the payment of bribes to foreign public officials recently received royal assent. The legislation to end the tax deductability of bribes was introduced into Parliament in June 1999 and was to be considered in August 1999.
Luxembourg	The Minister of Justice and Budget has prepared draft legislation that would criminalize bribes to foreign public officials as well as deny their tax deductibility.
New Zealand	Legislation was being prepared to disallow deductions for bribes paid to foreign public officials. The bill was presented to Parliament on 25 March 1999.
Sweden	A bill explicitly denying the deductibility of bribes and other illicit payments was passed by the Swedish Parliament. It came into force on 1 July 1999.
Switzerland	A proposal to deny deductibility of bribes has been elaborated. The Federal Council has approved this proposal in October 1997. The proposal was submitted in the spring of 1998 to cantons, political parties and other interested groups for consultation. The results of the consultations and the revised proposal should be discussed by the Parliament.

Source: OECD.

COUNTRY BOX — China

COUNTERFEITING AND PIRACY IN CHINA

The People's Republic of China is considered by many to be the world leader in counterfeiting and piracy. China's own Development and Research Center values the fake goods in the Chinese market in 1998 at more than $16 billion. Two out of five foreign MNEs in the country are losing more than 20 percent of their revenue to counterfeiters, which for a company like Procter & Gamble amounts to $150 million annually. Altogether, foreign MNEs lose almost $1 billion in sales annually. No product is safe: "They fake everything, from Rolls-Royce windshields to lemonade whipped up in top-loading washing machines," says the managing director for South China of Pinkerton, a security firm.[38] Almost 7 of the 11 million motorcycles sold in China annually are knock-offs of Japanese designs.[39]

Over the last few years, Chinese piracy levels have been relatively stable or showing a slight decline; however, counterfeiting has been soaring. According to some estimates, counterfeit goods now account for 15 to 20 percent of total sales in that country, with 90 percent of the products in some local markets being counterfeits. Large distribution centers coordinate the production and sale of counterfeit goods. Counterfeit goods are also exported from China to Southeast Asia, Africa, and Europe.[40] Large quantities of counterfeit items originating in China have been seized by U.S. customs, most recently in Honolulu.

Chinese firms have also been known to tinker with trademarks and brand-name goods by slightly altering their appearance. A Chinese manufacturer of knock-off motorcycles has registered in Japan Chinese brand names for "Nihon Honda" and "Nihon Suzuki." A Chinese beverage maker sells mineral water under its own brand name but in bottles that are a virtual replication of Perrier's. Another sells breakfast cereal in a box that looks marginally different from that of Kellogg's. Hong Kong-based Crocodile Garments has a crocodile for a logo, a take on the original Lacoste's alligator.

The table below shows counterfeiting trends in China across industrial categories. Some products, not listed in this exhibit, are especially hard hit. For instance, the level of piracy in motion picture, music and computer programs exceeds 90 percent, with annual damages approaching $2 billion.[41] Unfortunately, the problem is progressively worsening over time.

Industrial category	Improved	Unchanged	Worse	Much worse
Food manufacturing	14.29%	23.81%	40.47%	21.43%
Clothing, textiles, shoes	12.5%	18.75%	43.75%	25.0%
Daily-use products	0.0%	11.76%	41.18%	47.06%
Agricultural machinery	20.0%	0.0%	60.0%	20.0%
Transportation equipment	28.57%	0.0%	28.57%	42.86%
Ordinary machinery	0.0%	0.0%	31.35%	68.75%
Electric and electronics	13.04%	17.39%	39.13%	30.44%
Others	0.0%	30.77%	64.71%	11.76%
Overall	9.79%	16.08%	42.66%	31.47%

Note: Values shown are percentage of companies in each industrial category.
Source: From PRC State Council Research and Development Center, cited in D.C.K. Chow, *A Primer on Foreign Investment Enterprises and Protection of Intellectual Property in China.* The Hague: Kluwer, 2002.

CHAPTER SUMMARY

1. The MNE Code of Conduct defines the contours of ethical behavior in international business realms such as disclosure, employment, the environment, and corruption.

2. Corruption is correlated with developing or emerging status of an economy, higher level and scope of government intervention, and certain cultural dimensions.

3. Corruption is a serious impediment to economic development, trade, and FDI.

4. Corrupt practices in international business include smuggling, money laundering, piracy and counterfeiting, and bribe paying.

5. The Foreign Corrupt Practices Act (FCPA) penalizes U.S. firms and individuals who engage in corrupt practices.

6. The OECD Convention, once ratified, and if enforced, will level the playing field for U.S. firms that until recently were the only ones to be legally deterred from corrupt practices by their home country.

CHAPTER NOTES

[1] "Doing well by doing good," *The Economist*, April 22, 2000, 65; K. de Segundo, "Fight corruption," *Executive Excellence*, November 1998, 9–10; J. Mason, "Petty corruption set to move up agenda for multinationals," *Financial Times*, January 11, 2001, 13.

[2] Ford Motor Company press release, 1997.

[3] S. A. Aaronaon, "Corporate codes of conduct in an era of globalization," *Japan Economic Currents*, 9, June 2001, 3–4.

[4] A. J. Heidenheimer, M. Johnston and V. T. LeVine, *Political Corruption: A Handbook*. New Brunswick, NJ. Transaction Publishers, 1987.

[5] R. Kahana, *Corruption in Israeli Society*. Jerusalem: Academon, 1984.

[6] J. Macrae, 1982, 678, cited in Husted, B. W., "Wealth, culture and corruption," *Journal of International Business Studies*, 30, 2, 1999, 340.

[7] "Black hole," *The Economist*, August 28, 1999, 59, citing a study by Friedrich Schneider.

[8] "The termite hunter," *The Economist*, October 16, 1999, 72.

[9] "Crime, corruption and multinational business," *International Business*, July 1995.

[10] G. R. Simpson, "Bribes taint contract bids overseas often," *Wall Street Journal*, February 23, 1999, A3.

[11] J. Mason, "Petty corruption set to move up agenda for multinationals," *Financial Times*, January 11, 2001, 13.

[12] "U.S. government report on transnational bribery," *National Export Strategy Report*, September 24, 1996.

[13] A. Schleifer, and R. Vishny, "Corruption," *Quarterly Journal of Economics*, Autumn, 1993.

[14] Transparency International Web site, September 1999.

[15] J. R. Cohen, L. W. Pant, and D. J. Sharp, "A methodological note on cross-cultural accounting ethics research," *International Journal of Accounting*, 31, 1, 1996, 55–66.

[16] S. J. Vittell, S. L. Nwachukwo, and J. H. Barnes, "The effects of culture on ethical decision-making: An application of Hofstede's typology," *Journal of Business Ethics*, 12, 1993, 753–760.

[17] B. W. Husted, "Wealth, culture and corruption," *Journal of International Business Studies*, 30, 2, 1999, 340. A similar argument is made in terms of the lax internal control of Japanese corporations as in the infamous Sumitomo fiasco where one trader caused billions of dollars in losses while his colleagues by and large covered up his activities. See, for instance, S. Wudunn, "Big new loss makes Japan look inward," *The New York Times*, June 17, 1996.

[18] Asian Executive Poll, *The Far Eastern Economic Review*, July 1 1999, 31.

[19] "Pakistani stocks surge since military takeover amid hopes less corruption will lift economy," *Wall Street Journal*, February 24, 2000.

[20] P. Mauro, "Corruption and growth," *Quarterly Journal of Economics*, 110, 3, 1995, 681–712.

[21] G. P. Zachary, "Industrialized countries agree to adopt rules to curb bribery," *Wall Street Journal*, February 16, 1999, A18.

[22] "Who will listen to Mr. Clean?" *The Economist*, August 2, 1997, 52.

[23] "The termite hunter," *The Economist*, October 16, 1999, 72.

[24] "Black hole," *The Economist*, August 28, 1999, 59.

[25] *The World Competitiveness Yearbook, 2000*. Lawrence, Switzerland: IMD.

[26] "Beyond the Kremlin's walls," *The Economist*, May 20, 2000, 65.

[27] "Now exhale," *The Economist*, August 26, 2000, 19.

[28] R. G. Matthews, "Evasive maneuvers: Steel smugglers find many ways to enter lucrative U.S. market," *Wall Street Journal*, November A1.

[29] WTO Statistics on Globalization, 2001.

[30] E. Schmitt, "Chairman admits bank's 'lapse' in judgment in Russian laundering case," *The New York Times*, September 23, 1999 (Internet edition).

[31] J. Canute, and M. Peel, "Tax havens act to avoid sanctions," *Financial Times*, June 18, 2001, 4.

[32] T. McGirk, "Chasing shadows," *Time* magazine, June 11, 2001.

[33] U.S. government, report on transnational bribery, Fourth Annual National Export Strategy Report, September 24, 1996.

[34] J. Tagliabue, "Kazakhstan is suspected in 100 million of oil bribes," *The New York Times*, July 28, 2000, A5.

[35] *Business Week*, December 6, 1993.

[36] "Hong Kong business reveals the price of graft," *South China Morning Post*, July 25, 1993.

[37] G. P. Zachary, "Industrialized countries agree to adopt rules to curb bribery," *Wall Street Journal*, February 16, 1999, A18.

[38] T. McGirk, "Chasing shadows," *Time* magazine, June 11, 2001.

[39] AccessAsia, *Motorcycles in China: A Market Analysis*. March 2001

[40] D. C. K. Chow, "Counterfeiting in the People's Republic of China," *Washington University Law Quarterly*, 78, 1, 2000, 1–57; R. Jacob, "Businesses face genuine problem of Chinese fakes," *Financial Times*, April 4, 2000, 5.

[41] D. C. K. Chow, *A Primer on Foreign Investment Enterprises and Protection of Intellectual Property in China*. The Hague: Kluwer, 2002.

[42] C. H. Yee, "Asia takes the lead in total purchases in pirated software," *Asian Wall Street Journal*, May 23, 2001, 3.

THE OECD GUIDELINES FOR MULTINATIONAL ENTERPRISES (2000)

I. Concepts and Principles

1. The *Guidelines* are recommendations jointly addressed by governments to multinational enterprises. They provide principles and standards of good practice consistent with applicable laws. Observance of the *Guidelines* by enterprises is voluntary and not legally enforceable.

2. Since the operations of multinational enterprises extend throughout the world, international cooperation in this field should extend to all countries. Governments adhering to the *Guidelines* encourage the enterprises operating on their territories to observe the *Guidelines* wherever they operate, while taking into account the particular circumstances of each host country.

3. A precise definition of multinational enterprises is not required for the purposes of the *Guidelines*. These usually comprise companies or other entities established in more than one country and so linked that they may coordinate their operations in various ways. While one or more of these entities may be able to exercise a significant influence over the activities of others, their degree of autonomy within the enterprise may vary widely from one multinational enterprise to another. Ownership may be private, state or mixed. The *Guidelines* are addressed to all the entities within the multinational enterprise (parent companies and/or local entities). According to the actual distribution of responsibilities among them, the different entities are expected to cooperate and to assist one another to facilitate observance of the *Guidelines*.

4. The *Guidelines* are not aimed at introducing differences of treatment between multinational and domestic enterprises; they reflect good practice for all. Accordingly, multinational and domestic enterprises are subject to the same expectations in respect of their conduct wherever the *Guidelines* are relevant to both.

5. Governments wish to encourage the widest possible observance of the *Guidelines*. While it is acknowledged that small- and medium-sized enterprises may not have the same capacities as larger enterprises, governments adhering to the *Guidelines* nevertheless encourage them to observe the *Guidelines* recommendations to the fullest extent possible.

6. Governments adhering to the *Guidelines* should not use them for protectionist purposes nor use them in a way that calls into question the comparative advantage of any country where multinational enterprises invest.

7. Governments have the right to prescribe the conditions under which multinational enterprises operate within their jurisdictions, subject to international law. The entities of a multinational enterprise located in various countries are subject to the laws applicable in these countries. When multinational enterprises are subject to conflicting requirements by adhering countries, the governments concerned will cooperate in good faith with a view to resolving problems that may arise.

8. Governments adhering to the *Guidelines* set them forth with the understanding that they will fulfil their responsibilities to treat enterprises equitably and in accordance with international law and with their contractual obligations.

9. The use of appropriate international dispute settlement mechanisms, including arbitration, is encouraged as a means of facilitating the resolution of legal problems arising between enterprises and host country governments.

10. Governments adhering to the *Guidelines* will promote them and encourage their use. They will establish National Contact Points that promote the *Guidelines* and act as a forum for discussion of all matters relating to the *Guidelines*. The adhering Governments will also participate in appropriate review and consultation procedures to address issues concerning interpretation of the *Guidelines* in a changing world.

II. General Policies

Enterprises should take fully into account established policies in the countries in which they operate, and consider the views of other stakeholders. In this regard, enterprises should:

1. Contribute to economic, social and environmental progress with a view to achieving sustainable development.

2. Respect the human rights of those affected by their activities consistent with the host government's international obligations and commitments.

3. Encourage local capacity building through close cooperation with the local community, including business interests, as well as developing the enterprise's activities in domestic and foreign markets, consistent with the need for sound commercial practice.

4. Encourage human capital formation, in particular by creating employment opportunities and facilitating training opportunities for employees.

5. Refrain from seeking or accepting exemptions not contemplated in the statutory or regulatory framework related to environmental, health, safety, labor, taxation, financial incentives, or other issues.

6. Support and uphold good corporate governance principles and develop and apply good corporate governance practices.

7. Develop and apply effective self-regulatory practices and management systems that foster a relationship of confidence and mutual trust between enterprises and the societies in which they operate.

8. Promote employee awareness of, and compliance with, company policies through appropriate dissemination of these policies, including through training programs.

9. Refrain from discriminatory or disciplinary action against employees who make bona fide reports to management or, as appropriate, to the competent public authorities, on practices that contravene the law, the *Guidelines* or the enterprise's policies.

10. Encourage, where practicable, business partners, including suppliers and sub-contractors, to apply principles of corporate conduct compatible with the *Guidelines*.

11. Abstain from any improper involvement in local political activities.

III. Disclosure

1. Enterprises should ensure that timely, regular, reliable and relevant information is disclosed regarding their activities, structure, financial situation and performance. This information should be disclosed for the enterprise as a whole and, where appropriate, along business lines or geographic areas. Disclosure policies of enterprises should be tailored to the nature, size and location of the enterprise, with due regard taken of costs, business confidentiality and other competitive concerns.

2. Enterprises should apply high quality standards for disclosure, accounting, and audit. Enterprises are also encouraged to apply high quality standards for non-financial information including environmental and social reporting where they exist. The standards or policies under which both financial and non-financial information are compiled and published should be reported.

3. Enterprises should disclose basic information showing their name, location, and structure, the name, address and telephone number of the parent enterprise and its main affiliates, its percentage ownership, direct and indirect in these affiliates, including shareholdings between them.

4. Enterprises should also disclose material information on:

a) The financial and operating results of the company;

b) Company objectives;

c) Major share ownership and voting rights;

d) Members of the board and key executives, and their remuneration;

e) Material foreseeable risk factors;

f) Material issues regarding employees and other stakeholders;

g) Governance structures and policies.

5. Enterprises are encouraged to communicate additional information that could include:

a) Value statements or statements of business conduct intended for public disclosure including information on the social, ethical and environmental policies of the enterprise and other codes of conduct to which the company subscribes. In addition, the date of adoption, the countries and entities to which such statements apply and its performance in relation to these statements may be communicated;

b) Information on systems for managing risks and complying with laws, and on statements or codes of business conduct;

c) Information on relationships with employees and other stakeholders.

IV. Employment and Industrial Relations

Enterprises should, within the framework of applicable law, regulations and prevailing labor relations and employment practices:

1. a) Respect the right of their employees to be represented by trade unions and other bona fide representatives of employees, and engage in constructive negotiations, either individually or through employers' associations, with such representatives with a view to reaching agreements on employment conditions;

b) Contribute to the effective abolition of child labor;

c) Contribute to the elimination of all forms of forced or compulsory labor;

d) Not discriminate against their employees with respect to employment or occupation on such grounds as race, color, sex, religion, political opinion, national extraction or social origin, unless selectivity concerning employee characteristics furthers established governmental policies which specifically promote greater equality of employment opportunity or relates to the inherent requirements of a job.

2. a) Provide facilities to employee representatives as may be necessary to assist in the development of effective collective agreements;

b) Provide information to employee representatives which is needed for meaningful negotiations on conditions of employment;

c) Promote consultation and cooperation between employers and employees and their representatives on matters of mutual concern.

3. Provide information to employees and their representatives which enables them to obtain a true and fair view of the performance of the entity or, where appropriate, the enterprise as a whole.

4. a) Observe standards of employment and industrial relations not less favorable than those observed by comparable employers in the host country;

b) Take adequate steps to ensure occupational health and safety in their operations.

5. In their operations, to the greatest extent practicable, employ local personnel and provide training with a view to improving skill levels, in cooperation with employee representatives and, where appropriate, relevant governmental authorities.

6. In considering changes in their operations which would have major effects upon the livelihood of their employees, in particular in the case of the closure of an entity involving collective lay-offs or dismissals, provide reasonable notice of such changes to representatives of their employees, and, where appropriate, to the relevant governmental authorities, and cooperate with the employee representatives and appropriate governmental authorities so as to mitigate to the maximum extent practicable adverse effects. In light of the specific circumstances of each case, it would be appropriate if management were able to give such notice prior to the final decision being taken. Other means may also be employed to provide meaningful cooperation to mitigate the effects of such decisions.

7. In the context of bona fide negotiations with representatives of employees on conditions of employment, or while employees are exercising a right to organize, not threaten to transfer the whole or part of an operating unit from the country concerned nor transfer employees from the enterprises' component entities in other countries in order to influence unfairly those negotiations or to hinder the exercise of a right to organize.

8. Enable authorized representatives of their employees to negotiate on collective bargaining or labor-management relations issues and allow the parties to consult on matters of mutual concern with representatives of management who are authorized to take decisions on these matters.

V. Environment

Enterprises should, within the framework of laws, regulations and administrative practices in the countries in which they operate, and in consideration of relevant international agreements, principles, objectives, and standards, take due account of the need to protect the environment, public health and safety, and generally to conduct their activities in a manner contributing to the wider goal of sustainable development. In particular, enterprises should:

1. Establish and maintain a system of environmental management appropriate to the enterprise, including:

   a) Collection and evaluation of adequate and timely information regarding the environmental, health, and safety impacts of their activities;

   b) Establishment of measurable objectives and, where appropriate, targets for improved environmental performance, including periodically reviewing the continuing relevance of these objectives; and

   c) Regular monitoring and verification of progress toward environmental, health, and safety objectives or targets.

2. Taking into account concerns about cost, business confidentiality, and the protection of intellectual property rights:

   a) Provide the public and employees with adequate and timely information on the potential environment, health and safety impacts of the activities of the enterprise, which could include reporting on progress in improving environmental performance; and

   b) Engage in adequate and timely communication and consultation with the communities directly affected by the environmental, health and safety policies of the enterprise and by their implementation.

3. Assess, and address in decision-making, the foreseeable environmental, health, and safety-related impacts associated with the processes, goods and services of the enterprise over their full life cycle. Where these proposed activities may have significant environmental, health, or safety impacts, and where they are subject to a decision of a competent authority, prepare an appropriate environmental impact assessment.

4. Consistent with the scientific and technical understanding of the risks, where there are threats of serious damage to the environment, taking also into account human health and safety, not use the lack of full scientific certainty as a reason for postponing cost-effective measures to prevent or minimize such damage.

5. Maintain contingency plans for preventing, mitigating, and controlling serious environmental and health damage from their operations, including accidents and emergencies; and mechanisms for immediate reporting to the competent authorities.

6. Continually seek to improve corporate environmental performance, by encouraging, where appropriate, such activities as:

   a) Adoption of technologies and operating procedures in all parts of the enterprise that reflect standards concerning environmental performance in the best performing part of the enterprise;

   b) Development and provision of products or services that have no undue environmental impacts; are safe in their intended use; are efficient in their consumption of energy and natural resources; can be reused, recycled, or disposed of safely;

   c) Promoting higher levels of awareness among customers of the environmental implications of using the products and services of the enterprise; and

   d) Research on ways of improving the environmental performance of the enterprise over the longer term.

7. Provide adequate education and training to employees in environmental health and safety matters, including the handling of hazardous materials and the prevention of environmental accidents, as well as more general environmental management areas, such as environmental impact assessment procedures, public relations, and environmental technologies.

8. Contribute to the development of environmentally meaningful and economically efficient public policy, for example, by means of partnerships or initiatives that will enhance environmental awareness and protection.

VI. Combating Bribery

Enterprises should not, directly or indirectly, offer, promise, give, or demand a bribe or other undue advantage to obtain or retain business or other improper advantage. Nor should enterprises be solicited or expected to render a bribe or other undue advantage. In particular, enterprises should:

1. Not offer, nor give in to demands, to pay public officials or the employees of business partners any portion of a contract payment. They should not use subcontracts, purchase orders or consulting agreements as means of channelling payments to public officials, to employees of business partners or to their relatives or business associates.

2. Ensure that remuneration of agents is appropriate and for legitimate services only. Where relevant, a list of agents employed in connection with transactions with public bodies and state-owned enterprises should be kept and made available to competent authorities.

3. Enhance the transparency of their activities in the fight against bribery and extortion. Measures could include making public commitments against bribery and extortion and disclosing the management systems the company has adopted in order to honor these commitments. The enterprise should also foster openness and dialogue with the public so as to promote its awareness of and cooperation with the fight against bribery and extortion.

4. Promote employee awareness of and compliance with company policies against bribery and extortion through appropriate dissemination of these policies and through training programs and disciplinary procedures.

5. Adopt management control systems that discourage bribery and corrupt practices, and adopt financial and tax accounting and auditing practices that prevent the establishment of "off the books" or secret accounts or the creation of documents which do not properly and fairly record the transactions to which they relate.

6. Not make illegal contributions to candidates for public office or to political parties or to other political organizations. Contributions should fully comply with public disclosure requirements and should be reported to senior management.

VII. Consumer Interests

When dealing with consumers, enterprises should act in accordance with fair business, marketing and advertising practices and should take all reasonable steps to ensure the safety and quality of the goods or services they provide. In particular, they should:

1. Ensure that the goods or services they provide meet all agreed or legally required standards for consumer health and safety, including health warnings and product safety and information labels.

2. As appropriate to the goods or services, provide accurate and clear information regarding their content, safe use, maintenance, storage, and disposal sufficient to enable consumers to make informed decisions.

3. Provide transparent and effective procedures that address consumer complaints and contribute to fair and timely resolution of consumer disputes without undue cost or burden.

4. Not make representations or omissions, nor engage in any other practices, that are deceptive, misleading, fraudulent, or unfair.

5. Respect consumer privacy and provide protection for personal data.

6. Cooperate fully and in a transparent manner with public authorities in the prevention or removal of serious threats to public health and safety deriving from the consumption or use of their products.

VIII. Science and Technology

Enterprises should:

1. Endeavor to ensure that their activities are compatible with the science and technology (S&T) policies and plans of the countries in which they operate and as appropriate contribute to the development of local and national innovative capacity.

2. Adopt, where practicable in the course of their business activities, practices that permit the transfer and rapid diffusion of technologies and know-how, with due regard to the protection of intellectual property rights.

3. When appropriate, perform science and technology development work in host countries to address local market needs, as well as employ host country personnel in an S&T capacity and encourage their training, taking into account commercial needs.

4. When granting licenses for the use of intellectual property rights or when otherwise transferring technology, do so on reasonable terms and conditions and in a manner that contributes to the long-term development prospects of the host country.

5. Where relevant to commercial objectives, develop ties with local universities, public research institutions, and participate in cooperative research projects with local industry or industry associations.

IX. Competition

Enterprises should, within the framework of applicable laws and regulations, conduct their activities in a competitive manner. In particular, enterprises should:

1. Refrain from entering into or carrying out anti-competitive agreements among competitors:

   a) To fix prices;

   b) To make rigged bids (collusive tenders);

   c) To establish output restrictions or quotas; or

   d) To share or divide markets by allocating customers, suppliers, territories or lines of commerce;

2. Conduct all of their activities in a manner consistent with all applicable competition laws, taking into account the applicability of the competition laws of jurisdictions whose economies would be likely to be harmed by anti-competitive activity on their part.

3. Cooperate with the competition authorities of such jurisdictions by, among other things and subject to applicable law and appropriate safeguards, providing as prompt and complete responses as practicable to requests for information.

4. Promote employee awareness of the importance of compliance with all applicable competition laws and policies.

X. Taxation

It is important that enterprises contribute to the public finances of host countries by making timely payment of their tax liabilities. In particular, enterprises should comply with the tax laws and regulations in all countries in which they operate and should exert every effort to act in accordance with both the letter and spirit of those laws and regulations. This would include such measures as providing to the relevant authorities the information necessary for the correct determination of taxes to be assessed in connection with their operations and conforming transfer pricing practices to the arm's length principle.

CASES

Wienerberger Baustoffindustrie AG

*Department of Economics IV, University of Economics, Augasse 2-6, A-1090 Vienna, Austria

We would like to thank the management of Wienerberger and the investor's relations managers G. Bachmaier and Th. Melzer for their help and interest in the project. This case study was written under the umbrella of the international SMOPEC project on industrial firms in Small Open Economies.

1. SHORT HISTORY

Wienerberger, founded in 1820, underwent several periods of growth and decline, the latter being impacted partly by wars and partly by economic crises.

In the 1850s Wienerberger grew to be the largest brick manufacturer in the Austrian-Hungarian empire by acquiring several other producers and had about 4,700 employees. Wienerberger was founded in Vienna, but set up a production unit in Hungary as early as 1838. Further expansion and diversification (real estate/property, coal mines) made Wienerberger the world's largest brick manufacturer in the 1860s (10,000 employees). At that time it was an *entrepreneurial firm* in the Chandlerian sense (Chandler 1990).

Before the First World War its market share in Hungary was 54 per cent. This increased to 84 per cent during the war (Bellak 1997, p. 51). Eventually Wienerberger was sold to a few large shareholders ("syndicate") led by the Austrian bank *Creditanstalt*, who is a core shareholder still today. In 1917 Wienerberger became a quasi-monopoly by acquiring its largest competitor.

The loss of the First World War had two main consequences that led to a shrinking of the firm: first, demand was very low, and second, the loss of 65 per cent of Austria's territory led to divestments in most of its former home markets. Wienerberger therefore became a truly national firm. (The former home markets were by definition also "national" during the monarchy, but they were different from the Austrian market and thus in economic terms should be considered as foreign.) In 1924 Wienerberger had only 1,200 employees. The World Economic Crisis of 1929 led to further demand shortfall, and Wienerberger (now with 720 employees) became heavily indebted and almost ceased to exist. The *Creditanstalt* as the main creditor bought 76.5 per cent of the shares. After the Second World War, domestic expansion resumed quickly (3,000 employees in the mid-1950s), and in 1970, Wienerberger had 13 brick production units in Austria and a market share of 40 per cent. Diversification into construction materials like tiles, clay pipes, etc., fueled domestic growth, though Wienerberger remained a national firm until 1985.

Business Areas and Global Market Position

Wienerberger is the European market leader in hollow bricks (between 25 and 80 per cent in EU countries) and has a top position in plastic pipes (e.g., in Austria and Hungary: 50 per cent;

Table 1
Key figures of Wienerberger 1985–2001 (ATS or € mn and percentage)

Indicator	1985	1995	1996	1997	1998	1999	2000	2001
	ATS mn	€ mn						
Net sales	1,797	934.2	1,094.5	1,113.7	1,143.3	1,337.5	1,670.3	1,544.9
Operating Profit	14	121.7	116.4	131.1	162.6	187.8	254.3	−25.8
Earnings per Share	27	1.53	0.94	1.43	1.64	1.74	2.86	−0.29
Gearing (%)	17	51.3	58.3	19.0	29.7	62.2	54.5	66.9
Market Capitalization	339	1,009.5	1,325.0	1,530.0	1,471.3	1,499.5	1,328.7	1,093.9
Employees (total)	1,019	6,418	8,229	7,574	7,988	10.374	11,069	11,331

Source: *Annual Report,* 1985 and *Annual Report,* 2001: Ten Year Review; from 1997 onwards: IAS

Table 2
Share of Wienerberger divisions in sales and in operating profits in 1995, 1999, and 2001

Division	Share in Total Sales			Share in Operating Profits		
	1995	1999	2001	1995	1999	2001
Wall, ceiling, and roofing systems	38	60	71	59	58	n.a.
Pipe systems and sewage technology	25	27	28	11	14	n.a.
Treibacher +	33	—	—	10	—	—
Real estate / Property	4	13	1	19	28	n.a.

Sources: *Annual Report,* 1995, p. 24; *Annual Reports,* 1999, p. 45 and 2001, p. 48

n.a. ... not available

+ ... sold in 2000

Germany: 8 per cent; other EU countries: 7 to 20 per cent). In 1991 it held 15 per cent of the world's markets in ferro alloys and was the world leader in corundum, a natural aluminum oxide used as an abrasive. The latest available information (as of March 2002) shows that it is number 1 in hollow bricks worldwide, number 1 in facing bricks in Continental Europe, number 2 in facing bricks in the US, number 1 in roofing systems in Central-Eastern Europe, number 1 in clay pipes in Europe and number 4 in plastic pipes in Europe. Key financial data for Wienerberger for various years from 1985 to 2001 are provided in Table 1.

Today, the Wienerberger Group encompasses three divisions, namely bricks, pipes, and real estate.[i] See Table 2 for their shares in sales and profits, and Tables 9 and 10 for other main indicators and products. Two of them, namely bricks and real estate, are the traditional Wienerberger divisions of 1820, which have made dramatic changes over the years. The product range has widened enormously, and the company now serves markets throughout the world. Equally, the real estate division has been transformed from mainly private housing (most of it has been eventually sold) into commercial real-estate development. The brick division serves both private and public sectors.

The pipe division is a relatively young division and has been acquired "by chance" together with a number of brick companies in 1990 and has developed into the second core business within 5 years (see Tables 2 and 10). Several other acquisitions, joint-ventures (e.g., 50:50 with the Belgium Solvay Group) and "green field" investments in Asian markets followed. The customers in this market are public entities (65 per cent) and private customers (approximately 35 per cent). At the end of the 1990s, Wienerberger was ranked fourth among pipe systems suppliers in Europe.

2. AUSTRIA

Austria is a highly developed country, located in the centre of Europe, that performed at a high level, economically, when compared to most OECD members after the Second World War. The smallness of the country is one reason among many that dictated its openness to trade. However, the flow of outward direct investment (FDI) was modest until the mid-1980s (e.g., Bellak 1997). This is in sharp contrast to other small countries in Europe like Switzerland and the Netherlands. The few large industrial enterprises did not need to engage in FDI to serve customers outside Austria due to virtually free market access to EU countries. Economies of scale were achieved by exporting. Inward FDI played a substantial role in some sectors (e.g., electronics, pulp and paper industry). Table 3 provides key economic indicators for Austria.

In the early 1990s the picture changed dramatically and Austria's manufacturing sector experienced a "triple squeeze" from East and West, but new chances also emerged (cf. Bellak 1994, 1996). First, the opening of Eastern Europe created the opportunity for relocation of production units to take advantage of very low costs and the development of new markets but also resulted in new competition in some sectors. Second, the deepening integration of Austria into the European Community, which resulted in EU membership in 1995, made the country a favorable location for foreign firms (indeed, foreign takeovers started immediately) and an attractive market. Third, a tough currency policy which was pursued since the 1960s put Austria's industry under tough competitive pressure. Many firms are price takers in international markets due to their small size, and several competitor countries (e.g., Italy, Scandinavian countries) devalued their currencies substantially. In addition, the government started to privatize the large state-owned sector, which resulted in further structural market distortions.

Although Austria's economic performance has been positive in the past, the new imperative of the government that materialized through several national savings plans created higher unemployment and reduced public investment. On the other hand, this enabled Austria to eventually participate in the European Monetary Union, which was considered advantageous for both foreign and domestic firms acting internationally. Also, the opening of Central and Eastern Europe from 1989 onwards led to a sharp increase in Austrian exports and FDI into the region. Several Austrian firms became market leaders (e.g., in the banking sector) or had attained dominant market positions (e.g., in the pulp and paper industry, bricks industry).

Table 3
Main economic indicators of Austria, 1995 and 2001

Indicator	1995		2001	
	EU 15	Austria	EU15	Austria
Population (1000)	370,923+)	8,047	379,966	8,120
Area (sq km)	3,243,657	83,859	3,243,657	83,859
GDP per capita, current prices, PPPs, in USD	17,914+)	20,210+)	25,588	27,803
Real growth rate of GDP	2.5	1.8	1.6	1.0
Inflation rate	3.1	2.2	2.7	2.5
Current account as percent of GDP	+0.6	−2.6	−0.2	−2.3
Unemployment rate (standardized)	10.7	3.9	7.6	3.6

Source: WIFO, OECD
+) 1994

3. THE INDUSTRY

The structure, conduct and performance of the brick industry are analyzed briefly here for both home and foreign markets. The (private and public) *building and construction industry* is the main player on the demand side of the industry, while the supply side comprises the *brick and tiles industry* or more broadly defined, the *clay products industry*. In general, sales in the brick industry depend on (i) the general level of economic activity, (ii) the business of construction and construction-materials industries and (iii) the development of private residential construction (itself depending on interest levels and subsidies for private construction), since bricks are primarily used there. Established markets prevail such as Germany where 60 bn brick units sold annually for 60 mn inhabitants, which equals 500.000 flats in 1998), and the potential of *new* markets (like Poland with 40 mn inhabitants and sales in 1995 of only four billion brick-units) is significant.

Home Market

Demand

Wienerberger's home market is very small in absolute terms as the figures in Table 3 indicate. This applies also to the relative share of the home market to total turnover, which was less than 15 per cent in 1996. Yet, even the small size of Austria did not encourage Wienerberger to invest abroad until 1995 as many other companies in other small European countries did. In the mid-1980s the home market became too small, and Wienerberger started to "conquer" foreign markets. The upward trend in the Austrian building industry, which started in the mid-1980s and which created many opportunities for Wienerberger, came to an end in 1995 (0.7%). Table 4 records the actual and projected annual growth rates for key sectors of the Austrian construction industry for the years from 1991 to 2004 inclusive. Table 5 compares the growth rates in the industry for Austria with a number of other European nations for the same period.

In order to meet the fiscal criteria set up in the Maastricht treaty, public spending on housing and infrastructure has been scaled back. The tight budgetary situation of the government makes further cutbacks in public spending inevitable. The sectors developed differently, and public sector construction and civil engineering saw significant declines. Market potential in Austria relates only to the adaptation/renovation and modernization sectors, rather than to new (private or public) building. Yet, in the private sector elasticity of demand is much lower than in the public sector.

The home market is characterized by several structural changes: whereas traditionally, bricks have been used for high buildings, today and in the future they will be used primarily by private builders (as concrete is used more and more in pub-

Table 4
Construction industry in Austria (average annual growth at real prices)

Austria	1991	1992	1993	1994	1995	1996	1997	1998	1999	2000	2001	2002e	2003e	2004e
Residential construction	4.7	8.5	10.5	15.0	5.0	0.0	1.8	−2.0	−1.9	1.2				
Private non-residential c.	10.0	6.5	−10.0	−8.0	−4.5	−2.0	2.0	4.0	5.8	3.6	−4.4	−2.2	0.8	1.0
Public non-residential c.	3.0	1.6	2.0	0.5	−3.0	−3.0	0.0	2.0						
Civil Engineering	3.7	1.0	1.0	3.0	−5.0	−6.0	−3.0	5.0	2.8	3.9	1.6	2.6	3.6	2.8

Source: *Annual Report*, 1995, p. 21 and Czerny (1996–2002), based on Euroconstruct 2002; e ... estimate

Table 5
Output of the European construction industry (real average annual change at constant prices)

Country	1991	1992	1993	1994	1995	1996e	1997e	1998	1999	2000	2001	2002e	2003e	2004e
Germany	3.5	9.5	2.8	7.8	1.9	−0.6	−0.4	−1.0	1.5	−2.5	−5.2	−1.3	0.8	2.0
France	0.2	−3.0	−6.0	−0.2	1.0	1.8	1.5	1.9	6.5	7.3	1.5	0.2	−0.1	2.1
Italy	1.6	0.8	−5.7	−3.0	0.6	2.3	1.0	2.8	5.1	5.6	4.1	1.9	0.9	0.6
Switzerland	−5.6	−2.3	−2.0	2.0	−3.6	0.4	1.6	−0.4	−3.3	2.1	1.3	2.0	2.0	1.6
Hungary	−12.0	−3.0	−1.5	16.0	1.0	2.0	3.0	4.0	5.9	4.7	7.0	6.4	8.0	8.0
Czech Rep.	−23.9	19.7	−7.4	3.1	7.4	8.4	6.9	−8.2	−6.2	4.7	11.5	5.4	5.3	5.4
Slowak Rep.	−31.6	7.8	−26.8	−5.3	0.0	10.3	12.8	−4.0	−26.5	3.7	23.5	6.8	8.4	8.9
Poland	1.6	−0.6	4.3	2.0	4.0	5.5	5.5	12.4	6.2	−0.3	−7.8	−5.5	1.8	7.1
Austria	5.1	4.9	2.3	4.7	0.0	−1.0	−3.0	0.9	2.2	1.3	−3.0	−2.0	1.0	1.5
Western Europe	n.a.	n.a.	n.a.	n.a.	n.a.	n.a.	n.a.	1.8	3.6	2.7	0.1	0.5	1.3	1.8
Central Eastern Europe	n.a.	n.a.	n.a.	n.a.	n.a.	n.a.	n.a.	6.4	2.6	1.3	−2.2	−1.1	3.9	7.0

Source: *Annual Report,* 1995, p. 21; Czerny (var. iss.); Eurostat: Enterprises in Europe: Part 1, p. 289 and Euroconstruct, Rome, 2001, p. 144

lic buildings). The stagnating home market is also reflected by falling employment figures in the construction industry.

Supply and Employment

The development of brick production in Austria can be traced back more than 200 years. In general, the industry moved from small-scale sites (*Gewerbe*) to a large-scale industry, as found everywhere in the highly developed EU countries. The income tax register of the Austrian-Hungarian monarchy of 1856 mentioned 4,309 brickworks: the true number, however, was probably even higher. Of these brickworks, 700 were operating within today's territory of Austria, 1,464 in Bohemia and 532 in Hungary and many others in other provinces. After the boom triggered by the industrial expansion of the 19th century, the number of brickyards fell to about 300—in spite of the demand produced by the

Second World War. After the War about 420 production sites existed, of which almost half were considered small. In 1988 there were 56 firms with about 2,000 employees. By the mid-1990s, the number of production plants in Austria had fallen to 46. These were owned by 29 companies. In the future the number of firms is expected to fall to about ten. All domestic competitors are relatively small (between Euro 1.45 and 5.81 mn annual revenue). Only four of them surpass the threshold of Euro 7.26 mn, but nevertheless Wienerberger remains at least three times larger than its largest competitor in the end of the 1990s.

This structural change has gone hand in hand with a substantial production increase and energy savings. Output has increased six-fold during the last 50 years (based on *Bricks and Tiles International,* 1995), while the number of employees decreased to only 17 per cent of the 1953 level (see Figure 1).

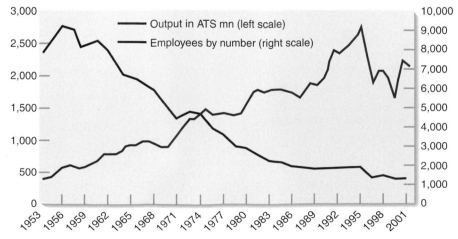

Figure 1. Output and employment in the Austrian bricks industry
Source: *Tiles and Brick International,* 19th Anniv. Issues, 1995 and Information of the Fachverband

Major EU Markets and EU Leading Suppliers

Demand

The building industry in the European Union has been a stable sector for many decades. While regional and sectoral developments differed substantially, production and productivity growth remained on a stable upward trend until 1990 or so. Between 1990 and 2000 apparent brick consumption remained stable. The efficiency of the industry was considerably improved, e.g., with employment falling by 21 per cent when output increased by 0.9 per cent annually between 1984 and 1989. Again, from 2000 onwards, the real growth rate is expected to remain well below 2 per cent in Western Europe. The structural shift of the building industry described below also affects its suppliers—the building material producers—directly and immediately.

By the mid-1990s the *West European building industry* had shifted from high growth during the last decade toward periods of stagnation and even decline. The average real growth (+1.6 per cent) fell below overall growth of GDP (+1.8 per cent) in 1995 for the first time in decades. (See Table 5 for single country figures.) This development had been predicted for several years, and the need to develop new markets led to a concentration process in the brick industry (see below the largest suppliers) as well as to a search for new markets abroad (geographical diversification).

In *Eastern Europe*, the building industry has increased its volume, thus offsetting the negative growth rates of the years after the transformation had started (see Table 5). Yet, growth is again forecast to remain sluggish as Table 5 shows. Growth is, however, very low and unstable still and varies considerably between the countries; e.g., the market share of Wienerberger rose substantially in some segments (e.g., tiles +65 per cent in the Czech Republic and a threefold increase in sales in Slovakia during 1995). The "super-normal" growth of market shares is, however, explained not only by rapid demand growth, which started from a very low level, but also by acquisitions. The shift of markets from West to Central and East Europe is a "chance" factor as it comes at a time when old markets show signs of stagnation.[ii]

The question arises, whether the new markets will be able to compensate for the loss of old ones in terms of prices, margins and quantity. In such an unstable environment, the strategy of a company like Wienerberger is particularly interesting, since it serves both markets.

Supply and Employment

The European brick industry underwent a dramatic restructuring process in search for the reduction of oversupply and higher efficiency. Supply was always slightly above apparent consumption, which implies the prevalence of strong price competition. Table 6 reveals the slow growth of the output price index relative to other cost components like wages. A good deal of foreign investment in the form of acquisitions led to the closing down of the less efficient production sites and those located far from the core markets in an effort to reduce overall capacity. As a result, the number of firms as well as production sites declined, pushing up industry concentration (see also main suppliers below). Table 6 and Figure 1 show that employment in

---

Table 6

Manufacture of bricks, tiles, and construction products (NACE group 26.4)—main indicators in the EU

	1990	1991	1992	1993	1994	1995	1996	1997	1998	1999	2000
Production (million Euro)	5,705	6,185	6,295	6,236	6,784	6,804	6,129	n.a.	6,330	6,907	n.a.
Purchases of goods and services (million Euro)	n.a.	n.a.	n.a.	n.a.	n.a.	3,685	3,493	n.a.	3,602	3,906	n.a.
Value added (million Euro)	2,766	2,958	3,084	3,053	3,324	3,395	2,950	n.a.	3,078	3,506	n.a.
Personnel costs (million Euro)	1,692	1,822	1,838	1,777	1,830	1,869	1,762	n.a.	1,732	1,828	n.a.
Number of persons employed (thousands)	84	83	78	74	73	73	66	n.a.	61	61	n.a.
Gross investment in tangible goods (million Euro)	n.a.	n.a.	n.a.	n.a.	n.a.	n.a.	n.a.	n.a.	n.a.	n.a.	n.a.
Gross operating rate (%)	18.0	17.3	18.7	19.4	20.5	21.4	18.7	n.a.	20.4	22.6	n.a.
App. labor productivity (1,000 Euro / person empl.)	32.8	35.7	39.5	41.2	45.3	46.5	45.0	n.a.	50.1	57.1	n.a.
Simple wage adjusted labor productivity (%)	163.5	162.3	167.8	171.8	181.6	181.6	167.4	n.a.	177.7	191.8	n.a.
Output price index (1995 = 100)	86.7	91.8	94.9	96.7	97.8	100.0	98.8	99.4	101.5	105.3	109.1

Source: Eurostat 2002, p. 183

n.a. ...not available

Table 7
Bricks & tiles exports and imports of EU at current values (mn ECU, selected years) and growth rates

Year	1984	1986	1988	1990	1992	1994	1995
EU-Exports to Third Countries	291.3	240.5	186.5	207.5	232.2	295.1	298.9
EU-Imports from Third Countries	6.4	6.8	12.4	15.4	38.4	63.5	68.0
Trade Balance	284.9	233.7	174.1	192.1	193.8	231.6	230.9
Coverage Ratio	45.5	35.4	15.0	13.5	6.0	4.6	4.4
average annual growth at real prices 1)	**1984–89**		**1989–93**		**1984–93**	**1992–93**	**1993–94**
EU-Exports to Third Countries	−8.68		3.74		−3.35	14.04	17.8
EU-Imports from Third Countries	11.03		32.41		20.07	35.28	21.2

Source: EU Panorama 95/96, p. 5–8 and 96/97, p. 9–28, Table 4 (1993–94) and EU Panorama 95/96, p. 5–8, and 96/97, p. 9–31, Tab. 5 (1995: Eurostat estimates)

1) For some countries estimates have been used for apparent consumption and production.

the brick industry decreased substantially due in part to the increase in innovation in the production process. From 1990 to 2000 value-added increased only slightly, but the number of persons employed fell again by one-fifth, which led to sharp productivity increases, thus offsetting some of the cost increases. Yet, in some years, wage-adjusted labor productivity even decreased industry-wide.

Overall, the industry improved its performance considerably from 1984 to 1994. Labor productivity increased by 33 per cent, while unit labor costs (+15.8 per cent) and total cost (+17.4 per cent) rose considerably less. This pushed the return on sales by 7.3 per cent, the outcome of the restructuring process that manifested itself in a concentration (decreasing number of firms) process and in improved efficiency of the firms themselves. Table 6 provides details of these trends.

Trade

Trade in the brick industry has been minimal as it is mainly a local business. Growth rates for EU exports even decreased over the decade 1984–1993, while those for imports increased heavily in real terms. Table 7 reflects both the current value of exports in the brick industry and the average annual growth rates in real prices for the period from 1984 to 1995.

Nature of Competition

The market structure in the brick industry is best described as an oligopoly. Contrary to a typical oligopoly, which normally tends to reduce competition between few suppliers, the reduced competition in the brick industry stems from the dominant position of each large supplier on its respective home market. Because of the local nature of the business, competition is mainly between local production units rather than at the group level. Since there are cultural and technical differences between countries in the construction industry, competition depends on two factors: These are, first, the share of bricks of total construction materials used, including substitutes such as concrete, and sec-

ond, the height of the buildings, since bricks can be used only for those edifices that are eleven stories or less. Therefore in highly developed countries like Germany, France, and the UK with their large towns, the brick industry is highly concentrated in order to stand the pressure of substitutes. On the other hand, in the less developed EU member states with large rural areas like Spain, Portugal, Southern Italy, or Greece, the role of substitutes is considerably less significant.

Main Suppliers

The ten largest suppliers (ranked by turnover) employed 55 per cent of total employees in the brick industry of the EU in 1993. The concentration rates are very high, and typically, there were dominant domestic suppliers in most countries. Table 8 lists these firms together with pertinent data on nationality, sales, and number of employees.

The UK seems to dominate the scene. Yet, a closer look reveals that the UK is a very competitive market, since the firms are very large and diversified. Stock market prices are too high for a foreign take-over. A comparison of the firms' efficiency in terms of sales per employee shows that the largest firms are not necessarily the most efficient (with the exception of Hanson Brick) and that Wienerberger was in second place in 1993. In Southern Europe the market is characterized by a large number of small suppliers, and a concentration and industrialisation process has not yet set in.

The largest global competitors of Wienerberger today are the Australian *Boral Group*, which is market leader in its home market and in the US and Asia (where Wienerberger is not present in the brick industry, so far).

Key Success Factors

The key success factor in the bricks industry is the mix of firm size and financial structure. The larger the firm, the higher the return on technology, since brick production sites are similar everywhere. The more financially sound a firm, the easier it can

Table 8
Main EU-brick industry suppliers, 1993

Company	Country	Sales (USD mn)	Employees (number)	Sales / Employee (USD mn)
Redland	UK	1,893	21,538	0.088
Wienerberger	A	950	5,629	0.169
Hanson Brick	UK	600	3,000	0.2
Ibstock	UK	201	3,681	0.055
Tarmack Building Materials	UK	139	2,406	0.058
Erlus Baustoff	D	88	529	0.166
Karl Bachl	D	88	924	0.095
Scheerders van Kerchove	B	68	798	0.085
RDB Edilizia	I	68	531	0.128
Roeben Tonbaustoffe	D	68	650	0.105

Source: EU Panorama 95/96, p. 5–11

play a role in the "M&A-game" in this industry (high cash flow). Both factors are crucial, since the first ensures efficient supply on the firm level and the second secures the market share necessary to reap profit from large fixed investments with relatively cheap products.

To sum up, then, the structure of the market is characterized by a high degree of concentration, segmented markets, and a competitively driven, firm-specific strategy. The good performance of the industry was based on the boom in the construction industry before the 1990s.

4. THE FIRM

Divisions and Products

The various products of each division are listed in Table 9, though market shares are only available for certain products. These products clearly reflect Wienerberger's concept of "concentration and consequence," as the number of products within each division has increased over time, with the number of divisions being quite small. Accordingly, Wienerberger constantly shifts its resources between its four divisions. This implies that Wienerberger may not support the divisions that are not their core businesses and are likely to engage in product development strategy primarily within the core business.

Market share in the "wall, ceiling and roofing systems" division in Austria remained at 40 per cent from 1970 until today (approximately 75 per cent in Eastern Austria). Wienerberger has not grown in relative terms for the last 25 years or so in Austria, and there have been no attempts to increase the market share here. In neighboring countries, Wienerberger has a dominant position in hollow bricks, as the substantial mar-

ket shares in the mid-1990s show: Germany 25 per cent, Hungary 44, Czech Republic 45, and Slovakia 30. In facing bricks, the respective market shares are in Eastern France 80 per cent and in Belgium, the Netherlands, and Northern France, between 29 and 38 per cent.

The relatively large number of products in the bricks and the pipes division are a result of Wienerberger's strategy of offering systems of related products. The "wall, ceiling and roofing systems" comprise all major components of the shell of a building. A minimum return on capital of at least 10 per cent must be indicated for Wienerberger to engage in a new investment. Since cost structures, markets, and prices are well known, the projected values have a high level of accuracy. As Wienerberger defines it: "We moved from the 'regional league' to the 'middle class' but now we are in the 'champions league.'"

In pursuit of growth, Wienerberger sometimes foregoes higher margins for market share gain. For example, in 1996, the margin in Germany decreased from 25 per cent to only 2 per cent, while the market share increased from 20 to 25 per cent. This was mainly a reaction to the aggressive pricing strategies of smaller firms trying to survive in stagnant or declining markets. Bricks are to a certain extent a price-sensitive product, which results in a quality premium of only approximately 5 per cent of the ordinary price. Thus, even if Wienerberger follows a "high quality–high price" strategy, it has to "follow the market" when price reductions by competitors become too large. The financial performance of the two major divisions is shown in Table 10.

Technology Acquisition, Absorption, and Creation, R&D

The long experience of Wienerberger in the brick business enables it to rely on 100 per cent in-house technology for heavy bricks. For light bricks (facing bricks), technology was acquired

Table 9
Product and market-related indicators, 1996

	Wall, ceiling and roofing systems	Pipe systems and sewage technology
No. of production plants mid-1996	118	31
Products	Wall Systems: Hollow Bricks, Clinkems: Brick Based Ceilings, Ceiling Elements Roofing Systems: Clay Tiles, Concrete Tiles; Paving Bricks; Concrete Products	Clay Pipes for Waste-Water Water Supply and Disposal; Irrigation, Gas Supply; Cables; Dreinage, Electric Installations and District Heating; Duroton Prefabricated Parts.
Market Shares	Hollow Bricks: A 44%, CZ 45%, H 44%, Slo 30%, E-FRA 80%, GER 25% Facing Bricks: B, NL, N-FRA 20–38%	Clay Pipes: EU approx. 20%; Plastic Pipes: EU 10%, A and H 50%, GER 8%, Other 7–20%

Source: *Annual Reports*

Table 10
Selected indicators of major Wienerberger divisions (currency million and percentages)

Division and Indicator	1993 ATS	1995 ATS	1997 ATS	1999 Euro	Central and Eastern Europe 2001 Euro	Western Europe 2001 Euro	USA 2001 Euro
Wall, ceiling and roofing systems							
Sales	3,395	4,917	8,598	857.8	287.1	522.9	291.2
Operating Profits	640	882	1,310	116.6	39.1	−6.6	27.5
Margin (%)	18.9	16.0	15.2	14.3	n.a.	n.a.	n.a.
Employment	1,819	3,285	5,154	8,129	3,109	3,527	2,091
Cash-flow / sales (%)	23.0	23.8	20.4	18.6	n.a.	n.a.	n.a.
Sales / employee	1.9	1.5	1.7	0.11	0.09	0.15	0.14
Pipe systems and sewage technology+)							
Sales	2,424	3,238	3,625	304.7	435.4		
Operating Profits	120	226	93	19.9	14.4		
Margin (%)	5.0	5.2	2.6	7.0	n.a.		
Employment	1,250	1,483	1,708	1,570	2,464		
Cash-flow / sales (%)	6.9	9.5	5.9	9.2	n.a.		
Sales / employee	1.9	2.2	2.1	0.19	0.18		

Source: *Annual Reports* 1993–2001

+) 2001: Bricks division; Pipe and Roofing Systems from 1997 onwards: IAS

through the acquisition of a competitor (e.g., Terca Bricks). In the bricks division there is applied R&D only. Wienerberger does not employ an R&D lab for basic research but organizes its R&D activities within flexible projects (localized technological change). The projects utilize engineers and local management from the larger plants and have different time horizons. For example, the development of the new production technology described in the following paragraphs has taken no less than ten years.

A recent development, a very efficient production process, was submitted for patent protection in 1996. Up to then, a multi-layered drying and burning process had been used, while the new technology introduced a drying and burning process on a brick-by-brick basis. This would result in a significant reduction in the amount of facilities to be handled and easier control of the process. This resulted not only in improved product quality, but also in a reduction of operating costs by 20 per cent. The cost-reduction stems from a reduction in production time of up to four-fifths (!) of the previously used technology, resulting in lower energy consumption, lower maintenance costs, and lower labor costs. Also, capital expenditure requirements are 20 per cent lower. These new brick plants require only one worker per shift for supervision, but actually two employees are there in order to comply with the Austrian law. In contrast, the number of employees in the production stage of a typical plant has been 25 up to now. The development of the new technology has been complicated by the high environmental standards (concerning exhaust fumes and energy consumption) in Europe among other things.

In addition, product technology and product development are advanced. As to bricks, the need for the reduction of construction costs is met by new brick designs as well as new materials, which are strong selling arguments given the heavy price competition. An example is the new "plain brick" for which the thin mortar bed used as a bonding agent between the individual brick courses is now barely one millimeter thick. Besides, walls made of plain bricks no longer require drying. This saves construction cost (up to 30 per cent) since it reduces the number of workers required considerably. The diffusion of such new construction processes takes a long time since there is strong mental resistance from the brick layers to apply new techniques.

Bricks are long-living products, and hence their quality requirements are high. Research is also focused on improvement of the insulating properties of bricks.

Firm-specific Assets

Wienerberger combines size and a sound financial structure, as these are the requirements of survival in the industry as described above. These factors are combined with firm-specific production and product technology (see above) and organizational know-how. The latter also refers to the restructuring of acquired firms and the efficient organization of independent subsidiaries. The restructuring experience gives Wienerberger an advantage (1) in cases when firms are taken over, when it is not willing to carry on or is not able to make the necessary investment; and (2) in cases when a whole group is taken over, which normally includes production sites of different degrees of efficiency. In these cases,

the know-how of local production managers makes up an important part of the competitive advantage. In addition, Wienerberger managers have helped to achieve efficiency in their own plants, and the key data for efficient brick production is well known. Newly acquired plants profit from the transfer of this know-how and the experience of the managers. Last, but not least, there exists the *will* of Wienerberger to grow internationally and to take risks in new markets (such as Asia).

The competitive advantages of Wienerberger today derive from a single fact, namely the *industrialization of brick production*. Out of the large number of local brick manufacturers which for a long time were associated with agriculture, Wienerberger created a firm with industrial activities like R&D, technological engineering, product development, and marketing. The concentration of the industry was the cause and effect of the internationalization of brick production. The competitive advantages of Wienerberger manifest themselves in the funding of large real investments which cannot be provided by family enterprises and a cost-effectiveness in the production of high-quality, innovative products with new technologies.[iii]

Organization

The "Wienerberger Group" regards itself as an international network. The group has been decentralized over the last decade and consists of a multitude of small, independent units and profit centers. The holding company itself employs a rather small number of people (about 40 only), which means that the whole group resembles an extremely "lean" organization. This meets best the requirements of a local business where economies of scope (synergy, see below) are the main competitive advantage. Moreover, this structure enabled Wienerberger to grow as fast as it did, without each acquisition affecting the whole organizational structure.

Normally, local management and local workers run the plants abroad autonomously. The Wienerberger holding company provides control but interferes only in cases where the figures deviate from those projected. The main difficulty associated with such a high degree of decentralization lies in the creation of a corporate identity and efficient information flows between the parent and its numerous subsidiary companies.

Ownership and Control—Nominal and Effective

As mentioned in the history section above, the *Wienerberger Holding* is controlled by *Creditanstalt*. This bank and *Koramic Building Products N.V.* each own 25 per cent of the Wienerberger *Baustoffindustrie AG* plus one share. Thus *Wienerberger Baustoffindustrie AG* is owned by *Wienerberger Holding* (50% +2 shares) and the rest (49.9%) is public shareholding (free float). The stock is owned 69 per cent by institutional investors and 30 per cent by private shareholders. Analysis of the nationality of shareholders reveals that Austrian owners declined to 51 per cent in 2002 (Annual Report 2001, p. 13). Taking into account that *Creditanstalt* has itself been bought by the *Bavarian HBV Group* recently, this means a substantial indirect increase in foreign ownership.

Table 11
Balance Sheet per 31.12.

	1993		1995		1997		1999		2001	
	Mn ATS	per cent	mn ATS	per cent	mn €	per cent	mn €	per cent	mn €	per cent
Assets										
Fixed and Financial Assets	8,337	54	11,004	57	892.6	55	1,446.8	62	1,556.3	64
Inventory	2,014	13	2,267	12	214.8	13	214.4	9	331.8	14
Current Assets	5,071	33	6,072	31	507.9	32	631.6	29	543.8	22
Total	15,422	100	19,343	100	1,615.3	100	2,343.8	100	2,431.9	100
Liabilities										
Equity	7,178	47	8,133	42	756.9	47	921.2	39	1,008.0	41
Reserves	1,991	13	1,812	9	239.5	15	311.9	13	283.1	12
Liabilities	6,253	40	9,398	49	619.0	38	1,110.7	48	1,140.8	47

Source: Based on *Annual Reports*

Financial Policies, Structure, and Performance

The financial structure of Wienerberger is sound. The share of equity on the balance sheet was 48 per cent in 1994, compared to an upper quartile of 43 per cent for the Austrian manufacturing sector total (OeNB 1995). All fixed assets are financed with long-term capital. The group's acid-test ratio (current liabilities to quick assets) shows a satisfying liquidity and the ability to meet all short-term obligations. Table 11 provides balance sheet information for the period from 1983 to 2001 inclusive.

Wienerberger is listed on the Vienna Stock Exchange, SEAQ (London), and ADR (New York). Average shareholder return (dividend + increase in share prices) between 1986 and 1997 was 19 per cent annually. A return on sales of 8.3 per cent (average 1993–1995) and on equity of 12.8 per cent gives evidence of the extraordinary performance and profits of the company.

5. INTERNATIONALIZATION

Back in 1869, Wienerberger had eight domestic plants and two in Hungary. In 1980 it had 18 plants in Austria. The takeoff came in 1986 because of the need for growth. As has been described above, the market share in the home market had already remained constant for two decades; hence growth could only be achieved abroad. Rather than internal growth, Wienerberger followed a consequent strategy of external growth abroad as about 90 per cent of growth abroad came through acquisitions, while the remaining 10 per cent came through organic growth (i.e., growth of market volume).

Was there a pressure for internationalization? First, there was the will to internationalize as the management consisted of entrepreneurs willing to take risks. Second, pressure to internationalize stemmed from the threat of competitors achieving first-mover advantages in this regard. Third, since the product is relatively cheap, a high input in technology pays only if this technology is used as often as possible (economies of scope). The technology can be transferred "at the price of one stamp" for sending the blueprints; i.e., transaction costs are very low. Of course, the new technology is introduced only gradually, but the principle applies at least to all new plants.

The forces governing key factors influencing the internationalization process included the following:

The spatial distribution of clay, the main input, determines the location of production, together with the relation between transport costs and the value of the product. Hence, the location of production depends on the proximity to markets. This, at the same time, restricts international trade to a minimum, especially in highly specialized bricks. Therefore, Wienerberger must have subsidiaries abroad, as production is required on the spot. Yet, in principle licensing would be a feasible alternative.

There also clearly exists a need to internalize technological and organizational know-how (see below). Externalization of product and process know-how would create strong positive externalities, as inputs (R&D etc.) are costly relative to the value of output (bricks). Only a maximization of turnover at the same time will reap profits. Second, the possibility to engage in practices such as cross-subsidization between markets as a competitive strategy is a strong incentive to engage in FDI to enter East European and Asian markets. Therefore, Wienerberger's internationalization takes the form of wholly-owned foreign production rather than contractual or trade options.

Wienerberger's competitive advantages are *partly* intangible asset advantages and are *mainly* advantages of common governance. The first, which comprises product and process know-how, has been described above. The second, which refers to the learning experience of Wienerberger and results in economies of scope, deserves closer examination. Brick production is a highly standardized process, and the product is highly standardized, too. When an innovatory shift occurs, the product can be produced by the new standard anywhere in the world. For example, a modern brick production site costs Euro 18–22 mn[iv] and an annual replacement investment of Euro 0.2–0.36 mn. The pay-back period (break even) lasts for seven to eight years in large sites (with an average service-life of 20 to 25 years) and already three to four years in smaller sites. Thus, the initial investment in a state-of-the-art technology deters entry by medium-sized firms.[v] This shows that the criteria for efficiency are very well known in this industry. The fact that these economies of scope exist does not sufficiently explain why Wienerberger acquired other firms (and not vice versa). One other competitive advantage is the financial capacity that Wienerberger developed in the home market.

Therefore, Wienerberger enjoys advantages over *new entrants* as well as *established* foreign competitors. This explains its success in internationalization. Summarizing, Wienerberger may not be a typical example of a multinational firm,[vi] yet a closer look reveals that the advantages of common governance are "the oil" in its internationalization process.

Target Markets

Wienerberger has attempted to create a market portfolio between *Western Europe, Eastern Europe,* and *overseas* (pipes) of 50 : 30 : 20. Since there are cultural differences in the construction industry in these markets, the market structures differ and require different strategies. In *Central Europe* heavy bricks are used, but the *Western markets* show overcapacities while in the *Eastern markets* capacities must rapidly be built up. Here the shortage of management and engineering capacity conflicts with excess demand. In these markets, Wienerberger can use its know-how best. In *Western Europe* the know-how must be acquired since mainly facing bricks are used.

Profits in *West European markets* have declined dramatically in the brick business, and in *East European markets* they are still low on an absolute level and differ substantially from country to country. The substitution of old by new markets causes several frictions which are reflected in a decline in the profitability of the bricks division as shown in Table 10, where Western Europe reveals an overall loss, while operations in the US and in Central and Eastern Europe are profitable. For example, sales increased by 65 per cent in the Czech Republic in 1995 (*Annual Report* 1995, p. 35), but the margins are lower than those in traditional markets. For example, in 2001, Central and Eastern Europe contributed no less than 65 per cent of the profits of the bricks division. So far, the decline of profits in the core markets has been counterbalanced by new acquisitions in France and Belgium (see description below).

But Eastern Europe itself is not a homogeneous market. In the *Commonwealth of Independent States (CIS)* and the *Ukraine* the "construction culture" differs again. Acquisitions in these markets are mainly resource oriented, and new Wienerberger technology has to be set up there. These markets require thorough preparations as the geographical distance widens and direct contacts between established Wienerberger plants become more difficult—in addition to the unstable economic and political environment.

Why is Wienerberger not active in *Southern Europe*? Product differentiation (heavy bricks and light bricks) and market structure are the main entry barriers, implying that a large market share cannot be achieved within a short period.[vii]

Operating Modes in Major Markets

The dominating operating mode is local production in wholly owned subsidiaries and production sites. Table 12 lists the major Wienerberger plants by country, division, and whether majority or minority owned.

The acquisition policy of Wienerberger is based on a "majority-ownership" principle, i.e., units which operate independently for the group without entailing problems of control. Many units acquired—with few exceptions—are rather small, thus not involving large financial outlays. Most acquisitions are market seeking, resource seeking, and rationalizing rather than strategic asset seeking. One recent example of such an acquisition is the *Sturm Group*, which entails—according to Wienerberger—the following advantages over a green-field investment: market entry into Eastern France, market leadership in southwest Germany, lean corporate structure, state of the art technology, low production costs, and above average earnings. Another example is the acquisition of *Terca Bricks*, which not only guarantees the stable ownership structure (see above its mother company *Koramic*) of Wienerberger, but also complements the product range of the bricks division in an optimal way in new markets. Moreover, this acquisition involves a transfer of technology from Wienerberger to Terca in hollow bricks and vice versa in light bricks.

In both cases the number of plants and the efficiency are high: Sturm owned 17 plants in 1996 and a profit-turnover ratio of 15.9 per cent, while for Terca the numbers were 28 in 1995 and 17.7 per cent, respectively.

The fact that no less than 15 of Wienerberger's acquisitions were shut down during the last few years reflects the pressure for rationalization and reduction of overcapacity in order to avoid price competition.

As with other firms and industries, some of Wienerberger's take-over attempts remained unsuccessful, e.g., the attempt to take over Redlands Bricks in 1995 (see Table 8) or the Salverson Group in 1994. The reason in both cases was mainly that take-over prices were too high: about three times the annual turnover. As a rule of thumb, even payment of a sum equal to twice the annual turnover normally is considered as too expensive and would justify a take-over only in exceptional cases.

The take-over of a brick producer abroad usually entails the following steps: vertical integration of resources (resource-oriented FDI) and markets (market-oriented FDI); the production process is normally not integrated, if the acquired plants are new, i.e., horizontal integration. Subsequently, the number of employees is drastically reduced, and at the same time capacity is extended. If an old plant exists, it is kept only as long as demand is high. Yet, in the stagnant markets of today they are quickly shut down, since they often feature unit production costs twice as high as new plants. Since such plants are relatively small, troubles with local authorities or with works councils remain limited.

Table 12
List of the major Wienerberger plants by country and ownership (April 1996) (n = 129)

Country	No of units					
	Bricks and Tiles		Pipes		Treibacher	
	majority	minority	majority	minority	majority	minority
Austria	18	3	2		2	
Belgium			2			
Croatia	1					
Czech Rep.	2	9	1			
France	15			5		
Germany	19	5	3			
Greece				1		
Hungary	8	6		2		
Italy	2	2			1	
Netherlands			1			
Poland	1					
Portugal	1					
Slovak Rep.	1					
Slovenia		2			1	
Spain			3			
Turkey				1		
Asia			2	3		
N. America					3	
Total	68	27	19	8	7	0

Source: based on *Annual Report* 1995, p. 15

Exports, Distribution, Service Policy

Bricks are a good example of non-tradable goods. The simple comparative advantage model of international trade (Ricardo) tells us that in an industry which uses labor (and forget about clay for a moment) as an input, trade is discouraged if transport costs are substantial. In such a case the comparative advantage is eroded and foreign markets may be served by the movement of factors rather than of goods. In order to build an average family house, between two and three truck loads of bricks are needed. These represent a value of about ATS 80,000 (approx. US$ 8,000) and demonstrates the local nature of the business. Bricks are supplied economically only over a range of 150 kilometers maximum.

Regional market segmentation requires also that Wienerberger uses the local brand names when firms are taken over. A global brand name would not create additional profits. Due to the regional nature of the market, it does not pay for Wienerberger to set up its own distribution outlets or to organise sales "ex works." Therefore, distribution is made by independent sales agents often belonging to large chains of construction materials warehouses.

Foreign Affiliates

The number of plants owned by Wienerberger in mid-1996 was 159, of which 27 were in Austria. The remaining 132 were dispersed in 21 countries. Almost all (148) are less than ten years old. The units are independent of each other and serve regional markets. The main marketing and product directives come from the holding company in Vienna (see Table 12).

Figure 2 shows clearly that expansion has taken place primarily abroad. As Table 12 shows, most of the units abroad are in the bricks division (95), while in the pipes division the number is considerably smaller (27). There is, however, a substantial difference in the size distribution of the units: While the bricks division accounts for a large number of small units, the units of the pipes division are considerably larger, which is explained by the different production process[viii] of both

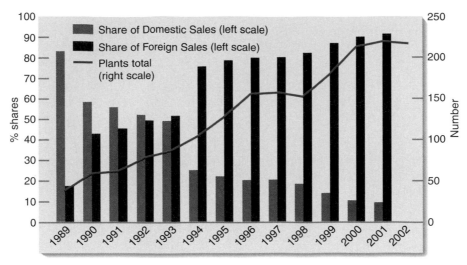

Figure 2. Operations at home and abroad
Source: Pinner 1996, p. 7 and *Annual Reports*

divisions. The latter can be much more regionally concentrated than the former.

Employment and Sales Abroad

The internationalization process led to a growing share of employment and sales abroad, while the number of domestic employees declined steadily (see Tables 13 and 14 and Figure 2). This meant a virtual reversal of foreign and domestic shares during the two decades, since internationalization had started.

International Strategic Alliances

International coalitions are seldom found in Wienerberger's bricks division, while they are more important in the pipes business.[ix] In facing bricks, however, the acquisitions of Sturm and Terca generate an important transfer of know-how which complements existing Wienerberger technology.

6. OUTLOOK

The *current position* of Wienerberger is characterized by the optimization of existing operations and preparation for further expansion. The former comprises activities like improved marketing of the new plain bricks, new technologies, cost-cutting programs, and local capacity reduction. Price wars have already begun and will exert further pressure on margins.

The problems Wienerberger faces in the *future* are many. Established markets are characterized by excess capacity, stagnating demand, and declining margins. After a decade of continued growth during which Wienerberger's sales have increased sevenfold and profits even 15-fold (see Table 1), constant sales (based on new acquisitions and market growth *per se*), but declining profits are expected as Wienerberger is entering a phase of consolidation.

New markets are difficult to enter,[x] but bear a high growth potential. A major advantage of Wienerberger has been the pos-

---

Table 13
Turnover, employment, and value-added of Wienerberger by domestic and foreign share, selected years

	1992	1993	1994	1995	2001
Sales	ATS mn				€ mn
total	11,711	12,120	10,553	12,855	1,544.9
— domestic	6,022	5,946	2,590	2,845	139.3
— abroad	5,689	6,174	7,963	10,010	1,405.6
Employees (no)					
Total	5,596	5,629	4,803	6,418	11,331
— domestic	1,950	2,675	2,382	2,302	906
— abroad	3,646	2,954	2,421	4,116	10,425

Source: *Annual Reports* 1992–1995 and internal information by Wienerberger

Table 14
Foreign sales and employment in selected countries (1996)

Country	Employment		Sales	
	Number	**% of Total**	**ATS mn**	**% of Total**
Germany	1,207	14.7	3,339	22.2
Belgium	982	11.9	1,527	10.1
France	871	10.6	1,705	11.3
Netherlands	500	6.1	1,327	8.8
Italy	157	1.9	521	3.5
Spain	109	1.3	409	2.7
USA/Canada	111	1.3	593	3.9
China	194	2.4	127	0.8
Czech Republic	678	8.2	573	3.8
Hungary	597	7.3	455	3.0
Foreign Total	6,036	73.4	12,107	80.4
Austria	2,193	26.6	2,954	19.6
Total	8,229	—	15,061	—

Note: Selected Countries do not add up to 100%
Source: *Annual Report* 1996, p. 31 and p. 72

sibility of cross-subsidizing markets. This will become even more important in the future, since new markets must counterbalance the decline of traditional core markets. In Eastern Europe, actual and potential growth substitutes for losses in old markets, but there are still problems with low productivity and market instability. Therefore, in the medium run, the new markets will not be able to compensate for either the volume or the margins of the traditional markets.

In the years to come, Wienerberger sees many opportunities to differentiate itself through cost leadership, technological leadership, full exploitation of market potential, and increasing synergies from the latest acquisitions. Besides, new large acquisitions are likely in the core business, since according to one Wienerberger manager: "We do not believe in the life-cycle of a firm—we believe that it constantly has to be re-born."

REFERENCES

Annual Reports of Wienerberger, various years.

Bank und Börse, various years.

Bellak, C. (1994) Outsiders' Response to EC'92—Evidence from Austria, *Multinational Business Review*, Fall, pp. 40-3.

Bellak, C. (1996) Foreign Direct Investment From Small States and Integration—Micro- and Macroeconomic Evidence from Austria, in: Hirsch, Seev, Tamar Almor (eds.) *Outsider's Response to the Unification of the European Community*, Munksgaard International Publishers Ltd., pp. 57–98.

Bellak, C. (1997) Austrian Manufacturing MNEs—Long Term Perspectives, *Journal of Business History*, Vol. 39, No. 1; pp. 47–71.

Bellak, C. et al. (1989) 17 aus 338—Internationalisierungsstrategien österreichischer Unternehmen, IWI Series "Internationalization," Vol. II, Vienna (especially: Ch. III, Wienerberger Baustoffindustrie AG, pp. 129–136).

Bellak, C. and Weiss, A. (1993) The Austrian Diamond, *Management International Review*, Special Issue, No. 2, pp. 109–118.

Chandler, A.D. (1990) *Scale and Scope*, Cambridge: Mass., Harvard University Press.

Czerny, M. (1996) Weitere Abschwächung der Baukonjunktur in Westeuropa, WIFO *Monatsberichte*, No. 2, pp. 117–121.

Czerny, M. (1998) Baukonjunktur erholt sich in Westeuropa nur schwach, WIFO *Monatsberichte*, No. 2, pp. 83–89.

Czerny, M. (1999) Leichte Belebung der Baukonjunktur in Westeuropa erwartet, WIFO *Monatsberichte*, No. 2, pp. 129–134.

Czerny, M. (2000) Wieder Dämpfung der Baukonjunktur in Westeuropa. WIFO *Monatsberichte*, No. 3, pp. 191–196.

Czerny, M. (2002) Nach Stagnation der Europäischen Bauwirtschaft leichte Erholung erst 2003/04, WIFO *Monatsberichte*, No. 3, pp. 161–166.

Dunning, J.H. (1993) *Multinational Enterprises and the Global Economy*, Addison-Wesley, Wokingham.

EU-Panorama 1995–6, Brussels.

EUROCONSTRUCT, various issues, Brussels.

Eurostat (2002) *European business—facts and figures*. Part 1: Industry and construction, Office for Official Publications of the European Communities; ISBN 92-894-3219-5, Luxembourg.

Fédération Européenne des Fabricants de Tuiles et de Briques, Zurich. (information about the latest sales figures)

Ghoshal, S. (1987) Global Strategy: An Organizing Framework, *Strategic Management Journal*, Vol. 8, pp. 425–440.

Gray, H.P. (1996) *Dunning's Eclectic Paradigm in1996*, mimeographed (Rutgers University, N.J.), 18p.

Markusen, J.R. (1995) The Boundaries of Multinational Enterprises and the Theory of International Trade, *Journal of Economic Perspectives*, Vol. 9, No. 2, Spring, pp. 169–189.

Mathis, F. *Big Business in Österreich*, Oldenburg, 1987.

OeNB (1995, ed.) *Bilanzkennzahlen österreichischer Industrieunternehmen 1991–1994*, No. 12 (Beilage zum statistischen Monatsheft), Vienna.

Pinner, W. (1996) *Unternehmensanalyse Wienerberger*, Die Erste, October, Vienna.

Porter, M.E. (1990) *The Competitive Advantage of Nations*, The Free Press, New York.

Tiles and Brick International, various issues.

Vince-Bsteh, C. and Kaltenbacher, S. (1996) Unternehmensanalyse Wienerberger AG, RZB, May, Vienna.

Wienerberger's homepage: www.wienerberger.at

WIFO; Euroconstruct, Rome (2001) The outlook for the European construction sector 2001–2004. Download address:

http://titan.wsr.ac.at/wifosite/wifosite.get_abstract_type?p_language=1&pubid=21004.

There are also analyses of the stock exchange and banks (analyst's reports of Bank Austria, Creditanstalt, and Erste Bank) and public institutions and all articles which appeared in newspapers and magazines about Wienerberger between 1988 and 2001.

ENDNOTES

i   *Treibacher* (ferro-alloys, corundum, and flints) was also owned by the *Creditanstalt* for many years and had been "in the red" until recently. It had been incorporated into Wienerberger so that the owners could take advantage of the latter's managerial competence. Contrary to the other divisions, its business was always global, and the customers are few and large (restricted monopoly), mainly in the steel industry. Due to the difficult market, *Treibacher* was considered to be the "venture field of Wienerberger" and was independent of the other divisions. Eventually, it was sold in 2000.

ii   In the pipes division, the booming Asian markets offer an additional growth potential but are more difficult to enter.

iii   At first sight this may sound like an advertisement of Wienerberger—but all the figures presented in this case study have to prove it.

iv   This sum corresponds to two to three annual turnovers only.

v   In the pipes industry, market entry is different, since a step-by-step expansion simply through adding more machines is possible, albeit a certain minimum output must be achieved in order to reap economies of scale. Sunk costs are higher than in the brick industry.

vi   As Markusen (1995, p. 172) points out, "multinationals tend to be important in industries and firms with four characteristics: high levels of R&D relative to sales; a large share of professional and technical workers in their workforces; products that are new and/or technically complex; and high levels of product differentiation and advertising. These characteristics appear in many studies, and I have never seen any of them contradicted in any study." Wienerberger—or the bricks industry in general—is certainly a "borderline case" in this context.

vii   In Asian markets where Wienerberger has some activities in the pipes business and where entry proved to be very difficult, an important decision lies ahead: the alternatives are either large-scale entry or total withdrawal of activities.

viii   With pipes economies of scale are much more important, since the raw material is transportable. With bricks, production often tends to be around the minimum efficiency scale, depending on the size of the local market. Expanding the output is therefore an important strategy of Wienerberger to move outwards along the horizontal part of the average cost function (i.e., constant average costs).

ix   Market entry by acquisition is more difficult in the latter, as there are few smaller firms which can be acquired. Moreover, the acquisition of know-how is more important than in the bricks division, given the relatively short period of Wienerberger's activities in this field.

x   E.g., Asian pipe market.

CASE DISCUSSION QUESTIONS

1. Do you agree with the companies' decision to internationalize? Justify your argument.

2. What other strategic options did the company have? Describe each fully and justify your choice as the most appropriate option.

3. Which entry modes would you choose? Why?

4. Do you agree with the companies' choice of geographic target markets? Why, or why not?

5. Which theories of trade and/or FDI best explain the companies' strategic actions? Justify your choice.

Elscint, Incorporated and the Worldwide Medical Imaging Industry

by Mona Makhija,
Uri Ben-Zion,
Gdaliahu Harel*

**The Ohio State University,
Ben-Gurion University,
Technion Institute of
Technology*

We wish to thank REMAS Limited and Giora Teltsch for their assistance in preparing this paper.

Elscint Ltd. was one of Israel's first high-technology companies, creating a niche for itself in computer-based medical diagnostic imaging technologies. Since its founding in 1969, Elscint has pioneered a number of technological innovations in the computer-based medical diagnostic imaging industry, which provides medical diagnostic information that helps to replace invasive diagnostic procedures. Elscint's line of products and systems can be grouped into four main modality groups: Computed Tomography (CT); Nuclear Medicine (NM); Magnetic Resonance Imaging (MRI); and Medical Ultrasound (ULS). The worldwide market for these imaging modalities grew from approximately $1 billion in 1980 to $5 billion 1990, and then to $10.2 billion in 1998. Elscint's sales grew from $111 million in 1990 to $ 209 million in 1998.

Elscint Ltd. started out as a subsidiary of Elron Ltd. It went public in 1978, listing its shares on the New York Stock Exchange. In 1985–6, Elscint was near bankruptcy, but was saved by government guaranteed loans. This resulted in approximately 45% of its shares held by its creditor banks. In 1990, another Elron-controlled company, Elbit Ltd., which at the time dedicated to military equipment systems, took over Elscint. It received 44% of the shares from the banks for $22 million, and 24.7% of the shares from Elron for $19 million.

In 1994, Elscint's parent company Elbit created a wholly owned subsidiary, Elbit Ultrasound Ltd. (EMI). Through EMI, the company acquired Diasonics Ultrasound, Inc., a California-based manufacturer of diagnostic ultrasound systems, for $81 million. One year later, Elbit took over Elscint's ultrasound division for $7.8 million and merged it into EMI.

In March 1998, EMI received an offer to sell all its ultrasound operations to GE Medical Systems (GEMS) for around $228 million. Later that same year, Elscint was given another opportunity to sell its net assets in its NM and MRI divisions and business to GEMS for approximately $100 million. At the same time, Picker (GEC) expressed the desire to take over Elscint's CT operations, in consideration of approximately $265 million.

Many in management opposed the divesting of main operative parts of the company. Nonetheless, the selling of these divisions of the corporation would achieve a much higher return than the market value of the whole company prior to these divestitures. Elscint was confronted with a difficult situation.

In many ways, Elscint exemplified the globally oriented, high-technology type of company that the Israeli government wanted to promote. The government believed that the higher value-added activities of such types of companies would be the engine of growth for the Israeli economy. Despite the government's assistance to such companies, small high-technology firms in Israel such as Elscint faced a number of obstacles in a highly competitive global industry. ∎

THE ISRAELI GOVERNMENT'S HIGH-TECHNOLOGY POLICIES

There has been growing recognition across nations that technology is a determining factor of economic development. Accordingly, many governments had begun to develop policies to foster greater technological innovation and progress in their countries. This had been particularly true in the case of Israel, which has actively pursued such policies for the last thirty years.

Since 1969, the Israeli government has had the goal of promoting a high technological orientation in the economy. The explicit objectives behind this goal were to create high-quality jobs, promote exports to reduce the trade deficit, and foster productivity and growth. In this regard, it had taken a variety of steps towards establishing national infrastructures associated with research and development, including the creation of research institutions. It had given priority to the goal of increasing support for research and development engaged in by small and large firms, as long as they have potential economic feasibility. In terms of the latter, the Israeli government has historically taken a number of actions to assist high technological firms. It provided low-cost loans to firms to support the development of new technologies through the Office of the Chief Scientist in the Ministry of Trade and Industry, and these loans were returned only out of the proceeds of the R&D. If there were no proceeds, the loan became a grant.

The governmental participation in R&D, and its criteria and mechanics, were developed through the 1970s and 1980s and were codified in 1985 in the Law for the Encouragement of Industrial R&D. This law has been revised many times since then. The goal of this law, and those of the bylaws which preceded it, was to develop science-based, export-oriented industries, which would promote employment and improve the balance of payments. This legislation was supposed to be the basis of expanding and exploiting the technological infrastructure of Israel, as well as making use of the country's high-skilled labor force. In line with this, the government has made available sizeable grants to support production processes related to such technologies. In the period 1987–94, the Office of the Chief Scientist paid out $1,400 million in subsidies to 1,200 firms, supporting $3,500 million in R&D.

There was evidence that the intent behind this law was realized, particularly in terms of Israel's exports and employment. In general, traditional and low value-added exports have been declining as a proportion of total exports, while high-technology exports have been increasing. In 1997, Israeli exports totaled $30 billion, of which more than 60% were technology-based.[1] The Bank of Israel noted that the growth rate of exports from advanced sectors (those employing highly skilled personnel such as scientists and engineers) grew at 18.5% in the years 1997 and 1998, while those from more traditional sectors (with less skilled personnel) generally declined by 1.4% in the same period. The number of technological startups in Israel has similarly been dramatic.[2]

The success of Israel's high-technology policies could also be seen in terms of their contribution to the nation's industrial development. In the period 1987–94, the $3,500 million of supported R&D generated estimated sales of over $31,000 million, creating 260,000 job-years. This constituted roughly 10% of industrial employment. In this same period, a dollar of R&D was found to increase total factor productivity by an additional $0.45, annually contributing $0.3 of GDP on average and earning a direct annual return of 13.4% of the economy. The impact of the subsidies also differed in terms of industrial sector. Electronics, communications, automation, and control equipment received roughly half the subsidies while generating nearly two-thirds of the gains. While small firms received one-sixth of the subsidies, they contributed to over a quarter of the gains.

The Office of the Chief Scientist

The Office of the Chief Scientist (OCS) in the Ministry of Trade and Industry is the chief administrator for the disbursement of funds to firms. The OCS generally funds up to 50% of R&D expenses in established companies and up to 66% for start-up firms. Successful projects repay in royalties on sales. At present, the OCS supports and administers a wide range of additional programs. These include programs that encourage (a) generic or basic research (entitled "magnet" research) through consortiums, (b) technological incubation, at a stage more advanced than that dealt with under the magnet programs, and (c) bilateral and multilateral international collaboration. In addition to these, the OSC also administers other minor programs targeted for more specific types of R&D or particular stages of development of R&D.

Despite the variety of R&D activities associated with it, support for R&D to firms is nonetheless the main activity of the Office of the Chief Scientist. In order to be entitled to receive funds from the OCS in the Ministry of Trade and Industry, a firm must meet certain eligibility criteria. It must have well-articulated plans for the development of innovative and export-oriented products. Qualifying firms submit grant applications for specific R&D projects, which are then reviewed by a committee headed by the Chief Scientist. The process of approval of a budget includes recommendation by a technical officer nominated to scrutinize the program and decision by the committee in the Chief Scientist's office on itemized expenditure and participation.

In the relevant period, if approved, the applicant receives a grant of up to 50% of the stated R&D budget for the project. Approximately 70% of the grant applications are generally approved.[3] If the grant is successful in generating R&D for commercial use and generates sales, the firm must pay back a proportion of its revenues from the sales of the products developed. Under the original terms of Israeli government participation, a royalty of 2% to 3% must be paid from revenues relating to sales of products developed with grant funds until the grant is repaid. If there are no sales, then there is no repayment. The payment is on an annual basis and as part repayment of expenditure. The terms of Israeli government participation also require that production of systems and products developed with government grants must be performed in Israel, unless a special concession has been granted. Separate Israeli government consent is required to transfer to third parties technologies developed through projects in which the government participates. Such restrictions do not apply to export from Israel of products incorporating such technologies.

As of 1998, the royalty amount has been increased, now ranging from 3 to 5% of sales, the percentage going up every three years. Many still consider this amount to be low, and there has been pressure to increase the percentage to be paid back to the government. Royalty is limited to 100% of the dollar value of the amount granted. In the case of the approved transfer of manufacturing rights out of Israel, the maximum to be repaid to the government was raised to 120% to 300% of the amount granted.

Elscint had been a major beneficiary of these forms of government support, repeatedly receiving grants from the Office of the Chief Scientist. In one particularly critical period in Elscint's history, in 1985, it almost went bankrupt due to a poor investment strategy. At that time as well, the government stepped in with additional funds, allowing it to continue to survive by granting government guarantees to the banks for Elscint's loans and pressing the banks to restructure Elscint's debt and forgive part of it.

ELSCINT'S PRODUCTS AND GLOBAL STRATEGY

The medical diagnostics imaging industry is an overwhelmingly global one, with both customers and competitors located across a large number of countries. In order to compete in this environment, Elscint had to focus outside of Israel for the majority of its customers. To this end, Elscint marketed its products worldwide through 16 wholly-owned marketing subsidiaries and various distributors, agents and representatives in Western, Central and Eastern Europe, North America, Commonwealth of Independent States, Latin America, the Middle East, the Pacific Rim (including People's Republic of China), South Africa, and Australia. Most of the company's revenues were generated by its own sales force, which consisted of about 260 people (plus nearly 600 in service). In addition, nearly all of its revenues were generated outside of Israel. In each of its major targeted markets, the company had a dedicated sales force, with different persons focusing on one or more of its four principal imaging modalities.

The Elscint line had products and systems in the following modalities:

1. Computed Tomography

Computed Tomography (CT) systems are based on rotating X-ray assembly that irradiates the body in transverse plane as it rotates around the patient. Data is collected from radiation detectors mounted on the opposite side of the assembly. This data is processed by a dedicated computer system to reconstruct a cross-sectional image of the body that is substantially more detailed than the simple projection image produced by conventional X-ray devices. Unlike conventional X-ray images, multiple CT images made along a longitudinal axis may then be combined to create a three-dimensional image of certain parts of the body without the interference of overlying tissue. This image can be manipulated by the physician to be viewed from any angle. The image can also be reconstructed to view any cross-section required. The three-dimensional and tissue-differentiation capabilities of CT make it especially useful for diagnosis of the central nervous system (head and spine), tumors and cysts, and the effects of trauma. It is also effective for reconstructive surgery and surgical planning. CT has experienced substantial market acceptance since the mid-1970s.

In 1994, the prices for the top-end systems of Elscint ranged from $600,000 to approximately $1,000,000, depending on system configuration and accessories. By 1996, these prices were from $500,000 to approximately $900,000. For Elscint's low-end systems, prices in 1994 ranged from $300,000 to $600,000, depending on system configuration and accessories. By 1996, these prices ranged from $300,000 to approximately $450,000, and in 1997, from $250,000 to approximately $400,000.

Beginning in December 1996, Elscint created an agreement with the Medical Engineering Group of Siemens AG to jointly develop and produce components. It also supplied subassemblies to Siemens.

2. Nuclear Medicine Imaging

Nuclear medicine (NM) imaging is based upon the detection of gamma radiation emitted by radiopharmaceuticals that are administered to a patient, concentrating in the organs to be examined. Gamma cameras using large sodium iodide detectors and dedicated nuclear medicine workstations trace the gamma particles emitted by the radiopharmaceutical. A complex electro-optical system detects their location within the patient's body or the examined organ. A distribution map of these particles is computer generated and displayed, forming a representation of the radiopharmaceutical distribution in the patient's body. This data is either directly used for diagnosis or further processed by the nuclear medicine workstation. NM systems can provide detailed diagnostic information relating to the function of the organs. These capabilities are especially useful in diagnosing coronary artery disease, cancer, and neurological functions that manifest themselves in normal and abnormal brain metabolism. In recent years, Single Photon Emission Computerized Tomography (SPECT), a technique which provides tomographic slices showing a three-dimensional distribution of radioisotope tracers, has become a standard capability in nuclear medicine imaging. Nuclear imaging began evolving as an important diagnostic imaging technology in the late 1960s.

In 1993, Elscint offered Positron Emission Tomography (PET) scanners to observe the consumption by cells of substances tagged with high-energy short half-life radioisotopes generated by cyclotrons. PET provides images of higher spatial resolution than NM SPECT images.

In 1994, prices for Elscint's NM gamma camera systems ranged from approximately $280,000 to $500,000, depending on the model selected and the system configuration. In 1996, the price range was from $150,000 to approximately $500,000 and from $40,000 to approximately $80,000 for a workstation.

Since July 1997 Elscint has had a joint venture with the Medical Systems division of GE—called ELGEMS—for development and production of systems sold by the two parent companies.

3. Magnetic Resonance Imaging

Magnetic resonance imaging (MRI) technology utilizes strong and homogeneous magnetic fields and the magnetic properties of various nuclei in the body to produce signals that can be measured, analyzed, and manipulated by a dedicated computer system to produce tomographic images. MRI provides good image contrast without the ionizing radiation exposure that is the basis of the conventional X-ray, CT, and NM modalities. The MRI modality enables the user to view a wide variety of tissue cross-sections at different angles along various axes, enhancing the resolution of three-dimensional images and making it particularly useful for imaging the central nervous system and for cardiac and muscular-skeletal diagnosis. This modality also permits diagnosis of the body's vascular system through magnetic resonance angiography, through which blood vessels are imaged and diagnosed. It has the potential to precisely determine metabolic function and dysfunction through magnetic resonance spectroscopy, a technique with varied applications which to date have not been integrated into routine clinical use. MRI began to achieve commercial acceptance in the early 1980s.

Elscint's MRI systems in 1994 ranged in price from $850,000 to $1,500,000, depending on the model selected and system configuration, from $650,000 to approximately $1,500,000 in 1996, and from $650,000 to approximately $1,400,000 in 1997.

4. Ultrasound Imaging

Ultrasound imaging (ULS) systems produce images by detecting and analyzing echoes of high-frequency sound waves focused on, and reflected back from, different organs within a patient's body. ULS has the ability to provide both static and dynamic images for analyzing an organ's function, as well as for tissue morphology. ULS also has the advantage of not using ionizing radiation, which makes it particularly suitable for the obstetrics/gynecology clinical segments. It is also widely used for cardiology and general radiology. ULS imaging was introduced as a practical imaging modality in the early 1970s.

5. Other Products

In addition to the major modalities discussed above, Elscint had a presence in several other medical imaging products as well, including mammography, connectivity solutions, and multi-imagers. These are discussed below.

Mammography

Mammography is used for the screening and diagnosis of patients for breast cancer, using an X-ray system that is customized for this application. Since 1993, Elscint has had a computer-controlled, low-dose mammography system. Prices for mammography units ranged from $55,000 to $125,000 in 1994, and from $65,000 to $90,000 in 1996–8.

Connectivity Solutions

Since 1994, Elscint has had a DICOM compliant independent multi-modality diagnostic workstation, which provides enhanced viewing, processing analysis, manipulation, storage and retrieval of images from different modalities. Virtual Endoscopy provides non-invasive, computer generated inner-body views similar to actual endoscopic procedures.

In 1996 Elscint introduced advanced WAN (Wide Area Network) solutions. These served to connect remote scanners to a central site for professional diagnostic services.

Multi-Imagers

Multi-imagers involve a multi-format camera that is used as an output device for all of Elscint's imaging systems. It features the high spatial resolution and linearity necessary for high-quality hard-copy reproduction of computer-generated images. The multi-imager is an essential part of most medical imaging equipment.

Elscint did not compete in the conventional X-ray market or in therapeutic equipment. In addition, it did not have a full line in other segments of the medical imaging field.

THE MEDICAL IMAGING INDUSTRY

The worldwide medical diagnostic imaging market (including conventional X-ray and customer support services) has been led by five major industrial companies: General Electric Corporation (U.S.A.), Siemens A.G. (Germany), Toshiba (Japan), Philips NV (the Netherlands), and the General Electric Company (U.K.). Other companies, including Hitachi Corporation, Ltd., Shimadzu Corporation, ADAC Laboratories, Elscint, Sopha Medical of ATL, Inc., Hewlett-Packard Corporation, Aloka Ltd., as well as many other smaller companies, share the remainder of the medical diagnostic imaging market.

The worldwide market for medical imaging has grown steadily. Between 1980 and 1990, this market grew from $1 billion to $5 billion. This market was estimated to be at $8.7 billion in 1995 and at $10.2 billion in 1998.[4] Sales are primarily to hospitals and clinics, which included teaching hospitals, community hospitals, private clinics, and hospital chains. These sales are made either directly or through unaffiliated leasing companies.

The maintenance of a long-term position in the market depends on the ability to introduce new technologically advanced products. Competition in the industry is primarily focused on providing advanced technological equipment with high-resolution imaging capability applicable to a wide variety of clinical procedures. Pricing, product reliability, and other performance indicators are all important competitive features. In addition, customers expect a high level of service and after-sales support.

Another feature of the medical imaging industry resulted from important changes in the structure of the healthcare all over the world, particularly in the large and influential market of the United States. The increasing costs of healthcare were no longer acceptable, and Health Management Organizations (HMOs) sprung up all over the United States to stem this increase. Other major economies in Europe faced recessionary pressures, which reduced the outlay of expenditures for public healthcare. These factors not only reduced growth, but also intensified competition in the medical equipment market.

Given the global nature of the medical imaging market, the ability to market across national boundaries was an important element. The ability to provide service to customers is also facilitated by a firm's global presence. Ongoing interaction with customers provides other important benefits, including information on medical developments that could provide the impetus for new products, adaptations required by hospitals due to infrastructural problems, and perspectives of the customers on competing products. Nonetheless, wide differences in marketing capabilities existed across competing firms.

Competition and Market Share

Within the overall dominance of the large companies, there were noticeable differences between the market shares in the various modalities (as well as in the various geographic regions). It is clear that market advantage could be translated into some price differential. Relative positions of market share in different modalities are given below.

Computed Tomography

World Market Share (%) held by companies providing CT equipment, based on revenues in 1996

Company	Market Share
GE Medical Systems	31
Siemens Medical Systems	17
Picker International	16
Philips Medical Systems	14
Toshiba Medical Systems	12
Others	10
TOTAL	100

Notes:
*Others include Elscint, Hitachi Medical Corporation, Medical High Technology International, Shimadzu Medical Systems. Hitachi distributes through Philips in all geographic regions except Japan. Hitachi has its own product line of CT scanners in Japan.
All figures are rounded.

Nuclear Medicine

World Market Share (%) held by companies in Gamma Camera Equipment, based on revenues in 1994

Company	Total Market Share	NonSPECT Share	Single-Head SPECT Share	Dual-Head SPECT Share
ADAC Laboratories	26	26	31	36
Siemens Medical Systems	19	19	25	13
GE Medical Systems Group	16	16	18	15
Picker	11	11	—	18
Sopha Medical	8	8	9	7
Elscint	6	6	8	5
Toshiba Medical Systems	5	5	—	—
Others	9	9	9	6
TOTAL	100	100	100	100

Notes:
*Others include (1) Total: Park Medical, Scinticor, Shimadzu, Summit Nuclear, Trionix. (2) Non SPECT: Park Medical, Scinticor, Shimadzu, Summit Nuclear, and Trionix. (3) Single-Head SPECT: Park Medical, Picker International, Scinticor, Shimadzu, Summit Nuclear, and Toshiba. (4) Dual-Head SPECT: Park Medical Systems, Shimadzu Medical Systems, Summit Nuclear/Hitachi, Toshiba Medical Systems, and Trionix Research Laboratory.
All figures are rounded.

Positron Emission Tomography (PET)

World Market Share (%) held by Positron Emission Tomography (PET) equipment manufacturers, based on revenues in 1994 and 1996

Company	Market Share 1994	Market Share 1996
Siemens/CTI PET Systems	45	42
GE Medical Systems	43	39
Shimadzu Medical Systems	8	10
Positron	4	6
Others*	3	3
TOTAL	100	100

Notes:
*Others include Pett Electronics, UGM Medical Systems.
All figures are rounded.

Diagnostic MRI Equipment Market

World Market Share (%) held by companies providing Diagnostic MRI Equipment, by revenues, 1996

Company	Market Share
GE Medical Systems	25
Siemens Medical Systems	24
Toshiba Medical Systems	15
Philips Medical Systems	12
Picker International	10
Hitachi Medical Corporation	7
Elscint	5
Others	2
TOTAL	100

Notes:
*Others include Advanced NMR, Asahi Chemical, Bruker Instruments, Fonar, Health Images, Metriflow Medical, Shimadzu Medical Systems, Sopha Medical Vision.
All figures are rounded.

Ultrasound Equipment

World Market Share (%) held by companies providing Diagnostic MRI Equipment, by revenues, 1996

Company	Market Share
Acuson	16
ATL	14
GE Medical Systems	13
Aloka	11
Toshiba Medical Systems	10
Elscint	6
Hitachi Medical Corporation	5
B&K Instruments	5
Others	20
TOTAL	100

Notes:
*Others include Acoustic Imaging, Alcon Laboratories (Surgical Products Division), Biosound, Canon USA, Cardiometrics, Carolina Medical Electronics, Dianostic Ultrasound, Esaote/Biomedica, Fukuda Denshi, Hoffrel Instruments, Humphreys Instruments, Hewlett-Packard Medical Products Group, Kontron Instruments, Medison, Mentor, Nidek, Perception, Philips Medical Systems, Pie Medical Equipment, Shimadzu Medical Systems, Siemens Medical Systems, Sonomed, Storz Instruments, Tetrad, Tomey Technology.
All figures are rounded.

Mammography

World Market Share (%) held by mammography equipment manufacturers, based on revenues, 1995 and 1996

Company	Market Share 1996	Market Share 1995
Trex Medical Corporation	48	35
GE Medical Systems	23	11
Siemens Medical Systems	5	9
Fischer Imaging		15
Continental		11
Others*	23	19
TOTAL	100	100

Notes:
*Others include (1996) Acoma Medical Imaging, Dentsply International, Dynarad, Elscint, Instrumentarium Imaging, Kramex, Philips Medical Systems, Picker International, (1995) Acoma, Dynarad, Dentsply International, International Medical Systems, Instrumentarium, Metaltronica SRL, Philips Medical Systems, Picker International, Planmed, Shimadzu, and TECHNOMED
All figures are rounded.

ELSCINT'S PERFORMANCE

1. Elscint's Sales

Although the worldwide industry for medical imaging modalities was driven by technological breakthroughs, by the 1990s cost considerations began to play a major role. Nonetheless, Elscint achieved a market share of 6% to 8% in some modalities. Despite its small size, this pointed to its strong technological capabilities in a number of product areas. The table below indicates Elscint's revenues by geographical area and modality. The breakdown of sales according to modalities will show that CT, the main modality of Elscint, has made a large gain, of about a third in sales as of 1995, and that the MRI has more than doubled in sales as of 1996.

Elscint's revenues by geographic markets, 1992–8 (in $ thousands)

	1992	1993	1994	1995	1996	1997	1998
N. America	$ 64,952	$ 79,721	$67,051	$71,282	$77,820	$69,861	$61,351
Europe	105,197	103,998	100,817	122,888	140,797	118,342	92,840
S. America	20,878	21,687	25,644	27,985	38,649	50,597	31,630
Pacific Rim	13,280	17,646	22,495	35,567	29,502	30,608	27,813
Israel	9,010	8,654	11,496	14,417	18,206	25,046	41,324
Others	7,604	6,098	7,372	9,767	6,446	8,537	7,100
Total	$220,891	$237,804	$234,875	$281,906	$311,420	$302,991	$262,058

System sales (including sub assemblies) by modality (in $'000,000)

	1993	1994	1995	1996	1997	1998
CT	66.3	74.1	100.9	109.4	92.4	100.4
MRI	32.6	22.8	22.6	49.5	49.1	22.9
NM	68.4	56.6	54.9	55.7	64.9	76.4
ULS	2.4	5.1	11	2.8	1.6	0.2
MAM	2.8	3.9	6.8	4.7	4.9	5.5
Others	1.6	1.6	5.1	4.7	3.2	3.9
Total	**174.1**	**164.1**	**201.3**	**226.8**	**216.0**	**209.3**

2. Research and Development

Elscint conducted extensive research and development activities in line with its strategy to develop products with enhanced features and improved performance. The company used information obtained through its sales and marketing operations (together with information obtained during test-trials of its products at major hospitals and universities worldwide) to focus its research and development activities to meet current and emerging market needs.

In many respects, Elscint was a technology leader and pioneered several innovations, including the first integrated digital NM camera, intravaginal scanning, and interactive three-dimensional presentations. Each of the company's products included a substantial amount of proprietary software. Purchasers of the company's products had access to the company's broad and comprehensive library of software programs developed and clinically tested over the past decade. The company had accumulated extensive experience both in the design of operating systems software and in the development of applications software. This enabled the company to provide its customers with new software versions which enhanced and extended the capabilities of systems purchased by such customers. While Elscint's research and development activities focused on its core modalities and on those technologies upon which its products are dependent, the company also closely monitored the technological advances related to the critical components and subassemblies that it did not manufacture. Elscint worked with manufacturers of such components to keep abreast of changing technologies to provide its customers with improved products. Such components included, for example, X-ray tubes, high voltage power supplies, RF amplifiers, and photomultipliers. Elscint also closely monitored emerging technologies for their application to future products that may be developed by the company. In this regard, it had purchased the assets of several ongoing operations which had significant research and development activities.

In the period of 1997–8, Elscint employed approximately 280 research and development employees for the purpose of developing new products and enhancing existing products. Of these personnel, approximately 240 were located in Israel. In earlier years, somewhat more researchers were engaged in R&D in the company.

Elscint regularly received royalty-bearing participation from the Office of the Chief Scientist of the Ministry of Trade and Industry for the development of systems, options, and products. As a participating company, Elscint received grants for 30% to 50% of its approved development expenditures for particular projects. The grant was called "participation" in an attempt to avoid entanglement (and punitive taxation) by United States customs authorities who consider subsidies to be a form of unfair competition.

Elscint typically sought patent or copyright protection for its products. As of December 31, 1997, the company held 328 patents related to diagnostic medical imaging (compared to 315 patents in 1994). In addition, numerous patent applications were also pending in the United States, Israel, Germany, the Netherlands, Japan, England, Canada, and France (this number was 244 in 1994). Elscint believed that its research orientation in medical imaging, a field of rapidly changing technology, increased the importance of its patents which were intended to

Elscint's R&D expenditures in $ Millions

	Total R&D	Chief Scientist's participation	Net R&D
1995 $mm	$26.4	$7.9	$18.5
1996 $mm	$28.3	$7.4	$20.9
1997 $mm	$24.2	$7.1	$17.1
1998 $mm	$15.8	$5.2	$10.7

R&D expenditure as % of
revenue and as % of
operating profit

	Total R&D	Chief Scientist's participation	Net R&D
As % of revenue			
1995	9.4	2.8	6.6
1996	9.1	2.4	6.7
1997	8.0	2.3	5.7
1998	6.0	2.0	4.0
As % of operating profit			
1995	240.9	72.1	168.8
1996	521.9	136.5	385.5
1997	434.9	127.6	307.3
1998	59.1	19.5	40.0

protect the company's ability to develop, manufacture, and market its products. The tables above provide a breakdown of Elscint's research and development expenditures for several years, as well as its proportion in relation to sales and profits.

THE ROAD AHEAD

By 1998, Elscint was a company at a crossroads. It was clear that many of its competitors posed formidable threats. The volume and complexity of its worldwide markets also made it difficult to compete. Although management understood that changes had to be made in their global strategy, it was unclear in what direction these should be. Should Elscint divest some of its businesses? If so, which ones? How could it leverage its limited financial resources? Could Elscint rationally expect any more assistance from the Israeli government? These difficult questions faced the management of Elscint as they pondered the future.

CASE DISCUSSION QUESTIONS

1. Does Elscint have a legal and/or ethical obligation to the government of Israel with respect to the disposition of its assets?

2. What factors should be considered in the decision to divest one, some, or all of Elscint's Strategic Business Units (SBUs)?

3. What factors support the retention of one, some or all of Elscint's SBUs?

4. What strategies should Elscint pursue?

5. Devise a plan of action designed to deal with all of Elscint's concerns.

ENDNOTES

1 Michael Eilan, "Less Is More: Israel's Technology Policies," National Institute for Research Advancement, 1998.

2 For an extensive discussion of such startups, see Yeheskel et al., "Cooperative Wealth Creation: Strategic Alliances in Israeli Medical Technology Ventures," Academy of Management Executive, 2001, pp. 16–25.

3 This description of OCS activities is drawn from the NBER Working Paper 7930 by Manuel Trajtenberg, entitled "R&D Policy in Israel: An Overview and Reassessment."

4 Estimates are from Medical Imaging Markets Report, Frost and Sullivan, Incorporated, 1999.

Troika Potato Chips (A)[1]

ST. PETERSBURG, RUSSIA

by Gene Gutenberg*

*Cornell University

John Mirren drummed his fingers impatiently on the dashboard as he sat in the usual Moscow traffic jam. He was a managing director of a British-owned, Moscow-based investment fund that made investments in various businesses throughout Russia. John saw many business plans, written with various degrees of competence, every week, and he had to decide which ones warranted further investigation. As part of his job, he visited companies that seemed especially promising.

John left his job at a London investment boutique in 1990 to take a job in Russia at a time when Russia was considered the land of unlimited opportunity. He had a background in the region because he had studied Russian history, literature, and language in university and had spent a year in St. Petersburg writing his senior thesis. As managing director of the investment fund, he had been extensively involved in evaluating and managing many projects, a few of which turned out to be spectacular successes, but many of them barely broke even and some were complete failures.

That week he was considering several plans. There was a furniture factory in Novosibirsk that was making good quality copies of Russian Empire furniture, as well as more modern furniture, and it needed investment money to expand operations. An interesting proposal—to open a fast food restaurant in Yekatrinburg—had come into the office last week. That seemed very promising since the potential manager had considerable restaurant experience, both domestic and international. There was also a proposal to open sorely needed self-service laundries in Moscow. However, that proposal needed careful examination since they were asking for a considerable sum of money.

A more modest business plan had come from St. Petersburg. Three different legal entities with experience and expertise in different fields had joined together to propose a company to produce and sell potato chips to the St. Petersburg market.

The formal business plan for this proposed startup follows. John had to decide if the business warranted his investment, given all he had learned about investing in Russia (see Appendix). ■

BUSINESS PLAN[2]

Summary

The proposed project envisions the establishment of a new enterprise that will produce high-quality, competitively-priced potato chips in the town of Komarovo, not far from St. Petersburg.[3] The initiators have formed a separate legal entity called "Troika" specifically for the purpose of realizing the project. The potato chips will be sold under the "Troika" brand name.

The initiators hope to attract an outside equity investor and use the invested funds to purchase specialized, high-quality, imported processing equipment that will enable them to produce and package world-class potato chips to be sold through both wholesalers and retailers in the Leningrad Oblast (region).

The preparatory stage has been completed, and practically all key aspects have been worked out by the initiators. The enterprise has acquired a production site (building and land) and a specialized potato storage facility. With the purchase and installation of processing equipment, and a complete renovation of the production site, production can begin. A preliminary agreement to purchase equipment has been reached with a Dutch firm considered a leading producer of food processing equipment.

The principal raw ingredient, potatoes, will be supplied by the agricultural consortium, Komarovo, which is one of the founding partners in Troika.

The financial requirements for the realization of the above project are as follows: an equity investment of $803,600 for the purchase of production equipment, and a short-term credit of $236,000 for startup capital.

The time frame for the realization of the project is 10.5 years. The expected net profit at the end of this period is $2,269,000. Profits will be reinvested to modernize or expand existing operations or used to start a new venture.

THE ENTERPRISE

General Information

Troika is registered as a closed joint-stock company in the town of Komarovo, Leningrad Oblast.[4] The venture's principal activity is the processing of agricultural products, specifically, the production of potato chips.

Troika's founding partners are three independently registered organizations. The first is the agricultural Consortium "Komarovo," a closed joint-stock company which was a state-owned farm until 1994. Komarovo owns 11,500 hectares of farm land, and it is the largest producer of potatoes in Russia's northwestern region. The second is "Baikal," a joint-stock company formed in 1995 by a group of producers, wholesalers, and retailers of food products.[5] Together, Baikal's shareholders make up a developed distribution network covering St. Petersburg and the surrounding region. The last is "Znamya," also a closed joint-stock company whose principal activity is processing agricultural products.

Contributed Capital

As of July 1, 1995, stockholders' equity totaled 100,000,000 rubles [US\$1 = 5,000 rubles at that time]. There were 100 shares of common stock, each with a nominal value of 1,000,000 rubles. Komarovo and Baikal each owned 40% of the shares, and the remaining 20% were held by Znamya.

The founders of Troika contributed the following assets, in lieu of cash, for shares in the enterprise:

Komarovo—building and land to be used for production, valued at 40,000,000 rubles;
Baikal—access to a distribution network covering the CIS, contribution valued at 40,000,000 rubles;
Znamya—potato storage facility valued at 20,000,000 rubles.

The initiators agreed that Baikal would withhold its cash contribution of 40 million rubles until the purchase and installation of production equipment. Thus, as of July 1, 1995, 60 out of 100 shares of common stock were paid for in full.

Appraising Market Value of Stockholder' Equity

Since Troika is a newly created enterprise, it has not incurred any debt or losses. The fixed assets owned by the company are as follows:

land	1.5 hectare
building	420 sq. meters
potato storage facility	480 sq. meters

In order to minimize taxes, the Founding Charter assigns to assets the lowest possible value allowed by Russian law. The actual market value of these assets is significantly higher.[6] For example, the cost of property in the area is between \$10,000 and \$15,000 per hectare. The cost of constructing a similar building is \$84,000, and the storage facility has been appraised at

\$60,000. Thus, the actual market value of Troika's fixed assets is approximately \$159,000, but that would fluctuate as the political and economic climate in Russia changes.

Decision Making

Regular shareholder meetings are to be held twice a year. Additional meetings can be initiated by a shareholder holding a minimum of 25% of common (voting) shares. Decisions can be approved provided shareholders holding a minimum of 50% of voting shares are present. Critical decisions, such as changing the Charter, re-organization, and liquidation of assets, require a 75% presence.

Troika will be managed by a Board of Directors, appointed by shareholders, with Alexander I. Ivanov serving as chairman.

Profit Sharing

Net profits will be distributed among shareholders as dividends. The dividends are to be approved at general shareholder meetings.

THE PRODUCT

Troika potato chips will be produced and packaged with equipment manufactured by a Dutch firm, Florigio Industrie, using only natural, high-quality ingredients. The principal raw ingredient is potatoes, not the customary processed potato concentrate, so as to give the finished product a more natural potato taste and smell. Florigio Industrie is a leading producer of food-processing technology. This technology will enable Troika to produce both regular chips and flavored chips up to the highest world standards. The chips will be packaged in 100 gram plastic packets bearing the company logo. Highest quality packaging materials (also Dutch) will be used, ensuring the chips remain fresh for up to six months. Package labeling will be in Russian.

Since potato chips are neither a staple nor a luxury product, demand is determined by price and quality. Troika chips will be cheaper than imported brands and of higher quality than domestic brands, so it is expected that they will be very popular.

ANALYSIS OF MARKET AND COMPETITION

Potato chips were produced locally in the 1960s and 1970s, then discontinued until 1992. Local market research indicates that the product currently enjoys a 90% awareness among the population.

In St. Petersburg, Western-style supermarkets selling brand name, imported products carry the widest assortment of potato chips. These supermarkets cater to consumers with high purchasing power. Potato chips are also available in food stores selling primarily Russian products and in 10 to 15% of all kiosks.[7] These stores offer a narrower range of products and usually carry no more than two brands of potato chips.

Market research shows that about 60% of the local population consumes potato chips with some regularity. A large segment of potato chip consumers is aged between 5 and 18. At the moment, the market has no obvious leader.

Since market research indicates that potato chips are a price elastic product in high demand, it could be concluded that expanding the consumer base by lowering the price would greatly increase sales. A consumer survey conducted by the St. Petersburg State University Economics Department confirms this fact, showing that 90% of potential buyers of potato chips refrain from buying due to high price. The remaining 10% choose not to buy because of perceived low quality or for some other reason. The survey also found that lowering the price of potato chips by 30% makes them affordable to 20 to 30% of potential consumers, compared to the 10% potential buyers who can afford to buy them at today's prices.

Troika's main competitors are foreign producers, followed by domestic producers. Domestic competition is not likely to become a factor for at least three to four years. Presently, the region is supplied by Finnish, Dutch, Israeli, and American producers. Retail prices for imported potato chips sold in elite supermarkets are between $.95 and $1.65 per 100 g package, making them affordable to only 7 to 10% of the population. Other stores sell chips at comparatively lower prices, from $.75 to $.90 per 100 g. These chips are produced by Russian, Baltic, and Polish companies.

Some widely distributed brands of potato chips and their prices per 100 g package are as follows:

SUPER	(Holland)	$1.12 to $1.52
SPECIAL SNACKS	(Moscow)	$.56
MINI SNACK	(Israel)	$1.43
RAFFLES	(Poland)	$1.74

Koloss, another major domestic brand, is also relatively inexpensive. Due to a number of factors, primarily high tariffs, retail prices of imported chips are kept relatively high. Thus, only a limited number of local wholesalers can afford to purchase potato chips from abroad. In fact, a survey of the wholesale market showed that imported potato chips are distributed by only three of the 15 largest wholesalers of food products in the area. Of the 20 largest supermarkets in St. Petersburg, only four sell potato chips. These figures demonstrate that choice and availability of potato chips in St. Petersburg and the surrounding area is limited.

At the moment, no local producers of potato chips use imported, high-quality equipment. In general, the simple, low-tech processes employed by these companies make them incapable of producing on a mass scale. Furthermore, the packaging of local chips is not consistent with world standards.

A careful pricing strategy, a high-quality product, and good packaging will enable Troika to successfully compete with local as well as foreign producers. Troika chips will differ from imports in price (30 to 40% cheaper), and from domestic substitutes in quality and packaging. Until more local mass-producers of potato chips enter the market, which is not likely to occur for the next three to four years, the demand for the product will remain unsatisfied. By the time equilibrium is reached, Troika is expected to have gained a 5% share of the local market, producing and selling 289 tons of chips per year.

In summary, the market situation can be characterized as follows:

- absence of a clear market leader
- limited choice and availability of high-quality potato chips
- high price elasticity for the product
- slowly but steadily increasing demand
- increased domestic competition in the next three to four years

MARKETING AND PRICING STRATEGY

The marketing plan consists of three general components: (1) pricing strategy, (2) advertising campaign, and (3) continuous analysis of the changing market situation and integration of new information into overall strategy.

The product's competitive advantage is based on its:
- high quality
- image (modern, eye-catching package design)
- low production cost (use of locally grown potatoes)
- being ahead of domestic competition

Since market research shows there is unmet local demand, Troika chips will be marketed initially in the St. Petersburg region using Baikal's distribution network of over 400 selling points. When the local market is saturated, other regions will be explored.

In the first five years, growth in sales will be based on the expansion of the consumer base rather than on the elimination of competition. Troika chips will be priced on average 35% cheaper than imports, and 10 to 20% cheaper than domestic substitutes, making them affordable to a larger segment of population.

The minimum wholesale price of $0.4125 allows retail prices to be maintained at competitive levels. The use of local potatoes minimizes expenditures on the principal raw ingredient, since potatoes supplied by other regions have a 10 to 15% mark-up reflecting added transportation costs. Raw material expenses (potatoes, oil, spices, etc.) constitute 80% of total production costs (Exhibit 6). Competitive pricing will allow Troika to realize its sales objectives.

Product image will play a significant role in attracting potential buyers. The chips will be packaged in multicolor polypropylene packages that prominently display the Troika brand name. The packaging will be modeled after Western standards both in quality and presentation and in guarantees of freshness. In order not to alienate Russian buyers, information and company logo displayed on the package will be in Russian.[8] The product weighs 100 g and will be distributed to retailers in cardboard boxes.

The product will be promoted through a multi-stage advertising campaign utilizing printed and electronic media. The first stage of the campaign will focus on gaining maximum exposure and creating brand awareness for Troika potato chips. The product will be introduced with printed advertisements placed in buses, metros, trains, and points of purchase. Promotions will be held at trade fairs, at local civic celebrations, and in schools. A qualified marketing manager will be hired to develop strategy and manage all marketing efforts.

It is estimated that within the first two years of the project, the cost of advertising will reach approximately $15,000 annually. As local competitors enter the market, advertising expenditures will be increased and the advertising strategy will be modified accordingly. At this stage, advertising will become more aggressive, focusing on maintaining market position as well as on attracting buyers of other brands. Advertisements on local radio and television will be added at this time. By the third year, advertising expenditures are expected to increase to about $25,000 annually.

Troika has obtained all necessary licenses, including certification from the Ministry of Agriculture, to produce and sell its products.

ORGANIZATION OF THE PRODUCTION PROCESS

The initiators have worked out all key operational aspects. All actions will be performed according to the schedule shown in Exhibit 1. The preparatory stage, during which equipment will be installed, building renovated, and personnel trained, will last six months. Full production capacity is expected to be reached four months after the start of production.

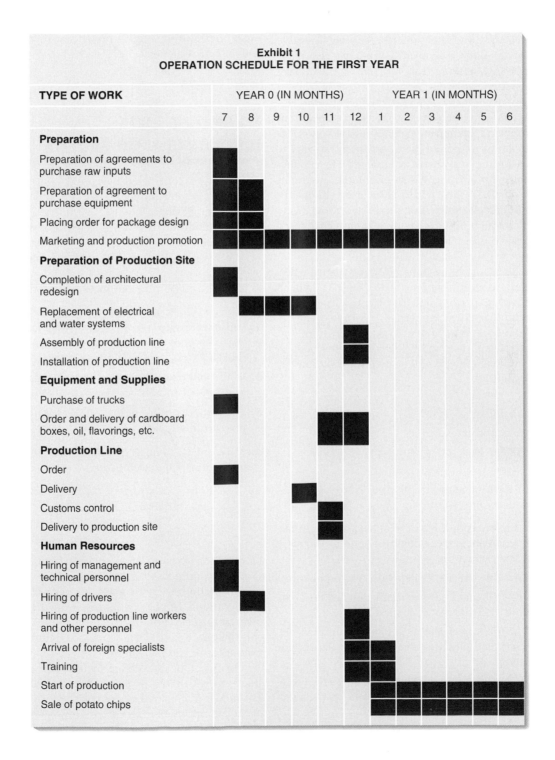

Exhibit 1
OPERATION SCHEDULE FOR THE FIRST YEAR

The production line requires a space measuring 200 square meters with a height of 3 meters. With the completion of renovation, which includes replacing electrical and water provision systems, the production site will satisfy all technical requirements. Beyond housing the production line, the building will contain an office, kitchen, bathrooms, and space for storing packaging materials. The site is easily accessible from a major highway.

An agrarian specialist will be hired to ensure that the potatoes purchased are of the highest quality. To prevent rotting, the potatoes will be stored in a specially adapted warehouse. A permanent contract with the potato supplier Komarovo is in effect. The Consortium owns 300 hectares of farmland, each producing between 16 and 18 tons of potatoes per year. Vegetable oil will be supplied by ARKO, a company located in a city about 400 miles south of St. Petersburg. The initiators of Troika have close ties with this supplier as well.

The production equipment supplied by the Dutch firm Florigio comes with enough spare parts for one year of operation. The choice of Florigio as equipment supplier is based on (1) its competitive price among imported analogues and (2) its higher quality compared to similar domestic equipment. The production line is capable of processing 400 kg of potatoes per hour, resulting in 100 kg of finished potato chips every hour. Approximately 5% of completed product is expected to be defective. Florigio would also supply packaging materials that come imprinted with the company logo and product information in Russian.

Production will go into recess during July and August when harvested potatoes are unsuitable for potato chips. The enterprise plans to hire a 22-person staff. The technical personnel will undergo a training session conducted by Florigio experts who will remain two months at the Troika production site. Training expense totals $7,500 and is included in the budget. All equipment maintenance work will be performed by specialists trained by Florigio.

RISK FACTORS

The following list identifies some of the risks facing the enterprise.

1. High rate of inflation, coupled with frequent changes in tax and licensing requirements, encumbers long-term financial planning and cost estimation.

2. The initiators have no experience in potato chip production.

3. A bad potato harvest could have a negative impact on quality, quantity, and price of potato supplies.

4. The break-up of the former Soviet Union has ruptured old inter-regional ties that formerly guaranteed a regular supply of raw materials.

5. The start of production could be postponed due to delays in delivery and installation of equipment or a delay in the completion of building renovation.

6. The initiators could encounter difficulties in obtaining financing.

7. Competition from domestic producers may have greater impact than expected.

All of the above factors are taken into consideration in making financial projections.

The organizers are engaged in a search for an additional source of potatoes in case there are problems with the contracted suppliers. Competition from local producers will not be a factor for at least three to four years and therefore will have no negative impact on the economics of the project in the first stages. When competitors do enter the market, Troika will have established a strong market presence with its products enjoying wide brand awareness.

FINANCING AND DISTRIBUTION OF PROFITS

The initiators considered two possible methods for financing the purchase of equipment: leasing and equity investment. Since leasing laws in Russia have not yet stabilized, they are seeking an outside investor. This investor will be offered newly issued stock in the enterprise. The total amount required of the investor is $837,100. The initiators will contribute $132,700.

Funds will be invested in the enterprise in the following order:

1. Baikal will contribute 40,000,000 as payment for its shares in the enterprise (40 shares at nominal price of 1,000,000 rubles).[9]

2. Redistribution of common shares: Komarovo and Baikal will purchase 10 and 5 shares each, in that order, from Znamya.

3. The second stock offering will be organized, and an equity investor brought in.

After the outside investor is brought in, common (voting) shares would be distributed as follows:

investor:	up to 40%
Baikal:	25–30%
Komarovo:	30%
Znamya:	up to 5%

Limiting the investors' share to a maximum of 40% of common stock is a condition set at the insistence of the Leningrad Oblast Administration, which is a 49% owner of Baikal.

All profits will be distributed as dividends in proportion to ownership stake. Priority will be given to shareholders whose contribution financed the purchase of equipment and the renovation of production site.

Troika proposes to issue 65 additional shares of common stock and 43 shares of preferred stock of Type A and Type B. The holder of preferred shares has no voice in the management of the enterprise, but has priority in dividend distribution.

Distribution of shares among
the stockholders after second
stock offering

	DISTRIBUTION OF COMMON SHARES BEFORE INVESTMENT		DISTRIBUTION OF COMMON SHARES AFTER INVESTMENT		DISTRIBUTION OF PREFERRED SHARES	
	Number of shares	%	Number of shares	%	Type A	Type B
Komarovo	40	40	50	30.3	—	—
Baikal	40	40	45	27.27	—	14
Znamya	20	20	5	3.03	—	—
Investor	—	—	65	39.39	29	—
TOTAL	100	100	165	100.00	43	

The face value of each share would remain 1,000,000 rubles. After the second stock offering, Troika's stockholders' equity will have a nominal value of 208,000,000 rubles.[10] Preferred stock would constitute 20.7% of total capital, well within the bounds of the law which places a 25% cap on preferred shares. Shares would be sold at a price of $8,905 per share. The investor would acquire 94 shares (65 common, 29 preferred) for a sum of $837,100; Baikal would purchase 14 newly issued preferred shares for $124,700.

Setting the actual price above the nominal price would have no tax implications. According to Russian securities law, when shares are sold to raise starting capital, the difference between nominal and actual price paid for each share is considered additional paid-in capital, not as taxable revenue.

Net profit will be distributed in the following order: (1) fixed dividends are paid to holders of preferred stock Type A, (2) dividends are paid to holders of Type B shares, (3) the remainder will be distributed among holders of common stock. Common and Type B stock holders will not receive any dividends until the holders of Type A stock are fully reimbursed the amount of investment ($837,100). After the fourth year, the 29 shares of preferred stock type A guarantee the investor a dividend income of $160,000 (Exhibit 9). Holders of Type B shares would receive yearly dividends of $9,000, starting in the fifth year of operation.

Since there is no undistributed income (retained earnings) at the end of the ten-year realization period, the value of owner's equity would equal the nominal price of shares plus additional paid-in capital. Initial stockholders' equity was formed with each partner's contribution (land, building, etc.). The maximum market value of stockholder's equity before the second stock offering is appraised at $159,000. Taking depreciation into account, this value is reduced to $123,000 at the end of 10 years. The total market value of Troika's assets is therefore $1,084,800: $123,000, the depreciated value of stockholders' equity before second offering, plus $961,800, the increase in stockholders' equity after second stock offering.

At the end of the 10-year operation period, the investors will have the option of selling back all preferred shares. Type A shares will be re-purchased for $692,000, and Type B shares,

held by Baikal, for $32,000. The subsequent market value of Troika's common shares will be $369,000.[11] Holders of preferred stock would also have the option to convert their holdings into common stock.

FINANCIAL PLANNING

All major expenditures will be made in accordance with the work schedule (Exhibit 1). Funds will be used primarily to:
- purchase equipment
- renovate the production site
- purchase transportation vehicles
- create a reserve fund

The three sources of financing are as follows: equity investment, initiators' contribution, and short-term credits. Short-term credit is needed to satisfy initial working capital requirements. The first credit, totaling $188,000, will be for three months and will be used to pay the VAT on the imported equipment. The second credit, totaling $48,000, will be for four months and will be used to purchase potatoes, oil, and other inputs. Principal and interest expense (30% annually) on these loans will be paid out of sales revenue.

The initiators will purchase automobiles for delivery of the product and pay the full cost of renovating the building out of their contributed funds. Equity investment will be used primarily for purchasing production equipment.

Financial projections are provided in attached Exhibits 2–9. Exhibit 6 shows production expenses with a 5% defect rate. Purchases of raw materials, particularly potatoes, make up the largest portion of expenses. Results of an analysis of potato price movements show that prices are stable, indicating that the market is in equilibrium. Potato prices in St. Petersburg reflect the average world price of the commodity.[12]

Prices of raw materials and maintenance costs are projected to rise 2% per year, beginning in the third year of production. Salaries are projected to rise 5% per year in the first four years, and 3% per year for the remainder of the ten-year period. By basing projections on rising cost for inputs and stable selling price for the product, the initiators compensate for the possibility of an unexpected adverse turn of events.

Break-even analysis shows that the enterprise must produce 121 tons of potato chips per year to break even, only 42% of its capacity. Cash flow projections (Exhibit 8) show that sales revenue will be sufficient to cover all production and dividend expenses and future preferred stock repurchase.

Troika's projected income statement (Exhibit 9) also shows positive results, even in the first year of production. Income is projected to grow from $126,000 in the first year to a $263,000 in the fourth year, and gradually decrease to $216,000 in the tenth year. Income grows as a result of increased production efficiency and then declines because projected expenses rise while selling price is maintained constant. The enterprise is expected to generate an average return of 23% on investment. A portion of these earnings can be reinvested to modernize and expand current operations, or as starting capital for a new enterprise.

Exhibit 2
General information

Project duration	10.5 years
Defects	5%
Prices:	
Potatoes (VAT not included)	$196/ton
Production cost (VAT not included)	$4,125/ton
Taxes:	
Revenue tax	34%
Tariff of imported equipment	0.0%
VAT on equipment	21.5%
Equity investment in overall long-term financing structure	86%
Short-term credits	
Interest rate	30%
Term	7%
Required equity investment	$837,100

Exhibit 3
Capital expenditures (in US$ thousands)

	INITIATORS	INVESTOR	TOTAL
CONSTRUCTION WORK			
Building and land			
1) Completion of architectural blueprints	2.5	0.0	2.5
2) Land and road improvement	3.0	0.0	3.0
3) Building renovation	21.3	0.0	21.3
4) Warehouse renovation	28.6	0.0	28.6
5) Additional construction expenses (heating, ventilation)	19.8	0.0	19.8
6) Total	75.2	0.0	75.2
7) Unexpected expenses (10%)	7.5	0.0	7.5
8) VAT (21% of 6+7)	17.8	0.0	17.8
9) Total for construction	**100.5**	**0.0**	**100.5**
EQUIPMENT			
Storage			
10) Sorting and control equipment	0.0	4.0	4.0
11) Dusting and spraying equipment	0.0	1.3	1.3
12) Total for storage	0.0	5.3	5.3
Production Line			
13) Washer	0.0	39.4	39.4
14) Cutter	0.0	107.2	107.2
15) Fryer	0.0	158.9	158.9
16) Heating unit	0.0	121.2	121.2
17) Control panel	0.0	52.0	52.0
18) Packaging equipment	0.0	152.0	152.0
19) Spare parts	0.0	42.2	42.2
20) Delivery and maintenance expense	0.0	50.3	50.3
21) Total for production line	0.0	723.2	723.2
22) Total for production and storage equipment (21+12)	0.0	728.5	728.5
23) Tariff	0.0	0.0	0.0
24) Delivery from port to site	0.0	2.0	2.0
25) Total (22+24)	**0.0**	**730.5**	**730.5**
TRANSPORT			
26) Trucks (2)	12.0	0.0	12.0
27) Insurance (18% of cost)	2.2	0.0	2.2
28) Total for transport	**14.2**	**0.0**	**14.2**
OTHER EXPENDITURES			
29) Office equipment	1.6	0.0	1.6
30) Maintenance and assembly fees (3 months)	13.5	0.0	13.5
31) Total for other expenditures	**15.1**	**0.0**	**15.1**
32) Total (25+28+31)	29.3	730.5	759.8
33) Unexpected expenses (10%)	2.9	73.1	76.0
34) Total for equipment (32+33)	**32.2**	**803.6**	**835.7**
35) VAT on domestic eq. (reimbursed 6 months from start of operation)	6.9	0.0	6.9
36) VAT on imported equipment (reimbursed at start of operation)	0.0	172.8	172.8
GRAND TOTAL	**132.7**	**803.6**	**936.2**

Exhibit 4
Fixed asset depreciation, insurance, and maintenance expense

	ORIGINAL PRICE US$1,000	LIFETIME IN YEARS	YEARLY DEPRECIATION		SALVAGE VALUE US$1,000	INSURANCE		MAINTENANCE	
			%	US$1,000		%	US$1,000	%	US$1,000
Building	100.5	40	2.5	2.5	75.4	1.7	1.7	2.0	2.0
Russian equipment	32.2	10	10.0	3.2	0.0	1.7	0.5	5.0	1.6
Imported equipment	803.6	10	10.0	80.4	0.0	1.7	13.7	5.0	40.2
Total	**936.3**	—	—	**86.1**	**75.4**	—	**15.9**	—	**43.8**

Exhibit 5
Operation plan

| | Number of shifts: | 2 | | Number of work days in a month: | | 20 | | | | | |
| | Number of hours in a shift: | 8 | | Number of work months in a year: | | 10 | | | | | |

YEAR	1	2	3	4	5	6	7	8	9	10	Total
First shift:											
Number of months	10	10	10	10	10	10	10	10	10	10	100
Number of work hours	160	160	160	160	160	160	160	160	160	160	1,600
	0	0	0	0	0	0	0	0	0	0	0
Second shift:											
Number of months	7	10	10	10	10	10	10	10	10	10	97
Number of work hours	112	160	160	160	160	160	160	160	160	160	1,552
	0	0	0	0	0	0	0	0	0	0	0
Work hours per year	272	320	320	320	320	320	320	320	320	320	3,152
Efficiency rate	0	0	0	0	0	0	0	0	0	0	0
Actual work hours per year	0.80	0.85	0.90	0.95	0.95	0.95	0.95	0.95	0.95	0.95	—
	217	272	288	304	304	304	304	304	304	304	2,905
	6	0	0	0	0	0	0	0	0	0	6
Raw potatoes (tons)	870	108	115	121	121	121	121	121	121	121	1,162
Finished goods (tons)		8	2	6	6	6	6	6	6	6	2
Defects (5% in tons)	218	272	288	304	304	304	304	304	304	304	2,906
Finished products net defects (tons)	11	14	14	15	15	15	15	15	15	15	145
	207	258	274	289	289	289	289	289	289	289	2,760
Sales revenue—without VAT at US$4,125 per ton	854	106	113	119	119	119	119	119	119	119	1,139
	4	0	2	2	2	2	2	2	2	2	2

Exhibit 6
Production costs

	AMOUNT	PRICE PER UNIT WITHOUT VAT, US$	TOTAL PRICE (WITHOUT VAT) US$
Variable costs for producing 1 ton of potato chips **(without defects)**			
Potatoes	4 tons	196	784
Chemicals	.25 liters	15	4
Oil	400 liters	1.25	500
Additives	20 kg	0.10	2
Packaging material	50 kg	8	400
Cardboard boxes	200	0.30	60
Electricity	800 kW	0.02	16
Total			1,766
Variable costs for producing 1 ton of potato chips **(with 5% defect rate)**			1,859
Variable costs for producing at **full capacity:** 289 tons of chips per year **(with 5% defect rate)**			537,160
Fixed annual costs			
Depreciation			86,100
Maintenance			43,800
Insurance			15,900
Utilities			
Water	10,000 cubic meters	0.01	100
Fuel	20,000 liters	0.15	3,000
Salary			
Manager	1	3,600	3,600
Accountant	1	3,000	3,000
Marketing director	1	3,000	3,000
Mechanic/electric	1	2,160	2,160
Agrarian specialist	1	2,160	2,160
Warehouse foreman	1	1,920	1,920
Sorter	2	1,680	3,360
Sales person	1	1,800	1,800
Driver	1	1,700	1,700
Manual worker (2 shifts)	2	1,440	2,880
Production controller (2 shifts)	2	1,680	3,360
Line operator	2	1,800	3,600
Packaging operator	2	1,800	3,600
Additional workers (2 shifts)	4	1,440	5,760
Total salary expense			**41,900**
Other fixed costs			
Advertising (first two years)		15,000	15,000
Advertising (subsequent years)		25,000	25,000
Training (first year)		7,500	7,500
Transport maintenance	2 trucks	1,550	3,100
Total other fixed costs			
First year			25,600
Second year			18,100
After			28,100

continued

	AMOUNT	PRICE PER UNIT WITHOUT VAT, US$	TOTAL PRICE (WITHOUT VAT) US$
Total fixed costs			
First year			216,400
Second year			208,900
After			218,900
Total operating expense at full capacity			
First year			753,560
Second year			746,060
After			756,060

Exhibit 7
Financing (US$1,000)

YEARS	0	1	Total
Investment	961.8	—	961.8
Short-term credit (3 months)	188	—	188
Interest payment	—	14	14
Debt repayment	—	188	188
Short-term credit (4 months)	48	—	48
Interest payment	—	5	5
Debt repayment	—	48	48
Total	1,197.8	(255)	942.8

Exhibit 8
Cash flow projections (US$1,000)

YEAR	0	1	2	3	4	5	6	7	8	9	10	Total
REVENUES												
Sales	0	854	1,064	1,130	1,192	1,192	1,192	1,192	1,192	1,192	1,192	11,392
Salvage value	0	0	0	0	0	0	0	0	0	0	75	75
Reimbursed VAT	0	180	0	0	0	0	0	0	0	0	0	180
Total	0	1,034	1,064	1,130	1,192	1,192	1,192	1,192	1,192	1,192	1,267	1,1647
EXPENSES												
Management cost	43	0	0	0	0	0	0	0	0	0	0	43
Investment activities	936	0	0	0	0	0	0	0	0	0	0	936
VAT on equipment	180	0	0	0	0	0	0	0	0	0	0	180
Other expenses	0	33	8	3	2	0	0	0	0	0	(46)	0
Variable costs	0	385	480	508	536	547	558	569	581	592	604	5,360
Maintenance (Exhibit 4)	0	44	44	45	45	46	46	47	47	48	49	461
Insurance (Exhibit 4)	0	16	15	14	13	12	11	10	9	8	7	115
Utilities	0	3	3	3	3	3	3	3	3	3	3	30
Salary	0	42	44	46	48	51	53	55	57	59	61	516
Other fixed costs	0	26	18	28	28	28	28	28	28	28	28	268
Total production expense	0	516	604	644	673	687	699	712	725	738	752	6,750
Income tax	0	74	115	124	135	131	128	124	120	116	112	1,179
Other taxes	0	29	31	31	31	29	28	26	25	23	22	275
Total expenses	1,159	652	758	802	841	847	855	862	870	877	840	9,363
Net income	(1,159)	382	306	328	351	345	338	330	322	315	427	2,284
Total before financing	(1,159)	(777)	(472)	(144)	207	552	889	1,219	1,542	1,857	2,284	—
Financing (Exhibit 7)	1206	(255)	0	0	0	0	0	0	0	0	0	951
Net income after financing	47	127	306	328	351	345	338	330	322	315	427	3,235
Total after financing	47	173	479	807	1,158	1,502	1,840	2,170	2,492	2,808	3,235	—
Dividend payments	0	123	219	236	257	250	243	235	228	221	212	2,224
Earnings after dividends	47	4	86	92	93	95	95	95	95	95	215	1,011
Total	47	50	173	229	322	417	512	607	701	796	1,011	—
Repurchase of preferred stock Type A	—	—	—	—	—	—	—	—	—	—	692	692
Repurchase of preferred stock Type B	—	—	—	—	—	—	—	—	—	—	32	32
Remainder												287

Exhibit 9
Income projections (US$1,000)

YEARS	0	1	2	3	4	5	6	7	8	9	10	Total
Sales revenue	0	854	1,064	1,130	1,192	1,192	1,192	1,192	1,192	1,192	1,192	1,1392
Expenses:												
Variable cost	0	385	48	508	536	547	558	569	581	592	604	5,360
Depreciation	0	86	86	86	86	86	86	86	86	86	86	860
Maintenance	0	44	44	45	45	46	46	47	47	48	49	461
Insurance	0	16	15	14	13	12	11	10	9	8	7	115
Utilities	0	3	3	3	3	3	3	3	3	3	3	30
Salary	0	42	44	46	48	51	53	55	57	59	61	516
Management fee	0	4	4	4	4	4	4	4	4	4	4	40
Other fixed costs	0	26	18	28	28	28	28	28	28	28	28	268
Total expenses	0	606	694	734	763	777	789	802	815	828	842	7,650
Earnings before interest and taxes	0	284	370	396	429	415	403	390	377	364	350	3,742
Taxes:												
Building and property tax	0		11	12	12	12	12	12	12	12	12	115
Tax on advertising	0	1	1	2	2	2	2	2	2	2	2	18
Road tax	0	3	4	5	5	5	5	5	5	5	5	47
Asset tax	0	16	15	13	10	10	9	7	6	4	3	95
Total tax	0	29	31	31	29	29	28	26	25	23	22	275
Income before taxes	0	219	339	365	398	386	375	364	352	341	328	3,467
Income tax	0	74	115	124	135	131	128	124	120	116	112	1,179
Income after taxes	0	145	224	241	263	255	248	240	232	225	216	2,288
Interest expense	0	19	0	0	0	0	0	0	0	0	0	19
Income after taxes and interest	0	126	224	241	263	255	248	240	232	225	216	2,269
Contribution to a reserve fund (2% of revenue)	0	3	4	5	5	5	5	5	5	5	4	45
Dividend payments—Type A	0	123	219	236	257	162	160	160	160	160	160	1,798
Dividend payments—Type B	0	0	0	0	0	7	9	9	9	9	9	52
Dividend payments—common	0	0	0	0	0	81	74	66	59	52	43	374
Total dividend payments	0	123	219	236	257	250	243	235	228	221	212	2,224
Retained earnings	0	0	0	0	0	0	0	0	0	0	0	0

APPENDIX
Cultural and Sociological Notes

THE RUSSIAN SENSE OF TIME

A Russian's sense of time may differ markedly from an American's. While Americans watch situation comedies where everything ends happily in a half-hour, the traditional Russian prefers three hour-long operas and theater pieces where a bad situation gets worse, people get emotional, and apparently nothing is resolved at the end. While Americans like to come quickly to the point and summarize their interests in a few sentences, Russian general managers usually choose to explain their corporate history and general philosophy before talking about specifics. This is often due to the Russian need to establish a relationship with a potential business partner. However, this differing sense of time can lead to confusion and a sense of distrust during initial meetings.

OPENNESS VERSUS SECRECY

Russia is a country that has been invaded many times during its history. Because of this legacy, Russians tend to keep their wealth and their business dealings secret. Just as a Russian peasant hid his grain, a Russian business tends to conceal its income, assets, and technological secrets. Russians are often reluctant to share information over the phone or in letters, and prefer at least a face-to-face meeting before going forward with details.

OBEDIENCE VERSUS AUTONOMY

Another painful legacy of Russian history is servitude. Up to the middle of the 19th century, the majority of Russians were peasants, who essentially were the property of local landowners. The peasants followed the landowner's orders and were not permitted to move or change jobs without his permission. Under the Soviet system, the entire economy was centrally planned. At the time of this case, Russian decision making, particularly in large organizations, still came from the top. The Russian employee traditionally had little or no autonomy, and, during this transition to capitalism, many Russians were still reluctant to make decisions without consulting superiors. This cultural difference baffles and frustrates many Americans. The Russian decision-making process will seem very slow to an American, with inexplicable starts, stops, and reversals. American managers often

must wait for months for a final decision to come from the top on matters already reviewed by layers of Russian managers. During the first few months working for a Western firm, new Russian employees often exasperate their American managers with their continual requests for precise instructions and direction.

ATTITUDE TOWARD LAW AND CONTRACTS

For many years, Soviet law viewed capitalism and business as a social evil. For many Russians, the idea that laws could actually help build companies is a relatively new concept. While Americans prefer to base their business relationships on legally enforceable contracts, many Russians still doubt the value of and lack respect for business laws and contracts. Many Russians prefer to keep their business dealings and accounts as far from government scrutiny as possible.

THE IMPORTANCE OF RELATIONSHIPS

Most Russians' business dealings are based on personal relationships. When making business decisions, Americans tend to focus on comparing contracts and prices. Russians, on the other hand, compare the depths of personal relationships. Most Russians prefer to do business with people who are close friends. Without a close personal relationship, often one that seems so close as to be claustrophobic to a Westerner, a Russian business deal is on shaky ground. For Americans, the contract is usually the centerpiece of negotiating sessions. For the Russian, the relationship is the focal point, and contracts and protocols are often merely thought of as polite ceremonies and starting points for further negotiation. Because Russians consider their business partners to be friends, Russian business leaders often have trouble saying no and will promise things they cannot—or do not want to—deliver.

Most deals are done on the basis of a verbal agreement, where both sides actually appear to be embarrassed to bring any formalities into the process. This is one of the major factors contributing to an enormous crisis in the early 1990s stemming from the failure of almost everyone to pay their debts. The combined debt that enterprises owed to each other amounted to trillions of rubles, and a significant part of that was not supported by proper documentation.

ORGANIZED CRIME

Dealing with organized crime is fundamental to doing business in Russia. Typically, banks have informers who tell the Mafia organs about incoming funds (sums above 10 million rubles). Equipped with this information, the Mafia attempts to extort money from the enterprise. Insistent young men approach the management, in teams of three or four people. Having made an appointment, they announce that they have come to discuss the topic of "protection" or are representatives of tax authorities or the police. They offer their "services" in the form of protecting the life of the firm's owners and safeguarding of goods and property of the firm. If the owner refuses, they start explaining, very politely, that they can provide very effective personal security, and then, depending on the reaction, they start giving out information about the company obtained from the bank, about the goods stored in the warehouse, his wife's place of work, the time his children are in school, and all sorts of compromising information. If there is still no reaction, direct threats are brought into play.

Ultimately, most enterprises conclude security agreements with organized crime groups. According to standard contracts, the director has to make a monthly payment on a strictly defined day to a particular person. The sum is set depending on the turnover and the amount of compromising information about the firm. In the event that representatives of other groups approach the firm, the directors must prove that they already have protection or krysha (roof), so that representatives of the Mafia groups sort out between themselves questions concerning turf and what belongs to whom.

If a company does not have a krysha, it becomes difficult to conduct business, especially receiving payments, and the company is totally exposed. But if one does have krysha, one is breaking the law, placing oneself outside of it in the realm of the informal and vague. The relationship with one's krysha is very important, but at the same time it makes one a part of a network, thereby severely restricting one's freedom.

WORKING WITH RUSSIAN PARTNERS

Although each investment opportunity presented its own unique set of characteristics and challenges, John found that there were many common elements and pitfalls when dealing with Russian partners as a foreign investor. For example:

- Most Russian entrepreneurs do not have a current, updated packet of information about their enterprise and/or project. At the initial meeting, they will most likely present old information and explain the project-at-hand orally, or as the Russians say, "using their fingers." Because written data seldom matches what is transmitted orally at the initial meeting, a foreign investor, upon reviewing the information packet, could become confused and distrustful.
- Russian citizens have grown accustomed to being secretive, a survival trait developed while living under a to-

talitarian regime. Consequently, the Russian entrepreneur is psychologically unprepared to reveal immediately all required information about his enterprise or project. He provides partial information, assuming that is sufficient for analysis. If obtaining information about a project or company begins to feel like pulling teeth, the investor may become suspicious and reluctant to proceed further.
- Russian entrepreneurs are not used to the language and protocol for attracting equity financing. They may ask potential investors to specify their requirements and then come up with a project to fit those requirements.
- Russian businessmen view unfavorably the Russian assistants employed by foreign consulting firms and investment funds. Most of these jobs are filled by young bilingual Russian "consultants" with some rudimentary knowledge of Western finance, but with virtually no experience in managing a business in Russia and a limited understanding of Russia's business climate. In worst cases, they become a buffer between the investor and the entrepreneur, filtering and sometimes misrepresenting information about the investment project. Generally, Russian businessmen prefer to stay in direct contact with the investor.
- The majority of Russian entrepreneurs are not accustomed to valuing other people's time, or paying for information or consulting services.

Working and investing in Russia is a continual learning process. The road to success is often paved with mistakes. During his stay, John made plenty of mistakes. He was able to identify the following lessons or "guidelines for practice" learned through his experience:

- At the initial meeting, set the tone and language for future discussions (whoever has the money gets to make the rules).
- Make a clear and firm request for all necessary information. If the requested information is not presented at the following meeting, end the meeting, clearly explaining the reasons for doing so.
- If you receive the necessary documents and, after evaluating them, refuse to finance the project, return the packet of information with an official letter explaining your decision.
- Before making any decision, consult a Russian expert. The most qualified experts are lawyers who are on top of current legal changes and know the system, or entrepreneurs who have had first-hand experience running a business in Russia. Some caution should be exercised in taking advice from foreign or Russian consultants who have no experience managing a business in Russia.
- The quality of management takes precedence over financial projections as the most important factor in evaluating potential projects in Russia. Because the instability of the Russian market makes long-term planning virtually impossible, most Russian entrepreneurs regard the business plan as a formality in attracting foreign capital rather than an actual blueprint for running their business. Therefore, the investor should concentrate on

those sections of the business plan which give some indication of management's style and degree of professionalism. These sections may deal with marketing research, risk assessment, sensitivity analysis, and project realization.

- In order to live through the years of economic transition, which is far from complete, Russian businesspeople developed certain survival traits and habits. A dearth of information, unfair taxation, and rampant corruption have made them very cautious, while an unstable legal and economic infrastructure has made them extremely competent in analyzing and quickly responding to new risks and obstacles. Consequently, a Russian entrepreneur can quickly assess and exploit any weakness or incompetence he perceives in a potential business partner.

CASE DISCUSSION QUESTIONS

1. What are some of the positive attributes of the proposed project?

2. What are the main negative features of this proposal?

3. What additional information would you request from the initiators?

4. Do you recommend that the project go ahead? Justify your argument.

ENDNOTES

1 This case is intended as a basis for class discussion rather than to illustrate either effective or ineffective handling of an administrative situation.

2 Actual business plan presented to investors. All names have been changed.

3 Second largest city in Russia with a population of 5.5 million.

4 Enterprise whose shares are not publicly traded. Similar to a limited partnership.

5 Enterprise whose shares are publicly traded.

6 It is beyond the scope of this case study to discuss the intricacies of the Russian accounting and tax systems. It is highly recommended that a qualified Russian lawyer be consulted in all commercial transactions.

7 A small street shop that primarily sells snacks, cigarettes, and alcoholic and non-alcoholic beverages.

8 Some products had actually been less successful with Russian labeling, as Russians equated Western products with higher quality. For example, Pepsi Cola's sales dropped when it labeled its products in Russian.

9 It was agreed that Baikal will hold its cash contribution until the purchase of equipment.

10 [(165+43) × 1,000,000].

11 These figures add up to $1.093 million, which contradicts the $1.084 million total stockholders' equity amount given in the previous paragraph. The amounts are taken from the actual business plan.

12 Potato prices on the London and Amsterdam commodity exchanges ranged between $215 and $271 per ton during the 1994–1995 season.

Hong Kong Disneyland

by Beatrice S. Leung,*
Yim-Yu Wong,* and
André M. Everett**

*San Francisco University
**University of Otago
(New Zealand)

INTRODUCTION

With its latest move to build Hong Kong Disneyland, Disney is taking a major step in opening up the vast Chinese market as part of its international expansion. Disney had learned some hard lessons from its Paris operations: Tokyo Disneyland's phenomenal success could, clearly, not be taken for granted in other theme parks outside the USA. For its third international foray, Disney has limited its risk exposure by experimenting with a joint ownership model involving local government and being more sensitive to the community responses in the host country. Michael Eisner, chairman and Chief Executive Officer of the Disney Company, remarked that their move to Hong Kong was the result of "an extensive worldwide review" and that they had come to "recognize Hong Kong as a unique city in an extraordinary nation at a remarkable time."

China has seen steady growth in its economy in recent years and is set for even more dramatic growth with its admission to the World Trade Organization (WTO). In locating its first Chinese venture in Hong Kong, Disney has sought to take advantage of both its central location in Southeast Asia and its role as gateway to Mainland China, allowing it to draw visitors from both Mainland China and neighboring countries, maximizing the potential revenue sources.

Now Disney was faced with additional strategic decisions relating to its choice of site and the most appropriate form of organizational structure, source of funding, and the degree to which the company needed to respond to local market requirements.

THEME PARKS AND DISNEY—A BRIEF STRATEGIC BACKGROUND

A theme park is a capital-intensive investment, with around half the capital normally spent on acquiring land and the remainder on equipment and operational funds. Most theme park operators reinvest the majority of their profit into upgrading and refurbishing park facilities and equipment in order to attract repeat customers. Admission fees usually make up 60% of park revenue, but some parks earn more from food, beverage and merchandise sales. Small parks usually charge on a pay-per-ride basis while large parks usually sell day passes with unlimited rides and access so as to keep customers in the park longer, spending more on site. The three distinct market segments for theme park business are local residents, regional or national visitors, and corporate customers. Each of these segments is most approachable through the use of distinct marketing efforts. Local residents, specifically annual-pass holders, are targeted through local advertisements, radio promotions, direct mail, and discounts. Many parks targeting the regional and national vacationer employ co-op advertising or marketing efforts with competing parks in the area or through a convention/tourism bureau to offer discount passes to all parks. Parks in the business-to-business segment offer their facilities as a location for company outings or promote purchase of admissions tickets as sales rewards or other employee incentives. In most cases, the key to any marketing program is sponsorship, which theme parks "relied upon to stretch promotion budget and advertising exposure."

Disney's seven theme parks dominated the rankings of the top ten amusement parks worldwide in 1999, which are listed in Table 1. A brief chronology of the parks is provided in Table 2, and the three international parks are summarily compared in Table 3.

Disney's corporate strategy for both domestic and international expansion reduces the impact of economic setbacks in any regional market while achieving long-term growth through international expansion. Its international growth is mainly achieved by selling Disney merchandise, setting up Disney cable channels, showing Disney's movies, and selectively building theme parks. Apart from its overwhelmingly successful Tokyo Disneyland and the improving Disneyland Paris (formerly Euro Disney), Disney has focused on Asia, China in particular, for its third non-US theme park. Eisner recognized that Disney's greatest opportunity for expanding the Disney brand lies overseas: "In addition to more aggressively exporting our movies and our consumer products, we are actively looking at several countries around the world—most notably China—as venues for our next full-scale theme park."

The theme park and resort business is an important growth engine for Disney. Bearing in mind that one of Disney's corporate strategies is to cross-promote each division's businesses, new theme parks will help promote consumer products as well as new animated pictures.

Hong Kong Disneyland is Disney's third effort towards internationalization. The Disneyland Paris experience does not necessarily prove that their successful service concept is not transferable. Rather, its failure highlights the vulnerability of the theme park business to economic, cultural, social, and political environmental factors. The key to success is to choose the right product to enter the right country or site at the right time with or without local adaptation. Among other things, one of the

Table 1

Top 10 theme parks in the world for the years 1995 and 1999

Rank in 1999	Attendance	Rank in 1995	Attendance	Park name and location	Country
1	17,459,000	1	15,509,000	TOKYO DISNEYLAND, Tokyo.	Japan
2	*15,200,000	3	12,900,000	MAGIC KINGDOM at Walt Disney World, Lake Buena Vista, Florida.	USA
3	*13,450,000	2	14,100,000	DISNEYLAND, Anaheim, California.	USA
4	12,500,000	4	10,700,000	DISNEYLAND PARIS, Marne-La-Vallee.	France
5	*10,100,000	4	10,700,000	EPCOT at Walt Disney World, Lake Buena Vista, Florida.	USA
6	8,700,000	6	9,500,000	DISNEY-MGM STUDIOS THEME PARK at Walt Disney World, Lake Buena Vista, Florida.	USA
7	8,640,000	8	7,300,000	EVERLAND, Kyonggi-Do.	South Korea
8	*8,600,000			DISNEY'S ANIMAL KINGDOM at Walt Disney World, Lake Buena Vista, Florida.	USA
9	*8,100,000	7	8,000,000	UNIVERSAL STUDIOS FLORIDA, Orlando.	USA
10	*6,900,000	9	7,200,000	BLACKPOOL PLEASURE BEACH.	England

*Estimate

Source: Amusement Business

Table 2

Chronological expansion of the Disney theme parks

Inauguration Dates	Theme Park	Domestic/ International
July 1955	Disneyland Resort	Domestic
October 1971	Magic Kingdom	Domestic
October 1982	Epcot	Domestic
April 1983	Tokyo Disneyland	International—Japan
May 1989	Disney-MGM Studios	Domestic
April 1992	Disneyland Paris	International—France
April 1998	Disney's Animal Kingdom	Domestic
Spring 2001	Disney's California Adventure	Domestic
Spring 2001	Tokyo DisneySea	International—Japan
Spring 2002	Disney Studios Paris	International—France
2005	Hong Kong Disneyland	International—China

Table 3

Comparison of the three non-U.S. Disney theme parks

	Hong Kong Disneyland	Disneyland Paris	Tokyo Disneyland
Opening	**2005**	**1992**	**1983**
Duration of negotiation	9 months	2.5 years	5 years
Total site area	180 ha of which 126 for Phase 1 2 hotels with 1,400 rooms	1,950 ha of which 500 for Phase 1 (including 250 for public infrastructure) 6 hotels	81 hectares
Land premium	$4 billion for Phase 1 $2.812 billion for Phase 2	Permitted to buy at 1971's agricultural land prices ($5,000 per acre)	Land owned by Oriental Land
Annual attendance	initial year target: 5 million after 15 years, 10 million visitors are expected each year	initial year target: 11 million but only 10 million visitors realized now at 12.5 million a year	17 million per year (only 500,000 are foreigners)
Disney investment	HK$ 320 million	$250 million	A token $2.5 million
Disney initial shareholding	43% of Hong Kong International Theme Parks	49% of Euro Disney S.C.A.	0%
Disney required minimum holding	33% of initial share capital for life of project	17% for 5 years	N/A
Debt/equity ratio	60:40	76:24	About 80:20
Disney's royalties (% of revenues)	Admission: 10% Participant: 10% Merchandise & food: 5% Hotel: 5%	))) Same)	Admission: 10% Merchandise & food: 5% Hotel: 5% Licensing (45 years): 5%
Base management fee	2%	3% for years 1–5 6% from year 6	
Variable management fee	2–8% of EBITDA (5% at Base Case)	0–50% of pre-tax cash flow above a pre-determined threshold	
Government Support			
Cash grant	$0	$250 million (1986 prices, French francs 200 million)	$0
Loan	$5.6 billion (1999 prices) @6.75-8.5% over 25 years from opening	$6 billion (1986 prices) @7.85% over 20 years from draw down	commercial loan from bank
Tax concessions	Nil	VAT at 5.5% instead of 18.6%. Accelerated depreciation	N/A

continued

	Hong Kong Disneyland	Disneyland Paris	Tokyo Disneyland
Opening	**2005**	**1992**	**1983**
Infrastructure	MTR extension Approach roads Water, Drainage, Sewage, Pier	MTR extension plus high speed rail station Approach roads Water, Drainage, Sewage, Solid Waste	
Target guests	70% Mainland Chinese; 30% Hong Kong people and other South-east Asians	French and Europeans	Mainly Japanese
Target experience	American experience with slight modification	American experience with minor European elements	Authentic American experience
Pricing (single adult one-day comprehensive admission)	HK$ 300 Mainlanders are expected to spend HK$ 1200 a day and local people to spend HK$ 680 a day	Expensive (skimming pricing) at 220 Francs (about HK$ 260)	5,200 Yen (about HK$ 394)
Cast members	Mostly Chinese	Diverse cast members from at least 35 different nations	Mostly Japanese
Community concern	Unfair deal, break down of laissez faire policy	American cultural imperialism	Widely accepted and welcomed
Weather	Sub-tropical. Cool and sunny in winter. Hot and humid in summer	Very cold and dry in winter. Cloudy half of the year.	Warm and rainy in summer. Cool in winter.

Source: http://www.info.gov.hk/tc/statement/doc/comparison.doc and Riding the Black Ship Japan and Tokyo Disneyland, Aviad E. Raz

major reasons for the early failure of Disneyland Paris was poor timing; it commenced operations at a time when the French economy was spiraling into a recession.

As for operational efficiency, it appears that Disney theme parks will not make any substantial gains through either integration or expansion of global operations. There is also little need to make substantial adaptation to local conditions. After all, the most valuable and inimitable asset of Disney is its brand name, synonymous with fantasy and closely integrated with cartoon characters from its popular animated movies and fantasy stories. It is basically an American product and therein lies its appeal. If Disney makes substantial adaptation to acculturate theme parks with host countries, offering a European face in Paris, a Japanese face in Tokyo, and a Chinese face in Hong Kong, the parks will lose their unique appeal to their guests, who are drawn precisely for the "foreign," meaning American, flavor.

Having balanced the force for local acculturation against the force for global integration, the best operational strategy for Disney is a global strategy. This means that decision-making is centralized at the corporate level and that knowledge and technology developed in the home country can be disseminated abroad without undue delay. The standard design of the theme park (the usual hub and spoke design), operational procedures, and staff training program will help to attain the goal of offering the same Disney theme park experience, regardless of location. It also helps to achieve greater economies of scale through the cross promotion of Disney's different business segments. Disney's core competence lies in its quality service. For this reason, it exercised tight operational control in Tokyo Disneyland and Disneyland Paris (through thick operating manuals), and plans the same approach for the forthcoming Hong Kong Disneyland. Equally, Disney plans the same centralized control when it moves forward to its next overseas theme parks in Latin America and other European countries.

DISNEY'S STRATEGIC CHOICE OF HONG KONG

China has been undergoing a series of structural, financial, and economic changes in recent years. The government has strived to privatize its giant state-owned enterprises and is opening more and more business sectors to foreign competition. An estimated extra US$80 billion in fresh capital is expected to flow into China during the first six years after joining the WTO. It is expected that leisure and travel operators will benefit from increasing international trade, and the presence of foreign businesspeople in China.

China also has a big domestic tourism market. As the economy grows, more people can afford domestic travel. In 1999, there were a total of 719 million domestic travelers spending a total of RMB 283 billion. To boost domestic consumption, the Chinese government mandated five-day workweeks in 1999 and increased the number of public holidays from 6 to 10 days in 2000. Many tourist destinations reported large revenue gains.

As for China's theme park business, the last five years have seen the failures of the American Dream Park, a $50 million project in Shanghai, and Frobelland, built as a German theme park by a Taiwanese investor. This led some analysts to predict an end to theme parks in China despite the anticipated explosive tourist growth in the new millennium. Investors' misjudgments have been many. Estimates of the number of customers were far too high, costs soared out of control, and bureaucracy weighed projects down. Other factors contributing to these failures include the rural location of the parks (which is customary in the West) and lack of clusters of middle-class residents in major cities. Chris Yoshii of Economic Research Associates on the other hand opined in 1998 that China was still "the theme park market for the new millennium."

Hong Kong, with about 7 million residents, is among the most populous cities in Asia. However, even this number is far too small to support a Disney theme park on its own. Disney also took into account the total number of visitors going in and out of Hong Kong and in particular the visitors from Mainland China. One of the biggest sources is the 72.7 million people, 5.8 percent of the total national population, living in Guang-

dong province, bordering Hong Kong. In terms of infrastructure, Guangdong has more than 51 state-approved ports and 7 civil airports, with the Guangzhou Baiyun International Airport providing international services. The province is a major railway hub and has a good network of highways linking major cities. Its telecommunication network is one of the most advanced in the country. Guangdong is also the largest light industrial base in China and has developed into a major export-processing base for investors from Hong Kong, Macau, and other markets. It is the largest consumer market in China, though its population ranks fifth largest among all provinces, municipalities and autonomous regions. It also ranked at the top in attracting foreign investment. Apart from the Pearl River Delta Open Economic Zone and three Special Economic Zones in Shenzhen, Zhuhai, and Shantou, Guangdong has 11 state-level economic and technological development zones, four bonded zones, and 59 provincial level economic and technological development zones. In the past 20 years, Guangdong has seen the largest GDP growth rate at 40.2% in 1993, and the GDP for the secondary sector gained over 60% in 1996. In short, Disney is stepping into one of the most affluent and densely populated areas of China with tremendous economic growth potential.

Hong Kong is also a great city for tourists from all over the world. It is ranked in second place, just behind China, in the top ten East Asia/Pacific destinations with 11,328,000 visitors in 1999, an increase of 18.3% over the previous year. The National Geographic Traveler, an authoritative publication in the United States, also put Hong Kong on its list of the top 50 tourist destinations of a lifetime. Each visitor spent an average of $975 per trip. Tourists from Southeast Asia who cannot afford a long trip to the United States Disneyland or the relatively expensive Tokyo Disneyland, will find Hong Kong Disneyland a convenient alternative for the American theme park experience.

A summary list of existing regional theme parks is provided in Table 4.

Table 4
Theme parks in Southern China and Hong Kong

Name	Cities	Theme	Description
Theme parks being planned/built in southern China			
Military Theme Park	Shenzhen of Guangdong	Military	■ Converted from the Minsk, a part of the former Soviet Union's Black Sea Fleet, 273 meters long. ■ Features an aircraft museum showing five Russian MiG fighters and military helicopters ■ The latest in virtual reality games and a soccer pitch on deck
Dinosaur Kingdom	Zigong of Chengdu, Sichuan	Dinosaurs	■ 8.1 square kilometers ■ RMB 400 million project

continued

Name	Cities	Theme	Description
Petrified Forest	Kunming of Yunan	High-tech	■ Add to the existing 'petrified forest' attraction. ■ A $6.4 million project. Overall concept is rooted in local folklore and the legend of Arshima, a beautiful young woman for whose hand a contest is held among local men.
Playa Maya Waterpark	Shenzhen	Waterpark	■ A seven-acre park with water slides and tropical landscaping.
Major theme parks in Shenzhen			
Splendid China	Shenzhen	Miniature of Chinese wonders	■ Largest miniature park in the world with more than 80 attractions
China Folk Culture Villages	Shenzhen	Cultural	■ 180,000 square meter park presenting the folk art, ethnic customs and traditional dwellings of the Chinese minorities
Windows of the World	Shenzhen	Miniature of world wonders	■ 480,000 square meter park featuring world wonders, historic sites, natural landscapes, folk customs, and international song and dance performance. ■ Adult: RMB 100, Child: RMB 50
Happy Valley	Shenzhen	Entertainment	■ A 170,000 square meter entertainment park featuring attractions and rides.
Overseas Chinese Town	Shenzhen	Cultural	■ Built in 1985
Existing Hong Kong theme parks			
Ocean Park	Aberdeen	Aquarium and water park	■ Ocean Park is planning to add a HK$500 million "Adventure Bay" attraction to their existing park. ■ $19.24 for adult, $9.62 for children.
Snoopy World	Sha Tin	Peanuts theme playground	■ 40,000-square-foot playground in the 15-year-old New Town Plaza (shopping center) undertaken by Sun Hung Kai Properties.
Theme Parks being planned/built in Hong Kong			
N/A	Ma Wan	Education	■ Planned by Sun Hung Kai Properties on 21.73 hectares as part of its residential project.
Space Island	Lok Ma Chau border	Indoor Space theme park	■ Planned by Concord Land Development ■ The theme park will be part of a 13 million-square-foot commercial/residential project ■ Construction cost is HK$10 billion.
N/A	Tai Po Kau	"Interactive" cultural theme park	■ Planned by Kerry Properties as part of a residential project ■ A 9 ha park will have an education center with a lake, rivers and mangroves.
N/A	Pak Mong and Ngau Kwu Long	Ecological	■ A 130 hectare ecological park planned by Swire Properties and Sun Hung Kai Property.

DISNEY'S BUSINESS STRATEGIES IN HONG KONG

Pursuing the Cautious and Growth Ownership Model

Despite early concern about its viability as the first Disney venture in Asia, Tokyo Disneyland has become the world's most popular amusement park. The Tokyo park was designed to closely resemble the Disney parks in America as the Japanese partner did not want Disney to do anything that was not Western. For instance, signs are in English, all but three of the park shows are in English, and there is virtually no Japanese food sold. The secret of its success is providing visitors with a slice of unadulterated Disney-style Americana, according to Oriental Land president Toshio Kagami. The park brought huge economic benefits to the Japanese economy in terms of tourism receipts and employment. In retrospect, Disney appears to have profited least because it handed over licensing rights in return for a paltry 10% of admissions earnings and 5% of food and souvenir sales. Disney's no-ownership position in Tokyo Disneyland is a result of Disney's initially cautious overseas investment policy and its heavy financial commitment to building the Epcot Center in Florida. The consequence, of course, is that Disney also limited its potential return from the venture.

To avoid repeating the same mistake, Disney was determined to be the primary owner for the European Disney theme park. In order to maximize its return, Disney took a 49% stake in the Paris project, but its high expectations foundered on the reality of economic recession and angry criticism from French intellectuals and social critics. French intellectuals called the project "a cultural Chernobyl" and disliked its promotion of an unhealthy American style of consumerism. However, the major cause of setbacks in Euro Disney lay in the economic recession and a miscalculation of revenue, i.e., visitors stayed in the park for much less time than was forecasted in the original projection. Disney also made operational mistakes such as serving no alcohol and underestimating the demand for breakfast. High employee turnover developed due to discontent over the strict Disney dress code and a "tough" Disney performance standard. In addition, the heavily leveraged Euro Disney needed to pay interest on its $2.9 billion of borrowed capital. For the fiscal year ending September 30, 1993, the amusement park lost $960 million. Disney quickly negotiated with its banks for debt restructuring, suspended 5 years' royalty payments, and streamlined its marketing and operations. As a results, its ownership fell from 49% to 39%.

Mindful of these costly missteps, Disney is "taking a new path" and trying out a third model for Hong Kong Disneyland. The partnership with the government will guarantee uninterrupted financial and governmental support to the construction of the project and in the park's initial years of operation. In addition, if there is any community concern or criticism to the project, the government, as the largest shareholder, will be as eager as Disney to fend it off. In fact, in view of the high capital layout, the high land price in Hong Kong and Disney's troubled consumer product and film business, it would be too risky for Disney to finance the project with its own capital. Under the current deal, Disney will totally control the operations of the park and have a 43% share of profits with small immediate cash investment. What Disney really needs is to display its expertise in the managing and marketing of its big brand in order to make the theme park a success.

Euro Disney proved to be an over-ambitious project at the time of opening because Disney underestimated the impact of a downsizing economy and was over-confident in its Disney magic and operational forecasts. Judson Green, chairman of Walt Disney Attractions, admitted that they were "risk averse" in the Hong Kong Disneyland project. The new theme park is being planned in stages, with 5.6 million visitors in the opening year and a plan to expand new attractions only when justified by attendance levels. However, it is evident that Disney is very cautious in avoiding over-investing while maintaining a solid share and control over the project.

Sensitivity to Community Concerns and Work Place Issues

Disneyland Paris has been criticized as a symbol of American cultural imperialism. Ariane Mnouchkin, a theater director, called Disney a "cultural Chernobyl." A Paris union official accused Disney of "suppressing French individualism through its strict employee dress code." The theme park was also a target for anti-Americanism, and hundreds of farmers blocked the roads to the park in June 1992 because the protestors believed the United States was responsible for the proposed cuts in European Community farm subsidies. It seemed to the French that Disney was just too obsessed in its insistence on the American Disney style and ignored local customs such as serving wine with meals.

Peter Murphy, a leading tourism scholar, emphasizes the importance of taking into consideration local attitudes and consultation with the community that includes local residents and tourism operators when developing tourism at the community level. In this context, Professor John Ap of the Hong Kong Polytechnic University conducted a pilot longitudinal study to monitor community perceptions and attitudes towards Hong Kong Disneyland and to assess its impact on tourism in the Pearl River Delta Region. As part of the study, two surveys were conducted in March and April 2000 (see Table 5). Of the 832 respondents, 75% indicated support for the project and 63% believed the benefits of Hong Kong Disneyland would outweigh the costs. Half of the respondents would tolerate the negative impact brought by the project. The social and cultural impact of the project also received positive ratings, while the environmental impact received the lowest rating. The major concern of the respondents appeared to be the fairness of the deal as about 39% of the interviewees tended to disagree with the arrangement and indicated the deal was not fair. Response to the influence of American culture upon Hong Kong society was also mixed. Professor Ap argued that for the project to be accepted, the community had to embrace, accept, and perceive it positively as well as to tolerate any negative impact of the project.

Environmentalists are lamenting the loss of a green belt, the accompanying pollution caused by the project, and the threat to the endangered nepenthes (i.e., pitcher plants), white dolphins, and the loss of a probable historical site. Mei Ng, di-

Table 5
Hong Kong's opinion polls on the Disneyland project

1. Dr. John Ap of Hong Kong Polytechnic University's Hotel and Tourism Management Department conducted a survey on the Hong Kong Disneyland project. Of the 832 respondents, 582 were polled randomly by telephone while the rest were Lantau and Peng Chau (both are outlying islands in Hong Kong) residents who gave lower ratings for the project than the first group. Other highlights are as follows:
   - Nearly 40 per cent of people disagreed with the statement that it was a fair deal for the government to provide a HK$5.6 billion low-interest loan for the project and HK$13.6 billion for reclamation and infrastructure works.
   - Between 53 and 69 per cent of respondents said they disliked the prospect of a negative impact on the environment and wildlife at Penny's Bay. The waters are the natural habitat for the Chinese white dolphin.
   - About half of the respondents said they would tolerate the negative impact, reschedule their activities, or avoid the area due to crowding.
   - 80 per cent of the people were positive about the revenue expected to be generated within the local economy.
   - Source: *South China Morning Post*, Hong Kong, July 13, 2000.

2. A survey conducted by the *Sun News* (with 234 respondents) on 11/3/1999 has the following results:
   - Does the HK Government's investment of $20 billion on Hong Kong Disneyland mean Disney is taking all the advantages while HK people foot the bill? Yes vote: 126 (53.8%), No: 44 (18.5%), no comment: 64 (27.4%).
   - Who is the biggest winner in the deal? Disney: 99 (42.3%), HK Government: 63(26.9%), Don't know: 72 (26.9%)
   - Do you agree to build Disneyland? Yes: 164 (70%), No: 64 (19.6%), No comment: 24 (10.4%)
   - What would be your ideal price for the ticket? HK$300 (190, 81.2%), $400 (32, 13.6%), $500 (12, 5.2%)
   - Source: http://www.the-sun.com.hk/channels/news/19991103/img/0311a1g3_big.jpg

3. An opinion poll conducted by the *Sun News* (with 4,553 respondents) as of 10/15/2000 has the following result:
   - 'Should Disneyland Hong Kong blend American and Chinese culture?' Yes: 27.7%, no: 34.8%, no comment: 1.8%
   - Source: http://www.the-sun.com.hk/cgi-bin/polling.cgi?input_polling_id=19991103033328_6288&dirsect=news)

4. Michael DeGolyer of Hong Kong Baptist University is conducting an academic study of political and economic change in Hong Kong between 1982 to 2007. As a part of the project, he discovered that an overwhelming 90 per cent of respondents to a survey knew of the multibillion-dollar project; 40 per cent described the deal with Disney as unfair, 33 per cent felt it was fair, with 15 per cent neutral and 12 per cent having no idea.

Source: Jimmy Cheung. "Tung deeper in doldrums," *South China Morning Post*, Hong Kong, November 24, 1999.

rector of the Friends of the Earth, asked for a "sustainable development" plan that could balance the environment, the economy, and social development. Environmentalists are also concerned about the cost and environmental impact caused by dredging and disposal of the contaminated mud at the Cheoy Lee shipyard that is necessary before reclamation work for the Disney site can commence. However, it appears that Hong Kong's environmentalists have less political influence over local issues than their Western counterparts. As such, the major community issues that remain to be resolved are whether the Disneyland project is a fair deal and whether the economic benefits are based on realistic projections.

Local Competition Enhancing the Growth of Hong Kong as a Recreation Destination

The primary competitor for Hong Kong Disneyland will be Hong Kong Ocean Park, a 23-year-old marine and amusement park in the southern part of Hong Kong Island. Ocean Park had 3.3 million guests in 2000, about 40% of whom were tourists, with 70% of those coming from Mainland China. Ocean Park planned major renovations over the next four years, including the addition of Pacific Pier, a viewing area fea-

turing 17 California sea lions, a United States Zamperla Mine Train coaster, a Turbo Drop Tower, and the Adventure Bay water park. According to Professor John Ap, Ocean Park's attendance will inevitably suffer in the initial years of Disneyland's operation. As the market settles down, the two competing parks in the area will increase Hong Kong's drawing power as a recreation destination and "result in attendance increases for all parks concerned." Randolph Guthrie, head of Ocean Park, commented that the key for their survival would be differentiating itself by "focusing on ecology and conservation issues." In fact, the not-for-profit Ocean Park is unique in providing educational opportunities on marine life and promoting animal conservation programs as well as amusement entertainment. In addition, its adult admission fee of US$19 is much more affordable than the premium price of about US$33 expected to be charged by Disney.

The small scale theme parks clustered in the Shenzhen area, across the Hong Kong border, are designed to provide entertainment experiences with a Chinese flavor and are therefore differentiated from the American Disney dream. Officials in the Pearl River Delta area and Guangdong province are confident that Hong Kong Disneyland will bring in more tourists from both within China and overseas.

As for other parts of Asia, Tokyo Disneyland is optimistic that Hong Kong Disneyland will not cannibalize its revenue as overseas tourists account for only 3% to 4% of its visitors. Tokyo Disneyland continued to perform well, and the Tokyo Disney-Sea park opened in fall 2001. Everland, part of the Samsung empire in Korea, is not worried about the competition from Hong Kong.

The Strategy of Differentiation

Disney theme parks are seen as places for family entertainment. Linda Warren, Disney World's senior vice president of marketing, noted that Disney was "about children and people who are children at heart. . . . We always have to be aware of our image." Tim O'Brien, editor for parks and attractions coverage at Amusement Business magazine in Nashville, agreed that "Disney's image is too squeaky clean to allow them to do Halloween right." Disney's appeal of fantasy and fun has proven to be very successful in bringing in millions of guests for Tokyo Disneyland and its Paris counterpart since their openings. Japanese love Disney's cuddly and adorable "wide-eyed" cartoon characters. Cries of "Kawaii" (cute) are often heard throughout the park. By the same token, Japanese and American cartoon characters also appeal to Chinese and other Asian kids. Disney is now a veteran in re-creating the "Pixie Dust" magic and American dream on foreign soil. This involves the use of the same theme park design and construction as well as attention to such details as maintaining a "no-fly" and a "no-anchor" zone as well as a green belt so that non-Disney construction and objects that may be distracting or incoherent with the theme park will not be seen at the site. The prime objective is to nourish an atmosphere of purity and innocence so that the Disney dream and the big stage concept remain undisturbed. This is the slice of Americana and Disney fantasy that will pull in millions of Mainlanders to experience first hand in Hong Kong.

One of the key success factors for Disney is its renowned quality service and efficiency. The so-called Disney look and Disney smile denote a unique service standard and practice that is built on a service oriented and pleasing culture. It is noted that Tokyo Disneyland is successful in instilling high service quality and the Disney spirit, due to a good source of young Japanese workers who are "generally comfortable wearing uniforms, obeying their bosses, and being part of a team."

As with its other theme parks, Disney would establish a Disney University in Hong Kong to provide on-the-job training and professional development for each theme park employee. This is also the place where its employees will learn about Disney's values, traditions, and standard of excellence. High-quality service is indeed essential to the success of a theme park, as it links directly to the visitors' intention to return.

International hotels and shopping malls in Hong Kong are able to offer on-the-job training for their staff or hire graduates from tertiary or technical institutes. However, most front-line sales personnel, janitors, or operators from other service providers receive little or no formal training. The quality of customer service may vary in different establishments. One of the biggest challenges for Disney is to instill the quality service concept among its locally recruited employees. All cast members have to commit themselves to "creating happiness" for all guests, irrespective of their color, race, and place of origin. With a projection of 70% of guests from Mainland China, Disney has to focus on establishing Disney's management practice and motto starting with hiring, training, and development of its cast members. John Ap remarked that education and training is critical to reduce prejudice toward the Mainlanders, and Disney has been good at training its staff.

Synergy in Disney's Operations

Synergy is very important for Disney, and its divisions have to promote each other. A writer commented that "Disney's method [is] conjuring value—in the form of Mickey Mouse and his sidekicks—from his own imagination and those of his viewers, and then fashioning a self-reinforcing cycle of promotion and sales." The main strategy for Disney's home operations is media-diversification while achieving synergy in operations. However, Disney will not replicate this strategy in Asia at this stage. Disney president Robert Iger said, "this market (Asia) has lots of potential for media companies . . . but our primary focus is on the Disney brand." He notes that Disney is developing a Disney.com for Hong Kong, but this is a means to help support the theme park by allowing customers to buy Disney merchandise on the web instead of offering full-fledged Internet services similar to what AOL and Yahoo! have been doing. Ultimately, there will be a Disney TV channel for China and Japan aiming to support Disney's operations in Asia. The three main operations, namely, theme park, merchandizing, and videos, will cross-promote each other's performance. One segment of operation serves as advertisement for the others, and most Asians are more familiar with Disney movies and merchandise than Disney's Internet operations. Disney is eager to exploit the enormous potential of its brand image to improve the corporation's overall performance.

Another method that Disney has developed in order to maximize its return on operations is DisneyQuest, a three- or four-hour amusement center experience. The first two were opened in Walt Disney World and Chicago in 1998. A third was scheduled to open in Philadelphia in the spring of 2001, but the project was abandoned. DisneyQuest offers a combination of storytelling and interactive entertainment for guests of all ages. Inside the facility, guests can enjoy virtual attractions such as Cyberspace Mountain (a roller coaster), ride in a 360-degree pitch and roll flight simulator, battle Hades in a 3D real-time video underworld, or draw their favorite Disney characters on computers. DisneyQuest is Disney's attempt to tap into extra revenues from city and neighboring kids whose families do not have the time or budget to afford a long trip to Disney's theme park resorts. Unless Disney proves to have overdone the DisneyQuest leading to cannibalization of theme park sales (attendance), the mini-scale amusement centers may well serve as an extra source of revenues and a big advertisement of Disney's brand in addition to being a testing ground for new rides and features.

It is therefore of strategic importance that Disney seeks more exposure of its products and names in Mainland Chinese cities to test the markets. The scale of investment and operations is easier to control and more affordable, while response and feedback are valuable for adjusting Disney's overall and long-term expansion plan into the Asian Pacific market in the future. This is particularly beneficial for the Chinese market since the business environment there is not mature enough to offer adequate information and legal infrastructure on which to venture an intensive and large-scale theme park at the current stage.

Strategic Alliance with the Hong Kong Government

Unlike Disneyland Paris and Tokyo Disneyland, Hong Kong Disneyland is meant to be a partnership between Disney and the local government right from the beginning. Even though the French government made significant concessions to the project in terms of extending highways and the railway, reduction in value-added tax, provision of $6 billion loans, and sale of land at agricultural value in 1971, the theme park was initially owned 49% by Walt Disney with the remaining 51% owned by a separate company called Euro Disney S.C.A. which traded on the French Bourse. There was French government support but not the strong support founded on co-ownership. As Disney prepares to take on the 1.2 billion Chinese market for its movies, cable channels, merchandise, and theme park, it must be more sensitive to the political environment and avoid irritating the Chinese government. The Hong Kong government may act as the intermediary to channel critical issues and concerns for Disney to reposition its overall expansion strategy and to make tactical adjustment while marching into the Chinese market.

By the same token, such a partnership will hopefully help divert any fallout from friction in Sino-American relations that are not directly related to Disney. These relations are experiencing ups and downs lately, with such thorny issues as human rights, Tibet independence, Taiwan, allegations of Chinese spying relating to nuclear weapons, and China's adhesion to its World Trade Organization commitments.

Stricter Copyright Enforcement and Development of Formal Distribution Channels

The main pillar supporting the Disney dream is its brand name. Disney has been very careful in managing and protecting its image and brand name. Apart from holding off scary Halloween celebrations and thrilling rides that are incongruent with its themes of fantasy and fun, Disney is aggressive in combating copyright infringement and protecting its image. Disney has strict codes for its licensees to follow so as to reduce the extent of damage such as the sweatshop problem that other multinationals experienced in recent years. However, intellectual property rights in China are a "different story." Since China's open door policy with respect to foreign investment began in the 1980s, efforts have been made to bring intellectual property rights protection in line with international standards. The Chinese government has revised its Trademark Law, Patent Law, and Copyright Law. However, the enforcement measures are less than effective, and pirated American consumer goods, including Mickey Mouse products, are openly sold to millions of Chinese.

In terms of intellectual rights protection, Hong Kong has been doing a better job recently. In February 1999, the United States removed Hong Kong from its international piracy watch list, and it has remained off the watch list since.

Promoting and Expanding Hong Kong's Inbound Tourism

The Special Administrative Region's (SAR) support in promoting and expanding Hong Kong's inbound tourism is a prerequisite to the success of the theme park. The SAR government is taking a number of steps to facilitate the development of tourism. Four major strategies have been identified and presented in the booklet, "2000 Policy Address, Tourism, Policy Objective for Economic Services Bureau." These measures are designed to develop and improve tourism infrastructure, facilities, and products, to improve Hong Kong's tourism friendliness and quality of service, to promote Hong Kong as an attractive tourism destination, and to enhance consumer protection. The Disney theme park and the accompanying development of Lantau Island are included as part of the major efforts in improving tourism attractiveness.

The SAR government is also negotiating with Guangdong officials with a view to increasing the quota of two-way permits from 1,500 to 2,000 daily in order to allow more Mainland tourists to visit Hong Kong. The Guangdong government has pledged to ease visa application for Mainlanders traveling to the SAR. In addition, both sides agreed to unify diesel standards for a better air quality and to reduce water pollution in Deep Bay. Another important step for Disney is to secure its resort hotels as one of the designated choices for Hong Kong tours.

Ensuring a Minimum One-Day Theme Park Experience

According to a survey conducted by the Hong Kong Tourist Association, 76% of Mainland vacation visitors and 80% of vacation visitors from all places of origin stayed in Hong Kong for three nights or less; 61% of the Mainlanders and 50% of all visitors chose an all-inclusive package to Hong Kong; 71% of the Mainlanders were on a multi-destination trip to Thailand, Macau, Singapore, or Malaysia for an average nine-day tour with Hong Kong as one of the main stops. As packaged tours for Mainlanders tend to use Chinese-owned or -operated hotels in Hong Kong that are cheaper, Disney's hotels, with higher rates, will have to target overseas visitors. Disney will therefore be in a better position if Mainland guests stay in the park for at least one whole day so that they will spend enough money on souvenirs and food before they move on to other city attractions or to Ocean Park.

Adaptations to Hong Kong and the Chinese Environment

Disney theme parks have a long-standing smoking ban policy in their stores, restaurants, queues for rides, and on their buses and monorails. Smoking is only allowed in restricted areas outside the main stream of traffic. However, given the wide use of cigarettes among Mainland Chinese, Disney is seriously considering being flexible about the rules on smoking in the Hong Kong theme park.

Another challenge lies in crowd management and maintaining cleanliness in the park. Again, Disney has to display its expertise in maintaining a clean and orderly environment in the park with a high volume of tourists.

As far as adapting to Chinese culture, it does not appear that Disney needed to make any significant adjustments as the Disney dream is basically a product of the American culture. Signs and restaurant menus will be in English as well as in Chinese. Cast members must be able to speak English, Cantonese, and preferably either Mandarin (the official language of China) or one other Chinese dialect to cater for the needs of the majority of the non-English speaking Mainlanders. Hong Kong people are being criticized for their deteriorating English ability and insufficient Mandarin skills. This touches on a much deeper and complicated social and educational phenomenon in Hong Kong where Cantonese is the daily communication tool of the people, although English and Mandarin are also official languages. To maintain competitiveness in international trade and tourism, Hong Kong has to revamp its educational system to train more capable bilingual people. To offer an authentic American experience to guests and to differentiate the theme park from its counterparts in the nearby Shenzhen area, it is not necessary for Disney to sell Chinese food. With growing numbers of McDonald's and KFC restaurants on the Mainland, American hamburgers, French fries, pizzas and Coke all help to make the Mainlanders' stay in the theme park a more Americanized experience.

Visitors from the Mainland or overseas go to Hong Kong mainly to enjoy its mix of East and West. They will be happy to see an American theme park on Chinese soil. If they want authentic Chinese culture and scenery, they can conveniently cross the border to Shenzhen or other Pearl River delta cities.

This does not imply that Chinese festivals should not be celebrated in the theme park. As a legacy of British rule, Hong Kong has been celebrating both Western and Chinese festivals. Public holidays tie in with New Year, Chinese New Year, Easter, Christmas, and several other traditional Chinese festivals such as the Dragon Boat and Ching Ming festivals. Local residents usually join overseas trips or board trains to the Mainland for short vacations during these holidays. Hong Kong Disneyland may be able to draw these locals as well as the Mainlanders and overseas visitors with its festival celebration events. After all, Hong Kong Disneyland is positioned as a family entertainment resort for both overseas and Mainland visitors.

Ensuring Top Theme Park Safety Operations

Lately, United States commentators have been highly critical of Disney's closed-door operations and silence on accident reports and figures. Disney's safety record made headlines three times in the second half of 2000 when a 37-year-old man died in the Splash Mountain ride at Disney World on November 6, a 4-year-old boy was critically injured in Disneyland's Roger Rabbit cartoon spin on September 22, and a separate accident in the Space Mountain roller coaster injured nine persons on July 31. Disney recently settled a lawsuit with an undisclosed sum paid to the family of a man killed and his wife's face shattered by flying metal ripped from the park's sailing ship Columbia in December 1998. "There is a clear pattern as to how Disney handles these matters. It is clear that Disney focuses first on image, not first-aid." Park officials said in October that Disneyland was updating its safety and emergency procedures, including employee training on 911 calls. Industry operators would argue that the fatality rate is still low compared to the number of person-rides per year. Although there are several years before Hong Kong Disneyland commences operations, Disney needs to improve its safety measures as well as to establish a responsible and open park operator image.

REFERENCES

Yoland Chung. "Making a Magic Kingdom." *Asiaweek,* November 12, 1999.

http://cnn.com/ASIANOW/asiaweek/magazine/99/1112/cover1.html

"Theme park promotions run the full marketing specturm." *Entertainment Marketing Letter,* 11 (4): 1+, April 1998.

Michael Eisner. *Work in Progress.* New York: Random House, 1998, pp. 415–416.

John D. Daniels, Lee. H. Radebaugh. *International Business Environments and Operations.* Addison-Wesley, 1998.

James Zoltak. "China: Theme park market for new millennium?" *Amusement Business.* New York, September 14, 1998.

Chester Dawson. "Tokyo's toon town," *Far Eastern Economic Review.* Hong Kong, November 11, 1999.

Robert F. Hartley. "Euro Disney: A Successful Format Stumbles in Europe." *Marketing Mistakes and Successes,* 7th Edition. New York, John Wiley & Sons, Inc. 1998. 143–159.

E. Scott Reckard. "Disney Discovering It's a Small World After All. Theme Parks: Mindful of some costly missteps, the company is taking a new path in Hong Kong as it pursues opportunities overseas." *Los Angeles Times,* C. December 19, 1999.

Bruce Gilley. "Aieeyaa! A mouse!" *Far Eastern Economic Review,* Hong Kong, November 11, 1999.

Elizabeth Anne Nestegard. *"Reading" Disneyland: A Historical Look at the Textual Interpretation of the Disney Parks and the Study of American Popular Culture."* A thesis presented to the faculty of California State University, Fullerton, 1994, pp 360–361.

Peter Murphy. *Tourism: A Community Approach,* New York, Methuen, 1985.

John Ap. "Hong Kong Disneyland—Community Reactions and Its Impacts on Tourism in the Pearl River Delta Region." Paper presented at the Leisure and Entertainment Asia Conference 2000, July 12–13, Hong Kong.

Chris Oliver. "Group urges caution on country park." *South China Morning Post,* Hong Kong, April 22, 2000.

Natasha Emmons. "Ocean Park Hong Kong prepares for the arrival of Disney themer." *Amusement Business,* New York, July 31, 2000.

Email from Professor John Ap to the author dated November 2, 2000.

Natasha Emmons. "Ocean Park Hong Kong prepares for the arrival of Disney theme," *Amusement Business,* New York, July 31, 2000.

Robert Johnson. "Cutthroat Business: How Universal Makes A Killing at Halloween—Disney Has No Axes to Grind, But Mickey Mouse

Operation Thinks Gore Isn't for Kids." *Wall Street Journal*, New York, October 31, 2000.

"Disney's Japan Venture Loses Some Lusters." *Los Angeles Times*, 7 April 1993.

Robert Anthony. "Euro Disney: The First 100 Days." *Harvard Business School 9-693-013.*

E-mail from Professor John Ap to the author dated November 2, 2000.

H.W. Brands. *Masters of Enterprise*. New York: The Free Press, 1999.

Joseph Lo. "What Disney focuses on brand building image more important than diversification as media giant readies theme park." *South China Morning Post*, Hong Kong, November 17, 2000.

The Walt Disney Company Annual Report 1999, pp. 21.

Jie Zhang. "A different story of intellectual property rights in China." *Asian Thought and Society*, Volume XXIV, Number 70 (January–April, 1999), pp 42–57.

"2000 Policy Address, Tourism, Policy Objective for Economic Services Bureau," http://www.info.gov.hk/esb/policy/index.htm

Chow Chung-yan. "Air and water quality deals sealed in cross-border talks." *South China Morning Post*, Hong Kong, September 26, 2000.

Richard Verrier and Pedro Ruz Gutierrez. "Disney death stirs debate; investigators said it was an accident, but ride-safety experts questioned whether restraints would have helped." *Orlando Sentinel*, Florida, November 7, 2000.

Kimi Yoshino and Meg James. "Disney updates safety policies; Company says the new emergency procedures and employee training are part of preparations for new Anaheim theme park, not because of recent accidents." *The Los Angeles* Times, Los Angeles, October 21, 2000.

Tony Saavedra. "Disneyland settles in '98 death, injury at ship ride." *Orange County Register*, Santa Ana, October 5, 2000.

Joseph J. Tobin. "Introduction: Domesticating the West," in *Remade in Japan*. New Haven: Yale University Press 1992

Paul Beamish, C. Dhanaraj, Y. S. Kim. "Samsung and the Theme Park Industry in Korea." Ivey Publication, Ontario, Canada, February 10, 2000.

CASE DISCUSSION QUESTIONS

1. Do you agree with Disney's decision with respect to market entry into HK/China? Justify your choice.

2. Disney plans to make certain adaptations to its previous strategies to enter the European (Paris) and Japanese markets. Do you agree with its decisions? Why or why not?

3. What are some of the key challenges Disney HK will face in implementing these strategies? Suggest methods of dealing with these challenges.

4. Do you agree with Disney's decision to pursue a "centralized control global strategy?" Discuss.

Frank Davis Comes to Madagascar[1]

by **Valeric VinCola***

*Emory University

ANATANANARIVO, MADAGASCAR

Frank Davis entered the cocktail lounge at the Madagascar Hilton Hotel, located in the nation's capital city of Antananarivo, and quickly scanned the room. Behind a cloud of cigarette smoke in the corner there was a table of boisterous French businessmen. A few other tables of two or three people were scattered throughout the lounge. Frank chose a seat at the bar next to a well-dressed white man who looked like he might be American. This was Frank's first visit to Madagascar, and he wanted to get the impressions of other Americans doing business there.

"What would you like?" asked the bartender in slightly accented English.

"A beer, please. What kind do you have?" Frank asked.

"Actually the THB isn't bad. It's the local beer," offered the well-dressed gentlemen next to Frank.

"Thanks. I'll try a THB," Frank told the bartender.

"Is this your first time in Madagascar?" asked the man after introducing himself as Jean-Paul, an American of French descent.

"Yes. I'm here evaluating the local business climate. I work for a U.S. food processing company, Summit Foods, that is interested in the local spice market. How about you?"

"I head up the operations of a textile company in Madagascar's free trade zone, Zone Franche. I've been here since right after the presidential election in 1993."

Frank was somewhat familiar with recent political history based on background material he had received from the U.S. State Department. Madagascar was a former French colony that had gained independence in 1960. Since independence, there have been four presidents: Tsiranana, from 1960 to 1972, and Ratsimandrava, assassinated in 1975, were both in power during the First Republic. Then came Ratsiraka, who introduced the country to the Second Republic and socialism, but he was forced to yield to a transitional government in 1991 after a six-month strike. In February 1993 the current president, Zafy, was elected after a popular referendum which adopted a new constitution establishing a mixed presidential-parliamentary regime. Since the late 1980s and particularly under Zafy's Third Republic, the country has been attempting to shift to a free-market economy from a centrally planned one.

"A textile company?" said Frank. "Then you must be pretty familiar with the general investment climate here.

My boss is convinced there's a lot happening in this country because he has a distant relative who made a fortune here. But I haven't had a chance to look around yet, except for the ride from the airport to the hotel, and that was pretty depressing. The poverty seems to be so pervasive, and yet we passed several Mercedes and sport utility vehicles that didn't seem to be driven by foreigners. I don't get it."

Jean-Paul laughed and shrugged his shoulders. Although he was smiling, his eyes seemed to be sad. "Investment climate? Investment climate . . . Well, I guess it depends on how you define it, and how badly you want to invest. It also depends on who you know and who you are willing to pay to get things done."

Frank's eyebrows shot up. "Pay to 'get things done'? Like what things?" he thought to himself. He let Jean-Paul continue.

"The Third Republic is about two years old. The present administration was elected after a general strike that brought the government and the economy to a standstill. Conditions were bad, wages were low and people got sick of socialism because it seemed to be benefiting only those in power, not the country. The new administration claims to support free-market capitalism, but according to many of my Malagasy business associates, this crew is almost as bad as the crew they voted out."

"But your company is still here. Obviously you are making money if you're still here, right?"

"Believe it or not, we're making money despite the local business climate and the Malagasy government, not because of it. Thanks to the Zone Franche, we pay no taxes on our export receipts and we can hold our profits in U.S. or French currency. Otherwise all the foreign exchange we earn would have to be directly deposited into local banks and then would be automatically converted and held in Malagasy currency. If we were not in the Zone Franche, each time we needed foreign exchange to do business outside the country, we would have to apply for it and, of course, pay a fee! Our firm is doing okay here due to the low barriers to entry in the textile industry, low labor costs and the ability of the Malagasy work force to master new skills quickly. But you would not believe all we've gone through to get where we are now." Jean-Paul fell silent and took a long drink of his beer.

Frank was thoughtful. "This guy doesn't seem too optimistic, but he himself said he's making money. I wonder what kinds of problems he ran into."

"Don't get me wrong. This is a beautiful country and the people work incredibly hard. When I first came here after President Zafy took office, I was full of optimism and could see lots of possibilities. I've been in operations management for 20 years. I've dealt with unions, weathered the effects of the energy crisis and foreign competition on the textile industry, as well as the relocation of our company to the southeastern United States from Massachusetts, my home state. I've even helped my company locate a facility in Taiwan. But it hasn't prepared me for some of the things I've dealt with here." He smiled ruefully and pushed back his chair. "Oh, and one more thing," Jean-Paul added.

"What's that?" Frank asked, eager for more information
"Do you have an umbrella?"

"An umbrella? No. Why?" Frank asked, puzzled by the amused expression on Jean-Paul's face.

"Buy one, you'll need it. We're getting into the rainy season here, complete with cyclones. You'll see what I mean soon enough. I wish you luck."

"Cyclones!" Frank thought to himself. "Thanks," he said to Jean-Paul's back as he headed towards the door. Frank wasn't sure whether Jean-Paul was wishing him luck with his assignment or in weathering the rainy season in Madagascar. He felt a bit discouraged, but at the same time his interest was piqued. He smelled a challenge and envisioned himself as an investment pioneer in rugged territory.

FRANK'S ASSIGNMENT

Frank Davis had been sent to Madagascar on an exploratory mission by his supervisor, Martin Herlihy, a regional vice president of a multinational food processing company, Summit Foods, based in the United States. Frank had been asked to identify potential opportunities for the company to either import agricultural products or set up a food processing operation in Madagascar. He was also asked to assess the country's general investment climate. Even if opportunities could be found, Frank's boss knew there could be several non-quantifiable costs of doing business in a developing country that could render an otherwise profitable project infeasible. Frank's foresight and good judgment had saved the company money in past expansion projects, and Martin knew Frank would be thorough in considering the many factors that could influence a potential investment. Martin was eagerly awaiting Frank's assessment of the situation.

Martin Herlihy was interested in expanding Summit Foods' product offerings to include spices. Due to the heightened health consciousness of U.S. and European consumers, spices were quickly replacing oils and heavy sauces as a natural flavor enhancer in both commercially processed and prepared-at-home foods. Given the increased numbers of dual-income families, consumers cooked at home less often than they did twenty years ago. However,

Exhibit 1
Spices of Madagascar

SPICES CURRENTLY EXPORTED			
English Name	**French Name**	**Malagasy Name**	**Latin Name**
Cinnamon	Cannelle	Kanela	Cinnamonum zeylanicum
Tumeric	Curcuma	Tamotamo	Cucuma longa
Ginger	Gingembre	Sakamalajirofoo	Zinngiber Oofficinale Roscoe
Clove	Girofle	Jirofo	
Hot or Chili pepper	Piment capsicum	Sakay	Capsicum frutescens
Black peppercorn	Poivre noir	Kipoavatra mainty	Piper nigrum
Green peppercorn	Poivre vert	Dioavatra maitso	Piper nigrum
Vanilla	Vanille	Lavanila	Vanilla fragrans

Source: May 1994 Study of Madagascar Exports for Horticultural Products, ATW Consultants for USAID.

SPICES WITH EXPORT POTENTIAL			
English Name	**French Name**	**Malagasy Name**	**Latin Name**
Pink Peppercorn	Baie rose	Voatsiperifery	Schirus terebenthifolius
Mace	Macis		Myristica fragrans
Nutmeg	Noix de muscade		Myristica fragrans

Source: May 1994 Study of Madagascar Exports for Horticultural Products, ATW Consultants for USAID.

they were using more volume and a greater variety of spices when they did cook at home. Ethnic cooking and ethnic restaurants were extremely popular, and that preparation required many nontraditional spices.

Madagascar was known for its spices, particularly vanilla and cloves. Martin asked Frank to find out about other types of spices grown in Madagascar and their current production levels. He felt strongly that the Malagasy government would encourage export of spices because he knew that cloves and vanilla were historically the main sources of foreign currency earnings in the country.

The restaurant at the Hilton did not serve dinner for another hour and a half. Frank decided to take a walk around the neighborhood of the hotel. Although he had researched Madagascar as thoroughly as possible before he left the States, he had not found much information beyond the official reports put out by government agencies such as the State Department and the Commerce Department. He had learned that Madagascar was the world's fourth largest island with a population of 12.5 million, 1 million of whom lived in the capital, Antananarivo, where he was staying. The annual population growth rate was estimated to be 3.19%, with a fertility rate of 6.68 children per woman. In economic terms, this could mean a largely untapped consumer market if the people had disposable income to spend. But Frank was not sure how to assess that yet. The annual per capita income was about $230, but he did not know what the median income was, or what the cost of living was.

He knew Madagascar was approximately the size of Texas and rich in natural resources such as graphite, chromite, coal, bauxite, titanium, salt, quartz, and tar sands, as well as semiprecious stones. His environmentally conscious friends in the States knew that the country was home to many species and even genuses of flora and fauna that were indigenous nowhere else in the world. He also knew that there was widespread soil erosion caused by deforestation and overgrazing, and that this was contributing to desertification of the island. Several species of plant and animal life were endangered. [Exhibit 3 omitted.]

Frank also knew a little about the Malagasy people. Their ethnic origin was a combination of Malay-Indonesian, African, Arab, French, Indian and Creole. The religious composition of the population was 7% Muslim, 41% Christian, and 52% indigenous beliefs. A strong emphasis on ancestor veneration characterized most spiritual belief in the country. Over 90% of the Malagasy work force was employed in the agricultural sector, including fishing and forestry, and the major exports included coffee, vanilla, cloves, shellfish, sugar and petroleum products. The chief industries were largely agricultural product processing (such as meat canneries, soap factories, breweries, tanneries and sugar refining plants) and textile factories, like the company Jean-Paul represented.

The first thing that struck Frank after leaving the grounds of the Hilton Hotel was the poor condition of the infrastructure—streets, sidewalks, and the storm drainage or sewer system (he was not quite sure what the purpose was

Exhibit 2
Exports of nontraditional spices from Madagascar 1993

Customs Code	Spices	Quantity in kg	Value FOB (1000 FMG)*	Price/kg OB (1000 FMG)*
090411100	Green peppercorns in brine	371,559	1,616,136	4,350
090411900	Other peppercorns, not ground	1,470,148	2,506,289	1,705
090412000	Peppercorns, ground or crushed	4,824	37,064	7,683
090420000	Chili peppers, dried or ground	20,022	96,635	4,826
090610000	Cinnamon, whole	1,169,319	1,704,081	1,457
090620000	Cinnamon, ground or crushed	46,724	86,310	1,847
090810000	Nutmeg	143	1,725	12,063
090930000	Cumin seeds	150	99	660
090950000	Fennel seeds	245	36	147
091010000	Ginger	17,461	8,682	497
091020000	Saffron	146	194	1,329
091030000	Tumeric	2,256	15,402	6,827
091040000	Thyme	48	81	1,688
091050000	Curry	232	1,518	6,543
0910099000	Other spices	476	6,619	13,905
	TOTAL	**3,103,753**	**6,080,871**	

Source: State Data Bank (BDE) Antananarivo

*Average rate of exchange in 1993: 1 US$ = 1,900 FMG
1 FF = 330 FMG

of the little streams that ran alongside the streets)—and the absence of traffic signals. Come to think of it, he did not remember stopping at a single red light on the way from the airport. An extensive and well-maintained transportation network certainly would contribute to the success of any agriculturally based economy where the producers were geographically dispersed throughout the country.

Frank also recalled that the Madagascar airport was served almost exclusively by Air Madagascar, a state-owned enterprise. The lack of competition would likely keep the cost of freight and passenger travel high, with little incentive to improve service efficiency. Despite the poor roads and lack of traffic signals, there was certainly no shortage of cars in the capital, and almost every third car seemed to be a taxi. The air was hot and hazy, thick with car exhaust. Frank noticed several buses so full of people that the back doors remained open and two or three people clung to the outside.

As he continued down the street, Frank was approached by several people selling a variety of items which they pushed at him: handicrafts, Ray Ban sunglasses, brooms, tire irons, a basketball, and some fruits or vegetables he did not recognize.

"*Non, merci,*" he said over and over again, but they continued to walk alongside him displaying their wares.

"*Bon marché! Combien, Monsieur?*" They were ready to bargain but Frank had no money and no need for a tire iron in Madagascar. He began to feel annoyed and a bit overwhelmed by the entourage of vendors. He decided to turn back after another several minutes of sales pitches in French and another language which he assumed was Malagasy. It occurred to him that he needed to change his money at the hotel before dinner anyway. As he came closer to the hotel, he was approached by a barefooted little boy in dirty rags carrying a baby on his back. "That boy can't be any more than 5 years old," Frank thought, shocked by the sight. "And the baby isn't even old enough to walk. Where are the parents?"

"*Monsieur, donnez-moi la monnaie? Donnez-moi la monnaie?*" the boy begged, thrusting his little hand forward. His big brown eyes implored Frank to give him some spare change. His face was dirty and his nose runny. Frank was torn inside but looked away and walked quickly back to the hotel, just as the sky was turning dark and threatening rain. Frank reminded himself to buy an umbrella as he took refuge in the air-conditioned lobby from both the rain and the pitiful scene he had confronted outside. He headed for the cashier to change his money.

THE FLOTTEMENT

The exchange rate was just under 4000 Malagasy francs (FMG) to a dollar. Frank recalled that when he left the United States two days before, the rate was about 3600 FMGs. "Could the rate have changed that much in three days?" Frank asked himself. Then he recalled what he had read about the monetary system. In May 1994 the FMG moved from a fixed exchange rate system to a floating exchange rate. The FMG was untied from the French franc to fluctuate on its own against hard currencies, but the French franc (FF) remained the main currency of reference. This step to liberalize the Malagasy currency was referred to as the flottement and was required by the International Monetary Fund (IMF) in fulfillment of a planned structural adjustment program. As a result of the flottement, the FMG lost about half of its value almost overnight, setting off wide-scale price increases. Because of the weak economy, Madagascar's currency was weak. It had consistently lost value relative to hard currencies since the flottement was instituted.

"Do you need to stamp this?" Frank pushed a small currency declaration form across the counter to the cashier. He had been given the form by the stewardess on his flight into Madagascar and told to declare all his currency, traveler's checks, credit card account numbers, and personal checks. The paper was barely large enough to contain all the information requested, but Frank complied. He did not want to be unnecessarily detained for not following procedures when he left the country. His tour book had warned him that airport officials would ask him how much he spent in the country and whether he was taking any Malagasy money outside the country with him.

"I'm sorry sir, we don't have a stamp. Only the banks stamp the form if you change money there," the cashier informed him.

"But aren't I required by law to have a stamp? How can the hotel exchange money for me but not stamp my form? I'm not sure I understand." Frank was genuinely puzzled.

"If you want your form stamped, you must go to a bank. But the banks are closed until Monday. If you want to exchange your money here, I'll give you a receipt, but I don't have a stamp. Do you want to change it here?"

Frank hesitated. He wanted to follow the rules but he did not quite understand them, and the cashier did not really clarify it for him. He needed the money now and the banks were closed. Was he expected to wait two days to exchange his money, or would he have to explain his predicament to the airport officials and risk being detained at the airport? He finally decided to exchange only as much money as he thought he would need for the weekend, and hope it would not be an issue later. He did not see any other option.

"For a country that is badly in need of foreign exchange, they certainly make it difficult to convert your money," he thought to himself as he left the counter.

GOVERNMENT APPROVALS

Frank entered the dining room and was seated promptly at a corner table set for one. A short time later Jean-Paul poked his head inside the restaurant and, seeing Frank, waved and approached his table.

"Mind if I join you?" he asked.

"Not at all." Frank gestured towards a chair, "Please, have a seat."

"How are you doing? I barely missed getting caught in the torrential downpour. It's coming down pretty hard out there."

Both men stared out the window at the pouring rain. The sky was dark and ominous. It was hard to believe that just 45 minutes ago the sun had been shining brightly with barely a cloud in the sky.

After giving their dinner orders to the waiter, Frank decided to broach the topic of Madagascar's investment climate again with Jean-Paul. He felt that although Jean-Paul seemed a bit cynical, there was probably a lot he could learn from his experiences. He planned to try to schedule appointments at the Ministry of Commerce, Ministry of Industry, Energy and Mining, and Ministry of Transport, Meteorology and Tourism during his one-month visit. He felt that an initial discussion with Jean-Paul would help him put things into a context and develop some meaningful questions for his interviews with the various Ministers.

"So Jean-Paul, I'm interested in hearing more about your experiences in Madagascar, if you don't mind sharing them with me. Tell me about some of the obstacles or problems your company encountered when trying to set up a facility," Frank asked.

"Well, the first thing any company interested in setting up business in Madagascar needs is an agrèment, or official approval of the government. The hard part is deciding who to approach to obtain this approval, and how to present your business proposal. You need some type of approval from every ministry which has jurisdiction over any part of your business. For example, in our case, we needed the okay of seven ministries, and each ministry has a set of questions that must be answered and documents that must be filed. Some ministries asked for the same information, others asked for information which seemed irrelevant or outside their jurisdiction. One ministry lost our dossier, but didn't bother to inform us—and maybe they didn't realize themselves—until we called to inquire about the status of the approval two months after submitting everything. The amount of red tape here is mind-boggling."

"Is there some sort of checklist or description of the type of documentation required? I mean, do they want a full-blown business plan? A letter from your financial institution? What do they base approval on?" Frank asked, trying to get a clearer picture of what the Malagasy government would request.

"That's just the problem. No one seems to know. It changes from ministry to ministry, day to day. To the first ministry we approached we gave every piece of documentation we thought they could possibly use. I figured that if I was forthcoming with information and demonstrated a serious willingness to do business in Madagascar, the review process would be shorter because they didn't have to keep asking for additional information. I even gave them the names and resumes of the managers we intended to bring in to manage the new facility," explained Jean-Paul.

"That seems like a reasonable approach. Did it help expedite things?" Frank asked.

"Expedite? That's not quite the word I would use. Try *mora mora*," responded Jean-Paul. "It means slowly, slowly in

Malagasy—and is often used to describe the 'Malagasy way,'" he grinned. "That first ministry was the ministry that lost it all. Or at least that's what they told us after two months."

Jean-Paul went on to explain that there seemed to be a great deal of overlap between the ministries, and even conflicting information about what types of business activities are encouraged. The laws of one ministry were often superseded by proclamations, decrees and statutes of that ministry or a different one. There was also a lack of communication between ministries, and Jean-Paul got the feeling there were little rivalries and power plays among the ministries.

"Reasons for denial or disapproval are not given, so it's difficult to address their concerns and try again. I heard from a friend that he knew someone who was denied an agrèment because they wouldn't offer an interest in their project to people high up in the ministry."

"It sounds like there's a problem with administrative efficiency and consistency. But you could probably find that sort of problem in any large organization in any country, really," Frank remarked.

"That may be true. But if you want to do business in this country and save yourself a lot of time and trouble, I'd suggest you find yourself an influential partner who is highly-placed in the government."

The waiter arrived with their dinner. As he laid the plate down in front of Frank, the lights went out and music stopped. The waiter immediately lit the candle on the table as other waiters circulated around the dining room to light those at other tables.

"*Bon appetit!*" the waiter said to the two men, as he walked back towards the dark kitchen. Dumbstruck, Frank watched the hotel employees for a few minutes waiting to see if someone would take control of the situation and explain to the customers what was going on. Jean-Paul and many of the other diners began eating as if nothing was awry.

"If you're waiting until the lights come back on to eat your dinner, it'll probably be cold. You might as well eat. The power will come back on eventually. It goes out just about every time there's a big rain. During rainy season, that could mean at least once a day."

Frank was surprised. Frequent power outages could obviously cause problems with production schedules and delivery dates. And what about information management? Companies which were highly dependent on data must have to take special precautions to safeguard it. Frank made a mental note to find out what provisions were made for back-up power sources, if any.

"What other types of problems have you dealt with?" Frank asked.

"The property rights laws," Jean-Paul answered. "It's been the policy of our company to purchase land and do the construction ourselves, to very exacting specifications. We have built two factories in other countries in the recent past and have found the best layout and configuration for our machinery and assembly lines. So we prefer to build from scratch rather than lease. But, as you may know, foreigners cannot own land in Madagascar. This posed a problem for us, and frankly our CEO took this to be a signal of distrust by the government."

Frank was not aware of this prohibition against foreign ownership of land. Jean-Paul went on to explain that the Malagasy culture considered the land to be sacred. He had even heard a man once say that to the Malagasy, the land is like their body. It was passed down through the generations from the ancestors, and the fact that Madagascar was an island nation probably contributed to their beliefs. Jean-Paul explained that many people get around this law by using Malagasy partners, but that this arrangement can be extremely costly and risky because the foreigner is beholden to the Malagasy. If there is ever a dispute or the relationship deteriorates, the foreigner has questionable legal recourse.

Jean-Paul's company solved the problem by leasing the land under a 99-year lease and constructing a building that would revert to the property owner at the end of the lease term. The rent was paid in foreign currency because of the high inflation rate. This eliminated the need to have the rents adjusted monthly as the value of the Malagasy franc declined.

"Is that legal? It seems like the government keeps very close tabs on the exchange of foreign currency," Frank remarked. Jean-Paul shrugged.

VISITS TO ASSESS THE POTENTIAL FOR EXPORTING SPICES

Over the next several days, Frank tried to make appointments to speak with government officials, agricultural membership organizations, food processors, exporters, and anyone else who he thought would have valuable information about the export potential for non-traditional spices. At the Ministry of Agriculture he hoped to obtain national production statistics but soon learned that the information available was inaccurate, outdated and incomplete. He also found out that the centralized or geographically concentrated cultivation of spices was declining in Madagascar, as the plantations once run by the French were either abandoned or extremely run down. Some spices were grown wild and harvested by independent peasants, so yields varied from year to year. Many plants from the large plantations had succumbed to disease, and those that grew wild often were damaged by severe weather and by the rampant deforestation taking place on the island, because they were not grown in a self-contained and protected area. The wide dispersion of spices also could pose a problem for processors, as the roads and communication infrastructure were almost nonexistent in many rural areas.

On the positive side, Frank was heartened to find out that spices were not restricted export products. Initially, he feared that they might be classified as protected flora, and therefore could not be exported except by special permit due to environmental regulations. Frank did have some concerns about the quality grade of the spices and whether it was comparable to those on the world market. He found out that there were government standards, set by the Ministry of Commerce, for most types of spices. However, these standards pertained to physical characteristics, such as the length and width of the vanilla bean, rather than the quality, growing and harvesting conditions. The majority of spices grown in Madagascar were exported, with 80% going to Europe. Frank hoped that boded well for the U.S. market and that the Malagasy spices would meet U.S. standards, which are typically the highest on the world market.

MEETING A MALAGASY BUSINESSMAN

Frank set up a meeting with the proprietor of a Malagasy spice processing company to learn more about the organization of spice production in Madagascar and to gauge preliminary receptivity to the idea of forming a partnership with Summit Foods. He hoped to gain a better understanding of how the agricultural sector functioned, and what types of concerns Malagasy operators might have about working with an American importer.

Frank was early for his 2:00 P.M. appointment despite the traffic jam caused by market day in Antananarivo. He was offered a seat in a crowded office where five employees appeared to share one telephone and one typewriter. He noticed the office workers used and reused sheets of carbon paper to make copies of their work. At 2:15 P.M., Frank asked if Mr. Rakotomanana knew he was here. The workers exchanged glances, and one of them told him he should be back shortly. Frank figured he might be tied up in traffic somewhere. All of the meetings he had attended so far had begun at least 20 minutes late. The Malagasy took lunch from noon until 2:00 P.M., and many returned home for the noon meal with their family.

At 2:55 P.M., Mr. Rakotomanana arrived. Frank was slightly annoyed because he realized he would probably miss his next meeting, scheduled for 3:30 P.M. He asked if he could use the phone briefly to call his next appointment. On his first few tries, there was no dial tone. One of the office workers volunteered to try calling for him so the meeting could begin.

After explaining who he was and Summit Foods' interest in spices, Frank spoke about his stay so far in Madagascar and asked for some recommendations about what tourist destinations he should visit. They discussed the weather, the local street market and the traffic, and Frank complimented Mr. Rakotomanana on his efficient staff. Frank was interested in touring Mr. Rakotomanana's processing plant, but he did not yet feel comfortable asking to do so. Mr. Rakotomanana's manner was friendly but still quite formal. Frank finally described in detail the techniques and processes used by Summit Foods, and asked Mr. Rakotomanana some basic questions about his operations. It was about 4:00 P.M. when Mr. Rakotomanana offered to take Frank on a tour.

The tour was brief, but Frank was impressed by how much they were able to produce in such small space with the unsophisticated equipment they used. He almost felt as though he were in a time warp. Many of the processes they used had been used in the United States in the 1940s and

Exhibit 3

Countries of destination for exports of nontraditional spices from Madagascar

Country	Quantity (kg)	%	Value FOB (1000 FMG)	%
			Ranked by Value of Freight on Board (FOB), 1993	
France	1,096,803	35	1,971,797	32
Germany	469,833	15	1,088,027	18
Great Britain	471,346	15	721,459	12
Belgium	149,473	5	583,252	10
Netherlands	367,213	12	568,748	9
Reunion	68,557	2	171,382	3
Spain	87,221	3	162,850	3
South Africa	73,036	2	146,562	2
Poland	83,515	3	130,993	2
Italy	32,268	1	114,219	2
Soviet Union	12,500	0	97,170	2
Singapore	53,850	2	79,017	1
Tunisia	36,050	1	53,921	1
Nigeria	25,000	1	51,447	1
Niger	24,000	1	33,557	1
Denmark	3,730	0	28,963	0
Egypt	18,000	1	25,366	0
Comoros	22,627	1	17,536	0
Ghana	6,462	0	15,386	0
Sweden	1,259	0	7,804	0
Switzerland	300	0	4,899	0
USA	297	0	3,448	0
Austria	360	0	3,047	0
Mauritius	50	0	16	0
Malta	2	0	4	0
Monaco	1	0	1	0
TOTAL	**3,103,753**	**100**	**6,080,871**	**100**

Source: State Data Bank (BDE) Antananarivo

Average rates of exchange in 1993:
1 FF = 330 FMG
1 US$ = 1,900 FMG
1 ECU = 2,200 FMG

1950s. Frank then asked some questions about the company's current customers and processing capacity: "You mentioned that your customers are all domestic. What is your current production capacity?"

"Yes. We like to produce for the Malagasy market. I cannot say for certain because our capacity depends on our customers. During harvest season, we hire temporary workers and they work longer hours until the work is finished," Mr. Rakotomanana explained.

"Are you interested in possibly producing for export as well?"

"Yes."

"Do you have the capacity to produce large quantities over a sustained period of time, for a large export customer such as Summit Foods, for example?"

"Yes. Of course." Mr. Rakotomanana seemed very definitive about that.

"Or would it be necessary to expand your operations, perhaps with the assistance of a partner like my company, through some sort of partnership agreement, to ensure you could meet demand?" Frank offered.

"Yes. I think that would be interesting," Mr. Rakotomanana eagerly replied.

"And your company would be willing to share in the capital expenses of such an expansion, if it were needed?"

Mr. Rakotomanana hesitated and did not look back up at Frank. "I cannot say. This must be discussed with my family."

"Of course. I understand. I am only exploring the possibilities at this point. Do you think you might be interested in discussing this further at a later date?" Frank asked hopefully. He did not want to push too hard, but wanted to get a clearer indication of what this processor could do for Summit Foods, and on what terms.

"Yes. I think it would be interesting."

"I am leaving in about three weeks. Would you like to set up a meeting next week, after you have a chance to discuss things with your family?"

"Oh, yes."

"When would be convenient for us to get together again?" Frank inquired. He was beginning to feel his approach may be too aggressive.

"I must talk with my family."

"Can you call me at the hotel, or should I phone you later to set up a meeting?" Frank at least wanted a definitive next step, since setting up the meeting had been so difficult to begin with.

"Yes."

Frank wasn't sure which question Mr. Rakotomanana was responding to.

"You can call me at the Madagascar Hilton?"

"Oh, yes."

"Or would you prefer that I call you?" Frank felt he might have a better chance of solidifying plans if he called Mr. Rakotomanana because he had already scheduled several meetings outside the hotel the next week.

"Oh, yes. I think that would be very interesting." The men shook hands and Frank departed.

As he left the building Frank thought to himself, "He certainly was an amiable guy, but a bit hard to read. Was he being realistic about his company's capabilities? He almost seemed too accommodating." Frank was not sure how well the meeting had gone.

ASSESSING THE CREDIT MARKET

Frank ran into Jean-Paul at the Hilton on his way into the dining room, so they decided to have a drink together before dinner. Frank wanted to know about the commercial loans market in Madagascar. If he were able to set up a partnership agreement or close a long-term deal with a Malagasy processor, the processor would most certainly need to expand in order to handle Summit Foods' business. Frank preferred to deal with one or two large suppliers rather than dozens of smaller ones, and he was fairly certain there were few, if any, with enough production capacity to take on a customer such as Summit Foods while continuing to serve their current customer base.

"What can you tell me about the credit situation here?" Frank asked. "I know the national government is far outspending its receipts and I'm sure that affects the availability of credit here. Did your company finance anything locally?"

"The banks here are extremely risk averse. Even so, they still have many nonperforming loans in their portfolio. We didn't need to use any local banks for financing, but we use a Mauritian-owned bank for our accounts payable and our payroll because we don't have a lot of faith in the local banking institutions. Two of the five banks are still partially owned by the Malagasy government, although they're in the process of privatizing. Until that happens, we'll stick with Union Commercial Bank."

Jean-Paul went on to explain that the prime rate was set by the Banque Centrale, which serves much the same purpose as the Federal Reserve Bank in the United States. The five commercial banks then set their rates accordingly.

"Just out of curiosity, what is the current rate to commercial borrowers?" Frank asked.

"Twenty-three percent," Jean-Paul answered, grinning.

"No, really." Frank laughed.

"I'm dead serious, Frank. And they require a 50% guarantee."

"A guarantee? What do you mean? How does that work?"

Jean-Paul explained that a borrower must deposit 50% of the total amount of the loan in the bank, or commit some other type of collateral that is acceptable to the bank.

Frank was incredulous. "That's crazy. If you had the money to begin with, you obviously wouldn't need the loan."

Jean-Paul shrugged. He went on to explain that banks and other funding institutions depended a great deal on a borrower's reputation through word of mouth. There are no formal credit bureaus in Madagascar. Knowing the "right" people was essential.

Frank now understood the capital constraints firms like Mr. Rakotomanana's were facing. After Frank described his earlier conversation with Mr. Rakotomanana, Jean-Paul explained the concept of *fihavanana*, or family harmony, which was central to Malagasy culture. "It is a critical decision-making factor in all family decisions. Preserving the *fihavanana* is of great importance in this culture, and it often leads to 'uneconomic' business decisions. You are not dealing with what economic theory traditionally refers to as "rational actors." What makes perfect business sense to you may not even be a consideration to your Malagasy colleague."

Jean-Paul had another appointment, so Frank ate alone that night. Over dinner he considered what he had learned about doing business in Madagascar during his first week, and what additional information he would need before he left the country in three weeks. He was scheduled to receive a call from Martin Herlihy tomorrow morning to give him a progress report.

Madagascar was eight hours ahead of the United States, so Martin would likely be calling around 6:00 A.M. local time. Frank wanted to think through the pros and cons tonight so he would be clear headed tomorrow morning when the call came through. He knew Martin would be interested in "the numbers," but there were so many other nonquantifiable factors that warranted as much if not more consideration than the numbers. He was not even at the stage where he could discuss production volume, profit margins and freight costs. Frank was not sure how to present what he learned thus far because, since Martin had not visited the country, he would not easily grasp the business environment nor see both the potential opportunities and obstacles to doing business in a developing country such as Madagascar.

Exhibit 4
Alternative sources of
supply for spices

Sales Prices Include Cost, Insurance and Freight			
Spices	**Origin**	**Unit**	**Price**
Cinnamon			
sticks	Madagascar	kg	
pieces	Madagascar	kg	5,75 to 6 FF
ground	Madagascar	kg	11 to 12 FF
Mace	Indonesia	ton	2,375 US$
	Nouvelle Guinée		
Chili pepper	Togo	kg	18 to 25 FF
	Central Africa		
	Republic of China		
	Madagascar		35 to 60 FF
	Martinique		35 to 100 FF
	Morocco		8 to 10 FF
Peppercorn			
I. white	Sarawak	ton	1,525–3,750 US$
	Sarawak DW		1,525–3,750 US$
	Muntok		1,525–3,750 US$
	Brazil		1,900–3,300 US$
II. black	Lampong	ton	1,050–1,895 US$
	Sarawak		1,000–1,835 US$
	Brazil		1,000–1,700 US$
	Madagascar		1,050–1,700 US$
Ginger	Brazil	kg	9–22 FF
	Thailand		12–19 FF
Chili pepper,	Morocco	kg	6–10 FF
green	Madagascar		30–60 FF
	Martinique		30–100 FF

Source: Marchés Tropicaux et Mediterranéens, 1993

CASE DISCUSSION QUESTIONS

1. What more could Frank and his employer, Summit Foods, have done to prepare for his visit to Madagascar?

2. How useful has Jean-Paul's advice been? Should Frank rely on the accuracy of all the information provided by Jean-Paul?

3. What different entry modes could Frank use to operate in Madagascar? What are the strengths and weaknesses of each?

4. If you were Frank, what would you tell Mr. Herlihy when you next speak to him?

5. What should Frank do next?

6. What other information does Frank need, and how should he try to obtain it?

7. If Frank does not get all the information that he is seeking, what company factors will affect the decision as to whether Summit will enter Madagascar?

8. What should Summit look out for if they decide to go ahead?

ENDNOTES

i   This case is intended as a basis for class discussion rather than to illustrate either effective or ineffective handling of an administrative situation.

Transforming Global Health Organizations— Reform at the World Health Organization (WHO)

by Richard Natzopoulos, with Leonard Lerer*

INSEAD

Copyright © 2000, INSEAD, Fontainebleau, France.

This case was written by Richard Natzopoulos, Visiting Research Associate at INSEAD, in collaboration with Leonard Lerer, Affiliate Professor At Large and Senior Research Fellow at the INSEAD Healthcare Management Initiative. It is intended to be used as the basis for class discussion rather than to illustrate either effective or ineffective handling of an administrative situation.

List of Institutional Abbreviations

DFID—Department for International Development
FAO—Food and Agricultural Organization of the United Nations
GAVI—Global Alliance for Vaccines and Immunization
ILO—International Labor Organization
NGO—Non-governmental Organization
UN—United Nations
UNAIDS—United Nations Programme on HIV/AIDS

UNDP—United Nations Development Programme
UNESCO—United Nations Educational Scientific and Cultural Organization
UNFPA—United Nations Family Planning Agency
UNICEF—United Nations Children's Fund
WHA—World Health Assembly
WHO—World Health Organization
WIPO—World Intellectual Property Organization

INTRODUCTION

What is our comparative advantage? Given our mandate and our human and financial resources, what are the functions that WHO is best placed to carry out more effectively than others? How can we shift the balance of our work to focus even more forcefully in areas where our comparative advantage really lies? And most important, how can we increase the impact of our contribution by engaging a variety of partners who can supplement and complement our contribution?

Dr. Gro Harlem Brundtland, Director-General of the World Health Organization (WHO), was addressing her Executive Board in Geneva at the opening of the 105th session on 24 January 2000. Brundtland was WHO's fifth Director-General and the first appointee from outside the WHO. The organization had been through considerable changes since Brundtland had taken office 18 months previously, and she was outlining her strategy for the 2002–2003 biennium. Her strategy for reform at headquarters had meant budgetary reorganization, the reallocation of funds, restructuring of WHO and review of managerial processes through which the organization planned and monitored its performance. Central to her address was the theme of "One WHO." She was developing new ways of working with donors and building stronger relationships, which made long-term planning possible.

The six regional offices—Africa, The Americas, Southeast Asia, Europe, the Eastern Mediterranean, and the Western Pacific—had for the first time collaborated with headquarters to produce a combined budget. They had also agreed, at the previous meeting of the Executive Board, to implement restructuring after the example set by headquarters. Brundtland had enhanced the transparency and accountability of the budget by allocating the appropriate funds from regular and extra-budgetary financing to

Exhibit 1

Summary by organizational level (US$ thousand)

	Total			Regular budget			Other sources		
	1998–1999	2000–2001	% change	1998–1999	2000–2001	% change	1998–1999	2000–2001	% change
Headquarters*	810 361	942 255	16.28	282 953	279 055	(1.38)	527 408	663 200	25.75
Regional offices*	417 176	422 350	1.24	237 871	231 816	(2.55)	179 305	190 534	6.26
Countries	419 620	436 249	3.96	321 830	331 783	3.09	97 790	104 466	6.83
Total	1 647 157	1 800 854	9.33	842 654	842 654	0.00	804 503	958 200	19.10

*Some of this funding is spent at country level.

Source: WHO 1999.

reflect WHO's organizational structure and to link it to the General Programme of Work. Among the changes in the budget were the allocation of more regular budget funds to Africa from the European allocation, and a greater proportion of funding at country level relative to headquarters and the regional offices. The stated budget allocation for general management and administrative costs had been reduced both at headquarters (by 13%) and in the regional offices and more funding was budgeted for projects. Spending for the 2000–2001 biennium compared to the 1998–1999 biennium increased from 7% in the case of health technology and pharmaceuticals to 98% for non-communicable diseases. Exhibits 1 and 2 provide a more detailed breakdown of the budget.

During the six months between Brundtland's nomination in January 1998 and the date that she took office on 21 July, a transition team reviewed the organization and advocated changes to the structure of WHO's senior administration. The seven Assistant Director-Generals, largely representative of the standing members of the UN Security Council, and two Executive Directors were replaced by a Cabinet of Executive Directors who represented nine clusters of WHO core activity. The clusters resulted from a redefinition of WHO programmes. Nineteen major and 52 specific programmes were reduced to 35 departments and allocated to the nine clusters. Brundtland had made a clear effort to recruit scientists of international repute to strengthen the technical base of the organization, especially to fill the Executive Director posts. A WHO manager described the move towards "technical" rather than "political" senior appointments:

> They were not there to play a geopolitical game. They owe their allegiance to Brundtland and you now have the right kind of politics in the organization.

A detailed breakdown of the WHO structure at headquarters and the allocation of the departments to the nine clusters are shown in Exhibit 3.

The Transition Team was led by Ambassador Jonas Gahr Store, who was later appointed to the Cabinet as Executive Di-

rector for the Office of the Director-General. The new Director-General's Office also comprised four senior policy advisers, a legal counsel and advisers for Internal Audit and Oversight and Strategies for Co-operation and Partnership. Store had served Brundtland previously as a Special Advisor, Director-General of International Affairs and finally as Ambassador in the Norwegian Mission to the United Nations when Brundtland had been Prime Minister of Norway. Among Brundtland's entourage, Store had been known as an intellectual and was regarded as an important contributor to many of her keynote political speeches.

Malaria was one of two flagship projects Brundtland had selected soon after taking office, where she felt potentially significant global advances could be made with cost-effective interventions. David Nabarro, an Englishman who had headed the health activities of the UK Department for International Development (DFID), was selected to manage *Roll Back Malaria* and Derek Yach, a South African who had been involved in the *Health for All* initiative, led the *Tobacco Free Initiative*. As a Brundtland adviser explained:

> She had picked two project managers who were important drivers of change. The idea behind the programmes was to get something that had no institutional baggage kick-started.

The projects were expected to be "pathfinders" for other projects. They would raise the profile of the organization internationally and act as catalysts for institutional reform within WHO. The projects interacted with several clusters within WHO, and the directors were given special support and status. For example, they attended Cabinet meetings with the Executive Directors and accompanied the Cabinet on management retreats.

The first step in the strategic planning process through which WHO would plan and monitor its performance was to clarify and articulate WHO's vision and values, formulate the mission and goals of clusters and regions, define priorities and allocate resources accordingly. Medium-term objectives were set for each area of work and managers at headquarters and in the regional offices were asked to define results expected at the end

Exhibit 2
Planned expenditure at headquarters (US$ thousand)

	Total			Regular budget			Other sources		
	1998–1999	2000–2001	% change	1998–1999	2000–2001	% change	1998–1999	2000–2001	% change
Communicable diseases	206 872	283 823	37.20	27 346	31 923	16.74	179 526	251 900	40.31
Noncommunicable diseases	7 207	14 305	98.49	5 005	10 305	105.89	2 202	4 000	81.65
Health systems and community health	120 116	145 022	20.73	21 274	21 622	1.64	98 842	123 400	24.85
Sustainable development and healthy environments	106 899	119 539	11.82	22 082	22 139	0.26	84 817	97 400	14.84
Social change and mental health	30 255	37 719	24.67	8 996	11 219	24.71	21 259	26 500	24.65
Health technology and pharmaceuticals	110 423	118 840	7.62	19 552	21 040	7.61	90 871	97 800	7.63
Evidence and information for policy	33 171	47 744	43.93	25 804	31 744	23.02	7 367	16 000	117.18
External relations and governing bodies	28 972	32 821	13.29	27 676	30 421	9.92	1 296	2 400	85.19
General management	138 122	119 610	(13.40)	105 344*	83 210	(21.01)	32 778	36 400	11.05
Director-General, Regional Directors and independent functions	28 324	22 832	(19.39)	19 874	15 432	(22.35)	8 450	7 400	(12.43)
Total	810 361	942 255	16.28	282 953	279 055	(1.38)	527 408	663 200	25.75

*Includes US$ 6.2 million for country activities.

Source: WHO 1999.

of the budgetary cycle (two years). For example, the *Roll Back Malaria* project's mission and goals included reducing the burden of disease associated with malaria, strengthening national systems to improve their response and supporting action taken by other groups. Some of the results expected by the end of 2001 were: the formulation of technical and implementation strategies in all participating countries; the establishment of resource support networks; the review and implementation of legal and policy instruments; the development and testing of models for facilitating access to care-providers; the mobilization of investment for the development and deployment of new malaria control tools and the establishment of a review mechanism.

Brundtland's election had followed a decision by Dr Hiroshi Nakajima not to seek a third five-year term. A series of contro-versies and charges of mismanagement and corruption had marked his tenure, and the United States was among several countries opposed to his leadership. The number of directors at WHO had almost doubled (all named at Nakajima's discretion without approval by the agency's senior selection committee) and three-quarters of its budget went on salaries and overheads. WHO had lost international esteem and donor countries suspicious of mismanagement would only provide funding earmarked for specific projects. Or, as one senior manager put it:

> Our AIDS money was to be allocated for HIV positive mothers in Lesotho.

There was a feeling both inside and outside the organization that WHO had "lost direction." Apart from the internal management concerns, Brundtland also felt that WHO had lost its

Exhibit 3
WHO organizational structure

WHO Structure at Headquarters

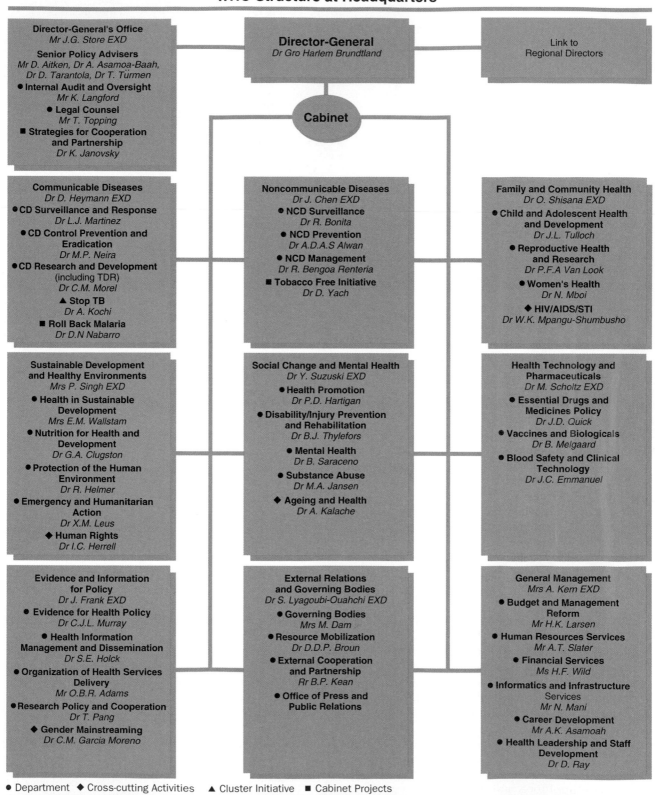

Director-General's Office
Mr J.G. Store EXD

Senior Policy Advisers
Mr D. Aitken, Dr A. Asamoa-Baah,
Dr D. Tarantola, Dr T. Türmen
● **Internal Audit and Oversight**
Mr K. Langford
● **Legal Counsel**
Mr T. Topping
■ **Strategies for Cooperation
and Partnership**
Dr K. Janovsky

Director-General
Dr Gro Harlem Brundtland

Link to
Regional Directors

Cabinet

Communicable Diseases
Dr D. Heymann EXD
●**CD Surveillance and Response**
Dr L.J. Martinez
● **CD Control Prevention and
Eradication**
Dr M.P. Neira
●**CD Research and Development**
(including TDR)
Dr C.M. Morel
▲ **Stop TB**
Dr A. Kochi
■ **Roll Back Malaria**
Dr D.N Nabarro

Noncommunicable Diseases
Dr J. Chen EXD
● **NCD Surveillance**
Dr R. Bonita
● **NCD Prevention**
Dr A.D.A.S Alwan
● **NCD Management**
Dr R. Bengoa Renteria
■ **Tobacco Free Initiative**
Dr D. Yach

Family and Community Health
Dr O. Shisana EXD
● **Child and Adolescent Health
and Development**
Dr J.L. Tulloch
● **Reproductive Health
and Research**
Dr P.F.A Van Look
● **Women's Health**
Dr N. Mboi
◆ **HIV/AIDS/STI**
Dr W.K. Mpangu-Shumbusho

**Sustainable Development
and Healthy Environments**
Mrs P. Singh EXD
● **Health in Sustainable
Development**
Mrs E.M. Wallstam
● **Nutrition for Health and
Development**
Dr G.A. Clugston
● **Protection of the Human
Environment**
Dr R. Helmer
● **Emergency and Humanitarian
Action**
Dr X.M. Leus
◆ **Human Rights**
Dr I.C. Herrell

Social Change and Mental Health
Dr Y. Suzuski EXD
● **Health Promotion**
Dr P.D. Hartigan
● **Disability/Injury Prevention
and Rehabilitation**
Dr B.J. Thylefors
● **Mental Health**
Dr B. Saraceno
● **Substance Abuse**
Dr M.A. Jansen
◆ **Ageing and Health**
Dr A. Kalache

**Health Technology and
Pharmaceuticals**
Dr M. Scholtz EXD
● **Essential Drugs and
Medicines Policy**
Dr J.D. Quick
● **Vaccines and Biologicals**
Dr B. Melgaard
● **Blood Safety and Clinical
Technology**
Dr J.C. Emmanuel

**Evidence and Information
for Policy**
Dr J. Frank EXD
● **Evidence for Health Policy**
Dr C.J.L. Murray
● **Health Information
Management and Dissemination**
Dr S.E. Holck
● **Organization of Health Services
Delivery**
Mr O.B.R. Adams
●**Research Policy and Cooperation**
Dr T. Pang
◆ **Gender Mainstreaming**
Dr C.M. Garcia Moreno

**External Relations
and Governing Bodies**
Dr S. Lyagoubi-Ouahchi EXD
● **Governing Bodies**
Mrs M. Dam
● **Resource Mobilization**
Dr D.D.P. Broun
● **External Cooperation
and Partnership**
Rr B.P. Kean
● **Office of Press and
Public Relations**

General Management
Mrs A. Kern EXD
● **Budget and Management
Reform**
Mr H.K. Larsen
● **Human Resources Services**
Mr A.T. Slater
● **Financial Services**
Ms H.F. Wild
● **Informatics and Infrastructure**
Services
Mr N. Mani
● **Career Development**
Mr A.K. Asamoah
● **Health Leadership and Staff
Development**
Dr D. Ray

● Department ◆ Cross-cutting Activities ▲ Cluster Initiative ■ Cabinet Projects

World Health: Organization

position of global leadership in health and international esteem. According to a senior Brundtland adviser:

> The challenge was to take WHO off the sidelines. . . It's a balancing act between high-profile projects—we need to get back into the mainstream, but need to get the headquarters into shape first.

Brundtland was unlike the former Director-General in that she made public appearances three or four times a week, wrote articles and was in constant contact with political and business leaders and the media. It was thought that the transition process was to a large extent "guided" by Brundtland's speeches. Her speeches were content-heavy and based on discussions with her Cabinet and Senior Policy Advisers. According to one "insider":

> The introduction of the collective decision had gone a long way to binding a fractured institution.

WHO was increasingly thought of as fairly unimportant by other groups competing for limited health funding, sometimes even in projects that WHO had helped to establish. UNICEF was now the lead UN agency dealing with children's health needs, and the AIDS portfolio had been moved to UNAIDS. The World Bank and other development banks were establishing leadership roles in health and, along with large private donors, such as the Bill and Melinda Gates Foundation, were funding important health and development projects. WHO had, in a sense, become a victim of its own advocacy. By saying that health was a multisectoral issue, it had encouraged the World Bank and UN agencies to develop progressive, proactive health interventions. After 10 years of poor performance, WHO was no longer setting the international public health agenda.

As a first step to regaining WHO's position in global health, Brundtland applied a project-orientated approach to the organization. *Roll Back Malaria* and the *Tobacco Free Initiative* were the first high-profile projects identified. Brundtland had highlighted nine priority areas in her opening address at the 105th Executive Board: improving health systems; fighting malaria, HIV/AIDS, and TB; curbing the tobacco epidemic; improving maternal health; campaigning for safe blood; preventing and improving treatment of mental disorders; working to reduce cancer, cardiovascular disease, diabetes, and chronic respiratory diseases; improving food safety; and investing in change in WHO.

WHO was also playing an important role in joint projects such as the Global Alliance for Vaccines and Immunization (GAVI). This alliance of business leaders, philanthropic foundations, development banks, UN agencies and national governments enjoyed a highly publicized launch at the World Economic Forum in Davos, Switzerland, and had received a US$750 million donation from the Bill and Melinda Gates Foundation. Although the Secretariat was housed at the UNICEF Offices in Geneva, WHO was an important and recognized player.

The Director-General's Office updated the political missions of all major countries based in Geneva about changes at WHO on a monthly basis. The year 2000 was seen as a "watershed year" as it would have been be the first time that people within the organization would see satisfied stakeholders and the rewards of the organization's improved profile.

STRUCTURE OF WHO

The No. 8 bus to WHO headquarters traveled through the international district of Geneva. It passed the Palais des Nations, headquarters of the United Nations in Geneva, the International Labor Organization (ILO), the Russian Embassy, the International Federation of Red Cross and Red Crescent Societies, and the World Intellectual Property Organization (WIPO), before arriving at the imposing WHO building. Headquarters was a formal environment, with the dress code for professionals being strictly "jacket (coat) and tie." The passages were full of reports and books on every health-related topic from acupuncture to xeno-transplants. The publications budget alone amounted to US$50 million per annum.

WHO was the UN's specialized agency on health and was similar in structure to ILO and WIPO. The organization remained independent of the UN so that it would not be threatened if the UN were dissolved. Membership was open to all members of the UN and other states approved by a simple majority at the World Health Assembly (WHA), as health concerns are not confined by national boundaries. The WHA was the WHO's plenary and legislative body. It met annually to determine the policy direction of WHO's six-year General Programme of Work and to review and approve reports and activities of the Executive Board. The WHA also had the authority to adopt regulations on sanitary and quarantine requirements, nomenclature for diseases, causes of death and public health practices; and standards with respect to the safety, purity and potency of biological, pharmaceutical and other products. Each member state was represented on the WHA by a delegation of no more than three delegates, while representatives of other international and non-governmental organizations were permitted to attend as observers. Each member state had one vote on the WHA, although in practice, most decisions were presented as resolutions and made by consensus.

The 32-member Executive Board oversaw the implementation of decisions made by the WHA. Membership of the Executive Board rotated, with each member serving a three year term and one-third of the members being retired each year. The Executive Board met twice yearly to prepare an agenda for the WHA, submit a draft of the General Programme of Work, review the proposed programme budget, advise on questions of constitutional and regulatory matters, submit advice on proposals of its own initiative and take emergency financial and administrative measures where necessary.

Representation of the Executive Board was seen to be problematic; its membership was based on regional representation and was not directly related to contributions. Some of WHO's biggest donors were not included, and the USA and France were the only larger industrialized countries represented on the 2000 Executive Board. The Scandinavian countries, WHO's largest donors of extra-budgetary funds, had no representatives on the 2000 Executive Board. Many of the UN agencies had revamped their governance structures in the past 10 years, but there had been no attempt to change that of the WHO. Furthermore, Brundtland's selection of a Transition Team on confirmation of sole-candidacy, and not after her election in July, demonstrated that decision-making was made at the Executive Board level and not at the WHA. The WHA had never failed to elect an official chosen by the Executive Board.

The Secretariat was the administrative and technical organ responsible for implementing the activities approved by the WHA. The Secretariat consisted of headquarters in Geneva and the six regional offices. The WHA appointed a Director-General, nominated by the Executive Board, to head the Secretariat for a five-year period. The Director-General's responsibilities included the appointment of Secretariat staff, the preparation of annual financial statements and the drafting of a proposed programme budget. The Regional Directors were elected by the member states through regional committees, subject to the overall authority of the Director-General and then appointed by the Executive Board. As well as the global headquarters and regional offices, country offices were located in selected states, headed by a WHO representative (WR). The country offices worked with health ministries to implement WHO policies and programmes and to support the development of the country's health system.

WHO's regular budget amounted to approximately US$1 billion, and contributions were determined by a complex formula which took into account the size of the country's economy. The maximum funding provided by a single country was 25% of the regular budget (the USA), while the minimum was 0.001%. Extra-budgetary funds were determined at the discretion of donor countries. The Scandinavian countries and the Netherlands accounted for almost 40% of these funds, which they had previously earmarked for specific projects, supposedly because they did not have confidence in WHO management and leadership. WHO became increasingly reliant on the extra-budgetary funding to finance projects. The funds were also regarded as a mechanism to circumvent the "one nation, one vote" principle in the WHA, and during the 1990s, 10 countries contributed more than 80% of these funds.

In Brundtland's 2000–2001 budget, extra-budgetary funding outweighed the regular funding. This was partly due to her extensive campaigning, but also due to a policy of zero real growth in regular budgetary funding which had been imposed on UN agencies from the early 1980s. Furthermore, 39% of the regular budget was still owing by member states, most notably the United States, which had adopted a 20% underpayment policy to selected organizations, including WHO, as a result of dissatisfaction with financial and budgetary reforms. Despite the imbalance, Brundtland was able to exert more control in allocating the contributions to her priority projects. This was due to the influence that she wielded among the major donors. The evolution of the WHO budget can be seen in Exhibit 4.

Targets were set to determine the professional staff complement of WHO. Member states were represented according to three criteria: the proportion of the donor country's contribution to the regular budget accounted for 70% of positions, 10% was allocated according to the size of the country's population and the remaining 20% was distributed proportionally among the member states. The Secretariat was expected to recruit professional staff to reflect this profile.

On 31 December 1999, WHO had a total of 3452 staff members holding fixed-term appointments of one to five years or career service appointments. Of these, 1259 (36.5%) were in the professional category (P levels), and 2193 (63.5%) in the general services (G levels). Since 1994 there had been a moratorium on career service appointments, which were held by 8.2% of the professional workforce and 15% of the general service staff in 2000. The number of staff holding such appointments had dropped by more than 600. Brundtland had just approved a further 224 mutually agreed separations in an attempt to decrease the average age of the staff, as more than half the professional staff were older than 50 years and the largest concentration of the general staff were in their forties. The short-term staff complement of consultants, professional and general service staff was more than 40%. At headquarters in the 1998–1999 biennium, there were 7315 contracts for short-term staff and consultants, more than there had ever been. The absence of Africans in senior positions had been widely noted prior to Brundtland's appointment. At the time Brundtland was elected, only one of WHO's 46 directorial posts was held by an African. After 18 months, Brundtland already had five Africans serving at a senior level. Within the organization, WHO was committed to

Exhibit 4
Evolution of WHO's Budget

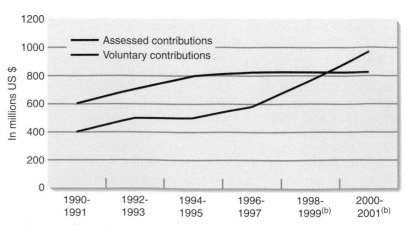

(a) Excluding Global Programme on AIDS
(b) Estimates/projections

achieving a goal of gender parity. Of the 3452 staff, 1806 were men (52%) and 1646 were women (48%). However, in the professional category, women only accounted for about 30% of the positions at headquarters and they were mainly concentrated at the lower grade levels of P1 to P4. The proportion of women was considerably lower in some of the regions, particularly Africa (21%) and the Eastern Mediterranean Region (23%). Forty-one percent of the newly recruited professional staff were women, whereas the stated recruitment target had been set at 60% in order to reach the parity goal by 2010.

HISTORY OF WHO

The World Health Organization was established in 1948. It was an amalgamation of organizations working in the health arena, such as the Office International d'Hygiène Publique, the Pan American Health Organization, the Health Organization of the League of Nations and the United Nations Relief and Rehabilitation Administration. These organizations played an important part in determining the regional structure of WHO. The regional emphasis was also due to the premise that health co-operation required global and local action. But the structure was controversial. Some argued that regionalization had been one of the factors contributing to WHO's success, while others felt that decentralization tipped the balance of power inappropriately away from the central administrative structures. Exhibit 5 shows a brief historical chronology of WHO. WHO's General Programme of Work had initially focused on the "Big Six": malaria, tuberculosis, sexually transmitted diseases, maternal and child health, environmental sanitation and nutrition. Experts were recruited and deployed to countries to work with the health administration on a project basis. Longer-term strategies soon followed, the most prominent of which were strategies for the prevention, control and elimination of selected diseases.

The Intensified Malaria Eradication Programme was initiated in 1955, targeting one of the world's most prevalent and endemic diseases. Extra-budgetary funds were paid into a special account, supplemented by the regular budget. The expectation was that the disease would be eradicated within a decade. However, by the end of the 1960s, operational, technical and budgetary problems had arisen and the project had to be re-evaluated. Mosquitoes had become resistant to the insecticides, which in turn were harmful to humans and the environment. Furthermore, growing conflict in Africa made cross-border eradication efforts impossible. Nevertheless, other diseases had been identified that could be tackled using the new technologies and, enabled by the spirit of international co-operation unique to the health sector in the Cold War environment, the Intensified Smallpox Eradication Programme was initiated in 1967. Unlike malaria, the nature of this disease favored eradication, and on 26 October 1977, the last naturally occurring case of smallpox was detected and contained. The Intensified Smallpox Eradication Programme remains the greatest achievement of WHO's history.

WHO also began to shift its strategy to technical co-operation activities, which supported more direct assistance to regions and member states. The organization had initially focused on information-oriented normative activities, such as the production of guidelines, the collection of health statistics and epidemiological information and the setting of global health standards. It had become apparent that in order to reform the health sector, countries needed financing to make basic services available to the poor. Dr. Halfdan Mahler, a Dane who had preceded Nakajima as Director-General, championed technical assistance. He was greatly respected by WHO staff who had worked under him, and who described him as a "priest, a visionary and a humanitarian." He was sympathetic to the demands of developing nations when they criticized the expensive and unsustainable solutions offered by Western development agencies. WHO led the UN system in being more responsive to the needs of less-developed countries, and the WHA approved a resolution that would ensure 60% of the regular budget was allocated to technical co-operation activities by 1980. Technical co-operation activities were centered on the principles of primary health care. They included health systems improvement through the transfer of skills and knowledge, practical projects, health resource planning and health programme co-ordination. Mahler's flagship project was *Health for All by the Year 2000*. The project's goal was "the attainment by all citizens of the world by the year 2000 of a level of health that will lead them to lead a socially and economically productive life." The focus was on low-technology community-based solutions such as the promotion of safe drinking water, nutrition, sanitation, essential drugs and maternal and child health.

When Brundtland was appointed, technical co-operation activities at WHO had grown in relative terms and accounted for 70% of the regular budget, partially as a result of an increasingly vocal number of developing countries becoming member states. The big financial donor countries had increasingly argued that WHO should focus on normative activities and consolidate its role in collecting, co-ordinating and disseminating scientific and technical information. At the core of the controversy was a growing feeling that much of the money disbursed for technical co-operation had been badly spent and that many programmes had produced little sustained improvement in the health of poorer countries. However, the transition was difficult, as one of Brundtland's policy advisors explained:

> From 1978, 60% of the regular budget was used for technical co-operation activities and WHO was the specialized agency most heavily oriented towards technical co-operation. You can't be a normative organization if you don't spend money on it.

Mahler had also not been scared to take on the private sector and the multinationals. An increase in malnourished children resulting from mothers using breast milk substitutes had prompted the WHA to adopt the International Code on the Marketing of Breast Milk Substitutes. Another area where WHO officials made their mark was in championing the Model List on Essential Drugs in 1977. This provided governments with a guide to the acquisition of appropriate pharmaceuticals in response to antibiotic resistance and overprescription, and the rapidly rising cost of drugs.

Based on its success in eradicating smallpox, WHO had initiated some high-profile joint projects in the 1980s, such as the Global Programme on AIDS, the Global Programme on Vaccines

Exhibit 5
WHO historical
chronology

1946

International Health Conference held in New York attended by 61 countries. Adopts and drafts WHO constitution. Interim Commission formed to prepare for establishment of permanent organization.

1948

WHO constitution ratified by 61 member states. The date is inaugurated as the annual World Health Day.
First World Health Assembly (WHA) opens in Geneva and is attended by 53 member states.
Dr. Brock Chisholm (Canada) elected as first Director-General.
Joint Committee on Health Policy (JCHP) created by WHO and UNICEF to coordinate health activities of the two organizations.
WHO and UNICEF provide support for mass treatment programmes for syphilis and other treponematoses.

1951

Creation of African Regional Office (AFRO) agreed by majority of member states. First session held in autumn of the same year and office opened in Brazzaville, Congo.

1952

WHA adopts resolution stating that no member state shall contribute more than one-third of regular budget funds.

1953

Dr. Marcelino Candau (Brazil) appointed as WHO's second Director-General.

1955

Intensified Malaria Eradication Programme is launched as the first and largest of WHO's mass campaigns.

1959

WHA resolves to undertake global eradication of smallpox.

1961

Executive Board is expanded from 18 to 24 members.

1962

Adverse reactions to the drug thalidomide leads WHO to establish international system to provide information on drug safety and efficacy. Codex Alimentarius created by WHO and the FAO.

1966

Inaugural ceremony held to celebrate the completion of WHO headquarters in Geneva, Switzerland.

1973

WHA decides that WHO should collaborate with, rather than assist, its member states in developing guidelines for national healthcare systems.
Dr. Halfdan Mahler (Denmark) is elected as WHO's third Director-General.

1974

WHA adopts Resolution WHA22.43 on breastfeeding and breast milk substitutes.

1975

Executive Board increases from 24 to 30 members.

continued

1976

WHA adopts resolution for WHO to spend 60% of regular budget funds on technical co-operation and provision of services by the end of the 1970s.

1977

WHA adopts Health for All by the Year 2000, which aims to achieve a basic level of health by the turn of the century that will enable all people to lead a socially and economically productive life.
WHO publishes Model List of Essential Drugs.

1978

Joint WHO/UNICEF International Conference is held at Alma-Ata, USSR. The Alma-Ata Declaration on Primary Health Care is signed by 134 countries as the key strategy for attaining the goal of Health for All by the Year 2000.

1979

A global commission declares that the worldwide eradication of smallpox has been achieved, with the last known case occurring in Ethiopia in 1977.

WHA endorses the Alma-Ata Declaration on Primary Health Care as the key to the strategy of Health for All by the Year 2000.

1980

A policy is adopted of zero real growth in the regular budgets of the UN specialized agencies, including WHO.

1981

Global strategy of Health for All by the Year 2000 adopted by WHO and endorsed by UN General Assembly.

1983

Consultative meeting on AIDS is held in Geneva to assess the international implications of the epidemic.

1986

WHO Control Programme on AIDS is established within the Division of Communicable Diseases.

1987

Special Programme on AIDS, later renamed the Global Programme, is created.
WHA declares HIV/Aids a worldwide emergency.

1988

WHA agrees to goal of global eradication of poliomyelitis by the year 2000, based on the Polio Eradication Initiative.
World No Tobacco Day is inaugurated as an annual event by the WHA.
Dr. Hiroshi Nakajima (Japan) is elected as WHO's fourth Director-General.
World AIDS Day is inaugurated as an annual event.

1990

Programme on Tobacco or Health is created.
Children's Vaccine Initiative is launched by WHO, UNICEF, UNDP, the World Bank and the Rockefeller Foundation.

1992

Director-General Nakajima initiates organizational reform under WHO Response to Global Change.
New control strategy for malaria launched at a meeting of health ministers held in Amsterdam, Holland.

continued

1993

World Bank publishes the *World Development Report: Investing in Health*.

1994

Global Programme for Vaccines and Immunization (GPV) is created.

1995

Process for Renewing the Health for All Strategy is launched.
WHO publishes its first *World Health Report*.

1996

A new UNAIDS programme replaces WHO Global Programme on AIDS. The programme is co-sponsored by five UN organizations: WHO, UNICEF, UNFPA, UNESCO and the World Bank.

1997

Development of global health charter to achieve a renewal of the Health for All strategy.

1998

Dr. Gro Harlem Brundtland is elected as WHO's fifth Director-General.
WHO celebrates its fiftieth anniversary.
Dr. Gro Harlem Brundtland takes office.

Source: Kelley Lee. Historical Dictionary of the World Health Organization: Historical Dictionaries of International Organizations, No. 15; The Scarecrow Press, Inc. Lanham, Md., & London 1998.

and Immunization and the Global Tuberculosis Programme. The organization worked in collaboration with UNICEF, the UNDP, prominent NGOs, the UNFPA, the ILO, the FAO, the World Food Programme, the UN High Commissioner for Refugees, regional organizations like the EU and the OAU, bilateral aid agencies, and the World Bank, which was becoming an increasingly important player in health and was, by 1990, the largest source of health financing. However, international funding was insufficient to maintain the increasing number of organizations operating in health-related fields, and co-operation soon turned to competition. Faced with decreasing funding, an archaic management structure and operational systems, WHO lost its leadership role. There was increasing pressure from donors, and also from within the organization, for structural and managerial reform.

In 1992, the Executive Board commissioned a working group to examine areas for reform. Their report included recommendations concerning the mission of WHO, its governing bodies, organizational levels and country offices, co-ordination with other UN organizations, technical expertise, research, communications, and budgetary and financial matters. In the mid-1990s, Nakajima announced that the recommendations would be implemented depending on the availability of funding. He had also started processes to re-examine the *Health for All* initiative and develop an appropriate strategy for WHO's new General Programme of Work in 2002.

Responses were varied, with the WHA and some of the donors (most notably Japan) commending Nakajima's efforts. However, the process was criticized for being driven by management (the Secretariat), while the governing bodies (WHA and Executive Board) had been bystanders. WHO's policy and mission had not been discussed, and no clear conclusions were reached on the priorities, organizational and work structure and strategic areas where WHO could make a difference.

A POLITICAL LEADER

Gro Harlem Brundtland was educated as a physician in Norway and graduated from the Harvard School of Public Health with a Master's of Public Health (MPH) degree. Brundtland held public office in Norway for more than 20 years, including the portfolio of Minister of Environment, followed by 10 years as Prime Minister. In the 1980s Brundtland chaired the World Commission on Environment and Development and gained international recognition for championing the principle of sustainable development. As described in her official WHO biography:

> Brundtland's first choice of career was neither environmentalist nor politician, but to become a doctor like her father. He was a specialist in rehabilitation medicine, a skill

much in demand following the Second World War. When Gro Harlem was 10 years old the family moved to the United States where her father had been awarded a Rockefeller scholarship. A few years later the family moved again, this time to Egypt where her father was serving as a United Nations expert on rehabilitation. The seeds of internationalism were sown in the young Gro.

And so were the seeds of political activism. Brundtland joined the children's section of the Norwegian Labor Movement at the age of seven. Her sense of global awareness matured when, as a young mother and newly qualified doctor, she won a scholarship to the Harvard School of Public Health. Working alongside distinguished public health experts, her vision of health extended beyond the confines of the medical world into environmental issues and human development.

Brundtland returned to Oslo and the Ministry of Health in 1965, where she worked on health issues such as breastfeeding and cancer prevention. After working in the National Hospital and Oslo City Hospital, she became Director of Health Services for Oslo's schoolchildren. In 1974, Brundtland was offered the job of Minister of the Environment and accepted the post with growing conviction of a link between health and the environment. In 1981, she was appointed Prime Minister of Norway for the first time. At the age of 41, she was the youngest person and the first woman to ever hold the office.

In 1983, the United Nations Secretary-General invited her to establish and chair the World Commission on Environment and Development. The Commission (also known as the "Brundtland Commission") published its report, *Our Common Future,* in April 1987, in which it developed the broad political concept of sustainable development. The Commission's recommendations led to the Earth Summit—the United Nations Conference on Environment and Development (UNCED) in Rio de Janeiro in 1992. Brundtland was re-elected Prime Minister of Norway for another two terms and finally stepped down in October 1996. In her successful bid to become Director-General of WHO, her skills as physician, politician, activist and manager had come together. She was nominated as Director-General by the Executive Board of WHO in January 1998, the World Health Assembly elected her to the position on 13 May and she took office on 21 July of the same year.

There had been seven candidates for the Director-General's post, four of whom were associated with WHO, but it was clear that the organization wanted new blood and someone who had not been tainted by the past. Brundtland's main rival was Dr. Nafis Sadik, a Pakistani, who had been gaining support among the developing countries, especially those from Africa. Among the criteria for the post were "strong technical and public health background, extensive experience in international health" and "proven historical evidence for public health leadership." This seemed to give Sadik the edge, as her whole career had been connected with public health administration. She had won widespread praise for running UNFPA with distinction and serving as Secretary-General of the 1994 International Conference on Population and Development.

Brundtland had also been mentioned prominently as a possible candidate for the position of UN Deputy Secretary-General, but she had made it clear that she preferred the Director-General's post at WHO. Among the major donor countries, critics of the organization had identified the need for a strong leader. Although Brundtland had not been directly involved in health for some time, her proven leadership abilities in the political arena, support within the European Union and her pioneering role in the global environmental movement won her support. Brundtland maintained that with her political knowledge she could transform the organization.

A TIME FOR CHANGE

Brundtland appointed a Transition Team in January 1998, after her candidacy for the Director-General's post was confirmed by the Executive Board. The Transition Team was expected to review the organization and advocate changes prior to her taking office on 21 July. Brundtland started a one-off extra-budgetary renewal fund, with a target amount of US$7.5 million, to finance the proposed changes. The Norwegian government had agreed to pay for the cost of the Transition Team. After extensive canvassing, Brundtland had also won the support of important donor countries, notably the UK. Some of the money continued to be used for studies on the corporate structure and management systems, 18 months after she took office.

Several members of the Transition Team had previous experience of WHO, but most were external experts with no history in the organization. The Team was based at an Ecumenical Center about 500 meters from WHO, as they wanted to be seen as retaining their independence. The Transition Team focused on "satellites," which included: the budget 2000–2001, in house, external relations (governing bodies, donors and interagency issues), communications, health and development, health sector development, *Roll Back Malaria,* tobacco, health and environment, mental health, emergencies, capacity building, collaborating centers, regional members. Each satellite developed a timetable for work, which consisted of relevant information and interviews. The Transition Team interviewed everyone from Director level up and selected others from within the organization. The directors had been driving for change in WHO, and the Transition Team had encouraged them to share their views. Generally the focus of the reports was on facts and evidence rather than on specific recommendations. Although Brundtland participated in some of the meetings, Store was the co-ordinator and interacted with the group. At the end of the process the satellites sent final reports to the co-ordinator.

The Transition Team devised broad objectives and a summary of responsibilities for new job positions within the organization, and senior staff were invited to apply. WHO managers were ensured that their contracts would be honored, although many would be reassigned to new duties. Although the rotation of the staff was traumatic, with approximately 750 employees moving offices, management's view was that the process had been quick. The message to observers was that the organization had changed. The Transitional Team policy was that the past was irrelevant and that the organization had turned over a new leaf. According to one of Brundtland's policy advisers:

It's as if a new government from a different party had come into power. The message had to be that anything that came before was bad.

There had been extensive canvassing for Brundtland within the organization, and the expectation of her integrity and leadership was considerable. However, many employees were shocked by the appointment of Transition Team members to senior positions. There had been a perception that they were an impartial external body, and many of the employees that they interviewed were uncompromising in their criticism of the organization and one another. As one employee said: "They really emptied their hearts and their knives on each other. It was suicidal."

The perception was that Brundtland had brought in academics of international repute, appointed several members of her inner circle and had divided the remaining posts among WHO staff. The appointments of the Executive Directors in particular seemed to be biased towards academics. In some quarters WHO was being referred to as "the Harvard on Lac Leman (Lake Geneva)."

Following the structural changes, Brundtland needed to address the procedural and cultural environment of the organization. A positive aspect of the transition in the eyes of the staff had been Brundtland's creation of a Career Development Service in the General Management Cluster. This was responsible for the overall direction and management of a career development programme, including succession planning, mobility and rotation of professional staff at headquarters and between the different levels of the organization. According to a senior WHO manager:

> The concept of human resource development in WHO mainly involved language courses and courses in effective business communication. We clearly recognize the need for human resource and management reform.

One of Brundtland's first steps was to cut down on the paperwork that was generated. Before she took office, there was considerable debate among her senior staff as to how the first budget of her directorship was going to be presented. They were unhappy with being associated with a budget that had been developed during the Nakajima era and decided to convert it to a completely different style. The budgets up to and including the 1998/1999 budget had been criticized for lacking detail, being unspecific and having no mechanisms for control. Each Assistant Director-General had been autonomous, and there was no common or standardized reporting mechanism. The budget was regarded as a one-off and rather tedious exercise.

The "new budget" (2000–2001) listed specific objectives, but rather than simply describing activities, provided specific outcomes or quantifiable deliverables in keeping with Brundtland's commitment to being accountable. Another major difference was in the implementation of the budget. A set of operational plans and guidelines was provided using a variant of the "LOGFRAME." The various Executive Directors operated autonomously, but adhered to a basic set of elements for deliverables. A computerized activity management system was set up

to link specific activities to work plans. The 2002–2003 budget also attempted to refine and clarify the role of WHO and its partners in specific programmes. The budget was seen as a tool for ensuring evaluation and accountability.

Brundtland supported the decentralization of some functions such as information technology, accounting and recruitment to the cluster level. A number of programmes, which had obtained extensive extra-budgetary funding, had developed strong administration cells, whereas programmes funded from the regular budget were totally reliant on the central administration. The Management Support Units (MSUs) were a cost-neutral system to devolve some of the administrative functions to the cluster level. However, the MSUs' structure was problematic. Each director had his own style of management, some favoring support and others control.

A MANAGEMENT MODEL

The strategies that the Transition Team proposed for WHO were strongly based on a paradigm that had emerged in the early 1990s. The World Bank's 1993 *World Development Report: Investing in Health* advocated a highly rational, evidence-based and programmatic approach to health policy for the governments of developing countries. The central tenet was that the global burden of disease measures quantifying disability and mortality provided a valid scientific indicator for designing interventions and allocating resources. The approach could be termed "selective" primary health care in that limited resources in developing countries only allowed specific health interventions to be targeted and delivered. Although other players such as UNICEF and the World Bank supported this approach, there was still considerable debate among health professionals as to its validity and ethical foundation.

The World Development Report's message to governments was that they should focus on three principles. They should facilitate economic growth, which would enable households to improve their own health; redirect spending towards low-cost effective solutions such as immunization, nutrition and treatment of infectious disease; and decentralize health services to encourage quality and competition. An implementation framework had even been developed by the Ad Hoc Committee on Health Research Relating to Future Intervention Options in 1996. The committee adopted a programmatic approach to health intervention that contained aspects of both normative and technical co-operation for priority projects. Brundtland later appointed several members of this committee to senior positions at WHO.

There was recognition that the health sector itself was becoming a minor player in the economic aspects that determined health. The major determinants were related to poverty, economic reform, social disparities, wars and conflict. The international focus was moving to developmental rather than health issues, and in order to be a player in development economics, WHO had to focus on poverty. This meant that WHO had to operate in an arena with many multilateral organizations and other UN agencies that were more experienced, more powerful and better funded. Towards the end of 1999, Brundtland established an international commission of eminent economists, chaired by Professor Jeffrey Sachs of Harvard University, to push health issues to the forefront of the global economic development agenda. The Commission on Macroeconomics and Health (CMH) would clarify over a two-year period the link between health and poverty. The Commission's report would consolidate evidence and provide practical examples on how investment in economic growth would reduce the health impacts of poverty and inequality.

Tobacco was regarded as the "hardest hitting" programme at WHO. Brundtland's predecessors had been slow to take on the giants of the tobacco industry, but WHO now led the UN Ad Hoc Agency Interagency Task Force on Tobacco Control. The Framework Convention on Tobacco Control was a legal instrument addressing issues as diverse as advertising and promotion, agricultural diversification, smuggling, taxes and subsidies. The Convention called for international, integrated efforts to put an end to tobacco use, with a view to protecting human health. It was the first time that WHO was exercising its constitutional right to negotiate a global Convention.

Another area in which Brundtland wanted to reaffirm WHO's position was AIDS, which she described as "the most dramatic" of the world's health problems. WHO would focus on three aspects of the epidemic: reduction in mother-to-child transmission, access to HIV/AIDS drugs and care for people currently living with HIV/AIDS. It was a brave move, as WHO had lost momentum with its AIDS portfolio after the resignation of the inspirational programme director, Jonathan Mann, and the transfer of international funding to the UNAIDS organization. The Global Programme on AIDS was formed in 1988 as a joint project of WHO and UNDP. WHO played a co-ordinating role in health policy, and technical and scientific matters, while UNDP provided expertise in socio-economic development. By securing an annual US$100 million in extra-budgetary funding, the Global Programme on AIDS had grown from a staff of three to more than 100 in a few years, and the work was extended beyond the traditional scope of WHO. Mann had developed an extensive and successful programme, but resigned after growing impatient with the lumbering WHO bureaucracy. Differences in approach between WHO and UNDP as to the most effective strategy to combat the disease jeopardized the alliance. In 1996 the Global Programme on AIDS was replaced with the Joint UN Programme on HIV/AIDS (UNAIDS), comprising WHO, UNESCO, UNICEF, the UNFPA, the UNDP and the World Bank. UNAIDS now shared a building within the WHO headquarters complex but managed its resources independently.

WHO also announced a plan for the expansion of its food safety programme, which would include the creation of a body to strengthen longstanding co-operation with the Food and Agriculture Organization of the United Nations (FAO). In 1963, the Sixteenth World Health Assembly had approved the establishment of a Joint FAO/WHO Food Standards Programme with the Codex Alimentarius as its principal organ. Codex Alimentarius was a reference source for food additives, contaminants, pesticide residues, hygiene and nutrition. However, WHO's role as a world player in food safety had recently been on the decline. Available data showed that foodborne illness was a growing public health problem both in developing and developed countries, threatening children, pregnant women and the elderly in particular, and Europe had been shaken by recent scandals concerning BSE, dioxin contamination and food-safety standards. WHO's function had initially been normative, involving international standard setting, health risk assessment, and the development of a risk analysis framework for the management of public health in the management of food and water. The FAO and the WTO were seen to have an increasing stake in international food safety. The WTO's involvement was largely attributed to an increase in globalization and integration of the agricultural and food industries, while the FAO had consolidated its position as the lead agency in food safety. In order to increase WHO's scientific and public health role in the work of Codex Alimentarius, a review of the current working relationship between WHO and FAO was suggested.

Brundtland's leadership also improved the relationship with UNICEF. WHO was alongside UNICEF in playing a leading role in the final push for polio eradication, which they hoped to achieve by the end of 2000. Major partners included technical agencies (the US Centers for Disease Control and Prevention); private foundations (United Nations Foundation, Bill & Melinda Gates Foundation); development banks (World Bank); donor governments (Australia, Belgium, Canada, Denmark, Finland, Germany, Italy, Japan, UK and the United States), and corporate partners, including De Beers and Aventis Pasteur.

There had been consensus among the diplomatic representatives of all the major industrialized countries that WHO had needed reform, particularly in the areas of management accountability and strategic re-evaluation. There was, however, some concern that Brundtland's focus on "hard-hitting, high-profile" projects was not sustainable and that WHO had retreated from dealing with difficult issues such as the provision of global primary health care. There was also a perception that WHO was sitting on the fence with regard to important political issues such as bioethics, genomics, cloning and the Internet. According to a senior diplomat:

> The problem is that it is not possible to get funding for these less glamorous projects and Brundtland has made funding her priority. The world is looking for WHO to take a stand on important issues. The most important issues that arose at the Executive Board were bioethics, food safety, AIDS, the use of languages and drugs and the Internet. WHO policy is still not clear after these discussions.

However, as WHO was the first specialized agency to be reformed, Brundtland did not have a model to follow. The ILO, which had the benefit of observing the early stages of WHO transformation, took a different approach. Instead of rapidly transforming the administrative structure of the organization, ILO spent considerable time on defining the strategic direction and objectives of the organization before making changes. Prior to Brundtland's election, the United States had withdrawn its candidate, so as not to split the vote of the industrialized countries. After 18 months in office, it appeared that, for some at least, Brundtland's period of grace was over. The United States was unexpectedly critical of the budget, her management style was attracting increasing scrutiny and criticism, and donors complained that the objectives, policy and governance of the organization were not clear.

CASE DISCUSSION QUESTIONS

1. What is WHO's comparative advantage?

2. Is the WHO utilizing its comparative advantage? Discuss.

3. What would you recommend that the WHO do to make better use of its comparative advantage?

4. Do you think that the Director General is suited to the role? Why or why not?

ExxonMobil Corporation: Implications of the Chad-Cameroon Pipeline

by Inna Francis*

*International Institute for Management

Research Associate Inna Francis prepared this case under the supervision of Professor Jean-Pierre Lehmann as a basis for class discussion rather than to illustrate either effective or ineffective handling of a business situation.

As part of a consortium, ExxonMobil Corporation started developing landlocked oil fields in southern Chad in 2000. When completed, the 1,000-km pipeline would link these fields to Cameroon's coastal export terminals.

The project, which was expected to produce one billion barrels of oil over its 25- to 30-year life, was estimated to cost US$3.5 billion. Esso Chad (an ExxonMobil affiliate) would have a 40% interest, Petronas would have 35% and Chevron 25%.

The consortium expected that benefits for Chad and Cameroon would amount to $8.5 billion and $900 million, respectively.

The governments of Chad and Cameroon received $200 million in loans from the World Bank to develop the necessary environmental and social expertise to deal with the project. The World Bank expected that by 2005 the pipeline would increase annual government revenues by up to 50% per year to be used for poverty-reducing investments in health, education, environment, infrastructure and rural development.

Oil pipelines can rupture, however, and slow leaks can contaminate the land, ground water, crops, residential areas, forests and tribal land, as well as releasing greenhouse gases and causing injuries from explosions and fires.

According to studies by environmentalists and human rights organizations in both countries, the development of the Chad-Cameroon pipeline involved significant social, economic and environmental risks not only for the peoples of Chad and Cameroon but also to the reputation of ExxonMobil.

Shareholders expressed concerns regarding the development of the pipeline project. They asked the company to come up with criteria for involvement in this project and report the results to shareholders by November 2001.

The NGO Transparency International rated the Cameroon government as the most corrupt government in the world in 1997/98.

The indigenous rain forest dwellers, the Pygmies (the Bakola people) are vulnerable to the effects of the pipeline. As experience shows in the Niger Delta area of Nigeria, leaking pipelines have caused a high level of water pollution and the death of fish, mangroves and tropical forests.[1]

The U.S. State Department's 1998 annual report on human rights states:

> Cameroon's human rights record continued to be poor, and the Government continued to commit serious human rights abuses. In October 1997, riots in Chad led to the massacre of eighty unarmed civilians by Chadian security forces.[2]

According to Amnesty International, parliamentarian Yorangar Ngarléjy was jailed for several months for publicly questioning how the pipeline project's revenue would be distributed:

> On 26 May, the Chadian National Assembly lifted the parliamentary immunity of Yorangar Ngarléjy, following a charge of defamation brought against him by President Déby. Following the lifting of parliamentary immunity, Yorongar Ngarléjy's house was surrounded—apparently as a form of intimidation—by members of the *Agence nationale de sécurité* (ANS), National Security Agency and on 3 June, Yorongar Ngarléjy was arrested.[3]

According to the World Bank, this project represented an unparalleled opportunity to create a much brighter future for Chad. The country could not afford to provide the minimum public services necessary to ensure a decent life for its people. James D. Wolfensohn, president of the World Bank Group, noted:

> The Chad-Cameroon project reflects an unprecedented collaborative effort between the Bank Group, the consortium of private companies and the two governments. While some may still have doubts, I believe that the hard work of specialists from the Bank Group, the private companies and the two countries, combined with the strong participation of civil society within Chad and Cameroon and around the world,

have made this a better, stronger project. The real challenge is about to begin. We intend to pursue it, with our partners, with the same openness and thoroughness we have brought to the process so far.[4]

An International Advisory Group consisting of independent international experts was set up to monitor the projects, with particular attention to social and environmental safeguards.

REQUIRED READING

The ExxonMobil consortium's website http://www.essochad.com

Exhibit 1

Economic justice now calls for halt to pipeline project

[*Exxon sent a small army of lobbyists to Washington, DC to put pressure on the World Bank to give its commitment to the project and it got it.*]

No Freedom: No Pipeline!

". . . The World Bank claims that the project will alleviate poverty because revenue from the oil development can be spent on poverty programs. But since both Governments have problems with corruption, the local communities have little faith that they will see any of the money from oil development.

These countries also suffer from human rights problems. The international press reports that Chadian government forces have resorted to indiscriminate killings and repression of the civilian population in the project area. A parliamentarian who spoke out against the project was recently jailed for three years in Chad.

The 600-mile underground pipeline through Cameroon will pass through ecologically fragile rainforest areas, including an area that is the home of a Pygmy minority of traditional hunters and gatherers. An uncontrollable influx of people in search of work will gather at the construction sites. As a result, deforestation, wildlife poaching, and the loss of farmland will be replaced by construction activities that will create a destructive environmental legacy. The pipeline itself, even with state-of-the-art equipment, poses a danger of groundwater contamination and pollution of important regional river systems as crude oil containing heavy metals leaks into the environment.

The project also promotes the development of fossil fuels and the release of greenhouse gas emissions, the leading cause of global climate change. The World Bank should not be financing the exacerbation of climate change, but should be financing projects that reduce carbon emissions and lead to more sustainable forms of energy development.

People in Chad and in Cameroon are poor and in need of assistance that will improve their livelihoods and chances for future development. The allocation of aid dollars for each country is limited and World Bank support for the oil project will divert scarce resources away from investments in health, education, environmental protection, and infra-structure that provides clean drinking water and sanitation.

The World Bank should not finance this project at this time as it cannot guarantee that human rights will be respected or that the environment will be protected. Once the money is flowing, the unholy trinity of oil, power and corruption will make corrective action difficult. Instead, the World Bank's resources should be used for projects which have direct, positive impacts on nutrition, health, education, the environment of the people of Chad and Cameroon.

Take action today to stop this corporate welfare project. Write the President of the World Bank, James Wolfensohn, and tell him that the World Bank should support human needs, not corporate wants! . . ."

Source: http://www.economicjustice.org/chadCameroon.html

Exhibit 2

The Chad-Cameroon petroleum development and pipeline project information

". . . Chad is one of the poorest countries in the world. About 80 percent of its 7 million people—or 5.6 million people—live on less than $1 a day. Chad also has very high infant mortality rates, limited access to basic social services, and extremely poor nutrition levels. Without oil, and despite recent growth of 5 percent a year, it could well take 35 years to double Chad's per capita income.

Ninety percent of the country is desert or semi-arid. Its very narrow economic base and lack of skilled people limit the opportunities for growth in most sectors. This project provides Chad with a unique opportunity to lift itself out of its extreme poverty. The additional revenues could remove the bottlenecks that constrain growth and create opportunity for the next generation of Chadians.

However, natural resource "booms" are difficult to manage. Drawing on its global knowledge, the Bank Group is seeking to ensure that the country's new wealth will be invested responsibly, for the well-being of all Chadians.

The project would increase Government spending on key economic and social services. Rather than displace social sector projects, the pipeline would support implementation of World Bank and other donor projects in these sectors by generating additional revenues to finance critical Government expenditures, such as teachers' salaries.

Managing the Oil Revenues. Chad and the Bank Group have applied the lessons of international experience to the proposed management of the oil resources. In fact, the Government has already taken unusual steps to target most of the oil revenues to poverty reduction and to ensure public oversight of the use of these resources.

On December 30, 1998, Chad's Parliament approved a law that sets out the Government's poverty reduction objectives and details arrangements for the use of the revenues. Under the law, 10 percent of the royalties and revenues will be held in trust for future generations, 80 percent of the remaining funds will be devoted to education, health and social services, rural development, infrastructure, and environmental and water resource management, and 5 percent will be earmarked for regional development in the oil-producing area (over and above its share of national spending). There will be annual published audits of the petroleum accounts, regular public expenditure reviews by the Government and the Bank, and special arrangements for channeling and accounting for the funds.

In addition, the law created an oversight committee to monitor the use of the oil revenues. This committee will include representatives of the Government, Parliament, the judiciary and civil society. A related IDA capacity-building credit will support the work of the oversight committee, as well as strengthen Chad's general accounting office and the dissemination of information about government expenditures.

In Cameroon, increased revenues from the project will be less significant: only 3 percent of the national budget, compared with 45–50 percent in Chad. Public disclosure of the use of oil revenues is already part of the Bank and IMF's economic reform program in the country.

Protecting the Environment. Any large project of this nature entails risks for the natural environment. From the start, the environmental risks of this project were seen to be significant but manageable. Numerous issues were identified, but in all cases adequate measures have been designed to deal with them. There was considerable work in studying alternative routings and induced—not just direct—impacts. National experts, Bank Group specialists, and consortium personnel walked the entire pipeline route to double-check data from aerial surveys. These analyses were summarized in a 19-volume Environmental Impact Assessment and Management

continued

Exhibit 2
(continued)

Plan, the first draft of which became available in June 1998. The final version was made public in June 1999 and additional information regarding the oil spill response plan was made available in October 1999. These documents were the subject of regular exchanges of views with local and international NGOs. Those discussions were aimed at ensuring that the project planners were studying the full range of potential risks and applying the appropriate standards of environmental protection.

Following 18 months of analysis, significant changes were made to the proposed right-of-way. As a result, the project will have only a minor net effect on the natural and human environments. The pipeline will be buried, rather than above-ground. For most of the route, it follows existing infrastructure. No one will need to be re-settled along the 1,070 km route—although a maximum of 150 families (probably many fewer) may be displaced where the oil itself will be produced. Construction may interrupt farmers' access to their land, but during a brief period. They will be compensated fully for lost income and lost fruit trees.

The final route complies with World Bank safeguard policies, including those on Environmental Assessments, Natural Habitats, Indigenous Peoples, Cultural Property, Resettlement, and Forests. Only a small amount of tropical forest (10–15 sq. km.) will be lost as a result of the construction. To compensate for this, two large new national parks (approximately 5,000 sq. km.) have been created in Cameroon, and will be managed for better biodiversity conservation in those areas.

Human Rights. Chad has had a troubled history. However, the country has made progress since the early 1990s towards a more inclusive and stable political environment. A democratic process and a program of national reconciliation have been launched. Opinions differ on how significant this progress has been. Military incidents in southern Chad two years ago and the temporary imprisonment of a parliamentarian from the project area created obvious concern. But everyone agrees—inside and outside Chad—that the success of the project will be enhanced by the free expression of community views. In itself, the preparation of the pipeline project has been a training ground for public debate. More information has been made available about this project than any other activity in the country.

Source: http://www.essochad.com/eaff/essochad/news/press 06jun00.html

Exhibit 3
Socioeconomic conditions in Chad

	Chad	World (avg.)	25 Highest GNP Countries (avg.)
Quality of Life			
GNP per capita	$160 (*5th poorest in the world*)	$5,130	$25,870
Infant mortality rate	115 per 1,000 births	54 per 1,000 births	6 per 1,000 births
Literacy rate (*age 15 +*) males	62%	79%	Near universal
Literacy rate (*age 15 +*) females	35%	62%	Near universal
Life expectancy at birth males	47	65	74
Life expectancy at birth females	50	69	81
Pupil-teacher ratio (*primary school*)	62	32	17
Population			
Total population	7 million	5,754 million	919 million
Avg. annual pop. growth	2.3%	1.2%	0.3%
Births per woman	5.6	2.8	1.7
Health and sanitation			
No access to health care	74%	n/a	n/a
People per physician	30,030	3,770	522
No access to safe water	76%	22%	6%
No access to sanitation	79%	53%	8%
Adult HIV-1 sero-prevalence	2.7%	0.6%	0.3%
Economy			
GDP avg. annual growth rate			
1980–90	6.1%	3.1%	3.2%
1990–95	1.5%	2.2%	2.0%
Inflation, avg. annual growth			
1980–90	1.1%	15.0%	4.8%
1990–95	8.9%	56.6%	2.4%
Agriculture	83%	49%	10%[1]
Industry	4%	20%	33%
Services	13%	31%	57%

[1]Data for "industrialized countries," UNDP, *Human Development Report,* 1997
Source: World Bank. World Development Indicators, 1997 and 1998

CASE DISCUSSION QUESTIONS

1. How should the board address shareholders' concerns about involvement in this project?

2. How important to the economic development of Chad and Cameroon are investments such as the ExxonMobil consortium?

3. What benefits do such projects bring to the host countries?

4. What are the costs that third world countries endure from such projects?

5. What can the consortium of MNEs do to minimize/eliminate "corruption," human rights violations, and degradation of the natural environment?

Exhibit 4
Socioeconomic conditions in Cameroon

	Cameroon	World (avg.)	25 Highest GNP Countries (avg.)
Quality of Life			
GNP per capita	$610 (*47th poorest in world*)	$5,130	$25,870
Infant mortality rate	54 per 1,000 births	54 per 1,000 births	6 per 1,000 births
Literacy rate (*age 15 +*) males	75%	79%	Near universal
Literacy rate (*age 15 +*) females	52%	62%	Near universal
Life expectancy at birth males	55	65	74
Life expectancy at birth females	58	69	81
Pupil-teacher ratio (*primary school*)	46	32	17
Population			
Total population	14 million	5,754 million	919 million
Avg. annual pop. growth	2.4%	1.2%	0.3%
Births per woman	5.5	2.8	1.7
Health and sanitation			
No access to health care	85%	n/a	n/a
People per physician	11,996	3,770	522
No access to safe water	59%	22%	6%
No access to sanitation	60%	53%	8%
Adult HIV-1 sero-prevalence	3%	0.6%	0.3%
Economy			
GDP avg. annual growth rate			
1980–90	3.3%	3.1%	3.2%
1990–95	−1.0%	2.2%	2.0%
Inflation, avg. annual growth			
1980–90	5.9%	15.0%	4.8%
1990–95	5.1%	56.6%	2.4%
Agriculture	70%	49%	10%[1]
Industry	9%	20%	33%
Services	21%	31%	57%

[1]Data for "industrialized countries," UNDP, *Human Development Report,* 1997
Source: World Bank. World Development Indicators, 1997 and 1998

ENDNOTES

1   *New York Times.* July 10, 2000.

2   http://www.state.gov/www/global/human rights/ 1998 hrp report/chad.html

3   http://web.amnesty.org/ai.nsf/Index/ AFR200091998?OpenDocument&of=COUNTRIES\CHAD

4   http://www.essochad.com/eaff/essochad/news/press 06jun00.html

Lobatse Clay Works[1]

by David Osgood*

*George Washington University

LOBATSE, BOTSWANA

Peter Williamson, the newly appointed General Manager of Lobatse Clay Works (LCW), looked out of his office window at the tangible evidence of his frustration. There, laying on the factory grounds, were over three million stockpiled bricks, and there were no reasonable prospects they would be sold anytime soon. The situation had grown so bad in recent months that the previous week he felt compelled to shut down the entire production line and lay off all 100 factory workers indefinitely. If these firings were not bad enough, he now faced the very real possibility of defaulting on the company's bank loans, due the upcoming week. With no revenues coming in from the company's principal buyer—now embroiled in a corruption scandal that had forced it to halt all purchases six months ago—the company's prospects looked very dim, quite different from the way things had seemed just nine months before when the company first began production.

Peter once thought he would be happy with a promotion to the role of General Manager. For over 25 years he had worked as a Production Manager for Interkiln Corporation of America (ICA), a parent company of the joint venture Lobatse Clay Works, which over the years had posted him to various production assignments throughout the developing world. In the past year, he had decided to leave ICA to work directly for its newly formed Botswana joint venture, Lobatse Clay Works, so that he could stay in one place and lead a "normal" life with his wife. After 20 years of infrequent visits to his family, Peter looked forward to being a full-time husband and father. He envisioned this production job as being his last overseas assignment before taking early retirement and moving back to England. To his surprise, however, within a few months on the job he was thrust into the General Manager role and asked to manage a crisis situation, clearly the biggest challenge of his professional career. Reflecting on his experience at LCW, he smiled ironically: everything was supposed to be relatively easy to manage; it looked good for the company, good for the country, and good for himself. Recent events, however, now made it seem that the entire joint venture was in question. The bank called him every day asking when they could expect their current loan repayment. ■

THE INTERKILN CORPORATION OF AMERICA

The Interkiln Corporation of America (ICA) was a privately held U.S.-based company headquartered inHouston, Texas. It constructed and managed ceramic manufacturing facilities around the world. The company was wholly owned by Elmer Salgo, its president of the past 45 years, and under his leadership it had found a niche for itself building "turn key" brick-making facilities for governments throughout the developing world. Beyond building and managing production facilities, the company provided technical and management support to train local personnel to take over management responsibility. By providing economically and politically viable industry to developing countries, ICA had become one of the premier construction companies in the world. ICA had built factories in China, Nigeria, Libya, Eastern Europe, and elsewhere.

ICA revenues were primarily generated from two sources. First, it earned fees for its management work, conducting feasibility studies for proposed new production facilities and providing technical assistance and onsite supervision before, during, and after the construction itself. Second, it earned a profit from the sale of equipment installed in these facilities, purchased from wholesalers or on the open market. While these business activities had been quite lucrative in years past, the company's cash flows from these agreements were always short-lived. Once the factory was complete and the new management trained, the "turn key" agreement ended and the company had to search for new opportunities. During times of worldwide recession, few countries showed much interest in the company's services. Recognizing its vulnerability to such unmanageable factors, the company for many years had been seeking a "good" longer-term investment opportunity: a deal that promised a steady cash flow over a longer period of time with a reasonable return on investment. Such deals were difficult to find given the firm's specialty in building facilities for developing countries. These environments were often politically volatile and economically unstable, so positive cash flows were not readily assured. At long last, however, ICA management thought they had found what they were looking for. A potential joint venture with the Botswana Development Corporation, a state-owned company of the newly prosperous country of Botswana, seemed like the perfect business opportunity.

HISTORY OF BOTSWANA

Botswana is located in southern Africa, surrounded by Namibia, Zambia, Zimbabwe, and the Republic of South Africa. It is approximately the size of the state of Texas, but with a population of only 1.3 million people. The country is situated primarily in the Kalahari Desert, giving it an arid landscape similar to northern Arizona or New Mexico. The temperature routinely reaches 120° during the summer months (December–February) and below freezing during the winter months. This harsh climate makes it close to impossible to obtain consistent agricultural crop yields. Historically, the people of Botswana relied on cattle and goat herding as their source of nutrition and wealth. Their semi-nomadic nature meant few urban centers were established prior to Botswanan independence from Great Britain in 1966. With no industrial base and no business centers, Botswana at the time was the fifth poorest country in the world, with gross domestic product (GDP) of $200 per person. The newly independent government made its primary focus the country's industrial development and the increased employment and wealth of its citizens. It aggressively searched for opportunities to exploit what they believed at the time to be the country's very few natural resources.

In 1969, the South African DeBeers Diamond Company discovered a vast diamond supply in the central region of Botswana. The diamond reserves were so large that it was estimated that the proposed mines could operate at full capacity through the year 2020. After negotiating mining rights for the excavation and handling of diamonds, Botswana found itself with vast economic wealth. The 1980s were marked by GDP growth of 12 to 15% per year and a general economic "boom" unseen in the area's history and, in fact, rarely seen in the world.

The construction sector could not keep pace with the newfound need for industrial and residential construction. Botswana's lack of natural resources and minimal industrial capabilities allowed foreign construction companies and products to enter the country and dominate the local marketplace. This became a source of concern for the government. They were wary of the country's complete dependence on South Africa. Botswana's landlocked position and lack of natural resources forced it to import 85% of all goods and services from South Africa. Even those goods and services originating from outside South Africa entered the country via South African ports and highways. The future political uncertainty in South Africa made it imperative that Botswana, and every other country in southern Africa, lessen its dependence on South Africa for its commercial needs.

Fortunately, Botswana was spared the racial tensions that had long strained social relations in South Africa and Zimbabwe. A unique feature of Botswana was the accepting relationship between the indigenous people, with family "roots" going back hundreds of years, and the "white" expatriate community that immigrated to the country during the twentieth century. The expatriates came primarily from South Africa and the United Kingdom but also from India, the United States, and Sweden. The mixing of people from different cultures was quite successful and even permeated the highest offices of government. The first freely elected President of Botswana was married to a Caucasian English woman. The appointed Governor of the Bank of Botswana was a Caucasian American. Expatriates dominated management positions in most private companies. The local people, the Batswana, lacked Western-style management experience, and people accepted that the country relied on foreign expertise to create an effective economic environment. Most Batswana wanted more of their own people in positions of power, but local businesspeople lacked the education and experience to manage large operations. Though the government now aggressively sponsored the overseas education and business experience of qualified local people, significant change would take some time. After all, rapid economic growth had transformed the country from a pastoral society to a thriving economy in less than one generation.

THE BOTSWANA DEVELOPMENT CORPORATION

The Government of Botswana attempted to use revenues from diamond mining to create indigenous industries. They formed the Botswana Development Corporation (BDC), a parastatal organization funded by the government, to create new business and industry within the country. The BDC had the freedom to search for projects that they believed would enhance the country's economic base. Over the years, they had made investments in a wide range of businesses, including a cement manufacturing plant, hotels, a furniture manufacturing company, and a variety of other businesses, all geared to diversifying the local economy.

Although it was an independent entity and expected to make a profit, the BDC had much latitude on how it conducted its mission. It was allowed to make decisions based on what it perceived to be long-term growth potential and not worry much about short-term financial losses. Though it aspired to live by free market principles, it did not always practice this ideal. The wealth generated from its diamond reserves allowed it to invest in projects that were far more risky than projects normally undertaken by developing countries. Inevitably, political and economic concerns shaped its decision-making. It developed a particular interest in challenging the foreign-owned companies that were operating within Botswana's borders.

The BDC felt that the country needed its own clay products facility to give entrenched South African companies some much-needed competition. For decades, foreign brick suppliers had received premium prices for their products, and the BDC was determined to break that monopoly. The housing industry was booming, and BDC officials felt it was time to encourage some domestic producer to supply needed construction materials.

THE BOTSWANA HOUSING CORPORATION

The main engine of growth in the construction industry in the country was the Botswana Housing Corporation (BHC). The

BHC, like the BDC, was a government parastatal created to build new residential housing for the rapidly growing population. This housing program consisted of high-cost, medium-cost and low-cost units. Low-cost housing for poor families was subsidized by high-cost housing sold at a profit to wealthier families. Because of this "mix" of residential building activity undertaken by the BHC, very little residential construction was done by private firms. The BHC had a virtual monopoly. To compete in the Botswana marketplace, any large construction materials manufacturer had to sell its products to the BHC.

FOREIGN COMPETITION

Once the government decided that a clay building products factory was needed in Botswana, the Botswana Development Corporation had to select a company that could build and manage the project to the satisfaction of both the public and private sectors. The public sector demanded that any new industry create employment for its citizens, introduce new job skills, and lessen dependence on foreign companies for essential building materials. The private sector wanted products that were competitive in quality, quantity, variety, and price compared to those of established foreign clay products suppliers.

There were risks with this plan of action, however. For years the primary supplier of clay building products was the South African company, Corobrik. The BDC was quite concerned as to how Corobrik and other brick manufacturers might react to new competition from a state-supported company. They knew quite well that Corobrik's large size—estimated to produce 150 million bricks per year—could easily overwhelm the much smaller plant planned for Botswana—expected to peak at 25 million bricks per year. The planned capacity for the new plant would supply nearly all the government's requirements for face-bricks, eliminating the need for a second major face-brick supplier in the country, and so either the BDC factory or Corobrik would have to abandon the face-brick market in Botswana. The stock brick market, on the other hand, would still require tens of millions of bricks per year, but the lower profit margins of that business made it much less lucrative than the higher-quality, higher-margin face-brick business. Neither company wanted to lose its most profitable market segment. There was fear Corobrik might "dump" its products on the Botswana market, selling at unfairly low prices, forcing the new manufacturer out of business.

THE FEASIBILITY STUDY

The economic growth of the 1980s created demand for all types of construction, and foreign-owned construction companies already dominated the contract-tendering process for new construction. Their projects required extensive import of bricks and other clay products. As part of its on-going search for new business, ICA approached the BDC about building a clay products plant in Botswana to respond to the growing demand for bricks. The BDC was delighted by their inquiry. Here was an opportunity to fulfill its goals of creating a new industry while adding employment in the country.

The BDC entered into negotiations with ICA to produce a feasibility study for a new clay products factory in Botswana. The study was extensive, including an analysis of the current market situation, projections of future demand, availability of raw materials, transportation issues, estimates of employment created, and assessments of costs for building the plant and supporting facilities. The Executive Summary of the report appears in Exhibit 1.

The feasibility study was conducted by ICA personnel with experience in constructing clay products facilities. It found that:

1. An indigenous plant could compete against foreign suppliers on quality and price. This was due to the quality of the clay and lower transportation costs associated with being situated near the capital city;

2. Future demand would slow but remain strong throughout the decade, due to world demand for diamonds and the resulting increased local wealth and growing demand for housing;

3. There was a large, high-quality clay deposit only 50 miles south of the capital city of Gaborone, in the vicinity of the town Lobatse;

4. The optimal size of the plant would produce 25 million units per year and employ nearly 200 factory workers plus administrative staff. This plant size would force it to utilize nearly 100% of its capacity to supply the Botswana Housing's needs for clay brick materials; and

5. The plant could be built for just over US$10 million.

Further details of the feasibility study appear in Exhibits 2 through 5. Exhibit 2 describes the technology planned for the facility, highlighting its state-of-the-art features. Exhibit 3 details the capital investment requirements, showing how anticipated costs were to be shared by the joint venture partners. Exhibit 4 shows the anticipated production volumes and operating costs once production began. Finally, Exhibit 5 shows in graph form the impressive cash flows anticipated from the operation in the ensuing years.

The results of the study made the project seem very attractive to the BDC. They were thrilled to learn that the BHC, the largest purchaser of building supplies in the country, would utilize nearly 100% of the plant's production output. That meant that BDC's "sister parastatal organization" would utilize almost *all* the production capacity of a proposed indigenous clay production facility. With such promising news, the biggest questions facing BDC management now became: (a) how to fund the project, and (b) who they should contact to request a bid to build and manage the new factory. There were not many companies in the world that could oversee the construction and management of a clay products factory, much less in a developing country like Botswana. The BDC realized its options for a business partnership were going to be limited.

Exhibit 1
Joint venture feasibility study: executive summary

This revised study appraises the technical and economic viability of the establishment of a high-quality facing brick and ceramic tile facility near the town of Lobatse, in Southeast Botswana. The study has been prepared by INTERKILN CORPORATION OF AMERICA utilizing previous detailed information provided by the BOTSWANA DEVELOPMENT CORPORATION, during recent meetings.

Over the last six years, Botswana has had an average annual consumption of building bricks and roofing the products of 90 million brick equivalent units. Demand is expected to grow by at least 5% per year, as Botswana's rapid economic development continues and the drought, which has affected the country since 1982, appears to have come to an end. The Government has introduced special measures to alleviate the shortage of serviced plots for housing and commercial construction. This would stabilize demand, should drought return.

Most of Botswana's building brick and roofing product requirements are being covered by locally made concrete blocks and, in the case of roofing materials, by imports. The market for clay bricks is presently catered for by either imported face bricks or locally produced low-quality stock bricks. A sound market potential is available in the manufacture of split tiles, ceramic pavers and clay roofing tiles, to displace current imports. The proposed plant has a modest production level of some 25 million units, which the market potential justifies.

The clay deposit near Lobatse is admirably suitable for the production range envisaged, and proven reserves are at least 1.2 million cubic meters, which is sufficient for over 20 years at full plant capacity. The land area and clay deposit are Government property, and a royalty of 3% will be paid on the annual turnover for the use of the land and the material.

The plant design is flexible and allows for the production of a wide variety of high-quality products at low cost. The plant will allow the production of the high-quality products with all local materials, thereby having a considerable impact on the economy. The plant will utilize known and proven technology and will be a combination of modern cost effective equipment linked with labor intensive handling operations.

The project as envisioned is a commercially sound investment, even with the conservative approach regarding revenues and costs. The operation would be profitable from the first year onwards and in the fifth year of operation, the return on equity is 40.1%. The break-even point is estimated at 54.2% in year 5 of operation. The financial projections allow for the payment of corporation tax from year 2 onwards. The projected net cash flow calculations show that the total indebtedness of the venture could be returned in 3.8 years with accelerated loan repayments.

The need for competent management for the operation has been recognized and it is envisaged that INTERKILN will provide competent knowledgeable on-site staff in key positions. INTERKILN will also provide an on-going management service to monitor the technical production and financial aspects of the operation.

Exhibit 2
Description of the proposed production system

TUNNEL KILN FIRING

The product, after drying on the dryer/kiln cars, will then be fed directly to the INTERKILN tunnel kiln. The kiln will be a continuous operation unit, which will utilize coal as the means of firing. The kiln will be complete with a coal handling system automatically linked to a temperature control system to ensure uniform firing of the product.

The kiln will incorporate the latest construction materials and technology, to ensure that the fuel consumption levels and the thermal gain in this department will be low, providing reasonable working conditions for the operatives.

The heating, firing and cooling cycles will be automatically controlled by both temperature and internal pressure, to ensure that the critical firing ranges associated with the firing of clay based products will be accurately maintained.

Exhibit 3

Projected capital investment for plant, equipment and services

Cost Category	Investment Foreign (USD)	Local (USD)
Site Preparation	—	46,000.00
Site Infrastructure	—	196,000.00
Plant Buildings	513,100.00	200,300.00
Machinery & Equipment	6,931,495.00	95,375.00
General Plant Services	217,680.00	—
Erection & Installation	—	383,600.00
Marine Freight & Insurance	578,450.00	200,000.00
Design & Engineering Services	660,000.00	—
Pre-Production Services	150,000.00	72,000.00
Technology Know-How	70,000.00	—
Construction Supervision	288,000.00	—
Commissioning Supervision	138,000.00	—
Pre-Commissioning Interest	1,160,000.00	—
Foreign Supervisor's Related Costs and Contingency	—	60,000.00
Fixed Capital Investment	10,706,725.00	1,253,275.00
Total Capital Investment	11,960,000.00	

Exhibit 4

Projected production volumes and operating costs

A. DESIGN CRITERIA:

   I.   ANNUAL PRODUCTION CAPACITY:

       i.)   25.0 Million Clay Brick and Tile Products or 60,000 M. Tons
       ii.)   Provision for 2.0 Million Glazed Split Tile Expansion

   II.   BASIC PRODUCTS:

       i.)   Face Brick 222 × 106 × 73mm @ 2.4 Kg. ea.
       ii.)   Semi-Face Brick 222 × 106 × 73mm @ 2.4 Kg. ea.
       iii.)   Split Tile 222 × 106 × 10mm @ 1.2 Kg./Pair
       iv.)   Split Paver 222 × 106 × 25mm @ 2.4 Kg./Pair
       v.)   Roofing Tile 420 × 240 × 15mm @ 2.6 Kg. ea.
       vi.)   Ridge Tile Shape 400 × 220 × 15mm @ 2.2 Kg. ea.

   III.   PRODUCTION PLAN:

Products	Year of Operation (Pcs. × 1000) First	Third	Fifth
i.) Face Brick	4,200	5,400	6,000
ii.) Semi-Face Brick	7,000	9,000	10,000
iii.) Split Tile	1,400	1,800	2,000
iv.) Split Paver	3,500	4,500	5,000
v.) Roofing Tile	1,260	1,620	1,000
vi.) Ridge Tile	140	180	200

continued

IV. SCHEME OF OPERATION:
- i.) Clay Preparation   8 Hrs/Day, 6 Days/Wk, 300 Days/Yr
- ii.) Forming & Pressing   8 Hrs/Day, 6 Days/Wk, 300 Days/Yr
- iii.) Drying & Firing   24 Hrs/Day, 7 Days/Wk, 365 Days/Yr
- iv.) Sorting, Packing & Storage   8 Hrs/Day, 6 Days/Wk, 300 Days/Yr
- v.) Services   8 Hrs/Day, 6 Days/Wk, 300 Days/Yr

V. RAW MATERIAL REQUIREMENT:

	Year of Operation (M Tons)		
	First	Third	Fifth
i.) Woodhall Clay Deposit	42,000	54,000	60,000

VI. FUEL, POWER AND WATER REQUIREMENTS:
- i.) Bituminous Coal   235 Kg/1000 pcs. or 5,900 M. Tons/Yr
- ii.) Diesel Fuel Oil   10 Liters/1000 pcs. or 25,000 Liters/Yr
- iii.) Electric Power   200 KWH/1000 pcs. or 5,000,000 KWH/Yr
- iv.) Water   100 Liters/1000 pcs. or 2,500,000 Liters/Yr

VII. MANPOWER REQUIREMENTS:

	Operating shifts		
	First	Second	Third
i.) Management & Office	21	0	0
ii.) Production	71	6	6
iii.) Maintenance & Laboratory	9	0	0
iv.) Total Personnel	101	6	6

VIII. FACTORY SITE AREA:
- i.) 27,000 Square Meters, Approx. Land Area

B. FINANCIAL CRITERIA:

I. PRODUCT SALES PRICE:
- i.) Face Brick   @ USD 220/1000 pcs or Pula 440/1000 pcs
- ii.) Semi-Face Brick   @ USD 125/1000 pcs or Pula 250/1000 pcs
- iii.) Split Tile   @ USD 275/1000 pcs or Pula 560/1000 pcs
- iv.) Split Paver   @ USD 330/1000 pcs or Pula 660/1000 pcs
- v.) Roofing Tile   @ USD 440/1000 pcs or Pula 880/1000 pcs
- vi.) Ridge Tile Shape   @ USD 880/1000 pcs or Pula 1760/1000 pcs

II. GROSS SALES REVENUES (USD × 1000):

	Year of Operation		
	First	Third	Fifth
i.) All Products	4,016.6	5,164.2	5,738.0

III. TOTAL INVESTMENT:
- i.) Total Fixed Assets — USD   11,960,000 (Incl. Interim Int.)
- ii.) Working Capital Needs — USD   500,000 (Overdraft)

IV. SHARE CAPITALIZATION AND FINANCING:
- i.) Initial Paid-in Capital
  - —55% Botswana Development Corp.   —   USD 2,375,000.00
  - —25% Interkiln Corp.   —   1,080,000.00
  - —20% Other American Investors   —   865,000.00
- ii.) Local Project Loan, BDC   —   3,575,000.00
- iii.) Local Project Loan   —   2,905,000.00
- iv.) Local Interim Interest Loan   —   1,160,000.00
- v.) Local Overdraft Loan   —   500,000.00

continued

V. OPERATING COSTS (USD × 1000):

		Year of Operation		
		First	Third	Fifth
i.)	Direct Operating Costs	783.80	989.75	989.75
ii.)	Factory Overhead Costs	175.00	175.00	175.00
iii.)	Admin. Overhead Costs	411.10	411.10	411.10
iv.)	Sales & Distribution Costs	38.37	38.37	38.37
v.)	Depreciation	1,185.88	1,185.88	1,185.88
vi.)	Finance Costs	843.15	592.69	293.47
	Total Production Costs	3,473.30	3,392.79	3,093.57

VI. PROFITABILITY (USD):

		Year of Operation		
		First	Third	Fifth
i.)	Net Sales Revenue	3,896,102	5,009,274	5,565,860
ii.)	Operational Margin	1,301,945	2,209,167	2,765,752
iii.)	Cost Finance	843,151	592,693	293,468
iv.)	Gross Profit	458,794	1,616,474	2,472,284
v.)	Taxes	—	161,647	741,685
vi.)	Net Profit	458,794	1,454,827	1,730,599
vii.)	% Return on Sales	11.42	28.17	30.16
viii.)	% Return on Equity	10.62	33.67	40.06
ix.)	IRR on Net Worth—25.06%			

Exhibit 5
Projected accumulated cash flows from operations

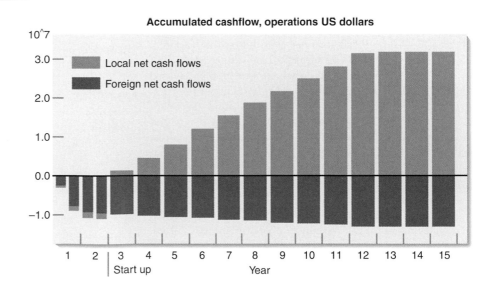

THE JOINT VENTURE DECISION

The BDC management decided that creating a joint venture with a private company would be the most effective and efficient way to get the new industry started. Although the goal of the BDC was to create employment for its own people, there were no Batswana with the experience or formal training to manage a state-of-the-art clay products factory. In fact, the entire upper management of the new company would have to be brought in from abroad by the joint venture partner. Given the Batswana's positive attitudes towards living and working with expatriates, there was little political concern about utilizing foreign expertise. Although the BDC did not like giving that much control to a joint venture partner, it saw no alternative. Maintaining oversight of the company would depend on the vigilance of the Board of Directors, of which the BDC would have majority representation proportional to its equity investment.

The BDC would actively oversee the operation, thus controlling its financial investment in the project. The actual amount of the investment would not be known until a joint venture partner was found to sign an agreement.

The large brick manufacturers located in neighboring South Africa were the easiest to contact as potential partners for the new joint venture. The BDC's main concern about contacting these companies, however, was their inherent conflict of interest: if any one became a partner, they would be helping to create a new competitor for their existing factories. The economic recession plaguing South Africa had already forced local brick companies to lay off thousands of workers and to stockpile hundreds of millions of bricks that could not be sold to the stalled South African construction sector. The logical move for the South African manufacturers was to sell their excess capacity to the strong construction sector in Botswana. But the BDC had made a conscious decision to reduce the country's reliance on foreign products. After reviewing the business and political ramifications of entering into an agreement with a South African company, the BDC decided to contact clay manufacturing experts outside the region regarding the possible joint venture agreement.

ICA Becomes Joint Venture Partner

The BDC contacted ICA about submitting a bid for the joint venture. The political and economic stability of Botswana seemed a perfect situation for ICA. They could profit short-term from the management fees and sale of equipment, and benefit longer-term by owning part of a clay products factory operating in a "booming" economy. The lack of prior long-term involvement by ICA in a venture did not affect the BDC's final decision. After all, the BDC and ICA had worked together well during the feasibility study, and both parties would have a financial stake in the project. ICA would supply the management expertise, specialized equipment, and nearly one-third of the total equity in the company—over $3 million. The BDC, utilizing its substantial financial resources, would supply the other two-thirds of equity and provide the loan guarantees necessary for the project to borrow from private financial institutions. The BDC's political clout might also be important if problems arose jeopardizing the company's attempt to become the major brick supplier in the country.

The arrangement seemed ideal for both parties. The BDC would meet its goals of creating new industry and employment while receiving technical assistance to get the project started. ICA would offer its management assistance, sell specialized equipment and benefit longer term from its equity infusion and semi-annual management fee. The long-term potential would more than make up for the initial capital expenditure, providing the company at last with an on-going income stream. Both partners thus felt confident that the joint venture would be the ideal way to achieve their individual goals.

FACTORY CONSTRUCTION BEGINS

Peter remembered that his first few weeks on the job as ICA's technical consultant were better than most of his previous assignments. He did not have to deal with the bureaucratic "red tape" or corruption that plagued other overseas experiences. The national and local officials whom he met seemed thrilled to have a new industry in their country. The town of Lobatse, where the company was to be located because of its ample clay deposits, had a population of 25,000. Its main industry, the national slaughterhouse, employed several thousand people. LCW would bring additional employment and revenue to the local economy. The joint venture partners had little trouble getting the land or improved utilities needed to begin the ground-breaking process.

With BDC and local government support, construction on the factory began in August 1990 and was completed less than 17 months later. The management team was able to get the factory built on-schedule despite a 20% cost overrun. The majority of these extra costs occurred during the first stages of construction. The concrete foundation for the factory floor was totally completed before it was discovered that the ground underneath the foundation could not support the weight of the factory equipment. The substantial weight of the equipment combined with the numerous bricks expected during production actually cracked the concrete floor. The entire floor had to be broken up, removed, and replaced with reinforced concrete. Two months of work and $2 million of unbudgeted expense were wasted correcting this oversight.

ICA's costly error with the floor did not make management at the BDC happy. Many people within the BDC felt that ICA should have realized that the floor needed reinforcement. After all, ICA's expertise was the main reason it was brought in to the joint venture project to begin with. Peter admitted to the BDC that the problems with the floor had been a major mistake, but he felt confident that ICA would make up for its oversight by producing an excellent quality product.

During the construction process, ICA argued for using coal-fired burners for the heating kiln instead of the more modern gas burners commonly used in other countries. ICA technicians reasoned that coal burners would take advantage of Botswana's plentiful supply of coal, and by utilizing an indigenous resource, they would further avoid importing natural gas from South Africa.

The overriding goal of building the factory, and the dream of locally produced goods dominating the construction materials market in Botswana, kept everyone focused on a common objective. Despite the problems with the floor, the factory was eventually ready for its Grand Opening. Lobatse Clay Works looked like a sure bet to be a good investment for both the country of Botswana and the Interkiln Corporation of America. The joint venture was ready to begin manufacturing its first clay building products to compete directly against the entrenched South African suppliers.

THE GRAND OPENING

The mood was festive throughout the factory grounds. The employees and guests at the Grand Opening of Lobatse Clay Works enjoyed the food and drink that accompanied a big celebration. The guests of honor, especially the Minister of Commerce and Industry, were very proud of Botswana's first state-of-the-art ceramics production facility. The past two years had been filled with intense negotiation over the joint venture agreement, the cost overruns, and the completion of the factory on-schedule, but each obstacle along the way had been conquered. The process had, at times, made both parties skeptical about the factory's eventual completion. But, today, they were all smiles and handshakes as the fruits of their labors finally ripened. Full-scale production was to begin the next day. During his speech to the assembled crowd, the Minister remarked:

> This new clay products facility will allow Botswana to manufacture its own clay bricks, roof tiles, floor tiles, and pavers, and not be dependent upon foreign manufactured construction materials to meet the increasing demand for new commercial and residential construction in our country. This is a great moment in the economic development of Botswana.

The Board of Directors and the management staff of Lobatse Clay Works had also been excited about the beginning of production, but each realized that they would soon be facing a highly competitive marketplace. The previous lack of a modern clay products manufacturing facility meant that foreign competition had been able to control the supply of brick and other clay products used throughout Botswana for the past 15 years. Breaking into the building materials market was not going to be easy for the new company. Many hurdles had to be overcome before the company would begin to show the sales revenues expected by the joint venture partners.

Nonetheless, LCW's prospects seemed bright. The feasibility study showed ample opportunity, and the full knowledge and experience of the expatriate management staff now onboard would likely steer the venture well. The country was experiencing an economic "boom" from its diamond deposits, with GDP rising over 10% a year. The construction craze was forecast to last through the year 2000. If all went according to plan, LCW would be well positioned to take advantage of the demand for construction materials and make a handsome profit for both joint venture partners.

PRODUCTION BEGINS

There were several stages to the production process. . . . Once the plant began operation, everyone immediately recognized the unfortunate consequences of installing coal-fired burners in the heating kiln. The low-grade coal used to heat the oven created excess ash when it was burned. The ash literally fell onto the bricks and cooked into their surface, creating ash "lines" and off-color marks on the brick faces. While the ash did not diminish the physical strength of the clay, it did leave a residue that made the bricks look "dirty." Architects and builders refused to use Lobatse Clay Works face-bricks for the external wall of buildings because the walls would not have the clean, classic look of red or brown clay. The BDC was upset that the kilns produced "inferior" face bricks. Until the problem could be corrected, material purchasers would continue to buy South African bricks. This made the BDC furious because they did not want to give construction companies any reason to continue pur-

chasing bricks from outside Botswana. It was clear that LCW would not achieve its full sales potential until its face bricks conformed to accepted building standards. The company began assigning crews of workers to scrub the bricks manually to remove as much ash as possible before shipping the bricks to customers.

Another drawback to using coal to fire the kiln was soon discovered. The products coming out of the oven were of inconsistent size. The coal did not burn in the kiln at even temperatures, so there were "hot" and "cold" areas in the kiln. This temperature variation caused the bricks to differ in size from one part of the kiln to another, producing unacceptable results. Current building standards in Botswana specified that face bricks be 222 mm +/−3 mm in length, whereas the LCW coal-fired kiln was creating variations up to +/−10 mm. These extremes in size made the bricks impossible to sell as face bricks. This quality problem also undermined the company's effort to sell its products to public and private construction material buyers. It also reinforced the notion held by many Batswana that products made in Botswana were simply inferior to those from other countries. Until a better heating system could be installed, LCW would lose market share to companies that supplied "clean" and properly sized bricks.

The inability to produce consistently proper face bricks also made it impossible for LCW to guarantee delivery of bricks to its customers.

As an emergency measure, the company had resorted to sending teams of employees to job sites to handsort previously delivered bricks to ensure that only "good" bricks were "supplied" to the customer. This quality control procedure was extremely expensive and time-consuming. The problem could have been avoided from the beginning if ICA had installed gas-fired burners in the kiln instead of the inconsistent coal-fired burners. The burner problem was the second mistake that ICA admitted to making during the construction phase of the project. The Board of Directors did not approve the conversion to gas-fired burners until November 1992.

DEPENDENCE ON THE BOTSWANA HOUSING CORPORATION

When conducting the feasibility study, ICA knew full well that the joint venture's survival was dependent on the BHC. Lobatse Clay Works had been created on the assumption that a majority of its overall production capacity would be dedicated to fulfilling the clay product needs of the BHC. Once the venture was underway, LCW management recognized the need to maintain close cooperation with the BHC. LCW could not prosper without the BHC buying up to 70% of the company's total production capacity. This reliance on a single entity for such a large percentage of sales had its positive and negative points. The positive side was that LCW did not have to search for market share from other sources; extensive marketing was not required to cultivate private sector sales. The negative side was the dependence on a single source for a majority of its sales; if anything happened to disrupt BHC construction projects, LCW would be very vulnerable in terms of lost demand and lost revenues. The BDC and ICA knew the risks of starting a company dependent upon a single state-owned organization. The feasibility study acknowledged LCW's vulnerability to one main purchaser, but the BDC and ICA decided to proceed nonetheless. The political issues of moving away from dependence on South African companies, of creating a new, indigenous industry, outweighed the strictly business decision that might have been made by a purely private company. ICA took the investment risk because it felt that the BDC would be able to influence the government in its favor if competition became too keen. The BDC and ICA each focused on overall potential for profit, not on the inherent risk of relying on a single buyer for the majority of its production. The management of LCW bet its very existence on the hope that the government of Botswana would provide some sort of assistance if times got really tough.

WORST-CASE SCENARIO: BHC SCANDAL

In April 1992, just three months after LCW began operations, a worse-case scenario happened to the company. A massive scandal was uncovered within the Botswana Housing Corporation. The National Legislature called a halt to every construction project in progress throughout the country. The construction stoppage was to remain in effect throughout the government's investigation of corruption in the upper management of the BHC. The Managing Director of the BHC, a Botswana, allegedly had taken pay-offs from construction companies and material suppliers to award them BHC contracts. The scandal shook the people of Botswana who had prided themselves on the honesty of their government officials and representatives. Botswana had not had the endemic corruption that plagued many developing countries throughout the world. The democratically elected government has been open about its operations, and allowed total freedom to the local press to fully investigate its operations.

The government investigation found several high-ranking managers guilty of taking bribes and vowed to "clean house." The BHC had been one of the few organizations that had a Batswana in a top leadership position, but now he was to be replaced by an expatriate. The National Legislative leaders involved with the investigation were so angered by the fact that one of their countrymen could take bribes that they declared: "There are no Motswana with the experience or education to properly manage the BHC." Until a suitable Batswana could be found to manage the Housing Corporation, a foreigner would be hired to keep the corporation operating. Though it disrupted the housing construction industry, this zeal to maintain a high standard of integrity within the government helped Botswana continue making steps towards becoming a more independent, politically stable nation.

The BHC scandal was uncovered just as LCW was beginning to receive sizable orders from the BHC, other government organizations, and the private sector. The decision by the National Parliament to stop BHC activities was a crippling blow to everyone at Lobatse Clay Works. No one had any idea how long it would be until the investigation was finished and the BHC resumed purchasing materials. Both joint venture partners were at risk of losing all their investment if sales did not materialize soon. The BDC faced the loss of a new industry that was important to the future of the national industrial base. ICA faced the possibility of accepting a devastating financial loss in its very first joint venture investment.

While the investigation was proceeding, the management of LCW was frantically searching for alternate markets. Unfortunately, not many markets were available. Other government organizations could not use more bricks for their buildings, and private builders were too small to make much of a dent in LCW's vast inventory. Even export markets were not promising. Botswana's robust economy, fueled by diamond exports, made its currency, the pula, strong against the other currencies in the area. Trade in the area was coordinated by the Southern Africa Development Commission (SADC) involving the countries of South Africa, Namibia, Zambia, Zimbabwe, Lesotho and Swaziland, as well as Botswana. The SADC was a regional organization that promoted free trade among member nations. The pula was approximately 30% stronger than the South African rand, for example, and twice as strong as the Zimbabwe dollar. The pula's appreciation against these currencies made it more expensive to sell Botswana products in these countries. Without domestic or international buyers, LCW found itself with an increasing stockpile of bricks on its factory grounds, no new prospects for sales, and an inability to pay its increasing debts.

PRESENT SITUATION

As Peter's thoughts came back to the present situation, he could not help but feel nostalgic about the euphoric expectations of the past. The current realities were much different. First, Peter had inherited his new position just three weeks previously because the former General Manager of the company, an American, and the Financial Manager, an Indian, had been fired for attempting to negotiate a deal to sell American cornmeal to the Zambian government. They were conducting personal business on company time and with company money. When their activities were discovered by ICA and the BDC, they were immediately fired, and Peter was asked to step in and fill their shoes.

Peter was eager to demonstrate that he was the best choice for the General Manager position and that the company could rebound from its present dilemma and produce the sales and revenues originally envisioned. The reality, however—almost no sales for the past six months, the loss of two top managers to scandal, the indefinite layoff of every factory worker, the stockpile of millions of bricks, and absence of any sign of future sales—was quite daunting. Peter would certainly be earning his "battle pay" during the current crisis.

Peter knew that ICA had been optimistic with its projected sales. The feasibility study based its conclusions on past economic strength, and Peter felt it had been "slanted" by ICA to make the project look as promising as possible. Peter felt ICA glossed over the fact that any construction materials manufacturer was almost totally dependent on the Botswana Housing

Corporation for its revenues. The joint venture partners assumed the BHC would continue to purchase construction materials at historic rates, and no unexpected situation would interrupt its purchasing schedule.

Year-to-date revenues were about 20% of what had been forecast in the feasibility study for the first year of operation. Though the company had not been expected to make a profit for the first three years, it was also not expected to face bankruptcy. Peter's immediate problem was how to meet his monthly loan payments. If he could not make the payments, the bank could foreclose on the company, closing the factory permanently. The country of Botswana would lose a new industry and jobs for its citizens, the bank would lose the millions of pula already loaned to the company and the BDC and ICA would lose its investment in the joint venture. Given the present situation, Peter felt that he had only three workable options from which to choose:

1. Get the joint venture partners to invest more equity to pay the monthly expenses;

2. Ask the bank for an additional loan to keep the company solvent until sales increased; or

3. Close the factory permanently.

Peter reached for the telephone. He had three phone calls to make to plan his next steps. He faced a tough decision—with major consequences both here and abroad—and he needed to know the wishes and flexibility of the key parties involved: the Botswana Development Corporation in Gaborone, the Interkiln Corporation of America in Texas, and his wife across town.

CASE DISCUSSION QUESTIONS

1. Why does Botswana need a domestic brick industry?

2. What should the government's role be in creating housing?

3. Did ICA make a good decision getting involved in this joint venture? Did the BDC?

4. How did South Africa react to the creation of Lobatse Clay Works?

5. Should the joint venture have relied so heavily on a single buyer for such a large percentage of sales?

6. What are the implications for other foreign-owned companies seeking joint ventures in Botswana and elsewhere in the developing world?

7. What could Lobatse Clay Works have done differently to prevent the loss of market share?

8. What should Peter say to the BDC, ICA, and his wife? What would you do if you were Peter?

ENDNOTES

1 This case is intended as a basis for class discussion rather than to illustrate either effective or ineffective handling of an administrative situation. Special gratitude goes to Dr. Richard Linowes who was extremely helpful and patient in editing and critiquing this work.

Tecnomatix–A Global Entrepreneurial Company

by Tamar Almor*

College of Management, Israel

(www.tecnomatix.com)

Shlomo Dovrat, Tecnomatix's Chairman of the Board, stated recently: *"Our biggest challenge at the moment is how to get from being a $100M company to being a half a billion company."*

Tecnomatix, an Israel-based company founded in 1983, is a world leader in computer-aided production engineering (CAPE). Its products are used in the design, simulation, and programming of automated manufacturing systems for a variety of production processes. The company's products are sold to large customers in the automotive, aerospace, and manufacturing industries worldwide.

In February 1993 the company went public on NAS-DAQ to raise capital for expanding its marketing activities and developing new products. In 1994 Tecnomatix acquired the California-based Valisys Corporation, a key rival, for $2.3 million, thereby enlarging its existing product line. In addition, the firm agreed to a joint marketing and development effort with EDS-Unigraphics, a major computer-aided-design company, and Computervision to integrate their designs into some of Tecnomatix's software products. That same year the company created a joint venture with Japan-based Nihon I-Tec, called Nihon Tecnomatix K.K., to distribute the software in Japan and Korea.

In 1997 Aesop, a German company which develops software used to create simulations of production lines, was acquired. In addition, Tecnomatix acquired Part, a Dutch company, for half a million USD.

During 1998 the company decided to buy back part of its shares. Harel Beit-On, the company's President and Chief Executive Officer, commented:

> We believe that purchasing the company's shares at this time is a productive use of company funds, and reflects management's confidence in the company's prospects. The company's consolidated cash, cash equivalents, short term and long term investments as of March 31, 1998 amounted to approximately $146 million which allow the company to maintain flexibility in funding both its business and the repurchase of its shares.

"Clearly," Dovrat explained, *"Tecnomatix is at a crossroads. While it is enlarging its product line, entering new market segments, and new geographical markets, it is also investing in a new conception, coined "the digital factory." The question is if these various activities will allow the company to reach its goal and turn it into a truly dominant global player."* ■

COMPANY BACKGROUND

Tecnomatix was founded in 1983. It evolved from the software and machinery operations of Oshap Technologies Ltd., an Israeli company that manufactures and markets automation systems, medical machinery, heavy machines, and automated software. In February 1993 the company went public to raise capital for expanding its marketing activities and developing new products. The company and its shares are traded on NASDAQ (ticker: TCNOF); in August 1998 Oshap held 27% of Tecnomatix's stock.

Tecnomatix Technologies Ltd., situated in Herzliya Pituah, north of Tel Aviv (Israel), is a world leader in the market for computer-aided production engineering (CAPE) products. The company develops, markets and supports software tools that enable production engineers to create an on-screen virtual manufacturing environment, which graphically displays and simulates a complete manufacturing plant, its production lines, manufacturing equipment and processes.

Tecnomatix products enable production engineers to evaluate the feasibility of manufacturing newly designed products: to design, visualize, simulate and optimize automated and manual manufacturing systems; and to create and debug programs for robotic and inspection machines using virtual machine models.

The CAPE products allow manufacturers to accelerate the introduction of new products, reduce engineering and manufacturing costs, minimize production downtime and increase productivity and product quality.

For instance, it used to take Volvo, the Swedish car manufacturer, about two to three months to adapt the production line to a new product. During that period, no cars could be produced while engineers would install new tools and program the robots operating the production line. Recently Volvo introduced the S-90; setup of this production line took only 48 hours because the company was able to use Tecnomatix off-line technology.

Tecnomatix's success story is closely related to the story of Shlomo Dovrat, a successful entrepreneur and currently Chairman of the Board.

In the beginning of the 1980s Dovrat, a software engineer, met Oded Polig, an IDF pilot who had a lot of experience with flight simulators. Polig suggested to Dovrat developing a simulator for robots that would operate on the production floor. Dovrat, who already worked for Oshap, liked the idea and decided to develop it.

After an initial investment, the company decided to study the market potential of this technology. In 1983 they hired an American consultant by the name of "Yankee Group" who came to the conclusion that the technology's market potential was huge. First, although companies did not yet have the computer graphics enabling simulation of robots, both Sun Micro systems and Silicon Graphics, which were start-ups at the time, were trying to develop such technologies. Second, CAD/CAM (Computer-Aided Design and Computer-Aided Manufacturing) technologies, which existed since the early seventies and which formed the basis for the use of simulators as developed by Tecnomatix, were starting to become three-dimensional instead of two-dimensional—a prerequisite for the use of simulators.

Still, the people of Tecnomatix were not sure about their timing. It was clear that timing was of essence, but they did not want to be too early. At the beginning of the 1980s, 95% of all potential clients were still using two-dimensional CAD/CAM technologies, thus ruling them out as actual consumers. On the other hand, various potential competitors were working on competing technologies.

The automotive industry is well known for its prolific use of robotics in its production processes; therefore management decided to target that industry. In early 1985 Tecnomatix's management entered the market with a prototype technology, which was sold to G.M., a large American car manufacturer. The product that was still in its development stage deeply disappointed G.M.'s management, and soon it terminated its contract with Tecnomatix. This unsuccessful try-out taught Tecnomatix's management an important lesson. As Dovrat stated: "*When serving key accounts, be completely sure that your product is stable and working and not a premature demo version.*"

In the meantime, Oshap had acquired a failing company in Belgium. Dovrat was sent over to Belgium to turn the company around and re-organize it so that it would answer to Oshap's needs in Europe. Being situated in Western Europe, Shlomo Dovrat decided to seize the opportunity and create intensive relationships with German car manufacturers, who are well known for their use of robotics. Dovrat:

> We established contacts with Volkswagen, BMW, and Audi. In 1986 we already had marketing people situated in Germany, we had good business contacts and our product was ready. Together with our German clients we developed the product further. Especially BMW gave us extensive support. Our first sale to them was in fact not yet a product, but rather a project.
>
> Right from the beginning we concentrated on large customers, who could function as opinion makers. It was always clear to me that we would be market leaders; in order to establish yourself as a leader you have to work closely with the largest clients right from the beginning.

In 1985 Oshap was taken public and its shares were offered on NASDAQ. The Initial Public Offering (IPO) enabled the company to raise $6M. During that time Tecnomatix was still a department within Oshap, and its activities were developed through the Belgium subsidiary.

Dovrat:

> In my view it is very important to be close to our customers, because that is the only way to understand what is important to them. We quickly found out that simulation tools are important only when customers encounter very complex situations, which are relatively rare. Therefore they were not really interested in simulators for robots. What they really needed was a tool that would enable them to engage in off-line programming of the production floor. You see, it is not enough to discover a need; in order to get a customer interested in your product, you have to make sure that the customer has a compelling reason to buy your product.
>
> We discovered that in the automotive industry the production floor has to be flexible. One of the main problems the automotive industry has is how to achieve maximum flexibility and maximum efficiency simultaneously. In other words, how to change the production line in such a way that one can offer various product options to consumers and at the same time minimize down time, which is always required when one adapts its line to different product options.
>
> Thus we came to the conclusion that we have to redefine our strategy; instead of concentrating on simulators we should develop off line programming tools. Subsequently we started working on the US market. We approached Ford and they decided to try us out. This was a very important break through, because quite soon they required their suppliers to start working with our technology.

As a result of Tecnomatix's close relations with its large (potential) clients, CAPE (computer-aided production engineering) tools were developed. CAPE tools allow engineers to plan production lines, workstations, and equipment layout early in the engineering cycle, before tangible products are manufactured. CAPE tools enable the engineer to evaluate products before spending money on manufacturing equipment. CAPE tools are used immediately after a model of the product is available on the CAD system. In other words, CAPE fills the gap that exists between CAD and CAM technology.

When Tecnomatix developed CAPE, it was still a vision of the future; no comparable product existed at the time. In order to sell this technology, Tecnomatix had to educate the market and its consumers. It had to convince its customers of CAPE's importance and show them that it is not only an instrument to control production processes but more important, it is a product which enables production run planning.

THE PRODUCT MARKET

For more than several decades, the drive for automation has pushed manufacturers to invest billions of dollars in computer-aided design (CAD) systems for the design of their products, as well as in the development of highly automated robots and other computer-controlled equipment for the production floor, also named computer-aided manufacturing (CAM). While product design and actual production became well automated, production engineering—the process of planning the manufacturing line of a product, including the equipment and processes to be used—remained a manually operated stage of the production process. Tecnomatix pioneered the automation of this part of the production process, thereby freeing the bottleneck between design and production. Since its inception, Tecnomatix has invested approximately 1000 man-hours in the development of the CAPE technology dedicated to the automotive industry.

The niche in which Tecnomatix operates traditionally is the automotive industry that uses CAD/CAM technology. Tecnomatix is the industry leader with a market share of over 60%, in an industry with an estimated size of $100 million and a growth rate of 25 to 30%. The market potential is huge when taking into account that the CAD/CAM industry is worth about $7 billion and every manufacturing engineer will eventually need a CAPE system.

Two financial analysts expressed the following opinions regarding market size and market potential.

Abe Finkelstein of the Barington Capital Group:

By year-end 2000, we expect the CAPE market to reach nearly $250 million, and over time to become a billion-dollar market. Tecnomatix, as the clear market leader, is best positioned to reap the rewards of this growth.

Sheila B. Ennis of Ambrecht & Quist:

We believe the market for CAPE tools is experiencing an acceleration in demand as companies move from pilot projects to mainstream adoption and that Tecnomatix is uniquely poised to benefit from this trend.

Dassault is Tecnomatix's major competitor. Dassault Systemes, a French company established in 1981, is a worldwide leading software developer for the CAD/ CAM market. Its products provide users with both process-centric and design-centric solutions for their product development needs. At the end of 1987, Dassault Systemes had a turn-over of $314.8 M and a net loss of $18.6 M. In December that same year it acquired Deneb, Tecnomatix's direct competitor, situated in the US.

Founded in 1985, Deneb is a recognized supplier of digital manufacturing leading solutions. It provides a comprehensive family of software and technical support for customers to virtually define and simulate their manufacturing activities, involving human beings, robots and machine tools within the factory shop floor.

Deneb's product line competes heads on with Tecnomatix's ROBCAD software. Acquisition of Deneb by Dassault has created a situation that allows customers to have seamless access to digital product definition and tooling definition from digital manufacturing applications, thus avoiding data re-entry or transfer and increasing productivity. Bernard Chales, President of Dassault Systemes, stated:

Our mission is to enable customers to build their digital enterprise. Customers are looking for global and simultaneous optimization of product definition, manufacturing process definition and plant definition. We believe this acquisition accelerates our ability to fulfill customers' digital manufacturing needs and, more globally, their end-to-end digital enterprise integration requirements.

In addition, 3D systems, Intergraph and Parametric Technology compete with Tecnomatix indirectly. Parametric Technology, for instance, is a billion dollar company that specializes in CAD/CAM and computer-aided engineering software. Intergraph, similar in size to Parametric, makes computers, workstations and peripherals for mapping and computer-aided design applications in the transportation and utilities industries. Although the companies do not compete with Tecnomatix head on, they do represent potential future competition.

PRODUCTS, MARKETING AND SALES

At present Tecnomatix's line includes six products: ROBCAD, VALISYS, EXALINE, PART, DYNAMO and SIMPLE++ (for short descriptions of each product, see appendix 2). All products are geared to automate that part of the production process that is situated between the CAD stage and the shop floor. Its central product, Robcad, is very profitable and has provided the basis for the company to broaden its product line.

So far Tecnomatix has invested 1000 man-years in the development of its products. Although its first sales were projects rather than products, the company basically sells off-the-shelf products and does not manufacture custom-made products.

Products are marketed directly to the end user through Tecnomatix's sales offices. Tecnomatix has offices in Belgium, France, Germany, Israel, Italy, Japan, the UK and the US. Furthermore it has distributors in Australia, Japan, South Korea, and Sweden.

In 1998 the company employed about 60 salespeople, who are specialized in specific industries and types of customers. Tecnomatix's customers are mostly large, well known, international companies (see appendix 3) and include, among others, Mazda, Ford, Fiat, General Motors and Renault. According to Yochanan Slonim Executive Vice President Products:

> Our customers are large and very conservative. Usually we work together with top management who take their time to decide if they want to use a system developed and marketed by a small Israeli company. We invest many months building up a relationship with each client, before it results in a sale. As software such as ours is considered high added value to most of our clients, they invest time and money in negotiations. On the other hand, once the contract is signed, our customers are very loyal and remain with us for many years.

Indeed, according to Dovrat, about 75% of all sales are repeat sales to existing customers. Moreover, once a lead customer decides to adopt the product, it is possible to address second- and third-tier manufacturers.

The company operates worldwide and has sales offices in Europe, the US and Japan. Most products are sold in Europe and the USA; sales to the Far East represented 15% of all sales at the end of 1996 (see appendix 4).

Tecnomatix's marketing strategy is explained as follows by Dovrat:

> You see I believe that in order to succeed you have to find the compelling reason for clients to buy. Once you know what your customers really need you can start educating the market. As I see it that is the way of the future. What you should realize that in order to be a market leader, time to market is very important, not only for us but also for our customers. What we offer them is a product that enables them to reduce their time to market significantly.
>
> However, it is also important to realize that as Israelis we can only target the high-end market, developing and marketing strategic products. I am a great believer in direct sales; this creates a barrier to entry which is difficult for others to break. Over the years we have established very strong ties with our customers and we have always enlarged our sales capacity by establishing additional ties in various industries.
>
> Nowadays we have people who are specialized in the automotive industry; we have others who are specialized in the aviation industry. In Japan we have an international joint venture and we have sales offices around the world. This enables us to be a multi product and a multi marketing company. Although we started out in the automotive industry, we have invested in seeding in other industries during the years, and this strategy enables us to continue growing.
>
> We are visionaries who will approach early adopters; in time those early adopters will form the basis for a wider audience or an early majority, which eventually will turn into a mass market for our products. At present we have 60 marketing people. Their task is to reach the executives of the companies that we want to target and convince those executives that they have to re-engineer their engi-

neering process. One of the problems we are encountering at the moment is that one needs different types of marketing people to reach the early adopters and to reach the early majority. As we have just switched stages we have to change and add sales people who can work with the early majority.

Slonim:

> Tecnomatix believes in short marketing channels and markets its products directly to the end user. Therefore, its sales organization is central to the organization's success. Recruiting large, medium or small sized prospective clients usually requires a similar investment in terms of hours and resources. Therefore, Tecnomatix has always invested most in its largest prospective clients. The fact that Tecnomatix markets directly to the end user has helped the company to build a body of knowledge that is unique. This knowledge allows the company to push additional products and create synergies for the customer. Thus, for instance, before Valisys was acquired it had a turnover of approximately $3m, today it has a turnover of $10m.

So far Tecnomatix has been extremely successful in the CAPE niche that it developed. Part of this success can be explained by Dovrat's business philosophy:

> In order to make sure you are on the right way you have to focus, focus, and focus. Therefore it is better to concentrate on one thing which you do right, than on seven things at the same time.

However, once the automotive CAPE niche started to become saturated and the company reached the size of $17 to 20 M, management understood that it had to start enlarging the market, so it decided to enter the aviation industry. Recently the company has expanded its activities in the aerospace, shipbuilding, train manufacturing and heavy industries. Management believes that these industries will follow the growth pattern of the automotive sector; i.e., initial point applications will evolve into more comprehensive mainstream applications, and industry suppliers will jump on the bandwagon and repeat sales will accelerate.

Also, the company is trying to enlarge its customer base in the automotive industry by targeting the OEM manufacturers of that industry. In addition, it is developing its global reach. So far the company has been successful mainly in the Western European and the North American market. At present Tecnomatix is developing the Eastern European market, as well as the South American market.

The company wants to leverage its installed customer base. Dovrat:

> We believe that the level of penetration is still very low considering the market potential. Therefore we try to concentrate on repeat sales as well as on developing new industries. Our repeat sales used to be 80%, however since we started developing additional industries, it has declined to 75%. On the other hand, the volume of each sale has increased tremendously. For instance, in March

1997 we sold systems at the tune of $30M of which $25M were product sales and $5M consulting services, to Ford. This however creates a problem for us as a company that is traded on NASDAQ. Once you start selling large projects, your income peaks unevenly, which in turn affects quarterly profitability.

THE ORGANIZATION

The company grew out of a small group of people who were all graduates of the same unit in the Israeli Defense Forces. This basis was slowly extended, and different people joined. In 1998 the company employed approximately 470 people; of these about 200 were employed in research and development (R&D) and 60 in marketing. The majority of the work force is located in Israel, although this ratio changes with each acquisition.

Tecnomatix senior management team is located in Israel and consists of Harel Beit-On, President and CEO and three Executive VPs—Products & Marketing, Finance & Administration and Business Development (see appendix 6—organizational chart). Four General Managers, each of whom heads a product line, as well as the VP Corporate Marketing, fall under Yochanan Slonim. GMs responsible for the various geographical markets as well as Exaline's GM report directly to the President. Although the formal organizational structure is in place, the organizational culture encourages flexibility and an open door policy.

R&D

Tecnomatix invests about 30% of its revenues in R&D. R&D is located mainly in Israel, because of financial as well as human resources considerations. The Ministry of Industry and Trade extends loans up to 50% of an approved project to Israeli high-tech companies that market their products outside Israel; therefore Israeli companies have a high incentive to leave the bulk of their R&D activities in Israel, even when other functions become global. In addition to these loans Tecnomatix also receives funds from the BIRD Foundation. The mission of this institution is to further cooperation between Israeli and US companies in various high-tech areas. Joint projects between Israel and the US can receive loans and grants. Tecnomatix's R&D activities are funded partially by these two institutions (see appendix 5).

It has become increasingly problematic to hire experienced engineers in Israel over the last few years. Still, Tecnomatix is considered an attractive company, and it has relatively little problem hiring people. Employees are considered very important to the company's success, and much effort is invested in their wellbeing and the establishment of a common organizational culture. For instance, employees go on trips and vacations together, paid for by the company. The company does not have a mess hall, but it picks up the tab when employees have their lunch in any of the restaurants situated in the neighborhood. While at work employees can spend their time in one of the cafes situated nearby Tecnomatix to talk, read, work or think. Everybody is allowed to order as much professional lit-

erature as needed. Also, state-of-the-art technology is used in R&D operations. Many resources are invested in updating computers and hardware used for development. The fact that R&D is slowly decentralizing as a result of the new acquisitions, provides an additional attraction. R&D engineers travel the world, meet people from different cultures and cooperate with engineers from various countries.

Marketing and Sales

While R&D is mainly situated in Israel, marketing is spread all over the world. Tecnomatix's marketing people are based close to the consumer, who is mostly situated in the automotive and other manufacturing industries. According to Tecnomatix's view, one should employ marketing and salespeople who are geographically as well as culturally close to the consumer. Therefore it mainly hires local salespeople who live in proximity to the potential customers, in cities such as Detroit. Tecnomatix employs people in the Netherlands, Germany, France, Spain, the UK and Italy as well as in the US. Once a year Tecnomatix organizes a kick-off for its entire marketing workforce.

Although the marketing function is spread out over the world, Tecnomatix wants its employees to identify with the organization and its products. Management has set the following goal: a client who is in contact with different parts of the organization should feel that he operates in a familiar context, where all parts know each other. Therefore the company organizes worldwide get-togethers and other events, which allows employees to meet each other and get acquainted with the whole organization.

TECNOMATIX'S GROWTH STRATEGY

In early 1997 Tecnomatix's management decided to move out from niche solutions into mainstream implementations. Thus Tecnomatix has started to establish the CAPE market by selling its products to a variety of customers outside the automotive and aviation industry and by focusing on the Far East and building and expanding its presence in other emerging areas such as South America, Central Europe and Eastern Europe. As stated in its 1996 annual report:

> Manufacturers are experiencing increased pressures to reduce costs, to improve quality and of even greater importance, to shorten time to market. For example, an automotive company's goal is to bring the development of a new car model down from the average of 60 months, as it has been until now, to 24 months by the end of the century.

Time to market is a strategic issue in most industries. Nowadays most manufacturers grapple with ways to shorten their time to market. Taking into account that an extremely low level of automation currently characterizes production engineering; CAPE technology can provide answers for a host of industries.

In order to develop the market further, Tecnomatix is pursuing alliances with leading CAD/CAM suppliers. Recently it has announced two significant strategic alliances with two large CAD/CAM companies. Tecnomatix will work with both companies to coordinate more tightly integrated product solutions, which will enable the company to provide a better answer to its main competitor, Dassault Systemes.

Tecnomatix tries to leverage its installed customer base by selling complete systems. The firm has appointed a group of consultants who will audit a client and help the client to implement the CAPE technology. As a result, the company has entered a new stage in its organizational life with sales of tens of millions USD per project.

Also, the company is developing a product line that will address small and medium-size customers and OEM manufacturers. Yochanan Slonim, Executive VP Products:

> We are developing a line of small and relatively cheap products that do not need support and will be targeted at small and medium-sized firms. Recently we identified PTC, a company that operates in the CAD industry and addresses only small and medium-sized companies. PTC employs approximately 900 salespeople who make thousands of sales every year. The products they sell are designed in such a way that they do not need additional support. We hope to develop a similar model in the CAPE market and approach that same market segment. Clearly, companies that have acquired the CAD technology are potential CAPE consumers.

Implementation of such a strategy is not that simple. At present Tecnomatix has not yet developed a product line that will enable the company to enter this market segment; moreover, it also does not have the sales force to implement the strategy. Not only does Tecnomatix not have the amount of salespeople needed for such a strategy, but its salespeople are specialized in customers who are large market leaders, who view purchasing a Tecnomatix system as a strategic procurement. Selling smaller, stand alone systems to small and medium-sized companies will need a different concept and a completely different market strategy. Still Slonim thinks the strategy is viable:

> We believe that we will be able to overcome the various problems because we have a strong competitive advantage, we have a good reputation, a lot of business contacts and strong financial backing. We will have to hire a lot of additional sales people, but overall our sales organization is strong and efficient and we are confident that we can manage such a large group.

As a start, the company hired about 20 new salespeople during the latter part of 1997 who are dedicated to the development of new markets.

Dovrat, however, is cautious:

> My major concern is that we are too quick bringing out new products that fit the line of our vision. We have reached an inflection point, and we have to consider carefully how to extend our basis without upsetting it.

THE DIGITAL FACTORY

In addition to the strategies presented, Tecnomatix is investing resources in the development of a "Digital Factory" concept. A digital factory means that a full simulation can be presented of all production processes starting from imaging of the planning process and ending with a full image of the production floor and the various processes taking place. The Tecnomatix Digital Factory will provide a set of software tools and methodologies that supports the development of manufacturing and assembly processes from the concept of a product to its actual production. The Tecnomatix Digital Factory is an integrated, computerized environment for designing, simulating and optimizing a complete factory, its production lines and processes, in all levels of detail.

Tecnomatix is developing its ability to design a complete "Digital Factory" through acquisitions. Shlomo Dovrat states:

> During 1997 we acquired the German Aesop. This company specializes in software that enables clients to simulate processes of a whole factory. Aesop specializes in simulations of processes, models that show how materials flow through a production process. It is a good technology which allows us to develop our vision further, where engineers will be able to plan a digital factory and simulate the whole thing before it is actually built. In other words, the whole production line is first planned at a holistic virtual level and only then implemented. This is a big step forward, because today these decisions are made at a detailed level, without understanding the process as a whole. The product we are developing will enable optimization of the digital factory by becoming a depository and a database from the whole factory. At present we have a demo which is shown to future customers, which we use to educate the market. You see, we are about eight steps further than our clients are; therefore we have to invest a lot of resources in market education.

The Digital Factory allows customers to concentrate on "time to customer" as well as "time to market." While "time to market" concerns new products, "time to customer" addresses the major issue of the existing product and the company's main business process. Companies find themselves competing on the time it takes them to bring their existing product to the customer. This process may take a long time because of the use of different data bases during the planning and the production processes.

Harel Beit-On, President and CEO:

> Delivering our expanded Digital Factory vision and creating a true Enterprise Manufacturing Solution is our primary R&D focus and we are very pleased with the positive feedback we have received from our customers.

Establishing a Digital Factory means creating a central data repository, which will allow for a much more efficient supply chain within the production process. Currently, the supply chain management market is estimated $3 to 4 million but eventually it will grow to approximately $2 billion. A central data repository will also allow for clear measurement of performance, and comparisons between production lines and systems. Eventually the Digital Factory will allow a company to manage its maintenance, logistics, floor management, production optimization, quality problems tracking and quality management automatically through its central data repository.

ACQUISITIONS AND GLOBAL MANAGEMENT

Tecnomatix's management believes that in order to implement its growth strategy it will have to rely on internal development as well as on acquisitions. As Shlomo Dovrat states:

> We would like to grow through acquisitions. In August 1996 we were able to raise $150M on Wall Street. Now we are looking for firms that are attractive to us to acquire. We already have an established market presence, and now we are looking to acquire firms that have products which will enlarge our product line.

Yigal Livne, Executive VP Business Development, observes that

Tecnomatix is looking for acquisitions that fit its business philosophy and strategy. Basically, we want to build a monolithic, coherent global business, by acquiring small successful companies that can supplement our product line. We are interested in companies that have a turnover up to $10 million, or compare to us at a 1:5 ratio. They should have a working product, a proven sales record and a good management team that can become an integral part of Tecnomatix. Their P&L and growth rate should be similar to Tecnomatix', so integration of the new acquisition will not hurt our EPS ratio.

Its acquisition strategy is forcing Tecnomatix to become a truly global player that has R&D centers spread over various continents, clients worldwide and a global sales force. For a small Israel-based company that has succeeded so far by being a niche player, this is not a small feat. Still, in a report published recently by Lehman Brothers the following recommendation could be found:

> Given indications of a healthy new business pipeline and the progress Tecnomatix is making in some of its newer markets we believe that there is upside to our estimates which call for a 22% increase in revenues in 1998 and a 38% increase in 1999.

APPENDIX 1

Financial data in thousands of dollars

Consolidated Statements of Operations

	1997	1996	1995	1994
Revenues:				
Software and system sales	41,533	32,495	24,812	16,721
Maintenance and engineering services	17,508	12,030	8,564	6,724
Total revenues	59,041	44,525	33,376	23,445
Cost of revenues:				
Software and systems sales	3,626	4,580	4,672	3,041
Maintenance and engineering services	3,114	1,947	1,006	935
Total cost of revenues	6,740	6,527	5,678	3,976
Gross profit	52,301	37,998	27,698	19,469
Gross R&D costs	16,565	13,210	10,510	8,334
Less—participation	2,728	2,031	1,578	1,555
Software and development costs capitalized	3,587	2,861	2,723	2,776
R&D costs, net	10,280	8,318	6,209	4,003
Selling expenses	26,593	19,812	14,618	10,545
General and Administrative expenses	4,283	3,250	2,952	2,419
Charge for purchased R&D	9,571	—	—	4,011
Write off goodwill		—	—	495
Operating profit (loss)	1,574	6,618	3,919	(2,004)
Financial income	3,378	2,046	784	394
Income (loss) before taxes on income	4,952	8,664	4,703	(1,610)
Income tax benefit	(1,687)	(435)	(24)	620
Income (loss) after taxes on income	3,265	8,229	4,679	(990)
Minority interest in net income of subsidiary	(93)	(267)	—	—
Share in income (loss) of joint venture operation	—	28	(192)	(143)
Net income (loss)	3,172	7,990	4,487	(1,133)
Earnings per share	0.32	0.82	0.55	(0.14)
Weighted average number of shares outstanding	10,711,793	9,694,326	8,173,200	7,950,355

Consolidated Balance Sheets
Financial data in thousands of dollars

	1997	1996	1995
Assets			
Current Assets			
Cash and cash equivalents	11,326	12,818	9,880
Short term investments	75,125	42,966	10,934
Receivables:			
Trade	20,960	12,844	10,915
Related parties	511	623	648
Other and prepaid expenses	6,937	3,715	3,018
Inventories	—	5	112
	114,859	**72,971**	**35,507**
Non current receivables	327	231	139
Long-term investments	61,000	—	—
Property and equipment			
Cost	15,469	11,328	9,098
Less-accumulated depreciation and amortization	8,439	6,351	5,170
	7,030	**4,977**	**3,928**
Other assets, net	13,005	8,559	7,232
Total assets	**196,221**	**86,738**	**46,806**

	1997	1996	1995
Liabilities and shareholders' equity			
Current liabilities			
Short term credits	—	973	500
Payables:			
Trade	2,738	1,423	1,673
Related parties	—	66	70
Other an accrued expenses	17,213	9,506	5,536
	19,951	**11,968**	**7,779**
Share in losses of joint venture company in excess of investment	—	—	306
Accrued severance pay	1,339	1,163	836
5 1/4% convertible subordinated notes	97,750	—	—
Minority interest	243	150	—
Commitments and contingent liabilities			
Shareholders' equity			
Share capital:			
Ordinary shares issued and outstanding	35	35	29
Additional paid in capital	58,596	56,711	28,874
Foreign currency translation adjustment	(1,121)	371	780
Unrealized gains (losses) on marketable securities	3	87	(61)
Retained earnings	19,425	16,253	8,263
	76,938	**73,457**	**37,885**
Total liabilities and shareholders' equity	**196,221**	**86,738**	**46,806**

APPENDIX 2
Description of product line

ROBCAD is a set of computer-aided production engineering (CAPE) tools for design, simulation, optimization and off-line programming of automated and manual manufacturing systems. ROBCAD improves quality, cuts cycle time, prevents design errors and ensures that the virtual manufacturing system that you see on the computer screen is what you will get on the production floor. ROBCAD provides seamless integration with multiple CAD systems, enabling production engineers to access and work on the master models residing in the CAD system while designing manufacturing processes.

VALISYS is a set of software tools to define, predict, measure and analyze tolerances throughout the industrial process. VALISYS helps ensure that tolerances are correctly specified during the design phase and fully adhered to during the manufacturing and assembly processes. At every stage of the industrial process, the broad range of VALISYS tools provides a dedicated solution to minimize variations, reduce engineering changes and help ensure that parts are manufactured according to the designer's intent.

EXALINE computer-aided process-engineering (CAPE) software tools provide a virtual manufacturing environment for electronics manufacturers. EXALINE graphically simulates assembly-line stations, including the printed circuit board itself. Powerful algorithms, called Machine Experts, analyze the components on each circuit board, balance the workload between assembly machines, and optimize the assembly sequence of individual machines in the production line.

PART automatically delivers the best process plan to manufacture parts based on cutting tools, machines and machining methods existing in your company and contained in the system's database. Each step of the process is planned automatically and can be reviewed or modified before proceeding to the next. PART improves machining efficiency by allowing you to attach manufacturing tolerance information to the geometric model. These tolerances determine the accuracy needed for machining and are a key factor in selecting the best machines and cutting tools to do the job.

DYNAMO, the dynamic digital mock-up software, enables users to catch design errors and to anticipate manufacturing process constraints before the product leaves the design room. DYNAMO is seamlessly integrated with major CAD systems and accesses the master product data without need for translation or duplication.

SIMPLE++ for planning, simulation and optimization of manufacturing plants, production systems and processes. The software helps you to develop optimal solutions for all levels of plant planning including global production facilities, local plants, and lines. The SIMPLE++ scalable plant model and simulation capabilities enable you to evaluate different scenarios and make fast and reliable decisions on relocation or closure of a plant. SIMPLE++ enables you to optimize the layout, capacity and performance of a local plant. The software's object-oriented technology enables you to create well-structured hierarchical models that take into account the external and internal supply chain, production resources and all aspects of production and business processes. Finally, you can design and verify the control and synchronization of components of each line or job shop, testing different strategies in order to optimize throughput. Real-time communication capabilities facilitate integration with enterprise information systems such as CAD, CAPE, and ERP.

APPENDIX 3
Tecnomatix Selected Customers

Automotive

BMW, Chrysler, Fiat, Ford, General Motors, Honda, Mazda, Mercedes Benz, Mitsubishi, Nissan Body, PSA, Renault, Rover, Saab, Subaru, Toyota, Volkswagen, Volvo

Aerospace

Aerospatiale, Boeing, European Space Agency, General Electric, Lockheed, McDonnell Douglas, Pratt & Whitney

Utilities

Electricite de France, Siemens, Westinghouse

Heavy industry

Caterpillar, J.I. Case, John Deere, Fuji heavy industries, Gec Alsthom, Giat, Komatsu, Mannesman, Mitsubishi heavy industries, Hyundai shipyards

Robotics & engineering companies

Abb Robotics, Classic Design, Comau, Efficient Engineering, Fanuc, J.S. McNamara, Kuka, Nachi robotics, Wisne design, Yaskawa

Electronics

Alcatel, Motorola, Tellabs, Telrad, U.S. Robotics

APPENDIX 4

Classification of total revenues by geographical distribution (in $thousands)

Year ended	1994	1995	1996
Europe	10,346	19,486	22,615
USA	12,136	12,323	15,317
Far East	818	1,544	6,508
Israel	145	23	85
Total revenues	23,445	33,276	44,525

APPENDIX 5

Research and development participation (in $thousands)

Year ended	1996	1995	1994
AIT	192	—	—
BIRD-F	192	28	64
The Government of Israel	1,647	1,550	1,491
Total R&D participation	2,031	1,578	1,555
Gross R&D expenses	13,210	10,510	8,334

APPENDIX 6
Tecnomatix's organizational chart

CASE DISCUSSION QUESTIONS

1. What is the core competence of Tecnomatix? Discuss.

2. Evaluate the growth strategy of Tecnomatix. Are there any elements of it that worry you? Discuss.

3. Critique the marketing strategy of Tecnomatix. Are there any elements of it that you would change?

4. Can you recommend any other prospective growth strategies that Tecnomatix does not seem to be pursuing?

BP–MOBIL and the Restructuring of the Oil Refining Industry

by Karel Cool,
Jeffrey Reuer,
Ian Montgomery,
and Francesca Gee*

*Insead

This case is intended to be used as a basis for classroom discussion rather than to illustrate either effective or ineffective handling of an administrative situation.

On February 29 1996, British Petroleum (BP) and Mobil surprised investors and competitors with an unexpected announcement: after six months of secret talks, the two oil companies had agreed to merge their refining and retail sales operations in a pan European joint venture.

The move was a new approach to confronting long-standing problems in the European oil market. In refining, international companies had been confronted with low returns, excess capacity and high exit costs; in retail, competition was heating up, especially from a new category of players: supermarkets. For years, major players had practiced increasingly stringent cost cutting. Yet, none had attempted anything as ambitious as Mobil and BP.

When presenting the deal, Mobil and BP stressed their shared focus on financial performance and discipline and said that the combination provided an excellent fit in terms of geographic spread and quality of assets, which would give them leadership in key markets. By pooling their US$5 billion in European assets, BP and Mobil figured they could save US$400–500m a year. They said their combined market share in Europe would amount to 12% in fuels, hard on the heels of market leaders Exxon and Shell, and 18% in lubricants.

While oil industry analysts praised BP and Mobil for acting decisively, they also expressed some doubts about the joint venture. Was an alliance the best response to the industry's troubles at a time when other players were leaving the market altogether? "It's an original deal," said an investment banker, "but it puts them right in the middle: they are not niche players but they are not the leaders either. I wonder whether they are quite big enough." To reap the dramatic savings they were announcing, Mobil and BP would have to close down more refineries and petrol stations and lay off thousands—an unpopular move in unemployment-stricken Europe. ■

THE OIL INDUSTRY VALUE CHAIN

Oil was the world's main source of energy. Its end products were used in a variety of ways: transport by land, water and air (petrol,[1] diesel, jet propulsion fuels), heating (heating oil), lubricants (mainly in rolling mills, car engines, machinery and precision instruments), building materials (asphalt), and so on. About 12% of crude oil was converted into plastics and synthetic fibers. Crude oils varied substantially in look, composition, density and flow properties due to their different formation conditions. Crude from Libya and Algeria, for instance, was thin-bodied and yellowish with virtually no sulphur content. Venezuelan heavy oils, by contrast, were viscous, almost solid and dark black in color with a lot of sulphur. Normal petroleum products could be made from all oils but good crude (thin-bodied, low-sulphur) was easier to refine.

Upstream Operations

Upstream operations, the generic name for all activities related to crude oil before refining, included exploration and production. Oil was found in underground reservoirs, surrounded by rock formations which geologists studied to identify the presence of oil. They used increasingly sophisticated and expensive tools, from surface mapping and aerial surveys to seismic soundings. Advanced drilling techniques had made it possible to explore new areas such as the seabed of the Gulf of Mexico and the North Sea. Exploratory wells could reach 2,500 meters below the surface of the ocean. By 1996, world production averaged 65m barrels per day (bpd).[2] While the world's largest oil fields were in the Middle East, part of production had moved to the North Sea and the Americas, the result of a switch to politically safer areas.

After a series of nationalizations, mostly in the 1970s, the upstream industry became dominated by major producers which owned most of the world's proven reserves. Aramco of Saudi Arabia was the biggest; other important players were Petroleos de Venezuela, Pemex of Mexico, the Kuwait Petroleum Company and Statoil of Norway. Exhibit 1 shows their share in world production.

Downstream Operations

Downstream included transportation and storage of crude oil, processing, refining and marketing of final products to customers. Refining (described in Exhibit 2) essentially breaks down crude into various components which are then reconfigured into new products. While refineries could handle different qualities of crude and produce various end products, the more sophisticated refineries were better able to upgrade crude into high-value products. Though the product mix could not be changed completely, the way plants were configured and the quality of crude afforded some flexibility.

Global refining capacity in 1996 stood at 78m bpd. Refining was carried out in about 700 refineries which were evenly distributed between North America, Europe, Asia and the rest of the world. The average capacity was 100,000 bpd.[3] Most of these plants had been planned before the 1973 oil shock when demand had been expected to grow almost indefinitely. Opening a new refinery took a long time and cost billions of dollars. Running it was comparatively inexpensive, but closing it down entailed substantial clean-up costs (estimated to be as high as US$100m) and redundancy costs. For these reasons, owners usually operated existing plants, even in a situation of overcapacity. Exhibit 3 shows the worldwide trend in refining.

Exhibit 1
Distribution of control of world oil production and refining

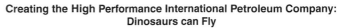

Creating the High Performance International Petroleum Company: Dinosaurs can Fly

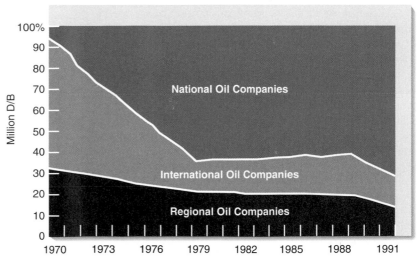

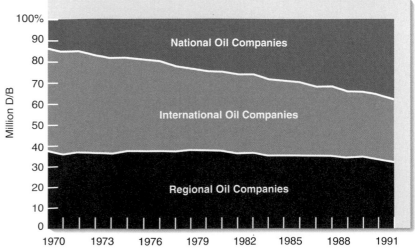

Source: Booz-Allen & Hamilton ("Dinosaurs can Fly")

Exhibit 2
Refining processes
and product flows

	Input	Intermediate	Output
Products	Crude oil	Kerosene, naphtha, gas oils, distillate	Gasoline, distillate, jet fuel, liquefied petroleum gas (LPG) and residuals
Processes	Crude distillation	Coker, hydrotreater, catalytic cracker, alkylation, hydrocracker, reformer	Distribution and retailing

In marketing, the largest volumes sold were petrol at the pump. Initially, service stations had been operated by large oil companies and by small independent operators. Lately, large out-of-town supermarkets had been joining the fray. Profitability was determined by the number and location of service stations and by supply logistics. Oil companies also offered specific services to industrial customers, supplies of jet fuel and bunkering (marine fuels, diesel oil and gas oil). These were usually delivered directly from the refinery.

Large integrated companies were dominating downstream operations. These included Shell, BP, Texaco, Gulf, Exxon, Mobil and Chevron. The last three had been formed after an antitrust decision to break up John D. Rockefeller's Standard Oil in 1911. These giant multinationals engaged in all aspects of the oil and gas business, from exploration and production to refining and marketing. Exhibit 4 shows their relative position in terms of reserves, output and sales.

Customer Demand

Historically, the main driver of demand for oil had been the rate of economic growth. Demand also followed an annual cycle, peaking during the Northern Hemisphere's winter and falling in summer, and stood at about 65m bpd in 1996. The global oil market was still growing, albeit at a slower pace than in the 1960s and 1970s. After World War II, demand had surged from 10m bpd in 1945 to 60m bpd in 1970. This had encouraged exploration, which soon unveiled large, accessible reserves in the Middle East.

The oil shock caused by OPEC's embargo in 1973–1974 and the second shock in 1979 wrought such havoc to Western economies that governments embarked on long-term programs to reduce oil dependence. Coal, liquefied natural gas and nuclear power were developed as substitutes; energy conservation and efficiency gains were encouraged. (Exhibit 5 shows the expected shift away from oil until 2005; Exhibit 6 shows fuel sav-

Exhibit 3
World refining capacity

Region	1980	1993	1994	1995	1996(est.)
Western Europe	1,000.0	704.5	706.7	701.4	704.1
Middle East	205.8	255.0	266.2	264.8	269.8
Africa	107.4	145.9	144.2	144.1	145.3
North America	1,025.0	851.1	861.3	860.1	864.2
Latin America	436.3	375.4	367.8	371.0	372.6
Far East	572.0	682.9	720.9	740.2	814.3
Eastern Europe and FSU	769.7	642.3	642.6	636.6	632.5
Total	4,116.2	3,657.1	3,709.7	3,718.2	3,802.8

millions of tonnes

Source: Union Francaise des Industries Petrolieres (Bilan 1996)

Exhibit 4

Relative positions of large companies at various stages of the oil industry value chain

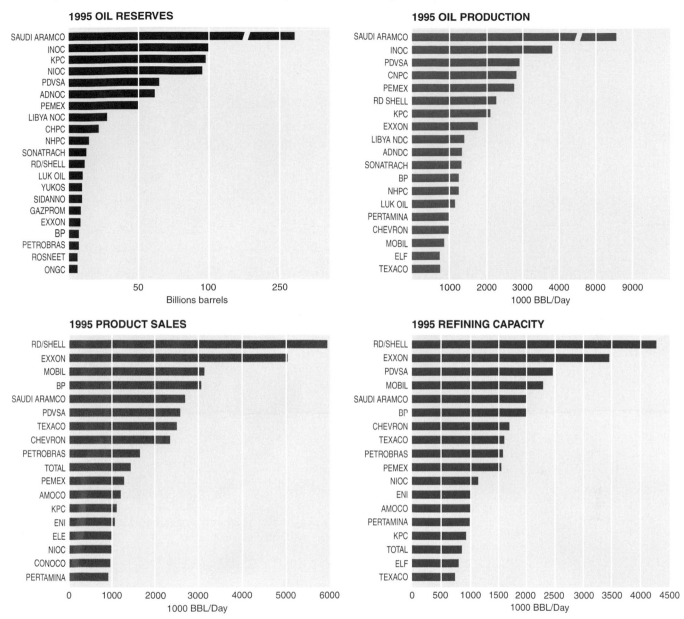

Source: National statistics, oil company annual reports

ings achieved by car manufacturers.) The result was that between 1978 and 1985, oil's share of the total energy market in industrial countries fell to 43% from 53%.

The oil shocks, government programs and the cyclical nature of demand caused wide swings in oil prices. After the 1973 shock, the price per barrel increased from US$2.9 in the summer to US$11.65 in December. By 1979, it had shot up to US$34.

In 1985, OPEC stopped protecting its prices to regain demand. The bellwether West Texas Intermediate futures contract immediately lost two-thirds of its value to trade below US$10. Internal conflict within OPEC and cheating on quotas led to overproduction. While more volatility ensued, prices stabilized in the mid-1990s within a US$15–18 range. Exhibit 7 plots spot prices in the 1990s.

Exhibit 5
European energy market
(existing and projected)

1995

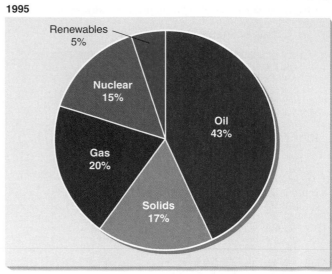

2005

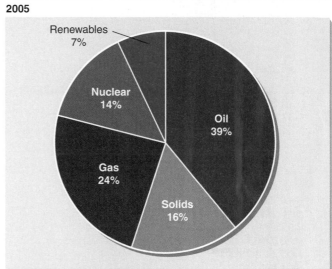

Source: Internal Marakon Analysis

Exhibit 6
Increase in automobile
fuel efficiency

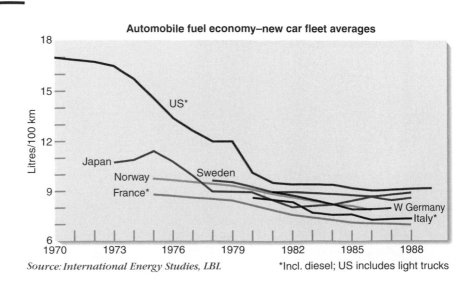

Automobile fuel economy—new car fleet averages

Source: International Energy Studies, LBL   *Incl. diesel; US includes light trucks

Exhibit 7
World-wide and European refining capacity and demand (throughput)

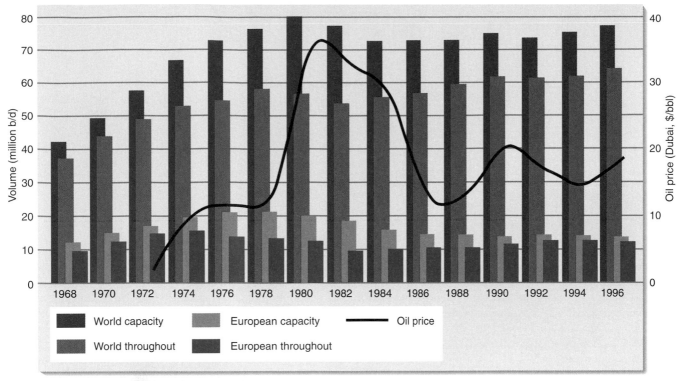

Source: BP Statistical Review of World Energy 1997

THE EUROPEAN DOWNSTREAM INDUSTRY

Refining

In recession-hit Europe in the mid-1990s, demand was nearly flat, with growth forecasts of 0.5% p.a. until 2005. The market was depressed by fuel efficiency gains, higher duties and taxes (which governments often justified on environmental grounds) and increased supplies of nuclear power and natural gas. This stagnation was in stark contrast with the optimistic development programs prior to 1973 when demand had been expected to grow exponentially. Because of the long lead times for planning and building refineries, new plants had come onstream, resulting in significant overcapacity in some parts of Europe. Exhibit 8 shows margins during the 1990s.

High exit costs as well as governments' industrial and employment policies were often blamed for the industry's failure to tackle overcapacity. There was also fragmented ownership of firms. The European refining industry had a mix of state-owned, integrated and independent companies. In most national markets, up to a dozen of these companies shared half the total capacity.

Exhibit 8
European refining margins

Dollar margin on a barrel of Complex NWE Brent						
	1991	1992	1993	1994	1995	1996
Quarter 1	6.28	2.2	1.81	2.17	1.35	1.56
Quarter 2	3.37	1.92	2.26	1.43	1.67	1.75
Quarter 3	2.88	1.94	2.34	1.74	1.64	
Quarter 4	−2.89	1.92	2.4	1.67	1.46	

Source: Woods Mackenzie

Exhibit 9
European refining margins
and utilisation

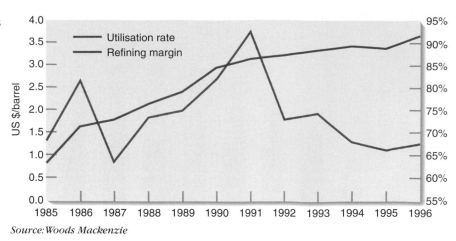

Source: Woods Mackenzie

Overcapacity was also exacerbated by productivity improvements. Until 1991, capacity utilization and margins had grown in parallel, but this was no longer true, as Exhibit 9 shows. Demanding new regulations, often dictated by environmental concerns, had resulted in capacity creep. As margins declined, all producers were working to incrementally increase their capacity. Exhibit 10 shows capacity utilization for major European oil companies.

The problem of overcapacity was aggravated by mismatches between the configuration of refineries (which had been planned for heavy Middle East crude) and actual supplies (often, lighter North Sea oil). Demand for diesel had also grown much faster than expected, so that many refineries operating at capacity for diesel had spare capacity for petrol. Demand for fuel oil had also declined as supplies of natural gas became available. Exhibit 11 shows changes in the European demand mix.

Although oil companies generally aggregated into their published accounts their refining and marketing results, it was known that refining was far less profitable than marketing. Geographic differences in refining margins persisted. Margins had been higher in Asia where refining units were larger and yielded greater market power. In Europe, they were lower than in the United States where cheap prices for divested plants had enabled independent refiners to acquire assets which they operated at about 15% return on capital (Tosco, for instance, had bought refineries and retail sites from both Exxon and BP). More lenient environmental laws, a flexible labor market, less price competition in a more consolidated industry and the absence of direct central government control also helped make U.S. downstream players more profitable than European ones.

Beyond these concerns, the European downstream industry was bracing itself for a huge bill following the European Commission's 1993 Auto-Oil program which aimed at reducing levels of urban atmospheric pollution by the year 2010. The industry would probably need huge investments to improve the quality of diesel and petrol. This was likely to cost the industry a total of US$16b over a 15-year period.

Marketing

Some 300 billion liters of petrol and other retail products were sold every year in Western Europe. The leaders, Shell and Exxon, each had about 12% market share. There were some 120,000 service stations operated by the major integrated companies, su-

Exhibit 10
Refining capacity
utilization rate

European refiners utilisation rate				
	1993	1994	1995	1996
Agip	78%	79%	74%	75%
Exxon	86%	84%	79%	89%
Repsol	86%	87%	87%	84%
Shell	100%	100%	98%	102%
Total	89%	94%	90%	104%
BP-Mobil	95%	92%	99%	94%
European average	86%	88%	88%	91%

Source: Woods Mackenzie

Exhibit 11
Demand mix

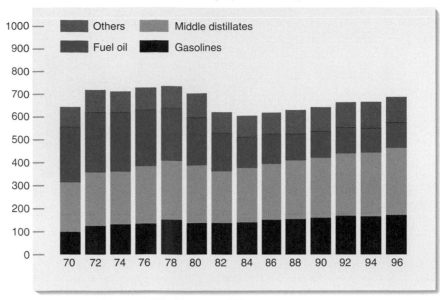

Regional consumption
OECD Europe (million tonnes)

Source: *BP statistical Review of World Energy 1997*
Note: "Middle distillates" refers to diesel.

permarkets and independent retailers. Their number was falling rapidly (as shown in Exhibit 12). In France, there were 18,000 petrol stations left, compared with 47,000 in 1976, and a further 5,500 were expected to close. Germany too had 18,000, down from a peak of 46,700. In the UK, their number was forecast to fall below 10,000 by 2005, from 16,000 in 1996.

The Western European market was characterized by weak brands and by changes in distribution channels where supermarkets increasingly displaced small dealer networks while integrated companies and national players were trying to turn ser-

vice station forecourts into convenience stores. (Exhibits 13 to 20 describe various characteristics of national markets.) Petrol was increasingly perceived as a commodity product with gross sales margins of 2 to 4%.

Consumers bought mainly on convenience (proximity) and price. Even the "majors" now competed on price. Brands remained weak and undifferentiated despite efforts to build them up: independent surveys showed that brand value, measured by the additional margin compared with an unbranded product, was minimal.

Exhibit 12
The trend in petrol retailing sites

	Average Number of Retail Sites			
	United Kingdom	**Germany**	**France**	**Benelux**
1987	20197	20751	31100	15510
1988	20016	20198	29000	15150
1989	19756	19802	27700	14699
1990	19465	19351	25700	13937
1991	19247	18898	23700	13211
1992	18549	18836	21700	12668
1993	17969	18464	20000	11820
1994	16971	18300	19013	11022
1995	16244	17957	18406	10490
1996	14748	17660	17974	10030

Source: Woods Mackenzie

Exhibit 13
Comparative average
throughput per site (1995)

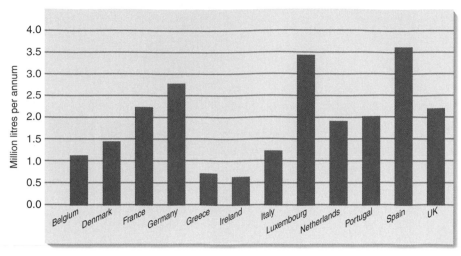

Source: Woods Mackenzie

The weakness of brands had favored the entry and growth of supermarkets. Huge shopping centers had sprung up near major cities and enjoyed many advantages. They had acres of free parking, and customers had become used to visiting them every week. Filling up was just part of "one-stop shopping." In 1996 their market share was already high in France (over 50%), the UK (over 20%) and Germany.

The average supermarket service station sold much more fuel than other service stations. In Britain, for example, the 664 supermarket stations had 20% of the whole market. As "bulk" buyers, they could negotiate lower prices for supplies. They could also take advantage of imbalances between supply and demand in their region. As a result, the supermarkets often paid lower wholesale prices than the integrated oil companies' own marketing divisions.

Supermarkets also seemed to operate on smaller margins than traditional service stations. Competitors grumbled that supermarkets didn't hesitate to sell at a loss in order to capture market share. In fact, French supermarkets had increased their prices as soon as they had established a degree of market power. While the growth of out-of-town supermarkets seemed to have peaked in the UK and France, it continued in Germany and Italy and was only starting up in Spain, Portugal and Ireland.

Independent retailers who could no longer compete went out of business. Other retailers tried to rise to the challenge: they consolidated their networks, keeping only the more profitable locations, and engaged in price wars. Others tried to turn old rivals into allies, opening their own branded outlets on supermarket premises. This was Repsol's strategy in Spain with El Corte and Shell's in the Netherlands with Ahold.

Exhibit 14
Retail petrol margins

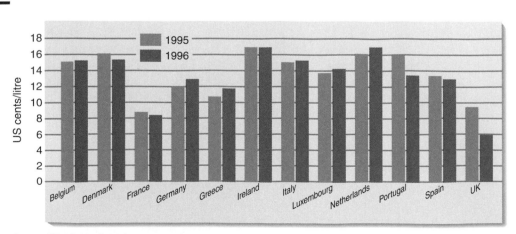

Source: Woods Mackenzie

Exhibit 15
Retail diesel margins

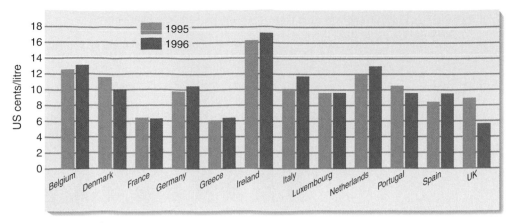

Source: Woods Mackenzie

Another strategy was to develop convenience stores in existing service stations. Taking advantage of long opening hours and dedicated car parks, these new "corner shops" offered goods and services such as cigarettes, newspapers, food and drinks, automated bank tellers, fax, photocopiers, post office, lottery and photo shops, reducing the dependence of retailers on petrol sales. It was hoped that, in the longer term, forecourts would become shopping areas in their own right, maybe in partnership with established food retailers.

Opportunities in Eastern Europe

The stagnation of the Western European retail market was encouraging oil companies to look east. The collapse of Communism in 1989 had left a dilapidated infrastructure and limited distribution networks, but upbeat forecasts for economic growth suggested that the downstream oil market would grow quickly. Oil companies could enter this new market in two ways. First, existing oil assets could be purchased at bargain-basement rates. However, their low prices often reflected poor quality and under-investment; cleaning up the sites and meeting potential environmental liabilities could turn out to be enormously costly. Second, firms could build new refineries and retail networks. This was less uncertain, but it would take a long time and be hugely expensive. While these risks had made investment slower than expected, all the integrated oil companies had plans for Eastern Europe, with Shell, Exxon and Total leading the pack.

Exhibit 16
Comparative total gross
margin per site (1995)

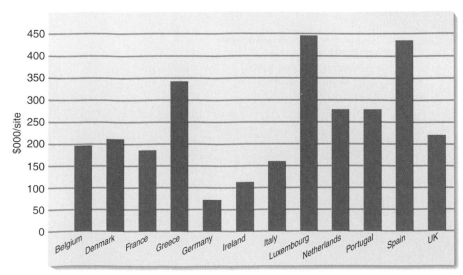

Source: Woods Mackenzie

Exhibit 17
Comparison of European countries—selected variables

Number of petrol stations and sales per station by country

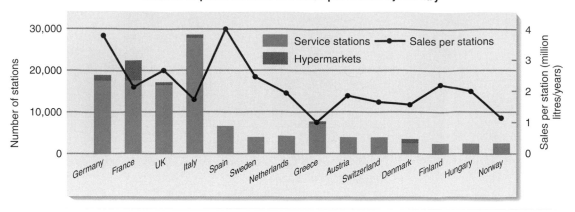

Market demand by country and fuel type

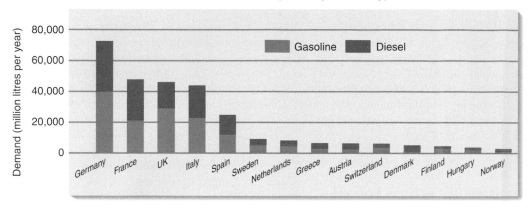

Source: Petroleum Review June 1997/UFIP/national oil industry associations

Exhibit 18
The economics of selling petrol across Europe

		Refining Net Profitability Analysis		
	United Kingdom	Italy	Germany	France
Retails costs				
Distribution	0.8	23.5	2.2	8
Advertising and promotion	0.5	15	1.4	4.5
Other marketing	1.3	33.5	3.4	11.5
Retail site costs	3.4	66	8.5	19
Retail revenue				
Unit margin	6.2	223	17.8	43
Non-fuel sources	1.5	12	4.3	4.5
	pence/litre	lire/litre	pfenning/litre	centimes/litre

Source: Woods Mackenzie

Exhibit 19
Market share data

| | Estimated Overall Market Share (1996) | | | | |
	United Kingdom	Italy	Germany	France	Benelux
Exxon	16%	10%	11%	11%	16%
Shell	16%	3%	13%	12%	19%
Total	5%	n/a	2%	21%	6%
Elf	3%	n/a	6%	21%	n/a
Agip	n/a	19%	2%	1%	n/a

Source: Woods Mackenzie

Exhibit 20
Western European oil consumption (1987–1996)

	1987	1988	1989	1990	1991	1992	1993	1994	1995	1996
Austria	9,359	9,145	8,948	9,489	10,158	9,913	9,984	10,074	10,136	10,816
Belgium	17,486	17,788	17,205	17,022	18,559	19,240	18,656	19,188	18,884	21,262
Denmark	8,997	8,351	7,898	7,704	7,879	7,648	7,665	8,100	7,847	8,128
Finland	9,810	9,561	9,410	9,371	9,058	8,786	8,541	8,913	8,664	8,960
France	77,528	77,616	80,518	79,636	84,124	84,337	82,718	82,984	84,234	85,871
Germany	120,020	120,172	112,954	117,617	125,062	126,134	127,451	126,102	126,210	128,358
Greece	10,351	10,948	11,379	11,328	12,133	12,190	12,072	12,541	13,273	14,212
Ireland	3,895	3,675	3,715	4,199	4,419	4,678	4,655	5,112	5,266	5,454
Italy	82,842	82,126	85,593	85,412	84,224	85,686	83,841	84,279	86,865	85,694
Luxembourg	1,285	1,316	1,450	1,585	1,848	1,897	1,892	1,884	1,736	1,808
Netherlands	17,902	18,680	18,293	17,537	18,038	17,840	16,923	17,365	18,264	17,295
Portugal	8,208	8,566	10,993	10,776	10,940	12,192	11,475	11,335	12,267	11,841
Spain	36,415	41,060	41,063	40,672	40,570	41,882	44,997	48,504	50,613	49,272
Sweden	15,032	16,119	15,122	13,735	13,941	14,570	14,161	15,058	15,330	17,719
United Kingdom	67,703	72,316	73,029	73,941	74,507	75,472	75,790	74,957	73,836	75,241
EU total	486,833	497,439	497,570	500,024	515,460	522,465	520,821	526,396	533,425	541,931
Iceland	608	596	538	540	565	561	718	729	731	780
Norway	7,402	7,087	6,909	6,737	6,599	6,560	6,147	6,407	6,442	7,171
Switzerland	12,211	12,247	11,774	12,612	12,790	12,969	12,117	12,508	11,577	11,923
Turkey	20,387	20,436	20,763	21,326	20,905	22,020	25,412	24,016	26,725	27,889
Western Europe total	527,441	537,805	537,554	541,239	556,319	564,575	565,215	570,056	578,900	589,694

Thousands of metric tonnes
Source: National statistics

BP AND MOBIL'S COMPETITORS IN EUROPE

Historically, integrated companies had been able to mitigate the impact of price variations as upstream and downstream hedged each other's risk. High crude prices which depressed downstream results, so the reasoning went, boosted upstream profits. Low oil prices supposedly had the opposite effect. However, from the mid-1980s, profitability fell both upstream (with lower crude prices) and downstream, where overcapacity and flat demand eroded margins.

Faced with these various challenges, downstream companies had taken steps to restructure, often in alliance with competitors. Overall, however, restructuring in Europe had remained less ambitious than in North America. The European players tended to only sell or swap assets. Their profitability was also lower as illustrated in Exhibit 21.

Exhibit 21
Comparative Financial Data

	ROACE (91–96)	ROE (91–96)	Average NI (91–96)	Average CAPEX (91–96)	Average Market Cap (91–96)	Average P/E (91–96)	Price to Book (91–96)	Net Income 1996	Balance Sheet 1996	
British Petroleum	6.8%	8.2%	1501	5092	38,378	15.4	2.1	3,025	12,914	(£ mln)
Mobil	8.6%	10.2%	1823	4288	34,886	21.7	2.0	3,043	19,118	(£ mln)
Royal Dutch/Shell	20.6%	10.7%	6028	9848	100,752	18.1	1.8	5,591	39,299	(£ mln)
Exxon	12.1%	15.4%	5788	7081	87849	15.3	2.3	6,975	45,456	($ mln)
Agip	6.9%	9.1%	1289	874	34,487	12.1	2.2	4,829	27,407	(LIT bn)
Elf	4.3%	4.6%	744	4167	19,592	24.0	1.3	7,518	99,709	(FF mln)
Total	7.0%	7.7%	713	2028	12,918	20.4	1.3	4,795	61,479	(FF mln)
Repsol	13.9%	15.7%	769	1332	8,967	12.1	1.9	120,932	986,886	(Ptas mln)
Norsk Hydro	8.4%	11.1%	548	1182	7681	1.9	1.7	6,991	42,808	(NKR mln)
Tosco	8.3%	7.5%	60	123	4127	34.9	6.1	146	1070	($ mln)
Lyondell	26.2%	61.9%	167	342	1858	37.4	4.1	96	1040	($ mln)
			($mln)	($mln)	($mln)					

Royal Dutch/Shell

Royal Dutch/Shell, the European market leader, had been founded in 1907 by merging a British and a Dutch group in order to counter the dominance of Standard Oil. With time, the group had become one of the world's largest corporations. Its operations in over 100 countries covered exploration and production of oil and natural gas, refining, marketing and chemicals, as well as coal mining, polymers, crop protection products and various metals.

In Europe, Shell was the second largest refiner after Exxon, with annual capacity of 70m tons and sales of 65m tons. In marketing, it had been the leader with a 12% market share and 8,500 retail sites. After the 1990–1991 Gulf War, Shell had found itself with large inventories just as prices fell. The drop in profits had prompted a round of internal restructuring that had left analysts generally unimpressed. In 1996 Shell was planning to sell its Swiss refinery, close down lubricant plants and reduce its retail workforce.

An early mover into Central and Eastern Europe, Shell had formed a joint venture with Agip and Conoco to take a 49% stake in two Czech refineries. In 1996, it had swapped 38 of its sites in western Germany for 44 Total sites in eastern Germany. It had also invested in some smaller markets such as Romania, Bulgaria and Slovenia.

Two recent public relation crises had damaged Shell's image. In 1995, it was forced to shelve plans to dump its used Brent Spar oil installation into the North Sea after vocal complaints led by Greenpeace and consumer boycotts orchestrated across Germany and the rest of Europe. And when Nigeria executed a leading dissident, human rights campaigners accused Shell of supporting a military dictatorship in contempt of minority rights.

Exxon

Exxon, the former Standard Oil of New Jersey (Esso), was the world's largest oil company in terms of revenue. After many of its Middle Eastern oil fields and facilities had been nationalized, Exxon had aggressively expanded exploration and production in safer regions in the 1980s. It suffered a major setback in 1989 when the *Exxon Valdez* tanker ran aground in Alaska, spilling 11m gallons of oil. The initial clean-up bill was US$3.6b, with a lawsuit seeking US$16.5b in compensatory and punitive damages still pending.

In Europe, Exxon had a retail market share of about 11%. It had cut back on refining investments and was focusing on reducing costs. In refining, the size and integration of its assets gave it a cost advantage. In marketing, it had started a fierce price war in Britain with its "Price Watch" campaign, which promised to match any competitor's prices within five kilometers.

Eastern Europe was a major area of new investment for Exxon. It had formed marketing joint ventures in Hungary (with state company AFOR) and in Poland (with a German partner). By 1996, 35 Esso stations were operating in Hungary, Poland, the Czech Republic and Slovakia.

National Companies

Agip, the leading Italian integrated oil company, was part of the ENI Group. It had production and downstream activities in 13 countries and downstream activities only in a further 13 countries. However, most of its refining and marketing operations were in Italy (which accounted for 41% of 1995 sales). Agip's strategy was to maintain a strong presence in the attractive Italian market while gradually expanding elsewhere in Europe. In Italy, it wanted to increase return on capital by reducing excess capacity in refining and by closing down less profitable retail sites.

Elf Aquitaine, France's largest industrial company, had been formed in 1965 by merging several small state companies. It was gradually being privatized; the government still had a 13.3% stake. Elf was a diversified conglomerate with interests in health and hygiene products and was refocusing on oil. Under a new chief executive, explicit goals had been set in terms of cost savings, debt reduction and return on capital; non-core assets were sold, resulting in a US$1b net loss for 1994 from write-downs. Its new strategy was to focus on the upstream business, limiting downstream operations to France, Spain and Germany where Elf had a strong position. There were plans to leave the British market. Elf was expanding in eastern Europe, although with mixed success. A joint venture with a Russian consortium and German public authorities to acquire 1,000 petrol stations in eastern Germany had proven expensive and unprofitable, and Elf now wanted to sell.

Repsol, Spain's largest industrial company, had a 60% share of the domestic oil market. The government, which had formed Repsol in 1987 to consolidate the fragmented Spanish oil industry, retained a 10% stake. The company was expanding its natural gas business through acquisitions, mostly, but not solely, in Spain. Repsol's strategy was to defend its domestic position while expanding natural gas exploration and production. Targets for international expansion included Latin America as well as Portugal, southern France and northern Africa.

Total, Europe's fourth largest oil and gas producer, had over 10,000 retail stations across the continent. It was quoted on the New York Stock Exchange. Yet the French government retained a 5% stake. The company had invested aggressively upstream in exploration, especially in the former Soviet Union. Efforts to restore downstream profitability had included cost cutting and selling off less profitable assets (e.g., refineries in Portugal and the Czech Republic were sold in 1995). In France, competition from the supermarkets had hurt profitability, prompting the company to trim retailing costs and to launch an aggressive effort to regain market share.

Total wanted to expand in high growth regions such as Central and Eastern Europe, Portugal and Turkey, with a focus on marketing and distributing motor fuel. Total had invested FF 700m in Hungary and the Czech Republic between 1992 and 1994. A joint venture with Benzina, owned by the Czech government, had been disappointing in terms of sites and mar-

ket share. In Hungary, Total had 25% of the LPG market after acquiring two marketing companies, Egaz and Kogaz, in 1993.

BP AND MOBIL

British Petroleum

One of the world's largest petroleum and petrochemicals groups, BP had operations in some 70 countries, more than 56,000 employees and annual revenues of US$79b. It had been fully privatized in 1987 when the British government sold its 51% stake and had gradually become more diversified and decentralized.

Upstream, BP focused on oil exploration, with production facilities in Alaska, the Gulf of Mexico, Colombia and the North Sea. (Exhibit 22 summarizes BP's upstream activities.) Downstream, BP had a weak position in the United States. Aggressive restructuring and asset disposals had not quite solved the problem of high costs and asset quality.

The company, however, had forced the admiration of industry watchers by staging a remarkable recovery under the successive CEOs David Simon and John Browne. In 1992, an unprecedented quarterly loss had caused it to nearly default on interest payments. Afterward, BP increased earnings to US$3.2b (from US$900m), while the share price had more than doubled (see Exhibit 22 for an overview of cumulative returns). By 1995, dividend payments were back above their 1992 level. (Exhibits 23 and 24 give financial data.) Analysts expected financial improvement to continue until at least the year 2000, thanks to higher output (by 5% p.a. on average) and a better product mix.

BP was seen as a leader in cutting costs: it had halved its total workforce to 56,500 in 1995 from 111,900 four years

Exhibit 22
Shareholder returns

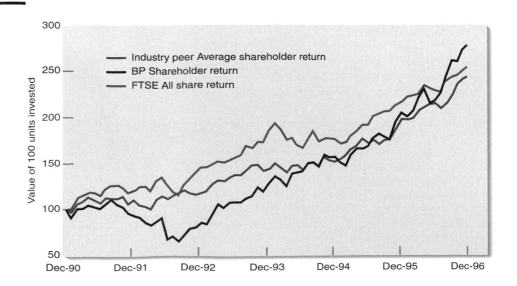

Exhibit 23
British petroleum earnings summary

	1991	1992	1993	1994	1995	1996E
Exploration & Production						
UK	870	795	1086	1527	1492	1636
Rest of Europe	423	483	399	257	330	304
US	1673	1607	1277	920	1251	1246
Rest of World	54	91	123	169	386	437
Total	3020	2976	2885	2873	3459	3623
Refining and Marketing						
UK	115	−132	36	119	92	13
Rest of Europe	407	175	245	189	−22	280
US	211	2	270	173	43	250
Rest of World	586	416	582	509	528	591
Total	1319	461	1133	990	641	1134
Chemicals						
US	−19	64	26	35	216	175
Non-US	76	−106	−128	350	−216	750
Total	57	−42	−102	385	0	925
Other & Corporate	−199	−60	−164	−79	−61	−13
Replacement cost operating profit	4197	3335	3752	4169	4039	5669
Gain/(loss) from asset sales	428	124	−60	55	−5	−11
Restructuring costs	−103	−1884	−300	0	−1525	0
Inventory gain/(loss)	−1113	−187	−426	95	4	95
Historical cost operating profit	3409	1388	2966	4319	2513	5753
Interest expense	−1280	−1190	−1013	−829	−787	−600
Pre-tax income	2129	198	1953	3490	1726	5153
Income tax	−1451	−1000	−1027	−1059	−1310	−1476
Minority interest	57	−9	−7	−18	8	−20
Historical cost income	735	−811	919	2413	424	3657
Exploration & Production						
US capital employed	7639	7237	7064	7017	7124	7480
US adjusted earnings	931	883	682	546	828	674
Foreign capital employed	11199	9912	9787	10594	11502	12422
Foreign adjusted earnings	843	784	969	1042	1322	1441
Refining and Marketing						
US capital employed	3697	3482	2802	2775	1571	1602
US adjusted earnings	139	1	176	112	59	162
Foreign capital employed	6317	5784	5476	5947	5663	5890
Foreign adjusted earnings	720	308	578	577	553	592

All numbers are in millions of dollars
Source: Merrill Lynch (1996)

("BP and Mobil—Similar in Size but Different in the Way They Are," Merrill Lynch 1996)

earlier. The company also sought greater efficiency through consolidation, re-organization and optimization of storage and logistics. In refining, its strategy was to sell or close unprofitable refineries, upgrade others and generally improve operating reliability. It had recently spent £171m on a five-year, worldwide re-branding effort, with mixed success.

Europe was BP's main market with 48% of refinery capacity and 49% of sales. The company had downstream operations in 18 countries. It employed some 15,500 people, including 4,000 service station staff, and owned wholly or in part eight European refineries with combined capacity of 760,000 bpd (the planned sale of the Lavera plant in southern France would reduce this to 575,000 bpd). BP and partner Texaco had also announced the closure of their Pernis refinery and the consolidation of their joint refining at BP's Europort plant in Holland. (Exhibit 25 has data on BP's refineries.)

Exhibit 24
BP refining and marketing profitability

	1992	1993	1994	1995	1996	Average
Net profit after tax (£ million)						
Refining	20	180	6	−68	194	66.4
Marketing	240	575	640	474	485	482.8
Total	260	755	646	406	679	549.2
Operating capital (£ million)						
Total	6,137	5,593	5,591	4,637	5,137	5,419
Refining	53%	56%	61%	54%	43%	53.4%
Marketing	47%	44%	39%	46%	57%	46.6%
Return on average capital employed (ROACE)						
Refining	0.6%	5.6%	0.2%	−2.3%	8.2%	2.5%
Maketing	8.3%	21.5%	27.6%	22.0%	19.2%	19.7%
Total	4.2%	12.9%	11.6%	7.9%	13.9%	10.1%

Source: BP Financial and Operating Information 1992–1996

BP sold 825,000 bpd of oil products through 5,600 retail sites. Its market share, 8% in both fuels and lubricants, had been steady for years. Exhibit 26 shows BP's market performance. In marketing, its two-pronged strategy was to upgrade facilities at prime retail sites to improve petrol throughput and increase non-fuel revenue and to pursue expansion in eastern Europe where it planned to quadruple its 100 service stations. In the last two years, BP had sold 90 service stations in southwestern France to Repsol, 60 other French sites to PetroFina and eight Austrian sites to Shell. In the UK, it had acquired independent fuel distributor Charringtons.

BP's success in cost cutting had spawned imitators and had not produced notable gains in its market share. Analysts believed that European oil companies (including BP) had cut "all the fat and some of the muscle" and doubted whether any further cost reductions were possible.

Exhibit 25
Summary BP downstream activity

Crude oil sources and sales					
Crude oil sources (i)	**thousand barrels per day**				
	1991	1992	1993	1994	1995
Produced from own reserves (ii)					
UK	359	364	370	429	403
Rest of Europe	81	87	88	81	69
USA	738	688	627	605	572
Rest of World	37	23	32	32	56
	1,215	1,162	1,117	1,147	1,100
Produced from associated undertakings					
Abu Dhabi	141	131	125	118	113
Total Production	1,356	1,293	1,242	1,265	1,213
Purchased					
USA	358	427	568	572	728
Rest of World	1,474	2,016	2,087	2,434	2,648
	1,832	2,443	2,655	3,006	3,376
Total	3,188	3,736	3,897	4,271	4,589

(i) Crude oil in respect of which royalty is taken in cash is shown as a purchase: royalty oil taken in kind
   is excluded from both production and purchased oil
(ii) Oil production includes natural gas liquids and condensate

continued

Crude oil sales	thousand barrels per day				
	1991	1992	1993	1994	1995
UK	1,167	1,301	1,378	1,860	2,004
Rest of Europe	40	88	82	90	116
USA	391	479	497	534	693
Rest of World	27	33	30	15	24
Total	1,625	1,901	1,987	2,499	2,837

Refinery throughputs and utilization

Refinery Throughputs(i)	thousand barrels per day				
	1991	1992	1993	1994	1995
UK	194	185	184	183	193
Rest of Europe	525	570	617	593	661
USA	701	711	717	621	713
Rest of World	297	307	327	339	332
	1,717	1,773	1,845	1,736	1,899
For BP by others	21	13	11	9	10
Total	1,738	1,786	1,856	1,745	1,909
Crude distillation capacity at 31 December	2,066	2,020	1,963	2,004	2,000
Crude distillation capacity utilisation (ii)	90%	94%	97%	94%	104%

(i) Includes actual crude oil and other feedstock input both for BP and third parties
(ii) Crude distillation capacity utilisation is defined as the percentage utilisation of capacity per calendar day over the year after making allowance for average annual shutdowns at BP refineries (net rated capacity)

Crude oil input	thousand barrels per day				
	1991	1992	1993	1994	1995
Low sulphur crude	69%	62%	63%	72%	71%
High sulphur crude	31%	38%	37%	28%	29%

Refinery yield (i)	thousand barrels per day				
	1991	1992	1993	1994	1995
Aviation fuels	171	186	184	192	194
Gasolines	659	712	676	668	704
Middle distillates	530	549	603	574	548
Fuel oil	220	245	282	214	215
Other products	212	218	230	196	286
Total	1,792	1,910	1,975	1,844	1,947

(i) Refinery yields exceed throughputs because of volumetric expansion

Mobil

Mobil, founded as Standard Oil of New York, was the world's third largest oil company after Exxon and Shell. It operated in over 100 countries with 50,000 employees and annual revenues of US$73b; it owned 21 refineries and 28 tankers and shared ownership in over 36,000 miles of pipeline. Its response to the 1970s oil shock had been to diversify. This had culminated in the acquisition of the Montgomery Ward department stores. Mobil later sold that business to concentrate once more on oil.

The company had worldwide earnings of US$2.9b in 1995, nearly double the 1992 level of US$1.5b. It had not suffered as badly as BP from the Gulf War, but its performance had not improved as dramatically either. Analysts saw potential for more cost-cutting and increased production. Exhibit 27 summarizes Mobil's financial results.

Upstream, Mobil was a major player in both oil and natural gas. Output, which had dropped in 1994, was expected to increase 2 to 3% annually in the medium term. A significant share of Mobil's revenue came from international exploration and production in Indonesia, Qatar, Nigeria, the North Sea and Canada where it had a share in the Hibernia offshore oilfield.

Mobil had a strong downstream position in the United States, especially in terms of market share and retail network. It was the world's leader in finished lubricants, with large market share in all regions. As part of its global strategy, Mobil had made considerable R&D investments in lubricants, and it was recognized as a quality brand in this business.

In Europe, Mobil's downstream operations had remained relatively weak despite extensive rationalization. Analysts wondered whether it would have to leave the market. Mobil owned,

Exhibit 26
BP's pre-alliance market share

	Estimated Market Share					
	1991	**1992**	**1993**	**1994**	**1995**	**Rank**
Benelux	21.1%	12.2%	12.0%	12.3%	12.6%	4
France	7.8%	8.1%	8.0%	8.5%	8.0%	5
Germany	8.2%	8.6%	8.5%	8.8%	8.8%	6
Italy						
Spain/Portugal	8.4%	8.1%	6.9%	6.9%	6.7%	3
UK	12.5%	12.0%	11.9%	11.5%	11.5%	3
Ireland	12.6%					
Austria	9.4%	8.9%	9.1%	9.2%	9.3%	4
Switzerland	13.5%	13.1%	12.4%	18.0%	18.6%	2
Denmark						
Norway						
Sweden	7.1%	2.6%	2.0%	0.1%	0.1%	
Finland						
Greece	12.8%	13.2%	13.4%	13.0%	13.5%	1
Turkey	8.0%	8.0%	8.0%	8.1%	8.1%	

Source: Woods Mackenzie

Exhibit 27
Mobil earnings summary

	1991	**1992**	**1993**	**1994**	**1995**	**1996E**
US Petroleum						
Exploration & Production	189	348	363	125	−107	444
Refining & Marketing	116	−145	151	241	226	448
Total	305	203	514	366	119	892
Foreign Petroleum						
Exploration & Production	1094	1042	1289	951	952	1150
Refining & Marketing	819	329	554	−33	447	846
Total	1913	1371	1843	918	1399	1996
Total Petroleum	2218	1574	2357	1284	1518	2888
Chemicals	217	136	44	102	1164	375
Financing	−385	−316	−127	−209	−295	−240
Other & Corporate	−130	−86	−190	−98	−11	−150
Accounting changes	0	−446	0	0	0	0
Net Income	1920	862	2084	1079	2376	2873
Exploration & Production						
US capital employed	6443	5670	4925	4420	4035	4116
US adjusted earnings	189	423	432	306	332	444
Foreign capital employed	3760	3621	3836	4076	4474	4832
Foreign adjusted earnings	1045	1066	1098	1018	1065	1150
Refining and Marketing						
US capital employed	4705	5286	5071	5155	5128	5231
US adjusted earnings	212	−17	296	273	330	448
Foreign capital employed	7362	7193	7464	7356	7770	8159
Foreign adjusted earnings	805	370	792	681	805	846

All numbers are in millions of dollars
Source: Merrill Lynch (1996)

("BP and Mobil—Similar in Size but Different in the Way They Are," Merrill Lynch 1996)

Exhibit 28
Mobil's pre-alliance market share

	Estimated Market Share					
	1991	**1992**	**1993**	**1994**	**1995**	**Rank**
Benelux	2.3%	2.2%	2.2%	2.3%	2.9%	8
France	5.5%	5.3%	4.5%	4.6%	4.3%	6
Germany	7.1%	7.4%	7.5%	7.3%	7.1%	7
Italy						
Spain/Portugal	2.2%	2.0%	2.1%	2.8%	2.6%	6
UK	5.0%	5.2%	4.9%	5.2%	5.3%	6
Ireland						
Austria	12.0%	12.4%	12.2%	13.0%	12.9%	3
Switzerland	2.7%	2.8%	2.8%	2.6%	2.0%	8
Denmark						
Norway	6.6%	3.1%	0.1%	0.1%	0.1%	
Sweden						
Finland						
Greece	11.9%	12.2%	11.2%	11.1%	11.4%	3
Turkey	10.9%	10.8%	12.6%	12.9%	12.6%	3

Source: Woods Mackenzie

wholly or in part, six European refineries with capacity of 350,000 bpd (about 16% of its total capacity) but was planning to close its Woerthe plant in Germany. It made 25% of its sales in Europe where its market share in fuels was only 4%. In lubricants, however, it had 10% share. (Exhibit 28 has details.) In 1996, Mobil's 8,000 workforce sold 550,000 bpd of oil products. About 2,000 service station staff operated 3,300 service stations in 22 European countries. In the last two years, Mobil had swapped 18 of its French service stations for eight Repsol stations in southern Spain.

In Germany, Mobil did not sell any retail fuels under its own brand, but it was a major supplier to Aral, a joint venture with German group Veba Oel in which Mobil had a 28% stake. Aral, which had by far the largest network of service stations in Germany, with a 20% market share, had been one of the first German retailers to open convenience stores. It was energetically expanding non-fuel retailing and considered selling McDonald's hamburgers. For some products, however, and in other countries, Mobil competed with Aral.

The Alliance

Discussions between Mobil and BP had begun in the summer of 1995; lawyers had become involved in October. The two companies had decided to form a partnership, with no changes in ownership of assets or equity. Setting up a traditional joint venture would have taken much longer because of the complex business of valuing assets, technologies and trademarks. Both BP and Mobil were familiar with using partnerships in their upstream activities.

The partnership would operate refineries, buy crude oil and other feedstocks for these refineries, refine and convert downstream products such as lubricants and market them, both to retail and to industrial and commercial customers, in western and eastern Europe (including west Russia) as well as in Turkey and Cyprus. The deal did not extend to international operations such as exploration and production, international trading, basic research and development. Aviation fuels and lubricants, marine fuels and lubricants and shipping, as well as natural gas marketing and chemicals, were also excluded.

In each country, Mobil and BP would combine their fuel and lubricant businesses through two separate partnerships, one for fuels, one for lubricants. BP would operate the fuels business as a whole, while Mobil would operate the lubricants business. All 8,000 service stations in the combined network would be re-branded with BP colors. They would display the alliance's logo and distribute Mobil oils. [Exhibit 29 omitted.]

BP as Fuels Operator and Mobil as Lubricants Operator would be controlled by a Supervisory Committee that would approve business plans, major acquisitions, closures, disposals and investments and oversee the national Fuels and Lubricants partnerships. BP and Mobil would have the power to veto any of the Committee's decisions. Exhibit 30 shows the alliance's organizational design.

BP and Mobil would have different equity stakes in each business: in fuels, BP would have 70% and Mobil 30%; in lubricants, Mobil would hold 51% and BP 49%. This reflected the value of the two partners' assets in February 1996 as well as their strength and expertise across Europe. Profits and losses in each partnership would be shared in the same proportion as the firms' equity stakes. If either partner contributed less assets than the agreed ratio in a given country, it would have to bridge the gap through cash.

BP and Mobil would hand over all relevant fuels and lubricants assets to the joint venture (including 10 refineries, terminals, retail sites, pipelines and truck fleets). BP would transfer its lubricants activities to Mobil, and Mobil would transfer its fuels activities to BP. Even though the ownership of assets would not be transferred, the joint venture would enjoy indef-

Exhibit 30
Structure of the BP-Mobil alliance

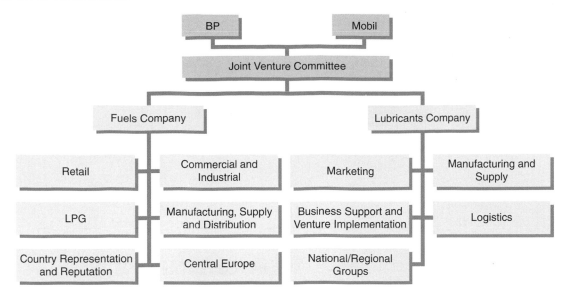

inite and exclusive use of those assets. Employees would transfer from one company to the other where appropriate. Central services (such as IT, human resources, legal and accounting management) would be merged under BP management. The new structure was expected to be fully implemented by mid-1998.

The Expected Benefits

The alliance would have US$5b assets (US$3.4b from BP) and sales of US$20b, with an estimated 12% market share in fuel retail (10% according to the European Commission) and 18% in lubricants. Combining the two retail networks would lead to redundant sites which could be sold without affecting overall sales volume. This and other asset disposals would produce one-off revenues of US$200m. However, this one-off benefit would be more than offset by exceptional charges to cover the costs of the alliance in its first year (US$490m for BP and US$330m for Mobil). The deal was also expected to produce annual savings of US$400-US$500m (most would come in the five largest markets) from three main sources:

Eliminating Duplication (60% of Expected Savings)

Most of the savings would come from operating as one business instead of two. This included operating a single accounting organization and computer system. In refining, BP and Mobil would consolidate their portfolio, selling assets where there was a clear overlap in capacity (this was the case for three refineries in Bavaria, among others), a move that would maximize capacity utilization. Both companies had found it difficult to find buyers for individual refineries in the past, but they hoped that a range of assets would be easier to sell.

Synergies (25%)

These would arise from the complementarity of the two partners' downstream organizations. In terms of geography, a bigger network of stations with the right spread across Europe would cut distribution costs. In the UK for instance, Mobil's network in the south of England complemented BP's strong presence in Scotland. In terms of product range, BP's strength in fuels complemented Mobil's leadership in lubricants. Duplicated storage and distribution facilities would be eliminated. The alliance would manage fuel storage at a pan-European level, ensuring a better balance relative to demand and reducing dependence on expensive external storage.

Thousands of jobs across Europe were earmarked for cuts, many from closing down overlapping service stations. In particular, between 2,000 and 3,000 non-service station jobs (out of a total 17,500) would be cut. BP and Mobil were already the industry's cost leaders in petrol retailing; they had built increasingly large self-service stations, and their combined network had lower costs than the small operators. Many competitors (especially national companies like Total, Elf, Agip and Repsol) were thought to be unable to match those cuts: their governments, opposed to lay-offs and fearing to lose control of a "strategic" industry, were unlikely to let them merge or enter cost-cutting alliances.

Scale (15%)

More refineries spread across major markets would reduce high transport costs to the retail site (shown in Exhibit 31). In many cases, this would obviate the need to buy from competitors.[4] In the United Kingdom, BP had been forced to buy from other refiners because its refinery at Grangemouth, in Scotland, was too

Exhibit 31
Transportation costs of petrol

Transportation	Cost
German rail	$4.34 per mt + $0.034 per km per mt
Polish rail	$2.38 per mt + $0.028 per km per mt
German road	$0.046 per km per mt
Czech pipe	$0.02 per km per mt
United Kingdom pipeline	$0.013 to $0.02 per km per mt
Rhine barge	$0.022 to $0.04 per km per mt

Mt = metric tonne
Source: BP

far from its retail network concentrated in the south of England. The alliance would now source from Mobil's refinery at Coryton. In France, the situation was similar: BP's refinery at Lavera served southern France and the Mediterranean market, but most of its petrol stations were in the Paris area. This forced it to buy from competitors. The alliance could use Mobil's refinery at Gravenchon to supply the Paris region. If buying from competitors was still necessary, at least BP and Mobil would have a stronger hand to negotiate.

The alliance could deliver better logistics, streamlined management processes, more efficient procurement and economies of scale, which BP saw as vital in the downstream industry. Together, Mobil and BP would be able to compete on prices with the largest European players. In particular, greater power in procurement, especially in lubricants packaging and non-fuel retail site supplies, was an obvious benefit.

Beyond Cash Savings

The two partners also expected other advantages from combining their operations. "The key issue is competitive performance," said John Browne, CEO of BP. "BP and Mobil were number three and four in the European market; now we will be up there with the big players." Together, they would be able to enter new markets, especially in Central and Eastern Europe. They would achieve economies of scale in investment and logistics to enter these attractive markets. They would be in a better position to buy privatized companies, since governments favored large investors.

A larger distribution network would also help attract food-retailing partners in new forecourt convenience stores and be better able to counter the supermarkets' negotiating power. Additional capacity to implement environmental investments would also be welcome. Finally, a wider geographic spread would make the joint venture less vulnerable to cyclical downturns as market conditions differed across Europe. For example, a strong, diversified pan-European player would be less affected by price wars in the UK or domineering supermarkets in France. Size was seen as an important advantage since it could smooth out some of the competitive conditions across Europe.

THE UNCERTAIN FUTURE

Analysts' initial reaction to the deal was largely favorable. Most saw the alliance as an innovative response to the industry's problems; they underlined the advantages in terms of market power and brand power as well as the complementary of the two businesses. Both partners would gain from the deal: BP would be able to cut costs further and continue its expansion. For Mobil, it was an opportunity to re-affirm its position in the European market. "The sub-text of this BP-Mobil deal is that you need a 10% market share to survive in the European market," commented investment bank Morgan Stanley.

But there were some negative interpretations as well. In a sense, the alliance was an admission of failure: BP and Mobil were acknowledging their inability to achieve economies of scale on their own. Since neither could grow big enough and neither wanted to leave the market, they had to compromise. Another concern was that the deal still left Mobil and BP in a middle position, stuck between the national players (each strong in its own domestic market) and overall leaders Shell and Exxon. Some analysts also questioned the extent of possible synergies, considering that the two companies were not a perfect fit. "A merger isn't a catch-all solution for the industry's fundamental problems," said one. "When you combine weak resources and low quality assets, you do not make a strong company."

While BP and Mobil had deliberately avoided an acquisition, the partnership still raised governance issues. Both partners had to give up a measure of control and flexibility. The Supervisory Committee had considerable operational independence, but it remained subject to a veto from either company. While Mobil and BP both had a lot of experience in managing upstream alliances, no oil company ever had attempted such an ambitious deal downstream. Initially, their interests seemed aligned, but questions about the longer term remained.

There was also the tricky Aral issue. Mobil was now allied with two competing groups. Given the strength of the BP-Mobil marketing network, Aral was the clear loser. Some analysts felt that Mobil should sell its stake to enable Aral to find another partner. Others criticizing Mobil's ability to manage complex alliances as the European Commission began investigating the two joint ventures.

The daunting task of actually merging operations still lay ahead. BP and Mobil executives were aware that most large mergers, no matter their strategic logic, failed to create value for shareholders. The challenges involved in bringing together different products, services, management systems and culture as well as workforces while competing in the marketplace often precluded benefits. These issues could be even more problematic in this deal because BP and Mobil continued to compete as independent corporations in petrol and other businesses elsewhere in the world.

Analysts also wondered how the relationship between the two partners would evolve over time. What if the deal turned out to be a half-hearted compromise that neither side was fully satisfied with? Also there was no guarantee that EU regulators would approve the deal. The combined market share of the two companies gave them a strong presence in several countries. Determined to root out anti-competitive behavior, the European Commission was targeting large, headline-grabbing mergers. If the alliance was shown to establish a dominant position which significantly restricted competition, the Commission could stop the deal. To overcome this hurdle, BP and Mobil had to provide enough information for the Commission to make a quick decision, and they had to demonstrate that there was no threat to competition.

Commentators were already speculating about how BP and Mobil's competitors would respond to the move. Was it the beginning of industry-wide re-alignment? The next few years could be crucial. What would the two companies have to do to turn their deal into a success? Was the deal a masterstroke or insufficient as some claimed? What would Mr. Browne have to do to keep the performance of BP on track?

ENDNOTES

1 Known as gasoline in the United States. We use the word "petrol" throughout to refer to retail motor fuels (petrol, diesel and other refinery products), unless otherwise specified.

2 One barrel equals 42 U.S. gallons, or 159 liters.

3 The world's largest refinery was at Yukong in South Korea (770,000 bpd).

4 Because even the integrated oil companies didn't have refineries near all their major markets, they were often faced with a difficult choice: either they bought fuels internally and paid the cost of shipment, or they purchased from competitors. For this reason major refining players such as Shell and Exxon often managed to extract high prices from retailers.

Developing a Global Mindset at Johnson & Johnson—1998

by Vladimir Pucik*

*International Institute for Management

This case was prepared by Professor Vladimir Pucik with the support of Cristina Duffy, Research Associate, as a basis for class discussion rather than to illustrate either effective or ineffective handling of a business situation.

In 1998, Johnson & Johnson (J&J) was the world's most comprehensive manufacturer of health care products. It was composed of more than 180 operating companies worldwide with three major business segments for consumer, pharmaceutical and professional markets. In the late 1980s, its total revenue was close to $10 billion, but it more than doubled to $22.6 billion by 1997, generated from sales activities in more than 175 countries (refer to Exhibit 1).

The company's sales were evenly distributed between the United States and the rest of the world, but only one-third of profits were earned abroad, compared to one-half of corporate profits almost a decade before—a consequence of several recent US acquisitions. By 1997, Europe accounted for 26% of J&J's total sales and 28% of operating profit. The Western Hemisphere (not including the US)

contributed 9% to the total sales, and J&J's sales in Africa, Asia and Pacific region accounted for 13% of sales (refer to Exhibit 2). Over the same decade, the company's number of employees grew from 83,500 to 90,500, and the percentage of J&J's total workforce outside the US had grown from half to two-thirds.

Before 1998, Johnson and Johnson had been organized around its operating companies established mostly on a country level (in some countries, J&J was represented by more than one operating company, and some companies operated in more than one country). The legacy of commitment to decentralized management was still evident in the company's customer-related functions. Marketing, sales and country management functions remained largely decentralized. However, support functions such as finance, human resources and information technology were increasingly shared among operating companies, and in an effort to streamline activities and reduce costs, J&J was moving toward a regional and global approach. ■

Exhibit 1
Regional sales as a percentage of total J&J sales

	1989	1997
Africa	1.1	1.2
Asia	8.9	11.6
United States	50.0	51.9
Europe	27.6	26.3
Western Hemisphere (not including U.S.)	12.4	9.0

Source: Johnson & Johnson

Exhibit 2
Number of J&J employees per region

	1989	1997
Africa	1,985	1,568
Asia	9,449	11,962
United States	37,465	42,946
Europe	19,939	23,581
Western Hemisphere (not including U.S.)	14,258	10,447
Total Number of Employees	83,096	90,504

Source: Johnson & Johnson

GLOBAL PLATFORMS

Due to the high cost of formulating new drugs, the company's pharmaceutical business segment had always used centralized research shared among operating companies worldwide. Johnson & Johnson's consumer and professional businesses were pursuing a similar approach in a large portion of their value chains. J&J was seeking to utilize fewer company resources by implementing coordinated strategies, for example, a single, common marketing strategy for a given region rather than several different marketing tactics.

Johnson & Johnson's three business segments were subdivided into franchises, which could best be described as "loose federations" of individual products integrated across the company's three major operating groups. This integration was achieved through the company's new global platforms defined as groupings of product franchises unified by use. J&J's new global platforms included such product franchise groups as wound care, skin care, women's health, and urology. The wound care global platform, for example, included a full range of Band-Aid products in the consumer business segment, and all types of surgical dressings in the professional business segment.

By 1998, the company's strategy had shifted from individual product-based operating companies to the new global platforms and integrated franchise management.

This shift to global platforms included shared marketing functions within geographic regions, consolidated production, and streamlining of product offerings to eliminate cost duplication. As recently as five years ago, J&J had marketed as many as 75 formulas for baby shampoo worldwide, but the product line had been streamlined to just a few formulas for differing hair types in world markets. Standardization of products within franchises allowed the company to make changes quickly to keep pace with global competition.

Consolidated production figured prominently in J&J's shift to global platforms. For example, rather than maintaining separate production facilities for different European markets, the company had started producing all its shampoo products for the European region *at a single efficient plant in Italy*. Globally, the company's Ethicon franchise (part of worldwide sutures platform) provided goods to Latin American markets from J&J's main facilities in Scotland, and Ethicon Brazil provided catgut and certain raw materials to Asia and Africa.

Before the shift to global platforms, individual manufacturing plants had been like silos of production activity—acting separately and producing different formulas. But the reduction of trade barriers and shipping costs in the era of globalization had increased opportunities to export, which allowed J&J to maximize plant capacities and increase efficiency.

J&J top management recognized that to compete in today's marketplace the company had to be nimble and agile and guided by a global mindset, defined by Allen C. Anderson, J&J's vice president of education and development, as "the ability to think globally and act locally, and to understand the impact of worldwide strategies." The company's global approach, fueled by the reduction of trade barriers and unification of regional markets, required more communication among employees, an increased emphasis on matrix management, and more shared responsibility between managers worldwide.

GLOBAL HUMAN RESOURCES STRATEGY

With the ongoing globalization of J&J businesses, the firm's human resources management had also become increasingly global. The external forces of globalization created new business opportunities for increased efficiency through global integration in R&D, production, and marketing, but were also reshaping the opportunities and challenges in human resource management.

The unification of the EU labor market and the decline in barriers to labor mobility facilitated the movement of J&J employees within EU countries, both influencing staffing decisions and broadening career opportunities. At the same time, the shift to global platforms created new human resource challenges and expectations of the skills and competencies required from J&J managers in a globally integrated business environment. J&J managers also had to be able to share responsibility with J&J managers in other parts of the world, and the compensation system was intended to mirror this shared responsibility.

Johnson & Johnson's human resources organization reflected the company's recent changes in business strategy. J&J's regional human resource vice presidents spanned the globe, with one human resource vice president for each of the company's three business segments in Europe, three human resource vice presidents in the Asia Pacific region, and two in Latin America. The 28 human resource vice presidents in the US represented each of J&J's companies operating in the US and were equivalent in scope of responsibilities to human resource directors in Johnson & Johnson's international operations. In 1997, all of the company's human resource vice presidents and directors had met to develop J&J's worldwide human resource strategic plan, which centered all management education and development initiatives around the company's Standards of Leadership developed in 1996.

Standards of Leadership

The company's Standards of Leadership had helped make leadership relevant to J&J employees by identifying 60 specific behaviors that contributed to business results (refer to Exhibit 3). These behaviors were grouped into categories: Customer/Marketplace Focus, Innovation, Interdependent Partnering, Masters Complexity, and Organizational and People Development. They were inextricably linked to the philosophy expressed in the well-known J&J Credo.

The J&J Credo (refer to Exhibit 4), which was periodically reviewed and updated, defined the company's view of its responsibility to customers, company employees, communities in which J&J operated, and finally, company stockholders. The values that underpinned Johnson & Johnson's Credo influenced how the company conducted its business. Upon this foundation, J&J's Standards of Leadership guided all aspects of the company's human resource function, from providing a basis for candidate assessment to evaluating managers' performance and potential.

International Recruitment

J&J's Standards of Leadership provided a basis for assessing an individual's potential fit with the company and helped the interviewer ask the right questions during the recruitment process. In the case of upper-level management positions, candidates' previous international experiences were assessed, and their savvy regarding the global mindset was evaluated through questions on cultural diversity. For lower-level managers, a global mindset was not considered immediately necessary; to rise to a leadership position, the candidate was expected to acquire this mindset "on the job."

However, recruiters did examine entry-level candidates' resumes for evidence of a global orientation. Candidates who had taken advantage of educational exchanges outside their home countries were of interest to J&J, and those who had undertaken internationally focused degree programs in another country were actively pursued by J&J's international recruiters. For example, an Italian student studying for an MBA at the

Exhibit 3
Standards of leadership

CREDO VALUES/BUSINESS RESULTS

Credo Values	Business Results
Behaves with honesty and integrity	Cash flow
Treats others with dignity and respect	Cost effectiveness
Applies Credo values	Customer satisfaction
Uses Credo Survey	Environmental/safety responsibility
results to improve the business	Income growth
Balances the interests	Market share
of all constituents	New product flow
Manages for the long-term	People development
	Product quality
	Productivity
	Regulatory compliance
	Volume growth

"Credo values represent the foundation stone upon which leadership is built. Certainly within Johnson & Johnson you cannot be a good leader if you don't believe in and try to live up to the Credo."

Ralph S. Larsen, Chairman and Chief Executive Officer

"Business results are in the center of the model because all five leadership competency areas influence business results."

Clark H. Johnson, Vice President, Finance

continued

Exhibit 3
(continued)

CUSTOMER / MARKETPLACE FOCUS

Creates Value for Customers

Projects a sense of passion
about customers
Recognizes the range of
customers and their needs
Serves as the voice of the
customer
Uses customer-perceived value
as the key criterion for the
design of current and future
products and services

Focuses Externally

Analyzes market
forces and positions
Johnson & Johnson
to capitalize on opportunities
Seizes the advantage of
being first
Benchmarks competitive
practices and performance

"Our raison d'étre, as the French say, is the customer. We tend to forget that we do not have any role to play if the customer is not there. Its place in this model is a way of reminding everyone that this is what we're here for."

Christian Koffmann, Worldwide Chairman, Consumer & Personal Care

INNOVATION

**Forges a Vision of
the Future**

Visualizes and communicates
the future
Develops strategies for growth
Inspires others to commit
to the vision
Executes vision and strategy

Fuels Business Growth

Acts and encourages others
to be entrepreneurial
Finds and exploits new
opportunities
Takes risks and manages
them intelligently
Demands the pursuit of stretch
goals for self and others

**Promotes Innovation and
Continuous Learning**

Generates and encourages
creative ideas
Finds new ways to do
things better and faster
Challenges and encourages
others to challenge the status
quo
Transfers ideas and successes
across boundaries
Promotes quality improve-
ment as a value and as
process
Finds new ways to use
technology more effectively
Learns from personal and
organizational experiences

"Our whole business is built on innovation and the ability to move rapidly ahead with new therapies, to be the first in a new treatment category. It is a key element of the Johnson & Johnson history and future, and a key competency of leaders within our company."

Robert N. Wilson, Vice Chairman, Board of Directors

INTERDEPENDENT PARTNERING

Builds Interdependent Partnerships

Cooperates across functions, business units and geographic boundaries
Leverages technology, products and services across boundaries
Establishes mutually beneficial objectives; clarifies roles and accountabilities with
partners
Fosters open communication with partners
Communicates commitment to the success of the partnership in both words and
actions

"We can no longer afford to be independent silos, not worrying about what's happening on your left or right or with other sister companies or other departments. It just isn't

continued

Exhibit 3
(continued)

going to work that way as the environment is changing. We need to do things differently and interdependent partnering is a very important part."

Ronald G. Gelbman, Worldwide Chairman, Pharmaceuticals & Diagnostics Group

MASTERS COMPLEXITY

Manages Complexity	Implements Positive Change
Thinks analytically and acts decisively	Recognizes and communicates the need for change
Thrives in uncertain circumstances	Embraces non-traditional ideas and practices
Knows when to act and when to wait	Engages in constructive conflict
Makes the complex clear and compelling	Drives the change process
Builds consensus and impacts outcomes with limited authority	Teaches and encourages others to deal with change

"As our business lives get more complex and we enter new businesses, we'll have to have a compass in the forest of all the information that comes at us every day and this model includes the leadership skills to handle it."

James T. Lenehan, Worldwide Chairman, Consumer Pharmaceuticals
& Professional Group

ORGANIZATIONAL AND PEOPLE DEVELOPMENT

Creates an Achievement Environment	Develops People for Optimal Performance
Challenges and motivates people to reach their highest potential	Fosters the continuous professional development and career growth of a diverse workforce
Creates an environment that encourages risk taking	Provides challenging work assignments and development opportunities
Promotes the business value of diverse perspectives, ideas, backgrounds, styles and cultures	Identifies and champions high potential talent as a Johnson & Johnson resource
Fosters organizational flexibility	Coaches and mentors future leaders
Sets clear performance standards and holds people accountable for results	Requires people to expand their capabilities, knowledge and skills
Values, recognizes and rewards the achievement of others	Functions as both team player and leader
Promotes teamwork	

"Our company is all about a large group of people engaged in a common endeavor. There's nothing more important than making our people better and better at what they do and at who they are."

Roger S. Fine, Vice President, General Counsel

"The organizational part is just as important. We need an environment in each of our business operations that encourages, fosters, and develops the kind of business activities and leadership we need to grow the business."

Russell C. Deyo, Vice President, Administration

Source: Johnson & Johnson

Exhibit 4
Credo

Our Credo

We believe our first responsibility is to the doctors, nurses and patients, to mothers and fathers and all others who use our products and services. In meeting their needs everything we do must be of high quality. We must constantly strive to reduce our costs in order to maintain reasonable prices. Customers' orders must be serviced promptly and accurately. Our suppliers and distributors must have an opportunity to make a fair profit.

We are responsible to our employees, the men and women who work with us throughout the world. Everyone must be considered as an individual. We must respect their dignity and recognise their merit. They must have a sense of security in their jobs.

Compensation must be fair and adequate, and working conditions clean, orderly and safe. We must be mindful of ways to help our employees fulfil their family responsibilities. Employees must feel free to make suggestions and complaints. There must be equal opportunity for employment, development and advancement for those qualified. We must provide competent management, and their actions must be just and ethical.

We are responsible to the communities in which we live and work and to the world community as well. We must be good citizens—support good works and charities and bear our fair share of taxes. We must encourage civic improvements and better health and

education. We must maintain in good order the property we are privileged to use, protecting the environment and natural resources.

Our final responsibility is to our stockholders. Business must make a sound profit. We must experiment with new ideas. Research must be carried on, innovative programmes developed and mistakes paid for. New equipment must be purchased, new facilities provided and new products launched. Reserves must be created to provide for adverse times. When we operate according to these principles, the stockholders should realise a fair return.

Source: Johnson & Johnson

International Institute for Management Development (IMD) in Switzerland might well have been considered a prime prospect for an international management career with J&J.

J&J's international recruiters, based at J&J headquarters in New Jersey, USA, sought candidates from the top US and European MBA schools for J&J's overseas companies. Each year, the operating companies sent requests to international recruiting with the number of MBAs they were seeking and descriptions of the positions they needed to fill. J&J international recruiters then made campus visits seeking suitable candidates from among the world's most competitive MBA programs.

J&J's international MBA recruitment programs included the Leadership Development Program Europe and the Asia Global Managers Program. The Leadership Development Program Europe focused on top MBA students in Europe. Usually, these graduates were not placed in their home countries, but rather in other European countries in which they were authorized to work. This program required that candidates be multilingual and mobile, since after their initial assignments of 12 to 18 months in one country, they were likely to be moved to other European countries. During their initial assignments, new hires in this program were assigned development mentors who worked with them to improve their management skills.

The Asia Global Managers Program recruited Asian candidates from top US and European MBA programs. J&J international recruiting manager Dina Da Silva explained: "After interviewing with the international recruiters, candidates were referred to top management for further interviews. Once selected, the new hires were trained for approximately 18 months

in the US and Asia, always outside their home countries." Training consisted of broad, multidisciplinary overview assignments that helped define the type of position for which the new hire was best suited. After the training period, new hires were placed in Asia, usually in their home countries or in other countries in which they were authorized to work and had language fluency. The company's experience had shown that placing new hires in their home countries for initial assignments often offered the best environment for career growth and development.

The company was satisfied with the success of these international recruitment programs, and the numbers of new hires through the programs had increased substantially over the last decade. By 1998, the programs were bringing in an average of 90 new hires a year, with about 45 in training at any given time.

Management Development

J&J's emerging regional and global strategies required managers to develop new skills to support the integration of the company's business segments. These skills included partnering with colleagues, sharing responsibility with managers in other units, cross-border communication, and matrix management, along with a broad global perspective and international experience. J&J's Anderson said, *"to develop these skills in J&J managers, the company depended largely on on-the-job training."*

J&J's new corporate structure based on global franchises promoted on-the-job training of employees, which the company viewed as 80% to 85% percent of an employee's overall development. Since J&J believed formal education and training could be difficult to apply directly to employees' jobs, development programs utilized on-the-job learning to develop managers, both individually and in the context of their organizational roles. Cross-functional teams in global franchises were one potential source of hands-on training, which strengthened global franchises and enhanced employees' matrix management skills.

Formal Training Programs

J&J also provided formal training programs to support leadership development. In the late 1980s, J&J sponsored in-company management development programs at Northwestern University in Chicago (for North American employees), the University of California at Berkeley (for the Asia-Pacific region), and IMD in Switzerland (for Europe). J&J had also developed relationships with several other universities in the US and the UK; however, since more and more training programs were being developed in-house, most of these relationships had disappeared.

After gaining experience through the earlier outside programs and opting not to invest in physical institutes of its own, J&J had developed in-house formal training programs which it viewed not only as more cost-effective and but also more flexible in teaching employees as needed and where needed. As Anderson reported, "Essentially, J&J had decided to build its own management program to "take on the road" as needed, which could be tailored for different regions and thereby minimized travel costs by bringing training to the most cost-effective location." In recent years, the company had offered an Advanced Manager Program in Antwerp for European employees and a smaller program in Sao Paulo and Miami for the South American region.

Ethics Training

As J&J grew from a $1 billion company with fewer than 10,000 employees in 1970 to a $23 billion company with over 90,000 employees in 1998, much of this through acquisitions, it had been challenged to maintain a high level of ethics in accordance with the long-standing Johnson & Johnson credo. Dedicated to upholding J&J's ethics standards, top management considered the Credo to be the "heart and soul" of their leadership, and took ownership of ethics development throughout the company. J&J's human resource personnel recruited individuals who shared Johnson & Johnson's values and then developed these new employees around the J&J's Standards of Leadership.

Adhering strictly to the company's ethical values throughout the global organization was difficult, considering the varying cultures of acquired companies and the varied countries in which J&J did business. To help employees deal with the variety of complex ethical issues that they might encounter in the company's extensive international operations, J&J's training organization had developed a case-based education program called "Ethics Toolkit" to help managers worldwide learn how to uphold the company's values regardless of prevailing cultural norms. Ethics Toolkit training examined front-line ethics situations (such as third-party payments), taught managers ethical decision-making processes, and advised them who to turn to for help and advice when ethical "gray areas" arose (refer to Exhibit 5).

Stretch Assignments

In order to accelerate development of high-potential managers, J&J used "stretch assignments" designed to extend a manager's range of skills by providing new challenges and career opportunities. "Stretch assignments" were the basis of J&J's succession planning, which focused on building dynamic leadership.

For example, the company might assign a manager who had performed particularly well in one turnaround situation to another turnaround assignment. However, J&J was aware of the limitation this could place on the employee's career development, and preferred to find an assignment in which the manager could gain additional experiences and skills. Still, international assignments were, by definition, well suited for a "stretch."

Global Coordination and Development Programs

The key J&J global coordination and development programs were the Executive Development programs and Executive Conference sessions.

The objective of the Executive Development program was to help managers develop global mindset through action learning. These high-impact programs, which were designed for high-potential managers, were driven by business needs (business issues addressed during the program were selected by each company's operating committee). Cross-border work groups, members of which were nominated by each company group chairman, were assigned to spend three weeks in the field abroad working on solutions for business issues and then present specific recommendations for action.

J&J's Executive Conference sessions were convened by global franchise leaders, who selected key franchise managers from around the world (usually numbering around 40 or 50, but as many as 130) and determined which specific business to address. Over a custom-developed session that lasted several days, the group worked to resolve specific business issues within the franchise with participants from across the globe. Executive Conferences provided opportunities for managers to broaden their global perspectives by working with colleagues from other regions, deepen the communication channels and relationships among franchise members, and advance partnering between employees and shared responsibility between managers. To demonstrate senior management commitment to managerial development, executive committee members actively participated in Executive Conferences.

International Mobility

Johnson & Johnson consistently worked to balance its use of in-country talent and expatriates. Since the 1980s, the number of expatriates had decreased, primarily to reduce costs. In addition, expatriate compensation packages had been reduced in recent years, making expatriate assignment less glamorous to many managers. However, expatriate assignments were still used when in-country talent was unavailable, or for the cross-cultural development of managers. Expatriate assignments were usually to a single country for a limited time period, although some expatriate managers moved from one foreign country to another.

J&J's reduction in the use of expatriate managers had achieved significant cost reductions without diminishing the

Exhibit 5
Ethics toolkit (sample case)

Applying Credo Values in the Real World—A Diagnostic Survey
Case: The Fine Line Between Custom and Corruption

You are the new general manager of Utopia, a recently acquired subsidiary that does business in a country with a tradition of corruption. It is customary for businesses to make payments and gifts to government officials. You have been briefed by the company's legal counsel about the Credo's statements about good citizenship and about the Foreign Corrupt Practices Act (a US law that makes the company criminally liable for improper payments to foreign officials). When you meet with the management to tell them that some of the practices they are used to may not be acceptable to the company, the reaction is disdain. One manager says flatly, "You don't understand what it takes to do business in this part of the world. If we can't make the traditional payments to politicians and bureaucrats we will be out of business within a year." You know that other US companies try to avoid the problem by hiring independent expediting firms who take care of all the details and shield management from direct knowledge or involvement. You ask an executive to make a list of the kinds of payments they are talking about. Each of the following was on the list and you are to determine whether you will permit continuation of the payments.

1 = Yes — there is nothing legally or ethically wrong with this action.
2 = Yes — this may not be proper elsewhere but it is acceptable under local standards.
3 = Yes — if the amounts are relatively small. Tell your people to proceed with caution.
4 = No — it is not consistent with Credo values or the Company's worldwide reputation.
5 = No — don't even think about it; this is foolish and probably illegal.

12345   When acquiring permits to ship goods internationally, it is customary to pay an unofficial service fee to the official in charge equal to 10% of the permit fees that go to the government.

12345   When goods arrive from outside the country, they must go through customs. It can take months to get release of the goods and the custom official exercises broad discretion in assessing duty. Officials are given monthly "gifts" during visits to the plant.

12345   When the electricity goes down, state-employed electrical workers expect to be "tipped" for performing their services. The more you tip, the faster the service.

12345   One of Utopia's largest customers is a state-run medical facility. It is customary to provide the buyers with free products, trips, and cash.

12345   The Minister of Health serves on the Company's "advisory council." A substantial fee is paid. The Company benefits from preferential treatment from the Ministry.

12345   During busy times one has to "tip" the train ticket agent to get a ticket.

12345   Occasionally, the local police stop Company vehicles for real or fictitious traffic violations. Employees are reimbursed for payments to avoid having the truck impounded.

Source: Johnson & Johnson

---

effectiveness of the organization. Still, maintaining the balance between using in-country talent and providing opportunities for cross-cultural experience through expatriate assignment remained a constant challenge. Expatriate assignments were often learning-driven, rather than solely driven by the demand for a manager in a foreign location, and were intended to develop managers' global mindsets and international experi-ence. Limiting the use of expatriate assignments to these development goals reflected the company's traditional preference for using in-country talent.

International experience was considered extremely important for young J&J managers, and international assignments were encouraged early in managers' professional careers. Ideally, the company tried to assign managers internationally when they were in their late 20s and early 30s, since young families usually relocated more easily than those already established in communities and schools. Johnson & Johnson also found that a global mindset was more readily adopted when managers were fairly young. To increase the likelihood of success of managers on international assignment, the company also worked to find challenging employment in the company for spouses in dual-career couples.

The International Recruitment and Development Program (IDP), J&J's broader umbrella development activity, also included career development programs for employees worldwide. Each year, the IDP moved 70 to 80 current J&J employees from different parts of the globe into one- to two-year assignments in the US. Since each operating company had to pay for the program, and accordingly had to justify the expense, the recurrent choice of the IDP program to develop managers reflected the value it provided. The company was pleased with this success: roughly the same number of participants took part in 1998 as ten years before, and the program had an excellent retention rate.

J&J had also launched a special program to globalize high-potential employees from the US. A formalized structure which can best be described as a "reverse IDP" program was used to give young US employees international exposure to prepare them for full-time international experience. Each year, five to ten US employees were sent abroad for up to 18 months for development purposes. These employees set out with clear individualized objectives specifically based on their own development requirements and the company's business needs. During the overseas assignment, the employee was expected to gain international experience through exposure to different cultures, markets, and products.

For example, a high-potential employee responsible for corporate compensation in the US might have been assigned for 18 months to work in corporate compensation in Belgium. After the assignment was completed, the employee returned to the US. J&J arranged work authorizations for employees in this program, since temporary assignments for current employees were easier to arrange than permanent assignments for new hires. Cost issues were always a factor in this program as well, since moving families, arranging spousal employment, and overall expatriate support were costly. This program was relatively new, and the company was watching the results closely to see if demonstrated success warranted expansion of the program.

Preparing for a Global Future

J&J top management believed that, from the point of view of doing business on a worldwide scale, "leaders are leaders, no matter where." Having found commonalties among excellent managers around the globe, the company was fine-tuning its global franchise corporate strategy.

J&J was also constantly searching for new methods to develop crucial cross-cultural business skills and to provide international management experiences that were driven by business needs. Anderson explained, "Rather than just providing classroom cross-cultural training, or arranging an international experience—which often amounted to "picking up" managers and moving them to foreign countries for a short time, only to have them then come back to sit at the same desk, unable to fully utilize their cross-cultural experience—J&J was focusing on increasing the opportunities for bringing managers together to work on specific business issues."

Through this international work integration, managers both developed cross-cultural management skills and accomplished business tasks. By partnering with international colleagues to solve specific operational problems, managers also developed the ability to share responsibility with others, improve cross-border communication, and operate in an international matrix organization. The company believed this "hands on" approach was well-suited to prepare managers for future global management activities because it supported global coordination while developing managers' international management skills.

CASE DISCUSSION QUESTIONS

1. What is a global mindset?

2. How important is it for Johnson & Johnson to sustain a global mindset in the twenty-first century?

3. Critique Johnson & Johnson's actions as they relate to sustaining and augmenting a global mindset for the organization.

4. What are your recommendations to Johnson & Johnson for sustaining and augmenting their global mindset in the future?

Ford Motor Company: Ford Automotive Operations

by **The Conference Board, Organizing for Global Competitiveness**

Focus: Reorganizing to a Global Product/Functional Matrix; Ford of Europe No Longer Exists

Ford Motor Company (Ford) is the world's largest producer of trucks and the second-largest producer of cars and trucks combined. It is also a major provider of financial services. Ford has manufacturing, assembly, or sales affiliates in 34 countries.

The company's two core businesses are Ford Automotive Operations and the Financial Services Group (Ford Credit, The Associates, and USL Capital). Ford is also engaged in a number of other businesses, including electronics, glass, electrical and fuel-handling products, plastics, climate control systems, automotive service and replacement parts, vehicle rental, and land development.

In 1995, Ford's sales totaled $137.1 billion and the company employed 346,990 individuals. Outside of the United States, Ford's sales revenue was $41.8 billion and the company had 161,030 employees. ∎

FORD IN EUROPE

In 1903, the year the company was founded, Ford exported Model A's to Britain. It began operating through its British subsidiary in 1909 and started assembling cars there in 1911. For decades, the firm's various European subsidiaries operated as virtually unconnected entities. But when the external conditions that had given rise to a multidomestic organization design began to change, so did Ford. In fact, Ford became one of the first U.S.-based MNCs to anticipate the evolution of a European economic region by grouping its operations under a common organizational umbrella:

> The formation of Ford of Europe in 1967 was the first step in the creation of a network of complementary plants stretching across the continent. . . . Over the next decade, Ford of Europe became an increasingly integrated regional division . . . the continent rather than the nation state became the geographic unit of strategic management and production.[1]

Automobiles were designed in the United Kingdom and in Germany, and manufactured in Belgium, France, Germany, Spain, and the United Kingdom. In due course, a common product range was developed. The company also entered into external alliances with Volkswagen, Nissan and other manufacturers to serve the European market. Functional executives in every country reported to their respective regional heads. The management information system consolidated cost, revenue, and profit at the European regional level. (For a depiction of the Ford of Europe organization prior to the global reorganization of 1995, see Chart 1.)

FORD AUTOMOTIVE OPERATIONS

Ford Automotive Operations (FAO), a new organization that was implemented on January 1, 1995, comprises all aspects of the company's core automotive business. FAO is responsible for the design, manufacture, assembly, and sale of cars, trucks, and related parts and accessories. It currently markets about 70 models of cars and trucks worldwide. These products are distributed through some 10,500 dealers in more than 200 countries and territories. More than 80 percent of FAO's unit car and truck sales are generated from six countries: the United States, the United Kingdom, Germany, Italy, Brazil, and Canada. While the company has production operations in 30 countries, more than 90 percent of its car and truck production is located in five countries: the United States, Germany, the United Kingdom, Spain and Canada.

FAO's major markets are in the United States and Europe, where it holds market shares of 25.6 percent and 12.3 percent, respectively. These two geographies represented 90 percent of FAO's total revenues in 1995. Despite its substantial U.S. and European presence, FAO has moved aggressively into the world's fast-growing emerging markets. In 1994, the company spent $1 billion in the Asia-Pacific region setting up wholly owned subsidiaries (Vietnam), investing in joint ventures (China), and purchasing equity interests in existing companies (India). The firm also leveraged its 25 percent ownership stake in Mazda Motors in order to gain a presence in the Malaysian and Indonesian markets. These examples demonstrate the company's commitment to serving the global marketplace.

FAO's sales in 1995 totaled $110.5 billion; $36.6 billion was generated from non-U.S. sources. (For more on why FAO was formed, see "FAO's Raison d'Être" on the next page.)

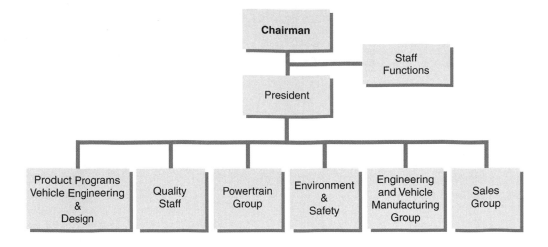

Chart 1
Ford of Europe
(March 1994)

Chairman

Staff Functions

President

- Product Programs Vehicle Engineering & Design
- Quality Staff
- Powertrain Group
- Environment & Safety
- Engineering and Vehicle Manufacturing Group
- Sales Group

THE FAO ORGANIZATION

FAO was created when Ford merged its North American Automotive Operations and its Ford of Europe unit, previously run as separate businesses, into a single organization. Management has since folded its Asia-Pacific, South American, and African affiliate operations into the same global organization effective January 1, 1996.

Important components of the new design include five vehicle centers, each of which produces particular sizes and types of vehicles. Four of the centers, located in the United States, focus on large four-wheel-drive vehicles, rear-wheel-drive cars, light trucks, and commercial trucks. The fifth center is jointly operated by Ford design centers in Dunton, England, and Merkenish, Germany, and concentrates on small and medium

vehicles. The five centers are responsible for the design, development, and launch of their respective lines of vehicles. They are also accountable for the production lifetime profitability and cash flow of each model.

The new organization is a global functional/product matrix. Approximately 10,000 managers report to both the specific vehicle center to which they are assigned and to their specific functional organization (e.g., product strategy, design, manufacturing engineering, and customer communications and satisfaction). Matrix managers are placed where the functions and the vehicle centers intersect. Their task is to integrate the work of both sides of the matrix and to mediate disputes.

The organization format is based on a team concept. Each FAO product is developed by a cross-functional team, whose members are permanently assigned to a vehicle center. Many of

---

FAO'S Raison d'Être

The reorganization of Ford's automotive activities is one of the largest MNC realignments ever to take place. A key reason why this was possible was that Ford in Europe had been operating as an integrated region, rather than as a collection of independent countries, since 1967.

By creating FAO, senior management seeks to achieve several goals:

- *To implement a strategy of global mass customization.* FAO intends to develop a "world car" that—appropriately modified to meet local tastes and governmental regulations—can be sold in large numbers around the world. The new organization also intends to produce a variety of cars and trucks for local markets throughout the globe. Ford acknowledges that achieving this strategy depends upon new technologies in telecommunications, advanced computers and linked computer networks, and satellite television, all of which enable FAO units to operate as global teams.

- *To serve the global market.* When the company operated through semi-autonomous regions, certain markets were underserved. The new global format is intended to expand Ford's presence in such areas—especially in the emerging markets of Asia and elsewhere.

- *To operate more cost effectively.* FAO hopes to reduce expenses by some $3 billion in five years by eliminating duplications (especially in product development), cutting the costs of materials, using fewer suppliers, and trimming bureaucracy. For example, Ford intends to reduce the numbers of basic designs (platforms) from 24 to 16 yet, at the same time, increase the number of models produced from these platforms by half—saving billions of dollars in the process.

Chart 2
Ford Automotive Operations

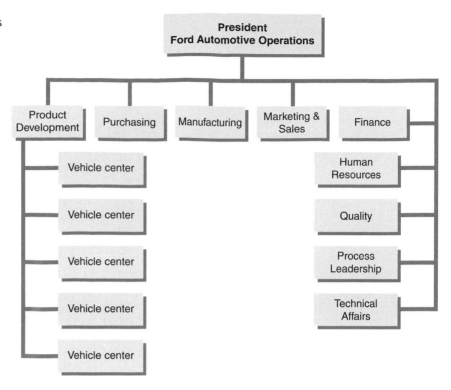

these members are also co-located at their respective vehicle centers. About 270 Europeans have relocated to the United States to join car and commercial truck centers, while about 200 have gone from the United States to Europe to work in the small and medium vehicle centers. There have also been relocations within the United States and Europe in order to get people to work more closely. For instance, individuals from several sites in the United Kingdom have been moved to a new center at Dunton.

The head of each vehicle center is ultimately responsible for the products that each local market will receive, since he or she is accountable for pleasing the majority of customers and meeting program volume and cost targets. His or her performance is measured by market acceptance of product design, costs, quality, and pricing. In a sense, these executives are running a global business since they are also provided staff support in areas such as quality, finance, employee relations, and process leadership. Nonetheless, the vehicle centers are considered cost centers. The various functional employees assigned to them, both line and staff, are on the budget of their respective global functions. The FAO itself is designated as the organization's only P&L center.

Other major global decisions within the FAO organization are overseen by company officers responsible for purchasing, manufacturing, and marketing and sales. Each of these executives, along with the head of product development—to whom the vehicle centers report—is directly accountable to the president of FAO (see Chart 2).

Business volume targets are set by the marketing function since the vehicle centers develop product specifications and costs based on information derived from marketing research and plans. Marketing and sales in Europe is organized on a country-by-country basis. The country managers report to a European marketing and sales executive who reports, in turn, to the head of the global marketing and sales function.

As most of Ford's joint ventures are alliances that build vehicles—such as the Ford-Volkswagen alliance, which manufactures an all-purpose minivan in Portugal—they are managed through the global manufacturing organization. Supplier relationships, on the other hand, are managed through global purchasing. FAO has sought to build worldwide affiliations with fewer suppliers than Ford has traditionally used and has rationalized several hundred different systems for parts numbering, purchasing, and supplier-related transactions.

Finally, many activities of central corporate staffs (such as finance and human resources) have been integrated into FAO. Since Ford of Europe no longer exists as an operating unit, there is no European regional staff. Certain corporate staff activities, such as legal, are represented in Europe and report back to corporate headquarters in Dearborn.

ORGANIZATIONAL STRENGTHS

The new FAO organization leverages Ford's worldwide resources to improve the quality and cost of its products and to grow by providing value to customers. By centralizing decision making, FAO can take a broad view of market opportunities. It can also develop products that serve multiple markets, thus increasing the return on product development-related expenditures.

The organization concentrates greater authority into the hands of those who run the individual car and truck development programs. This overcomes the problem of power being fragmented among functional groups (e.g., engine development), which could deny program leaders the funds they need to carry out their full responsibilities.

The organization has stimulated reengineering projects that seek to develop the most efficient practices. For example, a team from Europe and the United States reduced the task of machining a new engine prototype into stages that could be worked on simultaneously. It did this by taking the best internal practices from Europe and the United States as well by benchmarking best-in-class external competitors. FAO is also introducing a single set of worldwide processes and systems in product development, supply, production, and sales.

The new organization is reducing bureaucracy. This enhances the company's ability to serve the market faster, with a better product at less cost. Since the reorganization, FAO has been delayering levels of management, downsizing the numbers of senior managers, broadening spans of control, simplifying approval processes, and delegating greater authority further down the hierarchy. Ford has also reduced the number of standing corporate committees from 11 to 3.

By integrating European operations into a global organization, FAO allows the company to deal more effectively with Europe's unique competitive challenges. The recessionary and otherwise difficult European economic environment has affected the company's sales and margins for the past several years. Moreover, in the future, Europe is certain to feel the increasing impact of Japanese competition. Japanese automotive companies were allowed by the European Union to capture up to 16 percent of the market by 1999, and permitted unlimited access thereafter.

ORGANIZATIONAL CHALLENGES

FAO faces challenges to operating a global matrix design that are no different from those confronting other manufacturing MNCs. For example, firms that have traditionally managed by division of labor, specialization, hierarchical control, and conventional planning and budgeting systems have experienced difficulties in getting a matrix system to work effectively. Another common complication is diversity; a matrix operates best when the company is homogeneous and a strong national culture predominates. Finally, general managers everywhere have long complained about their inability to hold an individual or business activity accountable for successes and failures in a matrix organization.[2]

Ford has experienced some of these very same problems, and there have been reports that the company has taken certain actions to address them. Such actions include:

> . . . making doubly sure that objectives are agreed precisely between the vehicle centers and the functional side of the organization; specifying clearly the respective roles and responsibilities of individuals towards each side of the matrix; changing appraisal and reward systems accordingly; only appointing senior executives who have shown they can work collaboratively; training everyone involved in the art of developing a cooperative matrix "mindset" which largely replaces the need for policing; and introducing much more intensive and open communication than the organization is used to.[3]

A second set of challenges relates to the organization's size. Ford is the only world-class automotive company attempting to manage its operations through a unified global structure. This raises certain design questions that cannot be fully answered until several years have passed and a variety of business outcomes can be examined. Some of the questions are as follows: What is the correct balance of local and global influences for each function, and how should such balances be reflected in organization design? Are some of the functions too large? For example, can manufacturing, with plants on three continents, be effectively managed as a single global organization? Are certain spans of control too broad? Is the extent of empowerment in FAO too great? Will the customer's product requirements—especially in smaller markets—receive sufficient attention in the product design process? And finally, might a traditional geographic-based regional structure be easier to manage, operate closer to the customer, and produce competitive business results?

CASE DISCUSSION QUESTIONS

1. What are the strengths and weaknesses of Ford's regiocentric strategy?

2. What are the strengths and weaknesses of the global-product/functional matrix?

3. What other types of organizational structures would you consider for Ford?

4. Which organizational structure is best for Ford? Why?

ENDNOTES

1 Alan McKinlay and Ken Starkey, "After Henry: Continuity and Change in Ford Motor Company," *Business History*, January 1994, p. 22.
2 For an in-depth discussion of common matrix-related challenges supported with company examples, see Robert J. Kramer, *Organizing for Global Competitiveness: The Matrix Design*, Report No. 1088-94-RR, The Conference Board, 1994.
3 Christopher Lorenz, "Ford's Global Matrix Gamble," *Financial Times*, December 16, 1994, p. 13.

Hot Breads[1]

KATHMANDU, NEPAL

by **Julia Kreisinger Henker***

University of Massachusetts

This case is intended as a basis for class discussion rather than to illustrate either effective or ineffective handling of an administrative situation.

"Yes, yes, I've heard all of your arguments and you do have points. However, we must protect our procedures and our recipes," Mr. Sharma insisted. "If we hire locally, the workers will leave us after we have trained them and they will sell our secrets to our competitors. No, we must wait for Madras to send us more people." Mr. Sharma, the owner-manager of the most successful bakery in Kathmandu, was adamant about waiting for new Indian bakers to be assigned to Nepal, even though he was a bit unsure of himself. He sat at one of the tables in his store, discussing the most pressing problem of the moment—their shortage of trained bakers—with two of his executives.

"But we have been waiting more than two months, ever since Ramesh and Ali went back home. My bakers are complaining about the long hours, the customers are complaining that quality is down and that bread comes out later and later every day. We have to do something." Shubash, the executive chef, himself from India, was no less adamant and quite sure of himself, though of course he would eventually say, "Yes, sir," or risk continuing the conversation indefinitely. Mr. Sharma was unlikely to fire or even reproach him for his dissent; it was more the boss's style to wear down any opposition until the rebel agreed just to end the discussion.

"I realize that, of course. I will call Madras again soon, tomorrow perhaps," Sharma continued. "They have been very busy, but I am sure they will send us people as soon as they can spare them. You can manage for now, Shubash."

Subha Ratner, the customer service manager and the third member of the meeting, had been sitting quietly ever since he presented his argument some time ago. Realizing that once again they would take no action toward solving their ongoing problem, Subha had allowed himself to become absorbed in what was happening at the counter. The driver was preparing to make his second delivery to the local supermarket (because not enough products had been ready in the early morning to fill their daily order). He excused himself to supervise more closely. Shubash used the interruption to check on the kitchen. All three men knew that they would have to have another meeting on this issue tomorrow—and every day—until it resolved itself, so this meeting's sudden breakup was not unexpected or problematic. ∎

BACKGROUND ON NEPAL AND KATHMANDU

The Royal Kingdom of Nepal is a small country in South Asia, sandwiched between China and India. It is perhaps best known for its geography. The southern part of the country is flat and formerly a malaria-ridden jungle, a place where princes and Maharajas hunted tiger. Prince Siddhartha, the Buddha, was born here. The northern regions are dominated by Himalayas, including Mt. Everest, the tallest mountain in the world. The land in between, the "Middle Hills," harbors Kathmandu, Patan and Bhaktapur, cities that were once important stops on trade routes out of China, as well as home to numerous Hindu shrines. These hills are home to another source of Nepali fame: the Gurka soldiers of the British army. Famous for their bravery and toughness, they were recruited from the mountain villages of Nepal.

The Gurkas are not the only resilient inhabitants of this country. Hardship, in fact, is a way of life for most Nepali citizens. The country has the distinction of being among the five least developed countries in the world. The estimated per capita annual income is only US$160. Ninety-one percent of Nepal's population is involved in agriculture, most as subsistence farmers. Many of the children, especially the daughters, of these farmers work rather than attend school, and as a result the literacy rate is a paltry 40% (while literacy among women is only 25%). These conditions shorten the average life expectancy of Nepali men to 54.4 years, and women to 51.6 years.

Nepal is a country of extremes, and at the other extreme of the social spectrum is the elite, the former ruling classes. These few control most of the money in the country. They are concentrated in the capital city, Kathmandu. Their children are educated abroad, in Delhi, London and the United States. They, along with the diplomats and the expatriates from various

Exhibit 1
Map of Nepal

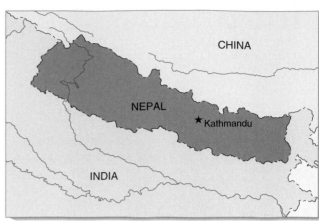

international aid agencies, give Kathmandu its unusual style, distinct from the poverty of the rest of the country.

Now, however, a middle class is emerging in Kathmandu. Domestic workers in expatriate homes, staff of various embassies, tourist and "trekking" guides and porters, carpet weavers and handicraft producers are developing wealth formerly unknown to their castes. This middle class, comprising less than 7% of the population, who work in manufacturing and service industries, is causing a change in the country. They have created a market for education, which entrepreneurs are more than happy to fill.

They also demand a more representative government. Nepal has been a constitutional monarchy since 1990. However, the Congresses have been supremely ineffective, leading the King to dissolve them repeatedly and call for new elections. The middle class is beginning to develop a taste for luxuries—imported fabrics and medicines, foods tasted in expatriate kitchens and movies and music from foreign countries. Nearly all of Nepal's imports come from India, its neighbor to the south.

Nepal's ties with India are stronger than just economic. Nepal is the only official Hindu state in the world, and about 80% of the population practices Hinduism. Many major Hindu shrines are located in Nepal, making it a pilgrimage spot for India's Hindus. Nepali, the official language of Nepal, is similar enough to Hindi that Nepal's cinemas feature Hindi movies and much of the populace understands and can communicate in Hindi.

The Hindu caste system is perhaps more salient in Nepal than in India. The prejudices that accompany the caste system are an omnipresent and socially acceptable aspect of everyday life in Nepal.

HOT BREADS

Hot Breads was the brand name of an Indian organization based in Madras. The company produced European quality pastries, both sweet and savory, and breads and cakes.

The bakers (breads and pastries) were required to go through a rigorous training procedure in Madras. Training lasted from three months to one year, depending on the needs of the organization

and the potential of the individual, and included general instruction on ingredients and baking techniques as well as specific recipes (confectioners, the men who baked the cakes, were trained in Calcutta). Bakers were then assigned to stores, where they continued learning as apprentices. A French baker visited each store at least once a year acting as a consultant, evaluating the baked goods, making suggestions and teaching new techniques.

The Hot Breads organization had stores in major cities all over India and was investigating possible new locations in Dubai and various African cities. The Nepal outlet is actually a franchise of the organization. Mr. Sharma, a Nepali, bought the exclusive right to use the Hot Breads logo in Nepal and set up a limited partnership which he called Himalayan Health Foods. Himalayan Health Foods pays a monthly royalty fee to use the Hot Breads brand name. They purchase certain supplies, including chemicals and packaging materials, from the parent organization, and receive consultation visits, advice and similar forms of support. [Exhibit 2 omitted.]

HIMALAYAN HEALTH FOODS AND ITS FOUNDER, SHARMA

The advice component was very important here, as prior to starting Himalayan Health Foods, Sharma had no experience in bakeries, or indeed in the food industry at all. He was an economist, a former Fulbright awardee to Cornell University and a former UN consultant. Friendly and urbane, he spoke flawless English. He belonged to a wealthy, powerful Brahmin family. As was traditional in Nepal, the Sharma family stored most of its wealth in land and consequently had large holdings in Kathmandu. The family owned many Western-style (and therefore luxurious) homes, which they rented to expatriates from various aid organizations.

Sharma sensed a change was underway in Nepal, however slow in coming. The social atmosphere was gradually shifting from unquestioning worship of the monarch to a more democratic ideal. To date, the Congresses had been supremely ineffective, but they were learning, and people continued campaigning for representation. In its periodic elections, the country enjoyed universal suffrage for those 18 years or older. They provided pictures on the ballot to accommodate the illiterate. More and more government-controlled businesses were being privatized, a movement encouraged by the aid agencies that were a significant source of funds for the government. (Aid agencies contributed in excess of US$286.5 million in 1990, or 40 per cent of the government's total expenditures.) The government further bolstered new enterprises by offering them a five-year tax holiday. Financing for new ventures was becoming more readily available, as banks loosened their lending regulations and the number of private finance companies increased monthly. Stocks in approximately ten companies were traded publicly, and Nepalis with a bit of discretionary money were enthusiastic, albeit somewhat unsophisticated, investors.

Interestingly, many of the entrepreneurs taking advantage of this atmosphere were not native Nepalis but Indian immigrants. In Nepali culture, family and religious obligations were much more important than business. As a result, Indian entrepreneurs dominated the private business scene. This caused a lot of resentment among the Nepalese. Sharma was careful to distance his business from the Indian organization, even though he capitalized on their superior recipes and technical training.

HOT BREADS BAKERY, KATHMANDU

A consequence of this distancing was that Nepali Hot Breads developed its own unique floor plan. Although most of his bak-

Exhibit 3

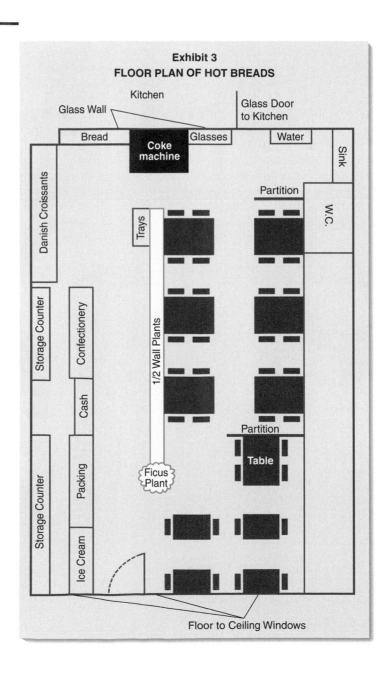

Exhibit 3
FLOOR PLAN OF HOT BREADS

ery and confectionery items mirrored those sold in Indian Hot Breads outlets, Sharma had different ideas for the presentation of breads and pastries. The usual Hot Breads formula called for breads and pastries to be kept behind the counters. Shoppers would tell a counter person what they wanted; he would then package it and tell the cashier what to charge. Sharma conceived of a new plan: a self-service area where customers could deliberate over their purchases without delaying others. In Hot Breads Kathmandu, customers used tongs to select items from attractive racks of baked goods, then carried their purchases to the counter where the cashier totaled their bill while a counter person packaged their selections.

In addition to the takeout bakery, Hot Breads Kathmandu also had a full-service restaurant, serving sandwiches and pizza in addition to baked goods and tea and soft drinks. Finally, the shop featured an ice cream counter equipped to serve sundaes as well as dishes and cones. The back wall of the shop was all glass, exposing the ovens and the counters where the bakers worked so that customers could see the condition of the kitchen. Other rooms in the kitchen area housed the confectioners, the sandwich grill, the bread cooling/slicing area, the staff kitchen and the storeroom. The executive office was in another building behind the shop. Located in the most expensive rent area in Kathmandu, Hot Breads made careful use of space.

The staff was an odd mix of Indians and Nepalese. The bakers were all South Indian, trained in Madras and sent to work in Kathmandu. The confectioners were North Indian, trained in Calcutta. All others—the waiters, cashiers and counter attendants, the bakers' helpers and the cleaners—were all Nepalese, most of them natives of Kathmandu. This made for an awkward working atmosphere in Nepal's extremely caste-conscious society. Differences in skills and in social castes created a pecking order that was frequently contradictory as well as counterproductive.

Finally, caste traditions caused another oddity for the organization. Both Sharma and Subha were Brahmin. Strict, practicing Brahmins were restricted in what foods they could eat, where and in whose presence they could eat, and by whom the food could be prepared. Though both men tasted the foods produced in the bakery, they seldom ate there and never took food home to their families. The rest of the staff similarly restricted their diets; most ate only traditional food provided by the staff cook. As a result, taste-testing and suggesting new products were done almost exclusively by customers.

BUSINESS AS USUAL

Apart from these difficulties, businesses in Kathmandu faced a myriad of crises. Electric power was unreliable, even with the expected load sharing (planned blackouts in different areas of the city during peak usage times). Supply lines were even less dependable, and on more than one occasion essential ingredients were held in customs for months. Time and strategic "gifts" eventually got them released, but due to storage conditions, many of the shipments were unusable when they finally did arrive. Local supplies were difficult to obtain with certainty, and their prices varied widely. As a result, Hot Breads was forced to carry large inventories of their most essential ingredients. At one time, for example, they had a six-month supply of margarine.

Exhibit 4
Average monthly sales

Year		Month	Average Daily Sales Total	Bakery
Opening	1994	Feb	13,562	7,866
		Mar	30,622	15,005
		Apr	28,996	13,918
		May	31,107	14,931
		June	24,897	14,938
		July	27,001	15,931
		Aug	39,521	20,551
		Sept	55,743	26,199
		Oct	60,142	25,861
		Nov	57,614	25,350
		Dec	52,882	25,912
	1995	Jan	47,203	26,906
		Feb	45,968	24,823
		Mar	49,925	22,966
		Apr	46,111	18,906
		May	37,565	14,275

To complicate matters further, the staff was capricious, particularly during the major holidays. Because of difficulties traveling around the country, staff members who returned home for holidays might return a few days or even a few weeks later than expected. Since Nepal has an inordinate number of holidays—the country celebrates Hindu holidays with week-long vacations, recognizes Buddhist holidays in similar fashion, and accommodates the important holidays of its numerous ethnic groups with additional days off—erratic absences could become a major disruption.

Equipment posed another problem, since the ovens, mixers and other special equipment were all imported. Repairing them and finding spare parts was a monumental task. These and other obstacles were dealt with somewhat haphazardly; management addressed them when they occurred, when they threatened the business, or, in the worst case, when they became big enough to overshadow all other concerns awaiting their attention.

TODAY'S CRISIS

The priority of the moment was a nagging production issue. Although within a month of its opening, Hot Breads had had a full complement of trained bake staff—ten Madras bakers assisted by three Nepali helpers—over time those numbers dwindled to just six bakers. For the South Indians, Kathmandu's climate, particularly its winters, was practically unbearable. Many found the separation from their wives and families difficult. The Nepali dislike of Indians was another sore point. These and other factors led to several bakers ending their contracts early, leaving the bake staff with a skeleton crew. For the past two months, this crew had been forced to work 11- and 12-hour days, seven days a week, to keep up with demand. Morale was low, quality was substandard, and the bakers were reporting for work later and later each day. This last trend was having a direct effect on sales.

Because of the unusual composition of Kathmandu's population, Hot Breads' customer base was about 45% local Nepali, 30% expatriate, and 25% tourist. Nepalis generally shop in the afternoons and early evenings, buying bread for the next day. Expats and especially tourists more likely visited the shop in the morning, buying bread for the day or eating in the cafe. Unfortunately, because of the bakers' late starts, very few products were ready when the shop opened at 8 A.M. Croissants and Danish were often not ready until 10 A.M., and breads did not come out of the ovens until 2 or 3 P.M. Consequently, foreign shoppers were often disappointed in the selection of goods available when they stopped in. In fact, a marketing survey showed that while many expats regarded Hot Breads' products superior to those of competitors in the city, they shopped there infrequently because of the irregular selection. The survey indicated that expat and tourist demand might increase by as much as 50% if more product was available before noon.

Although Subha, the customer service manager, was already aware of this issue, the results of the marketing survey made it much more salient in Sharma's mind. Evidence of a real loss of sales elevated this baker understaffing problem that Shubash (executive chef) had complained about for some time from a mere annoyance—("You can manage, Shubash," was his favorite refrain)—to a genuine crisis requiring immediate attention. In a series of meetings, the three men discussed possible solutions to the matter.

"I have some friends who are bakers in the Annapurna Hotel and the Everest Hotel (two five-star hotels in the city). Perhaps I can persuade them to leave the hotels and come to work

Exhibit 5
Indian bakers at Hot Breads, Kathmandu

Arrival and departure months for bakers from Madras, India

Name	Shubash	Ramesh	Sudeep	Sanjiv	Rajiv	Sudir	Sandeep	Pramod	Atul	Hari	Gopal	Sut	Subema	Rasheed	Raza	Sanjiv G.	Ali
Arrival	Nov-93	Nov-93	Feb-94	Feb-94	Feb-94	Feb-94	Mar-94	Mar-94	Mar-94	Mar-94	Jun-94	Jun-94	Jun-94	Oct-94	Oct-94	Oct-94	Oct-94
Departure		Mar-95	May-94	May-94	Dec-94	Jan-95	Aug-94	May-94	Nov-94		Oct-94		Feb-95				Mar-95

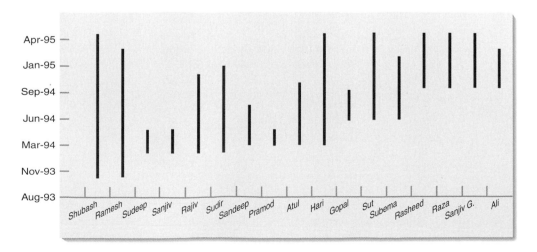

Exhibit 6
Hot Breads expenses
March 1995

		Sub-Totals
Salaries		**82,950 RPS**
Professional Staff	14,300 RPS	
Bakery (Bakers and Helpers)	23,100 RPS	
Confectionery	11,700 RPS	
Cooks	9,900 RPS	
Service	22,300 RPS	
Utility boys	1,650 RPS	
Rent		**60,500 RPS**
Durbar Marg (shop)	45,000 RPS	
Thamel (apartment housing Indian personnel— 10000 + 500/man)	15,500 RPS	
Royalty		**154,768 RPS**
Grindleys (Loan)		**135,420 RPS**
Utilities		**40,554 RPS**
Electricity		
Durbar Marg	20,216 RPS	
Thamel	750 RPS	
Gas		
Durbar Marg	15,203 RPS	
Thamel	225 RPS	
Water		
Durbar Marg	1,500 RPS	
Thamel	35 RPS	
Phone	2,625 RPS	
Suppliers		**462,595 RPS**
Bhat Bhateni	112,062 RPS	
Nirmal	24,500 RPS	
Rhabi Bhawan	150,365 RPS	
Dairy	90,850 RPS	
Bluebird Supermarket	45,183 RPS	
Hot Breads Corp.	39,635 RPS	
Services		**1,700 RPS**
Laundry Service	350 RPS	
Tailor (uniforms)	500 RPS	
Artist (sign)	850 RPS	
Travel		**14,780 RPS**
Cab in city	350 RPS	
Ramesh (one-way passage to Madras)	7,215 RPS	
All (one-way passage to Madras)	7,215 RPS	
Misc.		**6,000 RPS**
Gasoline	4,000 RPS	
Medicine (for Shubash)	2,000 RPS	
TOTAL EXPENSES MARCH 1995		**959,267 RPS**

Exhibit 7
Bakers' salaries
Nepali rupees

Baker	Current Monthly Salary	Comparable Nepali Salary
Shubash	3,000	4,500
Ramesh	2,800	4,500
Hari	2,500	3,500
Sut	2,500	3,500
Rasheed	1,600	2,500
Raza	2,500	3,500
Sanjiv G.	2,500	3,500
Ali	1,600	2,500
TOTAL	19,000	28,000
Average	**2,375**	**3,500**

for us. We could offer a lead baker position a slightly higher salary than they make now, maybe two weeks off for the Dasain holidays. Hiring them could solve our production problems immediately." Subha, himself highly skilled, knew skilled service people all over the city. Various friends of his had been helpful in solving past crises.

"They will have different methods, different recipes. My bakers will not work for Nepalis, and certainly not for Nepalis who have not been Hot Breads-trained," Shubash declared.

"We could set up a separate night shift, all Nepali or all Indian, to produce breads and pastries for the morning," Subha answered.

"Himalayan Health Foods cannot afford to pay the salaries they will expect," Sharma said. "The Indian bakers accept a much lower salary." For Sharma, committing money for anything other than capital investment was painful. "Besides, if we teach them our recipes, then they will go to work for someone else, or for themselves, selling products exactly like ours."

Because Hot Breads was such a success in Kathmandu, imitators were a serious concern. Nepal had very lax copyright laws and a host of people ready to copy any enterprise that was successful. A rival bakery had already surfaced, and the shop was laid out just as Hot Breads; it even had the words "Hot Bread" incorporated into its sign. Customers at the Hot Breads bakery frequently asked about the "other Hot Breads outlet" farther down the street. Since only Hot Breads recipes and techniques set Sharma's operation apart from imitators, he was very protective of them.

Shubash again advanced his plan. "We must recruit new, unskilled local workers. We can subject them to a trial phase, where they work as helpers and do not learn recipes. Then if they perform adequately, we can teach them as apprentices." Shubash had suggested this solution several times before.

"But the time that will take . . ." Subha worried.

"That is why we must start immediately," Shubash snapped.

"No, I do not trust Nepali workers. They do not work as hard as Indians," Sharma lamented. "They will learn what they need to know and then they will leave to work for someone else, or they will ask for more money. Madras must send us more bakers." Rightly or wrongly, Sharma was convinced that Nepalis would betray him.

"Sir, we asked for help three months ago, then two months ago, then again last month," Shubash reminded him. "The Hot Breads organization is expanding so rapidly that there simply are not enough trained bakers to go around. When they do finally get here, we have no assurance that they will have had any more than the most basic training. Worst of all, given our past experience, half of them will decide they cannot live here and will go home, requiring that Himalayan Health Foods pay travel expenses for yet another person. We must begin to become more self sufficient."

Shubash and Subha had previously discussed the situation at length. Though they had different solutions in mind, both agreed that waiting for help from the Indian organization was untenable. Since he was not Nepali, Shubash found it easier to disagree openly with Sharma.

"Yes, yes, I have heard all of your arguments . . ." The discussion broke off once again as each turned his attention to the immediate demands of operating the store.

CASE DISCUSSION QUESTIONS

1. Discuss the advantages and disadvantages of each of the recruitment options proposed by Hot Breads' management.

2. What other solutions could be considered?

3. What other issues are identified in the case?

4. What is the best solution from a cost perspective?

5. What would you recommend to the Hot Breads management team?

Idris S.A.[1]

SENOU, MALI

by Paula Goodman*

Case Western University

CASE A

Mr. Ahmed Idris, General Director of Idris S. A., a Malian commodities import/export firm, had been eager for many years to begin exporting the world famous West African mango to Europe. His friends in Europe faxed and wrote him regularly encouraging him to try his hand in this area.

Yet entering this business posed several problems, primarily logistical. Since his West African country is landlocked, exporters had no choice but to ship their goods by plane. He had yet to determine the costs. He also did not know where to buy cartons, where to store them, or how many men it would take to pack the mangos. He further had not determined how much time it would take to pack the goods and deliver them to the airport.

He did know the project would be labor intensive, however, and that he did not have the time to supervise the packing and follow up on the faxes, telexes and paperwork involved in exporting. Nonetheless, the business seemed tempting. He knew that one company, Fruitema, had at one time exported thousands of tons per season, primarily in the 1980s, and that they had found it consistently lucrative.

Exporting was attractive for another reason, too. In 1991 the government abolished all export taxes. Whereas importing involved complicated paperwork and heavy customs duties—sometimes as high as 75% of the cost of the good—exporting supposedly was tax-free and less bureaucratic.[2]

Fears of Currency Devaluation

All businessmen who imported goods into this country feared the possible devaluation of the F.CFA (Franc Communauté Financière Africaine), the currency used by as many as 14 West African nations and pegged to the French Franc (50 F.CFA equaling 1 FF). It was rumored that one day soon domestic austerity in France would mean the end of the expensive practice of intervening in the African currency to maintain its value. Economists at the USAID Mission in Senou estimated that the F.CFA in West Africa was overvalued by about 35%. World Bank and donor governments were pushing for this reform believing that a free-floating currency would encourage exports and help the economy.[3]

However, many businessmen in this country were quite concerned. About 80% of Mr. Idris's revenues came from importing grains, sugar, tea and powdered milk. It was daunting to think the costs of imported goods might skyrocket overnight.

Finally, importing was beginning to seem riskier financially. Merchandise always arrived two to four months after it was ordered, and market prices could fluctuate enough in the interim

to squeeze the importer's margin. Exported fruit, in contrast, would arrive in Europe the following day. The results of each transaction would be known almost overnight. Furthermore, payment by European clients was virtually guaranteed, he believed, and that was not always true with Malian clients.

Mr. Idris Takes on a Management Advisor

In 1991 Mr. Idris's father, Boubacar Idris, took a leave of absence from his business and left it completely in the hands of this son, Ahmed. The next summer, the 31-year-old new General Director of the company received a phone call from the United States Agency for International Development (USAID) Mission in Senou. The gentleman on the phone made an intriguing offer: would he like to have an American MBA student spend a year in his company to "give advice and help in various management areas"?

Mr. Idris had spent time in the United States and had fond memories of his undergraduate experiences at the University of San Francisco, where he graduated in 1985 with a degree in Business Administration. He wrote back agreeing to the offer, indicating he wanted assistance in establishing financial controls, motivating workers, and writing a business plan.

In September 1992, Rachel Steiner, a student from a Midwestern U.S. university, arrived in Senou, Mali. During her first few weeks, she made the rounds of the company and the community. She went to the market place to meet the major wholesalers, some of whom were important clients of Idris S.A. and who were known to buy hundreds of tons of grain, sugar, powdered milk, and tea at a time. She also met as many people as she could in the agricultural and development sectors of the foreign aid community.

One of the first people with whom she spoke was Jeff Colton, the director of the Cooperative League of the United States of America (CLUSA) in West Africa, who worked with villagers in a 90-kilometer radius around Senou, teaching them, among other things, how to manage their finances.

He told her that something that really bothered him in this country was how many mangos rotted in the countryside each year. He estimated the waste to be on the order of thousands of tons, and he encouraged her to think about buying the fruit cheaply for export. The mangos seemed to be of a very high quality, much better than anything he had ever eaten in the United States.

Beginning in October of 1992, Rachel began to meet businesspeople—Lebanese, African, and European—who had exported mangos out of West Africa. In the beginning she heard that West African mangos, of which the favorite varieties are Amelie and Kent, could be sold for as much as 1,000 F.CFA per kilo, or 20 French Francs, in Europe. This kept up her interest in the export idea, since early on she had learned that air freight cost only about 250 F.CFA per kilo. There was thus the potential to realize substantial profit margins.

Rachel's Projected Cash Budget

In mid-January Rachel presented Mr. Idris with her findings based on her interviews and meetings. She developed a spreadsheet that allowed her to do a sensitivity analysis using the following information:

1. Importers in Europe usually bought Amelie mangos at 600 F.CFA to 650 F.CFA per kilo in March, but prices fell to 550 F.CFA or lower by mid-April (when Ivoirien mangos arrived by boat and sold at more competitive prices than those arriving by plane). Prices went back up by June to 600 F.CFA for the Kent mango, and remained at this level through July. Nevertheless, even these prices were not guaranteed. The European importer could sell them to wholesalers for only as much as their quality merited.

2. Mango prices, set by the women who harvested them in this country, started at 70 F.CFA to 80 F.CFA in March and went down to 40 F.CFA by June for the Amelie. By April, however, the mango that Europeans most preferred was the Kent, and that would cost Idris S.A. a full 80 F.CFA per kilo. Normally, harvesting was women's work and the company would pay cash to the women who brought their harvested fruit to the warehouse every day.

3. European importers paid West African exporters anywhere from three weeks to several months after receiving the mangos and selling them.

4. The price per carton was 215 F.CFA and one carton held 5 kilos of mangos. The carton itself weighed 300 grams. The exporter paid freight for the weight of the mangos and cartons, but not for the weight of the pallet.[4]

5. She anticipated the company would export up to three pallets per week in the beginning. Each pallet held about 500 cartons, and each was considered a unit to be exported to a specific European importer. While boxing the mangos would be performed at the warehouse, palletization took place at the airport.

6. The importer's commission was between 6% and 8% of the selling price.

7. Airfreight would cost 250 F.CFA per kilo with Air Afrique, the airline which had control of all landing rights in this country and many parts of West Africa.

8. Transportation of the mangos to the airplane would cost about 7,500 F.CFA per delivery.

9. Laborers were paid 1,000 F.CFA per day whether or not they put in a full day's work. She heard that it would take one day for 10 to 14 men to manually wash and box a pallet of mangos. The company would need two to four men to take the mangos out to the airport and do the palletization. Overtime would cost between 250 F.CFA and 500 F.CFA per person.

10. She had heard that European importers passed their costs of handling and paperwork back to the exporter, but no one could tell her how much this would be. She looked at several possible numbers (expressed in percentages of the cost of airfreight) to see how sensitive the margins were to these variations.

11. The quality of the produce and the quality of its presentation greatly affected the price at which the mangos were sold in Europe.

The Company Decides to Export

After presenting Mr. Idris with the range of possible outcomes, Mr. Idris told her to proceed and start exporting in March. Ms. Steiner requested that she work in partnership with someone from the company. The choice, Mr. Male, was announced not long before exporting began in mid-March.

To box the mangos, the company used existing warehouse space. They already had a 10-ton truck and a large scale to weigh hundreds of kilos of mangos at a time, so there was almost no investment required. By mid-March the company was in the business of exporting mangos. There were some unexpected developments, however, and in response after a few weeks she wrote a letter to the head of the Project Reform for Economic Development project at the USAID Mission in Senou, requesting his assistance with some difficult unanticipated costs (see Exhibit 1).

Other than the problems described in this letter, there were a few challenges working with her partner, Mr. Male. He was normally in charge of exporting the local millet and sorghum to neighboring countries, and presumably that explained his selection as Rachel's partner in the effort to export mangos. He was a very smart, capable and equitable person, and also deeply religious. During their partnership he regaled her with tales of his exploits in the bush, where he often had to travel to export grain. As time went on, however, Rachel sensed that he was disinterested in this work. One day he informed her that exporting sorghum and millet was work well worth the heat and dust because the farmers gave him extra bags of grain (each worth about F.CFA 5,000) for his help with their recordkeeping. Working with mangos, he no longer had the opportunity to traverse the countryside and work with these farmers.

Rachel worked hard to get the business off the ground. At the end of the season, she looked forward to assessing the effort—comparing her company's actual performance to the mango exporting plans she so carefully crafted at the start of the season.

Exhibit 1
Letter to USAID

To: David Attenberry, Policy Reform for Economic Development, USAID
From: Rachel Steiner, Idris S.A.
Date: 26 April 1993
Re: Mango Exportation

I am a USAID subcontractor through the Institute of International Education, and part of a group of 16 student MBA advisors who have received a FMDAP (Free Market Development Adviser Program) grant to work with private enterprises in the third world.

The company with which I work, Idris S.A., has been extremely active in years past in the import and export of commodities such as rice, tea, sorghum and millet. This year we started exporting mangos, and between March 16 and April 25 we exported a total of 30 tons (compared to other major exporters who shipped 100 to 150 tons). This has been a good beginning, and we now know that we can make money during the brief window of time before Ivoirien mangos arrive by boat in mid-April.

As the lead person on this new project for Idris S.A, I have witnessed most of the difficulties involved in fruit exportation, which are many. The most frustrating problems, and the least necessary, have to do with the administrative stumbling blocks and extra "taxes" experienced at the airport. Air Afrique's presence as a monopoly also poses some major problems for exports of fruits and vegetables in West Africa.

(1) While exports have been officially declared exonerated of all taxes, the airport (Senou) has, as of this year, levied a duty of 15 F.CFA per kilo on mangos. Last year it was 5 F.CFA per kilo. We have yet to see any official document regarding this change of policy.

(2) In order for the client in Europe to take possession of the merchandise in Europe, he needs to have a form called the EURI dutifully signed by customs officials here. These signatures cost dearly: between 5,000 F.CFA and 15,000 F.CFA each. For us and other exporters who make a delivery almost every evening, this is costly both in terms of time and money.

(3) Finally, Air Afrique imposes landing rights on all airline companies of F.CFA 1.6 million (US$6,000). This means that any charter company offering to ship out mangos at 170 F.CFA per kilo (as opposed to Air Afrique's F.CFA 250) has difficulty recouping its investment. It is therefore impossible to export mangos after April 15 when prices in Europe drop drastically. I view these landing rights as a form of export tax.

I am requesting your office to pressure the Minister of Transport and other West African government officials to help exporters such as Idris S.A, by eliminating the official airport tax of 15 F.CFA per kilo as well as the unofficial tax levied for a signature on the EURI. Furthermore, can your office do anything about the landing rights imposed by Air Afrique? Your help, in any of these areas, would be of great service to private enterprise as well as to the fruit and vegetable growers of West Africa. Please let me know if we can meet to discuss these matters further.

Tel: 22.22.25/22.45.67.

CASE B

Problems and Anecdotes from the First Mango Season

Rachel wrote the above letter to Mr. Idris, and her eventual successor, describing what she learned during the mango exporting season, which lasted from 16 March to 24 April 1993.

Dear Mr. Idris,

I feel that it is important at this time to discuss some of the things which we have learned over the past six weeks. I hope that next season will prove more successful, given what we have learned during this one.

A. The Importance of Quality

(1) Each mango must be perfect (without scratches, holes, or bruises). Getting the workers to throw away imperfect mangos or ones too ripe was very difficult. Waste seemed to be more or less an anathema.

(2) Each box must weigh between 5 and 5.3 kg. If a box contained 14 equal-sized mangos, each mango would be considered calibre 14; if it contained 12 mangos, each would be considered caliber 12, etc. During our first season, a lot of boxes mixed calibre 8 mangos with calibre 12 ones. The additional work in Europe to sort them out raised our unit costs.

(3) The company can buy huge mangos from the women who harvest them. Europeans seem to feel the bigger the better, even though smaller mangos can be tastier. If the mangos have not finished developing when they are harvested, however, they will never ripen properly. This lowers their selling price per kilo in Europe.

(4) As the weather grows hotter, as high as 120° fahrenheit, we have to make sure that the mangos are dried after being wiped with a wet cloth, or their own heat and moisture will destroy them. Sometimes the workers did not dry the mangos.

My partner and colleague on the project, Mr. Male, later told me that he had not fully ensured the quality of the exported merchandise the way he should have, for a number of reasons.

The first problem had to do with the way he was assigned to the project. When he was originally called into the meeting to discuss this new business, he felt as though he had been ordered to do something that did not seem that lucrative for the company.

I am sure that I played a role in the mixed level of quality of our shipments. At the start of the season, I was largely responsible for the quality of the first few shipments. I assumed Mr. Male understood that such vigilance was required. I never explicitly told him why I was inspecting every box before it was shipped. In sum, it seems that we did not clarify his role in the project which to him may have seemed strange, dirty, and economically unviable.

B. Our Problems with Transportation

Paying the Airway Bill May Not Mean Mangos Reach Their Destination:

On 5 April 1993, Mr. Male went to the airport to send out 6 tons of mangos. The palletization was done properly and the freight was paid for in cash at the Air Afrique counter. With his work there done, he then left the airport.

The company found out two days later that three tons were actually never shipped out. It turns out that under very hot weather conditions, the planes cannot take off with a full load. So three of the six tons were taken off the plane and left on the runway.

As you recall, you and I went out to the airport on 7 April to settle the problem. The representative from Air Afrique explained that planes often cannot take off under a full load, and then he gave us our options.

Idris S.A. could either send the mangos to Europe, and the client there would take possession of the rotten mangos and through litigation recover his losses from Air Afrique. Alternatively, our company could open the boxes here in Mali and replace the rotten mangos, settling for reimbursement here in Senou.

We took the second option, and seven workers and I spent April 8 at the airport replacing the bad mangos (apparently to the amusement of the entire staff of Air Afrique). We believed the airline would then weigh what had gone bad and reimburse us. It turns out that since it was our people who did the sorting, Air Afrique was no longer liable. There was a third option that Air Afrique intentionally never told us: that Idris S.A. not touch the pallet and wait to be reimbursed for its replacement value.

Air Afrique Schedules Planes Which do not Come:

On 19 April we learned that a cargo plane would be passing through on 21 April and the company reserved space to ship a pallet (about 3 tons). Late in the afternoon of 20 April (after buying the mangos) we learned that the plane had been cancelled, but we were assured that there would be another plane coming through on 22 April. When this plane arrived in Senou from Dakar, it was already full of produce. Our mangos finally left on the 23rd, though they had been bought a full three days earlier. These mangos were ruined by the heat and so we did not break even on this shipment.

During this same week we made a confirmed reservation on 19 April for a flight with Air Algerie departing 22 April. We were subsequently told on 21 April that it would be impossible to export on this date; we would have to wait until the 24th. This time mangos bought on the 21st were finally sent on the 24th. This was again catastrophic given the heat of late April. We lost money on this shipment also.

C. Problematic European Importers

European importers can go broke and one of the biggest in France was in the midst of doing so in the spring of 1993. In all cases the importer pays the exporter anywhere from three weeks to several months after selling the merchandise. If an exporter is sending tens of tons of produce over a month, accounts receivable can balloon in a very short period of time. This situation becomes untenable if it means waiting for a bankruptcy court to sort out the priority of creditors.

D. Political Turmoil

On Friday 2 April, Senou had some of the worst violence it has had since the coup of 1991. The National Assembly was broken into and sacked. The president's mother's home was burned to the ground. Cars were burned and a few people died. Since then, the government has closed the schools. They realized that the youths organize themselves at school, and if they can't go to school, they can't organize.

During these days of violence it was difficult to travel back and forth between the home office and the warehouse. This was time consuming and sometimes dangerous for everyone.

These are a few thoughts, and they do not adequately tell the story of the complexity of doing business here.

Regards,

Rachel Steiner

The Outcome of the First Season Shows a Loss

Rachel learned that it was impossible to calculate exact unit costs and profit margins at the start of the season. The company did not even export throughout the anticipated 16 weeks. The season, which should have continued with the export of Kent mangos, could not be completed because the harvest was poor. In addition, quality played the greatest role in determining the sales price for the exported fruit.

At the end of the season, she calculated unit costs per delivery for the whole exporting season (see Exhibit 2). To do this, she took the amount of cash expended for the whole season (cash was used to pay the workers, purchase the mangos, and cover incidentals), and divided by the number of kilos (gross) sent with each delivery. Using the airfreight bills the company knew exactly how much each delivery weighed. The rest of Exhibit I shows start-up costs, how much the mangos were sold for, the net profit or loss on each shipment, and the overall season performance.

Exhibit 3 shows the cost per kilo of handling and paperwork in Europe, costs which were passed back to Idris S.A.

Gifts at the Airport and Calculation of Other Unit Costs

The cost per kilo of getting the EURI forms signed (mentioned in the letter to David Attenberry) also varied. Since one European importer may have one or more pallets delivered to him, it depends on the size of the delivery. That is, the signature will cost between 5,000 F.CFA and 15,000 F.CFA, but this cost will be lower when an increasing number of pallets are designated to a particular European importer. Sometimes the company paid nothing (usually when Rachel was around).

The biggest unknown had been the cost of handling in Europe, partially because fellow exporters were willing to share their experience to only a limited extent. As shown in Exhibit 3, the handling per kilo varied greatly.

Another surprise for the season had been the cost per kilo in airfreight, which went from the anticipated 250 F.CFA/kilo to 265 F.CFA because of the airport tax (also mentioned in the letter to David Attenbury).

The greatest cost to the company was the inability to assure a certain level of quality. This was the main reason for the fluctuations in the price at which mangos were sold in Europe.

Exhibit 2
Results of first season of mango exportation

Cash Spent at Warehouse	3,283,152		Cash was for mangos, labor and incidentals at warehouse				
Total Kilos Sent/Gross	29,804						
Unit Cost/Kilo Without Cartons	110.16						
Total Number Cartons Sent	5,561		Cartons weigh 300 Grams				
Cost/Carton	215						

SHIPMENTS

Date (Day/Month)	Importer	Kg	Cartons	Freight	Cost/Kilo	Sales Price	Net
16.03	CTR	604	139	COD	159.64	143.36	(9,831)
21.03	CTR	2430	493	COD	153.78	167.94	34,415
30.03	CTR	2430	486	646,500	419.21	458.48	95,432
5.04	CTR	6090	1157	1,768,850	441.46	453.77	74,991
8.04	Exotic	2670	480	COD	148.81	46.33	(273,621)
11.04	CTR	4920	850	1,308,800	413.32	401.34	(58,935)
16.04	Tropix	1100	200	COD	149.25	115.1	(37,564)
17.04	Exotic	2610	480	COD	149.70	135.45	(37,188)
19.04	CTR	2720	500	693,470	404.63	396.78	(21,358)
23.04	Tropix	2720	500	COD	149.68	93.9	(151,722)
24.04	Exotic	1510	276	405,150	417.77	376.89	(61,725)
Net Profit (Loss)							**(447,106)**

START-UP COSTS

Labels	70,000	
Forwarder	106,396	
AMELEF	50,000	Export association
Samples	78,100	
Cost of Freight	4,822,770	
Total Spent	9,606,033	Cash, Freight, Cartons + Start Up
Carton Inventory at End of Season	137,385	

Exhibit 3
Cost of handling and
paperwork incurred by
European importers

European Importer	Price/Kilo
CTR	69.91
CTR	36.48
CTR	59.44
CTR	66.13
Exotic	34.33
CTR	60.7
Tropix	89.2
Exotic	79.08
CTR	72.79
Tropix	24.31
Exotic	48.61
Average	58.27

Rachel and Mr. Male overestimated the amount of time the mangos could stay in the warehouse, especially as the weeks became increasingly hot. They also believed the workers could begin to supervise their own work, insuring that they packed similarly-sized mangos in each box, all well-cleaned and thoroughly dried. In fact, one of the leaders in the group, Dramane, assumed responsibility for checking the cartons. However, even this did not prove to be the right strategy.

Whether to Proceed in the Next Season

Despite the apparent failure of the first year's export season, Idris S.A. wanted to press on for the next season. One reason to go forward was that the other major exporters in the export association, revitalized in 1992, told Rachel that they had all lost money during their first season. She was told that it usually takes about three seasons before the company can begin to break even.

There was one exception. A cooperative in Sikasso, aided by an Italian nongovernmental organization (NGO) and which had never before exported to Europe (but had experience exporting out of Sikasso to Mopti and other outlying towns), made money during their first year on exports of 30 tons. Right from the beginning, they went to Europe to meet the client and wrote a fixed contract that guaranteed a minimum price per kilo.

Mr. Idris still had several problems. First of all, who would take over the supervision of this project? Mr. Male had said he was not particularly interested in the project, and the quality of the finished product hung in the balance if the supervisor was not committed. Profit margins were narrow as it was.

Rachel recommended Mr. Idris hire one of the foremen whom she had met who was in the export business and who was looking for a job because he was not very happy with his current boss. His name was Mr. Tele and he had been very help-ful at the airport where late nights were normal and tempers always flared. Mr. Idris did not seem too interested in this option.

Mr. Idris was also very worried about devaluation. Would this event help or hurt his profit margins? Mr. Idris basically liked mango exportation because it did not require heavy investment in infrastructure. Industrialists and factory owners told Rachel that they did not feel secure in this West African country and would leave if they could.

CASE DISCUSSION QUESTIONS

1. What is the unit cost of exporting mangos, and what would be the total profit given airfreight costs of F.CFA 250, and then F.CFA 265?

2. What are the important cost drivers? handling in Europe? air freight? labor? quality of mangos?

3. What actions can exporters undertake to address the problems Idris experienced at the airport?

ENDNOTES

1 This case is intended as a basis for class discussion rather than to illustrate either effective or ineffective handling of an administrative situation.

2 When Idris S.A. planned to import 5,000 metric tons of rice into West Africa, it had to declare its "intention to import" with the Economic Affairs Office. Before economic reforms and liberalization began in earnest in 1991, the government controlled prices and market share by limiting the number of "intentions to import." Now, almost no "intentions to import" were denied. When the goods arrived, importers were required by law to declare at the Customs Office whatever entered the country, and it then levied an import tax. Rice carried import duties of between 55% and 85% depending on the most recent ruling by the National Assembly.

3 The trade balance in this West African country is always negative. Figures for 1988 through 1990 were as follows (in millions of F.CFA):

	1988	1989	1990
Exports	250.7	268.9	410.2
Imports	507.5	483.3	610.1
Trade Deficit	(256.8)	(214.4)	(199.9)

Source: *Foreign Economic Trends and Their Implications for the United States,* West Africa, prepared by the American Embassy Senou.

4 A pallet is a metal platform on which the boxes of mangos are loaded. The platform measures about 12 feet by 12 feet. The platform is then lifted into the plane and rolled into the cargo space. Palletization involves stacking the boxes of mangos on top of each other, throwing a net over them, then tightly securing the bundle to prevent the boxes from capsizing in transit.

Riga Corporation: Collection or Corruption?

by Beverley Earle*

*Bentley College

In 1989, Riga Corporation was a closely held New Jersey corporation with one stockholder, Watson Riga. Riga had 15 employees and engaged in buying and selling commodities both domestically and internationally. Watson had met Ricardo Logo, of Verticales, a commodities broker in the Dominican Republic (DR), through a series of introductions of business acquaintances.

Logo proposed a sale of milk powder between Riga and the DR government in which Logo would receive the industry standard broker's commission. Watson Riga, on behalf of his corporation, entered into a contract to sell milk powder to the government of the DR. This was his first foray into this Caribbean nation, and he was unfamiliar with the country and its history. Riga had been warned about the Foreign Corrupt Practices Act by his lawyer, Darlene Trump, but this deal seemed straightforward.

Specifically, Riga agreed to sell 1500 tons (metric) of milk powder to the DR government for $2,200 a metric ton bringing the contract price to $3.3 million (US). Logo would get a commission of $102 per metric ton or $153,000. This was a standard clause and comparable to contracts around the world. Riga was to release the milk powder after payment was wired and received by his bank in New Jersey. Alternatively, Riga could choose to release the powder, and the government was obligated to pay within 60 days of delivery of the powder. They would pay an interest rate of prime rate plus one percent and after 60 days there would be late fees and additional penalties.

In October 1989 and January 1990, Riga shipped 870 tons of powder to the Dominican Republic pursuant to the contract. It was placed in a warehouse there until Riga received a wire transfer of funds at his designated bank in New Jersey. The government made full payment.

Riga shipped the final 630 tons of powder to the Dominican Republic warehouse between March and May 1990. Riga did not plan to release the powder until he was paid in New Jersey.

In May of 1990, just prior to an election in the Dominican Republic, government officials asked Riga for a favor. Before the election and without prepayment (as was done previously), they wanted him to release the remaining powder, which was in the local warehouse.

Riga discussed this with his wife. He understood that if he did release the powder giving the DR time to pay, there would no doubt be more business. If he didn't release it, he might as well say good bye to this new market.

His wife asked him, "Doesn't the contract protect you? If you give the DR the powder, don't they have to pay you? And if they are late, you will get even more money in penalties? So what's the problem?"

He wondered. After all, the DR had made the first payment with no problem. There had been no squawking about the quality of the powder—they seemed very satisfied. The contract supposedly protected him. If they were late in paying him, he would collect interest on the unpaid balance. It seemed like a win-win proposition. Logo had encouraged him to accede to the government's request too.

His lawyer, Darlene Trump, had not been as sanguine about the whole idea. She reminded him, "Riga, you can be legally correct and still not have the money in your pocket. It can cost you money to collect and everyone knows that—especially in international transactions. They can squeeze you by offering less money up front in settlement of the debt. They know it could take years to collect the full amount and then it is usually a pyrrhic victory because you have spent so much in legal fees trying to collect. That doesn't factor in the time value of money either. Think about it before you release that powder without money in your hand. But only you can gauge the value of the unspoken promise of future business in return for these delayed payment terms."

Riga was annoyed. Lawyers always seemed to be covering their backsides. Never a clear answer. But business involved risk, and he was ready to move forward.

Riga gave the go ahead to release the powder in May 1990. Two months passed and there was no payment from the DR.

By November 1990, the DR had made a payment, but still the DR owed Riga one million dollars in principal and interest. Riga was a small company and its customer, albeit a government, owed it a million dollars. This account had been due for seven months. Riga believed the account receivable was an intolerable drain on the cash flow of the business.

Riga began a campaign to collect the money. Riga called and wrote DR government officials. Nothing changed. By January 1991, Riga began focusing on US officials—trying Congressmen, the Ambassador and the American Chamber of Commerce in the Dominican Republic.

Finally in September 1991, over one year after Riga had completed his performance under the contract, the DR paid him $400,000. During this time, the Dominican government never disputed that it owed the money or that there was any problem with the powder delivered.

For the next year Riga continued to write letters to assorted officials of both countries trying to get some attention to this problem of his uncollected contract payment. He even wrote to the President of the DR, Dr. Joaquin Belaguer. By June of 1992, a full two years after delivery, Riga had received a few interim payments, but $163,000 was still due.

Riga's frustration was palpable. He regularly talked to Logo about what he could do to get paid. At some point in June 1992, Logo related that he had had a conversation with an unnamed Dominican official who said that for a "service fee" he could personally arrange the payment of what was owed on the contract.

Reluctantly but anxious to secure payment, Riga agreed to Logo's proposal. He made arrangements with a Dominican Bank on August 11, 1992 to transfer a portion of the money to be paid to a New Jersey bank and the rest to Logo's account. On August 12, the Dominican government deposited $100,000 in the DR bank which followed Riga's instructions transferring $70,000 to New Jersey and $30,000 to Logo's local account.

On August 17, 1992, Riga spoke with Robert Jenks, a Foreign Service officer in the US Embassy in Santo Domingo. Riga was recounting the two-year horror show of trying to collect his money, and Jenks commiserated with him. Riga mentioned the "service fee" request, and Jenks audibly gasped.

Jenks said very loudly, "Don't do it. Just say no. It ain't worth it, you know. What are you owed—$60,000 now? What, are you crazy?"

Riga tried to get off the phone. He mumbled, "Don't worry—I am not crazy. I have been around and can smell trouble. Oh. . . . O.K. Say Jenks, I have got a call on the other line about a deal in Nigeria. From the frying pan into the fire, eh? So I'll talk to you later—OK? Take care and stay out of those hurricanes' paths."

Jenks replied, "Right. Take care man. Stay out of trouble."

Riga heard the dial tone and cradled the receiver. He placed the phone down uttering softly, "They owe me, damn it. Why should I give up what amounts to years of college tuition when I don't have to?"

The next day Riga received a fax from Jenks. The fax stated:

> This will confirm our phone conversation of August 17, 1992. Any payment of a "service fee" to a "foreign official" will be deemed a violation of the Foreign Corrupt Practices Act. You are warned that any payment hereafter will be deemed a "knowing" violation of the law.

Five days later Riga responded by fax to Jenks:

> August 23
> Dear Robert,
>
> Thanks for your concern. As my contact in Jamaica always says—no problem—not to worry. I don't plan on setting myself up for a vacation at Lompoc Federal Prison. There are better ways to get to rest. Perhaps I will see you in DC this fall.
>
> Best,
>
> Watson

Riga wanted Jenks to forget they ever had a conversation in which the words "service fee" surfaced. For that matter, Riga wanted to forget HE had ever heard the word and he wanted to erase this two-year nightmare collection process from his memory. Riga consoled himself. How different was this from collecting delinquent accounts in the United States? He had allowed a middleman to take a percentage of money collected on overdue accounts. Isn't that what Logo was—a middleman? How did he really know or control what Logo was doing thousands of miles away? Riga had on file a form which Logo had signed which acknowledged that Logo would follow the FCPA. Riga knew he would never have paid a bribe to get the business in the DR. This was murky though. He did not agree with Jenks but he just was sick of the whole matter and wanted it to be over. After he was paid, he would have plenty of time to decide if he wanted to do business in the DR again.

On September 3, 1992, the Dominican Government made the last payment of $63,905 to the DR bank and following Riga's instructions transferred $20,000 to Logo's account and wired the remaining amount to Riga's New Jersey account.

A smile inched across Riga's face. Two years and it was over. He exhaled loudly. Riga felt he could finally close the book on the DR milk powder deal. He had learned some lessons. Business school had not fully prepared him for the dilemmas he had faced in his career. Everything seemed more clear-cut than when he was analyzing those cases in Philadelphia. But he was forty years old and still learning. He thought that was a good sign.

Three months later, Watson Riga was indicted for violations of the Foreign Corrupt Practices Act and faced a trial in New Jersey Federal District Court.

CASE DISCUSSION QUESTIONS

1. Do you believe that Mr. Riga violated the FCPA? Justify your decision (there is some material that can be handed out augmenting the case that is provided in the text).

2. Critique Mr. Riga's action with respect to the entire transaction. What would you have done differently? Did Mr. Riga have any other alternatives?

3. Given Robert Jenks' warning what would you have done next?

4. How would you deal with the indictment if you were Mr. Riga?

5. Outline a policy to deal with incidents such as this if you were engaged in international business.

Richard Ivey School of Business
The University of Western Ontario

IVEY

looks.com (A)—
A Grey Issue

by **Donna Everatt***
under the supervision
of Professor Kersi Anita

*The University of Western Ontario

Ian Smith, founder and managing director of looks.com—a soon-to-be-launched Hong Kong-based e-commerce site for brand name cosmetics, fragrances, skin care products and fashion aimed at Asian women—had run into a potentially serious issue in the implementation of his business plan. He had just finished a call with a high-profile buyer with over a decade of industry experience in Asia, Robbie Jessel. Jessel had stated in no uncertain terms that he would not compromise his hard-earned reputation to be associated with a parallel importer—regardless of his confidence in the concept.

Parallel importing, sourcing products wholesale from unauthorized distributors through the "grey" market, was a popular practice in Asia in most industries, including cosmetics. It allowed retailers to offer products at up to 70 per cent off retail, and, thus, consumers loved it. When authorized distributors complained about grey market intrusions and the consequent erosion of their margins, manufacturers took a tough stance against those responsible. Yet, driven by a desire to increase sales, at least in the short run, some brand owners looked the other way when it came to grey market sales. The "official" manufacturer disposition to grey markets was one of contempt.

According to Smith's business plan, looks.com would source products on the grey market. However, given Jessel's reticence, he now felt compelled to reconsider this decision—one of the most important strategic elements of the whole plan. Smith's business plan had been extraordinarily well received among the investment and Internet community. As a matter of fact, he had secured so much seed capital that his initial offering was oversubscribed, and in order to maintain his target equity level in the company, he was forced to return the last few subscriptions of US$100,000 each. Partnerships had been established with one of the most well-known Web sites in the region, China.com. The latest technology would support the site, and a locally renowned and award-winning design team had created an exciting site design and layout. Smith was poised to capitalize on a first-mover advantage—a critical success factor in the Internet industry—planning on launching the site just in time for the 1999 Christmas shopping season. "Dot-com fever" had caught on in Hong Kong, and e-commerce promised vast new opportunities, as Asian consumers adopted the Internet as a viable retail channel, repeating the pattern of rapid adoption of the Internet in the U.S. ∎

THE INTERNET INDUSTRY IN ASIA HEADING INTO THE NEXT MILLENNIUM

The e-commerce boom experienced in the U.S. was expected to hit Asia with full force in 2000. "While 1998 was the year that online shopping first rose to prominence in the U.S., the 1999 holiday season is shaping up to be the launching point for an expansion of global consumer e-commerce," according to a senior analyst for the Gartner Group, a high-profile Internet consulting firm.

It was estimated that in 1999 there were between 20 to 30 million Internet users throughout the Asia-Pacific region (almost half of whom were located in Japan) (see Exhibit 1). Though growth of the Internet had surged from a year earlier—up from 8.6 million users in 1997—this number accounted for only about 15 per cent of the world's total Internet-user population.[1] Internet usage in the region, however, was expected to rise significantly in the foreseeable future, coinciding with development of supporting infrastructure,[2] and as consumers overcame their initial skepticism and fears regarding security (a key concern globally with regard to e-commerce). Thus, in 1999 e-commerce in Asia accounted for just 7 per cent of the worldwide total of over US$12 billion (whereas the U.S. accounted for 70 per cent of online purchases and Europe 23 per cent). Asia, however, was forecast to be the second largest Internet growth opportunity in the world (after western Europe) and by 2002, the region was widely expected to have 50 million users, whose purchase activity would account for almost 10 per cent of the value of global e-commerce activity.

Exhibit 1

INDUSTRY STATISTICS

Growth in Number of Internet Users
- 1997 – 8.6 million
- 1998 – 14 million
- 1999 – 20 million
- 2000e – 26 million
- 2001e – 35 million
- 2002e – 48 million

Internet Spending in Asia
- 1998 – US$700 million
- 2003 – US$32 billion

Source: IDC, GS estimates

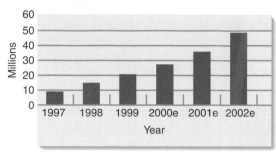

E-COMMERCE REVENUES IN ASIA

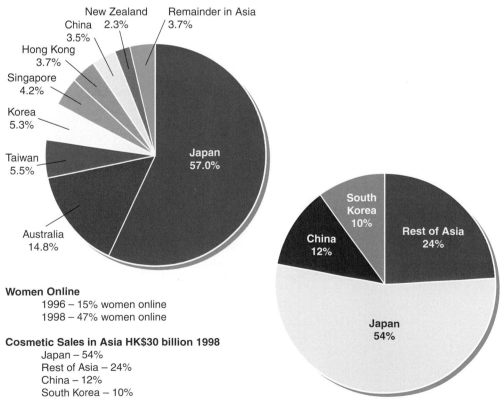

Women Online
- 1996 – 15% women online
- 1998 – 47% women online

Cosmetic Sales in Asia HK$30 billion 1998
- Japan – 54%
- Rest of Asia – 24%
- China – 12%
- South Korea – 10%

Source: Market Tracking International, Euromonitor

Several environmental factors would encourage increased e-commerce activity in Asia. Beyond the sheer size of several key markets,[3] regional governments were expected to gradually loosen restrictions, opening markets to foreign competition and paving the way for knowledge transfer of information technology (IT), as well as reducing tariffs. Public sector initiatives to strengthen the IT infrastructure[4] of many regional economies had also been developed. Pent-up demand among consumers and businesses alike for imported goods and services (especially those from the Western Hemisphere) would be unleashed over the next couple of years, aided by the increased adoption of e-commerce, making products and services readily available that had previously been sold predominantly in western markets.

Many Asian consumers and retailers alike welcomed this trend. Companies engaged in e-commerce were afforded several competitive advantages over their "bricks and mortar" competitors, including minimal leasing, leasehold improvement and overhead costs, centralized and highly efficient order processing and inventory controls, and lower cost, highly targeted marketing compaigns.[5] These competitive advantages, combined with a first-mover advantage, and the attractive margins associated with the cosmetic industry convinced Smith that looks.com was a tremendous opportunity.

LOOKS.COM

Smith's business plan stated that looks.com would offer a secure site[6] that sold "the most popular brands of cosmetics, fragrances, skin-care and fashion-related products at competitive prices." In addition to an "aggressive pricing strategy," Smith's approach for

building customer loyalty involved providing an extensive range of free give-aways, ranging from lipsticks and other cosmetic samples, to toiletry bags, perfumes and bigger ticket items. Smith planned on obtaining these give-aways "free of charge from the cosmetics companies as per standard industry practice." Looks.com offered "fast delivery to any destination around the world" (though Smith expected that at least 50 per cent of looks.com initial sales would be in the Hong Kong market). Taiwan and Singapore were other targeted key markets, though sales would come from other Southeast Asian countries as the site gained a higher profile throughout the region, and as Internet usage gained higher penetration among consumers throughout the Asia Pacific or as looks.com expanded into new markets.

One of the first market expansion plans was for Japan, where Smith planned on expanding in early 2000 with the development of a "mirror" site (in Japanese), with a company-owned server housed at a Japanese Internet service provider (ISP). Though he planned on organizing the Japanese site as a wholly or majority-owned subsidiary of Looks.com Holdings Limited, Smith did not rule out the possibility of the participation of a Japanese joint venture partner. In looking at initial target markets (including Singapore and Taiwan), Smith did not foresee duty and import tariffs as major constraints to sales. However, Japan was a high tariff market. Therefore, Smith planned on establishing a distribution center within Japan, which would also significantly reduce distribution costs and delivery times in that market.

According to Smith, while China remained another attractive market for the sale of consumer products, it remained a challenge for online sales. The combination of a lack of credit card processing facilities, post-sale distribution logistics, low

---

Exhibit 2
Sample pages from the looks.com site www.looks.com

Source: Company Web site, October 1999.

Exhibit 2 (continued)

URBAN DECAY

· [Gift Ideas] · [Makeup] ·

This is industrial-chic, super deluxe make-up in cutting edge colors for anyone who wants to rattle the notion of what beauty is. Express who you are (at any moment), decorate your body, defy convention -- or embrace it and put your own little twist on it. Be yourself, be someone else. Try it mild, try it wild. Just try it.

New Nail Graffiti - Urban Art for Fingers and Toes - Ironically, nail graffiti is our solution to nails that look vandalized by failed attempts at nail art. Ever tried to paint flowers on your toenails and ended up with worms instead? Or used nail decals and felt like you were reliving your cheesy sticker album days from the 7th grade? Nail Graffiti are foolproof art stencils that are easy to use. Just press a stencil onto your dry nail, stick on a couple coats of contrasting nail colour, and let it dry. When you peel it off, voila! Perfect nail art.

Eyeshadow - Manna for the disenchanted diva. Bold, iridescent shadows.

Lip gunk - More than gloss, its gunk.

Nails - The secret weapon of every glamazon warrior.

My Shopping Bag

Check My Order

Join Our Club

Delivery & Returns

looks' Guarantee

Site Map

Feedback

About Us

Legal

our partners
24/7 asia
aol
china.com
cww.com
hongkong.com
Meg-i.com
Redskirt.com
starz people
taiwan.com
the web connection
womenjapan.com

Internet penetration and adoption rates, and high tariffs, posed significant hurdles to effective penetration in the short term.

Though looks.com would initially focus on the markets in Hong Kong, Singapore, and Taiwan, Smith considered the five million women with middle to high incomes, aged 17 through 35 in the Asia Pacific region, to be looks.com's target market. Smith felt that this segment of women was more likely to have Internet access, and to be early adopters of on-line shopping. Smith grouped the target market into four market segments—"Trendies," "New Women," "Mothers," and "Sophisticates."

The so-called Trendies were at the younger end of target market demographic, sought new trends, and had a relatively high share of disposable income. Availability of new products, extensive choice and value were meaningful benefits to Trendies. The New Women had careers, relationships, and family commitments, with hectic lives and a wide range of interests and, thus, valued the benefits of convenience, quality and value. Mothers and Sophisticates were considered secondary target markets. Though the latter group gravitated toward the higher

end brands and was less concerned with value, they both sought quality and convenience. The design and functionality of the site would appeal to each of these market segments, offering two fully integrated and complementary components: the "looks.com Boutique" and the "LooksZone" (see Exhibit 2).

The Looks Boutique, the retail component of the site, would offer brand-name cosmetics and fragrances, and health and beauty products and fashions at competitive prices, with extensive product descriptions, photos, and where appropriate, digital demonstrations. The LooksZone was the entertainment component and was designed to promote repeat visits to "solidify looks.com as a Web-based community" by providing information on issues concerning Asian women, including, but not limited to, health and beauty. Various articles focusing on self-help and self-improvement, image consulting, fashion and trend reports would be written by looks.com in-house writers, and other articles would be written by contracted dermatologists, gynecologists, and other medical people, augmented with content that was aggregated from other sites. Smith's objective was to become a portal[7] for Asian women, selling health and beauty-related products—anything from baby and maternity products and services to vitamins and fashion accessories, for example. Beyond the spectacular forecast growth of e-commerce in Asia, looks.com's ability to evolve into a portal aimed at the lucrative and fast-growing market of Asian females was a key consideration in why Smith chose to sell cosmetics over the Internet in the first place.

WHY COSMETICS?

Smith explained that he had "no particular affinity for cosmetics" and no prior experience in the industry (or the Internet for that matter). However, he had been working in Asia for over a decade, since he was 24, and had been surfing the Net for almost as long. Most recently, Smith had worked for several years with a Hong Kong-based investment firm as an associate director, after a two-year term as the managing director (Asia) of a car park operation. Working in Asia was a natural move after having graduated with a degree in Asian Management Studies from the University of Hawaii. In 1998, Smith had enrolled in a two-year Executive MBA program at the Hong Kong campus of the Richard Ivey School of Business at The University of Western Ontario. Feeling a strong pull toward something entrepreneurial, Smith felt he wanted to "strike while the iron was hot" to capture a first-mover advantage in the rapidly growing e-commerce industry in Hong Kong and throughout Asia, and began research into what type of site he would launch. After examining "30 or 40 different site concepts, including pure portal plays, auction sites and e-commerce opportunities for products and services, such as real estate, Asian art, sporting goods and factory direct stuff out of China for example," Smith found that cosmetics offered the most promising e-commerce opportunities:

> In cosmetics, 80 per cent of the sales are repeat purchases—customers are highly brand loyal. Moreover, cosmetic brands are particularly recognizable—the industry spends about the highest percentage of revenue on promotion, so most of the products that would be listed on the site would already have a high profile in many other Asian markets. Fraud was not as much of an issue as with other e-commerce sites—you can't download cosmetics, and statistics have proven that sites catering to males were much more susceptible to fraud.
>
> Moreover, health and beauty products are very small generally, so they're easily shipped and received (a consideration especially in Asia where most people have very small mail boxes in apartment buildings) and they had a high value-to-weight ratio. Inventory management is made easier with such small products, and styles change each season so you don't have to carry products 10 years old (like Amazon does with books). One of the most enticing things attracting me to cosmetics was the fact that manufacturers are doing their damnedest to keep prices high; it was the profit margins that ultimately convinced me to sell cosmetics online.

Another important factor persuading Smith to launch a cosmetics Web site was the fact that in 1999, direct competition to looks.com was limited. Though several manufacturers of cosmetics and health and beauty products had created their own Web site, and a myriad of sites had been created that sold name brand cosmetics, none catered specifically to Asian women, and few U.S.-based sites shipped outside of North America. Smith considered traditional cosmetic retail outlets including department, drug, and variety stores as well as beauty salons, supermarkets and discount cosmetic outlets to be indirect (as opposed to direct) competition, as he felt that looks.com held a particular competitive advantage over more traditional distribution channels. Thus, Smith considered the concept behind looks.com an "overlooked Internet opportunity in Asia" and set out to develop a business plan. One of his most important considerations, therein, was whether he would source his products for sale on the site from the "grey" market or deal with authorized distribution channels.

THE GREY MARKET

Grey marketing activity—often confused with the illegal activity of counterfeiting, the sale of fake goods—was not universally illegal per se. However, the transport of goods between markets was often done cross-border, without proper licences or contrary to trade regulations.[8] By definition, grey marketing (also known as product diversion and parallel importing) occurred whenever the same product was sold at different prices in different markets, through authorized or unauthorized distribution channels. Thus, grey marketers were parties that capitalized on price differences between markets—their margins were made in the sales of those goods in the higher-priced markets, and as such grey market activity was arbitrage, conducted by parties outside the established supply-chain agreements.

Over the past decade, grey market activity had become ever more common across a variety of industries, ranging from watches, cameras, and health and beauty products to heavy industrial equipment. By some accounts, such unauthorized sales were increasing at a rate of over 20 per cent annually, in tandem with the increase in the level of cross-border trade, aided partly by the availability of market-by-market pricing information and crumbling trade barriers around the globe. While precise figures were difficult to come by, research suggested that grey market sales occurred to the tune of billions of dollars worldwide, and Asian markets accounted for some of the most prevalent grey marketing activity (see Exhibit 3).

There were several advantages in obtaining goods through the grey market. Being a parallel marketer would allow looks.com to offer deep discounts. Combined with the convenience of online shopping, Smith felt looks.com could gain a significant competitive advantage over "bricks and mortar" cosmetic retailers who dealt with authorized distribution channels (and, therefore, offered products within a narrowly defined range of the manufacturers suggested retail price [MSRP]. Smith felt, however, that as an online retailer, he could undercut not only full price competitors, but also the discounters. Smith felt this would be key in securing a leadership position.

Naturally, if Smith sourced products in the grey market, another key advantage was that he would not have to gain each

Exhibit 3
Estimated regional grey
market activity

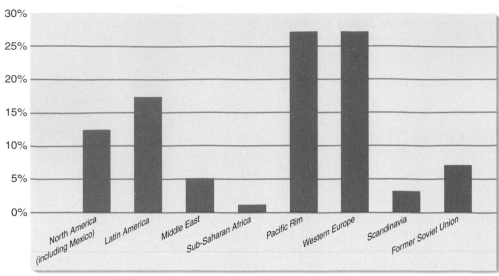

Source: *Business Horizons, Elsevier Science, Inc., NY, November-December 1999.*

manufacturer's permission to list their lines for sale on looks.com. Several positive consequences flowed from this. First, Smith would be free to set not only the price at which products were offered, but also the variety of products listed on the site. A key factor driving the success of the site was not only the breadth of product offerings, but also that looks.com offered many of the most sought-after brands. Another advantage in bypassing the manufacturer was that Smith could control the presentation and positioning of all products listed within the site. This meant that Smith was free to consider the overall branding of looks.com, without the particular positioning and branding of each individual product, allowing him to develop a more comprehensive looks.com brand. This was important, given that in Asia, e-commerce was not fully understood or adopted by the general public and Smith was eager to establish looks.com as "a premier, top-of-mind e-commerce site." The looks.com business plan also stated that looks.com would be "the lowest priced retailer in Asia in its category." By sourcing products through the grey market, Smith had more flexibility with regard to pricing as well. The business plan qualified this low pricing strategy, indicating:

> Because of the sheer number of products available, it will be impossible to ensure that looks.com is the price leader for all products. However, utilizing the customer and purchase analysis tools available on the Internet, looks.com will be able to ensure that it has the lowest prices on the products that are of the greatest interest to our customers.

A MODEL PARALLEL IMPORTER IN HONG KONG—SA SA COSMETICS

Products sourced in grey markets were sold at a significant discount on manufacturer's suggested retail prices to gain competitive advantage. Thus, even though Smith's costs would be lower, often his retail markup would be less than if he dealt with authorized dealers and sold items at close to full MSRP. Moreover, Smith explained that the added link (or links) added to the value chain (and, hence, another level of cost) would also decrease profit margins. Smith stated that if he chose to source his products through grey markets, "the game would be to drive up the volume, and get your profit that way". This was a key part of the business model of a very successful bricks and mortar cosmetics retailer—Sa Sa.[9]

Sa Sa's 25 locations throughout Hong Kong and the New Territories had the distinctive character of a discount retailer. Sa Sa's stores were located in very high pedestrian traffic locations, in a confined "no frills" environment, where cosmetics counters and bins brimmed with health and beauty products retailed at 25 per cent to 70 per cent off the MSRP. This business model had served the company well—1998 profits were HK$250 million on sales of HK$1.25 billion. With a 20 per cent after-tax profit, Smith referred to Sa Sa as "the best-known and most successful parallel importer in Asia."

Smith explained that Sa Sa obtained their products through a variety of channels, including manufacturers who were eager to get rid of last season's lines, products that were close to their expiry date, or excess inventory. Often, products were acquired in other regions and imported to Hong Kong, through either authorized distributors from a region outside of Hong Kong or an unauthorized party with access to the goods. They also bought product at retail at a bulk discount, or from a liquidation sale of another retailer (either in the region or internationally and then imported) or without the manufacturer's consent from the authorized distributor at a discounted rate. The UPC[10] code of products sold through parallel importers like Sa Sa had been covered or otherwise made illegible, making it impossible to trace the product's origin. The inventiveness of parallel importers left Sa Sa, and similar companies, with a myriad of sources to purchase their product, allowing them a distinct competitive advantage over drug and department stores and retailers who sourced their health and beauty products from locally authorized distributors.

Thus, Smith explained that the effect of parallel importing, which allowed retail sales at significantly below MSRP, had been hotly contested by brand name manufacturers of cosmetics for years. However, because parallel importing was "not really illegal," according to Smith, manufacturers had little recourse:

> Parallel importers pose a huge threat to manufacturers in Asia, and, therefore, most distributor contracts included a clause that forbade sales to discounters such as Sa Sa. If a manufacturer was to somehow find that a distributor was selling to Sa Sa (i.e., knowing that the product will be sold at a deep discount) in order to increase their numbers, they would likely run into trouble, but really, there is little that can be done to stop the practice.

Smith recounted the example of a large cosmetics manufacturer that took a parallel importer to court in Australia—and lost. According to Smith, the court said "hey, if you can't control the distribution of your product outside of Australia, then that's outside the jurisdiction of the Australian courts." The U.S. Supreme Court came to a similar conclusion when they ruled unanimously in favor of a distributor (Quality King Distributors, an $800 million company). The appellant was Robert L'anza, the founder and CEO of a US$20 million company, L'anza Research International. Though many other manufacturers had filed similar suits in lower courts in the U.S., L'anza was the first professional beauty product manufacturer to take his cause all the way to the Supreme Court and, thus, the case received extensive media coverage. Many interested parties across a myriad of industries viewed the decision of the case as a landmark, feeling that it would embolden Quality King and other grey marketers. In March 1998, L'anza summarized the court's decision saying:[11]

> A company that exports its U.S.-manufactured products is not protected under federal copyright laws from having them sold and shipped back into the country for sale by another firm.

This was certainly the case in Asia, where, according to Smith "there's essentially no such thing as MSRP for most products, not only cosmetics." He continued:

> When Sa Sa came to the market, it really caused problems. Local distributors would consistently be frustrated and angry at seeing their lines at their local Sa Sa store, knowing that they did not sell the products to Sa Sa. It gave a bad name to the industry—but the consumers love it.
>
> Many of the products bought on the grey market are highly sought after brands, including Christian Dior, Shiseido, and Lancome among others. Consumers don't really care about where the product came from if it means they can buy their favorite brands at significant discounts, for what appeared to be authentically branded products in their original wrapping, prior to (or close to) the date of expiry in most cases.

Smith described one perspective, saying that it's a good deal for consumers.

There's one school of thought that says "If Sa Sa can make money by parallel importing, then why not?" It's the manufacturer's responsibility to monitor the distribution, and if they can't do it, then in a highly entrepreneurial society as found throughout Southeast Asia, many people say "tough luck." Of course, in Asia, it is very difficult—if not impossible—to control distribution, given the widespread use and acceptance of parallel importing.

On the other hand, Smith stated that the practice could compromise a brand's quality positioning, as often (though not always) products were sold that were close to, or exceeded the suggested date of expiry, or that had not been stored or transported in optimal conditions, adversely affecting product quality. Moreover, the placement of the products on shelves or in bins, or the condition of its packaging, was generally at odds with the quality positioning that the manufacturers had invested heavily in to promote. Thus, manufacturers openly condemned Sa Sa and other parallel importers like them as a blight on the Asian retailing landscape. Smith was reluctant to position looks.com in this league, but was daunted by the considerable disadvantages in dealing directly with manufacturers and felt that on the whole, the advantages of parallel importing outweighed the disadvantages—at least while looks.com was becoming established. After the site had earned a reputation as an industry player and could meet minimum order lots, Smith planned on dealing directly with manufacturers. However, that day could come sooner than he had originally thought.

DECISIONS, DECISIONS

Smith felt compelled at this juncture to consider the implications of being a parallel importer. Would other highly sought-after industry professionals, as well as potential suppliers, strategic partners, and investors take the same stance as Jessel and refuse to deal with looks.com if they were a parallel marketer? Yet, so many issues arose if Smith decided to source products through authorized distribution channels. Not only would approaching each manufacturer be a time-consuming proposition, Smith expected that many manufacturers would not be interested in dealing with a relatively smaller player.[12]

Moreover, by supplying looks.com, there was a risk of antagonizing their distributors, fearing that sales through looks.com would cannibalize their existing distribution arrangements, even if Smith positioned the site as a duty-free retailer. If looks.com were to source its product line from local distributor(s), the firm's margins would decline precipitously. This extra layer could erode profit margins so that it could be virtually impossible to achieve an acceptable return on investment. However, if manufacturers were attracted to list with the site, looks.com's margins would be higher than if they dealt in the grey market, and they would establish themselves with arguably a more favorable reputation among manufacturers right from the beginning.

In the final analysis, though, there were clear advantages for manufacturers to list their products on the site, including increased sales and support of the brand. If several of the most sought-after brands decided not to sell to looks.com, it could be the ultimate demise of the site. Nonetheless, Smith felt strongly that Jessel's decade of industry experience managing the distribution in Asia of products from high-profile manufacturers such as Orlane, Club Monaco, Benetton, Ahava (a popular brand from Israel), Nina Ricci, Paco Robane, and Giorgio Fragrances would prove invaluable. Jessel would apply his knowledge of markets, pricing and the structure of deals to the looks.com venture, and would establish key contacts with various international suppliers through his extensive personal network.

During their discussions, Jessel had stated many times that his position would be the general sentiment of the most talented buyers in the industry, and Smith's initial inquiries seemed to support this. As Smith hung up from the videoconference, he mulled over whether he should revise the entire business model of looks.com. Smith considered the decision regarding whether of not to be a parallel importer, perhaps the single most important decision he could make, one that could have the largest impact on the success—or failure—of his dream.

CASE DISCUSSION QUESTIONS

1. What are the advantages of acquiring a line of cosmetics from the "grey" market?

2. What are the disadvantages of acquiring a line of cosmetics from the "grey" market?

3. Does the "grey" market appear to be "legal"? "ethical"? Discuss.

4. What should Smith do?

5. What would you do?

ENDNOTES

1 Despite the fact that almost half of the world's population lived in the region.

2 Specifically, many Asian-based Web sites still did not have payment gateways—electronic paths that directed credit card charges to the card's bank, from an electronic site, which made sites more secure. Without an electronic payment gateway, customer service representatives typed credit card numbers into a terminal, which then relayed the data to a bank.

3 Including Australia, China, Japan, Hong Kong, Taiwan, and South Korea for example.

4 Including Singapore's "wired island," Malaysia's "Multimedia Super Corridor," and Hong Kong's "Cyberport."

5 Web-based technologies allowed sites to capture a tremendous amount of knowledge on customer buying habits and preferences, as well as valuable demographic information that could be obtained through registration with the site.

6 Using an electronic payment gateway.

7 A portal is a Web site that is intended to be the first place people see when using the Web. Typically, a "portal site" has a catalogue of Web sites, a search engine, or both. A portal site may also offer e-mail and other services to entice people to use that site as their main "point of entry" (hence "portal") to the Web.

8 In 1999, legislation in the European Union (EU) banned grey market activity (resulting in an increase in legal actions taken against retailers and importers dealing in such activity) however, this is not the case in most other regions.

9 Though Sa Sa did purchase some brands directly from the manufacturer, they purchased the prestige brands—Lancome, Estée Lauder, and Polo Ralph Lauren, for example—on the grey market.

10 Uniform Product Code, a numerical sequence identifying individual products or SKUs (stock-keeping units).

11 Professional Beauty, Issue Number One, Creative Age Communications Inc., Van Nuys, CA., 1998.

12 Minimum wholesale orders for L'Oreal product lines were US$100,000 for example.

Seven-Eleven Japan: Venturing into e-Tailing

*The University of Hong Kong

Deric K.K. Tan prepared this case from public sources under the supervision of Dr. Ali Farhoomand for class discussion. This case is not intended to show effective or ineffective handling of decision or business processes.

This case is part of a project funded by a teaching development grant from the University Grants Committee (UGC) of Hong Kong.

Not content with nine million customers per day, Toshifumi Suzuki [see Exhibit 1], the Chairman and Chief Executive Officer of Seven-Eleven Japan Co. Ltd., was looking for ways to attract more customers and more sales. Fascinated by the market's optimistic outlook on the growth of business-to-consumer (B2C) e-commerce in Japan, he contacted several prominent Japanese companies to explore the possibility of working together to launch the biggest B2C e-commerce Website in Japan. Suzuki knew that successfully launching and operating a B2C e-commerce business in Japan, known for its citizens' hesitancy to buy on-line, could be a big coup for him. His challenge now was to convince his would-be partners that he had a potentially successful and lucrative business model. ■

Exhibit 1
Toshifumi Suzuki

The Japanese have Toshifumi Suzuki to thank for snack food at all hours. The name was especially familiar for those in the retailing sector as Suzuki, aged 67, was chairman and CEO of Seven-Eleven Japan Co., Ltd., the operator of the largest chain of convenience stores in Japan.

A country boy from the Nagano prefecture, Suzuki worked in publishing for a large publication sales agent before joining Japanese retailer Ito-Yokado Co. in 1963. At Ito-Yokado, he was involved in administration and human resources. In 1973, he led the fight to win a Seven-Eleven franchise in Japan from its US parent, Southland Company. As a result, Seven-Eleven Japan, Co., Ltd was established in 1973 with Ito-Yokado as its major shareholder. Suzuki helped open the first store in 1974, giving him the reputation of being the father of the Japanese convenience store concept. He led the drive to computerise operations, and had a reputation of forcefully maintaining his views and ideas through his top-down management style. After becoming President of Seven-Eleven Japan in 1978, he headed its team merchandising efforts. In 1992, he became the President of Ito-Yokado. Taking advantage of his experience at Seven-Eleven Japan, he tried to make the most of it at Ito-Yokado by implementing a series of reforms. Refuting criticisms that his top-down management style did not allow his staff to make their views reflected in the management of the company, Suzuki maintained that reform could only be done through the top-down line of command.

Sources:
1. "Asian Cover Story—Managers: Toshifumi Suzuki," *Business Week International Editions*, 3 July, 2000.

2. "Ito-Yokado Faces Its Limitations," *Nikkei Business*, 30 September, 1996, p. 22.

THE E-COMMERCE ENVIRONMENT IN JAPAN

In May 2000, the Economist Intelligence Unit (EIU) surveyed 60 countries and ranked them based on their readiness for e-commerce. This was assessed based on the general business environment and connectivity in each country. Factors taken into consideration included local government policies, the state of the existing telephone network, and Internet access-related issues such as dial-up costs and literacy rates. Based on these factors, Japan was placed in the 21st position, the lowest among the Group of Seven industrialised countries [see Exhibit 2].

Even though Internet usage was high in Japan, the growth of B2C e-commerce was slow compared to other G7 countries. According to a survey conducted jointly by the Ministry of International Trade and Industry (MITI) and Andersen Consulting (AC) in 1999, e-commerce transactions accounted for only 0.02 per cent of all the business-to-consumer transactions in 1998. This represented only about one thirty-fifth of the level in the US.[1] Numerous surveys were done to determine the reasons for the slow growth. In the March 2000 issue of *Japan Inc.* magazine, the authors of several articles attributed the relatively poor e-commerce environment in Japan to several reasons [see Appendix 1]. These included the phobia Japanese consumers had about submitting credit card information over the Internet and a relatively expensive connection charge. According to eMarketer, Japan had the world's highest combined telecommunication and ISP fees [see Figure 1]. In addition, endfulfilment of on-line orders was a problem for many people. Most consumers were not home during the day to receive parcels they had ordered on-line. Consumers were also doubtful about receiving their parcels from on-line stores, either due to mailing errors or non-fulfilment on the part of the stores.

In a bid to encourage the growth of e-commerce in Japan, the government deregulated stock commissions in 1999, enabling consumers to start trading via the Internet. That year was widely considered as "the first year of e-commerce" in Japan. The government also attempted to introduce competition into the telecommunications industry by splitting Nippon Tele-

Exhibit 2
The EIU e-business-readiness rankings

Rank	Country	Business Environment Ranking, 2000–04	Connectivity Ranking	E-business-Readiness Ranking
1	US	8.69	9	8.8
2	Sweden	8.26	9	8.6
3	Finland	8.21	9	8.6
4	Norway	8.00	9	8.5
5	Netherlands	8.84	8	8.4
6	UK	8.80	8	8.4
7	Canada	8.66	8	8.3
8	Singapore	8.55	8	8.3
9	Hong Kong	8.52	8	8.3
10	Switzerland	8.42	8	8.2
11	Ireland	8.42	8	8.2
12	Denmark	8.41	8	8.2
13	Germany	8.32	8	8.2
14	France	8.17	8	8.1
15	Belgium	8.17	8	8.1
16	Australia	8.14	8	8.1
17	New Zealand	8.10	8	8.1
18	Austria	7.96	8	8.0
19	Italy	7.68	8	7.8
20	Israel	7.61	8	7.8
*21	Japan	7.43	8	7.7
22	Spain	8.01	7	7.5
23	Chile	7.85	7	7.4
24	South Korea	7.30	7	7.2
25	Portugal	7.59	6	6.8
26	Argentina	7.22	6	6.6
27	Taiwan	8.13	5	6.6
28	Thailand	7.27	5	6.1
29	Poland	7.15	5	6.1
30	Hungary	7.09	5	6.0

Source: *The EIU ebusiness forum*, "Introducing the EIU's e-business-readiness rankings," 4 May, 2000.

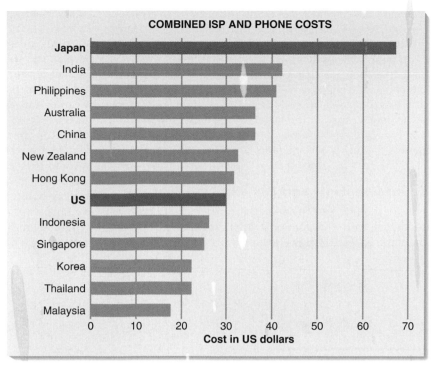

COMBINED ISP AND PHONE COSTS

Source: *Japan Inc*, URL: http: //www.japaninc.net/mag/comp/2000/06/ jun00_unwired _ispgraph.html, 15 November, 2000.

Figure 1. Combined ISP and phone costs

phone & Telegraph, the dominant telecommunication company, into three companies. Several research groups looked favourably upon the efforts taken by the government. For instance, in January 2000, Andersen Consulting projected that the market for B2C e-commerce in Japan would grow from 248 billion yen in 1999 to 3.5 trillion yen in 2003.[2]

Toward the end of 1999, e-commerce in Japan seemed to have evolved into a form that was different from the conventional US-style e-commerce practiced in most countries. The focus of e-commerce was on Japan's ubiquitous convenience stores, or *konbinis*, as they were known, each with an average floor space of 100 square metres.[3] The operators of these convenience stores had been racing to introduce e-commerce initiatives to capture the attention and business of the population. The most aggressive so far was Seven-Eleven Japan, with its investments into ambitious e-commerce ventures such as an on-line bookstore that allowed payment and pick-up at a 7-Eleven store. Others, such as Lawson Products Inc., the operator of the second-largest chain of convenience stores, were busy announcing e-commerce businesses of their own.[4] Up until February 2000, Lawson had invested US$60 million installing terminals in its over 7,200 stores nation-wide. These terminals allowed customers to browse on-line catalogues, download software or book package tours to overseas destinations, and to pay for their orders at the counter

in the store. The reason for the popularity of using convenience stores as a launch pad for e-commerce was that these stores offered a physical location for consumers to pay in cash and to pick up their orders, a method that the Japanese people were familiar and at ease with.

> "The Japanese would rather pick up their goods and pay for them at a konbini. "
>
> Morihiko Ida, Head of Equities Research,
> Century Securities, Japan.

SEVEN-ELEVEN JAPAN CO., LTD.

Since its establishment in 1973, Seven-Eleven Japan had taken on "Adapting to Change" as its business slogan, reflecting its focus on adapting to changing consumer trends. As such, its 7-Eleven convenience stores had earned the patronage of much of the population, far outstripping other companies in the convenience store sector as well as in the overall retail industry in terms of growth and profitability. For the fiscal year ended

29 February, 2000, while Japan was in the midst of an economic downturn, Seven-Eleven Japan opened an additional 423 stores and recorded the highest profits in the retail industry [see Table 1]. This impressive result and its rapid growth was due to its efforts at developing merchandise and services that met customers' needs and requirements. For example, it was the pioneer in providing ready-made meals such as sushi and spaghetti that had become popular among the Japanese population. In addition, the information and distribution systems played an especially large role in placing Seven-Eleven Japan in a leading position.

The Information and Distribution Systems

Since the inception of Seven-Eleven Japan, Suzuki had been preoccupied with the continual application of information technology to capture data so as to better meet customers

needs. Seven-Eleven Japan's first information system was introduced in 1978. Point of sale (POS) systems were introduced in 1982 and since then had been continuously upgraded. It formed the backbone of Seven-Eleven Japan's just-in-time ordering system. By showing real-time information such as merchandise sell-out schedules, shelf-stocking methods, the weather and local events, the POS systems allowed the stores to be extremely responsive to consumers' shifting tastes [Exhibit 3 omitted].[5] For example, if the weather was predicted to be bad, the systems would remind operators to put umbrellas next to the sales counter. In 1999, Seven-Eleven Japan completed the installation of the Fifth-Generation Total Information System [see Exhibit 4], representing a total investment of 60 billion yen. One of the largest information systems in the world, it linked all the 7-Eleven stores via satellite communications and ISDN telephone lines. The system could transmit

Table 1
Seven-Eleven Japan: non-consolidated financial information

	2000	1999	Fiscal Year 1998 (million yen)	1997	1996
Total store sales	1,963,972	1,848,147	1,740,961	1,609,007	1,477,127
Revenue from operations	327,014	297,993	277,186	254,617	231,227
Cost of sales	41,132	33,504	31,036	26,898	23,314
Selling, general and administrative expenses*	148,403	135,155	122,834	111,320	100,329
Operating income	137,477	129,334	123,316	116,399	107,584
Total shareholders'equity	529,822	482,516	439,411	397,744	N/A

* [see Table 2]

Source: *Seven-Eleven Japan Co., Ltd.,* Annual Reports 1998, 1999, and 2000.

Table 2
Major elements of selling, general and administrative expenses

	2000	1999	Fiscal Year 1998 (million yen)	1997	1996
Salaries and bonuses	26,211	23,319	21,712	19,665	17,569
Advertising expenses	19,322	20,073	18,141	14,039	11,630
Depreciation	24,394	22,865	16,234	14,734	14,245
Utilities expenses	20,220	19,144	19,492	17,358	16,612

Source: *Seven-Eleven Japan Co., Ltd.,* Annual Reports 1998, 1999, and 2000.

large volumes of information at high speed and had superior information-processing capability. Using this system, Seven-Eleven Japan was able to provide its stores with useful, easy-to-use data and visual information enabling reductions in missed sales opportunities and inventory write-offs through precise item-by-item management. As a result, inventory was kept at efficient levels [see Table 3].

The information system was used in tandem with Seven-Eleven Japan's distribution system, which served its network of stores with over 250 distribution centres, to deliver goods to stores

Exhibit 4
Fifth-generation total information system

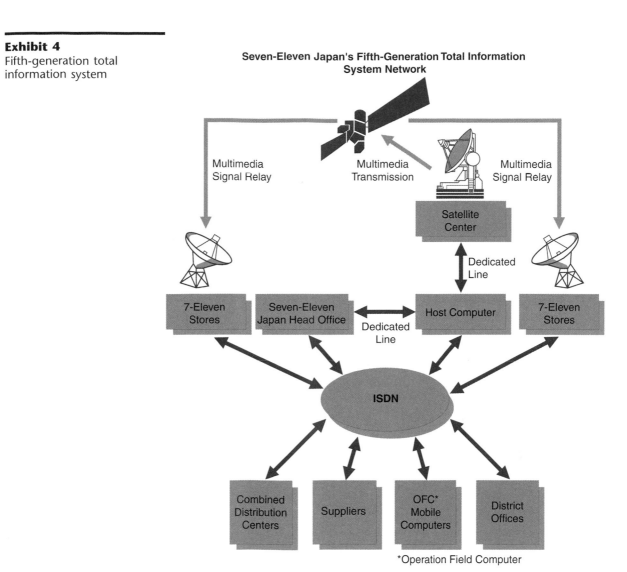

Seven-Eleven Japan's Fifth-Generation Total Information System Network

Source: Seven-Eleven Japan Co., Ltd., Annual Report 1998, p. 9.

Table 3
Inventory levels

| | Fiscal Year | | | |
| | 2000 | 1999 | 1998 | 1997 |
		(million yen)		
Processed food	491	400	346	304
Fast food	0	0	0	1
Daily/fresh food	70	48	42	40
Nonfood	755	596	551	459

Source: *Seven-Eleven Japan Co., Ltd.,* Annual Reports 1998, 1999 and 2000.

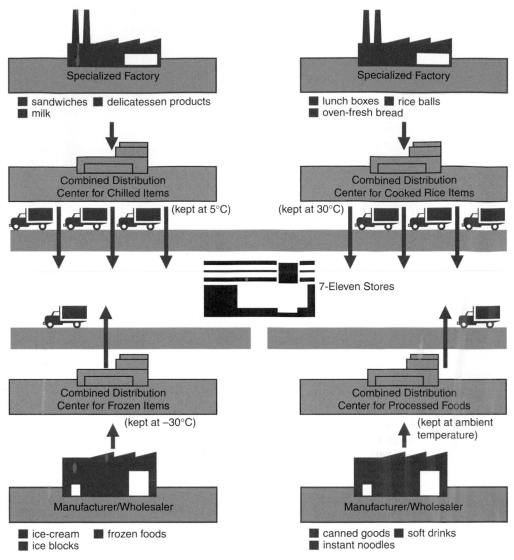

Source: Seven-Eleven Japan Co., Ltd., Annual Report 2000, p.8.

Figure 2. Seven-Eleven Japan's distribution system

efficiently. In 1999, Seven-Eleven Japan improved on its distribution system by creating one that allowed it to combine products that required the same temperature range control. Within this system, it was able to manage the delivery of temperature-sensitive food products to stores and better preserve their freshness. Cooked rice items and chilled foods, the bulk of total store sales, were delivered to 7-Eleven stores three times a day [see Figure 2]. As a result, daily supplies that would have taken 70 trucks to distribute in 1975 were being delivered using 10 trucks.[6]

E-Commerce Ventures

"Floor traffic at Seven-Elevens is about 9 million people daily, but basically they're seeing the same people and not generating a lot of new traffic."[7]

Mike Allen, a retail-sector analyst at ING Baring Securities (Japan)

By observing the average monthly sales trend per store and by listening to numerous complaints from franchisees, Suzuki was aware that the level of sales per store had reached a plateau [see Figure 3]. In order to increase sales, he recognized the need for Seven-Eleven Japan to venture into other avenues, notably e-commerce. As the operator of the largest chain of convenience stores in Japan, Suzuki was acutely aware of the fact that Seven-Eleven Japan had the distinct advantage of having more than 8,000 convenience stores to act as a payment and end-fulfilment network, both being important factors in e-commerce.

Instead of immediately fully diverting resources into a new e-commerce business though, Suzuki thought it was prudent to initially approach e-commerce based on two strategies. The first involved active investment in e-commerce joint ventures. In August 1999, Seven-Eleven Japan established e-Shopping! Books Corp., an on-line bookshop joint venture between Softbank

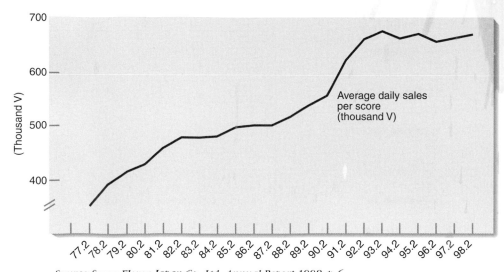

Source: Seven-Eleven Japan Co., Ltd., Annual Report 1998, p. 6.

Figure 3. Average daily sales per store

Corp. and Tohan Corp, in which Seven-Eleven Japan held a 30 per cent stake. In October 1999, it acquired a 10 per cent stake in CarPoint Japan KK, an on-line car broker set up in March 1999 by Softbank Corp., Yahoo Japan Corp. and Microsoft Corp. Seven-Eleven Japan did not deal with the daily operations of these joint ventures, opting instead for a pure investor approach.

The second strategy involved using its chain of stores as a distribution centre for various e-commerce businesses. In September 1999, it announced plans to use its stores as the payment and delivery stations for eight major on-line shop operators, including e-Shopping!, BIGLOBE, @nifty, Curio-city, Plala, Sofmap and So-net. These operators together operated more than 1,200 virtual shops. The premise was simple: the customer makes his purchase at the on-line store, pays at a 7-Eleven store, and a few days later, returns to the store to pick up the item. This service, launched in November 1999, was developed jointly with Nomura Research Institute based on the existing payment acceptance services for utilities.[8] Settlement between the on-line shops and Seven-Eleven Japan was through a settlement software module developed by several leading technology companies—NEC Corp., Hewlett-Packard Japan Ltd., Fujitsu Ltd. and Microsoft Co. Ltd.

A NEW B2C E-COMMERCE VENTURE

Buoyed by the optimistic outlook on the growth of B2C e-commerce in Japan and the success of previous e-commerce participatory-style undertakings, Suzuki decided that the time was ripe for Seven-Eleven Japan to fully venture into e-commerce. A pioneer by nature, he was the first to introduce the concept of a convenience store to Japan, was the first to install an electronic inventory and sales system, and the first to offer fast food. Noting that the obstacles to mainstream e-commerce in Japan were mainly culture-related, he recognised the need to introduce a unique e-commerce model that could entice Japan-

ese people to buy on-line. He began contacting the heads of several major Japanese companies, which included Sony Corp., Sony Marketing (Japan) Inc., NEC Corp., Nomura Research Institute, Mitsui & Co. Ltd., Japan Travel Bureau Ltd. and Kinotrope Inc., to convey his vision and to persuade them to join him into bringing e-commerce to Japanese consumers in a big way [see Exhibit 5]. The joint-venture, to be named 7dream.com to reflect the brand name of Seven-Eleven Japan, would be aimed at becoming the largest B2C e-commerce site in Japan and help Seven-Eleven Japan to realise its goal of becoming an on-line Japanese shopping behemoth.

Business

Suzuki envisioned that 7dream.com would offer services based on the technical expertise and industry knowledge of each founding member, including Seven-Eleven Japan. As such, he intended 7dream.com to offer services in eight content areas: travel; music; photographs; merchandise, gifts and mobile phones; tickets; books; car-related items; and information [see Exhibit 6]. This diverse range of merchandise was specially aimed at the buying pattern of most Japanese consumers and to complement the range of goods offered in the 7-Eleven stores. As the products to be offered on 7dream.com would not usually be found in convenience stores, due to limited space, Suzuki expected overall sales for Seven-Eleven Japan to grow. Also, the products to be offered were especially chosen for their ease of handling—if they were not viewable on screen or downloadable, they were small-sized. This was due to Suzuki's plans to utilise the existing Seven-Eleven Japan delivery system as 7dream.com's end-fulfilment system.

The Target Market

Convenience stores resembled centres of community life in Japan: consumers visited *konbinis* to pick up a meal or snack, to pay for their utilities, to socialise with friends and to look at the latest fashion accessories. In addition, the stores were easily ac-

Exhibit 5
Business of 7dream.com
partners

Company	Business
Seven-Eleven Japan Co., Ltd.	■ Operator of the largest chain of convenience store in Japan.
NEC Corporation	■ Recognised as a worldwide leader in high technology, NEC was one of the few companies capable of offering a full spectrum of products and systems in semiconductors, electron devices, communications, computer peripherals, imaging, and computers.
Nomura Research Institute, Ltd.	■ A leading Japanese research and consulting institute specialising in IT-related services.
Sony Corporation	■ A leading multinational company specialising in electronics-related items.
Sony Marketing (Japan) Inc.	■ The marketing arm of Sony Corp.
Mitsui & Co., Ltd.	■ It was Japan's largest general trading company and had two principal roles: to facilitate its clients' international trade-related activities and, making use of its substantial information, human, financial, and other resources, to create new trade flows, new enterprises, and new industries around the world.
Japan Travel Bureau	■ Founded in 1912, JTB was Japan's largest travel company.
Kinotrope Inc.	■ Kinotrope was reputed as one of the best independent Website content providers in Japan.

cessible as they were located in every conceivable location, at nearly every street corner, in every city or town in the country. Customers of 7-Eleven convenience stores alone numbered almost 10 million per day. Of these, most were mainly young people from their teens through their thirties. Recognising that this represented the portion of society that dictated shopping trends in the country, Suzuki intended to target this group of customers to get them to use 7dream.com to satisfy their shopping needs. In addition, this group represented the generation that had taken to the Internet most enthusiastically. In Suzuki's opinion, these characteristics made this group an ideal target to market an on-line shopping site.[9]

The Payment and Delivery System

Customers of 7dream.com could pay for their purchases by credit card over the Internet. However, recognising that many Japanese consumers were reluctant to reveal their credit card numbers on-line and preferred to settle their transactions by cash, Suzuki planned to give customers of 7dream.com the option of paying for their on-line purchases at a 7-Eleven store of their choice. After making a purchase at the 7dream.com Website, customers could select "Payment at a 7-Eleven store" as their payment method. Payment slips with bar codes would then be printed out from the customers' printers. Customers could then visit any 7-Eleven store in Japan with these slips to make their payments. Customers without printers could just state their assigned payment reference number to the cashier at the 7-Eleven store. Suzuki was confident that this payment system would work as the 7-Eleven stores were already equipped with the capability to accept payments on behalf of other businesses. For example, it was a common sight to see consumers pay their utility bills at convenience stores. Seven-Eleven Japan alone accepted about 70 million payments annually for a total of over 500 billion yen.[10] Besides, Seven-Eleven Japan already had a payment acceptance system with several major Japanese on-line stores in place.

Customers could choose to have their orders delivered to their home or other delivery address. Aware of the problem of end-fulfilment in Japan though, Suzuki planned to allow customers the option to pick up their purchases at a 7-Eleven store. This meant that a customer could pay for his or her purchase and later return to the same store, or another of his or her choice, to collect his or her merchandise. 7dream.com would utilise the existing logistics system that Seven-Eleven

Exhibit 6
Contents and services of 7dream.com

Content Area	Service
Travel (about 5,500 items)	A one-stop service combining an online, updated reservation and discount plan, original package tours, event and leisure contents, and hotel, airplane, train, and ship tickets.
Music (about 90,000 items)	Sales of CDs and supply of music-related information.
Photographs	Sales of celebrity, or special character, photographs.
Merchandise, gifts, mobile phones, etc. (about 1,800 items)	Sales of lifestyle-enhancing items.
Ticket sales	Sales of tickets to major events, and regionally oriented services.
Books	Sales of books via a tie-up with e-Shopping! Books Corp.
Car-related services (about 200 items)	Acting as agent for requests for automobile inspection, repairs and maintenance, driving school, and rent-a-car services.
Information services	Information on core services, like entertainment and photograph, and referral services for people wishing to take special qualification examinations.

Source: *Seven-Eleven Japan Co., Ltd.*, "Seven-Eleven Japan Establishes Joint Venture to Undertake Full-Scale Development of the Electronic Commerce Market," 6 January, 2000.

Japan employed for distribution of goods to its network of convenience stores. With over 8,000 stores spread throughout Japan, Suzuki thought that it would be unusual for the customer to have a long walk before seeing the familiar 7-Eleven sign. Furthermore, as the delivery system was already in place, orders on 7dream.com's site would probably only be charged a minimal cost, which would be signficantly lower than the shipping and handling charges levied by other e-commerce companies.

> "The Japanese person who doesn't pass a convenience store on the way home from the train station 'doesn't exist'."[11]
>
> Makoto Usui, Director, Seven-Eleven Japan

Combining the payment and pickup features offered by 7dream.com, Suzuki envisioned the following scenario:

A customer goes on-line via an Internet-enabled device to make a purchase at 7dream.com's Website and specifies pick up at the 7-Eleven store in his neighbourhood. The order is then processed and shipped by the 7dream.com Order Centre via Seven-Eleven Japan's distribution system to the specified store. The Order Centre then notifies the customer of the pick up date by e-mail. After receiving the e-mail, the customer brings a payment slip that he or she printed out when placing the order to the 7-Eleven store in his or her neighbourhood and picks up the purchased item after payment.

Marketing 7dream.com

Access to the services of 7dream.com would be initially tailored for consumers with Internet-accessible personal computers. However, the number of homes with personal computers in Japan was considered low. According to eMarketer, the penetration rate of personal computers in Japan was only about 20 per cent as opposed to 41 per cent in the US.[12] Moreover, getting on-line via wired dialup was expensive as Japan was considered to have the most expensive Internet dialup access fee in the world. Space was an issue too. Many Japanese homes were tiny and had no space to accommodate a personal computer.

Recognising that these factors were impediments to people's access to the Website, Suzuki envisioned other channels for consumers to utilise 7dream.com's services. One of the channels under consideration was Internet-enabled multimedia kiosks. Once 7dream.com's Website was enabled, Suzuki planned to start placing these multimedia kiosks in a few participating 7-Eleven stores in October 2000, aiming for a kiosk in all stores by June 2001.[13] The idea was to whet people's appetite for computers and the Internet.[14] These kiosks would enable consumers who did not wish to connect to the Internet at home, or did not have personal computers with Internet access, to access the full services of 7dream.com. Once consumers savoured what 7dream.com had to offer, it was expected that the utility-packed kiosks would offer enough value to attract the consumers into using the kiosks more often to access 7dream.com's services in order to satisfy their shopping needs. The kiosks would be equipped with a screen to access the services of 7dream.com, a digital printer for instant printing and delivery of pictures purchased or photographs taken with the in-built digital camera, and a MiniDisc drive and MemoryStick slot to allow customers to save purchased songs.

Suzuki was also looking ahead to a wireless capability. In Japan, nearly six million of Japan's 17.5 million Internet users, a full 34 per cent, were accessing the Web via Internet-enabled cellular phones.[15] This contrasted with the US, where nearly everyone accessed the Internet via a personal computer. One of the reasons for the popularity of wireless access in Japan was because subscribers were given continuous access to the Internet and paid based on the amount of data transmitted or received, not on airtime. This was evidently more advantageous than paying the expensive dialup fees associated with wired connections. In addition, there were thousands of Websites specially tailored for these phones, and many more were being developed. Citing statistical figures that indicated that the number of subscribers to Internet mobile services was on the rise, it seemed certain that wireless devices would be a key factor in promoting e-commerce in Japan. In the future, Suzuki planned to utilise other channels to market 7dream.com, such as digital broadcasting, television and magazines.

Projection of Sales

Convinced of the potential profitability of the 7dream.com model [see Figure 4], Suzuki projected 7dream.com to process seven billion yen in e-commerce transactions for the fiscal year ending February 2001, given that the 7dream.com Website could be launched by June 2000.[16] He further projected the amount to increase to 180 billion yen in 2003 and 240 billion yen in 2004. He also highlighted to his would-be partners that since 7dream.com would be dealing with wholesalers, it would be obtaining the goods directly from the warehouses of its suppliers. This meant that it would not have to hold inventory and incur warehousing costs. In addition, the 7dream.com model would be leveraging on an existing delivery system instead of building one from scratch, translating into more savings. As Seven-Eleven Japan was already making deliveries to 7-Eleven stores, the additional cost of delivering 7dream.com's orders to

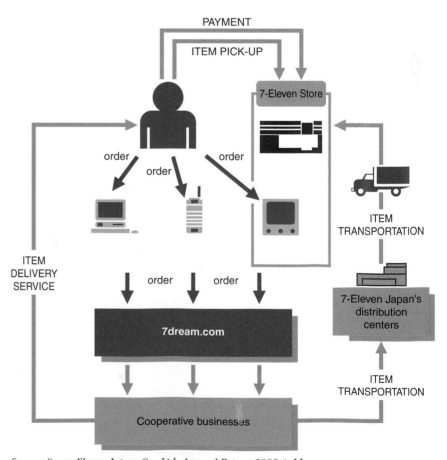

Source: Seven-Eleven Japan Co., Ltd., Annual Report 2000, p.11

Figure 4. Business model of 7dream.com

these stores using Seven-Eleven Japan's distribution system would be minimal to Seven-Eleven Japan. The low delivery charges meant that customers would not be charged exorbitant delivery rates, making it all the more attractive to consumers. These factors being two of the more challenging obstacles faced by many e-commerce companies, this meant that the 7dream.com had potentially huge savings in operating costs.

A BUSINESS DECISION

Suzuki was confident that he had the right business model to penetrate the B2C e-commerce market in Japan. Initial outlay was expected to be 5 billion yen, with Seven-Eleven Japan taking a 51 per cent stake in 7dream.com [see Table 4] and the others taking from 2 to 13 per cent. Not surprisingly though,

there were critics who believed that the e-commerce model proposed by Suzuki might be short-lived. As technology improved and new products such as debit cards and smart cards were introduced, Japanese consumers were expected to get accustomed to transacting and paying via on-line means. As such, the 7dream.com model, if it did not undergo any structural changes, would be vulnerable to shifts in cultural and shopping habits.

"In the short term, they'll be major players because of their networks, but the Japanese will begin using electronic cash and home delivery, like Americans."[17]

Hirokazu Ishii, analyst at Nikko Salomon Smith Barney in Tokyo

Nevertheless, Suzuki was still confident that he had a viable business model. He then put the question to his potential partners: will you invest in 7dream.com?

Table 4
Shareholding in
7dream.com

Company	Percentage of shareholding	Contributed capital (million yen)
Seven-Eleven Japan	51	2,550
NEC Corporation	13	650
Nomura Research Institute, Ltd.	13	650
Sony Corporation	6.5	325
Sony Marketing (Japan) Inc.	6.5	325
Mitsui & Co., Ltd.	6	300
Japan Travel Bureau	2	100
Kinotrope Inc.	2	100
Total	100	5,000

Source: *Seven-Eleven Japan Co. Ltd.,* "7dream.com established on February 1, 2000", 1 February, 2000.

APPENDIX 1

Factors Affecting the E-Commerce Environment in Japan

CONNECTION CHARGES

The state of the communications infrastructure in a country was very important towards e-business. The key to e-commerce was access to the Internet, which was usually through a telephone line and a personal computer. In Japan, the pricing of access charges to the Internet was decided upon by Nippon Telephone & Telegraph (NTT), of which the Government was a majority shareholder. Through its subsidiaries NTT East and NTT West, NTT controlled 95 per cent of Japan's telephone lines. Despite NTT's decision to cut monthly fixed charges by 50 per cent from May 2000, the price charged for connection to the Internet was considered to be high. Additionally, connection to the Internet was charged by the minute, deterring many people from browsing the Web, or staying at a Website for very long. In a move aimed at increasing the use of the Internet in Japan, the US government demanded that NTT lower access fees by 22.5 per cent over a two-year period starting from 2002, and ultimately by more than 40 per cent. The Japan government insisted that the reduction be limited to 22.5 per cent over a four-year period instead.[18]

GOVERNMENT POLICIES

Government policies played a crucial role in the promotion of e-commerce in a country. There was a general consensus among analysts that the system traditionally practised by the government of Japan ultimately cost the B2C e-commerce industry. Under the Japanese system, for the sake of international competitiveness, the government actively intervened in markets to promote producers' interests.[5] In the past, this system was laudable, but in the 1990s, when attention shifted towards satisfying customer requirements, it became evident that the system was maintained at the expense of consumers and could not adapt to the tides of change. For example, under what was termed as the *saihan* system, it was illegal for retailers and e-tailers based in Japan to sell music CDs at a discount because of a law that protected copyright holders.

However, since the mid-1990s, the government had been actively promoting deregulation and e-commerce. Recognising that competition was important in improving the general business environment, the government initiated steps such as splitting the telecom giant NTT into three companies—two regional carriers (NTT East and NTT West) and a long-distance and international one (NTT DoCoMo). Through MITI, the Electronic Commerce Promotion Council of Japan (ECOM) was established in January 1996 in order to develop a common platform to work for the realisation and expansion of e-commerce.

LOCAL CULTURE

The EIU surmised that even though the Internet was essentially a borderless network that facilitated global operations, the local culture was an important factor that had to be understood for the e-commerce company to survive and succeed.

Japan had traditionally been a cash-based society. It was not unusual to see salaries paid in bank notes. About 90 per cent of all mail-order sales were paid for with cash-on-delivery or by bank transfer, which were also the most commonly used methods of payment for on-line shopping. Cheques were not used. Credit card payment, the most common form of payment in e-commerce websites elsewhere, was not very popular, accounting for just over 10 per cent. Polls indicated that 70 per cent of Japanese disliked using credit cards for on-line purchases, being wary of the ease with which hackers hacked into servers to obtain credit card information and other personal data.[19]

> "It's part of the Japanese culture that people want to buy products, face-to-face."[20]
>
> —Minoru Matsumoto, spokesman for Seven-Eleven Japan

Japanese consumers were used to buying off-line. By doing their shopping off-line, they could see and touch the products, and perhaps obtain discounts. For example, if a consumer wanted to buy a personal computer in Tokyo, he could just visit Akihabara, a famous electric town, where all sorts of branded and non-branded systems and parts were offered at ever greater discounts by salespeople anxious to outdo their competitors. Furthermore, off-line shopping was very convenient in Japan. There was a long history of mail-order and catalogue shopping. There were also streets packed with stores selling daily necessities. A writer commented that "As long as one doesn't mind walking, which you do a lot of here, there's not much that isn't within 10 minutes."[21] In addition, convenience stores, or *konbinis* as they were known in Japan, were almost everywhere and, due to their small floor space that allowed them to be exempted from strict government rules requiring regular supermarkets to close by eight o'clock in the evening, most were open all night. Many Japanese consumers, with tiny homes that limited the size of refrigerators and storage space, frequented these stores for their daily necessities.

CASE DISCUSSION QUESTIONS

1. What are Seven-Eleven Japan's organizational strengths?

2. What are Seven-Eleven Japan's organizational weaknesses?

3. Discuss any external factors that must be considered by Seven-Eleven Japan in making the decision currently under consideration by Mr. Suzuki.

4. What is your opinion of Mr. Suzuki? Is he the right man to lead the proposed initiative?

5. Should Seven-Eleven go forward with the 7dream.com initiative? Justify your recommendation.

ENDNOTES

1   *Ministry of International Trade and Industry*, URL: http://www.jipdec.or.jp/chosa/MITIAE/sld013.htm, 4 July, 2000.

2   *Andersen Consulting*, "Total consumer electronic commerce market in Japan estimated at 336 billion yen, according to joint survey by ECOM and Andersen Consulting," 19 January, 2000.

3   "Seven-Eleven Japan takes two-pronged Net strategy," *The Nikkei Weekly,* 25 October, 1999.

4   Otsu, T.,"Lawson plans to go online," *China Daily (New York)*, 26 February, 2000.

5   Earl, M., "The Right Mind-set for Managing Information Technology", *Harvard Business Review*: September/October 1998.

6   *Seven-Eleven Japan Co., Ltd.*, Annual Report 2000, p. 8.

7   Nakada, G., "Seven-Eleven Japan's Web dream: Online mall goes live, multimedia kiosks to come". *CBS.MarketWatch.com,* 2 July, 2000.

8   The use of convenience stores to make utilities and other payments was popular in Japan.

9   "Seven-Eleven Japan takes two-pronged Net strategy," *The Nikkei Weekly*, 25 October, 1999.

10 *Seven-Eleven Japan Co., Ltd.*, "Seven-Eleven to Start Payment Acceptance Service for Internet Shopping," 3 September, 1999, URL: http://info.sej.co.jp/contents_e/news/index.html.

11 Kashiwagi, A., 8 February, 2000.

12 Scuka, D., "Unwired: Japan Has the Future in its Pocket," *Japan Inc,* June 2000.

13 Williams, M., "7-Eleven Japan Embraces E-Commerce," The Standard.com, 6 January, 2000.

14 Moshavi, S., "Online at the 7-Eleven—Japan Begins Embracing Internet Commerce Its Own Way: At Convenience Stores," *The Boston Globe,* 26 August, 2000.

15 Kashiwagi, A., "Japanese Going Online But Leaving PCs Behind," *eMarketer,* 8 February, 2000.

16 "Japan: Seven-Eleven's Success Multiplies," *IDEAadvisor,* 25 October, 2000.

17 Kunii, I.M., "From Convenience Store to Online Behemoth?," *Business Week* (New York), 10 April, 2000.

18 Anai, I., "U.S. pressure may give Japan IT industry boost," *The Daily Yomiuri (Tokyo),* 1 July, 2000, p. 13.

19 Kunii, I.M., "From Convenience Store to Online Behemoth?," *Business Week,* 10 April, 2000, p. 64.

20 Zielenziger, M., "7-Eleven Capitalizes on Japan Market Share with Wide Array of Services" *San Jose Mercury News,* 2 April, 2000.

21 Mollman, S., "How Convenient to Be a Konbini," *J@pan inc,* March 2000.

Glossary

A

Absolute PPP (Purchasing power parity) A theory that the exchange rate is determined by the relative prices of similar baskets of goods or services.

Absorptive capability A firm's ability to acquire, assimilate, integrate, and exploit knowledge and skills that are transferred from another firm.

Active role A subsidiary role in which many activities are located locally but carried out in close coordination with other subsidiaries.

Active or aggressive reciprocity The withdrawal of previous commitments and concessions from, or the undertaking of retaliatory measures against, a country until it reduces or eliminates its barriers to trade.

Adaptive system A system that imitates local HRM (human resources management) practices.

Advance pricing agreement An agreement between the tax authority and the taxpayer on the transfer pricing methodology to be applied to any apportionment or location of income, deductions, credits, or allowances between two or more members within an organization.

Affinity How closely aligned nations are, based on both history and political reality.

American depository receipts (ADRs) A means of trading foreign shares in the United States. Negotiable certificates issued by a U.S. bank in the U.S. to represent the underlying shares of a foreign stock held in trust in a foreign custodian bank.

Animosity How closely estranged nations are, based on both history and political reality.

Appreciation An increase in the foreign exchange value of a floating currency.

Arbitrage Temporary discrepancies that provide profit opportunities for simultaneously buying a currency in one market (at lower price) while selling it in another (at higher price).

Arm's-length principle Principle stating that the transfer price struck between related companies should be the same as that negotiated between two independent entities acting in an open and unrestricted market.

Autonomous role A subsidiary role where the subsidiary performs most activities of the value chain independently of headquarters.

Auto-stereotypes How we see ourselves as a group and as distinguished from others.

B

Back-to-back L/C (letter of credit) A letter of credit in which the exporter, as beneficiary of the first L/C (letter of credit), offers its credit as security in order to finance the opening of a second credit in favor of the exporter's own supplier of the goods needed for shipment under the first or original credit from the advising bank.

Balance of merchandise trade The value of a country's exports of goods minus the value of the country's imports of goods.

Balance-of-payments An accounting statement that reports the country's international performance in trading with other nations and the volume of capital flowing in and out of the country.

Balance of trade Exports minus imports of goods and services.

Bank guarantee A financial instrument that guarantees a specified sum of payment in the event of nonperformance by an exporter or by a foreign importer in the event of a payment default for goods purchased from a foreign supplier.

Bank line of credit The sum of money allocated to an exporter by a bank or banks that the exporter can draw from in order to finance its export business.

Bankers acceptance (BA) A time draft drawn on and accepted by banks with one branch in financing and the other in investment.

Barter The direct and simultaneous exchange of goods between two parties without a cash transaction.

Bid The exchange rate in one currency at which a dealer (e.g., bank) will buy another currency.

Bid-ask spread The compensation for transaction cost for the dealer.

Bill of lading (B/L) A document, issued by a shipping company or its agent as evidence of a contract for shipping the merchandise that lists the goods received for shipment.

Black hole subsidiaries Subsidiaries that operate in important markets where they barely make a dent, but their strong local presence is essential for maintaining global position.

Black markets Illegal markets in foreign exchange that exist as a response to business or private demand for foreign exchange.

Boycott The blanket prohibition on importation of all or some goods and services from a designated country.

Branch office A foreign entity in a host country in which it is not incorporated, but exists as an office of extension of the parent and is legally constituted as a branch.

Branding The process of creating and supporting positive perceptions associated with a product or service. In global markets, branding is especially complex given varying demand and environmental characteristics.

Bribery Payments to government officials, politicians, and political parties in order to gain favors that are otherwise not allowed by the law.

Build-operate-transfer (BOT) An investment in which a foreign investor assumes responsibility for the design and construction of an entire operation, and, upon completion of the project, turns the project over to the purchaser and hands over its total management to local personnel whom it has trained.

Bulldogs Foreign bonds sold in the United Kingdom.

Business-to-Business (B2B) Interfirm transactions, including government procurement, that drives 90% of the projected growth in the global E-commerce.

Business-to-Customer (B2C) Transactions between firms and individuals purchasing goods or services over the Internet (e.g., ordering a book online from a vendor).

Buyback A compensation arrangement through which a firm provides a local company with inputs for manufacturing products to be sold in international markets and agrees to take a certain percentage of the output produced by the local firm as partial payment for the contract.

Buyer credit Financing that exists where one of more financial institutions in an exporter's country extend credit to a foreign customer of the exporter.

Buy-local campaigns Efforts to curb all imports regardless of the country of origin.

C

Call option The purchase of a stated number of units of the underlying foreign currency at a specific price per unit during a specific period of time.

Capability building An MNE's capacity to learn and develop new capabilities.

Capability exploitation An MNE's capacity to extract economic returns from current resources.

Capital account In the balance of payments, records private and public investment or lending activities and is divided into portfolio and foreign direct investments.

Centers of excellence Foreign units equipped with the best practice of managing knowledge (e.g., GM small diesel center of excellence in Japan).

Channel decisions The length (number of levels or intermediaries employed in the distribution process) and width (number of firms in each level) of the channel used in linking manufacturers to customers.

Civil law Legal system that relies almost exclusively on the legal code and is applied universally.

Clean L/C (letter of credit) A L/C that does not require the presentation of documents.

Clearing House Interbank Payments System (CHIPS) Computerized system that provides for calculation of new balances owned by any one bank to another and for payment by 6:00 pm that same day in Federal Reserve Bank of New York funds.

Cluster When suppliers, manufacturers, and even distributors are located near each other or concentrated in the same area (e.g. Silicon Valley in California for the semiconductor and software industry).

Cluster format A format in which a business reports to a cluster headquarters that is accountable to corporate headquarters for business results.

Co-management arrangement A loosely structured alliance in which cross-national partners collaborate in training, production management, information systems development, and value-chain integration.

Co-marketing arrangement An arrangement that provides a platform in which each party can reach a larger pool of international consumers.

Commitment The extent to which each party will constantly and continuously contribute its resources and skills to joint operations and be dedicated to enhancing joint payoff.

Commodity cartel Group of producing countries that wish to protect themselves from the wild fluctuations that often occur in the prices of certain commodities traded internationally.

Common-law system Legal system, based on tradition, precedent, and custom, in which the independent judiciary relies on case precedents.

Common market A customs union that allows not only free trade of products and services but also free mobility of production factors across national member borders.

Comparative advantage The theory that a country should specialize in a good in which the opportunity cost for producing that good is lower at home than in the other country.

Comparative production cost A cost that depends on the commodity's production process (especially the state of technology) and on the prices of production factors.

Concentration ratio The proportion of FDI outward stock held by the 10 top investor countries.

Confirmed L/C (letter of credit) A letter of credit issued by one bank and confirmed by another, obligating both banks to honor any drafts drawn in compliance.

Confucian dynamism A cultural dimension renamed "long-term orientation" that is anchored in the Confucian value system.

Conglomerate FDI The activity of FDI abroad to manufacture products not manufactured by the parent company at home.

Contributor subsidiaries Subsidiaries that operate in small or strategically less important markets but have distinctive strategies.

Control A direct intervention into the operations of subsidiaries to ensure conformity with organizational goals.

Conversion The exchange of one currency for another.

Cooperative (or Contractual) joint venture A collaborative agreement whereby profits and other responsibilities are assigned to each party according to a contract.

Cooperative culture The extent to which each party's corporate culture is compatible, thus leading to a more cooperative atmosphere during GSA operations.

Cooperative joint venture A contractual agreement whereby profits and responsibilities are assigned to each party according to stipulations in a contract.

Coordination Linking different task units within the organization into a unified system.

Co-production (Co-service) agreement An agreement in which each partner is responsible for manufacturing a particular part of the product.

Core competence Skills within a firm that competitors cannot easily match or imitate.

Corporate guarantee The act of one company undertaking to pay if the principal debtor does not pay a matured debt obligation to a creditor.

Corporate socialization The processes through which the values and norms of subsidiary managers are aligned with those of the parent corporation. Such socialization is a powerful mechanism for building identification with and commitment to the organization as a whole.

Corruption An exchange between two partners (the "demander" and the "supplier") that (a) has an influence on the allocation of resources either immediately or in the future, and (b) involves the use or abuse of public or collective responsibility for private ends.

Corruption Perception Index (CPI) A broad measure of corruption that is calculated from multiple survey responses.

Counterfeiting The attempt to pass a copied product as an original, such as producing and selling a fake Gucci bag or a Rolex watch.

Counterpurchase A reciprocal buying agreement whereby one firm sells its products to another at one point in time and is compensated in the form of the other's products at some future time.

Countertrade A form of trade in which the seller and the buyer from different countries exchange merchandise without substantial cash involvement.

Country competitiveness The extent to which a country is capable of generating more wealth than its competitors do in world markets.

Country-of-origin effect The influence of the country of manufacturing image on the buying decision.

Crawling peg A system for revising the exchange rate, involving establishing a par value around which the rate can vary up to a given percent.

Cross rate The exchange rate between two infrequently traded currencies, calculated through a widely traded third currency.

Cultural or business etiquette The manners and behavior that are expected in a given situation, be it business negotiations, a supervisor-subordinate discussion, or outside the workplace and after business hours.

Cultural distance The extent to which cultures differ from each other.

Culture The art and other manifestations of human intellectual achievement regarded collectively; the customs, civilization, and achievement of a particular time or people; the way of life of a particular society or group.

Culture clustering The grouping of cultures based on relative similarity.

Current account The record of the export or import of goods and services.

Current/non-current method (of accounting) Current assets and liabilities are translated at the current rate, and non-current assets and liabilities at the applicable non-current rates.

Current rate The exchange rate in effect at the relevant financial statement date.

Current rate method (of accounting) All assets and liabilities, both monetary and non-monetary, are translated at the current or closing rate.

Currency valuation The extent to which a country's home currency is valued or priced properly to reflect the situation of market supply and demand pertaining to this currency.

Customer-to-Customer (C2C) Individual transactions online (e.g., online auction).

Customs union Similar to a free trade area except that member nations must conduct and pursue common external commercial relations such as common tariff policies on imports from non-member nations.

D

Defensive A motive that protects and holds a firm's market power or competitive position threatened by domestic rivalry or changes in government policies.

Depreciation A reduction in the foreign exchange value of a floating currency.

Devaluation A reduction in the foreign exchange value of a currency that is pegged to another currency.

Developing/Emerging Nation Multinational Enterprise (DMNE) A multinational enterprise from a developing or emerging economy.

Digital divide The difference in Internet hosts between developed countries and developing countries, developed countries having more Internet penetration.

Direct marketing Direct sales to customers via individual agents who typically make a commission not only on their sales but also on the sales of other agents they have recruited.

Direct quote A home currency price of a unit of foreign currency.

Discount When the forward exchange rate is below the current spot rate.

Discounting A short-term financing technique by which a local bank discounts a firm's trade bills.

Documentary (L/C) In a commercial transaction, the exporter must submit any necessary invoices and other documents such as the customs invoice, certificate of commodity inspection, packing list, and certificate of country of origin.

Documentary collection A payment mechanism that allows exporters to retain ownership of the goods until they receive payment or are reasonably certain that they will receive it.

Documents against acceptance (D/A) The act of the exporter's bank to hold the title documents until the importer accepts the obligation to pay the draft.

Documents against payment (D/P) The act of the exporter's agent (bank) to hold the title documents until the importer pays the draft.

Double-entry bookkeeping System in which every debit or credit in the account is represented as a credit or debit somewhere else.

Dumping The sale of imported goods either at prices below what a company charges in its home market or at prices below cost.

Dynamic capabilities A firm's ability to diffuse, deploy, utilize, and rebuild firm-specific resources in order to attain a sustained competitive advantage.

E

Early mover Firms that enter a market shortly after the first mover.

E-business Use of the Internet to conduct transactions of buying, selling, and distribution of goods or services over the Internet.

e-business climate The institutional and regulatory frameworks that facilitate or hinder e-commerce.

E-commerce The conduct of transactions to buy, sell, distribute or deliver goods and services over the Internet.

E-commerce readiness An index comprised of the three criteria of connectivity, information security, and e-business climate, plus e-leadership (the extent to which e-commerce is a national priority) and human capital (the availability of human resources to support e-commerce).

E-readiness The degree to which nations are prepared for e-commerce.

Economic exposure Foreign exchange risk, measured in the change in present value of the firm, determined by changes in the future operating cash flows of the firm caused by unexpected changes in exchange rates and macroeconomic factors.

Economic integration The abolition of trade barriers or impediments between national economies, such as within the EU.

Economic motives The intentions of a company to benefit from the differences in costs of labors, natural resources, and capital, as well as the differences in regulatory treatments, such as taxation between domestic and foreign countries.

Economic soundness The extent to which an economy has been equipped with all the economic prerequisites for sustained economic growth.

Economy of scale The reduction of manufacturing cost per unit as a result of increased production quantity during a given period.

Effective tax rate The statutory corporate rate, adjusted for all other taxes and subsidies affecting an MNE's taxable income; determines the company's net return from its revenues.

Efficiency-seeking FDI An MNE attempts to rationalize the structure of established resource-based or marketing-seeking investment in such a way that the firm can gain from the common governance of geographically dispersed activities.

e-leadership The extent to which e-commerce is a national priority.

Embargo The prohibition on exportation to a designated country.

EMS (European Monetary System) A system designed to create a zone of stability in Europe.

Entrepreneurs A special group or businesspeople taking risks in the development of new products, new markets, or new technologies.

Entry mode The manner in which a firm chooses to enter a foreign market through FDI.

Environmental dynamics The diversity that exists between countries with regard to their currency, inflation and interest rates, accounting practices, cultures, social customs, business practices, laws, government regulations, and political stability.

Equity joint venture (EJV) A legally and economically separate organizational entity created by two or more parent organizations that collectively invest financial as well as other resources to pursue certain objectives.

Escape clauses Special allowances permitted by the WTO (World Trade Organization) to safeguard infant industries or nourish economic growth for newly admitted developing countries.

Ethical behavior Not only following the rule of law but also attending to the values, norms and concerns of the home and host environments.

Ethnocentric The belief that one's own ethnic group or culture is superior; showing disregard for other countries.

Ethnocentric staffing The act of selecting PCNs (parent-country nations) regardless of location.

Euro The currency of European Union countries.

Eurobond A bond that is underwritten by an international syndicate of banks and other securities firms, and is sold exclusively in countries other than the country in whose currency the issue is denominated (e.g., a bond issued by a Japanese firm residing in Tokyo, denominated in Japanese yen but sold to investors in Europe and the United States).

Eurocurrency markets Countries not using the denomination currency (e.g., a Japanese firm obtained yen loans from banks in the United States and Europe).

Eurodollars U.S. dollar deposits in non-U.S. banks.

Euronote market The collective term used to describe short- to medium-term debt instruments sourced in the Eurocurrency market.

European Central Bank (ECB) The central bank in the euro zone based in Frankfurt. Sets interest rates for the euro zone.

Expatriate trainee An individual placed abroad for training purposes as part of initiation into an MNE (multinational enterprise).

Export controls Governmental limits on the type of products that can be exported to other countries, particularly those considered enemy nations or security risks.

Export intermediaries Third parties that specialize in facilitating imports and exports.

Export management company (EMC) An intermediary that acts as its client's export marketing department.

Export-Import Bank Financing A program whose primary function is to give U.S. exporters the necessary financial backing to compete in other countries.

Exportive system A system that replicates the HRM (human resources management) system in the home country and other affiliates.

Exposed Net Asset Position The excess of assets, that are measured or denominated in foreign currency and translated at the current rate, over liabilities that are measured or denominated in foreign currency and translated at the current rate.

Externality The extent to which the actions of one agent directly affect the environment of another agent.

F

Factoring houses Institutions that provide financing, perform credit investigations, guarantee commercial and political risks, assume collection responsibilities, and finance accounts receivable for small to medium-sized importers.

Factor-intensity reversal A change that occurs when the relative prices of labor and capital change over time, which affects the relative mix of capital and labor in the production process of a commodity from being capital-intensive to labor-intensive (or vice versa).

Familiarity theory Theory that supports the concept that firms would rather invest in host countries that are relatively close to it culturally and are likely to be more successful in such relatively familiar environments.

Financial capabilities Qualities of a global strategic alliance partner in risk management, exposure hedging, financing and cash flow management.

Financial risk The variability of the rate of return on an asset over time.

First mover First MNE to enter a specific foreign market.

First to file A patent system in which the first to file a patent in a given country is awarded the patent without the need to prove it has been the inventor.

First to invent A patent system in which patent protection is granted to the person or entity who first invented the technology or product.

Fixed or managed exchange rate system A system in which a country regulates the rate at which the local currency is exchanged for other currencies.

Fixed-rate system System under which governments buy or sell their currencies in the foreign-exchange market whenever their exchange rates threaten to deviate from their stated par values.

Floating exchange rate system (or Flexible exchange rate system) A system in which a rate of currency is determined by the laws of supply and demand rather than government intervention.

Flow of FDI (Foreign direct investment) The amount of FDI undertaken over a given time period (e.g., a year).

Foreign bond A bond that is underwritten by a syndicate composed of members from a single country, sold principally within that country, and denominated in the currency of that country (e.g., a Japanese firm issues corporate bonds in U.S. dollars and sells to U.S. investors by U.S. banks).

Foreign Corrupt Practices Act (FCPA) The act that criminalized the payment of bribes and other forms of special payment to foreign officials for the purpose of securing or retaining a deal (liability exists whether the deal has been consummated or not). It also required issuers of securities to meet accounting, record-keeping, and corporate control standards.

Foreign currency transaction Transactions (e.g., sales or purchases of goods or services or loans payable or receivable) whose terms are stated in a currency other than the entity's functional currency.

Foreign currency translation The process of expressing amounts denominated or measured in one currency in terms of another currency by use of the exchange rate between the two currencies.

Foreign direct investment (FDI) Direct investment in real or physical assets such as factories and facilities in a foreign country.

Foreign exchange The money of a foreign country, including foreign currency bank balances, banknotes, checks, and drafts.

Foreign exchange exposure The sensitivity of changes in the real domestic-currency value of assets, liabilities, or operating incomes to unanticipated changes in exchange rates.

Foreign exchange market A market where foreign currencies are bought and sold.

Foreign exchange rate The price of one currency expressed in terms of another currency.

Foreign exchange risk The variance of the domestic-currency value of an asset, liability, or operating income that is attributable to unanticipated changes in exchange rates.

Foreign exchange transaction An agreement between a buyer and seller that a certain amount of one currency be delivered at a specified rate for some other currency.

Foreign portfolio investment (FPI) Investment by individuals, firms, or public bodies (e.g., governments or nonprofit organizations) in foreign financial instruments such as government bonds, corporate bonds, mutual funds, and foreign stocks.

Foreign sales corporations Offshore corporations that market the products and/or services of firms in foreign countries.

Foreign subsidiaries Overseas units or entities created as a result of FDI.

Forfeiting A transaction in which an exporter transfers responsibility of commercial and political risks for the collection of a trade-related debt to a forfeiter (often a financial institution), and in turn receives immediate cash after the deduction of its interest charge (the discount).

Forward rate The exchange rate for a transaction that requires delivery of foreign exchange at specified future date.

Forward transaction Transaction between a bank and a customer (company, bank) calling for delivery, at a fixed future date, of a specified amount of foreign exchange at the fixed forward exchange rate.

Forward-forward swap Swap that involves two forward transactions.

Free trade area Country combination in which the member nations remove all trade barriers between themselves but retain their freedom concerning policy making vis-à-vis non-member countries.

Functional currency The primary currency in which an entity conducts its operation and generates and expends cash. It is usually the currency of the country in which the entity is located and the currency in which the books of record are maintained.

G

Geocentric staffing The act of recruiting the best managers worldwide regardless of nationality.

Global e-commerce The conduct of electronic commerce, whether B2B, B2C, or C2C, across national boundaries (e.g., a U.S. customer purchasing pharmaceuticals from a Canadian site).

Global firm A firm that integrates operations in international subsidiaries.

Global innovator A generic subsidiary role with high outflow and low inflow.

Global integration The coordination of activities across countries in an attempt to build efficient operation networks and take maximum advantage of internalized synergies and similarities across locations.

Global products Products that enjoy worldwide recognition and are relatively unaltered in terms of brand and appearance when sold abroad.

Global sourcing The procurement of production or service inputs and components in international markets. Global sourcing provides the MNE (multinational enterprise) with the opportunity to leverage its scale and competitive advantage in spotting procurement opportunities around the globe for use in its various divisions and locations.

Global strategic alliances Cross-border partnerships between two or more firms from different countries with an attempt to pursue mutual interests through sharing their resources and capabilities.

Global strategy Relative standardization across national markets, allowing strategic and operational control.

Global supply chain Activities in both logistics and operations such as: sourcing, procurement, order processing, manufacturing, warehousing, inventory control, servicing and warranty, custom clearing, wholesaling, and distribution.

Globalization of markets Trend toward one huge global market through the increasing volume and variety of cross-border transactions in goods, services, capital, information, and labor force.

Globalization of operations The standardization, in a marketing sense, of products (or services), brands, marketing, advertising, and the supply chain across countries and regions.

Globalization infrastructure Institutional frameworks and market efficiency that support fair and transparent transactions of products or services and streamline flows of commodities, capital, labor, knowledge, and information.

Globalizing R&D The process of distributing and operating R&D (research and development) laboratories in different countries, under a system coordinated and integrated by the company's headquarters, in order to leverage the technical resources of each facility to further the company's overall technological capabilities and competitive advantages.

Goal compatibility The congruence of strategic goals set for an alliance between parent firms.

Greenfield investment An initial establishment of fully owned new facilities and operations by the company without outside investment.

Group of Seven (G-7) A group of countries consisting of: the United States, Japan, West Germany, France, Britain, Canada, and Italy who meet periodically to make economic decisions.

H

Hard currency A currency that is expected to revalue or appreciate relative to major currencies.

Harmonization The process of increasing the compatibility of accounting practices by setting limits on how much they can vary.

Heckscher-Ohlin law of factor price equalization The international equalization of the prices of production factors under free trade.

Heckscher-Ohlin theorem Theorem that states that a country exports goods that make intensive use of locally abundant factors of production. Meanwhile, it would import commodities that make intensive use of locally scarce factors of production.

Hetero-stereotypes How we are seen by others.

Historical rate The foreign exchange rate that prevailed when a foreign currency asset or liability was first acquired or incurred.

Home-country compensation system A system that links base expatriate salary to the salary structure of the home country (e.g., the salary of a U.S. executive transferred to Japan will be based on the United States rather than the Japanese level).

Horizontal FDI (Federal direct investment) When a multinational enterprise (MNE) enters a foreign country to produce the same product(s) produced at home (or offer the same service that it does at home).

Host country-based (localized) compensation system A system that links base salary for an expatriate to the pay structure in the host country; however, supplemental compensation provisions are often connected to home-country salary structures.

Host Economy Transnationality Index A UNCTAD calculated average of FDI inflows as a percentage of gross capital formation, FDI inward stock as a percentage of GDP, value added of foreign affiliates as a percentage of GDP, and employment of foreign affiliates as a percentage of foreign employment.

Human capital Human resources that create economic value.

Human skills A factor of production in the conventional theory of trade that results in comparative advantage in terms of comparative abundance of professional skills and other high-level human skills.

Hybrid compensation system A system that blends features from the home- and host-based approaches.

Hypertext Transfer Protocol (HTTP or HTP) A set of rules for exchanging files (text, graphic images, sound, video, and other multimedia files) on the World Wide Web.

I

Imitation lag A strategy that prevents other countries from immediately duplicating the new products of the innovating country.

Implementor A generic subsidiary role with low outflow and high inflow.

Implementor subsidiaries Subsidiaries that operate in less strategically important markets but are competent to maintain local operations.

Independent float System under which an exchange rate is allowed to adjust freely to the supply and demand of a currency for another.

Indirect quote A foreign currency price of a unit of home currency.

Individualism/Collectivism (I/C) One of Hofstede's four dimensions of culture: the extent to which the self or the group constitutes the center point of identification for the individual.

Industrial policies All forms of conscious and coordinated government interventions to promote industrial development.

Infant industry argument An argument for tariffs that an industry new to a country, especially a developing country, needs to be protected by tariff walls or risk being squashed by global players before it can grow and develop.

Information security The existence of security and other protections pertaining to information dissemination.

Integrated player A generic subsidiary role with high outflow and high inflow.

Integrative system A system that emphasizes global integration while permitting some local variations.

Interest rate parity (IRP) Theory that provides an understanding of the way in which interest rates are linked between different countries through flows of capital.

Intermodal transportation The combination of ocean vessels (including short sea shipping), river transport, rail, road links, and air transport within a seamless supply chain.

Internalization The activity in which an MNE controls its foreign operations through a unified governance structure, primarily because it is less expensive to deal within the same corporation rather than contracting with external organizations.

International (or foreign) trade The exchange of goods and services to consumers in another country.

International accounting A system that involves accounting and taxation issues for companies that have internationalized their economic activities across countries in which accounting standards and practices vary.

International accounting information systems (IAIS) Accounting-related reporting systems, data management, and communication between various units under an intra-MNE (multinational enterprise) structure.

International acquisition A cross-border transaction in which a foreign investor acquires an established local firm and makes the acquired local firm a subsidiary business within its global portfolio.

International bond markets Markets where government bonds or corporate bonds are issued, bought, or sold in foreign countries.

International business Business activities that involve the transfer of resources, goods, services, knowledge, skills, or information involving two or more countries.

International cadres Individuals who move from one foreign assignment to another, seldom returning to their home country.

International entrepreneurs Companies or individuals that actively invest and operate in another country without a home base.

International entry strategies Strategies that concern where (location selection), when (timing of entry), and how (entry mode selection) international companies should enter and invest in a foreign territory during international expansion.

International firm Any firm, regardless of its size, that is engaged in international business.

International Fisher Effect The theory that addresses the relationship between the percentage change in the spot exchange rate over time and the differential between comparable interest rates in different national capital markets.

International franchising An entry mode in which the foreign franchiser grants specified intangible property rights to the local franchisee that must abide by strict and detailed rules as to how it does business.

International human resource management (IHRM) The procurement, allocation, utilization, and motivation of human resources in the international arena.

International investment The activity that occurs when a company invests resources in business activities outside its home country.

International leasing An entry mode in which the foreign firm (leaser) leases out its new or used machines or equipment to the local company.

International licensing An entry mode in which a foreign licensor grants specified intangible property rights to the local licensee for a specified period of time in exchange for a royalty fee.

International loan markets Markets that involve large commercial banks and other lending institutions providing loans to foreign companies.

International location selection Country and regional selection (e.g., state, province, or city) for an MNE's (multinational enterprise) foreign direct investment project(s).

International merger A cross-border transaction in which two firms from different countries agree to integrate their operations on a relatively co-equal basis because they have resources and capabilities that together may create a stronger competitive advantage in the global marketplace.

International monetary system Set of policies, institutions, practices, regulations, and mechanisms that determine foreign exchange rates.

International money markets The market in which foreign

monies are financed or invested. MNEs (multinational enterprises) may use international money markets to finance global operations at a lower cost than is possible domestically.

International stock (or equity) markets Markets in which company stocks are listed and traded on foreign stock exchanges.

International technology transfer The process by which one user's technology or knowledge is passed on to another in a different country for economic benefits.

International trade The activity that occurs when a company exports goods or services to consumers in another country.

International transactions Activities facilitated by companies crossing national boundaries.

Internationally committed company A firm with at least one majority-owned plant or a joint venture abroad but lacking representation in all three regions of the world (Asia, Europe, and the Americas).

Internationally learning firm Firm with foreign sales and possibly a representative office and or a licensing agreement, but with no ownership of foreign production sites.

Internet A worldwide network of computer networks known as the World Wide Web (WWW).

I-R paradigm (Integration-Responsiveness) A theoretical framework that suggests that participants in global industries develop competitive postures across two dimensions (global integration and local responsiveness).

Irrevocable L/C (letter of credit) A means of arranging payment that cannot be revoked without the specific permission of all parties concerned, including the exporter.

J

Joint exploration project A non-equity cooperative alliance whereby the exploration costs are borne by the foreign partner, with development costs later shared by a local entity.

L

Lags When a firm holding a hard currency with debts denominated in a soft currency decelerates by paying those debts late.

Laissez-faire The concept of freedom of enterprise and freedom of commerce with minimal government intervention in a society's economic activity.

Language A systematic means of communicating ideas or feelings by the use of conventionalized signs, gestures, marks, or especially articulate vocal sounds.

Late investor MNE that follows early movers into a new market.

Law-making treaty A multilateral treaty that is ratified by many countries with a joint interest in the issue at hand.

Leads When a firm holding a soft currency with debts denominated in a hard currency accelerates by using the soft currency to pay the hard currency debts before the soft currency drops in value.

Legal jurisdiction The laws of a particular country.

Legitimacy The acceptance of the MNE as a natural organ in the local environment.

Letter of credit (L/C) A contract between an importer and a bank that indicates that the bank will give credit to the importer and agrees to pay the exporter.

Liability of foreignness The costs of doing business abroad that result in a competitive disadvantage vis-à-vis indigenous firms.

Lingua franca A means of communication shared by people of different national and linguistic origin.

Local content The portion of a product (or service) that includes locally made and procured inputs.

Local currency Currency of a particular country; the reporting currency of a domestic or foreign operation.

Local innovator A generic subsidiary role with low outflow and low inflow.

Local responsiveness The attempt to respond to specific needs within a variety of host countries.

Location advantages The benefits arising from a host country's comparative advantages accrued for foreign direct investors.

Long position A position in which the initial transaction represents an asset or future ownership claim to foreign currency.

Long-term supply agreement An agreement in which the manufacturing buyer often provides the supplier with updated free information on products, markets, and technologies, which in turn helps ensure the input quality.

Louvre accords An agreement that calls for the G-7 (Group of Seven) to support the falling dollar by pegging exchange rates within a narrow, undisclosed range.

M

Managed float System designed to eliminate excess volatility and to preserve an orderly pattern of exchange rate changes in which some currencies are allowed to float freely, but the majority are either managed by a government or pegged to another currency.

Managerial control The process in which a party influences alliance activities or decisions in a way that is consistent with its own interests through various managerial, administrative, or social tools.

Market motives Firms conducting international business for reasons of seizing new market opportunities or protecting and holding their market power or competitive position.

Market-seeking FDI MNEs attempt to secure market share and sales growth in the target foreign market.

Masculinity/Femininity (M/F) One of Hofstede's four dimensions of culture: the extent to which traditional masculine values such as aggressiveness and assertiveness are emphasized.

Matching A mechanism whereby a company matches its foreign currency inflows with its foreign currency outflows in respect to amount, timing, and the currency unit.

Mental maps Our perceptions of the world around us and of geographic realities.

Mercantilism An economic philosophy based on beliefs that a country should simultaneously encourage exports and discourage imports in order to increase wealth.

Monetary/non-monetary method (of accounting) Monetary assets and liabilities are translated at the current rate. Non-monetary items are translated at historical rates.

Monetary items Obligations to pay or rights to receive a fixed number of currency units in the future.

Money laundering The act of concealing the source of ill-gotten funds by channeling them into legitimate business activities and bank deposits.

Monopolistic advantage The benefit incurred to a firm that maintains a monopolistic power in the market.

Moral hazard A hidden reckless action of external partners who know they will be saved if things go wrong.

Most Favored Nation (MFN) A clause in most treaties that requires a trade concession that is given to one country be given to all other countries.

Most favored nation treatment Any advantage, favor, or privilege granted by one country must be extended to all other member countries.

Multidomestic firms An enterprise with multiple international subsidiaries that are relatively independent of each other.

Multi-domestic strategy A strategy in which strategic and operating decisions are delegated to strategic business units in each country.

Multinational enterprise (MNE) A firm that has directly invested abroad and has at least one working affiliate in a foreign country (e.g., a factory, a branch office) over which it maintains effective control.

Mutualization The sharing of logistic facilities by two or more partners.

N

National treatment The principle that foreign goods in a member country should be treated the same as domestic goods, once the foreign goods have cleared customs.

Netting A practice by which subsidiaries or affiliates within a MNE (multinational enterprise) network merely settle inter-subsidiary indebtedness for the net amount owed during the post-transaction period.

New trade theory Countries do not necessarily specialize and trade solely in order to take advantage of their differences; they also trade because of increasing returns, which makes specialization advantageous per se.

Niche marketing Marketing that is narrowly directed toward a predefined segment of the market. In international markets, niche marketing may be directed not only to a product category (e.g., low end) but also to an ethnic or geographical segment.

Nominal exchange rate The exchange rate before deducting an inflation factor.

Non-tariff barriers Indirect measures that discriminate against the foreign manufacturers in the domestic market or otherwise distort or constrain trade.

O

Offensive A motive that seizes market opportunities in foreign countries through trade or investment.

Offer The exchange rate at which a dealer will sell the other currency.

Official reserves account A country's net holdings of the official reserves of monetary gold, special drawing rights (SDRs), reserve positions in the IMF, and convertible foreign currencies.

Offset An agreement whereby one party agrees to purchase goods and services with a specified percentage of its proceeds from an original sale.

OLI framework (Ownership, Location, Internalization) Framework that explains international production activities and recognizes the importance of three variables: Ownership-specific (O), Location-specific (L), and Internalization (I).

Openness The extent to which a country's national economy is linked to world economies through the flow of resources, goods, services, people, technologies, information, and capital.

Operational nature Organizational principles and managerial philosophies may differ widely across nations, thus heightening the complexity of operation and management of international business.

Operational risk Any change to the "rules of the game" under which the foreign firm operates (e.g., new and arbitrary taxation), especially when foreign firms are singled out.

Opportunity cost The activity or pathway that must be given up in order to pursue another activity or pathway. For a good X, the opportunity cost is the amount of other goods that have to be given up in order to produce one unit of X.

Optimal tariff theory An assumption that governments can capture a significant portion of the manufacturer's profit margin through the imposition of a tariff.

Organizational capabilities Qualities of a global strategic alliance partner in organizational skills, previous collaboration, learning ability, and foreign experience.

Original equipment manufacturing (OEM) A specific form of international subcontracting, in which a foreign firm supplies a local company with the technology and most sophisticated components so that the latter can manufacture goods that the foreign firm will market under its own brand in international markets.

Outflows of FDI The flow of FDI out of a country.

Outsourcing Buying of inputs outside the MNE's network.

Overdraft A line of credit against which drafts (checks) can be drawn (written) up to a specified maximum amount.

Overseas Assignment Inventory (OAI) Instrument that assists in the selection of expatriates using the following predictors of success on a foreign assignment: expectations, open-mindedness, respect for others' beliefs, trust in people, tolerance, locus of control, flexibility, patience, social adaptability, initiative, risk taking, sense of humor, and spouse communication.

Ownership risk Threat to the current ownership structure or to the ability of the MNE (multinational enterprise) to select or shift to a given structure.

Ownership structure The percentage of equity held by each parent in a global alliance.

P

Par value The rate at which a currency is fixed; the benchmark value of a currency.

Parallel loan (also known as **back-to-back loan)** An exchange of funds between firms in different countries, with the exchange reversed at a later date.

Parallel market An alternative market to the official exchange market.

Parent control The process through which a parent company ensures that the way an alliance is managed conforms to its own interest.

Passive reciprocity A position taken by a country in which it refuses to lower or eliminate its barriers to trade until the other party does the same.

Pegged exchange rate system A system in which a country's currency is tied to, or fixed with, another country's currency.

People skills Skills such as relational abilities, willingness to communicate, nonverbal communication, respect for others, and empathy for others.

Perception skills The cognitive processes that help executives understand the behavior of foreigners. This includes flexible attribution and breadth as well as being open-minded and nonjudgmental.

Permanent expatriates Individuals who stay in overseas assignments for extended periods of time, or even permanently.

Personal attachment Socialization and personal relations between senior GSA managers representing each party during their involvement in exchange activities between the same interacting organizations.

Personal skills Skills needed by expatriates that facilitate mental and emotional wellbeing (e.g., stress orientation, reinforcement, substitution, physical mobility, technical competence, dealing with alienation, isolation, realistic expectation prior to departure).

Physical assets Factories and facilities.

Piracy The use of illegal and unauthorized means to obtain goods, such as copying software.

Political behavior The acquisition, development, securing, and use of power in relation to other entities.

Political risk The unforeseen problems for the trader and investor that will adversely affect the profit and goals of a particular business enterprise.

Polycentric staffing (Ch. 17) The act of hiring HCNs (host-country nationals) for key positions in subsidiaries but not at corporate headquarters.

Portfolio theory The behavior of individuals or firms administering large amounts of financial assets in search of the highest possible risk-adjusted net return.

Predatory pricing The selling of goods below real cost so as to drive competition out of the market.

Power distance (PD) One of Hofstede's four dimensions of culture: the extent to which hierarchical differences are accepted in society and articulated, for example, in the form of deference to senior echelons.

Preference similarity A phenomenon in which the consumers and investors of two countries that have the same or similar demand structures demand the same goods with similar degrees of quality and sophistication.

Pricing The decision and process of setting a price to a product or service. In international markets, pricing is much more complex due to varying cost structures (e.g., transportation costs, tariffs) and market positioning.

Product origin The country in which a product was developed.

Production factors Activities involved in the production process, such as capital, labor, raw materials, and land.

Production function The amount of output that can be produced by using a given quantity of capital and labor.

Productivity The value of the output produced by a unit of labor or capital.

Prospector An instrument that assists in the selection of expatriates by assessing the potential of aspiring international executives on 14 dimensions: cultural sensitivity, business knowledge, courage, motivational ability, integrity, insight, commitment, risk taking, seeking feedback, using feedback, culturally adventurous, seeking learning opportunities, open to criticism, and flexibility.

Psychic distance Differences in language, culture, political systems, and such that disturb the flow of information between the firm and the market.

Purchasing power parity (PPP) A theory emphasizing the role of prices of goods and services in determining changes in exchange rates.

Put option The act of selling a stated number of units of the underlying foreign currency at a specific price per unit during a specific period of time.

Q

Quotas Quantitative limitations on the importation of goods typically spelled out in terms of units or value.

Quality-based (deployment) The distinctiveness of the resources allocated to a foreign market.

Quantity-based (deployment) The amount of critical resources deployed in a target foreign market.

R

R&D intensity Total R&D (research and development) expenditure relative to total sales during the same period.

Real exchange rate The exchange rate after deducting an inflation factor.

Receptive role A subsidiary role in which most subsidiary functions are highly integrated with headquarters or with other business units.

Regiocentric staffing The act of recruiting on a regional basis (e.g., recruit within Asia for a position in China).

Related divisional format A format in which product divisions report directly to headquarters.

Relative PPP (purchasing power parity) Theory that focuses on the relationship between the change in prices of two countries and the change in the exchange rate over the same period.

Religion Key values and norms that are reflected in adherents' way of life.

Reporting currency The currency in which an enterprise prepares its financial statement.

Research and development consortia A joint R&D project in which the costs may be allocated by an agreed-upon formula, but the revenue of each partner depends on what it does with the technology created.

Resource complementarity The extent to which one party's contributed resources are complementary to the other party's resources, resulting in synergies pursued by both parties.

Resource-seeking FDI MNEs attempting to acquire particular resources at a lower cost than could be obtained in the home country.

Revaluation An increase in the foreign exchange rate that is pegged to another currency or gold.

Revocable L/C (letter of credit) A letter of credit that can be revoked without notice, at any time up to the time a draft is presented to the issuing bank.

Revolving L/C The amount of the L/C is automatically renewed pursuant to its terms and conditions.

Risk The unpredictability of operational and financial outcomes.

Rule of origin The administration of tariffs and quotas based on the country of origin, not countries through which it passed, unless a product underwent material change in those countries.

S

Salary Base pay plus incentives (merit, profit sharing, bonus plans), determined via job evaluation or competency-based plans.

Samurai bonds Foreign bonds sold in Japan.

Services allowance and premiums Premiums paid to compensate for differences in expenditures between the home and host country.

Short position Position in which the cash market position represents a liability or a future obligation to deliver foreign currency.

Small and Midsize International Enterprises (SMIEs) Companies that engage in international business activities, but do not have substantial FDE presence and hence do not qualify as MNEs (multinational enterprises).

Smuggling The illegal trade and transportation of goods that is devised to circumvent custom duties, quotas, and other constraints on the movement of goods (e.g., safety transportation requirements that may add to cost at destination).

Society for Worldwide International Financial Telecommunications (SWIFT) A network of telephone, Internet, telex, and satellite communications that link banks in each country and throughout the world.

Soft or weak currency A currency that is anticipated to devaluate or depreciate relative to major trading currencies.

Special drawing right (SDR) A unit of account for the International Monetary Fund (IMF) to expand their official reserves bases.

Spot rate The exchange rate for a transaction that requires almost immediate delivery of foreign exchange.

Spot transactions Transactions between banks which are normally settled on the second working day after the date on which the transaction is concluded.

Spot-forward swap Situation where an investor sells forward the foreign currency maturity value of the bill, and simultaneously buys the spot foreign exchange to pay for the bill.

Standardization The imposition of a rigid and narrow set of rules; may even apply a single standard to all situations.

Statutory tax The rate that determines the general level of the tax burden shouldered by firms.

Stereotypes Our beliefs about others, their attitudes, and their behavior.

Stock of FDI (Federal direct investment) The total accumulated value of foreign-owned assets at a given time.

Strategic capabilities Expertise of a global strategic alliance partner in market power, marketing competence, technological skills, relationship building, industrial experience, and corporate image.

Strategic IHRM (SIHRM) Human resources, management issues, functions, and policies and practices that result from the strategic activities of MNEs (multinational enterprises) and impact the international concerns and goals of these enterprises.

Strategic leader The role played by a highly competent national subsidiary located in a strategically important market.

Strategic motives The intention of a company to capitalize on their distinctive resources or capabilities already developed at home (e.g., technologies and economy of scale).

Strategic orientation The indirect exercise of corporate direction.

Structural discrepancies Differences in industry structure attributes between home and host countries.

Subcontracting The process in which a foreign company provides a local manufacturer with raw materials, semi-finished products, sophisticated components, or technology for producing final goods that will be bought back by the foreign company.

Subsidies Payments provided by a government or its agencies to domestic companies in order to make them more competitive vis-à-vis foreign competitors at home or abroad.

Surge in imports A sudden and dramatic increase in imports or in market share that can cause material damage to the domestic industry.

Swap The exchange of interest or foreign currency exposures or a combination of both by two or more borrowers.

Swap transaction Transaction in which there is a simultaneous purchase and sale of a given amount for two different settlement dates.

Synergy Additional economic benefits (financial, operational, or technological) arising from cooperation between two parties that provide each other with complementary resources or capabilities.

T

Target-zone arrangement A system arranged by a group of nations sharing some common interest and goals. Countries adjust their national economic policies to maintain their exchange rates within a specific margin around an agreed-upon, fixed central exchange rate.

Tariff Surcharges that an importer must pay above and beyond taxes levied on domestic goods and services.

Tariff barriers Official constraints on the importation of certain goods and services in the form of a total or partial limitation or in the form of a special levy.

Tax equalization An adjustment to expatriate pay to reflect tax rates in the home country.

Tax havens Geographical locations in which taxation is substantially lower than that in a home country.

Technical standards Provisions made by government agencies in various countries that pertain to a large array of areas, for example, safety, pollution, and technical performance.

Temporal method (of accounting) Monetary items are translated at the current rate. Non-monetary items are translated at the rates that preserve their original measurement bases.

Technology gaps Relative scarcity of technology in a country that determines comparative disadvantage in technology-intensive products.

Temporaries Individuals who go on short assignments, up to one year.

Term loans Straight loans that are made for a fixed period of time and repaid in a single lump sum.

Terms of sale Conditions stipulating rights/responsibilities and costs/risks borne by exporter and importer.

Theocratic law Legal system that relies on religious codes.

Timing of entry When a firm enters a foreign market compared to other firms (e.g., early entry is when a firm enters a foreign market before the foreign MNEs and late entry when the firm enters after other international businesses have established themselves).

Traditional expatriate An older and experienced expatriate selected for his/her managerial or technical skills for a period of one to five years.

Transaction exposure Foreign exchange risk determined by changes in exchange rates affecting the value, in home currency terms, of anticipated cash flows denominated in foreign currency, relating to transactions already entered into.

Transfer pricing The pricing of goods and services that are transferred between members of a MNE (multinational enterprise) network.

Transfer risk Impediments to the transfer of production factors.

Transferability The extent to which MNE (multinational enterprise) resources or knowledge developed at home can be transferred to a foreign subunit resulting in competitive advantage or contributing to business success in the target foreign setting (industry, segmented market, or host country).

Transferable L/C (letter of credit) A letter of credit under which the beneficiary has the right to instruct the paying bank to make the credit available to one or more secondary beneficiaries.

Translation The process of restating accounting data recorded in one currency (e.g., the currency of a foreign subsidiary in Italy) into another currency (e.g., the currency of the parent company in the United States) for the purpose of aggregating data from different reporting entities.

Translation adjustments Translation adjustments result from the process of translating financial statements from the entity's functional currency into the reporting currency.

Translation exposure (Ch. 14) Foreign exchange risk that refers to the potential for accounting-derived changes in owners' equity to occur because of the need to consolidate foreign currency financial statements.

Transnational (or hybrid) strategy A strategy that seeks to achieve both global efficiency and local responsiveness.

Transnational firm A firm that consists of subsidiaries that fulfill varying roles.

Transnationality index The average of three ratios: (a) foreign assets to total assets, (b) foreign sales to total sales, and (c) foreign employment to total employment.

Treaties of Friendship, Commerce and Navigation (FCN) The treaty that provides firms from the signatory countries with the same rights and privileges enjoyed by domestic businesses in the other country.

U

Umbrella holding company An investment company that unites the firm's existing investments such as branch offices, joint ventures, and wholly-owned subsidiaries under one umbrella so as to combine sales, procurement, manufacturing, training, and maintenance within the host country.

Uncertainty The unpredictability of environmental or organizational conditions that affect firm performance.

Uncertainty avoidance One of Hofstede's four dimensions of culture: the extent to which uncertainty and ambiguity are tolerated.

Unconfirmed L/C (letter of credit) A letter of credit that is the obligation of only the issuing bank.

Unit of measure The currency in which assets, liabilities, revenue, and expense are measured.

Unrelated holdings company format A format in which businesses are managed as investment rather than profit centers with wide reporting variations.

Uppsala (or Scandinavian) model A perspective that views international expansion as a process involving a series of incremental decisions during which firms develop international operations in small steps (e.g., accumulated knowledge about country-specific markets help firms increase local commitment, reduce operational uncertainty, and enhance economic efficiency).

User/need model (Ch. 16) A model that assesses the needs of potential customers including the circumstances in which the product or service are likely to be used.

V

Vertical FDI When the MNE (multinational enterprise) enters a foreign country to produce intermediate goods that provide input into a company's domestic operations.

Virtual expatriate An individual who takes on foreign assignments without physically relocating.

W

Wholly-owned subsidiary An entry mode in which the investing firm owns 100 percent of the new entity in a host country.

Working capital The net position whereby a firm's current liability is subtracted from its current assets.

World Bank Group International institution comprised of the World Bank, the International Development Association, the International Finance Corporation, and the Multilateral Investment Guarantee Agency. Raises standards of living in developing countries by channeling financial resources from developed countries to them.

World Trade Organization (WTO) Multilateral trade organization aiming at international trade liberalization and which has the authority to oversee trade disputes among countries.

World Wide Web (WWW) A world-wide network of computer networks that constitutes all the resources and users on the Internet that use Hypertext Transfer Protocol (HTP or HTTP).

Y

Yankee bonds Foreign bonds sold in the United States.

Young, inexperienced expatriates Individuals sent for six months to five years, usually on local hire terms.

Indexes

ORGANIZATION INDEX

1 Line Long

NAME INDEX

SUBJECT INDEX

Photo Credits

COVER

Clockwise: Nik Wheeler/Corbis Images. Paul A. Sounders/Corbis Images. Carol Beck with Angela Fisher/HAGA/The Image Works. Bojan Brecelj/Corbis Images. Barbara A. Weightman. Jeremy Horner/Corbis Images. PhotoDisc, Inc./Getty Images. Barnabas Bosshart/Corbis Images.

PART OPENERS

Part 1 & 2 Openers: PhotoDisc, Inc./Getty Images. *Part 3 Opener:* Corbis Digital Stock. *Part 4 Opener:* Royalty-Free/Corbis Images. *Part 5 Opener:* Sami Sarkas/Alamy Images. *Part 6 Opener:* Stewart Cohen/Alamy Images.

CHAPTER 1

Opener: Chris Coxwell/Corbis Images. *Page 6:* Cartoonists & Writers Syndicate. http://www.cartoonweb.com. *Page 11:* Digital Vision/Getty Images.

CHAPTER 2

Opener: Kit Kittle/Corbis Images. *Page 18:* PhotoDisc, Inc./Getty Images.

CHAPTER 3

Opener: Lee Snider/Corbis Images. *Page 55:* ©The New Yorker Collection 1987 Frank Modell from cartoonbank.com. All Rights Reserved. *Page 84:* Carl & Ann Purcell/Corbis Images.

CHAPTER 4

Opener: Jeremy Horner/Corbis Images. *Page 119:* David Frazier/Corbis Images.

CHAPTER 5

Opener: Nik Wheeler/Corbis Images. *Page 133:* Cartoonists & Writers Syndicate. http://www.cartoonweb.com. *Page 136:* PhotoDisc, Inc./Getty Images. Page 142: Royalty-Free/Corbis Images.

CHAPTER 6

Opener: Barbara A. Weightman. *Page 150:* Charles Gupton/Stone/Getty Images. *Page 171:* Royalty-Free/Corbis Images.

CHAPTER 7

Opener: Carol Beck with Angela Fisher/HAGA/The Image Works. *Page 177:* Royalty-Free/Corbis Images. *Page 188:* ©The New Yorker Collection 1992 Mike Twohly from cartoonbank.com. All Rights Reserved.

CHAPTER 8

Opener: Michael S. Yamashita/Corbis Images. *Page 203:* Cartoonists & Writers Syndicate. http://www.cartoonbank.com. *Page 206:* AFP/Corbis Images. *Page 212:* ©AP/Wide World Photos.

CHAPTER 9

Opener: Barnabas Bosshart/Corbis Images. *Page 235:* Image State. *Page 251:* Jose Luis Pelaez, Inc/Corbis Images. *Page 253:* Cartoonists & Writers Syndicate. http://www.cartoonbank.com.

CHAPTER 10

Opener: Jack Hollingsworth/Corbis Images. *Page 271:* ©2003 The New Yorker Collection from cartoonbank.com. All Rights Reserved. *Page 279:* Norbert Schiller/Liaison Agency, Inc./Getty Images.

CHAPTER 11

Opener: Robert Holmes/Corbis Images. *Page 298:* AFP/Corbis Images.

CHAPTER 12

Opener: Dannielle Hayes/Omni-Photo Communications. *Page 330:* ©AP/Wide World Photos.

CHAPTER 13

Opener: Omni-Photo Communications. *Page 338:* AFP/Corbis Images. *Page 351:* Mug Shots/Corbis Images.

CHAPTER 14

Opener: Bojan Brecelj/Corbis Images.

CHAPTER 15

Opener: Michael Yamashita/Corbis Images.

CHAPTER 16

Opener: Bojan Brecelj/Corbis Images. *Page 423:* Joseph Sohm; ChromoSohm Inc./Corbis Images. *Page 434:* Corbis Images.

CHAPTER 17

Opener: Paul A. Sounders/Corbis Images.

CHAPTER 18

Opener: Lynn Goldsmith/Corbis Images. *Page 470:* PhotoDisc, Inc./Getty Images. *Page 475:* Kevin Lee/Getty Images.

CHAPTER 19

Opener: Philip & Karen Smith/SUPERSTOCK. *Page 500:* Reuters NewMedia Inc./Corbis Images. *Page 501:* Cartoonists & Writers Syndicate. http://www.cartoonweb.com.`